roget's
thesaurus

THE EVERYMAN EDITION

roget's thesaurus

OF ENGLISH WORDS AND PHRASES

THE EVERYMAN EDITION

REVISED FROM PETER ROGET BY

D. C. BROWNING MA (GLASGOW), BA, B. LITT (OXON)

Galley Press

Everyman's Thesaurus of English Words and Phrases was first published in
Great Britain in 1952, revised in 1971

This volume first published in Great Britain in 1982 by

Octopus Books Limited
Michelin House
81 Fulham Road
London SW3 6RB

under license from

J.M. Dent & Sons Limited
Aldine House
33 Welbeck Street
London W1

This edition published in 1988 for

Galley Press
An Imprint of W.H. Smith and Son Ltd. Registered number 237811, England

Trading as W.H. Smith Distributors
St Johns House, East Street, Leicester LE1 6NE.

ISBN 0 86136 618 2

This edition © 1982 by J.M. Dent & Sons Limited

Printed in Great Britain by
Richard Clay Ltd, Bungay, Suffolk

contents

'Proper words in proper places, make the true definition of a style.'

JONATHAN SWIFT
Letter to a young clergyman
9th January, 1720

Note

PETER ROGET'S UNIQUE *Thesaurus of English Words and Phrases* was first published in 1852. When J.M. Dent & Sons Ltd. decided to produce a single-volume edition for the Everyman Library, D.C. Browning was asked to undertake a complete revision of the work, bearing in mind the changes and developments of the English language which had inevitably taken place during the intervening period.

Every paragraph was carefully reviewed and over 10,000 words and phrases were added, following the logical order which agrees with the original plan. Since the first publication in 1952, several reprints and substantial revisions in 1962 and 1971 have taken account of recent developments in English vocabulary.

This edition includes the complete plan of classification as laid down by Peter Roget himself and explained in his original introduction to the 1852 edition.

Every effort has been made to ensure that the index is as complete as possible and cross-references have been included in many cases where one paragraph is closely associated in meaning with another.

Original Introduction

By Peter Roget

THE PRESENT WORK is intended to supply, with respect to the English language, a desideratum hitherto unsupplied in any language; namely, a collection of the words it contains and of the idiomatic combinations peculiar to it, arranged, not in alphabetical order, as they are in a dictionary, but according to the *ideas* which they express. The purpose of an ordinary dictionary is simply to explain the meaning of words; and the problem of which it professes to furnish the solution may be stated thus: The word being given, to find its signification, or the idea it is intended to convey. The object aimed at in the present undertaking is exactly the converse of this; namely, the idea being given, to find the word, or words, by which that idea may be most fitly and aptly expressed. For this purpose, the words and phrases of the language are here classed, not according to their sound or their orthography, but strictly according to their *signification*.

The communication of our thoughts by means of language, whether spoken or written, like every other object of mental exertion, constitutes a peculiar art, which, like other parts, cannot be acquired in any perfection but by long and continued practice. Some, indeed, there are, more highly gifted than others with a facility of expression, and naturally endowed with the power of eloquence; but to none is it at all times an easy process to embody in exact and appropriate language the various trains of ideas that are passing through the mind, or to depict in their true colours and proportions the diversified and nicer shades of feeling which accompany them. To those who are unpractised in the art of composition, or unused to extempore speaking, these difficulties present themselves in their most formidable aspect. However distinct may be our views, however vivid our conceptions, or however fervent our emotions, we cannot but be often conscious that the phraseology we have at our command is inadequate to do them justice. We seek in vain the words we need, and strive ineffectually to devise forms of expression which shall faithfully portray out thoughts and sentiments. The appropriate terms, notwithstanding out utmost efforts, cannot be conjured up at will, Like 'spirits from the vasty deep,' they come not when we call; and we are driven to the employment of a set of words and phrases either too general or too limited, too strong or too feeble, which suit not the occasion, which hit not the mark we aim at; and the result of our prolonged exertion is a style at once laboured and obscure, vapid and redundant, or vitiated by the still graver faults of affectation or ambiguity.

It is to those who are thus painfully groping their way and struggling with the difficulties of composition, that this work professes to hold out a helping hand. The assistance it gives is that of furnishing on every topic a copious store of words and phrases, adapted to express all the recognizable shades and modifications of the general idea under which those words and phrases are arranged. The inquirer can readily select, out of the ample collection spread out before his eyes in the following pages, those expressions which are best suited to his purpose, and which might not have occurred to him without such assistance. In order to make this selection, he scarcely ever need engage in any elaborate or critical study of the subtle distinctions existing between synonymous terms; for if the materials set before him be sufficiently abundant, an instinctive tact will rarely fail to lead him to the proper choice. Even while glancing over the columns of this work, his eye may chance to light upon a particular term, which may save the cost of a clumsy paraphrase, or spare the labour of a tortuous circumlocution. Some felicitous turn of expression thus introduced will frequently open to the mind of the reader a whole vista of collateral ideas, which could not, without an extended and obtrusive episode, have been unfolded to his view; and often will the judicious insertion of a happy epithet, like a beam of sunshine in a landscape, illumine and adorn the subject which touches it, imparting new grace, and giving life and spirit to the picture.

Every workman in the exercise of his art should be provided with proper implements. For the fabrication of complicated and curious pieces of mechanism the artisan requires a corresponding assortment of various tools and instruments. For giving proper effect to the fictions of the drama, the actor should have at his disposal a well-furnished wardrobe, supplying the costumes best suited to the personage he is to represent. For the perfect delineation of the beauties of nature, the painter should have within reach of his pencil every variety and combination of hues and tints. Now the writer, as well as the orator, employs for the accomplishment of his purposes the instrumentality of words; it is in words that he clothes his thoughts; it is by means of words that he depicts his feelings. It is therefore essential to his success that he be provided with a copious vocabulary, and that he possess an entire command of all the resources and appliances of his language. To the acquisition of this power no procedure appears more directly conducive than the study of a methodized system such as that now offered to his use.

The utility of the present work will be appreciated more especially by those who are engaged in the arduous process of translating into English a work written in another language. Simple as the operation may appear, on a superficial view, of rendering into English each of its sentences, the task of transfusing, with perfect exactness, the sense of the original, preserving at the same time the style and character of its composition, and reflecting with fidelity the mind and the spirit of the author, is a task of extreme difficulty. The cultivation of this useful department of literature was in ancient times strongly recommended both by Cicero and by Quintilian as essential to the formation of a good writer and accomplished orator. Regarded simply as a mental exercise, the practice of translation is the best training for the attainment of that mastery of language and felicity of diction which are the sources of the highest oratory and are requisite for the possession of a graceful and persuasive eloquence. By rendering ourselves the faithful interpreters of the thoughts and feelings of others, we are rewarded with the acquisition of greater readiness and facility in correctly expressing our own; as he who has best learned to execute the orders of a commander becomes himself best qualified to command.

In the earliest periods of civilization, translations have been the agents for propagating knowledge from nation to nation, and the value of their labours has been inestimable; but, in the present age, when so many different languages have become the depositories of the vast treasures of literature and of science which have been accumulating for centuries, the utility of accurate translations has greatly increased, and it has become a more important object to attain perfection in the art.

The use of language is not confined to its being the medium through which we communicate our ideas to one another; it fulfils a no less important function as an *instrument of thought*, not being merely its vehicle, but giving it wings for flight. Metaphysicians are agreed that scarcely any of our intellectual operations could be carried on to any considerable extent without the agency of words. None but those who are conversant with the philosophy of mental phenomena can be aware of the immense influence that is exercised by language in promoting the development of our ideas, in fixing them in the mind, and detaining them for steady contemplation. In every process of reasoning, language enters as an essential element. Words are the instruments by which we form all our abstractions, by which we fashion and embody our ideas, and by which we are enabled to glide along a series of premises and conclusions with a rapidity so great as to leave in the memory no trace of the successive steps of the process; and we remain unconscious how much we owe to this potent auxiliary of the reasoning faculty. It is on this ground, also, that the present work founds a claim to utility. The review of a catalogue of words of analogous signification will often suggest by association other trains of thought, which, presenting the subject under new and varied aspects, will vastly expand the sphere of our mental vision. Amidst the many objects thus brought within the range of our contemplation, some striking similitude or appropriate image, some excursive flight or brilliant conception, may flash on the mind, giving point and force to our arguments, awakening a responsive chord in the imagination or sensibility of the reader, and procuring for our reasonings a more ready access both to his understanding and to his heart.

It is of the utmost consequence that strict accuracy should regulate our use of language, and that every one should acquire the power and the habit of expressing his thoughts with perspicuity and correctness. Few, indeed, can appreciate the real extent and importance of that influence which language has always exercised on human affairs, or can be aware how often these are determined by causes much slighter than are apparent to a superficial observer. False logic, disguised under specious phraseology, too often gains the assent of the unthinking multitude, disseminating far and wide the seeds of prejudice and error. Truisms pass current, and wear the semblance of profound wisdom, when dressed up in the tinsel garb of antithetical phrases, or set off by an imposing pomp of paradox. By a confused jargon of involved and mystical sentences, the imagination is easily inveigled into a transcendental region of clouds, and the understanding beguiled into the belief that it is acquiring knowledge and approaching truth. A misapplied or misapprehended term is sufficient to give rise to fierce and interminable disputes: a misnomer has turned the tide of popular opinion; a verbal sophism has decided a party question; an artful watchword, thrown among combustible materials, has kindled the flames of deadly warfare, and changed the destiny of an empire.

In constructing the following system of classification of the ideas which are expressible by language, my chief aim has been to obtain the greatest amount of practical utility. I have accordingly adopted such principles of arrangement as appeared to me to be the simplest and most natural, and which would not require, either for their comprehension or application, any disciplined acumen, or depth of metaphysical or antiquarian lore. Eschewing all needless refinements and subtleties, I have taken as my guide the more obvious characters of the ideas for which expressions were to be tabulated, arranging them under such classes and categories as reflection and experience had taught me would conduct the inquirer most readily and quickly to the object of his search. Commencing with the ideas expressing mere abstract relations, I proceed to those which relate to the phenomena of the material world, and lastly to those in which the mind is concerned, and which comprehend intellect, volition, and feeling; thus establishing six primary Classes of Categories.

1. The first of these classes comprehends ideas derived from the more general and ABSTRACT RELATIONS among things, such as *Existence, Resemblance, Quantity, Order, Number, Time, Power.*

2. The second class refers to SPACE and its various relations, including *Motion,* or change of place.

3. The third class includes all ideas that relate to the MATERIAL WORLD; namely, the *Properties of Matter,* such as *Solidity, Fluidity, Heat, Sound, Light,* and the *Phemomena* they present, as well as the simple *Perceptions* to which they give rise.

4. The fourth class embraces all ideas of phenomena relating to the INTELLECT and its operations, comprising the *Acquisition,* the *Retention,* and the *Communication of Ideas.*

5. The fifth class includes the ideas derived from the exercise of VOLITION, embracing the phenomena and results of our *Voluntary and Active Powers,* such as *Choice, Intention, Utility, Action, Antagonism, Authority, Compact, Property,* etc.

6. The sixth and last class comprehends all ideas derived from the operation of our SENTIENT AND MORAL POWERS, including our *Feelings, Emotions, Passions,* and *Moral and Religious Sentiments.*

It must necessarily happen in every system of classification framed with this view, that ideas and expressions arranged under one class must include also ideas relating to another class; for the operations of the *Intellect* generally involve also those of the *Will,* and vice versa; and our *Affections* and *Emotions,* in like manner, generally imply the agency both of the *Intellect* and the *Will.* All that can be effected, therefore, is to arrange the words according to the principal or dominant idea they convey. *Teaching,* for example, although a Voluntary act, relates primarily to the Communication of Ideas, and is accordingly placed at No. 537, under Class IV, Division II. On the other hand, *Choice, Conduct, Skill,* etc., although implying the co-operation of Voluntary with Intellectual acts, relate principally to the former, and are therefore arranged under Class V.

It often happens that the same word admits of various applications, or may be used in different senses. In consulting the Index the reader will be guided to the number of the heading under which that word, in each particular acceptation, will be found, by means of *supplementary words,* printed in italics; which words, however, are not to be understood as explaining the meaning of the word to which they are annexed, but only assisting in the required reference. I have also, for shortness' sake, generally omitted words immediately derived from the primary one inserted, which sufficiently represents the whole group of correlative words referable to the same heading. Thus the number affixed to *Beauty* applies to all its derivatives, such as *Beautiful, Beauteous, Beautify, Beautifulness, Beautifully,* etc., the insertion of which was therefore needless.

The object I have proposed to myself in this work would have been but imperfectly attained if I had confined myself to a mere catalogue of words, and had omitted the numerous phrases and forms of expression, composed of several words, which are of such frequent use as to entitle them to rank among the constituent parts of the language. For example: To take time by the forelock; to turn over a new leaf; to show the white feather; to have a finger in the pie; to let the cat out of the bag; to take care of number one; to kill two birds with one stone, etc. Very few of these verbal combinations, so essential to the knowledge of our native tongue, and so profusely abounding in its daily use, are to be met with in ordinary dictionaries. These phrases and forms of expression I have endeavoured diligently to collect and to insert in their proper places, under the general ideas they are designed to convey. Some of these conventional forms, indeed, partake of the nature of proverbial expressions; but actual proverbs, as such, being wholly of a didactic character, do not come within the scope of the present work, and the reader must therefore not expect to find them here inserted.

The study of correlative terms existing in a particular language may often throw valuable light on the manners and customs of the nations using it. Thus Hume has drawn important inferences with regard to the state of society among the ancient Romans, from certain deficiencies which he remarked in the Latin language. 'It is an universal observation,' he remarks in his Essay on the Populousness of Ancient Nations, 'which we may form upon language, that where two related parts of a whole bear any proportion to each other, in numbers, rank, or consideration, there are always correlative terms invented which answer to both the parts and express their mutual relation. If they bear no proportion to each other, the term is only invented for the less, and marks its distinction from the whole. Thus *man* and *woman, master* and *servant, father* and *son, prince* and *subject, stranger* and *citizen,* are correlative terms. But the words *seaman, carpenter, smith, tailor,* etc., have no correspondent terms which express those who are no seamen, no carpenters, etc. Languages differ very much with regard to the particular words where this distinction obtains; and may thence afford very strong inferences concerning the manners and customs of different nations. The military government of the Roman emperors had exalted the soldiery so high, that they balanced all the other orders of the state: hence *miles* and *paganus* became relative terms; a thing, till then, unknown to ancient, and still so to modern, languages.' 'The term for a slave, born and bred in the family, was *verna.* As *servus* was the name of the genus, and *verna* of the species without any correlative, this forms a strong presumption that the latter were by far the least numerous: and from the same principles I infer that if the number of slaves brought by the Romans from foreign countries had not extremely exceeded those which were bred at home, *verna* would have had a correlative, which would have expressed the former species of slaves. But these, it would seem, composed the main body of the ancient slaves, and the latter were but a few exceptions. The warlike propensity of the same nation may in a like manner be inferred from the use of the word *hostis* to denote both a *foreigner* and an *enemy.*

In many cases, two ideas, which are completely opposed to each other, admit of an intermediate or neutral idea, equidistant from both: all these being expressible by corresponding definite terms. Thus, in the following examples, the words in the first and third columns; which express opposite ideas, admit of the intermediate terms contained in the middle column having a neutral sense with reference to the former:

Identity	*Difference*	*Contrariety*
Beginning	*Middle*	*End*
Past	*Present*	*Future*

In other cases, the intermediate word is simply the negative to each of two opposite positions; as, for example:

Convexity	*Flatness*	*Concavity*
Desire	*Indifference*	*Aversion*

Sometimes the intermediate word is properly the standard with which each of the extremes is compared; as in the case of

Insufficiency	*Sufficiency*	*Redundance*

For here the middle term, *Sufficiency,* is equally opposed on the one hand to *Insufficiency* and on the other to *Redundance.*

It often happens that the same word has several correlative terms, according to the different relations in which it is considered. Thus to the word *Giving* are opposed both *Receiving* and *Taking*; the former correlation having reference to the *persons* concerned in the transfer, while the latter relates to the *mode* of transfer. *Old* has for opposite both *New* and *Young,* according as it is applied to *things* or to *living beings. Attack* and *Defence* are correlative terms, as are also *Attack* and *Resistance. Resistance,* again, has for its other correlative *Submission. Truth in the abstract* is opposed to *Error,* but the opposite of *Truth communicated* is *Falsehood. Acquisition* is contrasted both with *Deprivation* and with *Loss. Refusal* is the counterpart both of *Offer* and of *Consent. Disuse* and *Misuse* may either of them be considered as the correlative of *Use. Teaching,* with reference to what is taught, is opposed to *Misteaching,* but with reference to the act itself, its proper reciprocal is *Learning.*

Words contrasted in form do not always bear the same contrast in their meaning. The word *Malefactor,* for example, would, from its derivation, appear to be exactly the opposite of *Benefactor,* but the ideas attached to these two words are far from being directly opposed; for while the latter expresses one who confers a benefit, the former denotes one who has violated the laws.

Many considerations, interesting in a philosophical point of view, are presented by the study of correlative expressions. It will be found, on strict examination, that there seldom exists an exact opposition between two words which may at first sight appear to be the counterparts of one another; for, in general, the one will be found to possess in reality more force or extent of meaning than the other, with which it is contrasted. The correlative term sometimes assumes the form of a mere negative, although it is really endowed with a considerable positive force. Thus *Disrespect* is not merely the absence of *Respect*; its signification trenches on the opposite idea, namely, *Contempt.* In like manner, *Untruth* is not merely the negative of *Truth*; it involves a degree of *Falsehood. Irreligion,* which is properly *the want of Religion,* is understood as being nearly synonymous with *Impiety.*

18

There exist comparatively few words of a general character to which no correlative term, either of negation or of opposition, can be assigned. The correlative idea, especially that which constitutes a sense negative to the primary one, may, indeed, be formed or conceived; but, from its occurring rarely, no word has been framed to represent it; for in language, as in other matters, the supply fails when there is no probability of a demand. Occasionally we find this deficiency provided for by the contrivance of prefixing the syllable *non*; as, for instance, the negatives of *existence, performance, payment,* etc., are expressed by the compound words, *non-existence, non-performance, non-payment,* etc. Functions of a similar kind are performed by the prefixes *dis-* (the word *disannul,* however, had the same meaning as *annul*), *anti-, contra-, mis-, in-,* and *un-.* In the case of adjectives, the addition to a substantive of the terminal syllable *less,* gives it a negative meaning: as *taste, tasteless; care, careless; hope, hopeless; friend, friendless; fault, faultless,* etc. With respect to all these great latitude is allowed according to the necessities of the case, a latitude which is limited only by the taste and discretion of the author.

On the other hand, it is hardly possible to find two words having in all respects the same meaning, and being therefore interchangeable; that is, admitted of being employed indiscriminately, the one or the other, in all their applications. The investigation of the distinctions to be drawn between words apparently synonymous forms a separate branch of inquiry which I have not presumed here to enter upon; for the subject has already occupied the attention of much abler critics than myself, and its complete exhaustion would require the devotion of a whole life. The purpose of this work, it must be borne in mind, is not to explain the signification of words, but simply to classify and arrange them according to the sense in which they are now used, and which I presume to be already known to the reader. I enter into no inquiry into the changes of meaning they may have undergone in the course of time.

Such changes are innumerable; for instance, the words *tyrant, parasite, sophist, churl, knave, villain,* anciently conveyed no opprobrious meaning. *Impertinent* merely expressed *irrelative,* and implied neither *rudeness* nor *intrusion,* as it does at present. *Indifferent* originally meant *impartial; extravagant* was simply *digressive;* and to *prevent* was properly to *precede* and *assist.* The old translations of the Scriptures furnish many striking examples of the alterations which time has brought in the signification of words. Much curious information on this subject is contained in Trench's *Lectures on the Study of Words.*

I am content to accept word meanings at the value of their present currency, and have no concern with their etymologies, or with the history of their transformations; far less do I venture to thrid the mazes of the vast labyrinth into which I should be led by any attempt at a general discrimination of synonyms. The difficulties I have had to contend with have already been sufficiently great without this addition to my labours.

The most cursory glance over the pages of a dictionary will show that a great number of words are used in various senses, sometimes distinguished by slight shades of difference, but often diverging widely from their primary signification, and even, in some cases, bearing to it no perceptible relation. It may even happen that the very same word has two significations quite opposite to one another. This is the case with the verb *to cleave,* which means *to adhere tenaciously,* and also *to separate by a blow. To propugn* sometimes expresses *to attack;* at other times, *to defend. To ravel* means both *to entangle* and *to disentangle.* The alphabetical index at the end of this work sufficiently shows the multiplicity of uses to which, by the elasticity of language, the meaning of words has been stretched so as to adapt them to a great variety of modified significations in subservience to the nicer shades of thought which, under peculiarity of circumstances, require corresponding expression. Words thus admitting of different meanings have therefore to be arranged under each of the respective heads corresponding to these various acceptations. There are many words, again, which express ideas compounded of two elementary ideas belonging to different classes. It is therefore necessary to place these words respectively under each of the generic heads to which they relate. The necessity of these repetitions is increased by the circumstance that ideas included under one class are often connected by relations of the same kind as the ideas which belong to another class. Thus we find the same relations of *order* and of *quantity* existing among the ideas of *Time* as well as those of *Space*. Sequence in the one is denoted by the same terms as sequence in the other, and the measures of time also express the measures of space. The cause and the effect are often designated by the same word. The word *Sound,* for instance, denotes both the impression made upon the ear by sonorous vibrations, and also the vibrations themselves, which are the cause or source of that impression. *Mixture* is used for the act of mixing, as well as for the product of that operation. *Taste* and *Smell* express both the sensations and the qualities of material bodies giving rise to them. *Thought* is the act of thinking, but the same word denotes also the idea resulting from that act. *Judgment* is the act of deciding, and also the decision come to. *Purchase* is the acquisition of a thing by payment, as well as the thing itself so acquired. *Speech* is both the act of speaking and the words spoken; and so on with regard to an endless multiplicity of words. Mind is essentially distinct from Matter, and yet, in all languages, the attributes of the one are metaphorically transferred to those of the other. Matter, in all its forms, is endowed by the figurative genius of every language with the functions which pertain to intellect; and we perpetually talk of its phenomena and of its powers as if they resulted from the voluntary influence of one body on another, acting and reacting, impelling and being impelled, controlling and being controlled, as if animated by spontaneous energies and guided by specific intentions. On the other hand, expressions of which the primary signification refers exclusively to the properties and actions of matter are metaphorically applied to the phenomena of thought and volition, and even to the feelings and passions of the soul; and in speaking of a *ray of hope,* a *shade of doubt,* a *flight of fancy,* a *flash of wit,* the *warmth of emotion,* or the *ebullitions of anger,* we are scarcely conscious that we are employing metaphors which have this material origin.

As a general rule, I have deemed it incumbent on me to place words and phrases which appertain more especially to one head also under the other heads to which they have a relation, whenever it appeared to me that this repetition would suit the convenience of the inquirer, and spare him the trouble of turning to other parts of the work; for I have always preferred to subject myself to the imputation of redundance, rather than incur the reproach of insufficiency. Frequent repetitions of the same series of expressions, accordingly, will be met with under various headings. For example, the word *Relinquishment,* with its synonyms, occurs as a heading at No. 624, where it applies to *intention,* and also at No. 782, where it refers to *property.* The word *Chance* has two significations, distinct from one another: the one implying the *absence of an assignable* cause, in which case it comes under the category of the relation of Causation, and occupies the No. 156; the other, the *absence of design,* in which latter sense it ranks under the operations of the Will, and has assigned to it the place No. 621. I have, in like manner, distinguished *Sensibility, Pleasure, Pain, Taste,* etc., according as they relate to *Physical* or to *Moral Affections*; the former being found at Nos. 375, 377, 378, 390, etc., and the latter at Nos. 822, 827, 828, 850, etc.

When, however, the divergence of the associated from the primary idea is suføiently marked, I have contented myself with making a reference to the place where the modified signification will be found. But in order to prevent needless extension, I have, in general, omitted *conjugate words* (different parts of speech from the same root exactly corresponding in point of meaning) which are so obviously derivable from those that are given in the same place, that the reader may safely be left to form them for himself. This is the case with adverbs derived from adjectives by the simple addition of the terminal syllable *-ly,* such as *closely, carefully, safely,* etc., from *close, careful, safe,* etc., and also with adjectives or participles immediately derived from the verbs which are already given. In all such cases, an 'etc.' indicates that reference is understood to be made to these roots. I have observed the same rule in compiling the index, retaining only the primary or more simple word, and omitting the conjugate words obviously derived from them. Thus I assume the word *short* as the representative of its immediate derivatives *shortness, shorten, shortening, shortened, shorter, shortly,* which would have had the same references, and which the reader can readily supply.

The same verb is frequently used indiscriminately either in the active or transitive, or in the neuter or intransitive sense. In these cases I have generally not thought it worth while to increase the bulk of the work by the needless repetition of that word, for the reader, whom I suppose to understand the use of the words, must also be presumed to be competent to apply them correctly.

There are a multitude of words of a specific character, which although they properly occupy places in the columns of a dictionary, yet, having no relation to general ideas, do not come within the scope of this compilation, and are consequently omitted. The names of objects in Natural History, and technical terms belonging exclusively to Science or to Art, or relating to particular operations, and of which the signification is restricted to those specific objects, come under this category. Exceptions must, however, be made in favour of such words as admit of metaphorical application to general subjects with which custom has associated them, and of which they may be cited as being typical or illustrative. Thus the word *Lion* will find a place under the head of *Courage,* of which it is regarded as the type. *Anchor,* being emblematic of *Hope,* is introduced among the words expressing that emotion; and, in like manner, *butterfly* and *weathercock,* which are suggestive of fickleness, are included in the category of *Irresolution.*

With regard to the admission of many words and expressions which the classical reader might be disposed to condemn as vulgarisms, or which he, perhaps, might stigmatize as pertaining rather to the slang than to the legitimate language of the day, I would beg to observe that, having due regard to the uses to which this work was to be adapted, I did not feel myself justified in excluding them solely on that ground, if they possessed an acknowledged currency in general intercourse. It is obvious that, with respect to degrees of conventionality, I could not have attempted to draw any strict lines of demarcation, and far less could I have presumed to erect any absolute standard of purity. My object, be it remembered, is not to regulate the use of words, but simply to supply and to suggest such as may be wanted on occasion, leaving the proper selection entirely to the discretion and taste of the employer. If a novelist or a dramatist, for example, proposed to delineate some vulgar personage, he would wish to have the power of putting into the mouth of the speaker expressions that would accord with his character, just as the actor, to revert to a former comparison, who had to personate a peasant, would choose for his attire the most homely garb, and would have just reason to complain if the theatrical wardrobe furnished him with no suitable costume.

Words which have, in process of time, become obsolete, are, of course, rejected from this collection. On the other hand, I have admitted a considerable number of words and phrases borrowed from other languages, chiefly the French and Latin, some of which may be considered as already naturalized; while others, though avowedly foreign, are frequently introduced in English composition, particularly in familiar style, on account of their being peculiarly expressive, and because we have no corresponding words of equal force in our own language. All these words and phrases are printed in italics. The rapid advances which are being made in scientific knowledge, and consequent improvement in all the arts of life, and the extension of those arts and sciences to so many new purposes and objects, create a continual demand for the formation of new terms to express new agencies, new wants, and new combinations. Such terms, from being at first merely technical, are rendered, by more general use, familiar to the multitude, and having a well-defined acceptation, are eventually incorporated into the language, which they contribute to enlarge and to enrich. *Neologies* of this kind are perfectly legitimate, and highly advantageous; and they necessarily introduce those gradual and progressive changes which every language is destined to undergo. Thus in framing the present classification I have frequently felt the want of substantive terms corresponding to abstract qualities or ideas denoted by certain adjectives, and have been tempted to invent words that might express these abstractions; but I have yielded to this temptation only in the four following instances: having framed from the adjectives *irrelative, amorphous, sinistral,* and *gaseous* the abstract nouns *irrelation, amorphism, sinistrality,* and *gaseity.* I have ventured also to introduce the adjective *intersocial* to express the active voluntary relations between man and man. Some modern writers, however, have indulged in a habit of arbitrarily fabricating new words and a new-fangled phraseology without any necessity, and with manifest injury to the purity of the language. This vicious practice, the offspring of indolence or conceit, implies an ignorance or neglect of the riches in which the English language already abounds, and which would have supplied them with words of recognized legitimacy, conveying precisely the same meaning as those they so recklessly coin in the illegal mint of their own fancy.

A work constructed on the plan of classification I have proposed might, if ably executed, be of great value in tending to limit the fluctuations to which language has always been subject, by establishing an authoritative standard for its regulation. Future historians, philologists, and lexicographers, when investigating the period when new words were introduced, or discussing the import given at the present time to the old, might find their labours lightened by being enabled to appeal to such a standard, instead of having to search for data among the scattered writings of the age. Nor would its utility be confined to a single language, for the principles of its construction are universally applicable to all languages, whether living or dead. On the same plan of classification there might be formed a French, a German, a Latin, or a Greek Thesaurus, possessing, in their respective spheres, the same advantages as those of the English model. Still more useful would be a conjunction of these methodized compilations in two languages, the French and the English, for instance; the columns of each being placed in parallel juxtaposition. No means yet devised would so greatly facilitate the acquisition of the one language by those who are acquainted with the other: none would afford such ample assistance to the translator in either language; and none would supply such ready and effectual means of instituting an accurate comparison between them, and of fairly appreciating their respective merits and defects. In a still higher degree would all those advantages be combined and multiplied in a *Polyglot Lexicon* constructed on this system.

Metaphysicians engaged in the more profound investigation of the Philosophy of Language will be materially assisted by having the ground thus prepared for them in a previous analysis and classification of our ideas, for such classification of ideas is the true basis on which words, which are their symbols. should be classified. It is by such analysis alone that we can arrive at a clear perception of the relation which these symbols bear to their corresponding ideas, or can obtain a correct knowledge of the elements which enter into the formation of compound ideas, and of the exclusions by which we arrive at the abstractions so perpetually resorted to in the process of reasoning and in the communication of our thoughts.

The principle by which I have been guided in framing my verbal classification is the same as that which is employed in the various departments of natural history. Thus the sectional divisions I have formed correspond to natural families in botany and zoology, and the filiation of words presents a network analogous to the natural filiation of plants or animals.

The following are the only publications that have come to my knowledge in which any attempt has been made to construct a systematic arrangement of Ideas with a view to their expression. The earliest of these, supposed to be at least nine hundred years old, is the AMERA CÓSHA, or *Vocabulary of the Sanscrit Language*, by Amera Sinha, of which an English translation, by the late Henry T. Colebrooke, was printed at Serampoor in the year 1808. The classification of words is there, as might be expected, exceedingly imperfect and confused, especially in all that relates to abstract Ideas or mental operations. This will be apparent from the very title of the first section, which comprehends '*Heaven, Gods, Demons, Fire, Air, Velocity, Eternity, Much*'; while *Sin, Virtue, Happiness, Destiny, Cause, Nature, Intellect, Reasoning, Knowledge, Senses, Tastes, Odours, Colours,* are all included and jumbled together in the fourth section. A more logical order, however, pervades the sections relating to natural objects, such as *Seas, Earth, Towns, Plants,* and *Animals,* which form separate classes, exhibiting a remarkable effort at analysis at so remote a period of Indian literature.

The well-known work of Bishop Wilkins, entitled *An Essay towards a Real Character and a Philosophical Language,* published in 1668, had for its object the formation of a system of symbols which might serve as a universal language. It professed to be founded on a 'scheme of analysis of the things or notions to which names were to be assigned'; but notwithstanding the immense labour and ingenuity expended in the construction of this system, it was soon found to be far too abstruse and recondite for practical application.

In the year 1797 there appeared in Paris an anonymous work, entitled *Pasigraphie, ou Premiers Éléments du nouvel Art-Science d'écrire et d'imprimer une langue de manière à être lu et entendu dans toute autre langue sans traduction,* of which an edition in German was also published. It contains a great number of tabular schemes of categories, all of which appear to be excessively arbitrary and artificial, and extremely difficult of application, as well as of apprehension.

Lastly, such analyses alone can determine the principles on which a strictly *Philosophical Language* might be constructed. The probable result of the construction of such a language would be its eventual adoption by every civilized nation, thus realizing that splendid aspiration of philanthropists—the establishment of a Universal Language. 'The languages,' observes Horne Tooke in his $E\pi\epsilon\alpha\ \Pi\tau\epsilon\rho\sigma\epsilon\nu\pi\alpha$, 'which are commonly used throughout the world, are much more simple and easy, convenient and philosophical, than Wilkins's scheme for a *real character*; or than any other scheme that has been at any other time imagined or proposed for the purpose.' However Utopian such a project may appear to the present generation, and however abortive may have been the former endeavours of Bishop Wilkins and others to realize it, its accomplishment is surely not beset with greater difficulties than have impeded the progress to many other beneficial objects which in former times appeared to be no less visionary, and which yet were successfully achieved, in later ages, by the continued and persevering exertions of the human intellect. Is there at the present day, then, any ground for despair that, at some future stage of that higher civilization to which we trust the world is gradually tending, some new and bolder effort of genius towards the solution of this great problem may be crowned with success, and compass an object of such vast and paramount utility? Nothing, indeed, would conduce more directly to bring about a golden age of union and harmony among the several nations and races of mankind than the removal of that barrier to the interchange of thought and mutual good understanding between man and man which is now interposed by the diversity of their respective languages.

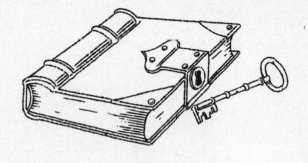

PLAN OF CLASSIFICATION

PLAN OF CLASSIFICATION

CLASS ONE
Abstract relations

Section 1
Existence

Abstract	1 EXISTENCE	2 INEXISTENCE
Concrete	3 SUBSTANTIALITY	4 UNSUBSTANTIALITY
	Internal	*External*
Formal	5 INTRINSICALITY	6 EXTRINSICALITY
	Absolute	*Relative*
Modal	7 STATE	8 CIRCUMSTANCE

Section 2
Relation

Absolute	9 RELATION	10 IRRELATION
	11 CONSANGUINITY	
	12 CORRELATION	
	13 IDENTITY	14 CONTRARIETY
		15 DIFFERENCE
Continuous	16 UNIFORMITY	16a NON-UNIFORMITY
	17 SIMILARITY	18 DISSIMILARITY
	19 IMITATION	20 NON-IMITATION
		20a VARIATION
	21 COPY	22 PROTOTYPE
General	23 AGREEMENT	24 DISAGREEMENT

Section 3
Quantity

	Absolute	*Relative*
Simple	25 QUANTITY	26 DEGREE
	27 EQUALITY	28 INEQUALITY
		29 MEAN
		30 COMPENSATION
	By Comparison with a Standard	
Comparative	31 GREATNESS	32 SMALLNESS
	By Comparison with a Similar Object	
	33 SUPERIORITY	34 INFERIORITY
	Changes in Quantity	
	35 INCREASE	36 NON-INCREASE
		DECREASE
	37 ADDITION	38 NON-ADDITION
		SUBDUCTION
	39 ADJUNCT	40 REMAINDER
		40a DECREMENT
Conjunctive	41 MIXTURE	42 SIMPLENESS
	43 JUNCTION	44 DISJUNCTION
	45 VINCULUM	
	46 COHERENCE	47 INCOHERENCE
	48 COMBINATION	49 DECOMPOSITION·

CLASS TWO
Space

CLASS THREE
Matter

CLASS FOUR
Intellect
Division I Formation of Ideas

CLASS FIVE
Volition
Division I Individual Volition

Division II Intersocial Volition

Monetary Relations

800 MONEY	
801 TREASURER	
802 TREASURY	
803 WEALTH	804 POVERTY
805 CREDIT	806 DEBT
807 PAYMENT	808 NON-PAYMENT
809 EXPENDITURE	810 RECEIPT
811 ACCOUNTS	
812 PRICE	813 DISCOUNT
814 DEARNESS	815 CHEAPNESS
816 LIBERALITY	817 ECONOMY
818 PRODIGALITY	819 PARSIMONY

CLASS SIX
Affections

Section 1
General

820 AFFECTIONS
821 FEELING
822 SENSIBILITY   823 INSENSIBILITY
824 EXCITATION
825 EXCITABILITY   826 INEXCITABILITY

Section 2
Personal

Passive

827 PLEASURE   828 PAIN
829 PLEASUREABLENESS   830 PAINFULNESS
831 CONTENT   832 DISCONTENT
                         833 REGRET
834 RELIEF   835 AGGRAVATION
836 CHEERFULNESS   837 DEJECTION
838 REJOICING   839 LAMENTATION
840 AMUSEMENT   841 WEARINESS
842 WIT   843 DULLNESS
844 HUMORIST

Discriminative

845 BEAUTY   846 UGLINESS
847 ORNAMENT   848 BLEMISH
                         849 SIMPLICITY
850 TASTE   851 VULGARITY
852 FASHION   853 RIDICULOUSNESS
                         854 FOP
                         855 AFFECTION
                         856 RIDICULE
                         857 LAUGHING-STOCK

Prospective

858 HOPE   859 HOPELESSNESS
                         860 FEAR
861 COURAGE   862 COWARDICE
863 RASHNESS   864 CAUTION
865 DESIRE   867 DISLIKE
           866 INDIFFERENCE
                         868 FASTIDIOUSNESS
                         869 SATIETY

Contemplative

870 WONDER   871 EXPECTANCE
872 PRODIGY

Extrinsic

873 REPUTE   874 DISREPUTE
875 NOBILITY   876 COMMONALTY
877 TITLE
878 PRIDE   879 HUMILITY
880 VANITY   881 MODESTY
882 OSTENTATION
883 CELEBRATION
884 BOASTING
885 INSOLENCE   886 SERVILITY
887 BLUSTERER

Section 3
Sympathetic

Social	888	FRIENDSHIP	889	ENMITY
	890	FRIEND	891	ENEMY
	892	SOCIALITY	893	SECLUSION
	894	COURTESY	895	DISCOURTESY
	896	CONGRATULATION		
	897	LOVE	898	HATE
	899	FAVOURITE	900	RESENTMENT
			901	IRASCIBILITY
	902	ENDEARMENT		
	903	MARRIAGE	904	CELIBACY
			905	DIVORCE
Diffusive	906	BENEVOLENCE	907	MALEVOLENCE
			908	MALEDICTION
			909	THREAT
	910	PHILANTHROPY	911	MISANTHROPY
	912	BENEFACTOR	913	EVILDOER
Special	914	PITY		
	915	CONDOLENCE		
Retrospective	916	GRATITUDE	917	INGRATITUDE
	918	FORGIVENESS	919	REVENGE
			920	JEALOUSY
			921	ENVY

Section 4
Moral

Obligations	922	RIGHT	923	WRONG
	924	DUENESS	925	UNDUENESS
	926	DUTY	927	DERELICTION
			927a	EXEMPTION
Sentiments	928	RESPECT	929	DISRESPECT
			930	CONTEMPT
	931	APPROBATION	932	DISAPPROBATION
	933	FLATTERY	934	DETRACTION
	935	FLATTERER	936	DETRACTOR
	937	VINDICATION	938	ACCUSATION
Conditions	939	PROBITY	940	IMPROBITY
			941	KNAVE
	942	UNSELFISHNESS	943	SELFISHNESS
	944	VIRTUE	945	VICE
	946	INNOCENCE	947	GUILT
	948	GOOD MAN	949	BAD MAN
	950	PENITENCE	951	IMPENITENCE
	952	ATONEMENT		
Practice	953	TEMPERANCE	954	INTEMPERANCE
	955	ASCETICISM		
	956	FASTING	957	GLUTTONY
	958	SOBRIETY	959	DRUNKENNESS
	960	PURITY	961	IMPURITY
			962	LIBERTINE

Institutions	963 Legality	964 Illegality
	965 Jurisdiction	
	966 Tribunal	
	967 Judge	
	968 Lawyer	
	969 Lawsuit	
	970 Acquittal	971 Condemnation
		972 Punishment
	973 Reward	974 Penalty
		975 Scourge

Section 5
Religious

Superhuman Beings and Objects	976 Deity	
	977 Angel	978 Satan
	979 Great Spirit	980 Demon
	981 Heaven	982 Hell
Doctrines	983 Theology	
	983a Christian Religion	984 Other Religions
	985 Christian Revelation	986 Other Sacred Books
	987 Piety	988 Impiety
		989 Irreligion
Acts	990 Worship	991 Idolatry
		992 Occult Arts
		993 Spell
		994 Sorcerer
Institutions	995 Churchdom	
	996 Clergy	997 Laity
	998 Rite	
	999 Vestments	
	1000 Temple	

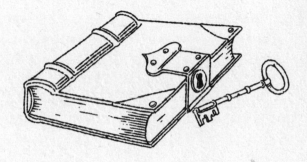

THESAURUS

CLASS ONE

Words relating to abstract relations

Section I – Existence

1 EXISTENCE

Substantives: being, life, vital principle, entity, ens, essence, quiddity, subsistence; coexistence (120).

Reality, actuality, positiveness, absoluteness, fact, truth (494); actualization.

Presence; existence in space (186).

Science of existence, ontology; existentialism.

Phrases: The sober reality; hard fact; matter of fact; the whole truth; no joke.

Verbs: To be, to exist, have being, subsist, live, breathe, stand, abide, remain, stay, obtain, occur, prevail, be so, find itself, take place, eventuate, consist in, lie in; to vegetate, pass the time.

To come into existence, arise, come out, emerge, come forth, appear (448).

To bring into existence, produce, bring forth, discover (161), objectify.

Adjectives: Existing, being, subsisting, subsistent, in being, in existence, extant, living, breathing, obtaining, prevailing, prevalent, current, afoot.

Real, actual, positive, absolute, essential, substantial, substantive, self-existing, self-existent; undestroyed, tangible, not ideal, not imagined, not suppositious, not potential, virtual, effective, unideal, true, authentic, genuine, mere, objective.

Adverbs: Actually, really, absolutely, positively, etc., in fact, *de facto, ipso facto.*

Phrase: *In esse; cogito ergo sum.*

2 INEXISTENCE

Substantives: non-existence, not-being, nonentity, *nihil*, nil, non-subsistence, nullity, vacuity, blank (4), negativeness, absence (187), removal (185).

Annihilation, abeyance, extinction (162); nirvana.

Philosophy of non-existence, nihilism.

Phrases: No such thing; Mrs. Harris; 'men in buckram.'

Verbs: Not to be, not to exist, etc.

To cease to be, pass away, perish, vanish, fade away, dissolve, melt away, disappear (449), to be annihilated, extinct, etc., to die (360), to die out.

Phrases: To have no being; to have no existence; to be null and void; *non est*; to be no more; 'to leave not a rack behind'; to disappear into thin air; to be brought out of existence.

Adjectives: Inexistent, non-existent, non-existing, etc., negative, blank, absent.

Unreal, potential, virtual, baseless, unsubstantial (4), imaginary, ideal, vain, fanciful, unpractical, shadowy, fabulous (515), suppositious (514).

Unborn, uncreated, unbegotten, unproduced, unmade.

Annihilated, destroyed, extinct, gone, lost, perished, melted, dissolved, faded, exhausted, vanished, missing, disappeared, departed, extinct, defunct (360).

Adverbs: Negatively, virtually, etc.

Phrase: *In nubibus.*

3 SUBSTANTIALITY
Substantives: hypostasis, person, thing, being, something, existence, entity, reification, corporeity, body, physique, substance, object, article, creature, matter, material, stuff (316), substratum, protoplasm.

Totality of existences, world (318), continuum, plenum.

Phrase: Something or other.

Adjectives: Substantive, substantial, personal, bodily, tangible, true, real, concrete, corporal, corporeal, material, objective, hypostatic.

Verbs: Substantialize, actualize, materialize, reify, embody.

Adverbs: Substantially, etc., essentially.

4 UNSUBSTANTIALITY
Substantives: insubstantiality, nothingness, nihility, nothing, naught, damn-all, *nihil*, nil, nix, love, zero, cipher, a duck, duck's-egg, pair of spectacles; nonentity, nobody, no one (187).

A shadow, phantom, phantasm, phantasmagoria, dream, mockery, air, thin air, idle dream, pipe dream, castle in Spain (515), idle talks, ignis fatuus, *fata morgana,* mirage.

Void, vacuum, vacuity, vacancy, voidness, vacuousness, inanity, emptiness, hollowness, blank, chasm, gap, hiatus (198); empty space, ether.

Phrases: Nothing at all; nothing whatever; nothing on earth; nothing under the sun; not a particle.

A man of straw; *vox et praetera nihil*; 'such stuff as dreams are made on.'

Verbs: To vanish, fade, dissolve, evaporate.

Adjectives: Unsubstantial, immaterial, void, vacant, vacuous, blank, null, inane, idle, hollow, airy, visionary (515).

5 INTRINSICALITY
Substantives: inbeing, immanence, inherence, inhesion, essence; essentiality, essentialness, subjectiveness, subjectivity, essential part, soul, quintessence, quiddity, gist, pith, core, backbone, marrow, sap, lifeblood; incarnation.

Nature, constitution, character, type, quality (157), temperament, temper, manner, spirit, ethos, habit, humour, grain, endowment, capacity, capability, moods, declensions, features, aspects, specialities, peculiarities (79), particularities, idiosyncrasy, idiocrasy, diagnostics.

Verbs: To be innate, inborn, etc.

Phrases: To be in the blood; to be born like that.

Adjectives: Derived from within, subjective, intrinsic, intrinsical, inherent, essential, natural, internal, implanted, inborn, innate, inbred, engrained, inherited, immanent, indwelling, radical, constitutional, congenital, connate, hereditary, instinctive, indigenous.

Phrases: In the grain; in the blood; bred in the bone.

Characteristic, peculiar, qualitative, special, diagnostic (79), invariable.

Adverbs: Intrinsically, subjectively, substantially, at bottom, *au fond,* at the core.

6 EXTRINSICALITY
Substantives: extraneousness, objectiveness, objectivity, accident, superficiality, incident.

Adjectives: Derived from without, objective, extrinsic, extrinsical, extraneous, modal, adventitious, adscititious, incidental, accidental, non-essential, outward (220).

Implanted, engrafted.

Adverbs: Extrinsically, etc.

7 STATE
Substantives: condition, category, class, kind, estate, lot, case, constitution, habitude, diathesis, mood, temper, morale.

Frame, fabric, structure, texture, contexture (329), conformation, organism.

Mode, modality, schesis, form, shape (240), figure, cut, cast, mould, stamp, set, fit, tone, tenor, trim, turn, guise, fashion, aspect, complexion, style, manner, character, kind, get-up, set-up, format, *genre*.

Verbs: To be in a state, to be in condition, to be on a footing, etc.

To do, fare; to have, possess, enjoy, etc., a state, condition, etc.

To bring into a state, etc. (144).

Adjectives: Conditional, modal, formal, structural, organic, textual.

Phrases: As the matter stands; as things are; such being the case.

Adverbs: Conditionally, etc.

8 CIRCUMSTANCE

Substantives: situation, phase, position, posture, attitude, place, point, bearings, terms, fare, regime, footing, standing, status, predicament, contingency, occasion, juncture, conjuncture, emergency, exigence, exigency, crisis, pinch, impasse, pass, push, plight, fix.

Phrases: How the land lies; how the wind blows; how the cat jumps.

Adjectives: Circumstantial; given, conditional, provisional, modal, critical, contingent, incidental (6, 151), circumstanced, placed.

Verb Phrases: To bow before the storm; to take things as they come; to cut one's coat according to the cloth.

Adverbs: In or under the circumstances, conditions, etc.; thus, so; in such a case, contingency, etc.; accordingly, such being the case; since, sith, seeing that, as matters stand, as things go.

Conditionally, provided, if, and if, if so, if so be, if it be so, if it so prove, or turn out, or happen; in the event of, provisionally, unless, without.

Phrases: According to circumstances; as it may happen, or turn out; as the case may be; *pro re nata*; wind and

weather permitting; D.V.; rain or shine; sink or swim; at all events; other things being equal; *ceteris paribus*.

Section II – Relation

9 RELATION

Substantives: relationship, bearing, reference, standing, concern, cognation, correlation (12), analogy, affinity, homology, alliance, homogeneity, connection, association, approximation, similarity (17), filiation, affiliation, etc. (11, 166), interest, habitude; relativity.

Relevancy, pertinency, fitness, etc. (646, 23).

Aspect, point of view, comparison (464); ratio, proportion.

Link, tie (45), homologue.

Verbs: To be related, have a relation, etc., to relate to, refer to, have reference to, bear upon, regard, concern, touch, affect, have to do with, pertain to, belong to, appertain to, answer to, interest.

To bring into relation with, correlate, associate, connect, affiliate, link (43), bring near (197), homologize; to bring to bear upon.

Phrase: To draw a parallel with.

Adjectives: Relative, correlative, cognate, relating to, relative to, relevant, in relation with, referable to, pertinent (23), germane, belonging to, pat, to the point, apposite, to the purpose, apropos, *ad rem*, just the thing, quite the thing; pertaining to, appertaining to, appurtenant, affiliated, allied, related, implicated, connected, associated, *en rapport*, in touch with, bound up with, homological, homologous.

Approximate, approximative, approximating, proportional, proportionate, proportionable, allusive, comparable, like, similar (17).

Adverbs: Relatively, thereof, as to, about, connecting, concerning, anent, touching, as relates to, with relation to, relating to, as respects, with respect to, in respect of, respecting, as regards, with regard to, regarding, in the matter of, with reference to, according to, while speaking of, apropos of, in connection with, inasmuch as, whereas, in consideration of, in point of, as far as, on the part of, on the score of, under the head of, *in re*; pertinently, etc. (23).

10 IRRELATION

Substantives: disconnection, dissociation, disassociation, misrelation, independence, isolation (44), multifariousness, disproportion; commensurability, irrelevancy; heterogeneity, irreconcilableness (24), impertinence.

Verbs: To have no relation with, or to, to have nothing to do with, to have no business there, not to concern, not to admit of comparison.

To isolate, separate, detach, disconnect, segregate (44).

Adjectives: Irrelative, irrespective, unrelated, without reference, etc., to, arbitrary, episodic, remote, farfetched, forced, out of place, out of tune (414), inharmonious, malapropos, irrelevant, foreign to, alien, impertinent, inapposite, extraneous to, strange to, stranger to, independent, parenthetical, incidental, outlandish, exotic, unallied, unconnected, disconnected, unconcerned, adrift, detached, isolated, insular.

Not comparable, incommensurable, inapplicable (24), irreconcilable, heterogeneous (83), unconformable.

Phrases: Foreign to the purpose; nothing to the purpose; having nothing to do with; *nihil ad rem*; neither here nor there; beside the mark; *à propos des bottes*; dragged in by the scruff of the neck.

Adverbs: Parentetically, by the way, by the by, *obiter dicta, en passant,* incidentally, irrespectively, irrelevantly, etc.

11 CONSANGUINITY

Substantives: relationship, kindred, blood, parentage (166), filiation, affiliation, lineage, agnation, connection, alliance, family connection, family tie, nepotism.

A kinsman, kinswoman, kinsfolk, kith and kin, relation, relative, friend, sibling, one's people, clan, connection, one's own flesh and blood, brother, sister, father, mother, uncle, aunt, nephew, niece, stepfather, etc., brother-in-law, etc., guid-brother, etc., cousin, cousin-german; first, second cousin; cousin once, twice, etc., removed; grand- or great-grandfather, etc., great-uncle, etc., a near relation, a blood-relation, a distant relation or relative, congener, collateral.

Family, issue, fraternity, sisterhood, brotherhood, parentage, cousinhood, etc.; race, stock, generation, sept, clan, tribe, strain.

Verbs: To be related, to have or claim relationship with.

Adjectives: Related, akin, consanguineous, congeneric, family, kindred, affiliated, allied, collateral, sib, agnate, agnatic, fraternal, of the same blood, nearly or close related, remotely or distantly related.

Phrase: Blood is thicker than water.

12 RECIPROCALNESS

Substantives: reciprocity, mutuality, correlation, correlativeness, interdependence, interchange, interaction, reciprocation, etc. (148), alternation (149), barter (794).

Verbs: To reciprocate, alternate, interchange, interact, exchange, counterchange, interdepend.

Adjectives: Reciprocal, mutual, common, correlative, alternate, alternative; interchangeable, interdependent, international.

Adverbs: Reciprocally, mutually, etc.

Phrases: *Mutatis mutandis*; each other; vice versa; turn and turn about.

13 IDENTITY

Substantives: sameness, oneness, coincidence, coalescence, convertibility; selfness, self, ego, oneself, number one; identification, monotony; equality (27), tautology (104).

Synonym; facsimile (21), counterpart (17).

Verbs: To be identical, to be the same, etc., to coincide, to coalesce.

To render the same.

To recognize the identity of, to identify, recognize.

Adjectives: Identical, identic, same, self, selfsame, very same, no other, ilk, one and the same, ditto, unaltered, coincident, coinciding, coessential, coalescing, coalescent, indistinguishable, tantamount, equivalent, equipollent, convertible, much the same.

Adverbs: All one, all the same, *ibidem*, ibid, identically, likewise.

Phrases: *Semper idem; toujours la même chose; alter ago*; on all fours; much of a muchness.

14 CONTRARIETY

Substantives: contrast, foil, set-off, antithesis, contradiction, opposition, oppositeness, antagonism (179, 708), distinction (15).

Inversion, reversion (218).

The opposite, the reverse, inverse, converse, antonym, the antipodes (237).

Phrases: The reverse of the medal; the other side of the shield; the tables being turned.

Verbs: To be contrary, etc., to contrast with, contradict, contravene, oppose, negate, antagonize, invert, reverse, turn the tables, to militate against.

Adjectives: Contrary, opposite, counter, converse, reverse, antithetical, opposed, antipodean, antagonistic, opposing, conflicting, inconsistent, contradictory, contrarious, contrariant, negative.

Phrases: Differing *toto caelo*; diametrically opposite; as black to white; light to darkness; fire to water; worlds apart; poles asunder.

Adverbs: Contrarily, contrariously, contrariwise, *per contra*, oppositely, *vice versa*, on the contrary, *tout au contraire*, quite the contrary, no such thing.

15 DIFFERENCE

Substantives: variance, variation, variety, diversity, modification, allotropy, shade of difference, nuance; deviation, divergence, divarication (291), disagreement (24), dissimilarity (18), disparity (28).

Distinction, contradistinction, differentiation, discrimination (465); a nice or fine or subtle distinction.

Phrases: A very different thing; *a tertium quid*; a horse of a different colour; another pair of shoes.

Verbs: To be different, etc., to differ, vary, mismatch, contrast, differ *toto caelo*.

To render different, etc., to vary, change, modify, varify, diversify, etc. (140).

To distinguish, differentiate, severalize (465), split hairs, discriminate.

Adjectives: Different, differing, disparate, heterogeneous, heteromorphic, allotropic, varying, distinguishable, discriminative, varied, modified, diversified, deviating, diverging, devious, disagreeing (24), various, divers, all manner of, multifarious, multiform, variform (81), variegated (440), diacritical.

Other, another, other-guess, not the same.

Unmatched, widely apart, changed (140).

Phrase: As different as chalk is from cheese.

Adverbs: Differently, variously, otherwise.

16 UNIFORMITY
Substantives: homogeneity, homogeneousness, consistency, connaturality, conformity (82), homology, accordance, agreement (23), regularity (58), routine, monotony, constancy.
Verbs: To be uniform, etc., to accord with, harmonize with, hang together, go together.

To become uniform, conform with, fall in with, follow suit.

To render uniform, to assimilate, level, smooth (255).
Adjectives: Uniform, homogeneous, homologous, of a piece, of a kind, consistent, connatural, monotonous, even, unvarying, flat, level, constant.
Adverbs: Uniformly, uniformly with, conformably (82), consistently with, in unison with, in harmony with, in conformity with, according to (23).

Regularly, at regular intervals, invariably, constantly, always, without exception.
Phrases: In a rut (or a groove); *ab uno disce omnes*; 'forty feeding like one.'

16A NON-UNIFORMITY
Substantives: variety, multiformity (81), diversity, unevenness, irregularity, unconformity (83).
Adjectives: Multiform, multifarious, various (81), diversified, inconsistent, of various kinds.

17 SIMILARITY
Substantives: resemblance, likeness, similitude, affinity, semblance, approximation, parallelism (216), analogy, brotherhood, family likeness; alliteration, head-rhyme, rhyme, pun, assonance, repetition (104), reproduction.

An analogue, copy (21), the like, facsimile, match, double, pendant, fellow, pair, mate, twin, *alter ego*, parallel, counterpart, brother, sister; simile, metaphor (521), resemblance, imitation (19).
Phrases: One's second self; *Arcades ambo*; birds of a feather; *et hoc genus omne*; a chip off the old block; the very spit (and image) of.
Verbs: To be similar, like, resembling, etc., to look like, resemble, bear resemblance, favour, approximate, parallel, match, imitate, take after (19), represent, simulate, personate, savour of, have a flavour of, favour, feature.

To render similar, assimilate, approximate, reproduce, bring near, copy, plagiarize.
Adjectives: Similar, like, alike, resembling, twin, analogous, analogical, parallel, allied to, of a piece, such as, connatural, congener, matching, conformable, on all fours with.

Near, something like, suchlike, mock, pseudo, simulating, representing, approximating, a show of, a kind of, a sort of.

Exact, accurate, true, faithful, close, speaking, lifelike, breathing.
Phrases: True to nature; to the life; for all the world like; like as two peas; *comme deux gouttes d'eau*; cast in the same mould; like father, like son.
Adverbs: As if, so to speak, as it were, quasi, as if it were, just as, after, in the fashion or manner of, *à la*.

18 DISSIMILARITY
Substantives: unlikeness, dissimilitude, diversity, divergence, difference (15), novelty (123), originality (515), disparity (28).
Verbs: To be unlike, etc., to vary (15, 20).

To render unlike, to diversify (140).
Phrase: To strike out something new.
Adjectives: Dissimilar, unlike, disparate, of a different kind, class, etc. (75); diversified, novel, new (123), unmatched, unique, unprecedented (83).
Phrases: Nothing of the kind; far from it; cast in a different mould; as different as chalk is from cheese.
Adverbs: Otherwise.

19 IMITATION
Substantives: assimilation, copying, transcription, transcribing, following, repetition (104), duplication, reduplication, quotation, reproduction.

Mockery, mocking, mimicry, mimicking, echoing, reflection, simulation, counterfeiting, plagiarism, forgery, fake, fakement, acting, personation, impersonation, representation (554), copy (21), parody, paraphrase, travesty, burlesque, semblance, mimesis.

An imitator, mimic, impersonator, echo, cuckoo, parrot, ape, monkey, mocking-bird.

Plagiary, plagiarist, forger, counterfeiter.
Phrase: *O imitatores, servum pecus.*
Verbs: To imitate, copy, plagiarize, forge, fake, reproduce, photograph, repeat (104), echo, re-echo, transcribe, match, parallel, emulate, do like, take off, hit off, reflect, mirror, model after (554).

To mock, mimic, ape, simulate, personate, impersonate (554), act, represent, adumbrate, counterfeit, parody, travesty, caricature, burlesque.
Phrases: To take or catch a likeness; to take after; to follow or tread in the steps of, or in the footsteps of; to take a leaf out of another's book; to follow suit; to go with the stream; to be in the fashion.
Adjectives: Imitated, copied, matched, repeated, paralleled, mock, mimic, parodied, etc., modelled after, moulded on, paraphrastic, imitative, mimetic, slavish, mechanical, synthetic, second-hand, imitable.
Adverbs: Literally, verbatim, to the letter, *literatim, sic, totidem verbis,* so to speak, in so many words, word for word, *mot à mot* (562).

20 NON-IMITATION
Substantives: originality, inventiveness, novelty.

Adjectives: Unimitated, uncopied, unmatched, unparalleled, inimitable, unique, original, novel.
Verb: To originate.

20A VARIATION
Substantives: alteration, modification, difference (15), change (140), deviation (279), divergence (291); moods and tenses.
Verbs: To vary, modify, change, alter, diversify (140).
Phrase: To steer clear of.
Adjectives: Varied, modified, diversified, etc.
Adverbs: Variously, in all manner of ways.

21 COPY
Substantives: facsimile, counterpart, effigies, effigy, form, likeness, similitude, semblance, reflex, portrait, photograph (556), photostat, microfilm, enlargement, miniature, study, cast, autotype, electrotype, imitation, replica, representation, adumbration.

Duplicate, transcript, transcription, repetition (104), réchauffé, reflection, shadow, record, recording.

Rough copy, fair copy, revise, carbon copy, tracing, rubbing, squeeze, draft or draught, proof, pull, reprint.

Counterfeit, parody, caricature, burlesque, travesty, paraphrase, forgery.
Phrases: A second edition; a twice-told tale.

22 PROTOTYPE
Substantives: original, model, pattern, standard, type, scale, scantling, archetype, protoplast, antitype, module, exemplar, example, ensample, protoplast, paradigm, fugleman, lay figure.

Text, copy, design, plan, blue-print, keynote.

Mould, matrix, last, plasm, proplasm, mint, die, seal, stamp, negative.
Verbs: To set a copy, to set an example.

23 AGREEMENT

Substantives: accord, accordance, unison, uniformity, harmony, union, concord, concert, concordance (714), cognation, conformity, conformance (82), consonance, consentaneousness, consensus, consistency, congruity, congruence, congeniality, correspondence keeping, parallelism.

Fitness, pertinence, suitableness, adaptation, meetness, patness, relevancy, aptness, aptitude, coaptation, propriety, apposition, appositeness, reconcilableness, applicability, applicableness, admissibility, commensurability, compatibility, adaptability.

Adaptation, adjustment, graduation, accommodation, reconciliation, reconcilement, concurrence (178), consent (488), co-operation (709).

Verbs: To be accordant, to agree, accord (714), correspond, tally, jibe, respond, harmonize, match, suit, fit, befit, hit, fall in with, chime in with, quadrate with, square with, cancel with, comport with, assimilate, unite with.

To render accordant, to adapt, accommodate, adjust, reconcile, fadge, dovetail, dress, square, regulate, comport, graduate, gradate, grade.

Phrases: To become one; to fit like a glove; to suit one to a T.

Adjectives: Agreeing, accordant, concordant, consonant, congruous, consentaneous, consentient, corresponding, correspondent, congenial, harmonizing, harmonious with, tallying with, conformable with, in accordance with, in harmony with, in unison with, in keeping with, squaring with, quadrating with, falling in with, of one mind, of a piece, consistent with, compatible, reconcilable with, commensurate.

Apt, apposite, pertinent, germane, relating to, pat, bearing upon (9), applicable, relevant, fit, fitting, suitable, happy, felicitous, proper, meet, appropriate, suiting, befitting, becoming, seasonable, deft, accommodating, topical.

Phrases: The cap fits; to the point; to the purpose; *rem acu tetigisti*; at home; in one's element.

24 DISAGREEMENT

Substantives: discord, discordance, dissonance, disharmony, dissidence, discrepancy, unconformity, disconformity, nonconformity, incongruity, incongruence, *mésalliance,* discongruity, jarring, clashing, jostling (713), inconsistency, inconsonance, disparity, disproportion, disproportionateness, variance, divergence, jar, misfit.

Unfitness, repugnance, unsuitableness, unsuitability, unaptness, ineptitude, inaptness, impropriety, inapplicability, inadmissibility, irreconcilableness, irreconcilability, incommensurability, inconcinnity, incompatability, inadaptability, interference, intrusion, irrelation (10).

Verbs: To disagree, belie, clash, jar, oppose (708), interfere, jostle (713), intrude.

Phrase: To have no business there.

Adjectives: Disagreeing, discordant, discrepant, jarring, clashing, repugnant, incompatible, irreconcilable, intransigent, inconsistent with, unconformable, incongruous, disproportionate, disproportioned, unproportioned, inharmonious, inconsonant, mismatched, misjoined, misjudged, unconsonant, incommensurable, incommensurate, divergent (291).

Unapt, inapt, inept, inappropriate, improper, unsuited, unsuitable, inapposite, inapplicable, irrelevant, not pertinent, impertinent, malapropos, ill-timed, intrusive, clumsy, unfit, unfitting, unbefitting, unbecoming, misplaced, forced, unseasonable, far fetched, inadmissible, uncongenial, ill-assorted, ill-sorted, repugnant to, unaccommodating, irreducible.

Phrases: Out of season; out of character; out of keeping; out of joint; out of tune; out of place; out of one's element; at odds; a fish out of water.

Adverbs: Discordantly, etc.; at variance with, in defiance of, in contempt of, in spite of, despite

Section III – Quantity

25 QUANTITY
Substantives: magnitude (192), amplitude, size, mass, amount, volume, area, quantum, measure, substance.

Science of quantity, mathematics.

Definite or finite quantity, handful, mouthful, spoonful, bucketful, pailful, etc.; stock, batch, lot.

Adjective: Quantitative.

Phrase: To the tune of.

26 DEGREE
Substantives: grade, gradation, extent, measure, ratio, stint, standard, height, pitch, reach, sweep, radius, amplitude, magnitude, water, calibre, range, scope, shade, tenor, compass, sphere, rank, station, standing, rate, way, sort.

Point, mark, stage, step, position, slot, peg; term (71).

Intensity, might, fullness, strength (31), conversion (144), limit (233).

Adjectives: Comparative, gradual, shading off.

Adverbs: By degrees, gradually, *gradatim*, inasmuch, *pro tanto,* however, howsoever, step by step, rung by rung, bit by bit, little by little, by inches, inch by inch, by slow degrees, by little and little, in some degree, to some extent.

27 EQUALITY
Substantives: parity, co-extension, evenness, equipoise, level, balance, equivalence, equipollence, equilib-rium, poise, equiponderance, par, quits.

Equalization, equation, equilibration, co-ordination, adjustment, symmetry.

A drawn game or battle, a dead heat, a draw, a tie.

A match, peer, compeer, equal, mate, fellow, brother (17), equivalent, makeweight.

Phrases: A distinction without a difference; a photo finish.

Verbs: To be equal, etc., to equal, match, come up to, keep pace with; come to, amount to, balance, cope with.

To render equal, equalize, level, balance, equate, acquiparate, trim, dress, adjust, fit, accommodate, poise, square; to readjust, equipoise, equilibrate, set against.

Phrases: To be or lie on a level with; to come to the same thing.

To strike a balance; to establish or restore equality; to stretch on the bed of Procrustes; to cry quits.

Adjectives: Equal, even, quit, level, coequal, co-ordinate, equivalent, synonymous, tantamount, convertible, equipollent, equiponderant, equiponderous, square.

Rendered equal, equalized, equated, drawn, poised, levelled, balanced, symmetrical, trimmed, dressed.

Phrases: On a par with; on a level with; much of a muchness; as broad as it is long; as good as; all the same; all one; six to one and half a dozen of the other; not a pin to choose between them; tarred with the same brush; diamond cut diamond.

Adverbs: *Pari passu,* equally, symmetrically, *ad eundem,* practically, to all intents and purposes, neck and neck.

28 INEQUALITY
Substantives: disparity, imparity, imbalance, odds, handicap, bisque, difference (15), unevenness.

Preponderance, preponderation, inclination of the balance, advantage, prevalence, partiality.

Superiority (33), a casting vote; inferiority (34).

Verbs: To be unequal, etc., to preponderate, outweigh, outbalance, overbalance, prevail, countervail, predominate, overmatch, outmatch (33).

To fall short of, to want (304), not to come up to.

Phrases: To have or give the advantage; to turn the scale; to kick the beam; to topple over.

Adjectives: Unequal, uneven, disparate, partial, unbalanced, overbalanced, top-heavy, lopsided, preponderating, outweighing, prevailing.

Phrases: More than a match for, above par; below par; *haud passibus aequis.*

29 MEAN

Substantives: medium, intermedium, compromise, average, norm, balance, middle (68), *via media, juste milieu.*

Neutrality, mediocrity, middle course, shuffling.

Phrases: The golden mean; the average man; the man in the street.

Verbs: To compromise, pair off, cancel out.

Phrases: To sit on the fence; split the difference; strike a balance; take the average; reduce to a mean; to take a safe course.

Adjectives: Mean, intermediate, middle, median, normal, average, mediocre, middling, ordinary (82), neutral.

Adverb phrases: On an average; in the long run; half-way; taking the one with the other; taking all things together; in round numbers.

30 COMPENSATION

Substantives: equation, commutation, compromise (774), idemnification, neutralization, nullification, counteraction (179), recoil (277), atonement (952).

A set-off, offset, makeweight, counterpoise, ballast, indemnity, hush-money, amends, equivalent.

Phrases: Measure for measure; give and take; *quid pro quo*; tit for tat.

Verbs: To compensate, make up for, indemnify, countervail, counterpoise, balance, compromise, outbalance, overbalance, counterbalance, counteract, set off, hedge, redeem, neutralize (27), cover.

Phrases: To make good; split the difference; fill up; make amends.

Adjectives: Compensating, compensatory, countervailing, etc., equivalent, equipollent (27).

Phrase: In the opposite scale.

Adverbs: However, yet, but, still, all the same, for all that, nevertheless, none the less, notwithstanding, be that as it may, on the other hand, although, though, albeit, *per contra.*

Phrases: As broad as it's long; taking one thing with another; it is an ill wind that blows nobody any good.

31 GREATNESS

Substantives: largeness, magnitude, size (192), multitude (102), fullness, vastness, immensity, enormity, infinity (105), intensity (26), importance (642), strength.

A large quantity, deal, power, world, macrocosm, mass, heap (72), pile, sight, pot, volume, peck, bushel, load, stack, cart-load, wagon-load, truck-load, ship-load, cargo, lot, flood, spring tide, mobs, bags, oodles, abundance (639), wholesale, store (636).

The greater part (50).

Verbs: To be great, etc., run high, soar, tower, transcend, rise, carry to a great height (305).

Phrases: To know no bounds; to break the record.

Adjectives: Great, gross, large, considerable, big, ample, above par, huge, full, saturated, plenary, deep, signal, extensive, sound, passing, goodly, famous, noteworthy, noble, heavy, precious, mighty (157), arch, sad, piteous, arrant, red-hot, downright, utter, uttermost, crass, lamentable, consummate, rank, thorough-paced, thorough-going, sovereign, unparalleled, matchless, unapproached, extraordinary, intense, extreme, pronounced, unsurpassed, unsurpassable.

Vast, immense, enormous, towering, inordinate, severe, excessive, monstrous, shocking, extravagant, exorbitant, outrageous, whacking, thumping, glaring, flagrant, preposterous, egregious, overgrown, stupendous, monumental, prodigious, marked, pointed, remarkable, astonishing, surprising (870), incredible, marvellous, transcendent, incomparable, tremendous, terrific, formidable, amazing, phenomenal, superhuman, titanic, immoderate.

Indefinite, boundless, unbounded, unlimited, incalculable, illimitable, immeasurable, infinite, unapproachable, unutterable, indescribable, unspeakable, inexpressible, beyond expression, swingeing, unconscionable, fabulous, uncommon, unusual (83).

Undiminished, unrestricted, unabated, unreduced, unmitigated, unredeemed, untempered.

Absolute, positive, decided staring, unequivocal, serious, grave, essential, perfect, finished, completed, abundant (639).

Adverbs: In a great degree, much, muckle, well, considerably, largely, grossly, greatly, very, very much, a deal, not a little, no end, pretty, pretty well, enough, richly, to a large extent, to a great extent, ever so, mainly, ever so much, on a large scale, insomuch, all lengths, wholesale, in a great measure.

In a positive degree, truly (494), positively, verily, really, indeed, actually, in fact, fairly, assuredly, decidedly, surely, clearly, obviously, unequivocally, purely, absolutely, seriously, essentially, fundamentally, radically, downright, in grain, altogether, entirely, completely.

In a comparative degree, comparatively, *pro tanto*, as good as, to say the least, above all, most, of all things, pre-eminently.

In a complete degree, completely (52), altogether, quite, entirely, wholly, totally, *in toto, toto coelo,* utterly, thoroughly, out and out, outright, out and away, fairly, clean, to the full, in every respect, *sous tous les rapports,* in all respects, on all accounts, nicely, perfectly, fully, amply, richly, wholesale, abundantly, consummately, widely, as . . . as . . . can be, every inch, *à fond, de fond,* far and wide, over head and ears, to the backbone, through and through, *ne plus ultra.*

In a greater degree, even, yea, *a fortiori,* still more.

In a high degree, highly, deeply, strongly, mighty, mightily, powerfully (157), profoundly, superlatively, ultra, in the extreme, extremely, exceedingly, excessively, consumedly, sorely, intensely, exquisitely, acutely, soundly, vastly, hugely, immensely, enormously, stupendously, passing, surpassing, supremely, beyond measure, immoderately, monstrously, inordinately, tremendously, over head and ears, extraordinarily, exorbitantly, indefinitely, immeasurably, unspeakably, inexpressibly, ineffably, unutterably, incalculably, infinitely, unsurpassably.

In a marked degree, particularly, remarkably, singularly, uncommonly, unusually, peculiarly, notably, *par excellence*, eminently, pre-eminently, superlatively, signally, famously, egregiously, prominently, glaringly, emphatically, strangely, wonderfully, amazingly, surprisingly, astonishingly, prodigiously, monstrously, incredibly, inconceivably, marvellously, awfully, stupendously.

In a violent degree, violently, severely, furiously, desperately, tremendously, outrageously, extravagantly, confoundedly, deucedly, devilishly, diabolically, with a vengeance, à outrance, like mad (173).

In a painful degree, sadly, grievously, woefully, wretchedly, piteously, sorely, lamentably, shockingly, frightfully, dreadfully, fearfully, terribly, horribly.

32 SMALLNESS

Substantives: littleness, minuteness (193), tenuity, scantness, scantiness, slenderness, meanness, mediocrity, insignificance (643), paucity, fewness (103).

A small quantity, modicum, atom, particle, molecule, corpuscle, microcosm, jot, iota, dot, speck, mote, gleam, scintilla, spark, ace, minutiae, thought, idea, suspicion, soupçon, whit, tittle, shade, shadow, touch, cast, taste, grain, scruple, spice, sprinkling, drop, droplet, driblet, globule, minim, dash, smack, nip, sip, scantling, dole, scrap, mite, slip, snippet, tag, bit, morsel, crumb, paring, shaving (51), trifle, thimbleful, toothful, spoonful, cupful, mouthful, handful, fistful.

Finiteness, a finite quantity.

Phrases: The shadow of a shade; a drop in a bucket or in the ocean.

Verbs: To be small, etc., to run low, diminish, shrink, decrease (36), contract (195).

Phrases: To lie in a nutshell; to pass muster.

Adjectives: Small, little, wee, scant, inconsiderable, diminutive, minute (193), tiny, minikin, puny, petty, sorry, miserable, shabby, wretched, paltry (643), weak (160), slender, feeble, faint, slight, scrappy, fiddling, trivial, scanty, light, trifling, moderate, low, mean, mediocre, passable, passing, light, sparing.

Below par, below the mark, under the mark, at a low ebb, imperfect, unfinished, partial (651), inappreciable, evanescent, infinitesimal, atomic, homoeopathic.

Mere, simple, sheer, bare.

Adverbs: In a small degree, on a small scale, to a small extent, a wee bit, something, somewhat, next to nothing, little, inconsiderably, slightly, so-so, minutely, faintly, feebly, lightly, imperfectly, scantily, shabbily, miserably, wretchedly, sparingly, weakly, slenderly, modestly.

In a limited degree, in a certain degree, to a certain degree or extent, partially, in part, some, somewhat, rather, in some degree, in some measure, something, simply, only, purely, merely, in a manner, at least, at most, ever so little, thus far, pro tanto, next to nothing.

Almost, nearly, well-nigh, all but, short of, not quite, close upon, near the mark.

In an uncertain degree, about, thereabouts, scarcely, hardly, barely, somewhere about, say, more or less, à peu près, there or thereabouts.

In no degree, noways, nowise, nohow, in no wise, by no means, not in the least, not at all, not a bit, not a bit of it, not a whit, not a jot, in no respect, by no manner of means, on no account.

Phrases: As little as may be; after a fashion; in a way.

Within an ace of; on the brink of; next door to; a close shave (or call).

33 SUPERIORITY

Substantives: majority, supremacy, primacy, advantage, preponderance, excess (641), prevalence, pre-eminence, championship.

Maximum, acme, climax, zenith,

summit, utmost height, record, culminating point (210), the height of, lion's share, overweight.

Phrases: A Triton among the minnows; cock of the walk; *ne plus ultra; summum bonum.*

Verbs: To be superior, etc.; to exceed, surpass, excel, eclipse, transcend, top, overtop, o'ertop, cap, beat, cut out, outclass, override, outmatch, outbalance, overbalance, overweigh, overshadow, outdo; preponderate, predominate, prevail.

To render larger, magnify (194).

Phrases: To have the advantage of; to have the upper hand; to bear the palm; to have one cold; to beat hollow; to take the shine out of; to throw into the shade; to be a cut above.

Adjectives: Superior, greater, major, higher, surpassing, exceeding, excelling, passing, ultra, vaulting, transcending, transcendent, unequalled, unsurpassed, peerless, matchless, unparalleled, without parallel.

Supreme, greatest, utmost, paramount, pre-eminent, foremost, crowning, sovereign, culminating, superlative, topmost, top-hole, highest, first-rate, champion, A1, the last word, the limit.

Phrases: *Facile princeps; nulli secundus; primus inter pares.*

Adverbs: Beyond, more, over and above the mark, above par, over and above, at the top of the scale, at its height.

In a superior degree, eminently, pre-eminently, egregiously, prominently, superlatively, supremely, above all, of all things, principally, especially, particularly, peculiarly, *par excellence, a fortiori.*

34 INFERIORITY

Substantives: minority, subordination, shortcoming (304); deficiency, minimum.

Verbs: To be less, inferior, etc., to fall or come short of, not to pass (304); to want, be wanting.

To become smaller, to render smaller (195); to subordinate.

Phrases: To be thrown into the shade; to hide one's diminished head; to give a person best; to play second fiddle.

Adjectives: Inferior, deficient, smaller, minor, less, lesser, lower, sub, subordinate, subaltern, secondary, second-rate, second-best.

Least, smallest, wee-est, minutest, etc., lowest.

Phrases: Weighed in the balance and found wanting; not fit to hold a candle to.

Adverbs: Less, under or below the mark, below par, at the bottom of the scale, at a low ebb, short of, at a disadvantage.

35 INCREASE

Substantives: augmentation, enlargement, extension, dilatation (194), increment, accretion, development, rise, growth, swell, swelling, expansion, aggrandizement, aggravation, exacerbation, spread, climax, exaggeration, diffusion (73), flood-tide; accession (37).

Verbs: To increase, augment, enlarge, amplify, extend, dilate, swell, wax, expand, grow, stretch, shoot up, mushroom, rise, run up, sprout, burgeon, advance, spread, gather head, aggrandize, add, superadd, raise, heighten, strengthen, greaten, exalt, enhance, magnify, redouble, aggravate, exaggerate, exasperate, exacerbate, escalate.

Phrases: To add fuel to the flame; to pour oil on the flames.

Adjectives: Increased, augmented, enlarged, etc., undiminished; cumulative; additional (37).

Adverb: Crescendo.

36 NON-INCREASE. DECREASE

Substantives: diminution, reduction,

63

depreciation, lessening, abatement, bating, declension, falling off, dwindling, contraction (195), shrinking, attentuation, extenuation, anticlimax, abridgment, curtailment (201), coarctation, narrowing; deduction (38). Subsidence, wane, ebb, decrement.

Verbs: To decrease, diminish, lessen, dwindle, decay, crumble, shrink, contract, shrivel, fall off, fall away, waste, wear, wane, ebb, subside, decline, languish, wear off, run low, grow downward.

To abridge, reduce, curtail, cut down, pare down, substract, shorten, cut short, dock (201), bate, abate, fritter away, attenuate, extenuate, lower, weaken, dwarf; to mitigate (174), to throw in the shade.

Phrase: To hide its diminished head.

Adjectives: Decreased, diminished, lessened, etc., shorn, short by, decreasing, on the wane.

Adverbs: *Diminuendo, decrescendo.*

37 ADDITION

Substantives: adjection, introduction, superinduction, annexation, superposition, superaddition, subjunction, supervention, increment, accession, superfetation, corollary, reinforcement, supplement, accompaniment (88), interposition (228), insertion (300).

Verbs: To add, annex, affix, superadd, supplement, reinforce, subjoin, superpose, throw in, clap on, tack to, append, tag, engraft, saddle on, saddle with, superinduce, introduce, work in, interleave, extra-illustrate, grangerize.

To become added, to accrue, advene, supervene.

Phrase: To swell the ranks of.

Adjectives: Added, annexed, etc., additional, supplementary, supplemental, suppletory, subjunctive, adscititious, additive, accessory, cumulative.

Adverbs: Additionally, in addition, more, *plus*, extra, and, also, likewise, too, furthermore, forby, item, and also, and eke, else, besides, to boot, etcetera, and so forth, into the bargain, over and above, moreover.

With, together with, withal, along with, including, inclusive, as well as, not to mention, to say nothing of; jointly, conjointly (43).

38 NON-ADDITION. SUBDUCTION

Substantives: subtraction, abstraction, deduction, deducement, retrenchment, removal, elimination, ablation (789), purgation, curtailment, etc. (36), garbling, mutilation, truncation, abscission, excision, amputation, detruncation, sublation, castration, apocope.

Subtrahend, minuend; decrement, discount.

Verbs: To subduct, exclude, deduct, subtract, abscind, retrench, remove, withdraw, eliminate, bate, detract, deduce, take away, deprive of, curtail (36), garble, truncate, mutilate, eviscerate, exenterate, detruncate, castrate, spay, geld, purge, amputate, cut off, excise, cut out, dock, lop, prune, pare, dress, clip, thin, shear, decimate, abrade (330).

Adjectives: Subtracted, deducted, etc., subtractive.

Adverbs: In deduction, etc., less, *minus*, without, except, excepting, with the exception of, but for, barring, save, exclusive of, save and except (83).

39 ADJUNCT

Substantives: additament, addition, affix, appendage, annex, suffix, postfix, inflexion, augment, increment, augmentation, accessory, item, garnish, sauce, supplement, extra, bonus (810), adjective, addendum, complement, corollary, continuation, increment, reinforcement, pendant, apanage.

Sequel (65), postscript, codicil, envoy, rider, corollary, heel-piece, tag, tab, skirt, flap, lappet, trappings, tail, tailpiece (67), queue, train, suite, cortège, accompaniment (88).

Phrase: More last words.

40 REMAINDER

Substantives: residue, remains, remnant, the rest, relics, leavings, heel-tap, odds and ends, cheese-parings, candle-ends, off-scourings, orts.

Residuum, *caput mortuum,* dregs, refuse (645), scum, recrement (653), ashes, dross, cinders, slag, sediment, silt, alluvium, stubble; slough, exuviae, result, educt.

Surplus, overplus, surplusage, superfluity, excess (641), balance, complement, fag-end, stump, butt, rump, wreck, wreckage, ruins, skeleton.

Verbs: To remain, be left, be left behind, exceed, survive.

Adjectives: Remaining, left, left behind, residual, exuvial, residuary, sedimentary, outstanding, net, cast off, odd, over, unconsumed, surviving, outlying.

Superfluous, over and above, exceeding, redundant (641), supernumerary.

41 MIXTURE

Substantives: admixture, commixture, commixtion, intermixture, alloyage, marriage, miscegenation.

Impregnation, infusion, infiltration, diffusion, suffusion, interspersion, transfusion, seasoning, sprinkling, interlarding, interpolation, interposition (228), intrusion; adulteration, sophistication.

Thing mixed, a touch, spice, tinge, tincture, dash, smack, sprinkling, seasoning, infusion, suspicion, *soupçon,* shade, bit, portion, dose.

Compound resulting from mixture, blend, alloy, amalgam, magma, *mélange,* half and half, hybrid, *tertium*

quid, miscellany, medley, pastiche, pasticcio, patchwork, odds and ends; farrago, jumble (59), mess, salad, sauce, hash, hodge-podge or hotch-potch or hotchpot, mash, mish-mash, job lot, omnium gatherum, gallimaufry, olla podrida, olio, salmagundi, pot-pourri, Noah's ark, cauldron, marquetry, mosaic (440), complex.

A cross, hybrid, mongrel, half-breed, Eurasian, mulatto, quadroon, octoroon, sambo.

Phrases: A mingled yarn; a scratch team.

Verbs: To mix, commix, immix, intermix, associate, join (43), mingle, commingle, intermingle, bemingle, interlard, intersperse, interpose, interpolate (228); shuffle together, hash up, huddle together, deal, pound together, stir up, knead, brew, jumble (59); impregnate with.

To be mixed, to get among, to be entangled with.

To instil, imbue, infuse, infiltrate, dash, tinge, tincture, season, sprinkle, besprinkle, suffuse, transfuse, attemper, medicate, blend, alloy, amalgamate, compound (48), adulterate, sophisticate, infect, cross, intercross, interbreed, interblend.

Adjectives: Mixed, mingled, intermixed, etc., motley, miscellaneous, promiscuous; complex, composite, mixed up with, half-and-half, linsey-woolsey, mongrel, heterogeneous; miscible.

42 SIMPLENESS

Substantives: singleness, purity, clearness, homogeneity.

Purification (652), elimination, sifting, winnowing.

Verbs: To render simple, simplify, sift, winnow, bolt, screen, sort, eliminate; to separate, disjoin (44).

To purify (652).

Adjectives: Simple, uniform, of a

65

piece, homogeneous, single, pure, clear, sheer, blank, neat, absolute, elemental, elementary; unmixed, unmingled, untinged, unblended, uncombined, uncompounded, undecomposed, unadulterated, unsophisticated, undiluted, straight.

Free from, exempt from.
Phrase: Pure and simple.

43 JUNCTION
Substantives: joining, joinder, union, connection, connecting, hook-up, conjunction, conjugation, annexion, annexation, annexment, attachment, compagination, astriction, ligation, alligation, colligation, fastening, linking, accouplement, coupling, matrimony (903), grafting; infibulation, inosculation, symphysis, anastomosis, association (72), concatenation, communication, approach (197).

Joint, join, juncture, pivot, hinge, suture, articulation, commissure, mitre, seam, stitch, meeting, reunion, mortise.

Closeness, firmness, tightness, compactness, attachment, communication.
Verbs: To join, conjoin, unite, connect, associate, put together, embody, re-embody, hold together, lump together, pack, fix together, attach, affix, saddle on, fasten, bind, secure, make fast, grapple, moor, clench (or clinch), catch, tie, pinion, strap, sew, lace, string, stitch, tack, knit, tat, crochet, knot, button, buckle, hitch, lash, truss, bandage, braid, splice, swathe, gird, tether, picket, harness, inspan, bridge over.

· Chain, enchain, shackle, pinion, fetter, manacle, handcuff, lock, latch, belay, brace, hook, clap together, leash, couple, link, yoke, bracket, hang together, pin, nail, bolt, hasp, clasp, clamp, screw, rivet, solder, weld, impact, wedge, rabbet, mortise, mitre, jam, dovetail, enchase, engraft, interlink, inosculate, entwine, enlace, interlace, intertwine, intertwist, interweave, interlock.

To be joined, etc., to hang or hold together, cohere (46).
Adjectives: Joined, conjoined, coupled, etc., bound up together, conjunct, corporate, compact.

Firm, fast, close, tight, taut, secure, set, fixed, impacted, jammed, locked, etc., intervolved, intertwined, inseparable, indissoluble, inseverable, untearable.

Phrases: Hand in hand; rolled into one.
Adverbs: Conjointly, jointly, etc.

With, along with, together with, in conjunction with.

Fast, firmly, closely, etc.

44 DISJUNCTION
Substantives: disconnection, disunity, disunion, disassociation, disengagement, abstraction, abstractedness, isolation, insularity, oasis, separateness, severalness, severality.

Separation, parting, detachment, divorce, sejunction, seposition, segregation, insulation, diduction, discerption, elision, caesura, division, subdivision, break, fracture, rupture, dismemberment, disintegration, dislocation, luxation, severance, disseverance, severing, fission, scission, rescission, abscission, laceration, dilaceration, wrenching, abruption, disruption, avulsion, divulsion, tearing asunder, section, cutting, resection, cleavage, fissure, breach, rent, split, crack, slit, tear, rip, dispersion (73), incision, dissection, vivisection anatomy.

Anatomist, prosector.
Phrase: *Disjecta membra.*
Verbs: To be disjoined, separated, etc., to come off, fall off, get loose, fall to pieces.

To disjoin, disconnect, disunite, part, dispart, detach, separate, space, space out, cut off, rescind, segregate, insulate, dissociate, isolate, disengage, set apart, liberate, loose, set free (750), unloose, unfasten, untie, unbind, disband, unfix, unlace, unclasp, undo, unbutton, unbuckle, unchain, unfetter, untack, unharness, ungird, unpack, unbolt, unlatch, unlock, unlink, uncouple, unpin, unclinch, unscrew, unhook, unrivet, untwist, unshackle, unyoke, unknit, unsolder, ravel out, unravel, disentangle, unpick, unglue, switch off, shut off.

Sunder, divide, subdivide, divorce, sever, dissever, abscind, cut, scissor, incide, incise, snip, nib, cleave, rive, slit, split, split in twain, splinter, chip, crack, snap, burst, rend, break or tear asunder, shiver, crunch, chop, cut up, rip up, hack, hew, slash, whittle, haggle, hackle, discind, tear, lacerate, mangle, mince, gash, hash, knap.

Dissect, cut up, carve, slice, castrate, detruncate, anatomize; take, pull or pick to pieces; unscam, tear to tatters, tear piecemeal, divellicate, disintegrate; dismember, disembowel, eviscerate, disbranch, dislocate, joint, disjoint, behead, mince, break up, crunch, gride, comminute (330), vivisect.
Phrase: To tear limb from limb.
Adjectives: Disjoined, disconnected, etc., snippety, disjointed, multipartite, abstract, disjunctive, isolated, insular, separate, discrete, apart, asunder, loose, free, liberated, disengaged, unattached, unannexed, distinct, unassociated, unconnected, adrift, straggling, dispersed, disbanded, segregated.

Cut off, rescinded, etc., rift, reft.

Capable of being cut, scissile, fissile, discerptible.
Adverbs: Separately, etc., one by one, severally, apiece, apart, adrift, asunder; in the abstract, abstractedly.

45 VINCULUM
Substantives: link, connective, connection, junction (43), conjunction, copula, intermedium, hyphen, bridge, stepping-stone, isthmus, span, girder.

Bond, filament, fibre (205), hair, cordage, cord, thread, string, packthread, twine, twist, whipcord, tape, ferret, raffia, line, snood, ribbon, riband, rope, cable, hawser, painter, halyard, guy, guy-rope, wire, chain.

Fastening, tie, tendril, tendon, ligament, ligature, strap, tackle, rigging, traces, harness, yoke, band, withe, withy, brace, bandage, roller, fillet, thong, braid, inkle, girth, cinch, cestus, girdle, garter, halter, noose, lasso, lariat, surcingle, knot, running-knot, slip-knot, reef-knot, sailor's knot, granny-knot, etc.

Pin, corking-pin, safety-pin, nail, brad, tack, skewer, staple, clamp, vice, bracket, cramp, screw, button, buckle, brooch, clasp, slide, clip, hasp, hinge, hank, bolt, catch, latch, latchet, tag, hook, tooth, hook and eye, lock, locket, holdfast, padlock, rivet, anchor, grappling-iron, stake, post, gyve, shackle (752).

Cement, adhesive, mucilage, glue, gum, paste, size, goo, solder, lute, putty, bird-lime, mortar, stucco, plaster, grout.

46 COHERENCE
Substantives: cohesion, adherence, adhesion, accretion, concretion, agglutination, conglutination, aggregation, consolidation, set, cementation, soldering, welding, grouting.

Sticking, clinging, adhesiveness, stickiness, gumminess, gummosity, glutinosity (352), cohesiveness, density (321), inseparability, inseparableness, tenaciousness, tenacity.

Clot, concrete, cake, lump, conglomerate (321).
Verbs: To cohere, adhere, stick, cling, cleave, hold, take hold of, hold fast, hug, grow or hang together, twine round.

To concrete, curdle, cake.

To glue, agglutinate, conglutinate,

agglomerate, consolidate, solidify (321); cement, lute, paste, gum, grout, stick, solder, weld.

Phrases: To stick like a leech; to stick like wax; to cling like ivy, like a bur, like a limpet.

Adjectives: Cohesive, adhesive, cohering, tenacious, sticky, tacky, glutinous, gluey, gooey, gummy, viscous (352), agglutinatory.

United, unseparated, sessile, inseparable, inextricable, infrangible (321).

47 INCOHERENCE

Substantives: non-adhesion, immiscibility, looseness, laxity, slackness, relaxation, freedom, disjunction.

Phrases: A rope of sand; *disjecta membra*.

Verbs: To loosen, make loose, slacken, relax, unglue, unsolder, etc., detach, untwist, unravel, unroll (44, 313), to comminute (330).

Adjectives: Incoherent, immiscible, detached, non-adhesive, loose, slack, lax, relaxed, baggy.

Segregated, flapping, streaming, dishevelled, unincorporated, unconsolidated, uncombined.

Phrase: Like grains of sand.

48 COMBINATION

Substantives: union, unification, synthesis, incorporation, amalgamation, coalescence, crasis, fusion, embodiment, conflation, absorption, blending, centralization; mixture (41).

Compound, composition, amalgam, impregnation, decompound, decomposite, resultant.

Verbs: To combine, unite, unify, incorporate, amalgamate, synthesize, embody, unify, re-embody, blend, merge, fuse, absorb, melt into one, consolidate, coalesce, centralize; to impregnate, to put together, to lump together.

Adjectives: Combined, compound, composite, coalescent, synthetic, synthetical, impregnated with, engrained.

49 DECOMPOSITION

Substantives: analysis, resolution, dissolution, disintegration, catalysis, electrolysis, corruption (653), dispersion (73), disjunction (44).

Verbs: To decompose, rot, disembody, analyse, electrolyse, decompound, resolve, take to pieces, separate into its elements, dissect, unravel (313), break up.

Adjectives: Decomposed, etc., catalytic, analytic, analytical, corrupted, dissolved.

50 WHOLE

Substantives: totality, integrity, integrality, allness, entireness, entirety, *ensemble,* collectiveness, individuality, unity (87), indivisibility, indiscerptibility, indissolubility; embodiment, integration.

All, the whole, total, aggregate, integer, gross amount, sum, sum total, *tout ensemble*, upshot, trunk, hull, skeleton, hulk, lump, heap (72).

The principal part, bulk, mass, tissue, staple, body, compages, the main, the greater part, major part.

Phrases: The whole caboodle; the whole boiling.

Verbs: To form or constitute a whole, to integrate, embody, aggregate, amass (72), to total, amount to, come to.

Adjectives: Whole, total, integral, entire, one, unbroken, uncut, undivided, seamless, individual, unsevered, unclipped, uncropped, unshorn, undiminished, undemolished, undissolved, unbruised, undestroyed, indivisible, indissoluble, indissolvable, indiscerptible.

Wholesale, sweeping.

Adverbs: Wholly, altogether, totally, entirely, all, all in all, as a whole, wholesale, in the aggregate, in the mass, *en masse,* in the lump, *en bloc,* on the whole, *in toto,* in the gross, *in extenso,* in the bulk, to the full, throughout, every inch.

Phrases: To long and short of it; nearly or almost all; root and branch; lock, stock, and barrel; hook, line and sinker; in the long run; in the main; neck and crop; from end to end; from beginning to end; from first to last; from head to foot; from top to toe; fore and aft; from alpha to omega.

51 PART

Substantives: portion, item, division, subdivision, section, chapter, verse, extract, passage, gobbet, sector, segment, fraction, fragment, frustum, detachment, piece, bit, lump, chunk, dollop, scrap, whit, swatch, morsel, mouthful, scantling, cantle, cantlet, slip, crumb (32), fritter, rag, tag, shred, tatter, splinter, snatch, cut, cutting, snip, snippet, snick, collop, slice, chip, chipping, shiver, sliver, matchwood, spillikin, smithereens, driblet, clipping, paring, shaving, debris, odds and ends, oddments, sundries, detritus, lamina, shadow, flotsam and jetsam, pickings.

Parcel, share, instalment, contingent, compartment, department, dividend, dose, particular, article, clause, paragraph.

Member, limb, lobe, lobule, arm, branch, scion, bough, joint, link, ramification (256), twig, bush, spray, sprig, offshoot, leaf, leaflet, stump, stub, butt, rump, torso.

Verbs: To part, divide, subdivide, break (44); to partition, parcel out, portion, apportion (786), to ramify, branch, branch out.

Adjectives: Part, fractional, fragmentary, scrappy, lobular, sectional, aliquot, divided, multifid, partitioned, isomeric.

Adverbs: Partly, in part, partially, piecemeal, in detail, part by part, by driblets, bit by bit, little by little, by inches, inch by inch, foot by foot, drop by drop, in snatches, by fits and starts.

52 COMPLETENESS

Substantives: entirety, fullness, impletion, completion (729), perfection (650), solidity, stop-gap, makeweight, padding, filling up, integration, absoluteness, sufficiency; complement, supplement (39).

Fill, load, bumper, brimmer, bellyful, skinful.

Verbs: To be complete, etc., suffice (639).

To render complete or whole, to complete, exhaust, perfect, finish, make up, fill up, charge, load, replenish, make good, piece out, eke out.

Phrases: To give the finishing touch; to supply deficiencies; to go to all lengths; to go the whole hog; to thrash out.

Adjectives: Complete, entire, whole (50), absolute, perfect, full, plenary, solid, undivided, with all its parts, supplementary, adscititious, thorough, exhaustive, radical, sweeping, searching; consummate, thorough-paced, regular, sheer, unmitigated, unqualified.

Crammed, saturated, brimful, chock-full.

Adverbs: Completely, entirely, to the full, outright, wholly, totally, thoroughly (31), *in toto, toto caelo,* in all respects.

Phrases: To the top of one's bent; up to the ears; *à fond;* from first to last; from beginning to end; *ab ovo usque ad mala.*

53 INCOMPLETENESS

Substantives: deficiency, defectiveness, shortcoming (304), unreadiness, defalcation, failure, imperfection (651), hollowness, patchiness.

Part wanting, omission, defect,

break, deficit, ullage, caret, lacuna, hiatus (198).
Verbs: To be incomplete, etc., to fail, fall short (304).

To dock, lop, mutilate, garble, truncate, castrate (38).
Adjectives: Incomplete, unfinished, imperfect, defective, deficient, wanting, failing, short by, hollow, meagre, insufficient, half-baked, perfunctory, sketchy, scrappy, patchy.

Mutilated, garbled, docked, lopped, truncated; proceeding, in progress.
Phrase: *Cetera desunt.*

54 COMPOSITION

Substantives: make-up, constitution, constituency, crasis.

Inclusion, admission, comprehension, reception.
Verbs: To be composed of, to consist of, be made of, formed of, made up of, be resolved into.

To contain, include, hold, comprehend, take in, admit, embrace, involve, implicate.

To compose, constitute, form, make, make up, fill up, build up, put together, embody.

To enter into the composition of, to be or form part of (51), to merge in, be merged in.
Adjectives: Comprehending, containing, including, comprising, etc.

Component, constituent, formative, forming, constituting, composing, etc., belonging to, appertaining to, inclusive.

55 EXCLUSION

Substantives: non-admission, omission, exception, rejection, proscription, repudiation, exile, banishment, excommunication.

Separation, segregation, elimination, seposition.
Verbs: To be excluded from, etc., to be out of it.

To exclude, shut out, bar, leave out,

omit, reject, repudiate, neglect, blackball; lay, put, or set apart or aside; segregate, pass over, throw overboard, slur over, neglect (460), excommunicate, banish, expatriate, extradite, deport, ostracize, relegate, rusticate, send down (297), rule out.

To eliminate, weed, winnow, screen, bar, separate (44), strike off.
Phrase: 'Include me out.'
Adjectives: Excluding, omitting, etc., exclusive.

Excluded, omitted, etc., unrecounted, inadmissible.
Adverbs: Except, save, bar, barring, excepting.

56 COMPONENT

Substantives: component part, integral part, element, constituent, ingredient, member, limb (51), part and parcel, contents (190), appurtenance, feature, personnel.

57 EXTRANEOUSNESS

Substantives: extrinsicality (5), exteriority (220).

A foreign body, alien, stranger, intruder, outsider, incomer, interloper, foreigner, dago, wop, *novus homo*, parvenu, immigrant, newcomer, new chum, pommy, greenhorn, tenderfoot.
Adjectives: Extraneous, foreign, alien, tramontane, ultramontane, interloping.
Adverbs: Abroad, in foreign parts, overseas.

Section IV – Order

58 ORDER

Substantives: regularity, orderliness, tidiness, uniformity, even tenor, symmetry.

Gradation, progression, pedigree, line, descent, subordination, course, series (69), array, routine.

Method, disposition, arrangement, system, economy, discipline, pattern, plan.

Rank, station, hierarchy, place, status, stand, scale, step, stage, period, term (71), footing; rank and file, pecking order.

Verbs: To be or become in order, to form, fall in, arrange itself, place itself, range itself, fall into its place, fall into rank.

Adjectives: Orderly, regular, in order, arranged, etc. (60), in its proper place, correct, tidy, shipshape, trim, *en règle,* well regulated, methodical, business-like, uniform, symmetrical, systematic, unconfused, undisturbed, untangled, unruffled, unravelled, still, etc. (265).

Phrases: In apple-pie order; Bristol fashion.

Adverbs: Systematically, methodically, etc., in turn, in its turn.

Step by step, by regular steps, gradations, stages, periods, or intervals, periodically (138).

At stated periods (138), *gradatim, seriatim.*

Phrase: Like clockwork.

59 DISORDER

Substantives: irregularity, asymmetry, anomaly, confusion, confusedness, disarray, untidiness, jumble, huddle, litter, lumber, farrago, mess, hash, clutter, pie, muddle, mix-up, upset, hotchpotch, hugger-mugger, anarchy, anarchism, imbroglio, chaos, tohubohu, omnium gatherum (41), derangement (61).

Complexness, complexity, complication, intricacy, intricateness, implication, perplexity, involution, ravelling, tangle, entanglement, snarl, knot, coil, skein, sleave, network, labyrinth, Gordian knot, jungle.

Turmoil, *mêlée,* tumult, ferment, stew, fermentation, pudder, pother riot, uproar, bobbery, rough-house,

rumpus, scramble, fracas, vortex, whirlpool, maelstrom, hurly-burly, bear-garden, Babel, Saturnalia, Donnybrook, pandemonium.

Tumultuousness, riotousness, inquietude (173), derangement (61), topsyturvydom (218).

Phrases: Wheels within wheels; confusion worse confounded; most admired disorder; *concordia discors;* hell broke loose.

A pretty kettle of fish; a fine state of things; a how-d'ye-do; the fat in the fire; a bull in a china shop; the devil to pay.

The cart before the horse; hysteron proteron.

Verbs: To be out of order, irregular, disorderly, etc., to ferment.

To derange, put out of order (61).

Phrases: To be at cross-purposes; to make hay of.

Adjectives: Disorderly, orderless, out of order, disordered, misplaced, out of place, deranged, disarranged (61), irregular, desultory, anomalous, untidy, sloppy, slovenly, tousled, straggling, unarranged, immethodical, unsymmetrical, unsystematic, unmethodical, undigested, unsorted, unclassified, unclassed, asymmetrical.

Disjointed, out of joint, out of gear, out of kilter, confused, tangled, involved, intricate, complicated, inextricable, irreducible.

Mixed, scattered, promiscuous, indiscriminate, casual.

Tumultuous, turbulent, riotous, troublous, tumultuary (173), rough-and-tumble.

Adverbs: Irregularly, etc., by fits and snatches, pell-mell; higgledy-piggledy, hugger-mugger; at sixes and sevens; helter-skelter, harum-scarum, anyhow.

60 ARRANGEMENT

Substantives: disposal, disposition, collocation, allocation, distribution, sorting, assortment, allotment, apportionment, marshalling, alignment, taxis, taxonomy, gradation, organization, ordination; plan (626).

Analysis, sifting, screening, classification.

Result of arrangement, digest, synopsis, analysis, table, register (551).

Instrument for sorting, sieve, riddle, screen (260).

Verbs: To order, reduce to order, bring into order, introduce order into.

To arrange, dispose, place, form; to put, set, place, etc., in order; to set out, collocate, pack, marshal, range, align (or aline), rank, group, parcel out, allot, distribute, assort, sort, sift, riddle.

To class, classify, categorize, file, string, thread, tabulate, pigeon-hole, catalogue, index, register, take stock.

To methodize, digest, regulate, size, grade, gradate, graduate, alphabetize, co-ordinate, systematize, organize, settle, fix, rearrange.

To unravel (246), disentangle, ravel, card, disembroil.

Phrases: To put or set to rights; to assign places to.

Adjectives: Arranged, methodical (58), embattled, in battle array.

Phrase: A place for everything, and everything in its place.

61 DERANGEMENT

Substantives: disarrangement, misarrangement, displacement, misplacement, dislocation, discomposure, disturbance, bedevilment, disorganization, perturbation, shuffling, rumpling, embroilment, corrugation (258), inversion (218), jumble, muddle, disorder (59).

Verbs: To derange, disarrange, misarrange, misplace, mislay, discompose, disorder, embroil, unsettle, disturb, confuse, perturb, jumble, tumble, huddle, shuffle, muddle, toss, hustle, fumble; to bring, put, or throw into disorder, trouble, confusion, etc., break the ranks, upset.

To unhinge, put out of joint, dislocate, turn over, invert; turn topsy-turvy; turn inside out (218), bedevil, throw out of gear.

To complicate, involve, perplex, tangle, entangle, embrangle (or imbrangle), ravel, ruffle, tousle, rumple, dishevel, muss, litter, scatter, make a mess of, monkey with, make hay of.

Adjectives: Deranged, etc., disordered (59).

62 PRECEDENCE

Substantives: coming before, antecedence, antecedency, anteposition, priority (116), anteriority, the *pas,* the lead.

Superiority (33), precession (280).

Verbs: To precede, come before, lead, introduce, usher in.

To place before; to prefix, affix, premise, prelude, preface, prologize.

Phrases: To have the *pas*; to take the lead; to have the start; set the fashion; to open the ball.

Adjectives: Preceding, precedent, antecedent, anterior, prior, previous, before, ahead of, leading.

Former, foregoing; coming or going before; precursory, precursive, prevenient, inaugural, prodromal, prodromic, preliminary, aforesaid, said, aforementioned, prefatory, introductory, prelusive, prelusory, proemial, preparatory, preambulatory.

Adverbs: In advance, ahead, in front of, before, in the van (234).

63 SEQUENCE

Substantives: coming after, consecution, succession, posteriority (117), secondariness; following (281).

Continuation, order of succession, successiveness; alternation (138).

Subordination, inferiority (34).

Phrase: *Proxime accessit.*

Verbs: To succeed, come after, follow, come next, ensue, come on, tread close upon; to alternate.

To place after, to suffix, append.

Phrases: To be in the wake or trail of; to tread on the heels of; to step into the shoes of; to assume the mantle of.

Adjectives: Succeeding, coming after, following, subsequent, ensuing, sequent, sequacious, consequent, next; consecutive, amoebean, alternate (138).

Latter, posterior.

Adverbs: After, subsequently, since, behind, in the wake of, in the train of, at the tail of, in the rear of (234).

64 PRECURSOR

Substantives: antecedent, precedent, predecessor, forerunner, pioneer, outrider, avant-courier, leader, bellwether, herald, harbinger.

Prelude, preamble, preface, foreword, prologue, prodrome, protasis, prolusion, overture, premise, proem, prolepsis, prolegomena, prefix, introduction, heading, advertisement, frontispiece, groundwork (673).

Adjectives: Precursory, prefatory (62).

65 SEQUEL

Substantives: afterpart, aftermath, suffix, successor, tail, runner-up, queue, train, wake, trail, rear, retinue, suite, appendix (39), postscript, epilogue, peroration, excursus, afterpiece, tailpiece, tag, colophon, afterthought, second thoughts, *arrière pensée,* codicil, continuation, sequela, apodosis.

Phrases: More last words; to be continued.

Adjectives: Subsequent, ensuing (63).

66 BEGINNING

Substantives: commencement, opening, outset, incipience, inception, inchoation, initiative, overture, exordium, introduction (64), inauguration, début, onset, brunt, alpha.

Origin, source, rise, conception, birth, infancy, bud, embryo, germ, egg, rudiment, *incunabula,* start, cradle, starting-point, starting-post (293); dawn, morning (125).

Van, vanguard, title-page, heading, front (234), fore-part, head (210).

Opening, entrance, entry, inlet, orifice, porch, portal, portico, gateway, door, gate, postern, wicket, threshold, vestibule, mouth, *fauces,* lips.

Alphabet, A B C, rudiments, elements.

Phrase: The rising of the curtain; the thin end of the wedge.

Verbs: To begin, commence, inchoate, rise, arise, originate, initiate, open, dawn, set in, take its rise, enter upon, embark on, set out (293), recommence, undertake (676).

To usher in, lead off, lead the way, take the lead or the initiative; head, stand at the head, stand first; broach, set on foot, set a-going, set abroach, set up, handsel, institute, launch, strike up.

Phrases: To make a beginning; to cross the Rubicon; to break ground; set the ball in motion; take the initiative; break the ice; fire away; open the ball; kick off; tee up; pipe up.

Adjectives: Beginning, commencing, arising, initial, initiatory, initiative, inceptive, incipient, proemial, inaugural, inchoate, inchoative, embryonic, primigenial, aboriginal, rudimental, nascent, natal, opening, dawning, entering.

First, foremost, leading, heading, maiden.

Begun, commenced, etc.

Adverbs: At, or in the beginning, at first blush, first, in the first place, *imprimis,* first and foremost, *in limine,* in the bud, in embryo.

From the beginning, *ab initio, ab ovo.*

67 END

Substantives: close, termination, desinence, conclusion, finish, finis, finale, period, term, terminus, limit, last, omega, extreme, extremity, butt-end, fag-end, stub, tail, nib, tip, after-part, rear (235), colophon, coda, tail-piece, tag, *cul-de-lampe,* peroration, swan-song.

Completion (729), winding-up, *dénouement,* catastrophe, consummation, expiration, expiry, finishing stroke, knock-out, K.O., death-blow, *coup de grâce,* upshot, issue, fate, doom, Day of Judgment, doomsday.

Phrases: The *ne plus ultra;* the fall of the curtain; *'le commencement de la fin.'*

Verbs: To end, close, finish, expire, terminate, conclude; come or draw to an end, close or stop, be all over, pass away, give out, peter out, run its course; to say one's say, perorate, be through with.

To come last, bring up the rear.

To bring to an end, close, etc., to put a period, etc., to; to make an end of; to close, finish, seal, wind up, complete, achieve (729), crown, determine.

Phrases: To cut the matter short; to shut up shop.

Adjectives: Ending, closing, etc., final, terminal, eschatological, desisive, definitive, crowning.

Last, ultimate, penultimate, antepenultimate, hindermost, rear, caudal, conterminal, conterminous.

Ended, closed, terminated, etc., through.

Unbegun, fresh, uncommenced.

Adverbs: Once for all, in fine, finally, at the end of the day, for good, for good and all.

68 MIDDLE

Substantives: midst, mean, medium, happy medium, *via media,* middle term, centre (223), *mezzo termine, juste milieu,* half-way house, hub, nave, navel, omphalos, bull's-eye, nucleus.

Equidistance, equator, diaphragm, midriff; bisection (91).

Intervenience, interjacence, intervention (228), mid-course (628).

Adjectives: Middle, medial, median, mesial, mean, mid, middlemost, midmost, mediate, intermediate (29), intervenient, interjacent (228), central (222), equidistant, embosomed, merged.

Mediterranean, equatorial.

Adverbs: In the middle, amid, amidst, midway, amidships, half-way.

Phrases: In the thick of; *in medias res.*

69 CONTINUITY

Substantives: consecution, consecutiveness, succession, suite, progression, series, train, chain, catenation, concatenation, scale, gradation, course, procession, column, retinue, cortège, cavalcade, rank and file, line of battle, array, pedigree, genealogy, lineage, race.

File, queue, echelon, line, row, rank, range, tier, string, thread, team, tandem, random, suit, flush, colonnade.

Verbs: To follow in, form a series, etc.; to fall in.

To arrange in a series, to marshal (60); to string together, file, thread, graduate, tabulate.

Adjectives: Continuous, sequent, consecutive, progressive, serial, successive, continued, uninterrupted, unbroken, entire, linear, in a line, in a row, etc., gradual, constant, unremitting, unintermitting, evergreen (110).

Adverbs: Continuously, consecutively, etc., *seriatum;* in a line, row, series, etc., in succession, etc., running, gradually, step by step; uninterruptedly, at a stretch, at one go.

Phrase: In Indian file.

70 DISCONTINUITY

Substantives: interruption, pause, period, interregnum, break, interval, interlude, episode, lacuna, cut, gap, fracture, fault, chasm, hiatus (198), caesura, parenthesis, rhapsody, anacoluthon.

Intermission, alternation (138); a broken thread, broken melody.

Verbs: To be discontinuous, etc.; to alternate, intermit.

To discontinue, pause, interrupt, break, interposte (228); to break in upon, disconnect (44); to break or snap the thread.

Adjectives: Discontinuous, inconsecutive, broken, interrupted, unsuccessive, desultory, disconnected, unconnected, fitful, spasmodic, sporadic, scattered.

Alternate, every other, intermitting, alternating (138).

Phrase: Few and far between.

Adverbs: At intervals, by snatches, *per saltum,* by fits and starts, *longo intervallo.*

71 TERM

Substantives: rank, station, stage, step, rung, round, degree (26), remove, grade, link, place, peg, mark, point, *pas,* period, pitch, stand, standing, status, footing, range.

Verbs: To hold, occupy, find, fall into a place, station.

72 ASSEMBLAGE

Substantives: collection, dozen, collocation, compilation, levy, gathering, ingathering, muster, round-up, colligation, contesseration, *attroupement,* association, concourse, conflux, convergence, meeting, assembly, congregation, at home (892), levee, club, reunion, gaudy, soirée, conversazione, accumulation, cumulation, array, mobilization.

Congress, convocation, convention, *comitium,* committee, quorum, conclave, synod, caucus, conventicle, eisteddfod, mass-meeting.

Miscellany, olla podrida, museum, *collectanea,* menagerie (636), Noah's ark, anthology, encyclopaedia, portfolio, file.

A multitude (102), crowd, throng, rabble, mob, press, crush, horde, posse, body, tribe, crew, gang, knot, band, party, swarm, school, shoal, bevy, galaxy, covey, flock, herd, drove, corps, troop, troupe, squad, squadron, phalanx, platoon, company, regiment, battalion, legion, host, army, division.

A sounder (of swine), skulk (of foxes), pride (of lions), charm (of finches), flush (of mallards), gaggle (of geese), wedge (of swans).

Clan, brotherhood, fraternity, sisterhood, party (712).

Volley, shower, storm, cloud, flood, deluge.

Group, cluster, clump, set, batch, battery, pencil, lot, pack, budget, assortment, bunch, parcel, packet, package, bundle, fascicle, fascicule, *fasciculus,* faggot, wisp, truss, tuft, rosette, shock, rick, fardel, stack, sheaf, stook, haycock.

Accumulation, congeries, heap, hoard, lump, pile, rouleau, tissue, mass, pyramid, bale, drift, snowball, acervation, cumulation, glomeration, agglomeration, conglobation, conglomeration, conglomerate, coacervation, coagmentation, aggregation, concentration (290), congestion, omnium gatherum.

Collector, tax-gatherer, whip, whipper-in.

Verbs: To assemble, collect, muster, meet, unite, cluster, swarm, flock, herd, crowd, throng, associate, congregate, conglomerate, concentrate, congest, rendezvous, resort, flock together, get together, reassemble.

To bring, get or gather together, collect, draw together, group, convene, convoke, convocate, collocate, colligate, round-up, scrape together, rake up, dredge, bring into a focus, amass, accumulate, heap up, pile, pack, do up, stack, truss, cram, pack together, congest, acervate, coagment, agglomerate, garner up, lump together, make a parcel of; to centralize; to mobilize.

Phrases: To heap Pelion upon Ossa; to collect in a drag-net.

Adjectives: Assembled, collected, etc., undispersed, met together, closely packed, dense, crowded, serried, huddled together, teeming, swarming, populous.

Phrases: Packed like sardines; crowded to suffocation.

73 NON-ASSEMBLAGE.
   DISPERSION

Substantives: scattering, dissemination, diffusion, dissipation, spreading, casting, distribution, apportionment, sprinkling, respersion, circumfusion, interspersion, divergence (291), demobilization.

Odds and ends, waifs and strays, flotsam and jetsam.

Verbs: To disperse, scatter, sow, disseminate, diffuse, shed, spread, overspread, dispense, disband, disembody, distribute, dispel, cast forth; strew, bestrew, sprinkle, sparge, issue, deal out, utter, resperse, intersperse, set abroach, circumfuse; to decentralize, demobilize; to hive-off.

Phrases: To turn adrift; to scatter to the four winds; to sow broadcast; to spread like wildfire.

Adjectives: Unassembled, uncollected, dispersed, scattered, diffused, sparse, spread, dispread, widespread, sporadic, cast, broadcast, epidemic, adrift.

Adverbs: *Sparsim,* here and there, *passim.*

74 FOCUS

Substantives: point of convergence, corradiation, rendezvous, home, headquarters, club, centre (222), gathering-place, meeting-place, trysting-place, rallying-ground, haunt, howff, resort, museum, repository, depot (636).

75 CLASS

Substantives: division, category, predicament, head, order, section, department, domain, province.

Kind, sort, variety, type, genus, species, family, phylum, race, tribe, caste, sept, clan, *gens,* phratry, breed, kith, sect, set, assortment, feather, stripe, suit, range, run.

Gender, sex, kin, kidney, manner, nature, description, denomination, designation, character, stamp, stuff, *genre.*

Adjectives: Generic, racial, tribal, etc.
Verbs: To classify, catalogue (60).

76 INCLUSION

Substantives: comprehension under a class, reference to a class, admission, comprehension, reception, subsumption.

Inclusion in a compound, composition (54).

Verbs: To be included in, to come under, to fall under, to range under; to belong, or pertain to, appertain; to range with, to merge in, to be of.

To include, comprise, comprehend, contain, admit, embrace, receive; to enumerate among, reckon among, reckon with, number among, refer to, place under, class with or among, arrange under or with, take into account, subsume.

Adjectives: Including, inclusive, all-embracing, congener, congeneric, congenerous, *et hoc genus omne,* etcetera.

Included, merged, etc.
Phrase: Birds of a feather.

77 EXCLUSION from a class

Substantives: Rejection, proscription.

Exclusion from a compound (55).
Verbs: To be excluded from, etc.; to exclude, proscribe, debar, rule out, set apart (55).

Phrase: To shut the door upon.
Adjectives: Exclusive, excluding, etc.

78 GENERALITY
Substantives: university, catholicism, catholicity.

Every man, every one, everybody, all, all hands.

Miscellaneousness, miscellany, encyclopaedia, generalization, prevalence, drag-net.
Phrases: The world and his wife; N or M.
Verbs: To be general, common, or prevalent, to prevail.

To render general, to generalize.
Adjectives: General, generic, collective, comprehensive, encyclopaedic, panoramic, bird's-eye, sweeping, radical, universal, world-wide, cosmopolitan, catholic, common, oecumenical, transcendental, prevalent, prevailing, all-pervading, epidemic, all-inclusive.

Unspecified, impersonal; every, all.
Adverbs: Whatever, whatsoever, to a man; generally, universally, on the whole, for the most part.

79 SPECIALITY
Substantives: particularity, peculiarity, individuality, haecceity, thisness, personality, characteristic, mannerism, idiosyncrasy, trick, gimmick, specificness, specificity, eccentricity, singularity (83).

Version, reading (522).

Particulars, details, items, counts.

I, myself, self, I myself, *moi qui vous parle.*
Phrases: *Argumentum ad hominem;* local colour.
Verbs: To specify, particularize, individualize, realize, specialize, designate, determine.
Phrases: To descend to particulars; to enter into detail.
Adjectives: Special, particular, individual, specific, proper, appropriate, personal, private, respective, several, definite, determinate, especial, certain, esoteric, endemic, partial, party, peculiar, characteristic, distinctive, typical, unique, diagnostic, exclusive, *sui generis,* singular, exceptional (83).

This, that, yonder, yon, such and such.
Adverbs: Specially, specifically, etc., in particular, respectively, personally, individually, *in propria persona.*

Each, apiece, one by one, severally, seriatim, namely, *videlicet,* viz., to wit.

80 RULE
Substantives: regularity, uniformity, constancy, standard, model, nature, principle, the order of things, routine, prevalence, practice, usage, custom, use, habit (613), regulation, precept (697), convention, *convenances*

Form, formula, law, canon, principle, keynote, catchword.

Type, archetype, pattern, precedent, paradigm, the normal, natural, ordinary or model state or condition; norm, control.
Phrases: A standing order; the bed of Procrustes; law of the Medes and Persians.
Adjectives: Regular, uniform, constant (82).

81 MULTIFORMITY
Substantives: variety, diversity, multifariousness, allotropy, allotropism.
Adjectives: Multiform, variform, polymorphic, multifold, manifold, multifarious, multigenerous, omnifarious, omnigenous, heterogeneous, motley, epicene, indiscriminate, desultory, irregular, diversified, allotropic; different (15).
Phrase: Of all sorts and kinds.

82 CONFORMITY
Substantives: conformance, observance, naturalization, harmony, convention (613).

Example, instance, specimen, sample, ensample, exemplar, exemplification, illustration, pattern (22), object lesson, case in point, quotation, the rule.

Phrases: The order of the day; the common or ordinary run of things (23); a matter of course.

Verbs: To conform to rule, be regular, orthodox, etc., to follow, observe, go by, bend to, obey rules; to be guided or regulated by, be wont, etc. (613), to comply or chime in with, to be in harmony with, follow suit; to standardize, naturalize.

To exemplify, illustrate, cite, quote, put a case, produce an instance, set an example.

Phrases: To go with the crowd; to do in Rome as the Romans do; to follow the fashion; to swim with the stream; to keep one in countenance.

Adjectives: Conformable to rule, regular, uniform, constant, steady, according to rule, *en règle, de rigueur,* normal, well regulated, formal, canonical, orthodox, conventional, strict, rigid, positive, uncompromising (23).

Ordinary, natural, usual, common, wonted, accustomed, habitual (613), household, average, everyday, current, rife, prevailing, prevalent, established, received, stereotyped, acknowledged, typical, accepted, recognized, representative, hackneyed, well-known, familiar, vernacular, commonplace, trite, banal, cut and dried, naturalized, orderly, shipshape, run of the mill.

Exemplary, illustrative, in point, of daily or everyday occurrence, in the order of things.

Phrases: Regular as clockwork; according to Cocker (or Hoyle).

Adverbs: Conformably, by rule, regularly, etc., agreeably to; in accordance, conformity, or keeping with.

Usually, generally, ordinarily, commonly, for the most part, as usual, *more solito, more suo, pro more;* of

course, as a matter of course, *pro forma.*

Always, uniformly (16), invariably, without exception, never otherwise.

For example, for instance, *exempli gratia, inter alia.*

Phrases: *Ab uno disce omnes; ex pede Herculem; ex ungue leonem;* birds of a feather.

83 UNCONFORMITY

Substantives: nonconformity, unconventionality, informality, arbitrariness, abnormity, abnormality, anomaly, anomalousness, lawlessness, peculiarity, exclusiveness; infraction, breach, violation, of law or rule; individuality, idiosyncrasy, mannerism, eccentricity, aberration, irregularity, unevenness, variety, singularity, rarity, oddity, oddness, exemption, salvo.

Exception, nondescript, a character, original, nonesuch, monster, monstrosity, prodigy (872), *lusus naturae, rara avis,* freak, curiosity, crank, queer fish; half-caste, half-breed, cross-breed, mongrel, hybrid, mule, mulatto (41), *tertium quid,* hermaphrodite, sport.

Phoenix, chimera, hydra, sphinx, minotaur, griffin, centaur, hippocentaur, hippogriff, basilisk, cockatrice, tragelaph, kraken, dragon, wyvern, roc, sea-serpent, mermaid, merman, cyclops, unicorn.

Phrases: Out of one's element; a fish out of water; neither one thing nor another; neither fish, flesh, nor fowl, nor good red herring; a law to oneself.

Verbs: To be unconformable to rule, to be exceptional, etc.; to violate a law or custom, to stretch a point.

Phrases: To have no business there; to beggar description.

Adjectives: Unconformable, exceptional, abnormal, anomalous, anomalistic, out of order, out of place, misplaced, irregular, unorthodox, uneven, arbitrary, informal, aberrant, stray, peculiar, funny, exclusive, unnatural, eccentric, unconventional, Bohemian, beatnick, hippy, yippy.

Unusual, unaccustomed, unwonted, uncommon, rare, singular, unique, curious, odd, extraordinary, strange, *outré*, out of the way, egregious, out of the ordinary, unheard of, queer, quaint, old-fashioned, unfashionable, nondescript, undescribed, unexampled, *sui generis,* unprecedented, unparalleled, unfamiliar, fantastic, newfangled, grotesque, bizarre, weird, eerie, outlandish, exotic, preternatural, unrepresentative, uncanny, denaturalized.

Heterogeneous, epicine, heteroclite, amorphous, out of the pale of, mongrel, amphibious, half-blood, hybrid (41), androgynous, betwixt and between.

Phrases: 'None but himself could be his parallel'; caviare to the general.
Adverbs: Unconformably, etc.; except, unless, save, barring, beside, without, but for, save and except, let alone, to say nothing of; however, yet, but.

Section V – Number

84 NUMBER
Substantives: symbol, numeral, figure, cipher, digit, integer, counter, a round number, notation, a formula; series.

Sum, difference, subtrahend, complement, product, factorial, multiplicand, multiplier, multiplicator, coefficient, multiple, least common multiple, dividend, divisor, factor, highest common factor, greatest common measure, quotient, sub-multiple, fraction, vulgar fraction, mixed number, numerator, denominator, decimal, circulating decimal, recurring decimal, repetend, common measure, aliquot part, reciprocal, prime number; permutation, combination, election.

Ratio, proportion, progression (arithmetical, geometrical, harmonical), percentage.

Power, root, exponent, index, function, logarithm, antilogarithm; differential, integral, fluxion, fluent; incommensurable, surd.
Adjectives: Numeral, complementary, divisible, aliquot, reciprocal, prime, fractional, decimal, factorial, fractional, mixed, incommensurable.

Proportional, exponential, logarithmic, logometric, differential, fluxional, integral.

Positive, negative, rational, irrational, surd, radical, real, imaginary, impossible.

85 NUMERATION
Substantives: numbering, counting, tale, telling, tally, calling over, recension, enumeration, summation, reckoning, computation, ciphering, calculation, calculus, algorism, dactylonomy, rhabdology.

Arithmetic, analysis, algebra, differential and integral calculus.

Statistics, dead reckoning, muster, poll, census, capitation, roll-call, muster-roll, account, score, recapitulation, demography.

Addition, subtraction, multiplication, division, proportion, rule of three, reduction, involution, evolution, practice, equations, extraction of roots, approximation, interpolation, differentiation, integration.

Abacus, logometer, ready-reckoner, slide-rule, sliding-rule, tallies, Napier's bones, calculating machine, tabulator, totalizator, totalizer, tote, cash-register.
Verbs: To number, count, tell, tally, call over, take an account of, enumerate, muster, poll, run over, recite, recapitulate; sum, sum up, cast up, tell off, score, cipher, compute, calculate, reckon, estimate, figure up, tot up; add, subtract, multiply, divide; amount to.

Check, prove, demonstrate, balance, audit, overhaul, take stock.

Adjectives: Numerical, arithmetical, logarithmic, numeral, analytic, algebraic, statistical, computable, calculable, commensurable, incommensurable, incommensurate.

86 LIST

Substantives: catalogue, inventory, schedule, register, census, return, statistics, record (551), account, registry, syllabus, roll, terrier, cadastre, cartulary, tally, file, muster-roll, roster, rota, bead-roll, panel, calendar, index, table, book, ledger, day-book, synopsis, bibliography, contents, invoice, bill of lading, bill of fare, menu, red book, peerage, baronetage, Almanach de Gotha, Debrett, Domesday Book, prospectus, programme, directory, gazetteer, who's who.

Registration, etc. (551).

87 UNITY

Substantives: unification, oneness, individuality, singleness, solitariness, solitude, isolation (893), abstraction; monism.

One, unit, ace, monad.

Someone, somebody, no other, none else, an individualist; monist.

Verbs: To be alone, etc.; to isolate (44), insulate, set apart.

To render one, unify.

Phrase: To dine with Duke Humphrey.

Adjectives: One, sole, single, individual, apart, alone, lone, isolated, solitary, lonely, lonesome, desolate, dreary, insular, insulated, disparate, discrete, detached; monistic.

Unaccompanied, unattended, *solus*, single-handed, singular, odd, unique, unrepeated, azygous.

Inseverable, irresolvable, indiscerptible, compact.

Adverbs: Singly, etc., alone, by itself, *per se,* only, apart, in the singular

number, in the abstract, one by one; one at a time.

One and a half, sesqui-.

88 ACCOMPANIMENT

Substantives: coexistence, concomitance, company, association, companionship, partnership, collaboration, copartnership, coefficiency.

Concomitant, adjunct, context, accessory (39), coefficient, companion, attendant, fellow, associate, consort, spouse, colleague, collaborator, partner, copartner, side-kick, buddy, satellite, escort, hanger-on, parasite, shadow; travelling tutor, chaperon, duenna.

Verbs: To accompany, chaperon, coexist, attend, associate or be associated with, keep company with, collaborate with, hang on, shadow, wait on, to join, tie together.

Phrases: To go hand in hand with; to be in the same boat.

Adjectives: Accompanying, coexisting, attending, attendant, concomitant, fellow, twin, joint, associated with, accessory.

Adverbs: With, withal, together with, along with, in company with, collectively, hand in hand, together, in a body, cheek by jowl, side by side; therewith, herewith, moreover, besides, also, and (37), not to mention.

89 DUALITY

Substantives: dualism, duplicity, twofoldness, doubleness, biformity; polarity.

Two, deuce, couple, brace, pair, dyad (or duad), twins, Siamese twins, Castor and Pollux, Damon and Pythias, fellows, gemini, yoke, span, file, conjugation, twosome; dualist.

Verbs: To unite in pairs, to pair, pair off, couple, match, mate, bracket, yoke.

Adjectives: Two, twain, dual, binary, dualistic, duplex (90), duplicate, dyadic, binomial, twin, tête-à-tête, Janus-headed, bilateral, bicentric, bifocal.

Coupled, bracketed, paired, etc., conjugate.

Both, both the one and the other.

90 DUPLICATION
Substantives: doubling, gemination, reduplication, ingemination, repetition, iteration (104), renewal.
Verbs: To double, redouble, geminate, reduplicate, repeat, iterate, re-echo, renew (660).
Adjectives: Double, doubled, redoubled, second.

Biform, bifarious, bifold, bilateral, bifacial, twofold, two-sided, two-faced, duplex, duplicate, ingeminate.
Adverbs: Twice, once more, over again, *da capo, bis, encore,* anew, as much again, twofold (104, 136).

Secondly, in the second place, again.

91 BISECTION
Substantives: bipartition, dichotomy, halving, dimidiation, bifurcation, forking, branching, ramification, divarication, splitting, cleaving.

Fork, prong, fold, branch, Y.

Half, moiety, semi-, demi-, hemi-.
Verbs: To bisect, halve, divide, split, cut in two, cleave, dimidiate, dichotomize.

To separate, fork, bifurcate, branch out, ramify.
Verbs: To go halves; to go fifty-fifty; to split the difference.
Adjectives: Bisected, halved, divided, etc., bipartite, bicuspid, bind, bifurcated, bifurcate, cloven, cleft, split, etc.

92 TRIALITY
Substantives: trinity.

Three, triad, triangle, triplet, trey, trio, tern, trinomial, leash, threesome, trefoil, triquetra, *terza rima,* trilogy.

Third power, cube.

Adjectives: Three, triform, trine, trinal, trinary, ternary, ternal, ternate (93), trinomial, tertiary, tri-.

93 TRIPLICATION
Substantives: triplicity, trebleness, trine.
Verbs: To treble, triple, triplicate, cube.
Adjectives: Treble, triple, tern, ternary, ternate, triplicate, trigeminal, threefold, third.
Adverbs: Three times, thrice, threefold, in the third place, thirdly.

94 TRISECTION
Substantives: tripartition, trichotomy, third part, third.
Verbs: To trisect, divide into three parts.
Adjectives: Trifid, trisected, tripartite, trichotomous, trisulcate, triform.

95 QUATERNITY
Substantives: four, tetrad, quadruplet, quad, quarter, quaternion, foursome, square, tetragon, tetrahedron, tessara, quadrature; tetralogy.
Verbs: To reduce to a square, to square.
Adjectives: Four, quaternary, quaternal, quadratic, quartile, tetractic, tetra-, quadri-.

96 QUADRUPLICATION
Verbs: To multiply by four, quadruplicate, biquadrate.
Adjectives: Fourfold, quadruple, quadruplicate, fourth.
Adverbs: Four times, in the fourth place, fourthly, to the fourth degree.

97 QUADRISECTION
Substantives: quadripartition, quartering, a fourth, a quarter.
Verbs: To quarter, to divide into four parts.
Adjectives: Quartered, etc., quadrifid, quadripartite.

98 FIVE, etc.
Substantives: cinque, cinqfoil, quint, quincunx, pentad, pentagon, pentahedron, quintuplet, quin, quintet.
Adjectives: Five, quinary, quintuple, fivefold, fifth.
SIX, half a dozen, hexad, hexagon, hexahedron, sextet.
Adjectives: Senary, sextuple, sixfold, sixth.
SEVEN, heptad, heptagon, heptahedron, septet.
Adjectives: Septenary, septuple, sevenfold, seventh.
EIGHT, octad, octagon, octahedron, octet, ogdoad.
Adjectives: Octonary, octonal, octuple, eightfold, eighth.
NINE, ennead, nonagon, enneagon, enneahedron, novena.
Adjectives: Enneatic, ninefold, ninth.
TEN, decad, decagon, decahedron, decade.
Adjectives: Decimal, denary, decuple, tenfold, tenth.
TWELVE, a dozen.
Adjectives: Duodenary, duodecimal, twelfth.
THIRTEEN, a long dozen, a baker's dozen.
TWENTY, a score, icosahedron.
Adjectives: Vigesimal, twentieth.
FORTY, twoscore.
Adjectives: Quadragesimal.
FIFTY, twoscore and ten.
Adjectives: Quinquagesimal.
SIXTY, threescore.
Adjectives: Sexagesimal, sexagenary.
SEVENTY, threescore and ten.
EIGHTY, fourscore.
NINETY, fourscore and ten.
HUNDRED, centenary, hecatomb, century. One hundred and forty-four, a gross.
Verbs: To centuriate.
Adjectives: Centesimal, centennial, centenary, centurial, centuple, centuplicate, hundredfold, hundredth.

THOUSAND, chiliad, millennium.
Adjective: Millesimal.
MYRIAD, lac, crore.
MILLION, billion, trillion, etc.

99 QUINQUESECTION, etc.
Adjectives: Quinquefid, quin-quarticular, quinquepartite.
Sexpartite.
Septempartite.
Octopartite.
DECIMATION, tithe.
Verb: To decimate.

100 PLURALITY
Substantives: a number, a certain number, a few, a wheen, a round number.
Adjectives: Plural, more than one, upwards of, some, a few, one or two, two or three, umpteen, certain.
Adverb: Etcetera.

101 ZERO
Substantives: nothing (4), nought (or naught), cipher; nobody, *nemo*.
Adjectives: None, not one, not any, not a soul.

102 MULTITUDE
Substantives: numerousness, numerosity, numerality, multiplicity, majority, profusion, legion, host, a great or large number, numbers, array, power, lot, sight, army, sea, galaxy, populousness (72), a hundred, thousand, myriad, million, etc.
A shoal, swarm, draught, bevy, flock, herd, drove, flight, covey, hive, brood, litter, mob, nest, crows (72).
Increase of number, multiplication, multiple; greater number, majority.
Verbs: To be numerous, etc., to swarm, teem, crowd, come thick upon, outnumber, multiply, to people.
Phrase: To swarm like locusts or bees.
Adjectives: Many, several, a wheen, sundry, divers, various, a great many, very many, full many, ever so many,

no end of, numerous, profuse, manifold, multiplied, multitudinous, multiple, multinomial, endless (105), teeming, populous, peopled.

Frequent, repeated, reiterated, outnumbering, thick, crowding, crowded; galore.

Phrases: Thick as hail; thick as leaves in Vallombrosa; plentiful as blackberries; in profusion; numerous as the sands on the seashore; their name is Legion.

103 FEWNESS
Substantives: paucity, a small number, handful, scantiness, rareness, rarity, thinness.

Diminution of number, reduction, weeding, elimination, thinning; smaller number, minority.

Verbs: To be few, etc.

To render few, reduce, diminish in number, weed, weed out, prick off, eliminate, thin, thin out, decimate.

Adjectives: Few, scanty, scant, rare, infrequent, sparse, scattered, hardly or scarcely any, reduced, thinned, etc.

Phrases: Few and far between; you could count them on the fingers of one hand.

104 REPETITION
Substantives: iteration, reiteration, harping, recapitulation, run, recurrence (136), recrudescence, tautology, monotony; cuckoo-note, chimes, repetend, echo, burden of a song, refrain, jingle, renewal, rehearsal, réchauffé, rehash, reproduction (19).

Cuckoo, mocking-bird, mimic, imitator, parrot.

Periodicity (138), frequency (136).

Phrase: A twice-told tale.

Verbs: To repeat, iterate, reiterate, recapitulate, renew, reproduce, echo, re-echo, drum, hammer, harp on, plug, rehearse, redouble, recrudesce, reappear, recur, revert, recommence.

Phrases: Do or say over again; ring the changes on; to harp on the same string; to din or drum in the ear; to go over the same ground; to begin again.

Adjectives: Repeated, repetitional, repetitionary, repetitive, recurrent, recurring, reiterated, renewed, ever-recurring, thick-coming, monotonous, harping, sing-song, mocking, chiming; above-mentioned, said, aforesaid.

Phrases: It's that man again; cut and come·again; *crambe repetita*.

Adverbs: Repeatedly, often (136), again, anew, over again, afresh, ditto, *encore, de novo, da capo, bis* (90).

Phrases: *Toties quoties*; again and again; in quick succession, over and over again; ever and anon; time after time; year after year; times out of number; *ad nauseam*.

105 INFINITY
Substantives: infiniteness, infinitude.

Adjectives: Infinite, numberless, innumerable, countless, sumless, untold, unnumbered, unsummed, incalculable, unlimited, limitless, illimitable, immeasurable, unmeasured, measureless, unbounded, boundless, endless, interminable, unfathomable, exhaustless, termless, indefinite, without number, without limit, without end, unending.

Adverbs: Infinitely, etc., without measure, limit, etc., *ad infinitum,* world without end.

Section VI – Time

106 DURATION
Substantives: time, period, term, space, span, spell, season, era, epoch, decade, century, chiliad, age, cycle, aeon.

Intermediate time, while, interval, interim, pendency, intervention, intermission, interregnum, interlude, recess, break, intermittence, respite (265).

Long duration (110).

Phrases: The enemy; the whirligig of time.

Verbs: To continue, last, endure, remain, go on; to take, take up, fill or occupy time, to persist, to intervene.

To pass, pass away, spend, employ, while away or consume time, waste time.

Adjectives: Continuing, lasting, enduring, remaining, persistent, perpetual, permanent (150).

Adverbs: While, whilst, so long as, during, pending, till, until, up to, during the time or interval, the whole time or period, all the time or while, in the long rung, all along, throughout, from beginning to end (52).

Pending, meantime, meanwhile, in the meantime, in the interim, *ad interim, pendente lite,* from day to day, for a time, for a season, for good, yet, up to this time.

107 TIMELESSNESS

Substantives: neverness, absence of time, no time, *dies non.*

Short duration (111).

Adverbs: Never, ne'er, at no time, on no occasion, at no period, nevermore, *sine die.*

Phrases: On Tib's eve; at the Greek Calends; *jamais de ma vie;* 'jam every other day.'

108 PERIOD

Substantives: second, minute, hour, day, week, fortnight, month, lunation, quarter, year, leap-year, lustrum, quinquennium, decade, lifetime, generation, century, age, millennium, *annus magnus.*

Adjectives: Hourly, horary; daily, diurnal, quotidian; weekly, hebdomadal, menstrual, monthly, annual, secular, centennial, bicentennial, etc., bissextile, seasonal.

Adverbs: From day to day, from hour to hour.

Once upon a time; Anno Domini, A.D.; Before Christ, B.C.

108a CONTINGENT DURATION.

During pleasure, during good behaviour, *quamdiu se bene gesserit.*

109 COURSE

Substantives: progress, process, succession, lapse, flow, flux, stream, tract, current, tide, march, step, flight, etc., of time.

Indefinite time, aorist.

Verbs: To elapse, lapse, flow, run, proceed, roll on, advance, pass, slide, press on, flit, fly, slip, glide, run its course.

Adjectives: Elapsing, passing, etc.; aoristic.

Adverbs: In course of time, in due time of season, in process of time, in the fullness of time.

Phrase: *Labuntur anni.*

110 DIUTURNITY

Substantives: a long time, an age, a century, an eternity, aeon.

Phrases: *Temporis longinquitas;* a month of Sundays.

Durableness, durability, persistence, lastingness, continuance, permanence (150), longevity, survival.

Distance of time, protraction, extension or prolongation of time, delay (133).

Verbs: To last, endure, stand, remain, continue, abide, tarry, protract, prolong, outlast, outlive, survive; spin out, draw out, eke out, temporize, linger, loiter, lounge (275), wait.

Phrase: To live to fight another day.

Adjectives: Durable, of long duration, permanent, enduring, chronic, intransient, intransitive, intransmutable, lasting, abiding, persistent; live-long, longeval, long-lived, macrobiotic, diuturnal, evergreen, perennial, unintermitting, unremitting, perpetual (112).

Protracted, prolonged, spun out, long-winded, surviving, lingering.

Adverbs: Long, a long time, permanently.

Phrases: As the day is long; all the day long; all the year round; the livelong day; hour after hour; morning, noon, and night; for good; for many a long day.

111 TRANSIENTNESS

Substantives: transitoriness, impermanence, evanescence, transitiveness, fugitiveness, fugacity, fugaciousness, caducity, mortality, span, shortness, brevity.

Quickness, promptness (132), suddenness, abruptness.

A *coup de main,* bubble, Mayfly, nine days' wonder.

Verbs: To be transient, etc., to flit, pass away, fly, gallop, vanish, fade, intromit.

Adjectives: Transitory, transient, transitive, passing, impermanent, evanescent, fleeting, momentary, fugacious, fugitive, flitting, vanishing, shifting, flying, temporary, temporal, makeshift, provisional, provisory, rough and ready, cursory, galloping, short-lived, ephemeral, deciduous, meteoric.

Brief, sudden, quick, prompt, brisk, abrupt, extemporaneous, summary, hasty, precipitate.

Adverbs: Temporarily, etc., *en passant, in transitu,* extempore.

In a short time, soon, at once, awhile, anon, by and by, briefly, presently, apace, eftsoons, straight, straightway, quickly, speedily, promptly, presto, slapdash, directly, immediately, incontinently, forthwith; suddenly, *per saltum,* at one bound.

Phrases: At short notice; the time being up; before the ink is dry; here to-day and gone to-morrow (149); *sic transit gloria mundi.*

112 PERPETUITY

Substantives: eternity, sempiternity, immortality, athanasy, everlastingness, perpetuation.

Verbs: To last or endure for ever, to have no end: to eternize, pertetuate.

Adjectives: Perpetual, eternal, everlasting, sempiternal, coeternal; endless, unending, ceaseless, incessant, unceasing, uninterrupted, interminable, having no end, unfading, evergreen, never-fading, amaranthine, ageless, deathless, immortal, undying, never-dying, imperishable, indestructible.

Adverbs: Always, ever, evermore, aye, for ever, for aye, for evermore, still, perpetually, eternally, etc., in all ages, from age to age.

Phrases: For ever and a day; *esto perpetua;* for ever and ever; world without end; time without end; *in secula seculorum;* to the end of time; till Doomsday; till hell freezes; to a cinder.

113 INSTANTANEITY

Substantives: instantaneousness, moment, instant, second, split second, minute, twinkling, trice, flash, breath, span, jiffy, flash of lightening, suddenness (111).

Verbs: To twinkle, flash, to be instantaneous.

Adjectives: Instantaneous, push-button, sudden, momentary, extempore.

Phrases: Quick as thought; quick as a flash; quick as lightening.

Adverbs: Instantly, momentarily, *subito,* presto, instanter, suddenly, plump, slap, slapdash, in a moment, in an instant, in a second, in no time, in a trice, in a twinkling, at one jump, in a breath, extempore, *per saltum,* in a crack, out of hand.

Phrases: Before one can say 'Jack Robinson'; in a brace of shakes; between the cup and the lip; on the spur of the moment; in the twinkling of an eye; in a jiffy; in two ticks; on the instant; in less than no time; at one fell swoop; no sooner said than done.

114 CHRONOMETRY

Substantives: chronology, horology, horometry, registry, date, epoch, style, era.

Greenwich, standard, mean, local, solar, sidereal time; summer time, double summer time.

Almanac, calendar, ephemeris, chronicle, annals, register, journal, diary, chronogram, time-book.

Instruments for the measurement of time, clock, watch, stop-watch, repeater, chronograph, chronometer, sextant, timepiece, dial, sun-dial, horologe, pendulum, hour-glass, water-clock, clepsydra; time signal.

Chronographer, chronologer, chronologist, time-keeper, annalist.

Verbs: To chronicle, to fix or mark the time, date, register, etc., to bear date, to measure time, to beat time, to make time, to time.

Adjectives: Chronological, chronometrical, chronogrammatical.

Adverb: O'clock.

115 ANACHRONISM

Substantives: error in time, prolepsis, metachronism, prochronism, parachronism, anticipation.

Disregard or neglect of time.

Verbs: To anachronize, misdate, antedate, postdate, overdate, anticipate.

Adjectives: Anachronistic, anachronous, misdated, undated, overdue, postdated, antedated.

Phrases: To take no note of time; to prophesy after the event.

116 PRIORITY

Substantives: antecedence, anteriority, precedence, pre-existence.

Precursor, predecessor, prelude, forerunner (64), harbinger, antecedent; the past (122).

Verbs: To precede, come before, fore-run, pre-exist, prelude, usher in, dawn, announce (511), foretell, anticipate, forestall.

Phrases: To be beforehand; to steal a march upon.

Adjectives: Prior, previous, preceding, precedent, anterior, antecedent, pre-existent, pre-existing, former, foregoing, aforesaid, said, above-mentioned, prehistoric, antediluvian, pre-Adamite.

Precursory, prelusive, prelusory, proemial, introductory, prefatory (62), prodromal, prodromic.

Adverbs: Before, prior to, previously, anteriorly, antecedently, aforetime, ere, ere now, erewhile, before now, heretofore, ultimo, yet, beforehand, above, *supra*.

Phrase: Before the flood.

117 POSTERIORITY

Substantives: succession, sequence, subsequence, supervention, sequel, successor (65), postlude.

Verbs: To follow, come or go after, succeed, supervene, ensue.

Phrases: To tread on the heels of; to follow in the footsteps of.

Adjectives: Subsequent, posterior, following, after, later, succeeding, post-glacial, post-diluvial, post-diluvian, puisne, posthumous, post-prandial, post-classical.

Adverbs: Subsequently, after, afterwards, since, later, later on, at a subsequent or later period, proximo, next, in the sequel, close upon, thereafter, thereupon, whereupon, upon which, eftsoons, below, *infra*.

118 THE PRESENT TIME

Substantives: the existing time, the time being, the present moment, juncture, crisis, epoch, day, hour; the twentieth century.

Age, time of life.

Verb: To strike while the iron is hot.

Adjectives: Present, actual, current, existing, that is.

Adverbs: At this time, moment, etc., now, at present, at this time of day, at the present time, day, etc., to-day, nowadays, instant, already, even now, but now, just now, upon which.

Phrases: For the time being; for the nonce; *pro hac vice*; on the nail; on the spot; on the spur of the moment; now or never.

119 DIFFERENT TIME

Substantives: other time.

Indefinite time, aorist.

Adjectives: Aoristic.

Adverbs: At that time, moment, etc., then, at which time, etc., on that occasion, upon, in those days.

When, whenever, whensoever, upon which, on which occasions, at another or a different time, etc., otherwhile, otherwhiles, at various times, ever and anon.

Phrases: Once upon a time; one day; some other time; one of these days.

120 SYNCHRONISM

Substantives: synchronization, coinstantaneity, coexistence, coincidence, simultaneousness, coevality, contemporaneousness, contemporaneity, concurrence, concomitance.

Having equal times, isochronism.

A contemporary, coeval, coetanean.

Verbs: To coexist, concur, accompany, synchronize.

Phrase: To keep pace with.

Verbs: Synchronous, synchronal, synchronistic, simultaneous, coexisting, coincident, concomitant, concurrent, coeval, coetaneous, contemporary, contemporaneous, coeternal, isochronous.

Adverbs: At the same time, simultaneously, etc., together, during the same time, etc., in the interim, in the same breath, in concert, *pari passu*; meantime, meanwhile (106), while, whilst.

121 FUTURITY

Substantives: the future, futurition, the approaching time, hereafter, the time to come, posteriority (117), after time, after age, the coming time, the morrow, after days, hours, years, ages; after life, millennium, doomsday, the day of judgment, the crack of doom.

The approach of time, the process of time, advent, time drawing on, the womb of time.

Prospection, anticipation, prospect, perspective, expectation (507), horizon, outlook, look-out.

Heritage, heirs, progeny, issue, posterity, descendants, heir apparent, heir presumptive.

Future existence, future state, post-existence, after-life, beyond.

Verbs: To look forward, anticipate, forestall (132), have in prospect, keep in view, expect (507).

To impend, hang over, lie over, approach, await, threaten, overhang, draw near, prepare.

Phrases: Lie in wait for; bide one's time; to wait impatiently; kick one's heels.

To be in the wind; to be cooking; to loom in the future.

Adjectives: Future, to come, coming, going to happen, approaching, impending, instant, at hand, about to be or happen, next, hanging, awaiting, forthcoming, near, near at hand, imminent, threatening, brewing, preparing, in store, eventual, ulterior, in view, in prospect, prospective, in perspective, in the offing, in the wind, on the cards, that will be, overhanging.

Unborn, in embryo, in the womb of time.

Adverbs: Prospectively, hereafter, by and by, some fine day, one of these days, anon, in future, to-morrow, in course of time, in process of time, sooner or later, *proximo*, in after time.

On the eve of, ere long, at hand,

near at hand, on the point of, beforehand, against the time.

After a time, from this time, henceforth, henceforwards, thence, thenceforth, thenceforward, whereupon, upon which.

Phrases: All in good time; in the fullness of time.

122 PRETERITION

Substantives: The past, past time, *status quo,* days of yore, time gone by, priority (116), former times, old times, the olden time, ancient times, antiquity, antiqueness, lang syne, time immemorial, prehistory.

Archaeology, palaeology, palaeontology, palaeography, archaism, retrospection, retrospect, looking back.

Archaeologist, antiquary, medievalist, palaeographer, palaeologist, Dr. Dryasdust.

Ancestry (166), pre-existence.

Phrases: The good old days; the golden age; the rust of antiquity.

Verbs: To pass, be past, lapse, go by, elapse, run out, expire, blow over; to look back, cast the eyes back, retrospect, trace back, dig up, exhume.

Phrases: To have run its course; to have had its day.

Adjectives: Past, gone, gone by, over, bygone, foregone, pristine, prehistoric, quondam, lapsed, elapsed, preterlapsed, expired, late, *ci-devant,* run out, blown over, that has been.

Former, foregoing, late, last, latter, recent, overnight, preterperfect, preterpluperfect, forgotten, irrecoverable, out of date.

Looking back, retrospective, retroactive, *ex post facto*; archaeological, etc.

Pre-existing, pre-existent.

Adverbs: Formerly, of old, erst, whilom, erewhile, before now, time was, ago, over, in the olden time, anciently, in days of yore, long since, retrospectively, ere now, before now,

till now, once, once upon a time, hitherto, heretofore, *ultimo.*

The other day, yesterday, last night, week, month, year, etc.; just now, recently, lately, of late, latterly.

Long ago, a long while or time ago, some time ago.

Phrases: Once upon a time; from time immemorial; in the memory of man; time out of mind.

Already, yet, at length, at last.

123 NEWNESS

Substantives: novelty, recentness, recency, modernity, freshness, greenness, immaturity, youth (127), rawness.

Innovation, renovation (660), renewal.

Nouveau riche, parvenu, upstart, mushroom; latest fashion, *dernier cri.*

Verbs: Renew, renovate, restore (660), modernize.

Adjectives: New, novel, recent, fresh, green, evergreen, raw, immature, untrodden, advanced, twentieth-century, modern, modernistic, avant-garde, neoteric, new-born, nascent, new-fashioned, up-to-date, new-fangled, vernal, renovated, brand-new, split-new, virgin.

Phrases: Fresh as a rose; fresh as a daisy; fresh as paint; just out; spick and span.

Adverbs: Newly, recently, lately, afresh, anew.

124 OLDNESS

Substantives: age (128), antiquity, eld, ancientry, primitiveness, maturity, decline, decay, obsolescence; seniority, eldership, primogeniture.

Archaism, relic, antique, fossil, eolith; elder, doyen.

Verbs: To be or become old, mature, mellow; to age, fade, decay.

Adjectives: Old, ancient, antique, antiquated, out-of-date, of long standing, time-honoured, venerable, hoary, primitive, diluvian, antediluvian, fossil, palaeozoic, preglacial, palaeolithic, neolithic, primeval, primordial, prime, pre-Adamite, prehistoric, antemundane, archaic, classic, medieval.

Immemorial, inveterate, rooted, traditional.

Senior, elder, eldest, oldest, first-born (128).

Obsolete, obsolescent, out-of-date, stale, time-worn, faded, decayed, effete, declining, played-out, crumbling, decrepit (128), *passé*.

Phrases: Nothing new under the sun; old as the hills; old as Methuselah; old as Adam; before the Flood; time out of mind; since the year one.

125 MORNING

Substantives: morn, morrow, forenoon, a.m., prime, dawn, daybreak, dayspring, peep of day, break of day, matins, aurora, first blush of the morning, prime of the morning, twilight, crepuscule, sunrise, sun-up, cockcrow.

Noon, midday, noontide, meridian, noonday, prime; spring, summer, midsummer.

Adjectives: Matutinal, auroral, vernal, midsummer.

126 EVENING

Substantives: eve, e'en, decline of day, close of day, eventide, nightfall, curfew, vespers, evensong, dusk, twilight, gloaming, eleventh hour, sunset, sundown, afternoon, p.m., bedtime, midnight; autumn, Indian summer, St. Martin's summer, St. Luke's summer, winter the fall.

Phrases: The witching time of night; the dead of night; blind-man's holiday.

Adjectives: Nocturnal, vespertine, autumnal, heimal, brumal.

127 YOUTH

Substantives: infancy, babyhood, boyhood, juvenility, childhood, youthhood, juniority, juvenescence, adolescence (131), minority, nonage, teens, tender age, bloom, heyday, boyishness, girlishness.

Cradle, nursery, leading strings, pupilage, pupilship, puberty.

Phrases: Prime or flower of life; the rising generation; salad days; school-days.

Adjectives: Young, youthful, juvenile, callow, sappy, beardless, under age, in one's teens, boyish, girlish, junior, younger.

Phrase: *In statu pupillari.*

128 AGE

Substantives: old age, senility, senescence, oldness, longevity, years, anility, grey hairs, climacteric, decrepitude, hoary age, caducity, crow's feet, superannuation, dotage, anecdotage, seniority, green old age, eldership.

Phrases: The vale of years; decline of life; the sere and yellow leaf; second childhood.

Adjectives: Aged, old, elderly, senile, matronly, anile, in years, ripe, mellow, grey, grey-headed, hoary, hoar, venerable, timeworn, declining, antiquated, *passé*, rusty, effete, decrepit, superannuated.

Patriarchal, ancestral, primitive, older, elder, senior; eldest, oldest, first-born, bantling, firstling.

Phrases: With one foot in the grave; marked with crow's feet; advanced in life, or in years; stricken in years; no chicken; long in the tooth; old as the hills.

129 INFANT

Substantives: babe, baby, nursling, suckling.

Child, baird, wean, little one, brat, toddler, kid, chit, urchin, bantling, bratling, papoose, elf, piccaninny.

Youth, boy, lad, laddie, stripling, youngster, teenager, callant, younker, gossoon, nipper, whipster, whippersnapper, schoolboy, young hopeful, hobbledehoy, cadet, minor.

Girl, lass, lassie, wench, miss, colleen, flapper, bobbysoxer, damsel, maid, maiden, *jeune fille*.

Scion, sapling, seedling, tendril, mushroom, nestling, chicken, larva, chrysalis, tadpole, whelp, cub, pullet, fry, foetus, calf, lamb, lambkin, colt, filly, pup, puppy, foal, kitten.

Adjectives: Infantine, infantile, puerile, boyish, girlish (127), virginal, childish, baby, babyish, unfledged, new-fledged, kittenish, callow.

Phrases: In leading-strings; at the breast; in arms; in one's teens; tied to mother's apron-strings.

130 VETERAN

Substantives: old man, seer, patriarch, greybeard, gaffer, grandsire, grandam, dowager, matron, crone, beldam, hag, sexagenarian, old-timer, old stager, old buffer, fogy, geezer.

Methuselah, Nestor; elders, forefathers, forbears, fathers, ancestors, ancestry.

Adjectives: Veteran, aged, old, greyheaded (128).

131 ADOLESCENCE

Substantives: puberty, pubescence, majority, adultness, maturity, ripeness, manhood, virility.

A man, adult (373), a woman, matron (374), *parti*; ephebe.

Phrases: Prime of life; man's estate; flower of age; meridian of life; years of discretion; *toga virilis*.

Adjectives: Adolescent, pubescent, of age, out of one's teens, grown up, mature, middle-aged, manly, virile, adult.

Womanly, matronly, nubile, marriageable, out.

132 EARLINESS

Substantives: timeliness, punctuality, readiness, promptness (682), promp-

titude, expedition, quickness, haste, acceleration, hastening, hurry, bustle, precipitation, anticipation, precociousness, precocity.

Suddenness, abruptness (111).

Phrases: A stitch in time saves nine; the early bird catches the worm.

Verbs: To be early, to be in time, keep time, be beforehand.

To anticipate, forestall, book, engage, bespeak, reserve.

To expedite, hasten, haste, quicken (274), press, dispatch, accelerate, precipitate, hurry, bustle (684).

Phrases: To take time by the forelock; to steal a march upon; to be beforehand with; to be pressed for time.

Adjectives: Early, prime, rathe, timely, timeous, punctual, matutinal, forward, ready, quick, expeditious, precipitate, summary, prompt, premature, precocious, prevenient, anticipatory, pre-emptive.

Sudden, abrupt, unexpected (508), subitaneous, extempore.

Adverbs: Early, soon, anon, betimes, apace, eft, eftsoons, in time, ere long, presently, shortly, punctually, to the minute, on time, on the dot.

Beforehand, prematurely, before one's time, in anticipation.

Suddenly, abruptly, at once, extempore, instanter.

Phrases: In good time; at sunrise; with the lark; early days.

On the point of; at short notice; on the spur of the moment; all at once; before you can say 'knife'; no sooner said than done.

133 LATENESS

Substantives: tardiness, slowness (275), delay, cunctation, procrastination, deferring, lingering, lagging, etc., postponement, dilatoriness, adjournment, shelving, prorogation, remand, moratorium.

Protraction, prolongation, leeway.

Phrase: Fabian tactics.

Verbs: To be late, etc., tarry, wait, stay, bide, take time, dally, dawdle, linger, loiter, lag, bide one's time, shuffle (275, 683).

To stand over, lie over, hang fire.

To put off, defer, delay, leave over, suspend, stave off, postpone, adjourn, carry over, shelve, procrastinate, temporize, stall, filibuster, prolong, protract, draw out, spin out, hold up, prorogue.

Phrases: To tide it over; to bide one's time; to let the matter stand over; to sleep on it; to kick (or cool) one's heels.

Adjectives: Late, tardy, slow, dilatory (275), posthumous, backward, unpunctual, procrastinatory, behindhand, belated, overdue.

Delayed, etc., suspended, pending, in abeyance.

Adverbs: Late, after time, too late, behind time; at length, at last.

Slowly, leisurely, deliberately.

Phrases: Late in the day; a day after the fair; at the eleventh hour; after death, the doctor.

134 OCCASION

Substantives: opportunity, chance, opening, break, show, room, suitable or proper time or season, high time, opportuneness, tempestivity, seasonableness, crisis, turn, juncture, conjuncture.

Spare time, leisure, holiday (685), spare moments, hours, etc., time on one's hands.

Phrases: Golden (or favourable) opportunity; the nick of time;

Verbs: To use, make use of, employ, profit by, avail oneself of, lay hold of, embrace, catch, seize, snatch, clutch, pounce upon, grasp, etc., the opportunity.

To give, offer, present, afford, etc., the opportunity.

To time well; to spend or consume time.

Phrases: To turn the occasion to account; to seize the occasion; to strike the iron while it is hot; to make hay while the sun shines; *carpe diem*; to take the tide at the flood; to furnish a handle for.

Adjectives: Opportune, timely, well-timed, timeful, timeous, seasonable, happy, lucky, providential, fortunate, favourable, propitious, auspicious, critical.

Adverbs: Opportunely, etc., on the spot, in proper or due time or season, high time, for the nonce.

By the way, by the by, *en passant, à propos,* parenthetically.

Phrases: In the nick of time; on the spur of the moment (612); now or never; at the eleventh hour; time and tide wait for no man.

135 INTEMPESTIVITY

Substantives: untimeliness, unsuitable time, improper time, unseasonableness, inopportuneness, evil hour.

Hitch, impediment (706), check, *contretemps*.

Verbs: To be ill-timed, etc., to mistime, intrude, come amiss.

To lose, omit, let slip, let go, neglect, pretermit, allow, or suffer the opportunity or occasion to pass, slip, go by, escape, lapse; to lose time, to fritter away time (683).

Phrases: to let slip through the fingers; to lock the stable door when the steed is stolen.

Adjectives: Ill-timed, untimely, untimeous, mistimed, unseasonable, out of season, unpunctual, inopportune, untoward, intrusive, too late (133), too early (132), malapropos, unlucky, inauspicious, unpropitious, unfortunate, unfavourable, unsuited, unsuitable.

Adverbs: Inopportunely, etc.

Phrases: As ill luck would have it; in evil hour; after meat, mustard; a day before (or after) the fair.

91

136 FREQUENCY

Substantives: oftness, recurrence, repetition (104), recrudescence, reiteration, iteration, run, reappearance, renewal, *ritornello, ritournelle,* burden.

Frequenter, *habitué,* fan, client.

Verbs: To recur, revert, return, repeat, reiterate, reappear, renew, reword.

To frequent, resort to, visit, attend, haunt, infest.

Adjectives: Frequent, common, not rare, repeated, reiterated, thickcoming, recurring, recurrent, incessant, everlasting, perpetual, rife; habitual (613).

Adverbs: Often, oft, oft-times, not infrequently, frequently, often-times, many times, several times, repeatedly.

Again, anew, afresh, *de novo,* ditto, over again, *da capo,* again and again, over and over, ever and anon, many times over, time after time, time and again, repeatedly (104).

Perpetually, continually, constantly, incessantly, everlastingly, without ceasing.

Sometimes, occasionally, at times, now and then, now and again, from time to time, at intervals, between whiles, once in a while, there are times when.

Most ofte, for the most part, generally, usually, commonly, most frequently, as often as not.

Phrases: A number of times; many a time (and oft); times out of number.

137 INFREQUENCY

Substantives: rareness, rarity, uncommonness, scarcity, fewness (103), seldomness.

Verbs: To be rare etc.

Adjectives: Infrequent, rare, scarce, unfrequent, uncommon, unprecedented, unheard-of.

Phrase: In short supply.

Adverbs: Seldom, rarely, scarcely, hardly, scarcely ever, ever, hardly ever, not often, unfrequently.

Once, once for all, once in a way.

Phrases: Once in a blue moon; angels' visits.

138 PERIODICITY

Substantives: intermittence, beat, ictus, pulse, pulsation, rhythm, lilt, swing, alternation, alternateness, bout, round, revolution, rotation, turn.

Anniversary, jubilee; silver, golden, wedding; centenary, bicentenary, tercentenary, etc.; feast, festival, birthday.

Regularity of return, rota, cycle, period, stated time, routine.

Phrase: The swing of the pendulum.

Verbs: To recur in regular order or succession, to come round, return, revolve, alternate, come in its turn, beat, pulsate, intermit; to regularize.

Adjectives: Periodic, periodical, recurrent, cyclical, revolving, intermittent, remittent, alternate, every other, alternating, rhythmic, rhythmical, steady, punctual.

Hourly, daily, diurnal, tertian, quotidian, weekly, hebdomadal, fortnightly, bi-monthly, monthly, biannual, annual, yearly, biennial, triennial, centennial.

Phrase: Regular as clockwork.

Adverbs: Periodically, at regular intervals, at stated times, at fixed periods, punctually, from day to day.

By turns, in turn, in rotation, alternately, in shifts, off and on, ride and tie, hitch and hike.

139 IRREGULARITY

Substantives: of recurrence, uncertainty, unpunctuality, fitfulness.

Adjectives: Irregular, uncertain, unpunctual, capricious, desultory, unrhythmic, unrhythmical, fitful, spasmodic, flickering, casual.

Adverbs: Irregularly, etc., by snatches, by fits and starts, skippingly, now and then, occasionally.

Section VII – Change

140 CHANGE

Substantives: alteration, mutation, permutation, variation, modification, modulation, inflexion, mood, qualification, innovation, metastasis, metabolism, deviation, turn, diversion, inversion, reversion, reversal, eversion, subversion (162), *bouleversement,* upset, organic change, revolution (146), substitution (147), transposition (148), transit, transition.

Transformation, transmutation, transfiguration, metamorphosis, transmigration, transubstantiation, transmogrification, metempsychosis, avatar.

Vicissitude, flux, unrest (149); change of mind, tergiversation (607).
Phrase: The wheel of fortune.
Verbs: To change, alter, vary, modify, modulate, diversify, qualify, tamper with, edit, turn, shift, veer, tack, chop, shuffle, swerve, warp, deviate, turn aside, turn topsy-turvy, upset, invert, reverse, introvert, subvert, evert, turn inside out.

Form, fashion, mould, model, vamp, warp, work a change, superinduce, resume, disturb (61), innovate, reform, remodel, refound, new-model, modernize, revolutionize.

Transform, transume, transmute, transfigure, transmogrify, metamorphose, pass to, leap to, transfer.
Phrases: To ring the changes; to turn over a new leaf; to introduce new blood; to shuffle the cards; to turn the corner; to wax and wane; to ebb and flow; *tempora mutantur; nous avons changé tout cela.*
Adjectives: Changed, altered, new-fangled, warped, etc.; transitional, metamorphic, metabolic, metastatic.
Adverb: *Mutatis mutandis.*

141 PERMANENCE

Substantives: persistence, endurance, *status quo*; maintenance, preservation, conservation, conservatism, *laissez-faire*, rest, sleep, establishment, truce, suspension, settledness (265), perdurability, stability (150).
Phrase: The law of the Medes and Persians.
Verbs: To remain, stay, stop, persist, tarry, hold, last, endure, continue, dwell, bide, abide, maintain, keep, hold on, stand, subsist, live, stand still, outlive, survive.

To let alone, let be.
Phrases: To keep one's footing; to hold one's ground; to stick to one's guns; to stand fast.
Adjectives: Persisting, etc., permanent, established, unchanged, unmodified, unrenewed, unaltered, fixed, settled, unvaried, intact, inviolate, persistent, stagnant, rooted, monotonous, unreversed, conservative, unprogressive, undestroyed, unrepelled, unsuppressed, unfailing, stationary (265), stereotyped, perdurable.
Adverbs: *In statu quo,* for good, finally, at a stand, at a standstill, *uti possidetis.*
Phrases: *J'y suis, j'y reste; plus cela change, plus cela est la même chose; esto perpetua.*

142 CESSATION

Substantives: discontinuance, desistance, quiescence.

Intermission, remission, suspension, interruption, suspense, stand, halt, closure, stop, stoppage, pause, rest, lull, breathing-space, respite, truce, drop, interregnum, abeyance.

Comma, colon, semicolon, period, full stop.
Verbs: To discontinue, cease, desist, break off, leave off, hold, stop, pause, rest, drop, lay aside, give up, have done with, stick, hang fire, pull up,

give over, shut down, knock off, relinquish (624), surcease.

To come to a stand, or standstill, suspend, cut short, cast off, go out, be at an end; intromit, interrupt, arrest, intermit, remit; put an end or stop to.

To pass away, go off, pass off, blow over, die away, wear away, wear off (122).

Phrases: To shut up shop; to stay one's hand; to rest on one's oars; to rest on one's laurels.

Interjections: Hold! hold on! stop! enough! avast! *basta!* have done! a truce to! stop it! drop it! cheese it! chuck it! stow it! cut it out!

143 CONTINUANCE in action

Substantives: continuation, perseverance, repetition (104), persistence, run.

Verbs: To continue, persist, go on, keep on, abide, keep, pursue, hold on, run on, follow on, carry on, keep up, uphold, sustain, perpetuate, persevere, keep it up, stick it, peg away, maintain, maintain one's ground, harp upon, repeat (104), take root.

Phrases: To keep the pot boiling; to keep the ball rolling.

Adjectives: Continual, continuous, continuing, etc., uninterrupted, inconvertible, unintermitting, unreversed, unstopped, unrevoked, unvaried, unshifting, perpetual (112).

144 CONVERSION

Substantives: reduction, transmutation, resolution, assimilation; chemistry, alchemy; growth, lapse, progress, becoming; naturalization.

Passage, transit, transition, transmigration, flux, shifting, sliding, running into, etc.; phase, conjugations; convertibility.

Laboratory, alembic, crucible (691).

Convert, pervert, vert, turncoat, renegade, apostate.

Verbs: To be converted into; to become, get, wax, come to turn to, turn into, assume the form of, pass into, slide into, glide into, lapse, shift, run into, fall into, merge into, melt, grow, grow into, open into, resolve itself into, settle into, mature, mellow; assume the form, shape, state, nature, character, etc., of; illapse.

To convert into; to make, render, form, mould, reduce, resolve into; transume (140), fashion, model, remodel, reorganize, shape, modify, transmogrify; assimilate to; reduce to; bring to; refound, re-form, reshape.

Adjectives: Converted into, become, etc., convertible, transitional.

Adverbs: Gradually, *gradatim,* by degrees, step by step, by inches, inch by inch, by little and little, by slow degrees, consecutively, seriatim, *in transitu.*

145 REVERSION

Substantives: return, reconversion, relapse (661), recidivism, atavism, throwback, reaction, recoil (277), backlash, rebound, ricochet, revulsion, alternation (138), inversion, regression (283).

Reinstatement, re-establishment (660).

Phrases: The turning-point; the turn of the tide; *status quo ante bellum.*

Verbs: To revert, turn back, return to, relapse, recoil, rebound, react; to restore (660), to undo, unmake.

Phrase: To turn the tables (719).

Adjectives: Reverting, etc., restored, etc., regressive, retrogressive, atavistic, revulsive, reactionary.

Interjection: As you were!

146 REVOLUTION

Substantives: counter-revolution, revolt, rebellion (742), transilience, jump, leap, plunge, jerk, start, spasm, convulsion, throe, storm, earthquake, catastrophe, cataclysm (173).

Legerdemain, conjuration, sleight of hand, hocus-pocus (545), harlequinade, witchcraft (992).

A revolutionary, revolutionist, counter-revolutionist, deviationist; the red flag.
Verbs: To revolutionize, remodel, recast, refashion, reconstruct.
Adjectives: Revolutionary, radical, extreme, intransigent, catastrophic, cataclysmic.
Adverbs: Root and branch.

147 SUBSTITUTION

Substantives: commutation, supplanting, replacement, supersession, enallage, metonymy, synecdoche, antonomasia.

Thing substituted, substitute (634), succedaneum, makeshift, shift, apology, stand-in, pinch-hitter, locumtenens, representative, proxy; understudy, deputy (759), vice, double, dummy, changeling, scapegoat, stooge; stop-gap, jury-mast, palimpsest, metaphor (521).
Phrase: Borrowing of or robbing Peter to pay Paul.
Verbs: To substitute, put in place of, commute, supplant, cut out, change for, supersede, take over from.

To give place to; to replace.
Phrases: To serve as a substitute, etc.; to do duty for; to stand in the shoes of; to take the place of.
Adjectives: Substituted, etc., vicarious, subdititious, makeshift, provisional.
Adverbs: Instead, in place of, in lieu of, in the room of, *faute de mieux*.

148 INTERCHANGE

Substantives: exchange, commutation, intermutation, reciprocation, transposition, permutation, shuffling, castling (at chess), hocus-pocus, interchangeableness, interchangeability.

Reciprocity (12), retaliation (718), barter (794).
Phrases: A Roland for an Oliver; tit for tat; *quid pro quo*.
Verbs: To interchange, exchange, bandy, transpose, shuffle, change hands, swap, dicker, permute, reciprocate, commute, counterchange.
Phrases: To play at puss in the corner; to play musical chairs; to return the compliment; to give and take; you scratch my back and I'll scratch yours.
Adjectives: Interchanged, etc., reciprocal, mutual, commutative, interchangeable, intercurrent.
Adverbs: In exchange, vice versa.

149 MUTABILITY

Substantives: changeableness, changeability, inconstancy, variableness, mobility, instability, unsteadiness, vacillation, unrest, restlessness, slipperiness, impermanence, fragility, fluctuation, vicissitude, alternation, vibration, oscillation (314), flux, ebbing and flowing, ebbs and flows, ups and downs, fidgets, fidgetiness, fugitiveness, disquiet, disquietude.

A Proteus, chameleon, quicksilver, weathercock, kaleidoscope, harlequin; the moon.
Phrases: April showers; shifting sands; the wheel of fortune; the Cynthia of the minute.
Verbs: To fluctuate, vary, waver, flounder, vibrate, flicker, flit, flitter, shift, shuffle, shake, totter, tremble, vacillate, ebb and flow, turn and turn about, change and change about.

To fade, pass away like a cloud, shadow, or dream.
Adjectives: Mutable, changeable, variable, ever-changing, inconstant, impermanent, unsteady, unstable, protean, proteiform, unfixed, fluctuating, vacillating, shifting, versatile, fickle, wavering, flickering, flitting, restless, erratic, unsettled, mobile, fluttering, oscillating, vibratory, vagrant, wayward, desultory, afloat, alternating, plastic, disquiet, alterable, casual, unballasted, volatile, capricious (608).

Frail, tottering, shaking, shaky, trembling, fugitive, ephemeral, transient (111), fading, fragile, deciduous, slippery, unsettled, irresolute (605), rocky, groggy.

Kaleidoscopic, prismatic, iridescent, opalescent, shot.

Phrases: Unstable as water; changeable as the moon, or as a weathercock; *sic transit gloria mundi*; here to-day and gone to-morrow.

150 IMMUTABILITY

Substantives: Stability, unchangeableness, unchangeability, constancy, permanence, persistence (106), invariableness, durability, steadiness (604), immobility, fixedness, stableness, settledness, stabiliment, firmness, stiffness, anchylosis, solidity, aplomb, ballast, incommutability, insusceptibility, irrevocableness.

Rock, pillar, tower, foundation, fixture.

Phrase: The law of the Medes and Persians.

Verbs: To be permanent, etc. (265), to stand, stand fast, stand pat, remain.

To settle, establish, stablish, perpetuate, fix, set, stabilitate, retain, keep, hold, make sure, nail, clinch, rivet, fasten (43), settle down, set on its legs.

Phrases: To build one's house on a rock; to weather the storm.

Adjectives: Immutable, incommutable, unchangeable, unaltered, unalterable, not to be changed, constant, permanent, invariable, undeviating, stable, durable (265), perennial (110), valid.

Fixed, steadfast, firm, fast, steady, confirmed, immovable, irremovable, rooted, riveted, stablished, established, incontrovertible, stereotyped, indeclinable, settled, stationary, stagnant.

Moored, anchored, at anchor, on a rock, firmly seated, deep-rooted, ineradicable.

Stranded, aground, stuck fast, high and dry.

Indefeasible, irretrievable, intransmutable, irresoluble, irrevocable, irreversible, inextinguishable, irreducible, indissoluble, indissolvable, indestructible, undying, imperishable, indelible, indeciduous, insusceptible of change.

Phrases: *J'y suis, j'y reste; stet*; can the Ethiopian change his skin, or the leopard his spots?

151 EVENTUALITY

Substantives: event, happening, occurrence, incident, affair, transaction, proceeding, fact, matter of fact, phenomenon, advent.

Business, concern, circumstance, particular, casualty, accident, adventure, passage, crisis, episode, pass, emergency, contingency, consequence (154).

The world, life, things, doings, course of things, the course, tide, stream, current, run, etc., of events.

Phrases: Stirring events; the ups and downs of life; a chapter of accidents; the cast of the dice (156).

Verbs: To happen, occur, take place, take effect, come, come of, become of, come about, come off, pass, come to pass, fall, fall out, run, be on foot, fall in, befall, betide, bechance, turn out, go off, prove, eventuate, draw on, turn up, crop up, supervene, survene, issue, arrive, ensue, arise, spring, start, come into existence, fall to one's lot.

To pass off, wear off, blow over.

To experience, meet with, go through, pass through, endure (821), suffer, fare.

Adjectives: Happening, occurring, etc., going on, current, incidental, eventful, stirring, bustling.

Phrase: The plot thickening.

Adverbs: Eventually, in the event of, on foot, on the *tapis,* as it may happen, happen what may, at all events, sink or swim, come what may.

Phrases: In the course of things; in the long run; as the world wags.

152 DESTINY
Substantives: fatality, fate, doom, destination, lot, fortune, star, planet, preordination, predestination, fatalism, inevitableness, kismet, karma, necessity (601), after life, futurity (121).
Phrases: The decrees of fate; the wheel of fortune.
Verbs: To impend, hang over, overhang, be in store, loom, threaten, await, come on, approach, stare one in the face, foreordain, preordain, predestine, doom, must be.
Phrase: To dree one's weird.
Adjectives: About to happen, impending, coming, destined, imminent, inevitable, ineluctable, inexorable, fated, doomed, devoted.
Phrases: On the cards; on the knees of the gods.
Adverbs: Necessarily, inevitably.
Phrases: What must be, must; *che sarà sarà*; 'It is written'; the die is cast.

Section VIII – Causation

153 CAUSE
Substantives: origin, source, principle, element, occasioner, prime mover, *primum mobile,* spring, mainspring, agent, seed, leaven, groundwork, basis (215), fountain, well, fount, fountain-head, spring-head, author (164), parent (166), *fons et origo, raison d'être.*

Pivot, hinge, turning-point, key, lever.

Final cause, proximate cause, immediate cause, ground, reason, the reason why, the why and the wherefore, rationale, occasion, derivation, provenance.

Rudiment, germ, embryo, bud, root, *radix,* radical, etymon, nucleus,

seed, ovum, stem, stock, trunk, taproot.

Nest, cradle, womb, *nidus,* birthplace, hot-bed, forcing-bed.

Causality, origination, causation, production (161), aetiology.

Theories of causation, creationism; evolution, Lamarckism, Darwinism, Spencerism, orthogenesis.
Verbs: To be the cause of, to originate, germinate, give origin to, cause, occasion, give rise to, kindle, suscitate, bring on, bring to pass, give occasion to, produce, bring about, institute, found, lay the foundation of, lie at the root of, procure, draw down, induce, realize, evoke, provoke, elicit, entail, develop, evolve, operate (161).

To conduce, contribute, tend to (176); to determine, decide.
Phrases: To have a hand in; to have a finger in the pie; to open the door to; to be at the bottom of; to sow the seeds of; to turn the scale.
Adjectives: Caused, occasioned, etc., causal, original, primary, primordial, having a common origin, connate, radical, embryonic, embryotic, in embryo.

Evolutionary, Darwinian; aetiological.
Phrase: Behind the scenes.

154 EFFECT
Substantives: consequence, product, result, resultant, resultance, upshot, issue, end (67), fruit, crop, aftermath, harvest, development, outgrowth, derivative, deriva-tion.

Production, produce, work, handiwork, performance, creature, creation, offshoot, fabric, offspring, first-fruits, firstlings, output, *dénouement,* derivation, heredity, evolution (161).
Verbs: To be the effect, work, fruit, result, etc., of; to be owing to, originate in or from, rise from, take its rise from, arise, spring, proceed, evolve, come of, emanate, come, grow, ger-

minate, bud, sprout, stem, issue, flow, result, follow, accrue, etc., from; come to; to come out of, be derived from, be caused by, depend upon, hinge upon, turn upon, result from, to be dependent upon, hang upon; to pan out.

Phrase: To take the consequences.

Adjectives: Owing to, due to, attributable to, ascribable to, resulting from, through, etc., all along of, hereditary, genetic, derivative.

Adverbs: Of course, consequently, necessarily, eventually.

Phrases: *Cela va sans dire*; thereby hangs a tale.

155 ATTRIBUTION

Substantives: theory, aetiology, ascription, reference to, rationale, accounting for, imputation to, derivation from, filiation, affiliation, genealogy, pedigree, paternity, maternity (166), explanation (522), cause (153).

Verbs: To attribute, ascribe, impute, refer to, derive from, lay to, point to, charge on, ground on, invest with, assign as cause, trace to, father upon, account for, theorize, ground, etc.

Phrases: To put the saddle on the right horse; to point out the reason of; to lay at the door of.

Adjectives: Attributable, imputable, assignable, traceable, ascribable, referable, owing to, derivable from.

Putative, attributed, imputed, etc.

Adverbs: Hence, thence, therefore, because, from that cause, for that reason, on that account, owing to, thanks to, forasmuch as, whence, *propter hoc,* wherefore, since, inasmuch as.

Why? wherefore? whence? how comes it? how is it? how happens it? how does it happen?

In some way, somehow, somehow or other, in some such way.

Phrase: *Hinc illae lacrimae.*

156 CHANCE

Substantives: indetermination, accident, fortune, hazard, hap, haphazard, chance-medley, luck, lot, fate (152), casualty, contingency, adventure, venture, pot-luck, lucky dip, treasure trove, hit.

A lottery, toss-up, game of chance, *sortes Virgiliance, rouge et noir,* heads or tails, gambling (621), sweepstake.

Possibility, probability, odds, long odds, a near shave, bare chance.

Phrases: The turn of the cards; a cast or throw of the dice; a pig in a poke, a blind date.

Verbs: To chance, hap, turn up; to fall to one's lot, to be one's fate (152); to light upon; stumble upon.

To game, gamble, cast lots, raffle, play for.

Phrases: To take one's chance; to toss up for; to chance one's arm; to take a flyer.

Adjectives: Casual, fortuitous, random, accidental, adventitious, causeless, incidental, contingent, uncaused, undetermined, indeterminate, suppositional, possible (470); aleatory.

Adverbs: By chance, by accident, perchance, peradventure, perhaps, maybe, mayhap, haply, possibly.

Casually, etc., at random, at a venture, as it may be, as it may chance, as it may turn up, as it may happen; as chance, luck, fortune, etc., would have it.

157 POWER

Substantives: potentiality, potency, prepotence, prepotency, propollence, puissance, strength (159), might, force, energy, metal, dint, right hand, ascendancy, sway, control, almightiness, ability, ableness, competency, efficiency, effectiveness, efficacy, efficaciousness, validity, cogency, enablement; agency (170), casualty (153), influence (175), authority (737).

Capability, capacity, faculty, quality, attribute, endowment, virtue, gift, property.

Pressure, high pressure, mechanical energy, applied force, motive power.
Verbs: To be powerful, etc., to gain power; to exercise power, sway, etc., to constrain.

To be the property, virtue, attribute, etc., of; to belong to, pertain to, appertain to, to lie or be in one's power.

To give or confer power, to empower, enable, invest, endue, endow, arm, render strong (159).
Adjectives: Powerful, high-powered, potent, puissant, potential, capable, able, equal to, cogent, valid, effective, effectual, efficient, efficacious, adequate, competent.

Forcible, energetic, vigorous, nervous, dynamic, sturdy, rousing, all-powerful, omnipotent, resistless, irresistible, vivid, inextinguishable, sovereign, invincible, unconquerable, indomitable.
Adverbs: Powerfully, etc., by virtue of, in full force.

158 IMPOTENCE
Substantives: inability, disability, disablement, impuissance, weakness (160), imbecility, paralysis, inaptitude, incapacity, incapability, invalidity, inefficacy, inefficiency, inefficaciousness, ineffectualness, disqualification, helplessness, incompetence.
Phrases: A dead letter; waste paper; *brutum fulmen*; blank cartridge.
Verbs: To be impotent, powerless, etc.; to collapse, fail, flunk, break down, fizzle out, fold up.

To render powerless, etc., to deprive of power, disable, disenable, incapacitate, disqualify, unfit, invalidate, nullify, deaden, cripple, cramp, paralyse, muzzle, hamstring, bowl over, render weak (160).
Phrases: To go by the board; to end in smoke.

To clip the wings of; spike the guns; to tie a person's hands; to put a spoke in one's wheel; to take the wind out of one's sails.
Adjectives: Powerless, impotent, unable, incapable, incompetent, inadequate, unequal to, inefficient, inefficacious, inept, ineffectual, ineffective, inoperative, nugatory, incapacitated, harmless, imbecile, disqualified, disabled, armless, disarmed, unarmed, weaponless, defenceless; unnerved, paralysed, palsied, disjointed, nerveless, adynamic, unendowed.
Phrases: Laid on the shelf; *hors de combat*; not having a leg to stand on.

159 STRENGTH
Substantives: energy (171), power (157), vigour, vitality, force, main force, physical force, brute force, spring, elasticity, tone, tension, tonicity.

Stoutness, sturdiness, lustiness, lustihood, stamina, physique, nerve, muscle, thews and sinews, backbone, pith, pithiness.

Feats of strength, athletics, gymnastics.

Strengthening, invigoration, bracing, recruital, recruitment, refreshment, refocillation (689).

Science of forces, dynamics, statics.

Adamant, steel, iron, oak, heart of oak.

An athlete, gymnast, acrobat; an Atlas, a Hercules, Sampson, Cyclops, Goliath.
Phrases: A giant refreshed; a tower of strength.
Verbs: To be strong, etc., to be stronger, to overmatch.

To render strong, etc., to give strength, tone, etc., to strengthen, invigorate, brace, buttress, sustain, fortify, harden, case-harden, steel, gird up, screw up, wind up, set up, tone up.

To reinforce, refit, recruit, vivify, restore (660), refect, refocillate (689).
Phrase: To set on one's legs.
Adjectives: Strong, mighty, vigor-

ous, stout, robust, sturdy, powerful, puissant, hard, adamantine, invincible, able-bodied, athletic, Herculean, muscular, brawny, sinewy, made of iron, strapping, well-set, well-knit, stalwart, doughty, husky, lusty, hardy, irresistible; strengthening, etc., invigorative, tonic.

Manly, manlike, masculine, male, virile, manful, full-blooded.

Unweakened, unallayed, unwithered, unshaken, unworn, unexhausted, unrelaxed, undiluted, unwatered, neat.
Phrases: Made of iron; as strong as a lion, as a horse; in great form; fit as a fiddle.
Adverbs: Strongly, forcibly, etc., by main force, *vi et armis*, by might and main, tooth and nail, hammer and tongs, for all one is worth.

160 WEAKNESS

Substantives: feebleness, impotence (158), debility, atony, relaxation, helplessness, languor, slackness, enervation, nervousness, faintness, languidness, infirmity, emasculation, effeminacy, feminality, femineity, flaccidity, softness, defencelessness.

Childhood, etc. (127, 129); orphan, chicken.

Declension, loss, failure, etc., of strength, invalidation, delicacy, delicateness, decrepitude, asthenia, neurasthenia, anaemia, bloodlessness, palsy, paralysis, exhaustion, collapse, prostration, faintness, cachexy (or cachexia).

A reed, thread, rope of sand, house of cards; a weakling, sissy, jellyfish.
Verbs: To be weak, etc., to droop, fade, faint, swoon, languish, decline, flag, fail, totter, drop, crock; to go by the board.

To render weak, etc., to weaken, enfeeble, debilitate, devitalize, deprive of strength, relax, enervate, unbrace, unman, emasculate, castrate, geld, hamstring, disable, unhinge, cripple,

cramp, paralyse, maim, sprain, exhaust, prostrate, blunt the edge of, deaden, dilute, water, water down.
Adjectives: Weak, feeble, debile, strengthless, nerveless, imbecile, unnerved, relaxed, unstrung, unbraced, enervated, nervous, sinewless, spineless, lustless, effeminate, feminine, womanly, unmanned, emasculated, castrated.

Crippled, maimed, lamed, shattered, broken, frail, fragile, flimsy, gimcrack, halting, shaken, crazy, shaky, paralysed, palsied, paralytic, decrepit, puny, shilpit, drooping, languid, faint, sickly, flagging, dull, slack, limp, spent, effete, weatherbeaten, worn, seedy, exhausted, deadbeat, all in, whacked, done up, languishing, wasted, washy, vincible, untenable, laid low, run down, asthenic, neurasthenic, neurotic, rickety, invertebrate, feckless.

Unstrengthened, unsustained, unsupported, unaided, unassisted, defenceless, indefensible, unfortified, unfriended, fatherless, etc.
Phrases: On one's last legs; the worse for wear; weak as a child, as a baby, as a kitten, as water; good or fit for nothing.

161 PRODUCTION

Substantives: creation, formation, construction, fabrication, manufacture, building, architecture, erection, edification, coinage, organization, putting together, establishment, setting up, performance (729), workmanship, output.

Development, breeding, evolution, flowering, genesis, generation, *epigenesis,* procreation, propagation, fecundation, impregnation, gestation, birth, bringing forth, parturition, growth, proliferation.

Theory of development, Mendelism, eugenics.
Verbs: To produce, effect, perform,

operate, do, make, form, construct, fabricate, frame, contrive, manufacture, weave, forge, coin, carve, sculp, chisel, build, raise, edify, rear, erect, run up, establish.

To constitute, compose, organize, institute, work out, realize, bring to bear, bring to pass, accomplish, bring off.

To create, generate, engender, beget, bring into being, breed, propagate, proliferate, conceive, bear, procreate, give birth to, bring forth, yield, flower, fructify, hatch, develop, bring up.

To induce, superinduce, suscitate (153).

Phrases: To be brought to bed of; to usher into the world.

Adjectives: Produced, etc., producing, productive of, etc., creative, formative, parturient, pregnant, *enceinte,* genetic; eugenic.

Phrase: In the family way.

162 DESTRUCTION

Substantives: waste, dissolution, breaking up, disruption, consumption, disorganization, falling to pieces, crumbling, etc.

Fall, downfall, ruin, perdition, crash, smash, havoc, desolation, *bouleversement, débacle,* upset, wreck, shipwreck, cataclysm, extinction, annihilation; doom, destruction of life (360), prang (716, 732).

Demolition, demolishment, overthrow, subversion, suppression, dismantling, cutting up, corrosion, erosion, crushing, upsetting, abolition, abolishment, sacrifice, immolation, holocaust, dilapidation, devastation, *razzia,* ravaging, extermination, eradication, extirpation, rooting out, averruncation, sweeping, etc., death-blow, *coup de grâce,* the crack of doom.

Verbs: To be destroyed, etc., to perish, waste, fall to pieces, break up, crumble, break down, crack.

To destroy, do or make away with, demolish, overturn, upset, throw down, overthrow, overwhelm, subvert, put an end to, uproot, eradicate, extirpate, root out, grub up, break up, pull down, do for, dish, ditch, crumble, smash, crash, crush, quell, quash, squash, squelch, cut up, shatter, shiver, batter, tear or shake to pieces, tear to tatters, pick to pieces, put down, suppress, strike out, throw or knock down, cut down, knock on the head, stifle, dispel, fell, sink, swamp, scuttle, engulf, submerge, wreck, corrode, erode, consume, sacrifice, immolate, burke, blow down, sweep away, erase, expunge, liquidate, wipe out, mow down, blast.

To waste, lay waste, ravage, dilapidate, dismantle, disorganize, devour, swallow up, desolate, devastate, sap, mine, blow up, stifle, dispatch, exterminate, extinguish, quench, annihilate, kill (361), unroot, root out, rout out, averruncate, deracinate.

Phrases: To go to the dogs, or to pot; to go to the devil, or to rack and ruin; to be all over with one.

To lay the axe at the root of; to make short work of; make a clean sweep of; to make mincemeat of; to scatter to the winds; cut up root and branch; knock on the head; to wipe the floor with; to knock into a cocked hat; to sap the foundations of; to nip in the bud; to strike at the root of; to pluck up by the root; to ravage with fire and sword.

Adjectives: Destroyed, done for, dished, etc.; destructive, subversive, pernicious, ruinous, deadly, indendiary, demolitionary.

163 REPRODUCTION

Substantives: renovation, restoration (660), reconstruction, revival, regeneration, revivication, resuscitation, reanimation, resurrection, resurgence, reappearance, palingenesis, reincarnation, multiplication; phoenix.

101

Verbs: To reproduce, revive, renew, renovate, rebuild, reconstruct, regenerate, revivify, resurrect, resuscitate, reanimate, reincarnate, quicken; come again into life, reappear.
Phrase: To spring up like a mushroom.
Adjectives: Reproduced, etc., renascent, reappearing; hydra-headed.

164 PRODUCER
Substantives: originator, author, artist, creator, prime mover, founder, workman, doer, performer, manufacturer, forger, agent (690), builder, architect, factor.

165 DESTROYER
Substantives: extinguisher, exterminator, assassin (361), executioner (975), ravager, annihilator, subverter, demolisher; iconoclast, vandal.

166 PATERNITY
Substantives: fatherhood, maternity, motherhood, parentage, parent, father, sire, paterfamilias, pater, dad, daddy, papa, pa; mother, mamma, ma, mummy, mum, dam, materfamilias, mater, procreator, progenitor, begetter, ancestor, ancestry, forefathers, forbears, grandsire; house, parent stem, trunk, stock, pedigree.
Adjectives: Paternal, maternal, parental, fatherly, motherly, family, ancestral, patriarchal.

167 POSTERITY
Substantives: progeny, breed, issue, offspring, brood, seed, litter, spawn, scion, offset, child, son, daughter, grandchild, grandson, granddaughter, etc., bantling, shoot, sprout, sprig, slip, branch, line, lineage, filiation, family, offshoot, ramification, descendant, heir, heiress, heir apparent, heir presumptive.
   Straight, descent, sonship, primogeniture, ultimogeniture.

Adjectives: Filial, daughterly, dutiful, lineal, hereditary.
Phrase: A chip off the old block; the rising generation.

168 PRODUCTIVENESS
Substantives: fecundity, fruitfulness, fertility, prolificness; creativeness, inventiveness.
   Pregnancy, gestation, pullulation, fructification, multiplication, propagation, procreation.
   A milch cow, rabbit, warren, hydra.
Phrase: A land flowing with milk and honey.
Verbs: To procreate (161), multiply, teem, pullulate, fructify, proliferate, generate, fertilize, impregnate, conceive.
Adjectives: Productive, prolific, teeming, fertile, fruitful, luxuriant, fecund, pregnant, great, gravid, *enceinte,* with child, with young.
   Procreant, procreative, generative, propagable, life-giving.

169 UNPRODUCTIVENESS
Substantives: infertility, barrenness, sterility, unfruitfulness, unprofitableness, infecundity, fruitlessness (645), non-agency.
Verbs: To be unproductive, etc., to come to nothing.
   To render unproductive, sterilize, castrate, spay, pasteurize.
Adjectives: Unproductive, inoperative, barren, addle, infertile, unprolific, sterile, unfruitful, fallow, fruitless, infecund, issueless, unprofitable (645).

170 AGENCY
Substantives: operation, force, working, strain, function, office, hand, intervention, intercession, interposition, exercise, work, swing, play, causation (153), impelling force, mediation (631), action (680).
   Modus operandi, quickening power, maintaining power.

Verbs: To be in action, to operate, function, work, act, perform, play, support, sustain, strain, maintain, take effect, quicken, strike, strike hard, strike home, bring to bear.

Phrases: To come into play; to make an impression.

Adjectives: Acting, operating, etc., operative, practical, efficient, efficacious, effectual, in force.

Acted upon, wrought upon.

171 PHYSICAL ENERGY

Substantives: force, power, activity, keenness, intensity, sharpness, pungency, vigour, strength, edge, point, raciness, metal, mettle, vim, dash, fire, punch, go, pep.

Seasoning, mordant, pepper, mustard, cayenne, caviare (392).

Mental energy (604), mental excitation (824), voluntary energy (682).

Exertion, activity, stir, bustle, hustle, agitation, effervescence, fermentation, ferment, ebullition, splutter, perturbation, briskness, voluntary activity (682), quicksilver.

Verbs: To give energy, energize, stimulate, invigorate, kindle, galvanize, electrify, intensify, excite, exert (173).

Adjectives: Strong, energetic, emphatic, forcible, forceful, active, keen, vivid, intense, severe, sharp, acute, pungent, poignant, racy, brisk, ebullient, mettlesome, enterprising, go-ahead, double-edged, double-barrelled, double-distilled, drastic, intensive, trenchant.

Phrases: *Fortiter in re*; with telling effect; with full steam; at high pressure; flat out.

172 PHYSICAL INERTNESS

Substantives: inertia, *vis inertiae,* inertion, passiveness, passivity, inactivity, torpor, latency, torpidity, dullness, stagnation, deadness, heaviness, flatness, slackness, tameness, slowness, languor, lentor, quiescence (265), sleep (683), intermission (141).

Mental inertness, indecision (605), placidity (826).

Verbs: To be alert, inactive, passive, etc.; to hang fire, smoulder.

Phrase: To sit on the fence.

Adjectives: Inert, inactive, passive, torpid, flaccid, limp, lymphatic, sluggish, dull, heavy, flat, slack, tame, slow, supine, slothful, stagnant, blunt, lifeless, dead.

Latent, dormant, smouldering, unexerted, unstrained, uninfluential.

Adverbs: Inactively, in suspense, in abeyance.

173 VIOLENCE

Substantives: inclemency, vehemence, might, impetuosity, boisterousness, abruptness, ebullition, turbulence, horseplay, bluster, uproar, shindy, row, riot, rumpus, fierceness, rage, wildness, fury, hear, exacerbation, exasperation, malignity, fit, paroxysm, orgasm, force, brute force, *coup de main,* strain, shock, spasm, convulsion, throe.

Outbreak, burst, outburst, dissilience, discharge, volley, explosion, blow-up, blast, detonation, rush, eruption, displosion, torrent.

Turmoil, tumult, storm, tempest, squall, hurricane, tornado, typhoon, cyclone, earthquake, volcano, thunder-storm.

A rowdy (949), berserk (or berserker), spitfire, fireater, hellhound, fury, termagant, virago, vixen, hellcat, dragon, demon, tiger, beldam, Tisiphone, Megaera, Alecto, Maenad.

Verbs: To be violent, etc., to run high, ferment, effervesce, run wild, run riot, run amuck, rush, tear, rush headlong, bluster, rage, rampage, riot, storm, boil, fume, let off steam, foam, wreak, bear down.

To break out, fly out, bounce, go off, explode, displode, fly, fulminate, detonate, blow up, flash, flare, burst, burst out, shock, strain.

To render violent, sharpen, stir up, quicken, excite, incite, stimulate, kindle, lash, suscitate, urge, accelerate, foment, aggravate, exasperate, exacerbate, convulse, infuriate, madden, lash into fury, inflame, let off, discharge.

Phrases: To break the peace; to see red; to out-herod Herod; add fuel to the flame.

Adjectives: Violent, vehement, warm, acute, rough, rude, wild, boisterous, impetuous, ungentle, tough, brusque, abrupt, rampant, knockabout, rampageous, bluff, turbulent, blustering, riotous, rowdy, noisy, thundering, obstreperous, uproarious, outrageous, frantic, phrenetic, headstrong, rumbustious, disorderly (59).

Savage, fierce, ferocious, fiery, fuming, excited, unquelled, unquenched, unextinguished, unrepressed, unbridled, unruly, boiling, boiling over, furious, outrageous, raging, running riot, storming, hysteric, hysterical, wild, running wild, ungovernable, unappeasable, immitigable, uncontrollable, insuppressible, irrepressible, raging, desperate, mad, rabid, infuriate, exasperated.

Tempestuous, stormy, squally, spasmodic, spastic, paroxysmal, convulsive, galvanic, bursting, explosive, detonating, volcanic, meteoric, seismic.

Phrases: Fierce as a tiger; all the fat in the fire.

Adverbs: Violently, etc., by force, by main force, like mad.

Phrases: By might and main; tooth and nail; *vi et armis*; at the point of the sword, or bayonet.

174 MODERATION

Substantives: gentleness, temperateness, calmness, mildness, composure, sobriety, slowness, tameness, quiet (740), restfulness, reason.

Relaxation, remission, measure, golden mean, mitigation, tranquillization, assuagement, soothing, allaying, etc., contemperation, pacification (723), restraint, check (751), lullaby, sedative, lenitive, demulcent, palliative, opiate, anodyne, balm, opium.

Mental calmness (826).

Verbs: To be moderate, etc., to keep within bounds or within compass, to settle down, to keep the peace, to sober down, remit, relent.

To moderate, soften, soothe, mitigate, appease, temper, attemper, contemper, mollify, lenify, tame, dull, take off that edge, blunt, obtund, tone down, subdue.

To tranquillize, assuage, appease, lull, cool, compose, still, calm, quiet, hush, quell, sober, pacify, damp, lay, allay, rebate, slacken, smooth, soften, alleviate, rock to sleep, deaden (376), check, restrain, slake, curb, bridle, rein in, hold in, repress, smother, counteract (179).

Phrases: To pour oil on the waves; to pour balm into; to throw cold water on.

Adjectives: Moderate, gentle, mild, sober, temperate, measured, reasonable, tempered, calm, unruffled, tranquil, smooth, untroubled; unexciting, unirritating, soft, bland, oily, demulcent, lenitive, cool, quiet, anodyne, hypnotic, sedative, peaceful, peaceable, pacific, lenient, tame, halcyon, restful.

Phrases: Gentle as a lamb; mild as milk.

Adverbs: Moderately, gently, temperately, softly, etc.

Phrases: Softly, softly, catchee monkey; *suaviter in modo; est modus in rebus.*

175 INFLUENCE

Substantives: weight, pressure, prevalence, sway, ascendancy (or ascendency), preponderance, predominance, predominancy, dominance, prepotency, importance (642), reign, ableness, capability (157).

Footing, hold, foothold, purchase, fulcrum, stance, *point d'appui, pou sto, locus standi,* leverage, vantage-ground; aegis, protection, patronage, auspices.
Phrases: A tower of strength; a host in himself.
Verbs: To have influence, etc., to have a hold upon, to have a pull, to gain a footing, work upon, take root, take hold, permeate, penetrate, infiltrate, prevail, dominate, predominate, outweigh, overweigh, carry weight, weigh, tell, to bear upon.
Phrases: To be in the ascendant; to cut some ice; to pull wires; to pull the strings; to set the fashion; to have a voice.
Adjectives: Influential, valid, weighty, prevailing, prevalent, dominant, regnant, predominating, predominant, prepotent, ascendant, rife.
Adverbs: With telling effect.

175A Absence of INFLUENCE
Substantives: impotence (158), weakness (160), inertness (172).
Verbs: To have no influence.
Phrase: To cut no ice.
Adjectives: Uninfluential.

176 TENDENCY
Substantives: aptness, proneness, proclivity, conduciveness, bent, bias, quality, inclination, trend, propensity, predisposition, leaning, drift, conducement, temperament, idiosyncrasy, vein, humour, mood.
Verbs: To tend, contribute, conduce, lead, dispose, incline, trend, verge, bend to, affect, carry, promote, redound to, subserve to (644), bid fair to, make for, gravitate towards.
Adjectives: Tending, contributing, conducing, conducive, working towards, calculated to, disposing, inclining, bending, leading, carrying to, subservient, subsidiary (644, 707);

apt, liable, prone, disposed, predisposed.
Adverbs: For, whither, in a fair way to.

177 LIABILITY
Substantives: subjection to, dependence on, exposure to, contingency, possibility (156), susceptivity, susceptibility.
Verbs: To be liable, etc., incur, to lay oneself open to, lie under, expose oneself to, stand a chance, to open a door to.
Phrase: To stick one's neck out.
Adjectives: Liable, apt, prone, subject, open to, incident to, exposed to, dependent on; answerable, accountable, responsible.

Contingent, incidental, possible, casual.
Phrases: Within range of; at the mercy of.

178 CONCURRENCE
Substantives: co-operation, collaboration (709), union, agreement, consent (488), pulling together, alliance; complicity, connivance, collusion.

Voluntary concurrence (709).
Verbs: To concur, co-operate, conspire, agree, conduce, contribute, unite, to pull together, hang together, join forces.
Phrases: To have a hand in; to be in the same boat; to go hand in hand (709).
Adjectives: Concurring, concurrent, conjoined, concomitant, associate, co-operating, conspiring, agreeing, correspondent, conformable, pulling together, etc., of one mind, in alliance with, with one consent, of one mind, with one accord,

179 COUNTERACTION
Substantives: opposition, antagonism, polarity, clashing, etc., collision, contrariety (14), resistance, interference, friction.

Neutralization, nullification, compensation (30).

Reaction, retroaction (277), repercussion, rebound, recoil, ricochet, counterblast.

Check, obstacle, hindrance (706); antidote, counter-irritant, preventive, corrective, remedy (662).

Voluntary counteraction (708).

Verbs: To counteract, oppose, cross, contravene, antagonize, interfere or conflict with, collide with, clash, neutralize, undo, nullify, render null; to militate against, withstand, resist (719), hinder (706), repress, control, curb, check, rein in (174).

To react (277), countervail, counterpoise (30), overpoise.

Adjectives: Counteracting, opposing, etc., counteractive, antagonistic, conflicting, reactionary, recalcitrant, opposite, retroactive, cohibitive, counter, contrary (14).

Adverbs: Counter, notwithstanding, nevertheless, nathless, none the less, yet, still, although, though, albeit, howbeit, maugre, at all events.

But, even, however, in defiance of, in the teeth of, in the face of, in spite of, in despite of (708).

Phrases: For all that; all the same; be that as it may; even so.

Words relating to space

Section 1 – Space in General

180 SPACE

Substantives: extension, extent, expanse, room, scope, range, purview, way, expansion, compass, sweep, play, amplitude, latitude, field, swing, spread, stretch; spare room, headway, elbow-room, freedom, house-room, stowage, roomage, margin.

Open space, void space, vacuity (4), opening, waste, wilderness, moor, moorland, campagna, tundra.

Abyss (198); unlimited space, infinity (105).

Adjectives: Spatial, two-dimensional, three-dimensional.

Spacious, roomy, commodious, extensive, expansive, capacious, ample.

Boundless, unlimited, unbounded, limitless, illimitable, infinite, uncircumscribed, shoreless, trackless, pathless.

Adverbs: Extensively, etc., wherever, everywhere.

Phrases: The length and the breadth of the land; far and near, far and wide; all over; all the world over; from China to Peru; from Land's End to John o' Groat's; in every quarter; in all quarters; in all lands; every hole and corner; here, there, and everywhere; from pole to pole; throughout the world; to the four winds; under the sun.

181 REGION

Substantives: sphere, ground, area, realm, quarter, district, orb, circuit, circle, compartment, domain, tract, department, territory, country, canton, county, shire, township, riding, hundred, parish, bailiwick, province, satrapy, *arrondissement*, commune, enclave, principality, duchy, kingdom, empire, dominion, colony, protectorate, mandate.

Arena, precincts, *enceinte*, walk, patch, plot, paddock, enclosure, field, compound.

Clime, climate, zone, meridian.

Adjectives: Regional, territorial, provincial, parochial, local, etc.

182 PLACE

Substantives: spot, point, nook, corner, recess, hole, niche, compartment, premises, precinct, station, pitch, venue, abode (189).

Indefinite place.

Adverbs: Somewhere, in some place, wherever it may be.

183 SITUATION

Substantives: position, locality, locale, status, latitude and longitude, footing, standing, post, stage, bearings, aspect, orientation, attitude, posture, lie, emplacement.

Place, site, station, pitch, seat, venue, whereabouts, direction, azimuth, etc. (278).

Topography, geography, chorography.

A map, chart, plan (554).

Verbs: To be situated, to lie, to have its seat in.

Adjectives: Local, topical; situate.

Adverbs: *In situ*, here and there, *passim*, whereabouts.

184 LOCATION

Substantives: localization, lodgment, deposition, reposition, stowage, establishment, settlement, fixation, grafting, insertion (300), lading, encampment, billet, installation.

A colony, settlement, cantonment.

A habitation, residence, dwelling (189).

Phrases: *Genius loci*; the spirit of the place.

Verbs: To place, situate, locate, localize, put, lay, set, seat, station, lodge, park, post, install, house, settle, stow, dump, establish, fix, root, plant, graft, stick in, tuck in, insert, wedge in, shelve, pitch, camp, posit, deposit, reposit, cradle, encamp, moor, pack, embed (or imbed), vest, stock, populate, people, colonize, domicile.

To billet on, quarter upon.

To pocket, pouch, put up, bag, load.

To inhabit, reside (186), domesticate, put up at, colonize.

Phrase: To pitch one's tent.

Adjectives: Placed, located, etc., situate, situated, ensconced, nestled, embosomed, housed, moored, rooted, unremoved.

185 DISPLACEMENT

Substantives: dislodgment, eviction, ejectment (297), deportation, extradition, expatriation, banishment, exile.

Removal, remotion, transposition, relegation (270).

Verbs: To displace, dislodge, unhouse, unkennel, break bulk, take off, eject, evict, chuck out, hoof out, expel, etc. (297), extradite, expatriate, banish, exile, relegate, oust, rusticate, ostracize, remove, transfer, transpose, transplant, transport (270), empty, clear, clear out, sweep off, sweep away, do away with, get rid of, root out, disestablish, unpeople, depopulate.

To vacate, leave (293), get out, heave out, bale out, lade out, pour out (297).

Phrase: To make a clean sweep of.

Adjectives: Displaced, etc., unhoused, houseless, homeless, stateless.

Phrase: Like a fish out of water.

186 PRESENCE

Substantives: occupancy, occupation, attendance, whereness.

Diffusion, permeation, pervasion, interpenetration, dissemination (73).

Ubiquity, ubiety, ubiquitousness, omnipresence.

Verbs: To exist in space, to be present, attend, remain.

To occur in a place, lie, stand, occupy, colonize.

To inhabit, dwell, reside, live, abide, sojourn, lodge, nestle, perch, roost, put up at, hang out at, stay at, stop at, squat, hive, burrow, camp, encamp, bivouac, anchor, settle, take up one's quarters, pitch one's tent, get a footing, frequent, haunt, tenant, take root, strike root, revisit.

To fill, pervade, permeate, penetrate, interpenetrate, infiltrate, be diffused through, be disseminated through, overspread, run through.

Adjectives: Present, occupying, inhabiting, etc., moored, at anchor, resident, residentiary, domiciled.

Ubiquitous, omnipresent.

Adverbs: Here, there, where? everywhere, in residence, aboard, on board, at home, afield, etc., on the spot.

Phrases: Here, there, and everywhere; at every turn.

187 ABSENCE

Substantives: non-existence (2), non-residence, non-attendance, alibi, absenteeism.

Emptiness, void, vacuum, voidness, vacuity, vacancy, vacuousness.

An absentee, truant, nobody, nobody on earth.

Verbs: To be absent, not present, etc., vacate, to keep away, to keep out of the way.

Phrases: Make oneself scarce; absent oneself; take oneself off; stay away; play truant; be conspicuous by one's absence.

Adjectives: Absent, not present, away, gone from home, missing, non-resident.

Empty, void, vacant, vacuous, blank, untenanted, tenantless, uninhabited, deserted, devoid, unoccupied, unpeopled.

Phrases: Nowhere to be found; AWOL (absent without leave); *non est inventus*; not a soul; nobody present; the bird being flown.

Adverbs: Without, minus, nowhere, elsewhere, sans.

Phrases: One's back being turned; behind one's back.

188 INHABITANT

Substantives: resident, residentiary, dweller, indweller, occupier, occupant, lodger, boarder, paying guest, inmate, tenant, sojourner, settler, squatter, backwoodsman, national, colonist, denizen, citizen, cit, cockney, townsman, burgess, countryman, villager, cottar, compatriot, garrison, crew, population, people.

Native, indigene, aborigines, autochthones, son of the soil.

A colony, settlement, household.

Newcomer (57).

Adjectives: Indigenous, native, aboriginal, autochthonous, domestic, domiciliated, domesticated, domiciliary.

189 ABODE

Substantives: dwelling, lodging, domicile, residence, address, habitation, berth, seat, lap, sojourn, housing, quarters, accommodation, headquarters, throne, ark, tabernacle.

Nest, nidus, lair, haunt, eyrie (or aerie), den, hole, earth, warren, rookery, hive, habitat, haunt, resort, retreat, nidification, perch, roost.

Bivouac, camp, encampment, cantonment, castrametation, tent, marquee, teepee, igloo.

Cave, cavern, cell, grove, grot, grotto, alcove, bower, arbour, cove, chamber (191).

Home, fatherland, motherland, native land, country, homestead, homestall, fireside, snuggery, hearth, Lares and Penates, household gods, roof, household, housing; 'dulce domum', Blighty.

Building, structure, edifice, fabric, erection, pile, tenement, messuage, farm, farmhouse, steading, grange.

Cot, cabin, hut, shack, chalet, croft, shed, hangar, penthouse, lean-to, booth, stall, hovel, outhouse, barn, kennel, sty, coop, hutch, cage, cote, stable, garage, offices.

House, mansion, villa, flat, flatlet, prefab, maisonnette, cottage, box, lodge, *pied-à-terre,* bungalow, hermitage, summer-house, gazebo, folly, rotunda, tower, temple (1000), château, castle, pavilion, court, hall, palace, kiosk, house-boat.

Inn, hostel, hotel, roadhouse, motel, tavern, caravansery, hospice, rest-house, dak-bungalow, barrack, loding-house, guest-house, doss-house, lodgings, apartments, diggings, digs.

Hamlet, village, clachan, thorp, dorp, kraal, borough, burgh, municipality, town, city, garden city, metropolis, suburb (227), conurbation, province, country.

Street, place, terrace, parade, road, avenue, row, lane, alley, court, wynd, close, yard, passage, rents, slum; square, polygon, quadrant, circus, crescent, mall, place, piazza, arcade, gardens.

Anchorage, roadstead, dock, basin, wharf, quay, port, harbour, haven.

Adjectives: Urban, civic, metropolitan, municipal, provincial, rural, rustic, countrified; home-like, homy.

190 CONTENTS
Substantives: cargo, lading, filling, stuffing, freight, load, burden, ware (798).

191 RECEPTACLE
Substantives: recipient, receiver, reservatory, compartment (636).

Cell, cellule, loculus, follicle, hole, corner, niche, recess, nook, crypt, stall, pigeon-hole, lodging (189), bed, berth, bunk, doss, etc. (215), store-room, strong-room.

Capsule, vesicle, cyst, bladder, pod.

Stomach, belly, paunch, ventricle, crop, craw, maw, gizzard, bread-basket, kyte, ovary, womb (221).

Pocket, pouch, sporran, fob, sheath, scabbard, socket, bag, sac, sack, wallet, scrip, poke, kit, knapsack, rucksack, haversack, sabretache, satchel, cigar-case, cigarette-case, reticule, powder-box, flapjack, compact, vanity-case, vanity-bag, portfolio, budget.

Chest, box, hutch, coffer, case, casket, caddy, pyx (or pix), caisson, desk, davenport, escritoire, bureau, cabinet, reliquary; trunk, portmanteau, saratoga, grip-sack, grip, bandbox, valise, hold-all, attaché-case, dispatch-case, dispatch-box, writing-case, suit-case, dressing-case, kit-bag, brief-bag, brief-case, gladstone bag, boot, creel, crate, packing-case, snuff-box, mull.

Vessel, vase, bushel, barrel, canister, jar, can, pottle, basket, pannier, corbeille, punnet, hamper, tray, hod.

For liquids: cistern, reservoir, tank, vat, cauldron, barrel, cask, keg, runlet, firkin, kilderkin, demijohn, carboy, amphora, bottle, jar, decanter, carafe, tantalus, ewer, cruse, crock, kit, canteen, flagon, flask, flasket, thermos flask, vacuum flask, stoup, noggin, vial (or phial), cruet, caster, urn, samovar, billy.

Tub, bucket, pail, pot, tankard, beaker, jug, pitcher, mug, noggin, pipkin, gallipot, matrass, receiver, alembic, retort, test-tube, pipette, capsule, kettle, spittoon.

Bowl, basin, jorum, punch-bowl, cup, goblet, chalice, quaich, tumbler, glass, horn, can, pan, pannikin, plate, dish, trencher, tray, salver, patera, calabash, porringer, saucepan, skillet, casserole, tureen, saucer, platter, hod, scuttle, baikie, shovel, trowel, spoon, spatula, ladle.

Closet, cupboard, cellaret, chiffonier, wardrobe, bunker, locker, bin, buffet, press, safe, sideboard, whatnot, drawer, chest of drawers, tallboy, lowboy, till.

Chamber, flat, storey, apartment, room, cabin, bower, office, court, hall, saloon, *salon*, parlour, state-room, presence-chamber, reception-room, drawing-room, sitting-room, living-room, gallery, cabinet, nursery, boudoir, library, study, snuggery, adytum, sanctum, den, phrontistery, lumber-room (636), dormitory, bedroom, dressing-room, refectory, dining-room, breakfast-room, billiard-room, smoking-room, pew, harem, seraglio, zenana.

Attic, loft, garret, cockloft, belfry, cellar, vault, hold, cockpit, ground-floor, *rez-de-chaussée*, basement, kitchen, kitchenette, pantry, scullery, bathroom, lavatory, water-closet, w.c., urinal, latrine, rear, toilet, convenience, comfort station, heads, thunder-box, offices.

Portico, porch, veranda, piazza, stoop, lobby, court, hall, vestibule, foyer, lounge, corridor, loggia, passage, anteroom, antechamber.

Adjectives: Capsular, saccular, sacculate, recipient, ventricular, cystic, vascular, celled, cellular, cellulous, cellulose, camerated, chambered, locular, multilocular, roomed, two-roomed, etc., polygastric, pouched, marsupial.

Section II – Dimensions

192 SIZE

Substantives: magnitude, dimension, bulk, volume, largeness, bigness, greatness (31), expanse, amplitude, mass, massiveness.

Capacity, capaciousness, tonnage (or tunnage), calibre, scantling.

Average size, stock size.

Corpulence, adiposity, obesity, chubbiness, plumpness, *embonpoint*, stoutness, out-size; corporation, flesh and blood, brawn, brawniness.

Hugeness, vastness, enormousness, enormity, immensity, monstrousness, monstrosity; expansion (194), infinity (105).

A giant, Goliath, Brobdingnagian, Antaeus, Gargantua, monster, whale, leviathan, elephant, mammoth, colossus, tun, lump, chunk, bulk, block, boulder, mass, bushel, whacker, thumper, whopper, spanker, behemoth.

A mountain, mound, heap (72).

Phrases: A Triton among the minnows; the lion's share.

Verbs: To be large, etc., to become large (194).

Adjectives: Large, big, great, considerable, bulky, voluminous, ample, massive, massy, capacious, comprehensive, mighty, king-sized.

Corpulent, obese, stout, fat, plump, rotund, buxom, sonsy, lusty, strapping, bouncing, portly, burly, brawny, fleshy, beefy, goodly, in good case, chopping, jolly, chubby, full-grown, chub-faced, lubberly, hulking, unwieldy, lumpish, husky, stalwart.

Squab, dumpy (202), tubby, rolypoly, pursy, blowsy.

Huge, immense, enormous, mighty, unbounded, vast, vasty, amplitudinous, stupendous, inordinate, herculean, thumping, whacking, whopping, spanking, thundering, monstrous, monster; gigantic, giant-like, colossal, titanic, mountainous, elephantine, mammoth, cyclopean, Antaean, Gargantuan, Falstaffian, Brobdingnagian; infinite, unbounded.

Phrases: Large as life; plump as a partridge; fat as a pig; fat as butter; fat as bacon.

193 LITTLENESS

Substantives: smallness (32), minuteness, diminutiveness, exiguity, inextension, puniness, dwarfishness, epitome, duo-decimo, rudiment, microcosm.

Leanness, emaciation, thinness, macilency, flaccidity, meagreness.

A dwarf, runt, pygmy, midget, Lilliputian, chit, bantam, urchin, elf, doll, puppet, skeleton, ghost, spindleshanks, shadow, Tom Thumb, manikin, *homunculus*.

Animalcule, mite, insect, emmet, fly, gnat, midge, shrimp, minnow, worm, grub, tit, tomtit, mouse, small fry, smout, mushroom, pollard, millet-seed, mustard-seed, grain of sand, molehill.

Atom, point, speck, dot, mote, ace, jot, iota, tittle, whit, particle, corpuscle, electron, molecule, monad, granule, grain, crumb, globule, nutshell, minim, drop, droplet, mouthful, thimbleful, sprinkling, dash, suspicion, *soupçon*, minimum, powder (330), driblet, patch, scrap, chip, inch, mathematical point; minutiae.

Phrases: The shadow of a shade; a drop in the ocean; chicken feed; tip of the ice-berg.

Verbs: To be small, etc., to become small, contract (195).

Adjectives: Little, small, minute, diminutive, inconsiderable, exiguous, puny, tiny, wee, weeny, teeny-weeny, petty, mini, minikin, hop-o'-my-thumb, miniature, bijou, *petite*, pygmy, undersized, half-pint, dwarf, stunted, dwarfed, dwarfish, pollard,

Lilliputian; pocket, thumb-nail, portative, portable, duodecimo.

Microscopic, infra-microscopic, evanescent, impalpable, imperceptible, invisible, inappreciable, infinitesimal, homoeopathic, atomic, corpuscular, molecular, rudimentary, rudimental.

Lean, thin, gaunt, meagre, emaciated, lank, macilent, ghostly, starved, starveling, fallen away, scrubby, reduced, shrunk, shrunken, attenuated, extenuated, shrivelled, tabid, flaccid, starved, skinny, wizen wizened, scraggy, lanky, raw-boned, scrawny, spindle-shanked, lantern-jawed (203).

Phrases: In a small compass; in a nutshell; on a small scale.

Worn to a shadow; skin and bone.

194   EXPANSION

Substantives: enlargement, extension, augmentation, increase of size, amplification, ampliation, aggrandisement, spread, increment, growth, development, pullulation, swell, dilatation, rarefaction, turgescence, turgidity, thickening, tumefaction, intumescence, swelling, tumour, diastole, distension, puffing, inflation.

Overgrowth, hypertrophy, overdistension, tympany.

Bulb, knot, knob (249).

Superiority of size.

Verbs: To become larger, to expand, widen, enlarge, extend, grow, increase, swell (202), gather, fill out, deploy, dilate, stretch, largen, spread, mantle, bud, burgeon, shoot, spring up, sprout, germinate, vegetate, pullulate, open, burst forth, put on flesh, outgrow.

To render larger, to expand, aggrandize, etc., distend, develop, open out, broaden, thicken, largen, amplify, tumefy, magnify, rarefy, inflate, puff, blow up, stuff, cram, pad, fill out.

To be larger than, to surpass, exceed, be beyond, cap, overtop (206, 33).

Adjectives: Expanded, enlarged, increased, etc., swelled out, swollen, distended, bulbous; exaggerated, bloated, tumid, turgid, puffy, full-blown, full-grown, full-formed, overgrown, hypertrophied, pot-bellied, swag-bellied, dropsical, oedematous.

Phrase: 'A-swellin' wisibly.'

195   CONTRACTION

Substantives: reduction, diminution, decrease of size, defalcation, lessening, decrement, shrinking, shrivelling, systole, collapse, emaciation, attenuation, tabefaction, tabes, consumption, marasmus, atrophy; hour-glass, neck (203).

Condensation, compression, squeezing.

Inferiority of size.

Corrugation, contractility, astringency.

Verbs: To become smaller, to lessen, diminish, decrease, dwindle, shrink, contract, shrivel, collapse, wither, wilt, lose flesh, wizen, fall away, decay, purse up, waste, wane, ebb, to grow less.

To render smaller, to contract, lessen, etc., draw in, to condense, reduce, clip, compress, constrict, cramp, squeeze, attenuate, chip, drawf, bedwarf, stunt, cut short (201), corrugate, crumple, crush, purse up, pinch (203), deflate.

To be smaller than, to fall short of, not to come up to.

Phrases: To grow 'small by degrees, and beautifully less' (659); to be on the wane; to hide its diminished head.

Adjectives: Contracting, etc., astringent, styptic, tabid, contracted, lessened, etc., shrivelled, wasted, wizened, stunted, waning, ebbing, etc., neap, condensed.

Unexpanded, contractile, compressible.

Phrase: *Multum in parvo.*

196 DISTANCE
Substantives: remoteness, farness, longinquity, elongation, offing, removedness, parallax, reach, span.

Antipodes, outpost, outskirts, aphelion, apogee, horizon.

Separation (44), transference (270).

Diffusion, disperson (73).

Phrases: *Ultima Thule; ne plus ultra*; the uttermost parts of the earth; the back of beyond.

Verbs: To be distant, etc.; to extend to, stretch to, reach to, spread to, go to, get to, stretch away to; outgo, outstep (303); to go to great lengths.

To remain at a distance, keep away, stand off, keep off, keep clear, stand aloof, hold off.

Adjectives: Distant, far, far off, remote, removed, distal, wide of, clear of, yon, yonder, at arm's length, apart, aloof, asunder, ulterior, transalpine, transatlantic, ultramundane, hyperborean, antipodean, hull down.

Inaccessible, un-get-at-able, out of the way, unapproachable, unreachable; incontiguous.

Adverbs: Far, away, far away, afar, off, a long way off, afar off, wide away, aloof, wide of, clear of, out of the way, a great way off, out of reach, abroad.

Apart, asunder, few and far between.

Yonder, farther, beyond, *longo intervallo,* wide apart, poles apart.

Phrases: Far and near; far and wide; over the hills and far away; a far cry to; from end to end; from pole to pole; from Indus to the Pole; from China to Peru; from Dan to Beersheba; to the ends of the earth; out of the sphere of; wide of the mark.

197 NEARNESS
Substantives: nighness, proximity, propinquity, vicinity, vicinage, neighbourhood, adjacency, closeness; perihelion, perigee.

A short distance, a step, an earshot, close quarters, a stone's throw, a hair's breadth, a span, bowshot, gunshot, pistol-shot.

Purlieus, neighbourhood, environs (227), vicinity, *alentours,* suburbs, whereabouts, *banlieue,* borderland.

A bystander, neighbour.

Approach, approximation, appropinquation, appulse (286), junction (43), concentration, convergence (290).

Meeting, *rencontre* (292).

Verbs: To be near, etc., to adjoin, hang about, trench on, border upon, stand by, approximate, tread on the heels of, cling to, clasp, hug, crowd, get near, etc., to aproach (287), to meet (290).

To bring near, to crowd, pack, huddle together.

Adjectives: Near, nigh, close, close at hand, neighbouring, proximate, approximate, adjacent, adjoining, intimate, bordering upon, close upon, hard upon, trenching on, treading on the heels of, verging on, at hand, handy, near the mark, home, at the point of, near run, in touch with, nearish.

Adverbs: Near, nigh, hard by, fast by, close to, next door to, within reach, within call, within hearing, within an ace of, close upon, at hand, on the verge of, near the mark, in the environs, round the corner, at one's door, at one's feet, at one's elbow, at close quarters; within range, pistol-shot, a stone's throw, etc.; cheek by jowl, beside, alongside, at the heels of, at the threshold.

About, hereabouts, thereabouts, in the way, in presence of, in round numbers, approximately, roughly, as good as, *à peu près* (32).

198 INTERVAL
Substantives: interspace (70), break, gap, opening (260), chasm, hiatus,

caesura, interstice, lacuna, cleft, fosse, mesh,

crevice, chink, creek, cranny, crack, slit, fissure, scissure, chap, rift, flaw, gash, cut, leak, dike (350), ha-ha, fracture, breach, rent, oscitation, gaping, yawning, pandiculation, insertion (300), pass, gorge, defile, ravine, canyon (or cañon), crevasse, chimney, couloir, *bergschrund,* gulf, gully, gulch, nullah, strait, sound, kyle, frith, furrow (*see* 259).

Thing interposed, go-between, interjacence (228).

Verbs: To separate (44), gape, yawn.

199 CONTIGUITY
Substantives: contact, proximity, apposition, juxtaposition, touching, tangency, tangent, osculation, meeting (292), syzygy, coincidence, register, co-existence, adhesion (46).

Confine, frontier, demarcation, border (233).

Verbs: To be contiguous, etc., to touch, meet, adhere (46), osculate, coincide, register, coexist, join, adjoin, abut on, graze, border, march with.

Adjectives: Contiguous, touching, bordering on, meeting, in contact, conterminous, osculating, osculatory, tangential, proximate.

Phrases: Hand to hand; end to end; tête-à-tête; next door to; with no interval; in juxtaposition, apposition, etc.; in register.

200 LENGTH
Substantives: longitude, span, stretch.

A line, bar, rule, stripe, spoke, radius.

Lengthening, elongation, prolongation, production, producing, protraction, extension, tension, stretching.

Verbs: To be long, etc., to extend to, reach, stretch to.

To render long, lengthen, extend, elongate, prolong, produce, stretch, draw out, protract, spin out, drawl.

Phrase: To drag its slow length along.

Adjectives: Long, longsome, lengthy, tedious, tiresome, wiredrawn, outstretched, lengthened, produced, etc., sesquipedalian, interminable, endless, unending, never-ending, there being no end of.

Linear, lineal, longitudinal, oblong.

Phrases: As long as my arm; as long as to-day and to-morrow.

Adverbs: Lengthwise, longitudinally, in a line, along, from end to end, endways, from stem to stern, fore and aft, from head to foot, from top to toe, cap-à-pie.

201 SHORTNESS
Substantives: brevity, briefness, a span, etc., *see* Smallness (193).

Shortening, abbreviation, abbreviature, abridgment, curtailment, reduction, contraction, compression (195), retrenchment, elision, ellipsis, compendium (596), conciseness (in style) (572).

Verbs: To be short, brief, etc.

To render short, to shorten, curtail, abridge, abbreviate, epitomize, reduce, contract, compress, scrimp, skimp, boil down.

To retrench, cut short, cut down, pare down, whittle down, clip, dock, lop, poll, prune, pollard, crop, bob, shingle, bingle, snub, truncate, cut, hack, hew, foreshorten.

Adjectives: Short, brief, curt, laconic, compendious, compact, stubby, squab, squabby, squat, chunky, stubby, stocky, dumpy, podgy, fubsy, skimpy, stumpy, pug, snub.

Oblate, elliptical.

Concise (572), summary.

202 BREADTH
Substantives: width, latitude, amplitude, diameter, bore, calibre, superficial, extent, expanse.

Thickness, crassitude (192), thickening, expansion, dilatation, etc. (194).

Verbs: To be broad, thick, etc.

To broaden, to swell, dilate, expand, outspread, etc. (194); to thicken, incrassate.

Adjectives: Broad, wide, ample, extended, fan-like, outstretched, etc.

Thick, corpulent, fat (192), squab, squabby, squat, chunky, stubby, stocky, dumpy, podgy, fulsy, thickset.

Phrases: Wide as a church door; thick as a rope.

203 NARROWNESS

Substantives: slenderness, closeness, scantiness, exility, lankness, lankiness, fibrousness.

A line (205), a hair's breadth, a finger's breadth, strip, streak, vein.

Thinness, tenuity, leanness, meagreness.

A shaving, a slip (205), a mere skeleton, a shadow, an anatomy.

A middle constriction, stricture, neck, waist, isthmus, wasp, hourglass, bottle-neck, ridge, ravine, defile, gorge, pass (198).

Narrowing, coarctation, tapering, compression, squeezing, etc. (195).

Phrases: A bag of bones; a living skeleton.

Verbs: To be narrow, etc., to taper, contract, shrink.

To render narrow, etc., to narrow, contract, coarctate, attenuate, constrict, constringe, cramp, pinch, squeeze, compress, tweak, corrugate, warp.

To shave, pare, shear, etc.

Adjectives: Narrow, strait, slender, thin, fine, tenuous, filiform, filamentary, filamentous, fibrous, funicular, capillary, stringy, wiredrawn, finespun anguine, taper, dapper, slim, slight, gracile, scanty, scant, spare, delicate.

Meagre, lean, emaciated, lank, lanky, weedy, rangy, gangling, starveling, attenuated, pinched, skinny, scraggy, gaunt, cadaverous, skin and bone, raw-boned, scrawny, spindle-shanked (193), hatchet-faced, wasp-waisted, herring-gutted, spidery, spindly, reedy.

Phrases: Thin as a lath; thin as a whipping-post; lean as a rake; thin as a thread-paper; thin as a wafer; thin as a shadow.

204 LAYER

Substantives: stratum, bed, zone, substratum, slab, escarpment, floor, flag, stage, course, storey, tier.

Plate, lamina, lamella, sheet, flake, scale, coat, pellicle, membrane, film, slice, shive, cut, shaving, rasher, board, plank, platter, trencher, spatula, leaf.

Stratification, scaliness, a nest of boxes, coats of an onion.

Verbs: To slice, shave, etc.

Adjectives: Lamellar, laminated, lamelliform, laminiferous, scaly, squamous, filmy, membranous, flaky, foliated, foliaceous, stratified, stratiform, tabular, nested.

205 FILAMENT

Substantives: line, fibre, fibril, tendril, hair, gossamer, wire, thread, cord, funicle, rope, yarn, string, twine (45), cilium, gimp.

Strip (51), shred, slip, spill, list, string, band, fillet, fascia, ribbon (or riband); roll, lath, slat, splinter, sliver, shiver, shaving; arborescence (256); strand.

A hair-stroke.

Adjectives: Filamentary, fibrous, hairy, capillary, thread-like, wiry, funicular, stringy.

206 HEIGHT

Substantives: altitude, elevation, eminence, pitch, loftiness, sublimity.

Stature, tallness, procerity, culmination (210).

A giant, grenadier, guardsman, colossus, giraffe.

Alp, mountain, mount, hill, butte, ben, brae, hillock, kopje, monticule, fell, moorland, hummock, knap, knoll, cape, headland, foreland, promontory, ridge, *arète,* peak, pike, uplands, highlands, rising ground, downs, dune, mound, mole, steep, bluff, cliff, crag, vantage-ground, tor, eagle's nest, aerie.

Orography, orology.

Tower, pillar, column, obelisk, monument, steeple, spire, *flèche,* campanile, belfry, minaret, turret, cupola, pilaster, skyscraper.

Pole, pikestaff, maypole, flagstaff, topmast, topgallant mast, crow's nest.

Ceiling, roof, awning, canopy (*see* 210), attic, loft, garret, housetop.

Growth, upgrowth (194).

Verbs: To be high, etc., to tower, soar, ride, beetle, hover, cap, overtop, culminate, overhang, hang over, impend, overlie, bestride, mount, surmount, to cover (222), perch.

To render high, to heighten, exalt (307).

To become high, grow, upgrow, soar, tower, rise (305).

Adjectives: High, elevated, eminent, exalted, lofty, supernal, tall, towering, beetling, soaring, colossal, gigantic (192), Patagonian, culminating, raised, elevated, etc., perched up, hanging (gardens), crowning, coronary.

Upland, moorland, hilly, mountainous, cloud-touching, heaven-kissing, cloud-topt, cloud-capt, Alpine, subalpine, aerial; orographical.

Upper, uppermost (210), topgallant.

Overhanging, impending, incumbent, overlying, superincumbent, supernatant, superimposed, hovering.

Phrases: Tall as a maypole; tall as a steeple; tall as a poplar.

Adverbs: On high, high up, aloft, above, upstairs, overhead, in the clouds, on tiptoe, on stilts, on the shoulders of, over head and ears.

Over, upwards, from top to bottom, from top to toe, from head to foot, cap-à-pie.

Interjection: Excelsior!

207 LOWNESS

Substantives: lowlands, depression, a molehill, recumbency, prostration.

Dwarf, pygmy, bantam, Lilliputian.

Lowlands; molehill.

A ground-floor, basement, cellar, *rez de chaussée* (191), hold.

Verbs: To be low, etc., lie low, grovel, wallow, crouch, slouch, lie flat.

To lower, depress (306), take down a peg, prostrate, subvert.

Adjectives: Low, low-lying, neap, nether, prostrate, flat, level with the ground, grovelling, crouched, crouching, subjacent, underground, underlying, squat.

Adverbs: Under, beneath, underneath, below, down, adown, downstairs, below stairs, over head and ears, downwards, underfoot, at the foot of, underground, at a low ebb.

208 DEPTH

Substantives: deepness, profundity, profoundness, depression, bathos, anti-climax, depth of water, draught.

A hollow, pit, shaft, well, crater, gulf, abyss, abysm, bottomless pit, hell.

Soundings, submersion, plunge, dive (310).

Plummet, lead, sounding-rod, probe; bathymetry.

Bathysphere, diving-bell, caisson, submarine; diver, frogman.

Verbs: To be deep, etc.

To render deep, etc., to deepen, sink, submerge, plunge, dip, dlive (310).

To dig, scoop out, hollow, sink, delve (252).

Adjectives: Deep, deep-seated, pro-

found, sunk, buried, submerged, etc.,
subaqueous, submarine, subterranean,
underground, subterrene, abysmal;
bathymetrical, bathymetric.

Bottomless, soundless, fathomless,
unfathomed, unsounded, unplumbed,
unfathomable.

Phrases: Deep as a well; ankle-deep;
breast-deep; chin-deep.

Adverbs: Beyond one's depth, out of
one's depth, underground.

Phrases: Over head and ears; to Davy
Jones's locker; in the bowels of the
earth.

209   SHALLOWNESS
Substantives: shoaliness, shoals.
Adjectives: Shallow, skin-deep,
superficial, shoaly.

210   SUMMIT
Substantives: top, vertex, apex,
zenith, pinnacle, acme, climax,
culminating, point, apogee, pitch,
meridian, sky, pole, watershed.

Tip, tiptop, crest, crow's nest, mast-
head, truck, peak, turning-point, pole.

Crown, brow, nib, head, nob,
noddle, pate.

Capital, cornice, sconce, architrave,
pediment, entablature, frieze.

Roof, ceiling, thatch, tiling, slating,
awning, canopy (222).

Adjectives: Top, topmost, uppermost, tiptop, culminating, meridian,
capital, head, polar, supreme, crowning, coronary.

Phrase: At the top of the tree.

211   BASE
Substantives: basement, plinth,
foundation, substratum, ground,
earth, pavement, floor, paving, flag,
ground floor, deck, substructure,
infrastructure, footing, groundwork.

The bottom, rock-bottom, nadir,
foot, sole, toe, root, keel.

Dado, wainscot, skirting-board.

Adjectives: Bottom, undermost,
nethermost, fundamental, basic.

212   VERTICALITY
Substantives: erectness, uprightness,
perpendicularity, aplomb, right angle,
normal, plummet, plumb-line,
azimuth, circle.

Wall, precipice, cliff.

Erection, raising, rearing.

Verbs: To be vertical, etc., to stand
up, to stand on end, to stand erect, to
stand upright, to stick up.

To render vertical, to set up, stick
up, erect, rear, raise up, cock up, prick
up, raise on its legs.

Adjectives: Vertical, upright, erect,
perpendicular, sheer, normal, straight,
standing up, etc., up on end, bolt
upright, rampant.

Adverbs: Up, vertically, etc., on end,
up on end, endways, endwise.

Phrase: Straight up and down.

213   HORIZONTALITY
Substantives: a level, plane, dead
level, flatness (251).

Recumbency, lying, lying down,
reclination, decumbence, decumbency,
supination, resupination, prostration;
spirit-level.

A plain, floor, level, flat, platform,
bowling-green, billiard-table, plateau,
terrace, estrade, esplanande, parterre,
table-land (204, 215).

Verbs: To be horizontal, recumbent,
etc., to lie, recline, lie down, couch, sit
down, squat, lie flat, lie prostrate,
sprawl, loll.

To render horizontal, etc., to lay, lay
down, lay out, level, flatten, prostrate,
knock down, fell, floor.

Adjectives: Horizontal, level, plane,
flat, even, discoid.

Recumbent, decumbent, lying,
prone, supine, couchant, couching,
jacent, prostrate, squat, squatting, sitting, reclining.

Adverbs: Horizontally, etc., on one's
back, on all fours, on one's hunkers.

Phrase: Like a millpond.

214 PENDENCY
Substantives: dependency, suspension, hanging.

A pendant, pedicel, peduncle, tail, train, flap, skirt, plait, pigtail, queue, tassel, earring, pendulum.

A peg, knob, button, stud, hook, nail, ring, fastener, zipper, clip, staple, knot (45), tenterhook.

Verbs: To be pendant, etc., to hang, swing, dangle, swag, daggle, flap, trail.

To suspend, append, hang, sling, hook up, hitch, fasten to.

Adjectives: Pendant, pendulous, pensile, hanging, dependent, swinging, etc., suspended, etc., loose, flowing, caudal.

Having a peduncle, etc., pedunculate, tailed, caudate.

Adverbs: Dingle-dangle.

Phrase: In the air.

215 SUPPORT
Substantives: ground, foundation, base, basis, *terra firma*, fulcrum, foothold, toehold, *point d'appui, pou sto, locus standi,* landing, landing-place, resting-place, ground-work, substratum, floor, bed, stall, berth, lap, mount.

A supporter, prop, stand, strut, stray, shore, boom, yard, outrigger, truss, sleeper, staff, stick, walking-stick, crutch, stirrups, stilts alpenstock, baton, anvil.

Post pillar, shaft, column, buttress, pedicle, pedestal, plinth (211), baluster, banister.

A frame, framework, scaffold, scaffolding, skeleton, cadre, beam, rafter, lintel, joist, jamb, mullion, cornerstone, stanchion, summer, girder, cantilever, sponson, tie-beam (45), columella, backbone, keystone, axle, axle-tree, axis, fuselage, chassis.

A board, form, ledge, platform, floor, stage, shelf, hob, bracket, arbor, rack, mantel, mantelpiece, mantel-shelf, counter, slab, console, dresser, flange, corbel, table, trestle, shoulder, perch, truss, horse, easel, desk.

A seat, throne, dais, divan, musnud, chair, arm-chair, easy-chair, *chaise longue,* hammock-chair, deck-chair, bench, sofa, davenport, lounge, settee, chesterfield, couch, *fauteuil,* stool, tripod, footstool, *tabouret,* trivet, woolsack, ottoman, settle, squab, bench, saddle, pillion, dicky, hassock, pouffe, cushion, howdah.

Bed, bedstead, chair-bedstead, bedding, pillow, bolster, mattress, shakedown, tester, pallet, hammock, bunk, stretcher, crib, cradle, cot, palliasse, donkey's breakfast, sleeping-bag, flea-bag.

Atlas, Persides, Atlantes, Caryatides, Hercules, Yggdrasil.

Verbs: To be supported, etc., to lie, sit, recline, lean, loll, lounge, abut, bear, rest, stand, step, repose, etc., on, be based on, bestride, straddle, bestraddle.

To support, bear, carry, hold, sustain, shoulder, uphold, hold on, upbear, prop, underprop, shore up, underpin, bolster up, pillow.

To give, furnish, afford, supply, lend, etc., support on foundations; to bottom, found, ground, base, embed.

Adjectives: Supported, etc., astride, astraddle; fundamental, basic.

216 PARALLELISM
Substantives: coextension.

Verbs: To be parallel, etc.

Adjectives: Parallel, coextensive.

Adverbs: Alongside, abreast, beside.

Phrases: Side by side; cheek by jowl.

217 OBLIQUITY
Substantives: inclination, slope, leaning, slant, crookedness, bias, bend, bevel, tilt, list, dip, swag, cant, lurch, skew, skewness, bevelling, squint.

Acclivity, uphill, rise, ascent, gradient, rising ground, bank, ramp.

Declivity, downhill, fall, devexity.

A gentle or rapid slope, easy ascent or descent, chute, helter-skelter, switchback, *montagnes russes*.

Steepness, precipitousness, cliff, precipice, talus, scarp, escarp, escarpment; measure of inclination, clinometer.

Diagonal, zigzag, distortion, hypotenuse, angle (244).

Phrase: The leaning tower of Pisa.

Verbs: To be or render oblique, etc., to slope, slant, tilt, lean, incline, shelve, stoop, descend, bend, heel, careen, sag, swag, slouch, cant, sidle, skew, scarp, escarp, bevel, distort.

Adjectives: Oblique, inclined, leaning, recumbent, sloping, shelving, skew, askew, skew-whiff, slant, aslant, slanting, slantendicular, plagioclastic, indirect, distorted, wry, awry, ajee, drawn, crooked, canted, tilted, biased, saggy, bevel, slouched, slouching, etc., out of the perpendicular, backhanded.

Uphill, rising, ascending, acclivitous.

Downhill, falling, descending, declining, declivitous, anticlinal.

Steep, abrupt, precipitous, breakneck.

Diagonal, transverse, athwart, transversal, antiparallel.

Adverbs: Obliquely, etc., on one side, askew, edgewise, askant, askance, sideways, aslope, slopewise, all on one side, crinkum-crankum, asquint, at an angle.

Phrase: *Facilis descensus Averni.*

218 INVERSION

Substantives: contraposition, overturn, somersault (or somerset), *culbute,* subversion, retroversion, reversion, reversal, introversion, eversion, transposition, pronation and supination.

Anastrophe, metathesis, hysteron, proteron, spoonerism, palindrome.

Verbs: To be inverted, etc., to turn turtle, loop the loop, bunt.

To render inverted, etc., to invert, reverse, upset, overset, overturn, turn over, upturn, subvert, retrovert, transpose, turn topsy-turvy, tilt over, *culbuter,* keel over, topple over, capsize.

Adjectives: Inverted, inverse, upside down, topsy-turvy, top-heavy.

Adverbs: Inversely, topsy-turvy, etc., inside out.

Phrases: To turn the tables; to put the cart before the horse; to the right about; bottom upwards; head over heels; the wrong side up; base over apex.

219 CROSSING

Substantives: intersection, decussation, transversion, convolution.

Reticulation, network, inosculation, anastomosis, interweaving, twining, intertwining, matting, plaiting, interdigitation, mortise (or mortice).

Net, knot, plexus, web, mesh, twill, skein, hank, felt, lace, tulle, wattle, wicker, basket-work, basketry, mat, matting, plait, trellis, lattice, grille, *cancelli,* grid, griddle, grating, gridiron, tracery, fretwork, filigree, reticle, diaper.

Cross, chain, wreath, braid, cat's cradle, dovetail, Greek cross, Latin cross, Maltese cross, cross of St. Anthony, St. Andrew's cross, cross of Lorraine, swastika, fylfot.

Verbs: To cross, lace, intersect, decussate, interlace, intertwine, intertwist, pleach, plash, entwine, enlace, enmesh, weave, interweave, inweave, twine, twist, wreathe, interdigitate, interlock, anastomose, inosculate, dovetail, splice (43).

To mat, plait, plat, braid, felt, twill, tangle, entangle, ravel, net, knot (43), dishevel, raddle.

Adjectives: Crossing, intersecting, etc., crossed, intersected, matted, etc., crucial, cruciform.

Retiform, reticulate, areolar,

areolate, cancellated, grated, barred, streaked, traceried.

Adverbs: Across, thwart, athwart, transversely, crosswise.

220 EXTERIORITY
Substantives: externality, outness, outside, exterior, surface, superficies, superstratum, eccentricity, extremity, frontage.

Disk, face, facet, front (234), skin (222).

Verbs: To be exterior, etc.

To place exteriorly, or outwardly, to turn out.

Adjectives: Exterior, external, outer, outward, outlying, outdoor, outside, extramural, superficial, skin-deep, frontal, discoid, eccentric, extrinsic.

Adverbs: Externally, etc., out, without, outwards, outdoors, abroad.

Phrases: Out of doors; *extra muros; ab extra*; in the open air; *sub Jove; à la belle étoile*; al fresco.

221 INTERIORITY
Substantives: inside, interior, hinterland, backblocks, interspace, substratum, subsoil.

Vitals, viscera, pith, marrow, heart, bosom, breast, entrails, bowels, belly, intestines, guts, inwards, womb, lap, backbone, *penetralia,* inmost recesses, cave, cavern (191).

Verbs: To be interior, internal, within, etc.

To place or keep within, to enclose, circumscribe (*see* 231, 232).

Adjectives: Interior, internal, inner, inside, intramural, inward, inlying, inmost, innermost, deep-seated, intestine, intestinal, splanchnic, intercostal, inland, interstitial, subcutaneous, intrinsic.

Home, domestic, indoor.

Adverbs: Internally, inwards, inwardly, within, inly, therein, *ab intra,* withinside, indoors, within doors, ben, at home, *chez soi,* up country.

222 COVERING
Substantives: cover, roof, ceiling, slates, tiles, thatch, cowling, canopy, baldachin, awning, tarpaulin, tilt, tent (189), lid, hatch, operculum (263), shed.

Integument, skin, tegument, pellicle, fleece, cuticle, scarf-skin, epidermis, hide, pelt, peel, crust, bark, rind, cortex, husk, scale, shell, carapace, capsule, coat, tunic, tunicle, sheath, case, casing, calyx, theca, sheathing, scabbard, wrapping, wrapper, envelope, tarpaulin, cloth, table-cloth, blanket, rug, quilt, eiderdown, coverlet (or coverlid), counterpane, carpet, drugget, oilcloth, wax-cloth, linoleum.

Superposition, coating, facing, veneer, paint, enamel, varnish, anointing, inunction, incrustation, plaster, stucco, wash, parget, patina.

Verbs: To cover, superpose, superimpose, overspread, over-canopy, wrap, lap, overlap, face, case, encase, veneer, pave, upholster.

To coat, paint, enamel, varnish, pave, plaster, beplaster, daub, bedaub, encrust, stucco, dab, smear, besmear, anoint, spray, do over, gild, japan, lacquer (or lacker), plate, electroplate, parget.

Phrase: To lay it on thick.

Adjectives: Covering, etc., cutaneous, dermal, cortical, cuticular, tegumentary, skinny, scaly, squamous, imbricated, epidermal, loricated, armour-plated, iron-clad.

223 CENTRALITY
Substantives: centre (68), middle, focus, epicentre, hub, core, kernel, marrow, pith, nucleus, nucleolus, heart, pole, axis, bull's-eye, nave, navel, umbilicus, omphalos; concentration, centralization.

Verbs: To be central, etc.

To render central, centralize, concentrate.

To bring to a focus.

Adjectives: Central, centrical, middle, middlemost, midmost, median, azygous, axial, focal, umbilical, concentric.

Adverbs: Midway, centrally, etc.

224 LINING

Substantives: coating, facing, internal incrustation, puddle, stalactite, stalagmite, wainscot, dado, wall.

Filling, stuffing, wadding, padding.

Verbs: To line, encrust, stuff, pad, wad, face, puddle, bush.

Adjectives: Lined, encrusted, etc.

225 INVESTMENT

Substantives: dress, clothing, raiment, drapery, costume, attire, toilet, trim, rig, rig-out, fig, habiliment, vesture, apparel, underwear, full dress, evening dress, soup-and-fish, glad rags, dinner-jacket, tuxedo, fancy dress, accoutrement, outfit, wardrobe, trousseau, uniform, regimentals, battle-dress, kit, equipment, livery, gear, harness, turn-out, caparison, suit, dress suit, lounge suit, bathing suit, swim-suit, tweeds, flannels, rigging, trappings, slops, traps, duds, togs, clobber, frippery, bloomers, haberdashery, housing.

Dishabille, morning dress, dressing-gown, undress, mufti, civvies, rags, _négligé,_ tea-gown.

Clothes, garment, garb, garniture, vestment, pontificals, robe, tunic, caftan, paletot, habit, gown, coat, dress-coat, claw-hammer, frock, stole, blouse, shirt-waist, toga, haik, smock-frock, kimono, bikini.

Cloak, opera-cloak, cape, mantle, mantlet, dolman, shawl, wrap, wrapper, veil, fichu, yashmak, tippet, kirtle, plaid, mantilla, tabard, burnous, overcoat, great-coat, British warm, duffle coat, surtout, spencer, rain-coat, ulster, mackintosh, water-proof, oilskin, slicker, burberry, poncho, surplice, alb, cassock, pallium, etc., mask,

domino, cardinal, pelerine.

Jacket, vest, under-vest, semmit, singlet, jerkin, lumberjacket, waistcoat, cardigan, sweater, jersey, pullover, slipover, jumper, windbreaker, windcheater, doublet, gaberdine, camisole, combinations, stays, corset, bodice, under-bodice, brassière, bra, corsage, cestus, petticoat, kilt, filibeg (or philibeg), stomacher, skirt, kirtle, crinoline, farthingale, underskirt, slip, apron, pinafore.

Trousers, trews, breeches, galligaskins, knickerbockers, plus-fours, knickers, drawers, scanties, pantaloons, pants, overalls, dungarees, boiler suit, rompers, unmentionables, inexpressibles, smalls, tights, bags, breeks, slacks, shorts, jeans, briefs.

Cap, hat, top-hat, silk hat, tile, bowler, panama, slouch-hat, trilby, Stetson, titfer, deerstalker, billycock, wide-awake, sou'wester, beaver, castor, bonnet, forage-cap, tam-o'-shanter, tammy, balmoral, glengarry, toque, sun-bonnet, hood, head-gear, head-dress, kerchief, scarf, muffler, comforter, boa, snood, coiffure, coif, skull-cap, calotte, biretta, cowl, chaplet, capote, calash, pelt, wig, peruke, periwig, toupee, transformation, chignon, turban, puggaree, fez, helmet, topi, shako, busby, képi, casque, beret.

Shirt, smock, shift, chemise, chemisette, nightshirt, nightgown, nightdress, pyjamas, bed-jacket, bedgown, collar, cravat, neck-cloth, necktie, stock, handkerchief.

Shoe, pump, high-low, Oxford shoe, sabot, brogue, sand-shoe, plimsoll, rubbers, sneakers, boot, jackboot, top-boot, Wellington, gumboot, slipper, mule, galosh, overshoe, legging, puttee, buskin, greaves, mocassin, gaiter, spatterdash, spat, stocking, sock, nylons, hose, sandal, clog, babouche.

Glove, gauntlet, mitten, sleeve, cuff, muff.

Outfitter, tailor, clothier, milliner, sempstress, costumier, hatter, hosier, shoemaker, cobbler.

Verbs: To invest, cover, envelop, lap, involve, drape, enwrap, wrap up, lap up, sheathe, vest, clothe, array, enrobe, dress, dight, attire, apparel, accoutre, trick out, rig, fit out, fig out, caparison, adonize, dandify, titivate, don, put on, wear, have on, huddle on, slip on, roll up in, muffle, perk up, mantle, swathe, swaddle, equip, harness.

Adjectives: Invested, clothed, arrayed, dight, etc., clad, shod, etc.; sartorial.

226 DIVESTMENT

Substantives: nudity, bareness, nakedness, baldness, undress, dishabille, threadbareness.

Denuding, denudation, stripping, uncovering, decortication, peeling, flaying, excoriation, desquamation, moulting, exfoliation.

Verbs: To divest, uncover, denude, bare, strip, unclothe, undress, unrobe, disrobe, disapparel, debag, disarray, take off, doff, cast off, peel, pare, decorticate, husk, uncoif, unbonnet, excoriate, skin, flay, expose, exfoliate, lay open, dismantle, unroof, uncase, unsheathe, moult, mew.

Adjectives: Bare, naked, nude, stripped, denuded, undressed, unclothed, unclad, undraped, uncovered, unshod, barefoot, bareheaded, unbonneted, exposed, in dishabille, in buff, bald, threadbare, ragged, callow, roofless.

Phrases: In a state of nature; stark-naked; *in puris naturalibus*; stripped to the buff; in one's birthday suit; bald as a coot; as bare as the back of one's hand; out at elbows.

227 CIRCUMJACENCE

Substantives: circumambiency, encompassment, surroundings, environment, atmosphere, medium, setting,

scene, outpost, skirt, outskirts, boulevards, suburbs, suburbia, rurbania, purlieus, precincts, faubourgs, environs, entourage, *banlieue,* green belt.

Verbs: To lie around, surround, beset, set about, compass, encompass, environ, enclose, encircle, embrace, lap, gird, begird, engirdle, orb, enlace, skirt, twine round, hem in (231).

Adjectives: Circumjacent, ambient, circumambient, surrounding, etc., circumfluent, circumferential, suburban, extramural, embosomed.

Adverbs: Around, about, without, on every side, on all sides, right and left, all around, round about.

228 INTERJACENCE

Substantives: interlocation, intervention, insertion, interposition, interspersion, interpenetration, interdigitation, interpolation, interlineation, intercurrence, intrusion, obtrusion, insinuation, intercalation, insertion, intertwinement, interference, permeation, infiltration.

An intermedium, intermediary, a go-between, bodkin, intruder, interloper; interlude, episode; parenthesis, gag, flyleaf, *entresol* (68).

A partition, septum, panel, diaphragm, midriff, party-wall.

A half-way house, no-man's- land.

Verbs: To lie, come, or get between, intervene, intrude, butt in, slide in, permeate, put between, put in, interpose, interject, chip in, throw in, wedge in, thrust in, foist in, insert, intercalate, interpolate, parenthesize, interline, interleave, interlard, interdigitate, dovetail, sandwich, worm in, insinuate, obtrude (300), intersperse, infiltrate; to gag.

Phrases: To put one's oar in; to stick one's nose into; to have a finger in the pie.

Adjectives: Interjacent, intervening, etc., intermediary, intermediate, intercalary, interstitial, parenthetical, mediterranean.

Adverbs: Between, betwixt, 'twixt, among, amongst, amid, amidst, midst, betwixt and between, sandwich-wise. parenthetically, between the lines, in the thick of.

229 OUTLINE

Substantives: circumference, perimeter, periphery, ambit, circuit, lines, tournure, contour, profile, silhouette, sky-line.

Zone, belt, girth, band, baldric, zodiac, cordon, girdle, cingulum, clasp (247).

230 EDGE

Substantives: verge, brink, brow, brim, margin, marge, border, skirt, rim, side, mouth, jaws, lip, muzzle, door, porch, portal (260), kerb; shore, coast.

Frame, flounce, frill, ruffle, jabot, list, fringe, valance, edging, trimming, hem, selvedge, welt, furbelow.

Verbs: To border, edge, skirt, coast, verge on.

Adjectives: Border, marginal, coastal, skirting.

231 CIRCUMSCRIPTION

Substantives: limitation, enclosure, confinement, shutting up, circumvallation, entombment.

Imprisonment, incarceration (751).

Verbs: To circumscribe, limit, delimit, localize, bound, confine, enclose, surround (227), compass about, impound, restrict, restrain (751), shut in , shut up, lock up, bottle up, dam, hem in, hedge in, wall in, rail in, fence, picket, pen, enfold, coop, corral, encage, cage, mew, entomb, bury, immure, encase, pack up, seal up, wrap up (225), etc.

Adjectives: Circumscribed, etc., imprisoned, pent up (754), landlocked.

Phrase: Not room to swing a cat.

232 ENCLOSURE

Substantives: envelope, case, box (191), pen, penfold, fold, sheep-fold, pound, paddock, enclave, *enceinte,* corral, ring fence, wall, hedge, hedgerow, espalier, exclosure, play-pen.

Barrier, bar, gate, gateway, door, barricade, cordon.

Dike (or dyke), ditch, fosse, moat.

Fence, pale, paling, balustrade, rail, railing, hurdle, palisade, battlement, rampart, embankment, breakwater, mole, groyne (717), circumvallation, contravallation.

233 LIMIT

Substantives: boundary, bounds, confine, term, bourne, line of demarcation, termination, stint, frontier, border, precinct, marches, line of circumvallation, pillars of Hercules, Rubicon, turning-point, last word, *ne plus ultra.*

Adjectives: Definite, conterminal, terminal, frontier.

Phrases: To cross the Rubicon; thus far and no farther.

234 FRONT

Substantives: face, anteriority, forepart, front rank, foreground, van, vanguard, advanced guard, outpost, proscenium, façade, frontage, foreword, preface, frontispiece (64).

Forehead, visage, physiognomy, phiz, countenance, mug, dial, puss, pan, beak, rostrum, bow, stem, prow.

Pioneer, avant-courier (64).

(In a medal) obverse; (in a coin) head.

Verbs: To be in front, etc., to front, face, envisage, confront, bend forward, etc.

Adjectives: Fore, anterior, front, frontal, facial.

Adverbs: Before, in front, ahead, right ahead, in the van, foremost, vis-à-vis, in the foreground, face to face, before one's eyes.

235 REAR

Substantives: back, posteriority, the rear rank, rearguard, the background, heels, tail, scut, rump, croup, crupper, breech, backside, posterior, fanny, catastrophe, buttocks, haunches, hunkers, hurdies, hind quarters, *dorsum*, dorsal region, stern, poop, after-part, tailpiece, wake.

(In a medal) reverse; (in a coin) tail.

Verbs: To be in the rear, behind, etc., to fall astern, to bend backwards, to back on.

Phrases: Turn the back upon; bring up the rear.

Adjectives: Back, rear, postern, hind, hinder, hindmost, sternmost, posterior, dorsal, after.

Adverbs: Behind, in the rear, aft, abaft, astern, aback, rearward.

Phrases: In the background; behind one's back; at the heels of; at the tail of; at the back of; back to back.

236 LATERALITY

Substantives: side, flank, quarter, hand, cheek, jowl, wing, profile, temple, loin, haunch, hip, broadside, lee-side, lee.

East, orient; West, occident.

Verbs: To be on one side, etc., to flank, outflank, to sidle, skirt.

Adjectives: Lateral, sidelong, collateral, sideling, bilateral, trilateral, quadrilateral, multilateral, many-sided, eastern, oriental, western, occidental, eastward, westward.

Adverbs: Sideways, side by side (216), sidelong, abreast, abeam, alongside, aside, by the side of, to windward, to leeward.

Phrases: Cheek by jowl; broadside on.

237 ANTIPOSITION

Substantives: opposite side, contra-position, reverse, inverse, antipodes, opposition, inversion (218).

Polarity, opposite poles, North and South.

Verbs: To be opposite, etc., subtend.

Adjectives: Opposite, reverse, inverse, antipodal, subcontrary.

Fronting, facing, diametrically opposite, vis-à-vis.

Northern, boreal, septentrional, arctic; southern, austral, antarctic.

Adverbs: Over, over the way, over against, facing, against, fronting (234), face to face, vis-à-vis.

238 DEXTRALITY

Substantives: right, right hand, dexter, offside, starboard, recto.

Adjectives: Dextral, right-handed; ambidextrous, ambidexter.

239 SINISTRALITY

Substantives: left, left hand, sinister, near side, port, larboard, verso.

Adjectives: Sinistral, left-handed.

Section III – Form

240 FORM

Substantives: figure, shape, configuration, make, formation, frame, construction, conformation, cut, set, trim, build, make, stamp, cast, mould, fashion, structure.

Feature, lineament, phase (448), turn, attitude, posture, pose.

Morphology, isomorphism.

Formation, figuration, efformation, sculpture.

Phrase: The cut of one's jib.

Verbs: To form, shape, figure, fashion, carve, cut, chisel, chase, emboss, hew, rough-hew, cast, rough-cast, hammer out, block out, trim, work, lick into shape, knock together, mould, sculpture, sculp, grave, stamp.

Adjectives: Formed, graven, etc., receiving form, plastic, fictile.

Giving form, formative, plastic, plasmatic, plasmic.

241 AMORPHISM
Substantives: amorphousness, formlessness, shapelessness, disfigurement, defacement, mutilation (846).

Vandalism, vandal, Goth.

Verbs: To destroy form, deform, deface, disfigure, disfeature (846), mutilate.

Adjectives: Shapeless, amorphous, formless, unhewn, rough, rude, Gothic, unfashioned, unshapen, misshapen, inchoate.

242 SYMMETRY
Substantives: shapeliness, eurhythmy, uniformity, finish, beauty (845), proportion, balance.

Adjectives: Symmetrical, regular, shapely, eurhythmic, well-set, uniform, finished, well-proportioned, balanced, chaste, classic.

Phrase: *Teres atque rotundus.*

243 DISTORTION
Substantives: twist, kink, wryness, asymmetry, gibbosity, contortion, malformation, ugliness, etc. (846), teratology.

Verbs: To distort, twist, wrest, writhe, wring, contort, kink, buckle.

Adjectives: Irregular, unsymmetrical, asymmetrical, distorted, twisted, wry, awry, askew, crooked, on one side, misshapen, deformed, ill-proprtioned, ill-made, round-shouldered, pigeon-chested, humpbacked, hunchbacked, gibbous, gibbose; knock-kneed, bandy-legged, bow-legged, club-footed, splay-footed.

Phrases: All manner of ways; all over the place.

244 ANGULARITY
Substantives: angulation, angle, cusp, bend, elbow, knee, knuckle, groin, crinkle-crankle, kink, crotch, crutch, crane, fluke, scythe, sickle, zigzag, anfractuosity, refraction; fold (258), corner (182).

Fork, bifurcation, dichotomy.

Right angle (212), salient angle, re-entrant angle, acute angle, obtuse angle.

A polygon, square, rectangle, triangle, pentagon, hexagon, heptagon, octagon, nonagon, decagon, lozenge, diamond, rhomb, rhombus, rhomboid, parallelogram, gore, gusset, wedge.

Cube, parallelepiped, pyramid, prism, rhombohedron, tetrahedron, pentahedron, hexahedron, octahedron, dodecahedron, icosahedron.

T-square, set-square, protractor, goniometer, theodolite, sextant, quadrant, clinometer.

Verbs: To bend, refract, diffract, fork, bifurcate, angulate, crinkle, crankle, splay.

Adjectives: Angular, triangular, quadrangular, rectangular, bent, crooked, hooked, aduncous, aquiline, jagged, serrated, falciform, falcated, furcated, forked, bifurcate, zigzag; dovetailed, knock-kneed, crinkled, akimbo, geniculated, polygonal, trigonal, pentagonal, etc., fusiform, sagittate, arrow-headed, wedge-shaped, cuneate, cuneiform, splayed, angulate, cubical, pyramidal, rhombohedral, tetrahedral, etc.

245 CURVATURE
Substantives: curvation, incurvity, incurvation, bend, flexure, flexion, hook, crook, camber, bending, deflexion, inflexion, arcuation, diffraction, turn, deviation, detour, sweep, sinuosity, curl, curling, winding, recurvature, recurvation, refraction, flexibility (324).

A curve, arc, circle, ellipse (247), parabola, hyperbola, catenary, festoon, arch, arcade, vault, bow, crescent, half-moon, lunette, horse-shoe, loop bight, crane-neck, conchoid, ogee.

Verbs: To be curved, etc., to bend, curve, etc., decline, turn, trend, deviate, re-enter, sweep.

To render curved; to bend, curve, incurvate, camber, deflect, inflect, crook, hook, turn, round, arch, arcuate, bow, curl, recurve, loop, frizzle.
Adjectives: Curved, vent, etc., curvilinear, curviform, recurved, recurvous, circular, oval (247), parabolic, hyperbolic, bowed, crooked, bandy, arched, vaulted, arcuated, camerated, hooked, falcated, falciform, crescent-shaped, semilunar, semicircular, conchoidal, lunular, lunulate, cordiform, heart-shaped, reniform, pear-shaped; bow-legged, bandy-legged, knock-kneed, devious.

246 STRAIGHTNESS
Substantives: rectilinearity, directness.
A straight line, a right line, a direct line; inflexibility (323).
Verbs: To be straight, etc.
To render straight, to straighten, rectify, set or put straight, take the curl out of, unbend, unfold, uncurl, uncoil, unroll, unwind, unravel, untwist, unwreathe, unwrap.
Adjectives: Straight, rectilinear (or rectilineal), direct, even, right, in a line; unbent; not inclining, not bending, not turning, not deviating to either side, undeviating, unturned, undistorted, unswerving.
Phrases: Straight as an arrow; as the crow flies; in a bee line.

247 CIRCULARITY
Substantives: roundness, rotundity (249).
A circle, circlet, ring, areola, hoop, roundlet, *annulus*, annulet, bracelet, bangle, armlet, anklet, ringlet, eye, loop, wheel, cycle, orb, orbit, rundle, zone, belt, cordon, band, sash, girdle, cestus, cincture, baldric, bandolier, fillet, cummerbund, fascia, wreath, garland, crown, corona, coronal, coronet, chaplet, necklace, rivière; noose, lasso.

An ellipse, oval, ovule, ellipsoid, cycloid, epicycloid, epicycle, semicircle, quadrant, sextant, sector, segment.
Verbs: To make round, round, circle, encircle, environ (227).
Adjectives: Round, rounded, circular, annular, orbicular.
Oval, elliptical, elliptic, ovate, egg-shaped; cycloidal, etc., moniliform.

248 CONVOLUTION
Substantives: winding, wave, undulation, circuit, tortuosity, anfractuosity, sinuosity, involution, sinuation, circumvolution, meander, circumbendibus, twist, twirl, squiggle, curl, curlicue, curlie-wurlie, tirlie-whirlie, crimp, frizz, frizzle, permanent wave, perm, windings and turnings, *ambages*, inosculation, peristalsis.
A coil, reel, roll, spiral, helix, corkscrew, worm, volute, scroll, cartouche, rundle, scallop (or scollop), escallop.
Serpent, eel, maze, labyrinth.
Verbs: To be convoluted, etc.
To wind, twine, twist, coil, roll, turn and twist, weave, twirl, wave, undulate, meander, scallop, curl, crimp, frizz, frizzle, perm, inosculate, entwine (219), enlace, twist together, goffer.
Adjectives: Convoluted, winding, twisting, contorted, waving, waved, wavy, curly, undulating, undulant, undulatory, undated, serpentine, anguilline, mazy, labyrinthine, Daedalian, tortuous, sinuous, flexuous, snaky, involved, sigmate, sigmoid, sigmoidal, vermiform, vermicular, peristaltic, meandrine; scalloped (or scolloped), wreathed, wreathy, crisped, crimped, frizzed, frizzy, frizzled, frizzly, ravelled, twisted, dishevelled (61).
Spiral, coiled, helical, turbinate.
Adverb: In and out.

249 ROTUNDITY

Substantives: roundness, cylindricity; cylinder, barrel, drum, cylindroid, roll, roller, rouleau, column, rolling-pin, rundle.

Cone, conoid; pear-shape, bell-shape.

Sphericity, spheroidity, globosity; a sphere, globe, ball, spheroid, ellipsoid, drop, spherule, globule, vesicle, bulb, bullet, pellet, pill, clue, marble, pea, knob, pommel.

Verbs: To form into a sphere, render spherical, to sphere, ensphere, to roll into a ball, round off, give rotundity, etc.

Adjectives: Rotund, round, cylindric, cylindrical, cylindroid, columnar, lumbriciform; conic, conical, conoidal.

Spherical, spheral, spheroidal, globular, globated, globous, globose, ovoid, egg-shaped, gibbous, bulbi-form, bulbous, bell-shaped, campaniliform, campaniform, campanulate, fungiform, bead-like, moniliform, pyriform, cigar-shaped.

Phrases: Round as an apple; round as a ball; *teres atque rotundus.*

250 CONVEXITY

Substantives: prominence, projection, swelling, gibbosity, bulge, protuberance, intumescence, tumour, cancer, tuberosity, tubercle, tooth, knob, excrescence, elbow, process, condyle, bulb, nub, nubble, node, nodule, nodosity, tongue, *dorsum,* hump, hunch, hunk, bunch, boss, embossment, bump, lump, clump, sugarloaf, point (253), bow, bagginess.

Pimple, wen, papula, pustule, carbuncle, corn, wart, polyp, boil, furuncle, fungus, fungosity, bleb, blister, blain, chilblain, bunion.

Papilla, nipple, teat, pap, breast, dug, udder, mamilla, proboscis, nose, neb, beak, snout, nozzle, belly, paunch, corporation, kyte, back, shoulder, elbow, lip, flange.

Peg, button, stud, ridge, rib, jetty, snag, eaves, mole, cupola, dome, balcony.

Cameo, high and low relief, bas-relief, *basso rilievo, alto rilievo*; repoussé work.

Mount, hill (206); cape, promontory, foreland, headland, ness, mull, salient, point of land, hummock, spur, hog's back, offset.

Verbs: To be prominent, etc., to project, bulge, belly, jut out, bristle up, to hang over, overhang, beetle, bend over, protrude, stand out, stick out, poke out, stick up, start up, cock up, shoot up, swell.

To render prominent; to raise (307), to emboss, chase, stud, bestud, ridge.

Adjectives: Convex, prominent, projecting, bulging, etc., bold, bossed, bossy, knobby, nubbly, lumpy, bumpy, nodose, embossed, chased, gibbous, salient, mamilliform, in relief, bowed, arched, bellied, baggy, cornute, odontoid, tuberous, tuberculous, ridged, ridgy.

251 FLATNESS

Substantives: plane; horizontality (213), layer (204), smoothness (255); plate, platter, slab, table, tablet; level.

Verbs: To render flat, flatten, smooth, level.

Adjectives: Flat, plane, even, level, etc. (213), flush, scutiform, scutellate.

Phrases: Flat as a pancake; flat as a flounder; flat as a board; flat as my hand; a dead flat; a dead level.

252 CONCAVITY

Substantives: depression, hollow, hollowness, indentation, intaglio, cavity, dent, dint, dimple, follicle, pit, sinus, alveolus, lacuna, honeycomb, excavation, trough (259).

Cup, basin, crater, etc. (191); socket, thimble.

Valley, vale, dale, dell, dingle, coombe, strath, bottom, corrie, glade,

glen, cave, cell, cavern, cove, grotto, grot, alcove, gully (198), cul-de-sac.
Verbs: To be depressed, etc., to cave in, subside, retire.

To depress, hollow, scoop, gouge, dig, delve, excavate, dent, dint, stave in, mine, undermine, burrow, tunnel.
Adjectives: Depressed, concave, hollow, stove in, retiring, retreating, cavernous, honeycombed, alveolar, cellular, funnel-shaped, infundibular, bell-shaped, campaniliform, porous (260).

253 SHARPNESS
Substantives: keenness, pointedness, acuteness, acuity, acumination, spinosity, prickliness.

A point, spike, spine, spicule, needle, bodkin (262), aiguille, pin, prickle, prick, prong, tine, caltrop, *chevaux de frise*, arrow, spear, bayonet, pike, sword, dagger (727), spur, rowel, barb, spit, cusp, horn, antler, snag, tag, jag, thorn, brier, bramble, thistle, nib, tooth, tusk, denticle, spoke, cog, ratchet, comb, bristle, beard, awn, *arête*, crest, cone, peak, spire, pyramid, steeple, porcupine, hedgehog.

Cutlery, blade, edge-tool, knife, jack-knife, penknife, clasp-knife, bowie, jocteleg, chisel, razor, scalpel, bistoury, lancet, axe, hatchet, pole-axe, pick-axe, pick, mattock, spade, adze, coulter, ploughshare, scythe, sickle, reaping-hook, bill, billhook, cleaver, scissors, shears, sécateurs.

Sharpener, knife-sharpener, strop, hone, grinder, grindstone, whet-stone, steel, emery, carborundum.
Verbs: To be sharp, etc., to taper to a point, to bristle with.

To render sharp, etc., to sharpen, point, aculeate, set, whet, strop, hone, grind, barb, bristle up.
Adjectives: Sharp, keen, pointed, conical, acute, acicular, aculeated, arrowy, needle-shaped, spiked, spiky,

spicular, spiculate, mucronate, mucronated, ensiform, peaked, acuminated, salient, cusped, cuspidate, cuspidated, cornute, prickly, spiny, spinous, thorny, jagged, bristling, muricate, pectinated, studded, thistly, briery, snaggy, digitated, barbed, spurred, two-edged, tapering, fusiform, dentiform, denticular, denticulated, toothed, odontoid, cutting, trenchant, sharp-edged.

Starlike, stellated, stelliform.
Phrases: Sharp as a needle, as a razor.

254 BLUNTNESS
Substantives: obtuseness, dullness.
Verbs: To be blunt, etc., to render blunt, etc., to obtund, dull, take off the point or edge, turn.
Adjectives: Blunt, obtuse, dull, bluff.

255 SMOOTHNESS
Substantives: evenness, level (213), polish, gloss, glossiness, sleekness, slipperiness, lubricity, lubrication (332), down, velvet, velveteen, velour, silk, satin, plush, glass, ice, enamel, macadam.

Burnisher, calender, mangle, iron, file, plane, sandpaper, emery-paper, roller.
Verbs: To smooth, smoothen, plane, polish, burnish, calender, mangle, enamel, glaze, iron, file, roll, lubricate, macadamize.
Adjectives: Smooth, even, level, plane, sleek, slick, polished, glazed, glossy, sleeky, silken, silky, satiny, velvety, glabrous, slippery, oily, soft, unwrinkled.
Phrases: Smooth as glass, as velvet, as satin, as soil; slippery as an eel.

256 ROUGHNESS
Substantives: unevenness, asperity, regosity, ruggedness, scabrousness, salebrosity, cragginess, craggedness, corrugation, nodosity, crispness, plumosity, villosity; grain, texture, nap, pile.

Arborescence, branching, ramification.

Brush, bur, beard, shag, whisker, dundreary, mutton-chop, sideboards, side-burns, down, goatee, imperial, moustache, feather, plume, crest, tuft, *panache*, byssus, hair, chevelure, toupee, wool, fur, mane, cilia, fringe, *fimbriae*, tress, moss, plush, velvet, velveteen, velour, stubble.

Verbs: To be rough, etc.

To render rough, to roughen, crisp, crumple, corrugate, rumple.

Adjectives: Rough, uneven, scabrous, gnarled, rugged, rugose, rugous, salebrous, unpolished, matt, frosted, rough-hewn, craggy, cragged, prickly, scrubby.

Arborescent, dendroid, dendriform, arboriform, branching, ramose, ramulose.

Feathery, plumose, plumous, plumigerous, tufted, fimbriated, hairy, ciliated, hirsute, flocculent, bushy, hispid, tomentous, downy, woolly, velvety, villous (or villose), bearded, pilous, shaggy, shagged, stubbly, fringed, befringed, setaceous, filamentous.

Phrases: Rough as a nutmeg-grater; like quills upon the fretful porcupine; against the grain.

257 NOTCH

Substantives: dent, dint, nick, cut, indent, indentation, dimple.

Embrasure, battlement, machicolation, machicoulis, saw, tooth, sprocket, crenelle, scallop (or scollop).

Verbs: To notch, nick, cut, dent, indent, dint, jag, scotch, slash, scallop (or scollop), crenelate.

Adjectives: Notched, etc., jagged, crenate, crenated, crenelated, dented, dentated, denticulated, toothed, palmated, indented, serrated.

258 FOLD

Substantives: plication, plait, ply,

crease, pleat, tuck, hem, flexion, flexure, joint, elbow, doubling, duplicature, gather, wrinkle, crow's-foot, rimple, crinkle, crankle, crumple, rumple, rivel, ruck, ruffle, ruche, dog's-ear, corrugation, flounce, frounce, lapel, pucker, crimp.

Verbs: To fold, double, plicate, plait, crease, wrinkle, crinkle, crankle, curl, cockle up, cocker, rimple, frizz, frizzle, rumple, flounce, frounce, rivel, twill, corrugate, ruffle, crimple, crumple, pucker, to turn down, turn under, tuck, ruck.

Adjectives: Folded, dog's-eared (or dog-eared), etc.

259 FURROW

Substantives: groove, rut, slit, scratch, streak, stria, crack, score, rib.

Channel, gutter, trench, ditch, dike, moat, fosse, trough, kennel, chamfer, ravine (198), fluting.

Verbs: To furrow, etc., flute, plough.

Adjectives: Furrowed, etc., ribbed, striated, striate, sulcated, fluted, canaliculate, bisulcate, trisulcate, etc., corduroy, corded, corrugated.

260 OPENING

Substantives: hole, foramen, perforation, eye, eyelet, keyhole, loophole, porthole, scuttle, mouse-hole, pigeonhole, eye of a needle, pinhole, peephole, puncture.

Aperture, hiatus, yawning, oscitancy, dehiscence, patefaction, slot, chink, crevice (198).

Window, light, fanlight, skylight, casement, lattice, embrasure.

Orifice, inlet, intake, outlet, mouth, throat, muzzle, gullet, weasand, nozzle, portal, porch, gate, lych-gate, wicket, postern, gateway, door, embouchure, doorway, exit, vomitory, hatch, hatchway, gangway, arcade.

Channel (350), passage, pass, tube, pipe, vessel, tubule, canal, thoroughfare, gut, fistula, ajutage, tap, faucet, chimney, flue, vent, funnel, gully, tunnel, main, adit, pit, shaft, gallery, alley, aisle, glade, vista, bore, mine, calibre, pore, follicle, porosity, porousness, lacuna.

Sieve, cullender, colander, strainer, tamis, riddle, screen, honeycomb.

Apertion, perforation, piercing, boring, mining, terebration, drilling, etc., impalement, pertusion, puncture, acupuncture, penetration (302).

Opener, tin-opener, key, master-key.

Verbs: To open, ope, gape, yawn.

To perforate, lay open, pierce, empierce, tap, bore, mine, drill, scoop out, canalize, tunnel, transpierce, transfix, enfilade, rake, impale, spike, spear, gore, stab, pink, stick, prick, lance, puncture, riddle, honeycomb, punch, jab; uncover, unrip, stave in.

Phrase: To cut a passage through.

Adjectives: Open, pierced, perforated, etc., perforate, wide open, ajar, unclosed, unstopped, patulous, gaping, yawning, patent.

Tubular, tubulous, tubulate, tubuliform, cannular, fistulous, fistular, fistulate, pervious, permeable, foraminous, porous, follicular, cribriform, honeycombed, infundibular, windowed, fenestrated.

Phrase: Open sesame!

261 CLOSURE

Substantives: occlusion, blockade, shutting up, filling up, plugging, sealing, obstruction, impassableness, blocking up, obstipation, constipation, blind alley, blind corner, cul-de-sac, impasse, caecum.

Imperforation, imperviousness, impermeability, imporosity.

Verbs: To close, occlude, steek, plug, block up, fill up, blockade, obstruct, bar, stop, bung up, seal, clinch, plumb, cork up, shut up, choke,

throttle, ram down, dam up, cram, stuff up.

Adjectives: Closed, shut, unopened, occluded, etc., impervious, imperforate, caecal, impassable, invious, pathless, untrodden, unpierced, unventilated, impermeable, imporous, operculated, tight, water-tight, air-tight, hermetic.

Phrase: Hermetically sealed.

262 PERFORATOR

Substantives: borer, auger, gimlet, stylet, drill, wimble, awl, bradawl, brog, scoop, corkscrew, dibble, trepan, probe, bodkin, needle, stiletto, lancet, punch, spike, bit, brace and bit, gouge, fleam.

Verbs: To spike, gouge, scoop, punch, lance.

263 STOPPER

Substantives: stopple, plug, cork, bung, spigot, spike, spile, vent-peg, stopcock, tap, stopgap, rammer, ramrod, piston, wad, dossil, wadding, tompion, stuffing, tourniquet.

Cover, lid, operculum, covering, covercle, door, etc. (222), valve.

A janitor, door-keeper, commissionaire, chucker-out, ostiary, concierge, porter, warder, beadle, Cerberus.

Section IV – Motion

264 MOTION

Substantives: movement, transit, transition, move, going, etc., passage, course, stir.

Step, gait, stride, tread, port, footfall, carriage, transference (270), locomotion, travel (266), voyage (267).

Mobility, restlessness, unrest, movability, movableness, inquietude, flux; kinematics.

Verbs: To be moving, etc., to move, go, stir, hie, gang, budge, pass, flit, shift, glide, roll, roll on, flow (347, 348), sweep along, wander (279), change or shift one's place or quarters, dodge, keep going.

To put in motion, impel, etc. (276); to propel, project (284); to mobilize, motorize.

Adjectives: Moving, in motion, on the move, going, transitional; kinematic.

Shifting, movable (270), mobile, restless, nomadic, wandering, vagrant, discursive, erratic (279), mercurial, unquiet.

Adverbs: *In transitu,* under way, on the move.

265 QUIESCENCE

Substantives: rest, stillness, stagnation, stagnancy, fixedness, immobility, catalepsy, paralysis.

Quiet, quietness, quietude, tranquillity, calm, calmness, sedentariness, peace; steadiness, balance, equilibrium.

Pause, suspension, suspense, lull, stop, stoppage, interruption, stopping, stand, standstill, standing still, lying to, repose (687), respite.

Lock, deadlock, dead stop, embargo.

Resting-place, anchorage, moorings, bivouac, port (189, 666), bed, pillow, etc. (215).

Verbs: To be quiescent, etc., to remain, stand, stand still, lie to, pull up, hold, halt, stop, anchor, stop short, stop dead, freeze, heave to, rest, pause, repose, keep quiet, take breath, stagnate, vegetate, settle; to mark time.

To stay, tarry, sojourn, dwell (186), pitch one's tent, cast anchor, settle, encamp, bivouac, moor, tether, picket, plant oneself, alight, land, etc. (292), ride at anchor.

Phrases: Not to stir a peg (or step or inch); *'j'y suis, j'y reste';* to come to a standstill; to come to a deadlock; to rest on one's oars or laurels.

To stop, suspend, arrest, lay to, hold one's hand, interrupt, intermit, discontinue (142), put a stop to, quell, becalm.

Phrases: To bring to a standstill; to lay an embargo on.

Adjectives: Quiescent, still, motionless, moveless, at rest, stationary, untravelled, stay-at-home, at a stand, at a standstill, stock-still, standing still, sedentary, undisturbed, unruffled, fast, stuck fast, fixed, transfixed, rooted, moored, aground, at anchor, tethered, becalmed, stagnant, quiet, calm, breathless, peaceful, unmoved, unstirred, immovable, immobile, restful, cataleptic, paralysed, frozen, irremovable, stable, steady, steadfast.

Phrases: Still as a statue; still as a post; quiet or still as a mouse.

Interjections: Soho! stop! stay! avast! belay! halt! as you were! hold hard! hold your horses! hold on! whoa!

266 JOURNEY

Substantives: travel, travelling, excursion, expedition, tour, trip, trek, circuit, peregrination, discursion, ramble, outing, pilgrimage, Odyssey, course, ambulation, march, route march, marching, walk, walking, promenade, stroll, saunter, dander, turn, trot, tramp, hike, stalk, noctambulation, perambulation, ride, equitation, drive, jog-trot, airing, constitutional, spin, jaunt, joy-ride, change of scene.

Roving, vagrancy, flit, flitting, migration, emigration, immigration, intermigration; *Wanderlust.*

Map, plan, itinerary, road-book, guide, Baedeker, Bradshaw, ABC.

Procession, caravan, cavalcade, column, cortège.

Organs and instruments of locomotion, legs, feet, pins, stilt, skate, ski, snow-shoe, locomotive, vehicle (272, 273), velocipede, penny-farthing, bone-shaker, bicycle, cycle, bike, push cycle, tandem, tricycle, fairy-cycle, scooter.

Phrase: Shanks's mare.

Verbs: To travel, journey, trek, walk, ramble, roam, rove, course, wander, itinerate, perambulate, stroll, straggle, expatiate, range, gad about, gallivant, knock about, to go or take a walk, journey, tour, turn, trip, etc.; to prowl, stray, saunter, tour, make a tour, knock about, emigrate, flit, migrate.

To walk, march, counter-march, step, tread, pace, wend, wend one's way, promenade, permabulate, circumambulate, take a walk, go for a walk, take the air, trudge, trapes, stalk, stride, straddle, strut, foot it, hoof it, stump, clump, plod, peg along, bundle, toddle, patter, shuffle on, tramp, hike, footslog, traverse, bend one's steps, thread one's way, make one's way, find one's way, tread a path, take a course, take wing, take flight, defile, file off.

Ride, jog on, trot, amble, canter, gallop, take horse, prance, frisk, tittup, caracole, have a run, ride and tie, hitch-hike, lorry-hop.

To drive, slide, glide, skim, skate, toboggan, ski.

To go to, repair to, resort to, hie to.

Phrases: To pad the hoof; to hump bluey.

Adjectives: Travelling, etc., ambulatory, itinerant, wayfaring, peripatetic, discursive, vagrant, migratory, nomadic, on the wing, etc., circumforanean, overland.

Adverbs: By the way, *chemin faisant,* on the road, *en passant, en route,* on foot, afoot.

267 NAVIGATION

Substantives: voyage, sail, cruise, Odyssey, circumnavigation, periplus, seafaring, yachting, boating; drifting, headway, sternway, leeway.

Natation, swimming, surf-riding.

Flight, flying, flip, volitation, aerostation, aeronautics, aerostatics, ballooning, aviation, gliding.

Space travel, astronautics.

Wing, pinion, fin, flipper; oar, scull, canvas, sail, rotor, paddle, punt-pole, paddle-wheel, screw, turbine, jet.

Verbs: To sail, make sail, warp, put to sea, navigate, take ship, get under way, spread sail, spread canvas, carry sail, plough the waves, plough the deep, scud, boom, drift, course, cruise, coast, circumnavigate, aviate.

To row, pull, paddle, scull, punt, steam.

To swim, float, buffet the waves, skim, *effleurer,* dive, wade.

To fly, aviate, hedge-hop, be wafted, hover, soar, glide, wing; to flush.

Phrases: To take wing; to take flight.

Adjectives: Sailing, etc., seafaring, under way, under sail, on the wing, volant, nautical; airborne, aeronautic, aeronautical, aerostatic; astronautical.

Phrases: In sail; under canvas.

268 TRAVELLER

Substantives: wayfarer, voyager, itinerant, passenger, commuter, tourist, tripper, excursionist, wanderer, rover, straggler, rambler, hiker, bird of passage, gad-about, globe-trotter, vagrant, tramp, hobo, bum, swagman, sundowner, vagabond, rolling-stone, nomad, pilgrim, hadji, palmer, runner, courier, pedestrian, peripatetic, emigrant, fugitive.

Rider, horseman, equestrian, cavalier, jockey, postilion, roughrider, scout, motorist.

Mercury, Iris, Ariel.

269 MARINER

Substantives: navigator, seaman, sailor, seafarer, shipman, tar, old salt, bluejacket, marine, jolly, boatman, *voyageur,* ferryman, waterman, lighterman, bargee, gondolier, longshoreman, crew, oarsman.

An aerial navigator, aeronaut, balloonist, aviator, airman, flying man, pilot.

Astronaut, cosmonaut, spaceman.

270 TRANSFERENCE
Substantives: transfer, displacement, metathesis, transposition (148), remotion, removal (185), relegation, deportation, extradition, conveyance, draft, carriage, carrying, convection, conduction, export, import.

Transmission, passage, transit, transition, ferry, transport, gestation, portage, porterage, cartage, carting, shovelling, shipment, transhipment, air lift, air drop, freight, wafture, transportation, transumption, transplantation, transfusion, translation, shifting, dodging, dispersion (73), traction (285).
Verbs: To transfer, convey, transmit, transport, transplant, transfuse, carry, bear, carry over, hand over, pass forward, remove (185), transpose (148), shift, export, import, convey, conduct, convoy, send, relegate, extradite, turn over to, deliver, waft, ship, tranship, ferry over.

To bring, fetch, reach, draft.

To load, lade, charge, unload, shovel, ladle, decant, empty, break bulk.
Adjectives: Transferred, etc., movable portable, portative.
Adverbs: From hand to hand, on the way, *en route, en passant, in transitu,* from pillar to post.

271 CARRIER
Substantives: porter, bearer, coolie, *hammal,* conveyer, transport-worker, stevedore (690), conductor, locomotive (285).

Beast of burden, cattle, horse, blood-horse, arab, steed, nag, palfrey, galloway, charger, destrier, war-horse, courser, racer, racehorse, hunter, pony, filly, colt, foal, barb, jade, hack,

bidet, pad, cob, tit, punch, roadster, goer, pack-horse, draught-horse, cart-horse, post-horse, shelty, jennet, bayard, mare, stallion, gelding, gee-gee, gee, stud.

Ass, donkey, moke, cuddy, jackass, mule, hinny, sumpter-mule.

Camel, dromedary, llama, zebra, reindeer, yak, elephant, carrier-pigeon.

272 VEHICLE
Substantives: conveyance.

Carriage, caravan, van, furniture van, pantechnicon, wagon, stage-wagon, wain, dray, cart, float, trolley, sledge, sleigh, bob-sleigh, *luge,* toboggan, truck, tumbril, pontoon, barrow, wheelbarrow, hand-barrow, lorry.

Train, railway train, goods train, freight train, rolling stock, Pullman car, parlour car, restaurant-car, dining-car, diner, buffet-car, sleeping-car, sleeper, horse-box, cattle-truck, rail-car, tender.

Equipage, turn-out, carriage coach, chariot, chaise, post-chaise, phaeton, curricle, tilbury, whisky, victoria, landau, brougham, clarence, gig, calash, dog-cart, governess-cart, trap, buggy, carriole, jingle, wagonette, jaunting-car, shandrydan, droshky, kibitka, berlin, stage, stage-coach, diligence, car, omnibus, bus, charabanc, brake, cabriolet, cab, hackney cab, four-wheeler, growler, fly, hansom.

Motor-car, motor, automobile, autocar, touring-car, tourer, sports car, torpedo, landaulette, limousine, saloon, sedan, two-seater, runabout, coupé, jalopy, tricar, motor-cycle, side-car, autocycle, moped, corgi, motor-bus, motor-coach, autobus, taxi-cab, taxi, motor-van, jeep; trolley-bus, tram-car, tram, street-car.

Tank, armoured car, half-track, amtrac, duck.

Bath-chair, wheel-chair, sedan chair, palanquin (or palankeen), litter, jinricksha (or rickshaw), brancard, stretcher, perambulator, pram, mail-cart, bassinette, baby-carriage.

Shovel, spoon, spatula, ladle, hod.

273 SHIP

Substantives: vessel, bottom, craft, shipping, marine, fleet, flotilla, squadron, three-master, barque (or bark), barquentine, brig, brigantine, schooner, sloop, cutter, skiff, yawl, ketch, smack, dogger, hoy, lugger, barge, wherry, lighter, hulk, buss, packet, clipper, rotor ship.

Navy, armada, warship, man-of-war, ironclad, capital ship, super-dreadnought, dreadnought, battle-ship, battle-cruiser, cruiser, frigate, corvette, gunboat, aircraft-carrier, monitor, torpedo boat destroyer, destroyer, torpedo boat, mine-sweeper, mine-layer, submarine, Q-boat, troop-ship, trooper, transport, hospital ship, flagship; ship of the line, first-rate, seventy-four, fireship.

Liner, merchantman, tramp, slaver, steamer, steamboat, steam-packet, paddle-steamer, stern-wheeler, screw-steamer, turbine, tender, tug, collier, whaler, coaster, tanker.

Argosy, bireme, trireme, quadrireme, quinquereme, galley, galleon, carrack, caravel, galliot, polacca, tartan, junk, praam, saic, dhow, proa, sampan, xebec.

Boat, motor-boat, long-boat, pinnace, launch, cabin cruiser, yacht, shallop, jolly-boat, gig, funny, dinghy, bumboat, fly-boat, wherry, coble, cock-boat, punt, cog, kedge, outrigger, catamaran, fishing-boat, coracle, hooker, life-boat, gondola, felucca, dahabeeyah, caique, canoe, dug-out, raft, float.

Adverbs: Afloat, aboard.

273A AIRCRAFT

Substantives: flying machine, aeroplane, monoplane, biplane, seaplane, hydroplane, plane, flyingboat, amphi-

bian, air-liner, flying wing, strato-cruiser, stratoliner, sky-master, jet aircraft, jet, turbo-jet, autogiro, helicopter, hoverplane, whirlybird, planicopter, glider; fighter, bomber, fighter-bomber, flying fortress, super-fortress.

Balloon, air-balloon, aerostat, Montgolfier, pilot balloon, blimp, kite, airship, dirigible, Zeppelin.

Space ship, rocket, sputnik, lunik, satellite.

Adjectives: Airborne; orbital.

274 VELOCITY

Substantives: speed, celerity, swiftness, rapidity, fleetness, expedition, speediness, quickness, nimbleness, briskness, agility, promptness, promptitude (682), dispatch, acceleration (684).

Gallop, full gallop, canter, trot, run, rush, scamper, scoot, scorch, hand-gallop, lope; flight, dart, bolt, dash, spurt, sprint.

Haste, hurry, scurry, bounce, bolt, precipitation, precipitancy (684), forced march, race, steeplechase, Marathon race.

Rate, pace, step, gait, course, progress.

Lightning, light, cannon-ball, bullet, wind, rocket, arrow, dart, quicksilver, telegraph, express train, clipper.

An eagle, antelope, doe, courser, racehorse, racer, gazelle, greyhound, hare, squirrel, bandersnatch.

Mercury, Ariel, Camilla.

Speed indicator, speedometer, tachometer, log, log-line.

Verbs: To move quickly; to trip, speed, haste, hie, hasten, hurry, fly, press, press on, press forward, post, push on, whip, scamper, run, sprint, race, scud, scour, scurry, scuttle, spin, scoot, scorch, rip, clip, shoot, tear, whisk, sweep, skim, brush, glance, cut along, dash on, dash forward, trot, gallop, lope, rush, bound, bounce, flounce, frisk, tittup, bolt, flit, spring, boom, dart.

To hasten, accelerate, expedite, dispatch, urge, whip, forward, buck up, express, speed-up, hurry, precipitate, quicken pace, gather way, ride hard.

To keep up with, keep pace with, race, race with, outpace, outmarch, distance, outdistance, lap, leave behind, outrun, outstrip, gain ground.
Phrases: To cover the ground; to clap on sail; take to one's heels; clap spurs to one's horse; to run like mad; ride hard; outstrip the wind; to make rapid strides; wing one's way; be off like a shot; run a race; stir one's stumps; do a scoot; get a move on; get cracking; step on it; give her the gun; let it rip.
Adjectives: Fast, speedy, swift, rapid, full-drive, quick, double-quick, fleet, nimble, agile, expeditious, prompt, brisk, frisky, hasty, hurried, flying, etc., precipitate, furious, light-footed, nimble-footed, winged, eagle-winged, mercurial, electric, telegraphic, light-legged; accelerative.
Phrases: Swift as an arrow, as a doe, as a lamplighter; off like a shot; quick as lightning; quick as thought.
Adverbs: Swiftly, with speed, speedily, trippingly, etc., full-tilt, full speed, apace, post-haste, *presto*, tantivy, by express, by telegraph, slap, slap-dash, headlong, hurry-scurry, hand over hand, at a round trot.
Phrases: Under press of sail, or canvas; *velis et remis*; on eagle's wings; at the double, in double-quick time; with giant, or gigantic steps; *à pas de géant*; in seven-league boots; whip and spur; *ventre à terre*; as fast as one's legs or heels will carry one; *sauve qui peut*; the devil take the hindmost; *vires acquirit eundo*; with rapid strides; at top speed; in top gear; flat out; all out; like greased lightning; like the wind.

275 SLOWNESS
Substantives: tardiness, dilatoriness, slackness, lentor, languor (683), drawl.

Hobbling, creeping, lounging, etc., shambling, claudication, halting, walk, amble, jog-trot, dog-trot, mincing steps, foot-pace, crawl.

A slow-goer, dawdle, dawdler, lingered, slow-coach, lame duck, drone, tortoise, snail, slug, sluggard, slacker.

Retardation, slackening, slowing down, delay (133).
Verbs: To move slowly, to creep, crawl, lag, slug, drawl, dawdle, linger, loiter (683), plod, trudge, flag, saunter, lounge, lumber, trail, drag, grovel, glide, laze, amble, steal along, inch along, jog on, rub on, bundle on, toddle, waddle, shuffle, halt, hobble, limp, claudicate, shamble, mince, falter, totter, stagger.

To retard, slacken, relax, check, rein in, curb, strike sail, reef, slow up, slow down.
Phrases: To 'drag its slow length along'; to hang fire; to march in slow time, in funeral procession; to lose ground.

To put on the drag; apply the brake; clip the wings; take in sail; take one's time; ca'canny; *festina lente*.
Adjectives: Slow, slack, tardy, dilatory, easy, gentle, leisurely, deliberate, lazy, languid, drawsy, sleepy, heavy, drawling, leaden, sluggish, snail-like, creeping, crawling, etc., dawdling, lumbering, hobbling, tardi-grade.
Adverbs: Slowly, etc., gingerly, softly, leisurely, deliberately, gradually, etc. (144) *piano, adagio, largo*.
Phrases: In slow motion; just ticking over; under easy sail; at a snail's pace; with mincing steps; with clipped wings; by degrees; little by little; inch by inch.

276 IMPULSE
Substantives: momentum, impetus, push, impulsion, thrust, shove, fling, jog, jolt, brunt, throw, volley, explosion (173), propulsion (284).

Percussion, collision, concussion, impact, clash, encounter, cannon, carom, carambole, appulse, shock, crash, bump, charge, tackle (716), foul.

Blow, stroke, knock, tap, fillip, pat, rap, dab, dig, jab, smack, slap, hit, putt, cuff, bang, crack, whack, thwack, slog, belt, wipe, clout, swipe, clip, squash, dowse, punch, thump, pelt, kick, lunge, buffet, beating (972).

Hammer, mallet, mall, maul, beetle, flail, cudgel, bludgeon, life-preserver, cosh, baton, truncheon, knobkerrie, shillelagh, staff, lathi, cane, stick, club, racket, bat, driver, brassy, baffy, spoon, putter, cleek, iron, mashie, niblick, ram, battering-ram, monkey-engine, catapult, pile-driver, rammer, sledge-hammer, steam hammer.

Dynamics; seismometer.

Verbs: To impel, push, give impetus, etc., drive, urge, hurtle, boom, thrust, elbow, shoulder, charge, tackle, jostle, justle, hustle, shove, jog, jolt, encounter, collide, clash, cannon, foul.

To strike,, knock, tap, slap, dab, pat, slam, hit, bat, putt, rap, prod, jerk, dig, cuff, smite, butt, impinge, thump, bethump, beat, bang, whang, biff, punch, thwack, whack, spank, skelp, swat, lay into, shin, slog, clout, wipe, swipe, batter, dowse, baste, pummel, pelt, patter, drub, buffet, belabour, cane, whip (972), poke at, hoof, jab, pink, lunge, kick, recalcitrate.

To throw, etc. (284), to set going, mobilize.

Adjectives: Impelling, etc., impulsive, impellent, impelled, etc., dynamic, dynamical.

Interjections: Bang! boom! wham!

277 RECOIL

Substantives: retroaction, revulsion, reaction, rebound, bounce, stot, repercussion, ricochet, rebuff, reverberation, reflux, reflex, kick, springing back, ducks and drakes.

A boomerang, spring (325).

Verbs: To recoil, react, spring back, fly back, bound back, rebound, stot, reverberate, repercuss.

Adjectives: Recoiling, etc., on the recoil, etc., refluent, repercussive, reactionary, retroactive.

Phrase: On the rebound.

278 DIRECTION

Substantives: bearing, course, route, bent, inclination, drift, tenor, tendency, incidence, set, leaning, bending, trend, dip, steerage, tack, steering, aim, alignment (or alinement), orientation, collimation.

A line, bee-line, path, road, aim, range, quarter, point of the compass, rhumb, great circle, azimuth, line of collimation.

Verbs: To tend towards, go to, point to, or at; trend, verge, align (or aline), incline, conduct to, determine.

To make for, or towards, aim at, take aim, level at, steer for, keep or hold a course, be bound for, bend one's steps towards, direct or shape one's course.

To ascertain one's direction, orient (or orientate) oneself, to see which way the wind blows.

Adjectives: Directed, etc., direct, straight, undeviating, unswerving, aligned (or alined) with, determinate, point-to-point.

Adverbs: Towards, to, *versus*, thither, directly, straight, point-blank, full tilt at, whither, in a line with, as the crow flies.

By way of, via, in all directions, *quaquaversum*, in all manner of ways, to the four winds.

279 DEVIATION

Substantives: swerving, aberration, obliquation, *ambages*, warp, bending, flexion, deflection, refraction, sidling, side-slip, skid, half-roll, barrel-roll, loop, straying, straggling, warping, etc., digression, circuit, detour, departure from, divergence (291), desultory motion; slice, pull, hook, leg-break, off-break, googly.

Motion sideways, side-step.

Verbs: To alter one's course, divert, deviate, depart from, turn, bend, swerve, break, switch, skid, side-slip, zoom, bank, loop, bunt, jib, shift, warp, stray, struggle, sidle, diverge (291), digress, wander, meander, veer, wear, tack, yaw, turn aside, turn a corner, turn away from, face about, wheel, wheel about, steer clear of, ramble, rove, go astray, step aside, shunt, side-track, jay walk.

Phrases: To fly off at a tangent; to face to the right-about; to go out of one's way; to lose one's way.

Adjectives: Deviating, etc., aberrant, discursive, devious, desultory, erratic, vagrant, stray, undirected, circuitous, roundabout, crab-like, zigzag.

Adverbs: Astray from, round about.

Phrases: To the right-about; all manner of ways; like the knight's move in chess.

280 PRECESSION

Substantives: leading, heading.

Precedence in order (62), priority (116), precursor (64), front (234).

Verbs: To precede, forerun, lead, head, herald, introduce, usher in (62), go ahead.

Phrases: Go in the van; take the lead; lead the way; open the ball; have the start; to get before; steal a march.

Adjectives: Preceding, leading, etc.

Adverbs: In advance, before (62), in the van, ahead.

281 SEQUENCE

Substantives: following, pursuit, chase, hunt (622).

A follower, pursuer, attendant, shadow, satellite, hanger-on, train.

Sequence in order (63), in time (117).

Verbs: To follow, pursue, chase, hunt, hound, shadow, dog, tail, trail, lag.

Phrases: Go in the rear, or in the wake of; tread in the steps of; tread on the heels of; go after; fly after; to follow as a shadow; to lag behind; to bring up the rear; to fall behind; to tail off.

Adjectives: Following, etc.

Adverbs: Behind, in the rear, etc.

282 PROGRESSION

Substantives: advance, advancement, progress (658), on-going, progressiveness, progressive motion, flood-tide, headway, advancing, etc., pursuit, steeplechase (622), journey, march (266).

Verbs: To advance, proceed, progress, go, move, bend or pass forward, go on, move on, pass on, get on, get along, jog on, push on, go one's way, go ahead, forge ahead, make head, make way, make headway, work one's way, press forward, edge forward, get over the ground, gain ground, make progress, keep or hold on one's course, keep up with, get forward, distance.

Phrases: To make up leeway; to go with the stream; to make rapid strides; to push or elbow or cleave one's way; to go full tilt at.

Adjectives: Advancing, etc., progressive, go-ahead, avant-garde, profluent, undeviating.

Adverbs: Forward, onward, forth, on, in advance, ahead, under way, straightforward.

Phrases: *Vestigia nulla retrorsum; en avant.*

283 REGRESSION

Substantives: regress, recess, retrogression, retrogradation, retreat, withdrawal, retirement, recession (287), refluence, reflux, retroaction, return, reflexion, reflex (277), ebb, countermovement, countermarch, veering, regurgitation, back-wash.

Verbs: To recede, retrograde, return,

rebound, back, fall back, fall or drop astern, lose ground, put about, go back, turn back, hark back, double, countermarch, turn tail, draw back, get back, retrace one's steps, wheel about, back water, regurgitate, yield, give.

Phrases: Dance the back step; beat a retreat.

Adjectives: Receding, etc., retrograde, retrogressive, regressive, refluent, reflex, recidivous, resilient.

Adverbs: Backwards, reflexively, to the right-about, about turn, *à reculons, à rebours.*

Phrase: *Revenons à nos moutons.*

284 PROPULSION

Substantives: push, pushing (276), projection, jaculation, ejaculation, throw, fling, fillip, toss, shot, discharge, shy.

Ballistics, gunnery; *vis a tergo.*

Missile, projectile, shot, shell, ball, bolt, dart, arrow, bullet, stone, shaft, brickbat, discus, quoit, caber.

Bow, sling, pea-shooter, catapult, etc. (727).

Verbs: To propel, project, throw, fling, cast, pitch, chuck, bung, toss, lob, loft, jerk, jaculate, ejaculate, hurl, boost, bolt, drive, sling, flirt, flip, flick, shy, dart, send, roll, send off, let off, discharge, fire off, shoot, launch, let fly, dash, punt, volley, heave, pitchfork.

To bowl, trundle, roll along (312).

To put in motion, start, give an impulse, impel (276), expel (297).

Phrases: To carry off one's feet; to put to flight.

Adjectives: Propelling, etc., propulsive, projectile, etc.

285 TRACTION

Substantives: drawing, draught, pull, pulling, towage, haulage.

Traction engine, locomotive; hauler, haulyer, tractor, tug; trailer.

Phrase: A long pull, a strong pull, and a pull all together.

Verbs: To draw, pull, haul, lug, drag, tug, tow, trail, train, wrench, jerk, twitch, yank.

Phrase: To take in tow.

Adjectives: Drawing, etc., tractile.

286 APPROACH

Substantives: approximation, appropinquation, access, appulse, afflux, affluxion, pursuit (622), collision (276), arrival (292).

Verbs: To approach, draw near, approximate, to near; to come, get, go, etc., near; to set in towards, make up to, snuggle up to, gain upon, gain ground upon.

Phrases: To tread on the heels of; to hug the shore.

Adjectives: Approaching, etc., approximative.

287 RECESSION

Substantives: retirement, withdrawal, retreat, retrocession (283), departure (293), recoil (277), decampment, flight, stampede, skedaddle.

A runaway, a fugitive.

Verbs: To recede, go, move or fly from, retire, retreat, withdraw, come away, go or get away, draw back, shrink, move away.

To move off, stand off, draw off, buzz off, fall back, turn tail, march off, decamp, absquatulate, skedaddle, vamoose, sheer off, bolt, scram, hop it, beat it, slip away, run away, pack off, fly, remove, abscond, sneak off, slink away.

Phrases: To take French leave; to cut and run; take to one's heels; to give leg-bail; take one's hook; *sauve qui peut*; the devil take the hindmost; beat a retreat; make oneself scarce; do a bolt; do a guy; make tracks; cut one's lucky.

Adjectives: Receding, etc., fugitive, runaway (671).

288 ATTRACTION
Substantives: drawing to, pulling towards, adduction, attractiveness, magnetism, gravity, gravitation.

A loadstone, magnet.

Verbs: To attract, draw, pull, drag, etc., towards, adduce.

Adjectives: Attracting, etc., adducent, attrahent, adductive, attractive, magnetic, gravitational.

Interjections: Come! come here! approach! come near!

289 REPULSION
Substantives: push (276), driving from, repulse, expulsion (297).

Verbs: To repel, repulse; push, drive, etc., from, drive away, cold-shoulder, send packing.

Phrases: To give the frozen mitt to; send away with a flea in one's ear; send to the right-about (678).

Adjectives: Repelling, etc., repellent, repulsive, forbidding.

Interjections: Get out! be off! scram! avaunt! (293, 297).

290 CONVERGENCE
Substantives: appulse, meeting, confluence, concourse, conflux, congress, concurrence, concentration.

Resort, assemblage, synod (72), focus (74), asymptote.

Verbs: To converge, come together, unite, meet, fall in with, close in upon, centre in, enter in, meet, come across, come up against.

To gather together, unite, concentrate, etc.

Adjectives: Converging, etc., convergent, confluent, concurring, concurrent, centripetal, asymptotical.

291 DIVERGENCE
Substantives: aberration, peregrination, wandering, divarication, radiation, ramification, separation (44), dispersion, diffusion, dissemination (73); deviation (279).

Verbs: To diverge, divaricate, deviate, wander, stray (279), radiate, branch off, ramify, file off, draw aside.

To spread, disperse, scatter, distribute, decentralize, diffuse, disseminate, shed, sow broadcast, broadcast, sprinkle.

To part, part company, turn away from, wander from, separate (44).

Phrase: To go or fly off at a tangent.

Adjectives: Diverging, etc., divergent, radiant, wandering, aberring, aberrant, centrifugal.

Adverb: Broadcast.

292 ARRIVAL
Substantives: advent, reception, welcome, return, disembarkation, debarkation, remigration.

Home, goal, resting-place, destination, journey's end, harbour, haven, port, dock, pier, landing-place, landing-stage, landing-ground, airfield, airstrip, airstop, airport, aerodrome, helidrome, terminus, station.

Meeting, rencontre, rencounter, encounter.

Caller, visitor, visitant, guest.

Verbs: To arrive, get to, come, come to, reach, attain, come up with, come up to, catch up, make, fetch, overtake, overhaul.

To light, alight, land, dismount, disembark, debark, detrain, outspan, debus, put in, put into, visit, cast, anchor.

To come upon, light upon, pitch upon, hit, drop in, pop upon, bounce upon, plump upon, bump against, run against, run across, close with.

To come back, return, get back, get home, sit down.

To meet, encounter, rencounter, contact, come in contact (199).

Phrase: To be in at the death.

Adjectives: Arriving, etc., homeward bound.

Adverbs: Here, hither.

Interjections: Welcome! hallo! hail! all hail! good day! good morrow! *ave!*

293 DEPARTURE
Substantives: outset, removal, exit, exodus, decampment, embarkation, flight, hegira.

Valediction, adieu, farewell, good-bye, leave-taking, send-off; stirrup-cup, doch-an-doris, one for the road.

A starting point or post, place of departure or embarkation, airfield, terminus, etc. (292).
Phrase: The foot being in the stirrup.
Verbs: To depart, go, set out, set off, start, start off, issue, go forth, sally, debouch, sally forth, set forward, be off, move off, pack off, buzz off, scram, begone, get off, sheer off, clear out, vamoose, skedaddle, absquatulate.

To leave a place, quit, retire, withdraw, go one's way, take wing, flit, embus, inspan, entrain, embark, go on board, set sail, put to sea, weigh anchor, slip cable, decamp (671).
Phrases: To take leave; bid or take adieu; bid farewell; to say good-bye; make one's exit; take a run-out powder.
Adjectives: Departing, etc., valedictory, outward bound.
Adverbs: Whence, hence, thence.
Interjections: Be off! get out! clear out! scram! buzz off! hop it! beat it! begone! get you gone! go along! off with you! avaunt! away with you! go about your business!

Good-bye! bye-bye! 'bye! ta ta! farewell! fare you well! adieu! *au revoir! auf wiedersehen! a rivederci! bon voyage! vale! hasta la vista! sayonara!* so long! cheerio! chin-chin! tinkety-tonk! pip-pip! tootle-oo! bung-ho!

294 INGRESS
Substantives: ingoing, entrance, entry, introgression, admission, admittance, intromission, introduction, insinuation, insertion (300), intrusion, inroad, incursion, influx, irruption, invasion, penetration, interpenetra-tion, infiltration, import, importation, illapse, immigration.

A mouth, door (260); an entrant.
Verbs: To enter, go into, come into, set foot in, intrude, invade, flow into, pop into, insinuate itself, penetrate, interpenetrate, infiltrate, soak into; to put into, etc., bring in, insert, drive in, run in, wedge in, ram in (300), intromit, introduce, import, smuggle.
Phrases: To find one's way into; creep into; worm oneself into; to darken one's door; have the *entrée*; to open the door to.
Adjectives: Ingoing, incoming, penetrative, penetrant.
Adverb: Inwards.

295 EGRESS
Substantives: exit, issue, emersion, emergence.

Exudation, extravasation, transudation (348), leakage, seepage, percolation, distillation, oozing, effluence, efflux, effusion, drain, dropping, dripping, dribbling, drip, dribble, drainage, filtering, defluxion, trickling, eruption, outbreak, outburst, outpouring, gush (348), emanation, aura.

Export, expatriation, emigration, remigration, repatriation, exodus (293).

An outlet, vent, spout, tap, faucet, sluice, flue, chimney, pore, drain, sewer (350).
Verbs: To emerge, emanate, issue, go, come, move, pass, pour, flow, etc., out of, find vent, pass off, evacuate.

To transude, exude, leak, seep, well out, percolate, transcolate, strain, distil, drain, ooze, filter, filtrate, dribble, trickle, drizzle, drip, gush, spout, run, flow out, effuse, extravasate, disembogue, debouch (348).
Adjectives: Dripping, outgoing, etc., oozy, leaky, trickly, dribbly.

296 RECEPTION
Substantives: admission, admittance,

importation, immission, introduction, ingestion, imbibition, absorption, resorption, ingurgitation, inhalation (300).

Eating, swallowing, deglutition, devouring, gulp, gulping, gorge, gorging, carousal.

Drinking, potation, sipping, supping, suction, sucking, draught, libation; smoking, snuffing.

Mastication, manducation, rumination, chewing; hippophagy, ichthyophagy, anthropophagy.

Verbs: To admit, receive, intromit, import, ingest, absorb, resorb, imbibe, inhale, let in, take in, readmit, resorb, reabsorb, snuff up, sop up, suck, suck in, swallow, take down, ingurgitate, engulf.

To eat, fare, feed, devour, tuck in, gulp, bolt, snap, get down, pick, peck, gorge, engorge, fall to, stuff, cram, gobble, guttle, guzzle, wolf, raven, eat heartily, do justice to, overeat, gormandize (957), dispatch, discuss.

To feed upon, live on, feast upon, regale, carouse, batten upon, fatten upon, dine, etc., browse, graze, crop, chew, champ, munch, gnaw, nibble, crunch, ruminate, masticate, manducate, mumble.

To drink, quaff, swill, swig, booze, drench, sip, sup, lap, drink up, drain up, toss off, drain the cup, tipple (959).

Phrases: To give entrance or admittance to; open the door to; usher in.

To refresh the inner man; restore one's tissues; play a good knife and fork; get outside of; wrap oneself round.

To drink one's fill; wet one's whistle; empty one's glass; crook or lift one's elbow; crack a bottle.

Adjectives: Admitting, etc., admitted, etc., admissible; absorbent, absorptive.

Hippophagous, ichthyophagous, anthropophagous, herbivorous, graminivorous, granivorous, omnivorous.

297 EJECTION
Substantives: emission, effusion, rejection, expulsion, detrusion, extrusion, eviction.

Discharge, egestion, evacuation, vomition, eructation, belch; bloodletting, venesection, phlebotomy, tapping.

Deportation, exile, rustication, banishment, relegation, extradition.

Phrases: The rogue's march; the bum's rush.

Verbs: To emit, eject, expel, export, reject, discharge, give out, let out, cast out, clear out, sweep out, clean out, gut, fillet, wipe off, turn out, chuck out, elbow out, kick out, hoof out, sack, dismiss, bounce, drive out, root out, pour out, ooze, shed, void, evacuate, disgorge, extrude, empty, detrude, throw off, spit, spit out, expectorate, spirt, spill, slop, drain.

To vomit, spue, cat, puke, cast up, keck, retch, spatter, splutter, slobber, slaver, slabber, squirt, eructate, belch, burp, give vent to, tap, broach, open the sluices, heave out, bale out, shake off.

To throw, project (284); to push, thrust (276).

To unpack, unlade, unload (270).

To banish, exile, extradite, deport; ostracize, boycott, send to Coventry.

Phrases: To send packing; to send to the right about; to send about one's business; to give the sack to; to show the door to; to turn out neck and crop; to make a clean sweep of; to send away with a flea in one's ear.

Adjectives: Emitting, etc., emitted, etc.

Interjections: Be off! get out! scram! (293), scat! fade! chase yourself! *allez-vous-en!*

298 FOOD
Substantives: pabulum, aliment,

nourishment, nutriment, sustenance, sustentation, nurture, subsistence, provender, fodder, provision, prey, forage, pasture, pasturage, keep, fare, cheer, rations, diet, regimen.

Comestibles, eatables, victuals, prog, grub, chow, chuck, toke, eats, meat, bread, breadstuffs, cake, pastry, viands, cates, delicacy, delicatessen, dainty, creature comforts, belly-timber, staff of life, dish, flesh-pots, pottage, pudding, ragout, omelet, sundae, kickshaws.

Table, board, commons, good cheer, bill of fare, menu, commissariat, table d'hôte, ordinary, cuisine.

Canteen, Naffy, restaurant, chop-house, café, cafeteria, eating-house, tea-room, tea-shop, coffee-house, coffee-stall, bar, milk bar, snack bar, public-house, pot-house, ale-house, wineshop, brasserie, bodega, tavern (189).

Meal, repast, feed, mess, spread, course, regale, regalement, entertainment, feast, banquet, junket, refreshment, refection; breakfast, *chota hazri*, elevenses, *déjeuner*, lunch, bever, luncheon, tiffin, tea, afternoon tea, five-o'clock tea, high tea, dinner, supper, whet, appetizer, aperitif, bait, dessert, *entremet, hors d'œuvre*, picnic, bottle-party, wayz-goose, beanfeast, blow-out, tuck-in, snack, pot-luck, table d'hôte, *déjeuner à la fourchette*.

Mouthful, bolus, gobbet, sip, sup, sop, tot, snort, hoot, dram, peg, cocktail (615), nip, *chasse*, liqueur.

Drink, hard drink, soft drink, tipple, beverage, liquor, broth, soup, etc., symposium.

Phrases: A good tuck-in; a modest quencher.

Adjectives: Eatable, edible, esculent, comestible, alimentary, cereal, culinary, nutritious, nutritive, nutrient, nutrimental, succulent, potable, drinkable.

298A TOBACCO

Substantives: the weed, bacca, baccy, honeydew, cavendish, bird's-eye, shag, virginia, latakia, perique, plug, twist.

Cigar, segar, cheroot, havana, manila, weed, whiff, cigarette, fag, gasper, stinker, coffin-nail.

Snuff, rappee.

A smoke, draw, puff, pinch, quid, chew, chaw.

Tobacco-pipe, pipe, briar, meerschaum, calabash, corncob, clay pipe, clay, churchwarden, dudeen (or dudheen), cutty, hookah, hubble-bubble, chibouque, narghile, calumet.

Verbs: To smoke, chew, take snuff.

Adjectives: Nicotian.

299 EXCRETION

Substantives: discharge, emanation, exhalation, exudation, secretion, extrusion, effusion, extravasation, evacuation, faeces, excrement (653), perspiration, sweat, saliva, salivation, spittle, diaphoresis; bleeding, haemorrhage, flux.

Verbs: To emanate, exhale, excern, excrete, exude, effuse, secrete, secern, extravasate, evacuate, urinate, discharge, etc. (297).

300 INSERTION

Substantives: putting in, implantation, introduction, interjection, insinuation, planting, intercalation, embolism, injection, inoculation, vaccination, importation, intervention (228), dovetailing, tenon, wedge.

Immersion, dip, plunge, bath (337), submergence, submersion, souse, duck, soak.

Interment, burying, etc. (363).

Verbs: To insert, introduce, intromit, put into, import, throw in, interlard, inject, interject, intercalate, infuse, instil, inoculate, vaccinate, pasteurize, impregnate, imbue, imbrue, graft, engraft, bud, plant, implant, embed, obtrude, foist in, worm in, thrust in, stick in, ram in, stuff in, tuck in, plough in, let in, dovetail, mortise (or mortice), insinuate, wedge in, press in, impact, drive in, run in, empierce (260).

To immerse, dip, steep, immerge, merge, submerge, bathe, plunge, drop in, souse, douse, soak, duck, drown.

To inter, bury, etc. (363).

Adjectives: Inserting, inserted, implanted, embedded, etc., ingrowing.

301 EXTRACTION

Substantives: taking out, removal, elimination, extrication, evulsion, avulsion, eradication, extirpation, wrench.

Expression, squeezing; ejection (297).

Extractor, corkscrew, pincers, pliers, forceps.

Verbs: To extract, take out, draw, draw out, pull out, tear out, pluck out, extort, wring from, prise, wrench, rake out, rake up, grub up, root up, uproot, eradicate, extirpate, dredge, remove, get out (185), elicit, extricate, eliminate.

To express, squeeze out, wring out, pick out, disembowel, eviscerate, exenterate.

Adjectives: Extracted, etc.

302 PASSAGE

Substantives: transmission, permeation, penetration, interpenetration (294), filtration, infiltration, percolation, transudation, osmosis (or osmose), capillary attraction, endosmosis (or endosmose), exosmosis (or exosmose), intercurrence; way, path (627); channel, pipe (350).

Terebration, impalement, etc. (260).

Verbs: To pass, pass through, traverse, terebrate, stick, pierce, impale, spear, spike, spit (260), penetrate, percolate, permeate, thread, thrid, enfilade, go through, cross, go across, go over, pass over, get over, clear, negotiate, cut across, pass and repass; work, thread or worm one's way, force a passage; to transmit.

Adjectives: Passing, intercurrent, penetrative, transudatory, etc.

303 TRANSCURSION

Substantives: Transilience, transgression, trespass, encroachment, infringement, extravagation, transcendence, enjambement, overrunning.

Verbs: To transgress, overstep, surpass, overpass, overrun, overgo, beat, outstrip, outgo, outstep, outrun, outdo, overreach, overleap, outleap, pass, go by, strain, overshoot the mark, overjump, overskip, overlap, go beyond, outpace, outmarch, transcend, distance, outdistance, lap, encroach, exceed, trespass, infringe, trench upon.

Phrases: To stretch a point; to steal a march on; to pass the Rubicon; to shoot ahead of; to throw into the shade.

Adverbs: Beyond the mark, out of bounds.

304 SHORTCOMING

Substantives: failure, falling short (732), defalcation, default, backlog, leeway, incompleteness (53); imperfection (651); insufficiency (640).

Verbs: To come or fall short of, not to reach, keep within bounds, keep within compass, to stop short, be wanting, lose ground, miss the mark.

Adjectives: Unreached, deficient (53), short, minus.

Adverbs: Within the mark, within compass, within bounds, etc., behindhand.

305 ASCENT

Substantives: rise, climb, ascension, upgrowth, leap (309).

A rocket, sky-rocket, lark, skylark; a climber, mountaineer, Alpinist, stegophilist.

Verbs: To ascend, rise, mount, arise, uprise, go up, get up, climb, clamber, swarm, shin, scale, scramble, escalade, surmount, aspire.

To tower, soar, zoom, hover, spire, plane, swim, float, surge.

Phrase: To make one's way up.

Adjectives: Rising, etc., scandent, buoyant, floating, supernatant, superfluitant.

Adverbs: Uphill, on the up grade.

Interjections: Excelsior!

306 DESCENT

Substantives: fall, descension, declension, declination, drop, cadence, subsidence, lapse, downfall, tumble, tilt, toppling, trip, lurch, *culbute,* spill, cropper, purler, crash.

Titubation, shamble, shambling, stumble.

An avalanche, landslip, landslide, debacle, slump.

Phrase: The fate of Icarus.

Verbs: To descend, come or go down, fall, sink, gravitate, drop, drop down, droop, decline, come down, dismount, alight, light, settle, subside, slide, slip, slither, glissade, toboggan, coast, volplane, dive (310).

To tumble, slip, trip, stumble, pitch, lurch, swag, topple, topple over, swoop, tilt, sprawl, plump down, measure one's length, bite the dust, heel over, careen (217), slump, crash.

To alight, dismount, get down.

Adjectives: Descending, etc., descendent, decurrent, decursive, deciduous.

Phrase: Nodding to its fall.

Adverbs: Downhill, on the down grade.

307 ELEVATION

Substantives: raising, lifting, erection, lift, uplift, upheaval, upcast.

Lift, elevator, hoist, escalator, crane, derrick, winch, windlass, jack, lever.

Verbs: To elevate, raise, lift, uplift, upraise, set up, erect, stick up, rear, uprear, upbear, upcast, hoist, uphoist, heave, upheave, weigh, exalt, promote, give a lift, help up, prick up, perk up.

To drag up, fish up, dredge.

To stand up, rise up, ramp.

Phrases: To set on a pedestal; to get up on one's hind legs.

Adjectives: Elevated, etc., rampant.

Adverbs: On stilts, on the shoulders of.

308 DEPRESSION

Substantives: lowering, abasement, abasing, detrusion, reduction.

Overthrow, upset, prostration, subversion, overset, overturn, precipitation.

Bow, curtsy (or curtsey), genuflexion, obeisance, kowtow, salaam.

Verbs: To depress, lower, let down, take down, sink, debase, abase, reduce, demote, detrude, let fall, cast down, to grass, send to grass.

To overthrow, overturn, upset, overset, subvert, prostrate, level, raze, fell; cast, take, throw, fling, dash, pull, cut, knock, hew, etc., down.

To stoop, bend, bow, curtsy (or curtsey), bob, duck, kneel, crouch, cower, lout, kowtow, salaam, bend the head or knee; to recline, sit, sit down, couch, squat.

Phrases: To take down a peg; to pull about one's ears; to trample in the dust.

Adjectives: Depressed, sunk, prostrate.

309 LEAP

Substantives: jump, hop, spring, bound, vault, saltation.

Dance, caper, curvet, caracole, *entrechat,* gambade, gambado, capriole, dido, demivolt.

Kangaroo, jerboa, chamois, goat, frog, grasshopper, flea, buck-jumper.

Phrases: Hop, skip, and jump; on the light fantastic toe.
Verbs: To leap, jump, bound, spring, take off, buck, buck-jump, hop, skip, vault, dance, bob, curvet, romp, caracole, caper, cut capers.
Adjectives: Leaping, etc., saltatory, Terpsichorean, frisky.

310 PLUNGE
Substantives: dip, dive, ducking, header.
Diver, frogman.
Verbs: To plunge, dip, souse, duck, dive, plump, plop, submerge, submerse, bathe, douse, sink, engulf, founder.

311 CIRCUITION
Substantives: turn, wind, circuit, curvet, detour, excursion, circumbendibus, circumvention, circumnavigation, north-west passage, circulation.
Turning, winding, twist, twisting, wrench, evolution, twining, coil, circumambulation, meandering.
Verbs: To turn, bend, wheel, put about, switch, circle, go round, or round about, circumnavigate, circumambulate, turn a corner, double a point, wind, meander, whisk, twirl, twist (248), twill; to turn on one's heel.
Phrases: To lead a pretty dance; to go the round; to turn on one's heel.
Adjectives: Turning, etc., circuitous, circumforaneous, circumfluent.
Adverb: Round about.

312 ROTATION
Substantives: revolution, gyration, roll, circumrotation, circumgyration, gurgitation, pirouette, circumvolution, convolution, turbination, whir, whirl, eddy, vortex, whirlpool, cyclone, anticyclone, tornado, typhoon, whirlwind, willy-willy, waterspout, surge, dizzy round, maelstrom, Charybdis.

A wheel, flywheel, screw, reel, whirligig, rolling stone, windmill, top, teetotum, merry-go-round, roundabout, gyroscope, gyrostat.
Axis, axle, spindle, pivot, pin, hinge, pole, swivel, gimbals, mandrel.
Verbs: To rotate, roll, revolve, spin, turn, turn round, circumvolve, circulate, gyre, gyrate, gimble, wheel, reel, whirl, twirl, birl, thrum, trundle, troll, twiddle, bowl, roll up, furl, wallow, welter.
Phrases: To box the compass; to spin like a top.
Adjectives: Rotating, etc., rotatory, rotary, circumrotatory, turbinate, trochoid, vortiginous, vortical, gyratory.
Phrase: Like a squirrel in a cage.
Adverbs: Clockwise, with the sun, deiseal (or deisil); counter-clock-wise, against the sun, withershins (or widdershins).

313 EVOLUTION
Substantives: unfolding, etc., development, introversion, reversion, eversion.
Verbs: To evolve, unfold, unroll, unwind, uncoil, untwist, unfurl, untwine, unravel, disentangle (44), develop, introvert, reverse.
Adjectives: Evolving, evolved, etc.
Adverbs: Against.

314 OSCILLATION
Substantives: vibration, undulation, pulsation, pulse, systole, diastole, libration, nutation, swing, beat, shake, seesaw, alternation, wag, evolution, vibratiuncle, coming and going, ebb and flow, flux and reflux; vibratility.
Fluctuation, vacillation, dance, lurch, dodge, rolling, pitching, tossing, etc.
A pendulum, seesaw, rocker, rocking-chair, rocking-horse, etc.
Verbs: To oscillate, vibrate, undulate, librate, wave, rock, swing, sway, pulsate, beat, wag, waggle, wiggle,

wobble, shoogle, nod, bob, tick, play, wamble, wabble, waddle, dangle, swag, curtsy.

To fluctuate, vacillate, alternate, dance, curvet, reel, quake, quiver, quaver, roll, top, pitch, flounder, stagger, totter, brandish, shake, flicker, flourish, seesaw, teeter, move up and down, to and fro, backwards and forwards, to pass and repass, to beat up and down.

Adjectives: Oscillating, etc., oscillatory, vibratory, vibratile, vibrant, vibrational, undulatory, pulsatory, pendulous, libratory, systaltic.

Adverbs: To and fro, up and down, backwards and forwards, seesaw, zigzag, wibble-wabble.

315 AGITATION

Substantives: stir, tremor, shake, ripple, jog, jolt, jar, succussion, trepidation, quiver, quaver, dance, jactitation, jactitancy, restlessness, shuffling, twitter, flicker, flutter, bobbing.

Disturbance, perturbation, commotion, turmoil, welter, bobbery; turbulence, tumult, tumultuation, bustle, fuss, flap, tirrivee, jerk, throw, convulsion, spasm (173), twitch, tic, staggers, St. Vitus's dance, epilepsy, writhing, ferment, fermentation, effervescence, ebullition, hurly-burly, hubbub, stramash, *tohu-bohu*; tempest, storm, whirlwind, cyclone (312), ground swell.

Verbs: To be agitated, to shake, tremble, quiver, quaver, shiver, dither, twitter, twire, writhe, toss about, tumble, stagger, bob, reel, sway, wag, waggle, wiggle, wobble, shoogle, dance, wriggle, squirm, stumble, flounder, shuffle, totter, dodder, shamble, flounce, flop, curvet, prance, cavort, throb, pulsate, beat, palpitate, go pit-a-pat, fidget, flutter, flitter, flicker, bicker, twitch, jounce, ferment, effervesce, boil.

To agitate, shake, convulse, toss, tumble, bandy, wield, brandish, flap, flourish, whisk, switch, jerk, hitch, jolt, jog, hoggle, jostle, hustle, disturb, shake up, churn.

Phrases: To jump like a parched pea; to be in a spin; to shake like an aspen leaf; to drive from pillar to post.

Adjectives: Shaking, etc., agitated, tremulous, shivery, tottery, jerky, shaky, shoogly, quivery, quavery, trembly, choppy, rocky, wriggly, desultory, subsultory, shambling, giddy-paced, saltatory.

Phrases: All of a tremble or twitter; like a pea on a drum; like a cat on hot bricks; like a hen on a hot griddle.

Adverbs: By fits and starts; subsultorily, *per saltum* (139).

146

CLASS THREE

Words relating to matter

Section 1 –
Matter in General

316 MATERIALITY
Substantives: corporeity, corporality, materialness, substantiality, physical, condition.

Matter, body, substance, brute matter, stuff, element, principle, parenchyma, material, substratum, frame, *corpus pabulum,* flesh and blood.

Thing, object, article, still life, stocks and stones.

Physics, somatology, somatics, natural philosophy, physiography, physical science, experimental philosophy, positivism, materialism.

Verbs: To materialize, embody, incarnate, objectify, externalize.

Adjectives: Material, bodily, corporeal, corporal, carnal, temporal, physical, somatic, somatological, materialistic, sensible, palpable, tangible, ponderable, concrete, impersonal, objective, bodied.

317 IMMATERIALITY
Substantives: incorporeity, spirituality, spirit, etc. (450), inextension.

Personality, I, me, myself, ego.

Spiritualism, spiritism, idealism, immaterialism.

Verbs: To disembody, spiritualize, immaterialize.

Adjectives: Immaterial, incorporeal, ideal, unextended, intangible, impalpable, imponderable, bodiless, unbodied, disembodied, extra-sensory, astral, psychical, psychic, extra-

mundane, unearthly, supernatural, supranatural, transcendent, transcendental, pneumatoscopic, spiritualistic, spiritual (450).

Personal, subjective.

318 WORLD
Substantives: nature, creation, universe; earth, globe, wide world, cosmos, sphere, macrocosm.

The heavens, sky, welkin, empyrean, starry heaven, firmament, ether; vault or canopy of heaven; celestial spaces, starry host, heavenly bodies, star, constellation, galaxy, Milky Way, *via lactea,* nebula, etc., sun, moon, planet, asteroid, planetoid, satellite, comet, meteor, meteorite, shooting star.

Zodiac, ecliptic, colure, orbit.

Astronomy, astrophysics, uranography, uranology, cosmology, cosmography, cosmogony; planetarium, orrery.

An astronomer, star-gazer, cosmographer; observatory.

Adjectives: Cosmic, cosmical, mundane, terrestrial, terraqueous, terrene, telluric, sublunary, under the sun, subastral, worldwide, global.

Celestial, heavenly, spheral, starry, stellar, nebular, etc., sidereal, sideral, astral, solar, lunar.

319 HEAVINESS
Substantives: weight, gravity, gravitation, ponderosity, ponderousness, avoirdupois, pressure, load, burden, ballast; a lump, mass, weight, counterweight, counterpoise; ponderability.

147

Lead, millstone, mountain.

Balance, spring balance, scales, steelyard, weighbridge.

Statics.

Phrase: Pelion on Ossa.

Verbs: To be heavy, to gravitate, weigh, press, cumber, load.

Adjectives: Weighty, heavy, ponderous, gravitating, weighing, etc., ponderable, lumpish, cumbersome, hefty, massive, unwieldy, cumbrous, incumbent, superincumbent; gravitational.

Phrase: Heavy as lead.

320 LIGHTNESS

Substantives: levity, imponderability, subtlety, buoyancy, airiness, portability, volatility.

A feather, dust, mote, down, thistledown, flue, ooss, fluff, cobweb, gossamer, straw, cork, bubble; float, buoy; featherweight.

Verbs: To be light, float, swim, be buoyed up.

Adjectives: Light, subtle, airy, vaporous, imponderous, astatic, weightless, imponderable, ethereal, sublimated, floating, swimming, buoyant, airborne, portable, uncompressed, volatile.

Phrases: Light as a feather; light as thistledown; 'trifles light as air'.

Section II --
Inorganic matter

321 DENSITY

Substantives: denseness, solidness, solidity, impenetrability, incompressibility, cohesion, coherence, cohesiveness (46), imporosity, impermeability, closeness, compactness, constipation, consistence, spissitude, thickness.

Specific gravity; hydrometer, araeometer.

Condensation, consolidation, solidi-

fication, concretion, coagulation, conglomeration, petrifaction, lapidification, vitrification, crystallization, precipitation, inspissation, thickening, grittiness, knottiness, induration (323).

Indivisibility, indiscerptibility, indissolubility.

A solid body, mass, block, knot, lump, concretion, concrete, cake, clot, stone, curd, coagulum, clinker, nugget; deposit, precipitate.

Verbs: To be dense, etc.

To become or render solid; solidify, solidate, concrete, set, consolidate, congeal, jelly, jell, coagulate, curdle, curd, fix, clot, cake, cohere, crystallize, petrify, vitrify, condense, incrassate, thicken, inspissate, compact, concentrate, compress, squeeze, ram down, constipate.

Adjectives: Dense, solid, solidified, consolidated, etc., coherent, cohesive, compact, close, thick-set, serried, substantial, massive, lumpish, impenetrable, incompressible, impermeable, imporous, constipated, concrete, knotted, gnarled, crystalline, crystallizable, vitreous, coagulated, thick, incrassated, inspissated, curdled, clotted, grumous.

Undissolved, unmelted, unliquefied, unthawed.

Indivisible, indiscerptible, infrangible, indissolvable, indissoluble, insoluble, infusible.

322 RARITY

Substantives: tenuity, absence of solidity, subtility, sponginess, compressibility; hollowness (252).

Rarefaction, expansion, dilatation, inflation, dilution, attenuation, subtilization.

Ether, vapour, air, gas (334).

Verbs: To rarefy, expand, dilate, dilute, attenuate, subtilize, thin out.

Adjectives: Rare, subtle, sparse, slight, thin, fine, tenuous, compressible.

Porous, cavernous, spongy, bibulous, spongious, spongeous.

Rarefied, expanded, dilated, subtilized, unsubstantial, hollow (252).

323 HARDNESS
Substantives: rigidity, rigescence, firmness, renitence, inflexibility, stiffness, starchiness, starchedness, temper, callosity, durity, induration, grittiness, petrifaction, etc. (321), ossification, sclerosis.

A stone, pebble, flint, marble, rock, granite, brick, iron, steel, corundum, diamond, adamant, bone, callus.
Verbs: To render hard, harden, stiffen, indurate, petrify, vitrify, temper, ossify.
Adjectives: Hard, horny, corneous, bony, osseous, rigid, rigescent, stiff, firm, starch, stark, unbending, unyielding, inflexible, tense, indurate, indurated, gritty, stony, proof, adamantean, adamantine.
Phrases: Hard as iron, etc.; hard as a brick; hard as a nail; hard as a deal board; 'as hard as a piece of the nether millstone'; stiff as buckram; stiff as a poker.

324 SOFTNESS
Substantives: tenderness, flexibility, pliancy, pliableness, pliantness, litheness, pliability, suppleness, sequacity, ductility, malleability, tractility, extensibility, plasticity, inelasticity, laxity, flaccidity, flabbiness, limpness.

Clay, wax, butter, dough; a cushion, pillow, featherbed, down, padding, wadding, cotton-wool.

Mollification, softening, etc.
Verbs: To render soft, soften, mollify, relax, temper, mash, pulp, knead, squash.

To bend, yield, give, relent, relax.
Adjectives: Soft, tender, supple, pliable, limp, limber, flexible, flexile, lithe, lissom, *svelte,* willowy, pliant, plastic, waxen, ductile, tractile, tract-

able, malleable, extensile, sequacious.

Yielding, bending, flabby, flaccid, lymphatic, flocculent, downy, flimsy, spongy, oedematous, doughy, argillaceous, mellow; emollient, softening, etc.
Phrases: Soft as butter; soft as down; soft as silk; yielding as wax; tender as a chicken.

325 ELASTICITY
Substantives: springiness, spring, resilience, buoyancy, renitency, contractility (195), compressibility.

Indiarubber, rubber, caoutchouc, whalebone, elastic.
Verbs: To be elastic, etc., to spring back, fly back, rebound, recoil (277).
Adjectives: Elastic, tensile, springy, resilient, buoyant.

326 INELASTICITY
Substantives: want or absence of elasticity, softness, etc. (324).
Adjectives: Inelastic, ductile, limber, etc. (324).

327 TOUGHNESS
Substantives: tenacity, strength, cohesion (46), stubbornness (606).

Leather, gristle, cartilage.
Verbs: To be tenacious, etc., to resist fracture.
Adjectives: Tenacious, tough, wiry, sinewy, stringy, stubborn, cohesive, strong, resisting, resistant, leathery, coriaceous.
Phrase: Tough as leather.

328 BRITTLENESS
Substantives: fragility, crispness, friability, frangibility, fissility.
Verbs: To be brittle, break, crack, snap, split, shiver, splinter, fracture, crumble, break short, burst, fly.
Adjectives: Brittle, frangible, fragile, frail, jerry-built, gimcrack, shivery, fissile, splitting, splintery, lacerable, crisp, friable, short, crumbling.

149

Phrases: Brittle as glass; a house of cards.

329 TEXTURE

Substantives: structure, construction, organization, set-up, organism, anatomy, frame, mould, fabric, framework, carcass, architecture, *compages*; substance, stuff, parenchyma, constitution, intertexture, contexture, tissue, grain, web, warp, woof, nap (256).

Fineness or coarseness of grain.

Histology.

Adjectives: Textural, structural, organic, anatomic, anatomical; fine, delicate, subtle, fine-grained; coarse, homespun, rough-grained, coarse-grained; flimsy, unsubstantial, gossamery, filmy, gauzy.

330 PULVERULENCE

Substantives: state of powder, powderiness, efflorescence, sandiness, friability.

Dust, stour (or stoor), powder, sand, shingle, sawdust, grit, meal, bran, flour, limature, filings, debris, detritus, moraine, scobs, crumb, seed, grain, spore, atom, particle (32), flocculence.

Reduction to powder, pulverization, comminution, granulation, disintegration, weathering, subaction, contusion, trituration, levigation, abrasion, detrition, filing, etc. (331).

Mill, quern, grater, nutmeg grater, rasp, file, pestle and mortar.

Verbs: To reduce to powder, to pulverize, comminute, granulate, triturate, levigate, scrape, file, abrade, rub down, grind, grate, rasp, mill, pound, bray, bruise, contuse, contund, beat, crush, crunch, scrunch, crumble, disintegrate, weather.

Adjectives: Powdery, granular, mealy, floury, branny, farinaceous, furfuraceous, flocculent, dusty, sandy, sabulous, arenaceous, gritty, efflores-cent, impalpable; pulverizable, pulverulent, friable, crumbly, shivery, pulverized, etc., attrite.

331 FRICTION

Substantives: attrition, rubbing, massage, abrasion, rub, scouring, limature, filing, rasping, frication, elbow-grease.

Grindstone, whetstone, buff, hone, strop (253).

Verbs: To rub, abrade, scratch, scrape, scrub, grate, fray, rasp, pare, scour, polish, massage, curry, shampoo, rub out.

332 LUBRICATION

Substantives: prevention of friction, oiling, etc., anointment.

Lubricant, oil, lard, grease, etc. (356); synovia, saliva.

Verbs: To lubricate, oil, grease, anoint, wax; smooth (255).

Adjectives: Lubricated, etc.

333 FLUIDITY

Substantives: fluid (including both inelastic and elastic fluids).

Liquidity, liquidness, aquosity, a liquid, liquor, lymph, humour, juice, sap, blood, serum, serosity, gravy, chyle, rheum, ichor, sanies; solubility.

Hydrology, hydrostatics, hydrodynamics.

Verbs: To be fluid or liquid, to flow, run (348).

Adjectives: Liquid, fluid, fluent, running, flowing, serous, juicy, succulent, sappy, lush.

Liquefied, uncongealed, melted, etc. (335).

334 GASEITY

Substantives: vaporousness, flatulence, flatulency; gas, air, vapour, ether, steam, fume, reek, effluvium.

Smoke, cloud (353).

Pneumatics, aerostatics, aerodynamics; gas-meter, gasometer.

Verbs: To emit vapour, evaporate, to steam, fume, reek, smoke, puff, smoulder.

Adjectives: Gaseous, aeriform, ethereal, aerial, airy, vaporous, vapoury, flatulent, volatile, evaporable.

335 LIQUEFACTION

Substantives: liquescence, fusion, melting, thaw, deliquation, deliquescence, lixiviation.

Solution, dissolution, decoction, infusion, apozem, flux.

Solvent, menstruum, alkahest.

Verbs: To render liquid, to liquefy, deliquesce, run, melt, thaw, fuse, solve, dissolve, resolve, to hold in solution.

Adjectives: Liquefied, melted, unfrozen, molten, liquescent, liquefiable, deliquescent, diffluent, soluble, dissoluble.

336 VAPORIZATION

Substantives: gasification, volatilization, evaporation, distillation, sublimation, exhalation, volatility.

Vaporizer, retort, still.

Verbs: To render gaseous, vaporize, volatilize, evaporate, exhale, distil, sublime, sublimate.

Adjectives: Volatilized, etc., volatile, evaporable, vaporizable.

337 WATER

Substantives: heavy water, serum, lymph, rheum, whey.

Dilution, immersion, maceration, humectation, infiltration, sprinkling, washing, spraying, aspersion, affusion, irrigation, douche, balneation, bath, shower-bath, inundation, deluge (348), a diluent.

Verbs: To be watery, etc., to reek.

To add water, to water, wet, moisten (339), dilute, dip, immerse, plunge, merge, immerge, steep, souse, duck, submerge, drown, soak, saturate, sop, macerate, pickle, blunge, wash, lave, sprinkle, asperge, asperse, dabble, bedabble, affuse, splash, splatter, spray, swash, douse, drench, slop, slobber, irrigate, inundate, deluge, flood.

To take a bath, to tub, bathe, bath, paddle.

To syringe, inject, gargle.

Adjectives: Watery (339), aqueous, aquatic, lymphatic, diluted, etc., reeking, dripping, sodden, drenched, soaking, sopping.

Wet, washy, sloppy, squashy, splashy, soppy, soggy, slobbery, diluent, balneal.

Phrases: Wet as a drowned rat; soaked to the skin; wet as a rag; wet through.

338 AIR

Substantives: common air, atmospheric air.

The atmosphere, troposphere, tropopause, stratosphere, ionosphere, Heaviside layer, Appleton layer; the sky, the ether, the open air, ozone, weather, climate.

Meteorology, climatology, isobar, barometer, aneroid barometer, weather-glass, weather-chart, weather station, weather ship

Exposure to the air or weather, airing, weathering (33o).

Verbs: To aerate, oxygenate, arterialize, ventilate, air-condition.

Adjectives: Containing air, windy, flatulent, aerated, effervescent.

Atmospheric, airy, open-air, *plein-air,* alfresco, aerial, aeriform; meteorological, barometric, weatherwise.

Adverbs: In the open air, *à la belle étoile, sub Jove.*

339 MOISTURE

Substantives: moistness, humidity, dampness, damp, wetness, wet, humectation, madefaction, dew, muddiness, march (345).

Hygrometer, hygrometry, hygrology.

Verbs: To be moist, etc.

To moisten, wet, humectate, sponge, damp, dampen, bedew, imbue, infiltrate, imbrue; soak, saturate (337).

Adjectives: Moist, damp, watery, humid, wet, dank, muggy, dewy, roral, rorid, roscid, juicy, swampy (345), humectant, sopping, dripping, sodden.

Phrase: Wringing wet.

340 DRYNESS

Substantives: siccity, aridity, drought.

Exsiccation, desiccation, arefaction, drainage.

Verbs: To be dry, etc.

To render dry, to dry, dry up, sop up, swab, wipe, blot, exsiccate, desiccate, dehydrate, drain, parch.

Adjectives: Dry, anhydrous, dehydrated, arid, dried, etc., unwatered, undamped, waterproof, husky, juiceless, sapless; siccative, desiccative.

Phrases: Dry as a bone; dry as dust; dry as a stick; dry as a mummy; dry as a biscuit; dry as a limekiln.

341 OCEAN

Substantives: sea, main, the deep, brine, salt water, blue water, high seas, offing, tide, wave, surge, ooze, etc. (348).

Hydrography, oceanography.

Neptune, Thetis, Triton, Oceanid, Nereid, sea-nymph, siren, mermaid, merman, dolphin; trident.

Phrases: The vasty deep; the briny; the ditch; the drink.

Adjectives: Oceanic, marine, maritime, thalassic, pelagic, pelagian, sea-going, hydrographic.

Adverbs: At sea, on sea, afloat.

342 LAND

Substantives: earth, ground, terra firma, continent, mainland, peninsula, delta, alluvium, polder, tongue of land, neck of land, isthmus, oasis.

Coast, shore, seaboard, seaside, seabank, strand, beach, bank, lea.

Cape, promontory, etc. (250), headland, point of land, highland (206).

Soil, glebe, clay, humus, loam, marl, clod, clot, rock, crag, chalk, gravel, mould, subsoil.

Adjectives: Terrene, continental, earthy, terraqueous, terrestrial.

Littoral, riparian, alluvial, midland.

Adverbs: Ashore, on shore, on land.

343 GULF

Substantives: bay, inlet, bight, estuary, roadstead, roads, arm of the sea, armlet, sound, frith, firth, fiord, lagoon, cove, creek, strait, belt, kyle, Euripus.

Adjectives: Estuarine.

343A LAKE

Substantives: loch, lough, mere, tarn, linn, plash, broad, pond, dew-pond, pool puddle, well, reservoir, standing water, dead water, a sheet of water, fish-pond, ditch, dike, backwater.

Adjectives: Lacustrine (or lacustrian), lacuscular.

344 PLAIN

Substantives: tableland, open country, the face of the country, champaign country, basin, downs, waste, wild, weald, steppe, pampas, savanna, llano, prairie, tundra, heath, common, wold, moor, moorland, the bush; plateau, flat (213).

Meadow, mead, haugh, pasturage, park, field, lawn, green, plot, plat, terrace, esplanade, sward, turf, sod, heather, lea, grounds, pleasure-grounds, playing-fields, campus.

Phrase: A weary waste.

Adjectives: Campestrian, champaign, lawny.

345 MARSH

Substantives: marish, swamp,

morass, moss, fen, bog, quag, quagmire, slough, sump, wash.

Adjectives: Marshy, marish, swampy, boggy, quaggy, fenny, soft, plashy, poachy, paludal.

346 ISLAND
Substantives: isle, islet, ait, eyot, inch, holm, reef, atoll; archipelago.
Adjectives: Insular, sea-girt.

347 STREAM
Substantives: flow, current, jet, undercurrent, course (348).
Verbs: To flow, stream, issue, run.

348 RIVER
Substantives: running water, jet, spurt, squirt, spout, splash, rush, gush, water-spout, sluice, linn, waterfall, cascade, force, catadupe, cataract, debacle, cataclysm, inundation, deluge, avalanche, spate.

Rain, shower, scud, driving rain, downpour, drencher, soaker, cloudburst, mizzle, drizzle, Scotch mist, smirr, dripping, stillicidium; flux, flow, profluence, effluence, efflux, effluxion, defluxion.

Irrigation (337).

Spring, fountain, fount, rill, rivulet, gill, gullet, rillet, streamlet, runnel, sike, burn, beck, brooklet, brook, stream, reach, torrent, rapids, race, flush, flood, swash.

Tide, spring tide, high tide, tidal wave, bore, eagre, freshet, current, indraught, reflux, eddy, whirlpool, vortex, maelstrom, regurgitation.

Tributary, confluent, effluent, billabong; corrivation, confluence, effluence.

Wave, billow, surge, swell, chop, ripple, ground swell, surf, breaker, roller, comber, white caps, white horses.

Irrigation (337); sprinkler, sprayer, spray, atomizer, aspergillum, aspersorium, water-cart, watering-pot, watering-can, pump, syringe, hydrant.

Hydraulics, hydrodynamics, hydrography; rain-gauge.
Verbs: To flow, run, meander, gush, spout, roll, billow, surge, jet, well, drop, drip, trickle, dribble, ooze (295), percolate, distil, transude, stream, sweat, perspire (299), overflow, flow over, splash, swash, guggle, murmur, babble, bubble, purl, gurgle, sputter, spurt, regurgitate, surge.

To rain, rain hard, pour with rain, drizzle, spit, mizzle, set in.

To flow into, fall into, open into, drain into, discharge itself, disembogue, disgorge, debouch.
Phrases: To rain cats and dogs; to rain in torrents.

To cause a flow, to pour, drop, distil, splash, squirt, spill, drain, empty, discharge, pour out, open the sluices or flood-gates; shower down, irrigate (337).

To stop a flow, to stanch, dam, dam up (261), intercept.
Adjectives: Fluent, profluent, affluent, confluent, diffluent, tidal, flowing, etc., babbling, bubbling, gurgling, meandering, meandrous.

Fluviatile, fluvial, riverine, streamy, showery, drizzly, rainy, pluvial, pouring.

349 WIND
Substantives: draught, current, breath, air, breath of air, puff, whiff, zephyr, blow, drift, aura.

Gust, blast, breeze, squall, gale, storm, tempest, hurricane, whirlwind, tornado, cyclone, typhoon, blizzard, simoom, samiel, harmattan, monsoon, trade wind, sirocco, mistral, *bise, tramontana, föhn,* pampero; windiness, ventosity.

Aeolus, Boreas, Auster, Euroclydon, the cave of Aeolus.

Bellow, blowpipe, fan, ventilator, punkah.

Anemometer, anemograph, wind-gauge, weathercock, vane.

Insufflation, sufflation, perflation, blowing, fanning, ventilation, blowing up, inflation, afflation; respiration, inspiration, expiration, sneezing, sternutation, cough, hiccup.

Phrase: A capful of wind.

Verbs: To blow, waft, blow hard, blow a hurricane, breathe, respire, inspire, expire, insufflate, puff, whiff, sough, whiffle, wheeze, gasp, snuffle, sniffle, sneeze, cough.

To fan, ventilate, inflate, perflate, blow up.

Phrase: To blow great guns.

Adjectives: Blowing, etc., rough, blowy, windy, breezy, gusty, squally, puffy, stormy, tempestuous, blustering.

350 CONDUIT

Substantives: channel, duct, watercourse, watershed, race, adit, aqueduct, canal, sluice, dike, main, gully, moat, ditch, lode, leat, rhine, trough, gutter, drain, sewer, culvert, cloaca, sough, kennel, siphon,, pipe (260), emunctory, gully-hole, artery, aorta, pore, spout, funnel, tap, faucet, scupper, adjutage (or ajutage), waste-pipe, hose, rose, gargoyle, artesian well.

Floodgate, dam, weir, levee, water-gate, lock, valve.

351 AIR-PIPE

Substantives: air-tube, shaft, flue, chimney, lum, funnel, smoke-stack, exhaust-pipe, exhaust, vent, blow-hole, nostril, nozzle, throat, weasand, trachea, larynx, windpipe, thrapple, spiracle, ventiduct.

Ventilator, louvre, register.

Tobacco-pipe, pipe, etc. (298A).

352 SEMILIQUIDITY

Substantives: pulpiness, viscidity, viscosity, ropiness, sliminess, gumminess, glutinosity, gummosity, siziness, clamminess, mucosity, spissitude, lentor, thickness, crassitude.

Inspissation, thickening, incrassation.

Jelly, mucilage, gelatine, mucus, chyme, phlegm, gum, glue, gluten, goo, colloid, albumen, size, milk, cream, emulsion, soup, broth, starch, treacle, squash, mud, clart, glaur, slush, slime, ooze, dope, glycerine; lava.

Pitch, tar, bitumen, asphalt, resin, rosin, varnish, copal, mastic, wax, amber.

Verbs: To inspissate, thicken, incrassate, jelly, jellify, mash, squash, churn, beat up, pulp.

Adjectives: Semi-fluid, semi-liquid, milky, emulsive, creamy, lacteal, lacteous, curdy, curdled, soupy, muddy, slushy, clarty, thick, succulent, squashy.

Gelatinous, albuminous, gummy, colloid, amylaceous, mucilaginous, glairy, slimy, ropy, stringy, clammy, glutinous (46), viscid, viscous, sticky, gooey, slab, slabby, sizy, lentous, tacky.

Tarry, pitchy, resinous, bituminous.

353 BUBBLE

Substantives: soda-water, aerated water, foam, froth, head, spume, lather, bleb, spray, spindrift, surf, yeast, barm, suds.

Cloud, vapour, fog, mist, smog, haze, steam, nebulosity (422); scud, rack, cumulus, cirrus, stratus, nimbus, mare's tail, mackerel sky.

Nephelology; Fido.

Effervescence, foaming, mantling, fermentation, frothing, etc.

Verbs: To bubble, boil, foam, froth, mantle, sparkle, guggle, gurgle, effervesce, fizz, ferment.

Adjectives: Bubbling, etc., frothy, yeasty, barmy, nappy, effervescent, fizzy, up, boiling, fermenting, sparkling, mantling, *mousseux*.

Cloudy, foggy, misty, vaporous, nebulous.

354 PULPINESS
Substantives: pulp, paste, dough, curd, pap, pudding, poultice, soup, squash, mud, slush, grume, jam, preserve.
Adjectives: Pulpy, pulpous, pultaceous, doughy, grumous.

355 UNCTUOUSNESS
Substantives: unctuosity, oiliness, greasiness, slipperiness, lubricity.
Lubrication (332), anointment, unction; ointment (356).
Verbs: To oil, grease, anoint, wax, lubricate (332).
Adjectives: Unctuous, oil, oleaginous, adipose, sebaceous, fat, fatty, greasy, waxy, butyraceous, soapy, saponaceous, pinguid, stearic, lardaceous.

356 OIL
Substantives: fat, butter, margarine, cream, grease, tallow, suet, lard, dripping, blubber, pomatum, pomade, stearin, lanoline, soap, soft soap, wax, beeswax, sealing-wax, ambergris, spermaceti, adipocere, ointment, unguent, liniment, paraffin, kerosene, gasolene, petroleum, petrol, mineral oil, vegetable oil, olive oil, castor oil, linseed oil, train oil.

Section III –
Organic matter

357 ORGANIZATION
Substantives: the organized world, organized nature, living nature, animated nature, living beings; protoplasm, protein.
Biology, ecology (or oecology), natural history, organic chemistry, zoology (368), botany (369).
Adjectives: Organic, animate.

358 INORGANIZATION
Substantives: the mineral world or kingdom; unorganized, inorganic, brute or inanimate matter.
Mineralogy, geognosy, petrology, lithology, geology, metallurgy, inorganic chemistry.
Adjectives: Inorganic, azoic, mineral, inanimate.

359 LIFE
Substantives: vitality, animation, viability, the vital spark or flame or principle, the breath of life, life-blood; existence (1).
Vicification, revivification.
Physiology, biology; metabolism.
Phrase: The breath of one's nostrils.
Verbs: To be living, alive, etc., to live, subsist (1), breathe, fetch breath, respire, draw breath, to be born, be spared.
To come to life, to revive, come to.
To give birth to (161); to bring, restore, or recall to life, to vivify, revive, revivify, quicken, reanimate, vitalize.
Phrases: To see the light; to come into the world; to walk the earth; to draw breath.
To keep body and soul together; to support life.
Adjectives: Living, alive, in life, above ground, breathing, animated, quick, viable.
Vital, vivifying, vivified, Promethean, metabolic.
Phrases: Alive and kicking; in the land of the living; on this side of the grave.

360 DEATH
Substantives: decease, dissolution, demise, departure, obit, expiration; termination, close or extinction of life, existence, etc.; mortality, fall, doom, fate, release, rest, end, quietus, loss, bereavement, euthanasia, katabolism.
Last breath, last gasp, last agonies, the death-rattle, dying breath, agonies of death, dying agonies.

Necrology, death-roll, obituary.

Phrases: The ebb of life; the king of terrors; the jaws of death; the swan-song; the Stygian shore; the sleep that knows no waking; a watery grave.

Verbs: To die, perish, expire.

Phrases: Breathe one's last; cease to live; depart this life; end one's days; be no more; go off; drop off; pop off; peg out; lose one's life; drop down dead; resign, relinquish, lay down, or surrender one's life; drop or sink into the grave; close one's eyes; break one's neck.

To give up the ghost; to be all over with one; to pay the debt to nature; to make the great change; to take one's last sleep; to shuffle off this mortal coil; to go to one's last home; to go the way of all flesh; to kick the bucket; to hop the twig; to turn up one's toes; to slip one's cable; to cross the Stygian ferry.

To snuff out; to go off the hooks; to go to one's account; to go aloft; to join the majority; to go west; to have had it; to be numbered with the dead; to die a natural death; to hand in one's checks; to pass away or over.

Adjectives: Dead, lifeless, deceased, demised, gone, departed, defunct, exanimate, inanimate, *kaput,* out of the world, mortuary; still-born.

Dying, expiring, moribund, *in articulo mortis, in extremis,* in the agony of death, etc., going, life ebbing, going off, life failing, *aux abois,* booked, having received one's death warrant.

Phrases: Dead and gone; dead as a door-nail, as mutton, as a door-post, as a herring; stone-dead; launched into eternity; gone to one's last home; gathered to one's fathers; gone to Davy Jones's locker; gone west; gone for a Burton; pushing up the daisies.

At death's door; on one's death-bed; in the jaws of death; death staring one in the face; one's hour being come; one's days being numbered; one's race being run; one foot in the grave; on one's last legs; life hanging by a thread; at one's last gasp.

Adverbs: Post-mortem, post-obit.

361 KILLING

Substantives: homicide, parricide, matricide, fratricide, sororicide, infanticide, regicide, tyrannicide, vaticide, genocide, manslaughter, murder, assassination, blood, gore, bloodshed, slaughter, carnage, butchery, massacre, immolation, holocaust, fusillade, *noyade,* thuggee, thuggery, thuggism; casualty, fatality.

Death-blow, kiss of death, *coup de grâce,* grace-stroke, mercy killing, euthanasia.

Suicide, felo-de-se, hara-kiri, happy dispatch, suttee, martyrdom, execution.

Destruction of animals, slaughtering, battue, hecatomb.

Slaughter-house, shambles, abattoir.

A butcher, slayer, murderer, homicide, parricide, matricide, etc., assassin, cut-throat, bravo, thug, executioner (975).

Verbs: To kill, put to death, do to death, slay, murder, assassinate, slaughter, butcher, immolate, massacre, decimate, take away or deprive of life, make away with, dispatch, burke, lynch, settle, do for, do in, bump off, brain, spiflicate.

To strangle, throttle, bowstring, choke, garrotte, stifle, suffocate, smother, asphyxiate, drown, hang, turn off, string up.

To cut down, sabre, cut to pieces, cut off, cut the throat, stab, knife, bayonet, shoot, behead, decapitate, stone, lapidate, execute (972).

To commit suicide, to make away with oneself.

Phrases: To put to the sword; put to the edge of the sword; give no quarter to; run through the body; knock on the head; give one the works; put one on the spot; blow the brains out; give the death blow, the *coup de grâce*; put out of one's misery; launch into eternity; give a quietus to.

Adjectives: Killing, etc., murderous, slaughterous, sanguinary, ensanguined, gory, bloody, blood-stained, blood-guilty, red-handed.

Mortal, fatal, deadly, lethal, internecine, suicidal, homicidal, fratricidal, etc.

362 CORPSE
Substantives: corse, carcass, bones, skeleton, carrion, defunct, relic, remains, ashes, earth, dust, clay, mummy.

Shade, ghost, *manes*; the dead, the majority, the great majority.

Phrases: All that was mortal; this tenement of clay; food for worms or fishes.

Adjectives: Cadaverous, corpse-like.

363 INTERMENT
Substantives: burial, sepulture, inhumation, obsequies, exequies, funeral, wake, lyke-wake, pyre, funeral pile, cremation.

Funeral rite or solemnity, knell, passing-bell, tolling, dirge, lament, coronach, keening (839), requiem, epicedium, obit, elegy, funeral oration, epitaph, death march, dead march, lying in state.

Grave-clothes, shroud, winding-sheet, cerecloth, cerement.

Coffin, casket, shell, sarcophagus, urn, pall, bier, hearse, catafalque.

Grave, pit, sepulchre, tomb, vault, catacomb, mausoleum, house of death, burial-place, cemetery, necropolis, churchyard, graveyard, God's acre, burial-ground, cromlech, dolmen, barrow, tumulus, cairn, ossuary, charnel-house, morgue, mortuary, crematorium, cinerator; Valhalla.

Monument, tombstone, gravestone, shrine, cenotaph.

Exhumation, disinterment; autopsy, necropsy, post-mortem.

Undertaker, mortician, mute, sexton, grave-digger.

Verbs: To inter, bury, lay in the grave, consign to the grave or tomb, entomb, inhume, cremate, lay out, embalm, mummify.

To exhume, disinter.

Adjectives: Buried, etc., burial, funereal, funebrial, funerary, mortuary, sepulchral, cinerary; elegiac.

Phrases: *Hic jacet*; RIP.

364 ANIMALITY
Substantives: animal life, animality, animation, breath, animalization.

Flesh, flesh and blood, physique.

Verbs: To animalize.

Adjectives: Fleshly, corporal, carnal.

365 VEGETABILITY
Substantives: vegetable life, vegetation.

Adjectives: Lush, rank, luxuriant.

366 ANIMAL
Substantives: the animal kingdom, brute creation, fauna, avifauna.

A beast, brute, creature, created being; creeping or living thing, dumb creature, flocks and herds, live-stock.

Cattle, kine, etc.

Game, *fera natura*, wild life.

Mammal, quadruped, bird, reptile, fish, mollusc, worm, insect, zoophyte, animalcule, etc.

Phrases: The beasts of the field; fowls of the air; denizens of the deep.

Adjectives: Animal, zoological, piscatory, fishy, molluscous, vermicular, etc., feral.

367 PLANT
Substantives: vegetable, the vegetable kingdom, flora.

Tree, fruit-tree, shrub, bush, creeper, herb, herbage, grass, fern, fungus, lichen, moss, weed, seaweed, alga; annual, biennial, perennial; exotic.

Forest, wood, hurst, holt, greenwood, woodland, brake, grove, copse, coppice, hedgerow, boscage, plantation, thicket, spinney, underwood, undergrowth, brushwood, clump of trees, park, chase, weald, scrub, jungle, prairie.

Foliage, florescence, flower, blossom, branch, bough, spray, twig, leaf.
Adjectives: Vegetable, vegetal, arboreal, herbaceous, herbal, botanic, sylvan, woodland, woody, wooded, well-wooded, shrubby, grassy, verdurous, verdant, floral, mossy.

368 ZOOLOGY
Substantives: zoography, anatomy, zootomy, comparative anatomy, physiology, morphology.

Ornithology, ichthyology, herpetology, ophiology, malacology, helminthology, entomology; palaeontology.

369 BOTANY
Substantives: phytography, phytology, vegetable physiology, herborization, dendrology, mycology, Pomona, Flora, Ceres.

Herbarium, herbal, *hortus siccus,* vasculum.
Verbs: To botanize, herborize.

370 TAMING
Substantives: domestication, domesticity; training, breaking-in, manège, breeding, pisciculture; veterinary art.

Menagerie, zoological garden, game reserve, aviary, apiary, vivarium, aquarium, fishery, fish-pond, duckpond.
Verbs: To tame, domesticate, train, tend, break in.
Adjectives: Pastoral, bucolic.

371 AGRICULTURE
Substantives: cultivation, culture, intensive cultivation, husbandry, agronomy, geoponics, hydroponics, georgics, tillage, gardening, horticulture, forestry, vintage, etc., arboriculture, floriculture, the topiary art.

Vineyard, vinery, garden, kitchen garden, market garden, nursery, bed, plot, herbaceous border, parterre, hothouse, greenhouse, conservatory, espalier, shrubbery, orchard, rock garden, rockery, winter garden, pinery, arboretum, allotment.

A husbandman, horticulturist, gardener, florist, agriculturist, agriculturalist, woodcutter, backwoodsman, forester, land girl, farmer, yeoman, cultivator.
Verbs: To cultivate, till, garden, farm; delve, dibble, dig, sow, plant, graft; plough, harrow, rake, reap, mow, cut, weed.
Adjectives: Agricultural, agrarian, arable, rural, country, rustic, agrestic.

372 MANKIND
Substantives: the human race or species; man, human nature, humanity, mortality, flesh, generation; Everyman.

Anthropology, anthropography, ethnology, ethnography, demography, sociology, social economics; civics.

Anthropomorphism.

Human being, person, individual, type, creature, fellow creature, mortal, body, somebody, one, someone, a soul, living soul, earthling, party personage, inhabitant; *dramatis personae.*

People, persons, folk, population, public, world, race, society, community, the million, commonalty (876), nation, state, realm, community, commonwealth, republic, commonweal, polity, nationality; civilized society, civilization.

Anthropologist, ethnologist, sociologist, etc.
Phrases: The lords of creation; the body politic.
Adjectives: National, civic, public, human, mortal, personal, individual,

social, cosmopolitan, ethnic, racial; sociological, anthropological, ethnological, anthropomorphic, anthropomorphous, anthropoid, manlike.

373 MAN
Substantives: manhood, manliness, virility, he, menfolk.

A human being, man, male, mortal, person, body, soul, individual, fellow creature, one, someone, somebody, so-and-so.

Personage, a gentleman, sir, master, yeoman, citizen, denizen, burgess, burgher, cosmopolite, wight, swain, fellow, blade, bloke, beau, chap, guy, bod, type, cove, gossoon, buffer, gaffer, goodman; husband (903).
Adjectives: Human, manly, male, masculine, manlike, mannish, virile, mannish, unwomanly, unfeminine.
Phrase: The spear side.

374 WOMAN
Substantives: female, feminality, femininity, womanhood, muliebrity, girlhood, she, womenfolk.

Womankind, the sex, the fair, the fair sex, the softer sex, the weaker vessel, a petticoat, skirt.

Dame, madam, madame, ma'am, mistress, lady, gentlewoman, donna, belle, matron, dowager, goody, gammer, good woman, goodwife; wife (903).

Damsel, girl, lass, lassie, maid (209), maiden, *demoiselle,* flapper, miss, missie, nymph, wench, bint, floosy, popsy, pusher, jade, dona, grisette, colleen.
Adjectives: Female, feminine, womanly, ladylike, matronly, maidenly, girlish; womanish, effeminate, unmanly, pansy.
Phrase: The distaff side.

375 PHYSICAL SENSIBILITY
Substantives: sensitiveness, sensitivity, feeling, perceptivity, acuteness; allergy, idiosyncrasy; moral sensibility (822).

Sensation, impression, consciousness (490).

The external senses.
Verbs: To be sensible of, to feel, perceive, be conscious of, respond to, react to.

To render sensible, to sharpen, cultivate, train, tutor, condition.

To cause sensation; to impress, excite, or produce an impression.
Adjectives: Sensible, conscious, sensitive, sensuous, aesthetic, perceptive.

Hypersensitive, thin-skinned, neurotic, hyperaesthetic, allergic.

Acute, sharp, keen, vivid, lively, impressive.
Adverb: To the quick.

376 PHYSICAL INSENSIBILITY
Substantives: obtuseness, dullness, paralysis, anaesthesia, analgesia, sleep, trance, stupor, coma, catalepsy; moral insensibility (823).

Anaesthetic, opium, ether, chloroform, chloral, cocaine, morphia, laudanum, nitrous oxide, laughing gas.

Anaesthetics.
Verbs: To be insensible, etc.

To render insensible, to blunt, dull, obtund, benumb, deaden, stupefy, stun, paralyse, anaesthetize, dope, hocus, gas.
Adjectives: Insensible, unfeeling, senseless, impercipient, impassable, thick-skinned, pachydermatous, hardened, proof, apathetic, obtuse, dull, anaesthetic, paralytic, palsied, numb, dead, unaffected, untouched.
Phrase: Having a rhinoceros hide.

377 PHYSICAL PLEASURE
Substantives: bodily enjoyment, gratification, titillation, comfort, luxury, voluptuousness, sensuousness, sensuality; mental pleasure (827).

Phrases: The flesh-pots of Egypt; creature comforts; a bed of roses; a bed of down; on velvet; in clover.
Verbs: To feel, experience, receive, etc., pleasure; to enjoy, relish, luxuriate, revel, riot, bask, wallow in, feast on, gloat over, have oneself a ball.

To cause or give physical pleasure, to gratify, tickle, regale, etc. (829).
Adjectives: Enjoying, etc., luxurious, sensual, voluptuous, comfortable, cosy, snug.

Pleasant, pleasing, agreeable, grateful, refreshing, comforting.

378 PHYSICAL PAIN
Substantives: bodily pain, suffering, sufferance, dolour, ache, aching, smart, smarting, shoot, shooting, twinge, twitch, gripe, headache, toothache, earache, sore, hurt, discomfort, malaise; mental pain (828).

Spasm, cramp, nightmare, crick, stitch, convulsion, throe.

Pang, anguish, agony, torment, torture, rack, cruciation, crucifixion, martyrdom.
Verbs: To feel, experience, suffer, etc., pain; to suffer, ache, smart, bleed, tingle, shoot, twinge, lancinate, wince, writhe, twitch.
Phrases: To sit on thorns; to sit on pins and needles.

To give or inflict pain; to pain, hurt, chafe, sting, bite, gnaw, pinch, tweak, grate, gall, fret, prick, pierce, gripe, etc., wring, torment, torture, rack, agonize, break on the wheel, put on the rack, convulse.
Adjectives: In pain, in a state of pain; uncomfortable, pained, etc.

Painful, aching, etc., sore, raw, agonizing, excruciating.

379 TOUCH
Substantives: taction, tactility, feeling, palpation, manipulation, tangibility, palpability.

Organ of touch: hand, finger, fore-finger, thumb, paw, feeler, antenna.
Verbs: To touch, feel, handle, finger, thumb, paw, fumble, grope, grabble, scrabble; pass, or run the fingers over, manipulate.
Phrase: To throw out a feeler.
Adjectives: Tactual, tangible, palpable, tactile.

380 SENSATIONS OF TOUCH
Substantives: itching, titillation, formication, etc., creeping, aura, tingling, thrilling.
Verbs: To itch, tingle, creep, thrill; sting, prick, prickle, tickle, kittle, titillate.
Adjectives: Itching, etc., ticklish, kittly.

381 NUMBNESS
Substantives: deadness, anaesthesia (376); pins and needles.
Verbs: To benumb, paralyse, anaesthetize; to chloroform, inject with cocaine, etc. (376).
Adjectives: Numb, bebumbed; intangible, impalpable.

382 HEAT
Substantives: caloric, temperature, warmth, fervour, calidity, incalescence, candescence, incandescence, glow, flush, hectic, fever, pyrexia, hyperpyrexia.

Fire, spark, scintillation, flash, flame, blaze, bonfire, firework, wildfire, pyrotechny, ignition (384).

Insolation, summer, dog-days, tropical heat, heat-wave, summer heat, blood heat, sirocco, simoom; isotherm.

Hot spring, thermal spring, geyser.

Pyrology, thermology, thermotics, calorimetry, thermodynamics; thermometer (389).
Phrase: The devouring element.
Verbs: To be hot, to glow, flush, sweat, swelter, bask, smoke, reek, stew, simmer, seethe, boil, burn, broil, bake, parch, fume, blaze, smoulder.

Phrases: To be in a heat, in a glow, in a fever, in a blaze, etc.

Adjectives: Hot, warm, mild, unfrozen, genial, tepid, lukewarm, blood-hot, thermal, thermotic, calorific, sunny, close, sweltering, stuffy, sultry, baking, boiling, broiling, torrid, tropical, aestival, canicular, glowing, piping, scalding, reeking, etc., on fire, afire, ablaze, alight, aglow, fervid, fervent, ardent, unquenched; isothermal, sotheral; feverish, pyretic, pyrexial, pyrexical.

Igneous, plutonic, fiery, candescent, incandescent, red-hot, white-hot, incalescent, smoking, blazing, unextinguished, smouldering.

Phrases: Hot as fire; warm as toast; warm as wool; piping hot; like an oven; hot enough to roast an ox.

383 COLD

Substantives: coldness, frigidity, coolness, coolth, gelidity, chill, chilliness, freshness, inclemency; cold storage.

Frost, ice, snow, snowflake, sleet, hail, hailstone, rime, hoar-frost, icicle, iceberg, ice-floe, glacier, winter.

Sensation of cold: chilliness, shivering, shuddering, goose-skin, goose-pimples, goose-flesh, rigor, horripilation, chattering of teeth.

Verbs: To be cold, etc., to shiver, quake, shake, tremble, shudder, dither, quiver, starve.

Adjectives: Cold, cool, chill, chilly, gelid, frigid, algid, bleak, raw, inclement, bitter, biting, cutting, nipping, piercing, pinching, clay-cold, fresh, keen; pinched, starved, perished, shivering, etc., aguish, frozen, frost-bitten, frost-nipped, frost-bound, unthawed, unwarmed; isocheimal, isochimenal.

Icy, glacial, frosty, freezing, wintry, brumal, hibernal, boreal, arctic, hiemal, hyperborean, icebound.

Phrases: Cold as a stone; cold as marble; cold as a frog; cold as charity; cold as Christmas; cool as a cucumber; cool as a custard.

384 CALEFACTION

Substantives: increase of temperature, heating, tepefaction.

Melting, fusion, liquefaction, thaw, liquescence (335), liquation, incandescence.

Burning, combustion, incension, accension, cremation, cautery, cauterization, roasting, broiling, frying, ustulation, torrefaction, scorification, branding, calcination, carbonization, incineration, cineration.

Boiling, coction, ebullition, simmering, scalding, decoction, smelting.

Ignition, inflammation, setting fire to, flagration, deflagration, conflagration, arson, incendiarism, fire-raising; *auto da fé,* suttee.

Inflammability, combustibility; incendiary, fire-bug, fire-ship, *pétroleur.*

Transmission of heat, diathermancy.

Verbs: To heat, warm, mull, chafe, fire, set fire to, set on fire, kindle, enkindle, light, ignite, relume, rekindle.

To melt, thaw, fuse, liquefy (335); defrost, de-ice.

To burn, inflame, roast, toast, broil, fry, grill, brander, singe, parch, sweal, scorch, brand, scorify, torrify, bake, cauterize, sear, char, carbonize, calcine, incinerate, smelt.

To boil, stew, cook, seethe, scald, parboil, simmer.

To take fire, catch fire, kindle, light, ignite.

Phrases: To stir the fire; blow the fire; fan the flame; apply a match to; make a bonfire of; to take the chill off.

To consign to the flames; to reduce to ashes; to burn to a cinder.

Adjectives: Combustible, inflammable, heating, etc., heated, warmed, melted, molten, unfrozen, boiled, stewed, sodden, adust.

385 REFRIGERATION
Substantives: infrigidation, reduction of temperature, cooling, freezing, congealing, congelation, glaciation.

Fire-brigade, fire-extinguisher, fire-engine, fireman; incombustibility.
Verbs: To cool, refrigerate, congeal, freeze, glaciate, ice, benumb, refresh, damp, slack, quench, put out, blow out, extinguish, starve, pinch, pierce, cut.

To go out.
Adjectives: Cooled, frozen, benumbed, etc., shivery, frigorific, refrigerant.

Incombustible, non-inflammable, fire-proof.

386 FURNACE
Substantives: Fire, gas fire, electric fire, stove, kiln, oven, bakehouse, hot-house, conservatory, fire-place, grate, hearth, radiator, register, reverberatory, range, hob, hypocaust, crematorium, incinerator, forge, blast-furnace, brasier, salamander, geyser, heater, hot-plate, hot-water bottle, electric blanket, warming-pan, stew-pan, boiler, cauldron, kettle, pot, urn, chafing-dish, gridiron, saucepan, frying-pan; sudatorium, sudatory, Turkish bath, *hammam,* vapour bath.

387 REFRIGERATORY
Substantives: refrigerator, frig, ice-pail, ice-bag, ice-house, freezing-mixture, cooler, freezer.

388 FUEL
Substantives: firing, coal, anthracite, coke, charcoal, briquette, peat, combustible, log, tinder, touchwood.

Lucifer, ingle, brand, match, vesuvian, vesta, safety-match, fusee, lighter, spill, embers, faggot, firebrand, incendiary, port-fire, fire-ball, fire-barrel.

389 THERMOMETER
Substantives: clinical thermometer, pyrometer, calorimeter, thermoscope, thermograph, thermostat, thermopile.

Fahrenheit, Centigrade, Celsius, Réaumur.

Thermometry, therm.

390 TASTE
Substantives: flavour, gust, gusto, zest, savour, sapor, tang, twang, smack, relish, aftertaste, smatch, sapidity.

Tasting, gustation, degustation.

Palate, tongue, tooth, sweet tooth, stomach.
Verbs: To taste, savour, smack, smatch, flavour, twang.
Phrases: To tickle the palate; to smack the lips.
Adjectives: Sapid, gustable, gustatory, saporific, strong, appetizing, palatable (394).

391 INSIPIDITY
Substantives: tastelessness, insipidness, vapidness, vapidity, mawkishness, wershness, mildness; wish-wash, milk and water, slops.
Verbs: To be void of taste, tasteless, etc.
Adjectives: Insipid, tasteless, savourless, mawkish, wersh, flat, vapid, *fade,* wishy-washy, watery, weak, mild; untasted.

392 PUNGENCY
Substantives: *haut-goût,* strong taste, twang, raciness, race, saltness, sharpness, roughness.

Ginger, caviare, cordial, condiment (393).
Verbs: To be pungent, etc.

To render pungent, to season, spice, salt, pepper, pickle, brine, devil.
Adjectives: Pungent, high-flavoured, high-tasted, high, sharp, strong, rough, stinging, piquant, racy, biting, mordant, spicy, seasoned, hot, pep-

pery, gingery, high-seasoned, gamy, salt, saline, brackish.
Phrases: Salt as brine; salt as a herring; salt as Lot's wife; hot as pepper.

393 CONDIMENT
Substantives: salt, mustard, pepper, cayenne, vinegar, curry, chutney, seasoning, spice, ginger, sauce, dressing, *sauce piquante,* caviare, pot-herbs, pickles, onion, garlic, sybo.

394 SAVOURINESS
Substantives: palatableness, toothsomeness, daintiness, delicacy, relish, zest.

A titbit, dainty, delicacy, ambrosia, nectar, *bonne-bouche.*
Verbs: To be savoury, etc.

To render palatable, etc.

To relish, like, fancy, be partial to.
Adjectives: Savoury, well-tasted, palatable, nice, good, dainty, delectable, toothsome, tasty, appetizing, delicate, delicious, exquisite, rich, luscious, ambrosial, meaty, fruity.

395 UNSAVOURINESS
Substantives: unpalatableness, bitterness, acridness, acridity, acrimony, roughness, acerbity, austerity; gall and wormwood, rue; sickener, scunner.
Verbs: To be unpalatable, etc.

To sicken, disgust, nauseate, pall, turn the stomach.
Adjectives: Unsavoury, unpalatable, ill-flavoured, bitter, acrid, acrimonious, unsweetened, rough, austere, uneatable, inedible.

Offensive, repulsive, nasty, fulsome, sickening, nauseous, nauseating, disgusting, loathsome, palling.
Phrases: Bitter as gall; bitter as aloes.

396 SWEETNESS
Substantives: dulcitude, dulcification, sweetening.

Sugar, saccharine, glucose, syrup, treacle, molasses, honey, manna, confection, confectionery, candy, conserve, jam, jelly, marmalade, preserve, liquorice, julep, sugar-candy, toffee, caramel, butterscotch, plum, sugar-plum, lollipop, bonbon, jujube, lozenge, pastille, comfit, fudge, chocolate, sweet, sweetmeat, marzipan, marchpane, fondant, nougat; mead, nectar, hydromel, honeysuckle.
Verbs: To be sweet, etc.

To render sweet, to sweeten, sugar, mull, edulcorate, candy, dulcify, saccharify.
Adjectives: Sweet, saccharine, sacchariferous, sugary, dulcet, candied, honeyed, luscious, edulcorated, nectarous, nectareous, sweetish, sugary.
Phrases: Sweet as a nut; sweet as honey.

397 SOURNESS
Substantives: acid, acidity, tartness, crabbedness, hardness, roughness, acetous, fermentation.

Vinegar, verjuice, crab, alum.
Verbs: To be sour, etc.

To render or turn sour, to sour, acidify, acidulate.
Phrase: To set the teeth on edge.
Adjectives: Sour, acid, acidulous, acidulated, sourish, subacid, vinegary, tart, crabbed, acerb, acetic, acetous, acescent, acetose, styptic, hard, rough.
Phrases: Sour as vinegar; sour as a crab.

398 ODOUR
Substantives: smell, scent, effluvium, emanation, fume, exhalation, essence; trail, nidor, redolence.

The sense of smell, act of smelling.
Verbs: To have an odour, to smell of, to exhale, to give out a smell, etc.

To smell, scent, snuff, sniff, inhale, nose, snowk.
Adjectives: Odorous, odorant, odoriferous, smelling, strong-scented, graveolent, redolent, nidorous, pungent.

Relating to the sense of smell: olfactory, keen-scented.

399 INODOROUSNESS
Substantives: absence or want of smell; deodorization.
Verbs: To be inodorous, etc., deodorize (652).
Adjectives: Inodorous, odourless, scentless, smell-less, wanting smell.

400 FRAGRANCE
Substantives: aroma, redolence, perfume, savour, bouquet.

Incense, musk, myrrh, frankincense, ambrosia, attar (or otto), eau-de-Cologne, civet, castor, ambergris, bergamot, lavender, sandalwood, orris root, balm, pot-pourri, pulvil; scent-bag, scent-bottle, sachet, nosegay.
Phrase: 'All the perfumes of Arabia.'
Verbs: To perfume, scent, embalm.
Adjectives: Fragrant, aromatic, redolent, balmy, scented, sweet-smelling, sweet-scented, ambrosial, perfumed, musky.

401 FETOR
Substantives: bad smell, empyreuma, stench, stink, mustiness, fustiness, frowziness, frowst, fug, rancidity, foulness, putrescence, putridity, mephitis.

A pole-cat, skunk, badger, teledu, asafoetida, cacodyl, stinkard, stink-bomb, stinkpot.
Verbs: To smell, stink, hum, niff, pong.
Phrase: To stink in the nostrils.
Adjectives: Fetid, strong-smelling, smelly, whiffy, malodorous, noisome, offensive, rank, rancid, reasty, mouldy, fusty, musty, stuffy, frowsty, fuggy, foul, frowzy, olid, nidorous, stinking, rotten, putrescent, putrid, putrefying, tainted, high (653), mephitic, empyreumatic.

402 SOUND
Substantives: sonance, noise, strain, voice (580), accent, twang, intonation, tone, resonance (408); sonority, sonorousness, audibleness, audibility.

Acoustics, phonics, phonetics, phonology, diacoustics.
Verbs: To produce sound; to sound, make a noise, give out or emit sound, to resound.
Adjectives: Sonorous, sounding, soniferous, sonorific, sonoriferous, resonant, canorous, audible, distinct, phonic, phonetic.

403 SILENCE
Substantives: stillness, quiet, peace, calm, hush, lull; muteness (581).

A silencer, mute, damper, sordine.
Verbs: To be silent, etc.

To render silent, to silence, still, hush, stifle, muffle, stop, muzzle, mute, damp, gag.
Phrases: To keep silence; to hold one's tongue; to hold one's peace.
Adjectives: Silent, still, stilly, noiseless, soundless, inaudible, hushed, etc., mute, mum, mumchance (581), solemn, awful, deathlike.
Phrases: Still as a mouse; deathlike silence; silent as the grave; one might hear a pin drop.
Adverbs: Silently, softly, etc., *sub silentio*.
Interjections: Hush! silence! soft! mum! whist! chut! *tace!*

404 LOUDNESS
Substantives: clatter, din, clangour, clang, roar, uproar, racket, hubbub, flourish of trumpets, tucket, tantara, taratantara, fanfare, blare, alarum, peal, swell, blast, boom, echo, fracas, shindy, row, rumpus, bobbery, clamour, hullaballoo, chorus, hue and cry, shout, yell, whoop, charivari, shivaree, vociferation; Stentor, Boanerges.

Speaking-trumpet, megaphone, loud-speaker, microphone, mike, amplifier, resonator.

Artillery, cannon, thunder.

Verbs: To be loud, etc., to resound, echo, re-echo, peal, swell, clang, boom, blare, thunder, fulminate, roar, whoop, shout (411).

Phrases: To din in the ear; to pierce, split, or rend the ears, or head; to shout, or thunder at the pitch of one's breath, or at the top of one's voice; to make the welkin ring; to rend the air; *faire le diable à quatre.*

Adjectives: Loud, sonorous, resounding, etc., high-sounding, big-sounding, deep, full, swelling, clamorous, clangorous, multisonous, noisy, blatant, plangent, vocal, vociferous, stunning, piercing, splitting, rending, thundering, deafening, ear-deafening, ear-piercing, obstreperous, blaring, deep-mouthed, open-mouthed, trumpet-tongued, uproarious, rackety, stentorian.

Phrases: Enough to split the head or ears; enough to wake the dead; enough to wake the Seven Sleepers.

Adverbs: Loudly, aloud, etc., *forte, fortissimo.*

Phrases: At the top of one's voice; in full cry.

405 FAINTNESS

Substantives: lowness, faint sounds, whisper, undertone, breath, underbreath, murmur, mutter, hum, susurration, tinkle, rustle.

Hoarseness, huskiness, raucity.

Verbs: To whisper, breathe, murmur, mutter, mumble, purl, hum, croon, gurgle, ripple, babble, tinkle.

Phrases: Steal on the ear; melt, float on the air.

Adjectives: Inaudible, scarcely audible, low, dull, stifled, muffled, hoarse, husky, gentle faint, breathed, etc., soft, floating, purling, etc., liquid, mellifluous, dulcet, flowing, soothing.

Adverbs: In a whisper, with bated breath, under one's breath, *sotto voce,* between the teeth, from the side of one's mouth, aside, *piano, pianissimo, à la sourdine.*

406 SNAP

Substantives: knock, rap, tap, click, clash, slam, clack, crack, crackle, crackling, crepitation, decrepitation, report, pop, plop, bang, thud, thump, ping, zip, clap, burst, explosion, discharge, crash, detonation, firing, salvo, atmospherics.

Squib, cracker, gun, pop-gun.

Verbs: To snap, knock, etc.

Adjectives: Snapping, etc.

407 ROLL

Substantives: rumble, rumbling, hum, humming, shake, trill, whirr, chime, tick, beat, toll, ticking, tick-tack, patter, tattoo, ding-dong, drumming, quaver, tremolo, ratatat, tantara, rataplan, rat-tat, clatter, clutter, rattle, racket, rub-a-dub; reverberation (408).

Phrases: The devil's tattoo; tuck of drum.

Verbs: To roll, beat, tick, toll, drum, etc., rattle, clatter, patter, shake, trill, whirr, chime, beat; to drum or din in the ear.

Adjectives: Rolling, rumbling, etc.

408 RESONANCE

Substantives: ring, ringing, jingle, chink, tinkle, ting, tink, tintinnabulation, gurgle, chime, toot, tootle, clang, etc. (404).

Reflection, reverberation, echo.

Verbs: To resound, reverberate, re-echo, ring, jingle, clink, chime, tinkle, etc.

Adjectives: Resounding, resonant, tintinnabular, ringing, etc.

Phrase: Clear as a bell.

BASS (*Substantives*), low, flat or grave note, chest-note, baritone, contralto.

Adjectives: Deep-toned, deep-sounding, deep-mouthed, hollow, sepulchral, *basso profondo.*

409 SIBILATION
Substantives: hiss, swish, buzz, whiz, rustle, fizz, fizzle, wheeze, whistle, snuffle, sneeze, sternutation.
Verbs: To hiss, buzz, etc.
Adjectives: Sibilant, hissing, buzzing, etc., wheezy.
SOPRANO (*Substantives*), high note (410).

410 STRIDOR
Substantives: jar, grating, creak, clank, twang, jangle, jarring, creaking, rustling, roughness, gruffness, sharpness, cacophony,
High note, shrillness, acureness, soprano, falsetto, treble, alto, countertenor, penny trumpet, head-note.
Verbs: To creak, grate, jar, burr, pipe, twang, jangle, rustle, clank; to shrill, shriek, screech, squeal, skirl (411), stridulate.
Phrases: To set the teeth on edge; to grate upon the ear.
Adjectives: Strident, stridulous, jarring, etc., harsh, hoarse, horrisonous, discordant, scrannel (414), cacophonous, rough, gruff, sepulchral, grating.
Sharp, high, acute, shrill, piping, screaming.

411 CRY
Substantives: voice (580), vociferation, outcry, roar, shout, bawl, bellow, brawl, halloo, hullaballoo, hoop, whoop, yell, cheer, hoot, howl, chorus, scream, screech, screak, shriek, squeak, squawk, squeal, skirl, yawp, squall, whine, pule, pipe, grumble, plaint, groan, moan, snore, snort.
Verbs: To vociferate, roar, shout, bawl, etc., sing out, thunder, raise or lift up the voice.
Adjectives: Vociferating, etc., clamant, clamorous, vociferous, stertorous.

412 ULULATION
Substantives: latration, cry, roar, bellow, reboation, bark, yelp, howl, bay, baying, yap, growl, grunt, gruntle, snort, neigh, nicker, whinny, bray, croak, snarl, howl, caterwauling, mew, mewl, miaow, miaul, purr, pule, bleat, baa, low, moo, boo, caw, coo, croodle, cackle, gobble, quack, gaggle, squeak, squawk, squeal, chuckle, chuck, cluck, clack, chirp, chirrup, crow, woodnote, twitter, peep.
Insect cry, drone, buzz, hum.
Cuckoo, screech-owl.
Verbs: To cry, bellow, rebellow, etc., bell, boom, trumpet, give tongue.
Phrases: To bay the moon; to roar like a bull or lion.
Adjectives: Crying, etc., blatant, latrant, remugient.

413 MELODY
Substantives: melodiousness, *melos*.
Pitch, note, interval, tone, intonation, timbre; high or low, acute or grave notes, treble, alto, tenor, bass, soprano, mezzo-soprano, contralto, counter-tenor, baritone, *basso profondo*.
Scale, gamut, diapason; diatonic, chromatic, enharmonic, whole-tone, etc., scales; key, clef; major, minor, Dorian, Phrygian, Lydian, etc., modes; tetrachord, hexachord, pentatonic scale; tuning, modulation, temperament; solmization, solfeggio, sol-fa.
Staff (or stave), lines, spaces, brace; bar, double bar, rest.
Notes of the scale: sharps, flats, naturals, accidentals; breve, semibreve, minim, crotchet, quaver, semiquaver, demisemiquaver, etc.
Tonic, keynote, supertonic, mediant, subdominant, dominant, submediant, leading note, octave; primes, seconds, triads, etc.
Harmonic, overtone, partial, fundamental, note, hum-note.
Harmony, harmoniousness, concord, concordance, unison,

homophony, chord, chime, consonance, concent, euphony; counterpoint, polyphony; tonality, atonality; thorough-bass, figured bass.

Rhythm, time, tempo; common, duple, triple, six-eight, etc., time; *tempo rubato,* syncopation, ragtime, jazz, swing, jive, boogie-woogie, bebop, skiffle, rock-and-roll.

Verbs: To harmonize, chime, be in unison; put in tune, tune, accord.

Adjectives: Harmonious, harmonic, harmonical, in harmony, in tune, etc., unisonant, unisonal, univocal, symphonic, homophonous; contrapuntal, chordal; diatonic, chromatic, enharmonic, tonal, atonal.

Measured, rhythmical, in time, on the beat, hot.

Melodious, musical, tuneful, tunable, sweet, dulcet, canorous, mellow, mellifluous, silver-toned, silvery, euphonious, euphonic, euphonical; enchanting, ravishing, etc., Orphean.

414 DISCORD

Substantives: discordance, dissonance, jar, jarring, caterwauling, cacophony.

Hoarseness, croaking, etc. (410).

Confused sounds, babel, Dutch concert, cat's concert, marrow-bones and cleavers, charivari (404).

Verbs: To be discordant, etc., to croak, jar (410).

Adjectives: Discordant, dissonant, out of tune, sharp, flat, tuneless, absonant, unmusical, inharmonious, unmelodious, untuneful, untunable, singsong.

Cacophonous, harsh, hoarse, croaking, jarring, stridulous, etc. (410).

415 MUSIC

Substantives: tune, air, lilt, melody, refrain, burden, cadence, theme, motive, motif, *leit-motiv,* subject, counter-subject, episode, modulation, introduction, finale, etc.

Solo, duet, trio, quartet, etc., concerted music, chorus, chamber music.

Instrumental music: Symphony, *sinfonietta,* symphonic poem, tone-poem, concerto, sonata, sonatina; *allegro, andante, largo,* scherzo, rondo, etc.; overture, prelude, intermezzo, postlude, voluntary; ballade, nocturne, serenade, aubade, barcarolle, *berceuse,* etc.; fugue, fugato, canon; variations, humoresque, rhapsody, caprice, *capriccio,* fantasia, impromptu; arrangement, pot-pourri; march, pibroch, minuet, gavotte, waltz, mazurka, etc. (840); accompaniment, *obbligato;* programme music.

Vocal music: Chant, plain-song, Gregorian music, neume, psalmody, psalm, hymn, anthem, motet, antiphon, canticle, introit, etc., service, song, ballad, *lied, chanson,* cavatina, canzonet, serenade, lullaby, ditty, chanty, folk-song, dithyramb; part-song, glee, catch, round, canon, madrigal, chorus, cantata, oratorio, etc.; opera (599).

Dirge, requiem, nenia, knell, lament, coronach, dead march.

Musical ornament; grace-note, appoggiatura, trill, shake, turn, beat, mordent, etc.; cadenza, roulade, bravura, colorature, *coloratura.*

Scale, run, arpeggio, chord; five-finger exercise, study, *étude,* toccata.

Performance, execution, technique, touch, expression, tone-colour, rendering, interpretation; voice-production, *bel canto; embouchure,* lipping, bowing.

Concert, recital, performance, ballad concert, etc., musicale, sing-song.

Minstrelsy, musicianship, musicality, musicalness, an ear for music; composition, composing, orchestration, scoring, filling in the parts.

Composer, harmonist, contrapuntist.

Apollo, the Muses, Erato, Euterpe, Terpsichore.

Verbs: To play, fiddle, bow, strike, strike up, thrum, strum, grind, touch, tweedle, scrape, blow, pipe, tootle, blare, etc.; to execute, perform, render, interpret, conduct, accompany, vamp, arrange, prelude, improvise (612).

To sing, chant, vocalize, warble, carol, troll, lilt, hum, croon, chirp, chirrup, twitter, quaver, trill, shake, whistle, yodel.

To compose, set to music, score, harmonize, orchestrate.

To put in tune, tune, attune, accord, string, pitch.

Adjectives: Musical, harmonious, etc. (413), instrumental, orchestral, pianistic, vocal, choral, operatic, etc.; musicianly, having a good ear.

Phrase: *Fanatico per la musica.*

Adverbs: *Adagio, largo, larghetto, andante, andantino, maestoso, moderato, allegretto, con moto, vivace, veloce, allegro, presto, prestissimo, strepitoso, etc.; scherzando, legato, staccato, crescendo, diminuendo, morendo, sostenuto, sforzando, accelerando, stringendo, più mosso, meno mosso, allargando, rallentando, ritenuto, a piacere, etc.; arpeggiando, pizzicato, glissando, martellato, da capo.*

416 MUSICIAN

Substantives: minstrel, performer, player, soloist, virtuoso, maestro.

Organist, pianist, violinist, fiddler, cellist, harper, harpist, flautist, fifer, clarinettist, trombonist, etc., trumpeter, bugler, piper, bagpiper, drummer, timpanist; campanologist; band, orchestra, brass band, military band, string band, pipe band, waits; conductor, bandmaster, drum-major, leader, *chef d'orchestre*, etc., accompanist.

Vocalist, singer, songster, songstress, chanter, chantress, *cantatrice*, *lieder*-singer, ballad-singer, etc.; troubadour, minnesinger, gleeman; nightingale, Philomel, thrush, throstle, Orpheus.

Choris, choir, chorister.
Phrase: The tuneful Nine.

417 MUSICAL INSTRUMENTS

1. Stringed instruments: Monochord, polychord, harp, lyre, lute, theorbo, mandolin, guitar, gittern, cithern, banjo, ukelele, balalaika.

Violin, fiddle, Cremona, Stradivarius (or Strad), kit, viola (or tenor), violoncello (or cello), double-bass (or bass-viol), viol, viola d'amore, viola da gamba, violone, rebeck, psaltery.

Pianoforte (or piano), harpsichord, clavier, clavichord, clavicembalo, spinet, cembalo, virginal, zither, dulcimer.

2. Wind instruments: Organ, siren, pipe, pitch-pipe, Pan-pipes; piccolo, flute, bass-flute, oboe (or hautboy), oboe d'amore, cor anglais, clarinet, basset-horn, bass-clarinet, bassoon, double-bassoon, saxophone, horn, French horn, tuba, trumpet, cornet, cornet-à-piston, fife, trombone, euphonium; flageolet, whistle, penny-whistle, ocarina, bugle, serpent, ophicleide, clarion, bagpipe, musette; harmonium, American organ, seraphina, concertina, accordion, melodeon, mouth-organ, etc.; great, swell, choir, solo and echo organs.

3. Vibrating surfaces: Cymbal, bell, carillon, gong, tabor, tambourine, timbrel, drum, side-drum, bass-drum, kettle-drum, timpano, military drum, tom-tom, castanet; musical glasses, harmonica, glockenspiel; sounding-board.

4. Vibrating bars: Tuning-fork, triangle, xylophone, Jew's harp.

5. Mechanical instruments: Musical box, hurdy-gurdy, barrel-organ, piano-organ, orchestrion, piano-player, pianola, etc.; gramophone, phonograph, tape recorder, juke box, nickelodeon.

Key, string, bow, drumstick, bellows, sound-box, pedal, stop; loud or sustaining pedal, soft pedal, mute, sordine, sourdine, damper, swell-box; keyboard, finger-board, console; organ-loft, concert platform, orchestra, choir, singing-gallery, belfry, campanile.

418 HEARING

Substantives: audition, auscultation, listening, eavesdropping; audibility.

Acuteness, nicety, delicacy, of ear.

Ear, auricle, acoustic organs, auditory apparatus, lug, ear-drum, tympanum.

Telephone, speaking-tube, ear-trumpet, audiphone, audiometer, earphone, phone, gramophone, phonograph, dictaphone, intercom, receiver.

Wireless telephony, broadcasting, wireless, radio, transmitter, walkie-talkie, radiogram, microphone, mike.

A hearer, auditor, listener, eaves-dropper, auditory, audience.

Verbs: To hear, overhear, hark, listen, list, hearken, give or lend an ear, prick up one's ears, give a hearing or audience to, listen in.

To become audible, to catch the ear, to be heard.

Phrases: To hang upon the lips of; to be all ears.

Adjectives: Hearing, etc., auditory, auricular, acoustic.

Interjections: Hark! list! hear! listen! oyez! (or oyes!)

Adverbs: *Arrectis auribus*; with ears flapping.

419 DEAFNESS

Substantives: hardness of hearing, surdity; inaudibility.

Verbs: To be deaf, to shut, stop, or close one's ears.

To render deaf, to stun, deafen.

Phrase: To turn a deaf ear to.

Adjectives: Deaf, stone deaf, tone deaf, hard of hearing, earless, surd, dull of hearing, deaf-mute, stunned, deafened, having no ear.

Inaudible, out of earshot.

Phrases: Deaf as a post; deaf as a beetle; deaf as an adder.

420 LIGHT

Substantives: ray, beam, stream, gleam, streak, pencil, sunbeam, moonbeam, starbeam.

Day, daylight, sunshine, sunlight, moonlight, starlight, the light of day, the light of heaven, noontide, noonday, noontide light, broad daylight.

Glimmer, glimmering, glow, afterglow, phosphorescence, lambent flame, play of light.

Flush, halo, aureole, nimbus, glory, corona.

Spark, sparkle, scintilla, sparkling, scintillation, flame, flash, blaze, coruscation, fulguration, lightning, flood of light, glint.

Lustre, shine, sheen, gloss, tinsel, spangle, brightness, brilliancy, refulgence, dazzlement, splendour, resplendence, luminousness, luminosity, luminescence, lucidity, lucidness, incandescence, radiance, illumination, irradiation, glare, flare, flush, effulgence, fulgency, fluorescence, lucency, lambency.

Optics, photology, photometry, dioptrics, catoptrics.

Radioactivity, radiography, radiograph, radiometer, radioscopy, radiotherapy.

Verbs: To shine, glow, glitter, glisten, glister, glint, twinkle, gleam, flicker, flare, glare, beam, radiate, shoot beams, shimmer, sparkle, scintillate, coruscate, flash, blaze, fizzle, daze, dazzle, bedazzle; to clear up, to brighten.

To illuminate, illume, illumine, lighten, enlighten, light, light up, irradiate, flush, shine upon, cast lustre upon; cast, throw, or shed a light upon, brighten, clear, relume.

Phrase: To strike a light.

Adjectives: Luminous, luminiferous, shining, glowing, etc., lambent, glossy, lucid, lucent, luculent, lustrous, lucific, glassy, clear, bright, scintillant, light, lightsome, unclouded, sunny, orient, noonday. noontide, beaming, beamy, vivid, alight, splendent, radiant, radiating, cloudless, unobscured; radioactive, fluorescent, phosphorescent.

Garish, resplendent, refulgent, fulgent, effulgent, in a blaze, ablaze, relucent, splendid, blazing, rutilant, meteoric, burnished.

Phrases: Bright as silver, as day, as noonday.

421 DARKNESS

Substantives: night, midnight, obscurity, dusk (422), duskiness, gloom, gloominess, murk, mirk, murkiness, shadow, shade, umbrage, shadiness, umbra, penumbra, Erebus.

Obscuration, adumbration, obumbration, obtenebration, obfuscation, black-out, extinction, eclipse, gathering of the clouds, dimness (422).

Phrases: Dead of night; darkness visible; darkness that can be felt; blind man's holiday.

Verbs: To be dark, etc.; to lour (or lower).

To darken, obscure, shade, shadow, dim, bedarken, overcast, overshadow, obfuscate, obumbrate, adumbrate, cast in the shade, becloud, overcloud, bedim, put out, snuff out, blow out, extinguish, dout, douse.

To cast, throw, spread a shade or gloom.

Phrase: To douse the glim.

Adjectives: Dark, obscure, darksome, darkling, tenebrous, tenebrific, rayless, beamless, sunless, moonless, starless, pitch-dark, pitchy; Stygian, Cimmerian.

Sombre, dusky, unilluminated, unillumined, unlit, unsunned, nocturnal, dingy, lurid, overcast, louring (or lowering), cloudy, murky, murksome, shady, shadowy, umbrageous.

Benighted, noctivagant, noctivagous.

Phrases: Dark as pitch; dark as a pit; dark as Erebus; dark as a wolf's mouth; the palpable obscure.

422 DIMNESS

Substantives: dim-out, brown-out, paleness, glimmer, glimmering, owl-light, nebulousness, nebulosity, nebula, cloud, film, mist, haze, fog, brume, smog, smoke, haziness, eclipse, dusk, cloudiness, dawn, aurora, twilight, crepuscule, cockshut time, gloaming, daybreak, dawn, half-light, moonlight; moonshine, moon-beam, starlight, starshine, starbeam, candle-light.

Verbs: To be dim, etc., to glimmer, loom, lour, twinkle.

To grow dim, to fade, to render dim, to dim, obscure, pale.

Adjectives: Dim, dull, lack-lustre, dingy, darkish, glassy, faint, confused.

Cloudy, misty, hazy, foggy, brumous, muggy, fuliginous, nebulous, lowering, overcast, crepuscular, muddy, lurid, looming.

Phrase: Shorn of its beams.

423 LUMINARY

Substantives: sun, Phoebus, star, orb, meteor, galaxy, constellation, blazing star, glow-worm, firefly.

Meteor, northern lights, aurora borealis, aurora australis, fire-drake, ignis fatuus, jack-o'-lantern, will-o'-the-wisp, friar's lantern.

Artificial light, flame, gas-light, incandescent gas-light, electric light, limelight, acetylene, torch, candle, flash-lamp, flashlight, flambeau, link, light, taper, lamp, arc-lamp, mercury vapour lamp, neon lighting, lantern (or lanthorn), rushlight, farthing rushlight, night-light, firework, rocket, Very light, blue lights, fizgig, flare.

Chandelier, gaselier, electrolier, candelabra, girandole, lustre, sconce, gas-bracket, gas-jet, gas-burner, batswing; gas-mantle, electric bulb, filament.

Lighthouse, lightship, pharos, beacon, watch-fire, cresset, brand.
Adjectives: Self-luminous, phosphoric, phosphorescent, radiant (420).

424 SHADE
Substantives: awning, parasol, sunshade, screen, curtain, veil, mantle, mask, gause, blind, shutter, cloud, mist.

A shadow, chiaroscuro, umbrage, penumbra (421).
Adjectives: Shady, umbrageous.

425 TRANSPARENCY
Substantives: clarity, transparence, diaphaneity, translucence, translucency, lucidity, pellucidity, limpidity.

Glass, crystal, mica, lymph, water.
Verbs: To be transparent, etc., to transmit light.
Adjectives: Transparent, pellucid, lucid, diaphanous, translucent, relucent, limpid, clear, crystalline, vitreous, transpicuous, glassy, hyaline.
Phrase: Clear as crystal.

426 OPACITY
Substantives: thickness, opaqueness, turbidity, turbidness, muddiness.

Cloud, film, haze.
Verbs: To be opaque, etc., to obfuscate, not to transmit, to obstruct the passage of light.
Adjectives: Opaque, turbid, roily, thick, muddy, opacous, obfuscated, fuliginous, cloudy, hazy, misty, foggy, impervious to light.

427 SEMITRANSPARENCY
Substantives: opalescence, pearliness, milkiness.

Film, gause, muslin.
Adjectives: Semitransparent, semi-diaphanous, semi-opaque, opalescent, gauzy, pearly, milky.

428 COLOUR
Substantives: hue, tint, tinge, dye, complexion, shade, spectrum, tincture, blazonry, cast, livery, coloration, glow, flush, tone, key.

Pure or positive colour, primary colour.

Broken colour, secondary or tertiary colour.

Chromatics; prism, spectroscope.

A pigment, colouring matter, medium, paint, dye, wash, stain, distemper, mordant.
Verbs: To colour, dye, tinge, stain, tinct, tincture, paint, wash, illuminate, blazon, emblazon, bedizen, imbur, distemper.
Adjectives: Coloured, colorific, chromatic, prismatic, full-coloured, lush, dyed; tinctorial.

Bright, deep, vivid, florid, fresh, high-coloured, unfaded, gay, showy, gaudy, garish, flaunting, vivid, gorgeous, glaring, flaring, flashy, tawdry, meretricious, raw, intense, double-dyed, loud, noisy.

Mellow, harmonious, pearly, light, quiet, delicate, pastel.

429 ACHROMATISM
Substantives: decoloration, discoloration, paleness, pallidity, pallidness, pallor, etiolation, anaemia, chlorosis, albinism, neutral tint, colourlessness; monochrome, black and white.
Verbs: To lose colour, to fade, pale, blanch, become colourless.

To deprive of colour, discolour, bleach, tarnish, decolour, decolorate, decolorize, achromatize, tone down.
Adjectives: Colourless, uncoloured, untinged, untinctured, achromatic, aplanatic, hueless, undyed, pale, pallid, pale-faced, pasty, etiolated, anaemic,

chlorotic, faint, faded, dull, cold, muddy, wan, sallow, dead, dingy, ashy, ashen, cadaverous, glassy, lacklustre, tarnished, bleached, discoloured.

Phrases: Pale as death, as ashed, as a witch, as a ghost, as a corpse.

430 WHITENESS

Substantives: milkiness, hoariness.

Albification, etiolation.

Snow, paper, chalk, milk, lily, sheet, ivory, silver, alabaster.

Verbs: To be white, etc.

To render white, whiten, bleach, whitewash, blanch, etiolate.

Adjectives: White, milk-white, snow-white, snowy, niveous, chalky, hoary, hoar, silvery, argent.

Whitish, off-white, cream-coloured, creamy, pearly, fair, blonde, etiolated, albescent.

Phrases: White as the driven snow; white as a sheet.

431 BLACKNESS

Substantives: darkness (421), swarthiness, dinginess, lividity, inkiness, pitchiness, nigritude.

Nigrification.

Jet, ink, ebony, coal, pitch, charcoal, soot, sloe, smut, raven, crow; negro, nigger, darkie, coon, blackamoor.

Verbs: To be black, etc.

To render black, to blacken, nigrify, denigrate, blot, blotch, smirch, smutch.

Adjectives: Black, sable, swarthy, swart, sombre, inky, ebon, livid, coal-black, jet-black, pitch-black, fuliginous, dingy, dusky, Ethiopic, nigrescent.

Phrases: Black as my hat; black as ink; black as coal; black as a crow; black as thunder.

432 GREY

Substantives: neutral, tint, dun.

Adjectives: Grey, etc., drab, dingy, sombre, leaden, livid, ashen, mouse-coloured, slate-coloured, stone-coloured, cinereous, cineritious, grizzly, grizzled.

433 BROWN

Substantives: bistre, ochre, sepia.

Adjectives: Brown, etc., bay, dapple, auburn, chestnut, nut-brown, umber, cinnamon, fawn, russet, olive, hazel, tawny, fuscous, chocolate, liver-coloured, tan, brunette, maroon, khaki, foxy, bronzed, sunburnt, tanned.

Phrases: Brown as a berry, as mahogany, as a gipsy.

Verbs: To render brown, embrown, to tan, bronze, etc.

434 REDNESS

Substantives: red, scarlet, vermilion, crimson, carmine, pink, lake, maroon, carnation, damask, ruby, rose, blush colour, peach colour, flesh colour, gules, solferino.

Rust, cinnabar, cochineal, madder, red lead, ruddle; blook, lobster, cherry, pillar-box.

Erubescence, rubescence, rubefaction, rosiness, rufescence, ruddiness, rubicundity.

Verbs: To become red, to blush, flush, mantle, redden, colour.

To render red, redden, rouge, rubefy, rubricate, incarnadine.

Adjectives: Red, scarlet, vermilion, carmine, rose, ruby, crimson, pink, etc., ruddy, rufous, florid, rosy, roseate, auroral, rose-coloured, blushing, mantling, etc., erubescent, blowzy, rubicund, stammel, blood-red, ensanguined, rubiform, cardinal, cerise, *sang-de-bœuf,* murrey, carroty, sorrel, brick-coloured, brick-red, lateritic, cherry-coloured, salmon-coloured.

Phrases: Red as fire, as blood, as scarlet, as a turkey-cock, as a cherry.

435 GREENNESS

Substantives: verdure, viridescence, viridity.

Emerald, jasper, verd-antique, verdigris, beryl, aquamarine, malachite, grass.

Adjectives: Green, verdant, pea-green, grass-green, apple-green, sea-green, turquoise-green, olive-green, bottle-green, glaucous, virescent, aeruginous, vert.

Phrase: Green as grass.

436 YELLOWNESS

Substantives: buff colour, orpiment, yellow ochre, gamboge, crocus, saffron, xanthin, topaz.

Lemon, mustard, jaundice, gold.

Adjectives: Yellow, citron, gold, golden, aureate, citrine, fallow, tawny, flavous, fulvous, saffron, croceate, lemon, xanthic, xanthous, sulphur, amber, straw-coloured, sandy, lurid, Claude-tint, luteous, primrose-coloured, cream-coloured, buff, chrome.

Phrases: Yellow as a quince, as a guinea, as a crow's foot.

437 PURPLE

Substantives: violet, plum, prune, lavender, lilac, peach colour, puce, gridelin, lividness, lividity, bishop's purple, magenta, mauve.

Amethyst, murex.

Verb: To empurple.

Adjectives: Purple, violet, plum-coloured, lilac, mauve, livid, etc.

438 BLUENESS

Substantives: bluishness, azure, indigo, ultramarine, Prussian blue, mazarine, bloom, bice.

Sky, sea, lapis lazuli, cobalt, sapphire, turquoise.

Adjectives: Blue, cerulean, sky-blue, sky-coloured, sky-dyed, watchet, azure, bluish, sapphire, Garter-blue.

439 ORANGE

Substantives: gold, flame, copper, brass, apricot colour; aureolin, nacarat.

Ochre, cadmium.

Adjectives: Orange, golden, ochreous, etc., buff, flame-coloured.

440 VARIEGATION

Substantives: dichroism, trichroism, iridescence, play of colours, *reflet*, variegatedness, patchwork, check, plaid, chess-board, tartan, maculation, spottiness, pointillism, parquetry, marquetry, mosaic, inlay, buhl, striae, spectrum.

A rainbow, iris, tulip, peacock, chameleon, butterfly, tortoise-shell, leopard, zebra, harlequin, motley, mother-of-pearl, nacre, opal, marble.

Verbs: To be variegated, etc.

To variegate, speckle, stripe, streak, chequer, bespeckle, fleck, freckle, inlay, stipple, spot, dot, damascene, embroider, tattoo.

Adjectives: Variegated, varicoloured, many-coloured, versicolour, many-hued, divers-coloured, particoloured, polychromatic, bicolour, tricolour, dichromatic.

Iridescent, prismatic, opaline, nacreous, pearly, opalescent, shot, watered, *chatoyant, gorge de pigeon,* all manner of colours, pied, piebald, skewbald, daedal, motley, mottled, veined, marbled, paned, dappled, clouded, cymophanous.

Mosaic, inlaid, tessellated, chequered, tartan, tortoiseshell.

Dotted, spotted, bespotted, spotty, speckled, bespeckled, punctate, maculated, freckled, fleckered, flecked, flea-bitten, studded, tattooed.

Striped, striated, streaked, barred, veined, brinded, brindled, tabby, roan, grizzled, listed, stippled.

Phrase: All the colours of the rainbow.

441 VISION

Substantives: sight, optics, eyesight.

View, espial, glance, glimpse, peep, peek, look, squint, dekko, gander, the once-over, gaze, stare, leer, perlustration, contemplation, sight-seeing, regard, survey, reconnaissance, introspection, inspection, speculation, watch, *coup d'œil*, œillade, glad eye, bo-peep, ocular demonstration, autopsy, visualization, envisagement.

A point of view, gazebo, vista, loophole, peep-hole, look-out, belvedere, field of view, watch-tower, observation post, crow's nest, theatre, amphitheatre, horizon, arena, commanding view, bird's-eye view, coign of vantage, observatory, periscope.

The organ of vision, eye, the naked or unassisted eye, retina, pupil, iris, cornea, white, optics, peepers.

Perspicacity, penetration, discernment.

Cat, hawk, lynx, eagle, Argus.

Evil eye; cockatrice, basilisk.

Verbs: To see, behold, discern, have in sight, descry, sight, catch a sight, glance, or glimpse of, spy, espy, to get a sight of.

To look, view, eye, open one's eyes, glance on, cast or set one's eyes on, clap eyes on, look on or upon, turn or bend one's looks upon, turn the eyes to, envisage, visualize, peep, peer, peek, pry, scan, survey, reconnoitre, contemplate, regard, inspect, recognize, mark, discover, distinguish, see through, speculate; to see sights, lionize.

To look intently, strain one's eyes, be all eyes, look full in the face, look hard at, stare, gaze, pore over, gloat on, leer, to see with half an eye, to blink, goggle, ogle, make eyes at; to play at bo-peep.

Phrases: To have an eye upon; keep in sight; look about one; glance round; run the eye over; lift up one's eyes; see at a glance, or with half an eye; keep a look-out for; to keep one's eyes skinned; to be a spectator of; to see with one's own eyes.

Adjectives: Visual, ocular, optic, optical, ophthalmic.

Seeing, etc., the eyes being directed to, fixed, riveted upon.

Clear-sighted, sharp-sighted, quick-sighted, eagle-eyed, hawk-eyed, lynx-eyed, keen-eyed, Argus-eyed, piercing, penetrating.

Phrase: The scales falling from one's eyes.

Adverbs: Visibly, etc., at sight, in sight of, to one's face, before one's face, with one's eyes open, at a glance, at first sight, at sight.

Interjections: Look! behold! see! lo! mark! observe! lo and behold!

442 BLINDNESS

Substantives: night-blindness, snow-blindness, cecity, amaurosis, cataract, ablepsy, nictitation, wink, blink.

A blinkard.

Verbs: To be blind, etc., not to see, to lose sight of.

Not to look, to close or shut the eyes, to look another way, to turn away or avert the eyes, to wink, blink, nictitate.

To render blind, etc., to put out the eyes, to blind, blindfold, hoodwink, daze, dazzle.

Phrase: To throw dust in the eyes.

Adjectives: Blind, eyeless, sightless, visionless, dark, stone-blind, sand-blind, stark-blind, mope-eyed, dazzled, hoodwinked, blindfolded, undiscerning.

Phrases: Blind as a bat, as a buzzard, as a beetle, as a mole, as an owl.

Adverbs: Blindly, etc., blindfold, darkly.

443 DIMSIGHTEDNESS

Substantives: purblindness, lippitude, confusion of vision, scotomy, failing sight, short-sightedness, near-sightedness, myopia, nictitation, long-sightedness, amblyopia, presbyopia, hypermetropia, nyctalopia (or nyctalopy), nystagmus, astigmatism, squint, strabismus, wall-eye, swivel-eye, cast of the eye, double sight; an albino, blinkard.

Fallacies of vision: *deceptio visus,* refraction, false light, phantasm, anamorphosis, distortion, looming, mirage, *fata morgana,* the spectre of the Brocken, ignis fatuus, phantasmagoria, dissolving views.

Colour-blindness, Daltonism.

Limitation of vision, blinker, screen.

Verbs: To be dim-sighted, etc., to see double, to have a mote in the eye, to squint, goggle, look askance (or askant), to see through a prism, wink, nictitate.

To glare, dazzle, loom.

Adjectives: Dim-sighted, half-sighted, short-sighted, near-sighted, purblind, myopic, long-sighted, hypermetropic, presbyopic, moon-eyed, mope-eyed, blear-eyed, goggle-eyed, wall-eyed, one-eyed, nictitating, winking, monoculous, amblyopic, astigmatic.

444 SPECTATOR

Substantives: looker-on, onlooker, watcher, sightseer, bystander, *voyeur,* inspector, snooper, rubberneck (455), spy, beholder, witness, eye-witness, observer, star-gazer, etc., scout.

Verbs: To witness, behold, look on at, spectate.

445 OPTICAL INSTRUMENTS

Substantives: lens, meniscus, magnifier, reading-glass, microscope, megascope, spectacles, specs, glasses, barnacles, goggles, pince-nez, lorgnette, folders, eye-glass, monocle, contact lens, periscope, telescope, spyglass, monocular, binoculars, fieldglass, night-glass, opera-glass, glass, view-finder, range-finder.

Mirror, reflector, speculum, looking-glass, pier-glass, cheval-glass, kaleidoscope.

Prism, camera, cine-camera, cinematograph (448), camera lucida, camera obscura, magic lantern, phantasmagoria, thaumatrope, chromatrope, stereoscope, pseudoscope, bioscope.

Photometer, polariscope, spectroscope, collimator, polemoscope, eriometer, actinometer, exposure meter, lucimeter.

446 VISIBILITY

Substantives: perceptibility, conspicuousness, distinctness, conspicuity, appearance, exposure.

Verbs: To be visible, etc., to appear, come in sight, come into view, heave in sight, open to the view, catch the eye, show its face, present itself, show itself, manifest itself, produce itself, discover itself, expose itself, come out, come to light, come forth, come forward, stand forth, stand out, arise, peep out, peer out, show up, turn up, crop up, start up, loom, burst forth, break through the clouds, glare, reveal itself, betray itself.

Phrases: To show its colours; to see the light of day; to show one's face; to tell its own tale; to leap to the eye; *cela saute aux yeux*; to stare one in the face.

Adjectives: Visible, perceptible, perceivable, discernible, in sight, apparent, plain, manifest, patent, obvious (525), clear, distinct, definite, well-defined, well-marked, recognizable, evident, unmistakable, palpable, naked, bare, barefaced, ostensible, conspicuous, prominent, staring, glaring, notable, notorious, overt; periscopic, panoramic, stereoscopic.

Phrases: Open as day; clear as day; plain as a pikestaff; there is no mistaking; plain as the nose on one's face; before one's eyes; above-board; exposed to view; under one's nose; in bold relief; in the limelight.

447 INVISIBILITY

Substantives: indistinctness, inconspicuousness, imperceptibility, non-appearance, delitescence, latency (526), concealment (528).

Verbs: To be invisible, escape notice, etc., to lie hidden, concealed, etc. (528), to be in or under a cloud, in a mist, in a haze, etc.; to lurk, lie in ambush, skulk.

Not to see, etc., to be blind to.

To render invisible, to hide, conceal (528).

Adjectives: Invisible, imperceptible, unseen, unbeheld, undiscerned, viewless, undiscernible, indiscernible, sightless, undescried, unespied, unapparent, non-apparent, inconspicuous, unconspicuous, hidden, concealed, etc. (528), covert, eclipsed.

Confused, dim, obscure, dark, misty, hazy, foggy, indistinct, ill-defined, indefinite, ill-marked, blurred, shadowy, nebulous, shaded, screened, veiled, masked.

Phrases: Out of sight; not in sight; out of focus.

448 APPEARANCE

Substantives: phenomenon, sight, spectacle, show, premonstration, scene, species, view, *coup d'Œil,* lookout, prospect, outlook, vista, perspective, bird's-eye view, scenery, landscape, seascape, streetscape, picture, tableau, *mise en scène,* display, exposure, exhibition, manifestation.

Pageant, pageantry, peep-show, raree-show, panorama, diorama, cosmorama, georama, *coup de théâtre, jeu de théâtre.*

Bioscope, biograph, magic lantern, epidiascope, cinematograph (or kinematograph).

Phantasm, phasma, phantom, spectrum, apparition, spectre, mirage, etc.

(4, 443).

Aspect, phase, *phasis,* seeming, guise, look, complexion, shape, mien, air, cast, carriage, manner, bearing, deportment, port, demeanour, presence, expression.

Lineament, feature, trait, lines, outline, contour, face, countenance, physiognomy, visage, phiz, mug, dial, puss, pan, profile, *tournure.*

Verbs: To seem, look, appear; to present, wear, carry, have, bear, exhibit, take, take on, or assume the appearance of; to play, to look like, to be visible, to reappear; to materialize.

To show, to manifest.

Adjectives: Apparent, seeming, etc., ostensible.

Adverbs: Apparently, to all appearance, etc., ostensibly, seemingly on the face of it, *prima facie,* at the first blush, at first sight.

449 DISAPPEARANCE

Substantives: evanescence, eclipse, occultation.

Dissolving views, fade-out.

Verbs: To disappear, vanish, dissolve, fade, melt away, pass, be gone, be lost, etc.

To efface, blot, blot out, erase, rub out, expunge (552).

Phrase: To go off the stage.

Adjectives: Disappearing, etc., lost, vanishing, evanescent, gone, missing.

Inconspicuous, unconspicuous (447).

Phrases: Lost in the clouds; leaving no trace; out of sight.

Interjections: Avaunt! vanish! disappear!

(297).

CLASS FOUR

Words relating to the intellectual faculties

I

Section I –
Operations of Intellect in General

450 INTELLECT
Substantives: mind, understanding, reason, thinking principle, nous, noesis, faculties, sense, common sense, consciousness, capacity, intelligence, percipience, intellection, intuition, instinct, conception, judgment, talent, genius, parts, wit, wits, shrewdness, intellectuality; the five senses; rationalism; ability, skill (698); wisdom (498).

Subconsciousness, subconscious mind, unconscious, id.

Soul, spirit, psyche, ghost, inner man, heart, breast, bosom.

Organ or seat of thought: *sensorium,* sensory, brain, head, headpiece, pate, noddle, nut, loaf, skull, brain-pan, grey matter, pericranium, cerebrum, cerebellum, cranium, upper storey, belfry.

Science of mind, phrenology, mental philosophy, metaphysics, psychology, psychics, psycho-analysis; ideology, idealism, ideality, pneumatology, immaterialism, intuitionism, realism; transcendentalism, spiritualism.

Metaphysician, psychologist, psychiatrist, psychotherapist, psychoanalyst.

Verbs: Appreciate, realize, be aware of, be conscious of, take in, mark, note, notice.

Adjectives: Intellectual, noetic, rational, reasoning, gnostic, mental, spiritual, subjective, metaphysical, psychical, psychological, noumenal, ghostly, immaterial (317), cerebral; subconscious, subliminal, Freudian.

450A ABSENCE OR WANT OF INTELLECT
Substantives: imbecility (499), materialism.

Adjectives: Material, objective, unreasoning.

451 THOUGHT
Substantives: reflection, cogitation, cerebration, consideration, meditation, study, lucubration, speculation, deliberation, pondering, head-work, brain-work, application, attention (457).

Abstraction, contemplation, musing, brown study, reverie (458); depth of thought, workings of the mind, inmost thoughts, self-counsel, self-communing, self-examination, introspection; succession, flow, train, current, etc., of thought or of ideas, brain-wave.

Afterthought, second thoughts, hindsight, reconsideration, retrospection, retrospect (505), examination (461), imagination (515).

Thoughtfulness, pensiveness, intentness.

Telepathy, thought-transference,

mind-reading, extra-sensory perception, retrocognition, telekinesis.

Verbs: To think, reflect, cogitate, excogitate, consider, deliberate, speculate, contemplate, mediate, introspect, ponder, muse, ruminate, think over, brood over, reconsider, animadvert, con, con over, mull over, study, bend or apply the mind, digest, discuss, hammer at, puzzle out, weigh, perpend, fancy, trow, dream of.

To occur, present itself, pass in the mind, suggest itself, strike one.

To harbour, entertain, cherish, nurture, etc., an idea, a thought, a notion, a view, etc.

Phrases: Take into account; take into consideration; to take counsel; to commune with oneself; to collect one's thoughts; to advise with one's pillow; to sleep on or over it; to chew the cud upon; revolve in the mind; turn over in the mind; to rack or cudgel one's brains; to put on one's thinking-cap.

To flash on the mind; to flit across the view; to enter the mind; come into the head; come uppermost; run in one's head.

To make an impression; to sink or penetrate into the mind; fasten itself on the mind; to engross one's thoughts.

Adjectives: Thinking, etc., thoughtful, pensive, meditative, reflective, ruminant, introspective, wistful, contemplative, speculative, deliberative, studious, abstracted, introspective, sedate, philosophical, conceptual.

Close, active, diligent, mature, deliberate, laboured, steadfast, deep, profound, intense, etc., thought, study, reflection, etc.

Intent, engrossed, absorbed, deep-musing, rapt (or wrapt), abstracted; sedate.

Phrases: Having the mind on the stretch; lost in thought; the mind or head running upon.

452 INCOGITANCY

Substantives: vacancy, inanity, fatuity (499), thoughtlessness (458).

Verbs: Not to think, to take no thought of, not to trouble oneself about, to put away thought; to inhibit, dismiss, discard, or discharge from one's thoughts, or from the mind; to drop the subject, set aside, turn aside, turn away from, turn one's attention from, abstract oneself, dream.

To unbend, relax, divert the mind.

Adjectives: Vacant, unintellectual (499), unoccupied, unthinking, inconsiderate, thoughtless, idealess, unidea'd, absent, *distrait,* abstracted, inattentive (458), diverted, distracted, distraught, unbent, relaxed.

Unthought-of, unconsidered, incogitable, undreamed-of, off one's mind.

Phrase: *In nubibus.*

453 IDEA

Substantives: notion, conception, apprehension, concept, thought, fancy, conceit, impression, perception, apperception, percept, ideation, image, eidolon, sentiment (484), fantasy, flight of fancy.

Point of view, light, aspect (448), field of view, standpoint; theory (514); fixed idea (481).

454 TOPIC

Substantives: subject, matter, theme, motif, thesis, text, subject-matter, point, proposition, theorem, business, affair, case, matter in hand, question, argument, motion, resolution, moot point (461), head, chapter; nice or subtle point, quodlibet.

Phrases: Food for thought; mental pabulum.

Adverbs: In question under consideration, on the carpet, *sur le tapis,* relative to, *re, in re* (9), concerning, touching.

Section 2 –
Precursory Conditions
and Operations

455 CURIOSITY
Substantives: curiousness, inquisitiveness, an inquiring mind.

A quidnunc, busybody, eavesdropper, snooper, rubberneck, Peeping Tom, Nosy Parker, Paul Pry, newsmonger, gosspi.

Verbs: To be curious, etc., to take an interest in, to stare, gape, pry, snoop, rubber, lionize.

Adjectives: Curious, inquisitive, inquiring, inquisitorial, all agog, staring, prying, snoopy, gaping, agape, over-curious, nosy.

Adverbs: With open mouth, on tiptoe, with ears flapping, *arrectis auribus.*

456 INCURIOSITY
Substantives: incuriousness, insouciance, nonchalance, want of interest, indifference (866).

Verbs: To be incurious, etc., to have no curiosity, take no interest in, not to care, not to mind; to mind one's own business.

Phrases: Not to trouble oneself about; one couldn't care less; the devil may care; san fairy ann.

Adjectives: Incurious, uninquisitive, indifferent, *sans souci,* insouciant, nonchalant, aloof, detached, apathetic, uninterested.

457 ATTENTION
Substantives: advertence, advertency, observance, observation, interest, notice, heed, look, regard, view, remark, inspection, introspection, heedfulness, mindfulness, look-out, watch, vigilance, circumspection, surveillance, consideration, scrutiny, revision, revisal, recension, review, revise, particularity (459).

Close, intense, deep, profound, etc., attention, application, or study.

Verbs: To be attentive, etc.; to attend, advert to, mind, observe, look, look at, see, view, look to, see to, remark, heed, notice, spot, twig, pipe, take heed, take notice, mark; give or pay attention to; give heed to, have an eye to; turn, apply, or direct the mind, the eye, or the attention to; look after, give a thought to, animadvert on, occupy oneself to, give oneself up to, see about.

To examine cursorily; to glance at, upon, or over; cast or pass the eyes over, run over, turn over the leaves, dip into, skim, perstringe.

To examine closely or intently, scrutinize, consider, give one's mind to, overhaul, pore over, perpend, note, mark, inspect, review, size up, take stock of, fix the eye, mind, thoughts, or attention on, keep in view, contemplate, revert to, etc. (451).

To fall under one's notice, observation, etc., to catch the eye; to catch, awaken, wake, invite, solicit, attract, claim, excite, engage, occupy, strike, arrest, fix, engross, monopolize, preoccupy, obsess, absorb, rivet, etc., the attention, mind, or thoughts; to interest.

To call attention to, point out, indicate (550).

Phrases: To trouble one's head about; lend or incline an ear to; to take cognizance of; to prick up one's ears; to have one's eyes open; to keep one's eyes skinned.

To have one's wits about one; to bear in mind; to come to the point; to take into account; to read, mark, learn.

Adjectives: Attentive, mindful, heedful, regardful, alive to, awake to, bearing in mind, occupied with, engaged, taken up with, interested, engrossed, wrapped in, absorbed, rapt.

Awake, watchful, on the watch (459), broad awake, wide awake, agape, intent on, with eyes fixed on,

179

open-eyed, unwinking, undistracted, with bated breath, breathless, upon the stretch.

Interjections: See! look! say! attention! hey! oy! mark! lo! behold! *achtung! nota bene!* NB.

458 INATTENTION

Substantives: inconsideration, inconsiderateness, inadvertence, inadvertency, non-observance, inobservance, disregard, oversight, unmindfulness, giddiness, respectlessness, thoughtlessness (460), in-souciance; wandering, distracted, etc., attention.

Absence of mind, abstraction, preoccupation, distraction, reverie, brown study, day-dream, day-dreaming, wool-gathering.

Phrases: The wits going wool-gathering; the attention wandering; building castle in the air, or castles in Spain.

Verbs: To be inattentive, etc., to overlook, disregard, pass by, slur over, pass over, gloss over, blink, miss, skim the surface, *effleurer* (460).

To call off, draw off, call away, divert, etc., the attention; to distract; to disconcert, put out, rattle, discompose, confuse, perplex, bewilder, bemuse, moider, bemuddle, muddle, dazzle, obfuscate, faze, fluster, flurry, flummox, befog.

Phrases: To take no account of; to drop the subject; to turn a deaf ear to; to come in at one ear and go out of the other; to reckon without one's host.

Adjectives: Inattentive, mindless, unobservant, unmindful, uninterested, inadvertent, heedless, regardless, respectless, careless (460), insouciant, unwatchful, listless, cursory, blind, deaf, etc.

Absent, abstracted, *distrait,* absent-minded, lost, preoccupied, bemused, dreamy, moony, napping.

Disconcerted, put out, etc., dizzy, muzzy (460).

Phrase: Caught napping.

Adverbs: Cavalierly, inattentively, etc.

459 CARE

Substantives: caution, heed, heedfulness, attention (457), wariness, prudence, discretion, watch, watchfulness, alertness, vigil, vigilance, circumspection, watch and ward, deliberation, forethought (510), predeliberation, solicitude, precaution (673), scruple, scrupulousness, scrupulosity, particularity, surveillance.

Phrases: The eyes of Argus; *l'œil du maître.*

Verbs: To be careful, etc., to take care, have a care, beware, look to it, reck, heed, take heed, provide for, see to, see after, keep watch, keep watch and ward, look sharp, look about one, set watch, take precautions, take tent, see about.

Phrases: To have all one's wits about one; to mind one's P's and Q's; to speak by the card; to pick one's steps; keep a sharp look out; keep one's weather eye open; to keep an eye on.

Adjectives: Careful, cautious, heedful, wary, canny, guarded, on one's guard, alert, on the alert, on the watch, watchful, on the look out, *aux aguets,* awake, vigilant, circumspect, broad awake, having the eyes open, Argus-eyed.

Discreet, prudent, sure-footed, provident, scrupulous, particular, meticulous.

Phrase: On the *qui vive.*

Adverbs: Carefully, etc., with care, etc., gingerly, considerately.

Phrases: Let sleeping dogs lie; catching a weasel asleep.

Interjections: Look out! mind your eye! watch! beware! cave! fore! heads!

460 NEGLECT

Substantives: negligence, omission, trifling, laches, heedlessness, carelessness, perfunctoriness, remissness, imprudence, secureness, indiscretion, *étourderie,* incautiousness, indiscrimination, rashness (863), recklessness, nonchalance, inattention (458); slovenliness, sluttishness.

Trifler, flibbertigibbet, Micawber; slattern, slut, sloven.

Verbs: To be negligent, etc., to neglect, scamp, pass over, cut, omit, pretermit, set aside, cast or put aside.

To overlook, disregard, ignore, slight, pay no regard to, make light of, trifle with, blink, wink at, connive at; take or make no account of; gloss over, slur over, slip over, skip, skim, miss, shelve, sink, jump over, shirk (623), discount.

To waste time, trifle, frivol, fribble (683).

To render neglectful, etc., to put or throw off one's guard.

Phrases: To give to the winds; take no account of; turn a deaf ear to; shut one's eyes to; not to mind; think no more of; set at naught; give the go-by to.

Adjectives: Neglecting, etc., unmindful, heedless, careless, *sans souci,* negligent, neglectful, slovenly, sluttish, remiss, perfunctory, thoughtless, unthoughtful, unheedful, off one's guard, unwary, incautious, unguarded, indiscreet, inconsiderate, imprudent, improvident, rash, headlong, reckless, heels over head, witless, hare-brained, giddy-brained, offhand, slapdash, happy-go-lucky, cursory, brain-sick, scatterbrained.

Neglected, missed, abandoned, shunted, shelved, unheeded, unperceived, unseen, unobserved, unnoticed, unnoted, unmarked, unattended to, untended, unwatched, unthought-of, overlooked, unmissed, unexamined, unsearched, unscanned, unweighed, unsifted, untested, unweeded, undetermined.

Phrases: In an unguarded moment; buried in a napkin.

Adverbs: Negligently, etc., anyhow, any old way.

Interjections: Let is pass! never mind! no matter! I should worry! san fairy ann! *nichevo!*

461 INQUIRY

Substantives: search, research, quest, pursuit (622), examination, review, scrutiny, investigation, perquisition, perscrutation, referendum, straw vote, Gallup poll; discussion, symposium, inquest, inquisition, exploration, exploitation, sifting, screening, calculation, analysis, dissection, resolution, induction; the Baconian method.

Questioning, asking, interrogation, interpellation, interrogatory, the Socratic method, examination, cross-examination, cross-questioning, third degree, quiz, catechism.

Reconnoitring, reconnaissance, feeler, *ballon d'essai,* prying, spying, espionage, the lantern of Diogenes, searchlight.

QUESTION, query, difficulty, problem, proposition, desideratum, point to be solved; point or matter in dispute; moot point, question at issue, bone of contention, plain question, fair question, open question, knotty point, vexed question, crux.

Enigma, riddle, conundrum, crossword, bone to pick, quodlibet, Gordian knot.

An inquirer, querist, questioner, heckler, inquisitor, scrutator, scrutineer, examiner, inspector, analyst, quidnunc, newsmonger, gossip (527, 532); investigator, detective, bloodhound, sleuth-hound, sleuth, inquiry agent, private eye, Sherlock Holmes, busy, dick, rozzer, flattie, G-man; secret police, Cheka, Ogpu, Gestapo.

Verbs: To inquire, seek, search, look for, look about for, look out for, cast about for, beat up for, grope for, feel for, reconnoitre, explore, sound, rummage, fossick, ransack, pry, snoop, look round, look over, look through, scan, peruse.

To pursue, hunt, track, trail, mouse, dodge, trace, shadow, tail, dog (622), nose out, ferret out, unearth, hunt up.

To investigate; to take up, follow up, institute, pursue, conduct, carry on, prosecute, etc., an inquiry, etc.; to overhaul, examine, study, consider, fathom, take into consideration, dip into, look into, calculate, pre-examine, dive into, to delve into, rake, rake over, discuss, canvass, thrash out, probe, fathom, sound, scritinize, analyse, anatomize, dissect, sift, screen, winnow, resolve, traverse, see into.

To ask, speer, question, query, demand; to put, propose, propound, moot, raise, stir, suggest, put forth, start, pop, etc., a question; to interrogate, catechize, pump, cross-question, cross-examine, grill, badger, heckle, dodge, require an answer.

Phrases: To look, peer, or pry into every hole and corner, to beat the bushes; to leave no stone unturned; to seek a needle in a bundle of hay; to scratch the head.

To subject to examination; to grapple with a question; to put to the proof; pass in review; take into consideration; to ventilate a question; seek a clue; throw out a feeler.

To undergo examination; to be in course of inquiry; to be under consideration.

Adjectives: Inquiring, etc., inquisitive, requisitive, requisitory, catechetical, inquisitorial, heuristic, analytic, in search of, in quest of, on the look out for, interrogative, zetetic.

Undetermined, untried, undecided, to be resolved, etc., in question, in dispute, under discussion, under consideration, *sub judice,* moot, proposed, doubtful.

Adverbs: Why? wherefore? whence? *quaere?* how comes it? how happens it?

how is it? what is the reason? what's in the wind? what's cooking?

462 ANSWER

Substantives: response, reply, replication, riposte, rejoinder, rebutter, surrejoinder, surrebutter, retort, comeback, repartee, rescript, antiphony, rescription, acknowledgment.

Explanation, solution, deduction, resolution, exposition, rationale, interpretation (522).

A key, master-key, open sesame, *passepartout,* clue.

Oedipus, oracle (513); solutionist.

Verbs: To answer, respond, reply, rebut, retort, rejoin, return for answer, acknowledge, echo.

To explain, solve, resolve, expound, decipher, spell, interpret (522), to unriddle, unlock, cut the knot, unravel, fathom, pick or open the lock, discover, fish up, to find a clue to, get to the bottom of.

Phrases: To turn the tables upon; QED

Adjectives: Answering, responding, etc., responsive, respondent.

Adverb: On the right scent.

Interjection: Eureka!

463 EXPERIMENT

Substantives: essay, trial, tryout, tentative method, *tâtonnement,* verification, probation, proof, criterion, test, acid test, reagent, check, control, touchstone, pyx, assay, ordeal; empiricism, rule of thumb method of trial and error.

A feeler, *ballon d'essai,* pilot-balloon, messenger-balloon: pilot-engine: straw to show the wind.

Verbs: To experiment, essay, try, explore, grope, angle, cast about, beat the bushes; feel or grope one's way; the thread one's way; to make an experiment, make trial of.

To subject to trial, etc., to experiment upon, try over, rehearse, give a trial to, put, bring, or submit to the test or proof; to prove, verify, test, assay, touch, practise upon.

Phrases: To see how the land lies; to see how the wind blows; to feel the pulse; to throw out a feeler; to have a try; to have a go.

Adjectives: Experimental, crucial, tentative, probationary, empirical, *sub judice,* under probation, on trial, on approval.

Adverbs: *A tâtons.*

464 COMPARISON

Substantives: collation, contrast, antithesis, identification.

A comparison, simile, similitude, analogy, parallel, parable, metaphor, allegory (521).

Verbs: To compare to or with; to collate, confront, place side by side or in juxtaposition, to draw a parallel, institute a comparison, contrast, balance, identify.

Adjectives: Comparative, metaphorical, figurative, allegorical, comparable, compared with, pitted against, placed by the side of.

465 DISCRIMINATION

Substantives: distinction, differentiation, perception or appreciation of difference, nicety, refinement, taste (850), judgment, discernment, nice perception, tact, critique.

Verbs: To discriminate, distinguish, differentiate, draw the line, sift, screen.

Phrases: To split hairs; to cut blocks with a razor; to separate the chaff from the wheat or the sheep from the goats.

Adjectives: Discriminating, etc., discriminative, distinctive, diagnostic, nice, judicial.

465A INDISCRIMINATION

Substantives: indistinctness, indistinction (460).

Verbs: Not to distinguish or discriminate, to confound, confuse; to neglect, overlook, lose sight of a distinction.

Adjectives: Indiscriminate, undistinguished, undistinguishable, sweeping, unmeasured, wholesale.

466 MEASUREMENT

Substantives: admeasurement, mensuration, triangulation, survey, valuation, appraisement, assessment, assize, estimation, reckoning, evaluation, gauging; mileage, voltage, horse power.

Geometry, geodetics, geodesy, orthometry, altimetry, sounding, surveying, weighing, ponderation, trutination, dead reckoning, metrology.

A measure, standard, rule, yardstick, compass, callipers, dividers, gauge, meter, line, rod, plumb-line, plummet, log, log-line, sound, sounding-rod, sounding-line, lead-line, index, flood-mark, Plimsoll line (or mark), check.

Scale, graduation, graduated scale, vernier, quadrant, theodolite, slide-rule, balance, spring balance, scales, steelyard, beam, weather-glass, barometer, aneroid, barograph, araeometer, altimeter, clinometer, graphometer, goniometer, thermometer, speedometer, tachometer, pedometer, ammeter, voltmeter, micrometer, etc.

A surveyor, geometer, leadsman, etc.

Verbs: To measure, mete, value, assess, rate, appraise, estimate, form an estimate, set a value on, appreciate, span, pace, step; apply the compass, rule, scale, etc., gauge, plumb, probe, sound, fathom, heave the log, survey, weigh, poise, balance, hold the scales, take an average, graduate, evaluate, size up, to place in the beam, to take into account, price.

Adjectives: Measuring, etc., metrical, ponderable, measurable, mensurable.

183

Section 3 –
Materials for Reasoning

467 EVIDENCE, on one side
Substantives: premises, data, grounds, *praecognita,* indication (550).

Oral, hearsay, internal, external, documentary, presumptive evidence.

Testimony, testimonial, deposition, declaration, attestation, testification, authority, warrant, warranty, guarantee, surety, handwriting, autograph, signature, endorsement, seal, sigil, signet (550), superscription, entry, fingerprint.

Voucher, credential, certificate, deed, indenture, docket, dossier, probate, affidavit, diploma; admission, concession, allegation, deposition, citation, quotation, reference; admissibility.

Criterion, test, reagent, touchstone, check, control, prerogative, fact, argument, shibboleth.

A witness, eye-witness, indicator, ear-witness, deponent, telltale, informer, sponsor, special pleader.

Assumption, presumption, show of reason, postulation, postulate, lemma.

Reason, proof (478), circumstantial evidence.

Ex-parte evidence, one-sided view.

Secondary evidence, confimation, corroboration, ratification, authentication, support, approval, compurgation.

Phrases: A case in point; *ecce signum; ex pede Herculem.*

Verbs: To be evidence, etc., to evidence, evince, show, indicate (550), imply, involve, entail, necessitate, argue, bespeak, admit, allow, concede, homologate, certify, testify, attest, bear testimony, depose, depone, witness, vouch for, sign, seal, set one's hand and seal to, endorse, confirm, ratify, corroborate, support, establish, uphold, bear upon, bear out, warrant, guarantee.

To adduce, cite, quote, refer to, appeal to, call, bring forward, produce, bring into court, confront witnesses, collect, bring together, rake up evidence, to make a case, make good, authenticate, substantiate, go bail for.

To allege, plead, assume, postulate, posit, presume; to beg the question.

Phrases: To hold good, hold water; to speak volumes; to bring home to; to bring to book; to quote chapter and verse; to speak for itself; tell its own tale.

Adjectives: Showing, etc., indicating, indicative, indicatory, evidential, evidentiary, following, deducible, consequential, collateral, corroborative, confirmatory, postulatory, presumptive.

Sound, logical, strong, valid, cogent, decisive, persuasive, persuasory, demonstrative, irrefragable, irresistible, etc. (578).

Adverbs: According to, witness, admittedly, confessedly, *a fortiori,* still more, still less, all the more reason for.

468 COUNTER-EVIDENCE
Substantives: disproof, contradiction, rejoinder, rebutter, answer (462), weak point, conflicting evidence, refutation (479), negation (536).

Phrases: A *tu quoque* argument; the other side of the shield.

Verbs: To countervail, oppose, rebut, check, weaken, invalidate, contradict, contravene.

Phrases: To tell another story; to cut both ways.

Adjectives: Countervailing, etc., contradictory; unauthenticated, unattested, unvouched-for.

Adverbs: Although, though, albeit, but, *per contra.*

Phrase: *Audi alteram partem.*

469 QUALIFICATION

Substantives: limitation, modification, allowance, grains of allowance, consideration, extenuating circumstance, condition, proviso, saving clause, penalty clause, exception (83), assumption (514).

Verbs: To qualify, limit, modify, tone down, colour, discount, allow for, make allowance for, take into account, introduce new conditions, admit exceptions, take exception.

Adjectives: Qualifying, etc., conditional, exceptional (83), contingent, postulatory, hypothetical, suppositious (514).

Adverbs: Provided, if, unless, but, yet, according as, conditionally, admitting, supposing, granted that; on the supposition, assumption, presumption, allegation, hypothesis, etc., of; with the understanding, even, although, for all that, at all events, after all.

Phrases: With a grain of salt; *cum grano salis*.

470 POSSIBILITY

Substantives: potentiality, contingency (156), what may be, what is possible, etc.

Practicability, feasibility (705), compatibility (23).

Verbs: To be possible, etc., to admit of, to bear.

To render possible, etc., to put into the way of.

Adjectives: Possible, contingent (475), conceivable, credible.

Practicable, feasible, achievable, performable, viable, accessible, surmountable, attainable, obtainable, compatible.

Adverbs: Possibly, by possibility, maybe, perhaps, mayhap, haply, perchance, peradventure, *in posse* (156).

Phrases: Wind and weather permitting; within the bounds of possibility; on the cards; DV.

471 IMPOSSIBILITY

Substantives: what cannot be, what can never be, imposs, no go, hopelessness (859).

Impracticability, incompatibility (704), incredibility.

Verbs: To be impossible, etc., to have no chance whatever.

Phrases: To make a silk purse out of a sow's ear; to wash a blackamoor white; to make bricks without straw; to get blood from a stone; to take the breeks off a highlandman; to square the circle; to eat one's cake and have it too.

Adjectives: Impossible, contrary to reason, inconceivable, unreasonable, absurd, incredible, visionary, chimerical, prodigious (870), desperate, hopeless, unheard-of, unthinkable.

Impracticable, unattainable, unachievable, unfeasible, infeasible, beyond control, unobtainable, unprocurable, insuperable, unsurmountable, inaccessible, inextricable.

Phrases: Out of the question; sour grapes; *non possumus*.

472 PROBABILITY

Substantives: likelihood, *vraisemblance*, verisimilitude, plausibility, show of, colour of, credibility, reasonable chance, favourable chance, fair chance, hope, prospect, presumption, presumptive evidence, circumstantial evidence, the main chance, a *prima facie* case.

Probabilism, probabiliorism.

Verbs: To be probable, likely, etc.; to think likely, dare say, expect (507).

Phrases: To bid fair; to stand fair for; to stand a good chance; to stand to reason.

Adjectives: Probable, likely, hopeful, well-founded.

Plausible, specious, ostensible, colourable, standing to reason, reasonable, credible, tenable, easy of belief, presumable, presumptive, *ben trovato*.

Phrases: Likely to happen; in a fair

185

way; appearances favouring; according to every reasonable expectation; the odds being in favour.

Adverbs: Probably, etc., belike, in all probability, or likelihood, apparently, to all appearance, on the face of it, in the long run, *prima facie,* very likely, like enough, arguably, ten to one.

Phrase: All Lombard Street to a china orange.

473 IMPROBABILITY
Substantives: unlikelihood, unfavourable chances, small chance, off-chance, bare possibility, long odds, incredibility.

Verbs: To be improbable, etc., to have or stand a small, little, poor, remote, etc., chance; to whistle for.

Adjectives: Improbable, unheard-of, incredible, unbelievable, unlikely.

Phrases: Contrary to all reasonable expectation; having scarcely a chance; a chance in a thousand.

474 CERTAINTY
Substantives: certitude, positiveness, a dead certainty, dead cert, infallibleness, infallibility, gospel, scripture, surety, assurance, indisputableness, moral certainty.

Fact, matter of fact, *fait accompli.*

Bigotry, dogmatism, *ipse dixit.*

Bigot, dogmatist, Sir Oracle.

Verbs: To be certain, etc., to believe (484).

To render certain, etc., to ensure, to assure, clinch, determine, decide.

To dogmatize, lay down the law.

Phrases: To stand to reason; to make assurance doubly sure.

Adjectives: Certain, sure, assured, solid, absolute, positive, flat, determinate, categorical, unequivocal, inevitable, unavoidable, avoidless, unerring, infallible, indubitable, indubious, indisputable, undisputed, uncontested, undeniable, incontestable, irrefutable, unimpeachable,

incontrovertible, undoubted, doubtless, without doubt, beyond a doubt, past dispute, unanswerable, decided, unquestionable, beyond all question, unquestioned, questionless, irrefragable, evident, self-evident, axiomatic, demonstrable (478), authoritative, authentic, official, unerring, infallible, trustworthy (939).

Phrases: Sure as fate; and no mistake; sure as a gun; clear as the sun at noonday; sure as death (and taxes); bet your life; you bet; *cela va sans dire*; it's in the bag; that's flat.

Adverbs: Certainly, assuredly, etc., for certain, *in esse,* sure, surely, sure enough, to be sure, of course, as a matter of course, yes (488), depend upon it, that's so, by all manner of means, beyond a peradventure.

475 UNCERTAINTY
Substantives: incertitude, doubt (485), doubtfulness, dubiety, dubiousness, suspense, precariousness, indefiniteness, indetermination, slipperiness, fallibility, perplexity, embarrassment, dilemma, ambiguity (520), hesitation, vacillation (605), equivoque, vagueness, peradventure, touch-and-go.

Phrases: A blind bargain; a pig in a poke; a leap in the dark; a moot point; an open question.

Verbs: To be uncertain, etc; to vacillate, hesitate, waver.

To render uncertain, etc., to perplex, embarrass, confuse, moider, confound, bewilder, disorientate.

Phrases: To be in a state of uncertainty; not to know which way to turn; to be at a loss; to be at fault; to lose the scent.

To tremble in the balance; to hang by a thread.

Adjectives: Uncertain, doubtful, dubious, precarious (665), chancy, casual, random, contingent, indecisive, dependent on circumstances, undecided, unsettled, undetermined, pending, pendent, vague, indeterminate, indefinite, ambiguous, undefined, equivocal, undefinable, puzzling, enigmatic, debatable, disputable, questionable, apocryphal, problematical, hypothetical, controvertible, fallible, fallacious, suspicious, fishy, slippery, ticklish.

Unauthentic, unconfirmed, undemonstrated, undemonstrable, unreliable, untrustworthy.

Section 4 – Reasoning Processes

476 REASONING
Substantives: ratiocination, dialectics, induction, deduction, generalization; inquiry (461).

Argumentation, discussion, *pourparler,* controversy, polemics, debate, wrangling, logomachy, apology, apologetics, ergotism, disputation, disceptation.

The art of reasoning, logic, process, train or chain of reasoning, analysis, synthesis, argument, lemma, proposition, terms, premises, postulate, data, starting-point, principle, inference, result, conclusion.

Syllogism, prosyllogism, enthymeme, sorites, dilemma, *perilepsis,* pros and cons, a comprehensive argument.

Correctness, soundness, force, validity, cogency, conclusiveness.

A thinker, reasoner, disputant, controversialist, logician, dialectician, polemic, wrangler, arguer, debater.
Phrases: A paper war; a war of words; a battle of the books; a full-dress debate.

The horns of a dilemma; *reductio ad absurdum; argumentum ad hominem; onus probandi.*
Verbs: To reason, argue, discuss, debate, dispute, wrangle; bandy words or arguments; hold or carry on an argument, controvert, contravene (536), consider (461), comment upon, moralize upon, spiritualize.
Phrases: To open a discussion or case; to moot; to join issue; to ventilate a question; to talk it over; to have it out; to take up a side or case.

To chop logic; to try conclusions; to impale on the horns of a dilemma; to cut the matter short; to hit the nail on the head; to take one's stand upon; to have the last word.
Adjectives: Reasoning, etc., rational, rationalistic, ratiocinative, argumentative, controversial, dialectic, polemical, discursory, discursive, debatable, controvertible, disputatious; correct, just, fair, sound, valid, cogent, logical, demonstrative (478), relevant, pertinent (9, 23).
Phrases: To the point; in point; to the purpose; *ad rem.*
Adverbs: For, because, for that reason, forasmuch as, inasmuch as, since, hence, whence, whereas, considering, therefore, consequently, *ergo,* then, thus, accordingly, wherefore, *a fortiori, a priori, ex concesso.*
Phrases: In consideration of; in conclusion; in fine; after all; *au bout du compte*; on the whole; taking one thing with another.

477 INTUITION
Substantives: instinct, association, presentiment, insight, second sight, sixth sense.

False or vicious reasoning, show of reason.

Misjudgment, miscalculation (481).
SOPHISTRY
Substantives: paralogy, fallacy, perversion, casuistry, jesuitry, quibble, equivocation, evasion, chicanery, special pleading, quiddity, mystification; nonsense (497).

Sophism, solecism, paralogism,

187

elenchus, fallacy, quodlibet, subterfuge, subtlety, quillet, inconsistency, antilogy.

Speciousness, plausibility, illusiveness, irrelevancy, invalidity; claptrap, hot air.

Quibbler, casuist, *advocatus diaboli*.

Phrases: Begging the question; *petitio principii*; *ignoratio elenchi*; reasoning in a circle; *post hoc, ergo propter hoc*; *ignotum per ignotius*.

The meshes or cobwebs of sophistry; a flaw in an argument; an argument falling to the ground.

Verbs: To envisage, to judge intuitively, etc.

To reason ill, falsely, etc.; to pervert, quibble, equivocate, mystify, evade, elude, gloss over, varnish, misjudge, miscalculate (481).

To refine, subtilize, cavil, sophisticate, mislead.

Phrases: To split hairs; to cut blocks with a razor; throw off the scent; to beg the question; reason in a circle; beat about the bush; prove that black is white; not have a leg to stand on; lose one's reckoning.

Adjectives: Intuitive, instinctive, impulsive, unreasoning, independent of or anterior to reason.

Sophistical, unreasonable, irrational, illogical, false, unsound, not following, not pertinent, inconsequent, inconsequential, unwarranted, untenable, inconclusive, incorrect, fallacious, inconsistent, groundless, fallible, unproved, indecisive, deceptive, illusive, illusory, specious, hollow, jesuitical, plausible, irrelevant.

Weak, feeble, poor, flimsy, trivial, trumpery, trashy, puerile, childish, irrational, silly, foolish, imbecile, absurd (499), extravagant, far-fetched, pettifogging, quibbling, fine-spun, hair-splitting.

Phrases: *Non constat*; *non sequitur*; not holding water; away from the point; foreign to the purpose or subject; having nothing to do with the matter; not of the essence; *nihil ad rem*; not bearing upon the point in question; not the point; beside the mark.

478 DEMONSTRATION

Substantives: proof, conclusiveness, probation, comprobation, clincher, *experimentum crucis*, test, etc. (463), argument (476).

Verbs: To demonstrate, prove, establish, show, evince, verify, substantiate; to follow.

Phrases: Make good; set at rest; settle the question; reduce to demonstration; to make out a case; to prove one's point; to clinch an argument; bring home to bear out.

Adjectives: Demonstrating, etc., demonstrative, probative, demonstrable, unanswerable, conclusive, final, apodictic (or apodeictic), irrefutable, irrefragable, unimpeachable, categorical, decisive, crucial.

Demonstrated, proved, proven, etc., unconfuted, unrefuted; evident, self-evident, axiomatic (474); deducible, consequential, inferential.

Phrases: *Probatum est*; it stands to reason; it holds good; there being nothing more to be said; QED.

Adverbs: Of course, in consequence, consequently, as a matter of course, no wonder.

479 CONFUTATION

Substantives: refutation, disproof, conviction, redargution, invalidation, exposure, exposition; demolition of an argument; answer, come-back, counter, retort.

Phrases: *Reductio ad absurdum*; a knock-down argument; a *tu quoque* argument.

Verbs: To confute, refute, disprove, redargue, expose, show the fallacy of, knock the bottom out of, rebut, parry, negative, defeat, overthrow, demolish, explode, riddle, overturn, invalidate, silence, reduce to silence, shut up, put down.

Phrases: To cut the ground from one's feet; to give one a set-down.

Adjectives: Confuting, etc., confuted, etc., capable of refutation, refutable, confutable, etc.; unproved, etc.

Phrases: The argument falls to the ground; it won't hold water; that cock won't fight.

Section 5 –
Results of Reasoning

480 JUDGMENT

Substantives: conclusion, determination, deduction, inference, result, illation, corollary, rider, porism, consectary.

Estimation, valuation, appreciation, judication, adjudication, arbitrament, arbitration, assessment, award, ponderation.

Decision, sentence, verdict, moral, ruling, finding; detection, discovery, estimate; *chose jugée*.

Criticism, critique, review, report, notice; plebiscite, casting vote.

A judge, umpire, arbiter, arbitrator, assessor, censor, referee, critic, connoisseur, reviewer. **Verbs:** To judge, deduce, conclude, draw a conclusion, infer, make a deduction, draw an inference, put two and two together; come to, arrive or jump at a conclusion; to derive, gather, collect.

To estimate, appreciate, value, count, assess, rate, account, rank, regard, review, settle, decide, pronounce, arbitrate, perpend, size up.

Phrases: To sit in judgment; to hold the scales; to pass an opinion; to pass judgment.

Adjectives: Judging, etc., deducible (467); impartial, unbiased, unprejudiced, unwarped, unbigoted, equitable, fair, sound, rational, judicious, shrewd.

480A DETECTION

Substantive: discovery.

Verbs: To ascertain, determine, find, find out, make out, detect, discover, elicit, recognize, trace, get at; get or arrive at the truth; meet with, fall upon, light upon, hit upon, fall in with, stumble upon, lay the finger on, spot, solve, resolve, unravel, fish out, worm out, ferret out, root out, nose out, disinter, unearth, grub up, fish up, investigate (461).

To be near the truth, to get warm, to burn.

Phrase: To smell a rat.

Interjection: Eureka!

481 MISJUDGMENT

Substantives: obliquity of judgment, misconception, error (495), miscalculation, miscomputation, presumption.

Prejudgment, prejudication, prejudice, prenotion, *parti pris,* prevention, preconception, predilection, prepossession, preapprehension, presentiment, *esprit de corps,* clannishness, party spirit, partisanship, partiality.

Bias, warp, twist, fad, whim, crotchet, fike; narrow-mindedness, bigotry, dogmatism, intolerance, tenacity, obstinacy (606); blind side; one-sided, partial, narrow or confined views, ideas, conceptions, or notions; *idée fixe,* fixed idea, obsession, monomania, infatuation.

Phrases: A bee in one's bonnet; a mote in the eye; a fool's paradise.

Verbs: To midjudge, misestimate, misconceive, misreckon, etc. (495).

To prejudge, forejudge, prejudicate, dogmatize, have a bias, etc., presuppose, presume.

To produce a bias, twist, etc.; to bias, warp, twist, prejudice, obsess, infatuate, prepossess.

Phrases: To have on the brain; to look only at one side of the shield; to view with jaundiced eye; to run away with the notion; to jump to a conclusion.

Adjectives: Prejudging, midjudging, etc., prejudiced, jaundiced, narrow-minded, dogmatic, intolerant, illiberal, blimpish, besotted, infatuated, fanatical, *entêté,* positive, obstinate (606), tenacious, pig-headed, having a bias, twist, etc., warped, partial, one-sided, biased, bigoted, hide-bound, tendentious, opinionated, opinionative, opinioned, self-opinioned, self-opinionated, crotchety, pernickety, faddy, fussy, fiky.

Phrases: Wedded to an opinion; the wish being father to the thought.

482 OVERESTIMATION

Substantive: exaggeration.

Phrases: Much ado about nothing; much cry and little wool; a storm in a tea-cup.

Verbs: To overestimate, estimate too highly, overrate, overvalue, overprize, overpraise, overweigh, outreckon; exaggerate, extol, puff, boost, make too much of, overstrain.

Phrases: To set too high a value upon; to make a mountain out of a molehill; *parturiunt montes, nascetur ridiculus mus;* to make two bites of a cherry; all his geese are swans.

Adjectives: Overestimated, etc.

483 UNDERESTIMATION

Substantives: depreciation, disparagement, detraction (934), underrating, undervaluing, etc.

Verbs: To depreciate, disparage, detract, underrate, underestimate, undervalue, underreckon, underprize, misprize, disprize, not to do justice to, make light of, slight, belittle, knock, slam, make little of, think nothing of, hold cheap, cheapen, disregard, to care nothing for, despise, set at naught, minimize, discount, deride, derogate, decry, cry down, crab, denigrate, smear, vilipend, run down (934).

To scout, deride, pooh-pooh, mock, scoff at, laugh at, whistle at, play with, trifle with, fribble, niggle, ridicule (856).

Phrases: To snap one's fingers at; throw into the shade; not to care a pin, rush, hoot, tinker's cuss, etc., for; to damn with faint praise.

Adjectives: Depreciating, etc., derogatory, cynical.

Depreciated, etc., unvalued, unprized.

484 BELIEF

Substantives: credence, faith, trust, troth, confidence, credit, dependence on, reliance, assurance.

Opinion, notion, idea (453), conception, apprehension, impression, conceit, mind, view, persuasion, conviction, convincement, sentiment, voice, conclusion, judgment (480), estimation, self-conviction.

System of opinions, creed, credo, religion (983, 987), doctrine, tenet, dogma, principle, school, ideology, articles of belief, way of thinking, popular belief, *vox populi,* public opinion, *esprit de corps,* partisanship; ism, doxy.

Change of opinion (607), proselytism, propagandism (537).

A convert, pervert, vert, proselyte.

Verbs: To believe, credit, receive, give faith to, give credit to, rely upon, make no doubt, reckon, doubt not, confide in, count upon, depend upon, build upon, calculate upon, take upon trust, swallow, gulp down, take one's word for, take upon credit, swear by.

To be of opinion, to opine, presume; to have, hold, possess, entertain, adopt, imbibe, embrace, foster, nurture, cherish, etc., a notion, idea, opinion, etc.; to think, look upon, view, consider, take, take it, hold, trow, ween, conceive, fancy, apprehend, regard, esteem, deem, account; meseems, methinks.

To cause to be believed, thought, or esteemed; to satisfy, persuade, assure, convince, convert, bring over, win over, indoctrinate, proselytize (537), evangelize; to vert.

Phrases: To pin one's faith to; to take at one's word.

To take it into one's head; to run away with the notion; to come round to an opinion.

To cram down the throat; to bring home to; to find credence; to carry conviction; pass current; pass muster; to hold water; to go down.

Adjectives: Believing, etc., impressed with, imbued with, wedded to, unsuspecting, unsuspicious, void of suspicion, etc., credulous (486), convinced, positive, sure, assured, cocksure, certain, confident.

Believed, etc., credited, accredited, unsuspected, received, current, popular.

Worthy of deserving of belief, commanding belief, believable, persuasive, impressive, reliable, dependable, trustworthy (939), credible, probable (572), fiducial, fiduciary; relating to belief, doctrinal.

Adverbs: In the opinion of, in the eyes of, on the strength of, to the best of one's belief, *me judice*.

485 UNBELIEF

Substantives: disbelief, misbelief, discredit, agnosticism, atheism (988), heresy (984), dissent (489).

Doubt, dubitation, scepticism, *diaporesis,* misgiving, demur, cliffhanging, suspense; shade or shadow of doubt, distrust, mistrust, misdoubt, suspicion, shyness, embarrassment, hesitation, uncertainty (475), scruple, qualm, dilemma; casuistry, paradox; schism (489), incredulity (487).

Unbeliever, sceptic (487); Doubting Thomas.

Verbs: To disbelieve, discredit, not to believe; refuse to admit or believe; misbelieve, controvert; put or set aside; join issue, dispute, etc.

To doubt, be doubtful, etc., diffide, distrust, mistrust, suspect, scent, jalouse; have, harbour, entertain, etc., doubts; demur, stick at, pause, hesitate, scruple, question, query, call in question, look askance (or askant).

To cause, raise, suggest, or start a doubt; to pose, stagger, floor, startle, embarrass, puzzle (704); shake or stagger one's faith or belief.

Phrases: Not to know what to make of; to smell a rat; to hang in doubt; to have one's doubts; to float in a sea of doubts.

Adjectives: Unbelieving, doubting, etc., incredulous, scrupulous, suspicious, sceptical, shy of belief, at sea, at a loss (487).

Unworthy or undeserving of belief, hard to believe, doubtful (475), dubious, unreliable, fishy, questionable, suspect, staggering, puzzling, etc., paradoxical, incredible, inconceivable.

Phrases: With a grain of salt; *cum grano salis; timeo Danaos et dona ferentes*; all is not gold that glitters; the cowl does not make the monk.

486 CREDULITY

Substantives: credulousness, gullibility, infatuation, self-delusion, self-deception, superstition, gross credulity, bigotry, dogmatism.

A credulous person, gull, gobemouche; dupe (547).

Verbs: To be credulous, etc., to follow implicitly, swallow, take on trust, take for gospel.

To impose upon, practise upon, palm off upon, cajole, etc., deceive (545).

Phrases: *Credo quia absurdum*; the wish being father to the thought.

Adjectives: Credulous, gullible, confiding, trusting; easily deceived, cajoled, etc.; green, verdant, superstitious, simple, unsuspicious, etc. (484), soft, childish, silly, stupid, overcredulous, over-confident.

191

487 INCREDULITY

Substantives: incredulousness, scepticism, pyrrhonism, nihilism, suspicion (485), suspiciousness, scrupulousness, scrupulosity.

An unbeliever, sceptic, misbeliever, pyrrhonist; nihilist.

Verbs: To be incredulous, etc., to distrust (485).

Adjectives: Incredulous, hard of belief, sceptical, unbelieving, inconvincible, shy of belief, doubting, distrustful, suspicious (485).

Phrases: Oh yeah? says you! a likely story! rats! that be hanged for a tale; tell that to the marines; it won't wash; that cock won't fight; *credat Judaeus Apella.*

488 ASSENT

Substantives: acquiescence, admission, assentation, nod, consent, concession, accord, accordance, agreement (23), concord (714), concordance, concurrence, ratification, confirmation, corroboration, approval, recognition, acknowledgment, acceptance, granting, avowal, confession.

Unanimity, chorus; affirmation (535), common consent, acclamation, consensus.

Yes-man, sycophant, echo.

Verbs: To assent, acquiesce, agree, yield assent, accord, concur, consent, nod assent, accept, coincide, go with, go along with, be at one with, chime in with, strike in with, close with, vote for, conform with, defer to; say yes, ay, ditto, amen, etc.

To acknowledge, own, avow, confess, concede, subscribe to, abide by, admit, allow, recognize, grant, endorse, ratify, countersign, OK, okay, approve, carry.

Phrases: To go or be solid for; to come to an understanding; to come to terms; one could not agree more.

Adjectives: Assenting, etc., acquiescent, content, consentient, willing; approved, agreed, carried; uncon-

tradicted, unchallenged, unquestioned, uncontroverted; unanimous.

Phrase: Of one mind.

Adverbs: Affirmatively, in the affirmative (535).

Yes, yea, yeah, yep, ay, aye, uh-huh, sure, very well, even so, just so, quite so, to be sure, all right, right oh! right you are, you said it, definitely, absolutely, exactly, precisely, truly, certainly, assuredly, no doubt, doubtless, verily, very true (494), *ex concesso.*

Be it so, so be it, by all means, granted, OK, okay, oke, okeydoke, by all manner of means, *à la bonne heure*, amen, willingly, etc. (602).

With one voice, with one accord, *una voce*, unanimously, in chorus, as one man, to a man, *nem. con.* or *nemine contradicente, nemine dissentiente, en bloc*, without a dissentient voice, one and all, on all hands.

489 DISSENT

Substantives: dissidence, discordance, denial (536), dissonance, disagreement; difference or diversity of opinion, recusancy, contradiction, nonconformity, schism (984), secession; protest.

A dissentient, dissenter, protestant, nonconformist, recusant, heretic; deviationist, nonjuror, schismatic seceder.

Verbs: To dissent, demur, deny, disagree, refuse assent, say no, differ, cavil, ignore, protest, contradict, secede, repudiate, refuse to admit.

Phrases: To shake the head; to shrug the shoulders; to join issue; to give the lie; to differ *toto caelo.*

Adjectives: Dissenting, etc., dissentient, dissident, discordant, protestant, nonconforming, recusant, nonjuring, non-content, schismatic, deviationist; unconvinced, unconverted, unavowed, unacknowledged.

Unwilling, reluctant, extorted, etc.

Adverbs: Negatively, in the negative (536), at variance with.

No, nay, nope, nit, na, not, not so, not at all, nohow, nowise, not in the least, not a bit, not a whit, not a jot, by no means, by no manner of means, not for the world, on no account, in no respect.

Phrases: Many men, many minds; *quot homines, tot sententiae; tant s'en faut;* the answer is in the negative; *il s'en faut bien.*

Interjections: No sir! God forbid! I'll be hanged first! I'll see you far enough! not bloody likely! not on your nelly! not if I know it! over my dead body! pardon me! I beg your pardon!

490 KNOWLEDGE
Substantives: cognizance, cognition, cognoscence, awareness, gnosis, acquaintance, experience, ken, privity, insight, familiarity, apprehension, comprehension, understanding, recognition; discovery (480), appreciation; knowability.

Intuition, clairvoyance, consciousness, conscience, perception, precognition, light, enlightenment, glimpse, inkling, glimmer, dawn, scent, suspicion; conception, notion, idea (453).

Self-consciousness, self-knowledge, apperception.

System or body of knowledge, science, philosophy, pansophy, pandect, doctrine, ideology, theory, aetiology, literature, *belles-lettres, literae humaniores,* the humanities, humanism; ology.

Erudition, learning, lore, scholarship, letters, book-learning, bookishness, bibliomania, bibliolatry, education, instruction, information, acquisitions, acquirements, accomplishments, attainments, proficiency, cultivation, culture; a liberal education, encyclopaedic knowledge, omniscience.

Elements, rudiments, abecedary (542), cyclopaedia, encyclopaedia, school, academy, etc.

Depth, extent, profoundness, profundity, stores, etc., solidity, accuracy, etc., of knowledge.

Phrases: The march of intellect; the progress, advance, etc., of science; the schoolmaster being abroad.

Verbs: To know, be aware of, savvy, ken, wot, ween, trow, have, possess, perceive, conceive, apprehend, ideate, understand, comprehend, make out, recognize, be master of, know full well, possess the knowledge of, experience, discern, perceive, see, see through, have in one's head.

Phrases: To know what's what; to know how the wind blows; to know the ropes; to have at one's fingertips or finger-ends.

Adjectives: Knowing, aware of, etc., cognizant of, acquainted with, privy to, conscious of, no stranger to, *au fait, au courant,* versed in, hep, up in, up to, alive to, wise to, conversant with, proficient in, read in, familiar with.

Apprised of, made acquainted with, informed of; undeceived.

Erudite, instructed, learned, well-read, lettered, literate, educated, cultivated, cultured, knowledgeable, enlightened, well-informed, shrewd, bookish, scholarly, scholastic, deep-read; self-taught, well-grounded, well-conned.

Known, etc., well-known, recognized, received, notorious, noted, proverbial, familiar; hackneyed, trite, commonplace; cognoscible, knowable; experiential.

Phrases: Behind the scenes; in the know; at home in; the scales fallen from one's eyes.

Adverbs: To one's knowledge, to the best of one's knowledge.

Phrase: *Experto crede.*

491 IGNORANCE
Substantives: nescience, nescientness, unacquaintance, unconsciousness, darkness, blindness, incomprehension, incognizance, inexperience, emptiness.

Imperfect knowledge, smattering, sciolism, glimmering; bewilderment, perplexity (475); incapacity.

Affectation of knowledge, pedantry, charlatanry, quackery, dilettantism.

Phrases: Crass ignorance; monumental ignorance.

A sealed book; unexplored ground; an unknown quantity; *terra incognita.*

Verbs: To be ignorant, etc., not to know, to know nothing of, not to be aware of, to be at a loss, to be out of it, to be at fault, to ignore, to be blind to, etc., not to understand, etc.

Phrases: To be caught tripping; not to know what to make of; to have no idea or notion; not to be able to make head or tail of; not to know a hawk from a handsaw; to lose one's bearings.

Adjectives: Ignorant, unknowing, unconscious, unaware, unwitting, witless, a stranger to, unacquainted, unconversant, unenlightened, unilluminated, incognizant, unversed, uncultivated, clueless.

Uninformed, uninstructed, untaught, unapprised, untutored, unschooled, unguided.

Shallow, superficial, green, verdant, rude, half-learned, illiterate, unread, uneducated, unlearned, uncultured, Philistine, unlettered, empty-headed, having a smattering, etc., pedantic.

Confused, puzzled, bewildered, bemused, muddled, bemuddled, lost, benighted, belated, at sea, at fault, posed, blinded, abroad, distracted, in a maze, misinformed, hoodwinked, in the dark, at a loss, *désorienté.*

Unknown, novel, unapprehended, unexplained, unascertained, uninvestigated, unexplored, untravelled, uncharted, chartless, unheard-of, unperceived, unknowable.

Phrases: Having a film over the eyes; wide of the mark; at cross purposes.

Adverbs: Ignorantly, unwittingly, unawares; for anything one knows; for aught one knows.

Phrase: 'A little learning is a dangerous thing.'

492 SCHOLAR

Substantives: student (541), savant, scientist, humanist, grammarian, intellectual, pundit, schoolman, don, professor, lecturer, reader, demonstrator, graduate, doctor, master of arts, licentiate, wrangler, gownsman, philosopher, philomath, clerk, encyclopaedist.

Linguist; *littérateur, literati, illuminati,* intelligentsia.

Pedant, pedagogue, bookworm, *helluo librorum,* bibliomaniac, bibliophile, blue-stocking, *bas-bleu,* high-brow, bigwig, bookman; swot, grind.

Phrases: Man of letters; man of learning; at the feet of Gamaliel; a walking dictionary.

Adjectives: Erudite, learned, scholarly (490).

493 IGNORAMOUS

Substantives: sciolist, smatterer, novice, greenhorn, half-scholar, schoolboy, booby, dunce (501); bigot (481); quack, mountebank, charlatan, dilettante, low-brow, amateur, Philistine, obscurant, obscurantist.

Phrase: The wooden spoon.

Adjectives: Bookless, shallow (499), ignorant, etc. (491), prejudiced (481), obscurantist.

494 TRUTH

Substantives: verity, actual, existence (1), reality, fact, matter of fact, actuality, nature, principle, orthodoxy, gospel, holy writ, substantiality, genuineness, authenticity, realism.

Accuracy, exactness, exactitude, precision, preciseness, nicety, delicacy, fineness, strictness, rigour, punctuality.

Phrases: The plain truth; the honest truth; the naked truth; the sober truth; the very thing; a stubborn fact; not a dream, fancy, illusion, etc.; the exact truth; 'the truth, the whole truth, and nothing but the truth'; 'a round unvarnished tale'; *ipsissima verba*; the real Simon Pure.

Verbs: To be true, real, etc., to hold good, to be the case.

To render true, legitimatize, legitimize, substantiate, realize, actualize, to make good, establish.

To get at the truth (480).

Phrases: *Vitam impendere vero; magna est veritas et praevalebit.*

Adjectives: True, real, veritable, veracious, actual, certain, positive, absolute, existing (1), substantial, categorical, realistic, factual; unrefuted, unconfuted, unideal, unimagined.

Exact, accurate, definite, precise, well-defined, just, correct, right, strict, hard-and-fast, literal, rigid, rigorous, scrupulous, conscientious, religious, punctilious, nice, mathematical, axiomatic, demonstrable, scientific, unerring, constant, faithful, *bona fide*, curious, delicate, meticulous.

Genuine, authentic, legitimate, pukka, orthodox, official, *ex officio*, pure, sound, sterling, hall-marked, unsophisticated, unadulterated, unvarnished; solid, substantial, undistorted, undisguised, unaffected, unflattering, unexaggerated, unromantic.

Phrases: Just the thing; neither more nor less; to a hair.

Adverbs: Truly, verily, veritable, troth, certainly, certes, assuredly, in truth, in good truth, of a truth, really, indubitably, in sooth, forsooth, in reality, in fact, in point of fact, as a matter of fact, strictly speaking, *de facto*, indeed, in effect, actually, *ipso facto*, definitely, literally, positively, virtually, at bottom, *au fond*.

Precisely, accurately, *ad amussim*, etc., mathematically, to a nicety, to a hair, to a T, to an inch; to the letter, *au pied de la lettre*.

In every respect, in all respects, *sous*

tous les rapports, at any rate, at all events, by all means.

Phrases: Joking apart; in good earnest; in sober earnest; sooth to say.

495 ERROR

Substantives: mistake, miss, fallacy, misconception, misapprehension, misunderstanding, inaccuracy, incorrectness, inexactness, misconstruction (523), miscomputation, miscalculation (481).

Fault, blunder, *faux pas*, bull, Irish bull, Irishism, bloomer, howler, floater, clanger, boner, lapse, slip of the tongue, *lapsus linguae,* Spoonerism, slip of the pen, malapropism, equivoque, cross purposes, oversight, flaw, misprint, erratum; heresy, misstatement, misreport, bad shot.

Illusion, delusion, self-deceit, self-deception, hallucination, monomania, aberration; fable, dream, shadow, fancy, bubble, false light (443), the mists of error, will-o'-the-wisp, jack-o'-lantern, ignis fatuus, chimera (515), *maya*.

Verbs: To be erroneous, false, etc., to cause error, to mislead, lead astray, lead into error, delude, give a false impression or idea, to falsify, misstate, misrelate, misinform, misrepresent (544), deceive (545), beguile.

To err, be in error, to mistake, to receive a false impression; to lie or labour under an error, mistake, etc., to blunder, be in the wrong, be at fault, to misapprehend, misconceive, misunderstand, misremember, misreckon, miscalculate, miscount, misestimate, misjudge, misthink, flounder, trip.

Phrases: To take the shadow for the substance; to go on a fool's errand; to have the wrong sow by the ear; to put one's foot in it; to pull a boner; to drop a brick.

Adjectives: Erroneous, untrue, false, fallacious, duff, unreal, unsubstantial, baseless, groundless, ungrounded,

195

unauthenticated, untrustworthy, heretical.

Inexact, incorrect, wrong, illogical, partial, one-sided. unreasonable, absonous, absonant, indefinite, unscientific, inaccurate, aberrant.

In error, mistaken, etc., tripping, floundering, etc.

Illusive, illusory, ideal, imaginary, fanciful, chimerical, visionary, shadowy, mock, futile.

Spurious, apocryphal, bogus, illegitimate, phoney, pseudo, bastard, meretricious, deceitful, sophisticated, adulterated.

Phrases: Wide of the mark; on the wrong scent; barking up the wrong tree; out of it; without a leg to stand upon.

496 MAXIM
Substantives: aphorism, apophthegm, dictum, saying, *mot*, adage, gnome, saw, proverb, wisecrack, sentence, precept, rule, formula, tag, code, motto, slogan, catchword, word, byword, moral, sentiment, phylactery, conclusion, reflection, thought, golden rule, axiom, theorem, scholium, lemma, truism.

Catechism, creed (484), profession of faith.

Adjectives: Aphoristic, gnomic, proverbial, phylacteric, axiomatic; hackneyed, trite.

Phrases: 'Wise saws and modern instances'; as the saying is or goes.

497 ABSURDITY
Substantives: absurdness, nonsense, folly, paradox, inconsistency, quibble, sophism (477), stultiloquy, stultiloquence, Irish bull, Irishism, Hibernicism, sciamachy, imbecility (499).

Jargon, gibberish, rigmarole, double-Dutch, fustian, rant, bombast, bathos, amphigouri, rhapsody, extravagance, rodomontade, romance; nonsense verse, limerick, clerihew.

Twaddle, claptrap, flapdoodle, bunkum, blah, fudge, rubbish, piffle, verbiage, trash, truism, stuff, balderdash, slipslop, *bavardage,* palaver, *baragouin,* moonshine, fiddlestick, wish-wash, platitude, cliché, flummery, inanity, fiddle-faddle, rot, tommy-rot, bosh, tosh, hot air, havers, blethers, tripe, bilge, bull, hooey, hokum, boloney.

Vagary, foolery, tomfoolery, mummery, monkey-trick, monkey-shine, dido, *boutade,* lark, escapade, ploy, rag.

Phrases: A cock-and-bull story; a mare's-nest; a wild-goose chase; talking through one's hat; 'a tale told by an idiot, full of sound and fury, signifying nothing'; clotted nonsense; arrant rot.

Adjectives: Absurd, nonsensical, foolish, senseless, preposterous (499), sophistical, inconsistent, extravagant, ridiculous, cock-and-bull, quibbling, trashy, washy, wishy-washy, twaddling, etc.; topsy-turvy, Gilbertian.

498 INTELLIGENCE
Substantives: capacity, nous, parts, talent, sagacity, sagaciousness, wit, mother-wit, *esprit*, gumption, comprehension, understanding, quick parts, grasp of intellect.

Acuteness, acumen, shrewdness, astuteness, arguteness, sharpness, aptness, aptitude, quickness, receptiveness, subtlety, archness, penetration, perspicacity, perspicaciousness, clearsightedness, discrimination, discernment, flair, refinement (850).

Head, brains, headpiece, a long head.

WISDOM
Substantives: sapience, sense, good sense, common sense, plain sense, horse-sense, reason, reasonableness, rationality, judgment, judiciousness, solidity, depth, profoundness, catholicity, breadth of view, enlarged views, reach or compass of thoughts.

Genius, inspiration, the fire of genius.

Wisdom in action, prudence, discretion, self-possession, aplomb (698), sobriety, tact, ballast.

Phrase: Discretion being the better part of valour.

Verbs: To be intelligent, wise, etc., to reason (476), to discern (441), discriminate (465), to penetrate, to see far into.

Phrases: To have all one's wits about one; to see as far through a brick wall as anybody.

Adjectives: Applied to persons: Intelligent, sagacious, receptive, quick, sharp, acute, fly, smart, shrewd, gumptious, canny, astute, sharp-sighted, quick-sighted, quick-eyed, keen, keen-eyed, keen-sighted, keen-witted, sharp-witted, quick-witted, needle-witted, penetrating, piercing, clear-sighted, perspicacious, discerning, discriminating, discriminative, clever (698), knowledgeable.

Wise, sage, sapient, sagacious, reasonable, rational, sound, commonsense, sane, sensible, judicious, judgmatic, enlightened, impartial, catholic, broad-minded, open-minded, unprejudiced, unbiased, unprepossessed, undazzled, unperplexed, judicial, impartial, fair, progressive.

Cool, cool-headed, long-headed, hard-headed, long-sighted, calculating, thoughtful, reflective, oracular, heaven-directed.

Prudent, discreet, sober, staid, deep, solid, considerate, provident, politic, diplomatic, tactful.

Applied to actions: Wise, sensible, reasonable, judicious, well-judged, well-advised, prudent, prudential, politic (646), expedient.

Phrases: Wise as a serpent; wise in one's generation; not born yesterday; up to snuff; no flies on him; wise as Solomon.

499 IMBECILITY

Substantives: incapacity, vacancy of mind, poverty of intellect, shallowness, dullness, stupidity, asininity, obtuseness, stolidity, hebetude, doltishness, muddleheadedness, vacuity, short-sightedness, incompetence.

Silliness, simplicity, childishness, puerility, babyhood; dotage, second childhood, anility, fatuity, idiocy, idiotism (503).

FOLLY

Substantives: unwisdom, absurdity, infatuation, irrationality, senselessness, foolishness, frivolity, inconsistency, lip-wisdom, conceit, vanity, irresponsibility, giddiness, extravagance, oddity, eccentricity (503), ridiculousness, desipience.

Act of folly (497), imprudence (699), rashness, fanaticism.

Phrases: A fool's paradise; apartments to let; one's wits going wool-gathering; the meanest capacity.

Verbs: To be imbecile, foolish, etc., to trifle, drivel, ramble, dote, *radoter*, blether, haver; to fool, to monkey, to footle.

Phrases: To play the fool; to play the giddy goat; to make an ass of oneself; to go on a fool's errand; to pursue a wild-goose chase; *battre la campagne*; Homer nods.

Adjectives: Applied to persons: Unintelligent, unintellectual, witless, reasonless, not bright, imbecile, shallow, *borné*, weak, soft, simple, sappy, spoony, weak-headed, weak-minded, feeble-minded, half-witted, short-witted, half-baked, not all there, deficient, wanting, shallow-pated, shallow-brained, dull, dumb, dense, crass, stupid, heavy, obtuse, stolid, doltish, asinine, addle-headed, dull-witted, blunt, dull-brained, dim-sighted, vacuous.

Childish, infantine, infantile, babyish, childlike, puerile, callow; anile.

Fatuous, idiotic, lack-brained, drivelling, blatant, brainless, blunt-witted, beef-witted, fat-witted, fat-headed, boneheaded, insulse, having

197

no head or brains, thick-skulled, ivory-skulled, blockish, Boeotian.

Foolish, silly, senseless, irrational, insensate, nonsensical, blunder-headed, chuckle-headed, puzzle-headed, muddle-headed, muddy-headed, undiscerning, unenlightened, unphilosophical; prejudiced, bigoted, purblind, narrow-minded, wrong-headed, tactless, crotchety, conceited, self-opinionated, pig-headed, mulish, unprogressive, one-ideaed, stick-in-the-mud, reactionary, blimpish, besot-ted, infatuated, unreasoning.

Wild, giddy, dizzy, thoughtless, eccentric, odd, extravagant, quixotic, light-headed, rantipole, high-flying, crack-brained, cracked, cranky, hare-brained, scatter-brained, scatter-pated, unballasted, ridiculous, frivolous, balmy (or barmy), daft (503).

Applied to actions: Foolish, unwise, injudicious, improper, imprudent, unreasonable, nonsensical, absurd, ridiculous, silly, stupid, asinine, ill-imagined, ill-advised, ill-judged, ill-devised, tactless, inconsistent, irra-tional, unphilosophical, extravagant, preposterous, egregious, footling, imprudent, indiscreet, improvident, impolitic, improper (645, 647).

Phrases: Dead from the neck up; concrete above the ears.

Without rhyme or reason; penny-wise and pound-foolish.

500 SAGE
Substantives: wise man, master-mind, thinker, *savant*, expert, lumi-nary, adept, authority, egghead.

Oracle, a shining light, *esprit fort,* intellectual, high-brow, pundit, academist, academician, philomath, schoolman, magi, a Solomon, Nestor, Solon, Socrates, a second Daniel.

Adjectives: Venerable, reverend, authoritative.

Phrases: 'A Daniel come to judg-ment'; the wise men of the East.

Ironically: Wiseacre, bigwig, know-all.

501 FOOL
Substantives: blockhead, bonehead, idiot, tom-fool, low-brow, simpleton, simp, sap, softy, sawney, witling, ass, donkey, goat, goose, ninny, dolt, booby, boob, noodle, muff, mug, muggins, juggins, owl, cuckoo, gowk, numskull, noddy, dumb-bell, gomeril, half-wit, imbecile, ninnyhammer, mutt, driveller, cretin, moron, natural, lackbrain, child, infant, baby, inno-cent, green-horn, zany, zombie, gaby.

Dunce, lout, loon, oaf, dullard, duf-fer, calf, colt, buzzard, block, stick, stock, clod-poll, clot-poll, clod-hopper, clod, lubber, bull-calf, bull-head, fat-head, thick-skull, dunder-head, addle-head, dizzard, hoddy-doddy, looby, Joe Soap, nincompoop, poop, put, *un sot à triple étage,* logger-head, sot, shallow-brain, jobbernowl, changeling, dotard, driveller, moon-calf, giddy-head, gobemouche, ran-tipole, muddler, stick-in-the-mud, old woman, April fool.

Phrases: One who is not likely to set the Thames on fire; one who did not invent gunpowder; one who is no con-jurer; *qui n'a pas inventé la poudre*; who could not say 'Bo' to a goose; one with his upper storey to let; no fool like an old fool.

Men of Gotham; men of Boeotia.

502 SANITY
Substantives: rationality; being in one's senses, in one's right mind, in one's sober senses; sobriety, lucidity, lucid interval, sound mind, *mens sana.*

Verbs: To be sane, etc., to retain one's senses, reason, etc.

To become sane, come to one's senses, sober down.

To render sane, bring to one's senses, to sober.

Adjectives: Sane, rational, reasonable,

compos, in one's sober senses, in one's right mind, sober-minded.

Phrase: In full possession of one's faculties.

Adverbs: Sanely, soberly, etc.

503 INSANITY

Substantives: lunacy, madness, unsoundness, derangement, psychosis, neurosis, alienation, aberration, schizophrenia, split personality, dementia, paranoia, mania, melancholia, hypochondria, calenture, frenzy, phrenitis, raving, monomania, megalomania, kleptomania, dipsomania, etc., disordered intellect, incoherence, wandering, delirium, hallucination, lycanthropy, eccentricity (499), dementation; Bedlam.

Phrases: The horrors; the jim-jams; pink spiders; snakes in the boots.

Verbs: To be or become insane, etc., to lose one's senses, wits, reason, faculties, etc., to run mad, run amuck, go off one's head, rave, dote, ramble, wander, drivel.

To render or drive mad; to madden, dementate, turn the brain, addle the wits, turn one's head, befool, infatuate, craze.

Phrases: *Battre la campagne; avoir le diable au corps.*

Adjectives: Insane, mad, lunatic, crazy, crazed, *non compos*, cracked, cranky, loco, touched, deficient, wanting, out of one's mind, off one's head or nut or onion, bereft of reason, unsettled in one's mind, unhinged, insensate, reasonless, beside oneself.

Demented, daft, dotty, potty, dippy, scatty, loopy, batty, bats, wacky, crackers, cuckoo, haywire, bughouse, bugs, nuts, possessed, maddened, moon-struck, mad-brained, maniac, maniacal, delirious, incoherent, rambling, doting, doited, gaga.

Wandering, frantic, phrenetic, paranoiac, schizophrenic, megalomaniacal, kleptomaniacal, etc., raving, corybantic, dithyrambic, rabid, pixillated, light-headed, giddy, vertiginous, wild, haggard, flighty, neurotic, distracted, distraught, hag-ridden, *écervelé, tête montée.*

Phrases: The head being turned; having a screw (or a tile) loose; far gone; stark staring mad; mad as a March hare; mad as a hatter; of unsound mind; up the pole; bats in the belfry; the devil being in one; dizzy as a goose; candidate for Bedlam; like one possessed.

The wits going wool-gathering or bird's-nesting.

504 MADMAN

Substantives: lunatic, maniac, bedlamite, energumen, raver, monomaniac, paranoiac, schizophrenic, nut, screwball, crack pot, madcap, megalomaniac, dipsomaniac, kleptomaniac, psychopath, hypochondriac, *malade imaginaire,* crank, maenad.

Section 6 – *Extension of Thought*

505 MEMORY

Substantives: remembrance, reminiscence, recognition, anamnesis, retention, retentiveness, readiness, tenacity.

Recurrence, recollection, retrospection, retrospect, flash-back, afterthought, hindsight.

Token of remembrance, reminder, memorial, memento, souvenir, keepsake, relic, reliquary, memorandum, aide-mémoire, remembrancer, prompter.

Things to be remembered, *memorabilia.*

Art of memory, artificial memory, *memoria technica,* mnemonics; Mnemosyne.

Phrases: The tablets of the memory; *l'esprit de l'escalier.*

199

Verbs: To remember, retain, mind, bear or keep in mind, have or carry in the memory, know by heart or by rote; recognize.

To be deeply impressed, live, remain, or dwell in the memory; to be stored up, bottled up, to sink in the mind, to rankle, etc.

To recollect, call to mind, bethink oneself, recall, call up, retrace, carry one's thoughts back, review, look back, rake up, brush up, think upon, call to remembrance, tax the memory.

To suggest, prompt, hint, recall to mind, put in mind, remind, whisper, call up, summon up, renew, commend to.

To say by heart, repeat by rote, say one's lesson, repeat as a parrot.

To commit to memory, get or learn by heart or rote, memorize, con, con over, repeat; to fix, imprint, impress, stamp, grave, engrave, store, treasure up, bottle up, embalm, enshrine, etc., in the memory; to load, store, stuff, or burden the memory with; to commemorate (883).

Phrase: To have at one's fingers' ends.

To jog or refresh the memory; to pull by the sleeve; to bring back to the memory; to keep the memory alive; to keep the wound green; to reopen old sores; to put in remembrance.

Adjectives: Remembering, etc., mindful, remembered, etc., fresh, green, unforgotten, present to the mind; living in, being in, or within one's memory; indelible, ineffaceable, green in remembrance, reminiscential, commemorative.

Adverbs: By heart, by rote, *memoriter*, without book; in memory of, in memoriam.

506 OBLIVION

Substantives: forgetfulness, amnesia, obliteration (552), a short memory; a lapse of memory; the memory failing, being in fault, or deserting one; the waters of Lethe, Nepenthe, *tabula rasa*.

Verbs: To forget, lose, unlearn, efface, expunge, blot out, etc. (552); discharge from the memory.

To slip, escape, fade, die away from the memory, to sink into oblivion.

Phrases: To cast behind one's back; to have a short memory; to put out of one's head; to apply the sponge; to think no more of; to consign to oblivion; to let bygones be bygones.

Adjectives: Forgotten, etc., lost, effaced, blotted out, obliterated, discharged, sponged out, buried or sunk in oblivion, out of mind, clean out of one's head or recollection, past recollection, unremembered.

Forgetful, oblivious, unmindful, mindless; Lethean.

507 EXPECTATION

Substantives: expectance, expectancy, anticipation, forestalling, foreseeing (510); reckoning, calculation.

Contemplation, prospect, look-out, outlook (121), perspective, horizon, vista, hope, trust (858), abeyance, waiting, suspense.

Phrase: The torments of Tantalus.

Verbs: To expect, look for, look out for, look forward to, anticipate, contemplate, flatter oneself, to dare to say, foresee (510), forestall, reckon upon, count upon, lay one's account to, to calculate upon, rely upon, build upon, make sure of, prepare oneself for, keep in view, not to wonder at.

To wait, tarry, lie in wait, watch for, abide, to bide one's time.

To hold out, raise, or excite expectation, to bid fair, to promise, to augur, etc. (511).

Phrases: To count one's chickens before they are hatched.

To have in store for; to have a rod in pickle.

Adjectives: Expectant, expecting, etc., prepared for, gaping for, ready for, agog, anxious, ardent, eager, breathless, sanguine.

Expected, anticipated, foreseen, etc., long expected, impending, prospective, in prospect.

Adverbs: With breathless expectation, on tenterhooks.

Phrases: On the tiptoe of expectation; on edge; looming in the distance; the wish father to the thought; we shall see; *nous verrons*.

508 INEXPECTATION

Substantives: non-expectation; blow, shock, surprise (870).

False or vain expectation, miscalculation.

Phrase: A bolt from the blue.

Verbs: Not to expect, not to look for, etc., to be taken by surprise, to start, come upon, to fall upon, not to bargain for, to miscalculate.

To be unexpected, etc., to crop up, pop up, to come unawares, suddenly, abruptly, like a thunderbolt, creep upon, burst upon, bounce upon; surprise, take aback, stun, stagger, startle.

Phrases: To reckon without one's host; to trust to a broken reed.

To drop from the clouds; you could have knocked me down with a feather.

Adjectives: Non-expectant, surprised, taken by surprise, unwarned, unaware, startled, etc., taken aback.

Unexpected, abrupt, unanticipated, unlooked-for, unhoped-for, unforeseen, beyond expectation, sudden, contrary to or against expectation, unannounced, unheralded; backhanded.

Adverbs: Suddenly, abruptly, unexpectedly, plump, pop, *à l'improviste*, unawares, without notice or warning (113).

Phrases: Like a thief in the night; who would have thought it?

509 DISAPPOINTMENT

Substantives: vain expectation, blighted hope, surprise, astonishment (870); balk, after-clap, miscalculation.

Phrase: 'There's many a slip 'twixt cup and lip.'

Verbs: To be disappointed, etc., to miscalculate; to look blank, to look blue, to look or stand aghast.

To disappoint, balk, bilk, tantalize, let down, play false, stand up, dumbfound, dash one's hope (859), sell.

Adjectives: Disappointed, disconcerted, aghast, blue, out of one's reckoning.

Happening, contrary to or against expectation.

Phrase: Parturiunt montes, nascetur ridiculus mus.

510 FORESIGHT

Substantives: prospiscience, prescience, foreknowledge, forethought, forecast, prevision, prognosis, precognition, second sight, clairvoyance.

Anticipation, foretaste, prenotion, presentiment, foregone conclusion, providence, discretion, prudence, sagacity.

Announcement, prospectus, programme, policy (626).

Verbs: To foresee, foreknow, forejudge, forecast, predict (511), anticipate, look forwards or beyond; look, peep, or pry into the future.

Phrases: To keep a sharp look out for; to have an eye to the future; *respice finem*.

Adjectives: Foreseeing, etc., prescient, weather-wise, far-sighted, far-seeing; provident, prudent, rational, sagacious, perspicacious.

511 PREDICTION

Substantives: announcement, prognosis, forecast, weird, prophecy, vaticination, mantology, prognostication, astrology, horoscopy, haruspicy, auguration, auspices, bodement, omination, augury, foreboding, abodement, aboding, horoscope, nativity, genethliacs, fortune-telling, crystal-gazing, palmistry, chiromancy, oneiromancy, sortilege, *sortes Virgilianae,* soothsaying, ominousness, divination (992).

Place of prediction, adytum, tripod.
Verbs: To predict, prognosticate, prophesy, vaticinate, presage, augur, bode, forebode, divine, foretell, croak, soothsay, auspicate, to cast a horoscope or nativity, tell one's fortune, read one's hand.

To foretoken, betoken, prefigure, portend, foreshadow, foreshow, usher in, herald, signify, premise, announce, point to, admonish, warn, forewarn, advise.
Adjectives: Predicting, etc., predictive, prophetic, fatidical, vaticinal, oracular, Sibylline.

Ominous, portentous, augural, auspicious, monitory, premonitory, significant of, pregnant with, weatherwise, bodeful, big with fate.
Phrase: 'Coming events cast their shadows before.'

512 OMEN
Substantives: portent, presage, prognostic, augury, auspice, sign, forerunner, precursor (64), harbinger, herald, monition, warning, avant-courier, pilot-balloon, handwriting on the wall, rise and fall of the barometer, a bird of ill omen, a sign of the times, gathering clouds.
Phrases: Touch wood! *absit omen.*

513 ORACLE
Substantives: prophet, seer, soothsayer, haruspex, fortune-teller, spaewife, palmist, gipsy, wizard, witch, geomancer, Sibyl, Python, Pythoness, *Pythia,* Pythian oracle, Delphic oracle, Old Moore, Zadkiel, Mother Shipton, Witch of Endor, Sphinx, Tiresias, Cassandra, Oedipus, Sibylline leaves.

Section 7 – Creative Thought

514 SUPPOSITION
Substantives: conjecture, surmise, presurmise, speculation, inkling, guess, guess-work, shot, divination, conceit; assumption, postulation, hypothesis, presupposition, postulate, *postulatum,* presumption, theory, thesis; suggestion, proposition, motion, proposal, allusion, insinuation, innuendo.
Phrases: A rough guess; a lucky shot.
Verbs: To suppose, conjecture, surmise, guess, divine, theorize, give a guess, make a shot, hazard a conjecture, throw out a conjecture, etc., presuppose, fancy, wis, take it, dare to say, take it into one's head, assume, believe, postulate, posit, presume, presurmise.

To suggest, hint, insinuate, put forth, propound, propose, start, allude to, prompt, put a case, move, make a motion.

To suggest, hint, insinuate, put forth, propound, propose, start, allude to, prompt, put a case, move, make a motion.

To suggest, itself, occur to one, come into one's head; to run in the head; to haunt (505).
Phrases: To put it into one's head; 'thereby hangs a tale.'
Adjectives: Supposing, etc., supposed, supposititious, suppositious, suppositive, reputed, putative, suggestive, allusive, conjectural, presumptive, hypothetical, theoretical, warranted, authorized, mooted, conjecturable, supposable.
Adverbs: If, if so be, an, gin, maybe, perhaps, on the supposition, in the event of, as if, *ex hypothesi, quasi.*

515 IMAGINATION
Substantives: fancy, conception, ide-

ality, idealism, inspiration, afflatus, verve, dreaming, somnambulism, frenzy, ecstasy, excogitation, reverie, *Schwärmerei,* trance, imagery, vision; Pegasus.

Invention, inventiveness, originality, fertility, romanticism, utopianism, castle-building.

Conceit, maggot, figment, coinage, fiction, romance, novel (594), myth, Arabian Nights, fairyland, faerie, the man in the moon, dream, day-dream, pipe-dream, nightmare, vapour, chimera, phantom, phantasy, fantasia, whim, whimsy, vagary, rhapsody, extravaganza, air-drawn dagger, bugbear, men in buckram, castle in the air, air-built castle, castle in Spain, will-o'-the-wisp, *ignis fatuus,* jack-o'-lantern, Utopia, Atlantis, Shangri-la, land of Prester John, millennium, golden age, *fata morgana* (443).

A visionary, romancer, rhapsodist, high-flyer, enthusiast, idealist, energumen, dreamer, seer, fanatic, knight-errant, Don Quixote.

Phrases: Flight of fancy; fumes of fancy; fine frenzy; thick-coming fancies; coinage of the brain; the mind's eye; a stretch of imagination; 'such stuff as dreams are made on.'

Verbs: To imagine, fancy, conceive, ideate, idealize, realize, objectify; fancy or picture to oneself; create, originate, devise, invent, coin, fabricate, make up, mint, improvise, excogitate, conjure up.

Phrases: To take into one's head; to figure to oneself; to strain or crack one's invention; to strike out something new; to give a loose to the fancy; to give the reins to the imagination; to set one's wits to work; to rack or cudgel one's brains.

Adjectives: Imagining, imagined, etc.; ideal, unreal, unsubstantial, imaginary, *in nubibus,* fabulous, fictitious, legendary, mythological, chimerical, *ben trovato,* fanciful, faerie, fairylike, air-drawn, air-built, original, fantastic, fantastical, whimsical, high-flown.

Imaginative, inventive, creative, fertile, romantic, flighty, extravagant, high-flown, fanatic, enthusiastic, Utopian, Quixotic.

II

Section 1 – Nature of Ideas Communicated

516 MEANING

Substantives: signification, sense, import, purport, significance, drift, gist, acceptation, acceptance, bearing, interpretation (522), reading, tenor, allusion, spirit, colouring, expression.

Literal meaning, literality, obvious meaning, grammatical sense, first blush, *prima facie* meaning; after-acceptation.

Equivalent meaning, synonym, synonymity.

Thing signified: Matter, subject, substance, pith, marrow, argument, text; sum and substance.

Verbs: To mean, signify, express, import, purport, convey, breathe, imply, bespeak, speak of, tell of, touch on, bear a sense, involve, declare (527), insinuate, allude to, point to, indicate, drive at; to come to the point, give vent to; to stand for.

To take, understand, receive, or accept in a particular sense.

Adjectives: Meaning, etc., significant, significative, significatory, literal, expressive, explicit, suggestive, allusive; pithy, pointed, epigrammatic, telling, striking, full of meaning, pregnant with meaning.

517 UNMEANINGNESS

Substantives: empty sound, a dead

letter, scrabble, scribble; inexpressive-
ness, vagueness (519).

Nonsense, stuff, balderdash (497),
jabber, gibberish, palaver, rigmarole,
twaddle, tosh, bosh, bull, rubbish, rot,
empty babble, empty sound, verbiage,
nugae, truism, moonshine, inanity.
Verbs: To mean nothing, to be
unmeaning, etc.; to scribble, jabber,
gibber, babble.
Adjectives: Unmeaning, meaningless, nonsensical, void of meaning, of
sense, etc., senseless, not significant,
undefined, tacit, not expressed.

Inexpressible, indefinable, undefinable, unmeant, unconceived.

Trashy, trumpery, twaddling, etc.
Phrases: *Vox et praeterea nihil*; 'a tale
told by an idiot, full of sound and fury,
signifying nothing'; 'sounding brass
and tinkling cymbal.'
Adverb: Tacitly.

518 INTELLIGIBILITY
Substantives: clearness, lucidity, perspicuity, explicitness, distinctness,
plain speaking, expressiveness, legibil-
ity, visibility (446); precision (494).

Intelligence, comprehension, understanding, learning (539).
Phrases: A word to the wise; *verbum
sapienti*.
Verbs: To be intelligible, etc.

To render intelligible, etc., to simplify, clear up, throw light upon.

To understand, comprehend, follow, take, take in, catch, catch on to,
twig, dig, get the hang of, get wise to,
grasp, sense, make out, get, collect;
master, tumble to, rumble.
Phrases: It tells its own tale; he who
runs may read; to stand to reason; to
speak for itself.

To come to an understanding; to see
with half an eye.
Adjectives: Intelligible, clear, lucid,
understandable, explicit, expressive,
significant, express, distinct, precise,
definite, well-defined, perspicuous,

transpicuous, striking, plain, obvious,
manifest, palpable, glaring, transparent, above-board, unambiguous,
ummistakable, legible, open, positive,
expressive (516), unconfused, unequivocal, pronounced, graphic, readable.
Phrases: Clear as day; clear as crystal;
clear as noonday; not to be mistaken;
plain to the meanest capacity; plain as a
pikestaff; in plain English.

519 UNINTELLIGIBILITY
Substantives: incomprehensibility,
inconceivability, darkness (421),
imperspicuity, obscurity, confusion,
perplexity, imbroglio, indistinctness,
mistiness, indefiniteness, vagueness,
ambiguity, looseness, uncertainty,
mysteriousness (526), paradox, inex-
plicability, incommunicability, spinosity.

Jargon, gibberish, rigmarole,
rodomontade, etc. (497); paradox,
riddle, enigma, puzzle (533).

Double or High Dutch, Greek, Heb-
rew, etc.
Verbs: To be unintelligible, etc., to
pass comprehension.

To render unintelligible, etc., to perplex, confuse, confound, bewilder,
darken, moither (475).

Not to understand, etc., to lose,
miss, etc., to lose the clue.
Phrases: Not to know what to make
of; not to be able to make either head
or tail of; to be all at sea; to play at cross
purposes; to beat about the bush.
Adjectives: Unintelligible, incognizable, inapprehensible, incomprehensible, inconceivable, unimaginable,
unknowable, inexpressible, undefinable, incommunicable, above or past
or beyond comprehension, inexplicable, illegible, undecipherable, inscrutable, unfathomable, beyond one's
depth, paradoxical, insoluble, impenetrable.

Obscure, dark, confused, indistinct,

indefinite, misty, nebulous, intricate, undefined, ill-defined, indeterminate, perplexed, loose, vague, ambiguous, disconnected, incoherent, unaccountable, puzzling, enigmatical, hieroglyphic, mysterious, mystic, mystical, at cross purposes.

Hidden, recondite, abstruse, crabbed, transcendental, far-fetched, *in nubibus,* searchless, unconceived, unimagined.

Phrases: Greek to one; without rhyme or reason; *obscurum per obscurius; lucus a non lucendo.*

520 EQUIVOCALNESS
Substantives: double meaning, quibble, equivoque, equivocation, *double-entendre,* paragram, anagram, amphibology, amphiboly, ambiloquy, prevarication, white lie, mental reservation, tergiversation, slip of the tongue,
lapsus linguae, a pun, play on words, homonym.

Having a doubtful meaning, ambiguity (475), homonymy.

Having a false meaning (544), *suggestio falsi.*

Verbs: To be equivocal, etc., to have two senses, etc., to equivocate, prevaricate, tergiversate, palter to the understanding, to pun.

Adjectives: Equivocal, ambiguous, amphibolous, amphibological, homonymous, double-tongued, double-edged, left-handed, equivocatory, paltering.

Adverb: Over the left.

521 METAPHOR
Substantives: figure, metonymy, trope, catachresis, synecdoche, figure of speech, figurativeness, image, imagery, metalepsis, type (22), symbol, symbolism (550), troplogy.

Personification, prosopopaeia, allegory, apologue, parable.

Implication, inference, allusion, application, adumbration, hidden meaning.

Allegorist, tropist, symbolist.

Verbs: To employ metaphore, etc., to personify, allegorize, adumbrate, shadow forth, imply, understand, apply, allude to.

Adjectives: Metaphorical, figurative, catachrestical, typical, tropical, parabolic, allegorical, allusive, symbolic (550), symbolistic, implied, inferential, implicit, understood.

Adverbs: So to speak, as it were.

Phrases: Where more is meant than meets the ear; in a manner of speaking; *façon de parler;* in a Pickwickian sense.

522 INTERPRETATION
Substantives: exegesis, explanation, meaning (516), explication, expounding, exposition, rendition, reddition.

Translation, version, rendering, construction, reading, spelling, restoration, metaphrase, literal translation, free translation, paraphrase.

Comment, commentary, inference, illustration, exemplification, definition, *éclaircissement,* elucidation, crib, cab, gloss, glossary, annotation, *scholium,* marginalia, note, clue, key, sidelight, master-key (631), rationale, denouement, solution, answer (462), object lesson.

Palaeography, dictionary, glossology, etc. (562), semantics, semasiology, oneirocritics, oneirocriticism, hermeneutics.

Verbs: To interpret, expound, explain, clear up, construe, translate, render, English, do into, turn into, transfuse the sense of.

To read, spell, make out, decipher, decode, unfold, disentangle, elicit the meaning of, make sense of, find the key of, unriddle, unravel, solve, resolve (480), restore.

To elucidate, throw light upon, illustrate, exemplify, expound, annotate,

comment upon, define, unfold.
Adjectives: Explanatory, expository, explicatory, explicative, exegetical, hermeneutic, constructive, inferential.

Paraphrastic, metaphrastic; literal, plain, simple, strict, synonymous; polyglot.
Adverbs: That is to say, *id est* (or i.e), *videlicet* (or viz.), in other words, in plain words, simply, in plain English.

Literally, word for word, verbatim, *au pied de la lettre,* strictly speaking (494).

523 MISINTERPRETATION
Substantives: misapprehension, misunderstanding, misacceptation, misconstruction, misspelling, misapplication, catachresis, mistake (495), cross-reading, cross-purpose.

Misrepresentation, perversion, falsification, misquotation, garbling, exaggeration (549), false colouring, abuse of terms, parody, travesty, misstatement, etc. (544).
Verbs: To misinterpret, misapprehend, misunderstand, misconceive, misdeem, misspell, mistranslate, misconstrue, misapply, mistake (495).

To misstate, etc. (544); to pervert, falsify, distort, misrepresent, torture, travesty; to stretch, strain, wring, or wrest the sense or meaning; to put a bad or false construction on; to misquote, garble, belie, explain away.
Phrases: To give a false colouring to; to be or play at cross-purposes; to put a false construction on.
Adjectives: Misinterpreted, etc., untranslated, untranslatable.
Phrase: *Traduttori traditori.*

524 INTERPRETER
Substantives: expositor, expounder, exponent, demonstrator, scholiast, commentator, annotator, metaphrast, paraphrast, palaeographer, spokesman, speaker, mouthpiece, guide, dragoman, cicerone, conductor, courier, showman, barker, oneirocritic; Oedipus (513).

Section 2 – Modes of Communication.

525 MANIFESTATION
Substantives: expression, showing, etc., disclosure (529), presentation, indication, exposition, demonstration, exhibition, production, display, showing off.

An exhibit, an exhibitor.

Openness, frankness, plain speaking (543), publication, publicity (531).
Verbs: To manifest, make manifest, etc., show, express, indicate, point out, bring forth, bring forward, trot out, set forth, exhibit, expose, produce, present, bring into view, set before one, hold up to view, set before one's eyes, show up, shadow forth, bring to light, display, demonstrate, unroll, unveil, unmask, disclose (529).

To elicit, educe, draw out, bring out, unearth, disinter.

To be manifested, etc., to appear, transpire, come to light (446), to come out, to crop up, get wind.
Phrases: Hold up the mirror; draw, lift up, raise, or remove the curtain; show one's true colours; throw off the mask.

To speak for itself; to stand to reason; to stare one in the face; to tell its own tale; to give vent to.
Adjectives: Manifest, clear, apparent, evident, visible (446), prominent, in the foreground, salient, signal, striking, notable, conspicuous, palpable, patent, overt, flagrant, stark, glaring, open.

Manifested, shown, expressed, etc., disclosed (529), frank, capable of being shown, producible.

Phrases: As plain as a pikestaff; as plain as the nose on one's face.

Adverbs: Openly, before one's eyes, face to face, above-board, in open court, in open daylight, in the light of day, in the open streets, on the stage, on show.

526 LATENCY

Substantives: secrecy, secretness, privacy, invisibility (447), mystery, occultness, darkness, reticence, silence (585), closeness, reserve, inexpression; a sealed book, a dark horse, an undercurrent.

Retirement, delitescence, seclusion (893).

Phrases: More is meant than meets the ear (or eye).

Verbs: To be latent, etc., to lurk, underlie, escape observation, smoulder; to keep back, reserve, suppress, keep close, etc. (528).

To render latent (528).

Phrases: Hold one's tongue; hold one's peace; leave in the dark; to keep one's own counsel; to keep mum; to seal the lips; not to breathe a syllable about.

Adjectives: Latent, lurking, secret, close, unapparent, unknown (491), dark, delitescent, in the background, occult, cryptic, snug, private, privy, *in petto*, anagogic, sequestered, dormant, smouldering.

Inconspicuous, unperceived, invisible (447), unseen, unwitnessed, impenetrable, unespied, unsuspected.

Untold, unsaid, unwritten, unpublished, unmentioned, unbreathed, untalked-of, unsung, unpronounced, unpromulgated, unreported, unexposed, unproclaimed, unexpressed, not expressed, tacit, implicit, implied, undeveloped, embryonic, unsolved, unexplained, undiscovered, untraced, untracked, unexplored.

Phrase: No news being good news.

Adverbs: Secretly, etc., *sub silentio*.

Phrases: In the background; behind one's back; under the table; behind the scenes; between the lines.

527 INFORMATION

Substantives: gen, pukka gen, low-down, enlightenment, communication, intimation, notice, notification, enunciation, announcement, annunciation, statement, specification, report, advice, monition, mention, acquaintance (490), acquainting, etc., outpouring, intercommunication, communicativeness.

An informant, teller, tipster, spy, nose, nark, stool-pigeon, intelligencer, correspondent, reporter, messenger, newsmonger, gossip (532).

Hint, suggestion (514), wrinkle, tip, pointer, insinuation, innuendo, wink, glance, leer, nod, shrug, gesture, whisper, implication, cue, office, by-play, eye-opener.

Phrases: A word to the wise; *verbum sapienti*; a broad hint; a straight tip; a stage whisper.

Verbs: To inform, acquaint, tell, mention, express, intimate, impart, communicate, apprise, post, make known, notify, signify to, let one know, advise, state, specify, give notice, announce, annunciate, publish, report, set forth, bring word, send word, leave word, write word, declare, certify, depose, pronounce, explain, undeceive, enlighten, put wise, set right, open the eyes of, convey the knowledge of, give an account of; instruct (537).

To hint, give an inkling of; give, throw out, or drop a hint, insinuate, allude to, glance at, touch on, make allusion to, to wink, to tip the wink, glance, leer, nod, shrug, give the cue, give the office, give the tip, wave, whisper, suggest, prompt, whisper in the ear, give one to understand.

To be informed, etc., of, made

acquainted with; to hear of, get a line on, understand.

To come to one's ear, to come to one's knowledge, to reach one's ears.

Adjectives: Informed, etc., of, made acquainted with, in the know, hep; undeceived.

Reported, made known (531), bruited.

Expressive, significant, pregnant with meaning, etc. (516), declaratory, enunciative, nuncupatory, expository, communicatory, communicative, insinuative.

Adverbs: Expressively, significantly, etc.

Phrases: A little bird told me; *on dit*; from information received.

528 CONCEALMENT

Substantives: hiding, occultation, etc., secrecy, stealth, stealthiness, slyness (702), disguise, incognito, privacy, masquerade, camouflage, smoke screen, mystery, mystification, freemasonry, reservation, suppression, secretiveness, reticence, reserve, uncommunicativeness; secret path.

A mask, visor, ambush, etc. (530), enigma, etc. (533).

Phrases: A needle in a bundle of hay; a nigger in the woodpile; a skeleton in the cupboard; a family skeleton.

Verbs: To conceal, hide, put out of sight, secrete, cover, envelop, screen, cloak, veil, shroud, enshroud, shade, muffle, mask, disguise, camouflage, ensconce, eclipse.

To keep from, lock up, bury, cache, sink, suppress, stifle, withhold, reserve, burke, hush up, keep snug or close or dark.

To keep in ignorance, blind, hoodwink, mystify, pose, puzzle, perplex, embarrass, flummox, bewilder, bamboozle, etc. (545).

To be concealed, etc., to lurk, skulk, smoulder, lie hid, lie in ambush, lie perdu, lie low, lie doggo, sneak, slink, prowl, gumshoe, retire, steal into, steal along.

To conceal oneself, put on a veil, etc. (530), masquerade.

Phrases: To draw or close the curtain; not breathe a word about; let it go no farther; keep it under your hat.

To play at bo-peep; to play at hide-and-seek; to hide under a bushel; to throw dust in the eyes.

Adjectives: Concealed, hid, hidden, etc., secret, clandestine, perdu, close, private, privy, furtive, surreptitious, stealthy, feline, underhand, sly, sneaking, skulking, hole-and-corner, undivulged, unrevealed, undisclosed, incognito, incommunicado.

Mysterious, mystic, mystical, dark, enigmatical, problematical, anagogical, paradoxical, occult, cryptic, gnostic, cabbalistic, esoteric, recondite, abstruse, unexplained, impenetrable, undiscoverable, inexplicable, unknowable, bewildering, baffling.

Covered, closed, shrouded, veiled, masked, screened, shaded, disguised, under cover, under a cloud, veil, etc., in a fog, haze, mist, etc., under an eclipse; inviolate, inviolable, confidential, under wraps.

Reserved, uncommunicative, secretive, buttoned up, taciturn (585).

Phrase: Close as wax.

Adverbs: Secretly, clandestinely, incognito, privily, in secret, *in camera,* with closed doors, *à huis clos, à la dérobée,* under the rose, *sub rosa,* privately, in private, aside, on the sly, *sub silentio,* behind one's back, under the counter, behind the curtain, behind the scenes.

Confidentially, between ourselves, between you and me, *entre nous, inter nos,* in strict confidence, on the strict q.t., off the record, it must go no farther.

Phrases: Like a thief in the night; under the seal of secrecy, of confession; between you and me and the gate-post;

'tell it not in Gath'; nobody any the wiser.

529 DISCLOSURE

Substantives: revealment, revelation, disinterment, exposition, show-down, exposure, effusion, outpouring.

Acknowledgment, avowal, confession; an *exposé,* denouement.

A telltale, talebearer, informer, stool-pigeon, nark, nose.

Verbs: To disclose, open, lay open, divulge, reveal, bewray, discover, unfold, let drop, let fall, let out, let on, spill, lay open, acknowledge, allow, concede, grant, admit, own, own up, confess, avow, unseal, unveil, unmask, uncover, unkennel, unearth (525).

To blab, peach, squeal, let out, let fall, let on, betray, give away, tell tales, speak out, blurt out, vent, give vent to, come out with, round on, split; publish (531).

To make no secret of, to disabuse, unbeguile, undeceive, set right, correct.

To be disclosed, revealed, etc., to come out, to transpire, to ooze out, to leak out, to creep out, to get wind, to come to light.

Phrases: To let into the secret; to let the cat out of the bag; to spill the beans; to unburden or disburden one's mind or conscience; to open one's mind; to unbosom oneself; to make a clean breast of it; to come clean; to give the show away; to own the soft impeachment; to tell tales out of school; to show one's hand; to turn Queen's (or King's or State's) evidence.

Murder will out.

Adjectives: Disclosed, revealed, divulged, laid open, etc., unriddled, etc.; outspoken, etc. (543).

Open, public, exoteric.

Interjection: Out with it!

530 AMBUSH

Substantives: hiding-place, hide, retreat, cover, lurking-hole, secret place, cubby-hole, recess, closet, priest's hole, crypt, cache, ambuscade, *guet-apens, adytum,* dungeon, oubliette.

A mask, veil, visor (or vizor), eyeshade, blinkers, cloak, screen, hoarding, curtain, shade, cover, disguise, masquerade dress, domino.

Verbs: To lie in ambush, lurk, couch, lie in wait for, lay or set a trap for (545).

531 PUBLICATION

Substantives: announcement, notification, enunciation, annunciation, advertisement, promulgation, circulation, propagation, edition, redaction, proclamation, hue and cry, the Press, journalism, wireless, radio, broadcasting, television.

Publicity, notoriety, currency, cry, bruit, rumour, fame, report (532), *on dit,* flagrancy, limelight, town-talk, small talk, table-talk, puffery, ballyhoo, *réclame,* the light of day, daylight.

Notice, notification, manifesto, propaganda, advertisement, blurb, circular, placard, bill, *affiche,* poster, newspaper, journal, daily, periodical, weekly, gazette; personal column, agony column.

Publisher (593), publicity agent, advertising agent: tout, barker, town crier.

Phrases: An open secret; *un secret de Polichinelle.*

Verbs: To publish, make known, announce, notify, annunciate, gazette, set forth, give forth, give out, broach, voice, ·utter, advertise, circularize, placard, *afficher,* circulate, propagate, spread, spread abroad, broadcast, edit, redact, rumour, diffuse, disseminate, celebrate, blaze about; blaze or noise abroad; bruit, buzz, bandy, hawk about, trumpet, proclaim, herald, puff, boost, splash, plug, boom, give tongue, raise a cry, raise a hue and cry, tell the world, popularize; bring, lay or drag before the public, give currency to, ventilate, bring out.

Phrases: To proclaim from the house-tops; to publish in the gazette; to send round the crier; with beat of drum.

To be published, etc., to become public, to go forth, get abroad, get about, get wind, take air, get afloat, acquire currency, get in the papers, spread, go the rounds, buzz about, blow about.

To pass from mouth to mouth; to spread like wildfire.

Adjectives: Published, etc., made public, in circulation, exoteric, rumoured, rife, current, afloat, notorious, flagrant, whispered, buzzed about, in every one's mouth, reported, trumpet-tongued; encyclical.

Phrases: As the story runs; to all whom it may concern.

Interjections: Oyez! O yes! notice is hereby given!

532 NEWS

Substantives: piece of information, intelligence, tidings, budget of news, word, advice, message, communication, errand, embassy, dispatch, bulletin.

Report, story, scoop, beat, rumour, canard, hearsay, *on dit,* fame, talk, gossip, tittle-tattle, *ouï-dire,* scandal, buzz, bruit, *chronique scandaleuse,* town talk.

Letter, postcard, airgraph, telegram, wire, cable, wireless message, radiogram.

Newsmonger, scandalmonger, scaremonger, alarmist, talebearer, tattler, gossip (527), local correspondent, special correspondent, reporter (590).

533 SECRET

Substantives: *arcanum, penetralia,* profound secret, mystery, crux, problem, enigma, teaser, poser, riddle, puzzle, conundrum, charade, rebus, logogriph, anagram, acrostic, cross-word, cipher, code, cryptogram, monogram,

paradox, maze, labyrinth, perplexity, chaos (528), the Hercynian wood; *terra incognita.*

Iron curtain, bamboo curtain, censorship, counter-intelligence.

Phrases: The secrets of the prison-house; a sealed book.

Adjectives: Secret, top secret, hush-hush, undercover, clandestine (528).

534 MESSENGER

Substantives: envoy, nuncio, inter-nuncio, intermediary, go-between, herald, ambassador, legate, emissary, *corps diplomatique.*

Marshal, crier, trumpeter, pursuivant, *parlementaire,* courier, runner, postman, telegraph-boy, errand-boy, bell-boy, bell-hop, Mercury, Hermes, Iris, Ariel, carrier pigeon.

Narrator, etc., talebearer, spy, secretservice agent, scout.

Mail, post (592), post office, telegraph, telephone, wireless, radio; grapevine, bush telegraph.

535 AFFIRMATION

Substantives: statement, predication, assertion, declaration, word, averment, asseveration, protestation, swearing, adjuration, protest, profession, deposition, avouchment, affirmance, assurance, allegation, acknowledgment, avowal, confession, confession of faith, oath, affidavit; vote, voice.

Remark, observation, position, thesis, proposition, saying, dictum, theorem, sentence.

Positiveness (474), dogmatism, *ipse dixit.*

A dogmatist, doctrinaire.

Phrase: The big bow-wow style.

Verbs: To assert, make an assertion, etc., say, affirm, predicate, enunciate, state, declare, profess, aver, avouch, put forth, advance, express, allege, pose, propose, propound, broach, set forth, maintain, contend, pronounce, pretend, pass an opinion, etc.; to re-assert, reaffirm, reiterate; quoth, *dixit, dixi.*

To vouch, assure, vow, swear, take oath, depose, depone, recognize, avow, acknowledge, own, confess, announce, hazard or venture an opinion.

To dogmatize, lay down, lay down the law; to call heaven to witness, protest, certify, warrant, posit, go bail for.

Phrases: I doubt not; I warrant you; I'll engage; take my word for it; depend upon it; I'll be bound; I am sure; I have no doubt; sure enough; to be sure; what I have said, I have said; faith! that's flat.

To swear till one is black in the face; to swear by all the saints in the calendar; to call heaven to witness.

Adjectives: Asserting, etc., dogmatic, positive, emphatic, declaratory, affirmative, predicable, pronounced, unretracted.

Positive, broad, round, express, explicit, pointed, marked, definitive, distinct, decided, formal, solemn, categorical, peremptory, absolute, flat, pronounced.

Adverbs: *Ex cathedra,* positively, avowedly, confessedly, broadly, roundly, etc.; ay, yes, indeed; by Jove, by George, by James, by jingo.

536 NEGATION

Substantives: abnegation, denial, denegation, disavowal, disclaimer, abjuration, contradiction, *démenti,* contravention, recusation, retraction, retractation, recantation, renunciation, palinode, recusancy, protest.

Qualification, modification (469); rejection (610); refusal (764).

Verbs: To deny, disown, contradict, negative, gainsay, contravene, dis-claim, withdraw, recant, disavow, retract, revoke, abjure, negate.

Phrases: To deny flatly; eat one's

words; go back from, or upon one's word.

To dispute, impugn, controvert, confute (479), question, call in ques-tion, give the lie to, rebut, belie.

Adjectives: Denying, etc., denied, etc., negative, contradictory, recusant.

Adverbs: No, nay, not, nohow, not at all, by no means (489), far from it, anything but, on the contrary, quite the reverse.

537 TEACHING

Substantives: instruction, direction, guidance, tuition, culture, inculcation, inoculation, indoctrination.

Education, co-education, initiation, preparation, practice, training, up-bringing, schooling, discipline, exer-cise, drill, exercitation, breaking in, taming, drilling, etc., preachment, persuasion, edification, proselytism, propagandism.

A lesson, lecture, prolusion, prelec-tion, exercise, task; curriculum, course.

Rudiments, ABC, elements, three Rs, grammar, text-book, vademecum, school-book (593).

Physical training, PT, gymnastics, callisthenics.

Verbs: To teach, instruct, enlighten, edify, inculcate, indoctrinate, instil, imbue, inoculate, infuse, impregnate, graft, infix, engraft, implant, sow the seeds of, infiltrate, give an idea of, cram, coach, put up to.

To explain, expound, lecture, hold forth, read a lecture or sermon, give a lesson, preach; sermonize, moralize, point a moral.

To educate, train, discipline, school, form, ground, tutor, prepare, qualify prime, drill, exercise, practise, bring up, rear, nurture, dry-nurse, breed, break in, tame, domesticate, condition.

To direct, guide, initiate, put in the way of, proselytize, bring round to an opinion, bring over, win over, brain-

211

wash, re-educate, persuade, convince, convict, set right, enlighten, give one new ideas, put one up to, bring home to.

Phrases: To teach the young idea how to shoot; to sharpen the wits; to enlarge the mind.

Adjectives: Teaching, etc., taught, etc., educational.

Didactic, academic, doctrinal, disciplinal, disciplinary, instructive, scholastic, persuasive.

538 MISTEACHING

Substantives: misdirection, misleading misinformation, misguidance, perversion, false teaching, sophistry.

Indocility, incapacity, misintelligence, dullness, backwardness.

Verbs: To misinform, misteach, mislead, misdirect, misguide, miscorrect, pervert, lead into error, bewilder, mystify (528), throw off the scent; to unteach.

Phrases: To teach one's grandmother; *obscurum per obscurius*; the blind leading the blind.

Adjectives: Misteaching, etc., unedifying.

539 LEARNING

Substantives: acquisition of knowledge, acquirement, attainment, scholarship, erudition, instruction, study, etc. (490).

Docility (602), aptitude (698), aptness to be taught, teachableness, persuasibility, capacity.

Verbs: To learn; to acquire, gain, catch, receive, imbibe, pick up, gather, collect, glean, etc., knowledge or information.

To hear, overhear, catch hold of, take in, fish up, drink in, run away with an idea, to make oneself acquainted with, master, read, spell, turn over the leaves, pore over, run through, peruse, study, grind, cram, mug, swot, go to school; to get up a subject; to serve one's time or apprenticeship.

To be taught, etc.

Adjectives: Docile, apt, teachable, persuasible, studious, industrious, scholastic, scholarly.

Phrase: To burn the midnight oil.

540 TEACHER

Substantives: instructor, apostle, master, director, tutor, preceptor, institutor, mentor, adviser, monitor, counsellor, expositor, dry-nurse, trainer, coach, crammer, grinder, governor, bear-leader, disciplinarian, martinet, guide, cicerone, pioneer, governess, duenna.

Orator, speaker, mouthpiece (582).

Professor, lecturer, reader, demonstrator, praelector, prolocutor, schoolmaster, schoolmistress, schoolmarm, usher, pedagogue, monitor, pupil-teacher, dominie, dame, moonshee; missionary, propagandist.

Adjectives: Tutorial, professorial.

541 LEARNER

Substantives: scholar, student, alumnus, disciple, pupil, *élève,* schoolboy, schoolgirl, beginner, tyro (or tiro), abecedarian, novice, neophyte, chela, inceptor, probationer, apprentice, tenderfoot, freshman, bejan (or bejant), undergraduate, undergraduette, sophomore.

Proselyte, concert, catechumen, sectator; class, form.

Pupilage, pupilarity, pupilship, tutelage, apprenticeship, novitiate, leading-strings, matriculation.

Phrases: Freshwater sailor; *in statu pupillari.*

542 SCHOOL

Substantives: day school, boarding school, public school, council school, national school, board school, private school, preparatory school, elementary school, primary school, secondary school, senior school, grammar school, high school, academy, university, Alma Mater, university extension, correspondence school, college, seminary, lyceum, polytechnic, nursery, institute, institution, palaestra, gymnasium, class, form, standard; nursery school, infant school, kindergarten, crèche; reformatory, Borstal, approved school.

Horn-book, rudiments, vademecum, abecedary, manual, primer, school-book, text-book.

Professorship, lectureship, readership, chair; pulpit, ambo, theatre, amphitheatre, forum, stage, rostrum, platform.

Adjectives: Scholastic, academic, collegiate.

543 VERACITY

Substantives: truthfulness, truth, sincerity, frankness, straightforwardness, ingenuousness, candour, honesty, fidelity, bona fides, openness, unreservedness, bluntness, plainness, plain speaking, plain dealing; simplicity, bonhomie, naïveté, artlessness (703), love of truth.

A plain-dealer, truth-teller, man of his word.

Verbs: To speak the truth, speak one's mind, open out, think aloud.

Phrases: Tell the truth and shame the devil; to deal faithfully with; to show oneself in one's true colours.

Adjectives: Truthful, true, veracious, uncompromising, veridical, veridicous, sincere, candid, frank, open, outspoken, unreserved, free-spoken, open-hearted, honest, simple, simple-hearted, ingenuous, blunt, plain-spoken, true-blue, straightforward, straight, fair, fair-minded, single-minded, artless, guileless, natural, unaffected, simple-minded, undisguised, unfeigned, unflattering, warts and all.

Adverbs: Truly, etc. (494), above-board, broadly.

Phrases: In plain English: without mincing the matter: honour bright: honest Injun; bona fide; *sans phrase.*

544 FALSENESS

Substantives: falsehood, untruthfulness, untruth (546), falsity, mendacity, falsification, perversion of truth, perjury, fabrication, romance, forgery, prevarication, equivocation, shuffling, evasion, fencing, duplicity, double-dealing, unfairness, dishonesty, fraud, misrepresentation, *suggestio falsi, suppressio veri,* Punic faith, giving the go-by, disguise, disguisement, irony, understatement.

Insincerity, dissimulation, dissembling, deceit (545), shiftiness, hypocrisy, cant, humbug, gammon, jesuitry, pharisaism, mental reservation, lip-service, simulation, acting, sham, malingering, pretending, pretence, crocodile tears, false colouring, art, artfulness (702).

Deceiver (548).

Verbs: To be false, etc., to play false, speak falsely, lie, fib, tell a lie or untruth, etc. (546), to mistake, misreport, misrepresent, misquote, belie, falsify, prevaricate, equivocate, quibble, palter, shuffle, fence, hedge, understate, mince the truth.

To forswear, swear false, perjure oneself, bear false witness.

To garble, gloss over, disguise, pervert, distort, twist, colour, varnish, cook, doctor, embroider, fiddle, wangle, gerrymander, put a false colouring or construction upon (523).

To invent, make up, fabricate, concoct, trump up, forge, fake, romance.

To dissemble, dissimulate, feign, pretend, assume, act or play a part, simulate, pass off for, counterfeit, sham, malinger, make believe, cant, put on.

Phrases: To play the hypocrite; to give the go-by; to play fast and loose; to play a double game; to blow hot and cold; to lie like a conjurer; sham Abraham; to look as if butter would not melt in one's mouth; to sail under false colours; to ring false.

Adjectives: False, dishonest, faithless, deceitful, mendacious, unveracious, truthless, trothless, unfair, uncandid, disingenuous, shady, shifty, underhand, underhanded, hollow, insincere, canting, hypocritical, jesuitical, sanctimonious, pharisaical, tartuffian, double, double-tongued, double-faced, smooth-spoken, smooth-tongued, plausible, mealymouthed, snide.

Artful, insidious, sly, designing, diplomatic, Machiavellian.

Untrue, unfounded, fictitious, invented, made up, *ben trovato*, forged, falsified, counterfeit, spurious, factitious, self-styled, bastard, sham, bogus, phoney, mock, pseudo, disguised, simulated, artificial, colourable, catchpenny, meretricious, tinsel, Brummagem, postiche, pinchbeck, illusory, elusory, supposititious, surreptitious, ironical, apocryphal.

Phrase: All is not gold that glitters.
Adverbs: Falsely, etc., slyly, stealthily, underhand.

545 DECEPTION

Substantives: falseness (544), fraud, deceit, imposition, artifice, juggle, juggling, sleight of hand, legerdemain, conjuration, hocus-pocus, jockeyship, trickery, coggery, fraudulence, imposture, *supercherie,* chicane, chicanery, covin, cozenage, circumvention, ingannation, prestidigitation, subreption, collusion, complicity, guile, gullery, hanky-panky, jiggery-pokery, rannygazoo.

Quackery, charlatanism, charlatanry, empiricism, humbug, hokum, eye-wash, hypocrisy, gammon, flapdoodle, bunkum, *blague,* bluff, mummery, borrowed plumes.

Stratagem, trick, cheat, wile, artifice, cross, deception, take-in, camouflage, make-believe, ruse, manœuvre, finesse, hoax, canard, hum, kid, chouse, bubble, fetch, catch, spoof, swindle, plant, sell, hocus, dodge, bite, forgery, counterfeit, sham, fake, fakement, rig, delusion, stalking-horse.

Snare, trap, pitfall, decoy, gin, spring, noose, hook, bait, net, meshes, mouse-trap, trap-door, false bottom, ambush, ambuscade (530), masked battery, mine, mystery-ship, Q-boat.
Phrases: A wolf in sheep's clothing; a whited (or painted) sepulchre; a pious fraud; a man of straw.
Verbs: To deceive, mislead, cheat, impose upon, practise upon, circumvent, play upon, put upon, bluff, dupe, mystify, blind, hoodwink, best, outreach, trick, hoax, kid, gammon, spoof, hocus, bamboozle, hornswoggle, juggle, trepan, nick, entrap, beguile, lure, inveigle, decoy, lime, ensnare, entangle, lay a snare for, trip up, stuff the go-by.

To defraud, fiddle, take in, jockey, do, do brown, cozen, diddle, have, have on, chouse, welsh, bilk, bite, pluck, swindle, victimize, outwit, over-reach, nobble, palm upon, work off upon, foist upon, fob off, balk, trump up.
Phrases: To throw dust in the eyes; to play a trick upon; to pull one's leg; to try it on; to cog the dice; to mark the cards; to live by one's wits; to play a part; to throw a tub to the whale.

Adjectives: Deceiving, cheating, etc.; hypocritical, Pecksniffian; deceived, duped, done, had, etc., led astray.

Deptive, deceitful, deceptious, illusive, illusory, delusory, prestigious, elusive, bogus, counterfeit, insidious, *ad captandum, ben trovato.*
Phrases: *Fronti nulla fides; timeo Danaos et dona ferentes.*

546 UNTRUTH
Substantives: falsehood, lie, falsity, fiction, fabrication, fib, whopper, bouncer, cracker, crammer, tarradiddle, story, fable, novel, romance, flam, bull, gammon, flim-flam, *guetapens,* white lie, pious, fraud, canard, nursery tale, fairy-tale, tall story.

Falsification, perjury, forgery, false swearing, misstatement, misrepresentation, inexactitude.

Pretence, pretext, subterfuge, irony, evasion, blind, disguise, plea, claptrap, shuffle, make-believe, shift, mask, cloak, visor, veil, masquerade, gloss, cobweb.

Phrases: A pack of lies; a tissue of falsehoods; a cock-and-bull story; a trumped-up story; all my eye and Betty Martin; a mare's-nest.

547 DUPE
Substantives: gull (486), gudgeon, gobemouche, cully, victim, sucker, flat, greenhorn, puppet, cat's-paw, April fool, simple Simon, Joe Soap, pushover, soft mark.

Phrases: To be the goat; to hold the baby; to carry the can; *qui vult decipi, decipiatur.*

548 DECEIVER
Substantives: liar, hypocrite, tale-teller, shuffler, shammer, dissembler, serpent, cockatrice; Janus, Tartuffe, Pecksniff, Joseph Surface, Cagliostro.

Pretender, impostor, knave, cheat, rogue, trickster, swindler, spiv, adventurer, humbug, sharper, jockey, welcher, leg, blackleg, rook, shark, confidence man, con man, confidence trickster, decoy, decoy-duck, stool-pigeon, gipsy.

Quack, charlatan, mountebank, empiric, quacksalver, *saltimbanco,* medicaster, *soi-disant.*

Actor, player, mummer, tumbler, posture-master, jack-pudding; illusionist, conjurer (994).

Phrases: A wolf in sheep's clothing; a snake in the grass; one who lives by his wits.

549 EXAGGERATION
Substantives: hyperbole, overstatement, stretch, strain, colouring, bounce, flourish, vagary, bombast (884), yarn, figure of speech, flight of fancy, *façon de parler,* extravagance, rhodomontade, heroics, sensationalism, highfalutin; tale of Baron Munchausen, traveller's tale.

Phrases: A storm in a teacup; much ado about nothing.

Verbs: To exaggerate, amplify, magnify, heighten, overcharge, overstate, overcolour, overlay, overdo, strain, stretch, bounce, flourish, embroider; to hyperbolize, aggravate, to make the most of.

Phrases: To make a song about; spin a long yarn; draw the long bow; deal in the marvellous; out-herod Herod; lay it on thick; pile it on; make a mountain of a molehill.

Adjectives: Exaggerated, etc., hyperbolical, turgid, tumid, fabulous, extravagant, magniloquent, bombastic, *outré,* highly coloured, high-flying, high-flown, high-falutin, sensational, blood-and-thunder, lurid.

Phrases: All his geese are swans; much cry and little wool.

Section 3 –
Means of Communicating Ideas

550 INDICATION
Substantives: symbolization, symbolism, typification, notation, connotation, prefigurement, representation (554), exposition, notice (527), trace (551), name (564).

A sign, symbol, index, placard,

exponent, indicator, pointer, mark, token, symptom, type, emblem, figure, cipher, code, device, epigraph, motto, posy.

Science of signs, sematology, semeiology, semeiotics.

Lineament, feature, line, stroke, dash, trait, characteristic, idiosyncracy, score, stripe, streak, scratch, tick, dot, point, notch, nick, asterisk, red letter, rubric, italics, print, stamp, impress, imprint, sublineation, underlining, display, jotting.

For identification: Badge, criterion, check, countercheck, countersign, stub, counterfoil, duplicate, tally, label, book-plate, *ex-libris,* ticket, billet, card, visiting-card, *carte de visite,* identity-card, passport, bill, bill-head, facia, sign-board, witness, voucher, coupon, trade mark, hall-mark, signature, hand-writing, sign manual, monogram, seal, sigil, signet, chop, autograph, autography, superscription, endorsement, *visé,* title, heading, caption, docket, watchword, password, shibboleth, *mot du guet,* catchword; fingerprint.

Insignia: Banner, banneret, flag, colours, bunting, streamer, standard, eagle, ensign, pennon, pennant, pendant, burgee, jack, ancient, labarum, oriflamme; gonfalon, banderole, Union Jack, Royal Standard, Stars and Stripes, Tricolour, etc.; crest, arms, coat of arms, armorial bearings, shield, scutcheon, escutcheon, uniform, livery, cockade, epaulet, chevron, cordon, totem.

Indication of locality: Beacon, cairn, post, staff, flagstaff, hand, pointer, vane, guide-post, finger-post, signpost, landmark, sea-mark, lighthouse, light-ship, pole-star, lodestar, cynosure, guide, address, direction, rocket, blue-light, watch-fire, blaze.

Indication of an event: Signal, nod, wink, glance, leer, shrug, beck, cue, gesture, gesticulation, deaf-and-dumb alphabet, by-play, dumb-show, pantomime, touch, nudge, freemasonry, telegraph, heliograph, semaphore.

Indication of time: Time-signal, clock (114), alarm-clock, hooter, blower, buzzer, siren; tattoo, reveille, last post, taps.

Indication of danger: Alarm, alarum, alarm-bell, alert, fog-signal, detonator, red light, tocsin, fire-hooter, maroon, S O S, beat of drum, fiery cross, sound of trumpet, war-cry, war-whoop, slogan.

Indication of safety: all-clear, green light.

Verbs: To indicate, point out, be the sign, etc., of, denote, betoken, connote, connotate, represent, stand for, typify, symbolize, shadow forth, argue, bear the impress of, witness, attest, testify.

To put an indication, mark, etc.; to note, mark, stamp, impress, earmark, brand, label, ticket, docket, endorse, sign, countersign; put, append, or affix a seal or signature; dot, jot down, book, score, dash, trace, chalk, underline, italicize, print, imprint, engrave, stereotype, rubricate, star, obelize, initial.

To make a sign, signal, etc., signalize; give or hang out a signal; give notice, gesticulate, beckon, beck, nod, wink, nudge, tip the wink; give the cue, tip, or office; wave, unfurl, hoist, or hang out a banner, flag, etc., show one's colours, give or sound an alarm, beat the drum, sound the trumpets, raise a cry, etc.

Adjectives: Indicating, etc., indicatory, indicative, sematic, semeiological, denotative, representative, typical, typic, symbolic, symbolical, diacritical, connotative, pathognomic, symptomatic, exponential, emblematic, pantomimic, attesting; armorial, totemistic.

Indicated, etc., typified, impressed, etc.

Capable of being denoted, denotable, indelible.
Phrases: *Ecce signum*; in token of.

551 RECORD
Substantives: trace, mark, tradition, vestige, footstep, footmark, footprint, footfall, wake, track, trail, slot, spoor, pug, scent.

Monument, relic, remains, trophy, hatchment, achievement, obelisk, monolith, pillar, stele, column, slab, tablet, medal, testimonial, memorial.

Note, minute, register, registry, index, inventory, catalogue, list (86), memorandum, jotting, document, account, score, tally, invoice, docket, voucher, protocol, inscription.

Paper, parchment, scroll, instrument, deed, indenture, debenture, roll, archive, schedule, file, dossier, cartulary, table, *procès verbal,* affidavit, certificate, attestation, entry, diploma, protest, round-robin, roster, rota, muster-roll, muster-book, notebook, commonplace-book, *adversaria,* portfolio.

Chronicle, annals, gazette, Hansard, history (594), newspaper, magazine, gazetteer, blue-book, almanac, calendar, ephemeris, diary, log, journal, day-book, ledger.

Registration, tabulation, enrolment, booking.
Verbs: To record, note, register, chronicle, calendar, make an entry of, enter, book, take a note of, post, enrol, jot down, take down, mark, sign, etc. (550), tabulate, catalogue, file, index, commemorate (883).
Adjectives: Registered, etc.
Adverbs: Under one's hand and seal, on record.

552 OBLITERATION
Substantives: erasure, rasure, cancel, cancellation, circumduction, deletion.
Verbs: To efface, obliterate, erase, raze, expunge, cancel, delete, blot out, take out, rub out, scrach out, strike out, elide, wipe out, wash out, black out, write off, render illegible.

To be effaced, etc., to leave no trace.
Phrases: To draw the pen through; to apply the sponge.
Adjectives: Obliterated, effaced, etc., printless, leaving no trace.

Unrecorded, unattested, unregistered, intestate.
Interjections: *Dele*; out with it!

553 RECORDER
Substantives: notary, clerk, registrar, registrary, register, prothonotary, secretary, stenographer, amanuensis, scribe, remembrancer, journalist, historian, historiographer, annalist, chronicler, biographer, book-keeper.

Recordership, secretaryship, secretariat, clerkship.

554 REPRESENTATION
Substantives: delineation, representment, reproduction, depictment, personification.

Art, the fine arts, the graphic arts, design, designing, illustration, imitation (19), copy (21), portraiture, iconography, photography.

A picture, drawing, tracing, photograph.

An image, likeness, icon, portrait, effigy, facsimile, autotype, imagery, figure, puppet, dummy, lay figure, figurehead, doll, manikin, *mannequin* mammet, marionette, *fantoccini* (599), statue (557), waxwork.

Hieroglyphic, hieroglyph, inscription, diagram, monogram, draught (or draft), outline, scheme, *schema,* schedule.

Map, plan, chart, ground-plan, projection, elevation, ichnography, atlas; cartography, chorography.
Verbs: To represent, present, depict, portray, photograph, delineate, design, figure, adumbrate, shadow forth, copy, draft, mould, diagrammatize, schematize, map.

217

To imitate, impersonate, personate, personify, act, take off, hit off, figure as; to paint (556); carve (557); engrave (558).

Adjectives: Representing, etc.; artistic, imitative, representative, illustrative, figurative, hieroglyphic, hieroglyphical, diagrammatic, schematic.

555 MISREPRESENTATION

Substantives: distortion (243), caricature, burlesque (856), a bad likeness, daub, scratch, sign-painting, anamorphosis; misprint, *erratum*.

Verbs: To misrepresent, distort, falsify, caricature, wrest the sense (or meaning).

556 PAINTING

Substantives: depicting, drawing; perspective, composition, treatment.

Drawing in pencil, crayon, pastel, chalk, water-colour, etc.

Painting in oils, in distemper, in gouache, in fresco; encaustic painting, enamel painting, scene-painting; wash (428), body-colour, impasto.

A picture, drawing, painting, sketch, illustration, scratch, *graffito*, outline, tableau, cartoon, fresco, illumination; pencil, pen-and-ink, etc., drawing; oil, etc., painting; photograph; silver print; POP, bromide, gaslight, bromoil, platinotype, carbon print; autochrome, Kodachrome; daguerreotype, calotype; mosaic, tapestry, etc., picture-gallery.

Portrait, portraiture, likeness, full-length, etc., miniature, kitcat, shade, profile, silhouette, still, snapshot.

Landscape, seascape, nocturne, view, still-life, *genre,* panorama, diorama.

Pre-Raphaelitism, impressionism, etc. (559).

Verbs: To paint, depict, portray, limn, draw, sketch, pencil, scratch, scrawl, block in, rough in, dash off, chalk out, shadow forth, adumbrate, outline, illustrate, illuminate; to take a portrait, take a likeness, to photograph, snap, pan.

Phrases: *Fecit, pinxit, delineavit.*

Adjectives: Painted, etc.; pictorial, graphic, picturesque, Giottesque, Raphaelesque, Turneresque, etc.; like, similar (17).

557 SCULPTURE

Substantives: insculpture, carving, modelling.

A statue, statuary, statuette, figure, figurine, model, bust, image, high relief, low relief, alto-rivievo, mezzo-rilievo, basso-rilievo, bas-relief, cast, marble, bronze, intaglio, anaglyph; medallion, cameo.

Verbs: To sculpture, sculp, carve, cut, chisel, model, mould, cast.

Adjectives: Sculptured, etc., sculptural, sculpturesque, anaglyphic, ceroplastic, ceramic.

558 ENGRAVING

Substantives: etching, wood-engraving, process-engraving, xylography, chalcography, cerography, glyptography; poker-work.

A print, engraving, impression, plate, cut, wood-cut, steel-cut, linocut, vignette.

An etching, dry-point, stipple, roulette; copper-plate, mezzotint, aquatint, lithography, chromolithograph, chromo, photo-lithograph, photogravure, anastatic-printing, collotype, electrotype, stereotype.

Matrix, flong.

Verbs: To engrave, etch, lithograph, print, etc.

559 ARTIST

Substantives: painter, limner, draughtsman, black-and-white artist, cartoonist, caricaturist, drawer, sketcher, pavement artist, screever, designer, engraver, copyist, photographer.

Academician; historical, landscape, portrait, miniature, scene, sign, etc., painter; an Apelles.

Primitive, Pre-Raphaelite, old master, quattrocentist, cinquecentist, impressionist, post-impressionist, futurist, vorticist, cubist, surrealist, Dadaist, pointillist.

A sculptor, carver, modeller, goldsmith, silversmith, *figuriste*; a Phidias, Praxiteles, Royal Academician, RA.

Implements of art: pen, pencil, brush, charcoal, chalk, pastel, crayon; paint (428); stump, graver, style, burin; canvas, easel, palette, maulstick, palette-knife; studio, *atelier*.

560 LANGUAGE
Substantives: tongue, speech, lingo, vernacular, mother-tongue, native tongue, standard English, King's (or Queen's) English, the genius of a language.

Dialect, local dialect, class dialect, provincialism, vulgarism, colloquialism, Americanism, Scotticism, Cockney speech, brogue, patois, patter, slang, cant, argot, Anglic, Basic English, broken English, pidgin English, lingua franca.

Universal languages: Esperanto, Volapük, Ido, Interglossa.

Philology, etymology (562), linguistics, glossology, dialectology, phonetics.

Literature, letters, polite literature, belles-lettres, the muses, humanities, the republic of letters, dead languages, classics, *literae humaniores*.

Scholarship (490), linguist, scholar (492), writer (593), glossographer.
Verbs: To express by words, to couch in terms, to clothe in language.
Adjectives: Literary, belletristic, linguistic, dialectal, vernacular, colloquial, slang, current, polyglot, pantomimic.
Adverbs: In plain terms, in common parlance, in household words.

561 LETTER
Substantives: alphabet, ABC, abecedary, spelling-book, horn-book, criss-cross-row; character (591), writing (590), hieroglyph, hieroglyphic; consonant, vowel, diphthong, triphthong; mute, liquid, labial, palatal, dental, guttural; spelling, orthography, phonetic spelling, misspelling; spelling-bee.

Syllable, monosyllable, dissyllable, trisyllable, polysyllable; anagram.
Verbs: To speel, spell out.
Adjectives: Literal, alphabetical, abecedarian, orthographic; syllabic, disyllabic, etc.

562 WORD
Substantives: term, vocable, terminology, part of speech (567), root, etymon.

Word similarly pronounced, homonym, homophone, paronym.

A dictionary, vocabulary, lexicon, index, polyglot, glossary, thesaurus, concordance, onomasticon, gradus; lexicography, lexicographer.

Derivation, etymology, glossology.
Adjectives: Verbal, literal, titular, nominal, etymological, terminological.

Similarly derived, conjugate, paronymous.
Adverbs: Nominally, etc., *verbatim*, word for word, in so many words, literally, *sic, totidem verbis, ipsissimis verbis, literatim*.

563 NEOLOGY
Substantives: neologism, slang, cant, byword, hard word, jaw-breaker, dog Latin, monkish Latin, loan word, vogue word, nonce word, Gallicism.

A pun, play upon words, paronomasia, *jeu de mots, calembour,* palindrome, conundrum, acrostic, anagram (533).

Dialect (560).

Neologian, neologist.

219

Verbs: To neologize, archaize, pun.
Phrase: To coin or mint words.
Adjectives: Neological, neologistic, paronomastic.

564 NOMENCLATURE
Substantives: nomination, naming, nuncupation.

A name, appellation, designation, appellative, denomination, term, expression, noun, byword, moniker, epithet, style, title, prenomen, forename, Christian name, baptismal name, given name, cognomen, agnomen, patronymic, surname, family name.

Synonym, namesake; euphemism, antonomasia, onomatopoeia.

Quotation, citation, chapter and verse.
Verbs: To name, call, term, denominate, designate, style, clepe, entitle, dub, christen, baptize, characterize, specify, label (550).

To be called, etc., to take the name of, pass under the name of; to quote, cite.
Phrases: To call a spade a spade; to rejoice in the name of.
Adjectives: Named, called, etc., hight, yclept, known as; nuncupatory, nuncupative, cognominal, titular, nominal.

Literal, verbal, discriminative.

565 MISNOMER
Substantives: missaying, malaprop, malapropism, antiphrasis, nickname, sobriquet, byname, assumed name or title, alias, *nom de guerre, nom de plume,* pen-name, pseudonym, pet name, euphemism.

So-and-so, what's-his-name, thingummy, thingumbob, thingumajig, dingus, *je ne sais quoi.*

A Mrs Malaprop.
Phrase: *Lucus a non lucendo.*
Verbs: To misname, missay, miscall, misterm, nickname.

To assume a name.
Adjectives: Misnamed, etc., malapropian, pseudonymous, *soi-disant,* self-called, self-styled, so-called.

Nameless, anonymous, without a name, having no name, innominate, unnamed.

566 PHRASE
Substantives: expression, phraseology, paraphrase, periphrasis, circumlocution (573), set phrase, round terms; mode or turn of expression; idiom, wording, *façon de parler,* mannerism, plain terms, plain English.

Sentence, paragraph, motto.

Figure, trope, metaphore (521), wisecrack, proverb (496).
Verbs: To express, phrase, put; couch, clothe in words, give words to; to word.
Adjectives: Expressed, etc., couched in, phraseological, idiomatic, paraphrastic, periphrastic, circumlocutory (573), proverbial.
Phrases: As the saying is; in good set terms; *sans phrase.*

567 GRAMMAR
Substantives: accidence, syntax, parsing, analysis, praxis, punctuation, conjugation, declension, inflexion, case, voice, person, number; philology (560), parts of speech.
Phrase: *Jus et norma loquendi.*
Verbs: To parse, analyse, conjugate, decline, inflect, punctuate.
Adjectives: Grammatical, syntactic, inflexional.

568 SOLECISM
Substantives: bad or false grammar, slip of the pen or tongue, bull, howler, floater, clanger, *lapsus linguae,* barbarism, vulgarism; dog Latin.
Verbs: To use bad or faulty grammar, to solecize, commit a solecism.
Phrases: To murder the king's English; to break Priscian's head.

Adjectives: Ungrammatical, barbarous, slipshod, incorrect, faulty, inaccurate.

569 STYLE
Substantives: diction, phraseology, wording, turn of expression, idiom, manner, strain, composition, authorship; stylist.
Adjectives: Stylistic, idiomatic, mannered.
Phrases: Command of language; a ready pen; *le style, c'est l'homme même.*

570 PERSPICUITY
Substantives: lucidity, lucidness, clearness, clarity, perspicacity, plain speaking, intelligibility (518).
Adjectives: Perspicuous, clear (525), lucid, intelligible, plain, transparent, explicit.

571 OBSCURITY
Substantives: ambiguity (520), unintelligibility (519), involution, involvedness, vagueness.
Adjectives: Obscure, confused, crabbed, ambiguous, vague, unintelligible, etc., involved, wiredrawn, tortuous.

572 CONCISENESS
Substantives: brevity, terseness, compression (195), condensation, concision, closeness, laconism, portmanteau word, telegraphese, pithiness, succinctness, quaintness, stiffness, ellipsis, ellipse, syncope.
Abridgment, epitome (596).
Verbs: To be concise, etc., to condense, compress, abridge, abbreviate, cut short, curtail, abstract.
Phrase: To cut the cackle and come to the horses.
Adjectives: Concise, brief, crisp, curt, short, terse, laconic, sententious, gnomic, snappy, pithy, nervous, pregnant, succinct, *guindé,* stiff, compact, summary, compendious (596), close,

cramped, elliptical, telegraphic, epigrammatic, lapidary.
Adverbs: Concisely, briefly, etc., in a word, to the point, in short.
Phrases: The long and short of it; *multum in parvo*; it comes to this; for shortness' sake; to make a long story short; to put it in a nutshell.

573 DIFFUSENESS
Substantives: prolixity, verbosity, macrology, pleonasm, tautology, copiousness, exuberance, laxity, looseness, verbiage, flow, flow of words, fluency, *copia verborum*, loquacity (584), redundancy, redundance, digression, amplification, *longueur*, padding, circumlocution, ambages, periphrasis, officialese, commercialese, gobbledygook, episode, expletive.
Verbs: To be diffuse, etc., to expatiate, enlarge, launch out, dilate, expand, pad out, spin out, run on, amplify, swell out, inflate, dwell on, harp on, descant, digress, ramble, maunder, rant.
Phrases: To beat about the bush; to spin a long yarn; to make a long story of.
Adjectives: Diffuse, wordy, verbose, prolix, copious, exuberant, flowing, fluent, bombastic, lengthy, long-winded, talkative (584), prosy, spun out, long-spun, loose, lax, slovenly, washy, slipslop, sloppy, frothy, flatulent, windy, digressive, discursive, excursive, tripping, rambling, ambagious, pleonastic, redundant, periphrastic, episodic, circumlocutory, roundabout.
Minute, detailed, particular, circumstantial.
Adverbs: In detail, at great length, *in extenso*, about it and about, *currente calamo, usque ad nauseam.*

574 VIGOUR
Substantives: energy, power, force,

221

spirit, point, vim, snap, punch, ginger, *élan,* pep, go, raciness, liveliness, fire, glow, verve, piquancy, pungency, spice, boldness, gravity, warmth, sententiousness, elevation, loftiness, sublimity, eloquence, individuality, distinction, emphasis, virility.

Phrase: 'Thoughts that glow and words that burn.'

Adjectives: Vigorous, energetic, powerful, strong, forcible, nervous, spirited, vivid, virile, expressive, lively, glowing, sparkling, racy, bold, slashing, incisive, trenchant, snappy, mordant, poignant, piquant, pungent, spicy, meaty, pithy, juicy, pointed, antithetical, sententious, emphatic, athletic, distinguished, original, individual, lofty, elevated, sublime, Miltonic, eloquent.

575 FEEBLENESS
Substantives: baldness, tameness, meagreness, coldness, frigidity, poverty, puerility, childishness, dullness, dryness, jejuneness, monotony.

Adjectives: Feeble, bald, dry, flat, insipid, tame, meagre, invertebrate, weak, mealy-mouthed, wishy-washy, wersh, banal, uninteresting, jejune, vapid, cold, frigid, poor, dull (843), languid, anaemic, prosy, prosaic, pedestrian, platitudinous, conventional, mechanical, decadent, trashy, namby-pamby (866), puerile, childish, emasculate.

576 PLAINNESS
Substantives: simplicity, homeliness, chasteness, chastity, neatness, monotony, severity.

Adjectives: Simple, unornamented, unvarnished, straightforward, artless, unaffected, downright, plain, unadorned, unvaried, monotonous, severe, chaste, blunt, homespun.

577 ORNAMENT
Substantives: floridness, floridity, flamboyance, richness, opulence, turgidity, tumidity, pomposity, inflation, altiloquence, spreadeagleism, pretension, fustian, affectation, euphuism, gongorism, mannerism, metaphor, preciosity, inversion, figurativeness, sesquipedalianism, *sesquipedalia verba,* rant, bombast, frothiness; flowers of speech, high-sounding words, well-rounded periods, purple patches.

A phrase-monger, euphuist.

Verbs: To ornament, overcharge, overlay with ornament, lard or garnish with metaphors, lay the colours on thick, round a period, mouth.

Adjectives: Ornamented, etc., ornate, florid, flamboyant, rich, opulent, golden-mouthed, figurative, metaphorical, pedantic, affected, pretentious, falsetto, euphuistic, Della Cruscan, pompous, fustian, high-sounding, mouthy, inflated, high-falutin (or high-faluting), bombastic, stilted, mannered, high-flowing, frothy, flowery, luscious, turgid, tumid, swelling, declamatory, rhapsodic, rhetorical, orotund, sententious, grandiose, grandiloquent, magniloquent, altiloquent, sesquipedalian, Johnsonian, ponderous.

Adverb: *Ore rotundo.*

578 ELEGANCE
Substantives: grace, ease, naturalness, purity, concinnity, readiness, euphony; a purist.

Phrases: A ready pen; flowing periods; *curiosa felicitas.*

Adjectives: Elegant, graceful, Attic, Ciceronian, classical, natural, easy, felicitous, unaffected, unlaboured, chaste, pure, correct, flowing, mellifluous, euphonious, rhythmical, puristic, well-expressed, neatly put.

Phrases: To round a period; 'to point a moral and adorn a tale.'

579 INELEGANCE
Substantives: stiffness, uncouthness,

barbarism, archaism, rudeness, crudeness, bluntness, brusquerie, ruggedness, abruptness, artificiality, cacophony.

Phrases: Words that dislocate the jaw, that break the teeth.

Verbs: To be inelegant, etc.

Phrase: To smell of the lamp.

Adjectives: Inelegant, ungraceful, stiff, forced, laboured, clumsy, contorted, tortuous, harsh, cramped, rude, rugged, dislocated, crude, crabbed, uncouth, barbarous, archaic, archaistic, affected (577), artificial, abrupt, blunt, brusque, incondite.

580 VOICE

Substantives: vocality, vocalization, utterance, cry, strain, articulate sound, prolation, articulation, enunciation, delivery, vocalism, pronunciation, orthoepy, euphony.

Cadence, accent, accentuation, emphasis, stress, tone, intonation, exclamation, ejaculation, vociferation, ventriloquism, polyphonism.

A ventriloquist, polyphonist.

Phonetics, phonology; voice-production.

Verbs: To utter, breathe, cry, exclaim, shout, ejaculate, vociferate; raise, lift, or strain the voice or lungs; to vocalize, prolate, articulate, enunciate, pronounce, accentuate, aspirate, deliver, mouth, rap out, speak out, speak up.

Phrase: To whisper in the ear.

Adjectives: Vocal, oral, phonetic, articulate.

Silvery, mellow, soft (413).

581 APHONY

Substantives: obmutescence, absence or want of voice, dumbness, muteness, mutism, speechlessness, aphasia, hoarseness, raucity; silence (585).

A dummy, a mute, deaf-mute.

Verbs: To render mute, to muzzle, muffle, suppress, smother, gag (585); to whisper (405).

Phrases: To stick in the throat; to close one's lips; to shut up.

Adjectives: Aphonous, dumb, speechless, mute, tongueless, muzzled, tongue-tied, inarticulate, inaudible, unspoken, unsaid, mum, mumchance, lips close or sealed, wordless; raucous, hoase, husky, sepulchral.

Phrases: Mute as a fish; hoarse as a raven; with bated breath; *sotto voce*; with the finger on the lips; mum's the word.

582 SPEECH

Substantives: locution, talk, parlance, verbal intercourse, oral communication, word of mouth, palaver, prattle, effusion, narrative (594), tale, story, yarn, oration, recitation, delivery, say, harangue, formal speech, speechifying, sermon, homily, discourse (998), lecture, curtain lecture, pi-jaw, address, tirade, pep-talk, screed; preamble, peroration; soliloquy (589).

Oratory, elocution, rhetoric, declamation, eloquence, gift of the gab, *copia verborum,* grandiloquence, magniloquence.

A speaker, spokesman, prolocutor, mouthpiece, lecturer, orator, stump-orator, speechifier; a Cicero, a Demosthenes.

Verbs: To speak, break silence, say, tell, utter, pronounce (580), open one's lips, give tongue, hold forth, make or deliver a speech, sheechify, harangue, talk, discourse, declaim, stump, flourish, spout, rant, recite, rattle off, intone, breathe, let fall, whisper in the ear, expatiate, run on; to lecture, preach, address, sermonize, preachify; to sililoquize (589); quoth he.

Phrases: To have a tongue in one's head; to have on the tip of one's tongue; to have on one's lips; to pass one's lips; to find one's tongue.

Adjectives: Speaking, etc., oral, spoken, unwritten, elocutionary, oratorical, rhetorical, declamatory, outspoken.

223

Adverbs: Viva voce; *ore rotundo*; by word of mouth.

583 STAMMERING

Substantives: inarticulateness, stuttering, impediment in one's speech, titubancy, faltering, hesitation, lisp, drawl, jabber, gibber, sputter, splutter, mumbling, mincing, muttering, mouthing, twang, a broken or cracked voice, broken accents or sentences, tardiloquence, falsetto, a whisper (405), mispronunciation.

Verbs: To stammer, stutter, hesitate, falter, hem, haw, hum and ha, mumble, lisp, jabber, gibber, mutter, sputter, splutter, drawl, mouth, mince, lisp, croak, speak through the nose, snuffle, clip one's words, mispronounce, missay.

Phrases: To clip the King's (or Queen's) English; *parler à tort et à travers*; not to be able to put two words together.

Adjectives: Stammering, etc., inarticulate, guttural, nasal, tremulous.

584 LOQUACITY

Substantives: loquaciousness, talkativeness, garrulity, flow of words, prate, gas, jaw, gab, gabble, jabber, chatter, prattle, cackle, clack, clash, blether (or blather), patter, rattle, twaddle, bibble-babble, gibble-gabble, talkee-talkee, gossip.

Fluency, flippancy, volubility, verbosity, *cacoethes loquendi,* anecdotage.

A chatterer, chatterbox, blatherskite, babbler, wind-bag, gas-bag, rattle, ranter, tub-thumper, sermonizer, proser, driveller, gossip.

Magpie, jay, parrot, poll; Babel.

Phrases: A twice (or thrice) told tale; a long yarn; the gift of the gab.

Verbs: To be loquacious, etc., to prate, palaver, chatter, prattle, jabber, jaw, rattle, twaddle, blether, babble, gabble, gas, out-talk, descant, dilate, dwell on, reel off, expatiate, prose, launch out, yarn, gossip, wag one's tongue, run on.

Phrases: To din in the ears; to drum into the ear; to spin a long yarn; to talk at random; to bum one's chat; to talk oneself out of breath; to talk nineteen to the dozen.

Adjectives: Loquacious, talkative, garrulous, gassy, gabby, open-mouthed, chatty, chattering, etc.

Fluent, voluble, glib, flippant, long-tongued, long-winded, verbose, the tongue running fast.

Adverb: Trippingly on the tongue.

585 TACITURNITY

Substantives: closeness, reverse, reticence (528), muteness, silence, curtness; aposiopesis; a clam, oyster.

Phrases: A Quaker meeting; a man of few words.

Verbs: To be silent, etc. (403), to hold one's tongue, keep silence, hold one's peace, say nothing, hold one's jaw, close one's mouth or lips, fall silent, dry up, shut up, stow it.

To render silent, silence, put to silence, seal one's lips, smother, suppress, stop one's mouth, gag, muffle, muzzle (581).

Adjectives: Taciturn, silent, close, reserved, mute, sparing of words, buttoned up, curt, short-spoken, close-tongued, tight-lipped, reticent, secretive, uncommunicative, inconversable.

Phrases: Not a word escaping one; not having a word to say.

Interjections: Hush! silence! mum! *chut!* hist! whist! wheesht!

586 ALLOCUTION

Substantives: address, apostrophe, interpellation, appeal, invocation, alloquialism, salutation, accost, greeting (894).

Feigned dialogue, imaginary conversation; inquiry (461).

Phrase: A word in the ear.

Verbs: To speak to, address, accost,

buttonhole, apostrophize, appeal to, invoke, hail, make up to, take aside, call to, halloo (or hallo), salute.

Phrases: To talk with one in private; to break the ice.

Adjectives: Accosting, etc., alloquial, invocatory, apostrophic.

Interjections: Hallo! hello! hullo! I say! hoy! oi! hey! what ho! psst!

587 RESPONSE
Substantives: answer, reply (462).
Verbs: To answer, respond, reply, etc.
Phrase: To take up one's cue.
Adjectives: Answering, responding, etc., responsive, respondent.

588 INTERLOCUTION
Substantives: collocution, colloquy, conversation, converse, confabulation, confab, talk, discourse, verbal intercourse, dialogue, duologue, logomachy, communication, intercommunication, commerce, debate.

Chat, chit-chat, crack, small talk, table-talk, tattle, gossip, tittle-tattle, babblement, clack, prittle-prattle, idle talk, town-talk, bazaar talk, *on dit, causerie, chronique scandaleuse.*

Conference, parley, interview, audience, tête-à-tête, reception, conversazione, palaver, pow-wow; council (686).

A talker, interlocutor, interviewer, gossip, tattler, chatterer, babbler (584), conversationalist, *causeur; dramatis personae.*

Phrases: 'The feast of reason and the flow of soul'; a heart-to-heart talk.
Verbs: To talk together, converse, collogue, commune, debate, discourse with, engage in conversation, interview; hold or carry on a conversation; chat, gossip, have a crack, put in a word, chip in, tattle, babble, prate, clack, prattle.

To confer with, hold conference, etc., to parley, palaver, commerce, hold intercourse with, be closeted with, commune with, have speech with, compare notes, intercommunicate.

Adjectives: Conversing, etc., interlocutory, verbal, colloquial, discursive, chatty, gossiping, etc., conversable, conversational.

589 SOLILOQUY
Substantives: monologue, apostrophe, aside.

Soliloquist, monologist, monologuist.

Verbs: To soliloquize, monologize; to say or talk to oneself, to say aside, to think aloud, to apostrophize.

Adjectives: Soliloquizing, etc.

590 WRITING
Substantives: chirography, pencraft, penmanship, long-hand, calligraphy, quill-driving, pen-pushing, typewriting, typing.

Scribble, scrawl, scratch, cacography, scribbling, etc., jotting, interlineation, palimpsest.

Uncial writing, court hand, cursive writing, picture writing, hieroglyphics, hieroglyph, cuneiform characters, demotic text, heiratic text, ogham, runes.

Pothooks and hangers.

Transcription, inscription, superscription, minute.

Shorthand, stenography, phonography, brachygraphy, tachygraphy, steganography.

Secret writing, writing in cipher, cryptography, polygraphy, stelography; cryptogram.

Automatic writing, planchette.

Composition, authorship, *cacoethes scribendi.*

Manuscript, MS, copy, transcript, rough copy, fair copy, carbon, black, duplicate, flimsy, handwriting, hand, fist, script, autograph, signature, signmanual, monograph, holograph, endorsement, paraph.

A scribe, amanuensis, scrivener, secretary, clerk, penman, calligraphist, copyist, transcriber, stenographer, typist.

Writer, author, scribbler, quill-driver, ink-slinger, pamphleteer, essayist, critic, reviewer, novelist (593), journalist, editor, subeditor, reporter, pressman, penny-a-liner, hack, free-lance; Grub Street, Fleet Street.

Pen, quill, fountain-pen, stylograph, stylo, ball-point, Biro, pencil, stationery, paper, parchment, vellum, tablet, slate, marble, pillar, table, etc.

Phrase: A dash or stroke of the pen.

Verbs: To write, pen, typewrite, type, write out, copy, engross, write out fair, transcribe, scribble, scrawl, scratch, interline; to sign, undersign, countersign, endorse (497), set one's hand to.

To compose, indite, draw up, draft, minute, jot down, dash off, make or take a minute of, put or set down in writing; to inscribe, to dictate.

Phrases: To take up the pen; to spill ink; to sling ink; set or put pen to paper; put on paper; commit to paper.

Adjectives: Writing, etc., written, in writing, penned, etc., scriptorial; uncial, cursive, cuneiform, runic, hieroglyphical; editorial, journalistic, reportorial.

Phrases: Under one's hand; in black and white; pen in hand; *currente calamo*.

591 PRINTING

Substantives: print, letterpress, text, context, note, page, proof, pull, revise; presswork.

Typography, stereotypography, type, character, black-letter, fount (or font), capitals, majuscules, lower-case letters, minuscules, etc.; roman, italic, type; braille.

Folio, quarto, octavo, etc.(593).

Printer, pressman, compositor, corrector of the press, proof-reader, copy-holder; printer's devil.

Printing-press, linotype, monotype, etc.

Verbs: To print, put to press, publish, edit, get out a work, etc.

Adjectives: Printed, etc.

592 CORRESPONDENCE

Substantives: letter, epistle, note, line, airgraph, postcard, chit, billet, missive, circular, favour, *billet-doux,* dispatch, bulletin, memorial, rescript, rescription.

Letter-bag, mail, post; postage.

Verbs: To correspond, write to, send a letter to.

Phrase: To keep up a correspondence.

Adjectives: Epistolary, postal.

593 BOOK

Substantives: writing, work, volume, tome, codex, opuscule, tract, manual, pamphlet, chap-book, booklet, brochure, enchiridion, circular, publication, part, issue, number, journal, album, periodical, magazine, digest, serial, ephemeris, annual, yearbook.

Writer, author, publicist, scribbler, pamphleteer, poet, essayist, novelist, fabulist, editor (590).

Book-lover, bibliophile, bibliomaniac, paperback.

Bibliography, *incunabula,* Aldine, Elzevir, etc.; library.

Publisher, bookseller, bibliopole, bibliopolist, librarian.

Folio, quarto, octavo, duodecimo, sextodecimo, octodecimo.

Paper, bill, sheet, leaf, fly-leaf, page, title-page.

Chapter, section, paragraph, passage, clause.

Adjectives: Auctorial, bookish, bibliographical, etc.

594 DESCRIPTION

Substantives: account, statement, report, return, delineation, specification, particulars, sketch, representation

(554), narration, narrative, yarn, relation, recital, rehearsal, annals, chronicle, saga, *adversaria,* journal (551), itinerary, log-book.

Historiography; historicity, historic muse, Clio.

Story, history, memoir, tale, tradition, legend, folk-tale, folk-lore, anecdote, ana, analects (596), fable, fiction, novel, novelette, thriller, whodunit, romance, short story, *conte, nouvelle,* apologue, parable; word-picture; local colour.

Biography, necrology, obituary, life, personal narrative, adventures, autobiography, confessions, reminiscences.

A historian, historiographer, narrator, *raconteur,* annalist, chronicler, biographer, fabulist, novelist, fictionist, story-teller.

Verbs: To describe, state (535), set forth, sketch, delineate, represent (554), portray, depict, paint, shadow forth, adumbrate.

To relate, recite, recount, sum up, run over, recapitulate, narrate, chronicle, rehearse, tell, give or render an account of, report, draw up a statement, spin a yarn, unfold a tale, novelize, actualize.

To take up or handle a subject; to enter into particulars, detail, etc., to characterize, particularize, detail, retail, elaborate, write up; to descend to particulars; to Boswellize.

Phrases: To plunge *in medias res;* to fight one's battles over again.

Adjectives: Descriptive, narrative, graphic, realistic, naturalistic, novelistic, historic, traditional, traditionary, legendary, storied, romantic, anecdotic, Boswellian, described, etc.

595 DISSERTATION

Substantives: treatise, tract, tractate, thesis, theme, monograph, essay, discourse, article, leading article, leader, leaderette, editorial, feuilleton, criticism, critique, review, memoir, prolusion, disquisition, exposition, exercitation, compilation, sermon, lecture, teach-in, homily, pandect, *causerie,* pamphlet (593).

Commentator, lecturer, critic, leader-writer, pamphleteer.

Verbs: To dissert, descant, treat of, discuss, write, compile, touch upon, ventilate, canvass; deal with, do justice to a subject.

Adjectives: Discursive, disquisitional, expository, compiled.

596 COMPENDIUM

Substantives: compend, summary, abstract, précis, epitome, *aperçu,* analysis, digest, sum and substance, *compte rendu, procès verbal,* draft, *exposé,* brief, recapitulation, résumé, conspectus, abridgment, abbreviation, minute, note, synopsis, argument, plot, syllabus, contents, heads, prospectus.

Scrap-book, album, note-book, commonplace-book, compilation, extracts, cuttings, clippings, text-book, analects, *analecta,* excerpts, flowers, anthology, *collectanea,* memorabilia.

Verbs: To abridge, abstract, excerpt, abbreviate, recapitulate, run over, make or prepare an abstract, etc. (201), epitomize, sum up, summarize, boil down, anthologize.

Adjectives: Compendious, etc., synoptic, abridged, etc., analectic.

Phrases: In a nutshell; in substance; in short.

597 POETRY

Substantives: poetics, poesy, the Muse, the Nine, Calliope, Parnassus, Helicon, the Pierian spring.

Verse, metre, measure, foot, numbers, strain, rhyme (or rime), head-rhyme, alliteration, rhythm, heroic verse, Alexandrine, octosyllables, *terza rima,* blank verse, free verse, *vers libre,* sprung rhythm, assonance, versification, macaronics, doggerel, jingle, prosody, orthometry, scansion.

Poem, epic, epopee, epic poem, ballad, ode, epode, idyll, lyric, eclogue, pastoral, bucolic, macaronic, dithyramb, anacreontic, sonnet, lay, roundelay, rondeau, rondel, ballade, villanelle, triolet, sestina, rhyme royal, madrigal, canzonet, libretto, posy, anthology; distich, stanza, stave, strophe, antistrophe, couplet, triplet, quatrain, cento, monody, elegy, *vers de société*.

Iambic (or iamb), trochee, spondee, dactyl, anapaest, amphibrach, amphimacer, tribrach, paeon, etc.

A poet, laureate, bard, scald, poetess, rhymer, rhymist, versifier, rhymester, sonneteer, poetaster, minor poet, minnesinger, meistersinger, troubadour, *trouvère*.

Phrase: *Genus irritabile vatum.*

Verbs: To rhyme, versify, sing, make verses, scan, poetize.

Adjectives: Poetical, poetic, Castalian, Parnassian, Heliconian, lyric, lyrical, metrical, epic, heroic; catalectic, dithyrambic, doggerel, macaronic, leonine; Pindaric, Homeric, Virgilian, Shakespearian, Miltonic, Tennysonian, etc.

598 PROSE

Substantives: prose-writer, proser, prosaist.

Verbs: To prose.

Adjectives: Prosaic, prosaical, prosing, prosy, rhymeless, unrhymed, unpoetical, commonplace, humdrum.

599 THE DRAMA

Substantives: stage, theatre, the histrionic art, dramatic art, histrionics, acting; stage effect, *mise en scène*, stage production, setting, scenery; buskin, sock, cothurnus; Melpomene, Thalia, Thespis; play-writing, dramaturgy.

Play, stage-play, piece, tragedy, comedy, tragi-comedy, morality, mystery, melodrama, farce, knockabout farce, comedietta, curtain-raiser, interlude, after-piece, vaudeville, extravaganza, *divertissement,* burletta, burlesque, variety show, revue; opera, grand opera, music-drama, comic opera, *opéra bouffe,* operetta, ballad opera, *singspiel,* musical comedy; ballet, pantomime, harlequinade, charade, wordless play, dumb-show, by-play; monodrama, monologue, duologue; masque, pageant, show; scenario, libretto, book of words, part, role; matinée, benefit; act, scene, prologue, epilogue.

Theatre, playhouse, music-hall, variety theatre; stage, the boards, the footlights, green-room, foyer, proscenium, flies, wings, stalls, box, pit, circle, dress-circle, balcony, amphitheatre, gallery.

An actor, player, stage-player, performer, artiste, comedian, comedienne, tragedian, tragedienne, Thespian, Roscius, clown, harlequin, pantaloon, *buffo,* buffoon, pierrot, pierrette, impersonator, entertainer, etc., strolling player; ballet dancer, *ballerina,* figurant, mime, star; prima donna, *primo tenore,* etc., leading lady, heavy lead, juvenile lead, *ingénue,* soubrette; supernumerary, super, walking, gentleman or lady, chorus girl; *dramatis personae,* cast, company, stock company, touring company, repertory company; a star turn.

Mummer, guiser, masquer; dancer, nautch-girl, bayadère, geisha.

Stage manager, impresario, producer, prompter, stage hands, call-boy, etc.

Dramatic writer, pantomimist, playwright, play-writer, dramatist, dramaturge, librettist.

Phrase: The profession.

Verbs: To act, enact, play, perform, personate (554), play or interpret a part, rehearse, spout, rant, gag, star, walk on.

To produce, present, stage, stage-manager.

Phrases: To strut and fret one's hour on the stage; to tread the boards.

Adjectives: Dramatic, theatre, theatrical, scenic, histrionic, comic, tragic, buskined, farcical, knock-about, slapstick, tragi-comic, melodramatic, transpontine, stagy, operatic.

599a CINEMA
Substantives: picture theatre, picture-drome, film, motion picture, pictures, movies, flicks, pix, silver screen; silent film, sound film, talkie, flattie; three-dimensional film, 3-D, wide-screen film, deepie; documentary, trailer.

Close-up, flash-back, fade-out.

Scenario, star, vamp; cinema-goer, cinemaddict, film fan.

Verbs: To feature, screen; dub.

599b RADIO
Substantives: wireless, receiving set, transistor, walkie-talkie; broadcast, radio play; teleprompter.

Announcer, listener.

Television, TV, video, telly; telecast, telefilm, newscast, script.

Looker-in, televiewer, viewer.

Verbs: To broadcast, televise, telecast.

To listen in, look in, view, teleview.

Phrase: On the air.

Adjective: Telegenic.

Words relating to the voluntary powers

I
Section 1 –
Volition in General

600 WILL
Substantives: volition, voluntariness, velleity, conation, free-will, spontaneity, spontaneousness, freedom (748).

Pleasure, wish, mind, animus, breast, mood, bosom, *petto*, heart, discretion, accord.

Libertarianism.

Determination (604), predetermination (611), intention (620), choice (609).
Verbs: To will, list, think fit, see fit, think proper, determine, etc. (604), settle, choose (609), to take upon oneself, to have one's will, to do as one likes, wishes, or chooses; to use or exercise one's own discretion, to volunteer, lend oneself to.
Phrases: To have a will of one's own; *hoc volo, sic jubeo, stet pro ratione voluntas*; to take the will for the deed; to know one's own mind; to know what one is about; to see one's way; to have one's will; to take upon oneself; to take the law into one's own hands.
Adjectives: Voluntary, volitional, willing, content, minded, spontaneous, free, left to oneself, unconstrained, unfettered, autocratic, bossy, unbidden, unasked, unurged, uncompelled, of one's own accord, gratuitous, of one's own head, prepense, advised, express, designed, intended, calculated, premeditated, precon-certed, predetermined, deliberate.
Adverbs: At will, at pleasure, *à volonté, à discrétion, ad libitum, ad arbitrium,* spontaneously, freely, of one's own accord, voluntarily, advisedly, designedly, intentionally, expressly, knowingly, determinately, deliberately, pointedly, in earnest, in good earnest, studiously, purposely, *proprio motu, suo motu, ex mero motu; quo animo.*
Phrases: With one's eyes open; in cold blood.

601 NECESSITY
Substantives: instinct, blind impulse, necessitation, ἀνάγκη, fate, fatality, destiny, doom, kismet, weird (152), foredoom, destination, election, predestination, preordination, fore-ordination, compulsion (744), subjection (749), inevitability, inevitableness.

Determinism, necessitarianism, fatalism, automatism.

A determinist, necessarian, necessitarian; robot, automaton.

The Fates, Parcae, the Three Sisters, fortune's wheel, the book of fate, the stars, astral influence, spell (152).
Phrases: Hobson's choice; what must be; a blind bargain; a *pis aller.*
Verbs: To lie under a necessity, to be fated, doomed, destined, etc. (152), to need be, have no alternative.

To necessitate, destine, doom, fore-doom, predestine, preordain.

To compel, force, constrain, etc. (744), cast a spell, etc. (992).
Phrases: To make a virtue of necessity; to be pushed to the wall; to dree one's weird.

Adjectives: Necessitated, fated, destined, predestined, foreordained, doomed, elect, spellbound.

Compelled, forced, etc., unavoidable, inevitable, irresistible, irrevocable.

Compulsory, involuntary, unintentional, undesigned, unintended, instinctive, automatic, blind, mechanical, impulsive, unconscious, reflex, unwitting, unaware.

Deterministic, necessitarian, fatalistic.

Phrase: Unable to help it.

Adverbs: Necessarily, needs, of necessity, perforce, forcibly, compulsorily; on or by compulsion or force, willy-nilly, *nolens volens*; involuntarily, etc., impulsively (612), unwittingly (491).

Phrases: It must be; it needs must be; it is written; one's fate is sealed; *che sarà sarà*; there is no help for it; there is no alternative; nothing for it but; necessity knows no law; needs must when the devil drives.

602 WILLINGNESS

Substantives: voluntariness, disposition, inclination, leaning, *penchant,* humour, mood, vein, bent, bias, propensity, proclivity, aptitude, predisposition, predilection (865), proneness, docility, pliability (324), alacrity, earnestness, readiness, assent (448).

Phrases: A labour of love; *labor ipse voluptas.*

Verbs: To be willing, etc., to incline to, lean to, not mind (865), to propend; to volunteer.

Phrases: To find in one's heart; to set one's heart upon; to make no bones of; have a mind to; have a great mind to; 'Barkis is willin'.'

Adjectives: Willing, fain, disposed, inclined, minded, bent upon, set upon, forward, predisposed, content, favourable, hearty, ready, wholehearted, cordial, genial, keen, prepense, docile, persuadable, persuasible, facile, tract-able, easy-going, easily led.

Free, spontaneous, voluntary, gratuitous, unforced, unasked, unsummoned, unbiased, unsolicited, unbesought, undriven.

Adverbs: Willingly, freely, readily, lief, heartily, with a good grace, without reluctance, etc., as soon, of one's own accord (600), certainly, be it so (488).

Phrases: With all one's heart, *con amore*; with heart and soul; with a right good will; with a good grace; *de bon cœur*; by all means; by all manner of means; nothing loth; *ex animo*; to one's heart's content.

603 UNWILLINGNESS

Substantives: indisposition, indisposedness, backwardness, disinclination, averseness, aversion, reluctance, repugnance, demur, renitence, remissness, slackness, lukewarmness, indifference, nonchalance.

Hesitation, shrinking, recoil, suspense, dislike (867), scrupulousness, scrupulosity, delicacy, demur, scruple, qualm.

A recusant, pococurante.

Verbs: To be unwilling, etc., to demur, stick at, hesitate (605), waver, hang in suspense, scruple, stickle, boggle, falter, to hang back, hang fire, fight shy of, jib, grudge.

To decline, reject, refuse (764), refrain, keep from, abstain, recoil, shrink, reluct.

Phrases: To stick in the throat; to set one's face against; to draw the line at; I'd rather not.

Adjectives: Unwilling, unconsenting, disinclined, indisposed, averse, reluctant, not content, laggard, backward, shy, remiss, slack, indifferent, lukewarm, frigid, scrupulous, repugnant, disliking (867).

Demurring, wavering, etc., refusing (764), grudging.

Adverbs: Unwillingly, etc., perforce.

Phrases: Against the grain; *invita Minerva; malgré lui; bon gré, mal gré; nolens volens*; in spite of one's teeth; with a bad grace; not for the world; willy-nilly.

604 RESOLUTION
Substantives: determination, decision, resolve, resolvedness, fixedness, steadiness, constancy, indefatigability, unchangeableness, inflexibility, decision, finality, firmness, doggedness, tenacity of purpose, pertinacity, perseverance, constancy, solidity, stability.

Energy, manliness, vigour, spirit, spiritedness, pluck, bottom, backbone, stamina, gameness, guts, grit, sand, will, iron will; self-reliance; self-mastery; self-control.

A devotee, zealot, extremist, ultra, enthusiast, fanatic, fan; bulldog, British lion.

Verbs: To be resolved, etc., to have resolution, etc., to resolve, decide, will, persevere, determine, conclude, make up one's mind; to stand, keep, or remain firm, etc., to come to a determination, to form a resolution, to take one's stand, to stand by, hold by, hold fast, stick to, abide by, adhere to, keep one's ground, persevere, keep one's course, hold on, hang on, not to fail.

To insist upon, to make a point of.

Phrases: To determine once for all; to form a resolution; to steel oneself; to pass the Rubicon; take a decisive step; to burn one's boats; to nail one's colours to the mast; to screw one's courage to the sticking-place; to take the bull by the horns; to mean business; to set one's teeth; to keep a stiff upper lip; to keep one's chin up.

Adjectives: Resolved, resolute, game, firm, steady, steadfast, staunch, constant; solid, manly, stout.

Decided, strong-willed, determined, uncompromising, purposive, self-possessed, fixed, unmoved, unshaken, unbending, unyielding, unflagging, unflinching, inflexible, unwavering, unfaltering, unshrinking, undiverted, undeterred, immovable, not to be moved, unhesitating, unswerving.

Peremptory, inexorable, indomitable, persevering, pertinacious, persistent, irrevocable, irreversible, reverseless, decisive, final.

Strenuous, bent upon, set upon, intent upon, proof against, master of oneself, steeled, staid, serious, stiff, stiff-necked, obstinate (606).

Phrases: Firm as a rock; game to the last; true to oneself; master of oneself; *in utrumque paratus.*

Adverbs: Resolutely, etc., without fail.

Phrases: Through thick and thin; through fire and water; at all hazards; sink or swim; *coûte que coûte; fortiter in re*; like grim death.

605 IRRESOLUTION
Substantives: indecision, indetermination, demur, hesitation, suspense, uncertainty (475), hesitancy, vacillation, unsteadiness, inconstancy, wavering, fluctuation, flickering changeableness, mutability, fickleness, caprice (608), levity, *légèreté*, trimming, softness, weakness, instability.

A weathercock, trimmer, timeserver, turncoat, shuttlecock, butterfly, harlequin, chameleon.

Verbs: To be irresolute, etc., to hesitate, hang in suspense, demur, waver, vacillate, quaver, fluctuate, shuffle, boggle, flicker, falter, palter, debate, dilly-dally, shilly-shally, dally with, coquette with, swerve, etc.

Phrases: To hang fire; to hum and ha; to blow hot and cold; not to know one's own mind; to leave 'ad referendum'; letting 'I dare not' wait upon 'I would.'

Adjectives: Irresolute, undecided, unresolved, undetermined, vacillating, wavering, hesitating, faltering, shuf-

VOLITION IN GENERAL 605–607

fling, etc., half-hearted, double-minded, indicisive.

Unsteady, unsteadfast, fickle, flighty, changing, changeable, versatile, variable, inconstant, mutable, protean, fluctuating, unstable, unsettled, unhinged, unfixed, weak-kneed, spineless.

Weak, feeble-minded, frail, soft, pliant, giddy, capricious, coquettish, volatile, fitful, frothy, freakish, lightsome, light-minded, invertebrate.

Revocable, reversible.

Phrases: Infirm of purpose; without ballast; waiting to see which way the cat jumps, or the wind blows.

Adverbs: Irresolutely, etc.; off and on.

606 OBSTINACY

Substantives: obstinateness, wilfulness, self-will, pertinacity, pertinaciousness, pervicacity, pervicaciousness, tenacity, tenaciousness, inflexibility, immovability, doggedness, stubbornness, steadiness (604), restiveness, contumacy, cussedness, obduracy, obduration, unruliness.

Intolerance, dogmatism, bigotry, opinionatedness, opiniativeness, fanaticism, zealotry, infatuation, monomania, indocility, intractability, intractableness (481), pig-headedness.

An opinionist, *opiniâtre,* crank, die-hard, blimp, stickler, enthusiast, monomaniac, zealot, dogmatist, fanatic, mule.

A fixed idea, rooted prejudice, blind side, obsession (481), King Charles's head.

Phrase: A bee in one's bonnet.

Verbs: To be obstinate, etc., to persist, stickle, opiniate.

Phrases: To stick at nothing; to dig in one's heels; not yield an inch.

Adjectives: Obstinate, opinionative, opinative, opinionated, opinioned, wedded to an opinion, self-opinioned, prejudiced (481), cranky, wilful, self-willed, positive, tenacious.

Stiff, stubborn, stark, rigid, stiff-necked, dogged, pertinacious, restive, pervicacious, dogmatic, arbitrary, bigoted, unpersuadable, mulish, unmoved, uninfluenced, hard-mouthed, unyielding, inflexible, immovable, pig-headed, wayward, intractable, hide-bound, headstrong, restive, refractory, unruly, infatuated, *entêté,* wrong-headed, cross-grained, obdurate, contumacious, fanatical, rabid, inexorable, impracticable.

Phrases: Obstinate as a mule; impervious to reason.

Adverbs: Obstinately, etc.

Phrases: *Non possumus; vestigia nulla retrorsum.*

607 TERGIVERSATION

Substantives: retractation, recantation, revocation, revokement, reversal, palinode, volteface, renunciation, disavowal (536), abjuration, abjurement, apostasy, relinquishment (624), repentance (950), vacillation, etc. (605).

A turncoat, rat, Janus, renegade, apostate, pervert, backslider, recidivist, trimmer, time-server, opportunist, Vicar of Bray, deserter, weathercock, etc. (605), Proteus.

Verbs: To change one's mind, etc., to retract, recant, revoke, forswear, unsay, take back, abjure, renounce, apostatize, relinquish, trim, straddle, veer round, change sides, rat, go over; pass, change, or skip from one side to another; back out, back down, swerve, flinch, balance.

Phrases: To eat one's words; turn over a new leaf; think better of it; play fast and loose; blow hot and cold; box the compass; swallow the leek; eat dirt.

Adjectives: Changeful, changeable, mobile, unsteady (605), trimming, double-faced, ambidexter, fast and loose, time-serving, facing both ways.

Fugacious, fleeting (111), revocatory.

233

608 CAPRICE

Substantives: fancy, fantasy, humour, whim, crotchet, fad, fike, craze, *capriccio,* quirk, freak, maggot, vagary, whimsy, whim-wham, kink, prank, shenanigans, fit, flim-flam, escapade, ploy, dido, contrariety, monkey-tricks, rag, monkey-shines, *boutade,* wild-goose chase, freakishness, skittishness, volatility, fancifulness, whimsicality, giddiness, inconsistency; a madcap.

Verbs: To be capricious, etc.

Phrases: To strain at a gnat and swallow a camel; to take it into one's head.

Adjectives: Capricious, inconsistent, fanciful, fantastic, whimsical, full of whims, etc., erratic, crotchety, faddy, maggoty, fiky, perverse, humoursome, wayward, captious, contrary, contrarious, skittish, fitful.

Phrases: The head being turned; the deuce being in him; by fits and starts.

609 CHOICE

Substantives: option, election, arbitrament, adoption, selection, excerption, co-optation, gleaning, eclecticism, lief, preference, predilection, preoption, discretion (600), fancy.

Decision, determination, adjudication, award, vote, suffrage, ballot, poll, plebiscite, referendum, verdict, voice, plumper.

Alternative, dilemma (704).

Excerpt, extract, cuttings, clippings; pick, *élite,* cream (650).

Chooser, elector, voter, constituent; electorate, constituency.

Verbs: To choose, decide, determine, elect, list, think fit, use one's discretion, fancy, shape one's course, prefer, have rather, have as lief, take one's choice, adopt, select, fix upon, pitch upon, pick out, single out, vote for, plump for, co-opt, pick up, take up, catch at, jump at, cull, glean, pick, winnow.

Phrases: To winnow the chaff from the wheat; to indulge one's fancy; to pick and choose; to take a decided step; to pass the Rubicon (604); to hold out; offer for choice; commend me to; to swallow the bait; to gorge the hook; to yield to temptation.

Adjectives: Optional, discretional, eclectic, choosing, etc., chosen, etc., decided, etc., choice, preferential; left to oneself.

Adverbs: Discretionally, at pleasure, *à plaisir, a piacere,* at discretion, at will, *ad libitum.*

Decidedly, etc., rather; once for all, either the one of the other, for one's money, for choice.

610 ABSENCE OF CHOICE

Substantives: Hobson's choice, necessity (601).

Indifference, indecision (605).

Phrase: First come, first served.

Adjectives: Neutral; indifferent, undecided.

Phrase: To sit on the fence.

REJECTION

Substantives: refusal (764); declining, repudiation, exclusion.

Verbs: To reject, refuse, etc., decline, give up, repudiate, exclude, lay aside, pigeon-hole, refrain, spare (678), abandon, turn down, blackball; to fail, plough, pluck, spin, cast.

Phrases: To lay on the shelf; to return to store; to throw overboard; to draw the line at.

Adjectives: Rejecting, etc., rejected, etc., not chosen, etc.

Phrases: Not to be thought of; out of the question.

Adverbs: Neither; neither the one nor the other, nothing to choose between them.

611 PREDETERMINATION

Substantives: premeditation, predeliberation, foregone conclusion, *parti pris.*

Verbs: To predetermine, premeditate, preconcert, resolve beforehand.

Adjectives: Prepense, premeditated, predetermined, advised, predesigned, aforethought, calculated, studied, designed (620).

Adverbs: Advisedly, deliberately, etc., with the eyes open, in cold blood.

612 IMPULSE

Substantives: sudden thought, improvisation, inspiration, flash, spurt.

Improvisator, improvisatore, improvisatrice, creature of impulse.

Verbs: To flash on the mind; to improvise, improvisate, make up, extemporize, vamp, ad-lib.

Adjectives: Extemporaneous, extemporary, impulsive, unrehearsed, unpremeditated (674), improvised, improvisatorial, improvisatory, unprompted, instinctive, spontaneous, natural, unguarded, unreflecting, precipitate.

Adverbs: Extempore, offhand, impromptu, *à l'improviste,* out of hand.

Phrases: On the spur of the moment, or of the occasion.

613 HABIT

Substantives: habitude, wont, rule, routine, jog-trot, groove, rut.

Custom, consuetude, use, usage, practice, trick, run, run of things, way, form prevalence, observance, fashion (852), etiquette, prescription, convention, *convenances,* red tape, red-tapery, red-tapism, routinism, conventionalism, vogue.

Seasoning, training, hardening, etc. (673), acclimatization, acclimation, acclimatation.

Second nature, *cocoethes,* taking root, diathesis.

A victim of habit, etc., an addict, junkie, *habitué.*

Verbs: To be habitual, etc., to be in the habit of, be wont, be accustomed to, etc.

To follow, observe, conform to, obey, bend to, comply with, accommodate oneself to, adapt oneself to; fall into a habit, convention, custom, or usage; to addict oneself to, take to, get the hang of.

To become a habit, to take root, to gain or grow upon one, to run in the blood.

To habituate, inure, harden, season, form, train, accustom, familiarize, naturalize, acclimatize, conventionalize, condition.

To acquire a habit, to get into the way of, to learn, etc.

Phrases: To follow the multitude; go with the current, stream, etc.; run on in a groove; do in Rome as the Romans do.

Adjectives: Habitual, accustomed, prescriptive, habituated, etc.; in the habit, etc., of; used to, addicted to, attuned to, wedded to, at home in; usual, wonted, customary, hackneyed, commonplace, trite, ordinary, set, stock, established, accepted, stereotyped, received, acknowledged, recognized; groovy, fixed, rooted, permanent, inveterate, ingrained, running in the blood, hereditary, congenital, innate, inborn, besetting, natural, instinctive, etc. (5).

Fashionable, in fashion, in vogue, according to use, routine, conventional, etc.

Phrases: Bred in the bone; in the blood.

Adverbs: Habitually; as usual, as the world goes, *more suo, pro more, pro forma,* according to custom, *de rigueur.*

614 DESUETUDE

Substantives: disuse, want of habit or of practice, inusitation, newness to.

Non-observance (773), infraction, violation, infringement.

Phrase: 'A custom more honoured in the breach than the observance.'

Verbs: To be unaccustomed, etc., to

be new to; to leave off, wean oneself of, break off, break through, infringe, violate, etc., a habit, usage, etc.; to disuse, to wear off.

Adjectives: Unaccustomed, unused, unusual, unwonted, unpractised, unprofessional, unfashionable, non-observant, lax, disused, weaned.

Unseasoned, uninured, untrained, green.

Unhackneyed, unconventional, Bohemian (83).

615 MOTIVE

Substantives: reason, ground, principle, mainspring, *primum mobile,* account, score, sake, consideration, calculation, *raison d'être.*

Inducement, recommendation, encouragement, attraction, allectation, temptation, enticement, bait, allurement, charm, witchery, bewitchment.

Persuasibility, softness, susceptibility, attractability, impressibility.

Influence, prompting, dictate, instance, impulse, impulsion, incitement, incitation, press, instigation, excitement, provocation, invitation, solicitation, advocacy, call, suasion, persuasion, hortation, exhortation, seduction, cajolery, tantalization, *agacerie,* seducement, fascination, blandishment, inspiration, honeyed words.

Incentive, stimulus, spur, fillip, urge, goad, rowel, provocative, whet, dram, cocktail, pick-me-up, appetizer.

Bribe, graft, sop, lure, decoy, charm, spell, magnetism, magnet, loadstone.

Prompter, tempter, seducer, seductor, siren, Circe, instigator, *agent provocateur.*

Phrases: The pros and cons; the why and wherefore.

The golden apple; a red herring; a sop for Cerberus; the voice of the tempter; the song of the sirens.

Verbs: To induce, move, lead, draw, draw over, carry, bring, to influence, to weigh with, bias, to operate, work upon, engage, incline, dispose, predispose, put up to, prompt, whisper, call, call upon, recommend, encourage, entice, invite, solicit, press, enjoin, entreat (765), court, plead, advocate, exhort, enforce, dictate, tantalize, bait the hook, tempt, allure, lure, seduce, decoy, draw on, captivate, fascinate, charm, bewitch, conciliate, wheedle, coax, speak fair, carny (or carney), cajole, pat on the back or shoulder, talk over, inveigle, persuade, prevail upon, get to do, bring over, procure, lead by the nose, sway, over-persuade, come over, get round, turn the head, enlist, retain, kidnap, bribe, suborn, tamper with.

To act upon, to impel, excite, suscitate, stimulate, key up, motivate, incite, animate, instigate, provoke, set on, urge, pique, spirit, inspirit, inspire, awaken, buck up, give a fillip, light up, kindle, enkindle, rekindle, quicken, goad, spur, prick, edge, egg on, hurry on, stir up, work up, fan, fire, inflame, set on fire, fan the flame, blow the coals, stir the embers, put on one's mettle, set on, force, rouse, arouse, lash into fury, get a rise out of.

Phrases: To grease the palm; to gild the pill; to work the oracle.

To follow the bent of; to follow the dictates of; to yield to temptation; to act on principle.

Adjectives: Impulsive, motive, persuasive, hortative, hortatory, seductive, carnying, suasory, suasive, honey-tongued, attractive, tempting, alluring, piquant, exciting, inviting, tantalizing, etc.

Persuadable, persuasible, suasible, soft, yielding, facile, easily persuaded, etc.

Induced, moved, disposed, led, persuaded, etc., spellbound, instinct with or by.

Adverbs: Because, for, since, on

account of, out of, from; by reason of, for the sake of, on the score of.

As, forasmuch as, therefore, hence, why, wherefore; for all the world.
Phrase: *Hinc illae lacrimae.*

616 ABSENCE OF MOTIVE
Substantives: caprice (608).
Adjectives: Aimless, motiveless, pointless, purposeless (621); uninduced, unmoved, unactuated, uninfluenced, unbiased, unimpelled, unswayed, impulsive, wanton, unprovoked, uninspired, untempted, unattracted.
Phrase: Without rhyme or reason.

DISSUASION
Substantives: dehortation, discouragement, remonstrance, expostulation, deprecation (766).

Inhibition, check, restraint, curb (752), bridle, rein, stay, damper, chill; deterrent, disincentive.

Scruple, qualm, demur (867), reluctance, delicacy (868); counterattraction.
Phrase: A wet blanket.
Verbs: To dissuade, dehort, discourage, disincline, indispose, dispirit, damp, choke off, dishearten, disenchant, disillusion, deter, keep back, put off, render averse, etc.

To withhold, restrain, hold, hold back, check, bridle, curb, rein in, keep in, inhibit, censor, repel (751).

To cool, blunt, calm, quiet, quench, slake, stagger, remonstrate, expostulate, warn, deprecate (766).

To scruple, refrain, abstain, etc. (603).
Phrases: To throw cold water on; to turn a deaf ear to.
Adjectives: Dissuading, etc., dissuasive, dehortatory, expostulatory, deprecatory.

Dissuaded, discouraged, etc.

Repugnant, averse, scrupulous, etc. (867), unpersuadable (606).

617 PLEA
Substantives: allegation, pretext, pretence, excuse, alibi, cue, colour, gloss, salvo, loophole, handle, shift, quirk, guise, stalking-horse, makeshift, white lie, evasion, get-out, special pleading (477), claptrap, advocation, soft sawder, blarney (933), moonshine; a lame excuse or apology.
Verbs: To make a pretext, etc., of; to use as a plea, etc.; to plead, allege, pretend, excuse, make a handle, etc., of, make capital of.
Adjectives: Ostensible, colourable, pretended, alleged, etc.
Phrases: *Ad captandum; qui s'excuse s'accuse*; playing to the gallery.

618 GOOD
Substantives: benefit, advantage, service, interest, weal, boot, gain, profit, velvet, good turn, blessing, boon; behoof, behalf.

Luck, piece of luck, windfall, strike, treasure trove, godsend, bonus, bunce, bonanza, prize; serendipity.

Goodness (648), utility (644), remedy (662).
Phrases: The main chance; *summum bonum; cui bono?*
Adjectives: Good, etc. (648), gainful (644).
Adverbs: Aright, well, favourably, satisfactorily, for the best.

In behalf of, in favour of.

619 EVIL
Substantives: harm, ill, injury, wrong, scathe, curse, detriment, hurt, damage, disservice, ill-turn, bale, grievance, prejudice, loss, mischief, devilry (or deviltry), gravamen.

Disadvantage, drawback, trouble, vexation (828), annoyance, nuisance, molestation, oppression, persecution, plague, corruption (659).

Blow, dunt, knock (276), bruise, scratch, wound, mutilation, outrage, spoliation, mayhem, plunder, pillage, rapine, destruction (791), dilapidation, havoc, ravage, devastation, inroad, sweep, sack, foray (716), desolation, *razzia,* dragonnade.

Misfortune, mishap, woe, disaster, calamity, affliction, catastrophe, downfall, ruin (735), prostration, curse, wrack, blight, blast; Pandora's box; a plague-spot.

Cause of evil, bane (663).

Phrases: Bad show; there's the devil to pay.

Adjectives: Bad, hurtful, etc. (649).

Adverbs: Amiss, wrong, evil, ill.

Section 2 – Prospective Volition

620 INTENTION

Substantives: intent, purpose, design, purport, mind, meaning, drift (516), animus, view, set purpose, point, bent, turn, proposal, study, scope, purview.

Final cause, object, aim, end, motive (615), *raison d'être*; destination, mark, point, butt, goal, target, prey, quarry, game, objective; the philosophers' stone.

Decision, determination, resolve, resolution (604), predetermination (611); set purpose.

A hobby, ambition, wish (865).

Study of final causes, teleology; study of final issues, eschatology.

Verbs: To intend, purpose, plan (626), design, destine, mean, aim at, propose to oneself.

To be at, drive at, be after, point at, level at, take aim, aspire at or after, endeavour after.

To meditate, think of, dream of, premeditate (611), contemplate, compass.

To propose, project, devise, take into one's head.

Phrases: To have in view; to have an eye to; to take upon oneself; to have to do; to see one's way; to find in one's heart.

Adjectives: Intended, etc., inten-tional, deliberate, advised, studied, minded, express, prepense (611), aforethought; set upon, bent upon, intent upon, in view, *in petto,* in prospect; teleological, eschatological.

Phrases: In the wind; *sur le tapis*; on the stocks; in contemplation.

Adverbs: Intentionally, etc., expressly, knowingly, wittingly, designedly, purposely, on purpose, with a view to, with an eye to, for the purpose of, with the view of, in order to, to the end that, on account of, in pursuance of, pursuant to, with the intent, etc.

Phrases: In good earnest; with one's eyes open; to all intents and purposes.

621 CHANCE

Substantives: fortune, accident, hazard, hap, haphazard (156), lot, fate (601), chance-medley, hit, fluke, casualty, contingency, exigency, fate, adventure, random shot, off chance, toss-up, gamble.

A godsend, luck, a run of luck, a turn of the dice or cards, a break, windfall, etc. (618).

Drawing lots, sortilege, *sortes Virgilianae.*

Wager, bet, flutter, betting, gambling; pitch-and-toss, *roulette, rouge-et-noir.*

Phrases: A blind bargain; a pig in a poke.

Verbs: To chance, hap, turn up; to stand a chance.

To risk, venture, hazard, speculate, stake; incur or run the risk; bet, wager, punt, gamble, plunge, raffle.

Phrases: To take one's chance; to chance it; to chance one's arm; try one's luck; shuffle the cards; put into a lottery; lay a wager; toss up; spin a coin; cast lots; draw lots; stand the hazard.

To buy a pig in a poke; *alea jacta est*; the die being cast; to go nap on; to put one's shirt on.

Adjectives: Casual, fortuitous, accidental, inadvertent, fluky, contingent, random, hit-or-miss, happy-go-lucky, adventitious, incidental.

Unintentional, involuntary, aimless, driftless, undesigned, undirected; purposeless, causeless, without purpose, etc., unmeditated, unpurposed, indiscriminate, promiscuous.

On the cards, possible (470), at stake.

Adverbs: Casually, etc., by chance, by accident, accidentally, etc., at haphazard, at a venture; heads or tails.

Phrase: As luck would have it.

622 PURSUIT

Substantives: pursuance, undertaking, enterprise (676), emprise, adventure, game, hobby, endeavour.

Prosecution, search, angling, chase, venery, quest, hunt, shikar, race, battue, drive, course, direction, wild-goose chase, steeplechase, point-to-point.

Pursuer, huntsman, hunter, Nimrod, shikari, hound, greyhound, foxhound, whippet, bloodhound, sleuth-hound, beagle, harrier.

Verbs: To pursue, undertake, engage in, take in hand, carry on, prosecute (461), endeavour.

To court, seek, angle, chase, give chase, course, dog, stalk, trail, hunt, drive, follow, run after, hound, bid for, aim at, take aim, make a leap at, rush upon, jump at, quest, shadow, tail, chivy.

Phrases: Take or hold a course; tread a path; shape one's course; direct or bend one's steps or course; run a race; rush headlong; rush head-foremost; make a plunge; snatch at, etc.; start game; follow the scent; to run or ride full tilt at.

Adjectives: Pursuing, etc., in hot pursuit; in full cry.

Adverbs: In order to, in order that, for the purpose of, with a view to, etc. (620); on the scent of.

Interjections: Yoicks! tally-ho!

623 AVOIDANCE

Substantives: forbearance, abstention, abstinence, sparing, refraining.

Flight, escape (671), evasion, elusion.

Motive for avoidance, counter-attraction.

Shirker, slacker, quitter, truant, fugitive, runaway.

Verbs: To avoid, refrain, abstain; to spare, hold, shun, fly, slope, flee, eschew, run away from, shrink, hold back, draw back (287), recoil from, flinch, blench, shy, elude, evade, shirk, blink, parry, dodge, let alone.

Phrases: To give the slip or go-by; to part company; to beat a retreat; get out of the way; to give one a wide berth; steer clear of; fight shy of; to take to one's heels.

Adjectives: Avoiding, etc., elusive, evasive, flying, fugitive, runaway, shy, retiring; unattempted, unsought.

Adverbs: Lest, with a view to prevent.

Phrases: *Sauve qui peut*; the devil take the hindmost.

624 RELINQUISHMENT

Substantives: dereliction, abandonment (782), renunciation, desertion (607), discontinuance (142).

Dispensation, riddance.

Verbs: To relinquish, give up (782); lay, set, or put aside; drop, yield, resign, abandon, renounce, discard, shelve, pigeon-hole, waive, desist from, desert, defect, leave, leave off, back out of, quit, throw up, chuck up, give over, forgo, give up, forsake, throw over, forswear, swerve from (279), put away, discontinue (681).

Phrases: To drop all idea of; to think better of it; to wash one's hands of; to turn over a new leaf; to throw up the sponge; to have other fish to fry; to draw in one's horns; to lay on the shelf; to move the previous question.

To give warning; to give notice; to ask for one's books.

Adjectives: Relinquishing, etc., relinquished, etc., unpursued.

Interjections: Hands off! keep off! give over! chuck it!

625 BUSINESS

Substantives: affair, concern, matter, task, work, job, job of work, assignment, darg, chore, stint, stunt, errand, agenda, commission, office, charge, part, duty, role; a press of business.

Province, department, beat, round, routine, mission, function, vocation, calling, avocation, profession, occupation, pursuit, cloth, faculty, trade, industry, commerce, art, craft, mystery, walk, race, career, walk of life, *métier*.

Place, post, orb, sphere, field, line, capacity, employment, engagement, exercise, occupation; situation, undertaking (676).

Verbs: To carry on or run a business, ply one's trade, keep a shop, etc.; to officiate, serve, act, traffic.

Phrases: To have to do with; have on one's hands; betake oneself to; occupy or concern oneself with; go in for; have on one's shoulders; make it one's business; go to do; act a part; perform the office of or functions of; to enter or take up a profession; spend time upon; busy oneself with, about, etc.

Adjectives: Business-like, official, functional, professional, workaday, commercial, in hand.

Adverbs: On hand, on foot, afoot, afloat, going.

Phrase: In the swim.

626 PLAN

Substantives: scheme, device, design, project, proposal, proposition, suggestion.

Line of conduct, game, card course,

tactics, strategy, policy, polity (692), craft, practice, campaign, platform, plank, ticket, agenda, orders of the day, gambit.

Intrigue, cabal, plot, conspiracy, complot, racket, machination, *coup d'état*.

Measure, step, precaution, proceeding, procedure, process, system, economy, set-up, organization, expedient, resource, contrivance, invention, artifice, shift, makeshift, gadget, stopgap, manœuvre, stratagem, fetch, trick, dodge, machination, intrigue, stroke, stroke of policy, masterstroke, great gun, trump card.

Alternative, loophole, counterplot, counter-project, side-wind, last resort, *dernier ressort, pis aller*.

Sketch, outline, blue-print, programme, draft (or draught), scenario, *ébauche*, rough draft, skeleton, forecast, prospectus, *carte du pays*, bill of fare, menu.

After-course, after-game, after-thought, *arrière-pensée*, under-plot.

A projector, designer, schemer, contriver, strategist, promoter, organizer, *entrepreneur*, artist, schematist, intriguant.

Verbs: To plan, scheme, devise, imagine, design, frame, contrive, project, plot, conspire, cabal, intrigue (702), think out, invent, forecast, strike out, work out, chalk out, rough out, sketch, lay out, lay down, cut out, cast, recast, map out, countermine, hit upon, fall upon, arrange, mature, organize, systematize, concert, concoct, digest, pack, prepare, hatch, elaborate, make shift, make do, wangle.

Phrases: To have many irons in the fire; to dig a mine; to lay a train; to spring a project; to take or adopt a course; to make the best of a bad job; to work the oracle.

Adjectives: Planned, etc., strategic; planning, scheming, etc.

Well-laid, deep-laid, cunning, well-devised, etc., maturely considered, well-weighed, prepared, organized, etc.

Adverbs: In course of preparation, under consideration, on the anvil, on the stocks, in the rough, *sur le tapis; faute de mieux.*

627 WAY

Substantives: method, manner, wise, form, mode, guise, fashion.

Path, road, gait, route, channel, walk, access, course, pass, ford, ferry, passage, line of way, trajectory, orbit, track, ride, avenue, approach, beaten track, pathway, highway, roadway, causeway, footway, pavement, sidewalk, subway, *trottoir*, footpath, bridle path, corduroy road, cinder-path, turnpike road, high road, arterial road, *autobahn*, clearway, boulevard, the King's (or Queen's) highway, thoroughfare, street, lane, alley, gangway, hatchway, cross-road, crossway, flyover, cut, short cut, royal road, cross-cut, *carrefour*, promenade.

Railway, railroad, tramway, tube, underground, elevated; canal.

Bridge, viaduct, stepping-stone, stair, corridor, aisle, lobby, staircase, moving staircase, escalator, companion-way, flight of stairs, ladder, step-ladder, stile, scaffold, scaffolding, lift, hoist, elevator; speedwalk, travolator.

Indirect way: By-path, by-way, by-walk, by-road, back door, backstairs.

Inlet, gate, door, gateway (260), portal, porch, doorway, adit, conduit, tunnel.

Phrase: *Modus operandi.*

Adverbs: How, in what way, in what manner, by what mode.

By the way, *en passant,* by the by, via, *in transitu, chemin faisant.*

One way or another, somehow, anyhow, by hook or by crook.

Phrases: All roads lead to Rome; *hae tibi erunt artes*; where there's a will there's a way.

628 MID-COURSE

Substantives: middle course, middle (68), mean (29), golden mean, *juste milieu, mezzo termine.*

Direct, straight, straightforward, course or path; great-circle sailing.

Neutrality, compromise.

Verbs: To keep in a middle course, etc.; to compromise, go half-way.

Adjectives: Undeviating, direct, straight, straightforward.

Phrases: *In medio tutissimus ibis*; to sit on the fence.

629 CIRCUIT

Substantives: roundabout way, zig-zag, circuition, detour, circumbendibus (311), wandering, deviation (279), divergence (291).

Verbs: To perform a circuit, etc., to deviate, wander, go round about, meander, etc. (279).

Phrases: To beat about the bush; to make two bites of a cherry; to lead one a pretty dance.

Adjectives: Circuitous, indirect, roundabout, tortuous, zigzag, etc.

Adverbs: By a roundabout way, by an indirect course, etc.

630 REQUIREMENT

Substantives: requisition, need, occasion, lack, wants, requisites, necessities, desideratum, exigency, pinch, *sine qua non,* the very thing, essential, must.

Needfulness, essentiality, necessity, indispensability, urgency, call for.

Phrases: Just what the doctor ordered; a crying need; a long-felt want.

Verbs: To require, need, want, have occasion for, stand in need of, lack, desire, be at a loss for, desiderate; not to be able to do without or dispense with; to want but little.

To render necessary, to necessitate,

to create a necessity for, demand, call for.

Adjectives: Requisite, required, etc., needful, necessary, imperative, exigent, essential, indispensable, irreplaceable, prerequisite, that cannot be spared or dispensed with, urgent.

631 INSTRUMENTALITY

Substantives: medium, intermedium, vehicle, channel, intervention, mediation, dint, aid (707), agency (170).

Minister, handmaid; obstetrician, midwife, *accoucheur*.

Key, master-key, passport, safe-conduct, passe-partout, 'open sesame'; a go-between, middleman (758), a cat's-paw, jackal, pander, tool, ghost, main-stay, trump card.

Phrase: Two strings to one's bow.

Verbs: To subserve, minister, intervene, mediate, devil, pander to.

Adjectives: Instrumental, intervening, intermediate, intermediary, subservient, auxiliary, ancillary.

Adverbs: Through, by, with, by means of, by dint of, *à force de,* along with, thereby, through the medium, etc., of, wherewith, wherewithal.

632 MEANS

Substantives: resources, wherewithal, appliances, ways and means, convenience, expedients, step, measure (626), aid (707), intermedium, medium.

Machinery, mechanism, mechanics, engineering, mechanical powers, automation, scaffolding, ladder, mainstay.

Phrases: Wheels within wheels; a shot in the locker.

Adjectives: Instrumental, accessory, subsidiary, mechanical.

Adverbs: How, by what means, by all means, by all manner of means, by the aid of, by dint of.

Phrases: By hook or by crook; somehow or other; for love or money; by fair means or foul; *quocumque modo.*

633 INSTRUMENT

Substantives: tool, implement, appliance, contraption, apparatus, utensil, device, gadget, craft, machine, engine, motor, dynamo, generator, mill, lathe.

Equipment, gear, tackle, tackling, rigging, harness, trappings, fittings, accoutrements, paraphernalia, equipage, outfit, appointments, furniture, material, plant, appurtenances.

A wheel, jack, clockwork, wheelwork, spring, screw, turbine, wedge, flywheel, lever, bascule, pinion, crank, winch, crane, capstan, windlass, pulley, hammer, mallet, mattock, mall, bat, racket, sledge-hammer, mace, club, truncheon, pole, staff, bill, crow, crowbar, poleaxe, handspike, crutch, boom, bar, pitchfork, etc.

Organ, limb, arm, hand, finger, claw, paw, talons, tentacle, wing, oar, paddle, pincer, plier, forceps, thimble.

Handle, hilt, haft, shaft, shank, heft, blade, trigger, tiller, helm, treadle, pummel, peg (214, 215), key.

Edge-tool, hatchet, axe, pickaxe, etc. (253), axis (312).

634 SUBSTITUTE

Substantives: shift, makeshift, succedaneum (147), stop-gap, expedient, *pis aller,* surrogate, understudy, pinch-hitter, stand-in, locum tenens, proxy, deputy (759).

635 MATERIALS

Substantives: material, matter, stuff, constituent, ingredient (56), pabulum, fuel, grist, provender, provisions, food (298).

Supplies, munition, ammunition, reinforcement, relay, contingents.

Baggage, luggage, bag and baggage, effects, goods, chattels, household stuff, equipage, paraphernalia, impedimenta, stock-in-trade, cargo, lading (780).

Metal, stone, ore, brick, clay, wood, timber, composition, compo, plastic.

636 STORE

Substantives: stock, fund, supply, reserve, relay, budget, quiver, *corps de réserve,* reserve fund, mine, quarry, vein, lode, fountain, well, spring, milch cow.

Collection, accumulation, heap (72), hoard, cache, stockpile, magazine, pile, rick, nest-egg, savings, bank (802), treasury, reservoir, repository, repertory, repertoire, album, depot, depository, treasure, thesaurus, museum, storehouse, promptuary, reservatory, conservatory, menagerie, aviary, aquarium, receptacle, warehouse, godown, *entrepôt,* dock, larder, cellar, garner, granary, store-room, box-room, lumber-room, silo, cistern, well, tank, gasometer, mill-pond, armoury, arsenal, coffer (191).

Verbs: To store, stock, stockpile, treasure up, lay in, lay by, lay up, file, garner, save, husband, hoard, deposit, amass, accumulate (72).

To reserve, keep back, hold back.

Phrase: To husband one's resources.

Adjectives: Stored, etc., in store, in reserve, spare, surplus, extra.

637 PROVISION

Substantives: supply, providing, supplying, sustentation (707), purveyance, purveying, reinforcement, husbanding, commissariat, victualling.

Forage, pasture, food, provender (298).

A purveyor, caterer, contractor, commissary, quartermaster, sutler, victualler, *restaurateur,* feeder, batman; bum-boat.

Verbs: To provide, supply, furnish, purvey, suppeditate, replenish, fill up, feed, stock with, recruit, victual, cater, find, fend, keep, lay in, lay in store, store, stockpile, forage, husband (636), upholster.

Phrase: To bring grist to the mill.

638 WASTE

Substantives: consumption, expenditure, exhaustion, drain, leakage, wear and tear, dispersion (73), ebb, loss, misuse, prodigality (818), seepage, squandermania.

Verbs: To waste, spend, expend, use, consume, spill, leak, run out, run to waste, disperse (73), ebb, dry up, impoverish, drain, empty, exhaust; to fritter away, squander.

Phrases: To cast pearls before swine; to burn the candle at both ends; to employ a steam-hammer to crack nuts; to break a butterfly on a wheel; to pour water into a sieve.

Adjectives: Wasted, spent, profuse, lavish, etc., at a low ebb.

Phrase: Penny wise and pound foolish.

639 SUFFICIENCY

Substantives: adequacy, competence; enough, satiety.

Fullness, fill, plenitude, plenty, abundance, copiousness, amplitude, affluence, richness, fertility, luxuriance, uberty, foison.

Heaps, lots, bags, piles, lashings, oceans, oodles, mobs.

Impletion, repletion, saturation.

Riches (803), mine, store, fund, (636); a bumper, a brimmer, a bellyful, a cart-load, truck-load, ship-load; a plumper; a charge.

A flood, draught, shower, rain (347), stream, tide, spring tide, flush.

Phrases: The horn of plenty; the horn of Amalthea; cornucopia; the fat of the land.

Verbs: To be sufficient, etc., to suffice, serve, pass muster, to do, satisfy, satiate, sate, saturate, make up.

To abound, teem, stream, flow, rain, shower down, pour, swarm, bristle with.

To render sufficient, etc., to make up, to fill, charge, replenish, pour in; swim in, wallow in, roll in.

Adjectives: Sufficient, enough,

adequate, commensurate, what will just do.

Moderate, measured.

Full, ample, plenty, copious, plentiful, plenteous, plenary, wantless, abundant, abounding, flush, replete, laden, charged, fraught; well stocked or provided, liberal, lavish, unstinted, to spare, unsparing, unmeasured; *ad libitum,* wholesale.

Brimful, to the brim, chock-full, saturated, crammed, up to the ears, fat, rich, affluent, full up, luxuriant, lush.

Unexhausted, unwasted, exhaustless, inexhaustible.

Phrases: Enough and to spare; cut and come again; full as an egg; ready to burst; plentiful as blackberries; flowing with milk and honey; enough in all conscience; enough to go round; *quantum sufficit.*

Adverbs: Amply, etc., galore.

640 INSUFFICIENCY

Substantives: inadequacy, inadequateness, incompetence.

Deficiency, stint, paucity, defect, defectiveness, default, defalcation, deficit, shortcoming, falling short (304), too little, what will not do, scantiness, slenderness, a mouthful, etc. (32).

Scarcity, dearth, shortage, want, need, lack, exigency, inanition, indigence, poverty, penury (804), destitution, dole, pittance, short allowance, short commons, a banian day, fast (956), a mouthful, starvation, malnutrition, famine, drought, depletion, emptiness, vacancy, flaccidity, ebb-tide, low water.

Phrase: 'A beggarly account of empty boxes.'

Verbs: To be insufficient, etc., not to suffice, to come short of, to fall short of, fail, run out of, stop short, to want, lack, need, require (630); caret.

To render insufficient, etc., to stint, grudge, hold back, withhold, starve, pinch, skimp, scrimp, famish.

Phrase: To live from hand to mouth.

Adjectives: Insufficient, inadequate, incompetent, too little, not enough, etc., scant, scanty, skimpy, scrimpy, deficient, defective, in default, scarce, empty, empty-handed, devoid, short of, out of, wanting, etc., hard up for.

Destitute, dry, drained, unprovided, unsupplied, unfurnished, unreplenished, unfed, unsorted, untreasured, bare, meagre, poor, thin, spare, skimpy, stinted, starved, famished, pinched, fasting, starveling, jejune, without resources (735), short-handed, undermanned, understaffed, etc.

Phrases: In short supply; not to be had for love or money; at the end of one's tether; at one's last gasp.

641 REDUNDANCE

Substantives: superabundance, superfluity, superfluence, glut, exuberance, profuseness, profusion, plethora, engorgement, congestion, surfeit, gorge, load, turgidity, turgescence, dropsy.

Excess, nimiety, overdose, over-supply, overplus, surplus, surplusage, overflow, inundation, deluge, extravagance, prodigality (818), exorbitance, lavishness, immoderation.

An expletive (908), pleonasm.

Phrases: *Satis superque*; a drug in the market; the lion's share.

Verbs: To superabound, overabound, run over, overflow, flow over, roll in, wallow in.

To overstock, overdose, overlay, gorge, engorge, glut, sate, satiate, surfeit, cloy, load, overload, surcharge, overrun, choke, drown, drench, inundate, flood, whelm, deluge.

Phrases: To go begging; it never rains but it pours; to paint the lily; to carry coals to Newcastle.

Adjectives: Redundant, superfluous, exuberant, superabundant, immoderate, extravagant, excessive, in excess, *de trop*, needless, unnecessary, uncalled-for, over and above (40), more than enough, buckshee, running to waste, overflowing, running over.

Turgid, gorged, plethoric, dropsical, replete, profuse, lavish, prodigal, supervacaneous, extra, spare, duplicate, supernumerary, supererogatory, expletive, surcharged, overcharged, sodden, overloaded, overladen, overburdened, overrun, overfed, overfull.
Phrase: Enough and to spare.
Adverbs: Over, over and above, too much, overmuch, over and enough, too far, without measure, without stint.
Phrase: Over head and ears.

642 IMPORTANCE
Substantives: consequence, moment, weight, gravity, seriousness, consideration, concern, significance, import, influence (175), pressure, urgency, instancy, stress, emphasis, interest, preponderance, prominence (250), greatness (31).

The substance, essence, quintessence, core, kernel, nub, gist, pith, marrow, soul, point, gravamen.

The principal, prominent, or essential part.

A notability, somebody, personage (875), VIP, bigwig, toff, big pot, big gun, his nibs; great doings, *notabilia,* a red-letter day.
Phrases: *A sine qua non*; a matter of life and death; no laughing matter.
Verbs: To be important, or of importance, etc., to signify, import, matter, boot, weigh, count, to be prominent, etc., to take the lead.

To attach, or ascribe importance to; to value, care for, etc. (897); overestimate, etc. (482), exaggerate (549).

To mark, underline, italicize, score, accentuate, emphasize, stress, rub in.
Phrases: To be somebody; to fill the bill; to make much of; to make a stir, a

fuss, a piece of work, a song and dance; set store upon; to lay stress upon; to take *au grand sérieux*.
Adjectives: Important, of importance, etc., grave, serious, material, weighty, influential, significant, emphatic, momentous, earnest, pressing, critical, preponderating, pregnant, urgent, paramount, essential, vital.

Great, considerable, etc. (31), capital, leading, principal, superior, chief, main, prime, primary, cardinal, prominent, salient, egregious, outstanding.

Signal, notable, memorable, remarkable, etc., grand, solemn, eventful, stirring, impressive; not to be despised, or overlooked, etc., unforgettable, worth while.
Phrases: Being no joke; not to be sneezed at; no small beer.

643 UNIMPORTANCE
Substantives: indifference, insignificance, triflingness, triviality, triteness; paltriness, emptiness, nothingness, inanity, lightness, levity, frivolity, vanity, frivolousness, puerility, child's play.

Poverty, meagreness, meanness, shabbiness, etc. (804).

A trifle, small matter, minutiae, bagatelle, cipher, moonshine, molehill, joke, jest, snap of the fingers, flea-bite, pinch of snuff, old song, *nugae;* fiddlestick, fiddlestick end, bubble, bulrush, nonentity, lay figure, nobody.

A straw, pin, fig, button, rush, feather, farthing, brass farthing, red cent, dime, dam, doit, peppercorn, pebble, small fry.

Trumpery, trash, codswallop, stuff, *fatras,* frippery, chaff, drug, froth, smoke, cobweb.

Toy, plaything, knick-knack, gimcrack, gewgaw, thingumbob, bauble, kickshaw, bric-à-brac, fal-lal, whimwham, whigmaleerie, curio, bibelot.

Refuse, lumber, junk, litter, orts,

tares, weeds, sweepings, scourings, off-scourings; rubble, debris, dross, scoriae, dregs, scum, flue, dust (653).

Phrases: 'Leather and prunella'; *peu de chose*; much ado about nothing; much cry and little wool; flotsam and jetsam; a man of straw; a stuffed shirt; a toom tabard.

Verbs: To be unimportant, to be of little or no importance, etc.; not to signify, not to deserve, merit, or be worthy of notice, regard, consideration, etc.

Phrases: To catch at straws; to make much ado about nothing; to cut no ice; *le jeu ne vaut pas la chandelle*.

Adjectives: Unimportant, secondary, inferior, immaterial, inconsiderable, inappreciable, insignificant, unessential, non-essential, beneath notice, indifferent; of little or no account, importance, consequence, moment, interest, etc.; unimpressive, subordinate.

Trifling, trivial, trite, banal, mere, common, so-so, slight, slender, flimsy, trumpery, foolish, idle, puerile, childish, infantile, frothy, trashy, catchpenny, fiddling, frivolous, commonplace, contemptible, cheap.

Vain, empty, inane, poor, sorry, mean, meagre, shabby, scrannel, vile, miserable, scrubby, weedy, niggling, beggarly, piddling, peddling, pitiful, pitiable, despicable, paltry, ridiculous, farcical, finical, finicking, finicky, finikin, fiddle-faddle, wishy-washy, namby-pamby, gimcrack, twopenny, twopenny-halfpenny, two-by-four, one-horse, piffling, jerry, jerry built.

Phrases: Not worth a straw; as light as air; not worth mentioning; not worth boasting about; no great shakes; nothing to write home about; small potatoes; neither here nor there.

Interjections: No matter! pshaw! pooh! pooh-pooh! shucks! I should worry! fudge! fiddle-de-dee! nonsense! boloney! hooey! nuts! rats! stuff! *n'importe!*

Adverbs: Meagrely, pitifully, vainly, etc.

644 UTILITY

Substantives: service, use, function, office, sphere, capacity, part, role, task, work.

Usefulness, worth, stead, avail, advantageousness, profitableness, serviceableness, merit, *cui bono,* applicability, adequacy, subservience, subserviency, efficacy, efficiency, help, money's worth.

Verbs: To be useful, etc., of use, of service.

To avail, serve, subserve, help (707), conduce, answer, profit, advantage, accrue, bedstead.

To render useful, to use (677), to turn to account, to utilize, to make the most of.

Phrases: To stand in good stead; to do yeoman service; to perform a function; to serve a purpose; to serve a turn.

Adjectives: Useful, beneficial, advantageous, serviceable, helpful, gainful, profitable, lucrative, worthwhile.

Subservient, conducive, applicable, adequate, efficient, efficacious, effective, effectual, seaworthy.

Applicable, available, handy, ready.

Adverbs: Usefully, etc.; *pro bono publico*.

645 INUTILITY

Substantives: uselessness, inefficacy, inefficiency, ineptness, ineptitude, inadequacy, inaptitude, unskilfulness, fecklessness, fruitlessness, inanity, worthlessness, unproductiveness, barrenness, sterility, vanity, futility, triviality, paltriness, unprofitableness, unfruitfulness, rustiness, obsoleteness, discommodity, supererogation, obsolescence.

Litter, rubbish, lumber, trash, junk, punk, job lot, orts, weeds (643), bilge, hog-wash. A waste, desert, Sahara, wild, wilderness.

Phrases: The labour of Sisyphus; the work of Penelope; a slaying of the slain; a dead loss; a work of supererogation.

Verbs: To be useless, etc., to be of no avail, use, etc. (644).

To render useless, etc.; to dismantle, disable, disqualify, cripple.

Phrases: To use vain efforts; to beat the air; to fish in the air; to lash the waves; to plough the sands.

Adjectives: Useless, inutile, inefficient, inefficacious, unavailing, inadequate, inoperative, bootless, supervacaneous, unprofitable, unremunerative, unproductive, sterile, barren, unsubservient, supererogatory.

Worthless, valueless, at a discount, gainless, fruitless, profitless, unserviceable, rusty, effete, vain, empty, inane, wasted, nugatory, futile, feckless, inept, withered, good for nothing, wasteful, ill-spent, obsolete, obsolescent, stale, dud, punk, dear-bought, rubbishy.

Unneeded, unnecessary, uncalled-for, unwanted, incommodious, discommodious.

Phrases: Not worth having; leading to no end; no good; not worthwhile; of no earthly use; a dead letter.

Adverbs: Uselessly, etc., to no purpose.

646 EXPEDIENCE

Substantives: expediency, fitness, suitableness, suitability, aptness, aptitude, appropriateness, propriety, pertinence, seasonableness (134), adaptation, congruity, consonance (23), convenience, eligibility, applicability, desirability, seemliness, rightness.

An opportunist, time-server.

Verbs: To be expedient, etc.

To suit, fit, square with, adapt itself to, agree with, consort with, accord with, tally with, conform to, go with, do for.

Adjectives: Expedient, fit, fitting, worth while, suitable, applicable, eligible, apt, appropriate, adapted, proper, advisable, politic, judicious, desirable, pertinent, congruous, seemly, consonant, becoming, meet, due, consentaneous, congenial, well-timed, pat, seasonable, opportune, apropos, befitting, happy, felicitous, auspicious, acceptable, etc., convenient, commodious, right.

Phrases: Being just the thing; just as well.

647 INEXPEDIENCE

Substantives: inexpediency, disadvantageousness, unserviceableness, disservice, unfitness, inaptitude, ineptitude, ineligibility, inappropriateness, impropriety, undesirability, unseemliness, incongruity, impertinence, inopportuneness, unseasonableness.

Inconvenience, incommodiousness, incommodity, discommodity, disadvantage.

Inefficacy, inefficiency, inadequacy.

Verbs: To be inexpedient, etc., to embarrass, cumber, lumber, handicap, be in the way, etc.

Adjectives: Inexpedient, disadvantageous, unprofitable, unfit, unfitting, unsuitable, undesirable, amiss, improper, unapt, inept, impolitic, injudicious, ill-advised, unadvisable, ineligible, objectionable, inadmissible, unseemly, inopportune, unseasonable, inefficient, inefficacious, inadequate.

Inconvenient, incommodious, cumbrous, cumbersome, lumbering, unwieldy, unmanageable, awkward, clumsy.

648 GOODNESS

Substantives: excellence, integrity (939), virtue (944), merit, value, worth, price, preciousness, estimation, rareness, exquisiteness.

Superexcellence, superiority, supereminence, transcendence, perfection (650).

Mediocrity (651), innocuousness, harmlessness, inoffensiveness.

Masterpiece, *chef d'œuvre,* flower, pick, cream, *crême de la crême, élite,* gem, jewel, treasure; a good man (948).

Phrases: One in a thousand (or in a million); the salt of the earth.

Verbs: To be good, beneficial, etc.; to be superior, etc., to excel, transcend, top, vie, emulate (708).

To be middling, etc. (651); to pass, to do.

To produce good, benefit, etc., to benefit, to be beneficial, etc., to confer a benefit, etc., to improve (658).

Phrases: To challenge comparison; to pass muster; to speak well for.

Adjectives: Good, beneficial, valuable, estimable, serviceable, advantageous, precious, favourable, palmary, felicitous, propitious.

Sound, sterling, standard, true, genuine, household, fresh, in good condition, unfaded, unspoiled, unimpaired, uninjured, undemolished, undamaged, unravaged, undecayed, natural, unsophisticated, unadulterated, unpolluted, unvitiated.

Choice, select, picked, nice, worthy, meritorious (944), fine, rare, unexceptionable, excellent, admirable, firstrate, splendid, swell, bully, wizard, priceless, smashing, super, topping, top-hole, clipping, ripping, nailing, prime, tiptop, crack, jake, cardinal, superlative, superfine, super-excellent, pukka, gradely, champion, exquisite, high-wrought, inestimable, invaluable, incomparable, transcendent, matchless, peerless, inimitable, unrivalled, *nulli secundus,* second to none, *facile princeps,* spotless, immaculate, perfect (650), *récherché,* first-class,

first chop.

Moderately good (651).

Harmless, innocuous, innoxious, unoffending, inoffensive, unobjectionable.

Phrases: The goods; the stuff to give them; a bit of all right; of the first water; precious as the apple of the eye; *ne plus ultra;* sound as a roach; worth its weight in gold; right as a trivet; up to the mark; an easy winner.

649 BADNESS

Substantives: hurtfulness, disserviceableness, injuriousness, banefulness, mischievousness, noxiousness, malignancy, malignity, malevolence, tender mercies, venomousness, virulence, destructiveness, scathe, curse, pest, plague, bane (663), plague-spot, evil star, ill wind; evildoer (913).

Vileness, foulness, rankness, depravation, depravity; injury, outrage, ill treatment, annoyance, molestation, oppression; sabotage; deterioration (659).

Phrases: A snake in the grass; a fly in the ointment; a nigger in the woodpile; a thorn in the side; a skeleton in the cupboard.

Verbs: To be bad, etc.

To cause, produce, or inflict evil; to harm, hurt, injure, mar, damage, damnify, endamage, scathe, prejudice, stand in the light of, worsen.

To wrong, molest (830), annoy, harass, infest, grieve, aggrieve, trouble, oppress, persecute, weigh down, run down, overlay.

To maltreat, abuse, ill use, ill treat, bedevil, bruise, scratch, maul, mishandle, man-handle, strafe, knock about, strike, smite, scourge (972), wound, lame, maim, scotch, cripple, mutilate, hamstring, hough, stab, pierce, etc., crush, crumble, pulverize.

To corrupt, corrode, pollute, etc. (659).

To spoil, despoil, sweep, ravage, lay

waste, devastate, dismantle, demolish, level, raze, consume, overrun, sack, plunder, destroy (162).

Phrases: To play the deuce with; to break the back of; crush to pieces; crumble to dust; to grind to powder; to ravage with fire and sword; to knock the stuffing out of; to queer one's pitch; to let daylight into.

Adjectives: Bad, evil, ill, wrong, prejudicial, disadvantageous, unprofitable, unlucky, sinister, left-handed, obnoxious, untoward, unadvisable, inauspicious, ill-omened.

Hurtful, harmful, injurious, grievous, detrimental noxious, pernicious, mischievous, baneful, baleful.

Morbific, rank, peccant, malignant, tabid, corroding, corrosive, virulent, cankering, mephitic, narcotic.

Deleterious, poisonous, venomous, envenomed, pestilent, pestilential, pestiferous, destructive, deadly, fatal, mortal, lethal, lethiferous, miasmal.

Vile, sad, wretched, sorry, shabby, scurvy, base, low, low-down (940), scrubby, lousy, stinking, horrid.

Hateful, abominable, loathsome, detestable, execrable, iniquitous, cursed, accursed, confounded, damnable, diabolic, devilish, demoniacal, infernal, hellish, Satanic, villainous, depraved, shocking (898).

Adverbs: Wrong, wrongly, badly, to one's cost.

Phrases: *Corruptio optimi pessima*; if the worst comes to the worst.

650 PERFECTION

Substantives: perfectness, indefectibility, impeccability, infallibility, unimpeachability, *beau idéal,* summit (210).

Masterpiece, *chef d'œuvre, magnum opus,* classic, model, pattern, mirror, phoenix, *rara avis*, paragon, cream, nonsuch (or nonesuch), nonpareil, *élite.*

Gem, bijou, jewel, pearl, diamond, ruby, brilliant.

A Bayard, a Galahad, an Admirable Crichton.

Phrases: The philosophers' stone; the flower of the flock; the cock of the roost; the pink or acme of perfection; the pick of the bunch; the *ne plus ultra.*

Verbs: To be perfect, etc., to excel, transcend, overtop, etc. (33).

To bring to perfection, to perfect, to ripen, mature, etc. (52, 729).

Phrases: To carry everything before it; to play first fiddle; bear away the bell; to sweep the board.

Adjectives: Perfect, best, faultless, finished, indeficient, indefectible, immaculate, spotless, impeccable, transcendent, matchless, peerless, unparagoned, etc. (648), inimitable, unimpeachable, superlative, superhuman, divine, classical.

Phrases: Right as a trivet; sound as a bell; *ad unguem factus; sans peur et sans reproche.*

651 IMPERFECTION

Substantives: imperfectness, unsoundness, faultiness, deficiency, disability, weak point, drawback, inadequacy, inadequateness (645), handicap.

Fault, defect, flaw, lacuna (198), crack, twist, taint, blemish, shortcoming (304), peccancy, vice.

Mediocrity, mean (29), indifference, inferiority.

Verbs: To be imperfect, middling, etc., to fail, fall short, lie under a disadvantage, be handicapped.

Phrases: To play second fiddle; barely to pass muster.

Adjectives: Imperfect, deficient, defective, faulty, dud, inferior, inartistic, inadequate, wanting, unsound, vicious, cracked, warped, lame, feeble, frail, flimsy, sketchy, botched, gimcrack, gingerbread, tottering, wonky, decrepit, rickety, ramshackle, rattletrap, battered, worn out, threadbare, seedy, wormeaten, moth-eaten, played out, used up, decayed, mutilated, unrectified, uncorrected.

Indifferent, middling, mediocre, below par, so-so, *couci-couci*, secondary, second-rate, third-rate, etc., second-best, second-hand.

Tolerable, passable, bearable, pretty well, well enough, rather good, decent, fair, admissible, not bad, not amiss, not so dusty, unobjectionable, respectable, betwixt and between.

Phrases: Having a screw loose; out of order; out of kilter; no great catch; milk and water; no great shakes; nothing to boast of; on its last legs; no class.

652 CLEANNESS
Substantives: cleanliness, asepsis, purity (960), neatness, tidiness, spotlessness, immaculateness.

Cleaning, purification, mundification, lustration, abstersion, depuration, expurgation, purgation, castration.

Washing, ablution, lavation, elutriation, lixiviation, clarification, defecation, edulcoration, filtration.

Fumigation, ventilation, antisepsis, decontamination, disinfection, soap; detergent, shampoo, antiseptic, disinfectant.

Washroom, wash-house, laundry; washerwoman, laundress, charwoman, cleaner, scavenger, dustman, sweep.

Brush, broom, besom, vacuum-cleaner, duster, handkerchief, napkin, face-cloth, towel, sponge, toothbrush, nail-brush; mop, sieve, riddle, screen, filter.

Verbs: To be clean, etc.

To render, clean, etc., to clean, to mundify, cleanse, wipe, mop, sponge, scour, swab, scrub, brush, sweep, vacuum, dust, brush up.

To wash, lave, sluice, buck, launder, steep, rinse, absterge, deterge, descale,

clear, purify, depurate, defecate, elutriate, lixiviate, edulcorate, clarify, drain, strain, filter, filtrate, fine, fine down.

To disinfect, deodorize, fumigate, delouse, ventilate, purge, expurgate, bowdlerize.

To sift, winnow, pick, screen, weed.

Phrase: To make a clean sweep of.

Adjectives: Clean, cleanly, pure, spotless, unspotted, immaculate, unstained, stainless, unsoiled, unsullied, taintless, untainted, sterile, aseptic, uninfected.

Cleansing, etc., detergent, detersive, abstersive, abstergent, purgatory, purificatory, etc., abluent, antiseptic.

Spruce, tidy, washed, swept, etc., cleaned, disinfected, purified, etc.

Phrases: Clean as a whistle; clean as a new penny; neat as ninepence.

653 UNCLEANNESS
Substantives: immundicity, uncleanliness, soilure, sordidness, foulness, impurity (961), pollution, nastiness, offensiveness, beastliness, muckiness, defilement, contamination, abomination, taint, tainture, corruption, decomposition (49).

Slovenliness, slovenly, untidiness, sluttishness, coarseness, grossness, dregginess, squalor.

Dirt, filth, soil, slop, dust, flue, ooss, cobweb, smoke, soot, smudge, smut, stour, clart, glaur, grime, *sordes*, mess, muck.

Slut, slattern, sloven, frump; mudlark, riff-raff.

Dregs, grounds, sediment, lees, settlement, dross, drossiness, precipitate, scoriae, slag, clinker, scum, sweepings, off-scourings, garbage, *caput mortuum,* residuum, draff, fur, scurf, scurfiness, furfur, dandruff, vermin.

Mud, mire, slush, quagmire, slough, sludge, alluvium, silt, slime, spawn, offal, faeces, excrement, ordure, dung, droppings, guano, manure, compost, dunghill, midden, bog, laystall, sink, cesspool, sump, sough, *cloaca,* latrine, lavatory, water-closet, w.c., toilet, urinal, rear, convenience, privy, jakes, comfort station, heads, thunder-box, drain, sewer; hog-wash, bilge-water.

Sty, pigsty, dusthole, lair, den, slum.

Rottenness, corruption, decomposition, decay, putrefaction, putrescence, putridity, purulence, pus, matter, suppuration, feculence, rankness, rancidity, mouldiness, mustiness, mucidness, mould, mother, must, mildew, dry-rot, fetor, (401).

Scatology, coprology.

Phrases: A sink of corruption; an Augean stable.

Verbs: To be unclean, dirty, etc., to rot, putrefy, corrupt, decompose, go bad, mould, moulder, fester, etc.

To render unclean, etc., to dirt, dirty, soil, tarnish, begrime, smear, besmear, mess, smirch, besmirch, smudge, besmudge, bemire, spatter, bespatter, splash, bedaggle, bedraggle, daub, bedaub, slobber, beslobber, beslime, to cover with dust.

To foul, befoul, sully, pollute, defile, debase, contaminate, taint, corrupt, deflower, rot.

Adjectives: Unclean, dirty, soiled, filthy, grimy, clarty, dusty, dirtied, etc., smutty, sooty, smoky, reechy, thick, turbid, dreggy, slimy, filthy, mucky.

Slovenly, untidy, sluttish, blowzy, draggle-tailed, dowdy, frumpish, slipshod, unkempt, unscoured, unswept, unwiped, unwashed, unstrained, unpurified, squalid.

Nasty, foul, impure, offensive, abominable, beastly, lousy.

Mouldy, musty, mildewed, fusty, rusty, mouldering, moth-eaten, reasty, rotten, rotting, tainted, rancid, high, fly-blown, maggoty, putrescent, putrid, putrefied, bad, festering, purulent,

feculent, fecal, stercoraceous, exrementitious.

Phrases: Wallowing in the mire; rotten to the core.

654 HEALTH

Substantives: sanity, soundness, heartiness, haleness, vigour, freshness, bloom, healthfulness, euphoria, incorruption, incorruptibility.

Phrases: *Mens sana in corpore sano*; a clean bill.

Verbs: To be in health, etc., to flourish, thrive, bloom.

To return to health, to recover, convalesce, recruit, pull through, to get the better of.

To restore to health, to cure, recall to life, bring to.

Phrases: To keep on one's legs; to take a new or fresh lease of life; to turn the corner.

Adjectives: Healthy, in health, well, sound, healthful, hearty, hale, fresh, whole, florid, staunch, flush, hardy, vigorous, chipper, spry, bobbish, blooming, weather-proof, fit.

Unscathed, uninjured, unmaimed, unmarred, untainted.

Phrases: Sitting up and taking nourishment; being on one's legs; sound as a bell, or roach; fresh as a daisy or rose; in fine or high feather; in good case; fit as a fiddle; in the pink of condition; in the pink; in good form.

655 DISEASE

Substantives: illness, sickness, ailment, ailing, indisposition, complaint, disorder, malady, distemper.

Attack, visitation, seizure, stroke, fit.

Sickliness, sickishness, infirmity, diseasedness, tabescence, invalidation, delicacy, weakness, cachexy, witheredness, atrophy, marasmus, incurableness, incurability, palsy, paralysis, decline, consumption, prostration.

251

Taint, pollution, infection, septicity, epidemic, endemic, murrain, plague, pestilence, virus, pox.

A sore, ulcer, abscess, fester, boil, gathering, issue, rot, canker, cancer, carcinoma, sarcoma, caries, gangrene, mortification, eruption, rash, congestion, inflammation, fever.

A valetudinarian, invalid, patient, case, cripple.

Pathology, aetiology, nosology.

Verbs: To be ill, etc., to ail, suffer, be affected with, etc., to complain of, to droop, flag, languish, halt, sicken, gasp; to malinger.

Phrases: To be laid up; to keep one's bed.

Adjectives: Diseased, ill, taken ill, seized, indisposed, unwell, sick, sickish, seedy, queer, crook, toutie, ailing, suffering, confined, bedridden, invalided.

Unsound, sickly, poorly, delicate, weakly, cranky, healthless, infirm, groggy, unbraced, drooping, flagging, withered, palsied, paralytic, paraplectic, decayed, decrepit, lame, crippled, battered, halting, worn out, used up, run down, off colour, moth-eaten, worm-eaten.

Morbid, tainted, vitiated, peccant, contaminated, tabid, tabescent, mangy, poisoned, immedicable, gasping, moribund (360).

Phrases: Out of sorts; good for nothing; on the sick-list; on the danger list; in a bad way; *hors de combat*; on one's last legs; at one's last gasp.

656 SALUBRITY

Substantives: healthiness, wholesomeness, innoxiousness.

Preservation of health, prophylaxis, hygiene, sanitation.

A health resort, spa, hydropathic, sanatorium (662).

Verbs: To be salubrious, etc., to agree with.

Adjectives: Salubrious, wholesome,

healthy, sanitary, hygienic, salutary, salutiferous, healthful, tonic, prophylactic, bracing, benign.

Innoxious, innocuous, harmless, uninjurious, innocent.

Remedial, restorative, sanatory (662), nutritious, alterative (660).

657 INSALUBRITY

Substantives: unhealthiness, unwholesomeness, deadliness, fatality.

Microbe, germ, virus, etc. (663).

Adjectives: Insalubrious, insanitary, unsanitary, unhealthy, ungenial, uncongenial, unwholesome, morbific, mephitic, septic, deleterious, pestilent, pestiferous, pestilential, virulent, poisonous, toxic, contagious, infectious, catching, epidemic, epizotic, endemic, pandemic, zymotic, deadly, pathogenic, pathogenetic, lowering, relaxing; innutritious (645).

Phrase: 'There is death in the pot.'

658 IMPROVEMENT

Substantives: melioration, amelioration, betterment, mend, amendment, emendation, advance, advancement, progress, elevation, promotion, preferment, convalescence, recovery, recuperation, curability.

Repair, reparation, cicatrization, correction, reform, reformation, rectification, epuration, purification, etc. (652), refinement, relief, redress, second thoughts.

New edition; *réchauffé, refacimento,* revision, revise, recension, rehash, redaction.

Verbs: To be, become, or get better, etc., to improve, mend, advance, progress (282), to get on, make progress, gain ground, make way, go ahead, pick up, rally, recover, get the better of, get well, get over it, pull through, convalesce, recuperate.

To render better, improve, amend, better, meliorate, ameliorate, advance, push on, promote, prefer, forward, enhance.

To relieve, refresh, restore, renew, redintegrate, heal (660); to palliate, mitigate.

To repair, refit, cannibalize, retouch, revise, botch, vamp, tinker, cobble, clout, patch up, touch up, cicatrize, darn, fine-draw, rub up, do up, furbish, refurbish, polish, bolster up, caulk, careen; to stop a gap, to staunch.

To purify, depurate (652), defecate, strain, filter, rack, refine, disinfect, chasten.

To correct, rectify, redress, reform, review, remodel, prune, restore (660), mellow, set to rights, sort, fix, put straight, straighten out, revise.

Phrases: To turn over a new leaf; to take a new lease of life; to make the most of; to infuse new blood into.

Adjectives: Improving, etc., improved, etc., progressive, corrective, reparatory, emendatory, revisory, sanatory, advanced.

Curable, corrigible, capable of improvement.

659 DETERIORATION

Substantives: wane, ebb, debasement, degeneracy, degeneration, degradation, degenerateness, demotion, relegation.

Impairment, injury, outrage, havoc, devastation, inroad, vitiation, adulteration, sophistication, debasement, perversion, degradation, demoralization, corruption, prostitution, pollution, contamination, alloy, venenation.

Decline, declension, declination, going downhill, recession, retrogression, retrogradation (283), caducity, decrepitude, decadence, falling off, pejoration.

Decay, disorganization, damage, scathe, wear and tear, mouldiness, rottenness, corrosion, moth and rust, dry-rot, blight, marasmus, atrophy, emaciation, falling to pieces, *délâbrement*.

Verbs: To be, or become worse, to deteriorate, worsen, disimprove, wane, ebb, degenerate, fall off, decline, go downhill, sink, go down, lapse, droop, be the worse for, recede, retrograde, revert (283), fall into decay, fade, break, break up, break down, fall to pieces, wither, moulder, rot, rust, crumble, totter, shake, tumble, fall, topple, perish, die (360).

To render less good; to weaken, vitiate, debase, alloy, pervert.

To spoil, embase, defile, taint, infect, contaminate, sophisticate, poison, canker, corrupt, tamper with, pollute, deprave, demoralize, envenom, debauch, prostitute, defile, degrade, downgrade, demote, adulterate, stain, spatter, bespatter, soil, tarnish (653), addle.

To corrode, erode, blight, rot, wear away, wear out, gnaw, gnaw at the root of, sap, mine, undermine, shake, break up, disorganize, dismantle, dismast, lay waste, do for, ruin, confound.

To embitter, acerbate, aggravate.

To wound, stab, maim, lame, cripple, mutilate, disfigure, deface.

To injure, harm, hurt, impair, dilapidate, damage, endamage, damnify, etc. (649).

Phrases: To go to rack and ruin; to have seen better days; to go to the dogs; to go to pot; to go on from bad to worse; to go farther and fare worse; to run to seed; to play the deuce with; to sap the foundations of.

Adjectives: Deteriorated, worse, impaired, etc., degenerate, *passé*, on the decline, on the down-grade, deciduous, unimproved, unrecovered, unrestored.

Decayed, etc., moth-eaten, worm-eaten, mildewed, rusty, time-worn, moss-grown, effete, wasted, worn, crumbling, tumbledown, dilapidated, overblown.

Phrases: Out of the frying-pan into the fire; the worse for wear; worn to a thread; worn to a shadow; reduced to a skeleton; the ghost of oneself; a hopeless case.

660 RESTORATION

Substantives: restoral, reinstatement, replacement, rehabilitation, instauration, re-establishment, rectification, revendication, redintegration, refection, reconstitution, cure, sanation, refitting, reorganization, recruiting, redress, retrieval, refreshment.

Renovation, renewal, reanimation, recovery, resumption, reclamation, reconversion, recure, resuscitation, revivification, reviviscence, revival, renascence, renaissance, rejuvenation, rejuvenescence, regeneration, regeneracy, regenerateness, palingenesis, redemption; a Phoenix.

Réchauffé, *rifacimento* (658), recast.

Phrases: A new lease of life; second youth; new birth; 'Richard's himself again.'

Verbs: To return to the original state, to right itself, come to, come round, rally, revive, recover.

To restore, replace, re-establish, reinstate, reseat, replant, reconstitute, redintegrate, set right, set to rights, sort, fix, rectify, redress, reclaim, redeem, recover, recoup, recure, retrieve, cicatrize.

To refit, recruit, refresh, refocillate, rehabilitate, reconvert, renew, renovate, revitalize, revivify, reinvigorate, regenerate, rejuvenesce, rejuvenate, resuscitate, reanimate, recast, reconstruct, rebuild, reorganize.

To repair, retouch, revise (658).

To cure, heal, cicatrize, remedy, doctor, physic, medicate.

Phrases: Recall to life; set on one's legs.

Adjectives: Restoring, etc., restored, etc., restorative, recuperative, reparative, sanative, remedial, curative (662).

Restorable, sanable, remediable, retrievable, recoverable.

Adverbs: *In statu quo*; as you were; Phoenix-like.

661 RELAPSE

Substantives: lapse, falling back, back-sliding, retrogression, reaction, set-back, recidivism, retrogradation, etc. (659).

Return to or recurrence of a bad state.

A recidivist, backslider, throwback.

Verbs: To relapse, lapse, backslide, fall back, slide back, sink back, return, retrograde.

662 REMEDY

Substantives: help, redress, cure, antidote, counterpoison, vaccine, antitoxin, antibiotic, antiseptic, specific, prophylactic, corrective, restorative, pick-me-up, bracer, sedative, anodyne, opiate, hypnotic, nepenthe, tranquillizer.

Febrifuge, diaphoretic, diuretic, carminative, purgative, laxative, emetic, palliative.

Physic, medicine, drug, tonic, medicament, nostrum, placebo, recipe, prescription, catholicon.

Panacea, elixir, *elixir vitae,* balm, balsam, cordial, cardiac, theriac, ptisan.

Pill, pilule, pellet, tablet, tabloid, pastille, lozenge, powder, draught, lincture, suppository.

Salve, ointment, plaster, epithem, embrocation, liniment, lotion, cataplasm, styptic, poultice, compress, pledget.

Treatment, diet, dieting, regimen.

Pharmacy, pharmacology, materia medica, therapeutics, homoeopathy, allopathy, faith healing, radiotherapy, actinotherapy, heliotherapy, thallassotherapy, hydrotherapy, hydropathy, osteopathy, dietetics, dietary, chirurgery, surgery, gynaecology, midwifery, obstetrics, paediatrics, geriatrics; psycho-analysis, psychiatry, psychotherapy.

A hospital, infirmary, pest-house, lazaretto, madhouse, asylum, lunatic asylum, mental hospital, *maison de santé,* ambulance, clinic, dispensary, sanatorium, spa, hydropathic, nursing home.

A doctor, physician, general practitioner, GP, surgeon, anaesthetist, dentist, aurist, oculist, specialist, alienist, psycho-analyst, psychiatrist, psycho-therapist; apothecary, druggist; midwife, nurse.

Verbs: To dose, physic, attend, doctor, nurse.

Adjectives: Remedial, medical, medicinal, therapeutic, surgical, chirurgical, sanatory, sanative, curative, salutary, salutiferous, healing, paregoric, restorative, tonic, corroborant, analeptic, balsamic, anodyne, sedative, lenitive, demulcent, emollient, depuratory, detersive, detergent, abstersive, disinfectant, antiseptic, corrective, prophylactic, antitoxic, febrifuge, alterative, expectorant; veterinary.

Dietetic, alexipharmic, nutritious, nutritive, peptic, alimentary.

663 BANE
Substantives: scourge, curse, scathe, sting, fang, gall and wormwood.

Poison, virus, venom, toxin, microbe, germ, bacillus, miasma, mephitis, malaria, pest, rust, canker, cancer, canker-worm.

Hemlock, hellebore, nightshade, henbane, aconite, upas-tree.

Sirocco.

A viper, adder, serpent, cobra, rattlesnake, cockatrice, scorpion, wireworm, torpedo, hornet, vulture, vampire.

Science of poisons, toxicology.

Adjectives: Poisonous, venomous, virulent, toxic, mephitic, pestilent, pestilential, miasmatic, baneful (649).

664 SAFETY
Substantives: security, surety,

impregnability, invulnerability, invulnerableness, escape (671).

Safeguard, guard, guardianship, chaperonage, protection, tutelage, wardship, wardenship, safe-conduct, escort, convoy, garrison.

Watch, watch and ward, sentinel, sentry, scout, watchman, patrol, vedette, picket, bivouac.

Policeman, policewoman, police officer, constable, cop, copper, bobby, peeler, slop, bull, dick, rozzer.

Watch-dog, bandog, Cerberus.

Protector, guardian, guard (717), defender, warden, warder, preserver, chaperon, tutelary saint, guardian angel, palladium.

Custody, safe-keeping (751).

Isolation, segregation, quarantine; insurance, assurance; cover.

Verbs: To be safe, etc.

To render safe, etc., to protect, guard, ward, shield, shelter, flank, cover, screen, shroud, ensconce, secure, fence, hedge in, entrench, house, nestel.

To defend, forfend, escort, convoy, garrison, mount guard, patrol, chaperon, picket.

Phrases: To save one's bacon; to light upon one's feet; to weather the storm; to bear a charmed life; to make assurance doubly sure; to take no chances.

To play gooseberry.

Adjectives: Safe, in safety, in security, secure, sure, protected, guarded, etc., snug, fireproof, waterproof, seaworthy, airworthy.

Defensible, tenable; insurable.

Invulnerable, unassailable, unattackable, impregnable, inexpugnable.

Protecting, etc., guardian, tutelary.

Unthreatened, unmolested, unharmed, scatheless, unhazarded.

Phrases: Out of harm's way; safe and sound; under lock and key; on sure ground; under cover; under the shadow of one's wing; the coast being clear; the danger being past; out of the wood; proof against.

Interjections: All's well! *salva est res!* safety first!

665 DANGER

Substantives: peril, insecurity, jeopardy, risk, hazard, venture, precariousness, slipperiness.

Liability, exposure (177), vulnerability, vulnerable point, Achilles heel.

Hopelessness (859), forlorn hope, alarm (860), defencelessness.

Phrases: The ground sliding from under one; breakers ahead; a storm brewing; the sword of Damocles.

Verbs: To be in danger, etc., to be exposed to, to incur or encounter danger, run the danger of, run a risk.

To place or put in danger, etc., to endanger, expose to danger, imperil, jeopardize, compromise, adventure, risk, hazard, venture, stake.

Phrases: To sit on a barrel of gunpowder; stand on a volcano; to engage in a forlorn hope.

Adjectives: In danger, peril, jeopardy, etc., unsafe, insecure, unguarded, unscreened, unsheltered, unprotected, guardless, helpless, guideless, exposed, defenceless, vulnerable, at bay.

Unwarned, unadmonished, unadvised.

Dangerous, perilous, hazardous, parlous, risky, chancy, untrustworthy, fraught with danger, adventurous, precarious, critical, touch-and-go, breakneck, slippery, unsteady, shaky, tottering, top-heavy, harbourless, ticklish, dicky.

Threatening, ominous, alarming, minacious (909).

Phrases: Not out of the wood; hanging by a thread; neck or nothing; in a tight place; between two fires; out of the frying-pan into the fire; between the devil and the deep sea; between Scylla and Charybdis; on the rocks; hard bested.

666 REFUGE

Substantives: asylum, sanctuary, fastness, retreat, ark, hiding-place, dugout, funk-hole, fox-hole, loophole, shelter, lee, cover.

Roadstead, anchorage, breakwater, mole, groyne, port, haven, harbour, harbour of refuge, pier.

Fort, citadel, fortification, stronghold, strong point, keep, shield, etc. (717).

Screen, covert, wing, fence, rail, railing, wall, dike, ditch, etc. (232).

Anchor, kedge, grapnel, grappling-iron, sheet-anchor, prop, stay, mainstay, jury-mast, lifeboat, lifebuoy, lifebelt, plank, stepping-stone, umbrella, parachute, lightning-conductor, safety-valve, safety curtain, safety-lamp.

667 PITFALL

Substantives: rocks, reefs, sunken rocks, snags, sands, quicksands, breakers, shoals, shallows, bank, shelf, flat, whirlpool, rapids, current, undertow, precipice, lee shore, air-pocket.

Trap, snare, gin, springe, deadfall, toils, noose, net, spring-net, spring-gun, masked battery, mine.

Phrases: The sword of Damocles; a snake in the grass; trusting to a broken reed; a lion's den; a hornet's nest; an ugly customer.

668 WARNING

Substantives: caution, *caveat,* notice, premonition, premonishment, lesson, dehortation, monition, admonition (864); alarm (669).

Beacon, lighthouse, lightship, pharos, watch-tower, signal-post, guide-post (550).

Sentinel, sentry, watch, watchman, patrol, vedette (664); monitor, Cassandra.

Phrases: The writing on the wall; the yellow flag; a red light; a stormy petrel; gathering clouds.

Verbs: To warn, caution, forewarn, premonish, give notice, give warning, admonish, dehort, threaten, menace (909).

To take warning; to beware; to be on one's guard (864).

Phrases: To put on one's guard; to sound the alarm.

Adjectives: Warning, etc., monitory, premonitory, dehortatory, cautionary, admonitory.

Warned, etc., careful, one one's guard (459).

Interjections: Beware! look out! mind what you are about! watch your step! let sleeping dogs lie! *foenum habet in cornu!* fore! heads! mind your back! cave!

669 ALARM
Substantives: alert, alarum, alarm-bell, horn, siren, maroon, fog-signal, tocsin, tattoo, signal of distress, SOS, hue and cry.

False alarm, cry of wolf, bugbear, bugaboo, bogy.

Verbs: To give, raise, or sound an alarm, to alarm, warn, ring the tocsin, dial 999; to cry wolf.

Adjectives: Alarming, etc., threatening.

Phrases: Each for himself; *sauve qui peut.*

670 PRESERVATION
Substantives: conservation, maintenance (141), support, upkeep, sustentation, deliverance, salvation, rescue, redemption, self-preservation, continuance (143).

Means of preservation, prophylaxis, preservative, preserver.

Verbs: To preserve, maintain, support, keep, sustain, nurse, save, rescue, file (papers).

To embalm, mummify, dry, dehydrate, cure, kipper, smoke, salt, pickle, marinade, season, kyanize, bottle, pot, can, tin.

Adjectives: Preserving, conservative, prophylactic, preservatory, hygienic.

Preserved, intact, unimpaired, uninjured, unhurt, unsinged, unmarred.

671 ESCAPE
Substantives: getaway, flight, elopement, evasion, retreat, reprieve, reprieval, deliverance, redemption, resuce.

Narrow escape, hair's-breadth, escape, close shave, close call, narrow squeak.

Means of escape: Bridge, drawbridge, loophole, ladder, plank, stepping-stone, trap-door, fireescape, emergency exit.

A fugitive, runaway, refugee, evacuee.

Verbs: To escape, elude, evade, wriggle out of, make or effect one's escape, make off, march off, pack off, skip, skip off, slip away, steal away, slink away, flit, decamp, run away, abscond, levant, skedaddle, scoot, fly, flee, bolt, bunk, scarper, scram, hop it, beat it, vamoose, elope, whip off, break loose, break away, get clear.

Phrases: To take oneself off; play truant; to beat a retreat; to give one the slip; to slip the collar; to slip through the fingers; to make oneself scarce; to fly the coop; to take to one's heels; to show a clean pair of heels; to take French leave; to do a bunk; to do a guy; to cut one's lucky; to cut and run; to live to fight another day; to run for one's life; to make tracks.

Interjections: *Sauve qui peut!* the devil take the hindmost!

Adjectives: Escaping, etc., escaped, etc., runaway.

Phrase: The bird having flown.

672 DELIVERANCE
Substantives: extrication, rescue, reprieve, respite, redemption, salvation, riddance, release, liberation (750); redeemableness, redeemability.

Verbs: To deliver, extricate, rescue, save, salvage, redeem, ransom, help out, bring off, *tirer d'affaire,* to get rid, to work off, to rid.

Phrases: To save one's bacon; to find a hole to creep out of.

Adjectives: Delivered, saved, etc., scot-free, scatheless.

Extricable, redeemable, rescuable.

673 PREPARATION

Substantives: making ready, providing, provision, providence, anticipation, preconcertation, rehearsal, precaution; laying foundations, ploughing, sowing, semination, cooking, brewing, digestion, gestation, hatching, incubation, concoction, maturation, elaboration, predisposition, premeditation (611), acclimatization (613).

Physical preparation, training, drill, drilling, discipline, exercise, exercitation, gymnastics, callisthenics, eurhythmics, athletics, gymnasium, *palaestra,* prenticeship, apprenticeship, qualification, inurement, education, novitiate (537).

Putting or setting in order, putting to rights, clearance, arrangement, disposal, organization, adjustment, adaptation, disposition, accommodation, putting in tune, tuning, putting in trim, dressing, putting in harness, outfit, equipment, accoutrement, armament.

Groundwork, basis, foundation, pedestal, etc. (215), stepping-stone, first stone, scaffold, scaffolding, cradle, sketch (626).

State of being prepared, preparedness, ripeness, maturity, readiness, mellowness.

Preparer, pioneer, avant-courier, sappers and miners.

Phrases: A stitch in time; clearing decks; a note of preparation; a breather; a trial bout; a practice swing.

Verbs: To prepare, get ready, make ready, get up, anticipate, forecast, pre-establish, preconcert, settle preliminaries, to found.

To arrange, set or put in order, set or put to rights, organize, dispose, cast the parts, mount, adjust, adapt, accommodate, trim, tidy, fit, predispose, inure, elaborate, mature, mellow, season, ripen, nurture, hatch, cook, concoct, brew, tune, put in tune, attune, set, temper, anneal, smelt, undermine, brush up, get up.

To provide, provide against, discount, make provision, keep on foot, take precautions, make sure, lie in wait for (507).

To equip, arm, man, fit out, fit up, furnish, rig, dress, dress up, furbish up, accoutre, array, fettle, vamp up, wind up.

To train, drill, discipline, break in, cradle, inure, habituate, harden, case-harden, season, acclimatize, qualify, educate, teach.

Phrases: To take steps; prepare the ground; lay or fix the foundations, the basis, groundwork, etc.; to clear the ground or way or course; clear decks; clear for action; close one's ranks; plough the ground; dress the ground; till the soil; sow the seed; open the way; pave the way; lay a train; dig a mine; prepare a charge; erect the scaffolding; *reculer pour mieux sauter.*

Put in harness; sharpen one's tools; whet the knife; shoulder arms; put the horses to; oil up; crank up; warm up.

To prepare oneself; lay oneself out for; get into harvest; gird up one's loins; buckle on one's armour; serve one's time or apprenticeship; be at one's post; gather oneself together.

To set on foot; to lay the first stone; to break ground.

To erect the scaffold; to cut one's coat according to one's cloth; to keep one's powder dry; to beat up for recruits; to sound the note of preparation.

Adjectives: Preparing, etc., in preparation, in course of preparation, in hand, in train, brewing, hatching, forthcoming, in embryo, afoot, afloat, on the anvil, on the carpet, on the stocks, *sur le tapis*.

Preparative, preparatory, provisional, in the rough, rough and ready (111).

Prepared, trained, drilled, etc., forearmed, ready, in readiness, ripe, mature, mellow, fledged, ready to one's hand, on tap, cut and dried, annealed, concocted, laboured, elabrated, planned (626).

Phrases: Armed to the teeth; armed cap-à-pie; booted and spurred; in full feather; *in utrumque paratus*; in working order.

Adverbs: In preparation, in anticipation of, etc., against.

674 NON-PREPARATION

Substantives: want or absence of preparation, inculture, inconcoction, improvidence.

Immaturity, crudeness, crudity, greenness, rawness, disqualification.

Absence of art, state of nature, virgin soil.

An embryo, skeleton, rough copy, draft (626); germ, rudiment (153), raw material, rough diamond.

Tyro, beginner, novice, neophyte, greenhorn, new chum, pommy, recruit, sprog.

Verbs: To be unprepared, etc., to want or lack preparation.

To improvise, extemporize (612).

To render unprepared, etc., to dismantle, dismount, dismast, disqualify, disable (645), unrig, undress (226).

Phrases: To put *hors de combat*; to put out of gear; to spike the guns; to remove the sparking-plug.

Adjectives: Unprepared, rudimentary, immature, embryonic, unripe, raw, green, crude, rough, roughcast, rough-hewn, unhewn, unformed, unhatched, unfledged, unnurtured, uneducated, unlicked, unpolished, natural, in a state of nature, *au naturel*, unwrought, unconcocted, undigested, indigested, unrevised, unblown, unfashioned, unlaboured, unleavened, fallow, uncultivated, unsown, untilled, untrained, undrilled, unexercised, unseasoned, disqualified, unqualified, out of order, unseaworthy.

Unbegun, unready, unarranged, unorganized, unfurnished, unprovided, unequipped, undressed, in dishabille, dismantled, untrimmed.

Shiftless, improvident, unguarded, happy-go-lucky, feckless, thoughtless, unthrifty.

Unpremeditated, unseen, off-hand (612), from hand to mouth, extempore (111).

Phrases: Caught on the hop; with their trousers down.

675 ESSAY

Substantives: endeavour, try, trial, experiment (463), probation, attempt (676), venture, adventure, tentative, *ballon d'essai, coup d'essai,* go, crack, whack, slap, shot, speculation.

Verbs: To try, essay, make trial of, try on, experiment, make an experiment, endeavour, strive, attempt, grope, feel one's way; to venture, adventure, speculate, take upon oneself.

Phrases: To put out or throw out a feeler; to tempt fortune; to fly a kite; to send up a pilot balloon; to fish for information, compliments, etc.; to have a crack at; to try one's luck; to chance it; to risk it.

Adjectives: Essaying, etc., experimental, tentative, empirical, on trial, probative, probatory, probationary.

Adverbs: Experimentally, etc., at a venture.

676 UNDERTAKING

Substantives: enterprise, emprise, quest, mission, endeavour, attempt, move, first move, the initiative, first step.

Verbs: To undertake, take in hand, set about, go about, set to, fall to, set to work, engage in, launch into, embark in, plunge into, take on, set one's hand to, tackle, grapple with, volunteer, take steps, launch out.

To endeavour, strive, use one's endeavours; to attempt, make an attempt, tempt.

To begin, set on foot, set agoing, take the first step.

Phrases: To break the neck of the business; take the initiative; to get cracking; to break ground; break the ice; break cover; to pass the Rubicon; to take upon oneself; to take on one's shoulders; to put one's shoulder to the wheel; *ce n'est que le premier pas qui coûte*; well begun is half done.

To take the bull by the horns; to rush *in medias res*; to have too many irons in the fire; to attempt impossibilities.

Adverbs: Undertaking, attempting, etc.

677 USE

Substantives: employment, employ, application, appliance, adhibition, disposal, exercise, exercitation.

Recourse, resort, avail, service, wear, usage, conversion to use, usufruct, utilization.

Agency (170); usefulness (644).

Verbs: To use, make use of, utilize, exploit, employ (134), apply, adhibit, dispose of, work, wield, manipulate, handle, put to use; turn or convert to use; avail oneself of, resort to, have recourse to, take up with, betake oneself to.

To render useful, serviceable, available, etc.; to utilize, draw, call forth, tax, task, try, exert, exercise, practise, ply, work up, consume, absorb, expend.

To be useful, to serve one's turn (644).

Phrases: To take advantage of; to turn to account; to make the most of; to make the best of; to bring to bear upon; to fall back upon; to press or enlist into the service; to make shift with; make a cat's-paw of.

To pull the strings or wires; put in action; set to work; set in motion; put in practice.

Adjectives: Used, employed, etc., applied, exercised, tried, etc.

678 DISUSE

Substantives: forbearance, abstinence, dispensation, desuetude (614), relinquishment, abandonment (624, 782).

Verbs: To disuse, not to use, to do without, to dispense with, neglect, to let alone, to spare, waive.

To lay by; set, put, or lay aside, to discard, dismiss (756); cast off, throw off, turn off, turn out, turn away, throw away, scrap, dismantle, shelve (133), shunt, side-track, get rid of, do away with; to keep back (636).

Phrases: To lay on the shelf; to lay up in a napkin; to consign to the scrapheap; to cast, heave, or throw overboard; to cast to the winds; to turn out neck and crop; to send to the right-about; to send packing.

Adjectives: Disused, etc., not used, unused, unutilized, done with, unemployed, unapplied, unspent, unexercised, kept or held back.

Unessayed, untouched, uncalled-for, ungathered, unculled, untrodden.

679 MISUSE

Substantives: misusage, misemployment, misapplication, misappropriation, abuse, profanation, prostitution, desecration.

Waste (818), wasting, spilling, exhaustion (638).

Verbs: To misuse, misemploy, misapply, misappropriate, desecrate, abuse, profane, prostitute.

To waste, spill, fritter away,

exhaust, throw or fling away, squander (818).

Phrases: To waste powder and shot; cut blocks with a razor; cast pearls before swine.

Adjectives: Misused, etc.

Section 3 –
Voluntary Action

680 ACTION

Substantives: performance, work, operation, execution, perpetration, proceeding, procedure, *démarche*, process, handiwork, handicraft, workmanship, manœuvre, evolution, transaction, bout, turn, job, doings, dealings, business, affair.

Deed, act, overt act, touch, move, strike, blow, *coup*, feat, stunt, exploit, passage, measure, step, stroke of policy, *tour de force, coup de main, coup d'état*.

Verbs: To act, do, work, operate, do or transact business, practise, prosecute, perpetrate, perform, execute (729), officiate, exercise, commit, inflict, strike a blow, handle, take in hand, put in hand, run.

To labour, drudge, toil, ply, set to work, pull the oar, serve, officiate, go about, turn one's hand to, dabble; to have in hand.

Phrases: To have a finger in the pie; to take or play a part; to set to work; to put into execution (729); to lay one's hand to the plough; to ply one's task; to get on with the job; to discharge an office.

Adjectives: Acting, etc., in action, in operation, etc., operative, in harness, in play, on duty, on foot, at work, red-handed.

Interjection: Here goes!

681 INACTION

Substantives: abstinence from action, inactivity (683), non-intervention, non-interference, neutrality, strike, Fabian tactics.

Verbs: Not to do, to let be, abstain from doing; let or leave alone, refrain, desist, keep oneself from doing; let pass, lie by, let be, wait.

To undo, take down, take or pull to pieces, do away with.

Phrases: To bide one's time; to let well alone; to cool one's heels; to stay one's hand; to wash one's hands of; to strike work; nothing doing; *nihil fit; dolce far niente*.

Adjectives: Not doing, not done, let alone, undone, etc.; passive, neutral.

682 ACTIVITY

Substantives: briskness, quickness, promptness, promptitude, expedition, dispatch, readiness, alertness, smartness, sharpness, nimbleness, agility (274).

Spirit, ardour, animation, life, liveliness, vivacity, eagerness, *empressement, brio*, dash, *élan*, abandon, pep, go, alacrity, zeal, push, vim, energy (171), hustle, vigour, intentness.

Wakefulness, *pervigilium*, insomnia, sleeplessness.

Industry, assiduity, assiduousness, sedulity, sedulousness, diligence; perseverance, persistence, plodding, painstaking, drudgery, busyness, indefatigability, indefatigableness, patience, Business habits.

Movement, bustle, commotion, stir, fuss, fluster, bother, pother, ado, fidget, restlessness, fidgetiness.

Officiousness, meddling, interference, interposition, intermeddling, tampering with, intrigue, *tripotage*, supererogation.

A man of action, busy bee, busybody, go-getter, zealot, devotee, meddler, hustler, whizz-kid.

Phrases: The thick of the action; *in medias res*; too many cooks; new brooms sweep clean; too many irons in the fire.

Verbs: To be active, busy, stirring, etc., to busy oneself in, stir, bestir oneself, bustle, fuss, make a fuss, speed, hasten, push, make a push, go ahead, hustle; to industrialize.

To plod, drudge, keep on, hold on, persist, persevere, fag at, hammer at, peg away, stick to, buckle to, stick to work, take pains; to take or spend time in; to make progress.

To meddle, moil, intermeddle, interfere, interpose, kibitz, tamper with, fool with, get at, nobble, agitate, intrigue.

To overact, overdo, overlay, outdo, ride to death.

Phrases: To look sharp; to lay about one; to have one's hands full; to kick up a dust; to stir one's stumps; to exert one's energies; to put one's best foot foremost; to do one's best; to do all one can; to leave no stone unturned; to have all one's eyes about one; make the best of one's time; not to let the grass grow under one's feet; to make short work of; to seize the opportunity; to come up to the scratch.

To take time by the forelock; to improve the shining hour; to make hay while the sun shines; to keep the pot boiling; to strike while the iron is hot; to kill two birds with one stone; to move heaven and earth; to go through fire and water; to do wonders; to go all lengths; to stick at nothing; to go the whole hog; to keep the ball rolling; to put one's back into it; to make things hum.

To have a hand in; to poke one's nose in; to put in one's oar; to have a finger in the pie; to mix oneself up with; steal a march upon.

Adjectives: Active, brisk, quick, prompt, alert, on the alert, stirring, spry, sharp, smart, quick, nimble, agile, light-footed, tripping, ready, awake, broad awake, wide awake, alive, lively, live, animated, vivacious, frisky, forward, eager, strenuous, zealous, expeditious, enterprising, pushing, pushful, spirited, in earnest, up in arms, go-ahead.

Working, on duty, at work, hard at work, intent, industrious, up and coming, assiduous, diligent, sedulous, painstaking, business-like, practical, in harness, operose, plodding, toiling, hard-working, fagging, busy, bustling, restless, fussy, fidgety.

Persevering, indefatigable, untiring, unflagging, unremitting, unwearied, never-tiring, undrooping, unintermitting, unintermittent, unflinching, unsleeping, unslumbering, sleepless, persistent.

Meddling, meddlesome, pushing, intermeddling, tampering, etc., officious, over-officious, intriguing, managing.

Phrases: Up and doing; up and stirring; busy as a bee; on the *qui vive*; nimble as a quirrel; the fingers itching; no sooner said than done; *nulla dies sine linea*; a rolling stone gathers no moss; the used key is always bright.

Adverbs: Actively, etc. (684).

Interjections: Look alive! look sharp! get a move on! get cracking! get busy! hump yourself! get weaving!

683 INACTIVITY

Substantives: inaction (681), idleness, sloth, laziness, indolence, inertness, inertia (172), lumpishness, supineness, sluggishness, segnitude, languor, torpor, quiescence, stagnation, lentor, limpness, listlessness, remissnes, slackness.

Dilatoriness, cunctation, procrastination (133), relaxation, truancy, lagging, dawdling, rust, rustiness, want of occupation, resourcelessness.

Somnolence, drowsiness, doziness, nodding, oscitation, sleepiness, hypnosis.

Hypnology.

Sleep, nap, doze, slumber, shut-eye, bye-bye, snooze, dog-sleep, cat-nap, siesta, dream, faint, swoon, coma, trance, hypnotic state, snore, a wink of sleep, lethargy, hibernation, aestivation.

An idler, laggard, truant, do-nothing, lubber, sluggard, sleepy-head, slumberer, faineant, *flâneur,* loafer, drone, dormouse, slow-coach, stick-in-the-mud, lounger, slug, sun-downer, bum, Weary Willie, lazy-bones, lotus-eater, slacker, trifler, dilettante.

Cause of inactivity (174), sedative, hypnotic, knock-out drops, hypnotism; lullaby.

Phrases: The Castle of Indolence; *dolce far niente;* the Land of Nod; the Fabian policy; *laissez aller; laissez faire;* masterly inactivity; the thief of time.

Sleeping partner; waiter on Providence.

Verbs: To be inactive, etc., to do nothing, let alone, lie by, lie idle, stagnate, lay to, keep quiet, hang fire, relax, slouch, loll, drawl, slug, dally, lag, dawdle, potter, lounge, loiter, laze, moon, moon about, loaf, hang about, stooge, mouch; to waste, lose, idle away, kill, trifle away, fritter away or fool away time; trifle, footle, dabble, fribble, peddle, fiddle-faddle.

To sleep, slumber, nod, close the eyes, close the eyelids, doze, drowse, fall asleep, take a nap, go off to sleep, hibernate, aestivate, vegetate.

To languish, expend itself, flag, hang fire.

To render idle, etc.; to sluggardize.

Phrases: To fold one's arms; to let well alone; play truant; while away the time; to rest upon one's oars; to burn daylight; to take it easy; slack off.

To get one's head down; to hit the hay; to have forty winks; to sleep like a top or like a log; to sleep like a dormouse; to swing the lead; to eat the bread of idleness; to twiddle one's thumbs.

Adjectives: Inactive, unoccupied, unemployed, unbusied, doing nothing (685), resourceless.

Indolent, easy-going, lazy, slothful, idle, thowless, fushionless, slack, inert, torpid, sluggish, languid, supine, heavy, dull, stagnant, lumpish, soul-less, listless, moony, limp, languorous, exanimate.

Dilatory, laggard, lagging, tardigrade, drawling, creeping, dawdling, faddling, rusty, lackadaisical, fiddlefaddle, shilly-shally, unpractical, unbusiness-like.

Sleepy, dozy, dopy, dreamy, drowsy, somnolent, dormant, asleep, lethargic, comatose, napping, somniferous, soporific, soporous, soporose, somnific, hypnotic, narcotic, unawakened.

Phrases: With folded arms; *les bras croisés,* with the hands in the pockets; at a loose end.

In the arms or lap or Morpheus.

684 HASTE

Substantives: dispatch, precipitancy, precipitation, spurt, precipitousness, impetuosity, posthaste, acceleration, quickness (274).

Hurry, flurry, drive, bustle, fuss, splutter, scramble, brusquerie, fidget, fidgetiness (682).

Verbs: To haste, hasten, urge, press on, push on, bustle, hurry, hustle, buck up, precipitate, accelerate; to bustle, scramble, scuttle, scurry, scoot, plunge, rush, dash on, press on, scorch, speed.

Phrases: To make the most of one's time; to lose not a moment; *festina lente.*

Adjectives: Hasty, hurried, precipitate, scrambling, etc., headlong, boisterous, impetuous, brusque, abrupt, slapdash, cursory.

Adverbs: Hastily, etc., headlong, in haste, slapdash, slap-bang, amain, hurry-scurry, helter-skelter, head and shoulders, head over heels, by fits and starts, by spurts.

Phrases: No sooner said than done; a word and a blow.

685 LEISURE

Substantives: leisureliness, spare time, breathing-space, off-time, slack time, holiday, bank holiday, Sunday, sabbath, vacation, recess, red-letter day, relaxation, rest, repose, halt, pause (142), respite.

Phrases: *Otium cum dignitate*; time to spare; time on one's hands.

Verbs: To have leisure, take one's ease, repose (687), pause.

Phrase: To shut up shop.

Adjectives: Leisurely, undisturbed, quiet, deliberate, calm, slow (683).

Adverbs: Leisurely, etc., at leisure.

686 EXERTION

Substantives: labour, work, toil, fag, exercise, travail, swink, sweat, exercitation, duty, trouble, pains, ado, drudgery, fagging, slavery, operoseness.

Effort, strain, grind, tug, stress, tension, throw, stretch, struggle, spell, heft.

Gymnastics, gym, physical jerks, PT.

Phrases: A stroke of work; the sweat of one's brow.

Verbs: To labour, work, exert oneself, toil, strive, use exertion, fag, strain, drudge, moil, take pains, take trouble, trouble oneself, slave, pull, tug, ply the oar, rough it, sweat, bestir oneself, get up steam, get a move on, fall to work, buckle to, stick to.

Phrases: To set one's shoulder to the wheel; to strain every nerve; to spare no pains; to do one's utmost or damnedest; to work day and night; to work one's fingers to the bone; to do double duty; to work double tides; to put forth one's strength; to work like a nigger or

a horse; to go through fire and water; to put one's best foot forward (682); to do one's level best, grub along; to lay oneself out, lean over backwards.

Adjectives: Labouring, etc., laborious, toilsome, troublesome, operose, herculean, gymnastic, palaestric.

Hard-working, painstaking, energetic, strenuous (682).

Adverbs: Laboriously, lustily, roundly.

Phrases: By the sweat of the brow; with all one's might; *totis viribus*; with might and main; *vi et armis*; tooth and nail; hammer and tongs; through thick and thin; heart and soul.

687 REPOSE

Substantives: rest, halt, pause, relaxation, breathing-space, respite (685).

Day of rest, *dies non*, sabbath, holiday.

Verbs: To repose, rest, relax, take rest, breathe, take breath, take one's ease, gather breath, recover one's breath, respire, pause, halt, stay one's hand, lay to, lie by, lie fallow, recline, lie down, go to rest, go to bed, go to sleep, etc., unbend, slacken.

Phrases: To rest upon one's oars, to take a holiday; to shut up shop.

Adjectives: Reposing, resting, etc., restful, unstrained; sabbatical.

688 FATIGUE

Substantives: lassitude, weariness (841), tiredness, exhaustion, sweat, collapse, prostration, swoon, faintness, faint, *deliquium,* syncope, yawning, anhelation; overstrain.

Verbs: To be fatigued, etc., to droop, sink, flag, wilt, lose breath, lose wind, gasp, pant, pech, puff, yawn, drop, swoon, faint, succumb.

To fatigue, tire, weary, fag, irk, jade, harass, exhaust, knock up, prostrate, wear out, strain, overtask, overwork, overburden, overtax, overstrain, drive, sweat.

Adjectives: Fatigued, tired, unrefreshed, weary, wearied, jaded; way-worn; overworked, hard-driven, toil-worn, done up.

Breathless, out of breath, windless, out of wind, blown, winded, broken-winded.

Drooping, flagging, faint, fainting, doneup, knocked up, exhausted, sinking, prostrate, spent, overspent, dead-beat, dog-tired, fagged out.

Worn out, played out, battered, shattered, weather-beaten, footsore, *hors de combat,* done for.

Fatiguing, etc., tiresome, irksome, wearisome, trying.

Phrases: Ready to drop; tired to death; on one's last legs; run off one's legs; all in.

689 REFRESHMENT
Substantives: recovery of strength, recruiting, repair, refection, refocillation, relief, bracing, regalement, bait, restoration, revival; pick-up.
Phrase: A giant refreshed.
Verbs: To refresh, recruit, repair, refocillate, give tone, reinvigorate, reanimate, restore, recover.

To recover, regain, renew, etc., one's strength; perk up.
Adjectives: Refreshing, etc., recuperative, tonic; refreshed, etc., untired, unwearied, etc. (682).

690 AGENT
Substantives: doer, performer, actor, perpetrator, practitioner, operator, hand, employee, commissionaire, executor, executrix, maker, effector, consignee, steward, broker, factor, middleman, jobber.

Artist, workman, workwoman, charwoman, worker, artisan, artificer, architect, craftsman, handicraftsman, mechanic, roustabout, machinist, machineman, manufacturer, operative, journeyman, labourer, navvy, stevedore, docker, smith, wright, day-labourer, co-worker; *dramatis personae.*

Drudge, hack, fag, man or maid of all work, hired man, hired girl, factotum, handy-man.
Phrase: Hewers of wood and drawers of water.

691 WORKSHOP
Substantives: laboratory, manufactory, mill, shop, works, factory, mint, forge, smithy, loom, cabinet, office, bureau, studio, atelier, hive, hive of industry, workhouse, nursery, hot-house, hotbed, kitchen, dock, slip, yard, foundry.

Crucible, alembic, cauldron, matrix.

692 CONDUCT
Substantives: course of action, practice, drill, procedure, business (625), transaction, dealing, ways, tactics, policy, polity, generalship, statesmanship, economy, strategy, husbandry, seamanship, stewardship, housekeeping, housewifery, *ménage,* regime, *modus operandi,* economy.

Execution, manipulation, handling, treatment, process, working-out, course, campaign, career, walk.

Behaviour, deportment, comportment, carriage, mein, air, demeanour, bearing, manner, observance.
Verbs: To conduct, carry on, run, transact, execute, carry out, work out, get through, carry through, go through, dispatch, treat, deal with, proceed with, officiate, discharge, do duty, play a part or game, run a race.

To behave; to comport, acquit, demean, carry, hold oneself.
Phrases: To shape one's course; to paddle one's own canoe.
Adjectives: Conducting, etc., strategical, business-like, practical, executive.

693 DIRECTION
Substantives: management, government, bureaucracy, statesmanship,

conduct (692), regulation, charge, agency, senatorship, ministry, ministration, managery, directorate, directorship, chairmanship, guidance, steerage, pilotage, superintendence, stewardship, supervision, surveillance, proctorship, chair, portfolio, statecraft, politics, *haute politique,* kingcraft, cybernetics; council (696).

Helm, rudder, compass, needle, radar.

Phrase: The reins of government.

Verbs: To direct, manage, govern, guide, conduct, regulate, order, prescribe, brief, steer, con, pilot, have or take the direction, take the helm, have the charge of, administer, superintend, overlook, supervise, look after, see to, control, boss, run, preside, hold office, hold the portfolio.

To head, lead, show the way, etc.

Phrase: To pull the wires.

Adjectives: Directing, etc., managerial, gubernatorial, executive; dirigible.

694 DIRECTOR

Substantives: manager, executive, master (745), prime minister, premier, governor, statesman, legislator, controller, comptroller, intendant, superintendent, rector, matron, supervisor, president, preses, chairman, headman, supercargo, inspector, moderator, monitor, overseer, overlooker, shopwalker, taskmaster, leader, ringleader, demagogue, conductor, precentor, fugleman; official, jack-in-office, bureaucrat, minister, officebearer, red-tapist, officer (726).

Conductor, steersman, helmsman, pilot, coxswain, guide, cicerone, guard, driver, engine-driver, motorman, whip, charioteer, coachman, Jehu, muleteer, teamster, chauffeur, postilion, *vetturino.*

Steward, factor, factotum, bailiff, landreeve, foreman, forewoman, gaffer, charge-hand, whipper-in,

shepherd, proctor, procurator, housekeeper, major-domo, chef, master of ceremonies, MC.

695 ADVICE

Substantives: counsel, suggestion, recommendation, advocacy, hortation, exhortation, dehortation, instruction, charge, monition, admonition (668), admonishment, caution, warning, expostulation (616), obtestation, injunction, persuasion.

Guidance, guide, handbook, chart, compass, manual, itinerary, roadbook, reference.

An adviser, senator, counsellor, counsel, consultant, specialist, monitor, mentor, Nestor, guide, teacher (540), physician, leech, doctor.

Referee, arbiter, arbitrator, referendary, assessor.

Verbs: To advise, counsel, give advice, recommend, advocate, admonish, submonish, suggest, prompt, caution, warn, forewarn.

To persuade, dehort, exhort, enjoin, expostulate, charge, instruct.

To deliberate, consult together, hold a council, etc., confer, call in, refer to take advice, be closeted with.

Phrases: To lay their heads together; to compare notes; to go into a huddle; to take counsel of one's pillow; to take one's cue from.

Adjectives: Monitory, monitive, admonitory, recommendatory, hortatory, dehortatory, exhortatory, exhortative, warning, etc.

Phrases: A word to the wise; *verb sap.*

Interjection: Go to!

696 COUNCIL

Substantives: conclave, court, chamber, cabinet, cabinet council, house, committee, subcommittee, board, bench, brains trust, *comitia,* staff.

Senate, *senatus,* parliament, synod, soviet, convocation, convention, congress, consistory, conventicle, chapter, chapel, witenagemot, junta, states-general, diet, Cortes, Riksdag, Thing, Storthing, Reichsrat, Reichstag, Duma, Politburo, Presidium, Comintern, Sobranje, Skupshtina, Tynwald, divan, durbar, kgotla, indala, Areopagus, sanhedrin, directory.

A meeting, assembly, sitting, session, séance, sederunt.

Adjectives: Senatorial, curule.

697 PRECEPT

Substantives: direction, instruction, charge, prescript, prescription, recipe, receipt, order (741).

Rule, canon, code, formula, formulary, law, statute, act, rubric, maxim, apophthegm, etc. (496).

698 SKILL

Substantives: skilfulness, cleverness, ability, talent, genius, ingenuity, calibre, capacity, competence, shrewdness, sagacity, parts, endowment, faculty, gift, forte, strong point, turn, invention, headpiece.

Address, dexterity, adroitness, aptness, aptitude, facility, felicity, knack, expertness, quickness, sharpness, resourcefulness, smartness, readiness, excellence, habilitation, technique, virtuosity, artistry, ambidexterity, ambidextrousness, sleight of hand (545), know-how, knowingness.

Qualification, proficiency, panurgy, accomplishment, attainment, acquirement, craft, mastery, mastership.

Tact, knowledge of the world, *savoir faire,* discretion, finesse, worldly wisdom.

Prudence, discretion (864).

Art, science, management, tactics, manœuvring, sleight, trick, policy, strategy, jobbery, temporization, technology.

A masterstroke, *chef-d'œuvre,* a masterpiece, *tour de force,* a bold stroke, *coup be maître,* a good hit (650).

Verbs: To be skilful, skilled, etc., to excel in, to specialize in, have the trick of, be master of; to temporize, manœuvre.

Phrases: To play one's cards well; to stoop to conquer; to have all one's wits about one; to keep one's hand in; to know your stuff; to cut one's coat according to one's cloth; to know what one is about; to know what's what; to know the ropes.

Adjectives: Skilled, skilful, etc., clever, able, accomplished, talented, versatile, many-sided, resourceful, ingenious, inventive, shrewd, gifted, hard-headed, sagacious, sharp-witted.

Expert, crack, dexterous, scientific, adroit, apt, sharp, handy, deft, fluent, facile, ready, quick, smart, slick, spry, yare, nimble, ambidextrous, neat-handed, fine-fingered.

Conversant, versed, proficient, efficient, capable, competent, qualified, good at, up to, master of, cut out for, at home in, knowing.

Experienced, practised, hackneyed, trained, initiated, prepared, primed, finished, schooled, thoroughbred, masterly, consummate.

Technical, artistic, workmanlike, business-like, daedalian.

Discreet, politic, tactful, diplomatic, sure-footed, felicitous, strategic.

Phrases: Up to snuff; sharp as a needle; no flies on him.

Adverbs: Skilfully, etc., aright.

699 UNSKILFULNESS

Substantives: inability, incompetence, incompetency, inproficience, improficiency, infelicity, inexpertness, indexterity, unaptness, ineptitude, lefthandedness, awkwardness, maladroitness, clumsiness, gaucherie, rawness, slovenliness, greenness, inexperience, disability, disqualification.

Bungling, blundering, etc., blunder (495), *bêtise;* unteachableness, dumbness, dullness, stupidity (499).

Indescretion, imprudence (863), thoughtlessness, giddiness, wildness, mismanagement, misconduct, maladministration, misrule, misgovernment, misapplication, misdirection.

Phrases: Rule of thumb; a bad show.

Verbs: To be unskilled, unskilful, etc.

To mismanage, bungle, blunder, botch, boggle, fumble, flounder, stumble, muff, foozle, miscue, muddle, murder, mistake, misapply, misdirect, misconduct; stultify.

Phrases: To make a mess or hash of; to begin at the wrong end; to make sad work or a bad job of; to put one's foot in it; to lose or miss one's way; to lose one's balance; to stand in one's own light; to quarrel with one's bread and butter; to pay dear for one's whistle; to cut one's own throat; to kill the goose which lays the golden eggs; to reckon without one's host.

Adjectives: Unskilled, etc., unskilful, bungling, etc., awkward, clumsy, unhandy, unworkmanlike, unscientific, shiftless, lubberly, *gauche,* maladroit, left-handed, hobbling, slovenly, sloppy, slatternly, giddy, gawky, dumb, dull, unteachable, at fault.

Unapt, unqualified, inhabile, incompetent, disqualified, untalented, ill-qualified, inapt, inept, inexpert, inartistic, raw, green, rusty.

Unaccustomed, unused, unhackneyed, unexercised, untrained, unpractised, undisciplined, uneducated, undrilled, uninitiated, unschooled, unconversant, unversed, inexperienced, unstatesmanlike, non-professional.

Unadvised, misadvised, ill-judged, ill-advised, unguided, misguided, foolish, wild, ill-devised, misconducted.

Phrases: His fingers are all thumbs; penny wise and pound foolish.

700 PROFICIENT

Substantives: adept, expert, special-ist, genius, dab, crack, whiz, master, *maître,* master-hand, virtuoso, champion, first string, first fiddle, protagonist, ace, artist, tactician, marksman, old stager, veteran, top-sawyer, picked man, cunning man, conjurer, wizard, etc. (994); connoisseur (850); prodigy (872), an Admirable Crichton.

Phrases: A man of the world; a practised hand; no slouch; a smart customer; an old file; an all-round man.

701 BUNGLER

Substantives: blunderer, marplot, greenhorn, lubber, landlubber, fumbler, muddler, duffer, butter-fingers, novice, no conjurer, flat, muff, babe.

Phrases: A poor hand at; no good at; a fish out of water; a freshwater sailor; the awkward squad; not likely to set the Thames on fire.

702 CUNNING

Substantives: craft, craftiness, wiliness, artfulness, subtlety, shrewdness, smartness, archness, insidiousness, slyness, opportunism, artificialness, artificiality.

Artifice, stratagem, wile, dodge, subterfuge, evasion, finesse, ruse, diplomacy, jobbery, backstairs influence.

Duplicity, guile, circumvention, chicane, chicanery, sharp practice, Machiavellism, legerdemain, trickery, etc. (545).

Net, toils, trap, etc. (667).

A slyboots, Ulysses, Machiavel, trickster, serpent, fox, intriguer, opportunist, time-server.

Verbs: To be cunning, etc., to contrive, design, manœuvre, gerrymander, finesse, shuffle, wriggle, wangle, intrigue, temporize, overreach (545), circumvent, get round, nobble, undermine.

Phrases: To play a deep game; to steal a march on; to know on which side one's bread is buttered.

Adjectives: Cunning, crafty, artful, knowing, wily, sly, fly, pawky, smooth, sharp, smart, slim, feline, subtle, arch, designing, intriguing, contriving, insidious, canny, downy, leery, tricky, deceitful (545), artificial, deep, profound, diplomatic, vulpine, Machiavellian, time-serving.

Phrases: Cunning as a fox; too clever by half; not born yesterday; not to be caught with chaff.

703 ARTLESSNESS

Substantives: nature, naturalness, simplicity, ingenuousness, *bonhomie*, frankness, naïveté, openness, *abandon*, candour, outspokenness, sincerity, straightforwardness, honesty (939), innocence (946).

Phrases: *Enfant terrible*; a rough diamond; a mere babe.

Verbs: To be artless, etc.

Phrases: To call a spade a spade; not to mince one's words; to speak one's mind; to wear one's heart upon one's sleeve.

Adjectives: Artless, natural, native, plain, simple-minded, ingenuous, candid, untutored, unsophisticated, simple, naïve, sincere, frank (543), open, frank-hearted, open-hearted, above-board, downright, unreserved, guileless, inartificial, undesigning, single-minded, honest, straightforward, outspoken, blunt, matter-of-fact.

Section 4 –
Antagonism.

704 DIFFICULTY

Substantives: hardness, toughness, hard work, uphill work, hard task, troublesomeness, laboriousness.

Impracticability, infeasibility, intractability, toughness, perverseness (471).

Embarrassment, awkwardness, perplexity, intricacy, intricateness, entanglement, knot, Gordian knot, labyrinth, net, meshes, maze, etc. (248).

Dilemma, nice point, delicate point, knotty point, stumbling-block, snag, vexed question, crux; *pons asinorum*, poser, puzzle, floorer, teaser, nonplus, quandary, strait, pass, critical situation, crisis, trial, pinch, emergency, exigency, scramble.

Scrape, hobble, fix, hole, lurch, contretemps, hitch, how-d'ye-do, slough, quagmire, hot water, pickle, stew, imbroglio, mess, ado, false position, stand, deadlock, encumbrance, cul-de-sac, impasse.

Phrases: A Herculean task; a labour of Sisyphus; a difficult role to play; a sea of troubles; horns of a dilemma; a peck of troubles; a kettle of fish; a pretty state of things; a handful; 'Ay, there's the rub.'

Verbs: To be difficult, etc.

To meet with, experience, labour under, get into, plunge into, be surrounded by, be encompassed with, be entangled by, struggle, contend against or grapple with difficulties.

To come to a stand, to stick fast, to be set fast, to boggle, flounder, get left.

To render difficult, etc., to embarrass, perplex, put one out, bother, pose, puzzle, floor, nonplus, ravel, entangle, gravel, faze, flummox, run hard.

Phrases: To come to a deadlock; to be at a loss; to get into hot water; to get into a mess; to be bunkered; to weave a tangled web; to fish in troubled waters; to buffet the waves; to be put to one's shifts; not to know which way to turn; to skate over thin ice.

To lead one a pretty dance; to put a spoke in one's wheel; to leave in the lurch.

Adjectives: Difficult, not easy, hard, stiff, troublesome, toilsome, formidable, laborious, onerous, operose,

269

awkward, unwieldy, beset with or full of difficulties, Herculean, Sisyphean.

Unmanageable, tough, stubborn, hard to deal with, *difficile,* trying, provoking, ill-conditioned, refractory, perverse, crabbed, intractable, against the grain.

Embarrassing, perplexing, delicate, ticklish, pernickety, complicated, intricate, thorny, spiny, knotty, tricky, critical, pathless, trackless, labyrinthine.

Impracticable, not possible, impossible (471), not practicable, not feasible, unachievable, un-come-at-able, inextricable, impassable, innavigable desperate, insuperable, insurmountable, unplayable.

In difficulty, perplexed, etc., beset, water-logged, put to it, hard put to it, run hard, hard pressed, thrown out, adrift, at fault, abroad, pushed.

Stranded, aground, stuck fast, at bay.

Phrases: At a standstill; at a stand; up against it; up a gum-tree; out of one's depth; at the end of one's tether; in a cleft stick; on the wrong scent; driven from pillar to post; things being come to a pretty pass; at a pinch; between two stools; in the wrong box; in a fix; in a hole; in a tight place; in the cart; in the soup.

Adverbs: With difficulty, hardly, etc., against the stream, against the grain, uphill.

705 FACILITY

Substantives: practicability, feasibility, practicableness (470).

Ease, easiness, smoothness, tractability, tractableness, ductility, flexibility, malleability, capability, disentanglement, freedom, advantage, vantage-ground.

A cinch, snap, cakewalk, walkover.

Phrases: Plain sailing; smooth water; fair wind; a clear coast; a holiday task; a royal road; child's play; a soft job; a piece of cake.

Verbs: To be easy, etc., to go, flow, swim, or drift with the tide or stream; to do with ease, to throw off.

To render easy, etc., to facilitate, popularize, smooth, ease, lighten, free, clear, disencumber, deobstruct, disembarrass, clear the way. smooth the way, disentangle, unclog, disengage, extricate, unravel, disburden, exonerate, emancipate, free from; to lubricate, etc. (332), relieve (834).

Phrases: To have it all one's own way; to have a walk-over; to win in a canter; to make light (or nothing) of.

To leave a loophole; to open the door to; to pave the way to; to bridge over; to grease the wheels.

Adjectives: Easy, facile, cushy, attainable, handy, practicable, feasible, achievable, performable, possible (470), superable, surmountable, accessible, come-at-able, get-at-able.

Easily managed or accomplished, etc., tractable, manageable, smooth, glib, pliant, yielding, malleable, ductile, flexible, plastic, submissive, docile.

At ease, free, light, unburdened, unencumbered, unloaded, disburdened, disencumbered, disembarrassed, exonerated, unrestrained, unobstructed, unimpeded, untrammelled, at home.

Phrases: The coast being clear; as easy as falling off a log; like taking candy from a child.

Quite at home; in one's element; in smooth water; on velvet.

Adverbs: Easily, etc., swimmingly.

706 HINDRANCE

Substantives: prevention, preclusion, impedance, retardment, retardation.

Obstruction, stoppage, interruption, interclusion, oppilation, interception, restriction, restraint, inhibition, embargo, blockade, embarrassment.

Interference, interposition, obtrusion, discouragement, chill.

An impediment, hindrance, obstacle, obstruction, bunker, hazard, let, stumbling-block, snag, check, impasse, countercheck, *contretemps,* set-back, hitch, bar, barrier, barrage, barricade, turnpike, wall, dead wall, bulkhead, portcullis, etc. (717), dam, weir, broom, turnstile, tourniquet.

Drawback, objection.

An encumbrance, impedimenta, onus, clog, skid, drag, weight, dead weight, lumber, top-hamper, pack, millstone, incubus, nightmare; trammel, etc. (752).

A hinderer, marplot; killjoy, interloper, passenger; opponent (710).

Phrases: A lion in the path; a millstone round one's neck; a wet blanket; the old man of the sea; *damnosa hereditas;* back to square one.

Verbs: To hinder, impede, prevent, preclude, retard, slacken, obviate, forefend, avert, turn aside, ward off, draw off, cut off, counteract, undermine.

To obstruct, stop, stay, let, make against, bar, debar, inhibit, scotch, squash, cramp, restrain, check, stonewall, set back, discourage, discountenance, foreclose.

To thwart, traverse, contravene, interrupt, intercept, interclude, frustrate, defeat, disconcert, embarrass, baffle, undo, intercept; to balk, unsight, cushion, stymie, spoil, mar.

To interpose, interfere, intermeddle, obtrude (682).

To hamper, clog, cumber, encumber, saddle with, load with, overload, overlay, lumber, block up, incommode, hustle; to curb, shackle, fetter; to embog.

Phrases: To lay under restraint; to tie the hands; to keep in swaddling bands.

To stand in the way of; to take the wind out of one's sails; to break in upon; to run or fall foul of; to put a spoke in the wheel; to throw cold water on; to nip in the bud; to apply the closure.

Adjectives: Hindering, etc., in the way of, impedimental, inimical, unfavourable, onerous, burdensome, cumbrous, intercipient, obstructive.

Hindered, etc., wind-bound, storm-stayed, water-logged, heavy-laden.

Unassisted, unaided, unhelped, unsupported, single-handed, unbefriended.

Phrase: Prevention is better than cure.

707 AID

Substantives: assistance, help, succour, support, advocacy, relief, advance, furtherance, promotion.

Coadjuvancy, patronage, interest, championship, countenance, favour, helpfulness.

Sustentation, subvention, subsidy, alimentation, nutrition, nourishment, ministration, ministry, accommodation.

Supplies, reinforcements, succours, contingents, recruits; physical support (215); relief, rescue.

Phrases: Corn in Egypt; a *deus ex machina.*

Verbs: To aid, assist, help, succour, support, sustain, uphold, subscribe to, finance, promote, further, abet, advance, foster, cherish, foment; to give, bring, furnish, afford or supply support, etc., to reinforce, recruit, nourish, nurture.

To favour, countenance, befriend, smile upon, encourage, patronize, make interest for.

To second, stand by, relieve, rescue, back, back up, take part with, side with, to come or pass over to, to join, to rally round, play up to.

To serve, do service, minister to, oblige, humour, cheer, accommodate, work for, administer to, pander to; to tend, attend, take care of, wait on, nurse, dry-nurse, entertain.

To speed, expedite, forward, quicken, hasten, set forward.

Phrases: To take the part of; consult the wishes of; to take up the cudgels for; to espouse the cause of; to enlist under the banners of; to lend or bear a hand; to hold out a helping hand; to give one a lift; to do one a good turn; to see one through; to take in tow; to pay the piper; to help a lame dog over the stile; to give a leg-up.

Adjectives: Aiding, helping, assisting, etc., auxiliary, adjuvant, ancillary, accessory, ministrant, subservient, subsidiary, helpful.

Friendly, amicable, favourable, propitious, well-disposed, neighbourly.

Adverbs: On or in behalf of; in the service of; under the auspices of; hand in hand.

Interjections: Help! save us! *à moi!*

708 OPPOSITION

Substantives: antagonism, oppugnancy, oppugnation, counteraction (179), contravention, impugnment, control, clashing, collision, competition, conflict, rivalry, emulation.

Absence of aid, etc., counterplot (718).

Phrase: A head wind.

Verbs: To oppose, antagonize, cross, counteract, control, contravene, countervail, counterwork, contradict, belie, controvert, oppugn, stultify, thwart, counter, countermine, run counter, go against, collide with, clash, rival, emulate, put against, militate against, beat against, stem, breast, encounter, compete with, withstand, to face, face down.

Phrases: To set one's face against; to make a dead set against; to match (or pit) oneself against; to stand out against; to fly in the face of; to fall foul of; to come into collision with; to be or to play at cross-purposes; to kick against the pricks; to buffet the waves; to cut one another's throats; to join issue.

Adjectives: Opposing, etc., adverse, antagonistic, opposed, conflicting, contrary, unfavourable, unfriendly,

hostile, inimical; competitive, emulous.

Phrases: Up in arms; at daggers drawn.

Adverbs: Against, versus, counter to, against the grain; against the stream, tide, wind, etc., in the way of, in spite of, in despite of, in the teeth of, in the face of, *per contra*; single-handed.

Across, athwart, overthwart.

Though, although (179), even, *quand même,* all the same.

Phrases: In spite of one's teeth; with the wind in one's teeth.

709 CO-OPERATION

Substantives: coadjuvancy, collaboration, concert, collusion, participation, complicity, co-efficiency, concurrence (178).

Alliance, colleagueship, freemasonry, joint-stock, co-partnership, coalition, combine, syndicate (778), amalgamation, federation, confederation (712).

Phrases: A helping hand; a long pull.

Verbs: To co-operate, combine, concur, conspire, concert, collaborate, draw or pull together, to join with, collude, unite one's efforts, club together, fraternize, be in league, etc., with, be a party to, to side with.

Phrases: To make common cause; to be in the same boat; to stand shoulder to shoulder; to play into the hands of; to hunt in couples; to hit it off together; to lay their heads together; to play ball.

Adjectives: Co-operating, etc., co-operative, co-operant, in co-operation, etc., in concert, allied, clannish; favourable (707).

Unopposed, unobstructed, unimpeded.

Phrase: Wind and weather permitting.

Adverbs: As one man (488).

710 OPPONENT

Substantives: antagonist, adversary, adverse party, opposition, rival, competitor, pacemaker, enemy, foe (891), assailant; malcontent.

711 AUXILIARY

Substantives: assistant, adjuvant, adjunct, adjutant, help, helper, helpmate, helpmeet, colleague, partner, side-kick, *confrère*, coadjutor, co-operator, collaborator, co-belligerent, ally, aide-de-camp, accomplice, accessory, stand-in, stooge.

Friend (890), confidant, champion, partisan, right hand, stand-by; adherent, *particeps criminis*, confederate, bottleholder, second, candle-holder, servant (746); *fidus Achates*.

Phrase: *Deus ex machina.*

712 PARTY

Substantives: side, partnership, fraternity, sodality, company, society, firm, house, establishment, body, corporation, corporate body, union, association, syndicate, guild, tong, joint concern, combine, trust, cartel.

Fellowship, brotherhood, sisterhood, denomination, communion, community, clan, clanship, club, friendly society, clique, junto, coterie, faction, gang, ring, circle, *camarilla*, cabal, league, confederacy, confederation, federation; *esprit de corps;* alliance, partisanship.

Band, staff, crew, team, set, posse, phalanx, *dramatis personae*.

Verbs: To unite, join, club together, join forces, federate, co-operate, befriend, aid, etc. (707), cement, form a party, league, etc., to be in the same boat.

Adjectives: In partnership, alliance, etc., federal, federated, bounded, banded, linked, cemented, etc., together, embattled.

713 DISCORD

Substantives: disagreement (24), variance, difference, divergence, dissent, dissension, misunderstanding, jar, jarring, clashing, friction, odds, dissonance, disaccord.

Disunion, schism, breach, falling out, division, split, rupture, disruption, open rupture, *brouillerie,* feud, vendetta, contentiousness, litigiousness, strife, contention (720); enmity (889).

Dispute, controversy, polemics, quarrel, tiff, spat, *tracasserie,* altercation, imbroglio, bickering, snip-snap, chicanery, squabble, row, shemozzle, rumpus, racket, fracas, brawl, bear garden, Donnybrook, debate (476).

Litigation, words, war of words, battle of the books, logomachy, wrangling, wrangle, jangle, breach of the peace, declaration of war (722).

Subject of dispute, ground of quarrel, disputed point, vexed question, bone of contention, apple of discord, *casus belli.*

Verbs: To be discordant, etc., to differ, dissent, disagree, clash, jar, to misunderstand one another.

To fall out, dispute, controvert, litigate, to quarrel, argue, wrangle, squabble, bicker, spar, jangle, nag, brawl; to break with; to declare war.

To embroil, entangle, disunite, set against, pit against; to sow dissension, disunion, discord, etc. among.

Phrases: To be at odds with; to fall foul of: to have words with; to have a bone to pick with; to have a crow to pluck with; to have a chip on one's shoulder; to be at variance with; to be at cross purposes; to join issue; to pick a quarrel with; to part brass rags; to chew the fat or rag; to go to the mat with; to live like cat and dog.

To set by the ears; to put the cat among the pigeons; to sow or stir up contention.

Adjectives: Discordant, disagreeing, differing, disunited, clashing, jarring, discrepant, divergent, dissentient, sectarian, at variance, controversial.

Quarrelsome, disputatious, litigious, litigant, factious, pettifogging, polemic, schismatic; unpacified, un-reconciled.

Phrases: At odds; on bad terms; in hot water; at daggers drawn; up in arms; out of tune; at sixes and sevens; at loggerheads; a house divided against itself; no love lost between them.

714 CONCORD

Substantives: accord, agreement (23), unison, unity, union, good understanding, quiet, peace, conciliation, unanimity (488), harmony, amity, sympathy (897), *entente cordiale, rapprochement,* alliance.

Phrases: The bonds of harmony; a happy family; kittens in a basket; a happy band of brothers.

Verbs: To agree, accord, be in unison, etc., to harmonize with, fraternize, stand in with.

Phrases: To understand one another; to see eye to eye with; to hit it off; to keep the peace; to pull together.

Adjectives: Concordant, congenial, agreeing, etc., united, in unison, etc., harmonious, allied, cemented, friendly (888), amicable, fraternal, at peace, peaceful, pacific, tranquil.

Phrases: At one with; with one voice.

715 DEFIANCE

Substantives: challenge, dare, cartel, daring, war-cry, slogan, college yell, war-whoop.

Verbs: To defy, challenge, dare, brave, beard, bluster, look big.

Phrases: To set at naught; snap the fingers at; to cock a snook at; to bid defiance to; to set at defiance; to hurl defiance at; to double the fist; to show a bold front; to brave it out; to show fight; to throw down the gauntlet or glove; to call out.

Adjectives: Defying, etc., defiant.

Adverbs: In defiance of; with arms akimbo.

Interjections: Come on! let 'em all come! do your worst!

Phrase: *Nemo me impune lacessit.*

716 ATTACK

Substantives: aggression, offence, assault, charge, onset, onslaught, battue, brunt, thrust, pass, passado, cut, sally, inroad, invasion, irruption, incursion, excursion, sortie, *camisade,* storm, storming, boarding, escalade, foray, raid, air raid, *razzia,* dragonnade (619); siege, investment.

Fire, volley, cannonade, barrage, blitz, broadside, bombardment, stonk, hate, raking fire, platoon-fire, fusillade.

Kick, punch (276), lunge, a run at, a dead set at, carte and tierce, a backhander.

An assailant, aggressor, invader.

Verbs: To attack, assault, assail, go for, fall upon, close with, charge, bear down upon, set on, have at, strike at, run at, make a run at, butt, tilt at, poke at, make a pass at, thrust at, stab, bayonet, cut and thrust, pitch into, kick, buffet, bonnet, beat (972), lay about one, lift a hand against, come on, have a fling at, slap on the face, pelt, throw stones, etc., to round on.

To shoot, shoot at, fire at, fire upon, let fly at, brown, pepper, bombard, shell, bomb, dive-bomb, blitz, strafe, prang.

To beset, besiege, lay siege to, invest, beleaguer, open the trenches, invade, raid, storm, board, scale the walls.

To press one hard, be hard upon, drive one hard.

Phrases: To draw the sword against; to launch an offensive; take the offensive; assume the aggressive; make a dead set at.

To give the cold steel to; to lay down a barrage; to pour in a broadside; to fire a volley.

Adjectives: Attacking, etc., aggressive, offensive, up in arms.

717 DEFENCE

Substantives: self-defence, self preservation, protection, ward, guard, guardianship, shielding, etc., resistance (719), safety (664).

Fence, wall, parapet, dike, ditch, fosse, moat (232), boom, mound, mole, outwork, trench, foxhole, dugout, shelter, Anderson shelter, Morrison shelter, entrenchment, fortification, embankment, bulwark, barbican, battlement, stockade, laager, zareba, abattis, turret, barbette, casemate, muniment, vallum, circumvallation, contravallation, barbed-wire entanglement, sunk fence, ha-ha, buttress, abutement, breastwork, portcullis, glacis, bastion, redoubt, rampart.

Hold, stronghold, keep, donjon, palladium, fort, fortress, blockhouse, pillbox, hedgehog, sconce, citadel, tower, castle, capitol, fastness, asylum (666).

Anchor, sheet-anchor.

Shield, armour, buckler, aegis, breastplate, coat of mail, cuirass, hauberk, habergeon, *chevaux de frise,* screen, etc. (666), helmet, tin hat, battle bowler, casque, shako, bearskin, gas-mask, panoply; fender, torpedonet, paravane, cow-catcher, buffer.

Defender, protector, guardian (664), champion, protagonist, knight errant; garrison, picket.

Verbs: To defend, shield, fend, fence, entrench, guard (664), keep off, keep at bay, ward off, beat off, parry, repel, bear the brunt of, put to flight.

Phrases: To act on the defensive; to maintain one's ground; to stand at bay; to give a warm reception to.

Adjectives: Defending, etc., defensive, defended, etc., armed, armoured, armour-plated, iron-clad, loopholed, sandbagged, castellated, panoplied, proof, bullet-proof, bomb-proof.

Phrases: Armed cap-à-pie; armed to the teeth.

Adverbs: Defensively, on the defence, on the defensive, at bay.

718 RETALIATION
Substantives: reprisal, retort, come-back, counter-stroke, reciprocation, *tu quoque,* recrimination, retribution, counterplot, counterproject, counterblast, *lex talionis,* revenge (919), compensation (30).

Phrases: Tit for tat; a *quid pro quo;* a Roland for an Oliver; diamond cut diamond; the biter bit; catching a Tartar; a game two can play at; hoist with his own petard.

Verbs: To retaliate, retort, cap, reciprocate, recriminate, counter, get even with one, pay off.

Phrases: To turn the tables; to return the compliment; to pay off old scores; to pay in one's own coin; to give as good as one got.

Adjectives: Retaliating, retaliatory, retaliative, recriminatory, recriminative.

Interjection: You're another!

719 RESISTANCE
Substantives: stand, oppugnation, reluctation, front, repulse, rebuff, opposition (708), disobedience (742), recalcitration.

Strike, industrial action, lockout, tumult, riot, pronunciamento, *émeute,* mutiny.

Revolt, rising, insurrection, rebellion, *coup d'état, putsch.*

Verbs: To resist, not to submit, etc., to withstand, stand against, stand firm, make a stand, repugn, reluct, reluctate, confront, grapple with, face down.

To kick, kick against, recalcitrate, lift the hand against (716), repel, repulse, rise, revolt, mutiny.

Phrases: To show a bold front; to make head against; to stand one's ground; to stand the brunt of; to hold one's own; to keep at bay; to stem the torrent; to champ the bit; to sell one's life dearly.

To fly in the face of; to kick against the pricks; to take the bit between one's teeth.

Adjectives: Resisting, etc., resistive, resistant, refractory, mutinous, recalcitrant, rebellious, up in arms, out.

Unyielding, unconquered, indomitable.

Interjections: Hands off! keep off!

720 CONTENTION

Substantives: contest, struggle, contestation, debate (476), logomachy, paper war, litigation, high words, rivalry, corrivalry, corrivalship, competition, *concours,* gymkhana, race, heat, match, tie, bickering, strife (713).

Wrestling, jiu-jitsu, pugilism, boxing, fisticuffs, spar, prize-fighting, athletics, sports, gymnastics, set-to, round, fracas, row, shindy, scrap, dust, rumpus, shemozzle, stramash, outbreak, clash, collision, shock, breach of the peace, brawl, Donnybrook (713).

Conflict, skirmish, rencounter, scuffle, encounter, velitation, tussle, scrimmage, scrummage, broil, fray, affray, *mêlée,* affair, brush, bout, fight, battle, combat, action, engagement, battle royal, running fight, free fight, joust, tournament, tourney, pitched battle, death struggle, Armageddon.

Naval engagement, naumachy, sea-fight; air duel, dogfight.

Duel, satisfaction, monomachy, single combat, passage of arms, affair of honour, a triangular duel.

Verbs: To contend, struggle, vie with, emulate, rival, race, race with, outvie, battle with, cope with, compete, join issue, bandy words with, try conclusions with, close with, square, buckle with, spar, box, tussle, fence, wrestle, joust, enter the lists, take up arms, take the field, encounter, struggle with, grapple with, tackle, engage with, pitch into, strive with, fall to, encounter, collide with.

Phrases: Join battle; fall foul of; have a brush with; break the peace; take up the cudgels; unsheath the sword; break a lance; to run a tilt at; give satisfaction; measure swords; exchange shots; lay about one; cut and thrust; fight without the gloves; go on the warpath.

Adjectives: Contending, etc., contentious, combative, bellicose (722); pugilistic, agnostic, competitive, rival, polemical (476), rough-and-tumble.

Phrases: A word and a blow; pull devil, pull baker.

721 PEACE

Substantives: amity, truce, armistice, harmony (714), tranquillity.

Phrases: Piping time of peace; a quiet life.

Verbs: To be at peace, etc., to keep the peace, etc. (714), pacify (723).

Adjectives: Pacific, peaceable, peaceful, tranquil, untroubled, bloodless, halcyon.

722 WARFARE

Substantives: war, hostilities, fighting, etc., arms, the sword, open war, *ultima ratio,* war to the knife.

Battle array, campaign, crusade, expedition, operation, mission, warpath.

Warlike spirit, military spirit, militarism, bellicosity.

The art of war, tactics, strategy, military evolutions, arms, service, campaigning, tented field; Mars, Bellona.

War-cry, slogan, fiery cross, trumpet, clarion, bugle, pibroch, war-whoop, beat of drum, tom-tom; mobilization.

Phrases: The mailed fist; wager of battle.

Verbs: To arm, fight, set to, spar, scrap, tussle, joust, tilt, box, skirmish, fight hand to hand, fence, measure swords, engage, combat, give battle, go to battle, join battle, engage in battle, raise or mobilize troops, declare war, wage war, go to war, come to blows, break a lance with, appeal to arms, appeal to the sword, give satisfaction, take the field, keep the field, fight it out, fight to a finish, spill blood, carry on war, carry on hostilities, to fight one's way, to serve, to fight like devils, to sell one's life dearly.

Phrases: To see service; to smell powder; to go over the top.

Adjectives: Contending, etc., unpeaceful, unpacific, contentious, beligerent, bellicose, jingo, chauvinistic, martial, warlike, military, militant, soldierly, soldierlike, gladiatorial, chivalrous, in arms, embattled.

Phrases: Together by the ears; sword in hand.

Adverbs: *Pendente lite*, the battle raging, in the cannon's mouth; in the thick of the fray.

Interjections: To arms! the Philistines be upon thee!

723 PACIFICATION
Substantives: reconciliation, accommodation, arrangement, *modus vivendi*, adjustment, terms, amnesty.

Peace-offering, olive-branch, calcumet or pipe of peace, preliminaries of peace.

Pacifism, pacificism, appeasement.

Truce, armistice, suspension of arms, of hostilities, etc., convention, *détente*.

Flag of truce, white flag, cartel.

Phrases: Hollow truce; cold war; *pax in bello*.

Verbs: To make peace, pacify, make it up, reconcile, reconciliate, propitiate, appease, tranquillize, compose, allay, settle differences, restore harmony, heal the breach.

Phrases: To put up the sword; to sheathe the sword; to beat swords into ploughshares; to bury the hatchet; to smoke the pipe of peace; to close the temple of Janus; to cry quits.

Adjectives: Pacified, etc., pacific, conciliatory.

724 MEDIATION
Substantives: intervention, interposition, interference, intermeddling, intercession, parley, negotiation, arbitration, conciliation, mediatorship,

good offices, diplomacy, peace-offering, eirenicon.

A mediator, intermediary, go-between, intercessor, peacemaker, diplomat, diplomatist, negotiator, troubleshooter, ombudsman.

Verbs: To mediate, intermediate, intercede, interpose, interfere, intervene, negotiate, arbitrate, compromise, meet half-way.

Phrase: To split the difference.

725 SUBMISSION
Substantives: surrender, non-resistance, appeasement, deference, yielding, capitulation, cession.

Homage, obeisance, bow, curtsy, kneeling, genuflexion, prostration, kow-tow.

Verbs: To surrender, succumb, submit, yield, give in, bend, cringe, crawl, truckle to, knuckle down or under, knock under, capitulate, lay down or deliver up one's arms, retreat, give way, cave in.

Phrases: Beat a retreat; strike one's flag or colours; surrender at discretion; make a virtue of necessity; to come to terms.

To eat humble pie; to eat dirt; to swallow the pill; to kiss the rod; to turn the other cheek; to lick a person's boots.

Adjectives: Surrendering, etc., non-resisting, unresisting, submissive, down-trodden.

Undefended, untenable, indefensible.

726 COMBATANT
Substantives: belligerent, champion, disputant, controversialist, litigant, competitor, rival, corrival, assailant, bully, bruiser, fighter, duellist, fighting-man, pugilist, pug, boxer, the fancy, prize-fighter, fighting-cock, gladiator, swashbuckler, fire-eater, berserker; swordsman, wrestler, Amazon, Paladin, son of Mars; staff, *état-major*, brass hats; militarist.

Warrior, soldier, campaigner, veteran, man-at-arms, redcoat, man in khaki, Tommy Atkins, tommy, doughboy, GI, *poilu,* trooper, dragoon, hussar, grenadier, fusilier, guardsman, lifeguard, lancer, cuirassier, spearman, musketeer, carabineer, rifleman, sniper, sharpshooter, *bersagliere*; ensign, standard-bearer, halberdier; private, subaltern, conscript, recruit, cadet; effectives, line, rank and file, cannon fodder, PBI.

Engineer, artilleryman, gunner, cannoneer, bombadier, sapper, miner; archer, bowman.

Paratrooper, aircraftman, erk, pilot, observer, aircrew.

Marine, jolly, leatherneck; seaman, bluejacket, tar, AB.

Guerrilla, Maquis, partisan, cossack, sepoy, gurkha, spahi, janizary, zouave, bashi-bazouk.

Armed force, the army, the military, regulars, soldiery, infantry, mounted infantry, fencibles, volunteers, territorials, yeomanry, cavalry, artillery, guns, tanks, armour, commando.

Militia, irregulars, *francs-tireurs,* Home Guard, train-band.

Legion, phalanx, myrmidons, squadron, wing, group, troop, cohort, regiment, corps, platoon, battalion, unit, mob, company (72), column, detachment, brigade, division, garrison, battle array, order of battle.

726 NON-COMBATANT

Substantives: civilian; passive resister, conscientious objector, conchy, Cuthbert, pacifist, pacificist; non-effective.

Quaker, Quirites.

Adjectives: Non-effective.

727 ARMS

Substantives: weapons, armament, armour, armoury, quiver, arsenal, magazine, armature.

Mail, chain-mail, lorication; ammunition, powder, gunpowder, gun-cotton, dynamite, gelignite, TNT, cordite, lyddite, cartridge, cartouche (635).

Artillery, park, ordnance piece, gun, cannon, swivel, howitzer, carronade, culverin, field-piece, machine-gun, Gatling, Maxim, submachine-gun, tommy-gun, mitrailleuse, pom-pom, mortar, grenade, petronel, petard, falconet.

Fire-arms, side-arms, stand of arms, musketry, musket, smooth-bore, muzzle-loader, firelock, match-lock, flint-lock, fowling-piece, rifle, revolver, six-shooter, carbine, blunderbuss, pistol, gat, rod, betsy, automatic pistol, derringer, Winchester, Lee-Metford, Mauser, Bren gun, Bofors, Sten gun, Lewis gun, bazooka.

Bow, arquebus (or harquebus), cross-bow, sling, catapult.

Missile, projectile, shot, round-shot, ball, shrapnel; grape, grape-shot, chain-shot, bullet, stone, shell, gas-shell, bomb, land-mine, block-buster, flying bomb, buzz-bomb, doodlebug, guided missile, V1, V2, atomic bomb, hydrogen bomb, torpedo, rocket, ballistics.

Pike, lance, spear, javelin, assagai, dart, arrow, reed, shaft, bolt, boomerang, harpoon.

Bayonet, sword, sabre, broadsword, cutlass, falchion, scimitar, rapier, skean, toledo, tuck, claymore, kris (or creese), dagger, dirk, hanger, poniard, stiletto, stylet, dudgeon, axe, bill, pole-axe, battle axe, halberd, tomahawk, bowie-knife, snickersnee, yataghan, kukri.

Club, mace, truncheon, staff, bludgeon, cudgel, knobkerrie, life-preserver, knuckle-duster, shillelagh, bat, cosh, sandbag, lathi.

Catapult, battering-ram; tank.

728 ARENA

Substantives: field, walk, battle-field, field of battle, lists, palaestra, campus, playing-field, recreation ground, playground, course, cinder-track, dirttrack, gridiron, diamond, pitch, links, rink, court, platform, stage, boards, racecourse, *corso,* circus, ring, cockpit, bear garden, scene of action, theatre of war, the enemy's camp, amphitheatre, hippodrome, coliseum (or colosseum), proscenium.

Section 5 –
Results of Voluntary Action

729 COMPLETION

Substantives: accomplishment, performance, fulfilment, fruition, execution, achievement, dispatch, work done, superstructure, finish, termination, denouement, catastrophe, conclusion, culmination, climax, consummation, *fait accompli,* winding up, the last stroke, finishing stroke, *coup de grâce,* last finish, final touch, crowning touch, coping-stone, end (67), arrival (292), completeness (52).

Verbs: To complete, effect, perform, do, execute, go through, accomplish, fulfil, discharge, achieve, compass, effectuate, dispatch, knock off, close, terminate, conclude, finish, end (67), consummate, elaborate, bring about, bring to bear, bring to pass, get through, carry through, bring through, bring off, pull off, work out, make good, carry out, wind up, dispose of, bring to a close, termination, conclusion, etc.

To perfect, bring to perfection, stamp, put the seal to, polish off, crown.

To reach, arrive (292), touch, reach, attain the goal; to run one's race.

Phrases: To give the last finish or finishing touch; to be through with; to get it over; to deliver the goods; to shut up shop.

Adjectives: Completing, final, terminal, concluding, conclusive, exhaustive, crowning, etc., done, completed, wrought.

Phrases: It is all over; *finis coronat opus; actum est.*

Adverbs: Completely, etc. (52), out of hand, effectually, with a vengeance, with a witness.

730 NON-COMPLETION

Substantives: inexecution, shortcoming (304), non-fulfilment, non-performance, neglect; incompleteness (53); a drawn battle or game, a draw, a stalemate.

Phrase: The web of Penelope; one swallow does not make a summer.

Verbs: Not to complete, perform, etc., to fall short of, leave unfinished, let slip, lose sight of, neglect, leave undone, etc., draw.

Phrases: To scotch the snake, not kill it; hang fire; do by halves.

Adjectives: Not completed, etc., uncompleted, incomplete, unfinished, left undone (53), short, unaccomplished, unperformed, unexecuted.

In progress, in hand, proceeding, going on, on the stocks.

Adverbs: *Re infecta; nihil fit.*

731 SUCCESS

Substantives: successfulness, speed, thrift, advance, luck, good fortune (734), godsend, prize, windfall, trump card, hit, stroke, lucky strike, break; lucky or fortunate hit; bold stroke, master-stroke, *coup de maître,* knockout blow (698), checkmate.

Continued success, run of luck, time well spent, tide, flood, high tide, heyday.

Advantage over, ascendancy, mastery, conquest, subdual, victory, subjugation, triumph, exultation (884).

A conqueror, victor, winner.

Phrase: A feather in one's cap.

Verbs: To succeed, to be successful, to come off successful, to be crowned with success, to come or go off well, catch on, to thrive, speed, prosper, bloom, blossom, flourish, go on well, be well off.

To gain, attain, carry, secure, or win a point or object; to triumph, be triumphant, etc.; to surmount, over-come, conquer, master, or get over a difficulty or obstacle; to score, make a hit.

To advance (282), come on, get on, gain ground, make one's way, make progress, progress, worry along, get by.

To bring to bear, to bring about, to effect, accomplish, complete (729), manage, contrive to, make sure; to reap, gather, etc., the benefit of.

To master, get the better of, con-quer, subdue, subjugate, quell, reduce, overthrow, overpower, vanquish, get under; get or gain the ascendancy, obtain a victory; to worst, defeat, beat, lick, drub, trim, settle, floor, knock out, put down, trip up, beat hollow, checkmate, non-suit, trip up the heels of, capsize, shipwreck, ruin, kibosh, do for, victimize, put to flight, drown, etc.; to roll in the dust, to trample under foot, to wipe the floor with.

To baffle, disconcert, frustrate, con-found, discomfit, dish, foil, out-gen-eral, outmanœuvre, outflank, outwit, overreach, balk, outvote, circumvent, score off, catch napping.

To answer, succeed, work well, turn out well.

Phrases: To sail before the wind; to swim with the tide; to stem the torrent; to turn a corner; to weather a point; to fall on one's legs or feet; *se tirer d'affaire*; to take a favourable turn; to turn up trumps; to have the ball at one's feet; to come off with flying colours; to win or gain the day; to win the palm; to win one's spurs; to breast the tape; to bear away the bell.

To get the upper hand; to gain an advantage; to get the whip-hand of; to have on the hip; to get the start of; to have a run of luck; to make a hit; to make a killing; to score a success; to reap or gather the harvest; to strike oil; to give a good account of oneself; to carry all before one; to put to rout; to cook one's goose; to settle one's hash.

Adjectives: Succeeding, etc., success-ful, home and dry, prosperous, felici-tous, blooming, etc., set up, tri-umphant, victorious, cock-a-hoop.

Unfoiled, unbeaten, unsubdued,etc. Effective, well-spent.

Phrases: Flushed with success; one's star being in the ascendant; the spoilt child of fortune.

Adverbs: Successfully, etc., tri-umphantly, with flying colours, in triumph, *à merveille,* to good purpose.

Phrase: *Veni, vidi, vici.*

732 FAILURE

Substantives: unsuccess, non-success, disappointment, blow, frustration, inefficacy, discomfiture, abortion, miscarriage, lost trouble; vain, ineffec-tual, or abortive attempt or effort.

A mistake, error, blunder, fault, miss, oversight, blot, slip, trip, stum-ble, claudication, breakdown, false step, wrong step, howler, floater, clanger, boner, *faux pas, bêtise,* tituba-tion, scrape, botch, bungle, foozle, mess, washout, stalemate, botchery, fiasco, flop, frost, sad work, bad job, bad show, want of skill.

Mischance, mishap, misfortune, misadventure, disaster, bad or hard luck (735).

Repulse, rebuff, set-down, defeat, fall, downfall, rout, discomfiture, col-lapse, smash, crash, wreck, perdition, shipwreck, ruin, subjugation, over-throw, death-blow, quietus, knock-out, destruction.

A victim, loser, bankrupt, insolvent (808).

Phrases: A losing game; a flash in the pan; a wild-goose chase; a mare's-nest; a fool's errand.

Verbs: To fail, to be unsuccessful, etc., to come off badly, go badly, go amiss, abort, go wrong, fall flat, flop, fall through, fizzle out, turn out ill, work ill, lose ground, recede (283), fall short of (304), prang (162, 176).

To miss, miss one's aim; to labour,

toil, etc., in vain; to lose one's labour, flounder, limp, miss one's footing, miscarry, abort; to make vain, ineffectual, or abortive efforts; to make a slip; to make or commit a mistake, commit a fault, make a mess of; to botch, make a botch of, bungle, foozle.

To be defeated, overthrown, foiled, worsted, let down, etc.; to break down, sink, drown, founder, go to ruin, etc., fall, slip, tumble, stumble, falter, be capsized, run aground, pack up, crock up, collapse.

Phrases: To come to nothing; to end in smoke; to slip through one's fingers; to hang fire; to miss fire; to miss stays; to flash in the pan; to split upon a rock; to go to the wall; to have had it; to take a back seat; to get the worst of it; to go to the dogs; to go to pot; to be all up with; to be in the wrong box; to stand in one's own light; to catch a Tartar; to get hold of the wrong sow by the ear; to burn one's fingers; to shoot at a pigeon and kill a crow; to beat the air; to tilt against windmills; to roll the stone of Sisyphus; to fall between two stools; to pull a boner; to come a cropper or mucker.

Adjectives: Unsuccessful, failing, etc., unfortunate, in a bad way, unlucky, luckless, out of luck, ill-fated, ill-starred, disastrous.

Unavailing, abortive, addle, still-born, fruitless, bootless, ineffectual, stickit, unattained, lame, hobbling, impotent, futile.

Aground, grounded, swamped, stranded, cast away, wrecked, on the rocks, foundered, capsized, torpedoed, shipwrecked.

Defeated, overcome, overthrown, overpowered, mastered, worsted, vanquished, conquered, subjugated, routed, silenced, distanced, foiled, unhorsed, baffled, befooled, dished, tossed about, stultified, undone, done for, down and out, ruined, circumvented, planet-struck, nonplussed.

Phrases: At a loss; wide of the mark; not having a leg to stand upon; ruined root and branch; the sport of fortune; bitched, bothered, and bewildered; hoist by one's own petard; left in the lurch; out of the running.

Adverbs: Unsuccessfully, etc., in vain, to no purpose, all up with.

Phrases: The game is up; all is lost.

733 TROPHY
Substantives: laurel, palm, crown, bays, wreath, garland, chaplet, civic crown, medal, ribbon, cup, scalp, prize, award, oscar, triumphal arch, ovation, triumph (883), flourish of trumpets, flying colours.

Phrase: A feather in one's cap.

734 PROSPERITY
Substantives: affluence (803), success (731), thrift, good fortune, welfare, well-being, felicity, luck, good luck, a run of luck, fair weather, sunshine, fair wind, a bed of roses, palmy days, the smiles of fortune, halcyon days, *Saturnia regna,* golden age.

An upstart, parvenu, *nouveau riche,* profiteer, skipjack, mushroom, self-made man.

A made man, a lucky dog.

Phrase: A roaring trade.

Verbs: To prosper, thrive, flourish, be well off; to flower, blow, blossom, bloom, fructify.

Phrases: To feather one's nest; to line one's pockets; to make one's pile; to bask in the sunshine; to rise in the world; to make one's way; to better oneself; to light on one's feet.

Adjectives: Prosperous, fortunate, lucky, well-off, well-to-do, bein, affluent, solvent (803), thriving, set up, prospering, etc., blooming, palmy, halcyon.

Auspicious, propitous, in a fair way.

Phrases: Born with a silver spoon in one's mouth; the spoilt child of fortune; in clover; on velvet; in luck's way.

Adverbs: Prosperously, etc., swimmingly.

735 ADVERSITY
Substantives: bad, ill, evil, adverse, etc., fortune, hap, or luck, tough luck, hard lines, reverse, set-back, comedown, broken fortunes, falling or going down in the world, hard times, iron age, evil day, rainy day.

Fall, ruin, ruination, ruinousness, undoing, mishap, mischance, misadventure, misfortune, disaster, calamity, catastrophe (619), failure (732); a hard life; trouble, hardship, blight, curse, evil star, evil genius, evil dispensation.
Phrases: The frowns of fortune; the ups and downs of life; a black look-out; the time being out of joint.
Verbs: To be ill off; to decay, sink, go under, fall, decline, come down in the world, lose caste; to have had it.
Adjectives: Unfortunate, unlucky, luckless, untoward, ill-off, badly off, decayed, ill-fated, ill-starred, impecunious, necessitous (804), bankrupt (808), unprosperous, adverse, untoward.

Disastrous, calamitous, ruinous, dire, deplorable, etc.
Phrases: Down on one's luck; in a bad way; in poor shape; having seen better days; born with a wooden ladle in one's mouth; one's star on the wane; from bad to worse; down and out.

736 MEDIOCRITY
Substantives: the golden mean, *aurea mediocritas,* moderation (174), moderate circumstances; the middle classes, bourgeoisie.
Adjectives: Tolerable, fair, middling, passable, average, so-so, ordinary, mediocre; middle-class, bourgeois.
Verbs: To keep a middle course, jog on, get along, get by.
Phrase: *Medio tutissimus ibis.*

II
Section 1 –
General Intersocial
Volition

737 AUTHORITY
Substantives: influence, patronage, credit, power, prerogative, control, jurisdiction, censorship, autoritativeness, absoluteness, despotism, absolutism, tyranny.

Command, empire, sway, rule, dominion, domination, supremacy, sovereignty, suzerainty, lordship, headship, seigniory, seigniorship, mastery, mastership, office, government, administration, gubernation, empire, body politic, accession.

Hold, grasp, gripe, grip, reach, fang, clutches, talons, helm, reins.

Reign, dynasty, regime, directorship, proconsulship, prefecture, caliphate, seneschalship, magistrature, magistracy, presidency, presidentship, premiership.

Empire, autocracy, monarchy, kinghood, kingship, royalty, regality, kingcraft, aristocracy, oligarchy, feudalism, republic, republicanism, democracy, socialism, demagogy, ochlocracy, mobocracy, mob-rule, dictatorship of proletariat, ergatocracy, collectivism, communism, Bolshevism, bureaucracy, bumbledom, syndicalism, militarism, stratocracy, *imperium in imperio,* dictatorship, protectorate, protectorship, directorate, directory, executive, raj.

Limited monarchy, constitutional government, representative government, home rule, diarchy (or dyarchy), duumvirate, triumvirate.

Vicarious authority (755, 759).

Gynarchy, gynaecocracy, petticoat government, matriarchy; patriarchy, patriarchism.
Verbs: To have, hold, possess, or exercise authority, etc.

To be master, etc.; to have the control, etc.; to overrule, override, overawe, dominate.

To rule, govern, sway, command, control, direct, administer, lead, preside over, boss; to dictate, reign, hold the reins; to possess or be seated on the throne; to ascend or mount the throne; to sway or wield the sceptre.

Phrases: To have the upper hand; to have the whip-hand; to bend to one's will; to have one's own way; to rule the roost; to lay down the law; to be cock of the roost; to have under the thumb; to keep under; to lead by the nose; to wear the breeches; to have the ball at one's feet; to play first fiddle.

Adjectives: Ruling, etc., regnant, dominant, paramount, supreme, authoritative, executive, gubernatorial, administrative, official.

Imperial, regal, sovereign, royal, royalist, kingly, monarchical, imperatorial, princely, baronial, feudal, seigneurial, seigniorial, aristocratic, democratic, etc.; totalitarian, ultramontane, absolutist.

Imperative, peremptory, arbitrary, absolute, overruling.

Adverbs: In the name of, by the authority of, in virtue of, at one's command, under the auspices of, under the aegis of, *ex officio, ex cathedra.*

738 LAXITY
Substantives: laxness, licence, licentiousness, relaxation, looseness, loosening, slackness, toleration, *laissez-faire,* remission, liberty (748).

Misrule, anarchy, interregnum.

Deprivation of power, dethronement, deposition, usurpation.

Denial of authority: anarchism, nihilism; insubordination, mutiny (742).

Anarchist, nihilist, usurper, mutineer.

Phrases: A dead letter; *brutum fulmen.*
Verbs: To be lax, etc., to hold a loose rein, tolerate, to relax, to misrule.

To dethrone.

Phrases: To give a loose rein to; to give rope enough.

Adjectives: Lax, permissive, loose, slack, remiss, relaxed, licensed, reinless, unbridled, anarchic, anarchical, nihilistic.

Unauthorized (925).

739 SEVERITY
Substantives: strictness, rigour, rigidity, rigidness, sternness, stringency, austerity, inclemency, harshness, acerbity, stiffness, rigorousness, inexorability.

Arbitrary power, absolutism, despotism, dictatorship, autocracy, domineering, tyranny; Moloch.

Assumption, usurpation.

A tyrant, disciplinarian, martinet, stickler, despot, oppressor, hard master; King Stork.

Phrases: Iron rule; reign of terror; mailed fist; martial law; blood and iron; tender mercies; red tape.

Verbs: To be severe, etc.; to assume, usurp, arrogate, take liberties; to hold or keep a tight hand; to bear or lay a heavy hand on; to be down on; to dictate; to domineer, bully, oppress, override, tyrannize.

Phrases: To lord it over; to carry matters with a high hand; to ride roughshod over; to rule with a rod of iron; to put on the screw; to deal faithfully with; to keep a person's nose to the grindstone.

Adjectives: Severe, strict, rigid, stern, stiff, dour, strait-laced, rigorous, exacting, stringent, hard and fast, peremptory, absolute, positive, uncompromising, harsh, austere, arbitrary, haughty, overbearing, arrogant, autocratic, bossy, dictatorial, imperious, domineering, tyrannical, masterful, obdurate, unyielding, inflexible, inexorable, exigent, inclement, Spartan, Rhadamanthine, Draconian.

Adverbs: Severely, etc., with a heavy hand.

740 LENITY
Substantives: mildness, lenience, leniency, gentleness, indulgence, clemency, tolerance, forbearance.

Verbs: To be lenient, etc., to tolerate, indulge, spoil, bear with, to allow to have one's own way, to let down gently.

Adjectives: Lenient, mild, gentle, soft, indulgent, tolerant, easy-going, clement.

Phrase: Live and let live.

741 COMMAND
Substantives: order, fiat, bidding, dictum, hest, behest, call, beck, nod, message, direction, injunction, charge, instructions, appointment, demand, exaction, imposition, requisition, requirement, claim, reclamation, revendication.

Dictation, dictate, mandate, caveat, edict, decree, decretal, enactment, precept, prescript, writ, rescript, law, ordinance, ordination, bull, regulation, prescription, brevet, placet, ukase, firman, warrant, passport, mittimus, mandamus, summons, subpoena, interpellation, citation, word of command.

Verbs: To command, to issue a command, order, give order, bid, require, enjoin, charge, claim, call for, demand, exact, insist on, make a point of, impose, entail, set, tax, prescribe, direct, brief, appoint, dictate, ordain, decree, enact; to issue or promulgate a decree, etc.

To cite, summon, call for, call up, send for, requisition, subpoena; to set or prescribe a task, to set to work, to give the word of command, to call to order.

Phrase: The decree is gone forth.

Adjectives: Commanding, etc., authoritative, peremptory, decretive, decretory (737).

Adverbs: By order, with a dash of the pen.

Phrase: *Le roy le veult.*

742 DISOBEDIENCE
Substantives: non-compliance, insubordination, contumacy, defection, infringement, infraction, violation; defiance (715), resistance (719), non-observance (773).

Rising, insurrection, revolt, *coup d'état, putsch,* rebellion, turn-out, strike, riot, riotousness, mutinousness, mutiny, tumult, sedition, treason, lese-majesty.

An insurgent, mutineer, rebel, rioter, traitor, apostate, renegade, seceder, quisling, fifth columnist; *carbonaro,* sansculotte, *frondeur;* agitator, demagogue, Jack Cade, Wat Tyler; ringleader.

Verbs: To disobey, violate, infringe, resist (719), defy (715), turn restive, shirk, kick, strike, mutiny, rise, rebel, secede, lift the hand against, turn out, come out, go on strike.

Phrases: To champ the bit; to kick over the traces; to unfurl the red flag.

Adjectives: Disobedient, resisting, rebellious, unruly, unsubmissive, ungovernable, uncomplying, uncompliant, restive, insubordinate, contumacious, mutinous, riotous, seditious, disaffected, recusant, recalcitrant, refractory, naughty.

Unbidden, unobeyed, a dead letter.

Phrase: The grey mare being the better horse.

743 OBEDIENCE
Substantives: submission, non-resistance, passiveness, resignation, cession, compliance, surrender (725), subordination, deference, loyalty, devotion, allegiance, obeisance, homage, fealty, prostration, kneeling, genuflexion, curtsy, kowtow, salaam, submissiveness, obsequiousness (886), servitorship, subjection (749).

Verbs: To be obedient, etc.; to obey,

submit, succumb, give in, knock under, cringe, yield (725), comply, surrender, follow, give up, give way, resign, bend to, bear obedience to.

To kneel, fall on one's knees, bend the knee, curtsy, kowtow, salaam, bow, pay homage to.

To attend upon, tend; to be under the orders of, to serve.

Phrases: To kiss the rod; to do one's bidding; to play second fiddle; to take it lying down; to dance attendance on.

Adjectives: Obedient, submissive, resigned, passive, complying, compliant, loyal, faithful, devoted, yielding, docile, tractable, amenable, biddable, unresisting, henpecked; restrainable, unresisted.

744 COMPULSION

Substantives: coercion, coaction, force, constraint, enforcement, press, *corvée,* conscription, levy, duress, brute force, main force, *force majeure,* the sword, club law, *ultima ratio, argumentum baculinum.*

Verbs: To compel, force, make, drive, coerce, constrain, steam-roller, enforce, put in force, oblige, force upon, press, conscribe, extort, put down, bind, pin down, bind over, impress, commandeer, requisition.

Phrases: To cram down the throat; to take no denial; to insist upon; to make a point of.

Adjectives: Compelling, etc., compulsory, compulsatory, obligatory, forcible, coercive, coactive, peremptory, rigorous, stringent, inexorable (739); being fain to do, having to do.

Adverbs: By force, perforce, under compulsion, *vi et armis,* in spite of one's teeth; *bon gré, mal gré*; willy-nilly, *nolens volens; de rigueur.*

745 MASTER

Substantives: lord, laird, chief, leader, captain, skipper, mate, protagonist, coryphaeus, head, chieftain, commander, commandant, director

(694), captain of industry, ruler, potentate, dictator, liege, sovereign, monarch, autocrat, despot, tyrant, *führer, duce,* demagogue, ring-leader, boss, big shot, fugleman.

Crowned head, emperor, king, majesty, tetrarch, *imperator,* protector, president, stadtholder, governor.

Caesar, czar, sultan, soldan, caliph, sophy, khan, cacique, inca, lama, mogul, imam, shah, khedive, pasha (or bashaw), dey, cham, judge, aga, hospodar, mikado, shogun, tycoon, exarch.

Prince, seignior, highness, archduke, duke, marquis, earl, viscount, baron (875), margrave, landgrave, palatine, elector, doge, satrap, rajah, maharajah, emir, bey, effendi, nizam, nawab, mandarin, sirdar, ameer, sachem, sagamore.

Empress, queen, czarina, sultana, princess, duchess, marchioness, countess, viscountess, baroness, infanta, ranee, maharanee, margravine, etc.

Military authorities, marshal, field-marshal, *maréchal,* generalissimo, commander-in-chief, admiral, commodore, general, lieutenant-general, major-general, brigadier, colonel, lieutenant-colonel, officer, captain, major, lieutenant, adjutant, midshipman, quartermaster, aide-de-camp, ensign, cornet, cadet, subaltern, non-commissioned officer, drum-major, sergeant-major, sergeant, corporal, air-marshal, group-captain, wing-commander, squadron-leader, flight-lieutenant, centurion, *seraskier,* hetman, subahdar, *condottiere.*

Civil authorities, mayor, prefect, chancellor, provost, magistrate, syndic, alcade (or alcayde), burgomaster, *corregidor,* sheik, seneschal, burgrave, alderman, warden, constable (965), beadle, alguazil, kavass, tribune, consul, proconsul, quaestor, praetor, aedile, archon, pole-march.

Statesman, politician, statist, legislator, lawgiver.

President, chairman, speaker, moderator, vice-president, comptroller, director (694), monitor, monitress.

746 SERVANT
Substantives: servitor, employee, attaché, secretary, subordinate, clerk, retainer, vassal, protégé, dependant, hanger-on, pensioner, client, emissary, *âme damnée.*

Retinue, cortège, staff, court, train, entourage, clientele, suite.

An attendant, squire, henchman, led captain, chamberlain, follower, usher, page, train-bearer, domestic, help, butler, footman, lackey, flunkey, parlour-man, valet, waiter, *garçon,* equerry, groom, jockey, ostler (or hostler), stable-boy, tiger, buttons, boot-boy, boots, livery servant, hireling, mercenary, underling, menial, gillie, under-strapper, journeyman, whipper-in, bailiff, castellan, seneschal, major-domo, cup-bearer, bottle-washer, scout, gyp.

Serf, villein, slave, galley-slave, thrall, peon, helot, bondsman, *adscriptus glebae,* wage-slave.

A maid, handmaid, abigail, chamber-maid, lady's maid, housekeeper, lady help, soubrette, *fille de chambre,* parlour-maid, housemaid, between-maid, kitchen-maid, nurse, *bonne,* scullion, laundress, bed-maker, skivvy, slavey, daily.
Verbs: To serve, attend upon, dance attendance, wait upon, squire, valet.
Adverbs: In one's pay or employ, in the train of.

747 SCEPTRE
Substantives: regalia, insignia (550), crown, coronet, rod of empire, orb, mace, *fasces,* wand, baton, truncheon, staff, insignia (550), portfolio.

A throne, chair, divan, dais, woolsack.

Diadem, tiara, ermine, purple, signet, seals, keys, talisman, cap of maintenance, toga, robes of state, decoration.

748 FREEDOM
Substantives: independence, liberty, licence (760), self-government, autonomy, scope, range, latitude, play, swing, free play, elbow-room, *lebensraum,* margin.

Franchise, immunity, exemption, emancipation (750), naturalization, denizenship.

Freeland, freehold, allodium (780).

A freeman, freedman, denizen.
Phrases: The four freedoms; *liberté, egalité, fraternité*; a place in the sun; Liberty Hall.
Verbs: To be free, to have scope, etc.

To render free, etc., to free, to emancipate, enfranchise (750), naturalize.
Phrases: To have the run of; to have one's own way; to have one's fling; to stand on one's own feet; to stand on one's rights; to have a will of one's own; to paddle one's own canoe; to play a lone hand.

To take a liberty; to make free with; to take the bit between one's teeth.
Adjectives: Free, independent, loose, at large, unconstrained, unrestrained, unchecked, unobstructed, unconfined, unsubdued, unsubjugated, self-governed, autonomous, self-supporting, untrammelled, unbound, uncontrolled, unchained, unshackled, unfettered, uncurbed, unbridled, unrestricted, unmuzzled, unbuttoned, unforced, uncompelled, unbiased, spontaneous, unhindered, unthwarted, heart-whole, uncaught, unenslaved, unclaimed, ungoverned, resting.

Free and easy, at ease, *dégagé,* wanton, rampant, irrepressible, unprevented, unvanquished, exempt, freehold, allodial, enfranchised, emancipated, released, disengaged (750), out of hand.
Phrases: Free as air; one's own master; *sui juris*; a law to oneself; on one's own; a cat may look at a king.

749 SUBJECTION
Substantives: dependence, thrall,

thraldom, subjugation, subordination, bondage, serfdom, servitude, slavery, vassalage, villeinage, service, clientship, liability (177), enslavement, tutelage, constraint (751).

Yoke, harness, collar.

Verbs: To be subject, dependent, etc., to fall under, obey, serve (743).

To subject, subjugate, enthral, enslave, keep under, control, etc. (751), to reduce to slavery, mediatize, break in.

Phrases: To drag a chain; not dare to call one's soul one's own; to be led by the nose; to be or lie at the mercy of.

To keep in leading strings.

Adjectives: Subject, subordinate, dependent, subjected, in subjection to, in thrall to, feudatory, feudal, enslaved, a slave to, at the mercy of, downtrodden, overborne, henpecked, enthralled, controlled, constrained (751).

Phrases: Under the thumb of; at the feet of; tied to the apron-strings of; the puppet, sport, plaything of.

750 LIBERATION

Substantives: disengagement, release, enlargement, emancipation, affranchisement, enfranchisement, manumission, discharge, dismissal.

Escape (671), deliverance (672), redemption, extrication, absolution, acquittance, acquittal (970).

Licence, toleration; parole, ticket of leave.

Verbs: To gain, obtain, acquire, etc., one's liberty, freedom, etc., to get off, get clear, to deliver oneself from.

To break loose, escape, slip away, make one's escape, cut and run, slip the collar, bolt (671).

To liberate, free, set free, set at liberty, release, loose, let loose, loosen, relax, unloose, untie, unbind, unhand, unchain, unshackle, unfetter, unclog, disengage, unharness (44).

To enlarge, set clear, let go, let out, disenchain, disimprison, unbar,

unbolt, uncage, unclose, uncork, discharge, disenthral, dismiss, deliver, extricate, let slip, enfranchise, affranchise, manumit, denizen, emancipate, assoil (748).

To clear, acquit, redeem, ransom, get off.

Phrases: To throw off the yoke; to burst one's bonds; to break prison.

To give one one's head.

Adjectives: Liberated, freed, etc.

751 RESTRAINT

Substantives: constraint, coercion, cohibition, repression, clamp down, control, discipline.

Confinement, durance, duress, detention, imprisonment, incarceration, prisonment, internment, blockade, quarantine, coarctation, mancipation, entombment, 'durance vile,' limbo, captivity, penal servitude.

Arrest, arrestation, custody, keep, care, charge, ward.

Prison, fetter (752); *lettre de cachet*.

Verbs: To be under restraint or arrest, to be coerced, etc.

To restrain, constrain, coerce, check, trammel, curb, cramp, keep under, enthral, put under restraint, restrict, repress, cohibit, detain, debar; to chain, enchain, fasten, tie up (43), picket, fetter, shackle, manacle, handcuff, bridle, muzzle, gag, suppress, pinion, pin down, tether, hobble.

To confine, shut up, shut in, clap up, lock up, cage, encage, impound, pen, coop, hem in, jam in, enclose, bottle up, cork up, seal up, mew, wall in, rail in, cloister, bolt in, close the door upon, imprison, incarcerate, immure, entomb, seclude, corral.

To take prisoner, lead captive, send or commit to prison, give in charge or in custody, arrest, commit, run in, lag; re-commit, remand.

Phrases: To put in irons; to clap under hatches; to put in a straitwaistcoat.

Adjectives: Restrained, coerced, etc., sewn up, pent up.

Held up, wind-bound, weather-bound, storm-stayed.

Coactive, stiff, restringent, strait-laced, hide-bound.

Phrases: In limbo; under lock and key; laid by the heels; 'cabined, cribbed, confined'; in quod; in durance vile; doing time; bound hand and foot.

752 PRISON

Substantives: jail (or gaol), prison-house, house of detention, lock-up, the cells, clink, glasshouse, brig, jug, quod, cooler, choky, stir, calaboose, cage, coop, den, cell, stronghold, fortress, keep, dungeon, bastille, oub-liette, bridewell, tollbooth, panopti-con, hulks, galleys, penitentiary, guard-room, hold, round-house, blackhole, station, enclosure, concentration camp, pen, fold, pound, paddock, stocks, bilboes, nick.

Newgate, King's Bench, Fleet, Marshalsea, Pentonville, Holloway, Dartmoor, Portland, Peterhead, Broadmoor, Sing Sing, the Bastille.

Fetter, shackle, trammel, bond, chain, irons, collar, cangue, pinion, gyve, fetterlock, manacle, handcuff, darbies, strait waistcoat; yoke, halter, harness, muzzle, gag, bridle, curb, bit, snaffle, rein, martingale, leading-strings, swaddling-bands, tether, hobble, picket, band, brake.

Bolt, bar, lock, padlock, rail, wall, paling, palisade (232), fence, corral, barrier, barricade.

753 KEEPER

Substantives: custodian, *custos,* warder, jailer (or gaoler), turnkey, castellan, guard, ranger, gamekeeper, watch, watchman, watch and ward, sentry, sentinel, coastguard, convoy, escort, *concierge,* caretaker, watch-dog.

Guardian, duenna, nurse, ayah, chaperon.

754 PRISONER

Substantives: prisoner-of-war, POW, kriegie, captive, *détenu,* convict, jail-bird, lag; ticket-of-leave man.

Adjectives: In custody, in charge, imprisoned, locked up, incarcerated, pent.

755 COMMISSION

Substantives: delegation, consignment, assignment, devolution, procuration, deputation, legation, mission, agency, clerkship, agentship; power of attorney; errand, embassy, charge, brevet, diploma, exequatur, committal, commitment.

Appointment, nomination, ordination, installation, inauguration, return, accession, investiture, coronation.

Vicegerency, regency, regentship.

Deputy (759).

Verbs: To commission, delegate, depute, devolve, send out, assign, consign, charge, encharge, entrust with, commit to, enlist.

To appoint, name, nominate, accredit, engage, bespeak, ordain, install, induct, inaugurate, invest, crown, return, enrol.

Employ, empower, set over.

To be commissioned, to represent.

Adverbs: *Per procurationem per pro.,* p.p.

756 ABROGATION

Substantives: annulment, cancel, cancellation, revocation, repeal, rescission, rescinding, deposal, deposition, dethronement, defeasance, dismissal, sack, *congé,* demission, disestablishment, disendowment.

Abolition, abolishment, counter-order, countermand, repudiation, nullification, recantation, palinode, retractation (607).

Verbs: To abrogate, annul, cancel, revoke, repeal, rescind, reverse, override, overrule, abolish, disannul, dissolve, quash, repudiate, nullify, retract, recant, recall, countermand, counter-order, break off, disclaim, declare null and void, disestablish, disendow, deconsecrate, set aside, do away with.

To dismiss, send off, send away, discard, turn off, turn away, cashier, sack, fire, bounce, oust, unseat, unthrone, dethrone, depose, uncrown, unfrock, disbar, disbench.

Phrases: Send about one's business; put one's nose out of joint; give one the mitten, the chuck, the sack, the boot, the push.

To get one's books or cards; to get the key of the street.

Adjectives: Abrogated, etc.; *functus officio*.

Interjections: Get along with you! clear out! be off! beat it!

757 RESIGNATION

Substantives: retirement, abdication, renunciation, abjuration.

Verbs: To resign, give up, throw up, retire, abdicate, lay down, abjure, renounce, forgo, disclaim, retract (756); to tender one's resignation, send in one's papers.

Phrases: To swallow the anchor; to be given one's bowler.

Adjectives: Emeritus.

Phrase: 'Othello's occupation's gone.'

758 CONSIGNEE

Substantives: delegate, commissary, commissioner, vice-regent, legate, representative, secondary, nominee, surrogate, functionary, trustee, assignee.

Corps diplomatique, plenipotentiary, emissary, embassy, ambassador, diplomat(ist), consul, resident, nuncio, internuncio.

Agent, factor, attorney, broker, factotum, bailiff, man of business, go-between, intermediary, middleman, salesman, commission agent, commercial traveller, bagman, drummer, colporteur, commissionaire, employee, attaché, curator, clerk, placeman.

759 DEPUTY

Substantives: substitute, vice, proxy, locum tenens, baby-sitter, *chargé d'affaires,* delegate, representative, *alter ego,* surrogate, understudy, stooge, stand-in, stopgap, pinch-hitter.

Regent, viceroy, vicegerent, vicar, satrap, exarch, vizier, minister, premier, commissioner, chancellor, prefect, warden, lieutenant, proconsul, legate.

Verbs: To deputize; to be deputy, etc., for; to appear for; to understudy; to take duty for.

Phrase: To hold a watching brief for.

Adjectives: Acting, deputizing, etc.

Adverbs: In place of, vice.

Section 2 –
Special Intersocial Volition

760 PERMISSION

Substantives: leave, allowance, sufferance, tolerance, toleration, liberty, law, licence, concession, grant, vouchsafement, authorization, sanction, accordance, admission, favour, dispensation, exemption, connivance.

A permit, warrant, brevet, precept, authority, firman, pass, passport, furlough, ticket, licence, charter, patent, *carte blanche,* exeat.

Verbs: To permit; to give leave or permission; to let, allow, admit, suffer, tolerate, concede, accord, vouchsafe, humour, indulge, to leave it to one; to leave alone; to grant, empower, charter, sanction, authorize, warrant, license; to give licence; to give a loose to.

To let off, absolve, exonerate, dispense with, favour, wink, connive at.

Phrases: To give *carte blanche*; to give rein to; to stretch a point; leave the door open; to let one have a chance; to give one a fair show.

To take a liberty; to use a freedom; to make so bold; to beg leave.

Adjectives: Permitting, etc., permissive, conceding, indulgent.

Allowable, permissible, lawful, legitimate, legal.

Unforbid, unforbidden, unconditional.

761 PROHIBITION

Substantives: inhibition, veto, disallowance, interdiction, estoppage, hindrance (706), restriction, restraints (751), embargo, an interdict, ban, injunction, taboo, proscription; *index librorum prohibitorum.*

Verbs: To prohibit, forbid, inhibit, disallow, bar, debar, interdict, ban, estop, veto, keep in, hinder, restrain (751), restrict, withhold, limit, circumscribe, keep within bounds.

To exclude, shut out, proscribe.

Phrase: To clip the wings of; to forbid the banns.

Adjectives: Prohibitive, restrictive, exclusive, prohibitory, forbidding, etc.

Not permitted, prohibited, etc., unlicensed, contraband, unauthorized.

Phrases: Under the ban of; on the Index.

Interjections: Hands off! keep off! God forbid!

762 CONSENT

Substantives: compliance, acquiescence, assent (488), agreement, concession, yieldingness, acknowledgment, acceptance.

Settlement, ratification, confirmation.

Verbs: To consent, give consent, assent, comply with, acquiesce, agree to, subscribe to, accede, accept.

To concede, yield, satisfy, grant, settle, acknowledge, confirm, homologate, ratify, deign, vouchsafe.

Phrase: To take at one's word.

Adjectives: Consenting, etc., having no objection, unconditional.

Adverbs: Yes (488); if you please, as you please, by all means, by all manner

of means, so be it, of course, certainly, sure, OK.

Phrases: Suits me; all right by me.

763 OFFER

Substantives: proffer, tender, present, overture, proposition, motion, proposal, invitation, candidature, presentation, offering, oblation, bid, bribe.

Sacrifice, immolation.

Verbs: To offer, proffer, tender, present, invite, volunteer, propose, move, make a motion, start, press, bid, hold out, hawk about.

To sacrifice, immolate.

Phrases: To be a candidate; to go abegging.

Adjectives: Offering, etc., in the market, for sale, on hire.

764 REFUSAL

Substantives: rejection, declining, non-compliance, declension, dissent (489), denial, repulse, rebuff, discountenance.

Disclaimer, recusancy, abnegation, protest.

Revocation, violation, abrogation (756), flat refusal, peremptory denial.

Verbs: To refuse, reject, deny, decline, disclaim, repudiate, protest, resist, repel, veto, refuse or withhold one's assent; to excuse oneself, to negative, turn down, rebuff, snub, spurn, resist, cross, grudge, begrudge.

To discard, set aside, rescind, revoke, discountenance, forswear.

Phrases: To turn a deaf ear to; to shake the head; not to hear of; to send to the right-about; to hang fire; to wash one's hands of; to declare off.

Adjectives: Refusing, etc., recusant, restive, uncomplying, unconsenting.

Refused, etc., out of the question, not to be thought of.

Adverbs: No, by no means, etc. (489).

Phrases: Excuse me; nix on that; not on your life; nothing doing.

765 REQUEST

Substantives: requisition, asking, petition, demand, suit, solicitation, craving, entreaty, begging, postulation, adjuration, canvass, candidature, prayer, supplication, impetration, imploration, instance, obsecration, obtestation, importunity, application, address, appeal, motion, invitation, overture, invocation, interpellation, apostrophe, orison, incantation, imprecation, conjuration.

Mendicancy, begging letter, round robin.

Claim, reclamation, revendication.

Verbs: To request, ask, sue, beg, cadge, crave, pray, petition, solicit, beg a boon, demand, prefer a request or petition, ply, apply to, make application, put to, make bold to ask, invite, beg leave, put up a prayer.

To beg hard, entreat, beseech, supplicate, implore, plead, conjure, adjure, invoke, evoke, kneel to, fall on one's knees, impetrate, imprecate, appeal to, apply to, put to, address, call for, press, urge, beset, importune, dun, tax, besiege, cry to, call on.

To bespeak, canvass, tout, make interest, court; to claim, reclaim.

Phrases: To send that hat round; to beg from door to door.

Adjectives: Requesting, asking, beseeching, etc., precatory, suppliant, supplicatory, postulant, importunate.

Phrases: Cap in hand; on one's knees.

Adverbs: Do, please, kindly, be good enough, pray, prithee, be so good as, have the goodness, vouchsafe.

For heaven's sake, for goodness' sake, for God's sake, for the love of Mike.

766 DEPRECATION
Substantives: expostulation, intercession, mediation.
Verbs: To deprecate, protest, expostulate; to enter a protest; to intercede for.
Adjectives: Deprecating, etc; deprecatory, expostulatory, intercessory; deprecated, protested.

Unsought, unbesought.
Interjections: God forbid! forbid it heaven! *Absit omen!*

767 PETITIONER
Substantives: solicitor, applicant, suppliant, supplicant, mendicant, beggar, mumper, suitor, candidate, aspirant, claimant, postulant, canvasser, tout, cadger, sponger.

Section 3 –
Conditional Intersocial
Volition

768 PROMISE
Substantives: word, troth, plight, profession, pledge, parole, word of honour, assurance, vow, oath.

Engagement, guarantee, undertaking, insurance, contract (769), obligation; affiance, betrothal, betrothment.
Verbs: To promise, give a promise, undertake, engage, assure; to give, pass, pledge or plight one's word, honour credit, faith, etc.; to covenant, warrant, guarantee (467); to swear, vow, be sworn; take oath, make oath, kiss the book; to attest, adjure; to betroth, plight troth, affiance.

To answer for, be answerable for, secure, give security (771).
Phrases: To enter on, make or form an engagement, take upon oneself; to bind, tie, commit, or pledge oneself; to be in for it; to contract an obligation; to be bound; to hold out an expectation.

To call heaven to witness; to swear by bell, book, and candle; to put on one's oath; to swear a witness.
Adjectives: Promising, etc., promised, pledged, sworn, etc.; votive, promissory.
Phrases: Under one's hand and seal; as one's head shall answer for.
Interjection: So help me God!

768a RELEASE FROM ENGAGEMENT
Substantives: disengagement, liberation (750).
Adjectives: Absolute, unconditional, uncovenanted, unsecured.

769 COMPACT
Substantives: contract, agreement, understanding, bargain, bond, deal, pact, paction, stipulation, covenant, settlement, convention, cartel, protocol, charter, treaty, indenture, concordat, *zollverein*.

Negotiation, transaction, bargaining, haggling, chaffering; diplomacy.

Ratification, settlement, signature, endorsement, seal, signet.

A negotiator, diplomatist, diplomat, agent, contractor, underwriter, attorney, broker (758).

Verbs: To contract, covenant, agree for, strike a bargain, engage (768); to underwrite.

To treat, negotiate, bargain, stipulate, haggle (or higgle), chaffer, stick out for, insist upon, make a point of, compound for.

To conclude, close, confirm, ratify, endorse, clench, come to an understanding, take one at one's word, come to terms.

To subscribe, sign, seal, indent, put the seal to, sign and seal.

Phrase: *Caveat emptor.*

770 CONDITIONS
Substantives: terms, articles, articles of agreement, clauses, proviso, provisions, salvo, covenant, stipulation, obligation, ultimatum, *sine qua non*.

Verbs: To make it a condition, make terms; to stipulate, insist upon; to tie up.

Adjectives: Conditional, provisional, guarded, fenced, hedged in.

Adverbs: Conditionally, on the understanding; provided (469).

Phrases: With a string tied to it; wind and weather permitting; God willing; DV; *Deo volente.*

771 SECURITY
Substantives: surety, guaranty, guarantee, mortgage, warranty, bond, debenture, pledge, tie, plight, pawn, lien, caution, sponsion, hostage, sponsor, bail, parole.

Deed, instrument, deed-poll, indenture, warrant, charter, cartel, protocol, recognizance; verification, acceptance, endorsement, signature, execution, seal, stamp, IOU.

Promissory note, bill of exchange, bill.

Stake, deposit, pool, kitty, jack-pot, earnest, handsel.

Docket, certificate, voucher, verification, authentication.

Verbs: To give security, go bail, pawn (787); guarantee, warrant, accept, endorse, underwrite, insure; execute, stamp.

To hold in pledge.

772 OBSERVANCE
Substantives: performance, fulfilment, satisfaction, discharge, compliance, acquittance, quittance, acquittal, adhesion, acknowledgment, fidelity (939).

Verbs: To observe, perform, keep, fulfil, discharge, comply with, make good, meet, satisfy, respect, abide by, adhere to, be faithful to, act up to, acquit oneself.

Phrase: To redeem one's pledge.

Adjectives: Observant, faithful, true, honourable (939), strict, rigid, punctilious.

Adverbs: Faithfully, etc., to the letter.

Phrase: As good as one's word.

773 NON-OBSERVANCE
Substantives: inobservance, evasion, omission, failure, neglect, laches, laxity, infringement, infraction, violation, forfeiture, transgression.

Retractation, repudiation, nullification, protest.

Informality, lawlessness, disobedience, bad faith (742).

Verbs: To break, violate, fail, neglect, omit, skip, cut, forfeit, infringe, transgress.

To retract, discard, protest, go back upon or from one's word, repudiate, nullify, ignore, set at naught, wipe off, cancel, etc. (552), to fob off, palter, elude, evade.

Phrases: To wash out; to shut one's eyes to; to drive a coach and six through.

Adjectives: Violating, etc., elusive, evasive, transgressive, unfulfilled; compensatory (30).

774 COMPROMISE

Substantives: composition, middle term, *mezzo termine, modus vivendi*; bribe, hush-money.

Verbs: To compromise, compound, commute, adjust, take the mean, split the difference, come to terms, come to an understanding, meet one half-way, give and take, submit to arbitration.

Section 4 –
Possessive Relations

775 ACQUISITION

Substantives: obtainment, gaining, earning, procuration, procuring, procurement, gathering, gleaning, picking, collecting, recovery, retrieval, totting, salvage, find.

Book-collecting, book-hunting, etc., philately, cartophily, phillumeny.

Gain, profit, benefit, emolument, the main chance, pelf, lucre, loaves and fishes, produce, product, proceeds, return, fruit, crop, harvest, scoop, takings, winnings.

Inheritance, bequest, legacy.

Fraudulent acquisition, subreption, stealing (791).

Profiteering, pot-hunting.

A collector, book-collector, etc., bird-fancier, etc., philatelist, cartophilist, phillumenist; a profiteer, money-grubber, pot-hunter.

Verbs: To acquire, get, gain, win, earn, realize, regain, receive (785), take (789), obtain, procure, derive, secure, collect, reap, gather, glean, come in for, step into, inherit, come by, rake in, scrape together, get hold of, scoop, pouch.

To profit, make profit, turn to profit, make money by, obtain a return, make a fortune, coin money, profiteer.

To be profitable, to pay, to answer.

To fall to, come to, accrue.

Phrases: To turn an honest penny; to earn an honest crust; to bring grist to the mill; to raise the wind; to line one's pockets; to feather one's nest; to reap or gain an advantage; to keep the wolf from the door; to keep the pot boiling.

Adjectives: Acquisitive, acquiring, acquired, etc., profitable, lucrative, remunerative, paying.

Phrase: On the make.

776 LOSS

Substantives: perdition, forfeiture, lapse.

Privation, bereavement, deprivation (789), dispossession, riddance.

Verbs: To lose; incur, experience, or meet with a loss; to miss, mislay, throw away, forfeit, drop, let slip, allow to slip through the fingers; to get rid of (782), to waste (638, 679).

To be lost, lapse.

Phrase: To throw good money after bad.

Adjectives: Losing, etc., lost, etc.

Devoid of, not having, unobtained, unpossessed, unblest with.

Shorn of, deprived of, bereaved of, bereft of, rid of, quit of, dispossessed, denuded, out of pocket, minus, cut off.

Irrecoverable, irretrievable, irremediable, irreparable.

Interjections: Farewell to! adieu to!

777 POSSESSION
Substantives: ownership, proprietorship, tenure, tenancy, seisin, occupancy, hold, holding, preoccupancy.

Exclusive possession, impropriation, monopoly, inalienability.

Future possession, heritage, heirship, inheritance, reversion.

Phrases: A bird in the hand; nine points of the law; the haves and the have-nots.

Verbs: To possess, have, hold, own, be master of, be in possession of, enjoy, occupy, be seized of, be worth, to have in hand or on hand; to inherit (775).

To engross, monopolize, corner, forestall, absorb, preoccupy.

To be the property of, belong to, appertain to, pertain to, be in the hands of, be in the possession of.

Adjectives: Possessing, etc., possessed of, seized of, worth, endowed with, instinct with, fraught, laden with, charged with.

Possessed, etc., proprietary, proprietorial; on hand, in hand, in store, in stock, unsold, unshared; inalienable.

778 PARTICIPATION
Substantives: joint stock, common stock, partnership, copartnership, possession in common, communion, community of possessions or goods, socialism, collectivism, communism, syndicalism.

Bottle party, share-out, picnic.

A syndicate, ring, corner, combine, cartel, trust, monopoly, pool.

A partner, co-partner, shareholder; co-tenant, co-heir; a communist, socialist.

Verbs: To participate, partake, share, communicate, go snacks, go halves, share and share alike; to have or possess, etc., in common; to come in for a share, to stand in with, to socialize, to pool.

Adjectives: Partaking, etc.; socialist, socialistic, communist.

Adverbs: Share and share alike, fifty-fifty, even Stephen.

779 POSSESSOR
Substantives: owner, holder, proprietor, proprietress, proprietary, master, mistress, heritor, occupier, occupant, landlord, landlady, landowner, lord of the manor, squire, laird, landed gentry; tenant, renter, lessee, lodger.

Future possessor, heir, heiress, inheritor.

780 PROPERTY
Substantives: possession, ownership, proprietorship, seisin, tenancy, tenure, lordship, title, claim, stake, legal estate, equitable estate, fee simple, fee tail, *meum et tuum*, occupancy.

Estate, effects, assets, resources, means, belongings, stock, goods, chattels, fixtures, plant, movables, furniture, things, traps, trappings, paraphernalia, luggage, baggage, bag and baggage, cargo, lading.

Lease, term, settlement, remainder, reversion, dower, jointure, apanage, heritage, inheritance, patrimony, heirloom.

Real property, land, landed estate, manor, demesne, domain, tenement, holding, hereditament, household, freehold, farm, ranch, *hacienda, estancia,* fief, feoff, seigniority, allodium.

Ground, acres, field, close.

State, realm, empire, kingdom, principality, territory, sphere of influence.

Adjectives: Predial, manorial, freehold, etc., copyhold, leasehold.

781 RETENTION
Substantives: keep, holding, keeping, retaining, detention, custody, grasp, gripe, grip, tenacity.

Fangs, teeth, clutches, hooks, tentacles, claws, talons, nails.

Forceps, pincers, pliers, tongs, vice. Incommunicableness, incommunicability.

Phrase: A bird in the hand.

Verbs: To retain, keep, keep in hand, secure, detain, hold fast, grasp, clutch, clench, cinch, gripe, grip, hug, withhold, keep back.

Adjectives: Retaining, etc., retentive, tenacious.

Unforfeited, undeprived, undisposed, uncommunicated, incommunicable, inalienable, not transferable.

782 RELINQUISHMENT

Substantives: cession, abandonment (624), renunciation, surrender, dereliction, rendition, riddance (776), resignation (758).

Verbs: To relinquish, give up, let go, lay aside, resign, forgo, drop, discard, dismiss, waive, renounce, surrender, part with, get rid of, lay down, abandon, cede, yield, dispose of, divest oneself of, spare, give away, throw away, cast away, fling away, maroon, jettison, chuck up, let slip, make away with, make way for.

Phrases: To lay on the shelf; to throw overboard.

Adjectives: Relinquished, etc., derelict, left, residuary (40), unculled.

783 TRANSFER

Substantives: interchange, exchange, transmission, barter (794), conveyance, assignment, alienation, abalienation, demise, succession, reversion; matastasis.

Verbs: To transfer, convey, assign, consign, make over, pass, transmit, interchange, exchange (148).

To change hands, change from one to another, alienate, devolve.

To dispossess, abalienate, disinherit.

Adjectives: Alienable, negotiable, transferable.

784 GIVING

Substantives: bestowal, donation, accordance, presentation, oblation, presentment, delivery, award, investment, granting.

Cession, concession, consignment, dispensation, benefaction, charity, liberality, generosity, munificence, almsgiving.

Gift, donation, bonus, boon, present, testimonial, presentation, fairing, benefaction, grant, subsidy, subvention, offering, contribution, subscription, whip-round, donative, meed, tribute, gratuity, tip, Christmas box, handsel, trinkgeld, *douceur, pourboire*, baksheesh, cumshaw, dash, bribe, free gift, favour, bounty, largess, allowance, endowment, charity, alms, dole, peace-offering, payment (807).

Bequest, legacy, demise, dotation.

Giver, grantor, donor, benefactor.

Phrase: *Panem et circenses.*

Verbs: To give, bestow, accord, confer, grant, concede, present, give away, deliver, deliver over, make over, consign, entrust, hand, tip, render, impart, hand over, part with, fork out, yield, dispose of, put into the hands of, vest in, assign, put in possession, settle upon, endow, subsidize.

To bequeath, leave, demise, devise.

To give out, dispense, deal, deal out, dole out, mete out.

To contribute, subscribe, put up a purse, send round the hat, pay (807), spend (809).

To furnish, supply, administer, afford, spare, accommodate with, indulge with, shower upon, lavish.

To bribe, suborn, grease the palm, square.

Adjectives: Giving, etc., given, etc., charitable, eleemosynary, tributary.

Phrase: *Bis dat qui cito dat.*

785 RECEIVING

Substantives: acquisition (775), reception, acceptance, admission.

A recipient, donee, assignee, legatee, grantee, stipendiary, beneficiary, pensioner, almsman.

Verbs: To receive, take (789), accept, pocket, pouch, admit, catch, catch at, jump at, take in.

To be received, etc.; to accrue, come to hand.

Adjectives: Receiving, etc., recipient; pensionary, stipendiary.

786 APPORTIONMENT

Substantives: distribution, dispensation, allotment, assignment, consignment, partition, division, deal, share-out.

Dividend, portion, contingent, share, whack, meed, allotment, lot, measure, dole, pittance, quantum, ration, quota, modicum, allowance, appropriation.

Phrase: Cutting up the melon.

Verbs: To apportion, divide, distribute, administer, dispense, billet, allot, cast, share, mete, parcel out, serve out, deal, partition, appropriate, assign.

Adjectives: Apportioning, etc., respective.

Adverbs: Respectively, severally.

787 LENDING

Substantives: loan, advance, mortage, accommodation, lease-lend, subsistence money, sub, pawn, pignoration, hypothecation, investment; pawnshop, *mont de piété*.

Lender, pawnbroker, uncle.

Verbs: To lend, loan, advance, mortgage, invest, pawn, impawn, pop, hock, hypothecate, impignorate, place or put out to interest, entrust, accommodate with.

Adjectives: Lending, etc., lent, etc., unborrowed.

Adverb: In advance; up the spout.

788 BORROWING

Substantives: pledging, replevin, borrowed plumes, plagiarism, plagiary; a touch.

Verbs: To borrow, hire, rent, farm, raise money, raise the wind; to plagiarize.

Adjectives: Borrowing, etc., borrowed, second-hand.

Phrases: To borrow of Peter to pay Paul; to run into debt.

789 TAKING

Substantives: appropriation, prehension, capture, seizure, abduction, ablation, catching, seizing, apprehension, arrest, kidnapping, round-up.

Abstraction, subtraction, deduction, subduction.

Dispossession, deprivation, deprival, bereavement, divestment, sequestration, confiscation, disendowment.

Resumption, reprise, reprisal, recovery (775).

Clutch, swoop, wrench, catch, take, haul.

Verbs: To take, capture, lay one's hands on; lay, take, or get hold of; to help oneself to; to possess oneself of, take possession of, make sure of, make free with.

To appropriate, impropriate, pocket, put into one's pocket, pouch, bag; to ease one of.

To pick up, gather, collect, round up, net, absorb (296), reap, glean, crop, get in the harvest, cull, pluck; intercept, tap.

To take away, carry away, carry off, bear off, hurry off with, abduct, kidnap, crimp, shanghai.

To lay violent hands on, fasten upon, pounce upon, catch, seize, snatch, nip up, whip up, jump at, snap at, hook, claw, clinch, grasp, gripe, grip, grab, clutch, wring, wrest, wrench, pluck, tear away, catch, nab, capture, collar, throttle.

To take from, deduct, subduct (38), subtract, curtail, retrench, abridge of, dispossess, expropriate, take away from, abstract, deprive of, bereave, divest, disendow, despoil, strip, fleece, shear, impoverish, levy, distrain, confiscate, sequester, sequestrate, commandeer, requisition, oust, extort, usurp, suck, squeeze, drain, bleed, milk, gut, dry, exhaust.

Phrases: To suck like a leech; to be given an inch and take an ell; to sweep the board; to scoop the pool.

Adjectives: Taking, etc., privative, prehensile, predatory, rapacious, raptorial, predial, ravenous.

790 RESTITUTION

Substantives: return, reddition, rendition, restoration, rehabilitation, remission, reinvestment, reparation, atonement.

Redemption, recovery, recuperation, release, replevin.

Verbs: To return, restore, give back, bring back, derequisition, denationalize, render, refund, reimburse, recoup, remit, rehabilitate, repair, reinvest.

To let go, disgorge, regorge, regurgitate.

Adjectives: Restoring, etc., recuperative.

Phrase: *Suum cuique.*

791 STEALING

Substantives: theft, thieving, thievery, abstration, appropriation, plagiarism, depredation, pilfering, rape, larceny, robbery, shop-lifting, burglary, house-breaking, abaction (of cattle), cattle-lifting, kidnapping.

Spoilation, plunder, pillage, sack, rapine, brigandage, foray, raid, hold-up, dragonnade, marauding.

Peculation, embezzlement, swindling (545), blackmail, *chantage,* smuggling, black market; thievishness, rapacity, kleptomania; den of thieves, Alsatia.

Licence to plunder, letter of marque.

Verbs: To steal, thieve, rob, abstract, appropriate, filch, pilfer, purloin, nab, nim, prig, grab, bag, lift, pick, pinch, knock off.

To convey away, carry off, make off with, run or walk off with, abduct, spirit away, kidnap, crimp, seize, lay violent hands on, etc. (789), abact, rustle (of cattle), shanghai.

To scrounge, wangle, win, crib, sponge, rook, bilk, diddle, swindle (545), peculate, embezzle, fiddle, flog, poach, run, smuggle, hijack.

To plunder, pillage, rifle, sack, ransack, burgle, spoil, spoliate, despoil, hold up, stick up, bail up, strip, fleece, gut, loot, forage, levy blackmail, pirate, plagiarize.

Phrases: To live by one's wits; to rob Peter to pay Paul; to obtain under false pretences; to set a thief to catch a thief.

Adjectives: Stealing, etc., thievish, light-fingered, larcenous, stolen, furtive, piratical, predaceous.

792 THIEF

Substantives: robber, spoiler, pickpocket, curpurse, dip, depredator, yegg, yeggman, footpad, highwayman, burglar, house-breaker, larcener, larcenist, pilferer, filcher, sneak-thief, shop-lifter, poacher, rustler; swell mob; the light-fingered gentry; kleptomaniac.

Swindler, crook, spiv, welsher, smuggler, bootlegger, hijacker, gangster, cracksman, magsman, mobsman, sharper, blackleg, shark, trickster, harpy, *chevalier d'industrie,* peculator, plagiarist, blackmailer; receiver, fence.

Brigand, freebooter, bandit, pirate, viking, corsair, buccaneer, thug, dacoit, picaroon, moss-trooper, rapparee, marauder, filibuster, wrecker, bushranger; Autolycus, Turpin, Macheath, Bill Sikes, Jonathan Wild.

Phrases: A snapper-up of unconsidered trifles; *homo triarum literarum.*

793 BOOTY

Substantives: spoil, plunder, swag,

loot, boodle, prey, pickings, grab, forage, blackmail, graft, prize.

794 BARTER

Substantives: exchange, truck, swop (or swap), chop, interchange, commutation.

Traffic, trade, commerce, dealing, business, custom, negotiation, transaction, jobbing, agiotage, bargain, deal, package deal, commercial enterprise, speculation, brokery.

Phrases: A Roland for an Oliver, a *quid pro quo*; payment in kind.

Verbs: To barter, exchange, truck, interchange, commute, swap (or swop), traffice, trade, speculate, transact, or do business with, deal with, have dealings with; open or keep an account with; to carry on a trade; to rig the market.

To bargain; drive, make, or strike a bargain; negotiate, bid for, haggle (or higgle), chaffer, dicker, stickle, cheapen, compound for, beat down, outbid, underbid, outbargain, come to terms, do a deal, quote, underquote.

Phrase: To throw a sprat to catch a whale.

Adjectives: Commercial, mercantile, trading, interchangeable, marketable, negotiable; wholesale, retail.

795 PURCHASE

Substantives: emption, buying, purchasing, shopping, hire-purchase, never-never; pre-emption, bribery, co-emption.

A buyer, purchaser, customer, emptor, shopper, patron, client, clientele.

Verbs: To buy, purchase, procure, hire, rent, farm, pay, fee, repurchase, buy in, keep in one's pay; pre-empt; bribe, suborn, square, buy over; shop, market.

Adjectives: Purchased, etc.

Phrase: *Caveat emptor.*

796 SALE

Substantives: disposal, custom.

Auction, Dutch auction, roup.

Lease, mortgage.

Vendibility, salability.

A vendor, seller (797).

To sell, vend, dispose of, retail, dispense, auction, auctioneer, hawk, peddle, undersell.

To let, sublet, lease, mortgage.

Phrases: Put up to sale or auction; bring under the hammer.

Adjectives: Vendible, marketable, salable; unpurchased, unbought, on one's hands, unsalable.

797 MERCHANT

Substantives: trader, dealer, tradesman, buyer and seller, vendor, monger, chandler, shopkeeper, shopman, salesman, saleswoman, changer.

Retailer, chapman, hawker, huckster, regrater, higgler, pedlar, cadger, sutler, bumboatman, middleman, coster, costermonger; auctioneer, broker, money-broker, bill-broker, money-changer, jobber, factor, go-between, cambist, usurer, money-lender.

House, firm, concern, partnership, company, guild, syndicate.

798 MERCHANDISE

Substantives: ware, mercery, commodity, effects, goods, article, stock, stock-in-trade, cargo (190), produce, freight, lading, ship-load, staple commodity.

799 MART

Substantives: market, change (or 'change), exchange, bourse, market-place, fair, hall, staple, bazaar, guildhall, tollbooth (or tolbooth), custom-house.

Office, shop, counting-house, bureau, counter, stall, booth, chambers.

Warehouse, depot, store (636), *entrepôt*, emporium, godown.

800 MONEY

Substantives: funds, treasure, capital,

stock, proceeds, assets, cash, bullion, ingot, nugget; sum, amount, balance.

Currency, soft currency; hard currency, circulating medium, legal tender, specie, coin, hard cash, sterling, pounds shillings and pence, LSD.

Ready, rhino, blunt, oof, lolly, splosh, chink, dibs, plunks, bucks, bones, siller, dust, tin, dough, jack, spondulicks, simoleons, mazuma, ducats, the needful, the wherewithal.

Gold, silver, copper, nickel, rouleau, dollar, etc.

Finance, gold standard, monometallism, bimetallism.

Pocket-money, pin-money, chicken feed, petty cash, change, small coin; doit, farthing, bawbee, penny, shilling, stiver, mite, sou; plum, grand, monkey, pony, tenner, fiver, quid, wheel, bob, tanner, two bits.

Sum, amount, balance.

Paper money, note, bank-note, treasury note, greenback, note of hand, promissory note, IOU.

Cheque (or check), bill, draft (or draught), order, remittance, postal order, money order, warrant, coupon, debenture, bill of exchange, exchequer bill, treasury bill, assignat.

A drawer, a drawee.

False money, base coin, flash note, kite, stumer.

Science of coins, numismatics.
Phrases: The sinews of war; the almighty dollar.
Verbs: To draw, draw upon, endorse, issue, utter; to amount to, come to.
Adjectives: Monetary, pecuniary, fiscal, financial, sumptuary; monometallic, bimetallic; numismatical.
Phrases: To touch the pocket; *argumentum ad crumenam*.

801 TREASURER
Substantives: purse-bearer, purser, bursar, banker, moneyer, paymaster, cashier, teller, accountant, steward, trustee, almoner.

Chancellor of the Exchequer, minister of finance, Queen's Remembrancer.

802 TREASURY
Substantives: bank, savings-bank, exchequer, coffer, chest, money-box, money-bag, strong-box, strong-room, safe, bursary, till, note-case, wallet, purse, *porte-monnaie*, purse-strings, pocket, fisc.

Consolidated fund, sinking fund, the funds, consols, government securities, war loan, savings certificates.

803 WEALTH
Substantives: fortune, riches, opulence, affluence, independence, solvency, competence, easy circumstances, command of money; El Dorado, Golconda, plutocracy.

Means, provision, substance, resources, capital, revenue, income, alimony, livelihood, subsistence, loaves and fishes, pelf, mammon, lucre, dower (810), pension, superannuation, annuity, unearned increment, pin-money.

A rich man, capitalist, plutocrat, financier, money-bags, millionaire, a Nabob, Dives, Croesus, Midas; *rentier*.
Phrases: The golden calf; a well-lined purse; the purse of Fortunatus; a mint or pot of money.
Verbs: To be rich, etc., to afford.

To enrich, fill one's coffers, etc.; to capitalize.
Phrases: To roll in riches; to wallow in wealth; to make one's pile; to feather one's nest; to line one's pockets; to keep one's head above water.
Adjectives: Wealthy, rich, well-off, affluent, opulent, flush, oofy, solvent (734), moneyed, plutocratic.
Phrases: Made of money; in funds; rich as Croesus; rolling in riches; one's ship come home.

804 POVERTY
Substantives: indigence, penury,

pauperism, destitution, want, need, lack, necessity, privation, distress, an empty purse; bad, reduced, or straitened circumstances; narrow means, straits, insolvency, impecuniosity, beggary, mendicancy, mendicity.

A poor man, pauper, mendicant, beggar, tramp, bum, vagabond, gangrel, starveling; the proletariat; *un pauvre diable*.

Poorhouse, workhouse, the institution.

Phrases: *Res angusta domi*; the wolf at the door.

Verbs: To be poor, etc., to want, lack, starve.

To render poor, etc., to reduce, to impoverish, reduce to poverty, depauperate, ruin; to pauperize.

Phrases: To live from hand to mouth; come upon the parish; not to have a penny; to have seen better days; to beg one's bread.

Adjectives: Poor, indigent, penniless, moneyless, impecunious, short of money, out of money, out of cash, out of pocket, needy, destitute, necessitous, distressed, hard up, in need, in want, poverty-stricken, badly off, in distress, pinched, straitened, dowerless, fortuneless, reduced, insolvent (806), bereft, bereaved, fleeced, stripped, stony broke, stony, stumped.

Phrases: Unable to make both ends meet; out at elbows; in reduced circumstances; not worth a sou; poor as Job; poor as a church mouse; down at heels; on one's uppers; on the rocks.

805 CREDIT

Substantives: trust, tick, score, account.

Letter of credit, duplicate, traveller's cheque (or check); mortgage, lien, debenture.

A creditor, lender, lessor, mortgagee, debenture-holder; a dun, usurer, gombeen-man, Shylock.

Verbs: To keep an account with, to credit, accredit.

To place to one's credit or account, give credit.

Adjectives: Crediting.

Adverbs: On credit, on tick, on account, to pay, unpaid-for.

806 DEBT

Substantives: obligation, liability, debit, indebtment, arrears, deficit, default, insolvency.

Interest, usance, usury.

Floating debt, bad debt, floating capital, debentures; deferred payment, hire system, never-never system.

A debtor, debitor, borrower, lessee, mortgagor; a defaulter (808).

Verbs: To be in debt, to owe, to answer for, to incur a debt, borrow (788).

Phrases: To run up a hill; to go on tick; to outrun the constable.

Adjectives: In debt, indebted, owing, due, unpaid, outstanding, in arrear, being minus, out of pocket, liable, chargeable, answerable for, encumbered, involved, in difficulties, insolvent, in the red.

Unrequited, unrewarded.

807 PAYMENT

Substantives: defrayment, discharge, quittance, acquittance, settlement, clearance, liquidation, satisfaction, remittance, instalment, stake, reckoning, arrangement, composition, acknowledgment, release.

Repayment, reimbursement, retribution, reward (973).

Bill, cheque, cash, ready money (800).

Phrase: A *quid pro quo*.

Verbs: To pay, defray, discharge, settle, quit, acquit oneself of, reckon with, remit, clear, liquidate, release; repay, refund, reimburse.

Phrases: To honour a bill; to strike a

balance; to settle, balance, or square accounts with; to be even with; to wipe off old scores; to satisfy all demands; to pay one's way or shot; to pay in full.

Adjectives: Paying, etc., paid, owing nothing, out of debt.

Adverbs: On the nail, money down, COD.

808 NON-PAYMENT

Substantives: default, defalcation, repudiation, protest.

Insolvency, bankruptcy, failure, whitewashing, application of the sponge.

Waste paper, dishonoured bills.

A defaulter, bankrupt, welsher, levanter, insolvent debtor, man of straw, lame duck.

Verbs: Not to pay, to fail, break, become insolvent or bankrupt, default, defalcate.

To protest, dishonour, repudiate, nullify; hammer.

Phrases: To run up bills; to tighten the purse-strings.

Adjectives: Not paying, in debt, behindhand, in arrear, insolvent, bankrupt, gazetted.

Phrases: Being minus or worse than nothing; plunged or over head and ears in debt; in the gazette; in Queer Street.

809 EXPENDITURE

Substantives: money going out; outgoings, expenses, disbursement, outlay.

Pay, payment, fee, hire, wages, perquisites, vails, allowance, stipend, salary, screw, divided, tribute, subsidy, batta, bat-money, shot, scot.

Remuneration, recompense, reward (973), tips, *pourboire,* largess, honorarium, refresher, bribe, *douceur,* hush-money, extras, commission, rake-off.

Advance, subsistence money, sub, earnest, handsel, deposit, prepayment, entrance fee, entrance.

Contribution, donation, subscription, deposit, contingent, dole, quota.

Investment, purchase (795), alms (748).

Verbs: To expend, spend, pay, disburse, lay out, lay or pay down, to cash, to come down with, brass up, shell out, fork out, bleed, make up a sum, to invest, sink money, prepay, tip.

Phrases: To unloose the purse-strings; to pay the piper; to pay through the nose.

Adjectives: Expending, expended, etc., sumptuary.

810 RECEIPT

Substantives: money coming in, incomings.

Income, revenue, earnings (775), rent, rental, rent-roll, rentage, return, proceeds, premium, bonus, gate-money, royalty.

Pension, annuity, tontine, jointure, dower, dowry, dot, alimony, compensation.

Emoluments, perquisites, recompense (809), sinecure.

Verbs: To receive, pocket (789), to draw from, derive from.

To bring in, yield, return, afford, pay, accrue.

Phrases: To get what will make the pot boil; keep the wolf from the door; bring grist to the mill.

Adjectives: Receiving, etc., received, etc.

Gainful, profitable, remunerative, lucrative, advantageous (775).

811 ACCOUNTS

Substantives: money matters, finance, budget, bill, score, reckoning, balance-sheet, books, account-books, ledger, day-book, cash-book, cash account, current account, deposit account, pass-book.

Book-keeping, audit, double entry.

301

An accountant, CA, auditory, actuary, book-keeper.

Verbs: To keep accounts, to enter, post, credit, debit, tot up, carry over; balance, make up accounts, take stock, audit.

To falsify, garble, cook, or doctor accounts.

812 PRICE

Substantives: cost, expense, amount, figure, charge, demand, damage, fare, hire.

Dues, duty, toll, tax, supertax, pay-as-you-earn, PAYE, rate, impost, cess, levy, gabelle, octroi, assessment, benevolence, custom, tithe, exactment, ransom, salvage, excise, tariff, brokerage, demurrage.

Bill, account, score, reckoning.

Worth, rate, value, valuation, evaluation, appraisement, market price, quotation; money's worth, pennyworth; price-current, price list.

Verbs: To set or fix a price, appraise, assess, value, evaluate, price, charge, demand, ask, require, exact.

To fetch, sell for, cost, bring in, yield, make, change hands for, go for, realize, run into, stand one in; afford.

Phrases: To run up a bill; to amount to; to set one back.

Adjectives: Priced, charged, etc., to the tune of, *ad valorem*; mercenary, venal.

Phrases: No penny, no paternoster; *point d'argent, point de Suisse.*

813 DISCOUNT

Substantives: abatement, reduction, deduction, depreciation, allowance, drawback, poundage, *agio,* percentage, rebate, set-off, backwardation, contango, tare and tret, salvage.

Verbs: To discount, bate, abate, rebate, reduce, take off, allow, give, discount, tax.

Adjectives: Discounting, etc.

Adverb: At a discount.

814 DEARNESS

Substantives: costliness, high price, expensiveness, rise in price, overcharge, surcharge, extravagance, exorbitance, extortion.

Phrase: A pretty penny.

Verbs: To be dear, etc., to cost much, to come expensive; to overcharge, surcharge, bleed, fleece (791).

To pay too much, to pay through the nose.

Adjectives: Dear, high, high-priced, expensive, costly, dear-bought, precious, unreasonable, extortionate, extravagant, exorbitant, steep, stiff.

Adverbs: Dear, at great cost, at a premium.

815 CHEAPNESS

Substantives: low price, inexpensiveness, drop in price, undercharge, bargain; absence of charge, gratuity, free admission.

Phrases: A labour of love; the run of one's teeth; a drug in the market.

Verbs: To be cheap, etc., to cost little, to come down or fall in price, to cut prices.

Phrase: To have one's money's worth.

Adjectives: Cheap, low, moderate, reasonable, inexpensive, unexpensive, low-priced, dirt-cheap, worth the money, half-price; catchpenny.

Gratuitous, gratis, free, for nothing, given away, free of cost, without charge, not charged, untaxed, scot-free, shot-free, expenseless, free of expense, free of all demands, honorary, unpaid.

Phrases: Cheap as dirt; for a mere song; given away with a pound of tea; at cost price; at a reduction; at a sacrifice.

816 LIBERALITY

Substantives: generosity (942), bounty, munificence, bounteousness, boutifulness, charity (906), hospitality.

Verbs: To be liberal, etc., spend freely, lavish, shower upon.

Phrases: To loosen one's purse-strings; to give *carte blanche*; to spare no expense.

Adjectives: Liberal, free, generous, charitable, hospitable, bountiful, bounteous, handsome, lavish, ungrudging, free-handed, open-handed, open-hearted, free-hearted, munificent, princely.

Overpaid.

817 ECONOMY
Substantives: frugality, thrift, thriftiness, care, husbandry, good housewifery, austerity, retrenchment; parsimony (819).

Verbs: To be economical, etc., to save, economize, skimp, scrimp, scrape, meet one's expenses, retrench; to lay by, put by, save up, invest, bank, hoard, accumulate.

Phrases: To cut one's coat according to one's cloth; to make ends meet; to pay one's way; to look at both sides of a shilling; to provide for a rainy day.

Adjectives: Economical, frugal, thrifty, canny, careful, saving, chary, spare, sparing, cheese-paring.

Phrase: Take care of the pence and the pounds will take care of themselves.

818 PRODIGALITY
Substantives: unthriftiness, thriftlessness, unthrift, waste, profusion, profuseness, extravagance, dissipation, squandering, squandermania, malversation.

A prodigal, spendthrift, squanderer, waster, wastrel.

Verbs: To be prodigal, etc., to squander, lavish, waste, dissipate, exhaust, run through, spill, misspend, throw away money, drain.

Phrases: To burn the candle at both ends; to make ducks and drakes of one's money; to spend money like water; to outrun the constable; to fool away, potter, muddle away, fritter away, etc., one's money; to pour water into a sieve; to go the pace.

Adjectives: Prodigal, profuse, improvident, thriftless, unthrifty, wasteful, extravagant, lavish, dissipated.

Phrases: Penny wise and pound foolish; money burning a hole in one's pocket.

819 PARSIMONY
Substantives: parsimoniousness, stint, stinginess, niggardliness, cheese-paring, extortion, illiberality, closeness, penuriousness, avarice, tenacity, covetousness, greediness, avidity, rapacity, venality, mercenariness, cupidity.

A miser, niggard, churl, screw, skinflint, money-grubber, codger, muckworm, hunks, curmudgeon, harpy.

Phrase: *Auri sacra fames.*

Verbs: To be parsimonious, etc., to grudge, begrudge, stint, pinch, screw, dole out.

Phrases: To skin a flint; to drive a hard bargain; to tighten one's purse-strings.

Adjectives: Parsimonious, stingy, miserly, mean, mingy, penurious, shabby, near, niggardly, cheese-paring, close, close-fisted, close-handed, chary, illiberal, ungenerous, churlish, sordid, mercenary, venal, covetous, avaricious, greedy, grasping, griping, pinching, extortionate, rapacious.

Phrases: Having an itching palm; with a sparing hand.

CLASS SIX

Words relating to the sentient and moral powers

Section 1 –
Affections in General

820 AFFECTIONS

Substantives: character, qualities, disposition, nature, spirit, mood, tone, temper, temperament; cast or frame of mind or soul; turn, bent, idiosyncrasy, bias, turn of mind, predisposition, diathesis, predilection, propensity, proneness, proclivity, vein, humour, grain, mettle.

Soul, heart, breast, bosom, the inner man, inmost heart, heart's core, heart-strings, heart's-blood, heart of hearts, *penetralia mentis*.

Passion, pervading spirit, ruling passion, master-passion.

Phrases: Flow of soul; fullness of the heart; the cockles of one's heart; flesh and blood.

Verbs: To have or possess affections, etc.; be of a character, etc.; to breathe.

Adjectives: Affected, characterized, formed, moulded, cast, tempered, attempered, framed, disposed, predisposed, prone, inclined, having a bias, etc., imbued or penetrated with; inbred, inborn, engrained (or ingrained).

821 FEELING

Substantives: endurance, experience, suffering, tolerance, sufferance, experience, sensibility (822), passion (825).

Impression, sensation, affection, response, emotion, pathos, warmth, glow, fervour, fervency, heartiness,

effusiveness, effusion, gush, cordiality, ardour, exuberance, zeal, eagerness, *empressement, élan,* enthusiasm, verve, inspiration.

Blush, suffusion, flush, tingling, thrill, kick, excitement (824), turn, shock, agitation (315), heaving, flutter, flurry, fluster, twitter, stew, tremor, throb, throbbing, panting, palpitation, trepidation, perturbation, hurry of spirits, the heart swelling, throbbing, thumping, pulsating, melting, bursting; transport, rapture, ecstasy, ravishment (827).

Verbs: To feel, receive an impression, etc.; to be impressed with, affected with, moved with, touched with, keen on.

To bear, bear with, suffer, endure, brook, tolerate, stomach, stand, thole, experience, taste, meet with, go through, put up with, prove; to harbour, cherish, support, abide, undergo.

To blush, change colour, mantle, tingle, twitter, throb, heave, pant, palpitate, go pit-a-pat, agitate, thrill, tremble, shake, quiver, wince, simmer, burble.

To swell, glow, warm, flush, redden, look blue, look black, catch the flame, catch the infection, respond, enthuse.

To possess, pervade, penetrate, imbue, absorb, etc., the soul.

Phrases: To bear the brunt of; to come home to one's feelings or bosom; to strike a chord.

Adjectives: Feeling, suffering, enduring; sentient, emotive, emotional.

Impressed, moved, touched, affected with, etc., penetrated, imbued.

Warm, quick, lively, smart, strong, sharp, keen, acute, cutting, incisive, piercing, pungent, racy, piquant, poignant, caustic.

Deep, profound, indelible, ineffaceable, impressive, effective, deep-felt, home-felt, heart-felt, warm-hearted, hearty, cordial, swelling, thrilling, rapturous, ecstatic, soul-stirring, emotive, deep-mouthed, heart-expanding, electric.

Earnest, hearty, eager, exuberant, gushing, effusive, breathless, glowing, fervent, fervid, ardent, soulful, burning, red-hot, fiery, flaming, boiling, boiling over, zealous, pervading, penetrating, absorbing, hectic, rabid, fanatical; the heart being big, full, swelling, overflowing, bursting.

Wrought up, excited, passionate, enthusiastic (825).
Phrase: Struck all of a heap.
Adverbs: Heartily, cordially, earnestly, etc.
Phrases: From the bottom of one's heart; de profundis; heart and soul; over head and ears.

822 SENSIBILITY
Substantives: impressibility, sensibleness, sensitiveness, hyperaesthesia (825), responsiveness, affectibility, susceptibleness, susceptibility, susceptivity, excitability, mobility, vivacity, vivaciousness, tenderness, softness, sentimentality, sentimentalism, schmalz.

Physical sensibility (375).
Verbs: To be sensible, etc., to shrink, have a tender heart.
Phrases: To be touched to the quick; to feel where the shoe pinches; to take it hard; to take to heart.
Adjectives: Sensible, sensitive, impressible, impressionable, suscep-

tive, susceptible, responsive, excitable, mobile, thin-skinned, touchy, alive, vivacious, lively, mettlesome, high-strung, intense, emotional, tender, soft, sentimental, maudlin, sloppy, romantic, enthusiastic, neurotic.
Adverbs: Sensibly, etc., to the quick.

823 INSENSIBILITY
Substantives: insensibleness, inertness, insensitivity, impassibility, impassibleness, impassivity, apathy, phlegm, dullness, hebetude, coolness, coldness, supineness, stoicism, insouciance, nonchalance, indifference, lukewarmness, frigidity, cold blood, sang-froid, dry eyes, cold heart, deadness, torpor, torpidity, ataraxia, pococurantism.

Lethargy, coma, trance, stupor, stupefaction, amnesia, paralysis, palsy, catalepsy, suspended animation, hebetation, anaesthesia (381), stock and stone, neutrality.

Physical insensibility (376).
Verbs: To disregard, be insensible, not to be affected by, not to mind, to vegetate, laisser aller, not to care; to take it easy.

To render insensible (376), numb, benumb, paralyse, deaden, render callous, sear, inure, harden, steel, caseharden, stun, daze, stupefy, brutalize, hebetate.
Phrases: To turn a deaf ear to; not care a straw (or a fig).
Adjectives: Insensible, unconscious, impassive, unsusceptible, insusceptible, impassible, unimpressionable, unresponsive, unfeeling, blind to, deaf to, dead to, passionless, spiritless, soulless, apathetic, listless, phlegmatic, callous, hard-boiled, thick-skinned, pachydermatous, obtuse, proof against, case-hardened, inured, steeled against, stoical, dull, frigid, cold, cold-blooded, cold-hearted, flat, inert, bovine, supine, sluggish, torpid, languid, tame, tepid, numb, numbed,

sleepy, yawning, comatose, anaesthetic.

Indifferent, insouciant, lukewarm, careless, mindless, regardless, disregarding, nonchalant, unconcerned, uninterested, pococurante; taking no interest in.

Unfelt, unaffected, unruffled, unimpressed, unmoved, unperturbed, uninspired, untouched, etc.; platonic, imperturbable, vegetative, automatic.

Adverbs: Insensibly, etc., *aequo animo,* with dry eyes, with withers unwrung.

Phrases: No matter; never mind; *n'importe*; it matters not; it does not signify; it is of no consequence or importance (643); it cannot be helped; nothing coming amiss; it is all the same or all one to; what's the odds? *nichevo.*

824 EXCITATION

Substantives: of feeling, excitement, galvanism, stimulation, provocation, calling forth, infection, animation, inspiration, agitation, perturbation, subjugation, fascination, intoxication, enravishment, unction; a scene, sensation, tableau, shocker, thriller.

Verbs: To excite, affect, touch, move, stir, wake, awaken, raise, raise up, evoke, call up, summon up, rake up.

To impress, strike, hit, quicken, swell, work upon.

To warm, kindle, stimulate, pique, whet, animate, hearten, inspire, impassion, inspirit, spirit, provoke, irritate, infuriate, sting, rouse, work up, hurry on, ginger up, commove.

To agitate, ruffle, flutter, fluster, flush, shake, thrill, penetrate, pierce, cut; to work oneself up, to simmer, bubble, burble.

To soften, subdue, overcome, master, overpower, overwhelm, bring under.

To shock, stagger, jar, jolt, stun, astound, electrify, galvanize, give one a shock, petrify.

To madden, intoxicate, fascinate, transport, ravish, enrapture, enravish, entrance, send.

Phrases: To come home to one's feelings; to make a sensation; to prey on the mind; to give one a turn; to cut to the quick; to go through one; to strike one all of a heap; to make one's blood boil; to lash to a fury; to make one sit up.

Adjectives: Excited, affected (825), wrought up, worked up, strung up, lost, *éperdu,* wild, haggard, feverish, febrile.

Exciting, etc., impressive, pathetic, sensational, provocative, piquant, aphrodisiac, dramatic, warm, glowing, fervid, swelling.

Phrases: Being all of a twitter; all of a flutter; the head being turned.

825 EXCITABILITY

Substantives: intolerance, impatience, wincing, perturbation, trepidation, disquiet, disquietude, restlessness, fidgets, fidgetiness, fuss, hurry, agitation, flurry, fluster, flutter, irritability (901), hypersensitiveness, hyperaesthesia.

Passion, excitement, vehemence, impetuosity, flush, heat, fever, fire, flame, fume, wildness, turbulence, boisterousness, tumult, effervescence, ebullition, boiling, boiling over, whiff, gust, storm, tempest, outbreak, outburst, burst, explosion, fit, paroxysm, brain-storm, the blood boiling.

Fierceness, rage, fury, furore, tantrum, hysteria, hysterics, raving, delirium, frenzy, intoxication, fascination, infection, infatuation, fanaticism, Quixotism, *la tête montée.*

Verbs: To be intolerant, etc., not to bear, to bear ill, wince, chafe, fidget, fuss, not to be able to bear, stand, tolerate, etc.

To break out, fly out, burst out, explode, run riot, boil, boil over, fly off, flare up, fire, take fire, fume, rage, rampage, rave, run mad, run amuck, raise Cain.

Phrases: To fly off at a tangent; to be out of all patience; to go off the deep end; to get the wind up; to make a scene; to go up in a blue flame.

Adjectives: Exitable, etc., excited, etc.

Intolerant, impatient, unquiet, restless, restive, fidgety, irritable, mettlesome, chafing, wincing, etc.

Vehement, boisterous, impetuous, demonstrative, fierce, fiery, flaming, boiling, ebullient, over-zealous, passionate, impassioned, enthusiastic, rampant, mercurial, high-strung, skittish, overwrought, overstrung, hysterical, hot-headed, hurried, turbulent, furious, fuming, boiling, raging, raving, frantic, phrenetic, rampageous, wild, heady, delirious, intoxicated, demoniacal; hypersensitive.

Overpowering, overwhelming, uncontrolled, madcap, reckless, stanchless, irrepressible, ungovernable, uncontrollable, inextinguishable, volcanic.

Phrases: More than flesh and blood can stand; stung to the quick; all hot and bothered.

Interjections: Pish! pshaw! botheration!

826 INEXCITABILITY

Substantives: hebetude, tolerance, patience.

Coolness, composure, calmness, imperturbability, sang-froid, collectedness, tranquillity, quiet, quietude, quietness, sedateness, soberness, poise, staidness, gravity, placidity, sobriety, philosophy, stoicism, demureness, meekness, gentleness, mildness.

Submission, resignation, sufferance, endurance, longanimity, long-sufferance, forbearance, fortitude, equanimity.

Repression, restraint (174), hebetation, tranquillization.

Phrases: Patience of Job; even temper; cool head; Spartan endurance; a sobersides.

Verbs: To be composed, etc., to bear, to bear well, tolerate, put up with, bear with, stand, bide, abide, aby, take easily, rub on, rub along, make the best of, acquiesce, submit, yield, bow to, resign oneself, suffer, endure, support, go through, reconcile oneself to, bend under; subside, calm down, pipe down.

To brook, digest, eat, swallow, pocket, stomach, brave, make light of.

To be borne, endured, etc., to go down.

To allay, compose, calm, still, lull, pacify, placate, quiet, tranquillize, hush, smooth, appease, assuage, mitigate, soothe, soften, temper, chasten, alleviate, moderate, sober down, mollify, lenify, tame, blunt, obtund, dull, deaden (823), slacken, damp, repress, restrain, check, curb, bridle, rein in, smother (174).

Phrases: To take things as they come; to submit with a good grace; to shrug the shoulders.

To set one's heart at rest or at ease.

Adjectives: Inexcitable, unexcited, calm, cool, temperate, composed, collected, placid, quiet, tranquil, unstirred, undisturbed, unruffled, serene, demure, sedate, staid, sober, dispassionate, unimpassioned, passionless, good-natured, easy-going, platonic, philosophic, stoical, imperturbable, cold-blooded, insensible (823).

Meek, tolerant, patient, submissive, unoffended, unresenting, content, resigned, subdued, bearing with, long-suffering, gentle, mild, sober-minded, cool-headed.

Phrases: Gentle or meek as a lamb; mild as milk; patient as Job; armed with patience; cool as a cucumber.

Section 2 –
Personal Affections

827 PLEASURE

Substantives: gratification, delectation, enjoyment, fruition, relish, zest, gusto, kick.

Well-being, satisfaction, complacency, content (831), ease, comfort, bed of roses, bed of down, velvet.

Joy, gladness, delight, glee, cheer, sunshine.

Physical pleasure (377).

Treat, refreshment, feast, luxury, voluptuousness, clover.

Happiness, felicity, bliss, beatitude, beatification, enchantment, transport, rapture, ravishment, ecstasy, heaven, *summum bonum,* paradise, Eden, Arcadia, nirvana, elysium, empyrean (981).

Honeymoon, palmy days, halcyon days, golden age, *Saturnia regna.*

Verbs: To be pleased, etc., to feel, receive, or derive pleasure, etc.; to take pleasure or delight in; to delight in, joy in, rejoice in, relish, like, enjoy, take to, take in good part.

To indulge in, treat oneself, solace oneself, revel, riot, luxuriate in, gloat over; to be on velvet, in clover, in heaven, etc.; to enjoy oneself; to congratulate oneself, hug oneself.

Phrases: To slake the appetite; to bask in the sunshine; to tread on enchanted ground; to have a good time; to make whoopee.

Adjectives: Pleased, enjoying, relishing, liking, gratified, glad, gladdened, rejoiced, delighted, overjoyed, charmed.

Cheered, enlivened, flattered, tickled, indulged, regaled, treated.

Comfortable, at ease, easy, cosy, satisfied, content (831), luxurious, on velvet, in clover, on a bed of roses, *sans souci.*

Happy, blest, blessed, blissful, over-joyed, enchanted, captivated, fascinated, transported, raptured, rapt, enraptured, in raptures, in ecstasies, in a transport, beatified, in heaven, in the seventh heaven, in paradise.

Phrases: With a joyful face; with sparkling eyes; happy as a king; pleased as Punch; in the lap of luxury; happy as the day is long; *ter quaterque beatus.*

Adverbs: Happily, etc.

828 PAIN

Substantives: suffering; physical pain (378).

Displeasure, dissatisfaction, discontent, discomfort, discomposure, malaise.

Uneasiness, disquiet, inquietude, weariness (841), dejection (837).

Annoyance, irritation, plague, bore, bother, botheration, worry, infliction, stew.

Care, anxiety, concern, mortification, vexation, chagrin, trouble, trial, solicitude, cark, dole, dule, load, burden, fret.

Grief, sorrow, distress, affliction, woe, bitterness, heartache, a heavy heart, a bleeding heart, a broken heart, heavy affliction.

Unhappiness, infelicity, misery, wretchedness, desolation, tribulation.

Dolour, sufferance, ache, aching, hurt, smart, cut, twitch, twinge, stitch, cramp, spasm, nightmare, convulsion, throe, angina.

Pang, anguish, agony, torture, torment, rack, crucifixion, martyrdom, purgatory, hell (982).

A sufferer, victim, prey, martyr.

Phrases: Vexation of spirit; a peck of troubles; a sea of troubles; the ills that flesh is heir to; *mauvais quart d'heure*; the iron entering the soul.

Verbs: To feel, suffer, or experience pain, etc.; to suffer, ache, smart, ail, bleed, twinge, tingle, gripe, wince, writhe.

To grieve, fret, pine, mourn, bleed,

worry oneself, chafe, yearn, droop, sink, give way, despair (859).

Phrases: To sit on thorns; to be on pins and needles; to labour under afflictions; to have a bad or thin time; to drain the cup of misery to the dregs; to fall on evil days.

Adjectives: In pain; feeling, suffering, enduring, etc., pain; in a state of pain, of suffering, etc., sore, aching, suffering, ailing, etc., pained, hurt, stung (830).

Displeased, annoyed, dissatisfied, discontented, weary (832), uneasy, ungratified, uncomfortable, ill at ease.

Crushed, stricken, victimized, ill-used.

Concerned, afflicted, in affliction, sorry, sorrowful, in sorrow, cut up, bathed in tears (839).

Unhappy, unfortunate, hapless, unblest, luckless, unlucky, ill-fated, ill-starred, fretting, wretched, miserable, careworn, disconsolate, inconsolable, woebegone, poor, forlorn, comfortless, a prey to grief, etc., despairing, in despair (859), heart-broken, broken-hearted, the heart bleeding, doomed, devoted, accursed, undone.

829 PLEASURABLENESS

Substantives: pleasantness, gratefulness, welcomeness, acceptableness, acceptability, agreeableness, delectability, deliciousness, daintiness, sweetness, luxuriousness, lusciousness, voluptuousness, eroticism.

Charm, attraction, attractiveness, sex-appeal, SA, It, oomph, fascination, witchery, prestige, loveliness, takingness, winsomeness, likableness, invitingness, glamour.

A treat, dainty, titbit, bonbon, *bonne bouche,* sweet, sweetmeat, sugar-plum, nuts, *sauce piquante.*

Verbs: To cause, produce, create, give, afford, procure, offer, present, yield, etc., pleasure, gratification, etc.

To please, take, gratify, satisfy, indulge, flatter, tickle, humour, regale, refresh, interest.

To charm, rejoice, cheer, gladden, delight, enliven (836), to transport, captivate, fascinate, enchant, entrance, bewitch, ravish, enrapture, enravish, beatify, enthral, imparadise.

Phrases: To do one's heart good; to tickle one to death; to take one's fancy.

Adjectives: Causing or giving pleasure, etc., pleasing, agreeable, grateful, gratifying, pleasant, pleasurable, acceptable, welcome, glad, gladsome, comfortable.

Sweet, delectable, nice, jolly, palatable, dainty, delicate, delicious, dulcet, savoury, toothsome, tasty, luscious, luxurious, voluptuous, genial, cordial, refreshing, comfortable, scrumptious.

Fair, lovely, favourite, attractive, engaging, winsome, winning, taking, prepossessing, inviting, captivating, bewitching, fascinating, magnetic, seductive, killing, stunning, ripping, smashing, likable.

Charming, delightful, exquisite, enchanting, enthralling, ravishing, rapturous, heart-felt, thrilling, beatific, heavenly, celestial, elysian, empyrean, seraphic, ideal.

Palmy, halcyon, Saturnian, Arcadian.

Phrases: To one's heart's content; to one's taste.

830 PAINFULNESS

Substantives: disagreeableness, unpleasantness, irksomeness, displeasingness, unacceptableness, bitterness, vexatiousness, troublesomeness.

Trouble, care, cross, annoyance, burden, load, nuisance, pest, plague, bore, bother, botheration, vexation, sickener, pin-prick.

Scourge, bitter pill, worm, canker, cancer, ulcer, curse, gall and wormwood, sting, pricks, scorpion thorn, brier, bramble, hornet, whip, lash, rack, wheel.

A mishap, misadventure, mischance, pressure, infestation, grievance, trial, crosses, hardship, blow, stroke, affliction, misfortune, reverse, infliction, dispensation, visitation, disaster, undoing, tragedy, calamity, catastrophe, adversity (735).

Provocation, infestation, affront, aggravation, indignity, outrage (900, 929).

Phrases: A thorn in one's side; a fly in the ointment; a sorry sight; a bitter pill; a crumpled rose-leaf.

Verbs: To cause, produce, give, etc., pain, uneasiness, suffering, etc.

To pain, hurt, wound, sting, pinch, grate upon, irk, gall, jar, chafe, gnaw, prick, lacerate, pierce, cut, cut up, stick, gravel, hurt one's feelings, mortify, horrify, shock, twinge, gripe.

To wring, harrow, torment, torture, rack, scarify, cruciate, crucify, convulse, agonize.

To displease, annoy, incommode, discompose, trouble, disquiet, grieve, cross, tease, rag, josh, bait, tire, vex, worry, try, plague, fash, faze, fret, haunt, obsess, bother, pester, bore, gravel, flummox, harass, importune, tantalize, aggravate.

To irritate, provoke, nettle, pique, rile, ruffle, aggrieve, enchafe, enrage.

To maltreat, bite, assail, badger, infest, harry, persecute, haze, roast.

To sicken, disgust, revolt, turn the stomach, nauseate, disenchant, repel, offend, shock.

To horrify, prostrate.

Phrases: To barb the dart; to set the teeth on edge; to stink in the nostrils; to stick in one's throat; to add a nail to one's coffin; to plant a dagger in the breast; to freeze the blood; to make one's flesh creep; to make one's hair stand on end; to break or wring the heart.

Adjectives: Causing, occasioning, giving, producing, creating, inflicting, etc., pain, etc., hurting, etc.

Painful, dolorific, dolorous, unpleasant, unpleasing, displeasing, unprepossessing, disagreeable, distasteful, uncomfortable, unwelcome, unsatisfactory, unpalatable, unacceptable, thankless, undesirable, untoward, unlucky, undesired, obnoxious.

Distressing, bitter, afflicting, afflictive, cheerless, joyless, comfortless, depressing, depressive, mournful, dreary, dismal, bleak, melancholy, grievous, pathetic, woeful, disastrous, calamitous, ruinous, sad, tragic, tragical, deplorable, dreadful, frightful, lamentable, ill-omened.

Irritating, provoking, provocative, stinging, biting, vexatious, annoying, unaccommodating, troublesome, fashious, wearisome, tiresome, irksome, plaguing, plaguy, teasing, pestering, bothering, bothersome, carking, mortifying, galling, harassing, worrying, tormenting, aggravating, racking, importunate, insistent.

Intolerable, insufferable, insupportable, unbearable, unendurable, shocking, frightful, terrific, grim, appalling, dire, heart-breaking, heart-rending, heart-wounding, heart-corroding, dreadful, horrid, harrowing, horrifying, horrific, execrable, accursed, damnable.

Odious, hateful, unpopular, repulsive, repellent, uninviting, offensive, nauseous, disgusting, sickening, nasty, execrable, revolting, shocking, vile, foul, abominable, loathsome, rotten.

Sharp, acute, sore, severe, grave, hard, harsh, bitter, cruel, biting, caustic, corroding, consuming, racking, excruciating, grinding, agonizing.

Phrase: More than flesh and blood can bear.

Adverbs: Painfully, etc.

831 CONTENT

Substantives: contentment, contentedness, satisfaction, peace of mind, complacency, serenity, sereneness, ease.

Comfort, snugness, well-being.

Moderation, patience (826), endurance, resignation, reconciliation.

Verbs: To be content, etc.; to rest satisfied, to put up with; to take up with; to be reconciled to.

To render content, etc., to set at ease, to conciliate, reconcile, disarm, propitiate, win over, satisfy, indulge, slake, gratify.

Phrases: To make the best of; to let well alone; to take in good part; to set one's heart at ease or at rest.

Adjectives: Content, contented, satisfied, at ease, easy, snug, comfortable, cosy.

Patient, resigned to, reconciled to, unrepining; disarming, conciliatory.

Unafflicted, unvexed, unmolested, unplagued, etc., serene, at rest, *sine cura, sans souci.*

Phrases: To one's heart's content; like patience on a monument.

Interjections: Very well, all right, suits me.

832 DISCONTENT

Substantives: discontentment, dissatisfaction, disappointment, mortification.

Repining, taking on, inquietude, heart-burning, regret (833).

Nostalgia, home-sickness, *maladie du pays.*

Grumbler, grouser, croaker.

Verbs: To be discontented, dissatisfied, etc.; to repine, regret (833), grumble (839).

To cause discontent, etc., to disappoint, dissatisfy, mortify.

Phrases: To take in bad part; to have the hump; to quarrel with one's bread and butter.

Adjectives: Discontented, dissatisfied, unsatisfied, malcontent, mortified, disappointed, cut up.

Repining, glum, grumbling, grous-

ing, grouchy, exigent, *exigeant,* exacting; nostalgic, home-sick; disgruntled.

Disappointing, unsatisfactory.

Phrases: Out of humour; in the dumps; in high dudgeon; down in the mouth.

833 REGRET

Substantives: bitterness, repining; lamentation (839); self-reproach, penitence (950).

Verbs: To regret, deplore, repine, lament, rue, repent (950).

Phrase: To rue the day.

Adjectives: Regretting, etc., regretful, regretted, regrettable, lamentable.

Phrase: What a pity!

834 RELIEF

Substantives: easement, alleviation, mitigation, palliation, solace, consolation, comfort, encouragement, refreshment (689), lullaby; deliverance, delivery.

Lenitive, balm, oil, restorative, cataplasm (662); cushion, pillow, bolster (215).

Phrases: A crumb of comfort; balm in Gilead.

Verbs: To relieve, ease, alleviate, mitigate, palliate, soften, soothe, assuage, allay, cheer, comfort, console, encourage, bear up, refresh, restore, remedy, cure.

Phrases: To dry the tears; to pour balm into; to lay the flattering unction to one's soul; to temper the wind to the shorn lamb; to breathe again; to breathe freely.

Adjectives: Relieving, etc., consolatory; balmy, balsamic, soothing, lenitive, anodyne (662), remedial, curative; easeful.

835 AGGRAVATION

Substantives: heightening, exacerbation, exasperation.

Verbs: To aggravate, render worse, heighten, intensify, embitter, sour,

311

acerbate, envenom, exacerbate, exasperate.

Phrase: To add fuel to the flame.

Adjectives: Aggravating, etc., aggravated, etc., unrelieved; aggravable.

Phrases: Out of the frying-pan into the fire; from bad to worse.

836 CHEERFULNESS

Substantives: gaiety, cheer, spirits, high spirits, high glee, light-heartedness, joyfulness, joyousness, good humour, geniality, hilarity, exhilaration, livliness, sprightliness, briskness, vivacity, buoyancy, sunniness, jocundity, joviality, levity, sportiveness, playfulness, jocularity.

Mirth, merriment, merrymaking, laughter (838), amusement (840); nepenthe, Euphrosyne.

Gratulation, rejoicing, exultation, jubilation, jubilee, triumph, paean, Te Deum, heyday; joy-bells.

Verbs: To be cheerful, etc.; to be of good cheer, to cheer up, perk up, brighten up, light up; take heart, bear up.

To rejoice, make merry, exult, congratulate oneself, triumph, clap the hands, crow, sing, carol, lilt, frisk, prance, galumph, rollick, maffick, frivol.

To cheer, enliven, elate, exhilarate, entrance, inspirit, animate, gladden, buck up, liven up.

Phrases: To drive dull care away; to make whoopee; to keep up one's spirits; care killed the cat; *ride si sapis*; laugh and grow fat.

Adjectives: Cheerful, gay, blithe, cheery, jovial, genial, gleeful, of good cheer, in spirits, in good or high spirits, *allegro*, light, lightsome, buoyant, debonair, bright, glad, light-hearted, hearty, free and easy, airy, jaunty, canty, perky, spry, chipper, saucy, sprightly, lively, vivacious, sunny, breezy, chirpy, hopeful (858).

Merry, joyous, joyful, jocund, playful, waggish, frisky, frolicsome, sportive, gamesome, jokesome, joky, jocose, jocular, jolly, frivolous.

Rejoicing, elated, exulting, jubilant, hilarious, flushed, rollicking, cock-a-hoop.

Phrases: In high feather; walking on air; with one's head in the clouds; gay as a lark; happy as a king or as the day is long; playful as a kitten; jolly as a sandboy; merry as a grig; full of beans.

Adverbs: Cheerfully, cheerily, cheerly, etc.

Interjections: Cheer up! never say die! hurrah! huzza!

837 DEJECTION

Substantives: depression, low spirits, lowness or depression of spirits, dejectedness, sadness.

Heaviness, dullness, infestivity, joylessness, gloom, dolefulness, dolesomeness, weariness (841), heaviness of heart, heart-sickness.

Melancholy, melancholia, dismals, mumps, dumps, doldrums, blues, mulligrubs, blue devils, megrims, vapours, accidie, spleen, hypochondria; *taedium vitae; maladie du pays.*

Despondency, despair, pessimism, disconsolateness, prostration; the Slough of Despond (859).

Demureness, seriousness, gravity, solemnity, solemnness, sullenness.

A hypochondriac, self-tormentor, *malade imaginaire*, kill-joy, Job's comforter, wet blanket, pessimist, futilitarian.

Verbs: To be dejected, sad, etc.; to grieve, take on, take to heart, give way, droop, sink, lour, look downcast, mope, mump, pout, brood over, fret, pine, yearn, frown, despond (859).

To depress, discourage, dishearten, dispirit, dull, deject, lower, sink, dash, unman, prostrate, over-cloud.

Phrases: To look blue; to hang down the head; to wear the willow; to laugh on the wrong side of the mouth; to get the hump.

To prey on the mind or spirits; to dash one's hopes.

Adjectives: Cheerless, unmirthful, mirthless, joyless, dull, glum, flat, dispirited, out of spirits, out of sorts, out of heart, in low spirits, spiritless, lowering, frowning, sulky.

Discouraged, disheartened, downhearted, downcast, cast down, depressed, chap-fallen, crest-fallen, dashed, drooping, sunk, heart-sick, dumpish, mumpish, desponding, pessimistic.

Dismal, melancholy, sombre, tristful, *triste,* pensive, *penseroso,* mournful, doleful, moping, splenetic, gloomy, lugubrious, funereal, woebegone, comfortless, forlorn, overcome, prostrate, cut up, care-worn, care-laden.

Melancholic, hipped, hypochondriacal, bilious, jaundiced, atrabilious, atrabiliar, saturnine, adust.

Disconsolate, inconsolable, despairing, in despair (859).

Grave, serious, sedate, staid, sober, solemn, grim, grim-faced, grim-visaged (846), rueful, sullen.

Depressing, preying upon the mind (830).

Phrases: Down in the mouth; down on one's luck; sick at heart; with a long face; a prey to melancholy; dull as a beetle; dull as ditch-water; as melancholy as a gib-cat; grave as a judge.

838 REJOICING
Substantives: exultation, heyday, triumph, jubilation, jubilee (840), paean (990).

Smile, simper, smirk, grin, broad grin.

Laughter, giggle, titter, snigger, crow, cheer, chuckle, guffaw, shout, hearty laugh, horse-laugh, cachinnation; a shout, burst, or peal of laughter.

Derision, risibility (856).

Momus, Democritus the Abderite.

Verbs: To rejoice, exult, triumph (884), hug oneself, sing, carol, dance with joy.

To smile, simper, smirk, grin, mock; to laugh, giggle, titter, snigger, chuckle, chortle, burble, crow, cackle; to burst out, shout, guffaw.

To cause, create, occasion, raise, excite, or produce laughter, etc.; to tickle, titillate.

Phrases: To clap one's hands; to fling up one's cap; to laugh in one's sleeve; to shake one's sides; to hold both one's sides; to split one's sides; to die with laughter.

To tickle one's fancy; to set the table in a roar; to convulse with laughter; to be the death of one.

Adjectives: Laughing, rejoicing, etc.; jubilant (836), triumphant.

Laughable, risible, ludicrous (853), side-splitting.

Phrases: Ready to burst or split oneself; 'Laughter holding both his sides.'

Interjections: Hurrah! three cheers!

839 LAMENTATION
Substantives: complaint, murmur, mutter, plaint, lament, wail, sigh, suspiration, heaving.

Cry, whine, whimper, sob, tear, moan, snivel, grumble, groan.

Outcry, scream, screech, howl, whoop, yell, roar, (414).

Weeping, crying, etc.; lachrymation, complaining, frown, scowl, sardonic grin or laugh.

Dirge (363), elegy, requiem, monody, threnody, jeremiad; coronach, wake, keen, keening.

Plaintiveness, querimoniousness, languishment, querulousness.

Mourning, weeds, willow, cypress, crape, sackcloth and ashes.

A grumbler, grouser, croaker, drip; Heraclitus, Niobe.

Phrases: The melting mood; wringing

of hands; weeping and gnashing of teeth.

Verbs: To lament, mourne, grieve, keen, complain, murmur, mutter, grumble, grouse, belly-ache, beef, squawk, sigh; give, fetch, or heave a sigh.

To cry, weep, sob, greet, blubber, blub; snivel, whimper; to shed tears; pule, take on, pine.

To grumble, groan, grunt, croak, whine, moan, bemoan, wail, bewail, frown, scowl.

To cry out, growl, mew, mewl, squeak, squeal, sing out, scream, cry out lustily, screech, skirl, bawl, howl, holloa, bellow, yell, roar, yammer.

Phrases: To melt or burst into tears; to cry oneself blind; to cry one's eyes out; to beat one's breast; to wring one's hands; to gnash one's teeth; to tear one's hair; to cry before one is hurt; to laugh on the wrong side of one's mouth.

Adjectives: Lamenting, complaining, etc.; mournful, doleful, sad, tearful, lachrymose, plaintive, plaintful, querulous, querimonious, elegiac.

Phrases: With tears in one's eyes; bathed or dissolved in tears; the tears starting from the eyes.

Interjections: O dear! ah me! alas! alack! heigh-ho! ochone! well-a-day! well-a-way! alas the day! woe worth the day! *O tempora, O mores!*

840 AMUSEMENT

Substantives: diversion, entertainment, sport, divertissement, recreation, relaxation, distraction, avocation, pastime.

Fun, frolic, pleasantry, drollery, jollity, joviality, jovialness, jocoseness, laughter (838).

Play, game, gambol, romp, prank, quip, quirk, rig, lark, fling, bat, spree, burst, binge, razzle-dazzle, escapade, dido, monkey-shines, ploy, jamboree.

Dance (309), ball, ballet (599), hop, shindig, jig, fling, reel, strathspey, cotillion, quadrille, lancers, rigadoon, saraband, lavolta, pavane, galliard, hornpipe, can-can, tarantella, cachucha, fandango, bolero, minuet, gavotte, polka, mazurka, schottische, waltz (or valse), fox-trot, tango, maxixe, rumba, samba, blues, two-step, one-step; folk-dance, morris-dance, square dance, round dance, country dance, step-dance, clog-dance, sworddance, egg-dance, cake-walk, breakdown.

Festivity, festival, jubilee, party (892), merrymaking, rejoicing, fête, gala, ridotto, revelry, revels, carnival, corroboree, saturnalia, high jinks, night out.

Feast, banquet, entertainment, carousal, bean-feast, beano, wayz-goose, jollification, junketing, junket, wake, field-day, regatta, fair, kermess, *fête champêtre*, symposium, wassail.

Buffoonery, mummery, tomfoolery, raree-show, puppet-show, masquerade.

Bonfire, fireworks, *feu de joie*.

A holiday, gala day, red-letter day.

A place of amusement, theatre, music-hall, concert-hall, cinema, circus, hippodrome, ballroom, dance hall, arena, auditorium, recreation ground, playground, playing field, park.

Toy, plaything, bauble, doll, puppet, teddy-bear.

A master of ceremonies or revels; a sportsman, sportswoman, gamester, reveller; devotee, votary, enthusiast, fan.

Phrases: A round of pleasure; a short life and a merry one; high days and holidays.

Verbs: To amuse, divert, entertain, rejoice, cheer, recreate, enliven, solace; to beguile or while away the time; to drown care.

To play, sport, disport, make merry, take one's pleasure, make holiday, keep holiday; to game, gambol, revel, frisk, frolic, romp, jollify, skylark, dally; to dance, hop, foot it, jump, caper, cut capers, skip.

To treat, feast, regale, carouse, banquet.

Phrases: To play the fool; to jump over the moon; to make a night of it; to make whoopee; to go on the bust; to have one's fling; *desipere in loco.*

Adjectives: Amusing, amusive, diverting, entertaining, etc., amused, etc.

Sportive, jovial, festive, jocose, tricksy, rompish.

Phrases: On with the dance! *vogue la galère! vive la bagatelle!*

841 WEARINESS

Substantives: tedium, ennui, boredom, lassitude, fatigue (688), dejection (837).

Disgust, nausea, loathing, sickness, disgust of life, *taedium vitae, Weltschmerz.*

Wearisomeness, irksomeness, tiresomeness, montony, sameness, treadmill, grind.

A bore, a buttonholer, proser, fossil, wet blanket.

Phrases: A twice-told tale; time hanging heavily on one's hands; a thin time.

Verbs: To tire, weary, fatigue, fag, jade, bore; set to sleep, send to sleep.

To sicken, disgust, nauseate.

Phrases: To harp on the same string; to bore to tears; never hear the last of.

Adjectives: Wearying, etc., wearisome, tiresome, irksome, uninteresting, devoid of interest, monotonous, humdrum, pedestrian, mortal, flat, tedious, prosy, prosing, slow, soporific, somniferous.

Disgusting, sickening, nauseating.

Weary, tired, etc.; aweary, uninterested, sick of, flagging, used up, blasé, bored, stale, fed up, browned off, brassed off, cheesed off, chokka, weary of life; drowsy, somnolent, sleepy (683).

Adverbs: Wearily, etc.

Phrase: *Ad nauseam.*

842 WIT

Substantives: humour, comicality, imagination (515), fancy, fun, drollery, whim, jocularity, jocosity, facetiousness, waggery, waggishness, wittiness, salt, Atticism, Attic wit, Attic salt, *esprit,* smartness, banter, chaff, persiflage, badinage, farce, *espièglerie.*

Jest, joke, jape, conceit, quip, quirk, quiddity, crank, wheeze, side-splitter, *concetto,* witticism, gag, wisecrack, repartee, retort, comeback, *mot, bon mot,* pleasantry, funniment, flash of wit, happy thought, sally, point, dry joke, idle conceit, epigram, quibble, play upon words, pun (563), conundrum, anagram (533), quodlibet, *jeu d'esprit, facetiae*; a chestnut, a Joe Miller; an absurdity (497).

A practical joke, a rag.

Phrases: The cream of the jest; the joke of it; *le mot pour rire.*

Verbs: To joke, jest, jape, retort; to cut jokes, crack a joke, perpetrate a joke or pun.

To laugh at, banter, rally, chaff, josh, jolly, jeer (856), rag, guy, kid; to make fun of, make merry with.

Phrase: To set the table in a roar.

Adjectives: Witty, facetious, humorous, fanciful, quick-witted, ready-witted, nimble-witted, imaginative (515), sprightly, *spirituel,* smart, jocose, jocular, waggish, comic, comical, laughable, droll, ludicrous, side-splitting, killing, funny, risible, farcical, roguish, sportive, pleasant, playful, sparkling, entertaining, arch.

Adverbs: In joke, in jest, in sport, for fun.

843 DULLNESS

Substantives: heaviness, stolidness, stolidity, dumbness, stupidity (499), flatness, prosiness, gravity (837),

solemnity; prose, matter of fact, platitude, commonplace, bromide.
Verbs: To be dull, prose, fall flat.

To render dull, etc., damp, depress.
Phrase: To throw cold water on.

Adjectives: Dull, prosaic, prosing, prosy, unentertaining, dismal (837), uninteresting, boring, flat, pointless, stolid, humdrum (841), pedestrian, literal, unimaginative, matter-of-fact, commonplace.

Slow, stupid, dumb, plodding, Boeotian.

Phrases: Dull as ditch-water; *Davus sum, non Oedipus; aliquando bonus dormitat Homerus.*

844 A HUMORIST
Substantives: wag, wit, funny man, caricaturist, cartoonist, epigrammatist, *bel esprit,* jester, joker, punster, wisecracker.

A buffoon (599), comedian, *farceur,* merry-andrew, jack-pudding, tumbler, mountebank, harlequin, punch, punchinello, scaramouch, clown, pantaloon.
Phrase: The life and soul of the party.

845 BEAUTY
Substantives: handsomeness, beauteousness, beautifulness, pulchritude, aesthetics.

Form, elegance, grace, symmetry, *belle tournure;* good looks.

Comeliness, seemliness, shapeliness, fairness, prettiness, neatness, spruceness, atractiveness, loveliness, quaintness, speciousness, polish, gloss, nattiness; a good effect.

Bloom, brilliancy, radiance, splendour, magnificence, sublimity.

Concinnity, delicacy, refinement, charm, style.

A beautiful woman, belle, charmer, enchantress, goddess; Helen of Troy, Venus, Hebe, the Graces, Peri, Houri; Cupid, Apollo, Hyperion, Adonis, Antinous, Narcissus.

Peacock, butteryfly, flower, rose, lily; the flower of, the pink of, etc.; a garden, a picture.
Phrases: *Je ne sais quoi; le beau idéal;* a sight for sore eyes.
Verbs: To be beautiful; to shine, beam, bloom.

To render beautiful, etc., to beautify, embellish, adorn, deck, bedeck, decorate, set out, set off, ornament (847), dight, bedight, array, garnish, furbish, smarten, trick out, rig out, fig out, dandify, dress up, prank, prink, perk, preen, trim, embroider, emblazon, adonize.

To polish, burnish, gild, varnish, japan, enamel, lacquer.

To powder, rouge, make up, doll up, titivate.
Adjectives: Beautiful, handsome, good-looking, fine, pretty, lovely, graceful, elegant, delicate, refined, fair, personable, comely, seemly, bonny, braw, well-favoured, proper, shapely, well-made, well-formed, well-proportioned, symmetrical, sightly, becoming, goodly, neat, dapper, tight, trig, spruce, smart, stylish, chic, dashing, swagger, dandified, natty, sleek, quaint, jaunty, bright-eyed, attractive, seductive, stunning.

Blooming, rosy, brilliant, shining, beaming, splendid, resplendent, dazzling, gorgeous, superb, magnificent, sublime, grand.

Picturesque, statuesque, artistic, aesthetic, decorative, photogenic, well-composed, well-grouped.

Passable, presentable, not amiss, undefaced, spotless, unspotted.
Phrases: Easy to look at; dressed up to kill.

846 UGLINESS
Substantives: deformity, inelegance, plainness, homeliness, uncomeliness, ungainliness, uncouthness, clumsiness, stiffness, disfigurement, distortion, contortion, malformation, monstros-

ity, misproportion, inconcinnity, want of symmetry, roughness, repulsiveness, squalor, hideousness, unsightliness, odiousness.

An eyesore, object, figure, sight, fright, guy, spectre, scarecrow, hag, harridan, satyr, sibyl, toad, baboon, monster, gorgon, Caliban, Hecate.
Phrases: A forbidding countenance; a wry face; a blot on the landscape; no oil-painting; *'monstrum horrendum, informe, ingens, cui lumen ademptum.'*
Verbs: To be ugly, etc.

To render ugly, etc., to deform, deface, distort, disfigure (241), disfeature, misshape, blemish, spot, stain, distain, soil, tarnish, discolour, sully, blot, daub, bedaub, begrime, blur, smear, besmear (653), bespatter, maculate, denigrate, uglify.
Phrase: To make faces.
Adjectives: Ugly, plain, homely, unsightly, unornamental, unshapely, unlovely, ill-looking, ordinary, unseemly, ill-favoured, hard-favoured, evil-favoured, hard-featured, hard-visaged, ungainly, uncouth, gawky, hulking, lumbering, slouching, ungraceful, clumsy, graceless, rude, rough, rugged, homespun, gaunt, raw-boned, haggard, scraggy.

Misshapen, shapeless, misproportioned, ill-proportioned, deformed, ill-made, ill-shaped, inelegant, disfigured, distorted, unshapen, unshapely, humpbacked, crooked, bandy, stumpy, dumpy, squat, stubby, bald, rickety.

Squalid, grim, grisly, gruesome, grooly, macabre, grim-faced, grim-visaged, ghastly, ghost-like, death-like, cadaverous, repellent, repulsive, forbidding, grotesque.

Frightful, odious, hideous, horrid, shocking, monstrous, unprepossessing.

Foul, soiled, tarnished, stained, distained, sullied, blurred, blotted, spotted, maculated, spotty, splashed, smeared, begrimed, spattered, bedaubed, besmeared; ungarnished.
Phrases: Ugly as sin; not fit to be seen.

847 ORNAMENT
Substantives: ornamentation, adornment, decoration, embellishment, enrichment, illustration, illumination, ornature, ornateness, flamboyancy.

Garnish, polish, varnish, gilding, japanning, enamel, lacquer, ormolu.

Cosmetic, rouge, powder, lipstick, mascara, hair-oil, brilliantine.

Jewel, jewellery, bijouterie, spangle, trinket, locket, bracelet, bangle, anklet, necklace, earring, brooch, chain, chatelaine, carcanet, tiara, coronet, diadem.

Gem, precious stone, diamond, brilliant, emerald, sapphire, ruby, agate, garnet, beryl, onyx, topaz, amethyst, opal; pearl, coral.

Embroidery, broidery, brocade, galloon, lace, fringe, trapping, trimming, edging, border, chiffon, hanging, tapestry, arras.

Wreath, festoon, garland, lei, chaplet, tassel, knot, epaulette, frog, star rosette, bow.

Feather, plume, *panache,* aigrette.

Nosegay, bouquet, posy, buttonhole.

Tracery, moulding, arabesque.

Frippery, finery, bravery, gewgaw, gaud, fal-lal, tinsel, spangle, clinquant, bric-à-brac, knick-knack.

Trope, flourish, flowers of rhetoric, purple patches (577).

Excess of ornament, tawdriness (851).
Verbs: To ornament, embellish, illustrate, illuminate, enrich, decorate, adorn, beautify, garnish, polish, gild, varnish, enamel, paint, white-wash, stain, japan, lacquer, fume, grain; bespangle, bedeck, bedizen (845), embroider, work, chase, emboss, fret, tool; emblazon, illuminate.
Adjectives: Ornamented, etc.,

beautified, rigged out, figged out, well-groomed, dolled up, ornate, showy, dressy, gaudy (851), garish, gorgeous, fine, gay, rich.
Phrases: Fine as fivepence; in full fig; in one's Sunday best; dressed up to the nines.

848 BLEMISH
Substantives: disfigurement, deface-ment, deformity, eyesore, defect, fault, deficiency, flaw, fleck.

Stain, blot, spot, speck, mote, blur, macula, blotch, speckle, spottiness; soil, tarnish, smudge, smut, dirt, soot (653); freckle, birthmark.

Excrescence, pimple, pustule (250).
Verbs: To blemish, disfigure, deface (846).
Adjectives: Blemished, disfigured, etc.; spotted, speckled, freckled, pitted.

849 SIMPLICITY
Substantives: plainness, undress, chastity, chasteness; freedom from ornament or affectation, homeliness.
Phrase: *Simplex munditiis.*
Verbs: To be simple, etc., to render simple, etc., to simplify.
Adjectives: Simple, plain, ordinary, household, homely, homespun, chaste, unaffected, severe, primitive.

Unadorned, unornamented, un-decked, ungarnished, unarrayed, untrimmed, unsophisticated, in dis-habille.

850 TASTE
Substantives: delicacy, refinement, gust, gusto, *goût*, virtuosity, virtuoso-ship, nicety, finesse, grace, culture, virtu, τò πρέπον, polish, elegance.

Science of taste, aesthetics.

A man of taste, connoisseur, judge, critic, *cognoscente*, virtuoso, dilettante, amateur, aesthete, purist, precision; an Aristarchus, Corinthian, *arbiter elegan-tiarum.*

Phrase: Caviare to the general.
Verbs: To appreciate, judge, discrimi-nate, criticize (465).
Adjectives: In good taste, tasteful, un-affected, pure, chaste, classical, attic, refined, aesthetic, cultivated, cultured, artistic, elegant.
Adverb: Elegantly, etc.
Phrases: To one's taste or mind; after one's fancy; *comme il faut.*

851 VULGARITY
Substantives: vulgarism, barbarism, Vandalism, Gothicism, *mauvais goût,* sensationalism, flamboyance.

Coarseness, grossness, indecorum, lowness, low life, *mauvais ton,* bad form, ribaldry, clownishness, rustic-ity, boorishness, brutishness, brutality, rowdyism, ruffianism, awkwardness, *gaucherie,* want of tact, tactlessness.

Excess of ornament, false ornament, tawdriness, loudness, gaudiness, flashiness, ostentation.

A rough diamond, a hoyden, tom-boy, slattern, sloven, dowdy, frump, cub, unlicked cub, clown, cad, gutter-snipe, ragamuffin (876); a Goth, Vandal.
Verbs: To be vulgar, etc., to misbe-have.
Adjectives: In bad taste, vulgar, coarse, unrefined, gross, ribald, heavy, rude, unpolished, indecorous, home-spun, clownish, uncouth, awkward, *gauche,* ungraceful, slovenly, slatternly, dowdy, frumpish.

Ill-bred, ungenteel, impolite, ill-mannered, uncivil, tactless, under-bred, caddish, ungentlemanly, unlady-like, unfeminine, unmaidenly, unseemly, unpresentable, unkempt, uncombed.

Rustic, countrified, boorish, provin-cial, barbarous, barbaric, brutish, blackguardly, rowdy, raffish, Gothic, unclassical, heathenish, outlandish, untamed (876).

Obsolete, out of fashion, *démodé,* out

of date, unfashionable, antiquated, fossil, old-fashioned, old-world, gone by.

New-fangled, odd, fantastic, grotesque, ridiculous (853), affected, meretricious, extravagant, sensational, monstrous, shocking, horrid, revolting.

Gaudy, tawdry, tinsel, bedizened, flamboyant, baroque, tricked out, gingerbread, loud, flashy, showy.
Phrase: A back number.

852 FASHION
Substantives: style, tonishness, *ton, bon ton,* mode, vogue, craze, rage, fad.

Manners, breeding, politeness, gentlemanliness, courtesy (894), decorum, *bienséance, savoir faire, savoir vivre,* punctilio, convention, conventionality, propriety, the proprieties, Mrs Grundy, form, formality, etiquette, custom, demeanour, air, port, carriage, presence.

Show, equipage, turn-out (882).

The world, the fashionable world, the smart set, the *beau monde,* high life, society, town, court, gentility (875), civilization, civilized life, the *élite.*
Phrases: The height of fashion; *dernier cri;* the latest thing.
Verbs: To be fashionable, etc.
Phrases: To cut a dash; to be in the swim.
Adjectives: Fashionable, in fashion, in vogue, *à la mode,* modish, tony, tonish, stylish, smart, courtly, *recherché,* genteel, aristocratic, conventional, punctilious, *comme il faut,* well-bred, well-mannered, polished, gentlemanlike, ladylike, well-spoken, civil, presentable, *distingué,* refined, thorough-bred, county, *dégagé,* jaunty, swell, swagger, posh, dashing, unembarrassed; trendy.
Phrases: Having a run; all the go.
Adverbs: Fashionably, in fashion.

853 RIDICULOUSNESS
Substantives: ludicrousness, risibility.

Oddness, oddity, whimsicality, comicality, drollery, grotesqueness,

fancifulness, quaintness, frippery, gawkiness, preposterousness, extravagance, monstrosity, absurdity (497).

Bombast, bathos, fustian, doggerel, nonsense verse, amphigouri, extravaganza, clerihew, bull, Irish bull, spoonerism.
Adjectives: Ridiculous, absurd, extravagant, *outré,* monstrous, preposterous, irrational, nonsensical.

Odd, whimsical, quaint, queer, rum, droll, grotesque, fanciful, eccentric, bizarre, strange, out-of-the-way, outlandish, fantastic, baroque, rococo.

Laughable, risible, ludicrous, comic, serio-comic, mock-heroic, comical, funny, derisive, farcical, burlesque, *pour rire,* quizzical, bombastic, inflated, stilted.

Awkward, gawky, lumbering, lumpish, hulking, uncouth.

854 FOP
Substantives: dandy, exquisite, swell, toff, dude, nut, masher, lady-killer, coxcomb, beau, macaroni, blade, blood, buck, spark, dog, popinjay, puppy, *petit-maître,* jackanapes, jack-a-dandy, tailor's dummy, man-milliner, man about town.

855 AFFECTATION
Substantives: mannerism, pretension, airs, dandyism, coxcombry, frills, side, swank, dog, conceit, foppery, affectedness, preciosity, euphuism, charlatanism, quackery, foppishness, pedantry, acting a part, pose, gush.

Prudery, Grundyism, demureness, coquetry, *minauderie,* sentimentality, lackadaisicalness, stiffness, formality, buckram, mock modesty, *mauvaise honte.*

Pedant, precisian, prig, square, bluestocking, *bas bleu,* formalist, *poseur,* mannerist, *précieuse ridicule;* prude, Mrs Grundy.
Phrases: A lump of affectation; prunes and prisms.

319

Verbs: To affect, to give oneself airs, put on side or frills, to swank, simper, mince, to act a part, overact, attitudinize, gush, pose.

Adjectives: Affected, conceited, precious, pretentious, stilted, pedantic, pragmatical, priggish, smug, puritanical, prim, prudish, starchy, up-stage, high-hat, stiff, formal, demure, goody-goody.

Foppish, namby-pamby, slip-slop, coxcombical, slipshod, simpering, mincing, niminy-piminy, la-di-da, sentimental, lackadaisical.

Exaggerated (549), overacted, overdone, high-falutin, gushing, stagy, theatrical.

856 RIDICULE

Substantives: derision, mockery, quiz, banter, chaff, badinage, irony, persiflage, raillery, send-up.

Jeer, gibe, quip, taunt, satire, scurrility, scoffing.

A parody, burlesque, travesty, skit, farce, comedy, tragi-comedy, doggerel, blunder, bull, *lapsus linguae,* slip of the tongue, malapropism, spoonerism, anticlimax.

Buffoonery, vagary, antic, mummery, tomfoolery, grimace, monkey-trick, escapade, prank, gambade, extravaganza, practical joke, booby-trap.

Verbs: To ridicule, deride, laugh at (929), laugh down, scoff, mock, jeer, banter, quiz, rally, fleer, flout, rag, rot, chaff, josh, guy, rib, razz, roast, twit, taunt, point at, grin at.

To parody, caricature, burlesque, travesty, pillory, take off.

Phrases: To raise a smile; to set the table in a roar; to make fun of; to poke fun at; to make merry with; to make a fool of; to make an ass of; to make game of; to make faces at; to make mouths at; to lead one a dance; to run a rig upon; to make an April fool of; to laugh out of court; to laugh in one's

sleeve; to take the micky out of.

Adjectives: Derisory, derisive, sarcastic, ironical, quizzical, mock, scurrilous, burlesque, Hudibrastic.

857 LAUGHING-STOCK

Substantives: gazing-stock, butt, stooge, target, quiz; an original, guy, oddity, card, crank, eccentric, monkey, buffoon, jester (844), mime, mimer (599), scaramouch, punch, punchinello, mountebank, golliwog.

Phrases: A figure of fun; a queer fish; fair game.

858 HOPE

Substantives: trust, confidence, reliance, faith, assurance, credit, security, expectation, affiance, promise, assumption, presumption.

Hopefulness, buoyancy, reassurance, optimism, enthusiasm, aspiration.

A reverie, day-dream, pipe-dream, Utopia, millennium.

Anchor, mainstay, sheet-anchor, staff (215).

Phrases: Castles in the air; castles in Spain; a ray, gleam, or flash of hope; the silver lining of the cloud.

Verbs: To hope; to feel, entertain, harbour, cherish, feed, nourish, encourage, foster, etc., hope or confidence; to promise oneself.

To trust, confide, rely on, build upon, feel or rest assured, confident, secure, etc.; to flatter oneself, expect, aspire, presume, be reassured.

To give or inspire hope; to augur well, shape well, bid fair, be in a fair way; to encourage, assure, promise, flatter, buoy up, reassure, embolden, raise expectations.

Phrases: To see daylight; to live in hopes; to look on the bright side; to pin one's hope or faith upon; to catch at a straw; to hope against hope.

Adjectives: Hoping, etc., in hopes, hopeful, confident, secure, buoyant, buoyed up, in good heart, sanguine, optimistic, enthusiastic, utopian.

Fearless, unsuspecting, unsuspicious; free or exempt from fear, suspicion, distrust, etc., undespairing.

Auspicious, promising, propitious, bright, rose-coloured, rosy, of good omen, reassuring.

Phrases: *Nil desperandum*; while there's life there's hope; *dum spiro spero*; never say die; all for the best.

859 HOPELESSNESS
Substantives: despair, desperation, despondency, pessimism (837); forlornness, a forlorn hope, the Slough of Despond.
Phrases: A black look-out; a bad business.
Verbs: To despair, despond, give up, be hopeless; to lose, give up, abandon, relinquish, etc., all hope; to yield to despair.

To inspire or drive to despair; to dash, crush, or destroy one's hopes.
Phrases: To trust to a broken reed; *'lasciate ogni speranza voi ch' entrate.'*
Adjectives: Hopeless, having lost or given up hope, losing etc., hope, past hope, despondent, pessimistic, forlorn, desperate, despairing.

Incurable, irremediable, irreparable, irrevocable, incorrigible, beyond remedy.

Inauspicious, unpropitious, unpromising, threatening, ill-omened.

860 FEAR
Substantives: cowardice (862), timidity, diffidence, nervousness, restlessness, inquietude, disquietude, solicitude, anxiety, care, distrust, mistrust, hesitation, misgiving, suspicion, qualm, want of confidence, nerves.

Apprehension, flutter, trepidation, tremor, shaking, trembling, palpitation, jitters, the jumps, the creeps, the needle, ague-fit, fearfulness, despondency; stage fright, cold feet, wind up.

Fright, affright, alarm, dread, awe, terror, horror, dismay, obsession, panic, funk, flap, stampede, scare, consternation, despair (859).

Intimidation, terrorism, reign of terror; an alarmist, scaremonger.

Object of fear, bugbear, bugaboo, bogy, scarecrow, goblin (980), *bête noire*, nightmare, Gorgon, ogre.
Phrases: Raw head and bloody bones; fee-faw-fum; butterflies in the stomach.
Verbs: To fear, be afraid, etc., distrust, hesitate, have qualms, misgiving, suspicions.

To apprehend, take alarm, start, wince, boggle, skulk, cower, crouch, tremble, shake, quake, quaver, quiver, shudder, quail, cringe, turn pale, blench, flutter, flinch, funk.

To excite fear, raise apprehensions, to give, raise, or sound an alarm, to intimidate, put in fear, frighten, fright, affright, alarm, startle, scare, haunt, obsess, strike terror, daunt, terrify, unman, awe, horrify, dismay, petrify, appal.

To overawe, abash, cow, browbeat, bully, deter, discourage.
Phrases: To shake in one's shoes; to shake like an aspen leaf; to stand aghast; to eye askance.

To fright from one's propriety; to strike all of a heap; to make the flesh creep; to give one the creeps; to cause alarm and despondency.
Adjectives: Fearing, timid, timorous, faint-hearted, tremulous, fearful, nervous, nervy, jumpy, funky, diffident, apprehensive, restless, haunted with the fear, apprehension, dread, etc., of.

Frightened, afraid, cowed, pale, alarmed, scared, terrified, petrified, aghast, awestruck, dismayed, horror-struck, horrified, appalled, panic-stricken.

Inspiring fear, fearsome, alarming, formidable, redoubtable, portentous, perilous (665), ugly, fearful, dreadful, dire, shocking, terrible, tremendous, horrid, horrible, horrific, ghastly, awful, awesome, horripilant, hair-raising, creepy, crawly.

Phrases: White as a sheet; afraid of one's shadow; the hair standing on end; letting 'I dare not' wait upon 'I would'; more frightened than hurt; frightened out of one's senses or wits; in a blue funk.

861 COURAGE

Substantives: bravery, value, boldness, spirit, moral fibre, spiritedness, daring, gallantry, intrepidity, contempt of danger, self-reliance, confidence, fearlessness, audacity.

Manhood, manliness, nerve, pluck, grit, guts, sand, mettle, gameness, heart, spunk, smeddum, virtue, hardihood, fortitude, firmness, resolution, sportsmanship.

Prowess, derring-do, heroism, chivalry.

A hero, heroine, ace, paladin, *preux chevalier,* Hector, Hotspur, Amazon, Joan of Arc, *beau sabreur,* fire-eater (863).

A lion, tiger, bulldog, gamecock, fighting-cock, sportsman.

Verbs: To be courageous, etc., to face, front, affront, confront, despise, brave, defy, etc., danger; to take courage; to summon up, muster up, or pluck up courage; to rally.

To venture, make bold, face, dare, defy, brave (715), beard, hold out, bear up against, stand up to.

To give, infuse, or inspire courage; to encourage, embolden, inspirit, cheer, nerve.

Phrases: To take the bull by the horns; to come up to the scratch; to face the music; to 'screw one's courage to the sticking-place'; to die game.

To pat on the back; to make a man of.

Adjectives: Courageous, brave, valiant, valorous, gallant, intrepid.

Spirited, high-spirited, high-mettled, mettlesome, plucky, manly, manful, resolute, stout, stout-hearted, lion-hearted, heart of oak, firm, indomitable, game, sportsmanlike.

Bold, daring, audacious, fearless, unfearing, dauntless, undaunted, indomitable, unappalled, undismayed, unawed, unabashed, unalarmed, unflinching, unshrinking, unblenching, unblenched, unapprehensive, confident, self-reliant.

Enterprising, venturous, adventurous, venturesome, dashing, chivalrous, heroic, fierce, warlike (722).

Unfeared, undreaded, etc.

Phrases: One's blood is up; brave as a lion; bold as brass; full of beans.

862 COWARDICE

Substantives: fear (860), pusillanimity, cowardliness, timidity, fearfulness, spiritlessness, faint-heartedness, softness, effeminacy, funk.

Poltroonery, baseness, dastardliness, yellow streak, a faint heart.

A coward, poltroon, dastard, recreant, funk, mollycoddle, milksop, cry-baby, 'fraid-cat, chicken, cowardy custard.

A runaway, fugitive, deserter, quitter.

Verbs: To be cowardly, etc.; to quail (860), to flinch, fight shy, shy, turn tail, run away, cut and run, fly for one's life, stampede.

Phrases: To show the white feather; to be in a sweat.

Adjectives: Coward, cowardly, yellow, pusillanimous, shy, fearful, timid, skittish, timorous, poor-spirited, spiritless, weak-hearted, faint-hearted, chicken-hearted, white-livered.

Dastard, dastardly, base, craven, recreant, unwarlike, unheroic, unsoldierly, unmanly, womanish.

Phrase: 'In face a lion, but in heart a deer.'
Interjections: *Sauve qui peut!* the devil take the hindmost!

863 RASHNESS
Substantives: temerity, audacity, presumption, precipitancy, precipitation, impetuosity, recklessness, overboldness, foolhardiness, desperation, knight-errantry, Quixotism; carelessness (460), want of caution, overconfidence.

Imprudence, indiscretion.

A desperado, madcap, bravo, daredevil, *enfant perdu,* gambler, adventurer, knight errant; Hotspur, Don Quixote, Icarus.
Phrases: A leap in the dark; a blind bargain; a wild-cat scheme.
Verbs: To be rash, incautious, etc.
Phrases: To buy a pig in a poke; to go on a forlorn hope; to go at it baldheaded; to play with fire; to tempt providence.
Adjectives: Rash, temerarious, headstrong, insane, foolhardy, slap-dash, dare-devil, devil-may-care, overbold, wild, reckless, desperate, hot-headed, hare-brained, headlong, hot-blooded, over-confident, precipitate, impetuous, venturesome, impulsive, Quixotic.

Imprudent, indiscreet, uncalculating, incautious, improvident.
Phrases: Without ballast; neck or nothing.
Interjections: *Vogue la galère!* come what may!

864 CAUTION
Substantives: cautiousness, discretion, prudence, reserve, wariness, heed, circumspection, calculation, deliberation (459).

Coolness, self-possession, aplomb, presence of mind, sang-froid, self-command, steadiness, the Fabian policy.

Phrases: The better part of valour; masterly inactivity.
Verbs: To be cautious, etc., to beware, take care, have a care, take heed, ca' canny, be on one's guard, look about one, take no chances.
Phrases: To look before one leaps; to think twice; to let sleeping dogs lie; to see which way the wind blows; to see how the land lies; to feel one's way; to count the cost; to be on the safe side; steady as she goes.
Adjectives: Cautious, wary, careful, heedful, cautelous, chary, canny, cagey, circumspect, prudent, prudential, reserved, discreet, politic, non-committal.

Unenterprising, unadventurous, cool, steady, self-possessed.
Phrases: Safety first; better be sure than sorry.

865 DESIRE
Substantives: wish, mind, inclination, leaning, bent, fancy, partiality, penchant, predilection, liking, love, fondness, relish.

Want, need, exigency.

Longing, hankering, solicitude, anxiety, yearning, yen, coveting, eagerness, zeal, ardour, aspiration, ambition, over-anxiety.

Appetite, appetence, appetency, the edge of appetite, keenness, hunger, stomach, thirst, thirstiness, drouth, mouth-watering, dispomania, itch, itching, prurience, lickerishness, *cacoethes,* cupidity, lust, libido, concupiscence, greed.

Avidity, greediness, covetousness, craving, voracity, bulimia, rapacity.

Passion, rage, furore, mania, kleptomania, inextinguishable desire, vaulting ambition, impetuosity.

A gourmand, gourmet, glutton, cormorant (957).

An amateur, votary, devotee, fan, aspirant, solicitant, candidate.

Object of desire, desideratum,

attraction, lure, allurement, fancy, temptation, magnet, loadstone, whim, whimsy (608), maggot, hobby, hobby-horse, pursuit.

Phrases: The height of one's ambition; *hoc erat in votis*; the wish being father to the thought; the torments of Tantalus.

Verbs: To desire, wish, long for, fancy, affect, like, have a mind to, be glad of, want, miss, need, feel the want of, would fain have, to care for.

To hunger, thirst, crave, lust after; to hanker after, itch for.

To desiderate, covet; to sigh, cry, gasp, pine, pant, languish, yearn for; to aspire after, catch at, jump at.

To woo, court, solicit, ogle, fish for.

To cause, create, raise, excite, or provoke, desire; to allure, attract, solicit, tempt, hold out temptation or allurement, to tantalize, appetize.

To gratify desire, slake, satiate (827).

Phrases: To have at heart; to take a fancy to; to set one's heart upon; to make eyes at; to set one's cap at; to run mad after.

To whet the appetite; to make one's mouth water.

Adjectives: Desirous, inclinded, fain, keen, wishful, wishing, optative, desiring, wanting, needing, hankering after, dying for, partial to.

Craving, hungry, esurient, sharp-set, keen-set, peckish, thirsty, athirst, dry, drouthy.

Greedy, voracious, lickerish, open-mouthed, agog, covetous, ravenous, rapacious, extortionate; unsated, unslaked, insatiable, insatiate, omnivorous.

Eager, ardent, avid, fervent, bent on, intent on, aspiring, ambitious.

Desirable, desired, desiderated (829).

Phrases: Pinched or perished with hunger; hungry as a hunter; parched with thirst; having a sweet tooth; nothing loth.

Interjections: O for! would that!

866 INDIFFERENCE

Substantives: coldness, coolness, unconcern, nonchalance, insouciance, inappetency, listlessness, lukewarmness, neutrality, impartiality; apathy (823), supineness (683), disdain (930).

Verbs: To be indifferent, etc.; to have no desire, wish, taste, or relish for; to care nothing about, take no interest in, not mind, make light of; to disdain, spurn (930).

Phrase: Couldn't care less.

Adjectives: Indifferent, undesirous, cool, cold, frigid, unconcerned, insouciant, unsolicitous, unattracted, lukewarm, half-hearted, listless, lackadaisical, unambitious, unaspiring, phlegmatic.

Unattractive, unalluring, uninviting, undesired, undesirable, uncared-for, unwished, uncoveted, unvalued.

Vapid, tasteless, insipid (391), wersh, unappetizing, mawkish, namby-pamby, flat, stale, vain.

Phrases: Never mind; all one to Hippocleides.

867 DISLIKE

Substantives: distaste, disrelish, disinclination, reluctance, backwardness, demur (603).

Repugnance, disgust, queasiness, turn, nausea, loathing, averseness, aversion, abomination, antipathy, abhorrence, horror, hatred, detestation (898), resentment (900); claustrophobia, agoraphobia, Anglophobia, Gallophobia.

Verbs: To dislike, mislike, disrelish, mind, object to.

To shun, avoid, eschew, withdraw from, shrink from, shrug the shoulders at, recoil from, shudder at.

To loathe, nauseate, abominate, detest, abhor, hate (898).

To cause or excite dislike; to disincline, repel, sicken, render sick, nauseate, disgust, shock, pall.

Phrases: Not to be able to bear or

endure or stand; to have no taste for; to turn up one's nose at; to look askance at.

To go against the grain; to turn one's stomach; to stink in the nostrils; to stick in one's throat; to make one's blood run cold.

Adjectives: Disliking, disrelishing, etc., averse to, adverse, shy of, sick of, fed up with, queasy, disinclined.

Disliked, disagreeable, unpalatable, unpopular, offensive, loathsome, loathly, sickening, nauseous, nauseating, repulsive, disgusting, detestable, execrable, abhorrent, abhorred (830), disgustful.

Adverbs: Disajeeably, etc.

Phrase: *Usque ad nauseam.*

Interjections: Faugh! Ugh!

868 FASTIDIOUSNESS

Substantives: nicety, daintiness, squeamishness, niceness, particularity, finicality, meticulosity, difficulty in being pleased, epicurism.

Excess of delicacy, prudery.

Epicure, gourmet, gourmand, *bon vivant,* gastronomer.

Verbs: To be fastidious, etc, to discriminate, differentiate, disdain.

Phrases: To split hairs; to mince one's words; to see spots in the sun.

Adjectives: Fastidious, nice, difficult, dainty, delicate, finicky, lickerish, pernickety, squeamish, queasy, difficult to please, particular, choosy, punctilious, fussy, hypercritical; prudish, straitlaced.

869 SATIETY

Substantives: fullness, repletion, glut, saturation, surfeit.

A spoilt child; too much of a good thing.

Verbs: To sate, satiate, satisfy, saturate, quench, slake, pall, glut, overfeed, gorge, surfeit, cloy, tire, spoil, sicken.

Adjectives: Satiated, sated, blasé,

used up, fed up, browned off, brassed off, cheesed off, chokka, sick of.

Phrases: Enough is enough; *Toujours perdrix.*

Interjections: Enough! that'll do!

870 WONDER

Substantives: surprise, marvel, astonishment, amazement, amazedness, wonderment, admiration, awe, bewilderment, stupefaction, fascination, thaumaturgy (992).

Verbs: To wonder, marvel, be surprised, admire; to stare, gape, start.

To surprise, astonish, amaze, astound, dumbfound, dumbfounder, strike, dazzle, startle, take by surprise, take aback, strike with wonder, electrify, stun, petrify, flabbergast, confound, stagger, stupefy, bewilder, fascinate, boggle.

To be wonderful, etc.

Phrases: To open one's mouth or eyes; to look blank; to stand aghast; not to believe one's eyes; not to account for; not to know whether one stands on one's head or one's heels.

To make one sit up; to take one's breath away.

To beggar description; to stagger belief; imagination boggles at it.

Adjectives: Surprised, astonished, amazed, astounded, struck, startled, taken by surprise, taken aback, struck dumb, awestruck, aghast, agape, dumbfounded, flabbergasted, thunderstruck, planet-struck, stupefied, openmouthed, petrified.

Wonderful, wondrous, surprising, astonishing, amazing, astounding, startling, stunning, unexpected, unforeseen, strange, uncommon, unheard-of, unaccountable, incredible, inexplicable, indescribable, inexpressible, ineffable, unutterable, unspeakable, monstrous, prodigious, stupendous, marvellous, miraculous, passing strange, uncanny, weird, phenomenal.

Phrases: Struck all of a heap; lost in

wonder; like a dying duck in a thunder-storm; you could have knocked me down with a feather.

Adverbs: Wonderingly, wonderfully, etc., with gaping mouth, all agog; *mirabile dictu*.

Interjections: What! indeed! really! hallo! humph! you don't say so! my stars! good heavens! my goodness! good gracious! bless my soul! bless my heart! my word! O gemini! great Scott! gee! *wunderbar!* dear me! well, I'm damned! well, I never! lo! heyday! who'd have thought it!

871 EXPECTANCE

Substantives: expectancy, expectation (507).

Verbs: To expect, not to be surprised, not to wonder, etc., *nil admirari*.

Phrase: To think nothing of.

Adjectives: Expecting, etc., blasé, unamazed, astonished at nothing, (841).

Common, ordinary (82); foreseen.

872 PRODIGY

Substantives: phenomenon, wonder, cynosure, marvel, miracle, monster (83), unicorn, phoenix, gazing-stock, curiosity, *rara avis,* lion, sight, spectacle, wonderment, sign, portent (512), eye-opener; wonderland, fairyland.

Thunderclap, thunderbolt, bursting of a shell or bomb, volcanic eruption.

Phrases: A nine days' wonder; *annus mirabilis*.

873 REPUTE

Substantives: distinction, note, notability, name, mark, reputation, figure, *réclame, éclat,* celebrity, vogue, fame, famousness, popularity, renown, memory, immortality.

Glory, honour, credit, prestige, kudos, account, regard, respect, reputableness, respectability, repectable-ness, good name, illustriousness, gloriousness.

Dignity, stateliness, solemnity, grandeur, splendour, nobility, nobleness, lordliness, majesty, sublimity.

Greatness, highness, eminence, supereminence, pre-eminence, primacy, importance (642).

Elevation, ascent (305), exaltation, superexaltation, aggrandisement.

Rank, standing, condition, precedence, *pas*, station, place, status, order, degree, *locus standi*.

Dedication, consecration, enshrinement, glorification, beatification, canonization, deification, posthumous fame.

Chief, leader (745), hero, celebrity, notability, somebody, lion, cock of the roost, cock of the walk, man of mark, pillar of the state, prima donna.

A star, sun, constellation, galaxy, flower, pearl, paragon (650); honour, ornament, aureole.

Phrases: A halo of glory; a name to conjure with; blushing honours; a feather in one's cap; the top of the tree; a niche in the temple of fame.

Verbs: To glory in, to be proud of (878), to exult (884), to be vain of (880).

To be glorious, distinguished, etc., to shine, to figure, to make or cut a figure, dash, or splash; to rival, outrival, surpass, emulate, outvie, eclipse, outshine, overshadow, throw into the shade.

To live, flourish, glitter, flaunt.

To honour, lionize, dignify, glorify, ennoble, nobilitate, exalt, enthrone, signalize, immortalize, deify.

To consecrate, dedicate to, devote to, to enshrine.

To confer or reflect honour, etc., on; to do, pay, or render honour to; to redound to one's honour.

Phrases: To acquire or gain honour, etc.; to bear the palm; to bear the bell; to take the cake; to win laurels; to make a noise in the world; to go far; to make a sensation; to be all the rage; to have a run; to catch on.

To exalt one's horn; to leave one's mark; to exalt to the skies.

Adjectives: Distinguished, *distingué,* noted, notable, respectable, reputable, celebrated, famous, famed, far-famed, honoured, renowned, popular, deathless, imperishable, immortal (112).

Illustrious, glorious, splendid, bright, brilliant, radiant, full-blown, heroic.

Eminent, prominent, conspicuous, kenspeckle, high, pre-eminent, peerless, signalized, exalted, dedicated, consecrated, enshrined.

Great, dignified, proud, noble, worshipful, lordly, grand, stately, august, imposing, transcendent, majestic, kingly, queenly, princely, sacred, sublime, commanding.

Phrases: Redounding to one's honour; one's name living for ever; *sic itur ad astra.*

Interjections: Hail! all hail! *vive! viva!* glory be to! honour be to!

874 DISREPUTE

Substantives: discredit, ingloriousness, derogation, abasement, degradation, odium, notoriety.

Dishonour, shame, disgrace, disfavour, disapprobation (932), slur, scandal, obloquy, opprobrium, ignominy, baseness, turpitude, vileness, infamy.

Tarnish, taint, defilement, pollution.

Stain, blot, spot, blur, stigma, brand, reproach, imputation, slur, black mark.

Phrases: A burning shame; *scandalum magnatum*; a badge of infamy; the bar sinister; a blot on the scutcheon; a byword of reproach; a bad reputation.

Verbs: To be conscious of shame, to feel shame, to blush, to be ashamed, humiliated, humbled (879, 881).

To cause shame, etc.; to shame, disgrace, put to shame, dishonour; to throw, cast, fling, or reflect shame, etc., upon; to be a reproach to, to derogate from.

To tarnish, stain, blot, sully, taint, discredit, degrade, debase, defile.

To impute shame to, to brand, stigmatize, vilify, defame, slur, run down, knock.

To abash, humiliate, humble, dishonour, discompose, disconcert, shame, show up, put out, put down, snub, confuse, mortify; to obscure, eclipse, outshine.

Phrases: To feel disgrace; to cut a poor figure; to hide one's face; to look foolish; to hang one's head; to laugh on the wrong side of the mouth; not to dare to show one's face; to hide one's diminished head; to lose caste; to be in one's black books.

To put to the blush; to put out of countenance; to put one's nose out of joint; to cast into the shade; to take one down a peg; to take the shine out of; to tread or trample under foot; to drag through the mud.

Adjectives: Feeling shame, disgrace, etc.; ashamed, abashed, disgraced, blown upon, branded, tarnished.

Inglorious, mean, base (940), shabby, nameless, unnoticed, unnoted, unhonoured.

Shameful, disgraceful, despicable, discreditable, unbecoming, degrading, humiliating, unworthy, disreputable, derogatory, vile, ribald, dishonourable, abject, scandalous, infamous, notorious.

Phrases: Unwept, unhonoured, and unsung; shorn of its beams; unknown to fame; in bad odour; under a cloud; down in the world.

Interjections: Fie! shame! for shame! *O tempora! O mores!*

875 NOBILITY

Substantives: noblesse, aristocracy, peerage, gentry, gentility, quality, rank, blood, birth, donship, fashionable world (852), the *haute monde,* high life, the upper classes, the upper ten, the four hundred.

A personage, notability, celebrity, man of distinction, rank, etc.; a nobleman, noble, lord, peer, grandee, magnate, magnifico, hidalgo, don, gentleman, squire, patrician, lordling, nob, swell, dignitary, bigwig, big gun.

House of Lords, Lords Spiritual and Temporal.

Gentlefolk, landed proprietors, squirearchy, *optimates.*

Prince, duke, marquis, earl, viscount, baron, thane, banneret, baronet, knight, count, armiger, laird, esquire; nizam, maharajah, rajah, nawab, sultan, emir (or ameer), effendi, sheik, pasha.

Princess, duchess, marchioness, marquise, countess, viscountess, baroness, lady, dame, maharanee, ranee, sultana, begum.

Verbs: To be noble, etc.

Adjectives: Noble, exalted, titled, patrician, aristocratic, high-born, well-born, genteel, *comme il faut,* gentlemanlike, ladylike, princely, courtly, fashionable (852).

Phrases: *Noblesse oblige*; born in the purple.

876 COMMONALTY

Substantives: the lower classes or orders, the vulgar herd, the crowd, the people, the commons, the proletariat, the multitude, Demos, οι πολλοί, the populace, the million, the masses, the mobility, the peasantry.

The middle classes, bourgeoisie.

The mob, rabble, rabble-rout, ruck, *canaille,* the underworld, riff-raff, *profanum vulgus.*

A commoner, one of the people, a proletarian, *roturier,* plebeian; peasant, yeoman, crofter, boor, carle, churl, serf, kern, tyke, (or tike), chuff, ryot, fellah, cottar.

A swain, clown, hind, clodhopper, bog-trotter, chaw-bacon, hodge, joskin, yokel, bumpkin, hayseed, rube, hick, ploughman, plough-boy, gaffer, loon, looby, lout, *gamin,* street arab, guttersnipe, mudlark, slubberdegullion.

A beggar, tramp, vagrant, gangrel, gaberlunzie, bum, hobo, sundowner, panhandler, pariah, muckworm, sans-culotte, raff, tatterdemalion, ragamuffin.

A Goth, Vandal, Hottentot, savage, barbarian, yahoo, rough diamond, unlicked cub.

An upstart, parvenu, skipjack, *novus homo, nouveau riche,* outsider, vulgarian, snob, mushroom.

Barbarousness, barbarism.

Phrases: The man in the street; the submerged tenth; ragtag and bobtail; the swinish multitude; hewers of wood and drawers of water; the great unwashed.

Verbs: To be ignoble, etc.

Adjectives: Ignoble, common, mean, low, plebeian, proletarian, vulgar, bourgeois, untitled, homespun, homely, Gorblimey.

Base, base-born, low-bred, beggarly, earth-born, rustic, agrestic, countrified, provincial, parochial; banausic, menial, sorry, scrubby, mushroom, dunghill, sordid, vile, uncivilized, loutish, boorish, churlish, rude, brutish, raffish, unlicked, barbarous, barbarian, barbaric.

877 TITLE

Substantives: honour, princedom, principality, dukedom, marquisate, earldom, viscounty, baronetcy, lordship, knighthood.

Highness, excellancy, grace, worship, reverence, esquire, sir, master, sahib, Mr, monsieur, signor, señor, Herr.

Decoration, laurel, palm, wreath, medal, gong, ribbon, cross, star, garter, feather, crest, epaulette, colours, cockade, livery; order, arms, shield, scutcheon.

Phrase: A handle to one's name.

878 PRIDE

Substantives: haughtiness, loftiness, hauteur, stateliness, pomposity, vainglory, superciliousness, assumption, lordliness, stiffness, primness, arrogance, *morgue,* starch, starchiness, side, swank, uppishness; self-respect, dignity.

A proud man, etc., a highflier.

Verbs: To be proud, etc., to presume, assume, swagger, strut, prance, peacock, bridle.

To pride oneself on, glory in, pique oneself, plume oneself, preen oneself.

Phrases: To look big; give oneself airs; to ride the high horse; to put on side; to put on dog; to hold up one's head; to get one's tail up.

To put a good face upon.

Adjectives: Proud, haughty, lofty, high, mighty, high-flown, high-minded, high-mettled, puffed up, flushed, supercilious, patronizing, condescending, disdainful, overweening, consequential, on stilts, swollen, arrogant, pompous.

Stately, dignified, stiff, starchy, prim, perked up, buckram, strait-laced, vainglorious, lordly, magisterial, purse-proud, stand-offish, up-stage, toffee-nose.

Unabashed (880).

Phrases: High and mighty; proud as a peacock; proud as Lucifer.

Adverbs: Proudly, haughtily, arrogantly, etc.

879 HUMILITY

Substantives: humbleness, meekness, lowness, lowliness, abasement, self-abasement, self-contempt, humiliation, submission, resignation, verecundity, modesty (881).

Verbs: To be humble, etc.; to deign; vouchsafe, condescend; to humble or demean oneself; stoop, submit, knuckle under, look foolish, feel small.

To render humble; to humble, humiliate, set down, abash, abase, shame, mortify, crush, take down, snub.

Phrases: To sing small; to pipe down; to draw in one's horns; to hide one's diminished head; to eat humble pie; to eat dirt; to kiss the rod; to pocket an affront; to stoop to conquer.

To throw into the shade; to put out of countenance; to put a person in his place; to put to the blush; to take down a peg, cut down to size; to send away with a flea in one's ear.

Adjectives: Humble, lowly, meek, sober-minded, submissive (725), resigned, self-contemptuous, under correction.

Humbled, humiliated, abashed, ashamed, chapfallen, crestfallen.

Phrases: Out of countenance; on one's bended knees; humbled in the dust; not having a word to say for oneself.

Adverbs: Humbly, meekly, etc.

880 VANITY

Substantives: conceit, conceitedness, self-conceit, self-confidence, self-sufficiency, self-esteem, self-approbation, self-importance, self-praise, self-laudation, self-admiration, complacency, self-complacency, swelled head, megalomania, *amour-propre.*

Pretensions, airs, mannerism, egotism, egoism, egomania, priggishness, coxcombry, gaudery, vainglory (943), elation, ostentation (882).

A coxcomb (854).

Verbs: To be vain, etc., to egotize.

To render vain, etc., to puff up, to inspire with vanity, turn one's head.

Phrases: To have a high or overweening opinion of oneself; to think no small beer of oneself; to thrust oneself forward; to give oneself airs; to show off; to fish for compliments.

Adjectives: Vain, conceited, overweening, forward, vainglorious, puffed up, high-flown, inflated, flushed, stuck-up.

Self-satisfied, self-confident, self-sufficient, self-flattering, self-admiring, self-applauding, self-opinionated, self-centred, egocentric, egoistic, egoistical, egotistic, egotistical, complacent, self-complacent, pretentious, priggish.

Unabashed, unblushing, unconstrained, unceremonious, free and easy.

Phrases: Vain as a peacock; wise in one's own conceit.

Adverbs: Vainly, etc., ostentatiously (882).

881 MODESTY

Substantives: humility (879), diffidence, timidity, bashfulness, shyness, coyness, sheepishness, *mauvaise honte,* shamefacedness, verecundity, self-consciousness.

Reserve, constraint, demureness.

Verbs: To be modest, humble, etc.; to retire, keep in the background, keep private, reserve oneself.

Phrases: To hide one's light under a bushel; to take a back seat.

Adjectives: Modest, diffident, humble (879), timid, bashful, timorous, shy, skittish, coy, sheepish, shamefaced, blushing, self-conscious.

Unpretending, unpretentious, unassuming, unostentatious, unboastful, unaspiring.

Abashed, ashamed, dashed, out of countenance, crestfallen (879).

Reserved, constrained, demure, undemonstrative.

Adverbs: Modestly, diffidently, quietly, privately, unostentatiously.

882 OSTENTATION

Substantives: display, show, flourish, parade, pomp, state, solemnity, pageantry, dash, splash, splurge, glit-

ter, veneer, tinsel, magnificence, pomposity, showing off, swank, swagger, strut, *panache, coup de théâtre,* stage effect.

Flourish of trumpets, fanfare, salvo of artillery, salute, fireworks, *feu de joie.*

Pageant, spectacle, procession, march-past, review, promenade, turn-out, set-out, build-up, fête, gala, regatta, field-day.

Ceremony, ceremonial, mummery; formality, form, etiquette, ritual, protocol, punctilio, puncitiliousness.

Verbs: To be ostentatious, etc.; to display, exhibit, posture, attitudinize, show off, swank, come forward, put oneself forward, flaunt, emblazon, prink, glitter; make or cut a figure, dash, or splash.

To observe or stand on ceremony, etiquette, etc.

Adjectives: Ostentatious, showy, gaudy, garish, flashy, dashing, pretentious, flaunting, jaunty, glittering, sumptuous, spectacular, ceremonial, stagy, theatrical, histrionic.

Pompous, solemn, stately, high-sounding, formal, stiff, ritualistic, ceremonious, punctilious.

Phrases: With flourish of trumpets; with beat of drum; with flying colours; in one's Sunday best; in one's best bib and tucker.

883 CELEBRATION

Substantives: jubilee, jubilation, commemoration, festival, feast, solemnization, ovation, paean, triumph.

Triumphal arch, bonfire, illuminations, fireworks, salute, salvo, *feu de joie,* flourish of trumpets, fanfare.

Inauguration, installation, presentation, coronation, fête (882).

Anniversary, silver wedding, golden wedding, diamond wedding, diamond jubilee, centenary, bicentenary, tercentenary, quartercentenary, quingentenary (or quincentenary), sexcentenary, etc., millenary.

Verbs: To celebrate, keep, signalize, do honour to, pledge, drink to, toast, commemorate, solemnize.

To inaugurate, install.

Phrase: To paint the town red.

Adjectives: Celebrating, etc., in honour of, in commemoration of, in memoriam.

Interjections: Hail! all hail! 'See the conquering hero comes.' 'For he's a jolly good fellow.'

884 BOASTING

Substantives: boast, vaunt, vaunting, brag, bounce, *blague,* swank, bluff, puff, puffing, puffery, flourish, fanfaronade, gasconade, braggadocio, bravado, tall talk, heroics, vapouring, rodomontade, bombast, exaggeration (549), self-advertisement, *réclame*; jingoism, Chauvinism, spread-eagleism.

Exultation, triumph, flourish of trumpets (883).

A boaster, braggart, braggadocio, Gascon, peacock; a pretender, charlatan.

Verbs: To boast, make a boast of, brag, vaunt, puff, flourish, vapour, blow, strut, swagger, swank, skite, gas.

To exult, crow, chuckle, triumph, gloat, glory.

Phrases: To talk big; to shoot a line; to blow one's own trumpet.

Adjectives: Boasting, vaunting, etc., thrasonical, vainglorious, braggart, jingo, jingoistic, chauvinistic.

Elate, elated, flushed, jubilant.

Phrases: On stilts; cock-a-hoop; in high feather.

885 INSOLENCE

Substantives: haughtiness, arrogance, imperiousness, contumeliousness, superciliousness, bumptiousness, bounce, swagger, swank.

Impertinence, sauciness, pertness, flippancy, petulance, malapertness.

Assumption, presumption, presumptuousness, nerve, forwardness, impudence, assurance, front, face, neck, cheek, lip, side, brass, shamelessness, hardihood, a hardened front, effrontery, audacity, procacity, self-assertion, gall, crust.

Verbs: To be insolent, etc.; to bluster, vapour, swagger, swank, swell, roister, arrogate, assume, bluff.

To domineer, bully, beard, snub, huff, outface, outlook, outstare, outbrazen, bear down, beat down, trample on, tread under foot, outbrave, hector.

To presume, take liberties or freedoms.

Phrases: To give oneself airs; to lay down the law; to put on side; to ride the high horse; to lord it over; *traiter, ou regarder de haut en bas*; to ride roughshod over; to carry with a high hand; to throw one's weight about; to carry it off; to brave it out.

Adjectives: Insolent, etc.; haughty, arrogant, imperious, dictatorial, highhanded, contumelious, supercilious, snooty, uppish, self-assertive, bumptious, overbearing, intolerant, assumptive.

Flippant, pert, perky, cavalier, saucy, cheeky, fresh, forward, impertinent, malapert.

Blustering, swaggering, swanky, vapouring, bluff, roistering, rollicking, high-flown, assuming, presuming, presumptuous, self-assertive, impudent, free, brazen, brazen-faced, barefaced, shameless, unblushing, unabashed.

886 SERVILITY

Substantives: obsequiousness, suppleness, fawning, slavishness, abjectness, prostration, prosternation, genuflexion (900), abasement, subjection (749).

Fawning, mealy-mouthedness,

sycophancy, flattery (833), humility (879).

A sycophant, parasite, gate-crasher, toad-eater, toady, spaniel, bootlicker, lickspittle, flunkey, sponger, snob, hanger-on, tuft-hunter, time-server, reptile, cur (941); Uriah Heep.
Verbs: To cringe, bow, stoop, kneel, fall on one's knees, etc.

To sneak, crawl, crouch, cower, truckle to, grovel, fawn.
Phrases: To pay court to; to dance attendance on; to do the dirty work of; to lick the boots of.

To go with the stream; to worship the rising sun; to run with the hare and hunt with the hounds.
Adjectives: Servile, subservient, obsequious, sequacious, soapy, oily, unctuous, supple, mean, crouching, cringing, fawning, slavish, grovelling, snivelling, beggarly, sycophantic, parasitical, abject, prostrate.
Adverb: Cap in hand.

887 BLUSTERER
Substantives: bully, swaggerer, braggart (884), fire-eater, daredevil, roisterer, puppy, sauce-box, hussy, minx, malapert, jackanapes, jack-in-office, jingo, Drawcansir, Captain Bobadil, Sir Lucius O'Trigger, Bombastes Furioso, Hector, Thraso, Bumble.
Phrases: The Great Panjandrum himself; a cool hand.

Section 3 –
Sympathetic Affections

888 FRIENDSHIP
Substantives: amity, amicableness, amicability, friendliness, friendly regard, affection (897), goodwill, favour, brotherhood, fraternity, sodality, comradeship, *camaraderie,* confraternity, fraternization, cordiality, harmony, good understanding, concord (714), *entente cordiale.*

Acquaintance, introduction, intimacy, familiarity, fellowship, fellow-feeling, sympathy, welcomeness, partiality, favouritism.
Verbs: To be friends, to be friendly, etc., to fraternize, sympathize with (897), to be well with, to be thick with, to befriend (707), to be in with, to keep in with.

To become friendly, to make friends with, to chum up with.
Phrases: To take in good part; to hold out the right hand of fellowship; to break the ice; to scrape acquaintance with.
Adjectives: Friendly, amical, amicable, brotherly, fraternal, harmonious, cordial, social, chummy, pally, neighbourly, on good terms, on a friendly footing, on friendly terms, well-affected, well-disposed, favourable.

Acquainted, familiar, intimate, thick, hand and glove, welcome.

Firm, staunch, intimate, familiar, bosom, cordial, devoted.
Phrases: In one's good books; hail fellow well met.
Adverbs: Friendly, amicably, etc., *sans cérémonie.*

889 ENMITY
Substantives: hostility, unfriendliness, antagonism, animosity, hate (898), dislike (867), malevolence (907), ill will, ill feeling, spite, bad blood, aversion, antipathy, alienation, estrangement; umbrage, pique.
Verbs: To be inimical, etc.; to estrange, to fall out, alienate.
Phrases: To keep at arms's length; to bear malice; to set by the ears.
Adjectives: Inimical, unfriendly, hostile, antagonistic, adverse, at variance, at loggerheads, at daggers drawn, on bad terms.

Estranged, alienated, irreconcilable.

890 FRIEND
Substantives: well-wisher, *amicus*

curiae, alter ego, bosom friend, *fidus Achates,* partner (711); *persona grata.*

Partisan, sympathizer, ally, backer, patron, good genius, fairy godmother.

Neighbour, acquaintance, associate, compeer, comrade, companion, *confrère, camarade,* mate, messmate, shopmate, shipmate, crony, cummer, confidant, chum, pal, buddy, side-kick, boon companion, pot-companion, school-fellow, playfellow, playmate, bed-fellow, bed-mate, bunkie, room-mate.

Arcades ambo, Pylades and Orestes, Castor and Pollux, Nisus and Euryalus, Damon and Pythias, David and Jonathan, *par nobile fratrum.*

Host, guest, visitor, *habitué,* protégé.

891 ENEMY
Substantives: foe, opponent (710), antagonist.

Public enemy, enemy to society, anarchist, terrorist, Ishmael.

892 SOCIALITY
Substantives: sociability, sociableness, social intercourse, companionship, companionableness, consortship, intercommunication, intercommunion, consociation.

Conviviality, good fellowship, hospitality, heartiness, welcome, the glad hand, joviality, jollity, *savoir vivre,* festivity, merrymaking.

Society, association, union, co-partnership, fraternity, sodality, coterie, clan, club (72), circle, clique, knot.

Assembly-room, casino, clubhouse, common-room.

Esprit de corps, nepotism (11).

An entertainment, party, social gathering, reunion, gaudy, levee, soirée, conversazione, rout, *ridotto,* at-home, house-warming, bee, tea-party, bun-fight, picnic, garden-party, festival (840), interview, assignation, appointment, date, tryst, call, visit, visiting, reception (588).

A good fellow, good scout, boon companion, good mixer, *bon vivant.*

Verbs: To be sociable, etc., to associate with, keep company with, to club together, sort with, hobnob with, consort, make advances, fraternize, make the acquaintance of.

To visit, pay a visit, interchange visits or cards, call upon, leave a card.

To entertain, give a party, dance, etc.; to keep open house; to receive, to welcome.

Phrases: To make oneself at home; to crack a bottle with.

To be at home to; to do the honours; to receive with open arms; to give a warm reception to; to kill the fatted calf.

Adjectives: Sociable, social, companionable, neighbourly, gregarious, clannish, clubbable, conversable, affable, accessible, familiar, on visiting terms, welcome, hospitable, convivial, jovial, festive.

Phrases: Free and easy; hail fellow well met.

Adverbs: *En famille;* in the family circle; in the social whirl; *sans façon; sans cérémonie; sans gêne.*

893 SECLUSION
Substantives: privacy, retirement, withdrawal, reclusion, recess, retiredness, rustication.

Solitude, singleness, estrangement from the world, loneliness, lonesomeness, retiredness, isolation; hermitage, cloister, nunnery (1000); study, den; ivory tower, Shangri-la.

Wilderness, depopulation, desolation.

Agoraphobia, claustrophobia.

EXCLUSION
Substantives: excommunication, banishment, expatriation, exile, ostracism, cut, cut direct, dead cut, inhospitality, inhospitableness, unsociability.

A recluse, hermit, cenobite, anchoret (or anchorite), stylite, santon, troglodyte, solitary, ruralist; displaced person, outcast, pariah; foundling, waif, wastrel, castaway; Timon of Athens, Simon Stylites.

Phrase: 'A lone lorn creetur.'

Verbs: To be secluded, etc., to retire, to live retired, secluded, etc.; to keep aloof, keep snug, shut oneself up, deny oneself.

To cut, refuse to associate with or acknowledge; repel, cold-shoulder, blackball, outlaw, proscribe, excommunicate, boycott, exclude, banish, exile, ostracize, rusticate, send down, abandon, maroon.

To depopulate, dispeople, unpeople.

Phrases: To retire from the world; to take the veil; to sport one's oak.

To send to Coventry; to turn one's back upon; to give one the cold shoulder.

Adjectives: Secluded, sequestered, retired, private, snug, domestic, claustral.

Unsociable, unsocial, aloof, eremitical, offish, stand-offish, unclubbable, inhospitable, cynical, inconversible, retiring, unneighbourly, exclusive, unforthcoming.

Solitary, lonely, lonesome, isolated, single, estranged, unfrequented, uninhabited, unoccupied, tenantless.

Unvisited, cut, blackballed, uninvited, unwelcome, friendless, deserted, abandoned, derelict, lorn, forlorn, homeless, out of it.

Phrase: Left to shift for oneself.

894 COURTESY

Substantives: good manners, good breeding, good form, mannerliness, manners, *bienséance,* urbanity, civilization, polish, politeness, gentility, comity, civility, amenity, suavity, discretion, diplomacy, good temper, easy temper, gentleness, mansuetude, gracious-ness, gallantry, affability, obligingness, *prévenance,* amiability, good humour.

Compliment, fair words, soft words, sweet words, honeyed phrases, attentions, *petits soins,* salutation, reception, presentation, introduction, *accueil,* greeting, regards, remembrances, welcome, *abord,* respect, devoir.

Obeisance, reverence, bow, curtsy, scrape, salaam, kowtow, capping, shaking hands, embrace, hug, squeeze, accolade, salute, kiss, buss, kissing hands, genuflexion, prostration, obsequiousness.

Mark of recognition, nod, wave, valediction (293).

Verbs: To be courteous, civil, etc., to show courtesy, civility, etc., to speak one fair; to make oneself agreeable; to unbend, thaw.

To visit, wait upon, present oneself, pay one's respects, kiss hands.

To receive, do the honours, greet, welcome, bid welcome, usher in, bid God speed; hold or stretch out the hand; shake, press, or squeeze the hand.

To salute, kiss, embrace, hug, drink to, pledge, hobnob; to wave to, nod to, smile upon, bow, curtsy, scrape, uncover, cap, present arms, take off the hat.

To pay homage or obeisance, kneel, bend the knee, prostrate oneself, etc.

To render polite, etc., to polish, civilize, humanize.

Phrases: To mind one's p's and q's; to do the polite; to greet with open arms; to speed the parting guest.

Adjectives: Courteous, courtly, civil, civilized, polite, Chesterfieldian, genteel, well-bred, well-mannered, mannerly, urbane, gentlemanly, ladylike, refined (850), polished, genial.

Gracious, affable, familiar, well-spoken, fair-spoken, soft-spoken, fine-spoken, suave, bland, mild, conciliatory, winning, obsequious, obliging, open-armed.

Phrases: With a good grace; *suaviter in modo; à bras ouverts.*
Interjections: Hail! welcome! good morning! good day! good afternoon! good evening! good night! well met! *pax vobiscum!*

895 DISCOURTESY
Substantives: ill-breeding; ill, bad, or ungainly manners; rusticity, inurbanity, impoliteness, ungraciousness, uncourtliness, insuavity, rudeness, incivility, tactlessness, disrespect, impertinence, impudence, cheek, barbarism, misbehaviour, *grossièreté,* brutality, blackguardism, roughness, ruggedness, brusqueness, brusquerie, bad form.

Bad or ill temper, churlishness, crabbedness, tartness, crossness, peevishness, moroseness, sullenness, sulkiness, grumpiness, grouchiness, acrimony, sternness, austerity, moodiness, asperity, captiousness, sharpness, snappishness, perversity, cussedness, irascibility (901).

Sulks, dudgeon, mumps, scowl, frown, hard words, black looks.

A bear, brute, boor, blackguard, beast, cross-patch, grouch, sorehead.
Verbs: To be rude, etc., frown, scowl, glower, lour, pout, snap, snarl, growl, nag; to cut, insult, etc.

To render rude, etc., to brutalize, decivilize, dehumanize.
Phrases: To turn one's back upon; to turn on one's heel; to look black upon; to give one the cold shoulder, or the frozen face, or the frozen mitt; to take liberties with.
Adjectives: Discourteous, uncourteous, uncourtly, ill-bred, ill-mannered, ill-behaved, unmannerly, mannerless, impolite, unpolished, ungenteel, ungentlemanly, unladylike, uncivilized.

Uncivil, rude, ungracious, cool, chilly, distant, stand-offish, offish, icy, repulsive, uncomplaisant, unaccommodating, ungainly, unceremonious, ungentle, rough, rugged, bluff, blunt, gruff, churlish, boorish, bearish, brutal, brusque, blackguardly, vulgar, stern, harsh, austere, cavalier.

Ill-tempered, out of temper or humour, cross, crusty, tart, sour, crabbed, sharp, short, snappish, testy, peevish, waspish, captious, grumpy, snarling, caustic, acrimonious, ungenial, petulant, pettish, pert.

Perverse, cross-grained, ill-conditioned, wayward, humoursome, naughty, cantankerous, intractable, curst, nagging, froward, sulky, glum, grim, morose, scowling, grouchy, glowering, surly, sullen, growling, splenetic, spleenful, spleeny, spleenish, moody, dogged, ugly.
Phrases: Cross as two sticks; sour as a crab; surly as a bear.
Adverbs: With a bad grace, grudgingly.

896 CONGRATULATION
Substantives: felicitation, wishing joy, the compliments of the season, good wishes.
Verbs: To congratulate, felicitate, give or wish joy, tender or offer one's congratulations.
Adjectives: Congratulatory, etc.
Phrases: Many happy returns of the day! merry Christmas! happy New Year!

897 LOVE
Substantives: fondness, liking, inclination (865), regard, good graces, partiality, benevolence (906), admiration, fancy, tenderness, leaning, penchant, predilection; amativeness, amorousness.

Affection, sympathy, fellow-feeling, heart, affectionateness.

Attachment, yearning, amour, romance, gallantry, love-affair, *affair de cœur,* passion, tender passion, *grande passion,* flame, pash, crush, rave,

335

devotion, enthusiasm, fervour, enchantment, infatuation, adoration, idolatry, idolization.

Eros, Cupid, Aphrodite, Venus, Freya, the myrtle.

Maternal love, στοργή.

Attractiveness, etc., popularity.

Abode of love, love-nest, agapemone.

A lover, suitor, follower, admirer, adorer, wooer, beau, fiancé, gallant, young man, boy friend, sweetheart, flame, love, true-love, leman, paramour, amorist, *amoroso, cavaliere servente, cicisbeo*; turtle-doves.

Girl friend, lady-love, fiancée, sweetie, cutie, mistress, *inamorata*, idol, doxy, dona, Dulcinea, goddess.

Betrothed, affianced.

Verbs: To love, like, affect, fancy, care for, regard, revere, cherish, admire, dote on, adore, idolize, fall for, hold dear, prize.

To bear love to; to take to; to be in love with; to be taken, smitten, etc., with; to have, entertain, harbour, cherish, etc., a liking, love, etc., for; to be fond of, be gone on.

To excite love; to win, gain, secure, etc., the love, affections, heart, etc.; to take the fancy of, to attract, attach, seduce, charm, fascinate, captivate, enamour, enrapture.

To get into favour; to ingratiate oneself, insinuate oneself, curry favour with, pay one's court to, *faire l'aimable*.

Phrases: To take a fancy to; to make a fuss of; to look sweet upon; to cast sheep's eyes at; to fall in love with; to set one's affections on; to lose one's heart to.

To set one's cap at; to turn one's head.

Adjectives: Loving, liking, etc., attached to, fond of, taken with, struck with, gone on, sympathetic, sympathizing with, charmed, captivated, fascinated, smitten, bitten, *épris,* enamoured, lovesick, love-lorn.

Affectionate, tender, sweet upon, loving, lover-like, loverly, amorous, amatory, amative, spoony, erotic, uxorious, motherly, ardent, passionate, devoted, amatorial.

Loved, beloved, etc., dear, precious, darling, favourite (899), pet, popular.

Lovely, sweet, dear, charming, engaging, amiable, winning, winsome, lovesome, attractive, adorable, enchanting, captivating, fascinating, bewitching, taking, seductive (829).

Phrases: Head over ears in love; to one's mind, taste, or fancy; in one's good graces; nearest to one's heart.

898 HATE

Substantives: hatred, disaffection, disfavour, alienation, estrangement, odium, dislike (867), enmity (899), animus, animosity (900).

Umbrage, pique, grudge, dudgeon, spleen, bitterness, ill feeling, acrimony, acerbity, malice (907), implacability.

Disgust, repugnance, aversion, averseness, loathing, abomination, horror, detestation, antipathy, abhorrence.

Object of hatred, abomination, *bête noir*.

Verbs: To hate, dislike, disrelish (867), loathe, nauseate, execrate, detest, abominate, shudder at, recoil at, abhor, shrink from.

To excite hatred, estrange, incense, envenom, antagonize, rile, alienate, disaffect, set against; to be hateful, etc.

Phrases: To make one's blood run cold; to have a down on; to hate one's guts.

To sow dissension among; to set by the ears.

Adjectives: Hating, etc., averse to, set against.

Unloved, disliked, unwept, unlamented, undeplored, unmourned, unbeloved, uncared-for, unvalued.

Crossed in love, forsaken, jilted, rejected, love-lorn.

Obnoxious, hateful, abhorrent, odious, repulsive, offensive, shocking, loathsome, sickening, nauseous, disgusting, abominable, horrid (830).

Invidious, spiteful, malicious (907), spleenful, disgustful.

Insulting, irritating, provoking.
Phrases: Not on speaking terms; there being no love lost between them; at daggers drawn.

899 FAVOURITE
Substantives: pet, cosset, dear, darling, honey, duck, moppet, jewel, idol, minion, spoilt child, blue-eyed boy, *persona grata*.
Phrases: The apple of one's eye; a man after one's own heart; the idol of the people; the answer to the maiden's prayer.

900 RESENTMENT
Substantives: displeasure, animus, animosity, anger, wrath, indignation.

Pique, umbrage, huff, miff, soreness, dudgeon, moodiness, acerbity, bitterness, asperity, spleen, gall, heartburning, heart-swelling, rankling; temper (901), bad blood, ill blood, ill humour.

Excitement, irritation, exasperation, warmth, bile, choler, ire, fume, dander, passion, fit, tantrum, burst, explosion, paroxysm, storm, rage, wax, fury, desperation.

Temper, petulance, procacity, angry mood, taking, snappishness.

Cause of umbrage, affront, provocation, offence, indignity, insult (929).

The Furies; the Eumenides.
Phrases: The blood being up or boiling; a towering passion; the vials of wrath; fire and fury.

A sore subject; a rap on the knuckles; *casus belli*.
Verbs: To resent, take amiss, take offence, take umbrage, take huff, bridle up, bristle up, frown, scowl, lour, snarl, growl, gnash, snap.

To chafe, mantle, redden, colour, fume, froth up, kindle; get, fall, or fly into a passion, rage, etc.; fly out, take fire, fire up, flare up, boil, boil over, rage, storm, foam.

To cause or raise anger; to affront, offend, give offence or umbrage; hurt the feelings; discompose, fret, ruffle, nettle, excite, irritate, provoke, rile, chafe, wound, sting, incense, inflame, enrage, aggravate, embitter, exasperate, rankle, infuriate, peeve.
Phrases: To take in bad part; to take it ill; to take exception to; to stick in one's gizzard; to take in dudgeon; to have a bone (or crow) to pick with one; to get up on one's hind legs; to show one's teeth; to lose one's temper; to stamp, quiver, swell, or foam with rage; to see red; to look as black as thunder; to breathe revenge; to cut up rough; to pour out the vials of one's wrath; to blaze up; to blow one's top; to go up in a blue flame; to go on the war-path; to raise Cain.

To put out of humour; to stir up one's bile; to raise one's dander or choler; to work up into a passion; to make one's blood boil; to lash into a fury; to drive one mad; to put one's monkey up; to get one's goat.
Adjectives: Angry, wroth, irate, ireful, warm, boiling, fuming, raging, etc., nettled, sore, bitter, riled, ruffled, chafed, exasperated, wrought up, worked up, snappish.

Fierce, wild, rageful, furious, infuriate, mad, fiery, savage, rabid, waxy, shirty, boiling over, rankling, bitter, virulent, set against.

Relentless, ruthless, implacable, unpitying, pitiless (919), inexorable, remorseless, stony-hearted, immitigable.
Phrases: One's back being up; up in arms; in a stew; the gorge rising; in the height of passion.

Interjections: Hell's bells! zounds! damme! For crying out loud!

901 IRASCIBILITY
Substantives: susceptibility, excitability, temper, bad temper, procacity, petulance, irritability, fretfulness, testiness, grouchiness, tetchiness, touchiness, frowardness, peevishness, snappishness, hastiness, tartness, huffiness, resentfulness, vindictiveness, acerbity, protervity, aggressiveness, pugnacity (895).

A shrew, vixen, termagant, virago, scold, spitfire, Xanthippe; a tartar, fire-eater, fury; *genus irritabile*.

Verbs: To be irascible, etc.; to take fire, fire up, flare up (900).

Adjectives: Irascible, susceptible, excitable, irritable, fretful, fretty, on the fret, fidgety, peevish, hasty, over-hasty, quick, warm, hot, huffish, huffy, touchy, testy, tetchy (or techy), grouchy, restive, pettish, waspish, snappish, petulant, peppery, fiery, passionate, choleric, short-tempered.

Ill-tempered, bad-tempered, cross, churlish, sour, crabbed, cross-grained, sullen, sulky, grumpy, fractious, splenetic, spleenful, froward, shrewish.

Quarrelsome, querulous, disputatious, contentious, cranky, cantankerous, sarcastic (932), resentful, vindictive, pugnacious, aggressive.

Phrases: Like touchwood or tinder; a word and a blow; as cross as two sticks.

902 ENDEARMENT
Substantives: caress, blandishment, fondling, billing and cooing, petting, necking, embrace, salute, kiss, buss, smack, osculation, deosculation.

Courtship, wooing, suit, addresses, attentions, *petits soins,* flirtation, coquetry, philandering, gallivanting, serenading, œillade, ogle, the glad eye, sheep's eyes, goo-goo eyes.

Love-tale, love-token, love-letter, *billet-doux,* valentine.

Flirt, coquette, gold digger, vamp; male flirt, masher, philanderer, lady killer, wolf, lounge lizard, cake eater, sheik.

Verbs: To caress, fondle, wheedle, dandle, dally, cuddle, cockle, cosset, nestle, nuzzle, snuggle, clasp, hug, embrace, kiss, salute, bill and coo.

To court, woo, flirt, coquette, philander, spoon, canoodle, mash, spark, serenade.

Phrases: To make much of; to smile upon; to make eyes et; to chuck under the chin; to pat on the cheek; to make love; to pay one's court or one's addresses to; to set one's cap at; to pop the question.

To win the heart, affections, love, etc., of.

Adjectives: Caressing, etc., caressed, etc., flirtatious, spoony.

903 MARRIAGE
Substantives: matrimony, wedlock, union, bridal, match, intermarriage, coverture, cohabitation, bed, the marriage bond, the nuptial tie.

Wedding, nuptials, Hymen, spousals, espousals; leading to the altar; the torch of Hymen; nuptial benediction, marriage song, epithalamium.

Bride, bridegroom, groom, bridesmaid, maid of honour, matron of honour, bridesman, groomsman, best man.

Honeymoon, honeymooner.

A married man, a husband, spouse benedick (or benedict), consort, goodman, lord and master, hubby.

A married woman, a wife, lady, matron, mate, helpmate, helpmeet, rib, better half, *femme couverte* (or *feme coverte*), squaw.

A married couple, wedded pair, Darby and Joan, man and wife.

A monogamist, bigamist, a Turk,

polygamist, a much-married man, a Bluebeard, a Mormon.

Monogamy, bigamy, digamy, deuterogamy, trigamy, polygamy, polygyny, polyandry, endogamy, exogamy.

A morgantic marriage, left-handed marriage, marriage of convenience, *mariage de convenance*, companionate marriage, trial marriage, misalliance, *mésalliance*.

Verbs: To marry, wed, espouse, wive.

To join, give away, handfast, splice.

Phrases: To lead to the altar; to take to oneself a wife; to take for better for worse; to give one's hand to; to get spliced.

To tie the nuptial knot; to give in marriage.

Adjectives: Matrimonial, conjugal, connubial, nuptial, wedded, hymeneal, spousal, bridal, marital, epithalamic.

Monogamous, bigamous, polygamous, etc.

904 CELIBACY

Substantives: singleness, misogamy; bachelorhood, bachelorship; virginity, maidenhood, maidenhead.

An unmarried man, bachelor, celibate, misogamist, misogynist.

An unmarried woman, spinster, maid, maiden, old maid, virgin, *feme sole,* bachelor girl.

Phrase: Single blessedness.

Verb: To live single.

Adjectives: Unwedded, unmarried, single, celibate, wifeless, spouseless, lone.

905 DIVORCE

Substantives: dissolution of marriage, separation, divorcement.

A divorcee, co-respondent, cuckold.

Verbs: To live separate, divorce, put away.

WIDOWHOOD, viduity, weeds.

Widow, relict, dowager, jointress, grass widow; widower, grass widower.

906 BENEVOLENCE

Substantives: goodwill, good nature, kindness, kindliness, benignity, brotherly love, beneficence, charity, humanity, fellow-feeling, sympathy, good feeling, kind-heartedness, amiability, complaisance, loving-kindness; toleration, consideration, generosity.

Charitableness, bounty, bounteousness, bountifulness almsgiving, philanthropy (910), unselfishness (942).

Acts of kindness, a good turn, good works, kind offices, attentions, good treatment.

Phrases: The milk of human kindness; the good Samaritan.

Verbs: To be benevolent, etc., to do good to, to benefit, confer a benefit, be of use, aid, assist (707), render a service, treat well, to sympathize with.

Phrases: To have one's heart in the right place; to enter into the feelings of others; to do a good turn to; to do as one would be done by.

Adjectives: Benevolent, well-meaning, kind, obliging, accommodating, kind-hearted, tender-hearted, charitable, generous, beneficent, bounteous, bountiful, humane, clement, benignant, benign, considerate.

Good-natured, *bon enfant, bon diable,* a good sort, sympathizing, sympathetic, responsive, complaisant, accommodating, amiable, gracious.

Kindly, well-meant, well-intentioned, brotherly, fraternal, friendly (888).

Adverbs: With a good intention, with the best intentions.

Interjections: Good luck! God speed!

907 MALEVOLENCE

Substantives: ill will, unkindness, ill nature, malignity, malice, maliciousness, spite, spitefulness, despite, despitefulness.

Uncharitableness, venom, gall, rancour, rankling, bitterness, acerbity, harshness, mordacity, acridity, virulence, *acharnement,* misanthropy (911).

Cruelty, hardness of heart, obduracy, cruelness, brutality, brutishness, hooliganism, savageness, savagery, ferocity, barbarity, blood-thirstiness, immanity, pitilessness, truculence, devilry (or deviltry), devilment.

An ill turn, a bad turn, outrage, atrocity, affront (929).

Phrases: A heart of stone; the evil eye; the cloven hoof.

Verbs: To be malevolent, etc.; to injure, hurt, harm, molest, disoblige, do harm to, ill treat, maltreat (649), do an ill office or turn to, (830), to wrong.

To worry, harass, bait, oppress, grind, haze, persecute, hunt down, dragoon, hound.

Phrases: To wreak one's malice on; to bear or harbour malice against; to do one's worst.

Adjectives: Malevolent, malicious, ill-disposed, evil-minded, ill-intentioned, maleficent, malign, malignant.

Ill-natured, disobliging, inofficious, unfriendly, unsympathetic, unkind, uncandid, unaccommodating, uncharitable, ungracious, unamiable.

Surley, churlish (895), grim, spiteful, despiteful, ill-conditioned, foul-mouthed, acrid, rancorous, caustic, bitter, acrimonious, mordacious, vitriolic, venomous.

Cold, cold-blooded, cold-hearted, hard-hearted, iron-hearted, flint-hearted, marble-hearted, stony-hearted.

Pitiless, unpitying, uncompassionate, without bowels, ruthless, merciless, unmerciful, inexorable, relentless, unrelenting, virulent, dispiteous.

Cruel, brutal, savage, ferocious, atrocious, untamed, ferine, inhuman, barbarous, fell, Hunnish, bloody, blood-stained, bloodthirsty, bloody-minded, sanguinary, truculent (919), butcherly.

Fiendish, fiendlike, infernal, demoniacal, diabolical, devilish, hellish.

Adverbs: Malevolently, etc., with bad intent or intention, despitefully.

908 MALEDICTION

Substantives: curse, malison, imprecation, denunciation, execration, anathema, ban, proscription, excommunication, commination, fulmination, *maranatha.*

Cursing, scolding, revilement, vilification, vituperation, invective, flyting, railing, Billingsgate, expletive, oath, bad language, unparliamentary language, ribaldry, scurrility.

Verbs: To censure, curse, imprecate, damn, scold, swear at, flyte on, rail at or against, execrate.

To denounce, proscribe, excommunicate, fulminate against, anathematize, blaspheme.

Phrases: To devote to destruction; to invoke or call down curses on one's head; to swear like a trooper; to rap out an oath; to curse with bell, book, and candle.

Adjectives: Cursing, etc., accursed, cursed, etc., blue-pencil, asterisk; maledictory, imprecatory, blasphemous.

Interjections: Curse! damn! blast! devil take it! dash! hang! blow! confound! plague on it! woe to! beshrew! *ruat coelum!* ill betide!

909 THREAT

Substantives: menace, defiance (715), abuse, minacity, intimidation, commination.

Verbs: To threaten, threat, menace, fulminate, thunder, bluster, defy, snarl; growl, gnarl, mutter; to intimidate (860).

Phrases: To hurl defiance; to throw down the gauntlet; to look daggers; to show one's teeth; to shake the fist at.

Adjectives: Threatening, menacing, minatory, comminatory, minacious, abusive, sinister, ominous, louring, defiant (715).

Interjections: Let them beware! You have been warned!

910 PHILANTHROPY

Substantives: humanity, humanitarianism, altruism, public spirit.

Patriotism, civicism, nationality, nationalism, love of country, *amor patriae,* sociology, socialism, utilitarianism.

A philanthropist, humanitarian, utilitarian, Benthamite, socialist, cosmopolitan, cosmopolite, citizen of the world, patriot, nationalist, lover of mankind.

Adjectives: Philanthropic, philanthropical, humanitarian, humane, utilitarian, patriotic, altruistic, public-spirited.

Phrases: '*Humani nihil a me alienum puto*'; *pro bono publico*; the greatest happiness of the greatest number.

911 MISANTHROPY

Substantives: egotism, egoism, incivism, want of patriotism, moroseness, selfishness (943); misogynism.

A misanthrope, egotist, cynic, man-hater, Timon, Diogenes.

Woman-hater, misogynist.

Adjectives: Misanthropic, misanthropical, antisocial, unpatriotic, fish, egotistical, morose, sullen, maladjusted.

912 BENEFACTOR

Substantives: saviour, good genius, tutelary saint, guardian angel, fairy godmother, good Samaritan.

Phrase: *Deus ex machina.*

913 EVILDOER

Substantives: wrong-doer, mischief-maker, marplot, anarchist, nihilist, terrorist, firebrand, incendiary, evil genius (980).

Frankenstein's monster.

Savage, brute, ruffian, blackguard, villain, scoundrel, cutthroat, barbarian, caitiff, desperado, jail-bird, hooligan, tough, rough, teddy boy, larrikin, hoodlum, gangster, crook, yegg, apache (949).

Fiend, tiger, hyena, bloodhound, butcher, blood-sucker, vampire, ogre, ghoul, serpent, snake, adder, viper, rattlesnake, scorpion, hell-hound, hag, hellbag, beldam, harpy, siren, fury, Jezebel.

Monster, demon, imp, devil (980), anthropophagi, Attila, vandal, Hun, Goth.

Phrases: A snake in the grass; a scourge of the human race; a fiend in human shape; worker of iniquity.

914 PITY

Substantives: compassion, commiseration, sympathy, fellow-feeling, tenderness, yearning.

Forbearance, mercy, humanity, clemency, leniency, ruth, long-suffering, quarter.

Phrases: The melting mood; *coup de grâce*; bowels of compassion; *argumentum ad misericordiam.*

Verbs: To pity, commiserate, compassionate, sympathize, feel for, yearn for, console, enter into the feelings of, have or take pity; show or have mercy; to forbear, relent, thaw, spare, relax, give quarter.

To excite pity, touch, soften, melt, propitiate, disarm.

To ask for pity, mercy, etc.; to supplicate, implore, deprecate, appeal to, cry for quarter, etc.; beg one's life, kneel, fall on one's knees, etc.

Phrase: To put one out of one's misery.

Adjectives: Pitying, commiserating, etc.

Pitiful, compassionate, tender, clement, merciful, lenient, relenting, etc.; soft-hearted, sympathetic, touched, weak, soft, melting, unhardened (740).

Piteous, pitiable, sorry, miserable.

Phrases: Tender as a woman; one's heart bleeding for.

Interjections: For pity's sake! mercy! God help you! poor thing! poor fellow!

915 CONDOLENCE

Substantives: lamentation, lament (839), sympathy, consolation.

Verbs: To condole with, console, solace, sympathize; express, testify, etc., pity; to afford or supply consolation, grieve for, lament with, weep with (839).

916 GRATITUDE

Substantives: gratefulness, thankfulness, feeling of obligation.

Acknowledgment, recognition, thanksgiving, giving thanks.

Thanks, praise, benediction, prace, paean, Te Deum (990).

Requital, thank-offering.

Verbs: To be grateful, etc.; to thank, to give, render, return, offer, tender thanks, acknowledgments, etc.; to acknowledge, appreciate, requite.

To lie under an obligation, to be obliged, beholden, etc.

Phrases: To overflow with gratitude; to thank one's stars; never to forget.

Adjectives: Grateful, thankful, obliged, beholden, indebted to, under obligation.

Interjections: Thanks! many thanks! ta! *merci!* gramercy! much obliged! thank heaven! heaven be praised!

917 INGRATITUDE

Substantives: ungratefulness, thanklessness, oblivion of benefits.

Phrases: 'Benefits forgot'; a thankless task.

Verbs: To be ungrateful, etc.; to forget benefits.

Phrases: To look a gift-horse in the mouth; to bite the hand that fed one.

Adjectives: Ungrateful, unmindful, unthankful, thankless, ingrate, inappreciative.

Forgotten, unacknowledged, unthanked, unrequited, unrewarded, ill-requited.

Phrase: Thank you for nothing.

918 FORGIVENESS

Substantives: pardon, condonation, grace, remission, absolution, amnesty, indemnity, oblivion, indulgence, reprieve.

Reconcilement, reconciliation, appeasement, mollification, shaking of hands, pacification (723).

Excuse, exoneration, quittance, acquittal, propitiation, exculpation.

Longanimity, forbearance, placability.

Verbs: To forgive, pardon, excuse, pass over, overlook, bear with, condone, absolve, pass, let off, remit, reprieve, exculpate, exonerate.

To allow for; to make allowance for.

To conciliate, propitiate, pacify, appease, placate, reconcile.

Phrases: To make it up; to forgive and forget; to shake hands; to heal the breach; to kiss and be friends; to bury the hatchet; to wipe the slate clean; to let bygones be bygones.

Adjectives: Forgiving, etc., unreproachful, placable, conciliatory.

Forgiven, etc., unresented.

919 REVENGE

Substantives: vengeance, revengement, avengement, vendetta, feud, retaliation.

Rancour, vindictiveness, implacability.

Revenger, avenger, vindicator, Nemesis, Furies.

Verbs: To revenge, take revenge, avenge.

Phrases: To wreak one's vengeance; to visit the sins on; to breathe vengeance; to have a bone to pick with; to have accounts to settle; to have a rod in pickle; to get one's knife into; to take one's change out of.

To harbour vindictive feelings; to rankle in the breast.

Adjectives: Revengeful, revanchist, vindictive, vengeful, rancorous, unforgiving, pitiless, ruthless, remorseless, unrelenting, relentless, implacable, rigorous.

920 JEALOUSY

Substantives: jealousness, heartburning.

Phrases: A jaundiced eye; the green-eyed monster.

Verbs: To be jealous, etc.; to view with jealousy.

Adjectives: Jealous, jaundiced, yellow-eyed.

Phrase: Eaten up with jealousy.

921 ENVY

Substantives: rivalry, emulation, covetousness; a Thersites, Zoilus.

Verbs: To envy, rival, emulate, covet.

Adjectives: Envious, invidious, covetous.

Phrase: Bursting with envy.

Section 4 – Moral Affections

922 RIGHT

Substantives: what ought to be, what should be; goodness, virtue (944), rectitude, probity (939).

Justice, equity, equitableness, fitness, fairness, fair play, impartiality, reasonableness, propriety.

Astraea, Themis.

Phrases: The scales of justice; even-handed justice; *suum cuique*; a fair field and no favour; *lex talionis*; 'Fiat justitia, ruat coelum.'

Morality, morals, ethics, duty (926).

Verbs: To stand to reason; to be right, just, etc.

To deserve, merit; to be worthy of, to be entitled to (924).

Phrases: To do justice to; to see justice done; to hold the scales even; to see fair play; to see one righted; to serve one right; to give the devil his due; to give and take; *audire alteram partem.*

Adjectives: Right, just, equitable, fair, equal, even-handed, impartial, judicial, legitimate, justifiable, rightful, reasonable, fit, proper, becoming, decorous, decent (926).

Deserved, merited, condign (924).

Adverbs: Rightly, in justice, in equity, fairly, etc., in reason, without distinction, without respect of persons.

Phrases: *En règle; de jure.*

923 WRONG

Substantives: what ought not to be, badness, evil (945), turpitude, improbity (940).

Injustice, unfairness, inequity, foul play, partiality, favour, favouritism, leaning, bias, party spirit, undueness (925), unreasonableness, tort, unlawfulness (964), encroachment, imposition.

Verbs: To be wrong, unjust, etc.; to favour, lean towards, show partiality, to encroach, impose upon.

Phrase: To rob Peter to pay Paul.

Adjectives: Wrong, wrongful, bad, unjust, unfair, undue, inequitable, unequal, partial, invidious, one-sided, improper, unreasonable, iniquitous, unfit, immoral (945).

Unjustified, unjustifiable, unwarranted, unauthorized, unallowable, unwarrantable.

Phrases: In the wrong; in the wrong box.

Adverbs: Wrongly, unjustly, etc., amiss.

Phrase: It won't do.

924 DUENESS

Substantives: due.

Right, privilege, prerogative, title,

claim, qualification, pretension, birthright, prescription, immunity, exemption, licence, liberty, franchise, enfranchisement, vested interest.

Sanction, authority, warranty, tenure, bond, security, lien, constitution, charter, warrant (760), patent, letters patent, copyright, *imprimatur.*

A claimant, pretender, appellant, plaintiff (938).

Women's rights, feminism; feminist, suffragist, suffragette.

Verbs: To be due, etc., to.

To have a right to, to be entitled to, to be qualified for, to have a claim upon, a title to, etc.; to deserve, merit, be worthy of.

To demand, claim, call upon, exact, insist on, challenge, to come upon one for, to revendicate, make a point of, enforce, put in force, use a right.

To appertain to, belong to, etc. (777).

To lay claim to, assert, assume, arrogate, make good, substantiate; to vindicate a claim, etc., to make out a case.

To give or confer a right; to entitle, authorize, warrant, sanction, sanctify, privilege, enfranchise, license, legalize, ordain, prescribe, allot.

Adjectives: Having a right to, a claim to, etc.; due to, entitled to, deserving, meriting, worthy of, claiming, qualified.

Privileged, allowed, sanctioned, warranted, authorized, permitted, licit, ordained, prescribed, chartered, enfranchised, constitutional, official.

Prescriptive, presumptive, absolute, indefeasible, unalienable, inalienable, imprescriptible, inviolable, unimpeachable, unchallenged, sacred, sacrosanct.

Condign, merited, deserved.

Allowable, permissible, lawful, legitimate, legal, legalized (693), proper, square, equitable, unexceptionable, reasonable (922), right, correct, meet, fitting (926).

Adverbs: Duly, by right, by divine right, *ex officio, Dei gratia, de jure.*

925 UNDUENESS

Substantives: unlawfulness, impropriety, unfitness, illegality (964).

Falseness, spuriousness, emptiness of invalidity of title, illegitimacy.

Loss of right, forfeiture, disfranchisement.

Usurpation, violation, breach, encroachment, stretch, imposition, relaxation.

Verbs: Not to be due, etc., to; to be undue, etc.

To infringe, encroach, violate, do violence to; to stretch or strain a point; to trench on, usurp.

To disfranchise, disentitle, disfrock, unfrock; to disqualify, invalidate, relax.

To misbecome, misbehave (945).

Adjectives: Undue, unlawful, illicit, unconstitutional.

Unauthorized, unwarranted, unsanctioned, unofficial, unjustified, unprivileged, illegitimate, bastard, spurious, supposititious, false, usurped, unchartered, unfulfilled, unauthorized.

Unentitled, disentitled, unqualified underprivileged; difranchised, forfeit.

Undeserved, unmerited, unearned.

Improper, unmeet, unbecoming, unfit, misbecoming, unseemly, preposterous.

Phrases: Not the thing; out of the question; not to be thought of; out of court.

926 DUTY

Substantives: what ought to be done; moral obligation, accountableness, accountability, liability, onus, responsibility, bounden duty; dueness (924).

Allegiance, fealty, tie, office, function, province, post, engagement (768).

Morality, morals, conscience,

accountableness, conscientiousness; the Decalogue, the Ten Commandments.

Dueness, propriety, fitness, decency, seemliness, decorum.

Observance, fulfilment, discharge, performance, acquittal, satisfaction, redemption, good behaviour.

Science of morals, ethics, deontology; moral or ethical philosophy, casuistry.

Phrases: The thing; the proper thing; a case of conscience; the still small voice.

Verbs: To be the duty of, to be due to, to be up to; ought to be; to be incumbent on, to behove, befit, become, beseem, belong to, pertain to, devolve on, to be on one's head; to be, or stand, or lie under and obligation; to have to answer for, to be accountable for, to owe it to oneself, to be in duty bound, to be committed to, to be on one's good behaviour.

To impose a duty or obligation; to enjoin, require, exact, bind, pin down, saddle with, prescribe, assign, call upon, look to, oblige.

To do one's duty, to enter upon a duty; to perform, observe, fulfil, discharge, adhere to; acquit oneself of an obligation.

Phrases: To be at one's post; to redeem one's pledge; to toe the mark or line.

Adjectives: Dutiful, duteous, docile, obedient, compliant, tractable.

Obligatory, binding, imperative peremptory, mandatory, behoving, incumbent on, chargeable on, meet, due to.

Being under obligation, under obedience, obliged by, beholden to, bound by, tied by, saddled with, indebted to.

Amenable, liable, accountable, responsible, answerable.

Right, proper, fit, due, correct, seemly, fitting, befitting, decent, meet.

Moral, ethical, casuistical, conscientious.

Adverbs: Conscientiously, with a safe conscience; as in duty bound; on one's own responsibility.

927 DERELICTION OF DUTY

Substantives: guilt (947), sin (945), neglect, negligence, non-observance, failure, evasion, dead letter.

Verbs: To violate, break, break through, infringe, set at naught, slight, neglect, trample on, evade, contravene, disregard, renounce, repudiate, quit, forswear, fail, transgress.

Phrase: To wash one's hands of.

927A EXEMPTION

Substantives: freedom, irresponsibility, immunity, liberty, licence, release, exoneration, excuse, dispensation, absolution, franchise, renunciation, discharge.

Verbs: To be exempt, free, at liberty, released, excused, exonerated, absolved, etc.

To exempt, release, excuse, exonerate, absolve, acquit, free, set at liberty, discharge, set aside, let off, remit, pass over, spare, excuse, license, dispense with; to give dispensation.

Phrase: To stretch a point.

Adjectives: Exempt, free, released, at liberty, absolved, exonerated, excused, let off, discharged, licensed, acquitted, unencumbered, dispensed, scot-free, immune.

Irresponsible, unaccountable, unanswerable, unbound.

928 RESPECT

Substantives: deference, reverence, regard, consideration, attention, honour, esteem, estimation, distance, decorum, veneration, admiration.

Homage, fealty, obeisance, genuflexion, kneeling, salaam, kowtow, presenting arms (896), prostration, obsequiousness, devotion, worship (990).

Verbs: To respect, honour, reverence,

regard, defer to, pay respect or deference to, render honour to, look up to, esteem, revere, think much of, think highly of, venerate, hallow.

To pay homage to, bow to, take off one's hat to, kneel to, bend the knee to, present arms, fall down before, prostrate oneself.

To command or inspire respect; to awe, overawe, dazzle.

Phrases: To keep one's distance; to make way for; to observe due decorum.

Adjectives: Respecting, etc., respectful, considerate, polite, attentive, reverential, obsequious, ceremonious, bare-headed, cap in hand, on one's knees, prostrate.

Respected, esteemed, honoured, hallowed, venerable, emeritus.

Phrases: Saving your presence; begging your honour's pardon.

929 DISRESPECT

Substantives: irreverence, dishonour, disparagement, slight, neglect, disesteem, disestimation, superciliousness, contumely, indignity, insult, rudeness.

Ridicule (856), sarcasm, derision, scurrility, mockery, scoffing, sibilation.

A jeer, gibe, taunt, scoff, sneer (930), hiss, hoot, fling, flout.

Verbs: To treat with disrespect, etc., to disparage, dishonour, misprise, vilipend, slight, insult, affront, disregard, make light of, hold in, no esteem, esteem of no account, set at naught, speak slightingly of, set down, pass by, overlook, look down upon, despise (930).

To deride, scoff, sneer at, laugh at, ridicule (856), roast, guy, rag, mock, jeer, taunt, twit, flout, gibe, hiss, hoot, boo.

Phrases: To make game of; to point the finger at; to make a fool of; to turn into ridicule; to laugh to scorn; to turn one's back upon.

Adjectives: Disrespectful, slighting, disparaging (934), dishonouring, scornful (940), irreverent, supercilious, contumelious, scurrilous, deriding, derisive, derisory.

Unrespected, unworshipped, unregarded, disregarded, ignored.

Adverbs: Disrespectfully, cavalierly, etc.

930 CONTEMPT

Substantives: disdain, scorn, contumely, despisal, slight, sneer, spurn, sniff; a byword.

Scornfulness, disdainfulness, haughtiness, contemptuousness, superciliousness, derision (929).

The state of being despised, despisedness.

Verbs: To despise, contemn, scorn, disdain, scout, spurn, look down upon, disregard, slight, make light of, not mind, hold cheap, hold in contempt, pooh-pooh, sneeze at, sniff at, whistle at, hoot, flout, trample upon.

Phrases: Not to care a straw, fig, button, etc., for (643); to turn up one's nose at; to shrug one's shoulders; to snap one's fingers at; to take no account of; to laugh to scorn; to make light of; to tread or trample under foot; to set at naught; to point the finger of scorn at.

Adjectives: Contemptuous, disdainful, scornful, contumelious, cavalier, derisive, supercilious, toplofty, upstage, sniffy, sardonic.

Contemptible, despicable, poor, paltry (643), downtrodden, unenvied.

Interjections: A fig for! hoots! bah! pshaw! pish! shucks! pooh-pooh! fiddlestick! fiddle-de-dee! tush! tut!

931 APPROBATION

Substantives: approval, approvement, endorsement, sanction, esteem, admiration, estimation, good opinion, appreciation, regard, account, popularity, kudos.

Commendation, praise, laud, laudation, advocacy, good word; meed or tribute of praise, encomium, eulogium, eulogy, *éloge,* panegyric, puff, blurb, homage.

Applause, plaudit, cheer, clap, clapping, clapping of hands, acclamation; paean, benediction, blessing, benison, hosanna; claque.

Phrases: A peal, shout, or chorus of applause; golden opinions; *succès d'estime.*

Verbs: To approve, think well or highly of, esteem, appreciate, value, prize, admire, countenance, endorse.

To commend, speak well of, recommend, advocate, praise, laud, belaud, compliment, bepraise, clap, clap hands, applaud, cheer, panegyrize, celebrate, eulogize, cry up, root for, crack up, write up, extol, glorify, magnify, puff, boom, boost, exalt, swell, bless, give a blessing to.

To deserve praise, etc., to be praised, etc.

Phrases: To set great store by; to sing the praises of; to extol to the skies; to applaud to the echo; to stick up for; to say a good word for; to pat on the back.

To redound to the honour or praise of; to do credit to.

To win golden opinions; to be in high favour; to bring down the house.

Adjectives: Approving, etc., commendatory, complimentary, benedictory, laudatory, panegyrical eulogistic, encomiastic.

Approved, praised, uncensured, unimpeached, admired, popular, deserving or worthy of praise, praiseworthy, commendable, estimable, plausible, meritorious.

Phrases: Lavish of praise; lost in admiration.

Interjections: Well done! good man! stout fellow! good show! atta-boy! bravo! bravissimo! *euge!* that's the stuff! hear, hear!

932 DISAPPROBATION

Substantives: disapproval, dislike (867), blame, censure, reprobation, obloquy, dispraise, contumely, odium, disesteem, depreciation, detraction (934), condemnation, ostracism.

Reprobation, exprobration, insinuation, innuendo, animadversion, reflection, stricture, objection, exception, criticism, critique, correction, discommendation.

Satire, sneer, fling, gibe, skit, squib, quip, taunt, sarcasm, lampoon, cavil, pasquinade, recrimination, castigation.

Remonstrance, reprehension, reproof, admonition, expostulation, reproach, rebuke, reprimand, talking-to, telling-off.

Evil speaking, hard words, foul language, personalities, ribaldry, Billingsgate, unparliamentary language.

Upbraiding, abuse, invective, vituperation, scolding, wigging, dressing-down, objurgation, jaw, railing, jobation, nagging, reviling, contumely, execration (908).

A set-down, trimming, rating, slap, snub, frown, scowl, black look.

A lecture, curtain lecture, diatribe, jeremiad, tirade, philippic; clamour, outcry, hue and cry, hiss, hissing, sibilation cat-call.

Phrases: A rap on the knuckles; a slap in the face; a left-handed compliment.

Verbs: To disapprove, dislike (867), dispraise, find fault with, criticize, glance at, insinuate, cut up, carp at, cavil, point at, peck at, nibble at, object to, take exception to, animadvert upon, protest against, frown upon, bar.

To disparage, depreciate, deprecate, crab, knock, traduce, smear, speak ill of, decry, vilify, vilipend, defame, detract (934), revile, satirize, sneer,

347

gibe, lampoon, inveigh against, write down, scalp.

To blame; to lay or cast blame upon, reflect upon, cast a slur upon, censure, pass censure on, impugn, show up, denounce, censure, brand, stigmatize, reprobate, improbate.

To reprehend, reprimand, admonish, remonstrate, expostulate, reprove, pull up, take up, set down, snub, twit, taunt, reproach, load with reproaches, rebuke, come down upon, sit on, pitch into, get on to, tell off, tick off.

To chide, scold, wig, rate, objurgate, upbraid, vituperate, recriminate, anathematize, abuse, call names, exclaim against, jaw, mob, trounce, trim, rail at, nag, nag at, bark at, blackguard, revile, ballyrag, rag, natter, blow up, roast, lecture; castigate, chastise, correct, lash, flay; to fulminate against, fall foul of.

To cry out against, cry down, run down, clamour, hiss, hoot; to accuse (938), to find guilty, ostracize, blacklist, blackball.

To scandalize, shock, revolt, incur blame, excite disapprobation.

Phrases: To set one's face against; to shake the head at; to take a poor or dim view of; to view with dark or jaundiced eyes; to pick holes in; to give a thing the bird; to damn with faint praise; to pluck a crow with; to have a fling at; to read a lecture; to put on the carpet (or mat); to take to task; to bring to book; to haul over the coals; to tear one off a strip; to shoot down in flames; to pull to pieces; to cut up; to cast in one's teeth; to abuse like a pickpocket; to speak or look daggers; to rail in good set terms; to give it one hot; to throw mud; to give a person the rough side of one's tongue.

To forfeit the good opinion of; to catch it; to be under a cloud; to carry the can; to stand corrected.

Adjectives: Disapproving, disparaging, etc., condemnatory, damnatory, denunciatory, reproachful, abusive, objurgatory, clamorous, vituperative, dyslogistic.

Censorious, critical, carping, satirical, sarcastic, sardonic, cynical, dry, hypercritical, captious; sharp, cutting, mordant, biting, withering, trenchant, caustic, severe, scathing; squeamish, fastidious, strait-laced (868).

Disapproved, chid, unapproved, blown upon, unblest, unlamented, unbewailed.

Blameworthy, uncommendable, exceptionable (649, 945).

Phrases: Hard upon one; weighed in the balance and found wanting; not to be thought of.

Interjections: Bad show! shame!

933 FLATTERY

Substantives: adulation, sycophancy, blandishment, cajolery, fawning, wheedling, coaxing, flunkeyism, toadeating, toadyism, tuft-hunting, back-scratching, blandiloquence, schmalz.

Incense, honeyed words, flummery, soft sawder, soft soap, butter, applesauce, blarney, malarkey; mouth-honour, lip-service.

Verbs: To flatter, wheedle, cajole, fawn upon, coax (615), humour, gloze, butter, toady, sugar, bespatter, beslaver, earwig, jolly, flannel, truckle to, pander to, court, pay court to.

Phrases: To curry favour with; to lay it on thick; to lay it on with a trowel; to ingratiate oneself with; to fool to the top of one's bent.

Adjectives: Flattering, adulatory, mealy-mouthed, smooth, honeyed, candied, soapy, oily, unctuous, fairspoken, plausible, servile, sycophantic, fulsome; courtier-like.

934 DETRACTION

Substantives: obloquy, scurrility, scandal, vilification, smear, defamation, aspersion, traducement, slander, calumny, back-biting, criticism, slating, personality, evil-speaking, disparagement, depreciation (932).

Libel, lampoon, skit, squib, sarcasm.

Verbs: To detract, criticize, asperse, depreciate, derogate, disparage, cheapen, blow upon, bespatter, blacken, denigrate, defame, brand, malign, decry, vilify, vilipend, backbite, libel, slate, lampoon, traduce, slander, calumniate, run down, write down.

Phrases: To speak ill of one behind one's back; to damn with faint praise; to sell oneself short.

Adjectives: Detracting, disparaging, libellous, scurrilous, abusive, cynical (932), foul-tongued, foul-mouthed, slanderous, defamatory, calumnious, calumniatory.

935 FLATTERER
Substantives: adulator, eulogist, encomiast, white-washer, toady, sycophant, toad-eater, *prôneur,* touter, booster, *claqueur,* spaniel, back-scratcher, flunkey, lick-spittle, pickthank, earwig, tuft-hunter, hanger-on, courtier, parasite, doer of dirty work, *âme damnée, Graeculus esuriens.*

936 DETRACTOR
Substantives: disapprover, critics, censor, caviller, carper, knocker, *frondeur,* defamer, backbiter, slanderer, traducer, libeller, calumniator, lampooner, satirist, candid friend, Thersites.

937 VINDICATION
Substantives: justification, exoneration, exculpation, acquittal, whitewashing.

Extenuation, palliation, mitigation, softening; extenuating circumstances.

Plea, excuse, apology, defence, gloss, varnish, salvo (617).

Vindicator, apologist, justifier, defender.

Verbs: To vindicate, justify, warrant, exculpate, acquit, clear, set right, exonerate, disculpate, whitewash.

To extenuate, palliate, excuse, soften, apologize, varnish, slur, gloze, gloss over, bolster up.

To plead, advocate, defend, stand up for, stick up for, speak for, make good, bear out, say in defence, contend for.

Phrases: To put in a good word for; to plead the cause of; to put a good face upon; to keep in countenance; to make allowance for.

Adjectives: Vindicatory, vindicative, palliative, exculpatory; vindicating, etc.

Excusable, defensible, pardonable, venial, specious, plausible, justifiable, warrantable.

Phrases: *'Honi soit qui mal y pense'; qui s'excuse s'accuse.*

938 ACCUSATION
Substantives: charge, imputation, inculpation, exprobration, delation, crimination, recrimination, invective, jeremiad (932).

Denunciation, denouncement, challenge, indictment, libel, delation, citation, arraignment, impeachment, appeachment, bill of indictment, true bill, condemnation (971), scandal (934), *scandalum magnatum.*

Accuser, prosecutor, plaintiff, pursuer, informer, appellant, complainant.

Accused, defendant, prisoner, panel, respondent.

Phrases: The gravamen of a charge; *argumentum ad hominem.*

Verbs: To accuse, charge, tax, impute, twit, taunt with, slur, reproach, brand with, stigmatize, criminate, incriminate, inculpate (932), implicate, saddle with.

To inform against; to indict, denounce, arraign, impeach, challenge, show up, pull up, cite, prosecute, summon.

Phrases: To lay to one's door; to lay to one's charge; bring home to; to call to account; to bring to book; to take to task; to trump up a charge; to brand with reproach.

Adjectives: Accusing, etc., accusatory, accusative, imputative, denunciatory, criminative, criminatory, incriminatory, accusable, imputable.

Indefensible, inexcusable, unpardonable, unjustifiable (945).

939 PROBITY

Substantives: integrity, uprightness, honesty, virtue (944), rectitude, faith, good faith, bona fides, fairness, honour, fair play, justice, principle, constancy, fidelity, incorruptibility.

Trustworthiness, trustiness, reliability, dependableness, grace, uncorruptedness, impartiality, equity, candour, veracity (545), straightforwardness, truth, equitableness, singleness of heart.

Conscientiousness, punctiliousness, nicety, scrupulosity, delicacy, sense of decency, strictness, punctuality.

Dignity, respectability, reputableness (873).

A man of honour, a gentleman, a man of his word, a sportsman, white man, trump, brick, *preux chevalier.*

Phrases: The court of honour; a fair field and no favour; 'a verray parfit gentil knight.'

Verbs: To be honourable, etc.; to keep one's word, to give and take, to deal honourably, squarely, impartially, fairly.

Phrases: To hit straight from the shoulder; to play the game.

Adjectives: Upright, honest, virtuous (944), honourable, fair, right, just, equitable, impartial, even-handed, square, constant, faithful, loyal, staunch, straight.

Trustworthy, trusty, reliable, dependable, tried, incorruptible, straightforward, ingenuous (703),

frank, open-hearted, candid.

Conscientious, tender-conscienced, high-principled, high-minded, high-toned, scrupulous, strict, nice, punctilious, correct, punctual, inviolable, inviolate, unviolated, unbroken, unbetrayed.

Chivalrous, gentlemanlike, respectable, unbought, unbribed, unstained, stainless, untarnished, unsullied, untainted, unperjured, innocent (946).

Phrases: Jealous of honour; as good as one's word; true to one's colours; *sans peur et sans reproche; integer vitae sceleris-que purus.*

Adverbs: Honourably, etc., bona fide; on the square; on the up and up.

940 IMPROBITY

Substantives: wickedness (945), bad faith, unfairness, infidelity, faithlessness, want of faith, dishonesty, disloyalty, falseness, falsity, one-sidedness, disingenuousness, shabbiness, littleness, meanness, caddishness, baseness, villainy, roguery, rascality, vileness, abjectness, turpitude, unreliability, untrustworthiness, insidiousness, knavery, knavishness, fraud (545), falsehood (544), shenanigans.

Disgrace, ignominy, infamy, tarnish, blot, stain, spot, slur, pollution, derogation, degradation (874).

Perfidy, perfidiousness, treason, high treason, perjury, apostasy (607), backsliding, breach of faith, defection, disloyalty, disaffection, foul play, sharp practice, graft, double-dealing, betrayal, treacherousness, treachery.

Phrases: The kiss of Judas; divided allegiance; Punic faith.

Verbs: To be of bad faith, dishonest, etc.; to play false, break one's word or faith, betray, forswear, shuffle (545).

To disgrace oneself, derogate, stoop, demean oneself, lose caste, dishonour oneself, sneak, crawl, grovel.

Phrases: To seal one's infamy; to sell oneself; to go over to the enemy.

Adjectives: Dishonest, unfair, one-sided, fraudulent (545), bent, knavish, wicked (945), false, faithless, unfaithful, foul, disingenuous, trothless, trustless, untrustworthy, unreliable, slippery, double-faced, double-tongued, crooked, tortuous, unscrupulous, insidious, treacherous, perfidious, false-hearted, perjured, rascally.

Base, vile, grovelling, dirty, scurvy, scabby, low, low-down, abject, shabby, caddish, mean, paltry, pitiful, inglorious, scrubby, beggarly, putrid, unworthy, disgraceful, dishonourable, derogatory, low-thoughted, disreputable, unhandsome, unbecoming (925), unbefitting, ungentlemanly, unmanly, unwomanly, undignified, base-minded, recreant, low-minded, blackguard, pettifogging, underhand, underhanded, unsportsmanlike.

Phrases: Lost to shame; dead to honour.

Adverbs: Dishonestly, etc., *mala fide,* on the crook.

941 KNAVE

Substantives: bad man (949), rogue, rascal, scoundrel, villain, spiv, sharper, shyster, blackleg, scab, trimmer, time-server, timist, turncoat, badmash, Vicar of Bray, Judas (607).

Apostate, renegade, pervert, black sheep, traitor, arch-traitor, quisling, fifth columnist, deviationist, betrayer, recreant, miscreant, cullion, outcast, mean wretch, slubberdegullion, snake in the grass, wolf in sheep's clothing.

942 UNSELFISHNESS

Substantives: selflessness, disinterestedness, generosity, high-mindedness, nobleness, elevation, liberality, greatness, loftiness, exaltation, magnanimity, chivalry, chivalrous spirit, heroism, sublimity, altruism, self-forgetfulness, unworldliness.

Self-denial, self-abnegation, self-sacrifice, self-restraint, self-control, devotion, stoicism.

Phrases: To put oneself in the background, in the place of others; to do as one would be done by.

Adjectives: Unselfish, selfless, self-forgetful, handsome, generous, liberal, noble, princely, great, high, high-minded, elevated, lofty, exalted, spirited, stoical, self-denying, self-sacrificing, self-devoted, magnanimous, chivalrous, heroic, sublime, unworldly.

Unbought, unbribed, pure, uncorrupted, incorruptible.

Adverb: *En prince.*

943 SELFISHNESS

Substantives: egotism, egoism, self-regard, self-love, self-indulgence, worldliness, worldly-mindedness, earthly-mindedness, self-interest, opportunism.

Illiberality, meanness, baseness.

A time-server, tuft-hunter, fortune-hunter, gold-digger, jobber, worldling, self-seeker, opportunist, hog, road-hog.

Phrase: A dog in the manger.

Verbs: To be selfish, etc., to indulge oneself, coddle oneself.

Phrases: To look after one's own interest; to take care of number one; to have an eye for the main chance.

Adjectives: Selfish, egotistical, egoistical, self-indulgent, apolaustic, self-regarding, self-centred, illiberal, self-seeking, mercenary, venal, mean, ungenerous, interested.

Worldly, earthly, mundane, time-serving, worldly-minded.

Phrases: To serve one's private ends; from interested motives; charity begins at home; I'm all right, Jack.

944 VIRTUE

Substantives: virtuousness, goodness, righteousness, morals, morality (926), rectitude, correctness, dutifulness, conscientiousness, integrity, probity

351

(939), uprightness, nobleness, nobility; innocence (946).

Merit, worth, worthiness, desert, excellence, credit, self-control, self-conquest, self-government, self-respect.

Well-doing, good actions, good behaviour, a well-spent life.

Verbs: To be virtuous, etc.; to act well; to do, fulfil, perform, or discharge one's duty, to acquit oneself well, to practise virtue; to command or master one's passions (926).

Phrases: To have one's heart in the right place; to keep in the right path; to fight the good fight; to set an example; to be on one's good behaviour.

Adjectives: Virtuous, good, innocent (946), meritorious, deserving, worthy, correct, dutiful, duteous (926), moral, ethical, righteous, right-minded, (939), laudable, well-intentioned, creditable, commendable, praiseworthy, excellent, admirable, sterling, pure, noble, well-conducted, well-behaved.

Exemplary, matchless, peerless, saintly, saint-like, heaven-born, angelic, seraphic, godlike.

Phrase: *Mens sibi conscia recti.*

Adverb: Virtuously, etc.

945 VICE

Substantives: evildoing, wrongdoing, wickedness, sin, iniquity, unrighteousness, demerit, unworthiness, worthlessness, badness.

Immorality, impropriety, indecorum, laxity, looseness of morals, want of principle, obliquity, backsliding, recidivism, gracelessness, infamy, demoralization, pravity, depravity, depravation, obduracy, hardness of heart, brutality (907), corruption, pollution, dissoluteness, debauchery, grossness, baseness, knavery, roguery, rascality, villainy (940), profligacy, abandonment, flagrancy, atrocity, devilry (or deviltry), criminality, guilt (947).

Infirmity, weakness, feebleness, frailty, imperfection, error, weak side or point, blind side, foible, failing, failure, defect, deficiency, indiscretion, peccability.

Phrases: The cloven hoof; the old Adam; the lowest dregs of vice; a sink of iniquity; the primrose path.

Verbs: To be vicious, etc.; to sin, commit sin, do amiss, misdo, err, transgress, go astray, misdemean or misconduct oneself, misbehave; to fall, lapse, slip, trip, offend, trespass.

To render vicious, etc., to demoralize, corrupt, seduce, debauch, debase, vitiate.

Phrases: To deviate from the line of duty or from the paths of virtue, rectitude, etc.; to blot one's copybook; to hug a sin or fault; to sow one's wild oats.

Adjectives: Vicious, bad, sinful, wicked, evil, evil-minded, immoral, iniquitous, unprincipled, demoralized, unconscionable, worthless, unworthy, good for nothing, graceless, heartless, virtueless, undutiful, unrighteous, unmoral, amoral, guilty (947).

Wrong, culpable, naughty, incorrect, indictable, criminal, dissolute, debauched, disorderly, raffish, corrupt, profligate, depraved, degenerate, abandoned, graceless, shameless, recreant, villainous, sunk, lost, obdurate, reprobate, incorrigible, irreclaimable, ill-conditioned.

Weak, frail, lax, infirm, spineless, invertebrate, imperfect, indiscreet, erring, transgressing, sinning, etc., peccable, peccant.

Blamable, reprehensible, blameworthy, uncommendable, discreditable, disreputable, shady, exceptionable.

Indecorous, unseemly, improper, sinister, base, ignoble, scurvy, foul, gross, vile, black, felonious, nefarious, scandalous, infamous, villainous, heinous, grave, flagrant, flagitious, atrocious, satanic, satanical, diabolic, diabolical, hellish, infernal, stygian, fiendlike, fiendish, devilish, miscreated, misbegotten, hell-born, demoniacal.

Unpardonable, unforgivable, indefensible, inexcusable, irremissible, inexpiable.

Phrases: Past praying for; of the deepest dye; not having a word to say for oneself; weighed in the balance and found wanting; *in flagrante delicto.*

Adverbs: Wrongly, etc.; without excuse, too bad.

946 INNOCENCE
Substantives: guiltlessness, harmlessness, innocuousness, incorruption, impeccability, inerrability, blamelessness, sinlessness.

A newborn babe, lamb, dove.

Phrases: Clean hands; a clear conscience.

Verbs: To be innocent, etc.

Adjectives: Innocent, guiltless, not guilty, faultless, sinless, clear, spotless, stainless, immaculate, unspotted, innocuous, unblemished, untarnished, unsullied, undefiled.

Inculpable, unblamed, blameless, unblamable, clean-handed, irreproachable, unreproached, unimpeachable, unimpeached, unexceptionable, inerrable, unerring.

Harmless, inoffensive, unoffending, dovelike, lamblike, pure, uncorrupted, undefiled, undepraved, undebauched, chaste, unhardened, unsophisticated, unreproved.

Phrases: Innocent as an unborn babe; in the clear; above suspicion; more sinned against than sinning.

Adverbs: Innocently, etc.

947 GUILT
Substantives: sin, guiltiness, culpability, criminality, criminousness, sinfulness.

Misconduct, misbehaviour, misdoing, malpractice, malefaction, malfeasance, misprision, dereliction, *corpus delicti.*

Indiscretion, peccadillo, lapse, slip, trip, *faux pas,* fault, error, flaw, blot, omission, failure.

Misdeed, offence, trespass, transgression, misdemeanour, delinquency, felony, sin, crime, enormity, atrocity.

Science of crime, criminology.

Phrases: Besetting sin; deviation from rectitude; a deed without a name.

948 GOOD MAN
Substantives: trump, brick, worthy, example, pattern, mirror, model, paragon, phoenix (650), superman, hero, demigod, seraph, angel, saint (987).

A good fellow, good sort, sportsman, white man.

Phrases: One of the best; one in a million; the salt of the earth.

949 BAD MAN
Substantives: wrong-doer, evildoer, culprit, delinquent, criminal, recidivist, malefactor, outlaw, felon, convict, lag, outcast, sinner (988).

Knave, rogue, rascal, scoundrel, spiv, scamp, scapegrace, black sheep, scallywag, spalpeen, varlet, *vaurien,* blighter, rotter, good-for-nothing, twerp, heel, jerk, creep, goon, son of a gun, dastard, blackguard, sweep, loose fish, bad egg, bad lot, hard case, lost soul, vagabond, bum, *mauvais sujet,* cur, sad dog, rip, rascallion, rapscallion, slubberdegullion, cullion, roisterer.

Mohock, rowdy, hooligan, larrikin, teddy boy, apache, thug, reprobate, *roué,* recreant, jail-bird, crook, tough, rough, roughneck, gangster, gunman, hoodlum, yegg, villain, ruffian, miscreant, caitiff, wretch, *âme damnée,* castaway, monster, Jonathan Wilde, Jack Sheppard, Lazarillo de Tormes, Scapin (941).

Cur, dog, hound, skunk, swine, rat,

viper, serpent, cockatrice, basilisk, reptile, urchin, tiger, imp, demon, devil, devil incarnate, Mephistopheles (978), hellhound, son of Belial, cut-throat, *particeps criminis,* incendiary.

Bad woman, hellcat, hellhag, bitch, witch, hag, harridan, trollop, jade, drab, hussy, minx, Jezebel.

Riff-raff, rabble, ragtag and bobtail, *canaille.*

Phrases: A fiend in human shape; scum of the earh; poor white trash.

Interjection: Sirrah!

950 PENITENCE
Substantives: contrition, compunction, regret (833), repentance, remorse.

Self-reproach, self-reproof, self-accusation, self-condemnation.

Confession, acknowledgment, shrift, apology, recantation (607).

A penitent, prodigal, Magdalen.

Phrases: The stool of repentance; the cutty-stool; sackcloth and ashes; qualms or prickings of conscience; a sadder and a wiser man.

Verbs: To repent, regret, rue, repine, deplore, be sorry for.

To confess (529), acknowledge, apologize, shrive oneself, humble oneself, reclaim, turn from sin.

Phrases: To have a weight on one's mind; to plead guilty; to sing small; to cry *peccavi*; to eat humble pie; to turn over a new leaf; to stand in a white sheet.

Adjectives: Penitent, repentant, contrite, repenting, remorseful, regretful, sorry, compunctious, self-reproachful, self-accusing, self-convicted, conscience-stricken, conscience-smitten.

Not hardened, unhardened, reclaimed.

Adverb: *Meâ culpâ.*

951 IMPENITENCE
Substantives: obduracy, recusance, irrepentance, hardness of heart, a seared conscience, induration.

Verbs: To be impenitent, etc.; to steel or harden the heart.

Phrases: To make no sign; to die game.

Adjectives: Impenitent, uncontrite, obdurate, hard, callous, unfeeling, hardened, seared, recusant, relentless, unrepentant, graceless, shiftless, lost, uncorrigible, irreclaimable, irredeemable, unatoned, unreclaimed, unreformed, unrepented.

952 ATONEMENT
Substantives: reparation, compromise, composition, compensation (30), quittance, quits; propitiation, expiation, redemption, conciliation.

Amends, *amende honorable,* apology, satisfaction, peace-offering, olive branch, sin-offering, scapegoat, sacrifice, burnt-offering.

Penance, fasting, maceration, flagellation, sackcloth and ashes, white sheet, lustration, purgation, purgatory.

Verbs: To atone, expiate, propitiate, make amends, redeem, make good, repair, ransom, absolve, do penance, apologize, purge, shrive, give satisfaction.

Phrases: To purge one's offence; to pay the forfeit or penalty.

Adjectives: Propitiatory, piacular, expiatory, expiational.

953 TEMPERANCE
Substantives: moderation, forbearance, abnegation, self-denial, self-conquest, self-control, self-command, self-discipline, sobriety, frugality, vegetarianism.

Abstinence, abstemiousness, teetotalism, prohibition, asceticism (955), gymnosophy, system of Pythagoras.

An abstainer, ascetic, gymnosophist, vegetarian, teetotaller, Pythagorean.

Phrases: The simple life; the blue ribbon.

Verbs: To be temperate, etc.; to abstain, forbear, refrain, deny oneself, spare.
Phrases: To sign the pledge; to go on the water wagon.
Adjectives: Temperate, moderate, sober, frugal, sparing, abstemious, abstinent, Pythagorean, vegetarian, teetotal, dry.

954 INTEMPERANCE

Substantives: excess, immoderation, unrestraint; epicurism, epicureanism, hedonism, sensuality, luxury, luxuriousness, animalism, carnality, effeminacy; the lap of pleasure or luxury; indulgence, self-indulgence, voluptuousness; drunkenness (959).

Dissipation, licentiousness, debauchery, dissolutenesss, crapulence, brutishness.

Revels, revelry, carousal, orgy, spree, jag, toot, drinking bout, debauch, jollification, saturnalia.

A sensualist, epicure, epicurean, voluptuary, rake, rip, *roué*, sybarite, drug addict, dope fiend, hophead.
Phrases: The Circean cup; a fast life; wine, women, and song.
Verbs: To be intemperate, sensual, etc.

To indulge, exceed, revel, dissipate; give a loose to indulgence, live hard.

To debauch, pander to, sensualize, animalize, brutalize.
Phrases: To wallow in voluptuousness, luxury, etc.; to plunge into dissipation; to paint the town red; to live on the fat of the land; to sow one's wild oats.
Adjectives: Intemperate, sensual, pampered, self-indulgent, fleshly, inabstinent, licentious, wild, dissolute, dissipated, fast, rakish, debauched, brutish, crapulous, hedonistic, epicurean, sybaritical, Sardanapalian, voluptuous, apolaustic, orgiastic, swinish, piggish, hoggish; indulged, pampered.

955 ASCETICISM

Substantives: austerity, puritanism, mortification, maceration, sackcloth and ashes, flagellation, martyrdom, yoga.

An ascetic, anchoret, yogi, martyr; a recluse, hermit (893); puritan, Cynic.
Adjectives: Ascetic, ascetical, austere, puritanical.

956 FASTING

Substantives: fast, spare diet, meagre diet, Lent, Quadragesima, a lenten entertainment, famishment, starvation, banian day, Ramadan.
Phrases: A Barmecide feast; a hunger strike; short commons.
Verbs: To fast, starve, clem, famish.
Phrases: To dine with Duke Humphrey; to perish with hunger.
Adjectives: Fasting, etc., unfed, famished, starved; lenten, Quadragesimal.

957 GLUTTONY

Substantives: epicurism, greediness, good cheer, high living, edacity, voracity, gulosity, crapulence, hoggishness, piggishness.

Gastronomy; feast, banquet, good cheer, blow-out.

A glutton, epicure, *bon vivant,* cormorant, gourmand, gourmet, belly-god, pig, hog, Apicius, gastronome, gastronomer, gastronomist.
Verbs: To gormandize, gorge, cram, stuff, guzzle, bolt, devour, gobble up, pamper.
Phrases: To eat out of house and home; to have the stomach of an ostrich; to play a good knife and fork.
Adjectives: Gluttonous, greedy, gormandizing, edacious, voracious, crapulent, swinish, piggish, hoggish, pampered, overfed; gastronomical.

958 SOBRIETY

Substantives: teetotalism, total abstinence, temperance (953).

355

Compulsory sobriety, prohibition.

A water-drinker, teetotaller, abstainer, total abstainer, blue-ribbonite, Rechabite, Band of Hope; prohibitionist.

Verbs: To abstain, to take the pledge.

Adjectives: Sober, abstemious, teetotal.

Phrases: Sober as a judge; on the water wagon.

959 DRUNKENNESS

Substantives: insobriety, ebriety, inebriety, inebriation, intoxication, ebriosity, bibacity, drinking, toping, tippling, sottishness, tipsiness, bacchanals, compotation, intemperance (954); dipsomania, alcoholism, delirium tremens, DT

A drunkard, sot, toper, tippler, hard drinker, winebag, winebibber, dramdrinker, soak, soaker, sponge, tun, tosspot, pub-crawler, reveller, carouser, Bacchanal, Bacchanalian, Bacchant, a devotee to Bacchus; a dipsomaniac.

Drink, hard drinks, intoxicant, alcohol, liquor, spirits, booze, blue ruin, grog, cocktail, highball, dram, peg, stirrup-cup, doch-an-doris.

Phrases: The flowing bowl; one for the road.

Verbs: To drink, tipple, tope, booze; to guzzle, swill, soak, swig, get or be drunk, etc.; to take to drinking, drink hard, drink deep.

To inebriate, intoxiate, fuddle.

Phrases: To liquor up; to wet one's whistle; to crack a bottle; to have a bucket; to look on the wine when it is red; to take a drop too much; to drink like a fish; to splice the main-brace; to crook or lift the elbow.

Adjectives: Drunk, drunken, tipsy, intoxicated, in liquor, inebriated, fuddled, mellow, boozy, high, fou, boiled, tiddly, stinko, blotto, lit up, groggy, top-heavy, pot-valiant, glorious, overcome, overtaken, elevated, whiffled, sozzled, screwed, corned, raddled, sewed up, lushy, squiffy, muddled, oiled, canned, muzzy, maudlin, dead-drunk, disguised, tight, beery.

Bibacious, bibulous, sottish, Bacchanal, Bacchanalian.

Phrases: In one's cups; *inter pocula*; the worse for liquor; half-seas-over; three sheets in the wind; under the table; drunk as a piper, as a fiddle, as a lord, as an owl, as David's sow; stewed to the eyebrows; pickled to the gills; one over the eight.

Interjections: Cheers! here's to you! down the hatch! mud in your eye! skin off your nose! *prosit! slainte! skoal!*

960 PURITY

Substantives: modesty, decency, decorum, delicacy, continence, chastity, honesty, pudency, virtue, virginity.

A virgin, maiden, maid, vestal; Joseph, Hippolytus, Lucrece.

Phrase: The white flower of a blameless life.

Adjectives: Pure, immaculate, undefiled, modest, delicate, decent, decorous.

Chaste, continent, honest, virtuous; Platonic.

961 IMPURITY

Substantives: immodesty, grossness, coarseness, indelicacy, impropriety, impudicity, indecency, obscenity, obsceneness, ribaldry, smut, smuttiness, bawdiness, bawdry, *double entendre*, equivoque, pornography.

Concupiscence, lust, carnality, flesh, salacity, lewdness, prurience, lechery, lasciviousness, voluptuousness, lubricity.

Incontinence, intrigue, gallantry, debauchery, libertinism, libertinage, fornication, liaison, wenching, whoring, whoredom, concubinage, hetaerism.

Seduction, defloration, violation, rape, adultery, defilement, *crim. con.,* incest, harlotry, stupration, procuration, white-slave traffic.

A seraglio, harem, brothel, bagnio, stew, bawdy-house, disorderly house, house of ill fame, red lamp district, Yoshiwara.

Phrases: The morals of the farmyard; the oldest profession.

Verbs: To intrigue, debauch, defile, seduce, abuse, violate, force, rape, ravish, deflower, ruin, prostitute, procure.

Adjectives: Impure, immodest, indecorous, indelicate, unclean, unmentionable, unseemly, improper, suggestive, indecent, loose, coarse, gross, broad, equivocal, risky, *risqué,* high-seasoned, nasty, smutty, scabrous, ribald, obscene, bawdy, lewd, pornographic, Rabelaisian, Aristophanic.

Concupiscent, prurient, lickerish, rampant, carnal, fleshy, sensual, lustful, lascivious, lecherous, libidinous, goatish, erotic, ruttish, salacious.

Unchaste, light, wanton, debauched, dissolute, carnal-minded, licentious, frail, riggish, incontinent, meretricious, rakish, gallant, dissipated, adulterous, incestous, bestial.

Phrases: On the streets; of easy virtue; no better than she should be.

Near the knuckle; not for ears polite; four-letter words.

962 A LIBERTINE

Substantives: voluptuary, man of pleasure, sensualist (954), rip, rake, *roué,* debauchee, loose fish, intriguant, gallant, seducer, fornicator, lecher, satyr, whoremonger, *paillard,* adulterer, a gay deceiver, Lothario, Don Juan, Bluebeard.

A prostitute, courtesan, tart, call-girl, strumpet, harlot, whore, punk, *fille de joie, cocotte, lorette,* woman of the town, streetwalker, pick-up, piece, the frail sisterhood, the *demi-monde,* soiled dove, demirep, wench, trollop, trull, baggage, hussy, drab, jade, quean, slut, harridan, an unfortunate, Jezebel, Messalina, Delilah, Thais, Aspasia, Phryne, Lais.

Concubine, odalisque, mistress, doxy, kept woman, *petite amie,* hetaera.

Pimp, pander, ponce, *souteneur,* bawd, procuress.

963 LEGALITY

Substantives: legitimateness, legitimacy, justice (922).

Law, legislature, code, constitution, pandect, enactment, edict, statute, charter, rule, order, ordinance, injunction, institution, precept, regulation, by-law, decree, firman, bull, ukase, decretal.

Legal process, form, formula, formality, rite.

Science of law, jurisprudence, legislation, codification.

Equity, common law, *lex non scripta,* unwritten law, law of nations, international law, *jus gentium,* civil law, canon law, statute law, *lex mercatoria,* ecclesiastical law.

Phrase: The arm of the law.

Verbs: To legalize, enact, ordain, enjoin, prescribe, order, decree (741); to pass a law, issue an edict or decree; to legislate, codify.

Adjectives: Legal, lawful, according to law, legitimate, constitutional, chartered, vested.

Legislative, statutable, statutory.

Adverbs: Legally, etc.

Phrases: In the eye of the law; *de jure.*

964 ILLEGALITY

Substantives: lawlessness, arbitrariness, antinomy, violence, brute force, despotism, outlawry.

Mob law, lynch law, club law, martial law.

Camorra, Ku Klux Klan, Judge Lynch.

357

Informality, unlawfulness, illegitimacy, bastardy, the baton or bar sinister.

Smuggling, poaching, bootlegging; black market, grey market.

Verbs: To smuggle, run, poach.

To invalidate, annual, illegalize, abrogate, void, nullify, quash.

Phrases: To take the law into one's own hands; to set the law at defiance; to drive a coach and six through the law.

Adjectives: Illegal, unlawful, illicit, illegitimate, injudicial, unofficial, lawless, unauthorized, unchartered, unconstitutional, informal, contraband, hot.

Arbitrary, extrajudicial, despotic, autocratic, irresponsible, unanswerable, unaccountable.

Adverbs: Illegally, with a high hand.

965 JURISDICTION

Substantives: judicature, soc (or soke), administration of justice.

Inquisition, inquest, coroner's inquest.

The executive, municipality, corporation, magistracy, police, police force, constabulary, posse, *gendarmerie.*

Lord lieutenant, sheriff, sheriff-substitute, deputy, officer, constable, policeman, state trooper, traffic warden, bailiff, tipstaff, bum-bailiff, catchpoll, beadle; *gendarme,* lictor, macebearer.

Adjectives: Juridical, judicial, forensic, municipal, executive, administrative, inquisitorial, causidical.

Phrases: *Coram judice; ex cathedra.*

966 TRIBUNAL

Substantives: court, guild, board, bench, judicatory, senate-house, court of law, court of justice, criminal court, police-court, Court of Chancery, of King's Bench; Probate, Divorce, Admiralty Court, Judicial Committee of the Privy Council, US Supreme Court, durbar.

City hall, town hall, theatre, bar, dock, forum, hustings, drum-head, wool-sack, jury-box, witness-box.

Assize, sessions, quarter sessions, petty sessions, eyre, court-martial, ward-mote.

967 JUDGE

Substantives: justice, justiciar, justiciary, chancellor, magistrate, beak, recorder, common serjeant, stipendiary, coroner, arbiter, arbitrator, umpire, referee, jury, Justice of the Peace, JP, Lord Chancellor, Lord Chief Justice, Master of the Rolls.

Mullah, ulema, mufti, cadi (or kadi), kavass.

Prosecutor, plaintiff, accuser, appellant, pursuer.

Defendant, panel, prisoner, the accused.

Verbs: Judge, try, pass judgment, give verdict.

968 LAWYER

Substantives: the bar, advocate, counsellor, counsel, queen's or king's counsel, QC, KC, pleader, special pleader, conveyancer, bencher, proctor, civilian, barrister, barrister-at-law, jurist, jurisconsult, publicist, draughtsman, notary, notary public, scrivener, attorney, solicitor, legal adviser, writer to the signet, writer, marshal, pundit; pettifogger.

Phrases: The gentlemen of the long robe; the learned in the law; a limb of the law.

Verbs: To practise law, plead.

Phrases: To be called to the bar; to take silk.

969 LAWSUIT

Substantives: suit, action, case, cause, trial, litigation.

Denunciation, citation, arraignment, prosecution, indictment, impeachment, apprehension, arrest, committal, imprisonment (751).

Pleadings, writ, summons, subpoena, plea, bill, affidavit, libel; answer, counterclaim, demurrer, rebutter, rejoinder, surrebutter, surrejoinder.

Verdict, sentence, judgment, finding, decree, arbitrament, adjudication, award, decision, precedent.

Verbs: To denounce, cite, apprehend, sue, writ, arraign, summons, prosecute, indict, contest, impeach, attach, distrain; to commit.

To try, hear a cause, sit in judgment.

To pronounce, find, judge, adjudge, sentence, give judgment; bring in a verdict; to doom, arbitrate, adjudicate, award, report.

Phrases: To go to law; to appeal to the law; to file a claim; to inform against; to lodge an information; to serve with a writ; to bring an action against; to bring to trial or the bar; to give in charge or custody; to throw into prison; to clap in jail.

Adjectives: Litigious, litigant, litigatory.

Adverbial phrases: *Sub judice; pendente lite.*

970 ACQUITTAL
Substantives: acquitment, absolution, exculpation, quietus, clearance, discharge, release, reprieve (918), respite, compurgation.

Exemption from punishment, impunity.

Verbs: To acquit, absolve, whitewash, extenuate, exculpate, exonerate, clear, assoil, discharge, release, reprieve, respite.

Adjectives: Acquitted, etc.

Uncondemned, unpunished, unchastised.

971 CONDEMNATION
Substantives: conviction, proscription, damnation, death-warrant.

Attainder, attainture, attaintment.

Verbs: To condemn, convict, cast, find guilty, proscribe, ban, outlaw, attaint, damn, doom, sentence, confiscate, sequestrate, non-suit.

Adjectives: Condemnatory, damnatory, condemned; self-convicted.

972 PUNISHMENT
Substantives: punition, chastisement, castigation, correction, chastening, discipline, infliction.

Retribution, requital (973), penalty (974), reckoning, Nemesis.

Imprisonment (751), transportation, exile (297), cucking-stool, ducking-stool, treadmill, crank, hulks, galleys, penal servitude, preventive detention.

A blow, slap, spank, skelp, swish, hit, knock, rap, thump, bang, buffet, stripe, stroke, cuff, clout, kick, whack, thwack, box, punch, pummel.

Beating, lash, flagellation, flogging, etc., dressing, lacing, tanning, knockout, spiflication, bastinado, strappado, pillory (975), running the gauntlet, *coup de grâce, peine forte et dure.*

Execution, capital punishment, hanging, beheading, decollation, decapitation, electrocution, guillotine, garrotte, *auto da fé, noyade,* crucifixion, impalement, *hara-kiri,* martyrdom.

Verbs: To punish, chastise, castigate, chasten, correct, inflict punishment, pay, do for, sever out, pay out, visit upon, give it to, strafe, spiflicate.

To strike, hit, smite, knock, slap, flap, rap, bang, thwack, whack, thump, kick, punch, pelt, beat, buffet, thrash, swinge, pummel, clapperclaw, drub, trounce, baste, belabour, lace, strap, comb, lash, lick, whip, flog, scourge, knout, swish, spank, skelp, birch, tan, larrup, lay into, knock out, wallop, leather, flagellate, horsewhip, bastinado, lapidate, stone.

To execute, hang, behead, decapitate, decollate, electrocute, guillotine, garrotte, shoot, gibbet; to hang, draw, and quarter; break on the wheel;

crucify, impale, torture, flay, keelhaul; lynch.

To banish, exile, transport, deport, expel, drum out, disbar, disbench, unfrock.

To be hanged, etc., to be spread-eagled.

Phrases: To make an example of; to serve one out; to give it one; to dust one's jacket; to tweak or pull the nose; to box the ears; to beat to a jelly; to tar and feather; to give a black eye; to lay it on.

To come to the gallows; to swing for it; to go to the chair; to die in one's shoes.

Adjectives: Punishing, etc., punitory, punitive, inflictive, penal, disciplinary, castigatory, borstal.

Interjection: *A la lanterne!*

973 REWARD

Substantives: recompense, remuneration, meed, guerdon, premium, indemnity, indemnification, compensation, reparation, requital, retribution, quittance, hush-money, acknowledgment, amends, solatium, sop, atonement, redress, consideration, return, tribute, honorarium, perquisite, tip, vail; salvage.

Prize, purse, crown, laurel, bays, cross, medal, ribbon, decoration (877).

Verbs: To reward, recompense, repay, requite, recoup, remunerate, compensate, make amends, indemnify, atone, satisfy, acknowledge, acquit oneself.

Phrase: To get for one's pains.

Adjectives: Remunerative, munerary, compensatory, retributive, reparatory.

974 PENALTY

Substantives: punishment (972), pain, penance.

Fine, mulct, amercement, forfeit, forfeiture, escheat, damages, deodand, sequestration, confiscation.

Phrases: Pains and penalties; the devil to pay.

Verbs: To fine, mulct, amerce, sconce, confiscate, sequester, sequestrate, escheat, estreat.

975 SCOURGE

Substantives: rod, cane, stick, rattan, switch, ferule, birch, cudgel.

Whip, lash, strap, thong, knout, cowhide, cat, cat-o'-nine-tails, sjambok, rope's end.

Pillory, stocks, cangue, whipping-post, ducking-stool, triangle, wooden horse, boot, thumbscrew, rack, wheel, treadmill.

Stake, tree, block, scaffold, gallows, halter, bowstring, gibbet, axe, maiden, guillotine, garrotte, electric chair, hot squat, lethal chamber.

Executioner, hangman, electrocutioner, firing squad, headsman, Jack Ketch.

Section 5 –
Religious Affections

976 DEITY

Substantives: Divinity, Godhead, Omnipotence, Omniscience, Providence.

Quality of being divine, divineness, divinity.

GOD, Lord, Jehovah, The Almighty; The Supreme Being; The First Cause, *Ens Entium*; The Author of all things, The Infinite, The Eternal, The All-powerful, The All-wise, The All-merciful, The All-holy.

Attributes and perfections, infinite power, wisdom, goodness, justice, mercy, omnipotence, omniscience, omnipresence, unity, immutability, holiness, glory, majesty, sovereignty, infinity, eternity.

The Trinity, The Holy Trinity, The Trinity in Unity, The Triune God.

GOD THE FATHER, The Maker, The Creator.

Functions: creation, preservation, divine government, theocracy, thearchy, providence; the ways, dispensations, visitations of Providence.

GOD THE SON, Christ, Jesus, The Messiah, The Anointed, The Saviour, The Redeemer, The Mediator, The Intercessor, The Advocate, The Judge, The Son of Man, The Lamb of God, The Word, The Logos, Emmanuel, The King of Kings and Lord of Lords, The King of Glory, The Prince of Peace, The Good Shepherd, The Way of Truth and Life, The Bread of Life, The Light of the World, The Sun of Righteousness, The Incarnation, the Word made Flesh.

Functions: salvation, redemption, atonement, propitiation, mediation, intercession, judgment.

GOD THE HOLY GHOST, The Holy Spirit, Paraclete, The Comforter, The Spirit of Truth, The Dove.

Functions: inspiration, unction, regeneration, sanctification, consolation.

Verbs: To create, uphold, preserve, govern.

To atone, redeem, save, propitiate, mediate.

To predestinate, elect, call, ordain, bless, justify, sanctify, glorify.

Adjectives: Almighty, all-powerful, omnipotent, omnipresent, omniscient, all-wise, holy, hallowed, sacred, divine, heavenly, celestial.

Superhuman, ghostly, spiritual, supernatural, theocratic.

977 ANGEL

Substantives: archangel.

The heavenly host; ministering spirits; the choir invisible.

Madonna, saint.

Seraphim, cherubim, thrones, principalities, powers, dominions.

Adjectives: Angelic, angelical, seraphic, cherubic, celestial, heavenly, saintly.

978 SATAN

Substantives: the Devil, Lucifer, Beelzebub, Belial, Mephistopheles, Mephisto, Abaddon, Apollyon, the Prince of the Devils.

His Satanic Majesty, the tempter, the evil one, the wicked one, the old Serpent, the Prince of darkness, the father of lies, the foul fiend, the archfiend, the common enemy, Old Harry, Old Nick, the Old Scratch, the Old Gentleman, Old Horny.

Diabolism, devilism, devilship; Satanism, the cloven hoof, the black mass.

Fallen angels, unclean spirits, devils, the powers of darkness, inhabitants of Pandemonium.

Adjectives: Satanic, diabolic, devilish.

979 GREAT SPIRIT

Substantives: deity, numen, god, goddess; Allah, Brahma, Vishnu, Siva, Krishna, Buddha, Mithra, Ormuzd, Isis, Osiris, Moloch, Baal, Asteroth.

Jupiter, Jove, Juno, Minerva, Apollo, Diana, Venus, Vulcan, Mars, Mercury, Neptune, Pluto; Zeus, Hera, Athena, Artemis, Aphrodite, Hephaestus, Ares, Hermes, Poseidon.

Odin or Woden, Frigga, Thor.

Good genius, demiurge, familiar; fairy, fay, sylph, peri, kelpie, nymph, nereid, dryad, hamadryad, naiad, merman, mermaid (341), undine; Oberon, Mab, Titania, Puck, Robin Goodfellow; the good folk, the little people.

Adjectives: Fairy, faery, fairy-like, sylph-like, sylphine.

Mythical, mythological, fabulous, legendary.

980 DEMON

Substantives: evil genius, fiend, unclean spirit, caco-demon, incubus, succubus, succuba, flibbertigibbet; fury, harpy, siren, faun, satyr, Eblis, Demogorgon.

Vampire, werewolf, ghoul, afreet (or afrite), ogre, ogress, gnome, djinn, imp, genie (or jinnee), lamia, bogy, bogle, nix, nixie, kobold, brownie, leprechaun, elf, pixy, troll, sprite, gremlin, spandule.

Supernatural appearance, ghost, spectre, apparition, shade, vision, goblin, hobgoblin, banshee, spook, wraith, *revenant, doppelgänger,* poltergeist.

Phrase: The powers of darkness.

Adjectives: Supernatural, ghostly, apparitional, elfin, elfish, unearthly, uncanny, eerie, weird, spectral, spookish, spooky, ghostlike, fiendish, fiendlike, impish, demoniacal, haunted.

981 HEAVEN

Substantives: the kingdom of heaven; the kingdom of God, the heavenly kingdom; the throne of God, the presence of God.

Paradise, Eden, Zion, the Celestial City, the New Jerusalem, the abode of the blessed; celestial bliss or glory.

Mythological heaven, Olympus; mythological paradise, Elysium, the Elysian Fields, the garden of the Hesperides; Valhalla, Nirvana, happy hunting grounds.

Translation, apotheosis, deification, resurrection.

Adjectives: Heavenly, celestial, supernal, unearthly, from on high, paradisaical, paradisical, paradisial, Elysian, beatific.

982 HELL

Substantives: bottomless pit, place of torment; the habitation of fallen angels, Pandemonium, Domdaniel.

Hell-fire, everlasting fire, the lake of fire and brimstone.

Purgatory, limbo, abyss.

Mythological hell, Tartarus, Hades, Pluto, Avernus, Styx, the Stygian creek, Acheron, Cocytus, Phlegethon, Lethe, Erebus, Tophet, Gehenna.

Phrases: The fire that is never quenched; the worm that never dies.

The infernal or nether regions; the shades below; the realms of Pluto.

Adjectives: Hellish, infernal, stygian, Tartarean, Plutonian.

983 THEOLOGY (natural and revealed)

Substantives: divinity, religion, monotheism, hagiology, hagiography, hierography, theosophy; comparative religion, comparative mythology.

Creed, belief, faith, persuasion, tenet, dogma, articles of faith, declaration, profession or confession of faith.

Theologian, divine, schoolman, the Fathers.

Adjectives: Theological, religious, patristic, ecumenical, denominational, sectarian.

983a CHRISTIAN RELIGION

Substantives: true faith, Christianity, Christianism, Christendom, Catholicism, orthodoxy.

A Christian, a true believer.

The Church, the Catholic or Universal Church, the Church of Christ, the body of Christ, the Church Militant.

The members of Christ, the disciples or followers of Christ, the Christian community.

Protestant, Church of England, Anglican, Church of Scotland; Church of Rome, Roman Catholic; Greek Church, Orthodox Church.

Adjectives: Christian, Catholic, orthodox, sound, faithful, true, scriptural, canonical, schismless.

984 OTHER RELIGIONS

Substantives: paganism, heathenism, ethnicism, polytheism, ditheism, tritheism, pantheism, hylotheism.

Judaism, Gentilism, Mohammedanism (or Mahometanism), Islam, Buddhism, Hinduism, Taoism, Confucianism, Shintoism, Sufism.

A pagan, heathen, paynim, infidel, unbeliever, pantheist, etc.

A Jew, Mohammedan (or Mahometan), Mussulman, Moslem, Brahmin (or Brahman), Parsee, Sufi, Magus, Gymnosophist, Fire-worshipper, Buddhist, Rosicrucian.

Adjectives: Pagan, heaten, ethnic, gentile, pantheistic, etc.

Judaical, Mohammedan, Brahminical, Buddhistic.

984a HERESY
Substantives: heterodoxy, false doctrine, schism, schismaticalness, latitudinarianism, recusancy, apostasy, backsliding, quietism, adiaphorism.

Bigotry, fanaticism, iconoclasm, bibliolatry, fundamentalism, puritanism, sabbatarianism.

Dissent, sectarianism, nonconformity, secularism, syncretism.

A heretic, deist, unitarian.

Adjectives: Heretical, heterodox, unorthodox, unscriptural, uncanonical, schismatic, sectarian, nonconformist, recusant, latitudinarian.

Credulous, bigoted, fanatical, idolatrous, superstitious, visionary.

985 CHRISTIAN REVELATION
Substantives: Word, Word of God, Scripture, the Scriptures, Holy Writ, the Bible, the Holy Book.

Old Testament: Septuagint, Vulgate, Pentateuch, Hagiographa, the Law, the Prophets, the Apocrypha.

New Testament: the Gospel, the Evangelists, the Epistles, the Apocalypse, Revelations.

Talmud, Mishna, Masorah, Torah.

A prophet, seer, evangelist, apostle, disciple, saint, the Fathers.

Adjectives: Scriptural, biblical, sacred, prophetic, evangelical, apostolic, apostolical, inspired, theopneustic, apocalyptic.

986 OTHER SACRED BOOKS
Substantives: the Koran (or Alcoran), Vedas, Upanishads, Puranas, Zend-Avesta.

Religious founders: Buddha (or Gautama), Zoroaster (or Zarathustra), Confucius, Lao-Tsze, Mohammed (or Mahomet).

Idols: Golden Calf, Baal, Moloch, Dagon.

Adjectives: Anti-scriptural, antichristian, profane, idolatrous, pagan, heathen, heathenish.

987 PIETY
Substantives: religion, theism, faith, religiousness, godliness, reverence, humility, veneration, devoutness, devotion, spirituality, grace, unction, edification, unworldliness, other-worldliness; holiness, sanctity, sanctitude, sacredness, consecration; virtue (944).

Theopathy, beatification, adoption, regeneration, conversion, justification, salvation, inspiration.

A believer, convert, theist, Christian, saint, one of the elect, a devotee.

The good, righteous, faithful, godly, elect, just.

Phrases: The odour of sanctity; the beauty of holiness; spiritual existence.

The children of God, of light.

Verbs: To be pious, etc., to believe, have faith; to convert, edify, sanctify, hallow, beatify, regenerate, inspire; to consecrate, enshrine.

Phrases: To work out one's salvation; to stand up for Jesus; to fight the good fight.

Adjectives: Pious, religious, devout, reverent, reverential, godly, humble, heavenly-minded, pure, holy, spiritual, saintly, saint-like, unworldly, other-worldly.

Believing, faithful, Christian.

Sanctified, regenerated, born again,

justified, adopted, elected, inspired, consecrated, converted, unearthly, sacred, solemn, not of the earth.

988 IMPIETY
Substantives: irreverence, profaneness, profanity, blasphemy, desecration, sacrilege, sacrilegiousness, sin (945); scoffing, ribaldry, reviling.

Assumed piety, hypocrisy, cant, pietism, lip-devotion, lip-service, lip-reverence, formalism, sanctimony, sanctimoniousness, pharisaism, precisianism, sabbatism, sabbatarianism, sacerdotalism, religiosity, religionism, *odium theologicum*.

Hardening, backsliding, declension, reprobation, perversion.

Sinner, outcast, castaway, lost sheep, reprobate.

A scoffer, hypocrite, pietist, pervert, religionist, precisian, formalist; son of darkness, son of Belial, blasphemer, Pharisee; bigot, devotee, fanatic, sabbatarian.

The wicked, unjust, ungodly, unrighteous.

Phrase: The unco guid.

Verbs: To be impious, etc., to profane, desecrate, blaspheme, revile, scoff, commit sacrilege.

To play the hypocrite, cant.

Adjectives: Impious, profane, irreverent, sacrilegious, desecrating, blasphemous; unhallowed, unsanctified, hardened, perverted, reprobate.

Bigoted, priest-ridden, fanatical, churchy.

Hypocritical, canting, pietistical, sanctimonious, unctuous, pharisaical, over-righteous, righteous overmuch.

Phrases: Under the mask, cloak, or pretence of religion.

989 IRRELIGION
Substantives: ungodliness, unholiness, gracelessness, impiety (988).

Scepticism, doubt, unbelief, disbelief, incredulity, incredulousness, faith-lessness, want of faith or belief (485, 487).

Atheism, hylotheism, materialism, positivism.

Deism, infidelity, freethinking, rationalism, agnosticism, unchristianness, antichristianity, antichristianism.

An atheist, sceptic, unbeliever, deist, freethinker, rationalist, agnostic, nullifidian, infidel, alien, giaour, heathen.

Verbs: To be irreligious, disbelieve, lack faith, doubt.

To dechristianize, rationalize.

Adjectives: Irreligious, undevout, godless, atheistic, atheistical, ungodly, unholy, unhallowed, unsanctified, graceless, without God, carnal-minded.

Sceptical, unbelieving, freethinking, agnostic, rationalistic, incredulous, unconverted, faithless, lacking faith.

Deistical, antichristian, unchristian, worldly-minded, mundane, carnal, earthly-minded.

Adverbs: Irreligiously, etc.

990 WORSHIP
Substantives: adoration, devotion, cult, homage, service, humiliation, kneeling, genuflexion, prostration.

Prayer, invocation, supplication, rogation, petition, orison, litany, the Lord's prayer, paternoster, collect.

Thanksgiving, giving or returning thanks, praise, glorification, benediction, doxology, hosanna, hallelujah, paean, Te Deum, Magnificat, Ave Maria, De Profundis, Nunc dimittis, Non nobis, Domine.

Psalmody, psalm, hymn, plainsong, chant, antiphon, response, anthem, motet.

Oblation, sacrifice, incense, libation, burnt-offering, votive offering; offertory, collection.

Discipline, self-discipline, self-examination, self-denial, fasting.

Divine service, religious service, office, duty, prime, terce, sext, matins, mass (998), angelus, nones, evensong, vespers, vigils, lauds, compline; prayer meeting, revival.

Worshipper, congregation, communicant, celebrant.

Verbs: To worship, adore, reverence, venerate, do service, pay homage, humble oneself, bow down, kneel, bend the knee, prostrate oneself.

To pray, invoke, supplicate, petition, put up prayers or petitions; to ask, implore (765).

To return or give thanks; to say grace; to bless, praise, laud, glorify, magnify, sing praises, lead the choir, pronounce benediction.

To propitiate, offer sacrifice, fast, deny oneself; vow, offer vows, give alms.

Phrases: To lift up the heart; to say one's prayers; to tell one's beads; to go to church; to attend divine service.

Adjectives: Worshipping, etc., devout, solemn, devotional, reverent, pure, fervent, prayerful.

Interjections: Hallelujah! alleluia! hosanna! glory be to God! *sursum corda!*

991 IDOLATRY

Substantives: idol-worship, idolism, demonism, demonolatry, fire-worship, devil-worship, fetishism.

Sacrifices, hecatomb, holocaust; human sacrifices, immolation, mactation, infanticide, self-immolation, suttee.

Idol, image, fetish, ju-ju, Mumbo-Jumbo, Juggernaut, joss.

Verbs: To worship idols, pictures, relics, etc.; to idolize, idolatrize.

Adjectives: Idolatrous, fetishistic.

992 OCCULT ARTS

Substantives: occultism, sorcery, magic, the black art, black magic, necromancy, theurgy, thaumaturgy, psychomancy, *diablerie,* bedevilment, withcraft, witchery, bewitchment,

wizardry, glamour, fetishism, vampirism, shamanism, voodooism, obeah (or obi), sortilege, conjuration, exorcism, fascination, mesmerism, hypnotism, animal magnetism, clairvoyance, telegnosis, telekinesis, psychokinesis, mediumship, spiritualism, extra-sensory perception, telepathy, parapsychology, second sight, spirit-rapping, table-turning, psychometry, crystal-gazing, divination, enchantment, hocus-pocus (545).

Verbs: To practise sorcery, etc.; to conjure, exorcize, charm, enchant, bewitch, bedevil, hoodoo, entrance, mesmerize, hypnotize, fascinate; to taboo, wave a wand, cast a spell, call up spirits.

Adjectives: Magic, magical, cabbalistic, talismanic, phylacteric, necromantic, incantatory, occult, mediumistic, charmed, exorcized, etc.

993 SPELL

Substantives: charm, fascination, incantation, exorcism, weird, cabbala, exsufflation, jinx, cantrip, runes, abracadabra, open sesame, mumbo-jumbo, taboo, counter-charm, evil eye, hoodoo, Indian sign.

Talisman, amulet, mascot, periapt, phylactery, philtre, fetish, wishbone, merrythought.

Wand, caduceus, rod, divining-rod, the lamp of Aladdin, magic ring, wishing-cap, seven-league boots.

994 SORCERER

Substantives: sorceress, magician, conjurer, necromancer, enchanter, enchantress, thaumaturgist, occultist, adept, Mahatma, seer, wizard, witch, warlock, charmer, exorcist, mage, archimage, soothsayer (513), shaman, medicine-man, witch-doctor, mesmerist, hypnotist, medium, spiritualist, clairvoyant; control.

Phrase: *Deus ex machina.*

995 CHURCHDOM

Substantives: ministry, apostleship, priesthood, prelacy, hierarchy, church government, Christendom, church; clericalism, sacerdotalism, priestcraft, theocracy, popery, papistry.

Monachism, monasticism, monkdom, monkhood, monkery.

Ecclesiastical offices and dignities: Pontificate, papacy, primacy, archbishopric, archiepiscopacy, bishopric, bishopdom, episcopate, episcopacy, see, diocese, prelacy, deanery, stall, canonry, canonicate, prebend, prebendaryship; benefice, incumbency, advowson, living, cure, rectorship, vicarship, vicariate, deaconry, deaconship, curacy, chaplaincy, chaplainship; cardinalate, abbacy.

Holy orders, ordination, institution, consecration, induction, preferment, translation.

Council, conclave, sanhedrim, synod, presbytery, consistory, chapter, vestry (696).

Verbs: To call, ordain, induct, install, prefer, translate, consecrate, canonize, beatify; to take the veil, to take vows.

Adjectives: Ecclesiastical, clerical, sacerdotal, priestly, prelatical, hierarchical, pastoral, ministerial, capitular, theocratic.

Pontifical, papal, episcopal, archidiaconal, diaconal, canonical; monastic, monachal, monkish; levitical, rabbinical.

996 CLERGY

Substantives: ministry, priesthood, presbytery.

A clergyman, cleric, parson, divine, ecclesiastic, churchman, priest, presbyter, hierophant, pastor, father, shepherd, minister, father in Christ, patriarch, padre, abbé, curé; sky-pilot, holy Joe, devil-dodger.

Dignitaries of the church: Primate, archbishop, bishop, prelate, diocesan, suffragan; dean, subdean, archdeacon, prebendary, canon, capitular, residentiary, beneficiary; rector, vicar, incumbent, chaplain, curate, deacon, subdeacon, preacher, reader, evangelist, revivalist, missionary, missioner.

Churchwarden, sidesman; clerk, precentor, choir, chorister, almoner, verger, beadle, sexton, sacrist, sacristan, acolyte.

Roman Catholic priesthood: Pope, pontiff, cardinal, confessor, spiritual director.

Cenobite, conventual, abbot, prior, father superior, monk, oblate, friar, lay brother, mendicant, Franciscan (or Grey Friars, Friars minor, Minorites), Observant, Capuchin, Dominican (or Black Friars), Carmelite (or White Friars), Augustin (or Austin Friars), Crossed or Crutched Friars, Benedictine, Jesuit (or Society of Jesus).

Abbess, prioress, canoness, mother, mother superior, *religieuse,* nun, novice, postulant.

Greek Church: Patriarch, metropolitan, archimandrite, pope.

Under the Jewish dispensation: Prophet, priest, high-priest, Levite, rabbi (or rabbin), scribe.

Moslem: Imam, mullah, mufti, dervish, fakir, santon, hadji; muezzin.

Hindu: Brahmin, pundit, guru, yogi.

Buddhist: Lama, bonze.

Phrase: The cloth.

Adjectives: Reverend, ordained, in orders.

997 LAITY

Substantives: flock, fold, congregation, assembly, brethren, people.

Temporality, secularization.

A layman, parishioner.

Verb: To secularize.

Adjectives: Secular, lay, laical, civil, temporal, profane.

998 RITE
Substantives: ceremony, ordinance, observance, cult, duty, form, formulary, ceremonial, solemnity, sacrament.

Baptism, immersion, christening, chrism, baptismal regeneration.

Confirmation, imposition or laying on of hands, ordination (995), consecration.

The Eucharist, the Lord's Supper, the communion, the sacrament, consubstantiation, celebration, consecrated elements, bread and wine.

Matrimony (903), burial (363), visitation of the sick, offertory.

Roman Catholic rites and ceremonies: Mass, high mass, low mass, dry mass; the seven sacraments, transubstantiation, impanation, extreme unction, viaticum, invocation of saints, canonization, transfiguration, auricular confession, maceration, flagellation, penance (952), telling of beads.

Relics, rosary, beads, reliquary, pyx (or pix), host, crucifix, *Agnus Dei*, thurible, censer, patera.

Liturgy, ritual, euchology, book of common prayer, litany, etc.; rubric, breviary, missal, ordinal; psalter, psalm book, hymn book, hymnal.

Service, worship (990), ministration, psalmody; preaching, predication; sermon, homily, lecture, discourse, exhortation, address.

Ritualism, ceremonialism, liturgics, liturgiology.

Verbs: To perform service, do duty, minister, officiate; to baptize, dip, sprinkle; to confirm, lay hands on; to give or administer the sacrament; to take or receive the sacrament, communicate.

To preach, sermonize, predicate, lecture, harangue, hold forth, address the congregation.

Adjectives: Ritual, ceremonial, baptismal, eucharistical, pastoral, liturgical.

999 VESTMENTS
Substantives: canonicals, robe, gown, pallium, surplice, cassock, alb, scapular (or scapulary), dalmatic, cope, soutane, chasuble, tonsure, cowl, hood, amice, calotte, bands, apron, biretta.

Mitre, tiara, triple crown, crosier.

1000 TEMPLE
Substantives: cathedral, pro-cathedral, minster, church, kirk, chapel, meeting-house, tabernacle, conventicle, bethesda, little Bethel, basilica, fane, holy place, chantry, oratory.

Synagogue, mosque, pantheon, pagoda, joss-house, dagobah, tope.

Parsonage, rectory, vicarage, manse, presbytery, deanery, bishop's palace, the Vatican.

Altar, shrine, sanctuary, *sanctum sanctorum*, the Holy of Holies, sacristy, communion table, holy table, table of the Lord; piscina, baptistery, font, aumbry.

Chancel, choir, nave, aisle, transept, vestry, crypt, apse, belfry, stall, pew, pulpit, ambo, lectern, reading-desk, confessional, prothesis, credence.

Monastery, priory, abbey, convent, nunnery, cloister.

Adjectives: Claustral, monastic, monasterial, conventual.

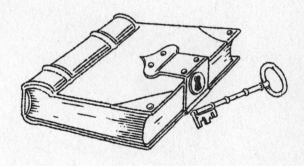

INDEX

Index

The numbers refer to the headings under which the words occur.

Abeyance
expectation, 507
extinction, 2
suspense, 142
Abhor
hate, 898
dislike, 867
Abide
continue, 141, 143
exist, 1
diuturnity, 110
endure, 821
dwell, 186
expect, 507
Abide by
resolution, 604
assent, 488
observance, 772
Abigail
servant, 746
Ability
power, 157
intellect, 450
skill, 698
Abject
servile, 886
vile, 874, 940
Abjure
renounce, 607
resign, 757
deny, 536
Ablation
subduntion, 38
taking, 789
Ablaze
heat, 382
light, 420
Able
skilful, 157, 698
Able-bodied
strength, 159
Ablepsy
blindness, 442
Ablution
cleanness, 652
Abnegation
denial, 536, 764
self-denial, 942
forbearance, 953
Abnormality
unconformity, 83
Aboard
ship, 273
present, 186

Abode
abode, 189, 182
Abodement
prediction, 511
Abolish
destroy, 162
abrogate, 756
Abominable
hateful, 898
bad, 649
foul, 653
painful, 830
Abominate
hate, 898
dislike, 867
Abomination
foulness, 653
Abord
courtesy, 894
Aboriginal
beginning, 66
native, 188
Aborigines
inhabitants, 188
Abortion
failure, 732
Abound
sufficiency, 639
About
relative to, 9
near, 32, 197
around, 227
Above
height, 206
priority, 116
Above all
greatness, 31
Above-board
visible, 446
plain, 518
artless, 703
true, 543
Above ground
alive, 359
Above par
greatness, 31
Abracadabra
spell, 993
Abrade
subduct, 38
Abrasion
pulverulence, 330
friction, 331

Abreast
lateral, 236
parallel, 216
Abridge
shorten, 201
conciseness, 572
lessen, 36
deprive, 789
in writing, 596
Abroach
dispersion, 73
Abroad
extraneous, 57
exterior, 220
distant, 196
ignorant, 491
perplexed, 704
Abrogation
abrogation, 756, 764
illegality, 964
Abrupt
sudden, 132
hasty, 684
violent, 173
transient, 111
steep, 217
unexpected, 508
style, 579
Abruption
separation, 44
Abscess
disease, 655
Abscission
retrenchment, 38
division, 44
Abscond
escape, 671
fly from, 287
Absence
non-existence, 2
non-presence, 187
inattention, 458
thoughtlessness, 452
Absent-minded
inattentive, 458
Absentee
absence, 187
Absit omen
deprecation, 766
Absolute
not relative, 1
certain, 474, 31
positive, 535
true, 494
unconditional, 768a

Accompaniment
musical, 415
adjunct, 37, 39

Accompanist
musician, 416

Accompany
coexist, 88
add, 37

Accomplice
auxiliary, 711

Accomplish
execute, 161
finish, 729

Accomplishment
talent, 698
learning, 490

Accord
agree, 23, 646
assent, 488
concord, 714
melody, 413
give, 784
grant, 760
spontaneous, 600

According to
relation, 9
conformably, 15
evidence, 467

Accordingly
reasoning, 476

Accordion
musical instrument, 417

Accost
allocation, 586

Accoucheur
instrument, 631

Account
money, 811
bill, 812
computation, 85
list, 86
record, 551
description, 594
value, 644
estimation, 484
judgment, 480
approbation, 931
fame, 873
sake, 615

Account for
attribution, 155

Accountable
duty, 926
liability, 177

Accountant
accounts, 811
treasurer, 801

Accouplement
junction, 43

Accoutre
dress, 225
equip, 673

Accoutrement
equipment, 633

Accredit
money, 805
honour, 873
commission, 755

Accretion
coherence, 46
increase, 35

Accrue
result, 154
add, 37
acquire, 775
receive, 785, 810
benefit, 644

Accueil
courtesy, 894

Accumulate
collect, 72
store, 636

Accurate
exact, 494
likeness, 17

Accursed
undone, 828
painful, 830
disastrous 649
cursed 908

Accuse
charge, 938
disapprove 932

Accuser
judge, 967

Accustom
habituate, 613
usual, 82

Ace
unit, 87
small in quantity, 32
small in size, 193
courage, 861

Acerbate
embitter, 659
aggravate, 835

Acerbity
sourness, 397
harshness, 739

spleen, 898, 900, 901
malevolence, 907

Acervate
assemblage, 72

Acetic
sour, 397

Acetous
sour, 397

Acharnement
malevolence, 907

Ache
physical pain, 378
moral pain, 838

Acheron
hell, 982

Achievable
possible, 470
easy, 705

Achieve
accomplish, 729
end, 67

Achievement
escutcheon, 551

Achromatism
achromatic, 429

Achtung
attention, 457

Acicular
sharpness, 253

Acid
sourness, 397

Acknowledge
avow, 535
disclose, 529
assent, 488
consent, 762
reward, 973
repent, 950
answer, 462
observe, 772
receive, 82

Acknowledged
habitual, 613

Acme
summit, 210
highest degree, 33
perfection, 650

Acolyte
clergy, 996

Aconite
bane, 663

Acoustics
sound, 402

Acquaint
information, 527

Acquaintance
knowledge, 490
friendship, 888
friend, 890

Acquiesce
assent, 488
consent, 762

Acquire
acquisition, 775

Acquirement
knowledge, 490
learning, 539
talent, 698

Acquisition
gain, 775
knowledge, 970

Acquit
absolve, 490
exempt, 927A
vindicate, 937
liberate, 750

Acquit oneself
of a duty, 926
of an agreement, 772

Acquittance
payment, 807

Acres
property, 780

Acrid
unsavouriness, 395

Acrimony,
taste, 395
hatred, 898
malevolence, 907
discourtesy, 895

Acrobat
athlete, 159

Across
transverse, 219
opposition, 708

Acrostic
neology, 563
puzzle, 533

Act
physical, 170
voluntary, 680
law, 697
to feign, 544
to personate, 599
deputize, 759
business, 625
to imitate, 19

Actinotherapy
remedy, 662

Action
physical, 170
voluntary, 680
battle, 720
at law, 969

Activity
physical, 171
voluntary, 682

Actor
impostor, 548
player, 599
doer, 690

Actual
existing, 1
real, 494
present, 118

Actualize
describe, 594
materialize, 3

Actuality
truly, 31

Actuary
accounts, 811

Actuate
motive, 615

Actum est
completion, 729

Acuity
sharpness, 253

Aculeated
sharpness, 253

Acumen
wisdom, 484

Acuminated
sharpness, 233

Acupuncture
opening, 260

Acute
pointed, 253
violent (physically),
173
sensible (physically),
375
painful (morally), 830
strong feeling, 820
musical tone, 410
perspicacious, 498

Acutely
much, 31

Ad arbitrium
will, 600

Ad captandum
plea, 617
deception, 545

Ad captandum vulgas
ostentation, 852

Ad eundem
equality, 27

Ad infinitum
infinity, 105

Ad interim
duration, 106

Ad-lib
improvise, 612

Ad libitum
will, 600
choice, 609
sufficiency, 639

Ad rem
reasoning, 473

Ad unguem
perfection, 650

Ad valorem
price, 812

Adage
maxim, 496

Adagio
slowness, 275
music, 415

Adamant
hard, 323
strong, 159

Adapt
fit, 646
adjust, 673
agree, 23

Add
addition, 37
increase, 35
numerically, 85

Addendum
adjunct, 39

Adder
viper, 663
maleficent being, 913

Addict
habit, 613

Addition
adjunction, 37
thing added, 39
arithmetical, 85

Addle
barren, 169
abortive, 732
to spoil, 659

Addle-headed
imbecile, 499

Address
speak to, 586
skill, 698
request, 765
residence, 189
direction, 550
lecture, 582
preach, 998

Addresses
courtship, 902

Adduce
bring to, 288
evidence, 467

Adept
proficient, 700
sorcerer, 994

Adequate
sufficient, 639
power, 157
strength, 159
for a purpose, 644

Adhere
stick, 46
fidelity, 772
resoluteness, 604

Adherent
follower, 711

Adhesive
coherence, 46
connective, 45

Adhibit
use, 677

Adiaphorism
heresy, 984A

Adieu
departure, 293

Andipose
unctuous, 355

Adiposity
corpulence, 192

Adit
conduit, 350
orifice, 260
way, 627

Adjacent
nearness, 197

Adjection
addition, 37

Adjective
adjunct, 39

Adjoin
nearness, 197
contiguity, 199

Adjourn
lateness, 133

Adjudge
lawsuit, 969

Adjudication
choice, 609
judgement, 480
lawsuit, 969

Adjunct
thing added, 39
accompaniment, 88
aid, 707

Adjuration
affirmation, 535

Adjure
request, 765
promise, 768

Adjust
fit, 27
preface, 673
settle, 723
compromise, 774

Adjutage (or ajutage),
pipe, 350
opening, 260

Adjutant
auxiliary, 711
military, 745

Adjuvant
helper, 707, 711

Admeasurement
measurement, 466

Administer
give, 784
apportion, 786
manage, 693
govern, 737

Administration
of justice, 965

Admirable
excellent, 648
virtuous, 944

Admiral
master, 745

Admire
approve, 931
love, 897
wonder, 870

Admissable
tolerable, 651

Admission
ingress, 294, 296
inclusion, 76

Admit
let in, 296
accept, 785
include, 76

composition, 54
concede in argument, 467
disclose, 529
allow, 760
assent, 488

Admit of
possibility, 470

Admixture
mixture, 41

Admonish
advise, 695
warn, 668
reprove, 932
predict, 511

Ado
exertion, 686
activity, 682
difficulty, 704

Adolescence
youth, 131

Adonis
beauty, 845

Adopt
choice, 609

Adore
love, 897
worship, 990

Adorn
beauty, 845

Adown
lowness, 207

Adrift
unrelated, 10
dispersed, 73
at fault, 704

Adroit
skill, 698

Adscititious
extrinsic, 6
added, 37
supplementary, 52

Adscriptus glebæ
servant, 746

Adulation
flattery, 933

Adulator
flatterer, 935

Adult
adolescence, 131

Adulterate
mix, 41
deteriorate, 659
falsify, 495

Adulterer
  libertine, 962
Adultery
  impurity, 961
Adumbrate
  sketch, 594
  representation, 554
  painting, 556
  faint likeness, 21
  imitate, 19
  personify, 521
Adust
  burnt, 384
  gloomy, 837
Advance
  progress, 282, 731
  to promote, 658
  forward, 707
  increase, 35
  lend, 787
  expenditure, 809
  assert, 535
Advanced
  progressive, 658
  modern, 123
Advantage
  good, 618
  utility, 644
  goodness, 648
  superiority, 33
  inequality, 28
  success, 705, 731
Advene
  addition, 37
Advent
  arrival, 292
  event, 151
  futurity, 121
Adventitious
  extrinsic, 6
  casual, 156, 621
Adventure
  event, 151
  chance, 156, 621
  pursuit, 622
  trial, 675
Adventurer
  deceiver, 548
  rashness, 863
Adventurous
  courageous, 861
  dangerous, 665
Adversaria
  register, 551
  chronicle, 594

Adversary
  opponent, 710
Adverse
  opposed, 708
  enmity, 889
  disliking, 867
  unprosperous, 735
Adversity
  adversity, 735
Advert
  attention, 457
Advertise
  publication, 531
Advertisement
  preface, 64
  information, 527
Advice
  counsel, 695
  notice, 527
  news, 532
Advisable
  expediency, 646
Advise
  inform, 527
  counsel, 695
  predict, 511
Advised
  voluntary, 600
  intentional, 620
Adviser
  counsellor, 695
  teacher, 540
Advocacy
  aid, 707
Advocate
  counsellor, 968
  advise, 695
  to prompt, 615
  commend, 931
  to vindicate, 937
  Saviour, 967
Advocatus diaboli
  sophistry, 477
Advowson
  churchdom, 995
Adytum
  secret place, 530
  room, 191
  prediction, 511
Aedile
  authority, 745
Aegis
  defence, 717
  patronage, 175
Aeolus

  wind, 349
Aeon
  duration, 106, 110
Aequiparate
  equate, 27
Aequo animo
  insensible, 823
Aerate
  air, 338
Aerial
  aeriform, 334, 338
  elevated, 206
Aerie
  abode, 189
  height, 206
Aeriform
  gaseity, 334, 338
Aerodrome
  destination, 292
Aeronautics
  navigation, 267
Aeroplane
  aircraft, 273A
Aerostat
  balloon, 273A
Aerostatics
  gaseity, 334
  navigation, 267
Aesthetic
  taste, 850
  beauty, 845
  sensibility, 375
Aestival
  morning, 125
Aestivate
  sleep, 68
Aetiology
  knowledge, 490
  attribution, 155
  disease, 655
Afar
  distance, 196
Affable
  courteous, 894
  sociable, 892
Affair
  business, 625, 680
  event, 151
  topic, 454
  battle, 720
Affaire de cœur
  love, 897
Affect
  desire, 865
  love, 897
  lend to, 176

377

touch, 824

Affectability
sensibility, 822

Affectation
pretension, 855
in style, 577

Affection
disposition, 820
love, 897
friendship, 888

Affiance
trust, 858
promise, 768

Affiche
publication, 531

Affidavit
evidence, 467
affirmation, 535
record, 551

Affiliation
relation, 9
kindred, 11
attribution, 155

Affinity
relation, 9
similarity, 17

Affirm
assert, 535
confirm, 488

Affirmatively
assent, 488

Affix
to join, 43
add, 37
sequel, 39
addition, 37

Afflatus
inspiration, 515

Afflict
painfulness, 830

Affliction
calamity, 619
pain, 828

Afflictive
painfulness, 830

Affluent
flowing, 348
sufficient, 639
prosperous, 734
wealthy, 803

Afflux
approach, 286

Afford
supply, 134, 784
wealth, 803

accrue, 810

Affranchise
liberation, 750

Affray
contention, 720

Affright
fear, 880

Affront
insult, 900, 929
courage, 861
molest, 830

Affuse
water, 337

Afire
heat, 382

Afloat,
at sea, 341
on shipboard, 273
unstable, 149
public, 531

Afoot
walking, 266
existing, 1
business, 625
in preparation, 673

Afore
priority, 116

Aforementioned
precedence, 62

Aforesaid
repetition, 104
precedence, 62
priority, 116

Aforethought
intention, 620
premeditation, 611

Afraid
fear, 860

Afreet
demon, 980

Afresh
new, 123
repeated, 104
frequent, 136

Aft
rear, 235

After
in order, 63
in time, 117

After all
qualification, 469

After-clap
disappointment, 509

After-course
plan, 626

After-game
plan, 626

After-life
futurity, 121

After-part
sequel, 65

After-piece
drama, 599

After-time
futurity, 121

Afterglow
light, 420

Aftermath
sequel, 65
effect, 154

Afternoon
evening, 126

Aftertaste
taste, 390

Afterthought
sequel, 65
thought, 451
memory, 505
plan, 626

Afterwards
posteriority, 117

Aga
master, 745

Agacerie
motive, 615

Again
repeated, 104
frequent, 136

Against
physical opposition, 179
voluntary opposition, 708
anteposition, 237
provision, 673

Agape
wonder, 870
curiosity, 455

Agate
ornament, 847

Age
period, 108
oldness, 124
duration, 106
present time, 118
advanced life, 128

Aged
veteran, 130

Ageless perpetual, 112

Agency
physical, 170
instrumentality, 157,

631, 755
direction, 693

Agenda
business, 625
plan, 626

Agent
physical, 153
voluntary, 690
consignee, 758, 769

Agentship
commission, 755

Agglomerate
assemblage, 72
coherence, 46

Agglutinate
coherence, 46

Aggrandize
in degree, 35
in bulk, 194
honour, 873

Aggravate
increase, 35
vehemence, 173
distress, 835
render worse, 659
exasperate, 900
exaggerate, 549
provoke, 830

Aggregate
whole, 50
collection, 72

Aggregation
coherence, 46

Aggression
attack, 716

Aggressive
pugnacious, 901

Aggrieve
distress, 830
injure, 649

Aghast
with wonder, 870
with fear, 860
disappointed, 509

Agile
swift, 274
active, 682

Agio
discount, 813

Agiotage
barter, 794

Agitate
motion, 315
activity, 682
to affect the mind, 821

to excite, 824

Aglow
hot, 382

Agnation
consanguinity, 11

Agnomen
nomenclature, 564

Agnosticism
unbelief, 485, 989

Agnus Dei
rite, 998

Ago
preterition, 122

Agog
curiosity, 455
expectation, 507
desire, 865

Agonstic
contention, 720

Agonize
painfulness, 830

Agony
physical, 378
mental, 828

Agoraphobia
seclusion, 893
dislike, 866

Agrarian
agriculture, 371

Agree
accord, 23
concur, 178
assent, 488
consent, 762
concord, 714

Agreeable
pleasant, 377, 829

Agreeably
conformably, 82

Agreement
bargain, 769

Agrestic
rural, 371
uncouth, 876

Agriculture
agriculture, 371

Agronomy
agriculture, 371

Aground
stranded, 265, 704
fixed, 150
failure, 732

Ague-fit
fear, 860

Anguish

cold, 383

Ahead
in front, 62, 234, 280

Ahead (go)
progression, 282
to improve, 658

Aid
to help, 707, 712
charity, 606

Aide-de-camp
auxiliary, 711
officer, 745

Aide-memoire
memory, 505

Aigrette
ornament, 847

Aiguille
sharp, 253

Ail
sick, 655
in pain, 828

Ailment
disease, 655

Aim
direction, 278
purpose, 620

Aimless
chance, 621
motiveless, 616

Air
gas, 334
atmospheric, 338
wind, 349
tune, 415
appearance, 448
conduct, 692
unsubstantial, 4
fashion, 852
affectation, 855
vanity, 880

Air-balloon
aircraft, 273A

Air-built
imagination, 515

Air-condition
air, 338

Airdrop
transference, 270

Airlift
transference, 270

Air-liner
aircraft, 273A

Air Marshal
master, 745

Air-pipe
air-pipe, 351

Air-pocket
pitfall, 667
Air-raid
attack, 716
Air-tight
closed, 261
Airborne
locomotion, 267
aircraft, 273A
lightness, 320
Aircraft
aeroplane, 273A
Aircraft-carrier
ship, 273
Aircraftman
fighter, 726
Aircrew
fighter, 726
Airfield
arrival, 292
Airgraph
news, 532
letter, 592
Airiness
levity, 320
Airing
journey, 266
Airman
navigation, 269
Airport
arrival, 292
Airship
aircraft, 273A
Airstop
arrival, 292
Airstrip
arrival, 292
Airworthy
safe, 664
Airy
atmosphere, 338
gay, 836
Aisle
passage, 260, 627
church, 1000
Ajutage
see, Adjutage
Akimbo
angular, 244
Akin
consanguinity, 11
Alabaster
whiteness, 430
Alack!

lamentation, 839
Alacrity activity, 682
cheerfulness, 836
Alarm
fear, 860
notice of danger, 669
signal, 550
threatening, 665
Alarmist
newsmonger, 532
Alarum
warning, 669
signal, 550;
loudness, 404
Alas!
lamentation, 839
Alb
dress, 225
vestments, 999
Albeit
counteraction, 179
counter-evidence, 468
compensation, 30
Albescent
white, 430
Albification
white, 430
Albinism
achromatism, 429
Albino
dim-sightedness, 443
Album
book, 553
compendium, 596
repertoire, 636
Albuminous
semiliquidity, 352
Alcade
master, 745
Alchemy
conversion, 144
Alcohol
drunkenness, 986
Alcoran
sacred books, 986
Alcove
cave, 252
dwelling, 189
Alderman
master, 745
Alembic
vessel, 191
laboratory, 691
Alentours
nearness, 197

Alert
active, 682
watchful, 459
alarm, 669
signal, 550
Alexandrine
verse, 597
Alexipharmic
remedy, 662
Alfresco
exterior, 220
air, 338
Algebra
numeration, 85
Algid
cold, 383
Algorism
numeration, 85
Alias
misnomer, 565
Alibi
absence, 187
Alien
irrelevant, 10
foreign, 57
Alienate
transfer, 783
estrange, 889
set against, 898
Alienation (mental)
insanity, 503
Alieni appetens
desire, 865
jealousy, 920
Alienist
doctor, 662
Alight
descend, 306
stop, 265
arrive, 292
light, 420
hot, 382
Align
arrange, 60
trend, 278
Alike
similarity, 17
Aliment
food, 298, 707
Alimentation
aid, 707
Alimony
dowry, 810
provision, 803

Aloud
loudness, 404
Alp
height, 206
Alpha
beginning, 66
Alphabet
letter, 561
beginning, 66
Alphabetize
arrange, 60
Alpinist
ascent, 305
Already
antecedently, 116
even now, 118
past time, 122
Also
addition, 37
accompaniment, 88
Altar
marriage, 903
church, 1000
Alter
vary, 20
change, 140
Alter ego
identity, 13
similarity, 17
deputy, 759
friend, 890
Alterable
mutability, 149
Alterative
salubrity, 656
Altercation
discord, 713
Alternate
reciprocal, 12
periodic, 63, 138
oscillating, 314
discontinuous, 70
Alternative
plan, 626
choice, 609
Although
counteraction, 179
compensation, 30
opposition, 708
counterevidence, 468
Altiloquence
floridity, 577
Altitude
height, 206

Alto
high note, 410
Alto rilievo
convexity, 250
sculpture, 557
Altogether
collectively, 50
entirely, 31
Altruism
disinterestedness, 942
philanthropy, 910
Alumnus
learner, 541
Alveolus
concavity, 252
Always
perpetuity, 112
uniformity, 16
conformity, 82
Amalgam
mixture, 41
compound, 48
Amanuensis
writing, 590
secretary, 553
Amaranthine
perpetual, 112
Amass
whole, 50
store, 636
to collect, 72
Amateur
desire, 865
taste, 850
ignoramus, 493
Amatory
love, 897
Amaurosis
blindness, 442
Amaze
wonder, 870
Amazingly
greatness, 31
Amazon
warrior, 726
courage, 861
Ambages
deviation, 279
Ambassador
messenger, 534
diplomat, 758
Amber
yellowness, 436
semiliquid, 352
Ambergris

oil, 356
fragrance, 400
Ambidexter
right, 238
clever, 678
fickle, 607
Ambient
circumscription, 227
Ambiguous
uncertain, 475, 520
obscure, 571
unintelligible, 519
Ambiloquy
double meaning, 520
Ambit
outline, 229
Ambition
desire, 865
intention, 620
Amble
pace, 266
slowness, 275
Amblyopia
dim-sighted, 443
Ambo
pulpit, 542, 1000
Ambrosial
savouriness, 394
fragrance, 400
Ambulance
remedy, 662
Ambulation
journey, 266
Ambuscade
ambush, 530
Ambush
ambush, 530
Âme damnée
servant, 746
flatterer, 935
bad man, 949
Ameer
master, 745
noble, 875
Ameliorate
improvement, 658
Amen
assent, 488
Amenable
duty, 926
obedient, 743
Amend
improvement, 658
Amende honorable
atonement, 952

Amends
  compensation, 30
  reward, 3973
  atonement, 952
Amenity
  courtesy, 894
Amerce
  penalty, 974
Americanism
  language, 560
Amethyst
  ornament, 847
  purple, 437
Amiable
  lovable, 897
  benevolent, 906
Amicable
  friendly, 888
  assisting, 707
Amice
  vestments, 999
Amicus curiae
  friend, 890
Amidst
  interjacent, 228
  middle, 68
  mixture, 41
Amiss
  wrong, 619, 923
  inexpedient, 647
Amity
  friendship, 888
  concord, 714
  peace, 721
Ammunition
  materials, 635
  warlike, 727
Amnesia
  oblivion, 506
  insensibility, 823
Amnesty
  forgiveness, 918
  pacification, 723
Amoebean
  sequence, 63
Among
  interjacence, 228
  mixture, 41
Amorist
  love, 897
Amoroso
  love, 897
Amorous
  love, 897
Amorphous

  formless, 241
  irregular, 83
Amount
  quantity, 25
  whole, 50
  numeration, 85
  sum of money, 800
  price, 812
Amour
  love, 897
Amour-propre
  vanity, 880
Amphibian
  aircraft, 273A
Amphibious
  unconformity, 83
Amphibology
  equivocality, 520
Amphibrach
  verse, 597
Amphigouri
  ridiculous, 853
  absurdity, 497
Amphimacer
  verse, 597
Amphitheatre
  arena, 728
  theatre, 599
  prospect, 441
  school, 542
Ample
  much, 31
  copious, 639
  large, 192
  broad, 202
  spacious, 180
Amplify
  enlarge, 35
  loudness, 404
  dilate, 194
  expatiate, 573
  exaggerate, 549
Amplitude
  degree, 26
  space, 180
  size, 192
  breadth, 202
Amputate
  subduction, 38
Amtrac
  vehicle, 272
Amuck, run
  violence, 173
  insanity, 503
  excitability, 825

Amulet
  spell, 993
Amuse
  amusement, 840
Amylaceous
  semiliquidity, 352
An
  if, 514
Ana
  description, 594
Anachronism
  anachronism, 115
Anacoluthon
  discontinuity, 70
Anacreontic
  poetry, 597
Anaemia
  pallor, 429
  weakness, 160
  feebleness, 575
Anaesthesia
  insensibility, 376, 381,
  823
Anaesthetist
  doctor, 662
'Ανάγκη,
  necessity, 601
Anaglyph
  sculpture, 557
Anagogic
  concealment, 528
Anagram
  letter, 561
  double meaning, 520
  puzzle, 533, 842
Analecta
  description, 594
Analeptic
  remedy, 662
Analgesia
  insensibility, 376
Analogy
  relation, 9
Analogy
  similarity, 17
  comparison, 464
Analysis
  decomposition, 49
  arrangement, 60
  compendium, 596
  grammar, 567
  algebra, 85
  inquiry, 461
  reasoning, 476

Anamnesis
memory, 505
Anamorphosis
optical, 443
misrepresentation, 555
Anapaest
verse, 597
Anarchist
enemy, 891
evildoer, 913
Anarchy
disorder, 59
social, 738
Anastomosis
junction, 43
crossing, 219
Anastrophe
inversion, 218
Anathema
malediction, 908
disapproval, 932
Anatomy
dissection, 44
skeleton, 329
inquiry, 461
Ancestor
paternity, 166
Anchor
safeguard, 666
hope, 858
fastening, 45, 150
Anchorage
roadstead, 189, 265
Anchoret
asceticism, 955
Anchylosis
immutability, 150
Ancient
oldness, 124
Ancillary
aid, 707
intermediate, 631
And
addition, 37
Andante
music, 415
Andantino
music, 415
Anderson
shelter, 717
Androgynous
unconformity, 83
Anecdotage
loquacity, 584
old age, 128
Anecdote

description, 594
Anemometer
wind, 349
Anent
relation, 9
Aneroid
measurement, 466
air, 338
Anew
newness, 123
Anfractuosity
angle, 244
convolution, 248
Angel
supernatural being, 977
object of love, 948
Angelic
virtue, 944
Angelus
worship, 990
Anger
resentment, 900
Angina
pain, 828
Angle
angularity, 244
pursuit, 622
explore, 463
Anglic
language, 560
Anglophobia
dislike, 867
Anguilline
narrow, 203
serpentine, 248
Anguish
physical, 378
moral, 828
Angular
angularity, 244
Anhelation
fatigue, 688
Anhydrous
dryness, 340
Anility
age, 128
silliness, 499
Animadvert
reprehend, 932
consider, 451
Animal
animal, 366
Animal cries
ululation, 412
Animalcule

minute, 193
Animalism
sensuality, 954
Animality
animality, 364
Animate
excite, 824
cheer, 836
stimulate, 615
living beings, 357
Animation
life, 359
animality, 364
activity, 682
excitation, 824
Animosity
enmity, 889
hatred, 898
anger, 900
Animus
will, 600
intention, 620
animosity, 898, 900
Anklet
ornament, 847
roundness, 247
Annalist
recorder, 114, 553
Annals
record, 551
history, 114
account, 551
Anneal
harden, 323
Annex
add, 37
adjunct, 39
join, 43
Annihilate
extinguish, 2
destroy, 162
Anniversary
period, 138
celebration, 883
Anno Domini
period, 108
Annotation
note, 550
glossary, 522
Annotator
interpreter, 524
Announce
inform, 527
publish, 531
predict, 511

384

assert, 535

Announcement
programme, 510

Announcer
radio, 599B

Annoyance
pain, 828
painfulness, 830
evil, 619
badness, 649

Annual
year, 108
periodic, 138
book, 593

Annuity
wealth, 803, 810

Annul
abrogation, 756, 964

Annular
circularity, 247

Annulet
circularity, 247

Annunciate
inform, 527
publish, 531

Annus mirabilis
period, 108
prodigy, 872

Anodyne
remedy, 174, 662, 834

Anoint
coat, 222
lubricate, 332
oil, 355

Anointed
deity, 976

Anomalistic
unconformity, 83

Anomaly
irregularity, 83
disorder, 59

Anon
ere long, 132
shortly, 111

Anonymous
misnomer, 565

Another
difference, 15

Answer
to an inquiry, 462
reply, 468, 587
confutation, 479
lawsuit, 969
to succeed, 731
serve, 644

Answer for
promise, 768

Answer to
correspond, 9

Answerable
duty, 926
liable, 177

Antaean
huge, 192

Antagonism
difference, 14
enmity, 889
hate, 898
voluntary, 708
physical, 179

Antagonist
opponent, 710
enemy, 891

Antecedence
in order, 62
in time, 116

Antecedent
in order, 64
in time, 116

Antechamber
room, 191

Antedate
anachronism, 115

Antediluvian
oldness, 124
priority, 116

Antelope
velocity, 274

Antemundane
oldness, 124

Antenna
touch, 379

Antepenultimate
end, 67

Anteposition
precedence, 62

Anterior
in order, 62
in time, 116
in place, 234

Ante-room
room, 191

Anthem
worship, 990

Anthology
poem, 597
collection, 72, 596

Anthropology
mankind, 372

Anthropomorphic
mankind, 372

Anthropophagi
evil-doer, 913

Anthropophagous
eat, 296

Antibiotic
remedy, 662

Antic
ridicule, 856

Antichristian
irreligion, 989

Anticipate
early, 132
future, 121
anachronism, 115
expect, 507
foresee, 510
prepare, 673
priority, 116

Anticlimax
depth, 208
bathos, 856
decrease, 36

Anticyclone
rotation, 312

Antidote
remedy, 662
counteraction, 179

Antilogarithm
number, 84

Antinomy
illegality, 964

Antinous
beauty, 845

Antiparallel
obliquity, 217

Antipathy
enmity, 889

Antiphon
music, 415
answer, 462
worship, 990

Antiphrasis
misnomer, 565

Antipodes
distance, 196
antiposition, 237
difference, 14
depth, 208

Antiposition
antiposition, 237

Antiquary
past, 122

Antiquated
vulgarity, 851
Antique
oldness, 124
Anti-scriptural
pagan, 986
Antiseptic
remedy, 662
cleanness, 652
Antisocial
misanthropy, 911
Antistrophe
poetry, 597
Antithesis
contrast, 14
comparison, 464
style, 574
Antitoxin
remedy, 662
Antitype
prototype, 22
Antler
sharpness, 253
Antonomasia
substitution, 147
nomenclature, 564
Antonym
opposite, 14
Anvil
support, 215
preparing, 673
(on the)
plan, 626
Anxiety
pain, 828
fear, 860
desire, 865
Anyhow
careless, 460
Aorist
indefinite time, 119
Apace
swift, 274
short time, 111
early, 132
Apache
ruffian, 913, 949
Apanage
adjunct, 39
property, 780
Apart
distance, 196
singleness, 87
difference, 15

Apartment
room, 191
abode, 189
Apathy
physical, 376
moral, 823
indifference, 456, 866
Ape
imitation, 19
Apelles
artist, 559
Aperçu
compendium, 596
Aperitif
food, 298
Aperture
opening, 260
Apex
summit, 210
Aphasia
aphony, 581
Aphelion
distance, 196
Aphony
aphony, 581
Aphorism
maxim, 496
Aphrodisiac
excitation, 824
Aphrodite
goddess, 979
love, 897
Apiary
domestication, 370
Apicius
gluttony, 957
Apiece
disjunction, 44
particularity, 79
Aplomb
vertical, 212
intelligence, 498
self-possession, 864
Apocalypse
revelation, 985
Apocryphal
uncertain, 475
false, 495, 544
Apodictic
demonstration, 478
Apogee
distance, 196
summit, 210
Apolaustic
self-indulgent, 943

Apollo
god, 979
music, 415
beauty, 845
Apologue
description, 521, 594
Apology
penitence, 950
vindication, 937
reasoning, 476
atonement, 952
substitute, 147
Apophthegm
maxim, 496
Apoplexy
weakness, 160
Aposiopesis
taciturnity, 585
Apostasy
palinode, 607
dishonour, 940
heterodoxy, 984A
Apostate
knave, 941
renegade, 144, 742
Apostatize
tergiversation, 607
Apostle
teacher, 540
Apostolic
revelation, 985
Apostrophe
appeal, 765
address, 586, 589
Apothecary
doctor, 662
Apotheosis
deification, 981, 991
Apozem
solution, 335
Appal
fear, 860
Appalling
painfulness, 830
Appanage
see Apanage
Apparatus
instrument, 633
Apparel
vestment, 225
Apparent
visible, 446
manifest, 525
Apparition
ghost, 980

appearance, 448

Appeal
request, 765
address, 586

Appear
come into being, 1, 448
come to light, 525
come into view, 446

Appear for
deputy, 759

Appearance
sight, 448
probability, 472

Appease
physically, 174
morally, 826
conciliate, 918

Appeasement
pacifism, 723
submission, 725

Appellant
plaintiff, 924, 938, 967

Appellation
nomenclature, 564

Append
addition, 37
sequence, 63
hang, 214

Appendage
adjunct, 39

Appendix
sequel, 65

Apperception
knowledge, 490
conception, 453

Appertain
belong, 777
related to, 9
right, 922
inclusion, 76

Appetence
desire, 865

Appetiser
whet, 298, 615

Appetite
desire, 865

Applaud
approbation, 931

Apple-green
greenness, 435

Apple of discord
discord, 713

Apple-sauce
flattery, 933

Appleton layer
air, 338

Appliance
means, 632
instrument, 633

Applicable
to use, 644
expedient, 646
relative, 23

Applicant
petitioner, 767

Application
use, 677
request, 765
metaphor, 521
study, 457

Appoggiatura
music, 415

Appoint
commission, 755
command, 741

Appointment
salary, 809
equipment, 633
interview, 892

Apportion
allot, 786
arrange, 60
portion, 51

Apportionment
dispersion, 73

Apposite
agreeing, 23
relative, 9

Apposition
agreement, 23
closeness, 199

Appraise
value, 812
estimate, 466

Appreciate
measure, 466
taste, 850
realize, 450
gratitude, 916
judge, 480
approve, 931

Apprehend
know, 490
believe, 484
fear, 860
seize, 789, 969

Apprehension
conception, 453

Apprentice
learner, 541

Apprenticeship
learning, 539
training, 673

Apprise
information, 527

Approach move, 286
nearness, 197
path, 627
of time, 121

Approbation
approbation, 931

Appropinquation
approach, 197, 286

Appropriate
fit, 23, 646
special, 79
to assign, 786
to take, 789
to steal, 791

Appropriation
stealing, 791

Approve
commend, 931
corroborate, 467
assent, 488

Approximate
approach, 286
nearness, 197
in mathematics, 85
resemble, 17
related to, 9

Appulse
convergence, 286, 290
collision, 276

Appurtenance
part, 51
component, 56

Apricot
colour, 439

April fool
fool, 501

Apron
dress, 225
vestments, 999

Apropos
relation, 9
expedience, 646
occasion, 134

Apse
church, 1000

Apt
consonant, 23
clever, 698

docile, 539
willing, 602
expedient, 646
tendency, 176
Aptitude
intelligence, 498
skill, 698
Aquarium
domestication, 370
collection, 636
Aquatic
water, 337
Aquatint
engraving, 558
Aqueduct
conduit, 350
Aqueous
water, 337
Aquiline
angularity, 244
Arabesque
ornament, 847
Arable
agriculture, 371
Araeometer
density, 321
measure, 466
Arbiter
judge, 480, 967
adviser, 695
Arbiter elegantiarum
taste, 850
Arbitrament
sentence, 969
judgment, 480
choice, 609
Arbitrary
without law, 964
authority, 737
obstinate, 606
severity, 739
irregular, 83
without relation, 10
Arbitrate
mediate, 724, 969
judge, 480
Arbor
support, 215
Arborescence
branching, 205, 242, 256
Arboretum
agriculture, 371
Arboriculture
agriculture, 371

Arbour
abode, 189
Arc
curvature, 245
Arc-lamp
light, 423
Arcade
arch, 245
passage, 189
Arcades ambo
similarity, 17
friend, 890
Arcadian
delightful, 829
Arcanum
secret, 533
Arch
curve, 245
great, 31
cunning, 702
roguish, 842
greatness, 31
Archaeology
preterition, 122
Archaic
oldness, 124
Archaism
inelegance, 579
Archangel
angel, 977
Archbishop
clergy, 996
Archdeacon
clergy, 996
Archduke
master, 745
Archetype
prototype, 22
model, 80
Arch-fiend
Satan, 978
Archiepiscopacy
churchdom, 995
Archimandrite
sorcerer, 994
Archimage
clergy, 996
Archipelago
island, 346
Architect
constructor, 164
agent, 690
Architecture
construction, 161
fabric, 329

Architrave
summit, 210
Archive
record, 551
Archness
cunning, 702
cleverness, 498
intelligence, 450
Archon
master, 745
Arch-traitor
knave, 941
Arctic
polar, 237
cold, 383
Arcuation
curvature, 245
Ardent
fiery, 382
feeling, 821
desire, 865
expectant, 507
Ardour
activity, 682
Arduous
difficulty, 704
Area
region, 181
quantity, 25
Arefaction
dryness, 340
Arena
field, 181, 728
amusement, 840
workshop, 691
Arenaceous
pulverulence, 330
Areolar
crossing, 219
Areopagus
council, 696
Area
god, 979
Arête
height, 206
sharpness, 253
Argent
whiteness, 430
Argillaceous
softness, 324
Argosy
ship, 273
Argot
language, 560

388

Arguably
probably, 471
Argue
reason, 476
evidence, 467
indicate, 550
discord, 713
Argument
evidence, 467
topic, 454
meaning, 516
compendium, 596
Argumentum ad crumenam
money, 800
Argumentum ad hominem
speciality, 79
accusation, 938
Argumentum ad misericordiam
pity, 914
Argumentum ad verecundiam
probity, 939
Argumentum baculinum
compulsion, 744
Argus-eyed
sight, 441
vigilant, 459
Argute
wisdom, 498
Aria
music, 415
Arid
dryness, 340
Ariel
messenger, 534
swift, 274
courier, 268
spirit, 979
Arietta
music, 415
Aright
goodness, 618, 648
Arise
begin, 66
mount, 305
appear, 446
happen, 151
proceed from, 154
exist, 1
Aristarchus
taste, 850

Aristocracy
power, 737
nobility, 875
Aristocratic
fashionable, 852
Arithmetic
numeration, 85
Ark
asylum, 666
Arm
instrument, 266, 633
part, 51
power, 157
to provide, 637
to prepare, 673
war, 722
Armada
ship, 273
Armageddon
contention, 720
Armament
arms, 727
Armature
arms, 727
Armiger
nobility, 875
Armistice
pacification, 721, 723
Armless
impotence, 158
Armlet
roundness, 247
inlet, 343
Armorial
indication, 550
Armour
arms, 727
defence, 717
soldier, 726
Armour-plated
covered, 222
Armoured car
vehicle, 272
Armoury
store, 636
Arms
blazon, 550
scutcheon, 877
war, 722
weapon, 727
See Arm
Army
troops, 726
multitude, 102
collection, 72

Aroma
fragrance, 400
Around
circumjacent, 227
Arouse
motive, 615
Arpeggio
music, 415
Arquebus
arms, 727
Arraign
accuse, 938
indict, 969
Arrange
order, 60
plan, 626
to prepare, 673
to settle, 723
Arrangement
order, 58
music, 415
Arrant
greatness, 31
Arras
ornament, 847
Array
order, 58
series, 69
dress, 225
prepare, 673
beauty, 845
multitude, 102
assemblage, 72
Arrears
debt, 806
Arrest
stop, 142, 265
seize, 789
imprison, 751
commit, 969
Arrière-pensée
plan, 626
sequel, 65
Arrive
reach, 292
approach, 286
happen, 151
complete, 729
Arrogant
insolent, 885
severe, 739
proud, 878
Arrogate
assume, 885
claim, 922

Arrondissement
region, 181
Arrow
swift, 274
missile, 284
arms, 727
Arrow-headed
angular, 244
Arrowy
sharp, 253
Arsenal
store, 636
military, 727
Arson
calefaction, 384
Art
skill, 698
cunning, 702
deception, 545
representation, 554
business, 625
Artemis
goddess, 979
Arterialize
to aerate, 338
Artery
conduit, 350
Artesian well
conduit, 348
Artful
cunning, 702
deceitful, 544
Article
thing, 3, 316
goods, 798
part, 51
conditions, 770
dissertation, 595
Articles
belief, 484, 983
Articulation
speech, 580
junction, 43
Artifice
cunning, 702
plan, 626
deception, 545
Artificer
agent, 690
Artificial
cunning, 702
fictitious, 544
style, 579
Artillery
arms, 727

corps of, 726
explosion, 404
Artisan
agent, 690
Artist
contriver, 626
producer, 164
painter, 559
agent, 690
Artiste
the drama, 599
Artistic
skilful, 698
beautiful, 845
tasteful, 850
Artless
natural, 703
veracious, 543
plain, 576
As
motive, 615
Ascend
ascent, 305
Ascendancy
Power, 157, 175
success, 731
Ascent
rise, 305
acclivity, 217
glory, 873
Ascertain
find out, 480A
Asceticism
asceticism, 955
temperance, 953
Ascribable
effect, 154
Ascribe
attribution, 155
Asepsis
cleanness, 652
Ash colour
grey, 432
Ashamed
shame, 874
humility, 879
modest, 881
Ashes
residue, 40
corpse, 362
Ashore
land, 342
Ashy
colourless, 429
Aside

laterally, 236
privately, 528
soliloquy, 589
Aside (to put)
relinquish, 624
disuse, 678
Asinine
imbecile, 499
Ask
inquire, 461
request, 765
as price, 812
supplicate, 990
Askance
obliquity, 217
doubt, 485
Askew
oblique, 217
distorted, 243
Aslant
obliquity, 217
Asleep
inactivity, 683
Aslope
obliquity, 217
Aspect
appearance, 448
state, 7
feature, 5
situation, 183
relation, 9
of thought, 453
Asperge
sprinkle, 337
Aspergillum
spray, 348
Asperity
roughness, 256
tartness, 895
anger, 900
Asperse
detraction, 934
Aspersorium
spray, 348
Asphalt
semiliquid, 352
Asphyxiate
killing, 361
Aspirant
petitioner, 767
Aspirate
voice, 580
Aspire
rise, 305
desire, 865

hope, 858
project, 620

Ass
beast of burden, 271
fool, 501

Assagai
arms, 727

Assail
attack, 716
plain, 830

Assailant
opponent, 710
attacker 716, 726

Assassinate
killing, 361

Assault
attack, 716

Assay
experiment, 463

Assemble
assemblage, 72

Assembly-room
sociality, 892

Assent
agree, 488
consent, 762

Assert
affirm, 535
claim as a right, 924

Assess
measure, 466
judge, 480
price, 812

Assessor
adviser, 695

Assets
property, 780
money, 800

Asseverate
affirm, 535

Assiduous
activity, 682

Assign
attribute, 155
transfer, 783
give, 784
commission, 755
allot, 786
duty, 926

Assignat
money, 800

Assignation
sociality, 892

Assignee
receive, 785

Assignment
allotment, 786
business, 625
commission, 755

Assimilate
resemble, 17, 144
imitate, 19
agree, 23

Assist
aid, 707
benefit, 906

Assistant
auxiliary, 711

Assize
measure, 466
tribunal, 966

Associate
accompany, 88
concur, 178
unite, 43
mixture, 41
assemble, 72
friend, 890
society, 892

Association
relation, 9
intuition, 477

Assoil
free, 750
acquit, 970

Assonance
similarity, 17
poetry, 597

Assort
arrange, 60

Assortment
class, 75
collection, 72

Assuage
physically, 174
morally, 826
relieve, 834

Assume
suppose, 514
evidence, 467
hope, 858
right, 924
insolence, 739, 885
pride, 878
falsehood, 544

Assumption
qualification, 469
severity, 739

Assurance
assertion, 535

promise, 768
certainty, 474
belief, 484
hope, 858
insolence, 885

Assuredly
positively, 31
assert, 488
safety, 664

Asterisk
indication, 550
expletive, 908

Astern
rear, 235

Asteroid
world, 318

Asteroth
deity, 979

Asthenia
weakness, 160

Astigmatism
dim-sightedness, 443

Astonish
wonder, 870

Astonishing
great, 31

Astound
surprise, 870
excite, 824

Astraea
right, 922

Astral
world, 318
immaterial, 317

Astray
deviation, 279

Astriction
junction, 43

Astride
support, 215

Astringent
contraction, 195

Astrology
prediction, 511

Astronaut
navigator, 269

Astronautics
navigation, 267

Astronomy
world, 318

Astrophysics
world, 318

Astute
wisdom, 498

Asunder
separate, 44
distant, 196
disjunction, 44

Asylum
retreat, 666
hospital, 662
defence, 717

Asymmetry
disorder, 59, 243

Asymptote
converge, 290

At-home
sociality, 892

At once
transientness, 111

At the end of the day
finally, 67

Ataraxia
insensibility, 823

Atavism
reversion, 145

Atelier
workshop, 691

Atheism
irreligion, 989
unbelief, 485

Athena
goddess, 979

Athirst
desire, 865

Athletic
strength, 159

Athletics
training, 673
contention, 720

Athwart
oblique, 217
crossing, 219
opposing, 708

Atlantis
visionary, 515

Atlas
support, 215
strength, 159;
maps, 554

Atmosphere
air, 338
circumstances, 227

Atoll
island, 346

Atom
small in degree, 32
in size, 193
particle, 330

Atomic bomb
arms, 727

Atomizer
spray, 348

Atonality
melody, 413

Atonement
atonement, 952
religious, 976
reward, 973

Atony
weakness, 160

Atrabilious
dejection, 837

Atrocious
vice, 945
guilt, 947
malevolence, 907

Atrophy
shrinking, 195
disease, 655
decay, 659

Attaboy
approval, 931

Attach
join, 43
love, 897
legal, 969

Attaché
servant, 746
consignee, 758

Attaché-case
receptacle, 191

Attachment
see Attach

Attack
attack, 716
disease, 655

Attain
arrive, 292
succeed, 731

Attainable
possible, 470
easy, 705

Attainder
condemnation, 971

Attainment
learning, 539
knowledge, 490
skill, 698

Attar
fragrance, 400

Attemper
mix, 41
moderate, 174

Attempt
undertaking, 676
try, 675

Attend
accompany, 88
follow, 281
treat, 662
apply the mind, 457
frequent, 136
be present, 186

Attendant
servant, 746

Attention
attention, 451, 457
respect, 928

Attentions
courtesy, 894
courtship, 902
kindness, 906

Attenuate
lessen, 36
rarefy, 322
contract, 195
narrow, 203

Attest
bear testimony, 467
indicate, 550
adjure, 768

Attestation
record, 551

Attic
garret, 191
high, 206
elegant, 578
wit, 842
taste, 850

Atticism
wit, 842

Attila
evildoer, 913

Attire
vestment, 225

Attitude
posture, 183, 240
circumstance, 8

Attitudinize
affectation, 855
ostentation, 882

Attorney
consignee, 758, 769
in law, 968

Attract
bring towards, 288
please, 829
allure, 865

Autocrat
master, 745
Autocratic
arbitrary, 739, 964
will, 600
Autocycle
vehicle, 272
Autogiro
aircraft, 273A
Autograph
warranty, 467
signature, 550
writing, 590
Autolycus
thief, 792
Automatic
mechanical, 601
insensible, 823
Automation
means, 632
Automobile
vehicle, 272
Autonomy
freedom, 748
Autopsy
vision, 441
disinter, 363
Autotype
copy, 21
Aux abois
death, 360
Aux aguets
care, 459
Auxiliary
aid, 707
helper, 711
intermediary, 631
Avail
use, 677
utility, 644
Avalanche
fall, 306
debacle, 348
Avant-courier
pioneer, 673
precursor, 64
Avant-garde
go-ahead, 282
Avarice
parsimony, 819
Avast
quiescence, 265
cessation, 142
Avaunt
disappear, 449
depart, 293

repulse, 289
Ave
arrival, 292
Avenge
revenge, 919
Avenue
street, 189
method, 627
Aver
affirmation, 535
Average
mean, 29
ordinary, 82, 736
Avernus
hell, 982
Averse
unwilling, 603
repugnant, 616
Aversion
dislike, 867
enmity, 889;
hate, 898
Avert
hindrance, 706
Aviary
collection, 636
taming, 370
Aviation
locomotion, 267
Avidity
desire, 865
avarice, 819
Avifauna
animals, 366
Avocation
business, 625
diversion, 840
Avoid
shun, 623, 867
Avoirdupois
weight, 319
Avouch
affirmation, 535
Avow
assert, 535
assent, 488
disclose, 529
Avulsion
separation, 44
extraction, 301
Await
future, 121
impend, 152
Awake
excite, 824

incite, 615
active, 682
attentive, 457
careful, 459
Award
lawsuit, 969
judgment, 480
decision, 609
giving, 784
trophy, 733
Aware
knowledge, 490
Away
absence, 187
Awe
wonder, 870
fear, 860
Aweary
weariness, 841
Awestruck
fear, 860
Awful
great, 31
fearful, 860
Awhile
transientness, 111
Awkward
unskilful, 699
vulgar, 851
ridiculous, 853
difficult, 704
Awl
perforator, 262
Awn
bristle, 253
Awning
tent, 222
shade, 424
top, 210
Awry
oblique, 217
distorted, 243
Axe
edge tool, 253
weapon, 727
for beheading, 975
Axiom
maxim, 496
Axiomatic
truth, 494
certain, 474
demonstrable, 469, 478
Axis
rotation, 312
length, 200

support, 215
centre, 223
Axle
rotation, 312
Ay
yes, 488
affirmation, 535
Ayah
keeper, 753
Aye
ever, 112
Azimuth
direction, 278
obliquity, 217
Azoic
inanimate, 358
Azure
blueness, 438
Azygous
unity, 87

Baa
animal sound, 412
Baal
divinity, 979
idol, 986
Babel
talk, 584
nonsense, 517
faint sound, 405
flow, 348
Babe
infant, 129
innocent, 946
novice, 701
Bable
confusion, 59
discord, 414
Baboon
ugliness, 846
Baby
fool, 501
Baby-sitter
deputy, 759
Babyhood
youth, 127
Babyish
folly, 499
Bacca
tobacco, 298A
Bacchanals
drunk, 959
Bacchus
drunkenness, 959
Bachelor

celibacy, 904
Bacillus
bane, 663
Back
rear, 235
convexity, 250
to recede, 283
to aid, 707
Back-blocks
interior, 221
Back down
revoke, 607
Back out
revoke, 607
relinquish, 624
Back to square one
hindrance, 706
Back-scratcher
flatterer, 935
Backbite
traduce, 932
detract, 934
Backbiter
detractor, 936
Backbone
frame, 215
interior, 221
strength, 159
decision, 604
intrinsic, 5
Backer
friend, 891
Backhanded
oblique, 717
unexpected, 508
Backhander
attack, 716
Backlash
recoil, 145
Backlog
leeway, 304
Backsheesh
see Baksheesh
Backsliding
dishonour, 940
delinquency, 945
relapse, 661
tergiversation, 607
heresy, 984A
Backward
regression, 283
traction, 285
unwilling, 603
Backwardation
discount, 813

Backwardness
unwillingness, 603
indocility, 538
dislike, 867
Backwoodsman
inhabitant, 188
forester, 371
Bacon, to save one's
escape, 671
Bad
badness, 649, 945
evil, 619
wrong, 923
putrid, 653
Bad blood
enmity, 889
Bad show
disapproval, 932
failure, 732
Badge
indication, 550
Badger
to maltreat, 830
question, 461
stink, 401
Badinage
wit, 842
ridicule, 856
Badmash
knave, 941
Baedeker
guide, 266
Baffle
thwart, 706
defeat, 731
Baffling
bewildering, 528
Baff
club, 276
Bag
receptacle, 191
to take, 789, 791
to receive, 810
to pocket, 184
Bagatelle
trifle, 643
Baggage
property, 780
materials, 634
hussy, 962
Baggy
loose, 47
bulging, 250
Bagman
agent, 758

Bagnio
impurity, 961
Bagpipe
musical instrument, 417
Bagpiper
musician, 416
Bags
greatness, 31
plenty, 639
Bah
contempt, 930
Baikie
receptacle, 191
Bail
security, 771
Bail up
rob, 791
Bailiff
director, 694
servant, 746
officer, 965
factor, 758
Bailiwick
region, 181
tribunal, 966
Bairn
infant, 129
Bait
allurement, 615
food, 298, 689
harass, 907, 830
Bake
heat, 384
Bakehouse
furnace, 386
Baker's dozen
thirteen, 98
Baksheesh
gratuity, 784
Balance
equality, 27
symmetry, 242
remainder, 40
numeration, 85
measure, 466
weight, 319
money, 800
accounts, 811
mean, 29
steadiness, 265
Balcony
convexity, 250
theatre, 599
Bald
bare, 226

ugly, 846
in style, 575
Baldachin
canopy, 222
Balderdash
absurdity, 497
nonsense, 517
Baldric
girdle, 247
Bale bundle, 72
evil, 619
Bale out
ejection, 297
Baleful
badness, 649
Balk
hinder, 706
fail, 731
disappoint, 509
deceive, 545
Ball
globe, 249
missile, 284, 727
dance, 840
Ball-point
pen, 590
Ballad
song, 415
poem, 597
Ballad opera
drama, 599
Ballade
poem, 597
music, 415
Ballast
weight, 319
compensation, 30
steadiness, 150
wisdom, 498
Ballet
amusement, 840
Ballistics
propulsion, 284
Ballon d'essai
feeler, 461, 463
Balloon
aircraft, 273A
Ballot
choice, 609
Ballyhoo
publicity, 531
Ballyrag
abuse, 932
Balm
fragrance, 400

relief, 834
lenitive, 174
remedy, 662
Balmoral
cap, 225
Balmy
foolish, 499
Balsam
see Balm
Balsamic
salubrious, 656
Baluster
support, 215
Balustrade
enclosure, 232
Bamboo curtain
secret, 533
Bamboozle
deception, 545
Ban
prohibition, 761
denunciation, 908
condemnation, 971
Banal
commonplace, 82, 643
feeble, 575
Banausic
menial, 876
Band
ligature, 45
assemblage, 72
party, 712
of music, 416
shackle, 752
Bandage
ligature, 45
to lie, 43
Bandbox
receptacle, 191
Banderole
flag, 550
Bandersnatch
swiftness, 274
Bandit
thief, 792
Bandog
warning, 668
Bandolier
roundness, 247
Bands
canonicals, 999
Bandy
agitate, 315
contest, 476, 720
exchange, 148

crooked, 245
deformed, 876
Bandy-legged
distorted, 243
curved, 245
Bane
badness, 649, 663
Bang
sound, 406
to impel, 276
to beat, 972
Bangle
ornament, 847
Banian day
fast, 956
scanty, 640
Banish
exclude, 55, 297
displace, 185
seclude, 893
punish, 972
Banister
support, 215
Banjo
musical instrument, 417
Bank
side of river, 342
acclivity, 217
store, 636
money, 802
deviate, 279
Banker
treasurer, 801
Bankruptcy
failure, 732
non-payment, 808
Banlieue
nearness, 197
Banner
indication, 550
Banneret
nobility, 875
Banquet
meal, 298
feast, 840
gluttony, 957
Banshee
demon, 980
Bantam
small, 193
low, 207
Banter
wit, 842
ridicule, 856
Bantling

child, 129
offspring, 167
Baptism
rite, 998
Baptistery
temple, 1000
Baptize
name, 564
Bar
hindrance, 706
line, 200
to exclude, 55
close, 261
enclosure, 232
prison, 752
prohibition, 761
tribunal, 966
legal profession, 968
drink, 298
Baragouin
absurdity, 497
Barb
spike, 253
horse, 271
Barbarian
evildoer, 913
Barbarism
discourtesy, 895
solecism, 568
Barbarous
maleficent, 907
vulgar, 851
rude, 876
style, 579
Barbette
defence, 717
Barbican
defence, 717
Bard
poetry, 597
Bare
mere, 32
nude, 226
scanty, 640
exposed to view, 446
Barefaced
visible, 446
shameless, 885
insolent, 886
Barefoot
divest, 226
Bareheaded
divest, 226
respect, 928
Barely

smallness, 32
Bargain
compact, 769
barter, 794
promise, 768
cheap, 813, 815
Bargain, into the
addition, 37
Barge
ship, 273
Bargee
mariner, 269
Baritone
deep-toned, 408
Bark
rind, 223
ship, 273
to yelp, 412
to censure, 932
Barker
interpreter, 524
publicity, 531
Barm
yeast, 353
Barmy
foolish, 499
Barn
abode, 189
Barnacles
spectacles, 445
Barometer
measurement, 466
air, 338
Baron
nobility, 875
master, 745
Baronet
nobility, 875
Baronetage
list, 86
Baronetcy
title, 877
Baroque
ridiculous, 853
Barque
ship, 273
Barquentine
ship, 273
Barrack
abode, 189
Barrage
obstacle, 706
Barred
crossed, 219
striped, 440

Barrel
 vessel, 191
 cylinder, 249
Barren
 sterile, 169
 useless, 645
Barricade
 fence, 232
 prison, 752
 obstacle, 706
Barrier
 fence, 232
 obstacle, 706
Barring
 except, 83
 save, 38
Barrister
 lawyer, 968
Barrow
 vehicle, 272
 grave, 363
Barter
 exchange, 794
Bas bleu
 affectation, 855
Bascule
 instrument, 633
Base
 lowest part, 211P
 support, 215
 bad, 649
 dishonourable, 940
 shameful, 874
 vicious, 945
 cowardly, 862
 plebeian, 876
Base-minded
 improbity, 940
Baseless
 unreal, 2
 erroneous, 495
Basement
 base, 211
Bashaw
 ruler, 745
Bashful
 modesty, 881
Basic
 support, 215
Basic English
 language, 560
Basilica
 temple, 1000
Basilisk
 serpent, 949
 monster, 83

 evil eye, 441
Basin
 hollow, 252
 vessel, 191
 plain, 344
 dock, 189
Basis
 preparation, 673
 foundation, 215
Bask
 warmth, 382
 physical enjoyment, 377
 moral enjoyment, 827
 prosperity, 734
Basket
 receptacle, 191
Basket-work
 plaiting, 219
Basketry
 plaiting, 219
Bas-relief
 convexity, 250
Bass
 deep-sounding, 408, 413
Bass/viol
 musical instrument, 417
Bassinette
 vehicle, 272
Basso rilievo
 convexity, 250P
 sculpture, 557
Bassoon
 musical instrument, 417
Bastard
 spurious, 544, 925
 erroneous, 495
Bastardy
 illegitimacy, 964
Baste
 beat, 276
 punish, 972
Bastille
 prison, 752
Bastinado
 punishment, 972
Bastion
 defence, 717
Bat
 club, 633, 727
 spree, 840
Batch
 assemblage, 72
 quantity, 25
Bate
 diminish, 36, 38

 reduce price, 813
Bath
 immersion, 300
 water, 337
Bath-chair
 vehicle, 272
Bath-room
 room, 191
Bathe
 immersion, 300
 plunge, 310
Bathing-suit
 dress, 225
Bathos
 depth, 208
 anticlimax, 497
 ridiculous, 853
Bathymetry
 depth, 208
Bathysphere
 depth, 208
Baton
 sceptre, 747
 impact, 276
Bats
 insane, 503
Battalion
 troop, 726
 assemblage, 72
Batten
 feed, 296
Batter
 beat, 276
 destroy, 162
Battered
 imperfect, 651
Battering-ram
 weapon, 276, 727
Battery
 instrument, 633
Battle
 contention, 720
Battle array
 warfare, 722
 arrangement, 60
Battle-axe
 arms, 727
Battle-bowler
 defence, 717
Battle-cruiser
 ship, 273
Battle-dress
 dress, 225
Battle-field
 arena, 728

Beautify
enrapture, 829
honour, 873
sanctify, 987, 995
Beating
impulse, 276
Beatnik
hippy, 183
Beatitude
pleasure, 827
Beau
fop, 854
man, 373
admirer, 897
Beau idéal
beauty, 845
perfection, 650
Beau monde
fashion, 852
nobility, 875
Beau sabreur
hero, 861
Beauty
beauty, 845
ornament, 847
symmetry, 242
Beaver
hat, 225
Bebop
melody, 413
Becalm
quiescence, 265
Because
attribution, 155
reasoning, 476
motive, 615
Bechance
eventuality, 151
Beck
rill, 348
signal, 550
mandate, 741
Beckon
signal, 550
Becloud
darkness, 421
Become
change to, 144
behove, 926
Become of
event, 151
Becoming
proper, 646
beautiful, 845
just, 922

apt, 23
Bed
layer, 204
support, 215
lodgment, 191
Bed-maker
servant, 746
Bedabble
splash, 337
Bedarken
darkness, 421
Bedaub
cover, 222
dirt, 653
deface, 846
Bedazzle
light, 420
Bedeck
beauty, 845
ornament, 847
Bedevil
derange, 61
bewitch, 992
Bedew
moisture, 339
Bedfellow
friend, 890
Bedight
beauty, 845
Bedim
darkness, 421
Bedizen
beautify, 845
ornament, 851
Bedlam
insanity, 503
Bedlamite
madman, 504
Bedraggle
soil, 653
Bedridden
disease, 655
Bedstead
support, 215
Bedtime
evening, 126
Bee
active, 682
party, 892
Bee-line
direction, 278
Bee-witted
folly, 499
Beef
complain, 839

Beefy
corpulent, 192
Beelzebub
Satan, 978
Beery
drunken, 959
Beeswax
oil, 356
Beetle
high, 206
projecting, 250
impact, 276
Befall
eventuality, 151
Befit
agree, 23
Befitting
right, 926
expedient, 646
Befool
deceive, 503, 545
baffle, 732
Before
precedence, 62
Before Christ
period, 108
Beforehand
prior, 116, 132
Befoul
uncleanness, 653
Beg
request, 765
Beg the question
evidence, 467
Beget
produce, 161
Begetter
father, 166
Beggar
petitioner, 767
poor, 804
Beggarly
mean, 643
vulgar, 876
servile, 886
vile, 940
Begilt
ornament, 847
Begin
beginning, 66
Begin again
repetition, 104
Beginner
learner, 541
novice, 674

400

Beginning to end, from,
whole, 50
completeness, 52
duration, 106
Begird
encircle, 227, 231
Begone
depart, 293
repel, 289
Begrime
soil, 653
deface, 846
Begrudge
refusal, 764
parsimony, 819
Beguile
deceive, 545
amuse, 840
Beguine
nun, 996
Begum
nobility, 875
Behalf
advantage, 618
aid, 707
Behave
conduct, 692
Behead
punish, 972
divide, 44
Behest
command, 741
Behind
in order, 63
in space, 235
Behindhand
late, 133
adversity, 735
insolvent, 808
shortcoming, 304
Behold
vision, 441
Beholden
grateful, 916
obligatory, 926
Behoof
good, 618
Behove
duty, 926
Bein
prosperous, 734
Being
abstract, 1
conduct, 3
Bejan

learner, 541
Bel canto
music, 415
Bel esprit
humorist, 844
Belabour
thump, 972
buffet, 276
Belated
late, 133
confused, 491
Belaud
approbation, 931
Belay
junction, 43
stop, 265
Belch
ejection, 297
Beldam
old woman, 130
hag, 913
Beleaguer
attack, 716
Belfry
height, 206
church, 1000
head, 450
Belie
falsify, 544
misinterpret, 523
deny, 536
disagreement, 24
oppose, 708
Belief
credence, 484
supposition, 514
religious creed, 983
Believer
piety, 987
Belike
probability, 472
Belittle
disparage, 483
Bell
sound, 417
cry, 412
funeral, 363
alarm, 669
Bell-boy
messenger, 534
Bell-shaped
globose, 249
concave, 252
Bell-washer
precursor, 64

Belle
woman, 374
beauty, 845
Belles-lettres
language, 560
knowledge, 490
Bellicose
warlike, 722
Belligerent
warfare, 722
Bellow
cry, 411, 412
complain, 839
Bellows
wind, 349
Belly
receptacle, 191
interior, 221
to bulge, 250
Belly-ache
complain, 839
Belly-god
glutton, 957
Belly-timber
food, 298
Bellyful
sufficiency, 639
fullness, 52
Belong
related, 9
property, 717
attribute, 157
duty, 926
inclusion, 76
Belongings
property, 780
Beloved
lover, 897, 899
Below
lowness, 207
posterior, 117
Belt
girdle, 247
gulf, 343
outline, 229
blow, 276
Belvedere
vision, 441
Bemire
soil, 653
Bemoan
lament, 839
Bemuddle
bewilder, 458
Bemuse
bewilder, 458

Ben
height, 206
interior, 221
Ben trovato
probable, 472
falsehood, 544
deception, 545
Bench
support, 215
council, 696
tribunal, 966
Bencher
lawyer, 968
Bend
curve, 245
angularity, 244
circle, 247
yield, 324, 725
circuit, 311
obliquity, 217
descent, 806
deviation, 279
bow, 308
humble, 879
Bend to
tend, 176
habit, 613
Bending
pliant, 324
Beneath
under, 207
unbecoming, 940
Benedick
marriage, 903
Benedictine
clergy, 996
Benediction
approval, 931
gratitude, 916
worship, 990
Benefaction
giving, 784
Benefactor
benevolence, 912
giver, 784
Benefice
churchdom, 995
Beneficent
benevolence, 906
Beneficial
useful, 644
good, 648
Beneficiary
clergy, 996

Benefit
advantage, 618
acquisition, 775
benevolence, 906
Benevolence
kindness, 906
love, 897;
tax, 812
Benighted
ignorance, 491
darkness, 421
Benignant
benevolence, 906
Benison
approbation, 931
Bent
direction, 278
inclination, 602
desire, 865
tendency, 176
intentions, 629
affections, 820
dishonest, 940
Bent on
willing, 602
resolved, 604, 620
desirous, 865
Benthamite
philanthropy, 910
Benumb
cold, 383
general insensibility, 376
tactual insensibility, 381
apathy, 823
Beplaster
cover, 222
Bepraise
approbation, 931
Bequeath
giving, 784
Bequest
gift, 784
acquisition, 775
Berceuse
music, 415
Bereave
take away, 789
Bereavement
loss, 789
Bereft
poor, 804
loss, 776
Bergschrund
interval, 198

Berlin
vehicle, 272
Berry
brown, 433
Bersagliere
combatant, 726
Berserker
combatant, 726
violence, 173
Berth
lodging, 189
bed, 191
repose, 215
Beryl
ornament, 847
Beseech
request, 765
Beseem
duty, 926
Beset
surround, 227
difficulty, 704
entreaty, 765
beshrew, 908
by the side of, 216
Besetting
habitual, 613
Beshrew
curse, 908
Beside
except, 83
accompaniment, 216
Beside, oneself
insanity, 503
Beside the mark
irrelation, 10
Besides
addition, 37, 88
Besiege
attack, 716
solicit, 765
Beslaver
flattery, 933
Beslime
uncleanness, 653
Beslobber
uncleanness, 653
Besmear
soil, 653
deface, 846
cover, 222
Besmirch
soil, 653
deface, 846

Besmudge
dirt, 653
Besom
cleanness, 652
Besotted
prejudiced, 481
foolish, 499
Bespangle
ornament, 847
Bespatter
soil, 653
spoil, 659
deface, 846
revile, 932
flatter, 933
Bespeak
indicate, 516
evidence, 467
commission, 755
earliness, 132
request, 765
Bespeckle
variegation, 440
Bespotted
variegation, 440
Besprinkle
mix, 41
wet, 337
Best
perfection, 650
to outwit, 545
Bestial
impurity, 961
Bestir
activity, 682, 686
Bestow
giving, 784
Bestraddle
sit, 215
Bestrew
disperse, 73
Bestride
mount, 206
sit, 215
Bestud
emboss, 250
Bet
chance, 621
Betake
business, 625
Bête noire
fear, 860
hate, 898
Bethink
memory, 505

Bethump
beat, 276
Betide
eventuality, 151
Betimes
earliness, 132
Bêtise
blunder, 699, 732
Betoken
indicate, 550
predict, 511
Betray
disclose, 529
deceive, 545
dishonour, 940
appear, 446
Betroth
promise, 768
Betrothed
affianced, 897
Betsy
gun, 727
Better (to)
improvement, 658
Between
interjacence, 228
Between-maid
servant, 746
Betwixt
interjacence, 228
Bevel
obliquity, 217
Bever
food, 298
Bevy
assemblage, 72, 102
Bewail
lamentation, 839
Beware
warn, 668
care, 459
afraid, 862
cautious, 864
Bewilder
confuse, 458
mislead, 538
perplex, 519, 528
astonish, 870
Bewildered
ignorant, 491
Bewitch
please, 829
exorcise, 992
influence, 615
Bewray

disclose, 529
Bey
master, 745
Beyond
distance, 196
Biannual
periodic, 138
Bias
slope, 217
prepossession, 481
unfairness, 923
inclination, 602
tendency, 176
motive, 615
disposition, 820
Biblacious
drunkenness, 959
Bibelot
trifle, 643
Bible
revelation, 985
Bibliography
list, 86
book, 593
Bibliolatry
heterodoxy, 984A
knowledge, 490
Bibliology
book, 593
Bibliomania
erudition, 490
book, 593
Bibliophile
book, 593
scholar, 492
Bibulous
spongy, 322
drunken, 959
Bicentenary
period, 138
celebration, 883
Bicentric
duality, 89
Bicker
flutter, 315
discord, 713
quarrel, 720
Bicuspid
bisection, 91
Bicycle
travel, 266
Bid
order, 741
offer, 763
Bid for
bargain, 794

Biddable
obedient, 743
Bide
tarry, 133
remain, 141
Bide one's time
future, 121
Biennial
periodic, 138
Bienséance
polish, 852
manners, 894
Bier
interment, 363
Bifacial
duplication, 90
Bifarious
duality, 89
Biff
impact, 276
Bifocal
duality, 89
Bifold
duplication, 90
Biform
duplication, 90
bisection, 91
Biformity
duality, 89
Bifurcation
bisection, 91
fork, 244
Big
in degree, 31
in size, 192
Big pot
importance, 642
Bigamy
marriage, 903
Bight
gulf, 343
bend, 245
Bigot
impiety, 989
Bigoted
imbecile, 499
prejudiced, 481
obstinate, 606
Bigotry
prejudice, 481
credulity, 486
certainty, 474
obstinacy, 606
heterodoxy, 984A

Bigwig
sage, 500
pedant, 492
notability, 642, 875
Bijou
gem, 650
little, 193
Bijouterie
ornament, 847
Bike
bicycle, 266
Bikini
dress, 225
Bilateral
duplication, 90
side, 236
Bilbo
arms, 727
Bilboes
prison, 752
Bile
resentment, 900
Bilge
trash, 645
Bilge-water
dirt, 653
Bilious
dejection, 837
Bilk
deception, 545
swindle, 791
disappointment, 509
Bill
money, account, 811
charge, 812
money-order, 800
security, 771
in law, 969
placard, 531
ticket, 550
instrument, 633
weapon, 727
sharpness, 253
Bill of fare
food, 298
list, 86
plan, 626
Billabong
river, 348
Billet
epistle, 592
ticket, 550
to apportion, 786
to locate, 184
Billet-doux

epistle, 592
endearment, 902
Billiard-table
level, 213
Billingsgate
scolding, 932
imprecatory, 908
Billion
numbers, 98
Billow
wave, 348
Billycock
hat, 225
Bimetallism
money, 800
Bimonthly
periodical, 138
Bin
receptacle, 191
Binary
duality, 89
Bind
connect, 43
compel, 744
obligation, 926
condition, 770
Binge
amusement, 840
Bingle
clip, 201
Binoculars
lens, 445
Binomial
duplication, 90
Bint
girl, 374
Biograph
spectacle, 448
Biographer
recorder, 553
Biography
description, 594
Biology
organization, 357
life, 359
Bioscope
spectacle, 448
Bipartition
duplication, 91
Biplane
aircraft, 273A
Birch
scourge, 975
to punish, 972

Bird
  animal, 366
Bird of passage
  traveller, 268
Bird-fancier
  collector, 775
Bird-lime
  vinculum, 45
Bird's-eye
  tobacco, 298A
  general, 78
Bird's-eye view
  sight, 448
Birds of a feather
  inclusion, 76
  conformity, 82
Bireme
  ship, 273
Biretta
  cap, 225
  vestments, 999
Biro
  pen, 590
Birth
  beginning, 66
  production, 161
  nobility, 875
Birthday
  anniversary, 138
Birthmark
  blemish, 848
Birthplace
  origin, 153
Birthright
  dueness, 924
Bis
  duplication, 89
  repetition, 104
Bise
  wind, 349
Bisection
  duality, 91
Bishop
  clergy, 996
Bishopric
  churchdom, 995
Bissextile
  period, 108
Bistoury
  sharpness, 253
Bistre
  brown, 433
Bisulcate
  fold, 258, 259
Bit

part, 51
mixture, 41
small quantity, 32
money, 800
curb, 752
Bit by bit
  part, 51
  degree, 26
Bitch
  bad woman, 949
Bite
  pain, 378
  painful, 830
  cheat, 545
Biting
  cold, 383
  pungent, 392
  painful, 830
Bitter
  taste, 395
  cold, 383
  animosity, 898
  wrath, 900
  malevolence, 907
  regret, 833
  painful, 830
Bitumen
  semiliquid, 352
Bivouac
  repose, 265
  to encamp, 186
  camp, 189;
  watch, 664
Bizarre
  ridiculous, 853
  unconformity, 83
Blab
  disclosure, 529
Black
  colour, 431
  crime, 945
  copy, 590
Black-and-white
  colourless, 429
Black art
  sorcery, 992
Black hole
  prison, 752
Black-letter
  printing, 591
Black looks
  discourtesy, 598
Black market
  illegality, 964
  theft, 791

Black-out
  darkness, 421
Black out
  obliterate, 552
Black sheep
  bad man, 949
Blackamoor
  blackness, 431
Blackball
  exclude, 55
  reject, 610
  seclude, 893
  disapprove, 932
Blacken
  disapprobation, 932
Blackguard
  rude, 895
  vulgar, 851
  vagabond, 949
  evildoer, 913
  to revile, 932
Blackleg
  sharper, 548
  thief, 792
  traitor, 941
Blacklist
  disapprove, 932
Blackmail
  theft, 791
  booty, 793
Bladder
  receptacle, 191
Blade
  instrument, 633
  sharpness, 253
  man, 372
  fop, 854
Blague
  humbug, 545
  boast, 884
Blah
  nonsense, 497
Blain
  swelling, 250
Blamable
  vice, 945
Blame
  disapprobation, 932
Blameless
  innocence, 946
Blameworthy
  vice, 945
  disapproval, 932
Blanch
  whiteness, 430

405

Bland
courteous, 894
mild, 174
Blandiloquence
flattery, 933
Blandishment
flattery, 902, 933
motive, 615
Blank
insubstantiality, 2, 4
simple, 42
vacant, 187
verse, 597
Blare
loudness, 404
Blarney
flattery, 933
plea, 617
Blasé
weariness, 841
satiety, 869
Blasphemy
impiety, 988
malediction, 908
Blast
wind, 349
sound, 404
evil, 619
curse, 908
explosion, 173
destroy, 162
Blast-furnace
furnace, 386
Blatant
cry, 412
loud, 404
silly, 499
Blatherskite
chatter, 584
Blaze
light, 420
heat, 382
Blaze abroad
publish, 531
Blazon
publication, 531
Blazonry
colour, 428
Bleach
discolour, 429
whiten, 430
Bleak
cold, 383
dreary, 830
Blear-eyed

dim-sighted, 443
Bleat
animal cry, 412
Bleb
swelling, 250
bubble, 353
Bleed
physical pain, 378
moral pain, 828
overcharge, 814
despoil, 789
Bleeding
excretion, 299
Blemish
ugly, 846
defect, 651, 848
Blench
avoid, 623
fear, 860
Blend
mix, 41
combine, 48
Bless
approbation, 931
Blessed
happy, 827
Blessing
good, 618
Blether
nonsense, 497, 499
loquacity, 584
Blight
evil, 619
adversity, 735
decay, 659
Blighter
knave, 949
Blighty
home, 189
Blimp
balloon, 273A
die-hard, 606
Blimpish
prejudiced, 481
foolish, 499
Blind
blindness, 442
ignorant, 491
screen, 424
falsehood, 546
deception, 545
concealment, 528
necessity, 601
heedless, 458
pretext, 617

imperforate, 261
Blind alley
closure, 261
Blind side
obstinacy, 606
prejudice, 481
Blindfold
sightless, 442
ignorant, 491
Blink
wink, 442
neglect, 460
overlook, 458
shirk, 623
Blinkard
dim-sighted, 443
Blinkers
mask, 530
Bliss
pleasure, 827
Blister
swelling, 250
Blithe
cheerfulness, 836
Blitz
attack, 716
Blizzard
wind, 349
Bloated
swollen, 194
Block
mass, 192
dense, 321
fool, 501
execution, 975
Block-buster
bomb, 727
Block in
sketch, 556
Block out
form, 240
Block up
plug, 261
impede, 706
Blockade
closure, 261
hindrance, 706
restraint, 751
Blockhead
fool, 501
Blockhouse
defence, 716
Blockish
folly, 499

Bloke
man, 373
Blonde
whiteness, 430
Blood
relation, 11
killing, 361
fluid, 333
affections, 820
nobility, 875
fop, 854
Blood-guilty
killing, 361
Blood-letting
ejection, 297
Blood-red
redness, 434
Blood-stained
murderous, 361P
maleficent, 907
Bloodhound
evil-doer, 913
detective, 461
Bloodless
weak, 160
peaceful, 721
Bloodshed
killing, 361
Bloodsucker
evildoer, 913
Bloodthirsty
malevolence, 907
Bloody
malevolence, 907
killing, 361
Bloom
youth, 127
prosperity, 734
success, 731
blueness, 438
Bloomer
error, 495
dress, 225
Blooming
beauty, 845
health, 654
Blossom
plant, 367
success, 731
prosperity, 734
Blot
obliterate, 552
dry up, 340
darken, 431
disappear, 449

discoloration, 429
forget, 506
ugly, 846
blemish, 848
disgrace, 874
dishonour, 940
guilt, 947
Blotch
blackness, 431
blemish, 848
Blotto
drunk, 959
Blouse
dress, 225
Blow
wind, 349
boast, 884
knock, 276
action, 680
evil, 619
expletive, 908
pain, 828
disappointment, 732
inexpectation, 508
mishap, 830
to prosper, 734
Blowdown
destruction, 162
Blow-hole
air-pipe, 351
Blow out
extinguish, 385, 421
gluttony, 957
Blow over
preterition, 122
cessation, 142
Blow up
fan, 615
wind, 349
inflame, 194
eruption, 173
objurgation, 932
Blow upon
censure, 934
Blower
signal, 550
Blown
fatigued, 688
Blowpipe
wind, 349
Blowzy
red, 434
sluttish, 653
Blubber
cry, 839

fat, 356
Bludgeon
club, 276
weapon, 727
Blue
colour, 438
learned, 490
Blue-book
record, 551
Blue devils
dejection, 837
Blue lights
firework, 423
Blue-pencil
expletive, 908
Blue-print
model, 22
plan, 626
Blue ruin
drunkenness, 959
Blue water
ocean, 341
Blues
dance, 840
Bluestocking
scholar, 492
affectation, 855
Bluff
high, 206
blunt, 254
insolent, 885
discourteous, 895
boasting, 884
deception, 545
Blunder
error, 495
folly, 499
awkwardness, 699
mistake, 732
ridiculous, 856
Blunderbuss
arms, 727
Blunderer
bungler, 701
Blunderheaded
folly, 499
Blunge
water, 337
Blunt
inert, 172
obtuse, 254
insensible, 376
inexcitable, 826
stupid, 499
cash, 800

discourteous, 895
inelegant, 579
plain, 576
frank, 543
to moderate, 174
to damp, 616
Blunt-witted
folly, 499
Blur
deformity, 846
blemish, 848
disrepute, 874
Blurb
commendation, 931
publicity, 531
Blurred
invisibility, 447
Blurt out
disclosure, 529
Blush
redden, 434
feel, 821
be ashamed, 874
Bluster
violence, 173
insolence, 885
defiance, 715
threat, 909
Blusterer
swagger, 887
Blustering
windy, 349
Boa
dress, 225
Board
layer, 204
food, 298
to attach, 716
council, 696
tribunal, 966
theatre, 599
Boast
brag, 884
Boat
ship, 273
navigation, 267
Bop
leap, 309
bow, 308
oscillate, 314
agitate, 315
Bob
money, 800
Bobadil
bluster, 887

Bobbery
disturbance, 315
row, 404
disorder, 59
Bobbish
healthy, 654
Bobby
police, 664
Bobbysoxer
youngster, 129
Bod
man, 373
Bode
prediction, 511
Bodega
drink, 298
Bodice
dress, 225
Bodily
substantiality, 3
Bodkin
perforator, 262
sharpness, 253
go-between, 228
Body
substance, 3
matter, 316
whole, 50
person, 373
assemblage, 72
party, 712
political, 737
Boeotian
dull, 843
foolish, 499
Bofors
gun, 727
Bog
swamp, 343
dunghill, 653
Boggle
demur, 603
hesitate, 605
difficulty, 704
awkward, 699
wonder, 870
Bogle
demon, 980
Bogus
false, 495, 544
deceitful, 545
Bogy
demon, 980
alarm, 669
Bohemian

oddity, 83, 614
Boil
heat, 382, 384
disease, 655
swelling, 250
bubble, 353
effervesce, 315
be excited , 825
be irate, 900
Boil down
shorten, 201, 596
Boiled
drunk, 959
Boiler
furnace, 386
Boiler suit
dress, 225
Boisterous
violent, 173
hasty, 684
excitable, 825
Bold
brave, 861
prominent, 250
Bolero
dance, 840
Boloney
nonsense, 497
trash, 643
Bolshevism
authority, 737
Bolster
support, 215
aid, 707
repair, 658
relief, 834
Bolt
fastening, 45
to fasten, 43
shackle, 752
sort, 42
to propel, 284
decamp, 287
swallow, 296
gluttony, 957
move rapidly, 274
escape, 671, 750
upright, 212
Bolus
mouthful, 298
Bomb
arms, 727
Bomb-proof
defence, 717

Bombard
attack, 716
Bombardier
combatant, 726
Bombast
absurd, 497
ridiculous, 853
boasting, 884
style, 549, 573, 577, 853
Bomber
aircraft, 273A
Bon enfant
benevolence, 906
Bon gré
willing, 602
Bon gré, mal gré
unwilling, 603
Bon mot
wit, 842
Bon ton
fashion, 852
Bon vivant
glutton, 957
epicure, 868
sociality, 892
Bon voyage
departure, 293
Bona fide
veracity, 543
probity, 939
Bonanza
good luck, 618
Bonbon
sweet, 396
pleasurable, 829
Bond
relation, 95
tie, 45
compact, 769
security, 771
right, 924
fetters, 752
Bondage
subjection, 749
Bondsman
servant, 746
Bone
hardness, 323
money, 800
Bone of contention
discord, 713
Bone-shaker
bicycle, 266
Bonehead
fool, 499, 501

Boner
error, 495, 732
Bones
corpse, 362
Bonfire
rejoicing, 838
Bonhomie
veracity, 543
candour, 703
Bonne
servant, 746
Bonne bouche
dainty, 829
savoury, 394
Bonnet
hat, 225
to assault, 716
Bonny
pretty, 845
cheerful, 836
Bonus
advantage, 618
gift, 784
money, 810
addition, 39
Bony
hard, 323
Bonze
clergy, 996
Boo
cry, 412
deride, 927
Boob
fool, 501
Booby
fool, 501
ignoramus, 493
Boodle
booty, 793
Boogie-woogie
rhythm, 413
Book
volume, 593
enter account, 811
to record, 551
to register, 86 ,
to bespeak, 132
Book-keeper
recorder, 553
Book-keeping
accounts, 811
Booked
dying, 360
Bookish
erudite, 490

scholarly, 492
Bookless
ignorant, 493
Bookworm
scholar, 492
Boom
bar, 633
defence, 717
obstacle, 706
support, 215
to sail, 267
rush, 274
cry, 402
sound, 404
impact, 276
praise, 931
Boomerang
arms, 727
recoil, 277
Boon
giving, 784
good, 618
Boor
clown, 876
discourteous, 895
ridiculous, 851
Boost
throw, 284
commend, 931
publicity, 531
Boot
addition, 37
dress, 225
advantage, 618
important, 642
punishment, 975
Boot-boy
servant, 746
Booth
abode, 189
shop, 799
Bootlegging
illegality, 964
Bootless
useless, 645
failing, 732
Bootlicker
toady, 886
Boots
servant, 746
Booty
plunder, 793
Booze
drunkenness, 959

Bo-peep
vision, 441
Border
edge, 230
limit, 233
ornament, 847
to be near, 197
Bore
hole, 260
diameter, 202
to trouble, 828
to plague, 830
to weary, 841
dull, 843
tide, 348
Boreal
polar, 237
cold, 383
Boreas
wind, 349
Borer
perforator, 262
Borné
folly, 499
Borough
abode, 189
Borrow
borrowing, 788
debt, 806
Borstal
school, 542
punishment, 972
Boscage
vegetation, 367
Bosh
nonsense, 517
Bosom
breast, 221
mind, 450
will, 600
affection, 820
Bosom friend
friend, 890
Boss
convexity, 250
to direct, 693, 737
master, 745
Bossy
will, 600
severity, 739
Botanic
plant, 367
Botany
botany, 369
Botch
to mend, 658

to fail, 732
unskilful, 699
inperfect, 651
Both
duality, 89
Bother
trouble, 828, 830
fuss, 682
Bottle
receptacle, 191
Bottle-neck
thinness, 203
Bottle-party
food, 298
sharing, 778
Bottle up
preserve, 670
enclose, 231
restrain, 751
remember, 505
Bottle-washer
servant, 746
Bottom
lowest part, 211
base, 215
valley, 252
ship, 273
pluck, 604
courage, 861
Bottom, at
intrinsicality, 5
Bottomless
depth, 208
Boudoir
room, 191
Bough
part, 51
plant, 367
curve, 245
Boulder
mass, 192
Boulevard
circumjacence, 227
way, 627
Bouleversement
change, 140
destruction, 162
Bounce
violence, 173
motion, 274
recoil, 277
eject, 297
dismiss, 756
boast, 884
insolence, 885

exaggeration, 549
Bounce upon
arrival, 292
surprise, 508
Bouncer
untruth, 546
Bouncing
large, 192
Bound
limit, 233
circumscribe, 231
speed, 274
leap, 309
Boundary
limit, 233
Bounder
upstart, 876
Boundless
great, 31
infinite, 105
space, 180
Bounteous
benevolent, 906
Bountiful
liberal, 816
Bounty
gift, 784
liberality, 816
benevolence, 906
Bouquet
fragrance, 400
ornament, 847
Bourgeois
middle class, 736, 876
Bourne
limit, 233
Bourse
mart, 799
Bout
turn, 138
job, 680
fight, 720
Boutade
absurdity, 497
caprice, 608
Bovine
inert, 172, 823
Bow
curve, 245
ornament, 847
fore-part, 234
shot, 284
arms, 727
to stoop, 308
reverence, 894

submission, 725
obeisance, 743
servility, 886
respect, 928
prominence, 250
Bow-legged
curvature, 245
distortion, 243
Bowdlerize
expurgate, 652
Bowels
interior, 221
of compassion, 914
Bower
alcove, 189
chamber, 191
Bowie-knife
arms, 727
sharpness, 253
Bowl
vessel, 191
hollow, 252
to propel, 284
Bowler
hat, 225
Bowling-green
horizontality, 213
Bowshot
nearness, 197
Bowstring
scourge, 975
Box
chest, 191
house, 189
theatre, 599
to strike, 972
to fight, 720
Boxer
combatant, 726
Boxing
contention, 720
Boy
infant, 129
Boy friend
love, 897
Boycott
exclude, 893
eject, 297
Boyhood
youth, 127
Bra
dress, 225
Brace
to tie, 43
fastening, 45

two, 89
to refresh, 689
to strengthen, 159
Brace and bit
perforator, 262
Bracelet
ornament, 847
circularity, 247
Bracer
remedy, 662
Brachygraphy
writing, 590
Bracing
strengthening, 159
refreshing, 689
Bracket
tie, 43
support, 215
vinculum, 45
couple, 89
Brackish
pungent, 392
Brad
vinculum, 45
Bradawl
perforator, 262
Brae
height, 206
Brag
boasting, 884
Braggadocio
boasting, 884
Braggart
boasting, 884
bully, 887
Brahma
god, 979
Brahmin
clergy, 996
religious, 984
Braid
to tie, 43
ligature, 45
intersection, 219
Braille
printing, 591
Brain
intellect, 450
skill, 498
Brain-sick
giddy, 460
Brain-storm
excitability, 825
Brainless
imbecile, 499

Brains trust
council, 696
Brainwash
teach, 537
Brake
copse, 367
curb, 752
vehicle, 272
Bramble
thorn, 253
painful, 830
Bran
pulverulence, 330
Bran-new
see Brand-new
Branch
member, 51
plant, 367
duality, 91
posterity, 167
ramification, 256
Branch off
divergence, 291
Branch out
style, 573
divide, 91
Brand
to burn, 384
fuel, 388
to stigmatize, 932
mark, 550
to accuse, 938
reproach, 874
Brand-new
new, 123
Brander
roast, 384
Brandish
oscillate, 314
flourish, 315
Bras croisés
inactive, 683
Brasier
furnace, 386
Brass
insolence, 885
colour, 439
Brass up
pay, 809
Brassed off
bored, 641
sated, 869
Brasserie
food, 298
Brassière
dress, 225

411

Brassy
club, 276
Brat
infant, 129
Bravado
boasting, 884
Brave
courage, 861
to defy, 715
Bravery
courage, 861
ornament, 847
Bravo
assassin, 361
applause, 931
Bravura
music, 415
Braw
handsome, 845
Brawl
cry, 411
discord, 713
contention, 720
Brawny
strong, 159
stout, 192
Bray
cry, 412
to grind, 330
Brazen-faced
insolent, 885
Breach
crack, 44
quarrel, 713
violation, 925
exception, 83
Bread
food, 298
Breadstuffs
food, 298
Breadth
thickness, 202
of mind, 498
Break
fracture, 44
shatter, 162
incompleteness, 53
interval, 70, 106, 198
opportunity, 134
luck, 621, 731
crumble, 328
violation, 773
bankruptcy, 808
to infringe, 927

to disclose, 529
to tame, 749
to decline, 659
to swerve, 311
Break down
fail, 158, 732
Break ground
undertaking, 676
Break in
teach, 537
train, 370, 673
Break loose
escape, 671
liberate, 750
Break off
a habit, 614
leave off, 142
abrogate, 756
Break out
fly out, 825
Break the ranks
derangement, 61
Break the record
superiority, 33
Break up
destroy, 162
deteriorate, 659
decompose, 49
Break with
discord, 713
Breaker
wave, 348
danger, 667
Breakfast
food, 298
Breakneck
perilous, 665
precipitous, 217
Breakwater
refuge, 666
enclosure, 232
Breast
interior, 221
convexity, 250
mind, 450
will, 600
soul, 820
to oppose, 708
Breastplate
defence, 717
Breastwork
defence, 717
Breath
air, 349
sound, 405

life, 359, 364
Breathe
exist, 1
live, 359
blow, 349
mean, 516
utter, 580, 582
repose, 687
Breather
preparation, 673
Breathing
lifelike, 17
Breathing-space
time, 106
pause, 141, 265
leisure, 685
Breathless
calm, 265
out of breath, 688
feeling, 821
Breech
rear, 235
Breeches
dress, 225
Breed
kind, 75
to multiply, 161
domesticate, 370
progeny, 167
Breeding
fashion, 852
Breeze
wind, 349
Breezy
lively, 836
Bren
gun, 727
Brevet
warrant, 741
commission, 755
permission, 760
Breviary
liturgy, 998
Brevity
space, 201
Brew
mix, 41
prepare, 673
impend, 121
Briar
tobacco, 298A
Bribe
buy, 795
offer, 763
gift, 784

fee, 809
tempt, 615
Bric-à-brac
trifle, 643
ornament, 847
Brick
materials, 635
hardness, 323
good man, 939, 946
Brickbat
missile, 284
Bride
marriage, 903
Bridegroom
marriage, 903
Bridewell
prison, 752
Bridge
intermedium, 45
way, 627
escape, 671
Bridge over
junction, 43
Bridle
curb, 752
to restrain, 751
to moderate, 174
to swagger, 878
Bridle up
resentment, 900
Brief
time, 111
space, 201
style, 572
compendium, 596
direct, 693, 741
Brief-case
receptacle, 191
Briefly
transientness, 111
Briefs
dress, 225
Brier
sharp, 253
painful, 830
Brig
ship, 273
prison, 752
Brigade
combatant, 726
Brigadier
master, 745
Brigand
thief, 792
Brigantine

ship, 273
Bright
shining, 420
colour, 428
cheerful, 836
auspicious, 858
glorious, 873
Brilliant
shining, 420
beautiful, 845
glorious, 873
perfect, 650
gem, 847
Brilliantine
ornament, 847
Brim
edge, 230
Brimful
sufficient, 639
fullness, 52
Brimmer
fullness, 52
Brindled
variegated, 440
Brine
salt, 392
sea, 341
Bring
transfer, 270
induce, 615
Bring about
cause, 153
achieve, 729
succeed, 731
Bring forth
produce, 161
Bring forward
manifest, 525
Bring home to
convince, 537
adduce, 467
Bring in
price, 812
Bring into
existence, 1
Bring off
deliver, 672
accomplish, 161, 729
Bring out
manifest, 525
publish, 531
Bring over
persuade, 484, 615
Bring to
restore, 658

Bring under
subdue, 824
Bring up
educate, 537
Brink
edge, 230
Brio
vivacity, 682
Briquette
fuel, 388
Brisk
quick, 274
energetic, 171
active, 682
prompt, 111
Bristle
sharpness, 253
Bristle up
resentment, 900
Bristle with
abound, 639
British warm
dress, 225
Brittle
brittleness, 328
Broach
begin, 66
tap, 297
put forth, 535
Broad
space, 292
indelicate, 961
meaning, 535
Broad-minded
wisdom, 498
Broadcast
scattered, 73
shed, 291
radio, 418, 599B
publication, 531
Broadmoor
prison, 752
Broadside
side, 236
cannonade, 716
Broadsword
arms, 727
Brobdingnagian
size, 192, 193
Brocade
ornament, 847
Brochure
book, 593
Brog
perforator, 262

Brogue
language, 560
shoe, 225
Broidery
ornament, 847
Broil
heat, 382
to fry, 384
fray, 720
Broken
weakness, 160
Broken-hearted
unhappy, 828
Broken-winded
fatigue, 688
Broker
agent, 690, 758, 769
merchant, 797
Brokerage
pay, 812
Bromide
photograph, 556
dull, 843
Bronze
brown, 433
sculpture, 557
Brooch
fastening, 45
ornament, 847
Brood
posterity, 167
Brood over
think, 451
mope, 837
Brook
stream, 348
to bear, 821, 826
Broom
cleanness, 652
Broth
food, 298
semiliquid, 352
Brothel
impurity, 961
Brother
kin, 11
similar, 17
equal, 27
friend, 888
Brother-in-law
kin, 11
Brougham
vehicle, 272
Brouillerie
discord, 713

Brow
summit, 210
edge, 230
Browbeat
intimidate, 860
swagger, 885
attack, 716
Brown
colour, 433
Brown-out
dim, 422
Brown study
reverie, 458
thought, 451
Browned off
bored, 841
sated, 869
Brownie
imp, 980
Browse
feed, 296
Bruise
hurt, 619
to injure, 649
pound, 330
Bruiser
fighter, 726
Bruit
publication, 531
news, 532
Brumal
cold, 383
evening, 126
Brummagem
spurious, 544
Brumous
foggy, 422
Brunette
brown, 433
Brunt
impulse, 276
attack, 716
Brush
rapid motion, 274
to clean, 652
painting, 559
fight, 720
rough, 256
Brush up
memo, 505
Brushwood
plant, 367
Brusque
discourteous, 895
inelegant, 579

rough, 173
Brutal
vicious, 945
ill-bred, 895
savage, 907
Brutalize
harden, 823, 895
Brute
animal, 366
rude, 895
maleficent, 913
Brute force
illegality, 964
Brute matter
materiality, 316
inanimate matter, 358
Brutish
vulgar, 851, 876
intemperate, 954
Brutum fulmen
impotence, 158
laxity, 738
Bubble
air, 353
light, 320
trifle, 643
error, 495
vision, 515
deceit, 545
excitement, 824
flow, 348
Buccaneer
thief, 792
Buck
leap, 309
to wash, 652
fop, 854
money, 800
Buck up
hasten, 274
stimulate, 615
cheer, 836
Bucket
receptacle, 191
Bucketful
quantity, 25
Buckle
to tie, 43
vinculum, 45
distort, 243
Buckle to
apply oneself, 682
Buckle with
grapple, 720

Buckler
defence, 666, 717
Buckram
hardness, 323
affectation, 855
Buckshee
superfluous, 641
Bucolic
domestication, 370
poem, 597
Bud
beginning, 66
to expand, 194
effect, 154
graft, 300
Buddha
deity, 979
religious founder, 986
Buddhism
religions, 984
Buddy
friend, 891
associate, 88
Budge
move, 264
Budget
heap, 72
store, 636
news, 532
accounts, 811
Buff
yellow, 436
grindstone, 331
Buffer
defence, 717
fellow, 373
Buffet
cupboard, 191
beat, 276, 972
Buffet car
vehicle, 272
Buffo
the drama, 599
Buffoon
humorist, 844
butt, 857
actor, 599
Buffoonery
amusement, 840
ridiculous, 856
Bugaboo
fear, 860
Bugbear
fear, 860

alarm, 669
imaginary, 515
Buggy
vehicle, 272
Bughouse
insane, 503
Bugle
instrument, 417
war-cry, 722
Bugs
insane, 503
Buhl
variegation, 440
Build
construct, 161
compose, 54
Build-up
display, 882
Build upon
expect, 507, 858
count upon, 484
Builder
producer, 164
Building
abode, 189
Bulb
knob, 249, 250
Bulbous
swollen, 194
rotund, 249
Bulge
convexity, 250
Bulimia
desire, 865
Bulk
whole, 50
size, 192
Bulkhead
hindrance, 706
Bulky
size, 192
Bull
absurdity, 497, 853
error, 495
solecism, 568
nonsense, 497, 517
law, 963
ordinance, 741
police, 664
Bull-calf
fool, 501
Bulldog
courage, 861
resolution, 604
Bullet

ball, 249
missile, 284
arms, 727
swiftness, 274
Bullet-proof
defence, 717
Bulletin
message, 532
Bullion
money, 800
Bull's-eye
middle, 68
Bully
bluster, 885
blusterer, 887
fight, 726
domineer, 739
frighten, 860
good, 648
Bulrush
unimportance, 643
Bulwark
defence, 717
refuge, 666
Bum
tramp, 268, 876
loafer, 683
pauper, 804
rascal, 949
Bumbledom
authority, 737
Bumboat
ship, 273
provision, 637
Bumboatman
trader, 797
Bump
projection, 250
thump, 276
Bump off
kill, 361
Bumper
sufficiency, 639
fullness, 52
Bumpkin
commonalty, 876
Bumptious
insolent, 885
Bun-fight
party, 892
Bunce
profit, 618
Bunch
protuberance, 250
collection, 72

Bundle
packet, 72
to move, 275
Bung
stopper, 263
throw, 284
Bung-ho
departure, 293
Bungalow
abode, 189
Bungle
unskilfulness, 699
failure, 732
Bungler
unskilful, 701
Bunion
swelling, 250
Bunk
bed, 191, 215
escape, 671
Bunker
receptacle, 191
obstruction, 706
Bunkie
friend, 891
Bunkum
humbug, 545
nonsense, 497
Bunt
inversion, 218
deviate, 279
Bunting
flag, 550
Buoy
float, 320
to raise, 307
to hope, 858
Buoyant
floating, 305
levity, 320
elastic, 325
hopeful, 858
cheerful, 836
Bur
rough, 256
clinging, 46
Burberry
dress, 225
Burden
weight, 319
clog, 706
chorus, 104, 415
frequency, 136
lading, 190
care, 830

oppresion, 828
Bureau
cabinet, 691
office, 799
Bureaucracy
direction, 693
authority, 737
Burgee
Flag, 550
Burgeon
expansion, 194
increase, 35
Burgess
citizen, 188, 373
Burgher
man, 373
Burglar
thief, 792
Burglary
stealing, 791
Burgomaster
master, 745
Burgrave
master, 745
Burial
corpse, 362
Buried
depth, 208
Burin
engraving, 559
Burke
kill, 361
destroy, 162
suppress, 528
Burlesque
imitation, 19
travesty, 21
drama, 599
ridicule, 856
ridiculous, 853
Burletta
the drama, 599
Burly
size, 192
Burn
heat, 382
consume, 384
detection, 480A
passions, 821
rivulet, 348
Burnish
polish, 255
beautify, 845
shine, 420
Burnous

dress, 225
Burp
belch, 297
Burrow
excavate, 252
lodge, 186
Bursar
treasurer, 801
Bursary
treasury, 802
Burst
explosion, 173
sound, 406
of anger, 900
paroxysm, 825
spree, 840
separate, 44
Burst forth
appear, 446
sprout, 194
Burst out
ejaculate, 580
Burst upon
inexpectation, 508
Bury
inter, 363
conceal, 528
Bus
vehicle, 272
Busby
hat, 225
Bush
branch, 51
shrub, 367
Bushel
receptacle, 191
Bushy
roughness, 256
Business
occupation, 625
event, 151
topic, 454
action, 680
barter, 794
Business-like
activity, 682
skilful, 698
order, 58
Buskin
dress, 225
drama, 599
Buss
ship, 272
kiss, 902

Bustle
activity, 682
agitation, 315
haste, 684
energy, 171
earliness, 132

Busy
activity, 682

Busybody
activity, 682
curiosity, 455

But
exception, 83, 179
counter-evidence, 468

Butcher
evildoer, 913

Butchery
killing, 361

Butler
servant, 746

Butt
aim, 620
laughing-stock, 857
remnant, 40
part, 51;
to push, 276
to attack, 716

Butt-end
end, 67

Butt in
intervene, 228

Butte
height, 206

Butter
softness, 324
oiliness, 356
to flatter, 933

Butter-fingers
bungler, 701

Butterfly
beauty, 845
fickleness, 605
fear, 860

Butterscotch
sweet, 396

Button
knob, 250
to fasten, 43
fasten, 43
fastening, 45
hanging, 214
trifle, 643

Buttoned up
reserved, 528
taciturn, 585

Buttonhole
ornament, 847
accost, 586

Buttonholer
weariness, 841

Buttons
servant, 746

Buttress
support, 215
defence, 717
strengthen, 159

Buxom
plump, 192
cheerful, 836

Buy
purchase, 795

Buzz
sound, 409, 412
to publish, 531
news, 532

Buzz-bomb
arms, 727

Buzz off
depart, 293

Buzzard
fool, 501

By and by
transientness, 111

By fits and starts
disorder, 59
irregularity, 139

By jingo
affirmation, 535

By-law
legality, 963

Byname
misnomer, 565

By the by
opportunity, 134

Bye-bye
departure, 293
sleep, 683

Bygone
former, 122
forgotten, 506

Bypath
road, 627

Byplay
gesture, 550

Byssus
roughness, 256

Bystander
spectator, 444
near, 197

Byway
road, 627

Byword
maxim, 496
cant term, 563
contempt, 930

C.A.
accounts, 811

C.O.D.
payment, 807

Ca' canny
caution, 864

Cab
vehicle, 272
translation, 522

Cabal
confederacy, 712
plan, 626

Cabbage
purloin, 791

Cabbala
spell, 993

Cabbalistic
mysterious, 528

Caber
missile, 284

Cabin
room, 189
receptacle, 191

Cabin cruiser
ship, 273

Cabinet
receptacle, 191
workshop, 691
council, 696

Cable
vinculum, 45

Cabriolet
vehicle, 272

Cache
hiding-place, 530
conceal, 528
store, 636

Cachexy
disease, 655
weakness, 160

Cachinnation
rejoicing, 838

Cachucha
dance, 840

Cacique
master, 745

Cackle
of geese, 412

talk, 588
laughter, 838
Cacodemon
demon, 980
Cacodyl
fetor, 401
Cacoethes
habit, 613
itch, 865
writing, 590
Cacoethes loquendi
loquacity, 584
Cacoethes scribendi
writing, 590
Cacography
writing, 590
Cacophony
stridor, 410
discord, 414
style, 579
Cad
vulgarity, 851
Cadastre
list, 86
Cadaverous
corpse, 362
pale, 429
thin, 203
hideous, 846
Caddish
mean, 940
Caddy
receptacle, 191
Cadence
accent, 580
music, 415
descent, 306
Cadenza
music, 415
Cadet
junior, 129
combatant, 726
officer, 745
Cadge
request, 765
Cadger
merchant, 797
Cadi
judge, 967
Cadmium
orange, 439
Cadre
framework, 215
Caduceus
spell, 993

Caducity
transientness, 111
Caecum
closure, 261
Caesar
master, 745
Caesura
break, 70
disjunction, 44
Caetera desunt
incomplete, 53
Caeteris paribus
circumstance, 8
equality, 27
Café
food, 298
Cafeteria
food, 298
Caftan
dress, 225
Cage
prison, 231, 752
to immure, 751
abode, 189
Cagey
cautious, 864
Caique
ship, 273
Cairn
grave, 363
sign, 550
Caisson
receptacle, 191
depth, 208
Caitiff
ruffian, 913
villain, 949
Cajole
persuade, 615
flatter, 933
Cake
cohesion, 46
density, 321
food, 298
Cake eater
philander, 902
Cakewalk
dance, 840
easy, 705
Calabash
receptacle, 191
tobacco-pipe, 298A
Calaboose
prison, 752
Calamity

evil, 619
adversity, 735
suffering, 830
Calash
vehicle, 272
cap, 225
Calcine
calefaction, 384
Calculate
reckon, 85
expect, 507
believe, 484
investigate, 461
Calculated,
tending to, 176
premeditated, 600, 611
Calculating
prudent, 498
Calculation
motive, 615
caution, 864
Calculus
numeration, 85
Caldron
see Cauldron
Calefaction
heating, 384
Calembour
pun, 563
Calendar
of time, 114
list, 86;
record, 551
Calender
to glaze, 255
Calf
fool, 501
Caliban
ugliness, 846
Calibre
size, 192
breadth, 202
degree, 26
opening, 260
intellectual capacity, 698
Calidity
heat, 382
Caliph
master, 745
Caliphate
authority, 737
Call
to name, 564
motive, 615
visit, 892

inspiration, 985
Call-boy
theatre, 599
Call down
malediction, 908
Call for
order, 741
ask, 765
require, 630
Call forth
resort to, 677
Call-girl
prostitute, 962
Call on
ask, 765
Call over
numeration, 85
Call up
memory, 505
summon, 741
Call upon
behove, 926
visit, 892
claim, 924
Callant
youth, 129
Caller
arrival, 292
Calligraphy
writing, 590
Calling
business, 625
Callipers
measurement, 466
Callisthenics
training, 537, 673
Callosity
hardness, 323
Callous
obtuse, 376
insensible, 823
impenitent, 951
Callow
infant, 129
young, 127
Calm
physical, 174
moral, 826
quiet, 265
dissuade, 616
Calorific
heat, 382
Calorimeter
thermometer, 389
Calotte

vestment, 225, 999
Caltrop
sharpness, 253
Calumet
pacification, 723
tobacco, 298A
Calumniator
detractor, 936
Calumny
detraction, 934
Calyx
integument, 222
Camarade
friend, 890
Camaraderie
friendship, 888
Camarilla
party, 712
Camber
curvature, 250
Cambist
merchant, 797
Camel
carrier, 271
Cameo
sculpture, 557
Camera
optical instrument, 445
Camerated
curved, 245
Camisade
attack, 716
Camisole
dress, 225
Camorra
illegality, 964
Camouflage
conceal, 528
deception, 545
Camp
to locate, 184
abode, 186
Campagna
space, 180
Campaign
warfare, 722
plan, 626
conduct, 692
Campaigner
combatant, 726
Campanile
tower, 206
Campaniliform
bell-shaped, 249
cupped, 252

Campanologist
musician, 416
Campus
field, 344
arena, 728
Can
power, 157
mug, 191
to preserve, 670
Canaille
commonalty, 876
rabble, 949
Canal
opening, 260
way, 627
Canard
deception, 545
news, 532
Can-can
dance, 840
Cancel
obliterate, 552, 773
abrogate, 756
Cancellated
crossing, 219
Cancelli
lattice, 219
Cancer
disease, 655
swelling, 250
foulness, 653
painful, 830
Candelabra
luminary, 423
Candescence
heat, 382
Candid
sincere, 543
ingenuous, 703
honourable, 939
Candidate
petitioner, 767, 865
Candidature
offer, 763
solicitation, 765
Candied
flattering, 933
Candle
luminary, 423
Candle-ends
remainder, 40
Candle-holder
auxiliary, 711
Candle-light
dimness, 422

Candlestick
  luminary, 423
Candour
  veracity, 543
  artlessness, 703
  honour, 939
Candy
  sweetness, 396
Cane
  scourge, 975
  to beat, 276
  punish, 972
Cangue
  shackle, 752
  stocks, 975
Canicular
  heat, 382
Canister
  receptacle, 191
Canker
  disease, 655
  bane, 663
  deterioration, 659
  pain, 830
Cankering
  badness, 649
Canned
  drunk, 959
Cannibal
  sinner, 949
Cannibalize
  repair, 658
Cannon
  arms, 727
  collision, 276
Cannonade
  attack, 716
Cannoneer
  combatant, 726
Canny
  cautious, 459, 864
  cunning, 702
  intelligent, 498
  thrifty, 817
Canoe
  ship, 273
Canon
  rule, 80
  music, 415
  precept, 697
  priest, 996
Canonical
  orthodox, 983A
Canonicals
  holy orders, 999

Canonize
  rites, 995, 998
  honour, 873
Canoodle
  endearment, 902
Canopy
  height, 206
  roof, 210
  covering, 222
Canorous
  resonant, 402
  melodious, 415
Cant
  neology, 563
  language, 560
  oblique, 217
  hypocrisy, 544, 988
Cantankerous
  discourtesy, 895
Cantata
  music, 415
Cantatrice
  musician, 416
Canted
  obliquity, 217
Canteen
  receptacle, 191
  feeding, 298
Canter
  move, 266
  gallop, 274
Canticle
  music, 415
Cantilever
  support, 215
Cantle
  part, 51
Canto
  poetry, 597
Canton
  region, 181
Cantonment
  location, 184
  abode, 189
Canty
  cheerfulness, 836
Canvas
  sail, 267
Canvass
  investigate, 461
  treat of, 595
  solicit, 765
Canyon
  ravine, 198
Canzonet

  song, 415
  poem, 597
Caoutchouc
  elasticity, 325
Cap
  hat, 225
  height, 206
  to be superior, 33, 194
  counter, 718
  to salute, 894
Cap-à-pie
  preparation, 673
  length, 200
Capability
  power, 157
  strength, 159
  skill, 698
  facility, 705
  endowment, 5
Capacity
  space, 180
  size, 192
  endowment, 5
  power, 157
  intellect, 450
  aptitude, 539
  talent, 698
  wisdom, 498
  utility, 644
  office, 625
Caparison
  vestment, 225
Cape
  land, 342
  projection, 250
  height, 206
  cloak, 225
Caper
  leap, 309
  dance, 840
Capillary
  thinness, 203, 205
Capital
  excellent, 648
  important, 642
  summit, 210
  money, 800
  wealth, 803
Capitalist
  wealth, 803
Capitation
  numeration, 85
Capitol
  defence, 717

Capitular
clergy, 996
Capitulate
submission, 725
Capote
vestment, 224
Capriccio
caprice, 608
Caprice
chance, 608
irresolution, 605
music, 415
Capricious
irregular, 139
changeable, 149
whimsical, 608
Capriole
leap, 309
Capsize
inversion, 218
wreck, 731
Capsized
failure, 732
Capstan
instrument, 633
Capsule
vessel, 191
tunicle, 222
Captain
master, 745
of industry, 745
Caption
indication, 550
Captious
capricious, 608
censorious, 932
discourteous, 795
Captivated
fascinated, 827, 897
induced, 615
Captivating
pleasing, 829
lovely, 897
Captive
prisoner, 754
Captivity
restraint, 751
Capture
taking, 789
Capuchin
clergy, 996
Caput mortuum
remainder, 40
unclean, 653
Car

vehicle, 272
Carabineer
combatant, 726
Caracole
leap, 309
journey, 266
Carafe
receptacle, 191
Carambole
impulse, 276
Caramel
sweet, 396
Carapace
covering, 222
Caravan
vehicle, 272
Caravansary
abode, 189
Caravel
ship, 273
Carbine
arms, 727
Carbon
copy, 590
Carbon print
photograph, 556
Carbonize
calefaction, 384
Carborundum
sharpener, 253
Carboy
receptacle, 191
Carcass
corpse, 362
Card
ticket, 550
plan, 626
oddity, 857
to unravel, 60
Cardiac
remedy, 662
Cardigan
dress, 225
Cardinal
important, 642
excellent, 648
red, 434
dress, 225
priest, 995, 996
Care
attention, 459
fear, 860
pain, 828, 830
custody, 751
Care for

desire, 865
love, 642, 897
Care-worn
pain, 828
Careen
slant, 217, 306
repair, 658
Career
business, 625
conduct, 692
Careful
caution, 864
Careless
inattentive, 458
neglectful, 460
insensible, 823
Caress
endearment, 902
Caret
incomplete, 53
to want, 640
Caretaker
keeper, 753
Cargo
goods, 798
contents, 190
property, 780
materials, 635
large quantity, 31
Caricature
likeness, 19
misrepresentation, 555
ridicule, 856
Caricaturist
humorist, 844
Caries
disease, 655
Carillon
musical instrument, 417
Carking
painful, 830
Carle
boor, 876
Carmelite
clergy, 996
Carminative
remedy, 662
Carmine
redness, 434
Carnage
killing, 361
Carnal
impure, 961
animality, 364
intemperate, 954

small quantity, 32
tinge, 428
squint, 443
aspect, 448
to peel, 226
reject, 610
Cast
to condemn, 971
to allot, 786
drama, 599
Cast about
inquiry, 461
Cast anchor
stop, 265
arrive, 293
Cast away
relinquish, 782
Cast down
dejection, 837
Cast forth
dispersion, 73
Cast off
remainder, 40
stop, 142
discard, 678
Cast out
ejection, 297
Cast up
add, 85
happen, 151
eject, 297
Castalian
poetry, 597
Castanet
musical instrument, 417
Castaway
lost, 732
outcast, 893
reprobate, 949
sinner, 949
Caste
class, 75
Castellan
keeper, 753
servant, 746
Castellated
defence, 717
Caster
receptacle, 191
Castigate
punish, 972
reprove, 932
Castle
defence, 717
edifice, 189

Castle building
imagination, 515
Castor
hat, 225
fragrance, 400
Castor oil
oil, 356
Castrate
mutilate, 38, 44, 53
sterilize , 169
Castrated
weakened, 160
purified, 652
Casual
by chance, 156, 621
irregular, 139
mutable, 149
liable, 177
uncertain, 475
unmethodical, 59
Casualty
event, 151
chance, 156, 621
killing, 361
Casuistry
sophistry, 477
scruple, 485
ethics, 926
Casus belli
discord, 713
resentment, 900
Cat
eye, 441
scourge, 975
to vomit, 297
Cat-call
abuse, 932
Cat-o'-nine-tails
scourge, 975
Catachresis
metaphor, 521
misinterpretation, 523
Cataclysm
deluge, 348
convulsion, 146
redundance, 641
Catacomb
interment, 363
Catafalque
interment, 363
Catalectic
poetry, 597
Catalepsy
quiescence, 265
insensibility, 376, 823

Catalogue
list, 86, 551
record, 551
arrangement, 60
classify, 75
Catalysis
decomposition, 49
Catamaran
vessel, 273
Cataplasm
remedy, 662
Catapult
projection, 276, 284
arms, 727
Cataract
river, 348
blindness, 442
Catastrophe
end, 67, 729
rear, 235
disaster, 619
adversity, 735
calamity, 830
convulsion, 146
Catch
take, 134, 789
receive, 785
learn, 539
gather meaning, 518
cheat, 545
vinculum, 45
Catch at
receiving, 785
Catch on
success, 731
Catch up
overtake, 292
Catching
infectious, 657
Catchpenny
trumpery, 643
cheap, 815
false, 544
Catchpoll
jurisprudence, 965
Catchword
formula, 80
maxim, 496
Catechetical
inquiry, 461
Catechize
inquiry, 461
Catechumen
learner, 541

Categorical
true, 494
positive, 474
demonstrative, 478
affirmative, 535
Category
class, 75
arrangement, 60
state, 7
Catenary
curve, 245
Catenation
continuity, 69
Cater
provision, 637
Caterwauling
cry, 412
discord, 414
Cates
food, 298
Cathedral
temple, 1000
Catholic
universal, 78
Christian, 983A
broad-minded, 448
Catholicity
generality, 78
broad-mindedness, 498
Catholicon
remedy, 662
Cat's-cradle
crossing, 219
Cat's-paw
instrument, 631
dupe, 547
Cattle-lifting
stealing, 791
Cattle-truck
vehicle, 272
Caucus
assemblage, 72
Caudal
end, 67
Caudate
pendency, 214
Cauldron
mixture, 41
vessel, 191
heating, 386
laboratory, 691
Caulk
repair, 658
Causality
cause, 153
power, 157

Causation
cause, 153
agency, 170
Cause
source, 153
final, 620
lawsuit, 969
Causless
casual, 156
aimless, 621
Causerie
chat, 588
Causeur
talker, 588
Causeway
road, 627
Causidical
juridical, 965
Caustic
feeling, 821
painful, 830
gruff, 895
disapproving, 932
malevolent, 907
Cautelous
caution, 864
Cauterize
calefaction, 384
Caution
care, 459
warning, 668
prudence, 864
advice, 695
security, 771
Cavalcade
continuity, 69
Cavalier
horseman, 268
insolent, 885
discourteous, 895
contemptuous, 930
Cavaliere servente
lover, 897
Cavalierly
inattention, 458
Cavalry
combatant, 726
Cavatina
music, 415
Cave
cavity, 252
cell, 91
dwelling, 189
warning, 668
care, 459

Cave in
submit, 729
Caveat
warning, 668
Cavendish
tobacco, 298A
Cavern
hollow, 252
cell, 191
dwelling, 189
Cavernous
hollow, 252
porous, 322
Caviare
pungent, 171, 392
Cavil
censure, 932
dissent, 489
split hairs, 477
Caviller
detractor, 936
Cavity
concavity, 252
Cavort
prance, 315
Caw
animal cry, 412
Cayenne
condiment, 393
pungent, 171
Cease
cessation, 142
Ceaseless
perpetuity, 112
Cecity
blindness, 442
Cede
relinquish, 782
Ceiling
height, 206
summit, 210
covering, 222
Cela va sans dire
conformity, 82
effect, 154
Celebrant
worship, 990
Celebrate
solemnize, 883
publish, 531
praise, 931
Celebration
fête, 883
rite, 998

Celebrity
repute, 873
nobility, 875

Celerity
velocity, 274

Celestial
physical, 318
moral, 829
religious, 976, 981
angelic, 977

Celibacy
bachelor, 904

Cell
cavity, 252
receptacle, 191
abode, 189
prison, 752

Cellar
room, 191
store, 636
lowness, 207

Cellaret
receptacle, 191

Cellular
concavity, 252

Cellule
receptacle, 191

Celsius
thermometer, 389

Cembalo
musical instrument, 417

Cement
connective, 45
to unite, 46
concord, 714

Cemetery
interment, 363

Cenobite
recluse, 893
anchoret, 996

Cenotaph
interment, 363

Censer
temple, 1000

Censor
detractor, 936
inhibit, 616

Censorious
disapprobation, 932

Censorship
authority, 737
secret, 533

Censure
disapprobation, 932

Census

counting, 85
list, 86

Centaur
unconformity, 83

Centenary
numbers, 98
celebration, 883

Centennial
numbers, 98
period, 108, 138

Centesimal
hundred, 98

Centigrade
thermometer, 389

Cento
· poetry, 597

Central
centrality, 223

Centralize
combine, 48
focus, 72
concentrate, 223

Centre
in order, 68
in space, 223

Centre in
convergence, 290

Centrifugal
divergence, 291

Centripetal
convergence, 290

Centuple
number, 98

Centurion
master, 745

Century
period, 108
duration, 106

Ceramic
sculpture, 557

Cerberus
janitor, 263
custodian, 664

Cerebration
thought, 451

Cerebrum
intellect, 450

Cerement
interment, 363

Ceremonious
respect, 928

Ceremony
parade, 882
religious, 998

Ceres

botany, 369

Cerise
red, 434

Cerography
engraving, 558

Certain
sure, 474, 484
special, 79
indefinite number, 100

Certainly
assent, 488

Certificate
voucher, 551
security, 771
evidence, 467

Certify
evince, 467
inform, 527
vouch, 535

Certitude
certainty, 474

Cerulean
blue, 438

Cess
tax, 812

Cessation
ceasing, 142

Cession
surrender, 725, 782
gift, 784

Cesspool
uncleanness, 633

Cestus
girdle, 225
ligature, 45
ring, 247

Chafe
warm, 384
pain, 378
irritate, 825, 828
vex, 830
incense, 900

Chaff
trash, 643
wit, 842
ridicule, 856
vulgar, 876

Chaffer
bargain, 769
sale, 794

Chafing-dish
furnace, 386

Chagrin
pain, 828

425

Chain
series, 69
to fasten, 43
vinculum, 45
ornament, 847
to imprison, 752
Chain-mail
arms, 727
Chain-shot
arms, 727
Chair
support, 215
vehicle, 272
direction, 693
professorship, 542
throne, 747
Chairman
director, 694, 745
Chairmanship
direction, 693
Chaise
vehicle, 272
Chaise longue
support, 215
Chalcography
engraving, 558
Chalet
abode, 189
Chalice
cup, 191
hollow, 252
Chalk
mark, 550
drawing, 556, 559
soil, 342
Chalk out
plan, 626
Chalky
white, 430
Challenge
defy, 715
accuse, 938
claim, 924
Cham
master, 745
Chamber
room, 191
council, 696
mart, 799
Chamber music
music, 415
Chamberlain
servant, 746
Chambermaid
servant, 746
Chameleon

variegation, 440
inconstancy, 149, 605
Chamfer
furrow, 259
Champ
eat, 296
Champaign
plain, 344
Champion
auxiliary, 711
proficient, 700
good, 648
defence, 717
combatant, 726
Championship
aid, 707
superiority, 33
Chance
absence of cause, 156
absence of aim, 621
opportunity, 134
Chance-medley
chance, 156
Chancel
temple, 1000
Chancellor
president, 745
judge, 967
Chancy
risky, 665
uncertain, 475
Chandelier
luminary, 423
Chandler
merchant, 797
Change
alteration, 140
mart, 799
small coin, 800
Changeable
mutable, 149, 607
irresolute, 605
Changeful
mutable, 149
volition, 607
Changeling
changed, 147
fool, 501
Channel
opening, 260
conduit, 350
instrumentality, 631
way, 627
passage, 302
furrow, 259

Chant
sing, 415
worship, 990
rites, 998
Chantage
blackmail, 791
Chanty
music, 415
Chaos
disorder, 59
secret, 533
Chap
man, 373
fissure, 198
Chap-book
book, 593
Chap-fallen
dejected, 837
humiliated, 879
Chapel
temple, 1000
council, 696
Chaperon
safety, 664, 753
accompaniment, 88
Chaplain
clergy, 996
Chaplet
circle, 247
dress, 225
ornament, 847
trophy, 733
Chapman
merchant, 797
Chaps
orifice, 66
Chapter
part, 51
topic, 454
book, 593
church, 995
council, 696
Char
calefaction, 384
Charabanc
vehicle, 272
Character
nature, 5
disposition, 820
state, 7
letter, 561
type, 591
drama, 599
class, 75
unconformity, 83

Characteristic
special, 79
feature, 550
intrinsic, 5

Characterize
name, 564
description, 594

Charade
secret, 533
drama, 599

Charcoal
fuel, 388
black, 431
artist, 559

Charge
business, 625
direction, 693
advice, 695
precept, 697
commission, 755
load, 52, 639
order, 741
accusation, 938
attack, 716
impact, 276
price, 812
custody, 751

Charge-hand
director, 694

Chargé d'affaires
deputy, 759

Chargeable
debt, 806

Charger
carrier, 271

Chariot
vehicle, 272

Charioteer
director, 694

Charity
giving, 784
benevolence, 906
bounty, 816

Charivari
loudness, 404
discordance, 413

Charlatan
imposter, 548
ignoramus, 493
boaster, 884

Charlatanism
quackery, 545, 855
ignorance, 491

Charm
to please, 829

love, 897
beauty, 845
motive, 615
to conjure, 992
spell, 993
flock, 72

Charnel-house
interment, 363

Chart
representation, 554

Charter
privilege, 924
legality, 963
permit, 760
compact, 769
security, 771
commission, 755

Charwoman
clean, 652

Chary
economical, 817
cautious, 864

Chase
pursue, 622
follow, 281
shape, 240
adorn, 847
convexity, 250
wood, 367

Chasm
discontinuity, 4, 70
interval, 198

Chassis
framework, 215

Chaste
simple, 576, 849
good taste, 850
symmetry, 242
pure, 960
innocent, 946
style, 576

Chasten
punish, 972
refine, 658
moderate, 826

Chastise
punish, 932, 972

Chasuble
vestments, 999

Chat
interlocution, 588

Château
abode, 189

Chatelaine
ornament, 847

Chatoyant
variegation, 440

Chattels
goods, 635
property, 780

Chatter
talk, 584
cold, 383

Chatterbox
loquacity, 584

Chauffeur
driver, 694

Chauvinistic
bellicose, 722
boasting, 884

Chaw
food, 298

Chaw-bacon
boor, 876

Cheap
low price, 815
worthless, 643

Cheapen
barter, 794
depreciate, 483

Cheat
deceiver, 548
to deceive, 545

Check
restrain, 174, 751
pacify, 826
slacken, 275
counteract, 179
hinder, 706
impediment, 135
dissuade, 616
test, 463
evidence, 467
ticket, 550
money order, 800
numerical, 85
variegate, 440

Checkmate
success, 731

Cheek
side, 236
insolence, 885
discourtesy, 895

Cheer
mirth, 836
rejoicing, 838

Cheer
amusement, 840
pleasure, 827
to give pleasure, 829

relief, 834
cry, 411
repast, 298
applaud, 931
aid, 707
inspirit, 861

Cheered
pleasure, 827

Cheerful
pleasurable, 836

Cheerio
departure, 293

Cheerless
dejection, 830, 837

Cheers
drink, 959

Cheese-parings
remainder, 40
parsimony, 819

Cheesed off
bored, 841
sated, 869

Chef
director, 694

Chef-d'œuvre
masterpiece, 650
capability, 648
master-stroke, 698

Cheka
detective, 461

Chela
novice, 541

Chemise
dress, 225

Chemistry
conversion, 144

Cheque
money, 800

Chequer
variegation, 440

Cherish
love, 897
aid, 707
entertain, 820

Cheroot
tobacco, 298A

Cherry
red, 434

Cherub
angel, 977

Chessboard
variegated, 440

Chest
box, 191
money-box, 802

Chest-note
resonance, 408

Chesterfield
seat, 215

Chesterfieldian
courtesy, 894

Chestnut
brown, 433
joke, 842

Cheval-glass
mirror, 445

Chevalier d'industrie
thief, 792

Chevaux-de-frise
defence, 717
spikes, 253

Chevelure
hair, 256

Chevron
indication, 550

Chew eat, 296
tobacco, 298A

Chew the cud
thought, 451

Chez soi
at home, 221

Chiaroscuro
shade, 424

Chibouque
tobacco-pipe, 298A

Chic
beauty, 845

Chicane
cunning, 702
deception, 545

Chicanery
sophistry, 477
deception, 545
wrangling, 713

Chicken
youth, 127
weakness, 160
cowardice, 862

Chicken feed
money, 800

Chicken-hearted
cowardice, 862

Chide
disapprobation, 932

Chief
principal, 642
master, 745

Chieftain
master, 745

Chiffon

ornament, 847

Chignon
head-dress, 225

Chilblain
swelling, 250

Child
youth, 129
fool, 501
offspring, 167

Childish
foolish, 499
banal, 575
trifling, 643

Child's play
unimportance, 643
easy, 705

Chiliad
numbers, 98
duration, 106

Chill
cold, 383
discouragement, 616,
706

Chilly
ungracious, 895

Chime
resonance, 408
roll, 407
repetition, 104
to harmonize, 413

Chime in with
agree, 23
conformity, 82
assent, 488

Chimera
monster, 83
error, 495
imaginary, 515

Chimerical
impossible, 471

Chimney
air-pipe, 351
fissure, 198
opening, 260
egress, 295

Chin-chin
departure, 293

Chink
gap, 198
opening, 260
sound, 408
money, 800

Chip
bit, 51
small part, 193

to detach, 44
to reduce, 195
Chip in
interpose, 228
conversation, 588
Chip of the old block
similarity, 17
Chipper
gay, 836
healthy, 654
Chirography
writing, 590
Chiromancy
prediction, 511
Chirp
bird cry, 412
sing, 415
Chirpy
cheerful, 836
Chirrup
see Chirp
Chisel
sculpture, 557
sharpness, 253
form, 240
fabricate, 161
Chit
infant, 129
small, 193
letter, 592
Chit-chat
colloquy, 588
Chivalrous
martial, 722
honourable, 939
bold, 861
generous, 942
Chivy
chase, 622
Chloral
anaesthetic, 376
Chlorosis
achromatism, 429
Chlorotic
achromatism, 429
Chock-full
sufficiency, 639
fullness, 52
Chocolate
brown, 433
sweet, 396
Choice
election, 609
excellent, 648
Choir

music, 415
orchestra, 416
church, 1000
Choke
close, 261
hinder, 706
surfeit, 641
suffocate, 361
Choke off
dissuade, 616
Chokka
bored, 841
sated, 869
Choky
prison, 752
Choler
resentment, 900
Choleric
irascible, 901
Choose
choice, 609
will, 600
Choosy
particular, 868
Chop
disjoin, 44
change, 140
barter, 794
wave, 348
sign, 550
Chop logic
reasoning, 476
Chopping
large, 192
Chops
orifice, 66
Choral
music, 415
Chord
harmony, 413
Chore
business, 625
Choreography
dance, 840
Chorister
musician, 416'
clergy, 996
Chorography
situation, 183, 554
Chortle
to laugh, 838
Chorus
sound, 404
voices, 411
musicians, 416

unanimity, 488
Chose jugée
judgment, 480
Chota hazri
food, 298
Chouse
deception, 545
Chrism
rite, 998
Christ
Deity, 976
Christen
nomenclature, 564
Christendom
Christianity, 983A
Christian
piety, 987
Christianity, 983A
Christianity
Christian religion, 983A
Christmas box
gift, 784
Chromatic
colour, 428
musical scale, 413
Chromatrope
optical instrument, 445
Chromolithograph
engraving, 558
Chronic
diuturnity, 110
Chronicle
annals, 551
measure of time, 114
account, 594
Chronicler
recorder, 553
Chronique scandaleuse
gossip, 532, 588
Chronology
time measurement, 114
Chronometry
time measurement, 114
Chrysalis
youth, 127, 129
Chubby
size, 192
Chuck
throw, 284
desist, 142
cry, 412
food, 298
Chuck out
expel, 297

Chuck up
abandon, 624
Chucker-out
doorkeeper, 263
Chuckle
laugh, 838
exult, 884
Chuckle-head
fool, 501
Chum
friend, 890
Chummy
friendly, 888
Chunk
size, 192
part, 51
Chunky
short, 201
broad, 202
Church
Christian religion,
983A
temple, 1000
Churchdom
churchdom, 995
Churchman
clergy, 996
Churchwarden
clergy, 996
tobacco-pipe, 298A
Churchy
bigoted, 988
Churchyard
interment, 363
Churl
boor, 876
rude, 895
irascible, 901
niggard, 819
Churn
agitation, 315, 352
Chute
obliquity, 217
Chutney
condiment, 393
Chyle
fluid, 333
Chyme
semiliquid, 352
Cicatrize
improvement, 658
Cicerone
teacher, 540
director, 694
Cicisbeo
love, 897

Ci-devant
preterition, 122
Cigar
tobacco, 298A
Cigar-case
receptacle, 191
Cigar-shaped
rotund, 249
Cigarette
tobacco, 298A
Cigarette-case
receptacle, 191
Ciliated
roughness, 256
Cimmerian
darkness, 421
Cinch
grip, 781
connection, 45
easy, 705
Cincture
circularity, 247
Cinders
remainder, 40
Cine-camera
lens, 445
Cinema
theatre, 599A
amusement, 840
Cinemaddict
cinema, 599A
Cinematograph
show, 448
Cinerary
burial, 363
Cineration
calefaction, 384
Cinerator
furnace, 386
Cinereous
grey, 432
Cingulum
belt, 229
Cinnabar
red, 434
Cinque
numbers, 98
Cipher
zero, 101
number, 84
to compute, 85
secret, 533
mark, 550
writing, 590
unimportant, 643

Circe
seductor, 615
sensuality, 954
Circle
form, 247
curvature, 245
space, 181
theatre, 599
party, 712
social, 892
Circuit
deviation, 279
indirect path, 629
winding, 248
turn, 311
tour, 266
space, 181
Circuitous
devious, 279
turning, 311
indirect, 629
Circular
round, 247
curved, 245
advertisement, 531
letter, 592
Circulate
rotate, 312
publish, 531
Circumambient
circumjacence, 227
Circumambulate
move, 266
wind, 311
Circumbendibus
winding, 248
circuit, 629
circuition, 311
Circumference
outline, 229
Circumfluent
circuition, 311
Circumfuse
dispersion, 73
Circumgyration
rotation, 312
Circumjacence
surrounding, 227
Circumlocution
phrase, 566, 573
Circumnavigation
navigation, 267
circuition, 311
Circumrotation
rotation, 312

Circumscribe
surround, 231
limit, 761
Circumspect
attentive, 457
careful, 459
cautious, 864
Circumstance
phrase, 8
event, 151
Circumstantial
diffuse, 573
evidence, 472
Circumvallation
enclosure, 232
defence, 717
Circumvent
cheat, 545
defeat, 731
cunning, 702
Circumvolution
rotation, 312
Circus
arena, 728
amusement, 840
edifice, 189
Cistern
receptacle, 191
store, 636
Citadel
fort, 666
defence, 717
Cite
quote as example, 82, 564
as evidence, 467
summon, 741
accuse, 938
arraign, 969
Cithern
musical instrument, 417
Citizen
inhabitant, 188
Citizen
man, 373
Citrine
yellow, 436
City
abode, 189
Civet
fragrance, 400
Civic
urban, 189
public, 372
Civicism

patriotism, 910
Civil
courteous, 894
laity, 997
Civilian
lawyer, 968
non–combatant, 726A
Civilization
courtesy, 894
mankind, 372
Civvies
dress, 225
Clachan
village, 189
Clack
talk, 588
snap, 406
animal cry, 412
Clad
dressed, 225
Claim
demand, 741, 765
property, 780
right, 924
Claimant
dueness, 924
petitioner, 767
Clairvoyance
occult arts, 992
insight, 490
foresight, 510
Clam
taciturn, 585
Clamant
cry, 411
Clamber
ascent, 305
Clammy
semiliquid, 352
Clamour
loudness, 404, 411
Clamp
to fasten, 43
fastening, 45
Clamp down
restrict, 751
Clan
class, 75
kindred, 11
clique, 892
Clandestine
concealment, 528
secret, 534
Clang
loudness, 404

resonance, 408
Clanger
error, 495, 732
solecism, 568
Clank
harsh sound, 410
Clannishness
prejudice, 481
co-operation, 709
Clap
explosion, 406
to applaud, 931
Clap on
addition, 37
Clap up
restraint, 751
Clapperclaw
beat, 972
Claptrap
plea, 617
pretence, 546
sophistry, 477
nonsense, 492
Claqueur
flatterer, 935
Clarence
vehicle, 272
Clarify
cleanness, 652
Clarinet
musical instrument, 417
Clarion
musical instrument, 417
Clarity
transparency, 425
perspicuity, 570
Clart
mud, 352
dirt, 653
Clash
oppose, 708
disagree, 24
discord, 713
contest, 720
concussion, 276
sound, 406
chatter, 584
Clasp
to unite, 43
fastening, 45
entrance, 903
come close, 197
Clasp-knife
sharpness, 253

Class
category, 75
to arrange, 60
learner, 541

Classic
masterpiece, 650
symmetry, 242
ancient, 124

Classical
taste, 578, 580

Classify
arrangement, 60
class, 75

Clatter
roll, 407
din, 404

Clause
part, 51
passage, 593
condition, 770

Claustral
secluded, 893

Claustrophobia
dislike, 867
seclusion, 893

Clavichord
musical, 417

Claw
hook, 633
to grasp, 789

Clay
earth, 342
corpse, 362
tobacco-pipe, 298A

Clay-cold
cold, 383

Claymore
arms, 727

Clean
unstained, 652
entirely, 31

Clean-handed
innocence, 946

Cleanse
purge, 652

Clear
transparent, 425
light, 420
visible, 446
intelligible, 518
perspicuous style, 570
to prepare, 673
to free, 750
to vindicate, 937
to acquit, 970
innocent, 946

simple, 42
easy, 705
to pay, 807
to pass, 302

Clear decks
prepare, 673

Clear of
distant, 196

Clear out
eject, 297
depart, 203

Clear-sighted
vision, 441
shrewd, 498

Clear up
interpret, 518, 522

Clearance
payment, 807

Clearway
way, 627

Cleave
adhere, 46
sunder, 44, 91

Cleek
club, 276

Clef
music, 413

Cleft
chink, 198

Clem
starve, 956

Clement
lenient, 740
kind, 906
pitiful, 914

Clench
see Clinch

Clepsydra
chronometry, 114

Clergy
clergy, 996

Clerical
churchdom, 995

Clerihew
drollery, 853
absurdity, 497

Clerk
scholar, 492
recorder, 553
writer, 590
servant, 746
agent, 758
church, 996

Clerkship
commission, 755

Clever
skill, 698

Cliché
platitude, 497

Click
snap, 406

Client
dependant, 746
buyer, 795
frequenter, 136

Clientship
subjection, 749

Cliff
height, 206
verticality, 212, 217

Cliff-hanging
suspense, 485

Climacteric
age, 128

Climate
region, 181
weather, 338

Climax
summit, 210
completion, 729
increase, 35
in degree, 33

Climb
ascent, 305

Clime
region, 181

Clinch
snatch, 789
fasten, 43
close, 261
an argument, 474, 478

Cling
cohere, 46

Clinic
medicine, 662

Clink
resonance, 408
prison, 752

Clinker
concretion, 321
dirt, 653

Clinometer
angularity, 244

Clinquant
ornament, 847

Clip
prune, 38
contract, 195
shorten, 201
stammer, 583

blow, 276
fastening, 45
hanging, 214
Clipper
ship, 273
swift, 274
Clipping
part, 51
extract, 596, 609
first-rate, 648
Clique
party, 712
sociality, 892
Cloaca
conduit, 350
foulness, 653
Cloak
dress, 225
conceal, 528
disguise, 546
Clock
chronometry, 114
Clockwise
rotation, 312
Clockwork
instrument, 633
Clod
earth, 342
fool, 591
Clod-pated
folly, 499
Clodhopper
boor, 876
Clodpoll
fool, 501
Clog
hindrance, 706
boot, 225
Clog-dance
dance, 840
Cloister
temple, 1000
seclusion, 893
Close
near, 197
short, 201
narrow, 203
dense, 321
tight, 43
similar, 17
warm, 382
to shut, 261
end, 67
to complete, 729
taciturn, 585

stingy, 819
piece of land, 780
house, 189
Close-fisted
parsimony, 819
Close in upon
converge, 290
Close quarters
nearness, 197
Close-up
cinema, 599A
Close with
arrive, 292
combat, 720
assent, 488
compact, 769
Closeness
junction, 43
Closet
room, 191
hide, 530
Closure
closing, 261
cessation, 142
Clot
concretion, 46
density, 321
earth, 342
Cloth
cover, 222
Clothes
dress, 225
Cloud
dimness, 422
shade, 424
opacity, 426
concealment, 528
crowd, 72
smoke, 334
Cloud-capt
height, 206
Clouded
variegated, 440
Cloudless
light, 420
Cloudy
opaque, 426
dark, 421
Clout
blow, 276
punishment, 972
to repair, 658
Cloven
bisection, 91
Cloven-footed

malevolent, 907
Clover
luxury, 377
comfort, 827
Clown
rustic, 876
buffoon, 844
pantomimic, 599
Clownish
vulgar, 851
Cloy
satiety, 641, 869
Club
bludgeon, 276
instrument, 633
weapon, 727
party, 712
to co-operate, 709
social meeting, 892
assemblage, 72
focus, 74
Club-footed
distorted, 243
Club-law
illegality, 964
compulsion, 744
Cluck
animal cry, 412
Clue
ball, 249
key, 462
Clueless
ignorant, 491
Clump
projecting mass, 250
assemblage, 72
trees, 367
to tread, 266
Clumsy
unskilful, 647, 699
graceless, 846
style, 579
Cluster
assemblage, 72
Clutch
seize, 134, 789
retain, 781
Clutches
authority, 737
Clutter
roll, 407
disorder, 59
Coacervation
crowd, 72

Coach
  carriage, 272
  to teach, 537
  tutor, 540
Coachman
  director, 694
Coaction
  compulsion, 744
Coadjutor
  auxiliary, 711
Coagency
  co-operation, 709
Coagment
  collect, 72
Coagulate
  density, 321
Coagulum
  density, 321
Coal
  fuel, 388
Coal-black
  blackness, 431
Coalesce
  identity, 13
  combine, 48
Coalition
  co-operation, 709
Coaptation
  agreement, 23
Coarctation
  narrow, 203
  decrease, 36
Coarse
  texture, 329
  vulgar, 851
  dirty, 653
  impure, 961
Coast
  land, 342
  to navigate, 267
  to skirt, 230
  to slide down, 306
Coaster
  ship, 273
Coastguard
  keeper, 753
Coat
  layer, 204
  exterior, 220
  habit, 225
  to paint, 222
  lining, 224
Coating
  lining, 224
Coax
  flatter, 933

persuade, 615
Cob
  horse, 271
Cobalt
  blue, 438
Cobble
  to mend, 658
Cobbler
  dress, 225
Co-belligerent
  helper, 711
Coble
  ship, 273
Cobra
  bane, 663
Cobweb
  light, 320
  flimsy, 643
  dirty, 653
  untruth, 546
Cochineal
  red, 434
Cock-a-hoop
  exulting, 731, 884
  gay, 836
Cock-and-bull
  absurdity, 497
Cock-crow
  morning, 125
Cock-sure
  belief, 484
Cock up
  stick up, 212
  project, 250
Cockade
  badge, 550
  title, 877
Cockatrice
  bane, 663
  monster, 83
  evil eye, 441
  miscreant, 949
Cockboat
  ship, 273
Cocker
  caress, 902
Cockle up
  fold, 258
Cockney
  townsman, 188
Cockpit
  arena, 728
  of a ship, 191
Cockshut time
  twilight, 422

Cocktail
  stimulus, 615
  drunkenness, 959
Cocotte
  prostitute, 962
Coction
  calefaction, 384
Cocytus
  hell, 982
Coda
  end, 67
Code
  law, 963
  precept, 697
  secret, 533
  signal, 550
Codex
  book, 593
Codger
  parsimony, 819
Codicil
  adjunct, 39
  sequel, 65
Codify
  legality, 963
Codswallop
  nonsense, 643
Coefficient
  co-operating, 709
  accompanying, 88
  factor, 84
Coemption
  purchase, 795
Coenobite
  seclusion, 893
Coequal
  equality, 27
Coerce
  restrain, 751
  compel, 744
  dissuade, 616
Coessential
  identity, 13
Coetaneous
  synchronism, 120
Coeternal
  perpetuity, 112
Coeval
  synchronism, 120
Coexist
  synchronism, 120
  accompany, 88
  contiguity, 199
Coextension
  equality, 27

434

parallelism, 216

Coffee-house
food, 298

Coffer
chest, 191
money-chest, 802
store, 636

Coffin
interment, 363

Coffin-nail
tobacco, 298A

Cog
tooth, 253
ship, 273
deceive, 545
flatter, 933

Cogent
powerful, 157
argument, 467, 476

Cogitate
thought, 451

Cognate
rule, 80
relation, 9

Cognation
relation, 9

Cognition
knowledge, 490

Cognizance
knowledge, 490

Cognomen
nomenclature, 564

Cognoscence
knowledge, 490

Cognoscente
taste, 850

Cognoscible
knowledge, 490

Cohabitation
marriage, 903

Co-heir
partner, 778

Cohere
unite, 46
dense, 321

Cohesive
uniting, 46
dense, 321
tenacious, 327

Cohibition
restraint, 751

Cohort
combatant, 726

Coif
dress, 225

Coiffure
dress, 225

Coil
convolution, 248
circuition, 311
disorder, 59

Coin
money, 800
to fabricate, 161
to imagine, 515

Coincidence
identity, 13
in time, 120
in place, 199
in opinion, 488

Coinstantaneity
synchronism, 120

Coke
fuel, 388

Colander
opening, 260

Cold
frigidity, 383
style, 575
insensible, 823
indifferent, 866

Cold-blooded
malevolent, 907
dispassionate, 823, 826

Cold-hearted
enmity, 889

Cold-shoulder
exclusion, 893
repulsion, 289

Cold war
truce, 723

Coliseum
arena, 728

Collaborate
accompany, 88
co-operate, 178, 709

Collapse
contraction, 195
prostration, 160
fatigue, 688
incapacity, 158
failure, 732

Collar
dress, 225
shackle, 749, 752
seize, 789

Collate
compare, 464

Collateral
relation, 11

lateral, 236
consequential, 467

Collation
food, 299
comparison, 464

Colleague
auxiliary, 711
co-operating, 709

Collect
assemble, 72
take, 789
acquire, 775
learn, 539
opine, 480
understand, 518
prayer, 990

Collectanea
assemblage, 72
compendium, 596

Collected
calm, 826

Collection
store, 636
offering, 990
assemblage, 72

Collectiveness
whole, 50

Collectivism
participation, 780
authority, 737

Collector
assemblage, 72

Colleen
woman, 374
girl, 129

College
school, 542

Collide
see Collision

Collier
ship, 273
man, 373

Colligate
assemblage, 72

Colligation
junction , 43

Collimation
direction, 278

Collimator
optical instrument, 445

Collision
approach, 286
percussion, 276
clashing, 179
opposition, 708

encounter, 720

Collocate
arrange, 60
assemble, 72

Collocution
interlocution, 588

Collogue
confer, 588

Colloid
semiliquid, 352

Collop
part, 51

Colloquialism
language, 560

Coloquy
interlocution, 588

Collotype
engraving, 558

Collusion
deceit, 545
concurrence, 178
conspiring, 709

Colon
stop, 142

Colonel
master, 745

Colonize
location, 184, 188

Colonnade
continuity, 69

Colony
region, 181
settlement, 184, 188

Colophon
end, 67
sequel, 65

Coloration
colour, 428

Coloratura
music, 415

Colossal
size, 192
height, 206

Colour
hue, 428
plea, 617
disguise, 545
qualify, 469
to blush, 434

Colourable
deceptive, 545
ostensible, 472

Colouring
meaning, 516
exaggeration, 549

Colourless
achromatism, 429

Colours
standard, 550
decoration, 877

Colporteur
agent, 758

Colt
fool, 501
horse, 271

Column
series, 69
height, 206
monument, 551
cylinder, 249
procession, 266
troop, 726

Colure
universe, 318

Coma
insensibility, 376, 823
inactivity, 683

Comb
sharpness, 253

Combat
contention, 720, 722

Combatant
contention, 726

Comber
wave, 348

Combination
union, 48

Combinations
arithmetical, 84
dress, 225

Combine
join, 48
co-operate, 709
union, 712
syndicate, 778

Combustible
heating, 384
fuel, 388

Come
arrive, 292
approach, 286
happen, 151

Come about
eventuality, 151

Come after
sequence, 63

Come-at-able
accessible, 705

Come away
recession, 287

Come-back
retort, 462, 479, 842
retaliation, 718

Come before
precedence, 62

Come by
acquisition, 775

Come down
descend, 306
cheapness, 815
pay, 809

Come-down
adversity, 735

Come forth
existence, 1

Come from
effect, 154

Come in for
obtain, 775

Come near
approach, 286

Come off
disjunction, 44
take place, 151

Come on
follow, 63
defy, 715
prosper, 731

Come out
egress, 294

Come over
induce, 615

Come to
whole, 50

Come up to
equal, 27

Come up with
arrival, 292

Come upon
arrival, 292

Comedian
the drama, 599
humorist, 844

Comedy
drama, 599
ridicule, 856

Comely
beauty, 845

Comestible
food, 298

Comet
wanderer, 268
universe, 318

Comfit
sweetness, 396

Comfort
pleasure, 377, 827
content, 831
relief, 834
Comfort station
toilet, 191, 653
Comfortable
pleased, 827
pleasing, 829
Comforter
deity, 976
dress, 225
Comfortless
unhappy, 828
painful, 830
dejected, 837
Comic
witty, 842
ridiculous, 853
Comintern
council, 696
Comitium
assemblage, 72
council, 696
Comity
courtesy, 894
Comma
stop, 141
Command
order, 741
authority, 737
Commandeer
impress, 744
take, 789
Commander
master, 745
Commanding
dignified, 873
Commando
combatant, 726
Comme il faut
taste, 850
fashion, 852
Commemorate
celebration, 883
record, 551
memory, 505
Commence
beginning, 66
Commend
approbation, 931
Commendable
virtuous, 944
Commensurate
accord, 23

adequate, 639
Comment
reason, 476
interpret, 522
dissertation, 595
Commerce
intercourse, 588
business, 625
barter, 794
Commercialese
verbiage, 573
Commination
threat, 909
Commingle
mixture, 41
Comminute
pulverulence, 330
disjunction, 44
incoherence, 47
Commiserate
pity, 914
Commissariat
provision, 298, 637
Commissary
consignee, 758
deputy, 759
Commission
business, 625
consignee, 755
fee, 809
Commissionaire
agent, 690
door-keeper, 263
Commissioner
consignee, 758
Commissure
junction, 43
Commit
act, 680
delegate, 755
imprison, 751
arrest, 969
Committee
council, 696
assemblage, 72
Commix
mixture, 41
Commodious
spacious, 180
expedience, 646
Commodity
merchandise, 798
Commodore
master, 745
Common

ordinary, 82
low, 876
unimportant, 643
general, 78
reciprocal, 12
frequent, 136
plain, 344
Common-room
sociality, 892
Common sense
intellect, 450
wisdom, 498
Commonalty
common, 876
people, 372
Commoner
commonalty, 876
Commonplace
unimportant, 643
habitual, 613
dull, 843
Commons
commonalty, 876
food, 298
Commonwealth
man, 373
Commotion
agitation, 315
Commune
muse, 451
converse, 588
territorial division, 181
Communicant
worship, 990
Communicate
tell, 527
participate, 778
join, 43
Communication
information , 527, 532
connection, 43
Communion
society, 712
participation, 778
sacrament, 998
Communism
participation, 778
authority, 737
Community
man, 373
fellowship, 712
participation, 778
Commute
barter, 794
substitution, 147

compensation, 30
compromise, 774
exchange, 148
Commuter
traveller, 268
Compact
close, 43
dense, 321
compendious, 201, 572
bargain, 769
unity, 87
receptacle, 191
Compages
whole, 50
texture, 329
Compagination
junction, 43
Companion
friend, 890
Companionable
sociality, 892
Companionship
accompaniment, 88
sociality, 892
Company
assembly, 72
accompaniment, 88
partnership, 797
Comparable
relation, 9
Comparative
degree, 26
magnitude, 31
Compare
comparison, 464
Compartment
cell, 191
region, 181
part, 51
place, 182
Compass
degree, 26
direction, 693
space, 180
surround, 227
measure, 466
to enclose, 231
achieve, 729
intend, 620
Compassion
pity, 914
Compatible
consentaneous, 23
possible, 470
Compatriot

inhabitant, 188
Compeer
equal, 27
friend, 890
Compel
compulsion, 744
Compendious
compendium, 596
concise, 572
Compendium
short, 201
writing, 596
Compensate
make up for, 30
requite, 973
Compensation
income, 810
Compete
oppose, 708
contend, 720
Competence
power, 157
sufficiency, 639
wealth, 803
skill, 698
Competition
opposition, 708
contention, 720
Competitor
opponent, 710
combatant, 726
Compilation
dissertation, 595
compendium, 596
assemblage, 72
Complacent
content, 831
pleased, 827
self-satisfied, 880
Complainant
accuser, 938
Complaint
murmur, 839
illness, 655
Complaisant
benevolent, 906
Complement
adjunct, 39
remainder, 40
part, 52
arithmetical, 84
Complete
entire, 52
great, 31
end, 67

to finish, 729
Complex
mixture, 41
disorder, 59
Complexion
state, 7
appearance, 448
Compliance
observance, 772
consent, 762
obedience, 743
duty, 926
Complicated
disorder, 59
difficult, 704
Complicity
deceit, 545
concurrence, 178
conspiring, 709
Compliment
courtesy, 894
praise, 931
Compline
worship, 990
Comply
consent, 762
obey, 743
observe, 772
Component
component, 56
Comport
conduct, 692
Comport with
agree, 23
Compos
sanity, 502
Compose
make up, 54
produce, 161
moderate, 174
pacify, 723
assuage, 826
music, 415
write, 590
Composed
self-possessed, 826
Composite
mixture, 41
Composition
constitution, 54
combination, 48
inclusion, 76
music, 415
painting, 556
writing, 590

Concise
conciseness, 572
Conclave
assembly, 72
council, 696
church, 995
Conclude
end, 67
infer, 476
opine, 480, 484
complete, 729
determine, 604
Conclusion (to try)
contention, 720
Conclusive
demonstration, 478
Concoct
prepare, 673
falsify, 544
plan, 626
Concomitant
synchronous, 120
concurring, 178
accompanying, 88
Concord
agreement, 23
in music, 413
assent, 488
harmony, 714
amity, 888
Concordance
dictionary, 562
Concordat
compact, 769
Concours
contention, 720
Concourse
assemblage, 72
convergence, 290
Concrete
mass, 46
material, 3, 316
density, 321
Concubine
libertine, 962
Concupiscence
desire, 865
impurity, 961
Concur
co-operate, 178
in concert, 709
converge, 290
assent, 488
Concurrence
agreement, 23

coexistence, 120
Concussion
impulse, 276
Condemn
censure, 932
convict, 971
Condense
contraction, 195
density, 321
style, 572
Condescend
humility, 879
Condescending
patronizing, 878
Condign
dueness, 922, 924
Condiment
condiment, 393
Condition
state, 7
rank, 873
term, 770
modification, 469
sensitiveness, 375
teach, 537
habit, 613
Conditional
circumstance, 8
Condole
condolence, 915
Condonation
forgiveness, 918
Condottiere
master, 745
Conduce
tend, 176
concur, 178
avail, 644
contribute, 153
Conduct
lead, 693
transfer, 270
procedure, 692
music, 415
Conductor
guard, 666
director, 694
interpreter, 524
musician, 416
conveyor, 271
Conduit
conduit, 350
Condyle
convexity, 250
Cone

round, 249
pointed, 253
Confabulation
interlocution, 588
Confection
sweetness, 396
Confederacy
party, 712
co-operation, 709
Confederate
auxiliary, 711
Confer
give, 784
converse, 588
advise, 695
Confess
avow, 529, 535
assert, 488
penitence, 950
rite, 998
Confessedly
affirmation, 535
admission, 467
Confessional
temple, 1000
Confidant
auxiliary, 711
friend, 890
Confide
trust, 484
credulity, 486
hope, 858
Confidence
courage, 861
Confidence man
cheat, 548
Confidential
concealment, 528
Configuration
form, 240
Confine
limit, 233
imprison, 751
circumscribe, 231
frontier, 199
Confined
ailing, 655
Confirm
corroborate, 467
consent, 762
rites, 998
Confirmed
fixed, 150
Confiscate
condemn, 971

take, 789
Conflagration
calefaction, 384
Conflation
combination, 48
Conflict
contention, 720
disagreement, 24
Conflicting
opposing, 14, 179, 708
Confluence
convergence, 290
Conflux
assemblage, 72
Conform
assent, 488
accustom, 613
concur, 178
agree, 646
Conformation
form, 240
frame, 7
Conformity
to rule, 16, 82
Confound
disorder, 61
injure, 649
perplex, 475
baffle, 731
confuse, 519
astonish, 870
indiscriminate, 465A
expletive, 908
Confoundedly
greatness, 31
Confraternity
friendship, 888
Confrère
friend, 890
Confront
face, 234
compare, 467
resist, 719
Confucianism
religion, 984
Confucius
religious founder, 986
Confuse
derange, 61
indiscriminate, 465A
obscure, 519
perplex, 458, 475
abash, 874
style, 571
Confusion

disorder, 59
shame, 874
Confutation
disproof, 479
Confute
deny, 536
Congé
dismissal, 756
Congeal
cold, 385
Congealed
dense, 321
Congener
consanguinity, 11
similar, 17
included, 76
Congenial
agreeing, 23, 714
expedient, 646
Congenital
intrinsic, 5
habitual, 613
Congeries
assemblage, 72
Congestion
collection, 72
redundance, 641
disease, 655
Conglobation
assemblage, 72
Conglomerate
assemblage, 72
density, 321
Conglutinate
coherence, 46
Congratulate
congratulation, 896
Congregate
assemblage, 72
Congregation
laity, 997
worship, 990
Congress
assemblage, 72, 290
council, 696
Congruous
agreeing, 23
expedient, 646
Conical
round, 249
pointed, 253
Conjecture
supposition, 514
Conjoin
junction, 43

concur, 178
Conjointly
together, 37, 43
Conjugal
marriage, 903
Conjugate
word, 562
Conjugation
junction, 43
pair, 89
phase, 144
grammar, 567
Conjunct
junction, 43
Conjunction
vinculum, 45
Conjuncture
contingency, 8
occasion, 134
Conjuration
deception, 545
sorcery, 992
Conjure
entreat, 765
exorcise, 992
Conjure up
imagine, 515
Conjurer
sorcerer, 994
adept, 700
Connate
cause, 153
intrinsic, 5
Connatural
uniform, 16
similar, 17
Connect
relate, 9
link, 43
Connection
kindred, 11
link, 45
Connective
link, 45
Connive
overlook, 460
concur, 178
allow, 760
Connoisseur
taste, 850
judge, 480
proficient, 700
Connotation
indication, 550

Connubial
marriage, 903
Conquer
success, 731
Conquered
failure, 732
Conquest
success, 731
Consanguinity
kindred, 11
Conscience
moral sense, 926
knowledge, 490
Conscience-smitten
penitence, 950
Conscientious
virtuous, 944
scrupulous, 726A, 939
true, 494
Consciousness
intuition, 450
knowledge, 490
Conscript
soldier, 726
Conscription
compulsion, 744
Consecrate
dedicate, 873
sanctify, 987, 995, 998
Consectary
corollary, 480
Consecution
sequence, 63
Consecutive
following, 63
continuous, 69
Consecutively
gradually, 144
Consensus
agreement, 23
assent, 488
Consent
grant, 762
concur, 178
assent, 488
agreement, 23
Consentaneous
agreeing, 23
expedient, 646
Consequence
effect, 154
event, 151
importance, 642
Consequent
sequence, 63
Consequential

arrogant, 878
deducible, 467, 478
Consequently
reasoning, 154, 476
Conservation
preservation, 670
Conservative
permanence, 141
Conservatoire
school, 542
Conservatory
store, 636
hothouse, 386
Conserve
sweet, 396
Consider
think, 451
attend to, 457
inquire, 461
Considerable
in degree, 31
in size, 192
important, 642
Considerate
judicious, 498
benevolent, 906
respectful, 928
Consideration
motive, 615
qualification, 469
importance, 642
requital, 973
respect, 928
Considering
reasoning, 476
Consign
transfer, 783
commission, 755
give, 784
allot, 786
Consignee
delegate, 758
Consignment
commission, 755
Consist in
existence, 1
Consist of
composition, 54
Consistence
density, 321
Consistency
uniformity, 16
Consistent
agreement, 23
Consistory

council, 696
church, 995
Consociation
sociality, 892
Console
relieve, 834
pity, 914
table, 215
keyboard, 417
Consolidate
unite, 46, 48
condense, 321
Consols
treasury, 802
Consonance
agreement, 23
expedience, 646
music, 413
Consonant
letter, 561
Consort
accompany, 88
associate, 892
spouse, 903
Consort with
fit, 646
Consortship
sociality, 892
Conspectus
compendium, 596
Conspicuous
visible, 446
eminent, 873
Conspiracy
plot, 626
Conspire
concur, 178
Constable
governor, 745
police, 664
officer, 965
Constant
uniformity, 16
immutable, 150
regular, 80, 82
continuous, 69
resolute, 604
True, 494
faithful, 939
Constantly
frequently, 136
Constellation
stars, 318, 423
glory, 873

Consternation
fear, 860
Constipate
density, 321
Constituent
component, 54, 56
voter, 609
Constitute
compose, 54, 56
produce, 161
Constitution
nature, 5
state, 7
texture, 329
charter, 924
law, 963
Constrain
power, 157
restrain, 751
compel, 744
abash, 881
Constrict
narrow, 203
contract, 195
Constringe
narrow, 203
Construct
production, 161
Construction
form, 240
structure, 329
meaning, 522
Construe
meaning, 522
Consubstantiation
rite, 998
Consul
diplomat, 758
Consult
advice, 695
Consume
destroy, 162
waste, 638
use, 677
ravage, 649
Consuming
painful, 830
Consummate
great, 31
complete, 52, 729
skill, 698
Consummation
end, 67
Consumption
shrinking, 195

waste, 638
disease, 655
use, 677
Contact
contiguity, 199
meet, 292
Contadino
peasant, 876
Contagious
insalubrious, 657
Contain
include, 76
be composed of, 54
Contaminate
spoil, 659
soil, 653
Contango
discount, 813
Contemn
contempt, 930
Contemper
moderation, 174
Contemplate
view, 441
think, 451
purpose, 620
expect, 507
Contemporaneous
synchronism, 120
Contemporary
synchronism, 120
Contempt
despise, 930
Contemptible
unimportant, 643
Contend
fight, 720
assert, 535
Content
satisfied, 827, 831
calm, 826
assentient, 488
patience, 821
will, 600
willing, 602
Contention
discord, 713
struggle, 720
Contentious
bad-tempered, 901
Contents
ingredients, 56
components, 190
list, 86
compendium, 596

end, 67
Conterminal
end, 67
limit, 233
Conterminous
adjoining, 199
Contest
contention, 720
lawsuit, 969
Context
printing, 591
accompaniment, 88
Contexture
state, 7
texture, 329
Contiguous
touching, 199
Continence
purity, 960
Continent
land, 342
Contingent
conditional, 8
qualifying, 469
eventual, 151
chance, 156
liable, 177
possible, 470
uncertain, 475
casual, 621
allotment, 786
part, 51
duration, 108A
Continually
frequency, 136
Continuation
sequence, 63
sequel, 65
adjunct, 39
Continue
persist, 141, 143
endure, 106, 110
Continued, to be
sequel, 65
Continuity
persistence, 69
Continuum
substantiality, 3
Contortion
distortion, 243
convolution, 246
deformity, 846
Contour
outline, 229, 448

443

Conversion
    change, 144
    religious, 987
Convert
    opinion, 484
    learner, 541
    piety, 987
    to change to, 144
    to use, 677
Convertible
    identical, 13
    equal, 27
Convex
    convexity, 250
Convey
    transfer, 270, 783
Conveyance
    vehicle, 272
Conveyancer
    lawyer, 968
Convict
    condemn, 971
    to convince, 537
    prisoner, 754
    condemned, 949
Conviction
    belief, 484
Convince
    teaching, 537
Convincement
    belief, 484
Convivial
    social, 892
Convocation
    council, 696, 995
Convoke
    asscmblage, 72
Convolution
    coil, 248
    rotation, 312
    crossing, 219
Convoy
    transfer, 270
    guard, 664, 753
Convulse
    violent, 173
    agitate, 315
    pain, 378
    torture, 830
Coo
    animal cry, 412
Cook
    heat, 384
    prepare, 673

    falsify, 544
    accounts, 811
Cool
    cold, 383
    to refrigerate, 385
    judicious, 498
    to moderate, 174
    to dissuade, 616
    to allay, 826
    indifferent, 866
    torpid, 826
Cool-headed
    torpid, 826
    judicious, 498
Cooler
    refrigerator, 387
    prison, 752
Coolie
    carrier, 271
Coombe
    valley, 252
Coon
    black, 431
Coop
    confine, 752
    restrain, 751
    abode, 189
Co-operate
    physically, 178
    voluntarily, 709
Co-operation
    agreement, 23
Co-operator
    auxiliary, 711
Co-ordinate
    equality, 27
    arrange, 60
Cop
    police, 664
Copal
    semiliquid, 352
Copartner
    participator, 778
    associate, 892
    accompanying, 88
Cope
    contend, 720
    equal, 27
    canonicals, 999
Copia verborum
    diffuseness, 573
    speech, 582
Coping-stone
    completion, 729

Copious
    abundant, 639
    style, 573
Copper
    money, 800
    colour, 439
    police, 664
Copperplate
    engraving, 558
Coppice
    plant, 367
Coprology
    impurity, 653
Copse
    see Coppice
Copula
    junction, 45
Copy
    imitation, 19, 21
    prototype, 22
    to write, 590
    represent, 554
Copyholder
    printing, 591
Copying
    imitating, 19
Copyist
    writing, 590
Copyright
    privilege, 924
Coquetry
    affectation, 855
Coquette
    flirt, 902
    vacillate, 605
Cor anglais
    musical, 417
Coracle
    boat, 273
Coral
    ornament, 847
Coram judice
    jurisdiction, 965
Corbeille
    receptacle, 191
Cord
    tie, 45
    filament, 205
    furrow, 259
Cordage
    junction, 45
Cordial
    grateful, 829
    warm, 821

willing, 602
friendly, 888
remedy, 662
Cordite
arms, 727
Cordon
outline, 229, 232
circular, 247
badge, 550
Corduroy
furrow, 259
Core
centrality, 223
importance, 642
Co-respondent
divorce, 905
Corgi
vehicle, 272
Coriaceous
tenacity, 327
Corinthian
taste, 850
Co-rival
see Corrival
Cork
lightness, 320
plug, 263
Cork up
closure, 261
restrain, 751
Corkscrew
extractor, 301
perforator, 262
spiral, 248
Cormorant
gluttony, 865, 957
Corn
projection, 250
Corncob
tobacco-pipe, 298A
Cornea
eye, 441
Corned
drunk, 959
Corneous
hard, 323
Corner
place, 182
receptacle, 191
angularity, 244
Corner-stone
support, 215
to engross, 777
syndicate, 778

Cornet
music, 417
officer, 745
Cornice
summit, 210
Cornucopia
sufficiency, 639
Cornute
sharp, 253
Corollary
deduction, 480
addition, 37, 39
Corona
circularity, 247
light, 420
Coronach
lamentation, 839
funeral, 363
Coronary
height, 206
summit, 210
Coronation
celebration, 883
Coronet
sceptre, 747
ornament, 847
Corporal
officer, 745
animality, 364
Corporality
materiality, 316
Corporate
junction, 43
Corporation
association, 712
convexity, 350
bulk, 192
Corporeal
materiality, 316
Corporeity
substantiality, 3
Corps
assemblage, 72
troops, 726
Corps de reserve
store, 636
Corps diplomatique
consignee, 758
Corpse
body, 362
Corpulent
size, 192
broad, 202

Corpus delicti
guilt, 947
Corpuscle
atom, 193
jot, 32
Corradiation
focus, 74
Corral
enclosure, 232, 752
Correct
true, 494
reason, 476
order, 58
virtuous, 939, 944
due, 924, 926
style, 570
elegant, 578
undeceive, 529
to improve, 658
to censure, 932
to punish, 972
Corrective
remedy, 662
counteraction, 179
Corregidor
master, 745
Correlation
relation, 9
reciprocity, 12
Correspond
agree, 23
concur, 178
write, 592
Correspondent
report, 527
Corridor
place, 191
passage, 627
Corrie
hollow, 252
Corrigible
improvement, 658
Corrival
combatant, 726
Corrivalry
contention, 720
Corrivation
river, 348
Corroborant
remedy, 662
assent, 488
Corroborate
evidence, 467

Corroboree
festivity, 840
Corrode
erode, 659
consume, 649
afflict, 830
Corrosion
evil, 619
Corrosive
destructive, 649
Corrugate
constrict, 195
narrow, 203
rumple, 258
derange, 61
Corrupt
foul, 653
noxious, 649
evil, 619
to spoil, 659
vicious, 945
Corruption
decomposition, 49
Corsage
dress, 225
Corsair
thief, 792
Corse
corpse, 362
Corset
dress, 225
Corse
arena, 728
Cortège
suite, 746
procession, 266
continuity, 39, 69
Cortes
council, 696
Cortex
covering, 222
Corundum
hardness, 323
Coruscate
light, 420
Corvée
compulsion, 744
Corvette
ship, 273
Corybantic
insanity, 503
Coryphaeus
leader, 745
Cosh

impact, 276
arms, 727
Cosmetic
ornament, 847
Cosmic
world, 318
Cosmogony
world, 318
Cosmography
world, 318
Cosmonaut
navigator, 269
Cosmopolitan
world-wide, 78
Cosmopolite
philanthropy, 910
Cosmorama
view, 448
Cossack
combatant, 726
Cosset
favourite, 899
Cost
price, 812
Costermonger
merchant, 797
Costly
dearness, 814
Costume
dress, 225
Cosy
comfortable, 377, 827, 829
Cot
abode, 189
Cote
hut, 189
Co-tenant
partner, 778
Coterie
party, 712
sociality, 892
Cotillion
amusement, 840
Cottage
abode, 189
Cottar
inhabitant, 188
peasant, 876
Cotton-wool
softness, 324
Couch
bed, 215
to lie, 213

recline, 308
lie in wait, 530
express, 566
Couchant
horizontal, 213
Couci-couci
imperfection, 651
Cough
puff, 349
Couloir
gully, 198
Coulter
sharpness, 253
Council
senate, 696
ecclesiastical, 995
Counsel
advice, 695
Counsellor
adviser, 695
lawyer, 968
Count
compute, 85
expect, 507
believe, 484
estimate, 480
signify, 642
lord, 875
Countenance
face, 234
favour, 707
appearance, 448
to approve, 931
Counter
contrary, 14
against, 179, 708
retort, 479
number, 84
token, 550
table, 215
shopboard, 799
to retaliate, 718
Counter-attraction
dissuasion, 616
avoidance, 623
Counter-claim
lawsuit, 969
Counter-evidence
contrary, 468
Counter-intelligence
secret, 533
Counter-irritant
counteraction, 179
Counter-movement
regression, 283

Counter-order
abrogation, 756
Counter-project
retaliation, 718
plan, 626
Counter-revolution
revolution, 146
Counter-stroke
retaliation, 718
Counter-subject
music, 415
Counter-tenor
melody, 413
high note, 410
Counteract
physically, 179
voluntarily, 708
hinder, 706
compensate, 30
Counterbalance
compensation, 30
Counterblast
counteraction, 179
retaliation, 718
Counterchange
reciprocality, 12, 148
Countercharm
spell, 993
Countercheck
hindrance, 706
Counterfeit
simulate, 544, 545
imitate, 19
copy, 21
Counterfoil
check, 550
Countermand
abrogation, 756
Countermarch
regression, 283
journey, 266
Countermark
indication, 550
Countermine
opposition, 708
Counterpane
covering, 222
Counterpart
copy, 21
match, 17
Counterplot
retaliation, 718
plan, 626
Counterpoint
harmony, 413

Counterpoise
compensation, 30
weight, 319
Counterpoison
remedy, 662
Countersign
indication, 550
assent, 488
Countervail
compensate, 28, 30
oppose, 179, 708
evidence, 468
Counterweight
weight, 319
Counterwork
opposition, 708
Countess
noble, 875
chief, 745
Counting-house
mart, 799
Countless
infinity, 105
Countrified
rural, 185
low, 876
Country
definite region, 181, 189
agriculture, 371
Countryman
inhabitant, 185
Counts
particulars, 79
County
region, 181
fashionable, 852
Coup
action, 680
Coup de grâce
death-blow, 361
destruction, 162
completion, 729
end, 67
pity, 914
punishment, 972
Coup de main
violence, 173
action, 680
Coup de maître
skill, 698
success, 731
Coup d'essai
essay, 675
Coup d'état
action, 680

plan, 626
revolt, 719, 742
Coup de théâtre
appearance, 448
ostentation, 882
Coup d'œil
vision, 441
appearance, 448
Coupé
vehicle, 272
Couple
two, 89
to unite, 43
Couplet
poetry, 597
Coupon
money, 800
ticket, 550
Courage
bravery, 861
Courier
messenger, 534
interpreter, 524
Course
order, 58
continuity, 69
of time, 109
layer, 204
direction, 278
motion, 264
locomotion, 266
effect, 154
rapidity, 274
pursuit, 622
teaching, 537
plan, 626
way, 627
conduct, 692
arena, 728
dinner, 298
Courser
carrier, 271
swift, 274
Court
house, 189
hall, 191
council, 696
arena, 728
to invite, 615
to pursue, 622
to solicit, 765
to wish, 865
to woo, 902
to flatter, 933
gentility, 852

tribunal, 966
retinue, 746
Court hand
writing, 590
Court-martial
tribunal, 966
Courtesan
libertine, 962
Courtesy
politeness, 894
manners, 852
Courtier
flatterer, 935
Courtier-like
flattery, 933
Courtly
fashion, 852
noble, 975
polite, 894
Courtship
endearment, 902
Cousin
consanguinity, 11
Coûte que coûte
resolution, 604
Cove
cell, 191
haunt, 189
hollow, 252
bay, 343
man, 373
Covenant
compact, 769, 770
promise, 768
Cover
dress, 225
superpose, 222
conceal, 528
retreat, 530
safety, 664, 666
to compensate, 30
stopper, 263
Coverlet
covering, 222
Covert
invisibility, 447
Coverture
marriage, 903
Covetous
miserly, 819
envious, 921
desirous, 865
Covey
assemblage, 72, 102
Cow

intimidate, 860
Cow-catcher
defence, 717
Coward
fearful, 860, 862
Cower
fear, 860
stoop, 308
grovel, 886
Cowl
dress, 225
sacerdotal, 999
Cowling
covering, 222
Co-worker
worker, 690
Coxcomb
fop, 854
Coxcombical
vain, 880
affected, 855
Coxswain
steersman, 694
Coy
modesty, 881
Cozen
deception, 545
Crab
sourness, 397
to depreciate, 932
Crab-like
deviation, 279
Crabbed
sour, 397
difficult, 704
inelegant, 579
uncivil, 895
testy, 901
Crack
split, 44
snap, 328
break up, 162
fissure, 198
furrow, 259
blow, 276
try, 675
sound, 406
chat, 588
excellent, 648
proficient, 698, 700
Crack, in a
instantaneity, 113
Crack-brained
imbecility, 499
Cracked

mad, 503
faulty, 651
Cracker
snap, 406
untruth, 546
Crackers
mad, 503
Crackle
snap, 406
Crackpot
madman, 504
Cradle
bed, 215
beginning, 66
origin, 153
infancy, 127
to place, 184
to train, 673
Craft
cunning, 702
skill, 698
plan, 626
apparatus, 633
business, 623
shipping, 273
Craftsman
doer, 690
Crag
height, 206
Cragged
rough, 256
Cram
stuff, 194
fill, 52, 639
collect, 72
gorge, 296, 957
teach, 537
choke, 261
Crambe repetita
repetition, 104
Crammer
teacher, 540
untruth, 546
Cramp
hinder, 706
restrain, 751
contract, 195
narrow, 203
fasten, 45
paralyse, 158
weaken, 160
spasm, 378, 828
Cramped
style, 572, 579

Crane
  instrument, 633
  raise, 307
Crane-neck
  curvature, 245
Cranium
  intellect, 450
Crank
  instrument, 633
  wit, 842
  eccentric, 83, 499
  punishment, 972
Crank up
  prepare, 673
Crankle
  to bend, 244
Cranky
  eccentric, 499
  opinionated, 606
  bad-tempered, 901
  insane, 503
Cranny
  interval, 198
Crape
  mourning, 839
Crapulence
  intemperance, 954
Crash
  sound, 406
  descent, 306
  destruction, 162, 732
  impulse, 276
Crasis
  coherence, 46
Crass
  great, 31
  ignorance, 491
  stupid, 499
Crassitude
  breadth, 202
  thickness, 352
Crate
  receptacle, 191
Crater
  hollow, 252
  depth, 208
  receptacle, 191
Cravat
  dress, 225
Crave
  ‘ask, 765
  desire, 865
Craven
  cowardice, 862
Craw

receptacle, 191
Crawl
  move, 275
  submission, 725
  servility, 886
  improbity, 940
Crayon
  painting, 556
  pencil, 559
Craze
  caprice, 608
  fashion, 852
Crazy
  weak, 160
  mad, 503
Creak
  stridor, 410
Cream
  emulsion, 354
  oil, 355
  perfection, 648, 650
  choice, 609
Cream-coloured
  white, 430
Creamy
  semiliquid, 352
Crease
  fold, 258
Create
  produce, 161
  cause, 153
  imagine, 515
Creation
  universe, 318
Creationism
  causation, 153
Creative
  productive, 168
Creator
  deity, 976
  producer, 164
Creature
  animal, 366
  thing, 3
  effect, 154
Creature comforts
  food, 298
Crèche
  nursery, 542
Credence
  belief, 484
Credential
  evidence, 467
Credible
  probable, 472, 484

possible, 470
Credit
  belief, 484
  authority, 737
  pecuniary, 805
  account, 811
  influence, 737
  hope, 858
  repute, 873
  desert, 944
Creditor
  credit, 805
Credo
  belief, 484
Credulity
  belief, 486
  superstition, 984A
Creed
  belief, 484, 496
  tenet, 983
Creek
  gulf, 343
Creep
  crawl, 275
  bad man, 949
Creeper
  plant, 367
Creeping
  sensation, 380
Creepy
  fearsome, 860
Cremation
  burning, 384
  of corpses, 363
Crème de la crème
  goodness, 648
Cremona
  musical instrument, 417
Crenated
  notch, 257
Crenelated
  notched, 257
Crepitate
  snap, 406
Crepuscule
  dawn, 125
  dimness, 422
Crescendo
  increase, 35
  music, 415
Crescent
  curve, 245
  street, 189
Cressset
  torch, 423

Crest
summit, 210
tuft, 256
armorial, 550, 877
Crestfallen
dejected, 837
humiliated, 879, 881
Cretin
fool, 501
Crevasse
interval, 198
Crevice
interval, 198
opening, 260
Crew
assemblage, 72
party, 712
inhabitants, 188
Crib
bed, 215
to steal, 791
interpretation, 522
Crick
pain, 378
Crier
messenger, 534
Crime
guilt, 947
Criminal
culprit, 949
vicious, 945
Criminality
guilty, 947
Criminate
accusation, 938
Criminology
crime, 947
Crimp
curl, 248
fold, 258
to steal, 791
Crimson
red, 434
Cringe
submit, 725, 743
servility, 886
fear, 860
Crinkle
fold, 258
angle, 244
Crinoline
dress, 225
Cripple
weaken, 160
disable, 158

injure, 649, 659
disease, 655
Crisis
conjuncture, 8
event, 151
difficulty, 704
opportunity, 134
Crisp
brittle, 328
rough, 256
rumpled, 248
concise, 572
Criss-cross-row
letter, 561
Criterion
trial, 463
evidence, 467
Critic
taste, 850
judge, 480
reviewer, 590
dissertation, 595
detractor, 936
Critical
opportune, 134
important, 642
difficult, 704
dangerous, 665
Criticism
disapprobation, 932
dissertation, 595
Criticize
taste, 850
Critique
discrimination, 465
dissertation, 595
disapprobation, 932
Croak
cry, 412
stammer, 583
complain, 839
discontent, 832
predict, 511
Croceate
yellow, 436
Crochet
knit, 43
Crock
weakness, 160
Crock up
failure, 732
Crocodile tears
falsehood, 544
Croesus
wealth, 803

Croft
hut, 189
Crofter
peasant, 876
Cromlech
interment, 363
Crone
veteran, 130
Crony
friend, 890
Crook
curvature, 245
evildoer, 913
swindler, 792
ill, 655
Crooked
angular, 244
distorted, 243, 846
sloping, 217
dishonourable, 940
Croon
to hum, 405, 415
Crop
stomach, 191
to shorten, 201
to gather, 775
to take, 789
to eat, 297
harvest, 154
Crop up
inexpectation, 508
event, 151
appear, 446
Cropper
fall, 306
Crosier
canonicals, 999
Cross
intersection, 219
passage, 302
swindle, 545
opposition, 179, 708
refusal, 572
vexation, 828
vexatiousness, 830
ill-tempered, 895
fretful, 901
failure, 732
mixture, 41
decoration, 877
reward, 973
rites, 998
Cross-breed
unconformity, 83

Cross-cut
method, 627
Cross-examine
inquiry, 461
Cross-grained
obstinate, 606
ill-tempered, 895, 901
Cross-purposes
error, 495
misinterpretation, 523
Cross-question
inquiry, 461
Cross-reading
misinterpretation, 523
Cross-road
way, 627
Crossbow
arms, 727
Crossing
crossing, 219
Crosspatch
ill-tempered, 895
Crossword
puzzle, 461, 533
Crotch
angularity, 244
Crotchet
music, 413
prejudice, 481
caprice, 608
Crotchety
folly, 499
Crouch
stoop, 308
lower, 207
servility, 886
fear, 860
Croup
rear, 235
Crow
cry, 412
laugh, 838
boast, 884
exult, 836
lever, 633
black, 431
Crowbar
instrument, 633
Crowd
assemblage, 72
multitude, 102
closeness, 197
the vulgar, 876
Crown
top, 210
end, 67

circle, 247
trophy, 733
sceptre, 747
reward, 973
to complete, 729
Crowning
superior, 33
Crow's nest
view, 441
Crucial
crossing, 219
experimental, 463
demonstrative, 478
Crucible
receptacle, 191
laboratory, 144, 691
Crucifix
rite, 998
canonicals, 999
Cruciform
crossing, 219
Crucify
torture (physical), 378
agony (mental), 828
painfulness, 830
execution, 972
Crude
unprepared, 674
inelegant, 579
Cruel
painful, 830
inhuman, 907
Cruet
receptacle, 191
Cruise
navigation, 267
Cruiser
ship, 273
Crumb
small part, 51
grain, 193
powder, 330
bit, 32
Crumble
pulverize, 330
destroy, 162
diminish, 36
spoil, 659
brittleness, 328
Crumple
ruffle, 256
crease, 258
contract, 195
Crunch
bruise, 44

masticate, 297
pulverize, 330
Crupper
rear, 235
Crusade
warfare, 722
Cruse
vessel, 191
Crush
pulverize, 330
destroy, 162
injure, 649
humiliate, 879
pain, 828
contract, 195
love, 897
Crust
covering, 222
insolence 885
Crusty
discourtesy, 895
Crutch
support, 215
angle, 244
instrument, 633
Crux
question, 461
mystery, 533
Cry
animal, 412
human, 411
loudness, 404
voice, 580
publish, 531
weep, 839
Cry down
disapprove, 932
Cry for
desire, 865
Cry to
beseech, 765
Cry up
praise, 931
Crypt
cell, 191
hide, 530
grave, 363
altar, 1000
Cryptic
latent, 526, 528
Cryptogram
cipher, 533
Cryptography
writing, 590

Crystal-gazing
prediction, 511
Crystalline
dense, 321
transparent, 425
Cub
young, 129
clown, 876
Cube
triality, 92
angularity, 244
Cubist
artist, 559
Cuckold
divorce, 905
Cuckoo
repetition, 104
imitation, 19
cry, 412
fool, 501
insane, 503
Cuddle
caress, 902
Cuddy
carrier, 271
Cudgel
beat, 975
bludgeon, 276, 727
Cue
hint, 527
watchword, 550
plea, 617
Cuff
beat, 276, 972
dress, 225
Cui bono
utility, 644
Cuirass
defence, 717
Cuirassier
combatant, 726
Cuisine
food, 298
Cul-de-lampe
tail-piece, 67
Cul-de-sac
concavity, 252
closure, 261
difficulty, 704
Culbute
inversion, 218
descent, 306
Culinary
food, 298
Cull

choice, 609
take, 789
Cullender
sieve, 260
Cullion
wretch, 941, 949
Cully
dupe, 547
Culminate
maximum, 33
height, 206, 210
Culmination
completion, 729
Culpability
guilt, 947
Culpable
vice, 945
Culprit
sinner, 949
Cult
worship, 990
rite, 998
Cultivate
improve, 658
sensitiveness, 375
taste, 850
till, 371
Culture
tillage, 371
taste, 850
teaching, 537
knowledge, 490
Culverin
arms, 727
Culvert
conduit, 350
Cum grano salis
qualify, 469
unbelief, 485
Cumber
load, 319
to incommode, 647
to obstruct, 706
Cummer
friend, 891
Cummerbund
girdle, 247
Cumshaw
gift, 784
Cumulation
assemblage, 72
Cumulative
increase, 35
addition, 37
Cumulus

cloud, 353
Cunctation
delay, 133
inactivity, 683
Cuneiform
angular, 244
writing, 590
Cunning
art, 702
sagacity, 698
well-planned, 626
Cup
hollow, 252
vessel, 191
Cupboard
receptacle, 191
Cupid
beauty, 845
love, 897
Cupidity
avarice, 819
desire, 865
Cupola
dome, 250
height, 206
Cur
knave, 949
Curable
improvement, 658
Curacy
churchdom, 995
Curate
clergy, 996
Curative
remedial, 834
Curator
consignee, 758
Curb
restrain, 751
hinder, 706
shackle, 752
moderate, 174
check, 826
dissuade, 616
counteract, 179
slacken, 275
Curd
mass, 46
density, 321
pulp, 354
Curdle
condense, 321
coagulate, 46, 352
Cure
remedy, 662, 834

reinstate, 660
religious, 995
preserve, 670
improve, 656
Curé
priest, 996
Curfew
evening, 126
Curio
toy, 643
Curiosa felicitas
elegance, 578
Curiosity
curiosity, 455
phenomenon, 872
Curious
true, 494
exceptional, 83
Curl
bend, 245, 248
cockle up, 258
Curlicue
convolution, 248
Curliewurlie
convolution, 248
Curmudgeon
parsimony, 819
Currency
publicity, 531
money, 800
Current
existing, 1
present, 118
happening, 151
stream, 347
river, 348
wind, 349
course, 109
danger, 667
opinion, 484
public, 531
prevailing, 82
Currente calamo
diffuseness, 573
Curricle
vehicle, 272
Curriculum
teaching, 537
Curry
condiment, 393
rub, 331
Curry flavour
flattery, 933
Curse
malediction, 908

bane, 663
evil, 619
adversity, 735
badness, 649
painfulness, 830
Cursive
writing, 590
Cursory
transient, 111
inattentive, 458
neglecting, 460
hasty, 684
Curst
perverse, 895
Curt
short, 201
taciturn, 585
concise, 572
Curtail
shorten, 201, 572
retrench, 38
decrease, 36
deprive, 789
Curtain
shade, 424
ambush, 530
Curtain lecture
speech, 582
Curtain-raiser
play, 599
Curtsy
obeisance, 743, 894
submission, 725
stoop, 308
Curule
council, 696
Curve
curvature, 245
Curvet
leap, 309
oscillate, 314
agitate, 315
Cushion
pillow, 215
softness, 324
to frustrate, 706
relief, 834
Cushy
easy, 705
Cusp
point, 253
angle, 244
Cussedness
obstinacy, 606
Custodian

keeper, 753
Custody
captivity, 664, 751, 781
captive, 754
Custom
rule, 80
habit, 613
fashion, 852
sale, 796
barter, 794
tax, 812
Custom-house
mart, 799
Customer
purchaser, 795
Cut
divide, 44
bit, 51
interval, 70, 198
sculpture, 557
curtail, 201
cultivate, 371
layer, 204
notch, 257
form, 240
road, 627
print, 558
attach, 716
pain, 828
to give pain, 830
affect, 824
ignore, 460, 893, 895
neglect, 773
state, 7
cold, 385
Cut across
passage, 302
Cut along
velocity, 274
Cut and dried
ready, 673
trite, 82
Cut and run
escape, 671
Cut capers
leap, 309
dance, 840
Cut down
diminish, 36
destroy, 162
shorten, 201
lower, 308
kill, 361
Cut down to size
humiliate, 879

Cut off
kill, 361
subduct, 38
impede, 706
disjunction, 44
Cut out
surpass, 33
retrench, 38
plan, 626
supplant, 147
Cut short
shorten, 201, 572
stop, 142
decrease, 36
contract, 195
Cut-throat
killing, 361
sinner, 913, 949
Cut up
divide, 44
destroy, 162
censure, 932
unhappy, 828, 837
Cutaneous
covering, 222
Cuthbert
pacifist, 726A
Cuticle
covering, 222
Cutie
sweetheart, 897
Cutlass
arms, 727
Cutlery
sharpness, 253
Cutpurse
thief, 792
Cutter
ship, 273
Cutting
cold, 383
affecting, 821
censorious, 932
extract, 596, 609
Cutty
tobacco, 298A
Cybernetics
statecraft, 693
Cycle
period, 138
duration, 106
circle, 247
travel, 266
Cycloid
circularity, 247

Cyclone
violence, 173
rotation, 312
agitation, 315
wind, 349
Cyclopaedia
knowledge, 490
Cyclopean
huge, 192
Cyclops
monster, 83
Cylinder
rotundity, 249
Cymbal
musical instrument, 417
Cynical
censorious, 932
detracting, 483
unsociable, 893
cross, 895
Cynosure
indication, 550
prodigy, 872
Cypher
see Cipher
Cypress
lamentation, 839
Cyst
receptacle, 191
Czar
master, 745

D.T.
drunkenness, 959
D.V.
conditions, 770
Da capo
repetition, 104
duplication, 90
frequency, 136
Dab
clever, 700
to paint, 222
to slap, 276
Dabble
action, 680
trifle, 683
moisten, 337
Dacoit
thief, 792
Dactyl
verse, 597
Dactylonomy
numeration, 85

Dad
paternity, 166
Dadaist
artist, 559
Dado
lining, 224
base, 211
Daedal
variegated, 440
Daedalian
skill, 698
convoluted, 248
Daft
insane, 503
silly, 499
Dagger
arms, 727
sharpness, 253
Daggers drawn
discord, 713
enmity, 889
Daggle
pendency, 214
Dago
alien, 57
Dagon
idol, 986
Daguerreotype
painting, 556
copy, 21
Dahabeeyah
ship, 273
Daily
routine, 138
publication, 531
servant, 746
Dainty
savoury, 394
pleasing, 829
fastidious, 868
Dais
support, 215
Dak-bungalow
inn, 189
Dale
concavity, 252
Dally
irresolute, 605
delay, 133
inactive, 683
amuse, 840
fondle, 902
Dalmatic
vestments, 999

Dam
parent, 166
lock, 350
close, 261
confine, 231
obstruct, 348, 706
trifle, 643
Damage
evil, 619
to injure, 649
to spoil, 659
payment, 812
Damages
penalty, 974
Damascene
variegate, 440
Damask
redness, 434
Dame
woman, 374
teacher, 540
Damn
condemn, 971
expletive, 908
Damn-all
nothing, 4
Damnable
execrable, 830
spoil, 659
Damnify
damage, 649
Damnosa hereditas
burden, 706
Damp
moist, 339
cold, 386
to moderate, 174
to dissuade, 616
depress, 837
calm, 826
Damper
silencer, 417
Damsel
youth, 129
lady, 374
Dance
oscillate, 314
agitate, 315
jump, 309
sport, 840
Dander
resentment, 900
journey, 266
Dandify
adorn, 845
dress, 225

Dandle
endearment, 902
Dandruff
uncleanness, 653
Dandy
fop, 854
Dandyism
affectation, 855
Danger
danger, 665
Dangle
hang, 214
swing, 314
Dank
moist, 339
Dapper
thin, 203
elegant, 845
Dapple
brown, 433
Dappled
variegation, 440
Darbies
fetter, 752
Dare
defy, 715
face danger, 861
Dare-devil
rashness, 863
blusterer, 887
Darg
work, 625
Daring
courage, 861
Dark
obscure, 421
dim, 422
invisible, 447
unintelligible, 519
mysterious, 528
ignorant, 491
blind, 442
latent, 526
Darkie
black, 431
Darling
favourite, 899
beloved, 897
Darn
improve, 658
Dart
missile, 727
to propel, 284
swift, 274
Darwinism

causation, 153
Dash
sprinkling, 32, 193
to mix, 41
throw down, 308
display, 882
depress, 837
shine, 873
mark, 550
expletive, 908
velocity, 274
energy, 171
vivacity, 682
gift, 784
Dash off
sketch, 556
Dash out
rush, 274
haste, 684
Dashing
brave, 861
smart, 845
fashionable, 852
Dastard
coward, 862
Data
evidence, 467
reasoning, 476
Date
chronometry, 114
party, 892
Daub
cover, 222
dirt, 653
bad painting, 555
to deform, 846
Daughter
posterity, 167
Daunt
frighten, 860
Dauntless
courage, 861
Davenport
receptacle, 191
support, 215
Dawdle
slow, 275
tardy, 133
inactive, 683
Dawn
morning, 125
precursor, 116
to begin, 66
dim, 422
glimpse, 490

Day
period, 108
light, 420
Day-book
list, 86
record, 551
accounts, 811
Day-dream
imagination, 515
hope, 858
inattention, 458
Day-labourer
workman, 690
Day of Judgment
end, 67
Daybreak
morning, 125
dim, 422
beginning, 66
Daylight
light, 420
publicity, 531
Dayspring
morning, 125
Daze
light, 420
confuse, 442
stupefy, 823
Dazzle
light, 420
confuse, 442
De bon cœur
willingly, 602
De facto
existence, 1
truth, 494
De haut en bas
contempt, 930
De jure
right, 922
legal, 963
dueness, 924
De novo
repetition, 104
frequency, 136
De omnibus rebus
multiformity, 81
De Profundis
worship, 990
De règle
rule, 80
De rigueur
rule, 80
De trop
redundance, 641

Deacon
clergy, 996
Dead
lifeless, 360
inert, 172
insensible, 376, 823
colourless, 429
Dead-beat
fatigue, 688
weak, 160
Dead-drunk
drunkenness, 959
Dead-heat
equality, 27
Dead weight
hindrance, 706
Deaden
weaken, 158, 160
moderate, 174, 826
benumb, 823
Deadfall
trap, 667
Deadlock
stoppage, 265
hindrance, 706
Deadly
mortal, 361, 657
destructive, 162
pernicious, 649
Deadness
numbness, 381
inertness, 172, 823
Deaf
deafness, 419
Deafening
loud, 404
Deal
quantity, 31
mingle, 41
give, 784
allot, 786
barter, 794
Deal out
distribute, 73, 784
Dealer
merchant, 797
Dealings
action, 680
Dean
clergy, 996
Deanery
office, 995
house, 1000
Dear
loved, 897, 899

high-priced, 814
Dear-bought
worthless, 645
Dearth
insufficiency, 640
Death
death, 360
Death-blow
end, 67
killing, 361
failure, 732
Deathless
perpetuity, 112
celebrated, 873
Deathlike
hideous, 846
silence, 403
Debacle
river, 348
descent, 306
destruction, 162
Debag
divest, 226
Debar
prohibit, 761
hinder, 751
exclude, 77
Debark
arrive, 292
Debase
depress, 308
deteriorate, 659
foul, 653
vicious, 945
Debatable
uncertain, 475
Debate
reason, 476
dispute, 713, 720
hesitate, 605
talk, 588
Debauch
spoil, 659
vice, 945
intemperance, 954
impurity, 961
Debenture
certificate, 551
security, 771
credit, 805
Debility
weakness, 160
Debit
debt, 806
accounts, 811

Debonair
cheerfulness, 836
Debouch
march out, 292
flow out, 295, 348
Debrett
list, 86
Debris
part, 51
pulverulence, 330
unimportance, 643
Debt
debt, 806
Debtor
debt, 806
Debus
arrival, 292
Début
beginning, 66
Decade
number, 98
period, 108
duration, 106
Decadence
deterioration, 659
Decadent
feeble, 575
Decagon
number, 98
angularity, 244
Decahedron
ten, 98
Decalogue
duty, 926
Decamp
move off, 287, 293
escape, 671
Decant
transfer, 270
Decanter
receptacle, 191
Decapitate
kill, 361, 972
Decay
spoil, 659
disease, 655
shrivel, 195
decrease, 36
Decayed
imperfect, 651
old, 124
adversity, 735
Decease
death, 360
Deceit

deception, 544, 545
Deceiver
deceiver, 548
Decent
modest, 960
tolerable, 651
seemly, 926
right, 922
Decentralize
disperse, 73
Deception
deception, 545
sophistry, 477
Decide
judge, 480
choose, 609
make certain, 474
cause, 153
Decided
resolved, 604
positive, 535
certain, 475
great, 31
Deciduous
transitory, 111
falling, 306
spoiled, 659
Decimal
number, 84, 98
Decimate
subduct, 38, 103
kill, 361
Decipher
interpret, 522
solve, 462
Decision
intention, 620
conclusion, 480
resolution, 604
verdict, 969
Decisive
final, 67
evidence, 467
resolution, 604
demonstration, 478
Decivilize
brutalize, 895
Deck
floor, 211
to beautify, 845
Declaim
speech, 582
Declamatory
florid, 577
Declare

assert, 535
inform, 516, 527
Declension
descent, 306
deterioration, 659
grammar, 567
intrinsicality, 5
Decline
decrease, 36
descent, 306
weaken, 160
decay, 735
disease, 655
become worse, 659
reject, 610
refuse, 764
be unwilling, 603
grammar, 567
Declivity
obliquity, 217
Decoction
calefaction, 384
Decode
interpret, 522
Decollate
punishment, 972
Decoloration
achromatism, 429
Decompose
decomposition, 49, 653
Decomposite
combination, 48
Decompound
combination, 48
Deconsecrate
cancel, 756
Decontamination
cleanness, 652
Decorate
embellish, 845, 847
Decoration
repute, 873
title, 877
insignia, 747
Decorous
decent, 960
befitting, 922
Decorticate
divest, 226
Decorum
politeness, 852
respect, 928
purity, 960
Decoy
entice, 615

deceive, 545
deceiver, 548
Decrease
in degree, 36
in size, 195
Decree
law, 963
judgment, 969
order, 741
Decrement
deduction, 38
Decrepit
old, 124, 128
weak, 160
frail, 651
Decrepitude
age, 128
feebleness, 160
Decrescendo
decrease, 36, 415
Decretal
law, 963
order, 741
Decry
depreciate, 483
censure, 932
defame, 934
Decumbent
horizontality, 213
Decuple
number, 98
Decurrent
descent, 306
Decursive
descent, 306
Decussation
crossing, 219
Dedicate
consecrate, 873
Deduce
infer, 480
retrench, 38
Deducible
evidence, 467, 478, 480
Deduct
retrench, 38
deprive, 789
Deduction
abatement, 813
decrease, 36
reasoning, 476
Deed
act, 680
record, 467, 551
security, 771

Deem
belief, 484
Deep
profound, 208, 451
the sea, 341
cunning, 702
prudent, 498
feeling, 821
sound, 404
colour, 428
greatness, 31
Deep-mouthed
loud, 404
Deep-rooted
fixed, 150
Deep-seated
interior, 221
deep, 208
Deep-toned
resonant, 408
Deepie
cinema, 599A
Deface
render ugly, 846
injure, 659
destroy form, 241
Defacement
blemish, 848
Defalcation
default, 304
contraction, 195
incompleteness, 53
insufficiency, 640
non-payment, 808
Defame
detract, 934
shame, 874
censure, 932
Defamer
detractor, 936
Default
insufficiency, 640
shortcoming, 304
non-payment, 806, 808
Defaulter
debtor, 806
Defeat
to confute, 479
master, 731
failure, 732
Defecate
clean, 652
improve, 658
Defect
incomplete, 53

imperfect, 651
failing, 945
to desert, 124
Defection
disobedience, 742
disloyalty, 940
Defective
incomplete, 53
imperfect, 651
insufficient, 640
Defence
resistance, 717
vindication, 937
safety, 664
Defenceless
weak, 158, 160
exposed, 665
Defendant
judge, 967
accusation, 938
Defer
put off, 133
Defer to
respect, 928
assent, 488
Deference
subordination, 743
submission, 725
respect, 928
Defiance
daring, 715
threat, 909
Deficiency
inferiority, 34
blemish, 848
frailty, 945
Deficient
incomplete, 53
imperfect, 651
insufficient, 640
inferior, 34
witless, 499
insane, 502
Deficit
debt, 806
Defile
ravine, 198, 203
march, 266
dirt, 653
spoil, 659
shame, 874
debauch, 961
Define
name, 564
explain, 522

Definite
exact, 494
special, 79
visible, 446
limited, 233
intelligible, 518
Definitely
assent, 488
Definitive
decided, 535
final, 67
Deflagration
calefaction, 384
Deflate
contract, 195
Deflection
curvature, 245
deviation, 279
Defloration
impurity, 961
soil, 653
Defluxion
river, 348
Deform
deface, 241, 846
Deformity
blemish, 848
Defraud
cheat, 545
non-payment, 808
Defray
pay, 807
Defrost
melt, 384
Deft
clever, 698
suitable, 23
Defunct
dead, 360
Defy
dare, 715
disobey, 742
threaten, 909
Dégagé
freedom, 748
fashion, 825
Degenerate
deterioration, 659
vice, 945
Deglutition
swallowing, 296
Degradation
shame, 874
dishonour, 940
deterioration, 659

Degree
quantity, 26
term, 71
honour, 873
Degustation
taste, 390
Dehortation
dissuasion, 616
advice, 695
warning, 668
Dehumanize
brutalize, 895
Dehydrate
dry, 340
preserve, 670
De-ice
melt, 384
Dei gratiâ
dueness, 924
Deification
heaven, 981
idolatry, 991
honour, 873
Deign
condescend, 879
consent, 762
Deiseal
rotation, 312
Deism
irreligion, 989
heresy, 984A
Deity
deity, 976
great spirit, 979
Dejection
sadness, 828, 837, 841
Déjeuner
food, 298
Dekko
look, 441
Délâbrement
deterioration, 659
Delation
accusation, 938
Delay
lateness, 133
protraction, 110
slowness, 275
Dele
obliteration, 552
Delectable
savoury, 394
agreeable, 829
Delectation
pleasure, 827

Delegate
consignee, 758, 759
to commission, 755
Deleterious
pernicious, 649
unwholesome, 657
Deletion
obliteration, 552
Deliberate
think, 451
cautious, 864
slow, 275
leisurely, 685
advised, 620, 695
Deliberately
slowly, 133
designedly, 600, 611
Delicacy
of texture, 329
slenderness, 203
weak, 160
sickly, 655
savoury, 394
dainty, 298
of taste, 850
fastidiousness, 868
exactness, 494
pleasing, 829
beauty, 845
honour, 939
purity, 960
difficulty, 704
scruple, 603, 616
Delicatessen
food, 298
Delicious
taste, 394
pleasing, 829
Delight
pleasure, 827
Delightful
pleasurableness, 829
Delilah
temptress, 615
Delimit
circumscribe, 231
Delineate
describe, 594
represent, 554
Delineavit
painting, 556
Delinquency
guilt, 947
Delinquent
sinner, 949

460

Delinquescent
liquid, 333
Delinquium
weakness, 160
fatigue, 688
Delirium
raving, 503
passion, 825
Delirium tremens
drunkenness, 959
Delitescence
latency, 526
Deliver
transfer, 270
give, 784
liberate, 750
relieve, 834
utter, 582
rescue, 672
escape, 671
Dell
concavity, 252
Delouse
disinfect, 652
Delta
land, 342
Delude
deceive, 495, 545
Deluge
flow, 337, 348
redundance, 641
multitude, 72
Delusion
error, 495
deceit, 545
Delve
dig, 252
cultivate, 371
depth, 208
Demagogue
leader, 745
director, 694
agitator, 742
Demagogy
authority, 737
Demand
claim, 924
ask, 765
require, 630
inquire, 461
order, 741
price, 812
Demarcation
limit, 199, 233
Démarche

procedure, 680
Dematerialize
immateriality, 317
Demean
humble, 879
dishonour, 940
Demeanour
conduct, 692
air, 448
fashion, 852
Dementation
insanity, 503
Démenti
contradiction, 536
Demerit
vice, 945
inutility, 645
Demesne
property, 780
Demi
bisection, 91
Demigod
hero, 948
Demijohn
receptacle, 191
Demi-rep
libertine, 962
Demise
death, 360
to transfer, 783
to give, 784
Demiurge
deity, 979
Demivolt
leap, 309
Demobilize
disperse, 73
Democracy
authority, 737
Démodé
obsolete, 851
Demogorgon
demon, 980
Demoiselle
woman, 374
Demolish
destroy, 162
confute, 479
damage, 649
Demolisher
destroyer, 165
Demon
devil, 980
wretch, 913
violent, 173

Demoniacal
wicked, 945
furious, 825
diabolic, 649, 980
Demonism
idolatry, 991
Demonolatry
idolatry, 991
Demonstrate
prove, 85, 478
manifest, 525
Demonstrative
evidential, 467, 478
excitable, 825
Demonstrator
scholar, 492
teacher, 540
Demoralize
vice, 945
degrade, 659
Demos
commonalty, 876
Demote
abase, 308
degrade, 659
Demotic
writing, 590
Demulcent
mild, 174
soothing, 662
Demur
unwillingness, 603
hesitation, 605
to disbelieve, 485
dissent, 489
dislike, 867
Demure
grave, 826
modest, 881
affected, 855
Demurrage
charge, 812
Demurrer
lawsuit, 969
Den
lair, 189
room, 191, 893
prison, 752
sty, 653
Denary
number, 98
Denationalize
restore, 790
Denaturalized
unconformity, 83

461

Dendriform
rough, 256
Denegation
negation, 536
Denial
negation, 536
Denigrate
blacken, 431
decry, 483, 934
Denization
liberation, 750
Denizen
inhabitant, 188
man, 373
Denominate
nomenclature, 564
Denomination
class, 75
party, 712
Denominational
theology, 983
Denominator
number, 84
Denote
indication, 550
Denouement
result, 154
end, 67
elucidation, 522
completion, 729
Denounce
accuse, 297
blame, 932
cite, 965
Dense
close, 321
crowded, 72
stupid, 499
Density
closeness, 46, 321
Dent
notch, 257
hollow, 252
Dental
letter, 561
Denticle
sharpness, 253
Denticulated
sharp, 253
Dentist
doctor, 662
Denude
divest, 226
deprive, 776
Denunciation

see Denounce
Deny
negative, 536
dissent, 489
refuse, 764
Deo volente
conditions, 770
Deodand
penalty, 974
Deodorize
disinfect, 652
Deontology
duty, 926
Depart
set out, 296
die, 360
Departed
gone, 2
Department
class, 75
part, 51
region, 181
business, 625
Depauperate
impoverish, 804
Depend
hang, 214
be contingent, 475
Depend upon
trust, 484
be the effect of, 154
affirm, 535
Dependable
belief, 484
probity, 939
Dependant
servant, 746
Dependence
subjection, 749
Dependent
liable, 177
Depict
paint, 556
represent, 554
describe, 594
Depletion
insufficiency, 640
Deplorable
bad, 649
disastrous, 735
painful, 830
Deplore
regret, 833
complain, 839
remorse, 950

Deploy
expansion, 194
Depone
affirm, 535
Deponent
evidence, 467
Depopulate
displace, 185
desert, 893
Deportation
displace, 185
exclusion, 55
transfer, 270
emigration, 297
punishment, 972
Deportment
conduct, 692
appearance, 448
Depose
evidence, 467
tell, 527
record, 551
dethrone, 738, 756
declare, 535
Deposit
place, 184
secure, 771
store, 636
expenditure, 809
solidify, 321
Depository
store, 636
Depot
store, 636
focus, 74
mart, 799
Deprave
spoil, 659
Depraved
bad, 649
vicious, 945
Deprecate
deprecation, 766
dissuade, 616
disapproval, 932
pity, 914
Depreciate
detract, 483
censure, 932
decrease, 36
Depreciation
discount, 813
stealing, 791
Depredation
stealing, 791

Depredator
thief, 792
Depression
lowering, 308
lowness, 207
depth, 208
concavity, 252
dejection, 837
Deprive
take, 789
subduct, 38
lose, 776
Depth
physical, 208
mental, 450, 490
Depurate
clean, 652
improve, 658
Depuratory
remedy, 662
Depute
commission, 755
Deputy
substitute, 147, 634, 759
jurisdiction, 965
Derangement
mental, 503
physical, 61
disorder, 59
Derelict
solitary, 893
Dereliction
relinquishment, 624, 782
guilt, 947
Derequisition
restore, 790
Deride
ridicule, 856
disrespect, 929
contempt, 930
trifle with, 643
scoff, 483
Derisive
ridiculous, 853
Derivation
origin, 153
verbal, 562
Derivative
effect, 154
Derive
attribute, 155
receive, 785
acquire, 755

income, 810
Dermal
covering, 222
Dernier cri
fashion, 852
newness, 123
Dernier ressort
plan, 626
Derogate
detract, 483, 934
demean, 940
shame, 874
Derrick
raise, 307
Derring-do
courage, 861
Derringer
arms, 727
Dervish
clergy, 996
Descale
clean, 652
Descant
dissert, 595
dwell upon, 584
diffuseness, 573
Descendant
posterity, 167
Descent
slope, 217
motion downwards, 306
order, 58
Describe
set forth, 594
Description
kind, 75
narration, 594
Descry
vision, 441
Desecrate
misuse, 679
profane, 988
Desert
solitude, 101, 893
waste, 645
merit, 944
to relinquish, 624
to escape, 671
Deserter
apostate, 607
coward, 862
Desertless
vice, 945
Deserve
merit, 944

right, 922, 924
Déshabillé
see Dishabille
Desiccate
dryness, 340
Desiderate
desire, 865
require, 630
Desideratum
desire, 865
inquiry, 461
requirement, 630
Design
intention, 620
cunning, 702
plan, 626
delineation, 554
prototype, 22
Designate
specify, 79, 564
Designation
kind, 75
Designed
intended, 600
Designer
artist, 559, 626
Designing
false, 544
artful, 702
Desirable
expedient, 646
Desire
longing, 865
Desist
discontinue, 142
relinquish, 624
inaction, 681
Desk
support, 215
receptacle, 191
Desolate
alone, 87
secluded, 893
afflicted, 828
to ravage, 162
Desolation
evil, 619
Désorienté
ignorance, 491
Despair
hopelessness, 859
dejection, 837
Despatch
see Dispatch
Desperado
rashness, 863

Desperate
  great, 31
  violent, 173
  rash, 863
  difficult, 704
  impossible, 471
Desperation
  hopelessness, 859
Despicable
  shameful, 874
  contemptible, 930
  trifling, 643
Despise
  contemn, 930
  deride, 483, 929
Despite
  notwithstanding, 179, 708
Despite
  malevolence, 907
Despoil
  take, 789
  rob, 791
  hurt, 649
Despondency
  sadness, 837
  fear, 860
  despair, 859
Despot
  master, 745
Despotism
  arbitrariness, 964
  authority, 737
  severity, 739
Desquamation
  divestment, 226
Dessert
  food, 298
Destination
  fate, 152, 601
  arrival, 292
  intention, 620
Destiny
  fate, 601
  chance, 152
Destitute
  insufficient, 640
  poor, 804
Destrier
  carrier, 271
Destroy
  demolish, 162
  injure, 649
  deface, 241

Destroyed
  inexistence, 2
Destroyer
  ship, 273
Destruction
  demolition, 162, 732
  evil, 619
Destructive
  hurtful, 649
Desuetude
  disuse, 614, 678
Desultory
  discontinuous, 70
  irregular in time, 139
  disordered, 59
  multiform, 81
  deviating, 149, 279
  agitated, 315
Detach
  separate, 10, 44, 47
Detached
  irrelated, 10, 47
  indifferent, 456
  unity, 87
Detachment
  part, 51
  army, 726
Detail
  to describe, 594
  special portion, 79
Detain
  retention, 781
Detection
  discovery, 480A
Detective
  inquiry, 461
Detention
  retention, 781
  imprisonment, 751
Détenu
  prisoner, 754
Deter
  dissuasion, 616
  fear, 860
Detergent
  remedy, 662
  remedial, 656
  cleanness, 652
Deteriorate
  deterioration, 659
Determinate
  special, 79
  exact, 474
  resolute, 604
Determination

resolution, 604
  will, 600
  judgment, 480
Determine
  find out, 480A
  intend, 620
  direction, 278
  make certain, 474
  cause, 153
  resolve, 604
  designate, 79
Determinism
  necessity, 601
Deterrent
  restraint, 616
Detersive
  cleanness, 652
Detest
  hate, 867, 898
Detestable
  bad, 649, 867
Dethrone
  abrogation, 756
Dethronement
  anarchy, 738
Detonate
  sound, 406
  explode, 173
Detonator
  signal, 550
Detour
  circuit, 629
  curvature, 245
  deviation, 279
Detract
  subduct, 38
  depreciate, 483
  censure, 932
  slander, 934
Detractor
  slanderer, 936
Detrain
  arrival, 292
Detriment
  evil, 619
Detrimental
  hurtful, 649
Detritus
  part, 51
  pulverulence, 330
Detrude
  cast out, 297
  cast down, 308
Detruncation
  subduction, 38

disjunction, 44

Deuce
duality, 89
demon, 980

Deuced
great, 31

Deux ex machina
helper, 707, 711
wonder-worker, 994

Deuterogamy
marriage, 903

Devastate
destroy, 162
injure, 649

Devastation
havoc, 659

Develop
cause, 153
produce, 161
increase, 35
expand, 194
evolve, 313

Development
effect, 154

Deviate
differ, 15
vary, 20
change, 140
turn, 279
diverge, 291
circuit, 629
bend, 245

Deviationist
revolutionary, 146
dissent, 489

Device
expedient, 626
instrument, 633
motto, 550

Devices
inclination, 602

Devil
Satan, 978
maleficent being, 913
mediate, 631
culprit, 949
seasoned food, 392

Devil-may-care
rash, 863

Devilish
great, 31
bad, 649
hell, 982

Devilry (or Deviltry)
evil, 619

cruelty, 907
wickedness, 945
sorcery, 992

Devious
deviating, 245, 279
different, 15

Devise
plan, 620, 626
imagine, 515
bequeath, 784

Devitalize
weaken, 160

Devoid
empty, 640
absent, 187
not having, 776

Devoir
courtesy, 894

Devolution
delegation, 755

Devolve
transfer, 783

Devolve on
duty, 926

Devote
attention, 457
curse, 908
employ, 677
consecrate, 873

Devoted
loving, 897
friendly, 888
doomed, 152, 735, 828

Devotee
pious, 987
resolute, 604
enthusiast, 682, 840

Devotion
piety, 987
worship, 990
respect, 928
love, 897
obedience, 743
disinterestedness, 942

Devour
eat, 296
gluttony, 957
destroy, 162

Devout
pious, 897

Dew
moisture, 339

Dew-pond
lake, 343

Dexter

right, 238

Dexterous
skill, 698

Dey
master, 745

Dhow
ship, 273

Diablerie
sorcery, 992

Diabolic
malevolent, 907
wicked, 945
bad, 649
satanic, 978

Diacoustics
sound, 402

Diacritical
distinctive, 550

Diadem
regalia, 747
ornament, 847

Diagnostic
intrinsicality, 5
speciality, 79
discrimination, 465

Diagonal
oblique, 217

Diagram
representation, 554

Diagraph
imitation, 19

Dial
clock, 114
face, 234, 448

Dialect
neology, 563

Dialectic
argumentation, 476
language, 560

Dialogue
interlocution, 588

Diameter
breadth, 202

Diamond
lozenge, 244
arena, 728
gem, 650
ornament, 847
hardness, 323

Diana
goddess, 979

Diapason
melody, 413

Diaper
reticulation, 219

Diaphanous
transparent, 425
Diaphoresis
excretion, 298
Diaphoretic
remedy, 662
Diaphragm
partition, 228
middle, 68
Diarchy
authority, 737
Diary
record, 551
journal, 114
Diastole
expansion, 194
pulse, 314
Diathermancy
calefaction, 384
Diathesis
state, 7
habit, 613
affections, 820
Diatonic
harmony, 413
Diatribe
disapprobation, 932
Dibble
perforator, 262
cultivate, 371
Dibs
money, 800
Dice
chance, 156
Dichotomy
bisection, 91
angularity, 244
Dichroism
variegation, 440
Dick
detective, 461
police, 664
Dicker
barter, 794
interchange, 148
Dicky
seat, 215
Dictaphone
hearing, 418
Dictate
command, 741
authority, 737
enjoin, 615
write, 590
Dictator

master, 745
Dictatorial
severe, 739
insolent, 885
Dictatorship
authority, 737
Diction
style, 569
Dictionary
word, 562
Dictum
maxim, 496
affirmation, 535
command, 741
Didactic
teaching, 537
Diddle
deception, 545
swindle, 791
Dido
leap, 309
prank, 840
foolery, 497
caprice, 608
Die
chance, 156
mould, 22
to expire, 2, 360
cease, 142
Die for
desire, 865
Die-hard
obstinacy, 606
Dies non
never, 107
repose, 687
Diet
food, 298
remedy, 662
council, 696
Dietetics
remedy, 662
Differ
dissent, 489
Difference
difference, 15
inequality, 28
dissimilarity, 18
discord, 713
numerical, 84
Differential
number, 84
Differentiation
numeration, 85
difference, 15

discrimination, 465
fastidiousness, 868
Difficile
troublesome, 704
Difficult
fastidious, 868
Difficulty
hardness, 704
question, 461
Diffident
modest, 881
fearful, 860
Diffluent
liquefaction, 335
flow, 348
Diffraction
curvature, 245
Diffuse
style, 573
disperse, 73, 291
publish, 531
permeate, 186
Dig
excavate, 252
Dig
cultivate, 371
deepen, 208
poke, 276
understand, 518
Dig up
past, 122
Digamy
marriage, 903
Digest
arrange, 60, 826
think, 451
plan, 626
book, 593
compendium, 596
Diggings
abode, 189
Dight
dressed, 225
Digit
number, 84
Digitated
pointed, 253
Dignify
honour, 873
Dignitary
cleric, 996
personage, 875
Dignity
glory, 873
pride, 878

honour, 939

Digress
deviate, 279
style, 573

Digs
abode, 189

Dike
ditch, 198, 232
defence, 666, 717

Dilaceration
disjunction, 44

Dilapidation
wreck, 162
deterioration, 659

Dilate
increase, 35
swell, 194
lengthen, 202
rarefy, 322
style, 573
discourse, 584

Dilatory
slow, 275
inactive, 683

Dilemma
difficulty, 704
logic, 476
doubt, 475, 485

Dilettante
ignoramus, 493
taste, 850
idler, 683

Diligence
coach, 272
activity, 682

Dilly-dally
irresolution, 605
lateness, 133

Dilution
weakness, 160
tenuity, 322
water, 337

Diluvian
old, 124

Dim
dark, 421
obscure, 422
invisible, 447

Dim-out
dim, 422

Dim-sighted
imperfect vision, 443
foolish, 499

Dime
trifle, 643

Dimension
size, 192

Dimidiation
bisection, 91

Diminish
lessen, 32, 36
contract, 195

Diminuendo
music, 415

Diminutive
in degree, 32
in size, 193

Dimness
dimness, 422

Dimple
concavity, 252
notch, 257

Din
noise, 404
repetition, 104
loquacity, 584

Dine
to feed, 297

Diner
vehicle, 272

Ding-dong
noise, 407

Dinghy
boat, 273

Dingle
hollow, 252

Dingus
euphemism, 565

Dingy
dark, 421, 431
dim, 422
colourless, 429
grey, 432

Dining-car
vehicle, 272

Dinner
food, 298

Dinner-jacket
dress, 225

Dint
power, 157
instrumentality, 631
dent, 257

Diocesan
clergy, 996

Diocese
churchdom, 995

Diorama
view, 448
painting, 556

Dip
plunge, 310
direction, 278
slope, 217
depth, 208
insert, 300
immerse, 337
thief, 792

Dip into
examine, 457
investigate, 461

Diphthong
letter, 561

Diploma
commission, 755
document, 551

Diplomacy
mediation, 724
artfulness, 702
courtesy, 894
negotiation, 769

Diplomatic
artful, 544, 702
tactful, 498, 698

Diplomat(ist)
messenger, 534
emissary, 758

Dippy
insane, 503

Dipsomania
drunkenness, 959
insanity, 503, 504
craving, 865

Dire
fearful, 860
grievous, 830
hateful, 649

Direct
straight, 246, 278, 628
to order, 737
to command, 741
to teach, 537
artless, 703

Direction
tendency, 278
course, 622
place, 183
management, 693
precept, 697

Directly
soon, 111
towards, 278

Director
manager, 694
master, 745

teacher, 540
Directorship
authority, 737
Directory
council, 696
list, 86
Dirge
song, 415
lament, 839
funeral, 363
Dirigible
airship, 273A
Dirk
arms, 727
Dirt
uncleanness, 653
trifle, 643
ugly, 846
blemish, 848
Dirt-cheap
cheap, 815
Dirt-track
arena, 728
Dirty
dishonourable, 940
Disability
impotence, 158
fault, 651
unskilfulness, 698
Disable
weaken, 158, 160, 674
Disabuse
disclosure, 529
Disadvantage
evil, 649
inexpedience, 647
badness, 649
Disaffection
hate, 898
disobedience, 742
disloyalty, 940
Disagreeable
unpleasant, 830
disliked, 867
Disagreement
incongruity, 24
difference, 15
discord, 713
dissent, 489
Disallow
prohibit, 761
Disannul
abrogate, 756
Disapparel
divest, 226

Disappear
vanish, 2, 449
Disappoint
discontent, 832
fail, 732
baulk, 509
Disapprobation
blame, 932
disrepute, 874
Disarm
incapacitate, 158
weaken, 160
conciliate, 831
propitiate, 914
Disarrange
derange, 61
Disarray
disorder, 59
undress, 226
Disaster
evil, 619
failure, 732
adversity, 735
calamity, 830
Disavow
negation, 536
retract, 607
Disband
disperse, 73
separate, 44
Disbar
punish, 972
dismiss, 756
Disbelief
doubt, 485
religious, 988
Disbench
punish, 972
dismiss, 756
Disbranch
disjunction, 44
Disburden
facilitate, 705
disclose, 529
Disburse
expend, 809
Disc
see Disk
Discard
dismiss, 624, 756
disuse, 678
refuse, 764
thought, 452
repudiate, 773
relinquish, 782

Discern
behold, 441
Discernible
visibility, 446
Discerning
wisdom, 498
Discernment
wisdom, 498
discrimination, 465
Discerption
disjunction, 44
Discharge
emit, 297
sound, 406
violence, 173
propel, 284
excrete, 299
flow, 348
duty, 926
acquit oneself, 692
observe, 772
pay, 807
exempt, 927A
accomplish, 729
liberate, 750
forget, 506
acquit, 970
Disciple
learner, 541
Disciplinarian
master, 540
martinet, 739
Discipline
order, 58
teaching, 537
training, 673
restraint, 751
punishment, 972
religious, 990
Disclaim
deny, 536
refuse, 764
repudiate, 756
abjure, 757
Disclose
disclosure, 529
Discoid
horizontally, 213
Discolour
achromatism, 429
to stain, 846
Discomfit
success, 731
Discomfiture
failure, 732

Discomfort
pain, 378, 828
Discommendation
blame, 932
Discommodious
inutility, 645
hindrance, 706
Discommodity
inexpedience, 647
Discompose
derange, 61
hinder, 706
put out, 458
to vex, 830
disconcert, 874
provoke, 900
Discomposure
pain, 828
Disconcert
hinder, 706
frustrate, 731
disappoint, 509
distract, 458
confuse, 874
Disconcerted
inattention, 458
Disconformity
disagreement, 24
Discongruity
disagreement, 24
Disconnect
disjunction, 44
irrelation, 10
Disconnected
confused, 519
Disconsolate
sad, 837
grief, 828
Discontent
dissatisfaction, 832
Discontented
pain, 828
Discontinuance
cessation, 142
Discontinue
interrupt, 70
relinquish, 624
Discord
disagreement, 24
dissension, 713
musical, 414
Discordance
incongruity, 24
sound, 410
dissent, 489

Discount
abatement, 813
deduction, 38
to anticipate, 673
disregard, 460, 483
qualify, 469
Discountenance
refuse, 764
disfavour, 706
rudeness, 895
Discourage
dissuade, 616
sadden, 837
disfavour, 706
fear, 860
Discourse
talk, 588
speech, 582
dissert, 595
Discourtesy
rudeness, 895
Discover
perceive, 441
find, 480a
solve, 462
Discredit
disbelief, 485
dishonour, 874
Discreditable
vice, 945
Discreet
careful, 459
cautious, 864
prudent, 498
clever, 698
Discrepancy
disagreement, 24
discord, 713
Discrete
separate, 44
single, 87
Discretion
wisdom, 498
foresight, 510
caution, 864
skill, 698
courtesy, 894
will, 600
care, 459
choice, 609
Discrimination
distinction, 465
difference, 15
taste, 850
fastidiousness, 868

wisdom, 498
Disculpate
vindicate, 937
Discursive
moving, 264
migratory, 266
wandering, 279
style, 573
chatty, 588
dissertation, 595
Discus
missile, 284
Discuss
reason, 476
inquire, 461
reflect, 451
treat of, 595
eat, 296
Disdain
contempt, 930
indifference, 866
fastidiousness, 868
Disdainful
proud, 878
Disease
illness, 655
Disembark
arrive, 292
Disembarrass
facilitate, 705
Disembodied
immaterial, 317
Disembody
decompose, 49
disperse, 73
Disembogue
flow out, 348
emit, 295
Disembowel
extraction, 300
disjunction, 44
Disenable
impotence, 158
Disenchant
dissuade, 616
Disencumber
facility, 705
Disendow
taking, 789
cancel, 756
Disengage
detach, 44
facilitate, 705
liberate, 750, 768a

469

derange, 61
destroy, 162
spoil, 659

Disown
negation, 536

Disparage
depreciate, 483
disrespect, 929
censure, 932

Disparate
different, 15
dissimilar, 18
single, 87
disagreeing, 24
unequal, 28

Disparity
dissimilarity, 18

Dispart
disjoin, 44

Dispassionate
calm, 826

Dispatch
speed, 274
activity, 682
haste, 684
earliness, 132
to conduct, 692
complete, 729
kill, 162, 361
eat, 296
epistle, 592
intelligence, 532

Dispatch-box
receptacle, 191

Dispatch-case
receptacle, 191

Dispel
destroy, 162
scatter, 73

Dispensable
disuse, 678

Dispensation
licence, 760
calamity, 830

Dispense
exempt, 927a
permit, 760
disuse, 678
relinquish, 624
give, 784
allot, 786
disperse, 73
retail, 796

Dispeople
seclusion, 893

Disperse
scatter, 73, 638
separate, 44
diverge, 291

Dispersion
removal, 270

Dispirit
sadden, 837
discourage, 616

Displace
remove, 185
transfer, 270
derange, 61

Display
show, 525
appear, 448
parade, 882

Displease
painfulness, 830

Displeasure
pain, 828
anger, 900

Displosion
violence, 173

Disport
amusement, 840

Dispose
arrange, 60
prepare, 673
tend, 176
induce, 615

Dispose of
sell, 796
give, 784
relinquish, 782
use, 677

Disposition
order, 58
arrangement, 60
inclination, 602
mind, 820

Dispossess
take away, 789
transfer, 783

Dispossessed
deprived, 776

Dispraise
disapprove, 932

Disprize
depreciate, 483

Disproof
counter-evidence, 468
confutation, 479

Disproportion
irrelation, 10

disagreement, 24

Disprove
confute, 479

Disputant
debater, 476
combatant, 726

Disputatious
irritable, 901

Dispute
discord, 713
denial, 485, 536
discussion, 476

Disqualified
incapacitated, 158
incompetent, 699

Disqualify
incapacitate, 158
weaken, 160
disentitle, 925
unprepared, 674

Disquiet
excitement, 825
uneasiness, 149, 828
to give pain, 830

Disquietude
apprehension, 860

Disquisition
dissertation, 595

Disregard
overlook, 458
neglect, 460, 927
indifferent, 823
slight, 483

Disrelish
dislike, 867
hate, 898

Disreputable
vicious, 945

Disrepute
disgrace, 874

Disrespect
irreverence, 929
discourtesy, 895

Disrobe
divestment, 226

Disruption
disjunction, 44
breaking up, 162
schism, 713

Dissatisfaction
discontent, 832
sorrow, 828

Dissect
anatomize, 44, 49
investigate, 461

Dissemble
  falsehood, 544
Dissembler
  liar, 548
Disseminate
  scatter, 73
  diverge, 291
  publish, 531
  pervade, 186
Dissension
  discord, 713
Dissent
  disagree, 489
  refuse, 764
  heterodoxy, 984a
  discord, 713
Dissertation
  disquisition, 595
Disservice
  disadvantage, 619
  inexpedience, 647
Dissever
  disjoin, 44
Dissidence
  disagreement, 24
  dissent, 489
Dissilience
  violent, 173
Dissimilar
  unlike, 18
Dissimulate
  falsehood, 544
Dissipate
  scatter, 73
  waste, 638
  prodigality, 818
  dissolute, 961
  licentiousness, 954
Dissociation
  irrelation, 10
  separation, 44
Dissolute
  intemperate, 954
  profligate, 945
  debauched, 961
Dissolution
  decomposition, 49
  liquefaction, 335
  death, 360
Dissolve
  vanish, 2, 4
  disappear, 449
  abrogate, 756
  liquefy, 335
Dissonance

disagreement, 24
  discord, 414
Dissuade
  dissuasion, 616
Distain
  ugliness, 846
Distance
  longinquity, 196
  swiftness, 274
  to overtake, 282
  to leave behind, 303, 732
  respect, 928
  of time, 110
Distant
  far, 196
  discourteous, 895
Distaste
  dislike, 867
Distasteful
  disagreeable, 830
Distemper
  disease, 655
  painting, 556
Distend
  expansion, 194
Distended
  swollen, 194
Distich
  poetry, 597
Distil
  evaporate, 336
  flow, 348
  drop, 295
Distinct
  visible, 446
  audible, 402
  intelligible, 518, 535
  disjoined, 44
Distinction
  difference, 15
  discrimination, 465
  fame, 873
  style, 574
Distinctive
  special, 75
Distingué
  repute, 873
  fashionable, 852
Distinguish
  perceive, 441
Distortion
  obliquity, 217
  twist, 243, 555
  falsehood, 544

of vision, 443
  perversion, 523
  ugliness, 846
Distracted
  insane, 503
  unthinking, 452
  confused, 491
Distraction
  inattention, 458
  amusement, 840
Distrain
  seize, 789, 969
Distrait
  incogitancy, 452
  inattention, 458
Distraught
  see Distracted
Distress
  affliction, 828
  cause of pain, 830
  poor, 804
Distribute
  disperse, 73
  arrange, 60
  allot, 786
  diverge, 291
District
  region, 181
Distrust
  disbelief, 485
  fear, 860
Disturb
  derange, 61
  alter, 140
  agitate, 315
Disunion
  separation, 44
  discord, 713
Disuse
  unemployment, 678
  desuetude, 614
Ditch
  conduit, 350
  hollow, 252
  trench, 259, 343
  defence, 717
  upset, 162
  sea, 341
Ditheism
  heathen, 984
Dither
  shiver, 315, 383
Dithyrambic
  poetry, 597

Ditto
repetition, 104, 136
Ditty
music, 415
Diuretic
remedy, 662
Diurnal
period, 108, 138
Diuturnal
diuturnity, 110
Divan
sofa, 215
council, 696
Divarication
divergence, 291
deviation, 279
difference, 15
Dive
plunge, 310
descent, 306
depth, 208
Divellicate
disjoin, 44
Divergence
variation, 20
dissimilarity, 18
difference, 15
discord, 713
dispersion, 73
separation, 291
disagreement, 24
deviation, 279
Divers
many, 102
different, 15
multiform, 81
Diversified
varied, 15, 16A, 18, 20, 81
Diversion
amusement, 840
change, 140
Diversity
difference, 15
dissimilarity, 18
multiform, 16A, 81
Divert
turn, 279
amuse, 840
abstract, 452
Divertissement
drama, 599
amusement, 840
Dives
wealth, 803

Divest
denude, 226
take, 789
Divest oneself of
leave, 782
Divide
separate, 44
part, 51, 91
apportion, 786
Dividend
part, 51
number, 84
portion, 786
Dividers
measure, 466
Divination
prediction, 511
occult arts, 992
Divine
Diety, 976
clergyman, 996
theologian, 983
to guess, 514
predict, 510, 511
perfect, 650
Diving-bell
depth, 208
Divining-rod
spell, 993
Divinity
Deity, 976
theology, 983
Division
separation, 44
part, 51
class, 75
troop, 72, 726
arithmetical, 85
discord, 713
distribution, 786
Divisor
number, 84
Divorce
matrimonial, 905
separation, 44
Divulge
disclose, 529
Divulsion
disjoin, 44
Dizzard
fool, 501
Dizzy
confused, 458
vertigo, 503
foolish, 499

Djinn
demon, 980
Do
act, 680
fare, 7
produce, 161
suffice, 639
complete, 729
cheat, 545
Do away with
remove, 185, 678
destroy, 162, 681
Do for
injure, 659
defeat, 731
kill, 361
suit, 646
punish, 972
Do in
kill, 361
Do into
interpret, 522
Do-nothing
inactivity, 683
Do over
cover, 222
Do up
repair, 658
pack, 72
Doch-an-doris
departure, 293
intoxicant, 959
Docile
teachable, 539
tractable, 705
willing, 602
obedient, 743
dutiful, 926
Dock
cut off, 38
diminish, 36
incompleteness, 53
shorten, 201
port, 189
yard, 636, 691
tribunal, 966
Docker
workman, 690
Docket
indication, 467, 550
record, 551
security, 771
Doctor
sage, 492
physician, 695

to restore, 660
amend, 658
remedy, 662
falsify, 544

Doctrinaire
ignoramus, 493

Doctrinal
teaching, 537

Doctrine
tenet, 484
knowledge, 490

Document
record, 551

Documentary
film, 599A

Dodecahedron
angle, 244

Dodge
oscillate, 314
pursue, 461
deceive, 545
avoid, 623
shift, 264
contrivance, 626
cunning, 702

Doe
swiftness, 274

Doer
agent, 690
originator, 164

Doff
put off, 226

Dog
to pursue, 622
follow, 281
affectation, 855

Dog-cart
vehicle, 272

Dog-days
heat, 382

Dog-ear
fold, 258

Dog Latin
solecism, 568

Dog-tired
fatigue, 688

Dog-trot
slowness, 275

Doge
master, 745

Dogfight
contest, 720

Dogged
obstinate, 606
discourteous, 895

Dogger
ship, 273

Doggerel
verse, 597
ridiculous, 853

Dogma
tenet, 484
theological, 983

Dogmatic
obstinate, 606
certainty, 474
assertion, 535
intolerant, 481

Dog's-eared
fold, 258

Doings
actions, 680
events, 151

Doit
trifle, 643
coin, 800

Doited
insane, 503

Dolce far niente
inactivity, 638

Doldrums
dejection, 837

Dole
small quantity, 32
to give, 784
to allot, 786
expenditure, 809
grief, 828

Dole out
parsimony, 819

Doleful
dejected, 837
lament, 839

Doll
plaything, 840
image, 554
small, 193

Doll up
beautify, 845
adorn, 847

Dollar
money, 800

Dollop
part, 51

Dolman
dress, 225

Dolmen
grave, 363

Dolorous
pain, 830

Dolour
physical, 378
moral, 828

Dolphin
ocean, 341

Dolt
fool, 501

Doltish
folly, 499

Domain
region, 181
class, 75
property, 780

Domdaniel
hell, 982

Dome
convexity, 250

Domesday Book
list, 86

Domestic
interior, 188, 221
servant, 746
secluded, 893

Domesticate
tame, 537

Domicile
abode, 189

Dominance
influence, 175

Dominant
prevailing, 737
note in music, 413

Domination
authority, 737

Domineer
tyrannize, 739
insolence, 885

Dominican
clergy, 996

Dominie
teacher, 540

Dominion
region, 181
spirit, 977

Domino
dress, 225
mask, 530

Don
to put on, 225
noble, 875
scholar, 492

Dona
woman, 374
sweetheart, 897

Donation
gift, 784, 804
Done
finished, 729
cheated, 547
Donee
receive, 785
Donjon
defence, 717
Donkey
ass, 271
fool, 501
Donkey's breakfast
bed, 215
Donna
woman, 374
Donnybrook
disorder, 59
discord, 713
contention, 720
Donor
giver, 784
Doodlebug
bomb, 727
Doom
fate, 152
necessity, 601
destruction, 162, 360
to sentence, 969
condemn, 971
end, 67
Doomed
undone, 828
fated, 152, 601
Doomsday
futurity, 121
end, 67
Door
opening, 260
passage, 627
brink, 230
entrance, 66, 294
barrier, 232
Door-keeper
janitor, 263
Doorway
opening, 260
Dope
semiliquid, 352
stupefy, 376
Dope fiend
intemperance, 954
Doppelgänger
ghost, 980
Dopy

sleepy, 683
Dormant
latent, 526
inert, 172, 683
Dormitory
room, 191
Dormouse
inactivity, 683
Dorsal
rear, 235
Dorsum
rear, 235
convexity, 250
Dose
part, 51
mixture, 41
remedy, 662
Doss-house
inn, 189
Dossier
record, 551
evidence, 461
Dossil
stopper, 263
Dot
speck, 32, 193
mark, 550
dowry, 810
Dotage
age, 128
folly, 499
Dotard
fool, 501
Dote
drivel, 499, 503
love, 897
Dotted
variegated, 440
Double
duplex, 90
turn, 283
fold, 258
false, 544
similarity, 17
Double-dealing
falsehood, 544
dishonour, 940
Double Dutch
jargon, 497
Double-edged
energy, 171
equivocal, 520
Double entendre
equivocalness, 520
indecency, 961

Double-faced
deceitful, 544
trimming, 607
Double-quick
speed, 274
Double-tongued
false, 544
equivocal, 520
Doublet
dress, 225
Doubt
disbelief, 485
scepticism, 989
Doubtful
uncertain, 475
incredulous, 485
Doubtless
certainty, 474
assent, 488
Douceur
expenditure, 809
giving, 784
Douche
water, 337
Dough
pulp, 354
inelastic, 324
money, 800
Doughboy
fighter, 726
Doughty
courageous, 861
strong, 159
Dour
severe, 739
Douse
immerse, 310
splash, 337
Dove
deity, 976
Dovelike
innocent, 946
Dovetail!
intervene, 228
intersect, 219
insert, 300
angular, 244
join, 43
agree, 23
Dowager
widow, 905
lady, 374
veteran, 130
Dowdy
vulgar, 851

dirty, 653
ugly, 846
Dower
wealth, 803, 810
property, 780
Dowerless
poverty, 804
Down
levity, 320
smoothness, 255
plumose, 256
bed of, 377
below, 207
Down-hearted
dejection, 837
Downcast
dejection, 837
Downfall
dejection, 837
calamity, 619
Downgrade
debase, 659
Downhill
obliquity, 217
Downright
absolute, 31
plain, 576
sincere, 703
Downs
plains, 344
uplands, 206
Downstairs
lowness, 207
Downtrodden
contemptible, 930
submission, 725
subject, 749
Downwards
lowness, 207
Downy
hairy, 256
soft, 324
cunning, 702
Dowry
wealth, 803, 810
Doxology
worship, 990
Doxy
belief, 484
Doyen
oldness, 124
Doze
inactivity, 683
Dozen
assemblage, 72

number, 98
Drab
colour, 432
hussy, 962, 949
Draconian
severe, 739
Draff
uncleanness, 653
Draft
copy, 21
transfer, 270
sketch, 554
write, 590
abstract, 596
plan, 626
cheque, 800
Drag
traction, 285
attract, 288
crawl, 275
brake, 752
Drag-net
generality, 78
assemblage, 72
Drag up
elevation, 307
Draggle
hang, 214
Dragoman
interpreter, 524
Dragon
fury, 173
monster, 83
Dragonnade
evil, 619, 791
Dragoon
combatant, 726
to persecute, 907
Drain
conduit, 350
to dry, 340
wash, 652
exhaust, 789
waste, 638
sewer, 653
dissipate, 818
flow out, 295
empty itself, 297, 348
drink up, 296
Dram
stimulus, 615
drink, 298
drunkenness, 959
Drama
the drama, 599

Dramatic
impressive, 824
Dramatis personae
the drama, 599
interlocution, 588
agent, 690
party, 712
Drapery
clothes, 225
Drastic
energy, 171
Draught
drink, 296
traction, 285
stream of air, 349
depth, 208
abundance, 639
remedy, 662
Draughtsman
artist, 559
Draw
pull, 285
attract, 288
extract, 301
tobacco, 298A
induce, 615
delineate, 556
equal, 27
unfinished, 730
money order, 800
Draw back
regress, 283, 287
avoid, 623
Draw in
contract, 195
Draw near
approach, 286
time, 121
Draw on
event, 151
entice, 615
Draw out
extract, 301
prolong, 200
protract, 110
exhibit, 525
Draw together
assemble, 72
Draw up
writing, 590
Drawback
hindrance, 706
imperfection, 651
discount, 813
evil, 619

476

Drawbridge
escape, 671
Drawcansir
blusterer, 887
Drawee
money, 800
Drawer
receptacle, 191
money, 800
Drawers
dress, 225
Drawing
sketch, 556
representation, 554
Drawing-room
room, 191
Drawl
creep, 275
prolong, 200
in speech, 583
sluggish, 683
Drawn
distorted, 217
Dray
vehicle, 272
Dread
fear, 860
Dreadful
great, 31
fearful, 860
calamitous, 830
Dreadnought
ship, 273
Dream
vision, 515
unsubstantial, 4
error, 495
inactivity, 683
Dream of
think, 451
intend, 620
Dreamy
inattentive, 458
sleepy, 683
Dreary
solitary, 87
melancholy, 830
Dredge
raise, 307
extract, 301
collect, 72
Dregs
refuse, 643
dirt, 653
remainder, 40

Drench
drink, 296
water, 337
redundance, 641
Dress
clothe, 225
prepare, 673
fit, 23
clip, 38
trim, 27
Dress-circle
theatre, 599
Dress up
adorn, 845
Dresser
support, 215
Dressing
punishment, 972
condiment, 393
Dressing-case
receptacle, 191
Dressing-down
reprimand, 932
Dressy
smart, 847
Dribble
flow out, 295
drop, 348
Driblet
part, 51
scanty, 193
small, 32
Drift
direction, 278
meaning, 516
intention, 620
tendency, 176
to float, 267
to accumulate, 72
Driftless
chance, 621
Drill
auger, 262
to train, 673
teach, 537
pierce, 260
procedure, 692
Drink
to swallow, 296
liquor, 298
to tipple, 959
sea, 341
Drink in
learn, 539
imbibe, 296

Drip
ooze, 295
flow out, 348
whirer, 839
Dripping
fat, 356
moist, 339
Drive
impel, 276
propel, 284
repel, 289
urge, 615
haste, 684
pursue, 622
fatigue, 688
compel, 744
airing, 266
Drive at
intend, 620
mean, 516
Drive in
insert, 300
ingress, 294
Drive out
ejection, 297
Drivel
folly, 499
fatuity, 503
Driveller
fool, 501
loquacious, 584
Driver
director, 694
Drizzle
distil, 295
rain, 348
Droll
witty, 842
odd, 853
Drollery
amusement, 840
ridiculousness, 853
Dromedary
carrier, 271
Drone
inactive, 683
slow, 275
sound, 412
Droop
sink, 306
flag, 688
weakness, 160
disease, 655
sorrow, 828
dejection, 837

decline, 659
Drop
  fall, 306
  discontinue, 142
  expire, 360
  relinquish, 624, 782
  lose, 776
  faint, 160
  fatigue, 688
  flow out, 348
  spherule, 249
  small quantity, 32, 193
Drop astern
  regression, 283
Drop in
  immerse, 300
  arrive, 292
Drop off
  die, 360
Droplet
  smallness, 32
Dropsical
  swollen, 194
  redundant, 641
Droshky
  vehicle, 272
Dross
  dirt, 653
  trash, 643
  remainder, 40
Drought
  insufficiency, 640
Drouth
  thirst, 865
Drove
  assemblage, 72, 102
Drown
  kill, 361
  immerse, 300
  water, 337
  surfeit, 641
  ruin, 731, 732
Drowsy
  slow, 275
  inactive, 683
  weary, 841
Drub
  beat, 276
  master, 731
  punish, 972
Drudge
  agent, 690
  to work, 680
  to plod, 682
Drug

remedy, 662
  superfluity, 641
  trash, 643
Drugget
  covering, 222
Drum
  cylinder, 249
  music, 417
  sound, 407
  to repeat, 104
Drum-major
  master, 745
Drum out
  punish, 972
Drumhead
  tribunal, 966
Drummer
  agent, 758
Drunk
  intoxication, 959
  intemperance, 954
Dry
  arid, 340
  jejune, 575
  thirsty, 865
  teetotal, 953
  scanty, 640
  wit, 844
  cynical, 932
Dry-nurse
  tend, 707
  teach, 537
  teacher, 540
Dry point
  engraving, 558
Dry rot
  deterioration, 653, 659
Dry up
  waste, 638
  silent, 585
Dryasdust
  past, 122
Duad
  duality, 89
Duality
  duality, 89
Dub
  name, 465
  cinema, 599A
Dubious
  uncertain, 475
Dubitation
  doubt, 485
Duce
  master, 745

Duchess
  noble, 875
Duchy
  region, 181
Duck
  immerse, 300
  plunge, 310
  wet, 337
  stoop, 308
  darling, 899
  nothing, 4
  vehicle, 272
Duck-pond
  taming, 370
Ducking-stool
  punishment, 975
Ducks and drakes
  recoil, 277
Duct
  conduit, 350
Ductile
  flexible, 324
  easy, 705
  useless, 645
Dud
  defective, 651
Dude
  fop, 854
Dudeen
  tobacco-pipe, 298A
Dudgeon
  anger, 900
  discourteous, 895
  club, 727
Duds
  clothes, 225
Due
  proper, 924, 926
  owing, 806
  effect, 154
  expedient, 646
Duel
  contention, 720
Duellist
  combatant, 726
Dueness
  right, 924
Duenna
  teacher, 540
  accompaniment, 88
  keeper, 753
Dues
  price, 812
Duet
  music, 815

Duff
false, 495
Duffer
fool, 501
bungler, 700
Duffle coat
dress, 225
Dug
convexity, 250
Dug-out
refuge, 666, 717
canoe, 273
Duke
noble, 875
ruler, 745
Dukedom
title, 877
Dulcet
sound, 405
melodious, 413
agreeable, 829
Dulcify
sweeten, 396
Dulcimer
musical instrument, 417
Dulcinea
favourite, 899
Dull
inert, 172
insensible, 376
tame, 575
callous, 823
blunt, 254
weak, 160
moderate, 174
colourless, 429
dejected, 837
inexcitable, 826
stolid, 699
prosing, 843
unapt, 499
Dull-brained
folly, 499
Dull-witted
folly, 499
Dullard
fool, 501
Duma
council, 696
Dumb
aphony, 581
stupid, 499, 843
unskilful, 699
Dumb-bell
fool, 501

Dumb show
the drama, 599
Dumbfound
astonish, 870
disappoint, 509
Dummy
aphony, 581
effigy, 554
Dump
deposit, 184
Dumps
sadness, 837
mortification, 832
Dumpy
broad, 202
short, 200
ugly, 846
Dun
colour, 432
to importune, 765
a creditor, 805
Dunce
ignoramus, 493
fool, 501
Dunderhead
fool, 501
Dundreary
whisker, 256
Dune
hillock, 206
Dung
uncleanness, 653
Dungarees
dress, 225
Dungeon
prison, 752
hide, 530
Dunghill
vulgar, 876
Dunt
blow, 619
Duodecimal
twelve, 98
Duodecimo
littleness, 193
book, 593
Duodenary
numbers, 98
Duologue
interlocution, 588
drama, 599
Dupe
to deceive, 545
deceived, 547
credulous, 486

Duplex
double, 89, 90
Duplicate
double, 89, 90
superfluous, 641
copy, 21, 590
pledge, 550, 805
Duplication
imitation, 19
Duplicity
false, 544, 702
Durable
lasting, 110
stable, 150
Durance
restraint, 751
Duration
period, 106
Durbar
tribunal, 966
assembly, 696
Duress
restraint, 751
compulsion, 744
During
lasting, 106
During pleasure
contingent, duration,
108a
Durity
hardness, 323
Dusk
evening, 126
obscurity, 422
Dusky
darkness, 421
Dust
powder, 330
corpse, 362
levity, 320
dirt, 653
trash, 643
to clean, 652
contest, 720
money, 800
Dustman
cleaner, 652
Duteous
virtue, 944
Dutiful
virtue, 944
filial, 167
Duty
obligation, 926
business, 625

work, 686
tax, 812
rite, 990, 998
Duumvirate
authority, 737
Dwarf
small, 193
low, 207
to lessen, 36
Dwell
tarry, 265
reside, 186
Dwell on
descant, 573, 584
Dweller
inhabitant, 188
Dwelling
location, 189
residence, 184
Dwindle
diminish, 32, 195
lessen, 36
Dyad
duality, 89
Dyarchy
authority, 737
Dye
colour, 428
Dying
death, 360
Dyke
see Dike
Dynamic
powerful, 157
Dynamics
force, 159, 276
Dynamite
arms, 727
Dynams
instrument, 633
Dynasty
authority, 737
Dyslogistic
disapproving, 932

Each
speciality, 79
Eager
ardent, 507, 821
desirous, 865
active, 682
Eagle
swift, 274
sight, 441

standard, 550
Eagre
tide, 348
Ear
hearing, 418
Ear-deafening
loudness, 404
Ear-phone
hearing, 418
Ear-piercing
loud, 404
Ear-trumpet
hearing, 418
Ear-witness
evidence, 467
Earache
pain, 378
Earl
nobility, 875
master, 745
Earldom
title, 877
Earless
deaf, 419
Early
earliness, 132
Earmark
sign, 550
Earn
acquire, 775
Earnest
intention, 620
strenuous, 682
emphatic, 642
pledge, 771
pay in advance, 809
eager, 821
Earring
pendant, 214
ornament, 847
Earshot
nearness, 197
Earth
land, 342
ground, 211
world, 318
den, 189
Earth-born
commonalty, 876
Earthly-minded
selfish, 943
worldly, 989
Earthquake
violence, 146, 173
Earwig

to flatter, 933
flatterer, 935
Ease
facility, 705
relief, 834
content, 831
pleasure, 827
in style, 578
Easel
frame, 215
painter's, 559
East
side, 236
Easy
slow, 275
Easy-going
inactive, 683
indulgent, 740
calm, 826
willing, 602
Eat
swallow, 296
Eatable
food, 298
Eaves
projection, 250
Eavesdropping
hearing, 418
prying, 455
Ébauche
plan, 626
Ebb
regress, 283
decrease, 36
contract, 195
waste, 638
spoil, 659
oscillation, 314
Eblis
demon, 980
Ebony
blackness, 431
Ebriety
drunkenness, 959
Ebullition
heat, 384
energy, 171
violence, 173
agitation, 315
excitation, 825
Ecce signum
evidence, 467
indication, 550
Eccentric
irregular, 83

Eftsoons
  soon, 111
  early, 132
Egg
  beginning, 66
Egg on
  urge, 615
Egg-shaped
  round, 247, 249
Egghead
  sage, 500
Ego
  self, 13
Egocentric
  vanity, 880
Egoism
  vanity, 880
  selfishness, 911
Egomania
  vanity, 880
Egotism
  vanity, 880
  selfishness, 911, 943
Egregious
  exceptional, 83
  important, 642
  extravagant, 499
Egregiously
  greatness, 31
Egress
  emergence, 295
Eiderdown
  covering, 222
Eidolon
  idea, 453
Eirenicon
  mediation, 724
Eisteddfod
  assemblage, 72
Either
  choice, 609
Ejaculate
  propel, 284
  utter, 580
Eject
  displace, 185
  emit, 297
Eke
  addition, 37
  to complete, 52
  spin out, 110
Elaborate
  preparation, 673
  complete, 729
  detail, 594

Élan
  ardour, 821
  vigour, 574
  activity, 682
Elapse
  pass, 122
  flow, 109
Elastic
  resilient, 325
  strong, 159
Elate
  to cheer, 836
  boast, 884
Elbow
  angle, 244, 258
  projection, 250
  to push, 276
Elbow-grease
  rubbing, 331
Elbow-room
  space, 180
  freedom, 748
Eld
  oldness, 124
Elder
  oldness, 124
  age, 128
  veteran, 130
Elect
  choice, 609
Election
  necessity, 601
  choice, 609
Elector
  master, 745
  voter, 609
Electric
  feeling, 821
Electric bulb
  light, 423
Electricity
  velocity, 274
Electrify
  excite, 824
  astonish, 870
  energize, 171
Electrocute
  punish, 972, 975
Electrolier
  light, 423
Electrolysis
  decomposition, 49
Electron
  atom, 193
Electroplate

  to cover, 222
Electrotype
  engraving, 558
  imitation, 19
Eleemosynary
  giving, 784
Elegance
  beauty, 845
  in style, 578
  taste, 850
Elegy
  dirge, 415
  funeral, 363
  plaint, 839
Element
  component, 56
  matter, 316
  cause, 153
  beginning, 66
  rudimental knowledge,
    490
Elemental
  simple, 42
Elementary
  simple, 42
Elenchus
  sophistry, 477
Elephant
  large, 192
  carrier, 271
Elevation
  height, 206
  raising, 307
  plan, 554
  improvement, 658
  of mind, 942
  style, 574
  glory, 873
Elevator
  lift, 627
Elevenses
  food, 298
Eleventh hour
  occasion, 134
Elf
  infant, 129
  little, 193
  demon, 980
Elicit
  manifest, 525
  discover, 480a
  cause, 153
  draw out, 301
Elide
  strike out, 552

Eligible
expedience, 646
Eliminate
exclude, 55
extract, 301
weed, 103
Elimination
subduction, 38
Elision
separation, 44
shortening, 201
Élite
perfection, 650
Elixir
remedy, 662
Elixir vitae
remedy, 662
Ellipse
circularity, 247
curvature, 245
conciseness, 572
Ellipsis
curtailment, 201
style, 572
Ellipsoid
circularity, 247
rotundity, 249
Elocution
speech, 582
Éloge
approval, 931
Elongation
lengthening, 200
distance, 196
Elope
escape, 671
Eloquence
of style, 574
speech, 582
Else
addition, 37
Elsewhere
absence, 187
Elucidate
interpret, 522
Elude
avoid, 623
escape, 671
palter, 773
sophistry, 477
succeed, 731
Elusory
falsehood, 544
Elysium
paradise, 981

bliss, 827
Emaciation
contraction, 193
smallness, 195
slenderness, 203
decay, 659
Emanate
go out of, 295
excrete, 299
proceed from, 154
Emanation
odour, 398
Emancipate
free, 750
facilitate, 705
Emasculate
weakness, 160
style, 575
Embalm
preserve, 670
bury, 363
memory, 505
to perfume, 400
Embankment
defence, 717
Embargo
prohibition, 706, 761
stoppage, 265
Embark
depart, 293
undertake, 676
Embarrass
render difficult, 704
hinder, 706
perplex, 475, 528
hesitation, 485
Embase
deterioration, 659
Embassy
errand, 532, 755
diplomat, 758
Embattled
arranged, 60
warfare, 722
Embed
locate, 184
insert, 300
Embellish
beautify, 845
ornament, 847
Embers
fuel, 388
Embezzle
steal, 791
Embitter

aggravate, 835
deteriorate, 659
acerbate, 900
Emblazon
colour, 428
beautify, 845, 847
display, 882
Emblem
indication, 550
Embody
combine, 48
compose, 54
join, 43
form a whole, 50
materialize, 3, 316
Embolden
encourage, 861
hope, 858
Embolism
insertion, 300
Embonpoint
size, 192
Embosomed
middle, 68
lodged, 184
circumjacence, 227
Emboss
form, 240
adorn, 847
Embossed
convex, 250
Embouchure
opening, 260
lipping, 415
Embrace
include, 76
compose, 54
enclose, 227
courtesy, 894
endearment, 902
Embrangle
derange, 61
Embrasure
notch, 257
opening, 260
Embrocation
remedy, 662
Embroider
beauty, 845
ornament, 847
variegate, 440
falsify, 544
exaggerate, 549
Embroil
discord, 713

derange, 61
Embrown
  brown, 433
Embryo
  cause, 153
  preparation, 673
  beginning, 66
Embryonic
  latent, 526
Embus
  depart, 293
Emendation
  improvement, 658
Emerald
  green, 435
  gem, 847
Emerge
  egress, 295
Emergency
  difficulty, 704
  conjuncture, 8
  event, 151
Emeritus
  retired, 757
  respected, 928
Emersion
  egress, 295
Emery
  sharpener, 253
Emery paper
  smooth, 255
Emetic
  remedy, 662
Émeute
  resistance, 716
Emigrant
  traveller, 268
Emigrate
  remove, 266
  egress, 295
Eminence
  height, 206
  fame, 873
Eminently
  superiority, 33
  greatly, 31
Emir
  master, 745
  noble, 875
Emissary
  messenger, 534
  consignee, 758
Emission
  ejection, 297
Emmet

little, 193
Emollient
  remedy, 662
  softness, 324
Emolument
  acquisition, 775
  receipt, 810
Emotion
  feeling, 821
Emotive
  feeling, 821
Emotional
  sensibility, 822
Empale
  see Impale
Emperor
  master, 745
Emphasis
  accent, 580
Emphatic
  positive assertion, 535
  style, 574
  energetic, 171
  important, 642
Empire
  region, 181
  dominion, 737
  domain, 780
Empirical
  tentative, 675
Empiricism
  experiment, 463
  quackery, 545
Employ
  use, 677
  commission, 755
  business, 625
Employee
  servant, 746
  agent, 690, 758
Emporium
  mart, 799
Empower
  power, 157
  commission, 755
  permit, 760
Empress
  chief, 745
Empressement
  activity, 682
  feeling, 821
Emprise
  undertaking, 676
Emption
  purchase, 795

Empty
  vacant, 187
  transfer, 270
  insufficient, 640
  unimportant, 643
  useless, 645
  drain, 297
Empty-handed
  insufficient, 640
Empty-headed
  ignorant, 491
Empurple
  purple, 437
Empyrean
  sky, 318
  blissful, 827, 829
Emulate
  rival, 708, 720
  envy, 921
  imitate, 19
  glory, 873
Emulsion
  semiliquidity, 352
Emunctory
  conduit, 350
En bloc
  assent, 488
  whole, 50
En famille
  sociality, 892
En garçon
  celibacy, 904
En passant
  method, 627
  transitoriness, 111
  irrelation, 10
  journey, 266
En prince
  generosity, 942
En rapport
  agreement, 23
  relation, 9
En règle
  conformity, 82
En revanche
  compensation, 30
En route
  journey, 266
Enable
  power, 157
Enact
  order, 741
  a law, 963
  drama, 599

Enamel
painting, 556
covering, 222
smooth, 255
adorn, 845, 847

Enamour
love, 897

Encage
circumscribe, 231
restrain, 751

Encamp
locate, 184, 265
inhabıt, 186

Encase
circumscribe, 231

Encaustic
painting, 556

Enceinte
region, 181
enclosure, 232
pregnant, 168

Enchain
bind, 43, 751

Enchant
please, 829
love, 897
conjure, 992, 994

Enchantress
beauty, 845
sorceress, 994

Encharge
consign, 755

Enchiridion
book, 593

Encircle
begird, 227

Enclave
enclosure, 232
region, 181

Enclose
circumscribe, 231

Enclosure
fence, 752
space, 181

Encomiast
flatterer, 935

Encomium
approval, 931

Encompass
begird, 227

Encore
repetition, 104

Encounter
meet, 292
clash, 276

contest, 720
withstand, 708

Encourage
animate, 615
aid, 707
embolden, 861
hope, 858
comfort, 834

Encroach
transgress, 303
infringe, 925

Encrust
line, 224
coat, 222

Encumbered
in debt, 806

Encumbrance
hindrance, 704, 706

Encyclical
publication, 531

Encyclopaedia
knowledge, 490
assembly, 72
generality, 78

End
termination, 67, 154
death, 360
object, 620

Endamage
injure, 659
harm, 649

Endanger
danger, 665

Endeavour
attempt, 675, 676
pursue, 622
intend, 620

Endemic
special, 79
disease, 655, 657

Endless
infinite, 105
multitudinous, 102
long, 200

Endogamy
marriage, 903

Endorsement
evidence, 467
sign, 550, 590
voucher, 771
ratification, 769
approval, 931

Endosmosis
passage, 302

Endow

confer power, 157

Endowment
gift, 784
capacity, 5
power, 157
talent, 698

Endue
empower, 157

Endure
time, 106
to continue, 141
to last, 110
event, 151
to bear, 821
to submit, 826

Endways
length, 200
vertical, 212

Enemy
enemy, 891

Energumen
madman, 503
fanatic, 515

Energy
physical, 171
strength, 159
style, 574
activity, 682
exertion, 686
resolution, 604

Enervate
weakness, 160

Enfant perdu
rashness, 863

Enfant terrible
artlessness, 703

Enfeeble
weaken, 160

Enfilade
pierce, 260
pass through, 302

Enfold
circumscribe, 231

Enforce
urge, 615
compel, 744
require, 924

Enfranchise
liberate, 748, 750, 924

Engage
induce, 615
the attention, 457
in a pursuit, 622
promise, 768, 769
commission, 755

undertake, 676
book, 132
Engagement
business, 625
contest, 720
promise, 768
duty, 926
Engaging
pleasing, 829
amiable, 897
Engender
produce, 161
Engine
instrument, 633
Engine-driver
director, 694
Engineering
means, 632
Engirdle
circumjacence, 227
English
translate, 522
Engorge
reception, 296
Engorgement
redundance, 641
Engraft
insert, 301
join, 43
add, 37
teach, 537
implant, 6
Engrained
imbued, 5
combined, 48
Engrave
mark, 550
on the memory, 505
Engraving
engraving, 558
Engross
possess, 777
write, 590
the thoughts, 451
the attention, 457
Engulf
destroy, 162
plunge, 310
swallow up, 296
Enhance
increase, 35
improve, 658
Enharmonic
harmony, 413
Enigma

secret, 533
question, 461
Enigmatic
concealed, 528
obscure, 519
uncertain, 475
Enjambement
transcursion, 303
Enjoin
command, 741
induce, 615
enact, 963
Enjoy
physically, 377
morally, 827
possess, 777
Enkindle
induce, 615
Enlace
surround, 227
entwine, 219, 248
join, 43
Enlarge
increase, 35
swell, 194
liberate, 750
in writing, 573
Enlighten
illuminate, 420
inform, 527
instruct, 537
Enlightened
wise, 498
Enlightenment
knowledge, 490
Enlist
commission, 755
engage, 615
Enliven
amuse, 840
cheer, 836
delight, 829
Enmesh
entwine, 219
Enmity
hostility, 889
hate, 898
discord, 713
Ennead
nine, 98
Enneagon
nine, 98
Ennoble
glorify, 873
Ennui

weariness, 841
Enormity
crime, 947
Enormous
in degree, 31
in size, 192
Enough
much, 31
sufficient, 639
satiety, 869
Enquiry
see Inquiry
Enrage
incense, 900
provoke, 830
Enrapture
excite, 824
beatify, 829
love, 897
Enravish
beatify, 829
Enrich
wealth, 803
ornament, 847
Enrobe
invest, 225
Enrol
record, 551
appoint, 755
Enrolment
list, 86
Ens
essence, 1
Ensanguined
red, 434
murderous, 361
Ensconce
settle, 184
render safe, 664
conceal, 528
Ensemble
whole, 50
Enshrine
memory, 505, 873
sanctify, 987
Enshroud
conceal, 528
Ensiform
sharpness, 253
Ensign
standard, 550
officer, 726
master, 745
Enslave
subjection, 749

Ensnare
cheat, 545
Ensue
follow, 63, 117
happen, 151
Ensure
certainty, 474
Entablature
summit, 210
Entail
cause, 153
involve, 467
impose, 741
Entangle
derange, 61
entwine, 219
disorder, 59
embroil, 713
perplex, 528
mixture, 41
Entente cordiale
friendship, 888
concord, 714
Enter
go in, 294
note, 551
accounts, 811
Enter in
converge, 290
Enter into
component, 56
Enter upon
begin, 66
Enterprise
pursuit, 622
attempt, 676
Enterprising
active, 682
energetic, 171
courageous, 861
Entertain
amuse, 840
support, 707
sociality, 892
an idea, 451, 484
Entertainment
repast, 298
Entêté
obstinate, 606
prejudiced, 481
Enthral
subdue, 749
delight, 829
Enthrone
repute, 873

Enthusiasm
feeling, 821
imagination, 515
love, 897
hope, 850, 858
Enthusiast
game, 840
zealot, 606
Enthusiastic
sensibility, 822
excitability, 825
Enthymeme
reasoning, 476
Entice
motive, 615
Enticing
pleasure, 829
Entire
whole, 50
complete, 52
Entirely
greatness, 31
Entitle
name, 564
give a right, 924
Entity
existence, 1
Entomb
inter, 231, 363
imprison, 751
Entourage
environment, 227
retinue, 746
Entr'acte
interval, 106
Entrails
interior, 221
Entrain
depart, 293
Entrance
beginning, 66
ingress, 294
fee, 809
to enrapture, 824, 829
to conjure, 992
Entrap
deceive, 545
Entre nous
concealment, 528
Entreat
request, 765
Entrechat
leap, 309
Entrée
ingress, 294

Entremet
food, 298
Entrench
defence, 717
Entrepôt
store, 636
mart, 799
Entrepreneur
organizer, 626
Entresol
interjacence, 228
Entrust
consign, 784
lend, 787
charge with, 755
Entry
ingress, 294
beginning, 66
record, 551
evidence, 467
Entwine
join, 43
intersect, 219
convolve, 248
Enumerate
number, 85
Enunciate
publish, 531
inform, 527
affirm, 535
voice, 580
Envelop
invest, 225
conceal, 528
Envelope
covering, 222
enclosure, 232
Envenom
poison, 649
deprave, 659
exasperate, 835, 898
Environs
nearness, 197
circumjacence, 227
Envisage
view, 441
confront, 234
intuition, 477
Envoy
messenger, 534
postscript, 39
Envy
jealousy, 921
Enwrap
invest, 225

Eolith
oldness, 124
Epaulet
badge, 550
decoration, 877
ornament, 847
Éperdu
excited, 824
Ephemeral
transient, 111
changeable, 149
Ephemeris
calendar, 114
record, 551
book, 593
Epic
poem, 597
Epicedium
interment, 363
Epicene
exceptional, 83
multiform, 81
Epicentre
focus, 223
Epicure
sensual, 954
glutton, 957
fastidious, 868
Epicycle
circularity, 247
Epicycloid
circularity, 247
Epidemic
disease, 655
dispersed, 73
general, 78
Epidermis
covering, 222
Epidiascope
spectacle, 448
Epigram
wit, 842
Epigrammatic
pithy, 516
concise, 572
Epigrammatist
humorist, 844
Epigraph
indication, 550
Epilepsy
convulsion, 315
Epilogue
sequel, 65
drama, 599
Episcopal

clergy, 995
Episode
event, 151
interjacence, 228
interruption, 70
Episodic
unrelated, 10
style, 573
Epistle
letter, 592
Epitaph
interment, 363
Epithalamium
marriage, 903
Epithem
remedy, 662
Epithet
nomenclature, 564
Epitome
compendium, 596
conciseness, 572
miniature, 193
Epizootic
insalubrity, 657
Epoch
time, 113
duration, 106
period, 114
Epode
poetry, 597
Epopee
poetry, 597
Épris
love, 897
Equable
right, 922
Equal
equality, 27
equitable, 922
Equanimity
inexcitability, 826
Equate
equality, 27
Equations
numeration, 85
Equator
middle, 68
Equerry
servant, 746
Equestrian
traveller, 268
Equidistant
Middle, 68
Equilibrium
equality, 27

steadiness, 265
Equip
dress, 225
prepare, 673
Equipage
vehicle, 272
instrument, 633
materials, 635
Equipoise
equal, 27
Equipollent
equal, 27
identical, 13
Equiponderant
equal, 27
Equitable
just, 922
fair, 480, 939
due, 924
Equitation
journey, 266
Equity
justice, 922
law, 963
honour, 939
Equivalence
equal, 27
Equivalent
identity, 13
compensation, 30
synonymous, 516
Equivocal
dubious, 475
double meaning, 520,
961
Equivocate
pervert, 477
prevaricate, 520
Equivoque
equivocal, 520
uncertainty, 475
impurity, 961
error, 495
Era
duration, 106
chronology, 114
Eradicate
destroy, 162
extract, 301
Erase
efface, 162, 499, 552
Ere
priority, 116
Ere long
earliness, 132

Erebus
dark, 421
hell, 982
Erect
raise, 307
build, 161
vertical, 212
Erection
house, 189
Eremitical
seclusion, 893
Erewhile
preterition, 122
priority, 116
Ergatocracy
rule, 737
Ergo
reasoning, 476
Ergotism
reasoning, 476
Eriometer
optical, 445
Erk
fighter, 726
Ermine
badge of authority, 747
Erode
destroy, 162
injure, 659
Erotic
amorous, 897
impure, 961
Eroticism
pleasantness, 829
Err
in opinion, 495
morally, 945
Errand
commission, 755
business, 625
message, 532
Erratic
capricious, 149, 608
wandering, 264, 279
Erratum
error, 495
misprint, 555
Error
false opinion, 495
failure, 732
vice, 945
guilt, 947
Erst
preterition, 122
Erubescence

redness, 434
Eructate
eject, 297
Erudite
scholar, 492
Erudition
knowledge, 490
Eruption
egress, 295
violence, 173
disease, 655
Escalade
mount, 305
attack, 716
Escalate
increase, 35
Escalator
way, 627
lift, 307
Escallop
convolution, 248
Escapade
freak, 608
prank, 840
vagary, 856
Escape
flight, 671
liberate, 750
evade, 927
forget, 506
Escarpment
slope, 217
Eschatology
intention, 620
end, 67
Escheat
penalty, 974
Eschew
avoid, 623
dislike, 867
Escort
to accompany, 88
safeguard, 664
keeper, 753
Escritoire
desk, 191
Esculent
food, 298
Escutcheon
indication, 550
Esoteric
private, 79
concealed, 528
Espalier
agriculture, 371

Especial
private, 79
Esperanto
language, 560
Espial
vision, 441
Espièglerie
wit, 842
Espionage
inquiry, 461
Esplanade
flat, 213
plain, 344
Espousal
marriage, 903
Esprit
shrewdness, 498
wit, 842
Esprit de corps
party, 712
misjudgment, 781
belief, 484
sociality, 892
Esprit fort
sage, 500
Espy
vision, 441
Esquire
title, 877
Essay
try, 463
endeavour, 675
dissertation, 595
Essayist
writing, 590
Essence
nature, 5
existence, 1
odour, 398
pith, 642
Essential
great, 31
requisite, 630
Establish
fix, 184
demonstrate, 478
evidence, 467
create, 161
substantiate, 494
settle, 150
Established
received, 82
habitual, 613
Establishment
fixture, 141

party, 712
location, 184
Estancia
property, 780
Estate
condition, 7
property, 780
Esteem
judge, 480
believe, 484
approve, 931
Estimable
good, 648
commendable, 931
Estimate
measure, 466
judge, 480
count, 85
Estimation
opinion, 484
respect, 928
good, 648
Estoppage
prohibition, 761
Estrade
horizontal, 213
Estrange
alienate, 449
hate, 898
seclude, 893
Estreat
penalty, 974
Estuary
gulf, 343
Esurient
hungry, 865
État-major
combatant, 726
Etcetera
addition, 37
inclusion, 76
plurality, 100
Etch
engraving, 558
Eternal
perpetuity, 112
Ether
sky, 313, 338
void, 4
vapour, 334
Ethical
virtue, 944
Ethics
duty, 926
Ethiopic

blackness, 431
Ethnic
heathen, 984
racial, 372
Ethnology
mankind, 372
Ethos
nature, 5
Etiolate
bleach, 429, 430
Etiquette
fashion, 852
custom, 613
ceremony, 882
Étude
music, 415
Etymology
word, 562
language, 560
Etymon
origin, 153
verbal, 562
Eucharist
rite, 998
Euchology
rite, 998
Eugenics
production, 161
Eulogy
approval, 931
Euphemism
misnomer, 565
Euphonious
musical, 413
style, 578
Euphony
harmony, 413
Euphoria
health, 654
Euphuism
ornament, 577
affectation, 855
Eurasian
mixture, 41
Eureka
judgment, 480
answer, 462
Eurhythmics
training, 673
Eurhythmy
symmetry, 242
Euroclydon
wind, 349
Euterpe
music, 415

Euthanasia
death, 360
killing, 361
Evacuate
emit, 297
excrete, 299
Evacuee
escape, 671
Evade
avoid, 623
escape, 671
sophistry, 477
dereliction, 927
Evaluate
appraise, 466, 812
Evanescent
transient, 111
minute, 32, 193
disappearing, 449
Evangelist
revelation, 985
Evangelize
convert, 484
Evaporate
vapour, 336
gas, 334
unsubstantiality, 4
Evasion
escape, 623, 671
sophistry, 477
plea, 617
falsehood, 544
untruth, 546
cunning, 702
dereliction, 927
Eve
evening, 126
priority, 116
Even
equal, 27
uniform, 16
level, 213
flat, 251
smooth, 265
straight, 246
although, 179, 469
Even-handed
equitable, 922
honourable, 939
Even so
assent, 488
Evening
evening, 126
Evening
worship, 990

evening, 126
Event
eventuality, 151
Eventful
stirring, 151
remarkable, 642
Eventide
evening, 126
Eventual
futurity, 121
Eventuate
occur, 1
Ever
always, 112
seldom, 137
Ever and anon
repetition, 104
Ever-changing
mutability, 149
Ever-recurring
repetition, 104
Evergreen
newness, 123
diuturnity, 110
continuous, 69
perpetuity, 112
Everlasting
perpetual, 112, 136
Evermore
perpetual, 112
Every
generality, 78
Everyday
conformity, 82
perpetuity, 112
Everyman
mankind, 372
Everywhere
space, 180, 186
Eviction
displacement, 185
Evidence
evidence, 467
Evident
visible, 446
certain, 474
demonstrable, 478
manifest, 525
Evil
harm, 619
wrong, 923
vice, 945
producing evil, 649
Evil day
adversity, 735

Evil eye
malevolence, 907
glance, 441
Evil-minded
malevolent, 907
vicious, 945
Evil-speaking
detraction, 934
Evildoer
maleficent, 913
badness, 649
culprit, 949
Evince
show, 467
prove, 478
Eviscerate
extract, 301
divide, 44
mutilate, 38
Evoke
call upon, 765
excite, 824
Evolution
numerical, 85
effect, 154
development, 161
turning out, 313
circuition, 311
Evulsion
extraction, 301
Ewer
receptacle, 191
Ex cathedra
affirmation, 535
insolence, 885
Ex concesso
reasoning, 476
assent, 488
Ex-libris
label, 550
Ex mero motu
will, 600
Ex necessitate rei
destiny, 152
Ex officio
truth, 494
authority, 737
dueness, 924
Ex parte
evidence, 467
Ex post facto
preterition, 122
Exacerbate
increase, 35
aggravate, 835

exasperate, 173
Exact
true, 494
similar, 17
require, 741
claim, 924
tax, 812
Exacting
severe, 739
Exactly
just so, 488
Exaggerate
increase, 35
overestimate, 482
misrepresent, 549
boast, 884
Exalt
increase, 35
elevate, 307
extol, 931
boast, 884
Exalted
heroic, 942
Examine
inquiry, 457, 461
Example
instance, 82
pattern, 22
model, 948
Exanimate
listless, 683
lifeless, 360
Exarch
ruler, 745
deputy, 759
Exasperate
increase, 35
exacerbate, 173
aggravate, 835
inflame, 900
Excavate
dig, 252
Exceed
surpass, 33
expand, 194
transgress, 303
Exceeding
remaining, 40
Exceedingly
greatness, 31
Excel
superiority, 33
goodness, 648, 650
Excellency
skill, 698

title, 877
Excellent
good, 648
virtuous, 944
Excelsior
ascent, 305
height, 206
Except
subduct, 38
exclude, 55
Exception
to a rule, 83
qualification, 469
censure, 932
Exceptionable
vicious, 945
blameworthy, 932
Exceptional
special, 79
irregular, 83
Excerpt
extract, 596
choice, 609
Excess
superiority, 33
remainder, 40
redundance, 641
intemperance, 954
Excessive
greatness, 31
Exchange
mutual change, 148
reciprocalness, 12
transfer, 783
barter, 794
mart, 799
Exchequer
treasury, 802
Excise
price, 812
Excision
subduction, 38
Excitability
excitement, 825
irascibility, 901
Excitation
excitation, 824
Excite
violent, 173
morally, 824
anger, 900
Exclaim
voice, 580
Exclosure
region, 181

enclosure, 232
Exclude
leave out, 55
prohibit, 761
ostracize, 893
subduction, 38
Exclusive
omitting, 55
special, 79
irregular, 83
unsociable, 893
Excogitation
thought, 451
imagination, 515
Excommunicate
exclude, 55, 893
hate, 898
curse, 908
Excoriate
flay, 226
Excrement
uncleanness, 653
Excrescence
projection, 250
blemish, 848
Excretion
excretion, 299
Excruciating
pain, 378, 830
Exculpate
forgive, 918
vindicate, 937
acquit, 970
Excursion
tour, 266
circuit, 311
attack, 716
Excursionist
traveller, 268
Excursive
style, 573
Excursus
appendix, 65
Excuse
plea, 617
exempt, 927
forgive, 918
vindicate, 937
Exeat
leave, 760
Exercrable
bad, 649
offensive, 830
nauseous, 867
Execrate

malediction, 908
hate, 898
Execute
conduct, 692
perform, 680, 739
in law, 771
music, 415
Executioner
killing, 361
Executive
jurisprudence, 965
directing, 693
director, 694
Executor
agent, 690
Exegesis
interpretation, 522
Exemplar
prototype, 22
Exemplary
virtue, 944
Exemplify
quote, 82
illustrate, 522
Exempt
absolve, 927
free, 748
permit, 760
Exemption
exception, 83
dueness, 924
Exenterate
extract, 301
mutilate, 38
Exequatur
commission, 755
Exequies
interment, 363
Exercise
employ, 677
act, 680
exert, 686
teach, 537
train, 673
task, 625
Exercitation
dissertation, 595
use, 677
Exert
exertion, 686
Exertion
physical, 171
Exfoliation
divestment, 226

Exhalation
vapour, 336
odour, 398
excretion, 299
Exhaust
drain, 638, 789
fatigue, 688
weaken, 160
misemploy, 679
squander, 818
complete, 52, 729
tube, 351
Exhaustless
infinite, 105
plentiful, 639
Exhibit
show, 525
display, 882
Exhilarate
cheer, 836
Exhort
advise, 695
induce, 615
preach, 998
Exhume
interment, 363
past, 122
Exigency
crisis, 8
chance, 621
difficulty, 704
requirement, 630
need, 865
dearth, 640
Exigent
severe, 640
exacting, 832
Exiguous
little, 193
Exile
displace, 185
send out, 297
seclude, 893
punish, 972
Exility
thinness, 203
Existence
being, 1
life, 359
thing, 3
in time, 118
in space, 186
Exit
departure, 293
egress, 295

escape, 671
Exodus
departure, 293
egress, 295
Exogamy
marriage, 903
Exonerate
exempt, 927
vindicate, 937
forgive, 918
acquit, 970
disburden, 705
absolve, 760
release, 756
Exorbitant
enormous, 31
redundant, 641
dear, 814
Exorcise
conjure, 992
Exorcism
theology, 993
Exorcist
heterodoxy, 994
Exordium
beginning, 66
Exosmosis
passage, 302
Exoteric
disclosed, 531
public, 529
Exotic
alien, 10
exceptional, 83
Expand
swell, 194
increase, 35
in breadth, 202
rarefy, 322
in writing, 573
Expanse
space, 180, 202
size, 192
Expansion
space, 180
Expatiate
in writing, 573
in discourse, 582, 584
Expatriate
deport, 295
displace, 185
exclude, 55, 893
Expect
look for, 121, 507
not wonder, 871

hope, 858
Expectorant
remedy, 662
Expectorate
eject, 296
Expedience
utility, 646
Expedient
means, 632
substitute, 634
plan, 626
Expedite
accelerate, 274
earliness, 132
aid, 707
Expedition
speed, 274
activity, 682
warfare, 722
march, 266
Expel
displace, 185
eject, 297
drive from, 289
punish, 972
Expend
use, 677
waste, 638
pay, 809
Expense
price, 812
Expensive
dear, 814
Experience
knowledge, 490
undergo, 821
event, 151
Experienced
skilled, 698
Experiment
trial, 463
endeavour, 675
Experimentum crucis
demonstration, 478
Expert
skill, 698
adept, 700
Experto crede
knowledge, 490
Expiate
atonement, 952
Expire
death, 360
end, 67
breathe out, 349

Explain
  expound, 522
  inform, 527
  teach, 537
  answer, 462
Explain away
  misinterpret, 523
Expletive
  redundance, 573, 641
  malediction, 908
Explication
  interpret, 522
Explicit
  distinct, 516, 518, 535
Explode
  burst, 3, 173
  sound, 406
  refute, 479
  passion, 825
  anger, 900
Exploit
  action, 680
  to use, 677
Explore
  investigate, 461
  experiment, 463
Explosion
  see Explode
Exponent
  index, 550
  numerical, 84
  interpreter, 522
Export
  transfer, 270
  send out, 297
  thing sent, 295
Exposé
  account, 596
  disclosure, 529
Expose
  show, 525
  interpret, 522
  confute, 479
  denude, 226
  endanger, 665
Exposition
  answer, 462
  disclosure, 529
Expositor
  interpreter, 524
  teacher, 540
Expository
  information, 527, 595
Expostulate
  deprecate, 766

  reprehend, 932
  dissuade, 616
  advise, 695
Exposure
  disclosure, 529
Exposure meter
  optical instrument, 445
Exposure to
  liability, 177
Expound
  interpret, 522
  teach, 537
  answer, 462
Expounder
  interpreter, 524
Express
  voluntary, 600
  intentional, 620
  declare, 525
  mean, 516
  inform, 527
  phrase, 566
  intelligible, 518
  name, 564
  squeeze out, 301
  rapid, 274
Expression
  aspect, 448
Expressive
  style, 574
Exprobation
  disapproval, 932
Exprobration
  accusation, 938
Expropriate
  take, 789
Expulsion
  see Expel
Expunge
  efface, 506, 552
  destroy, 162
  disappear, 449
Expurgation
  cleanness, 652
Exquisite
  excellent, 648
  pleasurable, 829
  savoury, 394
  fop, 854
Exquisitely
  great, 31
Exsiccate
  dryness, 340
Exsufflation
  sorcery, 992

Extant
  being, 1
Extempore
  instantly, 113
  early, 132
  off-hand, 612
  unprepared, 674
Extend
  prolong, 200
  expand, 194
  reach, 196
  increase, 35
Extensile
  pliable, 324
Extension
  space, 180
Extensive
  spacious, 180
  considerable, 31
Extent
  degree, 26
  space, 180
Extenuate
  decrease, 36
  diminish, 192
  excuse, 937
  acquit, 970
Exterior
  exteriority, 220
Exterminate
  destruction, 162
Exterminator
  destroyer, 165
External
  exteriority, 220
Externalize
  materialize, 316
Extinction
  destruction, 162
  non-existence, 2
  of life, 360
Extinguish
  destroy, 162
  darken, 421
  blow out, 385
Extinguisher
  destroyer, 165
Extirpate
  destruction, 162
  extraction, 301
Extol
  praise, 931
  over-estimate, 482
Extort
  despoil, 789

extract, 301
  compel, 744
Extortionate
  greedy, 865
  dear, 814
  parsimonious, 819
Extra
  additional, 37, 39
  supernumerary, 641
  store, 636
Extra muros
  exteriority, 220
Extra-sensory
  occult, 992
  thought, 451
  immaterial, 317
Extract
  take out, 301
  part, 51
  choice, 609
  quotation, 596
Extradite
  deport, 55, 270
  displace, 185
  eject, 297
Extrajudicial
  illegal, 964
Extramundane
  immateriality, 317
Extramural
  exterior, 220
Extraneous
  extrinsic, 6
  not related, 10
  foreign, 57
Extraordinary
  unconformity, 83
  greatness, 31
Extravagant
  exaggerated, 549
  irrational, 477
  absurd, 497
  ridiculous, 853
  foolish, 499
  redundant, 641
  high-priced, 814
  prodigal, 818
  vulgar, 851
  inordinate, 31
Extravaganza
  fanciful, 515
  burlesque, 853
  the drama, 599
Extravasate
  excretion, 299

Extreme
  greatness, 31
  revolutionary, 146
Extremist
  zealot, 604
Extremity
  end, 67
  exterior, 220
Extricate
  take out, 301
  liberate, 750
  deliver, 672
  facilitate, 705
Extrinsic
  extrinsicality, 6
Extrude
  eject, 297
Exuberant
  redundant, 641
  style, 573
  feeling, 821
Exude
  excretion, 299
  egress, 295
Exult
  crow, 836
  rejoice, 838
  boast, 873, 884
Exuviae
  remainder, 40
Eye
  organ of sight, 441
  opening, 260
  circle, 247
Eye-opener
  enlightenment, 527
  portent, 870
Eye-shade
  mask, 530
Eye-witness
  evidence, 467
  spectator, 414
Eyeglass
  optical instrument, 445
Eyeless
  blind, 442
Eyelet
  opening, 260
Eyesight
  vision, 441
Eyesore
  ugliness, 846
Eyewash
  deception, 545
Eyot

island, 346
Eyre
  jurisprudence, 965
Eyrie
  abode, 189

Fabian policy
  inactivity, 681, 683
  delay, 133
Fable
  fiction, 546
  error, 495
  description, 594
Fabric
  texture, 329
  house, 189
  effect, 154
  state, 7
Fabricate
  make, 161
  invent, 515
  forge, 544
  falsify, 546
Fabulous
  imagination, 515
  mythical, 979
  exaggerated, 549
  greatness, 31
  non-existent, 2
Façade
  front, 234
Face
  exterior, 220
  front, 234
  lining, 224
  impudence, 885
  confront, 861
  aspect, 448
Face about
  deviation, 279
Face-cloth
  wash, 652
Face down
  withstand, 719
Face to face
  manifestation, 525
Facet
  exterior, 220
Facetious
  wit, 842
Facia
  indication, 550
Facile
  irresolute, 605

persuasible, 602, 615
easy, 705
skilful, 698
Facile princeps
superiority, 33
goodness, 648
Facility
ease, 705
aid, 707
skill, 698
Facing
lining, 224
covering, 222
Façon de parler
meaning, 516
metaphor, 521
exaggeration, 549
phrase, 566
Facsimile
copy, 21
identity, 13
representation, 554
Fact
event, 151
truth, 494
existence, 1, 2
Faction
party, 712
Factious
discord, 713
Factitious
artificial, 544
Factor
numerical, 84
agent, 690
director, 694
consignee, 758
merchant, 797
Factory
workshop, 691
Factotum
manager, 694
employee, 758
Faculty
power, 157
intellect, 450
skill, 698
profession, 625
Fad
caprice, 608
prejudice, 481
fashion, 852
Fade
vanish, 2, 4, 111, 449
dim, 422

expel, 297
lose colour, 429
spoil, 659
droop, 160
change, 149
become old, 124
Fade
insipid, 391
Fade-out
cinema, 599A
Fadge
agreement, 23
Faeces
excretion, 298
foulness, 653
Faery
fabulous being, 979
imagination, 515
Fag
labour, 686
activity, 682
fatigue, 688, 841
drudge, 690
Fag-end
remainder, 40
end, 67
Faggot
bundle, 72
fuel, 388
Fahrenheit
thermometer, 389
Fail
incomplete, 53, 651
shortcoming, 304
non-observance, 732
non-payment, 808
dereliction, 927
droop, 160
break down, 158
reject, 610
vice, 945
Fain
wish, 865
willing, 602
compulsive, 744
Fainéant
idler, 683
Faint
weak, 160
sound, 405
colour, 429
small in degree, 32
swoon, 683, 688
Faint-hearted
coward, 862

fear, 860
Fair
in degree, 31
white, 430
just, 922
impartial, 498
honourable, 939
true, 543
tolerable, 651
pleasing, 829
beautiful, 845
mart, 799
festivity, 840
Fair play
justice, 922
honour, 939
Fair sex
woman, 374
Fair-spoken
courteous, 894
flattering, 933
Fairing
gift, 784
Fairly
great, 31
Fairy
fabulous being, 979
Fairy-cycle
bicycle, 266
Fairy godmother
friend, 891
benefactor, 912
Fairy-tale
lie, 546
Fait accompli
completion, 729
Faith
belief, 484
hope, 858
honour, 939
creed, 983
piety, 987
Faithful
likeness, 17
true, 494
obedient, 743
observant, 772
Christian, 983A
godly, 987
Faithless
false, 544
dishonourable, 940
sceptical, 989
Fake
imitation, 19

deception, 545
to forge, 544

Fakir
clergy, 996

Falcated
curved, 245
sharp, 244

Falchion
arms, 727

Falciform
angularity, 244
curvature, 245

Fall
descend, 306
destruction, 162
slope, 217
fail, 732
die, 360
adversity, 735
decline, 659
happen, 151
vice, 945
autumn, 126

Fall away
decrease, 36
shrink, 195

Fall back
recede, 283, 287
relapse, 661

Fall behind
sequence, 281

Fall down
descend, 306
worship, 990

Fall for
love, 897

Fall foul of
oppose, 708
encounter, 720
reprimand, 932

Fall in
marshal, 58, 60
happen, 151

Fall in with
find, 480A
uniformity, 16
agree, 23

Fall off
deterioration, 659
decrease, 36
disjunction, 44

Fall out
happen, 151
drop, 297

Fall short

shortcoming, 304, 730
fail, 53
insufficiency, 640

Fall through
failure, 732

Fall to
work, 686
devour, 296
fight, 722

Fall to pieces
disjunction, 44

Fall under
inclusion, 76

Fall upon
attack, 716
discover, 480A
devise, 626

Fallacy
error, 495
uncertainty, 475
sophistry, 477

Fal-lal
ornament, 847
trifle, 643

Fallible
uncertain, 475, 477

Fallow
yellow, 436
unproductive, 169
unready, 674

False
untrue, 544
error, 495
sophistry, 477
spurious, 925
dishonourable, 940

False-hearted
improbity, 940

Falsehood
lie, 546

Falsetto
music, 413
affected, 577

Falsify
misinterpret, 523
accounts, 811
deceive, 495
lie, 544

Falstaffian
fat, 192

Falter
stammer, 583
hesitate, 605
demur, 603
slowness, 275

Fame
renown, 873
rumour, 531
news, 532

Familiar
common, 82
habit, 613
known, 490
friendly, 888
affable, 892, 894
spirit, 979

Family
class, 75
consanguinity, 11
paternity, 166
posterity, 167

Famine
insufficiency, 640

Famished
fasting, 956

Famous
repute, 873
greatness, 31

Fan
blow, 349
excite, 615
enthusiast, 840, 865
frequenter, 136

Fanatic
extravagant, 515

Fanatical
feeling, 821

Fanaticism
folly, 499
obstinacy, 606
religious, 984A

Fanciful
capricious, 608
imaginative, 515
mistaken, 495
unreal, 2

Fancy
think, 451
believe, 484
wit, 842
idea, 453
suppose, 514
imagine, 515
caprice, 608
choice, 609
desire, 865
like, 394
love, 897
pugilism, 726

Fandango
dance, 840
Fane
temple, 1000
Fanfare
loudness, 404
ostentation, 882
Fanfaronade
boasting, 884
Fang
bane, 663
Fanlight
opening, 260
Fantasia
music, 415
imagination, 515
Fantastic
odd, 83
imaginary, 515
capricious, 608
ridiculous, 853
Fantasy
caprice, 608
imagination, 515
idea, 453
Fantoccini
marionettes, 554, 599
Far
distant, 196
Far-fetched
irrelation, 10
irrelevant, 24
irrational, 477
obscure, 519
Far from it
dissimilarity, 18
Far-seeing
foresight, 510
Farce
drama, 599
ridiculous, 856
Farceur
humorist, 844
Farcical
ridiculous, 856
witty, 842
trifling, 643
Fardel
assemblage, 72
Fare
circumstance, 8
event, 151
to eat, 296
food, 298
price, 812
Farewell

departure, 293
Farm
house, 189
property, 780
to rent, 788, 795
Farrago
mixture, 41
confusion, 59
Farthing
coin, 800
worthless, 643
Farthingale
dress, 225
Fasces
sceptre, 747
Fascia
band, 205
circle, 247
Fascicle
assemblage, 72
Fascinate
please, 829
excite, 824, 825
astonish, 870
love, 897
conjure, 992
Fascination
spell, 993
motive, 615
occult arts, 992
Fash
worry, 830
Fashion
form, 144, 240
custom, 613
mould, 140
mode, 627, 852
nobility, 875
Fast
rapid, 274
steadfast, 150
stuck, 265
joined, 43
dissolute, 954
not to eat, 640, 956
Fast and loose
false, 544
changeful, 607
Fasten
join, 45, 214
fix, 150
restrain, 751
Fastener
hanging, 214
Fastening

vinculum, 45
Fastidious
dainty, 868
squeamish, 932
Fasting
abstinence, 956
atonement, 952
insufficient, 640
Fastness
asylum, 666
defence, 717
Fat
oleaginous, 356
unctuous, 355
broad, 202
big, 192
Fat-head
fool, 501
Fat-witted
folly, 499
Fata morgana
phantasm, 4
dim sight, 443
imagination, 515
Fatal
lethal, 361
pernicious, 649
Fatalism
destiny, 152
necessity, 601
Fatality
killing, 361
Fate
necessity, 601
chance, 152, 621
end, 67, 360
Father
paternity, 166
priest, 996
theologian, 983
Father upon
attribute, 155
Fatherland
home, 189
Fatherless
unsustained, 160
Fathom
measure, 466
investigate, 461
answer, 462
Fathomless
depth, 208
Fatidical
prediction, 511
Fatigue

lassitude, 688
weariness, 841
Fatras
unimportance, 643
Fatten on
feeding, 296
Fatuity
folly, 499
Faubourg
suburb, 227
Fauces
beginning, 66
Faucet
opening, 260
channel, 350
outlet, 295
Faugh!
dislike, 867
Fault
imperfection, 651
blemish, 848
break, 70
vice, 945
guilt, 947
error, 495
failure, 732
ignorance, 491
Faultless
perfect, 650
innocent, 946
Fauna
animal, 366
Faute de mieux
shift, 147, 626
Fauteuil
support, 215
Faux pas
failure, 732
error, 495
vice, 945
Favour
aid, 707
permit, 760
friendship, 888
partiality, 923
gift, 784
letter, 592
to resemble, 17
Favourable
good, 648
willing, 602
friendly, 707, 888
co-operating, 709
Favourite
pleasing, 829

beloved, 897, 899
Favouritism
wrong, 923
Fawn
colour, 433
cringe, 886
flatter, 933
Fay
fairy, 979
Faze
worry, 830
discompose, 458
perplex, 704
Fealty
duty, 926
respect, 928
obedience, 743
Fear
fear, 860
cowardice, 862
Fearful
great, 31
Fearless
hopeful, 858
courageous, 861
Feasible
possible, 470
easy, 705
Feast
repast, 298
to devour, 296
gluttony, 957
revel, 840
enjoyment, 827
celebration, 883
anniversary, 138
Feast on
enjoy, 377
Feat
action, 680
Feather
tuft, 256
lightness, 320
trifle, 643
class, 75
ornament, 847
decoration, 877
Feather-bed
softness, 324
Feathery
roughness, 256
Feature
character, 5
form, 240
appearance, 448

lineament, 550
component, 56
to resemble, 17
cinema, 599A
Febrifuge
remedy, 662
Fecit
painting, 556
Feckless
feeble, 160
improvident, 674
useless, 645
Feculence
uncleanness, 653
Fecund
productive, 168
Fecundation
production, 161
Fed up
weariness, 841
dislike, 867
satiety, 869
Federation
co-operation, 709
party, 712
Fee
expenditure, 795, 809
Fee simple
property, 780
Feeble
weak, 160
imperfect, 651
scanty, 32
silly, 477
style, 575
Feeble-minded
foolish, 499
irresolute, 605
Feed
eat, 296
supply, 637
meal, 298
Feel
touch, 379
sensibility, 375
moral, 821
Feel for
seek, 461
sympathize, 914
Feeler
inquiry, 461
Feet
journey, 266
Feign
falsehood, 544

Feint
  deception, 545
Felicitate
  congratulate, 896
Felictious
  expedient, 646
  favourable, 648
  skilful, 698
  successful, 731
  happy, 827
  elegant, 578
  apt, 23
Felicity
  happiness, 827
  prosperity, 734
  skill, 698
Feline
  stealthy, 528
  sly, 702
Fell
  mountain, 206
  cut down, 308
  knock down, 213
  dire, 162
  wicked, 907
Fellah
  commonalty, 876
Fellow
  similar, 17
  equal, 27
  companion, 88
  man, 373
  dual, 89
Fellow creature
  man, 372, 373
Fellow-feeling
  love, 897
  friendship, 888
  sympathy, 906, 914
Fellowship
  sociality, 892
  partnership, 712
  friendship, 888
Felo-de-se
  killing, 361
Felon
  sinner, 949
Felonious
  vice, 945
Felony
  guilt, 947
Felt
  matted, 219
Felucca
  ship, 273

Female
  woman, 374
Feminality
  feebleness, 160
Feminine
  woman, 374
Feminism
  rights, 924
Femme couverte
  marriage 903
Femme de chambre
  servant, 746
Fen
  marsh, 345
Fence
  circumscribe, 231
  enclose, 232
  defence, 717
  fight, 720, 722P
  safety, 664
  refuge, 666
  prison, 752
  to evade, 544
Fencible
  combatant, 726
Fend
  defence, 717
  provision, 637
Fenestrated
  windowed, 260
Feoff
  property, 780
Ferine
  malevolence, 907
Ferment
  disorder, 59
  energy, 171
  violence, 173
  agitation, 315
  effervesce, 353
Fern
  plant, 367
Ferocity
  brutality, 907
  violence, 173
Ferret
  tape, 45
Ferret out
  inquiry, 461
  discover, 480A
Ferry
  transference, 270
  way, 627
Fertile
  productive, 168

  abundant, 639
Ferule
  scourge, 975
Fervent
  devout, 990
Fervour
  heat, 382
  animation, 821
  desire, 865
  love, 897
Fester
  disease, 655
  corruption, 653
Festina lente
  haste, 684
Festival
  celebration, 883
  anniversary, 138
Festive
  amusement, 840
  sociality, 892
Festoon
  ornament, 847
  curvature, 245
Fetch
  bring, 270
  arrive, 292
  stratagem, 626
  evasion, 545
  price, 812
Fête
  amusement, 840
  ostentation, 882
  celebration, 883
  convivial, 892
Fête champêtre
  amusement, 840
Fetid
  fetor, 401
Fetish
  spell, 993
Fetishism
  idolatry, 991P
  sorcery, 992
Fetter
  hinder, 706
  restrain, 751
  shackle, 752
  join, 43
Fettle
  preparation, 673
Fetus
  see Foetus
Feud
  discord, 713

revenge, 919

Feudal
authority, 737

Feudatory
subjection, 749

Feu de joie
firework, 840
salute, 882

Feuilleton
essay, 595

Fever
heat, 382
disease, 655
excitement, 825

Few
fewness, 103
plurality, 100

Fez
cap, 225

Fiancée
love, 897

Fiasco
failure, 732

Fiat
command, 741

Fib
falsehood, 544, 546

Fibre
link, 45
filament, 205

Fibrous
thin, 203

Fichu
dress, 225

Fickle
irresolute, 605

Fictile
form, 240

Fiction
untruth, 546
fancy, 515
story, 594

Fictitious
false, 544

Fiddle
to play, 415
violin, 417
deceive, 545
swindle, 791
falsify, 544

Fiddle-de-dee
trifling, 643
contemptible, 930

Fiddle-faddle
trifle, 643

dawdle, 683

Fiddler
musician, 416

Fiddlestick
contemptible, 930
absurd, 497
trifling, 643

Fiddling
trifling, 643

Fidelity
honour, 939
observance, 772

Fidget
excitability, 825
irascibility, 901
agitation, 315
activity, 682

Fidgety
changeable, 149

Fido
mist, 353

Fiducial
belief, 484

Fidus Achates
auxiliary, 711

Fie!
disrepute, 874

Fief
property, 780

Field
plain, 344
arena, 728
scope, 180
business, 625
property, 780

Field-day
pageant, 882
festivity, 840

Field-marshal
master, 745

Field of view
vista, 441
idea, 453

Field-piece
arms, 727

Fiend
demon, 980
ruffian, 913

Fiendish
malevolent, 907
wicked, 945

Fierce
violent, 173
passion, 825
daring, 861

angry, 900

Fiery
violent, 173
excitable, 825
hot, 382
fervent, 821

Fiery cross
warfare, 722

Fife
musical instrument, 417

Fifth columnist
traitor, 742

Fig
unimportant, 643
dress, 225
adorn, 845, 847

Fight
contention, 720, 722

Fighter
combatant, 726
aircraft, 273A

Fighter-bomber
aircraft, 273A

Figment
imagination, 515

Figurante
the drama, 599

Figuration
form, 240

Figurative
metaphorical, 521
style, 577
comparison, 464

Figure
state, 7
number, 84
price, 812
form, 240
metaphor, 521, 566
imagine, 515
represent, 550, 554
reputation, 873
ugliness, 846
parade, 882

Figurehead
effigy, 554
inaction, 683

Figurine
sculpture, 557

Fike
whim, 481

Filament
slender, 205
ligature, 45
light, 423

Filamentous
thin, 203
Filch
steal, 791, 792
File
to smooth, 255
to pulverize, 330
to string together, 60
row, 69
duality, 89
collection, 72
list, 86
store, 636
register, 551
File off
march, 266
diverge, 291
Filial
posterity, 167
Filiation
consanguinity, 11
posterity, 167
derivation, 155
Filibeg
dress, 225
Filibuster
thief, 792
delay, 133
Filigree
crossing, 219
Filings
pulverulence, 330
Fill
occupy, 186
fullness, 52
Fill out
expand, 194
Fill up
complete, 52
close, 261
satisfy, 639
composition, 54
compensate, 30
Fille de joie
libertine, 962
Fillet
band, 45
circle, 247
gut, 297
Filling
contents, 190
Fillip
stimulus, 615
impulse, 276
propulsion, 284

Filly
horse, 271
young, 129
Film
layer, 204
dimness, 421, 426
semitransparency, 427
cinema, 599A
Filmy
texture, 329
Filter
clean, 652
percolate, 295
amend, 658
Filth
uncleanness, 653
Filtration
passage, 302
Fimbriated
rough, 256
Fin
instrument, 267, 633
Final
end, 67
conclusive, 478
resolved, 604
Finale
music, 415
Finance
money, 800
accounts, 811
Find
discover, 480A
term, 71
provide, 637
sentence, 969
acquisition, 775
Fine
rare, 322
textural, 329
good, 648
beautiful, 845
adorned, 847
thin, 203
mulct, 974
to clarify, 652
Fine-draw
improve, 658
Fine-spoken
courtesy, 894
Fine-spun
thinness, 203
Finery
ornament, 847
Finesse

cunning, 702
manœuvre, 545
tact, 698
taste, 850
Finger
touch, 379
instrument, 633
Finger-post
indication, 550
Finger-print
evidence, 467
sign, 550
Finical
unimportant, 643
Finicky
fastidious, 868
Finikin
unimportant, 643
Finis
end, 67
Finish
complete, 52
achieve, 729
end, 67
symmetry, 242
Finished
perfect, 242, 650
accomplished, 698
greatness, 31
Finite
smallness, 32
Fiord
gulf, 343
Fire
heat, 382, 384
furnace, 386
vigour, 574
energy, 171
to excite, 825
to urge, 615
dismiss, 756
Fire at
attack, 716
Fire away
begin, 66
Fire-brigade
cooling, 385
Fire-bug
incendiary, 384
Fire-drake
light, 423
Fire-eater
blusterer, 887
Fire-eater
fury, 173, 901

cooling, 385
Fire-escape
escape, 671
Fireoff
propulsion, 284
Fire-place
furnace, 386
Fire-ship
ship, 273
burning, 384
Fireup
resentment, 900
Fire-worshipper
heathen, 984
Firebrand
brand, 388
incendiary, 913
Firefly
luminary, 423
Firelock
arms, 727
Fireman
cooling, 385
Fireproof
incombustible, 385
safe, 664
Fireside
abode, 189
Firework
fire, 382
light, 423
display, 882
celebration, 883
Firing
fuel, 388
explosion, 406
Firkin
receptacle, 191
Firm
hard, 323
junction, 43
stable, 150
resolute, 604
brave, 861
party, 712
partnership, 797
friendship, 888
Firmament
world, 318
Firman
order, 741
permit, 760
decree, 963
First
beginning, 66

First-born
age, 124, 128
First-rate
ship, 273
excellent, 648
superiority, 33
First string
proficient, 700
First to last, from
whole, 50
completeness, 52
duration, 106
Firth
gulf, 343
Fisc
treasury, 802
Fiscal
money, 800
Fish
animal, 366
Fish for
desire, 865
Fish out
discover, 480A
Fish out of water
disagreement, 24
Fish up
elevation, 307
Fishery
domestication, 370
Fishy
dubious, 475, 478
Fissile
brittle, 328
Fission
disjunction, 44
Fissure
chink, 198
Fist
writing, 590
Fistula
opening, 260
Fit
state, 7
paroxysm, 173
disease, 655
caprice, 608
to prepare, 673
equalize, 27
excitement, 825
anger, 900
duty, 926
agreement, 23
expedient, 646
right, 922

Fit out
preparation, 673
Fitful
capricious, 608
irresolute, 605
discontinuous, 70
irregular, 139
Fitness
agreement, 23
Fitting
expedient, 646
right, 922, 926
due, 924
instrument, 633
Five
number, 98
Fiver
money, 800
Fix
place, 150, 184
rectify, 658, 660
solidify, 321
arrangement, 60
situation, 8
difficulty, 704
Fix together
junction, 43
Fix upon
choose, 609
Fixed
determined, 604
permanent, 141, 150
quiescent, 265
Fixture
property, 780
stability, 150
Fizgig
firework, 423
Fizz
sibilation, 409
bubble, 353
Fizzle
hiss, 409
Fizzle out
failure, 158, 732
Fjord
see Fiord
Flabbergast
astound, 870
Flabby
soft, 324
Flaccid
shrivelled, 172, 193
soft, 324
empty, 640

503

Flag
streamer, 550
flat stone, 204
weakness, 160
floor, 211
droop, 688
inactive, 683
infirm, 160, 655
slowness, 275
Flagellation
flogging, 972
atonement, 952
asceticism, 955
Flageolet
musical, 417
Flagitious
vice, 945
Flagrant
notorious, 531
manifest, 525
great, 31
atrocious, 945
Flagstaff
sign, 550
high, 206
Flail
impulse, 276
Flair
intelligence, 498
Flake
layer, 204
Flam
untruth, 546
Flambeau
luminary, 423
Flamboyant
vulgar, 851
ornamented, 577, 847
Flame
light, 420
fire, 382
luminary, 423
passion, 825
love, 897
favourable, 899
Flame–coloured
orange, 439
Flaming
excited, 821, 825
Flâneur
idler, 683
Flange
support, 215
Flank
side, 236

safety, 664
Flannel
flattery, 933
Flannels
dress, 225
Flap
adjunct, 39
hanging, 214
move about, 315
beat, 972
fear, 860
Flapdoodle
deception, 546
nonsense, 497
Flapjack
receptacle, 191
Flapper
girl, 129, 374
Flapping
loose, 47
Flare
glare, 420
violence, 173
Flare up
kindle, 825
anger, 900
Flaring
colour, 428
Flash
instant, 113
fire, 382
light, 420
thought, 451
sudden act, 612
violence, 173
Flash-lamp
light, 423
Flash note
money, 800
Flashback
memory, 505
cinema, 599A
Flashy
gaudy colour, 428
bad taste, 851
ostentatious, 882
Flask
receptacle, 191
Flat
level, 251
uniform, 16
horizontal, 213
novice, 701
dupe, 547
low, 207

vapid, 391
inert, 172, 823
dull, 841, 843
insipid, 575
dejected, 837
sound, 408
indifferent, 866
positive, 535
abode, 189
apartment, 191
Flatlet
abode, 189
Flatter
pleasure, 829
encourage, 858
adulation, 933
servility, 886
Flatterer
eulogist, 935
Flattie
detective, 461
cinema, 599A
Flatulent
windy, 338
gaseous, 334
style, 573
Flaunt
display, 873, 882
gaudy, 428
ornament, 847
Flautist
musician, 416
Flavour
taste, 390
Flavous
yellow, 436
Flaw
crack, 198
error, 495
imperfection, 651
blemish, 848
fault, 947
Flay
divest, 226
punish, 972
Flea-bag
bed, 215
Flea-bite
trifle, 643
Flea-bitten
variegated, 440
Fleckered
variegation, 440
Fledged
preparation, 673

504

Flee
escape, 671
avoid, 623
Fleece
tegument, 222
to rob, 791
to strip, 789
impoverish, 804
Fleer
ridicule, 956
Fleet
swift, 274
ships, 273
Fleeting
transient, 111
changeful, 607
Flesh
mankind, 372
carnality, 961
Flesh colour
redness, 434
Flesh-pots
food, 298
Fleshly
sensual, 954, 961
Fleshy
corpulent, 192
Flexible
pliant, 324
tractable, 705
Flexion
bending, 245
deviation, 279
fold, 258
Flexuous
convolution, 248
Flexure
bending, 245
fold, 258
Flibbertigibbet
trifler, 460
Flick
propel, 284
cinema, 599A
Flicker
flutter, 315
oscillate, 314
waver, 149, 605
shine, 420
Flickering
irregular, 139
Flight
departure, 287, 293
escape, 671
volitation, 267

swiftness, 174
multitude, 102
Flight-lieutenant
master, 745
Flight of Fancy
imagination, 515
idea, 453
Flighty
insane, 503
fickle, 605
Flim-flam
lie, 546
caprice, 608
Flimsy
texture, 329
soft, 324
irrational, 477
trifling, 643
frail, 160, 651
manuscript, 590
Flinch
fear, 850, 862
avoid, 623
swerve, 607
Fling
propel, 284
censure, 932
attack, 716
jeer, 929
amusement, 840
Fling away
relinquish, 782
Flint
hardness, 323
Flint-hearted
malevolence, 907
Flip
propel, 284
aviation, 267
Flippant
pert, 885
fluent, 584
Flipper
fin, 267
Flirt
propel, 284
coquette, 902
Flit
move, 264, 266
fluctuate, 149
depart, 293
escape, 671
swift, 274
thought, 451
Flitter

flutter, 315
Flitting
evanescent, 111, 149
roving, 266
Float
navigate, 267
buoy up, 305
lightness, 320
Float
sound, 405
vehicle, 272
Floater
error, 495, 732
solecism, 568
Flocculent
soft, 324
pulverulent, 330
Flock
herd, 366
assemblage, 72, 102
laity, 997
Flog
punishment, 972
steal, 791
Flong
engraving, 558
Flood
water, 348
abundance, 639
multitude, 72
superfluity, 641
increase, 35
of light, 420
Floodgate
conduit, 350
Floor
base, 221
level, 23
horizontal, 213
support, 215
to puzzle, 485, 704
to overthrow, 731
Floosy
girl, 374
Flop
flutter, 315
failure, 732
Flora
plant, 367, 379
Florid
colour, 428
red, 434
health, 654
style, 577

Flotilla
ship, 273
Flotsam
fragments, 51
little, 643
Flounce
quick motion, 274
agitation, 315
trimming, 230
fold, 258
Flounder
toss, 315
waver, 314
mistake, 495
to blunder, 499, 699,
732
struggle, 704
Flourish
brandish, 314
succeed, 731, 734
display, 873, 882
boast, 884
exaggerate, 549
of speech, 577, 582
Flout
mock, 856, 929
sneer, 929
Flow
stream, 347
motion, 264
course, 109
result from, 154
Flow out
egress, 295
Flow over
run over, 348
abound, 641
Flower
plant, 367
beauty, 845
perfection, 648, 650
prosper, 734
produce, 161
of life, 127
of speech, 577P
honour, 873
Flowing
style, 573
sound, 405
abundant, 639
Fluctuate
oscillate, 314
wavering, 605
Flue
air-pipe, 351
egress, 295

opening, 260
down, 320
dross, 643, 653
Fluent
speech, 584
style, 573
flowing, 348
skilful, 698
Fluff
lightness, 320
Fluid
liquidity, 333
Fluke
angularity, 244
chance, 621
Flummery
vain, 643
flattery, 933
absurd, 497
Flummox
bewilder, 458
Flunk
break down, 158
Flunkey
lackey, 746
toady, 886
flatterer, 935
Fluorescence
light, 420
Flurry
hurry, 684
discompose, 458
agitation, 821, 825
Flush
flat, 251
flood, 348
heat, 382
light, 420
redness, 434
abundance, 639
feeling, 821
passion, 825
series, 69
flock, 72
rich, 803
in liquor, 959
Flushed
elated, 836, 884
vain, 880
proud, 878
Fluster
excitement, 824
fuss, 682
discompose, 458
Flustered

tipsy, 959
Flute
musical, 417
Fluted
furrow, 259
Flutter
move, 315
fear, 860
feeling, 821, 824, 825
Fluviatile
river, 348
Flux
flow, 109, 348
excretion, 299
motion, 264
oscillation, 314
changes, 140
Fly
depart, 293
take wing, 287
speed, 274
escape, 671
recede, 287
shun, 623
run away, 862
lose colour, 429
minute, 193
time, 109, 111
burst, 173, 328
vehicle, 272
clever, 498
cunning, 702
Fly at
attack, 716
Fly back
recoil, 277
elastic, 325
Fly-down
unclean, 653
Fly-leaf
insertion, 228
book, 593
Fly out
burst, 173
passion, 825
anger, 900
Fly-boat
ship, 273
Flying boat
aircraft, 273A
Flying bomb
arms, 727
Flying fortress
aircraft, 273A

Flying wing
aircraft, 273A
Flyover
way, 627
Flyte
curse, 908
Flywheel
instrument, 633
rotation, 312
Foal
young, 129
carrier, 271
Foam
spray, 353
passion, 173, 900
Fob
pocket, 191
to cheat, 545
evade, 773
Focus
reunion, 74
centre, 223
Fodder
food, 298
Foe
antagonist, 710
enemy, 891
Foetid
see Fetid
Foetus
infant, 129
Fog
cloud, 353
dimness, 422
Foggy
obscure, 447
shaded, 426
Fogy
veteran, 130
Föhn
wind, 349
Foible
vice, 945
Foil
contrast, 14
success, 731
Foiled
failure, 732
Foist in
insert, 228, 300
Foist upon
deception, 545
Fold
plait, 258
enclosure, 232

pen, 752
congregation, 996
bisect, 91
Foliaceous
layer, 204
Foliage
plant, 367
Foliated
layer, 204
Folio
book, 593
Folk
man, 373
Folk-dance
dance, 840
Folk-tale
legend, 594
Follicle
hollow, 252
opening, 260
cyst, 191
Follow
in order, 63
in time, 117
in motion, 281
to imitate, 19
pursue, 622
result from, 154
understand, 518
demonstration, 478
obey, 743
Follow on
continue, 143
Follow suit
conformity, 82
Follow up
inquiry, 461
Follower
sequence, 281
partisan, 746
Folly
irrationality, 499
nonsense, 497
building, 189
Foment
promote, 707
excite, 173
Fond
love, 897
Fondle
endearment, 902
Fondling
favourite, 899
Fondness
love, 897

desire, 865
Font
altar, 1000
Food
eatable, 298
materials, 635, 637
Fool
silly, 501
to deceive, 548
Foolhardy
rashness, 863
Foolish
unwise, 499
trifling, 643
irrational, 477, 497
misguided, 699
Foot
stand, 211
metre, 597
Foot it
walk, 266
dance, 840
Foot-pace
slowness, 275
Footfall
motion, 264
trace, 551
Foothold
influence, 175
support, 215
Footing
situation, 8, 183
state, 7
foundation, 211
place, 58
rank, 71
influence, 175
Footle
trifle, 683
Footlights
drama, 599
Footling
silly, 499
Footman
servant, 746
Footmark
record, 551
Footpad
thief, 792
Footpath
way, 627
Footprint
record, 551
Footslog
journey, 266

hinder, 706

Forge
produce, 161
furnace, 386
workshop, 691
trump up, 544

Forge ahead
advance, 282

Forgery
untruth, 546
imitation, 19

Forget
oblivion, 506

Forgive
foregiveness, 918

Forgo
relinquish, 624, 782
renounce, 757

Forgotten
unremembered, 506
ingratitude, 917

Fork
angularity, 244
bisection, 91

Fork out
give, 784
expend, 809

Forlorn
abandoned, 893
dejected, 837
woebegone, 828

Forlorn hope
hopeless, 859
danger, 665

Form
shape, 240
state, 7
arrange, 60
rule, 80
to make up, 54
produce, 161
educate, 537
habituate, 613
bench, 215
part, 569
fashion, 852
etiquette, 882
law, 963
rite, 998
fours, 58
manner, 627
beauty, 845
likeness, 21
pupils, 541

Formal

regular, 82
affected, 855
positive, 535

Formalism
hypocrisy, 988

Formality
ceremony, 852
parade, 882
law, 963

Format
style, 7

Formation
production, 161
shape, 240

Formed of
composition, 54

Former
in order, 62
in time, 122

Formication
itching, 380

Formidable
fear, 860
difficult, 704
great, 31

Formless
amorphism, 241

Formula
rule, 80
precept, 697
law, 963
number, 84

Fornication
impurity, 961

Fornicator
libertine, 962

Forsake
relinquish, 624

Forsooth
truth, 494

Forswear
renounce, 624
retract, 607
refuse, 764
perjure, 544, 940
violate, 927

Fort
defence, 717
refuge, 666

Forte
excellence, 698

Forte
loudness, 404

Forth
progression, 282

Forthcoming
futurity, 121, 673

Forthwith
transient, 111

Fortification
defence, 717
refuge, 666

Fortify
strength, 159

Fortitude
courage, 861
endurance, 826

Fortnight
period, 108, 138

Fortress
defence, 716
prison, 752

Fortuitous
chance, 156, 621

Fortunate
opportune, 134
prosperous, 734

Fortune
chance, 156
accident, 621
wealth, 803

Fortune-teller
oracle, 513

Fortune-telling
prediction, 511

Forum
tribunal, 966
school, 542

Forward
early, 132
to advance, 282
to help, 707
active, 682
willing, 602
vain, 880
impertinent, 885

Fosse
furrow, 259
gap, 198
defence, 717
enclosure, 232

Fossick
inquiry, 461

Fossil
antiquated, 851
old, 124
bore, 841

Foster
aid, 707

Fou
drunken, 959
Foul
bad, 649
corrupt, 653
odour, 401
offensive, 830
ugly, 846
vicious, 945
Foul-mouthed
malevolent, 907
Foul-tongued
scurrilous, 934
Found
cause, 153
prepare, 673
Foundation
base, 211
support, 215
Founder
originator, 164
sink, 310, 732
Foundling
outcast, 893
Fount
origin, 153
spring, 348
type, 591
Fountain
cause, 153
river, 348
store, 636
Fountain-pen
writing, 590
Four
number, 95
Four-square
number, 95
Fourfold
number, 96
Fourscore
number, 98
Fourth
number, 97
Fowl
animal, 366
Fowling-piece
arms, 727
Fox
cunning, 702
Fox-trot
dance, 840
Foxhole
refuge, 666
defence, 717
Foxhound

chase, 622
Foyer
room, 191
Fracas
contention, 720
brawl, 713
Fraction
part, 51
numerical, 84
Fractious
irascibility, 901
Fracture
disjunction, 44
discontinuity, 70, 198
to break, 328
Fragile
brittle, 328
frail, 149, 160
Fragment
part, 51
Fragrant
fragrant, 400
'Fraid-cat
coward, 862
Frail
brittle, 328
mutable, 149
weak, 160
irresolute, 605
imperfect, 651
unchaste, 961
failing, 945
Frame
condition, 7
support, 215
texture, 329
form, 240
substance, 316
to construct, 161
border, 230
Franc-tireur
fighter, 726
Franchise
right, 924
freedom, 748
exemption, 927
Franciscan
clergy, 996
Frangible
brittle, 328
Frank
artless, 703
open, 525
sincere, 543
honourable, 939

Frankincense
fragrant, 400
Frantic
delirious, 503
violent, 173
excited, 825
Fraternal
brotherly, 11
friendly, 888, 906
Fraternity
assemblage, 72
company, 712, 892
Fraternize
co-operate, 709
harmonize, 714
Fratricide
killing, 361
Fraud
deception, 544, 545
dishonour, 940
Fraught
having, 777
full of, 639
Fray
contention, 720
to abrade, 331
Freak
caprice, 608
unconformity, 83
Freakish
irresolution, 605
Freckle
blemish, 848
Freckled
variegation, 440
Free
detached, 44
at liberty, 748
spontaneous, 600, 602
exempt, 927
unobstructed, 705
liberal, 816
gratuitous, 815
insolent, 885
Free-born
freedom, 748
Free gift
giving, 784
Free play
freedom, 748
Free-spoken
veracity, 543
Free-thinking
religion, 989

Free will
will, 600
Freebooter
thief, 792
Freedom
liberty, 748
looseness, 47
full play, 705
exemption, 927
space, 180
Freehold
property, 780
freedom, 748
Freelance
writer, 590
Freemasonry
secrecy, 528
sign, 550
fraternity, 712
co-operation, 709
Freeze
frigefaction, 385
stop dead, 265
Freight
contents, 190
cargo, 798
transfer, 270
Freight train
vehicle, 272
Frenzy
insanity, 503
Frequency
repetition, 104
Frequent
in time, 136
in number, 102
in space, 186
Fresco
painting, 556
Fresh
new, 123
cold, 383
colour, 428
unforgotten, 505
healthy, 654
good, 648
cheeky, 885
tipsy, 959
Freshet
flood, 348
Freshman
learner, 541
Fret
suffer, 378
grieve, 828

to gall, 830
sadness, 837
to irritate, 900
adorn, 847
Fretful
irascibility, 901
Fretwork
crossing, 219
Freya
love, 897
Friable
pulverulence, 330
Friar
clergy, 996
Friar's lantern
light, 423
Fribble
trifle, 460, 643
dawdle, 683
Friction
rubbing, 331
obstacle, 179
discord, 713
Friend
well-wisher, 890
relation, 11
auxiliary, 711
Friendless
seclusion, 893
Friendly
amical, 714, 888
helping, 707
Friendship
amical, 714, 888
Frieze
summit, 210
Frig
refrigerator, 387
Frigate
ship, 273
Frigga
goddess, 979
Fright
alarm, 860
ugliness, 846
Frightful
great, 31
hideous, 846
dreadful, 830
Frigid
cold, 383
callous, 823
reluctant, 603
indifferent, 866
Frigorific

refrigeration, 385
Frill
border, 230
Frills
affectation, 855
Fringe
lace, 256
ornament, 847
Frippery
dress, 225
trifle, 643
ornament, 847
ridiculous, 853
Frisk
brisk, 682
gay, 836
amuse, 840
Frisky
nimble, 274
leap, 309
in spirits, 836
Frith
strait, 343
chasm, 198
Fritter
small part, 51
waste, 135, 638, 683
misuse, 679
diminish, 36
Frivol
trifle, 460
Frivolous
unimportant, 643
silly, 499
frisky, 836
Frizzle
curl, 248
fold, 258
Frock
dress, 225
Frog
ornament, 847
Frogman
depth, 208
dive, 310
Frolic
amusement, 840
Frolicsome
cheerful, 836
Front
fore-part, 234
precession, 280
beginning, 66
exterior, 220
resistance, 719

511

Frontal
beginning, 66
exterior, 220
Frontier
limit, 233
vicinity, 199
Fronting
antiposition, 237
Frontispiece
prefix, 64
front, 234
Frost
cold, 383
failure, 732
Froth
bubble, 353
trifle, 643
style, 577
Frounce
fold, 258
Froward
irascible, 901
discourteous, 895
Frown
disapprove, 932
anger, 900
scowl, 839, 895
lower, 837
Frowzy
fetor, 401
Fructify
production, 161
productiveness, 168
prosper, 734
Frugal
temperate, 953
economical, 817
Fruit
result, 154
acquisition, 775
Fruitful
productive, 168
Fruition
pleasure, 827
fulfilment, 729
Fruitless
useless, 645
unproductive, 169
abortive, 732
Frump
dowdy, 851
dirty, 653
Frustrate
defeat, 731
prevent, 706

Frustration
failure, 732
Frustrum
part, 51
Fry
young, 129
small, 193
heat, 384
Frying-pan
furnace, 386
Fubsy
short, 201
broad, 202
Fuddled
drunk, 959
Fudge
nonsense, 497
trivial, 643
sweet, 396
Fuel
combustible, 388
materials, 635
Fug
stink, 401
Fugacious
transitory, 111
Fugitive
escape, 287, 671
changeful, 149, 607
transitory, 111
evasive, 623
emigrant, 268
Fugleman
prototype, 22
director, 694
leader, 745
Fugue
music, 415
Führer
master, 745
Fulcrum
support, 215
Fulfil
observe, 772
duty, 926
complete, 729
Fulgent
light, 420
Fulguration
light, 420
Fuliginous
black, 422, 431
opaque, 426
Full
much, 31

complete, 52
sound, 404
abundant, 639
Full-blown
expansion, 194
Full-grown
expansion, 194
Fullness
satiety, 869
Fullness of time
occasion, 124
Fully
great, 31
Fulminate
loud, 404
violent, 173
malediction, 908
threat, 909
Fulsome
nauseous, 395
adulatory, 933
Fulvous
yellow, 436
Fumble
derange, 61
handle, 379
awkward, 699
Fumbler
bungler, 701
Fume
exhalation, 334
heat, 382
adorn, 847
odour, 398
violence, 173
excitement, 825
anger, 900
Fumigate
cleanness, 652
Fun
amusement, 840
Function
business, 625
duty, 926
utility, 644
number, 84
operate, 170
Functionary
consignee, 758
Fund
capital, 800
store, 636, 639
Fundamental
basis, 211, 215
note, 413

Fundamentalism
heterodoxy, 984A
Fundamentally
greatness, 31
Funds
money, 800
wealth, 803
treasury, 802
Funeral
interment, 363
Fungus
convexity, 250
Funicle
filament, 205
Funk
fear, 860
cowardice, 862
Funk-hole
refuge, 666
Funnel
opening, 260
channel, 350
air-pipe, 351
Funnel-shaped
concave, 252
Funny
witty, 842
ridiculous, 853
peculiar, 83
ship, 273
Fur
hair, 256
dirt, 653
Furbish
improve, 658
prepare, 673
beautify, 845
ornament, 847
Furfur
unclean, 653
Furfuraceous
pulverulent, 330
Furious
great, 31
violent, 173
passion, 825
enraged, 900
velocity, 274
Furl
roll up, 312
Furlough
permission, 760
Furnace
furnace, 386
Furnish

provide, 637
prepare, 673
give, 215, 784
Furniture
materials, 635
equipment, 633
goods, 780
Furor
excitement, 825
Furore
rage, 865
excitement, 825
Furrow
furrow, 198, 259
Further
aid, 707
Furthermore
addition, 37
Furtive
clandestine, 528
false, 544
stealing, 791
Fury
violence, 173
excitation, 825
anger, 900
temper, 901
demon, 980
revenge, 919.
evildoer, 913
Fuscous
brown, 433
Fuse
melt, 335
heat, 382, 384
combine, 48
Fusee
fuel, 388
Fushionless
lazy, 683
Fusiform
pointed, 253
angular, 244
Fusilier
combatant, 726
Fusillade
killing, 361
Fusion
liquefaction, 335
heat, 384
union, 48
Fuss
haste, 684
activity, 682
agitation, 315

hurry, 825
Fussy
fastidious, 868
faddy, 481
Fustian
nonsense, 497
ridiculous, 853
style, 477
Fusty
fetor, 401
dirt, 653
Futile
useless, 645
unavailing, 732
Futilitarian
pessimist, 837
Future
futurity, 121
Futurist
artist, 559
Fylfot
cross, 219

G.I.
fighter, 726
G-man
detective, 461
G.P.
doctor, 662
Gab
speech, 582
Gabble
loquacity, 584
Gabby
loquacious, 584
Gabelle
tax, 812
Gaberdine
dress, 225
Gaberlunzie
tramp, 876
Gaby
fool, 501
Gad about
journey, 266
Gadget
contrivance, 626
tool, 633
Gaffer
man, 373
veteran, 130
clown, 876
foreman, 694

Gag
 speechless, 581, 585
 muzzle, 403, 751
 interpolation, 228
 wit, 842

Gaga
 insane, 503

Gage
 security, 771

Gaggle
 flock, 72

Gaiety
 see Gay

Gain
 acquisition, 775
 advantage, 618
 to learn, 539

Gain ground
 improve, 658

Gain upon
 approach, 286
 become a habit, 613

Gainful
 utility, 644, 810

Gainless
 inutility, 645

Gainsay
 negation, 536

Gait
 walk, 264
 speed, 274
 way, 627

Gaiter
 dress, 225

Gala
 festival, 840
 display, 882

Galahad
 perfection, 650

Galaxy
 stars, 318
 assembly, 72
 luminary, 423
 multitude, 102
 glory, 873

Gale
 wind, 349

Gall
 bitterness, 395
 pain, 378
 to pain, 830
 insolence, 885
 malevolence, 907
 anger, 900

Gallant
 brave, 861

 courteous, 894
 lover, 897
 licentious, 961, 962

Gallantry
 love, 897

Galleon
 ship, 273

Galley
 room, 191
 theatre, 599
 passage, 260

Gallery
 ship, 273
 prison, 752

Galliard
 dance, 840

Gallicism
 neology, 563

Galligaskins
 dress, 225

Gallimaufry
 mixture, 41

Galliot
 ship, 273

Gallipot
 receptacle, 191

Gallivant
 travel, 266

Gallop
 ride, 266
 scamper, 274

Gallophobia
 dislike, 867

Galloway
 carrier, 271

Gallows
 scourge, 975

Gallup poll
 inquiry, 461

Galore
 multitude, 102
 sufficiency, 639

Galosh
 dress, 225

Galumph
 exult, 836

Galvanic
 violent, 173

Galvanism
 excitation, 824

Galvanize
 energize, 171

Gambade
 leap, 309
 prank, 856

Gamble
 chance, 156, 621

Gambler
 rashness, 863

Gambol
 amusement, 840

Game
 chance, 156
 pursuit, 622
 plan, 626
 intent, 620
 amusement, 840
 resolute, 604
 brave, 861

Game-cock
 courage, 861

Game reserve
 menagerie, 370

Gamekeeper
 keeper, 753

Gamesome
 cheerful, 836

Gamin
 commonalty, 876

Gammon
 untruth, 544, 546,
 to hoax, 545

Gamut
 harmony, 413

Gamy
 pungent, 392

Gander
 look, 441

Gang
 party, 712
 knot, 72

Gangling
 lank, 203

Gangrel
 tramp, 876
 pauper, 804

Gangrene
 disease, 655

Gangster
 evildoer, 913, 949
 swindler, 792

Gangway
 way, 627
 opening, 260

Gaol
 see Jail

Gap
 discontinuity, 70
 chasm, 4, 198

Gape
open, 260
wonder, 870
curiosity, 455
desire, 865
Garage
house, 189
Garb
dress, 225
Garbage
unclean, 653
Garble
retrench, 38
misinterpret, 523
falsify, 544
Garbled
incomplete, 53
Garçon
servant, 746
Garden
beauty, 845
Gardening
agriculture, 371
Gargantuan
size, 192
Gargle
water, 337
Gargoyle
spout, 350
Garish
colour, 428
light, 420
ornament, 847
display, 882
Garland
ornament, 847
trophy, 733
Garlic
condiment, 393
Garment
dress, 225
Garner
collect, 72
store, 636
Garnet
ornament, 847
Garnish
adorn, 845
ornament, 847
addition, 39
Garret
room, 191
high, 206
Garrison
combatant, 726

defend, 664, 717
Garrotte
killing, 361
punishment, 972
gallows, 975
Garrulity
loquacity, 584
Gas
rarity, 322
gaseity, 334
to chatter, 584
to boast, 884
Gas-bag
loquacity, 584
Gas-mantle
light, 423
Gasconade
boasting, 884
Gaselier
light, 423
Gash
disjunction, 44, 198
Gaslight print
photograph, 556
Gasolene
oil, 356
Gasometer
gas, 334
store, 636
Gasp
pant, 349, 688
desire, 865
droop, 655
Gastronomy
gluttony, 957
epicurism, 868
Gat
gun, 727
Gate
beginning, 66
way, 627
mouth, 260
barrier, 232
Gate-crasher
parasite, 886
Gather
collect, 72, 789
acquire, 775
enlarge, 194
learn, 539
conclude, 480
fold, 258
unite in a focus, 74
Gathering
disease, 655

Gatling
gun, 727
Gauche
unskilful, 699
ill-mannered, 851
Gaud
ornament, 847
Gaudery
vanity, 880
Gaudy
colouring, 428
ornamental, 847
Gaudy
vulgar, 851
flaunting, 882
party, 72, 892
Gauge
measure, 466
Gaunt
spare, 203
ugliness, 846
Gauntlet
defiance, 715
punishment, 972
glove, 225
anger, 909
Gautama
religious founder, 986
Gauze
shade, 424
Gauzy
filmy, 329
Gavotte
dance, 840
music, 415
Gawky
awkward, 699
ridiculous, 853
ugly, 846
Gay
cheerful, 836
adorned, 847
colour, 428
Gaze
vision, 441
Gazebo
look-out, 441
building, 189
Gazelle
velocity, 274
Gazette
publication, 531
record, 551
Gazetted
bankrupt, 808

Gazetteer
list, 86
Gazing-stock
prodigy, 872
Gear
clothes, 225
harness, 633
Gee!
wonder, 870
Gee-gee
carrier, 271
Geezer
veteran, 130
Gehenna
hell, 982
Geisha
dancer, 599
Gelatine
pulpiness, 354
Gelatinous
semiliquid, 352
Gelding
carrier, 271
Gelid
cold, 383
Gelignite
arms, 727
Gem
jewel, 650
ornament, 847
goodness, 648
Gemination
duplicate, 90
Gemini
duality, 89
Gen
information, 527
Gendarme
police, 965
Gender
class, 75
Genealogy
continuity, 69
filiation, 155
General
generic, 78
officer, 745
Generalissimo
master, 745
Generality
generic, 78
Generalship
conduct, 692
Generate
produce, 161, 168

Generation
mankind, 372
period, 108
Generic
general, 78
Generous
liberal, 816
benevolent, 906
giving, 784
unselfish, 942
Genesis
production, 161
Genial
warm, 382
cordial, 602, 829
courteous, 894
cheerful, 836
Geniculated
angular, 244
Genie
demon, 980
Genius
talent, 498
intellect, 450
skill, 698
spirit, 979
proficient, 700
Genius loci
location, 184
Genocide
killing, 361
Genre
class, 75
style, 7
painting, 556
Genteel
fashionable, 852
Gentile
heathen, 984
Gentility
rank, 875
politeness, 852, 894
Gentle
moderate, 174
slow, 275
meek, 826
lenient, 740
courteous, 894
sound, 405
Gentleman
person, 373
squire, 875
man of honour, 939
Gentlemanly
polite, 852

noble, 875
courteous, 894
Gentlewoman
woman, 374
Gently
slowly, 174, 275
Gentry
nobility, 875
Genuflexion
bow, 308
homage, 725, 743
respect, 928
servility, 886
worship, 990
Genuine
true, 494
real, 1
good, 648
Genus
class, 75
Geodesy
measurement, 466
Geography
place, 183
Geology
mineral, 358
Geometry
measurement, 466
Geriatrics
remedy, 662
Germ
rudiment, 153, 674
beginning, 66
bane, 663
insalubrity, 657
Germane
relation, 23
Germinate
sprout, 154, 194
produce, 153
Gerrymander
garble, 544
cunning, 702
Gestapo
detective, 461
Gestation
pregnancy, 168
production, 161
preparation, 673
Gesticulate
sign, 550
Gesture
hint, 527
indication, 550

Get
  acquire, 775
  understand, 518
  become, 144
Get about
  publication, 531
Get among
  mixture, 41
Get at
  tamper with, 682
  find out, 480A
Get-at-able
  attainable, 705
Get back
  arrival, 292
Get before
  precedency, 62
Get by
  succeed, 731
Get down
  descend, 306
Get home
  arrive, 292
Get off
  depart, 293
  liberate, 750
  escape, 927
Get on
  advance, 282
  succeed, 731
  improve, 658
Get on to
  blame, 932
Get out
  repulsion, 289
  ejection, 297
Get-out
  plea, 617
Get round
  circumvent, 702
Get the start
  precede, 62
Get to
  arrive, 292
Get together
  assemble, 72
Get up
  rise, 305
  prepare, 673
  style, 7
Get wind
  come to light, 525
Getaway
  escape, 671
Gewgaw

  trifle, 643
  ornament, 847
Geyser
  heat, 382
  furnace, 386
Ghastly
  tedious, 846
  frightful, 860
Ghost
  soul, 450
  apparition, 980
  shade, 362
  emaciated, 193
  Deity, 976
  instrumentality, 631
Ghoul
  demon, 980
  evildoer, 913
Giant
  tall, 206
  large, 192
Gibber
  stammer, 583
  unmeaning, 517
Gibberish
  jargon, 519
  nonsense, 517
  absurdity, 497
Gibbet
  gallows, 975
  to execute, 972
Gibbous
  globose, 249
  convex, 250
  distorted, 244
Gibe
  jeer, 856, 932
  taunt, 929
Giddiness
  caprice, 608
  inattention, 458
  bungling, 699
Giddy
  careless, 460
  irresolute, 605
  bungling, 699
  light-headed, 503
Gift
  given, 784
  power, 157
  talent, 698
Gig
  vehicle, 272
  ship, 273
Gigantic

  large, 192
  tall, 206
Giggle
  laugh, 838
Gild
  adorn, 845
  ornament, 847
  coat, 222
Gill
  river, 348
Gillie
  servant, 746
Gimbals
  rotation, 312
Gimble
  rotate, 312
Gimcrack
  brittle, 328
  weak, 160
  valueless, 645
  imperfect, 651
  ornament, 847
  whim, 865
Gimlet
  perforator, 262
Gimmick
  speciality, 79
Gin
  trap, 667
Ginger
  pungency, 392
  condiment, 393
  vigour, 574
Ginger up
  excite, 824
Gingerbread
  flimsy, 651
  ornament, 847
Gingerly
  carefully, 459
  slowly, 275
Gipsy
  deceiver, 548
  fortune-teller, 513
Girandole
  luminary, 423
Gird
  bind, 43
  surround, 227
  enclose, 231
  strengthen, 159
Girder
  bond, 45
  beam, 215

Girdle
circular, 247
outline, 229
connection, 45

Girl
young, 129
female, 374

Girl friend
sweetheart, 897

Girth
band, 45
outline, 229

Gist
essence, 5
important, 642
meaning, 516

Gittern
musical instrument, 417

Give
giving, 784
regress, 283
bend, 324

Give and take
probity, 939

Give back
restitute, 790

Give ear
listen, 418

Give entrance to
reception, 296

Give forth
publish, 531

Give in
submit, 725
obey, 743

Give notice
inform, 527
warn, 668

Give out
emit, 297
bestow, 784
publish, 531
teach, 537
end, 67

Give over
relinquish, 624
cease, 142
lose hope, 859

Give up
relinquish, 624
resign, 757
yield, 743
cease, 142
reject, 610
property, 782
despair, 859

Give way
yield, 725
obey, 743
despond, 837

Gizzard
receptacle, 191

Glabrous
smooth, 255

Glacial
cold, 383

Glaciate
frigefaction, 385

Glacier
cold, 383

Glacis
defence, 717

Glad
pressure, 827, 829
cheerful, 836

Glad eye
ogle, 441, 902

Glad hand
conviviality, 892

Glade
opening, 260
hollow, 252
thicket, 367

Gladiator
combatant, 726

Gladiatorial
warfare, 722

Gladsome
pleasurable, 829

Glairy
semiliquid, 352

Glamour
sorcery, 992

Glance
look, 441
rapid motion, 274
attend to, 457
hint, 527, 550

Glare
light, 420
visible, 446
colour, 428

Glaring
greatness, 31
manifest, 518, 525

Glass
vessel, 191
brittle, 328
smooth, 255
spectacles, 445

Glasshouse

prison, 752

Glassy
dim, 422
transparent, 425
colourless, 429

Glaucous
green, 435

Glaur
mud, 352
dirt, 653

Glazed
smooth, 255

Gleam
ray, 429
smallness, 32

Glean
choose, 609
take, 789
acquire, 775
learn, 539

Glebe
land, 342

Glee
satisfaction, 827
merriment, 836
music, 415

Gleeman
musician, 416

Glen
concavity, 252

Glengarry
cap, 225

Glib
valuble, 584
facile, 705

Glide
move, 266
aviation, 267
slowly, 275
course, 109

Glider
aircraft, 273A

Glimmer
light, 420
dimness, 422

Glimmering
slight knowledge, 490,
491

Glimpse
sight, 441
acknowledge, 490

Glint
shine, 420

Glissade
descent, 306

Glissando
music, 415

Glisten
shine, 420

Glitter
shine, 420, 873
display, 882

Gloaming
evening, 126
dimness, 422

Gloat
look, 441
revel, 377, 827
boast, 884

Global
worldwide, 318

Globe
sphere, 249
world, 318

Globe-trotter
traveller, 268

Globule
spherule, 249
minute, 32, 193

Glockenspiel
musical, 417

Glomeration
assembly, 72

Gloom
darkness, 421
sadness, 837

Glorify
approve, 931
worship, 990

Glory
honour, 873
light, 420
boast, 884
pride, 878

Gloss
light, 420
smoothness, 255
beauty, 845
plea, 617
falsehood, 546
interpretation, 522

Gloss over
neglect, 460
inattention, 458
sophistry, 477
vindication, 937
falsehood, 544

Glossary
interpretation, 522
verbal, 562

Glossy
smooth, 255

Glove
cartel, 715

Glow
shine, 420
colour, 428
warmth, 382
passion, 821
style, 574

Glow-worm
luminary, 423

Glower
scowl, 895

Gloze
flatter, 933
palliate, 937

Glucose
sweetness, 396

Glue
cement, 45
to stick, 46
viscosity, 352

Glum
discontented, 832
dejected, 837
sulky, 895

Glut
redundance, 641
satiety, 869

Glutinous
coherence, 46
semiliquid, 352

Gluttony
excess, 957
desire, 865

Glycerine
semiliquid, 352

Glyptography
engraving, 558

Gnarled
rough, 256

Gnash
anger, 900

Gnat
littleness, 193

Gnaw
eat, 296
corrode, 659
pain, 378
give pain, 830

Gnome
demon, 980
maxim, 496

Gnomic

sententious, 572

Gnosis
knowledge, 490

Gnostic
intellectual, 450
mystic, 528

Go
move, 264
depart, 293
vigour, 574
energy, 171, 682
try, 675

Go about
undertake, 676

Go across
passage, 302

Go ahead
advance, 282
improve, 658
activity, 682

Go-ahead
energetic, 171

Go bail
security, 771

Go-between
intermedium, 228, 631
messenger, 534
agent, 758

Go by
pass, 303

Go-by
evasion, 623

Go down
sink, 306
decline, 659

Go forth
depart, 293
publish, 531

Go-getter
activity, 682

Go halves
divide, 91

Go hand in hand with
accompany, 88

Go in for
business, 625

Go near
approach, 286

Go off
cease, 142
explode, 173
die, 360
fare, 151

Go on
continue, 143

Go over
change sides, 607
Go round
circuition, 311
Go through
pass, 302
complete, 729
endure, 821
Go to
direction, 278
remonstrance, 695
Go under
name, 564
sink, 310
ruin, 735
Go up
ascent, 305
Go with
assent, 488
suit, 646
Goad
motive, 615
Goal
object, 620
reach, 292
Goat
fool, 501
Goatish
impure, 961
Gobbet
piece, 51
Gobble
devour, 296
gluttony, 957
cry, 412
Gobbledygook
verbiage, 573
Gobemouche
credulous, 486
fool, 501
dupe, 547
Goblin
ghost, 980
bugbear, 860
God
Deity, 976
Goddess
great spirit, 979
favourite, 899
beauty, 845
Godless
irreligion, 989
Godlike
virtue, 944
Godliness

piety, 987
Godown
store, 636, 799
Godsend
luck, 621
advantage, 618
success, 731
Goer
horse, 271
Goggle
optical instrument, 445
to stare, 441
Goggle-eyed
dimsighted, 443
Golconda
wealth, 803
Gold
money, 800
Gold-digger
flirt, 902
selfishness, 943
Golden
yellow, 436
Golden age
pleasure, 827
prosperity, 734
imagination, 515
Golden calf
idols, 986
Golden-mouthed
ornament, 577
Golden wedding
celebration, 883
anniversary, 138
Goldsmith
artist, 559
Goliath
strength, 159
giant, 192
Gombeen-man
usurer, 805
Gomeril
fool, 501
Gondola
ship, 273
Gondolier
mariner, 269
Gone
non-extant, 2
absent, 187
dead, 360
Gone by
past, 123
Gone on
loving, 897

Gonfalon
flag, 550
Gong
resonance, 417
decoration, 877
Goniometer
angle, 244
measure, 466
Goo
adhesive, 45
viscid, 352
Good
advantage, 618
advantageous, 648
virtuous, 944
right, 922
tasty, 394
Good-bye
departure, 293
Good day
arrival, 292
salute, 894
Good-fellowship
892
Good-for-nothing
rascal, 949
Good humour
cheerfulness, 836
Good-looking
beauty, 845
Good manners
courtesy, 894
Good morning
salute, 894
Good nature
benevolence, 906
inexcitability, 826
Good show
approval, 931
Goodly
large, 192
beautiful, 845
Goods
effects, 780
Goods train
vehicle, 272
Goodwill
benevolence, 906
friendship, 888
merchandise, 798
materials, 635
Goody
woman, 374
Gooey
sticky, 46

Goo-goo eyes
ogle, 902
Goon
rascal, 949
Goose
fool, 501
Goose-skin
cold, 383
Gorblimey
vulgar, 876
Gordian knot
problem, 461
difficulty, 704
Gore
opening, 260
angularity, 244
Gorge
ravine, 198
narrowness, 203
to devour, 296
full, 641
satiety, 869
gluttony, 957
Gorgeous
colour, 428
splendid, 845
ornamented, 847
Gorgon
fear, 860
ugliness, 846
Gormandize
gluttony, 957
reception, 296
Gory
killing, 361
Gospel
scripture, 985
truth, 494
certainty, 474
Gossamer
texture, 329
slender, 205
light, 320
Gossip
conversation, 588
chatterer, 584
news, 532
Gossoon
boy, 129, 373
Goth
barbarian, 876
evildoer, 913
Gothic
vulgarity, 851
defacement, 241

Gouache
painting, 556
Gouge
concavity, 252
Gourmand
gluttony, 957
epicure, 868
Gourmet
desire, 865
epicure, 868
gluttony, 957
Goût
taste, 850
Govern
direct, 693
authority, 737
Governess
teacher, 540
Governess-cart
vehicle, 272
Governor
director, 694
master, 745
tutor, 540
Gowk
fool, 501
Gown
dress, 225
Grab
snatch, 789
steal, 791
booty, 793
Grabble
fumble, 379
Grace
elegance, 845
polish, 850
forgiveness, 918
honour, 939
title, 877
piety, 987
worship, 990
thanks, 916
style, 578
Grace-note
music, 415
Grace-stroke
killing, 361
Graceless
ungraceful, 846
vicious, 945
impenitent, 951
Gracile
slender, 203
Gracious

courteous, 894
good-natured, 906
Gradatim
degree, 26
order, 58
conversion, 144
Gradation
degree, 26
order, 58
arrangement, 60
continuity, 69
Grade
degree, 26
term, 71
Gradely
good, 648
Gradient
obliquity, 217
Gradual
degree, 26
continuity, 69
Graduate
to arrange, 60
to adapt, 23
to measure, 466
scholar, 492
Gradus
dictionary, 562
Graffito
drawing, 556
Graft
join, 300
insert, 43
cultivate, 371
locate, 184
teach, 537
bribe, 615
improbity, 940
Grain
essence, 5
minute, 32
particle, 193
texture, 329
roughness, 256
disposition, 820
adorn, 847
Graminivorous
eat, 296
Grammar
grammar, 567
Grammar school
school, 542
Grammarian
scholar, 492
Grammercy
gratitude, 916

521

Gramophone
reproduction, 19
music, 417
hearing, 418
Granary
store, 636
Grand
important, 642
beautiful, 845
glorious, 873
money, 800
Grandam
veteran, 130
Grandchild
posterity, 167
Grandee
master, 875
Grandeur
repute, 873
Grandiloquence
eloquence, 582
style, 577
Grandiose
style, 577
Grandsire
old, 130
ancestor, 166
Grandson
posterity, 167
Grange
abode, 189
Grangerize
addition, 36
Granite
hardness, 323
Granivorous
eat, 296
Grant
give, 784
allow, 760
consent, 762
disclose, 529
assent, 488
Grantee
receive, 785
Grantor
give, 784
Granulate
pulverulence, 330
Granule
littleness, 193
Grape-shot
arms, 727
Grapevine

news, 532
Graphic
painting, 556
description, 594
intelligible, 518
Grapnel
anchor, 666
Grapple
contend, 720
undertake, 676
join, 43
Grappling-iron
fastening, 45
safety, 666
Grasp
seize, 789
retain, 781
comprehend, 518
power, 737
Grasping
parsimony, 819
Grass
plant, 367
green, 435
Grass widow
divorce, 905
Grate
rub, 330
friction, 331
harsh, 410, 414
furnace, 386
pain, physical, 378
pain, moral, 830
Grateful
thanks, 916
agreeable, 377, 829
Gratification
animal, 377
moral, 827
Gratify
pleasure, 829
Grating
noise, 410
lattice, 219
Gratis
cheap, 815
Gratitude
thanks, 916
Gratuitous
spontaneous, 600, 602
cheap, 815
Gratuity
giving, 784
Gratulation
rejoicing, 836

Gravamen
importance, 642
grievance, 619
Grave
sad, 836
serious, 642
distressing, 830
heinous, 945
great, 31
engrave, 559
impress, 505
shape, 240
tomb, 363
sound, 408
Gravel
offend, 830
puzzle, 704
soil, 342
Graveolent
odour, 398
Graver
artist, 559
Gravestone
interment, 363
Graveyard
interment, 363
Gravid
pregnant, 168
Gravitate
descent, 306
Gravitation
attraction, 288
Gravity
weight, 319
attraction, 288
dullness, 843
seriousness, 837
importance, 642
composure, 826
Gravy
liquid, 333
Graze
browse, 296
touch, 199
Grease
oil, 332, 356
unctuous, 355
Great
much, 31
big, 192
importance, 642
glorious, 873
magnanimous, 942
pregnant, 168

Great circle
  direction, 278
Greatcoat
  garment, 225
Greaten
  enlarge, 35
Greaves
  garment, 225
Greedy
  voracious, 957
  desirous, 865
  avaricious, 819
Greek Church
  Christian religion, 983A
Green
  colour, 435
  meadow, 344
  new, 123
  unskilled, 699
  unprepared, 674
  unaccustomed, 614
  credulous, 484
  ignorant, 491
Green belt
  environs, 227
Green-eyed
  jealousy, 920
Green light
  signal, 550
Greenback
  money, 800
Greenhorn
  fool, 501
  dupe, 547
  novice, 493, 674
  stranger, 57
  bungler, 701
Greenroom
  the drama, 599
Greet
  hail, 894
  weep, 839
Gregarious
  social, 892
Gremlin
  demon, 980
Grenade
  arms, 727
Grenadier
  soldier, 726
  tall, 206
Grey
  colour, 432
  age, 128
Grey-headed

age, 128
veteran, 130
Grey market
  illegality, 964
Grey matter
  brain, 450
Greybeard
  veteran, 130
Greyhound
  swift, 274
Grid
  lattice, 219
Gridelin
  purple, 437
Gridiron
  lattice, 219
  arena, 728
Grief
  dejection, 837
Grievance
  injury, 619
  pain, 830
Grieve
  complain, 828, 839
  afflict, 830
  injure, 649
Griffin
  unconformity, 83
  keeper, 753
Grig
  cheerful, 836
Grill
  calefaction, 384
  question, 461
Grille
  lattice, 219
Grim
  ugly, 846
  frightful, 828
  discourteous, 895
  ferocious, 907
Grim-visaged
  grave, 837
Grimace
  ridicule, 856
Grime
  unclean, 653
Grin
  laugh, 838
  ridicule, 856
  scorn, 929
Grind
  pulverize, 330
  an organ, 415
  oppress, 907

learn, 539
sharpen, 253
scholar, 492
Grinder
  teacher, 540
Grinding
  painful, 831
Grip
  power, 737
  bag, 191
Grip-sack
  bag, 191
Gripe
  seize, 789
  retain, 781
  pain, 378, 828
  to give pain, 830
  power, 737
Griping
  avaricious, 819
Grisette
  woman, 374
Grisly
  ugliness, 846
Grist
  provision, 637
  materials, 635
Gristle
  toughness, 327
Grit
  pulverulence, 330
  determination, 604
  courage, 861
Gritty
  hard, 323
Grizzled
  variegation, 440
Grizzly
  grey, 432
Groan
  cry, 411
  lament, 839
Groggy
  drunk, 959
  ill, 655
Groin
  angular, 244
Grooly
  ugly, 845
Groom
  servant, 746
  marriage, 903
Groomsman
  marriage, 903

Groove
furrow, 259
habit, 613
Grope
feel, 379
experience, 463
inquire, 461
try, 675
Gross
whole, 51
greatness, 31
vulgar, 851
vicious, 945
impure, 961
Grossièreté
rudeness, 895
Grot
see Grotto
Grotesque
deformed, 846
ridiculous, 851, 853
outlandish, 83
Grotto
alcove, 189
hollow, 252
Grouchy
discourteous, 895
bad-tempered, 901
Ground
land, 342
support, 215
base, 211
region, 181
cause, 153
motive, 615
plea, 617
property, 780
arena, 728
teach, 537
Ground swell
surge, 348
agitation, 315
Grounded
knowing, 490
wrecked, 732
Groundless
erroneous, 495
sophistical, 477
Groundling
commonalty, 876
Grounds
lees, 653
Groundwork
basis, 211
support, 215
cause, 153

precursor, 64
preparation, 673
Group
cluster, 72
troop, 726
to marshal, 58
Group-captain
master, 745
Grouse
grumble, 832, 839
Grout
vinculum, 45
Grove
wood, 367
house, 189
Grovel
move slowly, 275
be low, 207
cringe, 886
base, 940
Grow
increase, 35
expand, 194
Grow from
effect, 154
Growl
cry, 412
complain, 839
threaten, 909
be rude, 895
anger, 900
Growler
vehicle, 272
Growth
in degree, 35
in size, 194
Groyne
refuge, 666
Grub
little, 193
food, 298
Grub up
extract, 301
destroy, 162
discover, 480A
Grudge
hate, 898
stingy, 640, 819
unwilling, 603
Gruelling
punishment, 972
Gruesome
ugly, 846
Gruff
morose, 895

sound, 410
Grumble
sound, 411
complain, 832, 839
Grumous
dense, 321
pulpy, 354
Grumpy
discourteous, 895
bad-tempered, 901
Grundyism
prudery, 855
Grunt
cry, 412
complain, 839
Guano
manure, 653
Guarantee
security, 771
evidence, 467
promise, 768
Guard
defend, 717
safety, 664
Guard-room
prison, 752
Guarded
circumspect, 459
conditional, 770
Guardian
safety, 664, 717
keeper, 753
Guardless
danger, 665
Guardsman
combatant, 726
Gubernatorial
directing, 693
authority, 737
Gudgeon
dupe, 547
Guerdon
reward, 973
Guerrilla
combatant, 726
Guess
suppose, 514
Guest
friend, 890
arrival, 292
Guet-apens
untruth, 546
ambush, 530
Guffaw
laughter, 834

524

Guggle
see Gurgle
Guide
direct, 693
director, 694
advice, 695
teach, 537
teacher, 540
road-book, 266
Guide-post
indicator, 550
warning, 668
Guideless
danger, 665
Guild
corporation, 712
tribunal, 966
partnership, 797
Guildhall
mart, 799
Guile
cunning, 702
deceit, 545
Guileless
artless, 703
sincere, 543
Guillotine
engine, 975
to decapitate, 972
Guilt
crime, 947
vice, 945
Guiltless
innocence, 946
Guindé
conciseness, 572
Guise
state, 7
appearance, 448
manner, 627
plea, 617
Guiser
the drama, 599
Guitar
music, 417
Gulch
gap, 198
Gules
redness, 434
Gulf
sea, 343
depth, 208
Gull
dupe, 547
credulous, 486

Gullet
throat, 260
rivulet, 348
Gullible
credulity, 486
Gully
conduit, 350
opening, 260
hollow, 252
ravine, 198
Gulosity
gluttony, 957
Gulp
swallow, 297
believe, 484
Gum
fastening, 45
coherence, 46
semiliquid, 352
Gum-boot
dress, 225
Gumption
capacity, 498
Gumshoe
prowl, 528
Gun
arms, 727
fighter, 726
Gun-cotton
arms, 727
Gunboat
ship, 273
Gunman
bad man, 949
Gunner
combatant, 726
Gurgitation
rotation, 312
Gurgle
sound, 405, 408
bubble, 353
Gurkha
soldier, 726
Guru
priest, 996
Gush
flow, 295
flood, 348
feeling, 821
affectation, 855
Gusset
angularity, 244
Gust
wind, 349
physical taste, 390

enjoyment, 826
moral taste, 850
Gustatory
taste, 390
Gusto
relish, 827
taste, 850
Gut
opening, 260
to sack, 789
vitals, 221
Guts
courage, 861
resolution, 604
Gutter
conduit, 350
groove, 259
Guttersnipe
commonalty, 876
vulgarity, 851
Guttle
devour, 296
Guttural
stammer, 583
letter, 561
Guy
rope, 45
ugliness, 846
man, 373
to ridicule, 842, 856
deride, 929
Guzzle
drink, 296
tipple, 959
gluttony, 957
Gymkhana
contention, 720
Gymnasium
school, 542
training, 673
Gymnast
strength, 159
Gymnastic
exertion, 686
contention, 720
teaching, 537
Gymnosophist
heathen, 984
temperance, 953
Gynaecocracy
rule, 737
Gynaecology
remedy, 662
Gyp
servant, 746

Gypsy
see Gipsy
Gyration
rotation, 312
Gyre
rotation, 312
Gyroscope
rotation, 312
Gyve
chain, 45
shackle, 752

Haberdashery
dress, 225
Habergeon
defence, 717
Habiliment
dress, 225
Habilitation
skill, 698
Habit
intrinsic, 5
custom, 613
coat, 225
Habitat
abode, 189
Habitation
abode, 189
location, 184
Habitual
regular, 82, 613
Habituate
accustom, 613
train, 673
Habitude
state, 7
relation, 9
habit, 613
Habitué
guest, 891
frequenter, 136
Hacienda
property, 780
Hack
cut, 44
shorten, 201
horse, 271
drudge, 690
writer, 590
Hackle
cut, 44
Hackneyed
regular, 82
trite, 496

habitual, 613
experienced, 698
Hades
hell, 982
Hadji
clergy, 996
pilgrim, 268
Haecceity
speciality, 79
Haemorrhage
excretion, 299
Haft
instrument, 633
Hag
ugly, 846
veteran, 130
wretch, 913
bad woman, 949
Haggard
ugly, 846
wild, 824
insane, 503
Haggle
bargain, 769, 794
Hagiography
theology, 983
Ha-ha
ditch, 198
defence, 717
Haik
dress, 225
Hail
call, 586
ice, 383
Hair
thread, 45
filement, 205
roughness, 256
Hair-oil
ornament, 847
Hair-raising
fear, 860
Hair's breadth
thin, 203
Halberd
arms, 727
Halberdier
combatant, 726
Halcyon
prosperous, 734, 829
joyful, 827
calm, 174
Hale
health, 654
Half

bisection, 91
Half a dozen
six, 98
Half and half
mixture, 41
Half-baked
incomplete, 53
witless, 499
Half-blood
unconformity, 83
Half-breed
unconformity, 83
Half-caste
mixture, 41
unconformity, 83
Half-hearted
indifferent, 866
irresolute, 605
timorous, 862
Half-moon
curvature, 245
Half-pint
little, 193
Half-seas-over
drunk, 959
Half-track
vehicle, 272
Half-way
middle, 68
Half-wit
fool, 501
Half-witted
folly, 499
Hall
chamber, 189
receptacle, 191
mart, 799
Hall-marked
genuine, 494
Hallelujah
worship, 990
Hallo!
call, 586
wonder, 870
arrival, 292
Halloo
cry, 411
Hallow
sanctify, 987
Hallowed
venerated, 928
Deity, 976
Hallucination
error, 495
delusion, 503

Halo
light, 420
glory, 873

Halt
stop, 142, 265
flag, 655
rest, 685, 687
limp, 275

Halter
rope, 45
fetter, 752
punishment, 975

Halting
lame, 160

Halve
bisect, 91

Halyard
rope, 45

Hamadryad
nymph, 979

Hamlet
abode, 189

Hammal
carrier, 271

Hammam
furnace, 386

Hammer
to knock, 276
instrument, 633
auction, 796
repetition, 104
bankrupt, 808

Hammer at
thought, 583
action, 682

Hammock
support, 215

Hamper
basket, 191
obstruct, 706

Hamstring
injure, 649
weaken, 160
incapacitate, 158

Hand
instrument, 633
indicator, 550
agent, 690
side, 236
writing, 590
to give, 784
agency, 170

Hand-barrow
vehicle, 272

Hand-gallop

velocity, 274

Hand-in-hand
accompaniment, 88

Hand over
transfer, 270

Handbook
advice, 695

Handcuff
tie together, 43
manacle, 751, 752

Handfast
marriage, 903

Handful
quantity, 25, 103
smallness, 32

Handicap
inequality, 28
disadvantage, 651

Handicraft
action, 680

Handicraftsman
agent, 690

Handiwork
action, 680
effect, 154

Handkerchief
dress, 225
clean, 652

Handle
instrument, 633
plea, 617
touch, 379
use, 677
describe, 594
dissert, 595
work, 680

Handling
treatment, 692

Handmaid
servant, 746
instrumentality, 631

Hands off!
resist, 719
prohibit, 761

Handsel
security, 771
give, 784
pay, 809
begin, 66

Handsome
beautiful, 845
liberal, 816
disinterested, 942

Handspike
instrument, 633

Handwriting
omen, 512
signature, 550
autograph, 590

Handy
near, 197
skilful, 698
useful, 644
attainable, 705

Hang
pendency, 214
kill, 361
execute, 972
expletive, 908

Hang about
loiter, 275

Hang back
hesitate, 603

Hang fire
reluctance, 603
vacillation, 605
stop, 142
refuse, 764
lateness, 133
slowness, 275
inactivity, 683

Hang out
reside, 188

Hang over
futurity, 121
destiny, 152
height, 206

Hang together
junction, 43

Hang up
defer, 133

Hangar
building, 189

Hanger
arms, 727

Hanger-on
servant, 746
accompany, 88
follow, 281
parasite, 886
flatterer, 935

Hangings
ornaments, 847

Hangman
executioner, 975

Hank
skein, 219

Hanker
desire, 865

Hanky-panky
fraud, 545
Hansard
record, 551
Hansel
see Handsel
Hansom
vehicle, 272
Hap
chance, 156, 621
Haphazard
chance, 156, 621
Hapless
hopeless, 859
miserable, 828
Haply
chance, 156
possibly, 470
Happen
event, 151
Happy
glad, 827
expedient, 646
agreement, 23
Happy-go-lucky
careless, 460
aimless, 621
improvident, 674
Happy medium
middle, 68
Happy thought
wit, 842
Hari-kiri
suicide, 361
execution, 972
Harangue
speech, 582
preach, 998
Harass
worry, 907
fatigue, 688
vex, 830
Harbinger
omen, 512
precursor, 64, 116
Harbour
anchorage, 189
refuge, 666
haven, 292
to cherish, 821
Harbourless
exposed, 665
Hard
dense, 323
difficult, 704
grievous, 830

strong, 159
obdurate, 951
sour, 397
Hard-and-fast
exact, 494
strict, 739
Hard-boiled
callous, 823
Hard case
bad man, 949
Hard currency
money, 800
Hard-favoured
ugly, 846
Hard-headed
skill, 698
wise, 498
Hard-hearted
cruel, 907
Hard lines
adversity, 735
Hard-mouthed
obstinacy, 606
Hard up
poverty, 804
Hard-working
exertion, 682, 686
Harden
accustom, 613
train, 673
render callous, 376, 823
impious, 988
impenitent, 951
Hardihood
courage, 861
insolence, 885
Hardly
scarcely, 32
infrequency, 137
Hardness of heart
vice, 945
Hardship
pain, 830
adversity, 735
Hardy
strong, 159
healthy, 654
Hare
velocity, 274
Hare-brained
rash, 460, 863
Harem
apartment, 191
impurity, 961
Hark

hearing, 418
Hark back
regression, 283
Harlequin
motley, 440
pantomimic, 599
humorist, 844
Harlot
libertine, 962
Harlotry
impurity, 961
Harm
evil, 619
badness, 649
malevolence, 907
Harmattan
wind, 349
Harmless
innocent, 946
innocuous, 648
impotent, 158
Harmonic
music, 413
Harmonica
musical, 417
Harmonium
musical instrument, 417
Harmonize
uniformity, 16
Harmony
agreement, 23
melody, 413
concord, 714
peace, 721
conformity, 82
friendship, 888
Harness
fasten, 43
fastening, 45
bond, 752
accoutrement, 225
instrument, 633
subjection, 749
Harp
musical instrument, 417
to repeat, 104
to weary, 841
Harper
musician, 416
Harpoon
arms, 727
Harpsichord
musical, 417
Harpy
demon, 980

evildoer, 913
thief, 792
miser, 819
Harquebus
arms, 727
Harridan
hag, 846
trollop, 962
bad woman, 949
Harrow
pain, 830
cultivate, 371
Harry
pain, 830
Harsh
severe, 739
morose, 895
disagreeable, 830
malevolent, 907
sound, 410
Harum-scarum
disorder, 59
Haruspex
oracle, 513
Harvest
acquisition, 775
effect, 154
Hash
mixture, 41
disorder, 59
to cut, 44
Hasp
lock, 45
to lock, 43
Hassock
support, 215
Hast la vista
departure, 293
Haste
in time, 132
in motion, 274
Haste
in action, 684
activity, 682
Hasten
to promote, 707
Hasty
transient, 111
irritable, 901
Hat
dress, 225
Hatch
produce, 161
plan, 626
prepare, 673

door, 66
opening, 260
Hatchet
instrument, 633
sharpness, 253
Hatchet-faced
thin, 203
Hatchment
record, 551
Hatchway
way, 627
opening, 260
Hate
hate, 898
enmity, 889
bombardment, 716
Hateful
noxious, 649
painful, 830
Hatter
dress, 225
Hauberk
arms, 717
Haughty
proud, 878
severe, 739
insolent, 885
Haul
traction, 285
catch, 789
Haunch
side, 236
Haunt
presence, 186
alarm, 860
abode, 189
resort, 74
frequent, 136
trouble, 830
Haut-goût
pungency, 392
Hautboy
musical instrument, 417
Haute monde
noble, 875
Haute politique
government, 693
Hauteur
pride, 878
Have
possession, 777
deceive, 545
Have it
belief, 484
Have oneself a ball

enjoy, 377
Haven
anchorage, 189
refuge, 292, 666
Havers
nonsense, 497
folly, 499
Haversack
receptacle, 191
Havoc
evil, 162, 619
Haw
stammering, 583
Hawk
sell, 796
publish, 531
Hawk-eyed
vision, 441
Hawker
merchant, 797
Hawser
rope, 45
Hay-cock
bundle, 72
Hayseed
peasant, 876
Haywire
insane, 503
Hazard
chance, 156, 621
danger, 665
obstacle, 706
Haze
mist, 353
dimness, 422
opacity, 426
to harass, 830, 907
Hazel
brown, 433
Hazy
indistinct, 447
Head
beginning, 66
class, 75
summit, 210
front, 234
to lead, 280
froth, 353
intellect, 450
wisdom, 498
master, 745
direction, 693
director, 694
topic, 454

Head and shoulders
whole, 50
Head-foremost
rash, 863
Head-rhyme
similarity, 17
poetry, 597
Head-work
thought, 451
Headache
pain, 378
Header
plunge, 310
Headgear
dress, 225
Heading
title, 550
precursor, 64
beginning, 66
Headlong
projection, 250
cape, 342
height, 206
Headlong
rashly, 460, 863
hastily, 684
swiftly, 274
Headpiece
intellect, 450, 498
skill, 698
Headquarters
focus, 74
abode, 189
Heads
compendium, 596
warning, 668
care, 459
toilet, 191, 653
Headship
authority, 737
Headstrong
rash, 863
obstinate, 606
violent, 173
Headway
space, 180
progress, 282
navigation, 267
Heal
repair, 658
forgive, 918
Health
health, 654
Healthy
salubrity, 656
Heap

collection, 72
store, 636
plenty, 639
much, 31, 50
Hear
audition, 418
learn, 539
Hearken
audition, 418
Hearsay
news, 532
Hearse
interment, 363
Heart
interior, 221
centre, 223
mind, 450
will, 600
affections, 820
courage, 861
love, 897
Heart-breaking
painful, 830
Heart-broken
pain, 828
Heart-felt
feeling, 821
Heart-rending
painful, 830
Heart-sick
dejected, 837
Heart-strings
affections, 820
Heart-swelling
resentment, 900
Heart-whole
free, 748
Heartache
pain, 828
Heartburning
resentment, 900
jealousy, 920
Hearten
inspirit, 824, 861
Hearth
abode, 189
fire, 386
Heartiness
feeling, 821
sociality, 892
Heartless
malevolent, 945
Hearty
healthy, 654
willing, 602

feeling, 821
cheerful, 831, 836
Heat
warmth, 382
calefaction, 384
contest, 720
violence, 173
excitement, 825
Heath
plain, 344
Heathen
pagan, 984, 986
irreligious, 988
Heathenish
vulgar, 851
Heave
raise, 307
pant, 821
throw, 284
Heave in sight
visibility, 446
Heave to
stop, 265
Heaven
paradise, 981
bliss, 827
Heaven-born
virtue, 944
Heaven-directed
wisdom, 498
Heavenly
divine, 976
rapturous, 829
celestial, 318
angelic, 977
Heavens
world, 318
Heaviness
inertia, 172
dejection, 837
dullness, 843
Heaviside layer
air, 338
Heavy
weighty, 319
inert, 172, 682
slow, 275
stupid, 499
rude, 851
large, 31
Hebdomadal
period, 108, 138
Hebe
beauty, 845

Hebetate
insensible, 823
Hecate
hag, 846
Hecatomb
killing, 361
Heckle
question, 461
Hectic
fever, 382
feeling, 821
Hector
courage, 861
bully, 885
Hedge
enclosure, 232
to shuffle, 544
to compensate, 30
Hedge-hop
fly, 267
Hedge in
enclose, 231
safe, 664
Hedgehog
sharpness, 253
defence, 717
Hedonism
intemperance, 954
Heed
attend, 457
care, 459
caution, 864
Heedless
inattentive, 458
neglectful, 460
Heel
slope, 217
rascal, 949
Heel-tap
remainder, 40
Heels
rear, 235
Heels over head
reckless, 460
Heft
handle, 633
exertion, 686
Hefty
heavy, 319
Hegemony
authority, 737
Hegira
departure, 293
Heigh-ho!
lamentation, 839

Height
altitude, 206
degree, 26
superiority, 33
Heighten
increase, 35
exalt, 206
exaggerate, 549
aggravate, 835
Heinous
vice, 945
Heir
possessor, 779
posterity, 167
futurity, 121
Heirloom
property, 780
Heirship
possess, 777
Helen
beauty, 845
Helicon
poetry, 597
Helicopter
aircraft, 273A
Helidrome
arrival, 292
Heliograph
signal, 550
Heliotherapy
remedy, 662
Helix
convolution, 248
Hell
gehenna, 982
abyss, 208
Hell-born
vice, 945
Hellcat
bad woman, 949
fury, 173
Hellebore
bane, 663
Hellhag
bad woman, 949
Hellhound
miscreant, 949
ruffian, 173, 913
Hellish
bad, 649
malevolent, 907
vicious, 945
Hello
see Hallo
Helm

handle, 633
direction, 693
authority, 737
Helmet
dress, 225
defence, 717
Helot
servant, 746
Help
aid, 707
auxiliary, 711
utility, 644
remedy, 662
servant, 746
Helpless
weak, 160
incapable, 158
exposed, 665
Helpmate
auxiliary, 711
wife, 903
Helter-skelter
disorder, 59
haste, 684
slope, 217
Hem
edge, 230
fold, 258
to stammer, 583
Hem in
enclose, 231
surround, 227
restrain, 751
Hemlock
bane, 663
Henbane
bane, 663
Hence
arising from, 155
deduction, 476
motive, 615
Henceforth
futurity, 121
Henchman
servant, 746
Henpecked
obedience, 743
subjection, 749
Hep
knowing, 490
informed, 527
Hephaestus
god, 979
Heptad
seven, 98

531

Heptagon
angularity, 244
seven, 98
Hera
goddess, 979
Herald
messenger, 534
precursor, 64
omen, 512
lead, 280
to predict, 511
to proclaim, 531
Herb
plant, 367
Herbarium
botany, 369
Herbivorous
eat, 296
Herculean
strength, 159
huge, 192
difficulty, 704
Herd
animal, 366
flock, 72, 102
Here
present, 186
Hereabouts
nearness, 197
Hereafter
futurity, 121
Hereditament
property, 780
Hereditary
derivative, 154
posterity, 167
habit, 613
intrinsic, 5
Heredity
paternity, 166
Heresy
error, 495
unbelief, 485
religious, 984A
Heretic
dissent, 489
heresy, 984A
Heretofore
preterition, 122
priority, 116
Herewith
accompaniment, 88
Heritage
futurity, 121
possession, 777

property, 780
Heritor
possessor, 779
Hermaphrodite
incongruity, 83
Hermeneutic
interpretation, 522
Hermes
god, 979
messenger, 534
Hermetically
closure, 261
Hermit
seclusion, 893
Hermitage
abode, 189
Hero
brave, 861
saint, 948
Heroic
brave, 861
glorious, 873
magnanimous, 942
verse, 597
Heroics
exaggeration, 549
boast, 884
Herr
title, 877
Herring-gutted
thin, 203
Hesitate
reluctant, 603
irresolute, 605
uncertainty, 475
fearful, 860
sceptical, 485
to stammer, 583
Hetaera
courtesan, 962
Heteroclite
incongruity, 83
Heterodox
heresy, 984A
Heterogeneous
mixed, 10, 15, 41
multiform, 81
exceptional, 83
Heteromorphic
difference, 15
Heuristic
inquiry, 461
Hew
cut, 44
shorten, 201

fashion, 240
Hexachord
melody, 413
Hexad
six, 98
Hexagon
numbers, 98
angularity, 244
Hexahedron
angularity, 244
six, 98
Hey
attention, 547
accost, 586
Heyday
wonder, 870
success, 731
exultation, 836, 838
youth, 127
Hiatus
interval, 198
opening, 260
unsubstantiality, 4
discontinuity, 70
Hibernal
cold, 383
Hibernate
sleep, 683
Hibernicism
absurdity, 497
Hic jacet
burial, 363
Hiccup
cough, 349
Hick
peasant, 876
Hid
invisible, 447
concealed, 528
Hidalgo
master, 875
Hide
conceal, 528
ambush, 530
skin, 222
Hide-bound
intolerant, 481
obstinate, 606
strait-laced, 751
Hideous
ugly, 846
Hiding-place
refuge, 666
ambush, 530

Hie
go, 264, 266, 274
Hiemal
cold, 383
evening, 126
Hierarchy
churchdom, 995
order, 58
Hieroglyphic
letter, 561
writing, 590
representation, 554
unintelligible, 519
Hierogram
revelation, 985
Hierography
theology, 983
Hierophant
churchman, 996
Higgle
chaffer, 794
bargain, 769
Higgledy-piggledy
disorder, 59
Higgler
merchant, 797
High
lofty, 206
pungent, 392
stinking, 401
proud, 878
magnanimous, 942
drunk, 959
High-born
master, 875
High-brow
scholar, 492
sage, 500
High-falutin
bombast, 549
affected, 855
florid, 577
High-flier
imagination, 515
pride, 878
High-flown
proud, 878, 880
insolent, 885
exaggerated, 549
High-handed
insolent, 885
High-hat
affected, 855
High jinks
festivity, 840

High life
fashion, 852
nobility, 875
High-mettled
spirited, 861
proud, 878
High-minded
proud, 878
generous, 942
honourable, 940
High-powered
power, 157
High-priced
dear, 814
High-seasoned
pungent, 932
obscene, 961
High-spirited
brave, 861
High-strung
excitable, 825
High-wrought
perfect, 650
finished, 729
excited, 825
Highball
intoxicant, 959
Higher
superiority, 33
Highland
land, 342
Highly
great, 31
Highness
title, 877
prince, 745
Hight
nomenclature, 564
Highway
road, 627
Highwayman
thief, 792
Hijack
rob, 791, 792
Hike
journey, 266
Hiker
traveller, 268
Hilarity
cheerfulness, 836
Hill
height, 206
Hillock
height, 206
Hilt

instrument, 633
Hind
back, 235
clown, 876
Hinder
back, 235; end, 67
to impede, 179
obstruct, 706
prohibit, 761
Hindrance
obstruction, 706
Hindsight
thought, 451
memory, 505
Hinduism
religions, 984
Hinge
depend upon, 154
cause, 153
rotate, 312
fastening, 43, 45
Hinny
beast of burden, 271
Hint
suggest, 505
inform, 527
suppose, 514
Hinterland
interior, 221
Hip
side, 236
Hipped
dejection, 837
Hippocentaur
oddity, 83
Hippodrome
arena, 728
amusement, 840
Hippogriff
incongruity, 83
Hippophagous
eat, 296
Hippy
unconformity, 83
Hire
commission, 755
fare, 812
purchase, 795
borrow, 788
Hire purchase
buy, 795
Hireling
servant, 746
Hirsute
rough, 256

Hispid
  rough, 256
Hiss
  sound, 409
  disrespect, 929, 932
Histology
  texture, 329
Historian
  recorder, 553, 594
Historic
  indication, 550
History
  record, 551
  narrative, 594
Histrionic
  the drama, 599
  ostentatious, 882
Hit
  strike, 276
  impress, 824
  punish, 972
  succeed, 731
  chance, 156, 621
  reach, 292
  agree, 23
Hit off
  imitate, 19, 554
Hit-or-miss
  chance, 621
Hit upon
  find, 480A
Hitch
  difficulty, 704
  impediment, 135
  jerk, 315
  hang, 43, 214
Hitch-hike
  travel, 266
Hither
  arrival, 292
Hitherto
  preterition, 122
Hive
  workshop, 691
  multitude, 102
  dwelling, 186
Hive-off
  distribute, 73
Hoar
  white, 430
  aged, 128
Hoar-frost
  cold, 383
Hoard
  store, 636

assemblage, 72
Hoarding
  screen, 530
Hoarse
  sound, 405, 410
  voice, 581
Hoary
  white, 430
  aged, 128
Hoax
  deception, 545
Hob
  support, 215
  fire, 386
Hobble
  limp, 275
  difficulty, 704
  lame, 732
  tether, 751
  bond, 752
  awkward, 699
Hobbledehoy
  youth, 129
Hobby
  pursuit, 622
  desire, 865
Hobgoblin
  demon, 980
Hobnob
  courtesy, 894
Hobo
  traveller, 268
  tramp, 876
Hobson's choice
  necessity, 601
  absence of choice, 610
Hock
  pawn, 787
Hocus
  deceive, 545
  stupefy, 376
Hocus-pocus
  cheat, 545
  conjuration, 992
Hod
  receptacle, 191
  vehicle, 272
Hodge
  clown, 876
Hodge-podge
  mixture, 41
  confusion, 59
Hog
  sensuality, 954
  gluttony, 957

selfishness, 943
Hog-wash
  uncleanness, 653
Hoist
  elevate, 307
  lift, 627
Hoity-toity!
  wonder, 870
Hokum
  humbug, 497
  deception, 545
Hold
  possess, 777
  believe, 484
  retain, 781
  cohere, 46
  fix, 150
  stop, 265
  discontinue, 142
  continue, 141, 143
  refrain, 623
  contain, 54
  influence, 175
  prison, 752
  in a ship, 207
  term, 71
Hold forth
  declaim, 582
  teach, 537
Hold good
  truth, 494
Hold in
  moderation, 174
Hold on
  move, 264
  continue, 141, 143
  determination, 604
Hold out
  resist, 718
  offer, 763
Hold the tongue
  silence, 403, 585
Hold together
  junction, 43
Hold up
  sustain, 707
  continue, 143
  delay, 133
  plunder, 791
Holder
  possessor, 779
Holdfast
  vinculum, 45
Holding
  property, 780

535

Hooliganism
brutality, 907
Hoop
circle, 247
Hoot
cry, 411
deride, 929, 930, 932
drink, 298
Hooter
indication, 550
Hoots
contempt, 930
Hop
leap, 309
dance, 840
Hop it
go away, 293, 287
escape, 671
Hop the twig
die, 360
Hope
hope, 858
probability, 472
Hopeful
probable, 472
Hopeless
desperate, 859
impossible, 471
Hophead
intemperance, 954
Horde
assemblage, 72
Horizon
distance, 196
view, 441
prospect, 507
futurity, 121
Horizontal
horizontality, 213
Horn
sharpness, 253
musical, 417
alarm, 669
Horn-mad
jealousy, 920
Horn of plenty
sufficient, 639
Hornbook
school, 542
Hornet
bane, 663, 830
Hornpipe
dance, 840
Hornswoggle
deceive, 545

Horny
hard, 323
Horology
chronometry, 114
Horoscope
prediction, 511
Horrible
great, 31
fearful, 860
Horrid
noxious, 649
ugly, 846
dire, 830
vulgar, 851
fearful, 860
hateful, 898
Horripilation
cold, 383
terror, 860
Horrisonous
strident, 410
Horror
dislike, 867
hate, 898
fear, 860
Hors de combat
impotence, 158
disease, 655
Hors-d'œuvre
food, 298
Horse
animal, 271
cavalry, 726
stand, 215
Horse-box
vehicle, 272
Horse-laugh
laugh, 838
Horse-power
measure, 466
Horse-sense
wisdom, 498
Horse-shoe
curvature, 245
Horseman
traveller, 268
Horseplay
violence, 173
Horsewhip
punishment, 972
Hortation
advice, 615, 695
Horticulture
agriculture, 371
Hortus siccus

botany, 369
Hosanna
worship, 990
Hose
dress, 225
conduit, 350
Hospice
abode, 189
Hospitable
social, 892
liberal, 816
Hospital
remedy, 662
Hospodar
master, 745
Host
multitude, 100
collection, 72
friend, 890
religious, 999
Hostage
security, 771
Hostel
inn, 189
Hostile
adverse, 708
Hostilities
warfare, 722
Hostility
enmity, 889
Hot
warm, 382
pungent, 392
irascible, 901
rhythm, 413
contraband, 964
Hot air
sophistry, 477
Hot-bed
workshop, 691
cause, 153
Hot-blooded
rash, 863
Hot-brained
rash, 863
excited, 825
Hot-headed
rash, 863
excited, 825
Hot-plate
heater, 386
Hot water
difficulty, 704
Hot-water bottle
heater, 386

536

Hotchpotch
mixture, 41
confusion, 59
Hotel
inn, 189
Hothouse
conservatory, 386
workshop, 691
Hotspur
rashness, 863
courage, 861
Hottentot
boor, 876
Hough
maltreat, 649
Hound
pursue, 281, 622
oppress, 907
wretch, 949
Hour
period, 108
Hour-glass
time, 114
form, 203
Houri
beauty, 845
Hourly
routine, 138
House
abode, 189
to locate, 184
safety, 664
party, 712
senate, 696
partnership, 797
House-warming
sociality, 892
Houseboat
abode, 189
Housebreaker
thief, 792
Household
abode, 189
conformity, 82
plain, 849
property, 780
Housekeeper
director, 694
servant, 746
Housekeeping
conduct, 692
Houseless
displaced, 185
Housemaid
servant, 746

Housewifery
conduct, 692
economy, 817
Housing
lodging, 189
Hovel
abode, 189
Hover
soar, 267
rise, 305
high, 206
Hoverplane
aircraft, 273A
How
in what way, 627
by what means, 632
How-d'ye-do
difficulty, 704
Howbeit
counteraction, 179
Howdah
seat, 215
However
except, 83
notwithstanding, 179
degree, 23
compensation, 30
Howff
resort, 74
Howitzer
arms, 727
Howl
ululation, 411, 412,
839
Howler
error, 495
solecism, 568
Howsoever
degree, 26
Hoy
ship, 273
salutation, 586
Hoyden
vulgarity, 851
Hub
centre, 223
middle, 68
Hubble-bubble
tobacco-pipe, 298A
Hubbub
din, 404
discord, 713
agitation, 315
Huckster
merchant, 797

Huddle
mix, 41
disorder, 59
derange, 61
collect, 72
don, 225
nearness, 197
Hue
colour, 428
Hue and cry
noise, 404
outcry, 931
alarm, 669
proclamation, 531
Hueless
achromatism, 429
Huff
anger, 900
insolence, 885
Huffiness
irascibility, 901
Hug
cohere, 46
retain, 781
endearment, 894, 902
Hug oneself
rejoice, 838
Hug the shore
approach, 286
Huge
in degree, 31
in size, 192
Hugger-mugger
confusion, 59
Hulk
whole, 50
ship, 273
Hulking
big, 192
awkward, 853
ugly, 846
Hull
whole, 50
Hullabaloo
noise, 404
cry, 411
Hullo
see Hallo
Hum
faint sound, 405
continued sound, 407,
412
to sing, 415
deceive, 545
stink, 401

Hum and ha
hesitate, 583
demur, 605
Hum-note
melody, 413
Human
mankind, 372
Humane
benevolent, 906
philanthropic, 910
Humanism
knowledge, 490
Humanist
scholar, 492
Humanitarian
philanthropist, 906
Humanities
letters, 560
Humanity
human nature, 372
benevolence, 906
Humanize
courtesy, 894
Humble
meek, 879
modest, 881
to abash, 874
pious, 987
Humbug
deception, 545
falsehood, 544
Humdrum
dull, 843
Humectate
moisten, 339
Humid
moist, 339
Humiliate
humble, 879
shame, 874
worship, 990
Humility
piety, 987
Humming-top
musical, 417
Hummock
height, 206, 250
Humoresque
music, 415
Humorist
humorist, 844
Humour
essence, 5
liquid, 333
disposition, 602

tendency, 176
caprice, 608
indulge, 760
affections, 820
to please, 829
wit, 842
Humoursome
capricious, 608
discourteous, 895
Hump
convexity, 250
Hump bluey
journey, 266
Hump yourself
activity, 682
Humpbacked
distortion, 243
ugliness, 846
Humph!
wonder, 870
Humus
soil, 342
Hun
evildoer, 913
Hunch
convexity, 250
Hundred
number, 99
region, 181
Hunger
desire, 865
Hunks
parsimony, 819
Hunnish
malevolent, 907
Hunt
follow, 281
pursue, 622
inquire, 461
Hunter
carrier, 271
Hunting grounds
heaven, 981
Hurdle
fence, 232
Hurdy-gurdy
musical, 417
Hurl
propel, 284
Hurly-burly
confusion, 59
turmoil, 315
Hurrah!
cheerfulness, 836
rejoicing, 838

Hurricane
tempest, 349
violence, 173
Hurried
excitability, 825
Hurry
haste, 684
swiftness, 274
earliness, 132
to urge, 615
to excite, 824
Hurst
plant, 367
Hurt
evil, 619
physical pain, 378
moral pain, 828
to injure, 649, 907
to molest, 830
Hurtful
badness, 649
Hurtle
impulse, 276
Husband
spouse, 903
to store, 636
Husbandman
agriculture, 371
Husbandry
agriculture, 371
conduct, 692
economy, 817
Hush
silence, 403
latent, 526
moderate, 174
assuage, 826
pacify, 723
Hush-hush
secret, 534
Hush-money
bribe, 809
compensation, 30
Hush up
conceal, 526, 528
Husk
covering, 222
to strip, 226
Husky
dry, 340
big, 192
strong, 159
faint sound, 405, 501
Hussar
combatant, 726

Hussy
libertine, 962
bad woman, 949
impertinent, 887
Hustings
tribunal, 966
platform, 542
Hustle
push, 276
disarrange, 61
agitate, 315
bustle, 171, 682
haste, 684
Hut
abode, 189
Hutch
abode, 189
Huzza!
cheerfulness, 836
Hyaline
transparency, 425
Hybrid
mixture, 41
nondescript, 83
Hydra
unconformity, 83
Hydra-headed
reproduction, 163
Hydrant
spray, 348
Hydraulics
fluids, 348
Hydrogen bomb
arms, 727
Hydrographic
sea, 341
Hydrology
water, 333
Hydromel
sweetness, 396
Hydrometer
density, 321
Hydropathic
salubrity, 656
remedy, 662
Hydropathy
remedy, 662
Hydrophobia
dislike, 867
Hydroplane
aircraft, 273A
Hydroponics
agriculture, 371
Hydrostatics
water, 333

Hydrotherapy
remedy, 662
Hyena
evildoer, 913
Hygiene
salubrity, 656
Hygrology
moisture, 339
Hygrometer
moisture, 339
Hylotheism
heathen, 984
Hymen
marriage, 903
Hymn
worship, 990
Hymnal rite, 998
Hyperaesthesia
excitability, 825
sensibility, 376, 822
Hyperbole
exaggeration, 549
Hyperborean
cold, 383
Hypercritical
disapprobation, 932
fastidious, 868
Hyperion
beauty, 845
Hypermetropia
vision, 443
Hyperpyrexia
heat, 382
Hypersensitive
sensitive, 375, 825
Hypertrophy
expansion, 194
Hyphen
vinculum, 45
Hypnology
inactivity, 683
Hypnosis
inactivity, 683
Hypnotic
remedy, 662
sedative, 683
Hypnotize
occult, 992, 994
Hypocaust
furnace, 386
Hypochondriac
dejection, 837
insanity, 503, 504
Hypocrisy
deception, 545

religious, 988
Hypocrite
deceiver, 548
Hypocritical
falsehood, 544
Hypostasis
substantiality, 3
Hypostatic
Deity, 976
Hypothecation
lending, 787
Hypothesis
supposition, 514
Hysterical
violence, 173
excitement, 825
Hysteron proteron
inversion, 218
i.e. meaning, 516

IOU
security, 771
money, 800
Iambic
verse, 597
Ibidem
identity, 13
Icarus
ascent, 305
Ice
cold, 383
cool, 385
smooth, 255
Ice-house
refrigeratory, 387
Ice-pail
cooler, 387
Ichnography
representation, 554
Ichor
liquidity, 333
Ichthyophagous
eat, 296
Icicle
cold, 383
Icon
representation, 554
Iconoclasm
heresy, 984A
Iconoclast
destroyer, 165
Icosahedron
angularity, 244
twenty, 98

Ictus
rhythm, 138
Icy
discourteous, 895
Id
mind, 450
Id est
interpretation, 522
Idea
notion, 453
belief, 484
knowledge, 490
small degree, 32
small quantity, 192
inexistence, 2
Ideal
erroneous, 495
unreal, 2, 515
immaterial, 317
pleasurable, 829
Ideality
intellect, 450
imagination, 515
Ideate
imagine, 515
apprehend, 490
Idée fixe
misjudgment, 481
Identify
comparison, 464
Identity
identity, 13
Identity-card
sign, 550
Ideologist
doctrinaire, 493
Ideology
intellect, 450
knowledge, 490
belief, 484
Idiocy
folly, 499
Idiom
phrase, 566
style, 569
Idiosyncrasy
essence, 5
speciality, 79
characteristic, 550
abnormality, 83
tendency, 176
temperament, 820
sensitiveness, 375
Idiot
imbecile, 501

foolish, 499
Idle
slothful, 683
trivial, 643
Ido
language, 560
Idol
favourite, 899
Idolatry
superstition, 984A
heathen, 986
impious worship, 991
love, 897
Idolize
love, 897
Idyll
poetry, 597
If
supposition, 514
qualification, 469
Igloo
abode, 189
Igneous
heat, 382
Ignis fatuus
light, 423
phantom, 515
unsubstantial, 4
dim sight, 443
error, 495
Ignite
calefaction, 384
Ignition
heat, 382
Ignoble
base, 876, 945
Ignominy
dishonour, 940
shame, 874
Ignoramus
ignoramus, 493
Ignorant
ignorance, 491
Ignore
repudiate, 773
slight, 460, 929
dissent, 489
Ilk
identity, 13
Ill
sick, 655
evil, 619
Ill-advised
foolish, 499, 699
inexpedient, 647

Ill-assorted
disagreement, 24
Ill-bred
discourtesy, 895
vulgar, 851
Ill-conditioned
discourteous, 895
malevolent, 907
vicious, 945
Ill-favoured
ugliness, 846
Ill feeling
enmity, 889
hate, 898
Ill-flavoured
unsavouriness, 395
Ill humour
resentment, 900
Ill-judged
foolish, 499
ill-advised, 699
Ill-looking
ugliness, 846
Ill-made
distortion, 243
Ill-natured
malevolence, 907
Ill-off
adversity, 735
Ill-omened
evil, 649
disagreeable, 858
hopeless, 859
Ill-proportioned
distortion, 243
Ill-sorted
disagreement, 24
Ill-starred
adversity, 735
Ill-tempered
discourtesy, 895
irascibility, 901
Ill-timed
inappropriate, 24
untimely, 135
Ill-treat
injure, 649, 907
Ill turn
evil, 619
Ill-used
hurt, 828
Ill will
enmity, 889
malevolence, 907

Illapse
  entry, 294
Illation
  judgment, 480
Illegal
  illegality, 964
Illegible
  unintelligible, 519
Illegitimate
  undue, 925
  illegal, 964
  erroneous, 495
Illiberal
  selfish, 943
  stingy, 819
  intolerant, 481
Illicit
  illegality, 964, 925
Illimitable
  infinite, 105
  great, 31
Illiterate
  ignorance, 491
Illness
  disease, 655
Illogical
  sophistical, 477
  erroneous, 495
Illuminate
  enlighten, 420
  colour, 428
  adorn, 847
Illuminati
  scholar, 492
Illumination
  drawing, 556
  ornament, 847
  celebration, 883
Illusion
  error, 495
  deceit, 545
Illusionist
  conjurer, 548
Illusive
  erroneous, 495
  sophistical, 477
  deceitful, 544
Illusory
  see Illusive
Illustration
  interpretation, 522
  drawing, 556
  representation, 554
  ornament, 847
  example, 82

Illustrious
  repute, 873
Image
  representation, 554
  idea, 453
  statue, 557
  idol, 991
  likeness, 17
Imagery
  metaphor, 521
  fancy, 515
Imaginary
  non-existing, 2
  erroneous, 495
  quantity, 84
Imagination
  fancy, 515
  wit, 842
Imam
  clergy, 996
  master, 745
Imbalance
  inequality, 28
Imbecile
  foolish, 477, 499
  absence of intellect, 450A
  weak, 160
  incapable, 158
Imbed
  see Embed
Imbibe
  receive, 296
  learn, 539
Imbrangle
  derange, 61
Imbricated
  covering, 222
Imbroglio
  unintelligibility, 519
  discord, 713
Imbrue
  moisten, 339
  impregnate, 300
Imbue
  mix, 41
  tinge, 428
  impregnate, 300
  moisten, 339
  teach, 537
  feel, 821
Imitate
  to copy, 19
  repetition, 104
  to represent, 554
Imitation

  copy, 21
Immaculate
  excellent, 648
  spotless, 652
  faultless, 650
  innocent, 946
  pure, 960
Immanent
  inherent, 5
Immanity
  malevolence, 907
Immaterial
  unsubstantial, 4
  spiritual, 317
  mental, 450
  trifling, 643
Immature
  new, 123
  unprepared, 674
Immeasurable
  infinite, 105
  great, 31
Immediate
  transient, 111
Immedicable
  incurable, 655, 659
Immemorial
  old, 124
Immense
  in degree, 31
  in size, 192
Immerse
  introduce, 300
  dip, 337
  baptism, 998
Immethodical
  disorder, 59
Immigrant
  stranger, 57
Immigration
  migration, 266
  entrance, 294
Imminent
  futurity, 121
  destiny, 152
Immiscibility
  incoherence, 47
Immission
  reception, 296
Immitigable
  ire, 900
  violence, 173
Immobility
  immutability, 150
  quiescence, 265

resolution, 604
Immoderately
  greatness, 31
Immoderation
  intemperance, 954
Immodest
  impurity, 961
Immolate
  destroy, 162
  kill, 361
  offer, 763
Immolation
  sacrifice, 991
Immoral
  vicious, 945
  wrong, 923
Immortal
  perpetual, 112
  glorious, 873
  celebrated, 883
Immovable
  unchangeable, 150
  resolved, 604
  obstinate, 606
Immunity
  exemption, 927A
  right, 924
  freedom, 748
Immure
  enclose, 231
  imprison, 751
Immutable
  immutability, 150
Imp
  demon, 980
  ruffian, 913
  wretch, 943
Impact
  contact, 43
  impulse, 276
  insertion, 300
Impair
  deterioration, 659
Impale
  transfix, 260
  pierce, 302
  execute, 972
Impalpable
  small, 193
  powder, 330
  immaterial, 317
  intangible, 381
Impanation
  rite, 998
Imparity

inequality, 28
Impart
  give, 784
  inform, 527
Impartial
  just, 922
  wise, 498
  indifferent, 866
  honourable, 939
Impassable
  closed, 261, 704
Impasse
  hindrance, 706
  situation, 8
  difficulty, 704
Impassible
  insensible, 376, 823
Impassion
  excite, 824
Impassive
  insensible, 823
Impasto
  painting, 556
Impatient
  excitable, 825
Impawn
  lending, 787
Impeach
  accuse, 938
Impeccability
  perfection, 650
Impecunious
  adversity, 735
  poverty, 804
Impede
  hindrance, 706
Impedimenta
  hindrance, 706
  baggage, 635
Impel
  push, 276, 284
  move, 264
  induce, 615
Impend
  future, 121
  expectation, 507
  height, 206
  destiny, 152
Impenetrable
  latent, 526
  hidden, 528
Impenitence
  impenitence, 951
Imperative
  authority, 737

duty, 926
  requirement, 630
Imperator
  master, 745
Imperceptible
  invisible, 447
  minute, 193
Impercipient
  insensibility, 376
Imperfect
  incomplete, 53
  failing, 651
  shortcoming, 304
  vicious, 945
  small, 32
Imperforate
  closure, 261
Imperial
  authority, 737
  beard, 256
Imperil
  endanger, 665
Imperious
  stern, 739
  insolent, 885
Imperishable
  external, 112, 150
  glorious, 873
Impermanent
  transitory, 111
Impermeable
  closed, 261
  dense, 321
Impersonal
  generality, 78
  material, 316
Impersonate
  represent, 554
  imitate, 19
Impertinence
  inexpedience, 647
Impertinent
  irrelevant, 10
  disagreeing, 24
  insolent, 885
  discourteous, 895
Imperturbable
  unruffled, 823, 826
Impervious
  closure, 261
Impetrate
  beseech, 765
Impetuous
  boisterous, 173
  hot, 825

hasty, 684
rash, 863
eager, 865
Impetus
impulse, 276
Impiety
impiety, 988
irreligion, 989
Impignorate
lending, 787
Impinge
impulse, 276
Impish
supernatural, 980
Implacable
hatred, 898
wrath, 900
unforgiving, 919
Implant
insert, 300
teach, 537
Implanted
adventitious, 6
inborn, 5
Implement
instrument, 633
Impletion
sufficiency, 639
fullness, 52
Implicate
accuse, 938
involve, 54
Implication
inference, 521
Implicit
understood, 516
metaphorical, 521
untold, 526
Implore
beseech, 765
pray, 990
pity, 914
Imply
mean, 516
latent, 526
evidence, 467
metaphor, 521
Impolite
rude, 895
vulgar, 851
Impolitic
folly, 499
inexpedient, 647
Imponderable
light, 320

immaterial, 317
Import
ingress, 294
transfer, 270
insert, 300
mean, 516
be of consequence, 642
receive, 296
Importance
greatness, 31
Important
importance, 642
repute, 873
Importunate
painfulness, 830
Importune
ask, 765
pester, 830
Impose
order, 741
cheat, 545
be unjust, 923, 925
palm off upon, 486
Imposing
grand, 873
Impossible
incredible, 471
impracticable, 704
Impost
price, 812
Impostor
deceiver, 548
Imposture
deception, 545
Impotence
impotence, 158
weakness, 160
failure, 732
Impound
enclose, 231
imprison, 751
Impoverish
drain, 638
fleece, 789
render poor, 804
Impracticable
difficult, 704
impossible, 471
obstinate, 606
Imprecation
request, 765
malediction, 908
Impregnable
safety, 664
Impregnate

insert, 300
produce, 161, 168
mix, 41
teach, 537
Impresario
drama, 599
Imprescriptible
dueness, 924
Impress
mark, 550
memory, 505
excite, 375, 824
compel, 744
Impressible
sensibility, 822
motive, 615
Impression
belief, 375, 484
idea, 453
feeling, 821
engraving, 558
Impressionist
artist, 559
Impressive
exciting, 824
notable, 642
Imprimatur
sanction, 924
Imprimis
beginning, 66
Imprint
indication, 550
Imprison
shut up, 751
circumscribe, 231
Improbable
improbability, 473
Improbity
improbity, 940
wrong, 923
Improficiency
unskilfulness, 699
Impromptu
impulse, 612
music, 415
Improper
wrong, 923, 925
inexpedient, 499, 647
incongruous, 24
unseemly, 961
Impropriate
take, 789
possess, 777
Improve
improvement, 658

Improvident
careless, 460
not preparing, 674, 863
prodigal, 818P
Improvise
impulse, 612
imagine, 515
Imprudent
rash, 863
unwise, 699
neglectful, 460
Impudent
insolence, 885
discourtesy, 895
Impudicity
impurity, 961
Impugn
blame, 932
deny, 536
oppose, 708
Impuissance
impotence, 158
Impulse
push, 276
unpremeditation, 612
necessity, 601
Impulsive
instinctive, 477
motive, 615
motiveless, 616
rash, 863
Impunity
acquittal, 970
Impure
foul, 653
licentious, 961
Imputation
disrepute, 874
Impute
ascribe, 155
accuse, 938
In esse
existence, 1
In extenso
whole, 50
diffuse, 573
In extremis
death, 360
In fine
end, 67
In hand
possession, 777
business, 625
In limine
beginning, 66

In loco
agreement, 23
In mediis rebus
middle, 68
In nubibus
inexistence, 2
incogitancy, 452
imagination, 515
unintelligibility, 519
In propria persona
speciality, 79
In puris naturalibus
divestment, 226
In re
relation, 9
In saecula saeculorum
perpetuity, 112
In statu pupillari
youth, 127
learner, 541
In statu quo
permanence, 141
restoration, 660
In terrorem
threat, 909
In toto
whole, 50
greatness, 31
In transitu
transient, 111
conversion, 144
motion, 264
transference, 270
method, 627
Inability
want of power, 158
want of skill, 699
Inaccessible
distance, 196
impossible, 471
Inaccurate
error, 495, 568
Inaction
inaction, 681
Inactivity
inactivity, 172, 683
Inadaptability
disagreement, 24
Inadequate
insufficient, 640, 645
imperfect, 651
weak, 158, 160
Inadmissible
inexpedient, 647
incongruous, 24

excluded, 55
Inadvertence
inattention, 458
unintentional, 621
Inalienable
right, 924
possession, 777
retention, 781
Inamorata
love, 897
Inane
trivial, 643
useless, 645
void, 4
Inanimate
dead, 360
inorganic, 358
Inanition
insufficiency, 640
Inanity
inutility, 645
absence of thought, 452
absence of meaning, 517
insignificance, 643
Inappetence
indifference, 866
Inapplicable
irrelation, 10
disagree, 24
Inapposite
disagree, 24
irrelevant, 10
Inappreciable
in size, 193
in degree, 32
unimportant, 643
Inappreciative
ungrateful, 917
Inapprehensible
unknowable, 519
Inappropriate
discordant, 24
inexpedient, 647
Inapt
inexpedient, 647
incongruous, 24
Inaptitude
impotence, 158
Inarticulate
stammering, 583
Inartificial
artlessness, 703
Inartistic
unskilled, 699
imperfect, 651

Inattention
 indifference, 458
Inaudible
 silent, 403, 405
 mute, 581
Inaugurate
 begin, 66
 precedence, 62
 celebrate, 883
Inauguration
 commission, 755
Inauspicious
 hopeless, 859
 untimely, 135
 untoward, 649
Inbeing
 intrinsicality, 5
Inborn
 intrinsic, 5, 820
 habitual, 613
Inbred
 intrinsic, 5, 820
Inca
 master, 745
Incalculable
 infinite, 105
 much, 31
Incalescence
 heat, 382
Incandescence
 heat, 382
 light, 420
Incantation
 invocation, 765
 spell, 993
Incapable
 weak, 160
 unable, 158
Incapacity
 impotence, 158
 weakness, 160
 stupidity, 499
 indocility, 538
Incarcerate
 imprison, 751
 surround, 231
Incarnadine
 red, 434
Incarnate
 materialize, 316
Incarnation
 intrinsic, 5
 Deity, 976
Incautious
 neglectful, 460

 rash, 863
Incendiary
 evildoer, 913
 destructive, 162
Incense
 fragrance, 400
 to provoke, 900
 hatred, 898
 flattery, 933
 worship, 990
Incentive
 motive, 615
Inception
 beginning, 66
Inceptor
 learner, 541
Incertitude
 uncertain, 475
Incessant
 perpetual, 112
 frequency, 136
Incest
 impurity, 961
Inch
 littleness, 193
 slowness, 275
 island, 346
Inch by inch
 degree, 26
Inchoate
 amorphous, 241
Inchoation
 beginning, 66
Incidence
 direction, 278
Incident
 event, 151
Incidental
 extrinsic, 6, 8
 irrelative, 10
 liable, 177
 casual, 156, 621
Incinerate
 calefaction, 384
Incipient
 beginning, 66
 style, 574
Incision
 cut, 44
Incisive
 style, 574
 feeling, 821
Incite
 urge, 615
 exasperate, 173

Incivility
 rudeness, 895
Incivism
 misanthropy, 911
Inclement
 cold, 383
 severe, 739
Incline
 slope, 217
 direction, 278
 tendency, 176
 willing, 602
 desire, 865
 love, 897
 induce, 615
Inclusive
 in a compound, 54
 in a class, 76
Incogitable
 incogitancy, 452
Incognito
 concealment, 528
Incognizable
 unknowable, 519
Incognizance
 ignorance, 491
Incoherent
 physical, 47
 mental, 503
 meaning, 519
Incombustible
 fire-proof, 385
Incomer
 receipt, 810
 wealth, 803
Income
 stranger, 57
Incoming
 ingress, 294
Incommensurable
 quantity, 84, 85
 irrelation, 10
 disagreeing, 24
Incommode
 to hinder, 706
 annoy, 830
Incommodious
 inconvenient, 647
Incommunicable
 retention, 781
 unintelligible, 519
Incommunicado
 concealed, 528
Incommutable
 unchangeable, 150

Incomparable
goodness, 648
Incompatible
disagree, 24
Incompetence
inability, 158
incapacity, 499
insufficiency, 640
unskilfulness, 699
Incomplete
defective, 53
not completed, 730
Incomprehensible
unintelligible, 519
Incomprehension
ignorance, 491
Incompressible
density, 321
Inconceivable
unintelligible, 519
incredible, 485
Inconcinnity
ugliness, 846
Inconclusive
sophistry, 477
Incondite
inelegant, 579
Incongruous
disagreement, 24
Inconsecutive
discontinuous, 70
Inconsequential
unreasonable, 477
Inconsiderable
in size, 193
in degree, 32
unimportant, 643
Inconsiderate
thoughtless, 452
heedless, 460
foolish, 699
Inconsistent
contrary, 14
unreasonable, 477
disagreeing, 24
multiform, 16A
absurd, 497
capricious, 608
Inconsolable
pain, 828
dejection, 837
Inconsonance
disagreement, 24
Inconspicuous
invisible, 447

latent, 526
Inconstant
irresolution, 605
Incontestable
certainty, 474
Incontinent
impurity, 961
Incontinently
transient, 111
Incontrovertible
certainty, 474
unchangeable, 150
Inconvenient
inexpedient, 647
Inconvincible
incredulity, 487
Incorporate
combination, 48
Incorporeal
immaterial, 317
Incorrect
erroneous, 495, 568
sophistical, 477
Incorrigible
vicious, 945
impenitent, 951
irremediable, 649
hopeless, 859
Incorruptible
honourable, 939
pure, 942
Incorruption
health, 654
innocence, 946
Incrassate
thickness, 202
density, 321
Increase
in degree, 35
in size, 194
Incredible
impossible, 471
improbable, 473, 485
much, 31
wonderful, 870
Incredulity
unbelief, 485, 487
religious, 989
Increment
increase,
in degree, 35
in size, 194
addition, 37, 39
Incrustation
covering, 222

Incubation
preparation, 673
Incubus
hindrance, 706
Inculcate
teach, 537
Inculpate
accuse, 938
Incumbent
height, 206
weight, 319
duty, 926
clergyman, 996
Incunabula
beginning, 66
book, 591
Incur
liable, 177
Incurable
disease, 655
Incuriosity
incurious, 456
Incursion
ingress, 294
attack, 716
Incurvation
curvature, 245
Indaba
council, 696
Indebted
owing, 806
duty, 926
gratitude, 916
Indecent
impure, 961
Indecision
irresolute, 605
absence of choice, 610
Indecisive
uncertain, 475
inconclusive, 477
Indeclinable
immutable, 150
Indecorum
vice, 945
impurity, 961
vulgarity, 851
Indeed
very, 31
wonder, 870
truth, 494
assertion, 535
Indefatigable
activity, 682
resolute, 604

reasoning, 476
of a priest, 995
appointment, 755
Indulge
allow, 760
give, 784
lenity, 740
pleasure, 827
pleasing, 829
intemperance, 954
satisfy, 831
Induration
hardening, 323
impenitence, 951
Industrial action
strike, 719
Industry
activity, 682
learning, 539
business, 625
Indweller
inhabitant, 188
Inebriety
drunkenness, 959
Inedible
unsavoury, 395
Ineffable
wonder, 870
Ineffably
greatness, 31
Ineffaceable
memory, 505
feeling, 821
Ineffectual
incapable, 158
weak, 160
useless, 645
failing, 732
Inefficacious
see Ineffectual
Inefficient
see Ineffectual
Inelastic
not elastic, 326
soft, 324
Inelegant
ugly, 846
in style, 579
Ineligible
inexpedience, 647
Ineluctable
destiny, 152
Inept
incapable, 158, 699
useless, 645

unsuitable, 24
Inequality
inequality, 28
Inequitable
wrong, 923
Ineradicable
fixed, 150
Inerrable
innocence, 946
Inert
physically, 172, 683
morally, 823
Inertia
inertness, 172
inactivity, 683
Inestimable
goodness, 648
Inevitable
destiny, 152, 601
certain, 474
Inexact
error, 495
Inexactitude lie, 546
Inexcitability
inexcitability, 826
Inexcusable
vice, 938, 945
Inexecution
non-completion, 730
Inexhaustible
sufficiency, 639
Inexistence
inexistence, 2
Inexorable
resolved, 604
stern, 739
compelling, 744
wrathful, 900
relentless, 907
Inexpectation
inexpectation, 508
Inexpedient
inexpedience, 647
Inexpensive
cheapness, 815
Inexperience
ignorance, 491
disqualification, 699
Inexpert
unskilfulness, 699
Inexpiable
vice, 945
Inexplicable
unintelligible, 519
wonderful, 870

Inexpressible
unmeaning, 517
wonder, 870
great degree, 31
Inexpressive
unmeaning, 517, 519
Inexpugnable
safety, 664
Inextinguishable
immutable, 150
uncontrollable, 825
energetic, 157
Inextricable
difficult, 704
impossible, 471
disorder, 59
coherence, 46
Infallible
certainty, 474
perfect, 650
Infamy
dishonour, 940
shame, 874
vice, 945
Infancy
beginning, 66
youth, 127
Infant
infant, 129
Infanta
master, 745
Infanticide
killing, 361
Infantile
puerile, 643
foolish, 499
Infantry
combatant, 726
Infatuation
folly, 499
misjudgment, 481
obstinacy, 606
credulity, 486
passion, 825
love, 897
Infeasible
impossible, 471
difficult, 704
Infect
mix, 41
Infection
disease, 655
contamination, 659
excitation, 824

Infectious
insalubrity, 657
Infecund
unproductiveness, 169
Infelicity
unhappiness, 828
inexpertness, 699
Infer
judgment, 480
Inference
judgment, 480
interpretation, 522
Inferential
deducible, 478
Inferior
less, 34
imperfect, 651
Infernal
bad, 649
wicked, 945
malevolent, 907
Infertility
unproductiveness, 169
Infest
annoy, 649, 830
frequent, 136
Infibulation
junction, 43
Infidel
heathen, 984
Infidelity
dishonour, 940
irreligion, 989
Infiltrate
intervene, 228
influence, 175
imbue, 339
teach, 537
mixture, 41
Infiltration
ingress, 294
passage, 302
presence, 186
Infinite
in quantity, 105
in degree, 31
in size, 192
Infinitesimal
in degree, 32
in quantity, 193
Infinity
infinitude, 105
space, 180
Infirm
weak, 160

irresolute, 605
vicious, 945
Infirmary
remedy, 662
Infirmity
weakness, 160
disease, 655
failing, 945
Infix
teaching, 537
Inflame
burn, 384
stir up, 173
incense, 900
incite, 615
Inflammation
disease, 655
Inflate
expend, 194
rarefy, 322
blow, 349
style, 573, 577
ridiculous, 853
vanity, 880
Inflect
curvature, 245
grammar, 567
Inflexible
hard, 323
resolved, 604
obstinate, 606
stern, 739
Inflexion
curvature, 245
change, 140
appendage, 39
grammar, 567
Inflict
condemn, 971
act upon, 680
give pain, 830
Infliction
pain, 828
Influence
physical, 175
authority, 737
inducement, 615
importance, 642
Influential
important, 642
Influx
ingress, 294
Inform
information, 527
Inform against

accusation, 938
Informal
irregular, 83
lawless, 964
Information
knowledge, 490
communication, 527
Informer
witness, 467
Infra
posterior, 117
Infra dignitatem
disrepute, 874
Infra-microscopic
little, 193
Infraction
non-observance, 773
unconformity, 83
exemption, 927
disobedience, 742
violation, 614
Infrangible
coherence, 46, 321
Infrastructure
base, 211
Infrequency
infrequency, 137
fewness, 103
Infringe
transgress, 303
violate, 742, 773, 925, 927
break through, 614
Infundibular
concavity, 252
Infuriate
wrathful, 900
excite, 824
violent, 173
Infuse
mix, 41
insert, 300
teach, 537
Infusible
solid, 321
Ingeminate
duplication, 90
Ingenious
skill, 698
Ingénue
actress, 599
Ingenuous
artless, 703
sincere, 543
guileless, 939

Ingest
absorb, 296
Ingle
fuel, 388
Inglorious
disrepute, 874
base, 940
Ingoing
ingress, 294
Ingot
money, 800
Ingraft
see Engraft
Ingrate
ingratitude, 917
Ingratiate
love, 897
Ingratitude
ingratitude, 917
Ingredient
component, 56
Ingress
ingress, 294
Ingrowing
insertion, 300
Ingurgitate
reception, 296
Inhabile
unskilfulness, 699
Inhabit
presence, 186
Inhabitant
inhabitant, 188
Inhale
reception, 296
sniff, 398
Inharmonious
discordant, 414
incongruity, 24
Inherence
intrinsicality, 5
Inherit
acquire, 775
possess, 777
Inheritance
property, 780
Inhesion
intrinsicality, 5
Inhibit
prohibit, 761
not think of, 452
dissuade, 616
hinder, 706
Inhospitable
seclusion, 893

Inhuman
malevolence, 907
Inhume
interment, 363
Inimical
hostile, 708, 889
unfavourable, 706
Inimitable
perfect, 650
good, 648
Iniquitous
bad, 649
Iniquity
wrong, 923
vice, 945
Initiate
begin, 66
teach, 537
Initiated
skilful, 698
Initiative
enterprise, 676
beginning, 66
Inject
insertion, 300
Injudicious
folly, 499
inexpedient, 647
Injunction
command, 741
prohibition, 761
advice, 695
decree, 963
Injure
to damage, 659
malevolence, 907
Injury
harm, 649
Injustice
wrong, 923
Ink
blackness, 431
Ink-slinger
writer, 590
Inkle
connection, 45
Inkling
information, 527
supposition, 514
knowledge, 490
Inlaid
variegation, 440
Inland
interiority, 221
Inlay

variegation, 440
Inlet
opening, 260
way, 627
beginning, 66
of the sea, 343
Inly
interiority, 221
Inmate
inhabitant, 188
Inmost
interiority, 221
Inn
abode, 189
Innate
intrinsicality, 5
Innavigable
difficulty, 704
Inner
interiority, 221
Innocence
innocence, 946
probity, 939
virtue, 944
Innocuous
harmless, 648
wholesome, 656
Innominate
misnomer, 565
Innovation
newness, 123
change, 140
Innoxious
innocent, 946
salubrious, 656
harmless, 648
Innuendo
information, 527
insinuation, 932
Innumerable
infinity, 105
Inobservance
non-observance, 773
Inoculate
insert, 300
teach, 537
Inodorous
inodorousness, 399
Inoffensive
harmless, 648, 946
Inofficious
malevolence, 907
Inoperative
unproductive, 169
useless, 645

Inopportune
untimely, 135
inexpedient, 647
Inordinate
size, 192
superfluous, 641
excessive, 31
Inorganic
inorganization, 358
Inosculate
intersect, 219
convoluted, 248
joined, 43
Inquest
inquiry, 461
jurisdiction, 965
Inquietude
uneasiness, 828
apprehension, 860
discontent, 832
restlessness, 264
disorder, 59
Inquiry
search, 461
curiosity, 455
Inquisition
inquiry, 461
jurisdiction, 965
Inroad
ingress, 294
invasion, 716
devastation, 619
Insalubrity
insalubrity, 657
Insane
mad, 503
rash, 863
Insanitary
insalubrious, 657
Insatiable
desire, 865
Inscribe
write, 590
label, 551
represent, 554
Inscrutable
unintelligibility, 519
Insculpture
sculpture, 557
Insect
animal, 366
minute, 193
Insecure
danger, 665
Insensate

foolish, 499
mad, 503
Insensibility
physical, 376
moral, 823
Inseparable
cohering, 46
attached, 43
Insert
put in, 300
locate, 184
interpose, 228
enter, 294
Inseverable
junction, 43
unity, 87
Inside
interiority, 221
Insidious
false, 544
cunning, 702
dishonourable, 940
Insight
knowledge, 490
intuition, 477
Insignia
indication, 550
Insignificance
smallness, 32
Insignificant
unimportance, 643
Insincere
falsehood, 544
Insinuate
intervene, 228
ingress, 294
mean, 516
suppose, 514
hint, 527
blame, 932
insert, 300
Insipid
tasteless, 391
dull, 575
indifferent, 866
Insist
command, 741
Insistent
importunate, 830
Insobriety
drunkenness, 959
Insolence
insolence, 885
Insoluble
dense, 321

unintelligible, 519
Insolvent
non-payment, 808
Insomnia
wakefulness, 680
Insomuch
greatness, 31
Insouciance
thoughtlessness, 458
supineness, 823
indifference, 866
Inspan
harness, 43
depart, 293
Inspect
look, 441
attend to, 457
Inspector
spectator, 444
director, 694
inquirer, 461
Inspiration
breathing, 349
impulse, 612
excitation, 824
prompting, 615
imagination, 515
wisdom, 498
piety, 987
Inspire
prompt, 615
animate, 824
Inspirit
urge, 615
animate, 824
cheer, 836
courage, 861
Inspissation
semiliquidity, 352
Instability
mutability, 149
Install
locate, 184
commission, 755
celebrate, 883
ordain, 995
Instalment
portion, 51
payment, 807
Instance
example, 82
solicitation, 765
motive, 615
Instancy
urgency, 642

Instant
moment, 113
present, 118
future, 121
Instanter
earlier, 132
instantaneity, 113
Instauration
restoration, 600
Instead
substitution, 147
Instigate
motive, 615
Instil
insert, 300
teach, 537
mix, 41
Instinct
intellect, 450
intuition, 477
impulse, 601
innate, 5
Instinctive
habitual, 613
impulsive, 612
Institute
school, 542
beginning, 66
cause, 153
organize, 161
Institution
legality, 963
poorhouse, 804
Institutor
teacher, 540
Instruct
teach, 537
advise, 695
precept, 697
command, 741
Instructor
teacher, 540
Instrument
implement, 633
record, 551
security, 771
Instrumental
means, 632
music, 415
subservient, 631
Instrumentality
medium, 631
Insubordinate
disobedience, 742
anarchy, 738

Insubstantiality
nothingness, 4
Insufferable
painfulness, 830
Insufficient
insuffiency, 640
shortcoming, 304
Insufflation
wind, 349
Insular
island, 346
detach, 44
single, 87
Insulate
separate, 44
Insult
rudeness, 895
disrespect, 929
offence, 900
Insuperable
difficulty, 704
impossible, 471
Insupportable
painfulness, 830
Insuppressible
violence, 173
Insurance
promise, 768
security, 771
precaution, 664
Insurgent
disobedience, 742
Insurmountable
difficulty, 704
impossible, 471
Insurrection
disobedience, 742
resistance, 719
Insusceptible
insensibility, 823
Intact permanence, 141
preserve, 669
Intaglio
concavity, 252
sculpture, 557
Intake
inlet, 260
Intangible
numbness, 381
immaterial, 317
Integer
whole, 50
Integral calculus
number, 84
Integral part

component, 56
Integrate
consolidate, 50
complete, 52
Integration
number, 84
Integrity
whole, 50
virtue, 944
probity, 939
Integument
overing, 222
Intellect
intellect, 450
Intelligence
mind, 450
news, 532
wisdom, 498
Intelligible
intelligibility, 518, 570
Intemperate
intemperance, 954
drunkenness, 957
Intempestivity
unseasonableness, 135
Intend
design, 620
Intendant
director, 694
Intended
will, 600
Intensify
energize, 171
aggravate, 835
Intensity
degree, 26
greatness, 31
energy, 171
Intent
active, 682
thoughtful, 451, 457
Intention
design, 620
Intentional
will, 600
Intentness
attention, 457
thought, 451
Inter
bury, 363
insert, 300
Inter alia
conformity, 82
Interaction
reciprocal, 12

Interblend
  mix, 41
Interbreed
  mix, 41
Intercalate
  insert, 300
  intervene, 228
Intercede
  mediate, 724
  deprecate, 766
Intercept
  hinder, 706
  take, 789
Intercession
  deprecation, 766
Interchange
  interchange, 148
  reciprocate, 12
  barter, 794
  transfer, 783
Intercipient
  hinder, 706
Interclude
  hindrance, 706
Intercom
  hearing, 418
Intercommunicate
  interlocution, 588
  information, 527
Intercommunion
  society, 892
Intercostal
  interiority, 221
Intercourse
  converse, 588
Intercross
  mix, 41
Intercurrence
  passage, 302
Interdict
  prohibition, 761
Interdigitate
  intervene, 228
  intersect, 219
Interest
  advantage, 618
  concern, 9
  importance, 642
  curiosity, 455
  attention, 457
  aid, 707
  to please, 829
  debt, 806
Interested
  selfish, 943

Interesting
  style, 574
Interfere
  intervene, 228
  meddle, 682
  disagree, 24
  counteract, 179
  thwart, 706
  mediate, 724
  activity, 682
Interglossa
  language, 560
Interim
  duration, 106
  synchronism, 120
Interior
  interiority, 221
Interjacence
  coming between, 228
  middle, 68
Interject
  insert, 300
  interpose, 228
Interlace
  twine, 219
  join, 43
Interlard
  interpose, 228
  mix, 41
  insert, 300
Interleave
  interjacence, 228
  addition, 37
Interline
  insert, 228
  write, 590
Interlink
  junction, 43
Interlocation
  interjacence, 228
Interlock
  cross, 219
  join, 43
Interlocution
  interlocution, 588
Interloper
  intervene, 228
  obstruct, 706
  extraneous, 57
Interlude
  dramatic, 599
  time, 106
  interjacence, 228
  interruption, 70
Intermarriage

  marriage, 903
Intermeddle
  hinder, 706
  interfere, 682
Intermeddling
  mediation, 724
Intermediary
  messenger, 534
Intermediate
  mean, 29
  middle, 68
  intervening, 228
Intermedium
  link, 45
  instrument, 631
  intervention, 228
Interment
  interment, 300, 363
Intermezzo
  interlude, 106
  music, 415
Interminable
  infinite, 105
  eternal, 112
  long, 200
Intermingle
  mixture, 41
Intermission
  discontinuance, 142
Intermit
  interrupt, 70
  discontinue, 142
  recur, 138
  suspend, 265
  in time, 106
Intermix
  mixture, 41
Intermutation
  interchange, 148
Intern
  restrain, 751
Internal
  interior, 221
  intrinsic, 5
International
  reciprocal, 12
  law, 963
Internecine
  slaughter, 361
  war, 722
Internuncio
  messenger, 534
  consignee, 758
Interpellation
  inquiry, 461

evolve, 313
Intrude
intervene, 228
enter, 294
inopportune, 135
interfere, 24
Intruder
extraneous, 57, 228
Intrusion
mixture, 41
Intuition
mind, 450
instinct, 477
knowledge, 490
Intuitive
instinctive, 477
Intumescence
expansion, 194
convexity, 250
Inunction
covering, 222
Inundate
effusion, 337
flow, 348
redundance, 641
Inurbanity
discourteous, 895
Inure
habituate, 613
train, 673
harden, 823
Inutility
inutility, 645
Invade ingress, 294
attack, 716
Invalid
disease, 655
Invalidate
disable, 158
disentitle, 925
illegalize, 964
confute, 479
rebut, 468
Invalidity
confutation, 479
Invaluable
goodness, 648
Invariable
intrinsic, 5
immutability, 150
Invasion
ingress, 294
attack, 716
Invective
accusation, 938

malediction, 908
abuse, 932
Inveigh
blame, 932
Inveigle
deceive, 546
seduce, 615
Invent
imagine, 515
devise, 626
falsehood, 544
Inventive
skilful, 698
productive, 168
original, 20
Inventory
list, 86
record, 551
Inversion
reversion, 145
of position, 218, 237
of relation, 14
of order, 59, 61
Invertebrate
feeble, 160, 575
vicious, 945
irresolute, 605
Invest
give, 784
lend, 787
empower, 157, 755
ascribe, 155
clothe, 225
besiege, 716
Investigate
inquiry, 461
Investiture
see Invest
Investment
see Invest
Inveterate
habit, 613
old, 124
Invidious
envy, 921
hatred, 898
unfair, 923
Invigorate
stimulate, 171
Invigoration
strength, 159
Invincible
strength, 159
Inviolable
right, 924

honour, 939
concealment, 528
Inviolate
unchanged, 141
concealed, 528
Invisible
not to be seen, 447
small, 193
latent, 526
Invite
ask, 765
offer, 763
induce, 615
Inviting
pleasing, 899
alluring, 615
Invoice
list, 86
record, 551
Invoke
implore, 767
pray, 990
address, 586
curse, 908
Involuntary
compulsory, 601
unintentional, 621
Involution
disorder, 59
convolution, 248
numerical, 85
style, 571
Involve
derange, 61
include, 54
wrap, 225
evidence, 467
meaning, 516
Involved
disorder, 59
in debt, 806
Invulnerable
safety, 664
Inward
interiority, 221
Inweave
crossing, 219
Ionosphere
air, 338
Iota
particle, 32
minute, 193
Ipse dixit
certainty, 474

Ipsissimis verbis
word, 562
Ipso facto
being, 1
truth, 494
Irascible
anger, 901
Irate
resentment, 900
Ire
resentment, 900
Iridiscent
variegation, 440
changeable, 149
Iris
variegation, 440
eye, 441
Irish bull
ridiculousness, 853
error, 495
Irishism
absurdity, 497
error, 495
Irk
oppress, 830
tire, 688
Irksome
tiresome, 688
tedious, 841
oppressive, 830
Iron
strength, 159
hardness, 323
club, 276
to smooth, 255
Iron age
adversity, 735
Iron curtain
secret, 533
Iron-hearted
malevolence, 907
Ironclad ship, 273
covering, 222
defence, 717
Irons
fetters, 752
Irony
ridicule, 856
untruth, 544, 546
Irradiate
light, 420
Irrational
number, 84
silly, 477, 499
ridiculous, 853
Irreclaimable

vile, 945
impenitent, 951
Irreconcilable
discordant, 24
unrelated, 10
hostile, 889
Irrecoverable
lost, 776
past, 122
Irredeemable
impenitent, 951
Irreducible
out of order, 59
discordant, 24
fixed, 150
Irrefragable
certain, 475
proved, 478
Irrefutable
certain, 475
proved, 467, 478
Irregular
out of order, 59
against rule, 83
in time, 139
distorted, 243
multiform, 16A, 81
fighter, 726
Irrelation
unrelated, 10
disagreement, 24
Irrelevant
unrelated, 10
unaccordant, 24
sophistical, 477
Irreligion
atheism, 989
Irremediable
lost, 776
hopeless, 859
bad, 649
Irremissible
vice, 945
Irremovable
immutable, 150
quiescence, 265
Irreparable
loss, 776
bad, 649
hopeless, 859
Irrepentance
impenitence, 951
Irreplaceable
indispensable, 630
Irrepressible

violent, 173
excitement, 825
free, 778
Irreproachable
innocence, 946
Irresistible
strength, 159
compulsory, 601
evidence, 467
Irresolute
irresolution, 149, 605
Irresolvable
unity, 87
Irrespective
irrelation, 10
Irresponsible
exempt, 279A
arbitrary, 964
silly, 499
Irretrievable
lost, 776
Irreverence
disrespect, 929
impiety, 988
Irreversible
past, 122
immutable, 150
Irrevocable
immutable, 150, 601,
604
hopeless, 859
Irrigate
water, 337
Irritable
excitable, 825
irascible, 901
Irritate
provoke, 898
incense, 900
fret, 828
pain, 830
Irruption
ingress, 294
invasion, 716
Ishmael
enemy, 891
Isis
deity, 979
Islam
religions, 984
Island
island, 346
Isobar
air, 338

Jasper-coloured
green, 435
Jaundiced
prejudiced, 481
jealous, 920
dejected, 837
yellow, 436
Jaunt
journey, 266
Jaunting-car
vehicle, 272
Jaunty
fashionable, 852
pretty, 845
showy, 882
Javelin
arms, 727
Jaw
mouth, 230
loquacity, 584
to scold, 932
Jaw-breaker
neology, 563
Jay
loquacity, 584
Jazz
melody, 413
Je ne sais quoi
euphemism, 565
Jealousy
envy, 920
Jeans
dress, 225
Jeep
vehicle, 272
Jeer
gibe, 856, 929
joke, 842
Jehovah
Deity, 976
Jehu
director, 694
Jejune
scanty, 640
style, 575
Jell
set, 321
Jelly
pulpiness, 354
sweet, 396
Jellyfish
weakness, 160
Jennet
carrier, 271
Jeopardy
danger, 665

Jeremiad
invective, 932, 938
lamentations, 839
Jerk
throw, 146, 284
draw, 285
agitate, 315
bad man, 949
Jerry
flimsy, 643
Jerry-built
fragile, 328
Jersey
dress, 225
Jest
wit, 842
trifle, 643
Jester
humorist, 844
buffoon, 857
Jesuit
clergy, 996
Jesuitry
deception, 544
sophistry, 477
Jesus
Deity, 976
Jet
water, 347
stream, 348
aircraft, 273A
blackness, 431
Jetsam
fragments, 51
little, 643
Jettison
abandon, 782
Jetty
convexity, 250
Jeu d'esprit
wit, 842
Jeu de mots
neology, 563
Jeu de théâtre
appearance, 448
Jeune fille
girl, 129
Jew
religions, 984
Jewel
gem, 650
ornament, 847
goodness, 648
favourite, 899
Jew's harp

musical, 417
Jezebel
wretch, 949
courtesan, 962
Jib
deviation, 279
demur, 603
Jibe
accord, 23
Jiffy
instant, 113
Jig
dance, 840
Jilt
deception, 545
lovelorn, 898
Jimjams
insanity, 503
Jingle
resonance, 408
vehicle, 272
Jingo
warlike, 722
boasting, 884
blusterer, 887
Jinnee
demon, 980
Jinx
spell, 993
Jitters
fear, 860
Jiu-jitsu
contention, 720
Jive
rhythm, 413
Job
business, 625
action, 680
unfairness, 940
Jobation
upbraiding, 932
Jobber
merchant, 797
agent, 690
trickster, 943
Jobbernowl
fool, 501
Jobbery
cunning, 702
Jobbing
skill, 698
barter, 794
Jockey
horseman, 268
servant, 746

to deceive, 545
deceiver, 548

Jocose
witty, 836, 840, 842

Jocular
gay, 836
amusing, 840

Jocund
cheerful, 836

Joe Soap
fool, 501
dupe, 547

Jog
push, 276
shake, 315

Jog on
advance, 282
slowness, 275
trudge, 266

Jog-trot
routine, 613

Joggle
agitation, 315

Johnsonian
style, 577

Join
junction, 43
contiguity, 199

Joint
part, 44, 51
junction, 43
flexure, 258
accompanying, 88

Joint stock
share, 778

Jointly
addition, 37

Jointress
widow, 905

Jointure
receipt, 810
property, 780

Joist
support, 215

Joke
wit, 842
trifle, 643

Jollification
spree, 954

Jollity
amusement, 480

Jolly
gay, 836
conviviality, 892
pleasing, 829

plump, 192
joke, 842
flatter, 933

Jolly-boat
ship, 273

Jolt
impulse, 276
agitation, 315
shock, 824

Jonathan Wild
thief, 792

Jorum
receptacle, 191

Josh
tease, 830
joke, 842
ridicule, 856

Joskin
clown, 876

Joss
idolatry, 991

Joss-house
temple, 1000

Jostle
clash, 24
push, 276
agitate, 315

Jot
small quantity, 32
particle, 193
to record, 551

Jotting
writing, 590

Jounce
agitation, 315

Journal
annals, 114
record, 551
description, 594
book, 593

Journalism
publication, 531

Journalist
recorder, 553
writer, 590

Journey
journey, 266
progression, 282

Journeyman
agent, 690
servant, 746

Joust
contention, 720

Jove
god, 979

Jovial
gay, 836
convivial, 892
amusement, 840

Jowl
laterality, 236

Joy
pleasure, 827

Joy-ride
journey, 266

Joyful
cheerful, 836

Joyless
dejection, 830, 837

Joyous
cheerful, 836

Jubilant
joyous, 836
boastful, 884

Jubilation
celebration, 882

Jubilee
rejoicing, 836, 838
festival, 840
anniversary, 138
celebration, 883

Judaism
religions, 984

Judge
arbitrator, 967
master, 745
taste, 850

Judgmatic
wisdom, 498

Judgment
decision, 480
intellect, 450
belief, 484
wisdom, 498
sentence, 969

Judgment-seat
tribunal, 966

Judicature
law, 965

Judicial
discriminative, 465
impartial, 922

Judicious
wisdom, 498
expedient, 646

Jug
receptacle, 191
prison, 752

Juggernaut
idol, 991

Juggle
deception, 545

Juice
liquid, 333

Juicy
moist, 339
style, 574

Ju-ju
idol, 991

Jujube
sweet, 396

Juke box
mechanical instrument, 417

Julep
sweet, 396

Jumble
confusion, 59
derangement, 61
mixture, 41

Jump
leap, 309, 146
dance, 840

Jump at
seize, 789
pursue, 622
desire, 865
conclusion, 480

Jump over
neglect, 460

Jumper
dress, 225

Jumpy
fear, 860

Junction
join, 43

Juncture
period, 134
circumstance, 8
junction, 43

Jungle
plant, 367
disorder, 59

Junior
youth, 127

Junk
ship, 273
trumpery, 643, 645

Junket
merry-making, 840
dish, 298

Junkie
addict, 613

Juno
goddess, 979

Junta
party, 712
council, 696

Jupiter
god, 979

Jure divino
dueness, 624

Jurisconsult '
lawyer, 958

Jurisdiction
law, 965
authority, 737

Jurisprudence
law, 963

Jurist
lawyer, 968

Jury
judge, 967

Jury-mast
resource, 666

Jus gentium
law, 963

Just
accurate, 494
reasonable, 476
right, 922
equitable, 939

Just as
similarity, 17

Just so
assent, 488

Juste milieu
mean, 29

Justice
right, 922
legality, 963
magistrate, 967

Justiciar
judge, 967

Justification
religious, 987
vindication, 937

Justify
deity, 976

Jut out
convexity, 250

Juvenescence
youth, 127

Juvenile
youth, 127

Juxtaposition
contiguity, 199

K.C.
lawyer, 968

K.O.
end, 67

Kadi
judge, 967

Kaleidoscope
optical, 445
changeable, 149

Kaput
done for, 360

Karma
destiny, 152

Katabolism
dissolution, 360

Kavass
authority, 745
jurisdiction, 965

Keck
ejection, 297

Kedge
anchor, 666
ship, 273

Keel
base, 211

Keelhaul
punish, 972

Keen
sharp, 253
cold, 383
energetic, 171
poignant, 821
desirous, 865
lament, 363, 839

Keen-witted
wisdom, 498

Keep
retain, 781
custody, 751
prison, 752
refuge, 666
to observe, 772
to celebrate, 883
to continue, 141, 143
food, 298
provision, 637
preserve, 670

Keep back
conceal, 528
disuse, 678
dissuade, 616

Keep from
refrain, 603

Keep off
distance, 196

Kiss
endearment, 902
courtesy, 894
of death, 361

Kit
bag, 191
accoutrements, 225
fiddle, 417

Kitcat
painting, 556

Kitchen
workshop, 691
room, 191

Kitchen garden
agriculture, 371

Kitchen-maid
servant, 746

Kite
flying, 273A
bill, 800

Kith and kin
consanguinity, 11

Kittle
sensation, 380

Kitty
stake, 771

Kleptomania
desire, 865
insanity, 503, 504

Knack
skill, 698
toy, 840

Knap
ridge, 206
to break, 44

Knapsack
receptacle, 191

Knave
deceiver, 548
rouge, 941
dishonour, 949

Knavish
improbity, 940

Knead
mix, 41
soften, 324

Knee
angularity, 244

Kneel
beg, 765
respect, 928
submission, 725
stoop, 308
pray, 990
servility, 886

Knell
interment, 363

Knick-knack
unimportant, 643
ornament, 847

Knife
sharpness, 253
kill, 361

Knight
noble, 875

Knight errant
defence, 717
rash, 863

Knighthood
title, 877

Knit
junction, 43

Knob
protuberance, 250
ball, 249

Knobkerrie
arms, 727
club, 276

Knock
blow, 276, 619
sound, 406
beat, 972
disparage, 483, 932
vilify, 874

Knock about
maltreat, 649
wander, 266
boisterous, 173

Knock down
destroy, 162
overthrow, 308

Knock-kneed
curved, 245
distorted, 243

Knock off
finish, 729
cease, 142
steal, 791

Knock out
beating, 972
end, 67
combine, 778

Knock under
yield, 725
obey, 743

Knock up
fatigue, 688
distorted, 243

Knoll
height, 206

Knot
ligature, 45
to fasten, 43
entanglement, 59
group, 72, 892
intersection, 219
difficulty, 704
ornament, 847

Knotted
crossing, 219

Knotty
difficult, 704
dense, 321

Knout
scourge, 972, 975

Know-all
sage, 500

Know-how
skill, 698

Know no bounds
greatness, 31

Knowing
skill, 698
cunning, 702

Knowingly
intentionally, 620

Knowledge
know, 490

Knuckle
angularity, 244

Knuckle-duster
arms, 727

Knuckle under
submit, 725
humble, 879

Kobold
gnome, 980

Kodachrome
photograph, 556

Kopje
height, 206

Koran
sacred books, 986

Kowtow
bow, 308, 894
respect, 928
submission, 725
obedience, 743

Kraal
abode, 189

Kraken
monster, 83

Kriegie
prisoner, 753

Kris
knife, 727
Ku Klux Klan
illegality, 964
Kudos
repute, 873, 931
Kukri
arms, 727
Kyanize
preserve, 670
Kyle
gap, 198
gulf, 343
Kyte
belly, 191
convexity, 250

L.S.D.
money, 800
Laager
defence, 717
Labarum
flag, 550
Label
indication, 550
Labial
letter, 561
Laboratory
workshop, 691
Labour
exertion, 686
work, 680
difficulty, 704
Labourer
agent, 690
Labyrinth
secret, 533
difficulty, 704
disorder, 59
convolution, 248
Lace
tie, 43
net, 219
to beat, 972
Lacerable
fragile, 328
Lacerate
disjunction, 44
pain, 830
Laches
neglect, 460
omission, 773
Lachrymation
lamentation, 839

Lack
insufficiency, 640
destitution, 804
requisition, 630
number, 98
Lack-brain
fool, 501
Lack-lustre
dim, 423
discoloured, 429
Lackadaisical
affected, 855
indifferent, 866
Lacker
see Lacquer
Lackey
servant, 746
Laconic
conciseness, 572
shortness, 201
Lacquer
varnish, 22
adorn, 845, 847
Lacteal
semiliquid, 352
Lacuna
orifice, 260
pit, 252
deficiency, 53
interval, 198
break, 70
Lacuscular
lake, 343
Lacustrine
lake, 343
Lad
infant, 129
Ladder
method, 627
Lade
transfer, 270
Laden
charged, 639
La-di-da
foppish, 855P
Lading
cargo, 190, 635
baggage, 780
Ladle
spoon, 272
vessel, 191
Lady
woman, 374
wife, 903
noble, 875

Lady help
servant, 746
Lady-killer
fop, 854
philanderer, 902
Lady-love
sweetheart, 897
Ladylike
fashion, 852
courteous, 894
noble, 875
Lag
linger, 275
follow, 281
dawdle, 683
lateness, 133
imprison, 751
prisoner, 754
Laggard
slack, 603, 683
Lagoon
lake, 343
Laical
laity, 997
Lair
den, 189
sty, 653
Laird
nobility, 875
possessor, 779
Laissez aller
inactivity, 683
Laissez faire
laxity, 738
inactivity, 683
permanence, 141
Laity
laity, 997
Lake
lake, 343
Lama
priest, 996
master, 745
Lamarckism
causation, 153
Lamb
innocent, 946
nursling, 129
Saviour, 976
saint, 948
Lambent flame
light, 420
Lamblike
innocent, 946

Lame
    weak, 160
    bad, 649
    imperfect, 65
    failing, 732
    laxity, 738
Lamella
    layer, 204
Lament
    complain, 839
    regret, 833
    funeral, 363
    pity, 914
Lamentable
    greatness, 31
    painful, 830
    regret, 833
Lamia
    demon, 980
Lamina
    layer, 204
    part, 51
Lamp
    luminary, 423
Lampoon
    disparage, 932
    libel, 934
Lance
    perforate, 260
    javelin, 727
Lancer
    combatant, 726
Lancet
    perforator, 262
    sharpness, 253
Lancinate
    pain, 378
Land
    ground, 342
    to arrive, 292
    to stop, 265
    estate, 780
Land girl
    agriculture, 371
Land-mine
    arms, 727
Landau
    vehicle, 272
Landaulette
    vehicle, 272
Landgrave
    master, 745
Landing-ground
    arrival, 292
Landing-place
    support, 215

    destination, 292
Landing-stage
    arrival, 292
Landlocked
    circumscribed, 231
Landlord
    possessor, 779
Landlubber
    bungler, 701
Landmark
    indicate, 550
Landowner
    possessor, 779
Landscape
    view, 448
    delineation, 556
Landslide
    fall, 306
Landslip
    fall, 306
Lane
    street, 189
    way, 627
Language
    words, 560
Languid
    weak, 160
    slow, 275
    torpid, 683, 823
    style, 575
Languish
    desire, 865
    illness, 655
    decline, 36
Languor
    weakness, 160
    inactivity, 683
Lank
    little, 193
Lanolin
    oil, 356
Lantern
    light, 423
Lantern-jawed
    lean, 193
Lao-Tsze
    religious founder, 986
Lap
    support, 215
    interior, 221
    to wrap, 222
    encompass, 227
    speed, 274
    surpass, 303
    drink, 296

Lapel
    fold, 258
Lapidary
    concise, 572
Lapidate
    kill, 361
Lapis lazuli
    blue, 438
Lappet
    adjunct, 39
Lapse
    of time, 109, 135
    past time, 122
    fall, 306
    be lost, 776
    degeneracy, 659
    guilt, 947
    error, 495
Lapsus linguae
    solecism, 568
    ridicule, 856
    error, 495
    equivocal, 520
Larboard
    left, 239
Larcener
    thief, 792
Larceny
    theft, 791
Lard
    unctuousness, 353, 256
Larder
    store, 636
    food, 298
Lares and Penates
    abode, 189
Large
    in quantity, 31
    in size, 192
Largess
    giving, 784, 809
Largo
    slowness, 275, 415
Lariat
    vinculum, 45
Lark
    mount, 305
    frolic, 840
Larrikin
    rowdy, 949
    evildoer, 913
Larrup
    strike, 972
Larva
    youth, 127

Larynx
air-pipe, 351
Lascivious
impure, 961
Lash
tie together, 43
punish, 972
scourge, 830, 975
censure, 932
violence, 173
Lashings
plenty, 639
Lass
girl, 129, 374
Lassitude
fatigue, 688
weariness, 841
Lasso
vinculum, 45
Last
in order, 67
endure, 106
continue, 141
durable, 110
model, 22
Last post
signal, 550
Latakia
tobacco, 298A
Latch
vinculum, 45
Latchet
vinculum, 45
Late
tardy, 133
past, 122
new, 123
Latent
concealed, 526
Latent
implied, 516
inert, 172
Later
posterior, 117
Lateral
side, 236
Lath
strip, 205
Lathe
instrument, 633
Lather
foam, 353
to flog, 972
Lathi
impact, 276

arms, 727
Latitude
scope, 180
situation, 183
breadth, 202
freedom, 748
Latitudinarian
heterodoxy, 984A
Latrine
room, 191
Latter
sequent, 63
past, 122
Lattice
crossing, 219
opening, 260
Laud
praise, 931
worship, 990
Laudable
virtue, 944
Laudanum
anaesthetic, 376
Laudation
approval, 931
Laudator temporis acti
oldness, 124
permanence, 141
discontent, 832
lamentation, 839
Lauds
worship, 990
Laugh
rejoice, 838
Laugh at
ridicule, 856
sneer, 929
underestimate, 483
joke, 842
Laughable
ridiculous, 853
Laughing gas
anaesthetic, 376
Laughing-stock
ridicule, 857
Laughter
rejoice, 836, 838, 840
Launch
propel, 284
begin, 66
adventure, 876
Launch out
expatiate, 584
style, 573
Laundress

servant, 746
Laundry
cleanness, 652
Laureate
poetry, 597
Laurel
trophy, 733
reward, 973
glory, 873
decoration, 877
Lava
semiliquid, 352
Lavatory
room, 191
privy, 653
Lave
cleanness, 652
water, 337
Lavender
colour, 437
fragrance, 400
Lavish
prodigal, 818
giving, 784
profuse, 639, 641
liberal, 816
Lavolta
dance, 840
Law
rule, 80, 697
ordination, 963
command, 741
permission, 760
Lawful
dueness, 924
allowable, 760
Lawless
arbitrary, 964
irregular, 83
Lawn
plain, 344
Lawsuit
law, 969
Lawyer
lawyer, 968
Lax
incoherent, 47
soft, 324
diffuse, 573
disuse, 614
remiss, 738
licentious, 945
Laxative
remedy, 662

Lay
place, 184
assuage, physically, 174
assuage, morally, 826
bet, 151
poetry, 597
music, 415
level, 213
secular, 997
Lay aside
relinquish, 624
give up, 782
cease, 142
reject, 610
Lay bare
manifest, 525
Lay brother
clergy, 996
Lay by
store, 636
economize, 817
Lay down
assert, 535
renounce, 757
Lay figure
prototype, 22
effigy, 554
nonentity, 643
Lay in
store, 636
Lay into
punish, 972
buffet, 276
Lay open
disclose, 529
show, 525
divest, 226
Lay out
level, 213
Lay to
stop, 265
be inactive, 683
repose, 687
Lay up
illness, 655
store, 636
Lay waste
ravage, 649
disorganize, 659
Layer
layer, 204
Layman
laity, 997
Laystall
unclean, 653

Lazaretto
remedy, 662
Lazy
inactive, 683
slow, 275
Lea
plain, 342, 344
Lead
to precede in order, 62
precede in motion, 280
to tend, 176
to direct, 693
to induce, 615
authority, 737
heaviness, 319
depth, 208
Lead-line
measurement, 466
Lead off
begin, 66
precursor, 64
Leader
master, 745
director, 694
dissertation, 595
Leading
important, 642
Leading strings
subjection, 749
Leaf
part, 51
plant, 367
layer, 204
of a book, 593
Leaflet
part, 51
League
party, 712
Leak
dribble, 295
waste, 638
Lean
thin, 193
narrow, 203
oblique, 217
recline, 215
Lean-to
building, 189
Leaning
direction, 278
tendency, 176
willingness, 602
Leap
jump, 309
Leap to

change, 140
Learned
knowledge, 490, 492
Learner
learner, 541
Learning
acquiring, 539
erudition, 490
Lease
sale, 796
property, 780
Lease-lend
lend, 787
Leash
tie, 43
three, 92
Least
inferiority, 34
Leat
conduit, 350
Leather
to beat, 972
toughness, 327
Leatherneck
fighter, 726
Leave
quit, 293
vacate, 185
relinquish, 624
permission, 760
bequeath, 784
Leave off
cessation, 142, 614, 624
Leave out
exclusion, 55
Leave over
postpone, 133
Leaven
cause, 153
Leavings
remainder, 40
Lebensraum
freedom, 748
Lecher
libertine, 962
Lechery
impurity, 961
Lectern
church, 1000
Lecture
teach, 537
censure, 932
discourse, 582, 595
Lecturer
learner, 541

Ledge
support, 215
Ledger
accounts, 811
record, 551
list, 86
Lee
laterality, 236
refuge, 666
Lee shore
pitfall, 667
Leech
suck, 789
physician, 695
Leer
vision, 441
signal, 550
Leery
cunning, 702
Lees
uncleanness, 653
Leeway
navigation, 267
shortcoming, 304
Left
remaining, 40
sinistral, 239
Left-handed
unskilful, 699
equivocal, 520
sinister, 649
Leg
swindler, 548
Leg-break
deviation, 279
Legacy
gift, 784
acquisition, 775
Legal
legitimate, 924
relating to law, 963
allowable, 760
Legate
consignee, 750
messenger, 534
deputy, 759
Legatee
receive, 785
Legation
commission, 755
Legend
narrative, 594
record, 551
Legendary
mythical, 979

imaginary, 515
Legerdemain
trick, 545, 702
cunning, 702
Legèreté
irresolution, 605
Legging
dress, 225
Legible
intelligible, 518
Legion
army, 726
multitude, 102
assemblage, 72
Legislate
legality, 963
Legislator
director, 694
Legislature
legality, 963
Legitimate
true, 494
allowable, 760
just, 922
due, 924
legal, 963
Legs
journey, 266
Lei
garland, 847
Leisure
unoccupied, 685
opportunity, 134
Leisurely
slowly, 133, 275
Leit-motiv
music, 415
Leman
favourite, 899
Lemma
evidence, 467
maxim, 496
Lemon
yellow, 430
Lend
lending, 787
credit, 805
Length
length, 200
Lengthy
diffuse, 573
Lenient
compassionate, 914
moderate, 174
mild, 740

Lenify
moderate, 174
Lenitive
remedy, 662
relief, 834
Lenity
lenity, 740
Lens
optical instrument, 445
Lent
fasting, 956
Lenticular
curvature, 245
Lentor
inertness, 172
inactivity, 683
Lentous
viscid, 352
Leopard
variegation, 440
Leprechaun
sprite, 980
Lese-majesty
disobedience, 742
Less
inferior, 34
subduction, 38
Lessee
debt, 806
possessor, 779
Lessen
in quantity or degree, 36
in size, 195
Lesson
teaching, 537
warning, 668
Lessor
credit, 805
Lest
avoidance, 623
Let
hindrance, 706
sell, 796
permit, 760
Let down
depress, 308
disappoint, 509
Let fall
depression, 308
speak, 582
Let fly
propulsion, 284
Let go
liberate, 750
relinquish, 782

unclutch, 790

Let in
admit, 296
insert, 300

Let loose
release, 750

Let off
exempt, 927A
forgive, 918
explode, 173

Let out
eject, 297
release, 750
disclose, 529

Let slip
lose, 776
neglect, 730

Lethal
deadly, 361
pernicious, 649

Lethal chamber
gallows, 975

Lethargy
insensibility, 823
inactivity, 683

Lethe
oblivion, 506
hell, 982

Letter
character, 561
epistle, 592

Lettered
knowledge, 490

Letterpress
printing, 591

Letters
language, 560
knowledge, 490

Lettre de cachet
restraint, 751

Levant
abscond, 671
default, 808

Levee
sociality, 892
dam, 350

Level
horizontal, 213
flat, 251
smooth, 16, 255
to equalize, 27
to direct, 278
to lower, 308
to raze, 649

Level at

intention, 620

Lever
instrument, 633
raise, 307

Leverage
influence, 175

Leviathan
size, 192

Levigate
pulverulence, 330

Levite
clergy, 996

Levity
lightness, 320
trifle, 643
irresolution, 605
jocularity, 836

Levy
demand, 812
assemblage, 72
distrain, 789
conscription, 744

Lewd
impurity, 961

Lewis
gun, 727

Lex non scripta
legality, 963

Lex talionis
right, 922

Lexicography
word, 562

Lexicon
word, 562

Liable
subject to, 177
apt, 176
debt, 806
duty, 926

Liaison
impurity, 961

Liar
deceiver, 548

Libation
potation, 296
worship, 990

Libel
detraction, 934
censure, 932
lawsuit, 969

Liberal
generous, 816
disinterested, 942
ample, 639
giving, 784

Liberate
release, 672, 750
disjoin, 44

Libertarianism
will, 600

Libertinage
impurity, 961

Libertine
libertine, 962

Libertinism
impurity, 961

Liberty
freedom, 748
right, 924
exemption, 927A
permission, 760

Libidinous
impurity, 961

Libido
desire, 865

Library
book, 593
room, 191

Librate
oscillation, 314

Libretto
poetry, 597

Licence
permission, 760
laxity, 738
right, 924
exemption, 927A
toleration, 750

License
permit, 760
exempt, 927A

Licentiate
scholar, 492

Licentious
dissolute, 954
debauched, 961

Lich-gate
see Lych-gate

Lichen
plant, 367

Licit
dueness, 924

Lick
beat, 972

Lickerish
fastidious, 868
greedy, 865
licentious, 961

Lickspittle
flatterer, 935

component, 56
instrument, 633
Limber
flexible, 324
Limbo
incarceration, 751
purgatory, 982
Lime
deception, 545
Limelight
publicity, 531
Limerick
absurdity, 497
Limit
boundary, 233
end, 67
to circumscribe, 231
qualify, 469
prohibit, 761
Limitless
infinity, 105
space, 180
Limn
painting, 556
Limner
artist, 559
Limousine
vehicle, 272
Limp
halt, 275
fail, 732
weak, 160
inert, 172, 683
soft, 324
Limpid
transparent, 425
Lincture
remedy, 662
Line
length, 200
filament, 205
to coat, 224
band, 45
order, 58
contour, 229
continuity, 69
direction, 278
business, 625
soldier, 726
feature, 550
appearance, 448
posterity, 167
epistle, 592
Lineage
posterity, 167

series, 69
kindred, 11
Lineament
appearance, 448
mark, 550
Linear
length, 200
Linger
loiter, 275
delay, 133
protract, 110
Lingo
language, 560
Lingua franca
neology, 563
Linguist
scholar, 492
language, 560
Liniment
unctuous, 355
remedy, 662
Lining
lining, 224
Link
relation, 9
connecting, 45
to connect, 43
part, 51
term, 71
flambeau, 423
Links
arena, 728
Linn
lake, 343
Linocut
engraving, 558
Linoleum
covering, 222
Linotype
printing, 591
Linsey-woolsey
mixed, 41
Lion
courage, 861
prodigy, 872
celebrity, 873
Lip
edge, 230
beginning, 66
prominence, 250
impudence, 885
Lip-devotion
impiety, 988
Lip-service
insincerity, 544

flattery, 933
impiety, 988
Lip-wisdom
folly, 499
Lipogram
misnomer, 565
Lippitude
dim sight, 443
Lipstick
ornament, 847
Liquation
calefaction, 384
Liquefaction
soluble, 335
calefaction, 384
Liquescence
calefaction, 384
Liquescent
soluble, 335
Liquid
fluid, 333
letter, 561
sound, 405
Liquidate
pay, 808
destroy, 162
Liquor
liquid, 333
intoxicant, 959
potable, 299
Liquorice
sweet, 396
Lisp
stammering, 583
Lissom
soft, 324
List
catalogue, 86
record, 551
strip, 205
fringe, 230
obliquity, 217
hear, 418
will, 600
choose, 609
Listed
variegation, 440
Listen
hearing, 418
Listen in
radio, 599B
Listless
inattentive, 458
inactive, 683
impassive, 823

indifferent, 866
Lists
  arena, 728
Lit up
  drunk, 959
Litany
  rite, 998
Literae humaniores
  language, 560
Literal
  exact, 19, 494
  meaning, 516
  unimaginative, 843
Literate
  knowledge, 491
Literati
  scholar, 492
Literatim
  imitation, 19
  word, 562
Literature
  learning, 490
  language, 560
Lithe
  softness, 324
Lithograph
  engraving, 558
Litigant
  combatant, 726
  lawsuit, 969
Litigate
  discord, 713
  contention, 720
Litigious
  discord, 713
  lawsuit, 969
Litter
  disorder, 59
  to derange, 61
  trash, 643
  useless, 645
  vehicle, 272
  offspring, 167
Little
  in degree, 32
  in size, 193
Littoral
  land, 342
Liturgy
  rite, 998
Live
  exist, 1
  continue, 141
  dwell, 186
  fame, 873

Livelihood
  wealth, 803
Livelong
  perpetuity, 110
Lively
  sprightly, 836
  acute, 821
  sensitive, 375, 822
  active, 682
  style, 574
Liver-coloured
  brown, 433
Livery
  badge, 550, 877
  colour, 428
  suit, 225
Livid
  dark, 431
  purple, 437
Living
  life, 359
  benefice, 995
Lixiviate
  cleanness, 652
  liquefaction, 335
Lixivium
  liquidity, 333
Llama
  carrier, 271
Llano
  plain, 344
Lo!
  see, 441
  wonder, 870
Load
  weight, 319
  cargo, 190
  quantity, 31
  redundance, 641
  hindrance, 706
  anxiety, 828
  fill up, 52
  to oppress, 830
Loadstone
  attraction, 289, 865
  motive, 615
Loaf
  head, 450
Loafer
  idler, 683
Loam
  soil, 342
Loan
  lending, 787
Loathe

dislike, 867
hate, 898
Loathing
  nausea, 841
Loathsome
  hateful, 649, 898
  abhorrent, 867
  nauseous, 395
Lob
  toss, 284
Lobby
  room, 191
  passage, 627
Lobe
  part, 51
Lobster
  red, 434
Local
  situation, 183
  regional, 180
Locality
  situation, 183
Localize
  location, 184
  limit, 231
Locate
  location, 184
Loch
  lake, 343
Lock
  fasten, 43
  confine, 229
  rest, 265
  enclose, 232
  barrier, 706
  canal, 350
  tuft, 256
Lock up
  concealment, 528
  restraint, 751
Lock-up
  jail, 752
Locker
  receptacle, 191
Locket
  ornament, 847
Lockout
  resistance, 719
Loco
  insane, 503
Locomotion
  motion, 264
Locomotive
  traction, 285

572

vista, 441
plea, 617
refuge, 666, 717
escape, 671
feint, 545
Loopy
insane, 503
Loose
detach, 44
free, 748
liberate, 750
incoherent, 47
vague, 519
style, 573
lax, 738
dissolute, 961
Loosen
disjoin, 47, 750
Loot
stealing, 791
booty, 793
Lop
retrench, 38
shorten, 53, 201
Lope
velocity, 274
Loquacity
talk, 584
prolixity, 573
Lord
nobleman, 875
ruler, 745
GOD, 976
Lord it over
insolence, 885
Lordling
bluster, 875
Lordly
proud, 878
grand, 873
Lordship
title, 877
Lore
knowledge, 490
Lorn
seclusion, 893
Lorry
vehicle, 272
Lorry-hop
travel, 266
Lose
opportunity, 135
property, 776
time, 683
Loser

victim, 732
Loss
privation, 776
waste, 638
evil, 619
Lost
invisible, 449
non-existing, 2
bewildered, 491
inattentive, 458
demoralized, 945
Lot
destiny, 152
chance, 156, 621
group, 72
state, 7
allotment, 786
quantity, 25, 639
multitude, 102
Lotion
remedy, 662
Lottery
chance, 156, 621
Lotus-eater
inactivity, 683
Loud
loudness, 404
showy, 428
vulgar, 851
Lough
lake, 343
Lounge
inactive, 683
to loiter, 275
room, 191
seat, 215
Lounge lizard
flirt, 902
Lour
darken, 421, 422
mope, 837
frown, 895
threaten, 511, 908
resent, 900
Lousy
bad, 649
Lout
clown, 876
fool, 501
to stoop, 308
Love
attachment, 897
favourite, 899
nothing, 4
Love-nest

love, 897
Lovelorn
love-sick, 897
rejected, 898
Lovely
dear, 897
pleasing, 829
beautiful, 845
Lover
love, 897
Low
depressed, 207
debased, 940
vulgar, 876
cry, 412
price, 815
bad, 649
sound, 403
smallness, 32
Low-bred
commonalty, 876
Low-brow
ignoramus, 493
fool, 501
Low-down
information, 527
Low-lying
low, 207
Low-thoughted
improbity, 940
Lowboy
receptacle, 191
Lower
depress, 308
decrease, 36
inferior, 34
Lowering
unhealthy, 657
Lowlands
lowness, 207
Lowly
humility, 879
Lowness
see Low
Loyal
probity, 939
obedient, 743
Lozenge
angularity, 244
sweet, 396
Lubber
slow, 683
awkward, 699
fool, 501
big, 192

573

Lubricate
smooth, 255, 332
facilitate, 705
Lubricity
slippery, 255
impurity, 961
Lucid
luminous, 420
intelligible, 518
style, 570
sane, 502
Lucifer
Satan, 978
match, 388
Luck
chance, 156, 621
good, 618
success, 731
prosperity, 734
Luckless
failure, 732
adversity, 735
distressed, 828
Lucky
prosper, 134, 734
Lucrative
receipt, 810
useful, 644
profitable, 775
Lucre
gain, 775
wealth, 803
Lucubration
thought, 451
Luculent
light, 420
Ludicrous
laughable, 838
ridiculous, 853
witty, 842
Lug
traction, 285
Luggage
baggage, 635, 780
Lugger
ship, 273
Lugubrious
dejection, 837
Lukewarm
temperate, 382
unwilling, 603
indifferent, 866
torpid, 823
Lull
assuage, 174

mitigate, 826
silence, 403
quiescence, 142, 265
Lullaby
soothing, 174
sleep, 683
song, 415
relief, 834
Lum
funnel, chimney, 351
Lumber
useless, 645
slow, 275
trash, 643
disorder, 59
hindrance, 647, 706
Lumber-room
receptacle, 191, 636
Lumbering
ugly, 846
Lumberjacket
dress, 225
Luminary
light, 423
sage, 500
Luminous
light, 420
Lump
mass, 192
density, 321
concrete, 46
totality, 50
to amass, 72
Lumpish
heavy, 319
massive, 192
sluggish, 683
awkward, 853
Lunacy
insanity, 503
Lunar
world, 318
Lunatic
madman, 504
Lunation
period, 108
Luncheon
food, 298
Lunette
curvature, 245
Lunge
impulse, 276
attack, 716
Lunik
space ship, 273A

Lurch
sink, 306
difficulty, 704
deception, 545
oscillation, 314
slope, 217
Lure
entice, 615
allurement, 865
deception, 545
Lurid
dim, 422
dark, 421
yellow, 436
sensational, 549
Lurk
latent, 526
concealed, 528
hide, 530
unseen, 447
Luscious
savoury, 394, 396
grateful, 829
style, 577
Lush
succulent, 333
vegetation, 365
luxuriant, 639
Lushy
drunkenness, 959
Lust
desire, 865
concupiscence, 961
Lustily
exertion, 686
Lustration
purification, 652
atonement, 952
Lustre
brightness, 420
chandelier, 423
Lustrum
period, 108
Lusty
size, 192
strong, 159
Lusus naturae
unconformity, 83
Lute
cement, 45
to cement, 46
guitar, 417
Luxation
disjunction, 44

Magnate
  nobility, 875
Magnet
  attraction, 288, 829
  desire, 865
  motive, 615
Magnificat
  worship, 990
Magnificent
  grand, 882
  fine, 845
  magnanimous, 942
Mangifico
  nobility, 875
Magnifier
  optical instrument, 445
Magnify
  increase, 35
  enlarge, 194
  exaggerate, 549
  praise, 990
  approve, 931
Magniloquent
  ornament, 577
  extravagant, 549
  speech, 582
Magnitude
  quantity, 25
  size, 192
Magpie
  loquacity, 584
Magsman
  thief, 792
Magus
  heathen, 984
Maharajah
  master, 745
  noble, 875
Maharanee
  noble, 875
  chief, 745
Mahatma
  sorcerer, 994
Mahogany colour
  brown, 433
Mahomet
  religious founder, 986
Mahometanism
  religions, 984
Maid of honour
  marriage, 903
Maiden
  girl, 129, 374
  servant, 746
  spinster, 904

purity, 960
  guillotine, 975
  first, 66
Mail
  letters, 592
  news, 532
  defence, 717
  armoury, 727
Mail-cart
  vehicle, 272
Maim
  injure, 649, 659
  weaken, 160
Main
  whole, 50
  tunnel, 260
  conduit, 350
  ocean, 341
  principal, 642
Mainland
  land, 342
Mainly
  greatness, 31
Mainspring
  cause, 153
  motive, 615
Mainstay
  instrument, 631
  refuge, 666
  hope, 858
Maintain
  continue, 141, 143
  preserve, 670
  sustain, 170
  assert, 535
Maison de santé
  remedy, 662
Maître
  expert, 700
Majestic
  repute, 873
Majesty
  king, 745
  rank, 873
  Deity, 976
Major
  greater, 33
  officer, 745
Majordomo
  director, 694
  commissary, 746
Majority
  age, 131
  greater number, 102
  dead, 362

Majuscules
  printing, 591
Make
  produce, 161
  constitute, 54
  form, 240
  arrive at, 292
  price, 812
Make-believe
  untruth, 546
Make fast
  vinculum, 43
Make for
  tend, 176
Make good
  compensation, 30
  substantiate, 467
Make it up
  forgive, 918
Make known
  information, 527
Make loose
  incoherence, 47
Make out
  decipher, 522
  understand, 518
  discover, 480A
Make over
  transfer, 783
Make up
  complete, 52
  compose, 54
  imagine, 515
  invent, 544
  improvise, 612
Make up for
  compensate, 30
Make up to
  accost, 586
  approach, 286
Make way
  progress, 282
  improve, 658
Maker
  artificer, 690
  Deity, 976
Makeshift
  substitute, 147
  temporary, 111
  plan, 626
  plea, 617
Makeweight
  compensate, 30
  equality, 27
  completeness, 52

Mala fide
  improbity, 940
Malachite
  green, 435
Malade imaginaire
  madman, 504
  dejection, 837
Maladie du pays
  discontent, 832
  dejection, 837
Maladjusted
  antisocial, 911
Maladministration
  unskilful, 699
Maladroit
  unskilful, 699
Malady
  disease, 655
Malaise
  pain, 378, 828
Malapert
  jackanapes, 887
  insolent, 885
Malaprop
  misnomer, 565
Malapropism
  ridicule, 856
  error, 495
Malapropos
  irrelevant, 10
  discordant, 24
  inopportune, 135
Malaria
  disease, 657
Malarkey
  flattery, 933
Malcontent
  discontent, 832
Male
  strength, 159
Malediction
  curse, 908
Malefactor
  evildoer, 949
Maleficent
  malevolence, 907
Malevolent
  malevolence, 907
  badness, 649
  enmity, 889
Malfeasance
  guilt, 947
Malformation
  ugliness, 846
Malice

spite, 907
hate, 898
Malign
  detraction, 934
Malignant
  malevolent, 907
  pernicious, 649
Malignity
  violence, 173
  badness, 649
Malinger
  falsehood, 544
  disease, 655
Mall
  club, 633
  impact, 276
  street, 189
Malleable
  soft, 324
  facile, 705
Mallet
  hammer, 276, 633
Malodorous
  fetor, 401
Malpractice
  guilt, 947
Maltreat
  injure, 649
  aggrieve, 830
  molest, 907
Malversation
  waste, 818
Mamilla
  convexity, 250
Mamma
  mother, 166
Mammal
  animal, 366
Mammet
  representation, 554
Mammon
  wealth, 803
Mammoth
  size, 192
Man
  mankind, 372P
  person, 373
  to arm, 673
Man-handle
  maltreat, 649
Man of straw
  defaulter, 808
Man-of-war
  ship, 273
Manacle

shackle, 751, 752
to fetter, 43
Manage
  direction, 693
  succeed, 731
Manageable
  facility, 705
Management
  skill, 698
Manager
  director, 694
Managing
  active, 682
Mancipation
  restraint, 751
Mandamus
  command, 741
Mandarin
  master, 745
Mandate
  command, 741
  region, 181
Mandatory
  obligatory, 926
Mandolin
  musical instrument, 417
Mandrel
  rotation, 312
Manducation
  feeding, 296
Mane
  rought, 256
Manège
  training, 370
Manes
  corpse, 362
Manful
  strong, 159
  brave, 861
Mangle
  disjunction 44
  smooth, 255
Mangy
  disease, 655
Manhood
  virility, 131, 373
  bravery, 861
Mania
  insanity, 503
  desire, 865
Maniac
  mad, 504
Manifest
  visible, 446
  obvious, 518

to show, 525
to appear, 448
Manifesto
publication, 531
Manifold
multitude, 102
Manikin
image, 554
dwarf, 193
Manila
tobacco, 298A
Manipulate
handle, 379
use, 677
conduct, 692
Mankind
man, 372
Manlike
strength, 159
Manly
adolescent, 131
resolute, 604
brave, 861
Manna
sweetness, 396
Mannequin
image, 554
Manner
intrinsic, 5
way, 627
appearance, 448
conduct, 692
kind, 75
Mannerism
singularity, 79, 83
phrase, 566
ornament, 577
affectation, 855
vanity, 880
Mannerly
courtesy, 894
Manners
breeding, 852
politeness, 894
Manœuvre
scheme, 626
operation, 680
skill, 698
stratagem, 545, 702
Manor
property, 780
Manse
temple, 1000
Mansion
abode, 189

Mansuetude
courtesy, 894
Mantel
support, 215
Mantilla
dress, 225
Mantle
cloak, 225
kindle, 900
flush, 821
spread, 194
Mantlet
dress, 225
Mantology
prediction, 511
Manual
book, 542, 593
reference, 695
Manufactory
workshop, 691
Manufacture
production, 161
Manufacturer
agent, 690
producer, 164
Manumit
liberate, 750
Manure
unclean, 653
Manuscript
writing, 590
Many
multitude, 102
Many-coloured
variegation, 440
Many-sided
accomplished, 698
Map
representation, 554
journey, 266
Maquis
fighter, 726
Mar
spoil, 649
obstruct, 706
Maranatha
malediction, 908
Marasmus
atrophy, 655
shrinking, 195
Marauder
thief, 792
Marauding
stealing, 791
Marble

ball, 249
hard, 323
sculpture, 557
Marble-hearted
malevolence, 907
Marbled
variegated, 440
March
journey, 266
progression, 282
March-past
display, 882
March with
contiguity, 199
Marches
limit, 233
Marchioness
noble, 875
chief, 745
Marchpane
sweet, 396
Marconigram
message, 532
Mare
carrier, 271
Maréchal
master, 745
Mare's nest
absurdity, 497
failure, 732
Mare's tail
cloud, 353
Margin
edge, 230
space, 180
latitude, 748
Marginalia
commentary, 522
Margrave
master, 745
Marinade
pickle, 670
Marine
oceanic, 341
fleet, 273
soldier, 726
Marish
marsh, 345
Marital
marriage, 903
Maritime
oceanic, 341
Mark
indication, 550
record, 551

repute, 873
object, 620
degree, 26, 71
observe, 441, 450
attend to, 457

Marked
great, 31

Market
mart, 799
buy, 795

Market garden
agriculture, 371

Marketable
trade, 794, 796

Marksman
proficient, 700

Marl
land, 342

Marmalade
sweet, 396

Maroon
seclusion, 893
abandon, 782
signal, 550, 669

Marplot
bungler, 701
obstacle, 706
malicious, 913

Marquee
tent, 189

Marquetry
mixture, 41
variegation, 440

Marquis
noble, 875
master, 745

Marquisate
title, 877

Marriage
marry, 903
union, 41

Marriageable
adolescence, 131

Marrow
essence, 5
interior, 221
central, 223
gist, 516
essential, 642

Mars
god, 979

Marsh
marsh, 345
moisture, 339

Marshal

arrange, 60
officer, 745
in law, 968
messenger, 534

Mart
mart, 799

Martellato
music, 415

Martial
contention, 720

Martinet
tyrant, 739
teacher, 540

Martingale
bridle, 752

Martyr
pain, 828

Martyrdom
torture, 378
agony, 828
killing, 361
asceticism, 955

Marvel
wonder, 870
prodigy, 872

Marvellous
great, 31
impossible, 471

Marzipan
sweet, 396

Mascara
ornament, 847

Mascot
talisman, 993

Masculine
strength, 159
man, 373

Mash
mix, 41
knead, 324

Masher
fop, 854

Mashie
club, 276

Mask
concealment, 528
ambush, 530
untruth, 546
shade, 424
dress, 225

Masked
invisible, 447

Masorah
revelation, 985

Masque

drama, 599

Masquerade
frolic, 840
concealment, 528
ambush, 530
deception, 546

Mass
quantity, 25
degree, 31
whole, 50
heap, 72
size, 192
weight, 319
density, 321
rites, 990, 998

Massacre
killing, 361

Massage
friction, 331

Masses
lower classes, 876

Massive
huge, 192
heavy, 319
dense, 321

Mast-head
summit, 210

Master
ruler, 745
director, 694
proficient, 700
of arts, 492
teacher, 540
to succeed, 731
possessor, 779
to learn, 539
to understand, 518
to overpower, 824

Master-hand
skilled, 698

Master-key
explanation, 462
opener, 260
instrumentality, 631

Master-mind
sage, 500

Mastered
failure, 732

Masterful
domineering, 736

Masterly
skill, 698

Masterpiece
perfection, 650, 698

Mayhem
evil, 619
Mayor
master, 745
Maypole
height, 206
Mazarine
blue, 438
Maze
convolution, 248
bewilderment, 491
enigma, 533
Mazuma
money, 800
Mazurka
dance, 840
music, 415
Me
personality, 317
Me judice
belief, 484
Mea culpa
penitence, 950
Mead
plain, 344
sweet, 396
Meadow
plain, 344
Meagre
thin, 193
narrow, 203
scanty, 640
style, 575
Meal
powder, 330
repast, 298
Mealy-mouthed
false, 544
servile, 886
Mean
average, 29
middle, 68, 628
small, 32
contemptible, 643
shabby, 874
base, 940
humble, 879
sneaking, 886
selfish, 943
stingy, 819
intend, 620
to signify, 516
Meander
circuition, 311
convolution, 248

river, 348
wander, 279, 629
Meaningless
nonsense, 517
Means
appliances, 632
fortune, 803
property, 780
Meantime
period, 106, 120
Meanwhile
duration, 106, 120
Measure
extent, 25
degree, 26
moderation, 174, 639
to compute, 466
proceeding, 626, 680
to apportion, 786
in music, 413
in poetry, 597
Measure, in a great
greatness, 31
Measure for measure
compensation, 30
Meat
food, 298
Meaty
savoury, 394
Mechanic
agent, 690
Mechanical
automatic, 601
style, 575
imitative, 19
Mechanics
force, 159
machinery, 632
Mechanism
means, 632
Medal
reward, 973
record, 551
palm, 733
decoration, 877
Medallion
sculpture, 557
Meddle
interpose, 682
act, 680
Meddlesome
interpose, 682
Medial
middle, 68
Median

mean, 29
Mediation
mediation, 724
deprecation, 766
Mediator
Saviour, 976
Medicament
remedy, 662
Medicaster
deceiver, 548
Medicate
heal, 660
compound, 41
Medicine
remedy, 662
Medieval
oldness, 124
past, 122
Mediocrity
moderate, 32
mean, 29
of fortune, 736
imperfect, 648, 651
Meditate
think, 451
purpose, 620
Mediterranean
middle, 68
interjacent, 228
Medium
mean, 29
pigment, 428
instrument, 631
spiritualist, 994
Medley
mixture, 41
Meed
reward, 973
gift, 784
share, 786
praise, 931
Meek
humble, 879
gentle, 826
Meerschaum
tobacco-pipe, 298A
Meet
contact, 199, 292
agreement, 23
converge, 290
assemble, 72
expedient, 646
proper, 924, 926
fulfil, 772

Meet with
find, 480A
happen, 151
Meeting-place
focus, 74
Megalomania
insanity, 503
vanity, 880
Megalomaniac
madman, 504
Megaphone
loudness, 404
Megascope
optical instrument, 445
Megrims
dejection, 837
Melancholia
insanity, 503
Melancholy
distressing, 830
dejection, 837
Mélange
mixture, 41
Mêlée
contention, 720
disorder, 59
Meliorate
improve, 658
Mellifluous
sound, 405
melody, 413
style, 578
Mellow
sound, 413, 580
mature, 144, 673
old, 124
soft, 324
tipsy, 959
Melodeon
wind instrument, 417
Melodrama
the drama, 599
Melody
music, 413
Melpomene
the drama, 599
Melt
liquefy, 335
fuse, 384
change, 144
disappear, 449
pity, 914
Melt away
disappear, 2, 449
Member
part, 51

component, 56
Membrane
layer, 204
Memento
memory, 505
Memento mori
interment, 363
Memoir
description, 594
dissertation, 595
Memorabilia
memory, 505
Memorable
importance, 642
Memorandum
memory, 505
record, 551
Memorial
record, 551
epistle, 592
Memoriter
memory, 505
Memory
reminiscence, 505
fame, 873
Menace
threat, 908
Ménage
conduct, 692
Menagerie
taming, 370
collection, 72
store, 636
Mend
improve, 658
Mendacity
falsehood, 544
Mendelism
production, 161
Mendicant
beggar, 767
monk, 996
Mendicity
beggar, 804
Menial
servant, 746
servile, 876
Menstrual
period, 108
Mensuration
measure, 466
Mental
intellect, 450
Mention
information, 527

Mentor
adviser, 695
teacher, 540
Menu
list, 86
food, 298
plan, 626
Mephistopheles
Satan, 978
miscreant, 949
Mephitic
fetid, 401
pernicious, 649
deleterious, 657
poison, 663
Mercantile
merchant, 794
Mercenary
parsimonious, 819
price, 812
servant, 746
self-seeking, 943
Merchandise
goods, 798
Merchant
merchant, 797
Merchantman
ship, 273
Merci
thanks, 917
Merciful
pity, 914
Merciless
malevolence, 907
Mercurial
excitable, 825
mobile, 264
quick, 274
Mercury
god, 979
messenger, 534
Mercy
mercy, 914
Mercy-seat
tribunal, 966
Mere
simple, 32
unimportant, 643
lake, 343
Meretricious
false, 495, 544
vulgar, 851
licentious, 961
colour, 428

Merge
  plunge, 337
  insert, 300
  include, 76
  combine, 48
  midst, 68
Meridian
  summit, 210
  noon, 125
  desert, 944
  to deserve, 922, 924
  usefulness, 644
Merit
  goodness, 648
Mermaid
  ocean, 341
  monster, 83
Merry
  cheerful, 836
Merry-andrew
  humorist, 844
Merry-go-round
  rotation, 312
Merrymaking
  amuse, 836, 840
  sociality, 892
Merrythought
  spell, 993
Merum sal
  wit, 842
Mésalliance
  ill-assorted, 24
  marriage, 903
Meseems
  belief, 484
Mesh
  crossing, 219
  interval, 198
Mesial
  middle, 68
Mesmerism
  occult arts, 992, 994
Mess
  mixture, 41
  disorder, 59
  dirt, 653
  failure, 732
  meal, 298
Message
  command, 741
  intelligence, 532
Messenger
  message, 534
Messiah
  Deity, 976

Messmate
  friend, 890
Messuage
  abode, 189
Metabolism
  change, 140
  life, 369
Metachronism
  anachronism, 115
Metal
  material, 635
Metallurgy
  mineral, 358
Metamorphosis
  change, 140
Metaphor
  metaphor, 521
  comparison, 464
  analogy, 17
Metaphorical
  style, 557
Metaphrase
  interpret, 522, 524
Metaphysics
  intellect, 450
Metastasis
  change, 140
Metathesis
  transference, 270
  inversion, 218
Mete
  measure, 466
  give, 784
  distribute, 786
Metempsychosis
  change, 140
Meteor
  luminary, 423
  light, 420
  universe, 318
Meteoric
  violent, 173
  refulgent, 420
  transient, 111
Meteorology
  air, 338
Methinks
  belief, 484
Method
  order, 58
  way, 627
Methodize
  arrange, 60
Meticulous
  careful, 459

Metonymy
  metaphor, 521
  substitution, 147
Metre
  poetry, 597
Metrical
  measurement, 466
Metropolis
  abode, 189
Mettle
  spirit, 820
  courage, 861
Mettlesome
  excitable, 822, 825
  brave, 861
Mew
  enclose, 231
  restrain, 751
  divest, 226
  complain, 839
Mewl
  ululation, 412
Mezzo-rilievo
  sculpture, 557
Mezzo-soprano
  melody, 413
Mezzo termine
  middle, 68
  mid-course, 628
Mezzotint
  engraving, 558
Miasma
  bane, 663
Miasmal
  morbific, 649
Micawber
  careless, 460
Microbe
  bane, 663
  insalubrity, 657
Microcosm
  little, 32, 193
Microfilm
  copy, 21
Microphone
  loudness, 404
  hearing, 418
Microscope
  optical, 445
Microscopic
  little, 193
Mid
  middle, 68
Mid-course
  middle, 628

Midas
wealth, 803
Midday
course, 125
Midden
uncleanness, 653
Middle
in order, 68
in degree, 29
in space, 223
Middleman
agent, 690
go-between, 631
salesman, 797
Middling
imperfect, 651
mean, 29
Midge
littleness, 193
Midget
dwarf, 193
Midland
land, 342
Midnight
evening, 126
darkness, 421
Midriff
interjacence, 228
Midshipman
master, 745
Midst
central, 223
Midsummer
morning, 125
Midway
middle, 68
Midwife
doctor, 662
Mien
appearance, 448
conduct, 692
Miff
resentment, 900
Might
power, 157
degree, 26
violence, 173
Mighty
much, 31
large, 192
powerful, 159
haughty, 878
Migrate
journey, 266
Mikado

master, 745
Mike
loudness, 404
hearing, 418
Milch cow
store 636
Mild
moderate, 174
insipid, 391
lenient, 740
calm, 826
courteous, 894
warm, 382
Mildew
unclean, 653
Mileage
measurement, 466
Militant
contention, 720
Militarism
warfare, 722
authority, 737
Military
combatant, 726
Militate
opposition, 179, 608
Militia
combatant, 726
Milk
to despoil, 789
Milk-and-water
inperfect, 651
Milk-white
whiteness, 430
Milksop
coward, 862
Milky
semitransparent, 427
emulsive, 252
Milky Way
world, 318
Mill
machine, 330, 633
workshop, 691
Mill-pond
store, 636
Millenary
celebration, 883
Millennium
period, 108
thousand, 98
futurity, 121
Utopia, 515
hope, 858
Millesimal

thousand, 98
Millet-seed
littleness, 193
Milliner
dress, 225
Million
number, 98
Millionaire
wealth, 803
Millstone
incubus, 706
weight, 319
Miltonic
sublime, 574
poetry, 597
Mime
player, 599
buffoon, 856
Mimeograph
imitation, 19
Mimesis
imitation, 19
Mimic
imitation, 19
repeat, 104
Minacity
threat, 909
Minaret
height, 206
Minatory
threatening, 909
dangerous, 665
Minauderie
affected, 855
Mince
disjoin, 44
stammer, 583
Mincing
slow, 275
affected, 855
Mind
intellect, 450
will, 600
desire, 865
dislike, 867
purpose, 620
to attend to, 457
believe, 484
remember, 505
Minded
willing, 602
Mindful
attentive, 457
remembering, 505

Mindless
  inattentive, 458
  forgetful, 506
Mine
  store, 636
  abundance, 639
  to hollow, 252
  open, 260
  snare, 545
  sap, 162
  damage, 659
Mine-layer
  ship, 273
Mine-sweeper
  ship, 273
Mineral
  inorganic, 358
Mineralogy
  inorganic, 358
Minerva
  goddess, 979
Mingle
  mix, 41
Mingy
  parsimony, 819
Mini
  small, 193
Miniature
  portrait, 556
  small, 193
Minikin
  small, 193
Minim
  small, 32, 193
Minimize
  moderate, 174
  underestimate, 483
Minumum
  small, 32, 193
Mining
  opening, 260
Minion
  favourite, 899
Minister
  deputy, 759
  instrumentality, 631
  director, 694
  to aid, 707
  rites, 998
Ministry
  direction, 693
  church, 995
Minnow
  littleness, 193
Minor

inferior, 34
  infant, 129
Minority
  fewness, 103
Minotaur
  unconformity, 83
Minster
  temple, 1000
Minstrel
  music, 416
Minstrelsy
  musician, 415
Mint
  workshop, 691
  mould, 22
  wealth, 803
Minuend
  deduction, 38
Minuet
  dance, 840
  music, 415
Minus
  less, 38
  in debt, 806
  deficient, 304
Minuscules
  printing, 591
Minute
  in quantity, 32
  in size, 193
  of time, 108
  instant, 113
  compendium, 596
  record, 551
  in style, 573
Minutest
  inferior, 34
Minutiae
  small, 32
  little, 193
  unimportant, 643
Minx
  impertinent, 887
  bad woman, 949
Mirabile dictu
  wonder, 870
Miracle
  prodigy, 872
Miraculous
  wonder, 870
Mirage
  dim sight, 443
  appearance, 448
  shadow, 4
Mire

uncleanness, 653
Mirk
  darkness, 421
Mirror
  reflector, 445
  perfection, 650
  saint, 948
  imitate, 19
Mirth
  cheerful, 836
Mirthless
  dejected, 837
Misadventure
  failure, 732
  adversity, 735
  misfortune, 830
Misalliance
  marriage, 903
Misanthrope
  recluse, 893, 911
Misapply
  misuse, 679
  misinterpret, 523
  mismanage, 699
Misapprehend
  mistake, 495
  misinterpret, 523
Misappropriate
  misuse, 679
Misarrange
  derange, 61
Misbecome
  vice, 945
Misbegotten
  vice, 945
Misbehaviour
  discourtesy, 895
  vulgarity, 852
  guilt, 947
Misbelief
  doubt, 495
Miscalculate
  sophistry, 477
  disappoint, 509
Miscall
  misnomer, 565
Miscarriage
  failure, 732
Miscegenation
  mixture, 41
Miscellany
  mixture, 41
  collection, 72
  generality, 78

Mischance
  misfortune, 830
  adversity, 735
  failure, 732
Mischief
  evil, 619
Mischievous
  badness, 649
Miscible
  mix, 41
Miscompute
  mistake, 495
Misconceive
  mistake, 495
  misinterpret, 481, 523
Misconduct
  guilt, 947
  bungling, 699
Misconstrue
  misinterpret, 523
Miscount
  error, 495
Miscreant
  wretch, 949
  apostate, 941
Miscreated
  vice, 945
Miscue
  unskilfulness, 699
Misdate
  anachronism, 115
Misdeed
  guilt, 947
Misdeem
  misinterpret, 523
Misdemean
  vice, 945
Misdevotion
  impiety, 988
Misdirect
  misteaching, 538
  bungle, 699
Misdoing
  guilt, 947
Mise en scène
  appearance, 448
Misemploy
  misuse, 679
Miser
  parsimony, 819
Miserable
  contemptible, 643
  unhappy, 828
  pitiable, 914
  small, 32
Miserly

  parsimony, 819
Misery
  pain, 828
Misestimate
  error, 495
Misfit
  disparity, 24
Misfortune
  evil, 619
  failure, 732
  adversity, 735
  unhappiness, 830
Misgiving
  fear, 860
  doubt, 485
Misgovern
  unskilful, 699
Misguide
  misteaching, 538
Misguided
  foolish, 699
Mishandle
  maltreat, 649
Mishap
  evil, 619
  failure, 732
  adversity, 735
  disaster, 830
Mishmash
  mixture, 41
Misinform
  misteach, 538
  ignorance, 491
  error, 495
Misintelligence
  misteach, 538
Misinterpret
  misinterpret, 523
Misjoined
  disagreement, 24
Misjudge
  err, 495
  sophistry, 477
Mislay
  lose, 776
  derange, 61
Mislead
  deceive, 477, 545
  misteach, 538
  error, 495
Mislike
  dislike, 867
Mismanage
  unskilful, 699
Mismatch

  difference, 15
Mismatched
  disagreement, 24
Misname
  misnomer, 565
Misnomer
  misnomer, 565
Misogamy
  celibacy, 904
Misogynist
  celibacy, 904
Misplace
  disorder, 59
  unconformity, 83
Misplaced
  unsuitable, 24
Misprint
  error, 495
Mispronounce
  speech, 583
Misproportioned
  ugliness, 846
Misquote
  misinterpret, 523
  false, 544
Misreckon
  error, 495
Misrelate
  error, 495
Misremember
  error, 495
Misreport
  err, 495
  falsify, 544
Misrepresent
  untruth, 546
Misrepresentation
  perversion, 523
  falsehood, 544
  caricature, 555
Misrule
  misconduct, 699
  laxity, 738
Miss
  lose, 776
  fail, 732
  inattention, 458, 460
  want, 865
  girl, 374
Missal
  rite, 998
Missay
  stammer, 583
  misnomer, 565

Misshapen
ugliness, 846
distortion, 243
Missile
thing thrown, 284
arms, 727
Missing
absence, 187
Mission
commission, 755
undertaking, 676
business, 625
warfare, 722
Missionary
clergy, 996
Missive
correspond, 592
Misspell
misinterpret, 523
Misspend
prodigal, 818
Misstate
misinterpret, 523
falsify, 544
Misstatement
error, 495
falsehood, 544
untruth, 546
perversion, 523
Mist
dimness, 422
Mistake
error, 495
failure, 732
mismanagement, 699
misconstrue, 523
Misteach
misteach, 538
Misterm
misnomer, 565
Misthink
error, 495
Mistime
intempestivity, 135
Mistral
wind, 349
Mistranslate
misinterpret, 523
Mistress
lady, 374
sweetheart, 897
concubine, 962
Mistrust
doubt, 485
Misty

opaque, 426
dim, 422
invisible, 447
Misunderstanding
error, 495
misinterpretation, 523
discord, 713
Misuse
misuse, 679
waste, 638
Mite
small, 193
bit, 32
money, 800
Mitigate
abate, 36, 174
relieve, 834
calm, 826
improve, 658
extenuate, 937
Mitrailleuse
gun, 727
Mitre
canonicals, 999
joint, 43
Mitten
dress, 225
Mittimus
command, 741
Mix
mix, 41
Mixed
disorder, 59
Mixture
mix, 41
Mizzle
rain, 348
Mnemonics
memory, 505
Mnemosyne
memory, 505
Moan
lamentation, 411, 839
Moat
enclosure, 232
ditch, 350
defence, 717
Mob
crowd, 31, 72
multitude, 102
troop, 726
plenty, 639
vulgar, 876
to scold, 932
Mob law

illegal, 964
Mobile
movable, 264
sensible, 822
inconstant, 607
Mobility
commonalty, 876
move, 264
Mobilization
warfare, 722
Mobocracy
authority, 737
Mobsman
thief, 792
Moccasin
dress, 225
Mock
imitate, 17
repeat, 104
erroneous, 495
false, 544
to ridicule, 483, 856
laugh at, 838
Mock-heroic
ridiculous, 853
Modal
extrinsic, 6
state, 7
circumstance, 8
Mode
fashion, 852
method, 627
Model
prototype, 22
to change, 140, 144
rule, 80
example, 82
to copy, 19
sculpture, 557
perfection, 650
saint, 948
Modeller
artist, 559
Moderate
small, 32
to allay, 174
to assuage, 826
temperate, 953
cheap, 815
Moderation
temperateness, 174
mediocrity, 736
Moderato
music, 415

587

Moderator
 master, 745
 director, 694
Modern
 newness, 123
Modernize
 change, 140
Modesty
 humility, 881
 purity, 960
Modicum
 little, 33
 allotment, 786
Modification
 difference, 15
 variation, 20
 change, 140
 qualification, 469
Modify
 convert, 144
Modish
 fashion, 852
Modulation
 change, 140
 harmony, 413
Modus operandi
 method, 627
 conduct, 692
Modus vivendi
 arrangement, 723
 compromise, 774
Mogul
 master, 745
Mohammed
 religious founder, 986
Mohammedanism
 religions, 984
Mohock
 roisterer, 949
Moider
 bewilder, 475
 inattention, 458
Moiety
 bisection, 91
Moil
 action, 680
 work, 686
Moist
 wet, 337
 humid, 339
Moke
 carrier, 271
Molasses
 sweetness, 396
Mole
 mound, 206

 defence, 717
 refuge, 666
Molecule
 small, 32, 193
Molehill
 lowness, 207
 trifling, 643
Molestation
 evil, 619
 damage, 649
 malevolence, 907
Mollify
 allay, 174
 soften, 324
 conciliate, 918
 assuage, 826
Mollusc
 animal, 366
Mollycoddle
 cowardice, 862
Moloch
 tyranny, 739
 divinity, 979
 idol, 986
Molten
 liquid, 335
Moment
 of time, 113
  importance, 642
Momentary
 transient, 111
Momentum
 impulse, 276
Momus
 rejoicing, 838
Monachism
 church, 995
Monad
 littleness, 193
 unity, 87
Monarch
 master, 745
Monarchy
 authority, 737
Monastery
 temple, 1000
Monastic
 churchdom, 995 5
Monetary
 money, 800
Money
 money, 800
Money-bag
 treasury, 802
Money-changer

 merchant, 797
Money-grubber
 miser, 819
 acquisition, 775
Moneyed
 wealth, 803
Moneyer
 treasurer, 801
Moneyless
 poverty, 804
Monger
 merchant, 797
Mongrel
 mixture, 41
 anomalous, 83
Moniker
 name, 564
Moniliform
 circular, 247
Monism
 unity, 87
Monition
 advice, 695
 warning, 668
 information, 527
 omen, 512
Monitor
 teacher, 540
 director, 694
 master, 745
 ship, 723
Monitory
 prediction, 511
 warning, 668
Monk
 clergy, 996
Monkery
 churchdom, 995
Monkey
 imitative, 19
 engine, 276
 ridiculous, 856
 laughing-stock, 857
 to play the fool, 499
 money, 800
Monkey-shines
 prank, 840
 foolery, 497
 caprice, 608
Monkish
 clergy, 995
Monochord
 musical, 417
Monochrome
 colourless, 429

Monocular
lens, 445
Monody
lamentation, 839
Monogamy
marriage, 903
Monogram
sign, 550
cipher, 533
diagram, 554
Monograph
dissertation, 595
Monolith
record, 551
Monologue
soliloquy, 589
Monomania
insanity, 503
error, 495
obstinacy, 606
Monomaniac
madman, 504
Monometallism
money, 800
Monoplane
aircraft, 273a
Monopolize
possess, 777
engross, 457
Monopoly
syndicate, 778
Monosyllable
letter, 561
Monotheism
theology, 983
Monotonous
unchanging, 141
Monotony
identity, 13
uniformity, 16
repetition, 104, 141
in style, 575
weariness, 841
Monotype
printing, 591
Monsieur
title, 877
Monsoon
wind, 349
Monster
exception, 83
prodigy, 872
size, 192
ugly, 846
evildoer, 913

ruffian, 949
Monstrous
greatness, 31
huge, 192
wonderful, 870
ugly, 846
ridiculous, 853
Mont de piété
lending, 787
Montgolfier
balloon, 273a
Month
period, 108
Monthly
periodical, 138
Monticule
height, 206
Monument
record, 551
interment, 363
tallness, 206
Monumental
great, 31
Mood
nature, 5
state, 7
temper, 820
will, 600
tendency, 176
disposition, 602
affections, 820
variations, 20
change, 140
Moody
sullen, 895
fretful, 900
furious, 825
Moon
inaction, 681
changeable, 149
Moon-eyed
dim sight, 443
Moonbeam
light, 420
dimness, 422
Mooncalf
fool, 501
Moonless
dark, 421
Moonlight
light, 420
Moonshine
nonsense, 497, 517
excuse, 617
trumpery, 643

dimness, 422
Moonstruck
insanity, 503
Moony
dreamy, 458
foolish, 499
listless, 683
Moor
open space, 180
plain, 344
locate, 184
join, 43
rest, 265
Moorland
space, 180
plain, 344
Moot
inquire, 461
argue, 476
conjecture, 514
Moot point
topic, 454, 461
Mop
clean, 652
Mope
dejection, 837
Mope-eyed
dim sight, 443
Moped
vehicle, 272
Moppet
darling, 899
Moraine
debris, 330
Moral
right, 922
duty, 926
virtuous, 944
maxim, 496
Moral fibre
courage, 861
Morale
state, 7
Moralize
reason, 476
teach, 537
Morality
drama, 599
Morass
marsh, 345
Moratorium
delay, 133
Morbid
bad, 649
diseased, 655

noxious, 657
Morbific
  bad, 649
  diseased, 655
  noxious, 657
Mordacity
  malevolence, 907
Mordant
  pungent, 392
  vigorous, 574
  sarcastic, 932
Mordent
  grace-note, 415
More
  addition, 37
  superiority, 33
More or less
  smallness, 32
  equality, 27
More suo
  conformity, 82
Moreover
  addition, 37
  accompaniment, 88
Morganatic
  marriage, 903
Morgue
  pride, 878
  dead-house, 363
Moribund
  dying, 360
  sick, 655
Mormon
  polygamist, 903
Morning
  morning, 125
Moron
  fool, 501
Morose
  discourtesy, 895
Morphia
  anaesthetic, 376
Morphology
  form, 240
Morris-dance
  dance, 840
Morrison
  shelter, 717
Morrow
  futurity, 121
  morning, 125
Morsel
  small quantity, 32
  portion, 51
Mortal

man, 373
  fatal, 361
  bad, 649
  weariness, 841
Mortality
  death, 360
  evanescence, 111
  mankind, 372
Mortar
  cement, 45
  artillery, 727
  pulverization, 330
Mortgage
  sale, 796
  lend, 787
  security, 771
  credit, 805
Mortgagee
  credit, 805
Mortgagor
  debt, 806
Mortice
  see Mortise
Mortician
  interment, 363
Mortify
  pain, 828
  to vex, 830
  to discontent, 832
  to humiliate, 874, 879
  disease, 655
  asceticism, 955
Mortise
  unite, 43
  insert, 300
  intersect, 219
Mortuary
  interment, 363
Mosaic
  mixture, 41
  variegation, 440
  painting, 556
Moslem
  religions, 984
Mosque
  temple, 1000
Moss
  marsh, 345
  tuft, 256
Moss-grown
  deterioration, 659
Moss-trooper
  thief, 792
Most
  greatness, 31

Most part, for the
  general, 78
  conformity, 82
Mot
  maxim, 496
Mote
  particle, 193
  smallness, 32
  blemish, 848
  light, 320
Motel
  inn, 189
Motet
  music, 415
  worship, 990
Moth
  decay, 659
Moth-eaten
  imperfect, 651
Mother
  parent, 166
  mould, 653
  nun, 997
Mother-of-pearl
  variegation, 440
Mother tongue
  language, 560
Mother wit
  wisdom, 498
Motherland
  abode, 189
Motherly
  love, 897
Motif
  music, 415
  theme, 454
Motion
  change of place, 264
  proposition, 514
  topic, 454
  request, 765
  offer, 763
Motion picture
  drama, 599
Motionless
  quiescence, 265
Motive
  reason, 615
  music, 415
Motiveless
  absence of motive, 616
Motley
  multiform, 81
  mixed, 41
  variegated, 440

Motor
machine, 633
vehicle, 272
Motor-boat
ship, 273
Motor-bus
vehicle, 272
Motor-car
vehicle, 272
Motor-coach
vehicle, 272
Motor-cycle
vehicle, 272
Motor-van
vehicle, 272
Motorize
move, 264
Motorman
director, 694
Mottled
variegated, 440
Motto
device, 550
maxim, 496
phrase, 566
Mouch
inactivity, 688
Mould
form, 240, 329
condition, 7
earth, 342
mildew, 653
to model, 554
carve, 557
matrix, 22
Moulder
deterioration, 659
Moulding
ornament, 847
Mouldy
decayed, 653
fetid, 401
Moult
divestment, 226
Mound
defence, 717
hillock, 206
Mount
to rise, 305
hill, 206, 250
support, 215
to prepare, 673
Mountain
hill, 206
size, 192

weight, 319
Mountaineer
climber, 305
Mountebank
quack, 548
ignoramus, 493
buffoon, 844, 857
Mourn
grieve, 828
lament, 839
Mournful
sad, 837
aflicting, 830
Mouse
little, 193
to search, 461
Mouse-coloured
grey, 432
Mouse-hole
opening, 260
Mousseux
bubble, 353
Moustache
hair, 256
Mouth
entrance, 66
opening, 260
brink, 230
voice, 580
stammer, 583
Mouth-honour
flattery, 933
Mouth-watering
desire, 865
Mouthful
portion, 51, 193
Mouthpiece
speaker, 524, 540
speech, 582
Mouthy
style, 577
Movable
transference, 270
Movables
property, 780
Move
be in motion, 264
induce, 615
excite, 824
act, 680
undertaking, 676
propose, 514
Move off
recede, 287
depart, 293

Move on
progression, 282
Moved
impressed, 827
Moveless
quiescence, 265
Movement
motion, 264
stir, 682
Movie
cinema, 599a
Mow
cultivate, 371
destruction, 162
Mr.
title, 877
Much
greatness, 31
Mucilage
semiliquid, 352
adhesive, 45
Muck
uncleanness, 653
Muckle
greatness, 31
Muckworm
miser, 819
baseborn, 876
Mucronate
sharpness, 253
Mucus
semiliquid, 352
Mud
unclean, 653
Muddle
disorder, 59
derange, 61
bungle, 699
Muddled
confused, 458
tipsy, 959
foolish, 499
Muddy
opaque, 426
Mudlark
commonalty, 876
Muezzin
clergy, 996
Muff
bungler, 701
to bungle, 699
Muffle
silent, 403, 581
conceal, 528
taciturn, 585

wrap, 225
Muffler
dress, 225
Mufti
clergy, 996
judge, 966
dress, 225
Mug
receptacle, 191
fool, 501
face, 448
to study, 539
Muggy
dim, 422
moist, 339
Mulatto
unconformity, 83
mixture, 41
Mulct
penalty, 974
Mule
beast, 271
mongrel, 83
obstinate, 606
fool, 499
slipper, 225
Muleteer
director, 694
Muliebrity
woman, 374
Mull
cape, 250
sweeten, 396
Mull over
think, 451
Mullah
judge, 967
priest, 996
Mulligrubs
depression, 837
Mullion
support, 215
Multifarious
multiform, 81
various, 15
Multifid
divided, 51
Multifold
multiform, 16A, 81
Multiform
diversified, 16A, 81
Multigenerous
multiform, 81
Multilateral
side, 236

Multipartide
disjunction, 44
Multiple
numerous, 102
product, 84
Multiplicand
number, 84
Multiplication
arithmetical, 85
reproduction, 163
Multiplicator
number, 84
Multiplicity
multitude, 102
Multiplier
number, 84
Multisonous
loud, 404
Multitude
number, 102
greatness, 31
mob, 876
assemblage, 72
Multitudinous
multitude, 102
Multum in parvo
contraction, 195
conciseness, 572
Mum
silence, 403
aphony, 581
mother, 166
Mumble
eat, 296
mutter, 405, 583
Mumbo Jumbo
idol, 991
spell, 993
Mumchance
silent, 403
mute, 581
Mummer
the drama, 599
Mummery
absurdity, 497
ridicule, 856
parade, 882
imposture, 545
masquerade, 840
Mummify
preserve, 670
bury, 363
Mummy
corpse, 362
dryness, 340

mother, 166
Mump
dejection, 837
Mumper
beggar, 767
Mumps
sullenness, 895
Munch
eat, 296
Munchausen
exaggerate, 549
Mundane
world, 318
selfishness, 943
irreligion, 989
Munerary
reward, 973
Municipal
law, 965
distinct, 189
Munificent
liberality, 816
giving, 784
Muniment
record, 551
defence, 717
refuge, 666
Munition
material, 635
Murder
killing, 361
to bungle, 699
Murex
purple, 437
Muricate
sharpness, 253
Murky
darkness, 421
Murmur
sound, 405
complaint, 839
flow, 348
Murrain
disease, 655
Murrey
redness, 434
Muscle
strength, 159
Muse
to reflect, 451
poetry, 597
language, 560
Musette
musical instrument, 415

592

Museum
store, 636
collection, 72
focus, 74
Mushroom
small, 193
newness, 123
low-born, 876
upstart, 734
increase, 35
Music
music, 415
Music-hall
theatre, 599
amusement, 840
Musical
melodious, 413
Musician
usician, 416
Musk
fragrance, 400
Musket
arms, 727
Musketeer
combatant, 726
Muslin
semitransparent, 427
Muss
dishevel, 61
Mussulman
religions, 984
Must
mucor, 653
necessity, 152
obligation, 926
compulsion, 744
essential, 630
Mustard
condiment, 393
yellow, 436
Mustard-seed
little, 193
Muster
collect, 72
numeration, 85
Muster-roll
record, 551
list, 86
Musty
foul, 653
rank, 401
Mutable
changeable, 149
irresolute, 605
Mutation

change, 140
Mutatis mutandis
reciprocalness, 12
substitution, 147
Mutato nomine
substitution, 147
Mute
silent, 403
letter, 561
silencer, 417
speechless, 581
taciturn, 585
interment, 363
Mutilate
retrench, 38
deform, 241
garble, 651
incomplete, 53
injure, 649, 659
spoliation, 619
Mutineer
disobey, 742
Mutiny
disobey, 742
misrule, 738
revolt, 719
Mutt
fool, 501
Mutter
speak, 583
murmur, 405
threaten, 909
Mutual
reciprocal, 12, 148
Muzzle
opening, 260
edge, 230
to silence, 403, 581
taciturn, 585
to incapacitate, 158
restrain, 751
imprison, 752
Muzzle-loader
gun, 727
Muzzy
confused, 458
in liquor, 959
Myopic
dim sight, 443
Myriad
number, 98
multitude, 102
Myrmidon
troop, 726
Myrrh

fragrance, 400
Myrtle
love, 897
Mysterious
concealed, 528
obscure, 519
Mystery
secret, 533
latency, 526
concealment, 528
craft, 625
drama, 599
Mystery-ship
deception, 545
Mystic
concealed, 528
obscure, 519
Mystify
to deceive, 545
hide, 528
falsify, 477
misteach, 538
Myth
imagination, 515
Mythological
god, 979
imaginary, 515

N.B.
attention, 457
N or M
generality, 78
Na
dissent, 489
Nab
seize, 789
Nabob
wealth, 803
Nacreous
variegation, 440
Nadir
base, 211
Naffy
food, 298
Nag
carrier, 271
be rude, 895
discord, 713
to scold, 932
Naiad
mythological, 979
Nail
to fasten, 43
fastening, 45

Nail-brush
clean, 652
Nailing
good, 648
Naïveté
artless, 703
Naked
denuded, 226
visible, 446
Namby-pamby
affected, 855
insipid, 866
trifling, 643
style, 575
Name
appellation, 564
fame, 873
to appoint, 755
Nameless
anonymous, 565
obscure, 874
Namely
conformity, 82
specifically, 79
Namesake
name, 564
Nap
sleep, 683
down, 256
texture, 329
Napkin
clean, 652
Napping
inattentive, 458
Nappy
frothy, 353
Narcissus
beauty, 845
Narcotic
noxious, 649
somniferous, 683
Narghile
tobacco-pipe, 298A
Nark
informer, 527, 529
Narrate
description, 594
Narrow
thinness, 203
Narrow-minded
bigoted, 499
prejudiced, 481
Nasal
accent, 583
Nascent

begin, 66
new, 123
Nasty
foul, 653
unsavoury, 395
offensive, 830
ugly, 846
Natal
beginning, 66
Natation
navigation, 267
Nathless
counteraction, 179
Nation
mankind, 372
National
inhabitant, 188
Nationality
philanthropy, 910
Native
inhabitant, 188
artless, 703
Nativity
prediction, 511
Natter
nag, 932
Natty
spruce, 845
Natural
intrinsic, 5
regular, 82
true, 543
artlessness, 703
a fool, 501
style, 578
Natural history
organize, 357
Natural philosophy
materiality, 316
Naturalistic
description, 594
Naturalization
conversion, 144
Naturalized
habitual, 613
established, 82
Nature
essence, 5
world, 318
organization, 357
affections, 820
reality, 494
rule, 82
artless, 703
unfashioned, 674

spontaneous, 612
class, 75
style, 578
Naught
nothing, 4
zero, 101
Naughty
vicious, 945
disobedient, 742
perverse, 895
Naumachy
conflict, 720
Nausea
disgust, 867
weariness, 841
hatred, 898
unsavoury, 395
Nautch-girl
dancer, 599
Nautical
navigation, 267
Nave
middle, 68
centre, 223
church, 1000
Navel
middle, 68
centre, 223
Navigation
ship, 267
Navigator
mariner, 269
Navvy
workman, 690
Navy
ship, 273
Nawaub
master, 745
Nay
negation, 536
Ne plus ultra
greatness, 31
end, 67
distance, 196
superiority, 33
goodness, 648
perfection, 650
Neap
lowness, 207
Near
in space, 197
in time, 121
approach, 286
stingy, 817
likeness, 17

Nestling
infant, 129
Nestor
veteran, 130
Net
intersection, 219
snare, 667, 702
to capture, 789
difficulty, 704
remainder, 40
Nether
lowness, 207
Nettle
to sting, 830
incense, 900
Network
crossing, 219
disorder, 59
Neurasthenia
weakness, 160
Neurosis
insanity, 503
Neurotic
sensitive physically, 375
morally, 822
Neutral
mean, 29, 628
indifferent, 610, 866
non-interference, 681
Neutral tint
grey, 432
Neutralize
counteract, 179
compensate, 30
Never
neverness, 107
Never-ending
long, 200
Never-never
purchase, 795
debt, 806
Nevertheless
counter, 179
compensation, 30
New
newness, 123
New-born
newness, 123
New-fashioned
new, 123
Newcomer
extraneous, 57
Newfangled
new, 123
strange, 83

Newcast
barbarous, 851
News
news, 532
Newscast
radio, 599B
Newspaper
record, 551
Next
after, 63, 117
Nib
point, 253
summit, 210
disjunction, 44
end, 67
Nibble
carp at, 932
eat, 296
Niblick
club, 276
Nice
savoury, 394
good, 648
exact, 494
pleasing, 829
honourable, 939
fastidious, 868
Nicely
greatness, 31
Nicety
taste, 850, 868
discrimination, 465
exactness, 494
Niche
recess, 182
receptacle, 191
Nichevo
indifference, 460, 823
Nick
notch, 257
mark, 550
deceive, 545
of time, 134
prison, 752
Nickelodeon
juke box, 417
Nicker
animal sound, 412
Nickname
misnomer, 565
Nicotian
tobacco, 298A
Nictitate
blind, 442
dim sight, 443
Nidification

abode, 189
Nidus
nest, 189
cradle, 153
Niff
stink, 401
Niggard
parsimony, 819
Nigger
blackness, 431
Niggle
trifle, 643
depreciate, 483
Nigh
nearness, 197
Night
darkness, 421
Night-glass
lens, 445
Nightfall
evening, 126
Nightgown
dress, 225
Nightingale
music, 416
Nightmare
pain, 378, 828
imagination, 515
hindrance, 706
Nightshade
bane, 663
Nightshirt
dress, 225
Nigrification
black, 431
Nihilism
non-existence, 1
scepticism, 487
anarchism, 738
Nihilist
evildoer, 913
Nihility
unsubstantiality, 4
Nil admirari
expectance, 871
Nil desperandum
hope, 858
Nil ultra
superiority, 33
Nimble
swift, 274
active, 682
skilful, 698
Nimbus
cloud, 353

light, 420

Nimiety
redundance, 641

Niminy-piminy
affectation, 855

N'importe
unimportance, 643

Nimrod
chase, 622

Nincompoop
fool, 501

Nine
number, 98

Nine days' wonder
transientness, 111

Ninny
fool, 501

Ninnyhammer
fool, 501

Niobe
lament, 839

Nip
cut, 44
destroy, 162
smallness, 32

Nip up
taking, 789

Nipper
youngster, 129

Nipping
cold, 383

Nipple
convexity, 250

Nirvana
extinction, 2
happiness, 827
heaven, 979

Nit
dissent, 489

Nitrous oxide
anaesthetic, 379

Niveous
white, 430

Nix
nothing, 4

Nixie
fairy, 980

Nizam
master, 745

No
dissent, 489
negation, 536

No go
impossible, 471

Nob

summit, 210
nobility, 875

Nobble
deceive, 545
tamper with, 682
circumvent, 702

Nobility
nobleness, 875

Noble
rank, 873
greatness, 31
generous, 942
virtue, 944

Nobleman
nobleness, 875

Noblesse
nobility, 875

Nobody
absence, 187
zero, 101
unimportant, 643
ignoble, 876

Noctivagant
darkness, 421

Nocturnal
dark, 421
black, 431

Nocturne
music, 415
picture, 556

Nod
sleep, 683
signal, 550
assent, 488
order, 741
information, 527
bow, 894;
to wag, 314

Noddle
head, 450
summit, 210

Noddy
fool, 501

Node
convexity, 250

Nodosity
roughness, 256
convexity, 250

Nodule
convexity, 250

Noetic
intellect, 450

Noggin
receptacle, 191

Nohow

negation, 536

Noise
sound, 402

Noiseless
silence, 403

Noisome
fetor, 401

Noisy
loud, 404
showy, 428

Nolens volens
compulsion, 744
necessity, 601

Nom de guerre
misnomer, 565

Nom de plume
misnomer, 565

Nomad
vagrant, 264
traveller, 268
locomotive, 266

No-man's-land
interjacence, 228

Nomenclature
name, 564

Nominate
commission, 755
name, 564

Nominee
consignee, 758

Non constat
sophistry, 477

Non est
non-existence, 2

Non nobis Domine
worship, 990

Non possumus
impossible, 471
obstinacy, 606

Non sequitur
sophistry, 477

Non-adhesion
incoherence, 47

Non-admission
exclusion, 55

Nonage
youth, 127

Nonagon
angularity, 244
nine, 98

Non-appearance
invisible, 447

Non-attendance
absence, 187

Nonce
present time, 118

Nonce word
neologism, 563
Nonchalance
neglect, 460
indifference, 456, 823,
866
unwillingness, 603
Non-coincidence
contrariety, 14
Non-combatant
non-combatant, 726A
Non-committal
cautious, 864
Non-completion
non-complete, 730
Non-compliance
disobey, 742
Nonconformity
dissent, 489
unconformity, 81
sectarianism, 984A
Non-content
dissent, 489
Nondescript
unconformity, 83
None
zero, 101
Non-effective
non-combatant, 726A
Nonentity
inexistence, 2
unimportance 643
Nones
worship, 990
Non-essential
unimportance, 643
Nonesuch
see Nonsuch
Non-existence
inexistence, 2
Non-expectance
inexpectation, 508
Non-fulfilment
incomplete, 730
Non-inflammable
fireproof, 385
Non-intervention
inaction, 681
Nonjuror
dissent, 489
Non-observance
non-observance, 773
Nonpareil
perfection, 650

Nonpayment
non-payment, 808
Non-performance
non-completion, 730
Nonplus
difficulty, 704
failure, 732
Non-preparation
non-preparation, 674
Non-residence
absence, 187
Non-resistance
submission, 725
obedience, 743
Nonsense
unmeaningness, 517
absurdity, 497
ridiculousness, 853
folly, 499
trash, 643
Nonsuch
perfection, 650
unconformity, 83
Nonsuit
to cast, 731
to fail, 732
condemn, 971
Non-uniformity
variety, 16A
Noodle
fool, 501
Nook
place, 182
receptacle, 191
Noon
midday, 125
light, 420
Noose
ligature, 45
loop, 247
snare, 667
Nope
dissent, 489
• **Norm**
type, 80
mean, 29
Normal
regular, 82
vertical, 212
North
opposite, 237
Northern lights
light, 423
Nose
smell, 398

informer, 527, 529
prominence, 250
Nose out
detect, 480A
Nosegay
fragrance, 400
ornament, 847
Nosology
disease, 655
Nostalgia
discontent, 832
Nostril
air-pipe, 351
Nostrum
remedy, 662
Nosy
curiosity, 455
Not
dissent, 489
Not on your nelly
dissent, 489
Not-being
inexistence, 2
Nota bene
care, 457
Notability
personage, 642, 875
repute, 873
Notable
visible, 446
manifest, 525
important, 642
famous, 873
Notably
greatness, 31
Notary
recorder, 553
lawyer, 968
Notch
nick, 257
mark, 550
Note
sign, 550
record, 551
letter, 592
precursor, 64
music, 413
fame, 873
notice, 450, 457
minute, 596
money, 800
Note-book
compendium, 596
Note-case
purse, 802

Noted
known, 490
Noteworthy
greatness, 31
Nothing
nihility, 4
zero, 101
trifle, 643
Notice
observe, 457
mark, 450, 550
criticism, 480
warning, 668
Notify
inform, 527
publish, 531
Notion
idea, 453
belief, 484
knowledge, 490
Notoriety
disrepute, 874
publication, 531
Notorious
known, 490
seen, 446
Notwithstanding
counteraction, 179
compensation, 30
Nought
zero, 101
Noumenal
intellect, 450
Noun
nomenclature, 564
Nourish
aid, 707
Nourishment
food, 298
Nous
intellect, 450
wisdom, 498
Nous verrons
expectation, 507
Nouveau riche
newness, 123
prosperity, 734
Novel
new, 18, 123
fiction, 515
description, 594
unknown, 491
false, 546
Novena
nine, 98

Novice
learner, 541, 674
ignoramus, 493
bungler, 701
religious, 996
Novitiate
learner, 541
training, 674
Novus homo
extraneous, 57
commonalty, 876
Now
present time, 118
Now or never
occasion, 134
Nowadays
present time, 118
Nowhere
absence, 187
Nowise
in no degree, 32
dissent, 489
Noxious
badness, 649
Noyade
killing, 361
execution, 972
Nozzle
projection, 250
air-pipe, 351
opening, 260
Nuance
difference, 15
Nub
importance, 642
Nubble
lump, 150
Nubile
adolescence, 131
Nucleus
centre, 223
middle, 68
cause, 153
Nudge
indication, 550
Nudity
divestment, 226
Nugae
unmeaning, 517
unimportant, 643
Nugatory
inexistence, 2
useless, 645
inoperative, 158
Nugget

lump, 321
Nuisance
annoyance, 830
evil, 619
Null
unsubstantiality, 4
Nullah
gap, 198
Nulli secundus
superiority, 33
goodness, 648
Nullifidian
atheist, 988
Nullify
counteract, 179
repudiate, 773
invalidate, 964
compensate, 30
Numb
morally, 823
physically, 376, 381
Number
abstract, 84
plurality, 100
grammar, 568
publication, 593
to count, 85
Numberless
infinity, 105
Numbers
poetry, 597
Numbness
physical, 381
moral, 823
Numen
great spirit, 979
Numeral
number, 84
Numeration
numeration, 85
Numerator
number, 84
Numerous
multitude, 102
Numismatics
money, 800
Numskull
fool, 501
Nun
clergy, 996
Nunc dimittis
worship, 990
Nuncio
messenger, 534
consignee, 758

Nuncupatory
naming, 564
informing, 527
Nunnery
temple, 1000
seclusion, 893
Nuptials
marriage, 903
Nurse
servant, 746
treat, 662
to help, 707
preserve, 670
Nursery
room, 191
school, 542
workshop, 691
for plants, 367
Nurseryman
horticulture, 371
Nursling
infant, 129
Nurture
food, 298
to support, 707
prepare, 673
Nut
head, 450
fop, 854
madman, 504
Nut-brown
brown, 433
Nutation
oscillation, 314
Nutmeg-grater
rough, 256
Nutriment
food, 298
Nutrition
aid, 707
Nuts
insane, 503
rubbish, 643
Nutshell
littleness, 193
compendium, 596
Nuzzle
endearment, 902
Nyctalopia
dim-sighted, 443
Nylons
dress, 225
Nymph
woman, 374
goddess, 979

Nystagmus
dim-sighted, 443

O.K.
assent, 488
consènt, 762
Oaf
fool, 501
Oak
strength, 159
Oar
instrument, 633
paddle, 267
Oasis
land, 342
Oath
promise, 768
assertion, 535
expletive, 908
Obbligato
music, 415
Obduracy
sin, 945
impenitence, 931
obstinacy, 606
severity, 739
malevolence, 907
Obeah
occult arts, 992
Obedience
obedience, 743
duty, 926
Obeisance
bow, 894
reverence, 928
submission, 725
worship, 990
fealty , 743
Obelisk
monument, 551
tall, 206
Obelize
indicate, 550
Oberon
sprite, 980
Obesity
size, 192
Obey
obedience, 743, 749
Obfuscate
darken, 421, 426
bewilder, 458
Obit
death, 360

Obiter dictum
irrelation, 10
Obituary
description, 594
death, 360
Object
thing, 3, 316
intention, 620
ugly, 846
to disapprove, 932
Object lesson
explanation, 522
Object to
dislike, 867
Objectify
existence, 1
Objective
extrinsic, 6
material, 316, 450A
Objurgate
disapprobation, 932
Oblate
shortness, 201
monk, 996
Oblation
gift, 789
proffer, 763
worship, 990
Obligation
duty, 926
promise, 768
conditions, 770
debt, 806
gratitude, 916
Oblige
compel, 744
benefit, 707
Obliging
kind, 906
courteous, 894
Oblique
obliquity, 217
Obliquity
vice, 945
Obliterate
efface, 552
Oblivion
oblivion, 506
Oblong
length, 200
Obloquy
censure, 932
disgrace, 874
Obmutescence
aphony, 581

Obnoxious
  hateful, 898
  unpleasing, 830
  pernicious, 649
Oboe
  musical instrument, 417
Obscene
  impurity, 961
Obscurantist
  ignoramus, 493
Obscure
  dark, 421
  unseen, 447
  unintelligible, 519
  style, 571
  to eclipse, 874
Obscurum per obscurius
  unintelligibility, 519
  misteaching, 538
Obsecration
  request, 765
Obsequies
  interment, 363
Obsequious
  respectful, 928
  courteous, 894
  servile, 886
Observance
  fulfilment, 772
  rule, 82
  habit, 613
  practice, 692
  rites, 998
Observatory
  universe, 318
Observe
  note, 457
  conform, 926
  remark, 535
Observer
  spectator, 444
  fighter, 726
Obsess
  preoccupy, 457
  worry, 830
  haunt, 860
Obsession
  misjudgment, 481
  fixed idea, 606
Obsolete
  old, 124
  effete, 645
  vulgar, 851
Obstacle
  physical, 179

  moral, 706
Obstetrician
  instrumentality, 631
Obstinate
  stubborn, 606
  resolute, 604
  prejudiced, 481
Obstreperous
  violent, 173
  loud, 404
Obstruct
  hinder, 706
  close, 261
Obtain
  exist, 1
  acquire, 775
Obtainable
  possibility, 470
Obtestation
  entreaty, 765
  injunction, 695
Obtrude
  intervene, 228
  insert, 300
  obstruct, 706
Obtund
  blunt, 254
  deaden, 376
  paralyse, 826
Obtuse
  blunt, 254
  stupid, 499
  dull, 823
Obverse
  front, 234
Obviate
  hindrance, 706
Obvious
  visible, 446
  clear, 518
Ocarina
  musical instrument, 417
Occasion
  juncture, 8
  opportunity, 134
  cause, 153
Occasionally
  frequency, 136
Occidental
  lateral, 236
Occlusion
  closure, 261
Occult
  latent, 526
  hidden, 528

  supernatural, 992
Occupancy
  presence, 18
  property, 780
  possession, 777
Occupant
  dweller, 188
  proprietor, 779
Occupation
  business, 625
  presence, 186
Occupier
  dweller, 188
  possessor, 779
Occupy
  station, 71
  place, 186
  attention, 457
Occur
  exist, 1
  happen, 151
  be present, 186
  to the mind, 451
Ocean
  ocean, 341
  plenty, 639
Ochlocracy
  authority, 737
Ochone
  lamentation, 839
Ochre
  brown, 433
  orange, 439
O'clock
  time, 114
Octad
  number, 98
Octagon
  angularity, 244
  eight, 98
Octahedron
  angularity, 244
  eight, 98
Octavo
  book, 593
Octodecimo
  book, 593
Octonary
  eight, 98
Octoroon
  mixture, 41
Octroi
  tax, 812
Octuple
  number, 98

Oiled
drunk, 959
Oilskin
dress, 225
Okay
assent, 488
Old
oldness, 124
veteran, 130
Old-fashioned
obsolete, 851
quaint, 83
Old Harry, Old Horny, Old Nick
Satan, 978
Old-timer
veteran, 130
Oleaginous
unctuous, 355
Olfactory
odour, 398
Olid
fetor, 401
Oligarchy
authority, 737
Olio
mixture, 41
Olive
brown, 433
Olive-branch
pacify, 723
Olive-green
greenness, 435
Olla podrida
mixture, 41
miscellany, 72
Olympus
heaven, 981
Ombudsman
mediator, 724
Omega
end, 67
Omelet
food, 298
Omen
omen, 512
Ominous
prediction, 511
danger, 665
threat, 909
Omission
neglect, 460
exclusion, 55
incomplete, 53
non-fulfilment, 773

guilt, 947
Omnibus
vehicle, 272
Omnifarious
multiformity, 81
Omnigenous
multiform, 81
Omnipotence
Deity, 976
Omnipotent
powerful, 157
Omnipresence
presence, 186
Deity, 976
Omniscience
knowledge, 490
divine, 976
Omnium gatherum
mixture, 41
confusion, 59
assemblage, 72
Omnivorous
voracious, 865
Omphalos
middle, 68
centre, 223
On
forwards, 282
On end
verticality, 212
On dit
publication, 531
news, 532
interlocution, 588
Once
preterition, 122
infrequency, 137
Once for all
end, 76, 137
Once-over
look, 441
Once upon a time
different time, 119
period, 108
One
unity, 87
One by one
disjunction, 44
unity, 87
One-ideaed
folly, 499
One-sided
prejudiced, 481
partial, 940
incorrect, 495

One-step
dance, 840
Oneiromancy
prediction, 511
Oneness
unity, 87
identity, 13
Onerous
difficulty, 704
Onion
condiment, 393
Onlooker
spectator, 444
Onomasticon
dictionary, 562
Onset
attack, 716
beginning, 66
Onslaught
attack, 716
Ontology
existence, 1
Onus
duty, 926
Onus probandi
reasoning, 476
Onward
progression, 282
Onyx
ornament, 847
Oodles
greatness, 31
plenty, 639
Oof
money, 800
Oomph
charm, 829
Ooss
lightness, 320
dirt, 653
Ooze
distil, 295, 297
river, 348
sea, 341
transpire, 529
Opacity
opacity, 426
Opal
ornament, 847
Opalescent
variegation, 440
changeable, 149
Opaque
opacity, 426
Ope
open, 260

Open
  begin, 66
  expand, 194
  unclose, 260
  manifest, 518, 525
  reveal, 529
  frank, 543
  artless, 703

Open-air
  air, 338

Open-eyed
  attention, 457

Open-handed
  liberal, 816

Open-hearted
  sincere, 543
  frank, 703
  honourable, 939

Open-minded
  intelligence, 498

Open-mouthed
  loud, 404
  loquacious, 584
  gaping, 865

Open sesame
  interpretation, 522

Opening
  aperture, 198, 260
  occasion, 134
  beginning, 66

Opera
  drama, 599
  music, 415

Opéra bouffe
  drama, 599

Operate
  incite, 615
  work, 170, 680

Operation
  warfare, 722

Operative
  agent, 690

Operator
  agent, 690

Operculum
  covering, 222
  stopper, 263

Operose
  difficult, 704
  active, 683
  exertive, 686

Ophicleide
  musical, 417

Ophthalmic

  vision, 441

Opiate
  remedy, 174
  sedative, 174

Opine
  belief, 484

Opiniâtre
  obstinacy, 606

Opinion
  belief, 484

Opinionative
  obstinacy, 606

Opium
  moderation, 174

Oppilation
  hindrance, 706

Opponent
  antagonist, 710
  enemy, 891

Opportune
  well-timed, 134
  expedient, 646

Opportunism
  cunning, 702

Opportunist
  time server, 607, 646,
   943

Opportunity
  occasion, 134

Oppose
  antagonize, 179
  clash, 708
  resist, 719
  evidence, 468

Opposite
  contrary, 14
  antiposition, 237

Oppress
  molest, 649
  domineer, 739

Oppression
  injury, 619, 649
  dejection, 837

Opprobrium
  disrepute, 874

Oppugn
  oppose, 708

Optative
  desire, 865

Optics
  light, 420
  sight, 441

Optimates
  nobility, 875

Optimism

  hope, 858

Option
  choice, 609

Opulence
  wealth, 803

Opus
  music, 415

Opuscule
  book, 593

Oracle
  prophet, 513
  sage, 500

Oracular
  wise, 498
  prophetic, 511

Oral
  voice, 580

Orange
  orange, 439

Oration
  speech, 582

Orator
  speaker, 582
  teacher, 540

Oratorio
  music, 415

Oratory
  speech, 582
  temple, 1000

Orb
  circle, 247
  region, 181
  luminary, 423
  sphere of action, 625
  insignia, 747

Orbicular
  circularity, 247

Orbit
  path, 627
  world, 318

Orbital
  space ship, 273A

Orchestra
  musician, 416

Orchestration
  music, 415

Orchestrion
  musical, 417

Ordain
  command, 741
  churchdom, 976

Ordained
  prescribed, 924
  clergy, 996

Ordeal
experiment, 463
sorcery, 992

Order
regularity, 58
subordinate class, 75
rule, 80
law, 963
command, 741
direct, 693, 697
rank, 873, 875
of the day, 82

Orderless
disorder, 59

Orderly
conformity, 82

Orders, holy
churchdom, 995

Ordinal
rite, 998

Ordinance
command, 741
law, 963
rite, 998

Ordinary
usual, 82, 613
plain, 849
mean, 29, 736
ugly, 846

Ordination
command, 741
arrangement, 60
rite, 998

Ordure
uncleanness, 653

Ore
materials, 635

Ore rotundo
ornament, 577
speech, 582

Organ
instrument, 633
music, 417

Organic
state, 7
living beings, 357

Organism
state, 7
structure, 329

Organist
musician, 416

Organization
structure, 329

Organize
arrange, 60

plan, 626
prepare, 673
produce, 161

Organized
organization, 357

Orgasm
violence, 173

Orgy
intemperance, 954

Orient
light, 420
direction, 278

Orientate
direction, 278

Orientation
situation, 183

Orifice
opening, 66, 260

Oriflamme
indication, 550

Origin
cause, 153
beginning, 66

Original
model, 22
oddity, 83, 857
invented, 515
vigorous, 574

Originate
cause, 153
begin, 66
invent, 515

Originator
producer, 164

Orison
request, 765
prayer, 990

Ormolu
ornament, 847

Ormuzd
deity, 979

Ornament
ornament, 847
glory, 873
style, 577

Ornate
ornament, 847
style, 577

Orography
height, 206

Orotund
style, 577

Orphan
weakness, 160

Orpiment

yellow, 436

Orris root
fragrance, 400

Orthodox
true, 494
conformity, 82
in religion, 983A

Orthoepy
voice, 580

Orthogenesis
causation, 153

Orthography
writing, 590

Orthometry
measurement, 466
poetry, 597

Orts
remnants, 40
refuse, 643
useless, 645

Oscar
trophy, 733

Oscillation
oscillation, 314

Osculate
contiguity, 199
kiss, 902

Osmosis
percolation, 302

Osseous
hard, 323

Ossification
hardness, 323

Ossuary
interment, 363

Ostensible
visible, 446
apparent, 448
probable, 472
plea, 617
explicit, 576

Ostentation
ostentation, 882
vanity, 880
vulgarity, 851

Osteopathy
remedy, 662

Ostiary
door-keeper, 263

Ostler
servant, 746

Ostracize
exclude, 55
displace, 185
seclude, 893

censure, 932
Other
difference, 15
Other-guess
difference, 15
Other-worldliness
piety, 987
Otherwise
difference, 15
dissimilarity, 18
O'Trigger
blusterer, 887
Otto
see Attar
Ottoman
support, 215
Oubliette
prison, 752
hide, 530
Ought
duty, 926
Oui-dire
news, 532
Oust
displace, 185
deprive, 789
dismiss, 756
Out
exteriority, 220
up in arms, 719
Out and out
greatness, 31
Out-herod
bluster, 173
exaggerate, 549
Out of bounds
transcursion, 303
Out of date
old, 124
past, 122
obsolete, 851
Out of place
disorder, 59
unconformity, 83
Out-talk
loquacity, 584
Outbalance
superiority, 28, 33
Outbid
barter, 794
Outbrave
insolence, 885
Outbrazen
insolence, 885
Outbreak

egress, 295
violence, 173
contest, 720
passion, 825
Outburst
egress, 295
violence, 173
passion, 825
Outcast
secluded, 893
sinner, 949
apostate, 941
Outclass
superiority, 33
Outcome
result, 154
Outcry
noise, 411
complaint, 839
censure, 932
Outdistance
speed, 274
surpass, 303
Outdo
activity, 682
surpass, 303
superiority, 33
Outdoor
exteriority, 220
Outer
exteriority, 220
Outface
insolence, 885
Outfit
preparation, 673
equipment, 633
Outfitter
dress, 225
Outflank
baffle, 731
Outgeneral
success, 731
Outgo
transgress, 303
distance, 196
Outgoings
expenditure, 809
Outgrow
expansion, 194
Outhouse
abode, 189
Outing
journey, 266
Outlandish
irregular, 83

foreign, 10
barbarous, 851
ridiculous, 853
Outlast
diuturnity, 110
Outlaw
reprobate, 949
exclude, 893
condemn, 971
Outlawry
illegality, 964
Outlay
expenditure, 809
Outleap
transcursion, 303
Outlet
egress, 295
opening, 260
Outline
contour, 229
sketch, 554
features, 448
plan, 626
Outlive
survive, 110
continue, 141
Outlook
insolence, 885
futurity, 121
prospect, 507
view, 448
Outlying
exteriority, 220
remainder, 40
Outmanœuvre
success, 731
Outmarch
speed, 274
Outmatch
inequality, 28
superiority, 33
Outnumber
multitude, 102
Outpace
velocity, 274
transcursion, 303
Outpost
distance, 196
circumjacent, 227
front, 234
Outpouring
information, 527
Outrage
evil, 619, 649
malevolence, 907

Overgrown
size, 31
swollen, 194
Overhang
height, 206
jut out, 250
impend, 121
Overhaul
inquire, 461
attend to, 457
number, 85
overtake, 292
Overhead
height, 206
Overhear
hear, 418
learn, 539
Overjoyed
pleasure, 827
Overjump
transcursion, 303
Overland
journey, 266
Overlap
cover, 222
go beyond, 303
Overlay
excess, 641
oppress, 649
hinder, 706
style, 577
Overleap
transcursion, 303
Overload
excess, 641
obstruct, 706
Overlook
disregard, 458
neglect, 460
superintend, 693
forgive, 918
slight, 929
Overlooker
director, 694
Overmatch
inequality, 28, 149
Overmuch
redundance, 641
Overnight
preterition, 122
Overpass
exceed, 33
transgress, 303
Overplus
excess, 641

remainder, 40
Overpower
subdue, 731
emotion, 824
Overpowered
failure, 732
Overpowering
excitability, 825
Overprize
overestimation, 482
Overrate
overestimation, 482
Overreach
pass, 303
deceive, 545
cunning, 702
baffle, 731
Override
pass, 303
cancel, 756
overrule, 737
domineer, 739
be superior, 33
Overrule
control, 737
cancel, 736
Overrun
ravage, 649
pass, 303
excess, 641
Overseas
extraneous, 57
Overseer
director, 694
Overset
level, 308
invert, 218
subvert, 731
Overshadow
darkness, 421
superiority, 33
repute, 873
Overshoe
dress, 225
Overshoot
transcursion, 303
Oversight
error, 495
inattention, 458
failure, 732
Overspread
cover, 222
pervade, 73, 186
Overstate
exaggeration, 549

Overstep
transcursion, 303
Overstrain
overrate, 482
fatigue, 688
Overstrung
excitability, 825
Overt
visible, 446
manifest, 525
Overtake
arrive, 292
Overtaken
tipsy, 959
Overtask
fatigue, 688
Overtax
fatigue, 688
Overthrow
destroy, 162
level, 308
confute, 479
vanquish, 731, 732
Overtone
melody, 413
Overtop
surpass, 33
height, 206
perfection, 650
Overture
beginning, 66
precursor, 64
offer, 763
music, 415
request, 765
Overturn
destroy, 162
level, 308
confute, 571
invert, 218
Overvalue
overestimation, 482
Overweening
conceit, 880
pride, 878
Overweight
overrate, 482
exceed, 33
influence, 175
Overwhelm
destroy, 162
affect, 824
Overwhelming
excitability, 825

Overwork
fatigue, 688
Overwrought
excited, 825
Ovoid
rotundity, 249
Ovule
circularity, 247
Owe
debt, 806
Owing to
attribution, 155
Owl-light
dimness, 422
Own
assent, 488, 535
divulge, 529
possess, 777
Owner
possessor, 779
Ownership
property, 780
Oxygenate
air, 338
Oy
attention, 457
Oyez
hearing, 418
Oyster
taciturnity, 585

P.A.Y.E.
tax, 812
P.B.I.
soldier, 725
p.m.
evening, 126
P.O.P.
photograph, 556
P.O.W.
prisoner, 754
p.p.
commission, 755
P.T.
Teaching, 537
Exertion, 686
Pa
father, 166
Pabulum
food, 298
Pace
speed, 274
step, 266
measure, 466

Pachydermatous
insensible, 376, 823
Pacific
concord, 714, 721
Pacifism
pacification, 723
Pacifist
non-combatant, 726A
Pacify
allay, 174
compose, 826
give peace, 723
forgive, 918
Pack
to join, 43
arrange, 60
bring close, 197
locate, 184
assemblage, 72
Pack-horse
carrier, 271
Pack off
depart, 293
recede, 287
decamp, 671
Pack up
circumscribe, 231
fail, 732
Package
parcel, 72
Packet
parcel, 72
ship, 273
Packing-case
receptacle, 191
Packthread
vinculum, 45
Pact
agreement, 769
Pactolus
wealth, 803
Pad
carrier, 271
line, 224
expand, 194
diffuse, 573
Padding
softness, 324
Paddle
oar, 267, 633
to bathe, 337
Paddle-steamer
ship, 273
Paddle-wheel
navigation, 267

Paddock
arena, 181
enclosure, 232, 752
Padlock
fastening, 45
fetter, 752
Padre
clergy, 996
Paean
thanks, 916
rejoicing, 836
worship, 990
Paediatrics
remedy, 662
Paeon
verse, 597
Paganism
heathen, 984, 996
Page
attendant, 746
of a book, 593
Pageant
spectacle, 448
the drama, 599
show, 882
Pagoda
temple, 1000
Pail
receptacle, 191
Pailful
quantity, 25
Paillard
libertine, 962
Pain
physical, 378
moral, 828
penalty, 974
Painful
painfulness, 830
Pains
exertion, 686
Painstaking
active, 682
laborious, 686
Paint
coat, 222
colour, 428
adorn, 847
delineate, 556
describe, 594
Painter
artist, 559
rope, 45
Painting
painting, 556

Pair
couple, 89
similar, 17
Pair off
average, 29
Pal
friend, 890
Palace
abode, 189
Paladin
courage, 861
Palaeography
interpretation, 522
Palaeolithic
oldness, 142
Palaeology
preterition, 122
Palaeontology
zoology, 368
past, 122
Palaestra
school, 542
arena, 728
training, 673
Palaestric
exertion, 686
Palanquin
vehicle, 272
Palatable
savoury, 394
pleasant, 829
Palatal
letter, 561
Palate
taste, 390
Palatine
master, 745
Palaver
speech, 582
colloquy, 588
council, 696
nonsense, 497, 517
loquacity, 584
Pale
dim, 422
colourless, 429
enclosure, 232
Palfrey
carrier, 271
Palimpsest
substitution, 147
writing, 590
Palindrome
neology, 563
inversion, 218

Paling
prison, 752
enclosure, 232
Palingenesis
restore, 660
Palinode
denial, 536
recantation, 607
Palisade
prison, 752
enclosure, 232
Pall
funeral, 363
disgust, 395, 867
satiate, 869
Palladium
defence, 664, 717
Pallet
support, 215
Palliasse
support, 215
Palliate
mend, 658
relieve, 834
moderate, 174
extenuate, 937
Palliative
remedy, 662
Pallid
achromatism, 429
Palling
unsavouriness, 395
Pallium
dress, 225
canonicals, 999
Pally
friendship, 888
Palm
trophy, 733
glory, 873
laurel, 877
deceive, 545
impose upon, 486
Palmer
traveller, 268
Palmist
fortune-teller, 513
Palmistry
prediction, 511
Palmy
prosperous, 734
halcyon, 827, 829
Palpable
tactile, 379
tangible, 316

obvious, 446, 525
intelligible, 518
Palpitate
tremble, 315
emotion, 821
fear, 860
Palsy
disease, 655
weakness, 160
incapacity, 158
insensibility, 376, 823
Palter
falsehood, 544
shift, 605
elude, 773
Paltry
mean, 940
despicable, 643, 930
little, 32
Paludal
marsh, 345
Pampas
plain, 344
Pamper
indulge, 954
gorge, 957
Pampero
wind, 349
Pamphlet
book, 593
Pamphleteer
writing, 590
dissertation, 595
Pan
receptacle, 191
face, 234, 448
Panacea
remedy, 662
Panache
plume, 256
ornament, 847
Pandect
code, 963
compendium, 596
erudition, 490
Pandemic
insalubrity, 657
Pandemonium
hell, 982
disorder, 59
Pander
flatter, 933
indulge, 954
mediate, 631
help, 707

Pandora
evil, 619
Paned
variegation, 440
Panegyric
approbation, 931
Panel
list, 86
partition, 228
accused, 938
legal, 967
Panem et circenses
giving, 784
Pang
physical, 378
moral, 828
Panhandler
tramp, 876
Panic
fear, 860
Pannier
receptacle, 191
Panoply
defence, 717
Panopticon
prison, 752
Panorama
view, 448
painting, 556
Panoramic
general, 78
Pansophy
knowledge, 490
Pansy
effeminate, 374
Pant
breathless, 688
desire, 865
agitation, 821
Pantaloon
buffoon, 844
dress, 225
Pantechnicon
vehicle, 272
Pantheism
heathen, 984
Pantheon
temple, 1000
Pantograph
imitation, 19
Pantomime
sign, 550
language, 560
drama, 599
Pantry

receptacle, 191
Pap
pulp, 354
teat, 250
Papa
father, 166
Papacy
churchdom, 995
Paper
writing, 590
book, 593
record, 551
white, 430
Paperback
book, 593
Papilla
convexity, 250
Papoose
infant, 129
Pappy
semiliquidity, 352
Par
equality, 27
Parable
metaphor, 521
analogy, 464
story, 594
Parabolic
metaphor, 521
curve, 245
Parachronism
anachronism, 115
Parachute
refuge, 666
Paraclete
Deity, 976
Parade
walk, 189
ostentation, 882
Paradigm
prototype, 22
example, 80
Paradise
heaven, 981
bliss, 827
Paradox
obscurity, 519
absurdity, 497
mystery, 528
enigma, 533
Paragon
perfection, 650
saint, 948
glory, 873
Paragraph

phrase, 566
part, 51
article, 593
Paralipsis
neglect, 460
Parallax
distance, 196
Parallel
position, 216
similarity, 17
to imitate, 19
agreement, 23
comparison, 464
Parallelepiped
angularity, 244
Parallelogram
angularity, 244
Paralogism
sophistry, 477
Paralyse
weaken, 160
benumb, 381
deaden, 823
insensibility, 376
impassivity, 823
stillness, 265
disqualify, 158
disease, 655
Paramount
essential, 642
in degree, 33
authority, 737
Paramour
love, 897
Paranoia
insanity, 503, 504
Parapet
defence, 717
Paraph
writing, 590
Paraphernalia
machinery, 633
materials, 635
property, 780
Paraphrase
interpretation, 522, 524
phrase, 566
imitation, 19, 21
Paraplectic
disease, 655
Parapsychology
occult, 992
Parasite
flatterer, 935
servile, 886

follow, 88
Parasol
shade, 424
Paratrooper
fighter, 726
Paravane
defence, 717
Parboil
calefaction, 384
Parcel
group, 72
portion, 51
Parcel out
arrange, 60
allot, 786
Parch
dry, 340
heat, 382
bake, 384
Parchment
manuscript, 590
record, 551
Pardon
forgiveness, 918
Pardonable
vindication, 937
Pare
scrape, 38, 226, 331
shorten, 201
decrease, 36
Paregoric
salubrity, 656
Parenchyma
texture, 329
Parent
paternity, 166
Parentage
kindred, 11
Parenthesis
interjacence, 228
discontinue, 70
Parenthetical
irrelation, 10
occasion, 134
Par excellence
greatness, 31
superiority, 33
Pari passu
equality, 27
Pariah
commonalty, 876
outcast, 892
Paring
part, 51
smallness, 32

Parish
region, 181
Parishioner
laity, 997
Parity
equality, 27
Park
plain, 344
vegetation, 367
amusement, 840
artillery, 727
locate, 184
Parlance
speech, 582
Parlementaire
messenger, 534
Parley
talk, 588
mediation, 724
Parliament
council, 696
Parlour
room, 191
Parlour-car
vehicle, 272
Parlourmaid
servant, 746
Parnassus
poetry, 597
Parochial
regional, 181
ignoble, 876
Parody
imitation, 19
copy, 21
travesty, 856
misinterpret, 523
Parole
promise, 768
Paronomasia
pun, 563
Paronymous
word, 562
Paroxysm
violence, 173
emotion, 825
anger, 900
Parquetry
variegation, 440
Parricide
killing, 361
Parrot
imitation, 19
loquacity, 584
repetition, 104

Parry
avert, 623
confute, 479
defend, 717
Parse
grammar, 567
Parsee
religions, 984
Parsimony
parsimony, 819
Parson
clergy, 996
Parsonage
temple, 1000
Part
portion, 51
component, 56
to diverge, 291
to divide, 44
business, 625
function, 644
Part with
relinquish, 782
give, 784
Partake
participation, 778
Parterre
agriculture, 371
Parti
adolescence, 131
Parti pris
prejudgment, 481
predetermination, 611
Partial
unequal, 28
special, 79
one-sided, 481
unjust, 923
love, 897
friendship, 888
desire, 865
erroneous, 495
smallness, 32
harmonic, 413
Particeps criminis
auxiliary, 711
bad man, 949
Participation
participation, 778
co-operation, 709
Particle
quantity, 32
size, 193
Particoloured
variegation, 440

Pastime
  amusement, 840
Pastor
  clergy, 996
Pastoral
  domestication, 370
  poem, 597
  religious, 995, 998
Pastry
  food, 298
Pasturage
  plain, 344
Pasture
  food, 298
Pasty
  semiliquid, 352
  colourless, 429
Pat
  expedient, 646
  pertinent, 9
  to strike, 276
Patagonian
  height, 206
Patch
  region, 181
  smallness, 193
  repair, 658
Patchwork
  mixture, 41
  variegation, 440
Patchy
  imperfect, 53
Pate
  head, 450
Patent
  open, 260
  visible, 446
  manifest, 525
  permit, 760
  privilege, 924
Patera
  plate, 191
  church, 1000
Paternity
  parent, 155, 166
Path
  way, 627
  passage, 302
  direction, 278
Pathetic
  painful, 830
  affecting, 824
Pathless
  closure, 261
  difficult, 704
  spacious, 180

Pathogenic
  unhealthy, 657
Pathognomonic
  indication, 550
Pathology
  disease, 655
Pathos
  feeling, 821
Pathway
  way, 627
Patience
  endurance, 826
  content, 831
  perseverance, 682
Patient
  invalid, 655
Patois
  language, 560
Patriarch
  veteran, 130
Patriarchal
  paternity, 166
Patriarchy
  authority, 737
Patrician
  nobility, 875
Patrimony
  property, 780
Patriot
  philanthropy, 910
Patristic
  theological, 983
Patrol
  safeguard, 664
  warning, 668
Patron
  friend, 891
  buyer, 795
Patronage
  aid, 707
  protection, 175
  authority, 737
Patronize
  aid, 707
Patronizing
  condescending, 878
Patronymic
  nomenclature, 564
Patter
  to strike, 276
  step, 266
  sound, 407
  chatter, 584
  patois, 560
Pattern

  model, 22
  order, 58
  type, 80
  example, 82
  perfection, 650
  saint, 948
Patulous
  opening, 260
Paucity
  fewness, 103
  scantiness, 640
  smallness, 32
Paul Pry
  curiosity, 455
Paunch
  receptacle, 191
  convexity, 250
Pauperism
  poverty, 804
Pause
  stop, 265
  discontinuance, 142
  rest, 685, 687
  disbelief, 485
Pavane
  dance, 840
Pave
  prepare, 673
  cover, 222
Pavement
  base, 311
  footway, 627
Pavilion
  abode, 189
Paving
  base, 211
Paw
  touch, 379
  finger, 633
Pawky
  cunning, 702
Pawn
  security, 771
  lending, 787
Pax vobiscum
  courtesy, 894
Pay
  expend, 809
  defray, 807
  condemn, 971
  punish, 972
Pay-as you earn
  tax, 812
Paymaster
  treasury, 801

Paynim
heathen, 984
Pea
rotundity, 249
Pea-green
greenness, 435
Pea-shooter
propulsion, 284
Peace
silence, 403
amity, 721
concord, 714
Peace-offering
pacify, 723
atonement, 952
Peaceable
gentle, 174
Peach
disclosure, 529
Peach colour
redness, 434
Peacock
variegation, 440
beauty, 845
pride, 878
boaster, 884
Peak
summit, 210
height, 206
Peaked
sharpness, 253
Peal
loudness, 404
laughter, 838
Pear-shaped
rotundity, 249
curved, 245
Pearl
gem, 650
ornament, 847
glory, 873
Pearly
nacreous, 440
semitransparent, 427
white, 439
Peasant
commonalty, 876
Peat
fuel, 388
Pebble
hardness, 323
trifle, 643
Peccability
vice, 945
Peccadillo

guilt, 947
Peccancy
disease, 655
imperfection, 651
badness, 649
Peccant
wrong, 945
Pech
pant, 688
Peck
quantity, 31
eat, 296
Pecking-order
precedence, 58
Peckish
desire, 865
Pecksniff
hypocrite, 548
Pectinated
sharpness, 253
Peculate
stealing, 791
Peculator
thief, 792
Peculiar
special, 5, 79
exceptional, 83
Peculiarly
greatness, 31, 33
Pecuniary
money, 800
Pedagogue
scholar, 492
teacher, 540
Pedant
scholar, 492
affected, 855
teacher, 540
Pedantic
affected, 855
Pedantic
half-learned, 491
style, 577
Peddle
trifle, 683
sell, 796
Pedestal
support, 215
Pedestrian
traveller, 268
dull, 842, 843
style, 573
Pedicel
pendency, 214
Pedigree

ancestry, 155, 166
continuity, 69
Pediment
capital, 210
base, 215
Pedlar
merchant, 797
Peduncle
pendency, 214
Peek
look, 441
Peel
skin, 222
to uncover, 226
Peeler
police, 664
Peep
vision, 441
Peep-hole
opening, 260
view, 441
Peep out
visibility, 446
Peep-show
spectacle, 448
Peeping Tom
curiosity, 455
Peer
equal, 27
nobleman, 875
pry, 441
inquire, 461
appear, 446
Peerage
list, 86
Peerless
perfect, 650
excellent, 648, 873
superior, 33
virtuous, 944
Peeve
irritate, 900
Peevish
cross, 895
irascible, 901
Peg
degree, 26, 71
project, 250
hang, 214
jog on, 266
drink, 298
intoxicant, 959
Peg away
persist, 143
activity, 682

Peg out
die, 360
Pegasus
imagination, 515
Peine forte et dure
punishment, 972
Pejoration
deterioration, 659
Pelagic
ocean, 341
Pelerine
dress, 225
Pelf
money, 803
materials, 635
gain, 775
Pellet
rotundity, 249
remedy, 662
Pellicle
film, 205
skin, 222
Pell-mell
disorder, 59
Pellucid
transparency, 425
Pelt
skin, 222
throw, 276
attack, 716
beat, 972
Pen
surround, 231
enclose, 232
restrain, 751
imprison, 752
draw, 559
write, 590
Pen-and-ink
drawing, 556
Pen-name
misnomer, 565
Penal
punishment, 972
Penalty
penalty, 974
Penance
atonement, 952
rite, 998
penalty, 974
Penchant
inclination, 865
love, 897
Pencil
bundle, 72

of light, 420
artist, 556, 559, 590
Pencraft
writing, 590
Pendant
adjunct, 39
flag, 550
pendency, 214
match, 17
Pendent
during, 106
hanging, 214
uncertain, 485
Pendente lite
warfare, 722
lawsuit, 969
Pending
duration, 106
lateness, 133
uncertain, 475
Pendulous
pendency, 214
Pendulum
clock, 114
oscillation, 314
Penetralia
interiority, 221
secret, 533
Penetrate
fill, 186
influence, 175
Penetrating
affecting, 821
Penetration
ingress, 294
passage, 302
discernment, 441
sagacity, 498
Penfold
enclosure, 232
Peninsula
land, 342
Penitent
penitence, 950
Penitentiary
prison, 752
Penmanship
writing, 590
Penniless
poverty, 804
Pennon
indication, 550
Penny-a-liner
writer, 590
Penny-farthing

bicycle, 266
Pennyworth
price, 812
Penseroso
dejection, 837
Pensile
pendency, 214
Pension
wealth, 803, 810
Pensioner
servant, 746
recipient, 785
Pensive
thoughtful, 451
sad, 837
Pent
imprisoned, 754
Pentad
five, 98
Pentagon
angularity, 244
five, 98
Pentahedron
angularity, 244
five, 98
Pentatonic
melody, 413
Penthouse
building, 189
Penultimate
end, 67
Penumbra
darkness, 421, 424
Penurious
parsimony, 819
Penury
poverty, 804
scantiness, 640
People
man, 373
inhabitant, 188
commonalty, 876
to colonize, 184
Pep
energy, 171, 682
vigour, 574
Pep-talk
speech, 582
Pepper
hot, 171
pungent, 392
condiment, 393
attack, 716
Peppercorn
unimportance, 643

Peppery
irascibility, 901
Peptic
remedy, 662
Per contra
contrariety, 14
opposition, 708
Per procurationem
commission, 755
Per saltum
discontinuity, 70
transientness, 111
instantaneity, 113
Per se
unity, 87
Peradventure
chance, 156
possibly, 470
uncertainty, 475
Perambulate
journey, 266
Perceivable
visible, 446
Percentage
proportion, 84
discount, 813
Perceptible
visibility, 446
Perception
idea, 453
of touch, 380
Perceptivity
sensibility, 375
Perch
support, 215
to alight, 186
tall, 206
habitation, 189
Perchance
chance, 156
possibly, 470
Percipience
intellect, 450
Percolate
distil, 295
Percolation
passage, 302
Percussion
impulse, 276
Perdition
ruin, 732
loss, 776
Perdu
concealment, 528
Perdurable

permanence, 141
Peregrination
journey, 266
Peremptory
assertion, 535
denial, 536
firm, 604
rigorous, 739
authoritative, 737
compulsory, 744
obligatory, 926
order, 740, 741
Perennial
diuturnity, 110, 150
Perfect
entire, 52
complete, 729
excellent, 650
Perfectly
greatness, 31
Perfidy
improbity, 940
Perforate
opening, 260
Perforator
perforator, 263
Perforce
compulsion, 744
Perform
do, 170, 680
achieve, 729
produce, 161
act, 599
fulfil, 772
duty, 926
Performable
facility, 705
possible, 470
Performance
effect, 154
Performer
musician, 416
actor, 599
workman, 164
agent, 690
Perfume
fragrance, 400
Perfunctory
neglect, 460
incomplete, 53
Perhaps
possibly, 470
chance, 156
supposition, 514
Peri

fairy, 979
Periapt
spell, 993
Perigee
nearness, 197
Perihelion,
nearness, 197
Peril
danger, 665
Perimeter
outline, 229
Period
end, 67
of time, 106, 108
stop, 142
point, 71
recurrence, 138
Periodical
book, 593
publication, 531
Peripatetic
traveller, 268
ambulatory, 266
Periphery
outline, 229
Periphrasis
phrase, 566
diffuseness, 573
Perique
tobacco, 298A
Periscope
vision, 441
optical instrument, 445
Perish
vanish, 2
be destroyed, 162
die, 360
decay, 659
Peristaltic
convolution, 248
Periwig
dress, 225
Perjured
false, 940
Perjury
falsehood, 544
untruth, 546
Perk
lift, 307
smarten, 845
Perk up
recover 689
Perky
saucy, 885
gay, 836

Perlustration
vision, 441
Perm
convolution, 248
Permanent
unchanged, 141
unchangeable, 150
lasting, 106, 110
Permeable
opening, 260
Permeate
pervade, 186
influence, 175
insinuate, 228
pass through, 302
Permissible
dueness, 924
Permissive
lax, 738
Permit
permission, 760
Permutation
change, 140
numerical, 84
Pernicious
badness, 649
destructive, 162
Pernickety
fastidious, 868
faddy, 481
difficult, 704
Peroration
end, 67
sequel, 65
speech, 582
Perpend
thought, 451
attend, 457
Perpendicular
verticality, 212
Perpetrate
action, 680
Perpetrator
doer, 690
Perpetual
perpetuity, 112
duration, 106, 110
frequent, 136
continual, 143
Perpetuate
immutable, 150
Perplex
to derange, 61
bewilder, 458, 519

bother, 830
embarrass, 475
puzzle, 528
Perplexity
disorder, 59
difficulty, 704
ignorance, 491
doubt, 475
unintelligibility, 519
maze, 533
Perquisite
receipt, 810
reward, 973
Perquisition
inquiry, 461
Persecute
worry, 830, 907
oppress, 619, 649
Perseverance
firmness, 604
activity, 682
continuance, 143
Persiflage
ridicule, 856
wit, 842
Persist
endure, 106, 143, 606
Persistence
continuance, 110, 141
resolution, 604
activity, 682
Person
man, 373
grammar, 567
Personable
beauty, 845
Personage
nobility, 875
important, 642
Persona grata
favourite, 899
friend, 890
Personal
special, 79, 317, 372
bodily, 3
Personalities
abuse, 932
Personate
imitate, 17
act, 554
Personify
metaphor, 521
Personnel
component, 56
Perspective

view, 448
painting, 556
futurity, 121
sagacity, 498
sight, 441
Perspicacious
foreseeing, 510
Perspicacity
intelligence, 498
Perspicuity
Perspicuity, 518, 570
Perspiration
excretion, 299
Perstringe
attention, 457
Persuade
induce, 609, 615
teach, 537
advise, 695
Persuasible
learning, 539
willing, 602
Persuasion
opinion, 484
creed, 983
Pert
vain, 880
saucy, 885
discourteous, 895
Pertain
belong, 76, 777
relate to, 9
behove, 926
Pertinacious
obstinacy, 606
determination, 604
Pertinent
relative, 9
congruous, 23
Pertinent
relevant, 476
applicable, 646
Perturb
derange, 61
agitate, 315
emotion, 821
excitability, 825
ferment, 171
Peruke
dress, 225
Peruse
learning, 539
examine, 461
Pervade
extend, 186

affect, 821
Perverse
  crotchety, 608
  difficult, 704
  wayward, 895
Perversion
  injury, 659
  sophistry, 477
  falsehood, 544
  misinterpretation, 523
  misteaching, 538
  impiety, 988
Pervert
  apostate, 144, 941
  turncoat, 607
  blasphemer, 988
Pervicacious
  obstinacy, 606
Pervigilium
  activity, 682
Pervious
  opening, 260
Pessimism
  dejection, 837
  hopelessness, 859
Pest
  bane, 663
  badness, 649
  bother, 830
Pest-house
  remedy, 662
Pester
  painfulness, 830
Pestiferous
  insalubrity, 657
Pestilent
  badness, 649
  poison, 663
Pestle
  pulverulence, 330
Pet
  plaything, 840
  favourite, 899
  passion, 900
  to love, 897
  to fondle, 902
Petard
  arms, 727
Peter out
  end, 67
Peterhead
  prison, 752
Petit-maître
  fop, 854
Petite

little, 193
Petite amie
  mistress, 962
Petitio principii
  sophistry, 477
Petition
  ask, 765
  pray, 990
Petitioner
  petitioner, 767
Petits soins
  courtesy, 894
  courtship, 903
Pétri
  feeling, 821
Petrify
  dense, 321
  hard, 323
  affright, 860
  astonish, 870
  thrill, 824
Petroleum
  oil, 356
Pétroleur
  incendiary, 384
Petronel
  arms, 727
Petticoat
  dress, 225
Pettifogger
  lawyer, 968
Pettifogging
  discord, 713
  hair-splitting, 477
Pettish
  irascibility, 895, 901
Petty
  in degree, 32
  in size, 193
Petulant
  insolent, 885
  snappish, 895
  angry, 900
  irascible, 901
Pew
  temple, 1000
Phaeton
  carriage, 272
Phalanx
  army, 726
  party, 712
  assemblage, 72
Phantasm
  unreal, 4
  appearance, 448

delusion, 443
Phantasmagoria
  optical, 445
Phantom
  vision, 448
  unreal, 4
  imaginary, 515
Pharisaical
  falsehood, 544
Pharmacology
  remedy, 662
Pharmacy
  remedy, 662
Pharos
  warning, 668
  indication, 550
Phase
  aspect, 8
  appearance, 448
  change, 144
  form, 240
Phenomenal
  great, 31
  apparent, 448
  wonderful, 870
Phenomenon
  appearance, 448
  event, 151
  prodigy, 872
Phial
  receptacle, 191
Phidias
  artist, 559
Philanderer
  flirt, 902
Philanthropy
  philanthropy, 910
Philatelist
  collector, 775
Philibeg
  dress, 225
Philippic
  disapproval, 932
Philistine
  uncultured, 491, 493
Phillumenist
  collector, 775
Philology
  grammar, 567
Philomath
  scholar, 492
  sage, 500
Philomel
  musician, 416

Philosopher
scholar, 492
Philosophy
calmness, 826
thought, 451
knowledge, 490
Philtre
charm, 993
Phiz
appearance, 448
Phlebotomy
ejection, 297
Phlegethon
hell, 982
Phlegm
insensibility, 823
semiliquid, 352
Phoenix
prodigy, 872
exception, 83
paragon, 650
saint, 948
renovation, 163, 660
Phonetics
sound, 402
speech, 580
Phoney
fasle, 495, 544
Phonic
sound, 402
Phonograph
musical instrument, 417
hearing, 418
Phonography
shorthand, 590
Phosphorescent
light, 420, 423
Photo-lithograph
engraving, 558
Photogenic
beauty, 845
Photograph
copy, 21
representation, 554
Photography
painting, 556
Photogravure
engraving, 558
Photology
light, 420
Photometer
optical instrument, 445
Photostat
copy, 21
Phrase
phrase, 566

Phrase-monger
floridity, 577
Phraseology
style, 569
Phratry
class, 75
Phrenetic
see Frantic
Phrenitis
insanity, 503
Phrenology
intellect, 450
Phrontistery
room, 191
Phylactery
spell, 993
Phylum
class, 75
Physic
remedy, 662
to cure, 660
Physical
materiality, 316
Physician
advice, 695
Physics
materiality, 316
Physiognomy
appearance, 448
face, 234
Physiology
life, 359
Physique
substance, 3
animality, 364
Phytography
botany, 369
Phytology
botany, 369
Piacular
atonement, 952
Pianissimo
faint, 405
Pianist
musician, 416
Piano
instrument, 417
slowly, 275
faint sound, 405
Pianola
instrument, 417
Piazza
street, 189
veranda, 191
Pibroch

music, 415
Picaroon
thief, 792
Piccaninny
child, 129
Piccolo
musical instrument, 417
Pick
select, 609
goodness, 648
extract, 301
eat, 296
clean, 652
sharpness, 253
Pick-me-up
stimulant, 615
remedy, 662
Pick-thank
flatterer, 935
Pick up
learn, 539
improve, 658
acquire, 775
Pickaxe
sharpness, 253
Picket
join, 43
tether, 265
fence, 231
defence, 717
guard, 664
imprison, 752
Pickings
part, 51
booty, 793
Pickle
difficulty, 704
preserve, 670
pungent, 392
condiment, 393
macerate, 337
Pickpocket
thief, 792
Picnic
food, 298
party, 892
Picture
painting, 556
representation, 554
fancy, 515
Picturesque
beautiful, 845
graphic, 556
Piddling
paltry, 643

Pidgin English
language, 560
Pie
type, 591
disorder, 59
Piebald
variegation, 440
Piece
bit, 51
cannon, 727
drama, 599
Piece out
completeness, 42
Piecemeal
part, 51
Pied
variegation, 440
Pied à terre
abode, 189
Pier
refuge, 666
Pier-glass
optical instrument, 445
Pierce
perforate, 260, 302
pain, 378, 830
affect, 824
Piercing
cold, 383
sound, 404
sagacious, 498
feeling, 821
sight, 441
Pierian spring
poetry, 597
Pierrot
actor, 599
Pietism
impiety, 988
Piety
piety, 987
Piffle
absurdity, 497
Pig
gluttony, 957
Pig-headed
prejudiced, 481
obstinate, 606
stupid, 499
Pigeon-chested
distorted, 243
Pigeon-hole
receptacle, 191
aperture, 260
arrange, 60

discard, 624
reject, 610
Piggish
intemperance, 954
gluttony, 957
Pigment
colour, 428
Pigmy
see Pygmy
Pigsty
uncleanness, 653
Pigtail
pendant, 214
Pi-jaw
speech, 582
Pike
arms, 727
sharpness, 253
hill, 206
Pikestaff
height, 206
Pilaster
height, 206
Pile
heap, 72
nap, 256
building, 189
store, 636
wealth, 803
Pile-driver
hammer, 276
Pilfer
stealing, 791, 792
Pilgrim
traveller, 268
Pilgrimage
journey, 266
Pill
rotundity, 249
remedy, 662
Pill-box
defence, 717
Pillage
rob, 971
rapine, 619
devastation, 649
Pillar
support, 150, 215
monument, 551
lofty, 206
Pillar-box,
red, 434
Pillion
support, 215
Pillory

scourge, 975
to ridicule, 856
Pillow
support, 215, 265
soft, 324
ease, 831
Pilot
director, 694
mariner, 269
to guide, 693
balloon, 273
fighter, 726
trial, 463
Pilous
roughness, 256
Pimp
libertine, 962
Pimple
tumour, 250
blemish, 848
Pin
fastening, 45
to fasten, 43
axis, 312
sharp, 253
trifle, 643
Pin down
restrain, 751
compel, 744
Pin-prick
annoyance, 830
Pinafore
dress, 225
Pincers
extraction, 301
grip, 781
Pinch
emergency, 8
difficulty, 704
to contract, 195
narrow, 203
chill, 385
pain, 378
stint, 640, 819
to hurt, 830
to steal, 791
Pinch-hitter
substitute, 147, 634
deputy, 759
Pinchbeck
spurious, 544
Pinched
chilled, 383
thin, 203
indigent, 804

Pinching
  miserly, 819
Pine
  desire, 865
  grieve, 828
  droop, 837
Ping
  sound, 406
Pinguid
  unctuousness, 355
Pinhole
  opening, 260
Pinion
  instrument, 633
  wing, 267
  fetter, 752
  to fasten, 43
  to restrain, 751
Pink
  colour, 434
  perfection, 650
  beauty, 845
  glory, 873
  to pierce, 260
Pinnace
  ship, 273
Pinnacle
  summit, 210
Pinxit
  painting, 556
Pioneer
  precursor, 64
  preparer, 673
  teacher, 540
Pious
  piety, 987
Pip-pip
  departure, 293
Pipe
  conduit, 350
  passage, 302
  vent, 351
Pipe
  tobacco, 298A
  tube, 160
  sound, 510
  cry, 411
  music, 415
  instrument, 417
  observe, 457
Pipe down
  subside, 826
Pipe-dream
  hope, 858
  imagination, 515

Piper
  musician, 416
Piping
  sound, 410
  hot, 382
Pipkin
  receptacle, 191
Piquant
  pungent, 392
  style, 574
  motive, 615
  feeling, 821
  exciting, 824
Pique
  enmity, 889
  hate, 898
  anger, 900
  irritate, 830
  stimulate, 615, 824
Pique oneself
  pride, 878
Pirate
  thief, 792
  to steal, 791
Pirouette
  rotation, 312
Pis aller
  substitute, 634
  necessity, 601
  plan, 626
Piscatory
  animal, 366
Pisciculture
  taming, 370
Piscina
  church, 1000
Pistol
  arms, 727
Pistol-shot
  nearness, 197
Piston
  stopper, 264
Pit
  hole, 252
  opening, 260
  deep, 208
  grave, 363
  hell, 982
  theatre, 599
Pit against
  opposition, 708
Pit-a-pat
  feeling, 821
Pitch
  degree, 26

  term, 51
  station, 182
  arena, 728
  height, 206
  descent, 306
  summit, 210
  musical note, 413
  dark, 421
  black, 431
  semiliquid, 352
  to throw, 294
  to reel, 314
  to place, 184
Pitch-and-toss
  gambling, 621
Pitch into
  contention, 720
Pitch-pipe
  musical, 417
Pitch tent
  settle, 265
Pitch upon
  choose, 609
  reach, 292
Pitcher
  receptacle, 191
Pitchfork
  propel, 284
Piteous
  painfulness, 830
  greatness, 31
Pitfall
  pitfall, 667
Pith
  gist, 5, 516
  strength, 159
  interior, 221
  central, 223
  important, 642
Pithy
  significant, 516
  concise, 572
Pitiable
  unimportance, 643
Pitiful
  unimportant, 643
  compassionate, 914
  paltry, 940
Pitiless
  malevolent, 907
  revengeful, 900, 919
Pittance
  allotment, 786
Pitted
  blemished, 848

Pity
  compassion, 914
  regret, 833
Pivot
  cause, 153
  axis, 312
Pix
  cinema, 599A
Pixillated
  mad, 503
Pixy
  sprite, 980
Pizzicato
  music, 415
Placable
  forgiveness, 918
Placard
  notice, 550
  to publish, 531
Placate
  pacify, 826
Place
  situation, 182, 183
  circumstances, 8
  rank, 873
  term, 71
  in order, 58
  abode, 189
  to locate, 184
  substitution, 147
  office, 625
Placebo
  remedy, 662
Placeman
  consignee, 758
Placet
  command, 741
Placid
  calm, 826
Placket
  dress, 225
Plagiarism
  stealing, 791
  borrowing, 788
  imitation, 19
Plagiarist
  thief, 792
Plagioclastic
  oblique, 217
Plague
  disease, 655
  pain, 828
  to worry, 830
  evil, 619
  badness, 649

Plaid
  dress, 225
  variegated, 440
Plain
  horizontal, 213
  country, 344
  obvious, 446, 518
  simple, 849
  artless, 703
  ugly, 846
  style, 576
Plain dealing
  veracity, 543
Plain-song
  worship, 990
  music, 415
Plain speaking
  veracity, 543
  perspicuity, 570
Plain-spoken
  veracity, 543
Plaint
  cry, 411
  lamentation, 839
Plaintiff
  accuser, 938, 967
Plaintive
  lamentation, 839
Plait
  fold, 258
  pendant, 214
  interlace, 219
Plan
  project, 626
  intention, 620
  order, 58
  model, 22
  diagram, 554
Planchette
  writing, 590
Plane
  flat, 251
  smooth, 255
  horizontal, 213
  to soar, 305
  aircraft, 273A
Planet-struck
  failure, 732
Planetarium
  universe, 318
Plangent
  loud, 404
Planicopter
  aircraft, 273A
Plank

board, 204
  safely, 666
  plan, 626
Plant
  vegetable, 367
  cultivate, 371
  to insert, 300
  place, 184
  stop, 265
  swindle, 545
  equipment, 633
  effects, 780
Plantation
  plant, 367
Plash
  lake, 343
  plait, 219
Plashy
  marshy, 345
Plasm
  prototype, 22
Plasmic
  form, 240
Plaster
  cement, 45
  remedy, 662
  mend, 658
  cover, 223
Plastic
  soft, 324
  form, 240
  mutable, 149
  materials, 635
Plat
  crossing, 219
  plain, 344
Plate
  layer, 204
  engraving, 558
  to cover, 222
Plateau
  horizontality, 213
  height, 206
Platform
  support, 215
  stage, 542
  arena, 728
  horizontal, 213
  plan, 626
Platinotype
  photograph, 556
Platitude
  absurdity, 497
  dull, 843
Platitudinous
  feeble, 575

Platonic
cold, 823
chaste, 960
Platoon
army, 726
assemblage, 72
Platter
receptacle, 191
layer, 204
Plaudit
approbation, 931
Plausible
probable, 472
sophistical, 477
false, 544
specious, 937
Play
operation, 170
scope, 180, 748
chance, 186
drama, 599
amusement, 840
music, 415
oscillation, 314
appear to be, 448
to act, 680
Play a part
falsehood, 544
Play of colours
variegation, 440
Play-pen
enclosure, 232
Play upon
deception, 545
Play with
deride, 483
Played out
fatigue, 688
old, 124
imperfect, 651
Player
actor, 599
deceiver, 548
musician, 416
Playfellow
friend, 890
Playful
cheerfulness, 836
Playground
amusement, 840
arena, 728
Playhouse
the drama, 599
Playmate

friend, 890
Plaything
toy, 840
trifle, 643
dependence, 749
Plea
excuse, 617
vindication, 937
falsehood, 546
in law, 969
Pleach
plait, 219
Plead
argue, 467
lawyer, 968
encourage, 615
request, 765
vindicate, 937
Pleader
lawyer, 968
Pleasant
agreeable, 377, 829
witty, 842
amusing, 840
Please
pleasurableness, 829
Pleasure
will, 600
physical, 377
moral, 827
Pleat
fold, 258
Plebeian
commonalty, 876
Plebiscite
judgment, 480
choice, 609
Pledge
security, 771
promise, 768
to borrow, 788
drink to, 894
Pledget
remedy, 662
Plein-air
air, 338
Plenary
full, 31
complete, 52
abundant, 639
Plenipotentiary
consignee, 758
Plenitude
sufficiency, 639
Plenty

sufficiency, 639
Plenum
substantiality, 3
Pleonasm
diffuseness, 573
Pleonastic
diffuseness, 573
Plethora
redundance, 641
Plexus
crossing, 219
Pliable
softness, 324
Pliant
soft, 324
facile, 705
irresolute, 605
Plication
fold, 258
Pliers
extraction, 301
grip, 781
Plight
predicament, 8
to promise, 768
security, 771
Plimsoll
shoe, 225
Plimsoll line
measure, 466
Plinth
base, 211
rest, 215
Plod
trudge, 275
journey, 266
work, 682
Plodding
dull, 843
Plop
plunge, 310
sound, 406
Plot
plan, 626
of ground, 181, 344
agriculture, 371
Plough
preparation, 673
to furrow, 259
reject, 610
Plough in
insertion, 300
Ploughman
commonalty, 876
Ploughshare

Pointless
dullness, 843
motiveless, 616
Poise
balance, 27
measure, 466
composure, 826
Poison
bane, 663
to injure, 659
Poisonous
deleterious, 657
injurious, 649
Poke
push, 276
project, 250
pocket, 191
Poker
stiff, 323
Polacca
ship, 273
Polar
summit, 210
Polariscope
optical, 445
Polarity
duality, 89
antagonism, 179, 237
Polder
land, 342
Pole
lever, 633
axis, 223
summit, 210
tallness, 206
Pole-axe
arms, 727
Pole-star
indication, 550
sharpness, 253
Polecat
fetor, 401
Polemarch
master, 745
Polemics
discussion, 476
discord, 713
Polemoscope
optical, 445
Police
jurisdiction, 965
safety, 664
Policy
plan, 626
conduct, 692
skill, 698

Polish
smooth, 255
to rub, 331
urbanity, 894
furbish, 658
beauty, 845
ornament, 847
taste, 850
Politburo
council, 696
Politeness
manners, 852
urbanity, 894
respect, 928
Politic
wise, 498
expedient, 646
skilful, 698
cautious, 864
cunning, 702
Politician
statesman, 745
Politics
government, 693
Polity
plan, 626
conduct, 692
community, 372
Polka
dance, 840
Poll
count, 85
choice, 609
crop, 201
parrot, 584
Pollard
clip, 201
Pollute
corrupt, 659
soil, 653
disgrace, 874
dishonour, 940
Pollution
vice, 945
disease, 655
Poltergeist
demon, 980
Poltroon
cowardice, 862
Polychord
musical, 417
Polychromatic
variegation, 440
Polygamy
marriage, 903

Polyglot
word, 562
interpretation, 522
Polygon
figure, 244
building, 189
Polygraphy
writing, 590
Polygyny
marriage, 903
Polymorphic
multiform, 81
Polyp
convexity, 250
Polyphonism
voice, 580
Polyphony
melody, 413
Polysyllable
letter, 561
Polytechnic
school, 542
Polytheism
heathen, 984
Pomade
oil, 356
Pomatum
oil, 356
Pommel
rotundity, 249
Pommy
stranger, 57
greenhorn, 674
Pomp
ostentation, 882
Pom-pom
gun, 727
Pomposity
pride, 878
style, 577
Ponce
libertine, 962
Poncho
dress, 225
Pond
lake, 343
Ponder
thought, 451
Ponderation
judgment, 480
Ponderous
gravity, 319
style, 577
Pong
stink, 501

Poniard
arms, 727
Pons asinorum
difficulty, 704
Pontiff
clergy, 996
Pontifical
churchdom, 995
Pontificals
dress, 225
Pony
carrier, 271
money, 800
Pooh-pooh
trifle, 643
contempt, 930
to make light of, 483
Pool
lake, 343
participation, 778
Poop
rear, 235
fool, 501
Poor
indigent, 804
afflicted, 828
weak, 160
insufficient, 640
trifling, 643
contemptible, 930
style, 575
Poor-spirited
cowardice, 862
Poorly
disease, 655
Pop
noise, 406
unexpected, 508
pawn, 787
Pop upon
arrive, 292
find, 480
Pope
clergy, 996
Popgun
snap, 406
Popinjay
fop, 854
Popsy
girl, 374
Populace
commonalty, 876
Popular
current, 484
favourite, 897

celebrated, 873
Popularize
facilitate, 705
Populate
to stock, 184
Population
mankind, 373
inhabitants, 188
Populous
crowded, 72
Porch
entrance, 66
opening, 260
mouth, 230
way, 627
receptacle, 191
Porcupine
sharpness, 253
Pore
opening, 260
conduit, 350
look, 441
learn, 539
apply the mind, 457
Porism
corollary, 480
Pornography
impurity, 961
Porous
foraminous, 260
concavity, 252
light, 322
Porpoise
size, 192
Porringer
receptacle, 191
Port
harbour, 666
gait, 264
resting-place, 265
arrival, 292
carriage, 448
demeanour, 852
Port-hole
opening, 260
Portable
movable, 268, 270
light, 320
little, 193
Portage
transference, 270
Portal
entrance, 66
mouth, 230
opening, 260

way, 627
Portative
transference, 270
small, 193
Portcullis
defence, 706, 717
Porte-monnaie
purse, 802
Portend
prediction, 511
Portent
omen, 512
prodigy, 872
Portentous
prophetic, 511
fearful, 860
Porter
carrier, 271
janitor, 263
Porterage
transference, 270
Portfolio
record, 551
miscellany, 72
receptacle, 191
badge, 747
direction, 693
Portico
entrance, 66
room, 191
Portion
piece, 51, 41
allotment, 786
Portland
prison, 752
Portly
size, 192
Portmanteau
receptacle, 191
Portmanteau word
conciseness, 572
Portrait
painting, 556
copy, 21
Portray
describe, 594
represent, 554
paint, 556
Pose
puzzle, 485
hide, 528
difficulty, 704
affirm, 535
embarrassment, 491
attitude, 240

affectation, 855
Poseidon
  god, 979
Poser
  secret, 533
Poseur
  affectation, 855
Posh
  fashion, 852
Posit
  locate, 184
  assume, 467, 514
  affirm, 535
Position
  circumstance, 7
  situation, 183
  assertion, 535
  degree, 26
Positive
  certain, 474
  real, 1
  true, 494
  unequivocal, 518
  absolute, 739
  obstinate, 481, 606
  assertion, 535
  quantity, 84
Positively
  great, 31
Positivism
  materiality, 316
  irreligion, 989
Posse
  party, 712
  jurisdiction, 965
Possess
  have, 777
  feel, 821
Possessed
  insane, 503
Possession
  property, 780
Possessor
  possessor, 779
Possible
  feasible, 470, 705
  casual, 156, 177, 621
Post
  support, 215
  place, 184
  beacon, 550
  swift, 274
  employment, 625
  office, 926
  to record, 551

accounts, 811
  mail, 592
  news, 532
  inform, 527
Post-chaise
  vehicle, 272
Post-classical
  posterior, 117
Post-date
  anachronism, 115
Post-diluvian
  posterity, 117
Post-existence
  futurity, 121
Post-haste
  fast, 274
Post hoc
  sophistry, 477
Post-impressionist
  artist, 559
Post-mortem
  death, 360
  disinter, 363
Post-obit
  death, 360
Postcard
  news, 532
  epistle, 592
Poster
  notice, 531
Posterior
  in time, 117
  in order, 63
  in space, 235
Posterity
  in time, 117, 121
  descendants, 167
Postern
  back, 235
  portal, 66
  opening, 260
Postfix
  appendage, 39
Posthumous
  late, 133
  subsequent, 117
Postiche
  artificial, 544
Postilion
  director, 694
Postlude
  music, 415
  posterior, 117
Postman
  messenger, 534

Postpone
  lateness, 133
Postscript
  sequel, 65
  appendix, 39
Postulant
  petitioner, 767
  request, 765
  nun, 997
Postulate
  supposition, 514
  evidence, 467
  reasoning, 476
Postulation
  request, 765
Posture
  circumstance, 8
  attitude, 240
  display, 882
Posy
  motto, 550
  poem, 597
  flowers, 847
Pot
  mug, 191
  stove, 386
  greatness, 31
  ruin, 732
Pot-companion
  friend, 890
Pot-hooks
  writing, 590
Pot-hunting
  acquisition, 775
Pot-luck
  food, 298
Pot-pourri
  mixture, 41
  fragrance, 400
  music, 415
Pot-valiant
  drunk, 959
Potable
  drinkable, 298
Potation
  drink, 296
Potency
  power, 157
Potentate
  master, 745
Potential
  virtual, 2
  possible, 470
  power, 157

Pother
to worry, 830
fuss, 682
confusion, 59
Pottage
food, 298
Potter
idle, 683
Pottle
receptacle, 191
Potty
mad, 503
Pou sto
influence, 175
Pouch
receptacle, 191
insert, 184
receive, 785
take, 789
acquire, 775
Pouffe
support, 215
Poultice
soft, 354
remedy, 662
Pounce upon
taking, 789
Pound
bruise, 330
mix, 41
enclose, 232
imprison, 752
Poundage
discount, 813
Pounds
money, 800
Pour
egress, 295
Pour out
eject, 185, 297, 248
Pour rire
ridicule, 853
Pourboire
giving, 784
expenditure, 809
Pourparler
discussion, 476
Pout
sullen, 895
sad, 837
Poverty
indigence, 804
scantiness, 640
trifle, 643
Powder

pulverulence, 330
ornament, 845, 847
Powder-box
receptacle, 191
Power
efficacy, 157
physical energy, 171
authority, 737
spirit, 977
much, 31
multitude, 102
numerical, 84
of style, 574
Powerful
strength, 159
Powerless
weakness, 160
Pow-wow
conference, 588
Pox
disease, 655
expletive, 908
Praam
ship, 273
Practicable
possible, 470
easy, 705
Practical
activity, 672
agency, 170
Practice
act, 680
conduct, 692
use, 677
habit, 613
teaching, 537
rule, 80
proceeding, 626
Practise
deceive, 645
Practised
skill, 698
Practitioner
agent, 690
Praecognita
evidence, 467
Praenomen
name, 564
Praetor
master, 745
Pragmatical
pedantic, 855
vain, 880
Prairie
plain, 344

plaint, 367
Praise
commendation, 931
thanks, 916
worship, 990
Praiseworthy
commendable, 931
virtuous, 944
Prance
dance, 315
swagger, 878
move, 266
Prang
bomb, 162, 716, 732
Prank
caprice, 608
amusement, 840
vagary, 856
to adorn, 845
Prate
babble, 584, 588
Prattle
talk, 582, 588
Pravity
badness, 649
Pray
request, 765
Prayer
request, 765
worship, 990
Preach
teach, 537
speech, 582
predication, 998
Preacher
clergy, 996
Preachify
speech, 582
Preamble
precursor, 64
speech, 582
Preapprehension
misjudgment, 481
Prebendary
clergy, 996
Prebendaryship
churchdom, 995
Precarious
uncertain, 475
perilous, 665
Precatory
request, 764
Precaution
care, 459
expedient, 626

preparation, 673

Precede
in order, 62
in time, 116
lead, 280

Precedence
rank, 873

Precedent
rule, 80
verdict, 969

Precentor
clergy, 996
director, 694

Precept
maxim, 697
order, 741
rule, 80
permit, 760
decree, 963

Preceptor
teacher, 540

Precession
in order, 62
in motion, 280

Précieuse ridicule
affectation, 855
style, 577

Precincts
environs, 227
boundary, 233
region, 181
place, 182

Preciosity
affectation, 855

Precious
excellent, 648
valuable, 814
beloved, 897

Precipice
slope, 217
vertical, 212
danger, 667

Precipitancy
haste, 274, 684

Precipitate
rash, 863
impulse, 612
early, 132
transient, 111
to sink, 308
refuse, 653
consolidate, 321
swift, 274

Precipitous
obliquity, 217

Précis
compendium, 596

Precise
exact, 494
definite, 518

Precisely
assent, 488

Precisian
formalist, 855
taste, 850

Preclude
hindrance, 706

Precocious
early, 132
immature, 674

Precognition
foresight, 510
knowledge, 490

Preconception
misjudgment, 481

Preconcert
preparation, 673
predetermine, 611

Preconcerted
will, 600

Precursor
forerunner, 64
precession, 280
harbinger, 512

Precursory
in order, 62
in time, 116

Predacious
stealing, 791

Predatory
stealing, 791

Predecessor
in order, 64
in time, 116

Predeliberation
care, 459

Predestination
fate, 152
necessity, 601

Predetermination
predetermination, 611

Predetermined
will, 600
predetermination, 611

Predial
property, 780

Predicament
situation, 8
class, 75

Predicate

affirmation, 535

Predication
rite, 998

Prediction
prediction, 511

Predilection
love, 897
desire, 865
choice, 609
prejudice, 481
inclination, 602
affections, 820

Predisposition
proneness, 602
tendency, 176
motive, 615
affection, 820
preparation, 673

Predominance
influence, 175
inequality, 28
superiority, 33

Pre-eminent
famed, 873
superior, 31, 33

Pre-emption
purchase, 795

Pre-emptive
early, 132

Preen
adorn, 845

Pre-establish
preparation, 673

Pre-examine
inquiry, 461

Pre-exist
priority, 116
past, 122

Prefab
abode, 189

Preface
precedence, 62
precursor, 64
front, 234

Prefatory
in order, 62, 64
in time, 106

Prefect
ruler, 745
deputy, 759

Prefecture
authority, 737

Prefer
choose, 609
a petition, 765

Preferment
improvement, 658
ecclesiastical, 995
Prefiguration
indication, 550
prediction, 510
Prefix
precedence, 62
precursor, 64
Pregnant
productive, 161, 168
predicting, 511
important, 642
concise, 572
Prehension
taking, 789
Prehistoric
preterition, 122
old, 124
Prejudge
misjudgment, 481
Prejudice
evil, 619
detriment, 649
Prelacy
churchdom, 995
Prelate
clergy, 996
Prelection
teaching, 537
Prelector
teacher, 540
Preliminary
preceding, 62
precursor, 64
priority, 116
Prelude
preceding, 62
precursor, 64
priority, 116
music, 415
Prelusory
preceding, 62
precursor, 64
priority, 116
Premature
earliness, 132
Premeditate
intend, 630
predetermine, 611
Premeditated
will, 600
Premier
director, 694, 759
Premiership

authority, 737
Premise
prefix, 62
precursor, 64
announce, 511
Premises
ground, 182
evidence, 467
Premisses
see Premises
Premium
reward, 973
receipt, 810
Premonition
warning, 668
Prenticeship
preparation, 673
Preoccupied
inattentive, 458
Preoccupy
possess, 777
the attention, 457
Preoption
choice, 609
Preordain
necessity, 601
Preordination
destiny, 152
Preparatory
precedence, 62
Prepare
mature, 673
plan, 626
instruct, 537
Prepared
ready, 698
Prepay
expenditure, 809
Prepense
advised, 611
spontaneous, 600
intended, 620
Prepollence
power, 157
Preponderant
unequal, 28
superior, 33
important, 642
influential, 175
Prepossessing
pleasurableness, 829
Prepossession
misjudgment, 481
Preposterous
in degree, 31

ridiculous, 853
absurd, 497, 499
Prepotency
power, 157
Pre-Raphaelite
artist, 559
Prerequisite
requirement, 630
Prerogative
right, 924
authority, 737
Presage
omen, 512
to predict, 511
Presbyopic
dim-sightedness, 443
Presbytery
parsonage, 1000
Prescient
foresight, 510
Prescribe
order, 741
direct 693
entitle, 924
duty, 926
Prescript
decree, 741
precept, 697
law, 963
Prescription
remedy, 662
convention, 613
Prescriptive
dueness, 924
Presence
in space, 186
existence, 1
appearance, 448
carriage, 852
Presence of mind
caution, 864
Present
in time, 118
in place, 186
in memory, 505
give, 784
offer, 763
show, 525
represent, 554
introduce, 894
to the mind, 451
Presentable
fashion, 852
beauty, 845

Presentation
offer, 763
manifestation, 525
gift, 784
celebration, 883
Presentiment
prejudgment, 481
instinct, 477
foresight, 510
Presently
soon, 111, 132
Preservation
continuance, 141
conservation, 670
Preserve
sweet, 396
Preses
director, 694
Preside
command, 737
direct, 693
Presidency
authority, 737
President
master, 694, 745
Presidium
council, 696
Press
hasten, 132, 684
beg, 765
compel, 744
offer, 763
weigh, 319
solicit, 615
crowd, 72
closet, 191
velocity, 274
Press in
insertion, 300
Pressing
urgent, 642
Pressman
writer, 590
printer, 591
Pressure
weight, 319
influence, 175
urgency, 642
affliction, 830
Prestidigitation
deception, 545
Prestige
attractiveness, 829
repute, 873
Prestigious
delusive, 545

Prestissimo
music, 415
Presto
transientness, 111
velocity, 274
music, 415
Presume
suppose, 514
hope, 858
believe, 484
prejudge, 481
take liberties, 885
Presumption
probable, 472
right, 924
rashness, 863
insolence, 885
Presumptive
conjectural, 514
rightful, 924
probable, 472
indicative, 467
Presumptuous
rash, 863
insolent, 885
Presuppose
prejudge, 481
conjecture, 514
Presurmise
prejudge, 481
conjecture, 514
Pretence
untruth, 544, 546
excuse, 617
Pretend
simulate, 544
assert, 535
Pretender
boaster, 884
claimant, 924
deceiver, 548
Pretension
claim, 924
affectation, 855
vanity, 880, 884
ostentation, 882
Preterition
preterition, 122
Preterlapsed
preterition, 122
Pretermit
omit, 460
Preternatural
irregular, 83
Pretext

excuse, 617
falsehood, 546
Pretty
beauty, 845
Pretty well
much, 31
imperfect, 651
Prevail
influence, 175
be general, 78
be superior, 33
exist, 1
Prevail upon
motive, 615
Prevailing
preponderating, 28
usual, 82
Prevalence
influence, 175
usage, 613
superiority, 33
Prevaricate
falsehood, 544
equivocate, 520
Prévenance
courtesy, 894
Prevenient
precedence, 62
Prevention
hindrance, 706
counteraction, 179
prejudice, 481
Previous
in order, 62
in time, 116
Prevision
foresight, 510
Prey
food, 298
booty, 793
object, 620
victim, 828
Price
money, 812
value, 648
Priceless
goodness, 648
Prick
sharpness, 253
to incite, 615
sensation, 380
pain, 378, 830
Prick off
weed, 103

Prick up
raise, 212
Prickle
sharpness, 253
sensation, 380
Pride
loftiness, 878
Priest
clergy, 996
Priest-ridden
impiety, 988
Priestcraft
churchdom, 995
Priesthood
clergy, 996
Prig
affectation, 855
to steal, 791
Priggish
affectation, 855
vanity, 880
Prim
affectation, 855, 878
Prima donna
the drama, 599
repute, 873
Prima facie
appearance, 448
Primacy
churchdom, 995
pre-eminence, 33
repute, 873
Primary
importance, 642
Primate
clergy, 996
Prime
early, 132
primeval, 124
excellent, 648, 650
important, 642
to prepare, 673
teach, 537
number, 84
worship, 990
Primed
prepared, 698
Primer
school, 542
Primeval
oldness, 124
Primigenial
beginning, 66
Primitive
old, 124

simple, 849
Primogeniture
posterity, 167
Primordial
oldness, 124
Primrose-coloured
yellowness, 436
Primum mobile
cause, 153
Prince
master, 745
noble, 875
Princedom
title, 877
Princely
authoritative, 737
liberal, 816
generous, 942
noble, 873, 875
Princess
noble, 875
Principal
importance, 642
money, 800
Principality
property, 780
spirit, 977
title, 877
Principle
element, 316
cause, 153
truth, 494
reasoning, 476
law, 80
tenet, 484
motive, 615
Prink
adorn, 845
show off, 882
Print
mark, 550
record, 551
engraving, 558
letterpess, 591
Printless
obliteration, 552
Prior
in order, 62
in time, 116
religious, 996
Prioress
clergy, 996
Priory
temple, 1000
Prise

extract, 301
Prism
optical instrument, 445
angularity, 244
Prismatic
colour, 428, 440
changeable, 149
Prison
prison, 752
restraint, 751
Prisoner
captive, 754
defendant, 967
Pristine
preterition, 122
Prithee
request, 765
Prittle-prattle
interlocution, 588
Privacy
secrecy, 526
concealment, 528
seclusion, 893
Private
special, 79
Private eye
inquiry agent, 461
Privateer
combatant, 726
Privation
loss, 776
poverty, 804
Privative
taking, 789
Privilege
dueness, 924
Privity
knowledge, 490
Privy
concealed, 528
Prize
booty, 793
reward, 973
success, 731
palm, 733
good, 618
love, 897
approve, 931
Prize-fighter
combatant, 726
Pro and con
reasoning, 476
Pro bono publico
utility, 644
philanthropy, 910

633

Pro forma
habit, 613
Pro hac vice
present, 118
Pro more
conformity, 62
habit, 613
Pro rata
relation, 9
Pro re nata
circumstance, 8
occasion, 134
Pro tanto
greatness, 31
smallness, 32
Proa
ship, 273
Probable
probability, 472
chance, 156
Probate
evidence, 467
Probation
trial, 463
essay, 675
demonstration, 478
Probationer
learner, 541
Probe
stiletto, 262
measure, 466
depth, 208
investigate, 461
Probity
virtue, 944
right, 922
integrity, 939
Problem
enigma, 533
Problem
inquiry, 461
Problematical
uncertain, 475
hidden, 528
Proboscis
convexity, 250
Procedure
conduct, 692
action, 680
plan, 626
Proceed
advance, 282
from, 154
elapse, 109
happen, 151

Proceeding
action, 680
event, 151
plan, 626
incomplete, 53
Proceeds
money, 800
receipts, 810
gain, 775
Procerity
height, 206
Procès-verbal
compendium, 596
Process
projection, 250
plan, 626
action, 680
conduct, 692
engraving, 558
time, 109
Procession
train, 69
ceremony, 882
Prochronism
anachronism, 115
Proclaim
publication, 531
Proclivity
disposition, 602
proneness, 176, 820
Proconsul
deputy, 759
master, 745
Proconsulship
authority, 737
Procrastination
delay, 133, 683
Procreant
productiveness, 168
Procreate
production, 161
Procreator
paternity, 166
Proctor
officer, 694
law, 968
Proctorship
direction, 693
Procumbent
horizontality, 213
Procuration
commission, 755
pimping, 961
Procurator
director, 694

Procure
get, 775
cause, 153
buy, 795
pimp, 962
Prod
poke, 276
Prodigal
extravagant, 818
lavish, 641
penitent, 950
Prodigious
wonderful, 870
much, 31
Prodigy
prodigy, 872
Prodromal
precedence, 62
Prodrome
precursor, 64
Produce
cause, 153
create, 161
prolong, 200
show, 525, 599
evidence, 467
result, 154
fruit, 775
ware, 798
Product
effect, 154
acquisition, 775
multiple, 84
Productive
productiveness, 168
Proem
precursor, 64
Proemial
preceding, in order, 62
in time, 106
beginning, 66
Profane
impious, 988
pagan, 986
desecrate, 679
laical, 997
Profess
affirmation, 535
Profession
business, 625
promise, 768
Professor
teacher, 540
Proffer
offer, 763

Proficiency
skill, 698
Proficient
adept, 700
knowledge, 490
skilful, 698
Profile
lateral, 236
outline, 229
appearance, 448
Profit
acquisition, 775
advantage, 618
Profitable
useful, 644
gainful, 810
Profiteer
acquisition, 775
upstart, 734
Profitless
inutility, 645
Profligacy
vice, 945
Profluent
advancing, 282
flowing, 348
Profound
deep, 208
sagacity, 702
feeling, 821
thought, 451
Profoundly
great, 31
Profuse
prodigal, 818
lavish, 641
Prog
food, 298
Progenitor
paternity, 166
Progeny
posterity, 121, 167
Prognostic
omen, 512
Prognosticate
prediction, 511
Programme
catalogue, 86
announcement, 510
plan, 626
Progress
advance, 282
speed, 274
of time, 109
improvement, 658

success, 731
Progression
series, 69
gradation, 58
numerical, 84
motion, 282
Prohibit
forbid, 761
Prohibition
sobriety, 953, 958
Project
bulge, 250
propel, 284
eject, 297
move, 264
plan, 626
intend, 620
Projectile
missile, 284
weapon, 727
Projection
map, 554
Prolegomena
precursor, 64
Prolepsis
anachronism, 115
Prolétaire
commonalty, 876
Proletarian
commonalty, 876
Proliferate
reproduction, 161
Prolific
productive, 168
Prolix
diffuse, 573
Prolocuter
teacher, 540
speaker, 582
Prologue
precursor, 64
drama, 599
Prolong
lengthen, 200
protract, 110, 133
Prolusion
beginning, 64
lesson, 537
dissertation, 595
Promenade
journey, 266
causeway, 627
display, 882
Promethean
life, 359

Prominent
convex, 250, 252
conspicuous, 446, 525
important, 642
famous, 873
Prominently
great, 31
Promiscuous
irregular, 59
casual, 621
Promise
engage, 768
augur, 507
hope, 858
Promissory
pledged, 768
Promissory note
security, 771
money, 800
Promontory
cape, 206, 342
projection, 250
Promote
aid, 707
plan, 626
Promotion
improvement, 658
Prompt
in time, 111
early, 132
quick, 274
suggest, 514, 695
tell, 527
remind, 505
induce, 615
active, 682
Promptuary
store, 636
Promulgate
publication, 531
Pronation
inversion, 218
Prone
horizontal, 213
tending, 176
inclined, 602
disposed, 820
Prong
sharpness, 253
Pronounce
articulate, 580
speak, 582
assert, 535
judge, 480
sentence, 969

Pronounced
great, 31
obvious, 518
emphatic, 535
Pronunciamento
revolt, 719
Proof
demonstration, 478
test, 463
copy, 21
defence, 717
insensible, 376
Prop
support, 215
help, 707
refuge, 666
Propagable
productive, 168
Propaganda
publicity, 531
Propagandism
teaching, 537
proselytism, 484
Propagate
produce, 161
publish, 531
Propel
propulsion, 284
move, 264
Propensity
tendency, 176
disposition, 602
affections, 820
Proper
special, 79
right, 922, 926
expedient, 646
consonant, 23
handsome, 845
Property
possession, 780
power, 157
Prophecy
prediction, 511
scriptural, 985
Prophesy
predict, 511
Prophet
oracle, 513
Prophylactic
remedy, 662
preservative, 670
Prophylaxis
preservation, 670
salubrity, 656

Propinquity
nearness, 197
Propitiate
conciliate, 831, 918
pacify, 723
atone, 952
pity, 914
religious, 976
worship, 990
Propitious
favouring, 707
opportune, 134
prosperous, 734
auspicious, 858
Proplasm
prototype, 22
Proportion
relation, 9
mathematical, 84, 85
symmetry, 242
Proposal
plan, 626
Propose
offer, 763
intend, 620
suggest, 514
broach, 535
ask, 461
Proposition
reasoning, 476
problem, 461
supposition, 454
Propound
broach, 535
inquire, 461
suggest, 514
Propria persona
speciality, 79
Proprietary
possessor, 779
Proprietor
possessor, 779
Proprietorship
possession, 777
property, 780
Propriety
consonance, 23
expedience, 646
taste, 850
duty, 922, 926
Proprio motu
will, 600
Propter hoc
attribution, 155
Propulsion

propulsion, 284
impulse, 276
Prorogue
lateness, 133
Prosaic
dull, 843
style, 575, 598
Proscenium
front, 234
Proscribe
interdict, 761
curse, 908
condemn, 971
denounce, 938
exclude, 77, 893
Prose
not verse, 598
dullness, 843
to prate, 584
to weary, 841
Prosector
anatomist, 44
Prosecute
pursue, 622
accuse, 938
arraign, 969
action, 680
Prosecutor
judge, 967
Proselyte
learner, 541
convert, 484
Proselytism
teaching, 537
belief, 484
Prosit
drink, 959
Prosody
poetry, 597
Prosopopoeia
metaphor, 521
Prospect
view, 448
probability, 472
futurity, 121, 507
Prospectus
scheme, 626
compendium, 596
programme, 86
Prosperity
success, 731, 734
Prostitute
to corrupt, 659
misuse, 679
dishonour, 961, 962

Prostrate
low, 207
level, 213
to depress, 308
weak, 160
exhausted, 688
laid up, 655
dejected, 837
heart-broken, 830

Prostration
ruin, 619
disease, 655
servility, 886
obeisance, 725, 743,
  928
worship, 990

Prosy
diffuse, 573
dull, 575, 843

Prosyllogism
reasoning, 476

Protagonist
leader, 745
champion, 711
proficient, 700

Protasis
precursor, 64

Protean
mutable, 149, 605

Protect
shield, 664
defend, 717

Protection
influence, 175

Protector
master, 745

Protectorate
region, 181
authority, 737

Protégé
servant, 746
friend, 890

Protein
living beings, 357

Protervity
petulance, 901

Protest
dissent, 489
denial, 536
affirmation, 535
refusal, 764
deprecate, 766
censure, 932
non-observance, 773
non-payment, 808

Protestant
Christian religion, 983A

Proteus
change, 149

Prothonotary
recorder, 553

Protocol
document, 551
compact, 769
warrant, 771
etiquette, 613
ceremony, 882

Protoplasm
substance, 3
living beings, 357

Protoplast
prototype, 22

Prototype
thing copied, 22

Protract
time, 110, 133
length, 200

Protractor
angularity, 244

Protrude
convexity, 250

Protuberance
convexity, 250

Proud
lofty, 878
dignified, 873

Prove
demonstrate, 85, 478
try, 463
turn out, 151
affect, 821

Provenance
cause, 153

Provender
food, 298
materials, 635
provision, 637

Proverb
maxim, 496

Proverbial
knowledge, 490

Provide
furnish, 637
prepare, 673

Provided
qualification, 469
condition, 770
conditionally, 8

Providence
foresight, 510

divine government, 976

Provident
careful, 459
foresight, 510
wise, 498
prepared, 673

Providential
opportune, 134

Province
region, 181
department, 75
office, 625
duty, 926

Provincialism
language, 560
vulgarity, 851, 876

Provision
supply, 637
materials, 635
preparation, 673
wealth, 803
food, 298

Provisional
preparing, 673
substituted, 147
temporary, 111
conditional, 8

Proviso
qualification, 469
condition, 770

Provoke
incite, 615
cause, 153
excite, 824
vex, 830
hatred, 898
anger, 900

Provoking
difficult, 704

Provost
master, 745

Prow
front, 234

Prowess
courage, 861

Prowl
journey, 266
conceal, 528

Proximity
nearness, 197
contiguity, 199

Proximo
futurity, 121
posterior, 117

Proxy
deputy, 759
substitute, 634
Prude
affectation, 855
Prudent
cautious, 864
foresight, 510
careful, 459
wise, 498
discreet, 698
Prudery
affectation, 855
Prune
shorten, 201
correct, 658
purple, 437
Prunella
unimportance, 643
Prurient
desire, 865
lust, 961
Pry
inquire, 461
curiosity, 455
look, 441
Psalm
worship, 990
Psalmody
music, 415
Psalter
rite, 998
Pseudo
spurious, 495
sham, 544
Pseudonym
misnomer, 565
Pseudoscope
optical, 445
Pshaw
contempt, 930
Psst
accost, 586
Psyche
soul, 450
Psychiatrist
mind, 450
remedy, 662
Psychical
immaterial, 317
intellectual, 450
Psycho-analysis
remedy, 662
Psychokinesis
occult, 992
Psychology

intellect, 450
Psychomancy
divination, 992
Psychopath
madman, 504
Psychosis
insanity, 503
Psycho-therapist
intellect, 450
remedy, 662
Ptisan
remedy, 662
Pub-crawler
drunkard, 959
Puberty
youth, 127
Public
people, 373
open, 529, 531
Public-house
drink, 298
Public-spirited
philanthropy, 910
Publication
promulgation, 531
showing, 525
printing, 591
book, 593
Publicist
writer, 593
lawyer, 968
Publicity
publication, 531
Publish
inform, 527
Puce
purple, 437
Puck
imp, 980
Pucker
fold, 258
Pudder
disorder, 59
Pudding
food, 298
Puddle
lakelet, 343
lining, 224
Pudency
purity, 960
Puerile
boyish, 127, 129
trifling, 643
foolish, 499
weak, 477, 575

Puff
wind, 349
vapour, 334
tobacco, 298A
inflate, 194
commendation, 931
advertisement, 531
boast, 884
pant, 688
Puffed up
vain, 770
proud, 878
Puffy
swollen, 194
wind, 349
Pug
shortness, 201
footprint, 551
boxer, 726
Pugilism
contention, 720
Pugilist
combatant, 726
Pugnacity
anger, 901
Puisne
posterior, 117
Puissant
strong, 157, 159
Puke
ejection, 297
Pukka
true, 494
goodness, 648
Pulchritude
beauty, 845
Pule
cry, 411, 412
weep, 839
Pull
draw, 285
attract, 288
row, 267
swerve, 279
advantage, 33
proof, 21, 591
Pull down
destroy, 162
lay low, 308
Pull off
accomplish, 729
Pull out
extract, 301
Pull through
recover, 658

Pull together
concord, 714
Pull up
stop, 142, 265
accuse, 938
Pullet
infant, 129
Pulley
instrument, 633
Pullman car
vehicle, 272
Pullover
dress, 225
Pullulate
grow, 194
multiply, 168
Pulp
pulpiness, 354
soften, 324
semiliquid, 352
Pulpit
rostrum, 542
church, 1000
Pulsate
see Pulse
Pulse
oscillate, 314
agitate, 315
periodically, 138
Pultaceous
pulpy, 354
Pulverize
maltreat, 649
Pulverulence
powder, 330
Pulvil
fragrance, 400
Pummel
handle, 633
beat, 276, 972
Pump
inquire, 461
spray, 348
reservoir, 636
Pun
verbal, 520, 563
wit, 842
similarity, 17
Punch
to perforate, 260
perforator, 262
to strike, 276
punish, 972
energy, 171
vigour, 574

buffoon, 857
humorist, 844
puppet, 599
horse, 271
Punctate
spotted, 440
Punctilio
ostentation, 882
Punctilious
correct, 494
fashionable, 852
observant, 772
fastidious, 868
scrupulous, 939
Punctual
early, 132
periodical, 138
scrupulous, 939
Punctuation
grammar, 567
Puncture
opening, 260
Pundit
scholar, 462
sage, 500
clergy, 996
Pungent
taste, 392
caustic, 171
feeling, 821
Punic faith
improbity, 940
Punish
punishment, 972
Punk
prostitute, 962
trash, 645
Punka
fan, 349
Punnet
receptacle, 191
Punster
humorist, 844
Punt
ship, 273
propel, 267, 284
gamble, 621
Puny
in degree, 32
in size, 193
weak, 160
Pup
infant, 129
Pupil
learner, 541

eye, 441
Puppet
subjection, 749
effigy, 554
plaything, 840
dupe, 547
little, 193
Puppet-show
the drama, 599
amusement, 840
Puppy
fop, 854
blusterer, 887
Puranas
sacred books, 986
Purblind
dim-sighted, 443
undiscerning, 499
Purchase
buy, 795
leverage, 175
Pure
simple, 42
true, 494
good taste, 850
clean, 652
innocent, 946
virtuous, 944
Purely
smallness, 32
greatness, 31
Purgation
cleansing, 652
atonement, 952
Purgative
remedy, 662
Purgatory
suffering, 828
atonement, 952
hell, 982
Purge
clean, 652
improve, 658
atone, 952
subduction, 38
Purify
cleanse, 652
improve, 658
Purist
style, 578
taste, 850
Puritanical
ascetic, 955
pedantic, 855

Puritanism
heterodoxy, 984A
Purity
purity, 960
of style, 578
Purl
gargle, 405
flow, 348
Purler
fall, 306
Purlieus
suburbs, 197, 227
Purloin
steal, 791
Purple
purple, 437
insignia, 747
Purport
meaning, 516
intent, 620
Purpose
intention, 620
Purposeless
chance, 621
motiveless, 616
Purposely
will, 600, 620
Purr
animal sound, 412
Purse
money-bag, 802
wealth, 803
to shrivel, 195
prize, 973
Purse-bearer
treasurer, 801
Purse-proud
pride, 878
Purse-strings
treasury, 802
Purser
treasurer, 801
Pursuant to
intention, 620
Pursue
follow, 281
continue, 143
aim, 622
inquire, 461
Pursuer
prosecutor, 938, 967
Pursuit
hobby, 865
business, 625
Pursuivant
messenger, 534

Pursy
size, 192
Purulent
unclean, 653
Purvey
provision, 637
Purview
extent, 180
intention, 620
Pus
dirt, 653
Push
exigency, 8
accelerate, 274
impel, 276
propel, 284
repel, 289
activity, 682
dismissal, 756
Push on
progress, 282, 684
Push-button
instant, 113
Pusher
girl, 374
Pushover
dupe, 547
Pusillanimity
cowardice, 862
Puss
face, 234, 448
Pustule
pimple, 250
blemish, 848
Put
place, 184
a question, 461
fool, 501
Put about
turn back, 283
circuition, 311
Put away
relinquish, 624
Put by
economy, 817
Put down
destroy, 162
confute, 479
coerce, 744;
baffle, 731
humiliate, 874
Put forth
assert, 535
suggest, 514
Put in

interject, 228
Put into
insert, 300
arrive, 292
Put off
delay, 133
deter, 616
Put on
clothe, 225
deceive, 544
Put out
quench, 385
darken, 421
perplex, 458
difficulty, 704
Put up to
teach, 537
Put up with
feeling, 821
Put upon
deception, 545
Putative
attribution, 155, 514
Putid
improbity, 940
Putrefy
unclean, 653
Putrid
unclean, 653
Putsch
revolt, 719, 742
Putt
impel, 276
Puttee
dress, 225
Putty
vinculum, 45
Puzzle
enigma, 533
obscurity, 519
mystify, 528
stagger, 485
bewilder, 491
Puzzle-headed
fool, 499
Puzzling
uncertain, 475
Pygmy
little, 193
low, 207
Pylades
friend, 890
Pyramid
point, 253
heap, 72

Pyre
interment, 363
Pyretic
hot, 382
Pyrexia
heat, 382
Pyrometer
thermometer, 389
Pyrotechny
heat, 382
Pyrrhonism
incredulity, 487
Pythagorean
temperance, 953
Python
oracle, 513
Pyx
receptacle, 191
assay, 463
ritual, 998

Q-boat
ship, 273
deception, 545
Q.C.
lawyer, 968
Q.E.D.
answer, 462
Quack
impostor, 548
ignoramus, 493
cry, 412
Quackery
deception, 545
ignorance, 491
affectation, 855
Quacksalver
deceiver, 548
Quadragesima
fasting, 956
Quadragesimal
forty, 98
Quadrangular
angularity, 244
Quadrant
measure, 466
angularity, 244
Quadrate with
agreement, 23
Quadratic
number, 95
Quadrifid
number, 97
Quadrilateral

side, 236
Quadrille
dance, 840
Quadripartition
number, 97
Quadrireme
ship, 273
Quadrisection
number, 97
Quadruped
animal, 366
Quadruple
number, 96
Quaere
inquiry, 461
Quaestor
master, 745
Quaff
reception, 296
Quag
bog, 345
Quagmire
bog, 345
mire, 653
difficulty, 704
Quaich
bowl, 191
Quail
fear, 800, 862
Quaint
odd, 83
ridiculous, 853
pretty, 845
Quake
shake, 315
fear, 860
cold, 383
Qualification
modification, 469
accomplishment, 698
change, 140
retraction, 536
training, 673
right, 924
Qualify
train, 673
modify, 469
change, 140
teach, 537
Quality
power, 157
nature, 5
tendency, 176
character, 820
nobility, 875

Qualm
fear, 860
scruple, 603, 616
disbelief, 485
penitence, 950
Quandary
difficulty, 704
Quand même
opposition, 708
Quantitative
amount, 25
allotment, 786
Quantity
amount, 25
Quantum
amount, 25
apportionment, 786
Quantum sufficit
sufficiency, 639
Quaquaversum
direction, 278
Quarantine
safety, 664
confinement, 751
Quarrel
discord, 713
Quarrelsome
enemy, 901
Quarry
mine, 636
object, 620
Quarter
fourth, 97
region, 181
side, 236
direction, 278
to place, 184
mercy, 914
Quartering
number, 97
Quartermaster
provision, 637
master, 745
Quarters
abode, 189
Quartet
number, 95
Quarto
book, 593
Quash
destroy, 162
annul, 756, 964
Quasi
similarity, 17

Quatercentenary
celebration, 883
Quaternal
number, 95
Quaternity
number, 95
Quatrain
poetry, 597
Quaver
oscillate, 314
shake, 315
sound, 407
music, 413
hesitate, 605
fear, 860
shiver, 383
Quay
abode, 189
Quean
libertine, 962
Queasiness
dislike, 867
fastidious, 868
Queen
master, 745
Queenly
majestic, 873
Queer
unconformity, 83
sick, 655
whimsical, 853
Quell
destroy, 162
hush, 265
calm, 826
moderate, 174
subdue, 732
Quench
cool, 385
dissuade, 616
extinguish, 162
satiate, 869
Querimonious
lament, 839
Querist
inquiry, 461
Quern
mill, 330
Querulous
complaining, 839
quarrelsome, 901
Query
inquiry, 461
to doubt, 485
Quest
inquiry, 461

pursuit, 622
undertaking, 676
Question
inquiry, 461
topic, 454
to doubt, 485
to deny, 536
Questionable
uncertainty, 475, 485
Questionless
certainty, 474
Questor
treasurer, 801
Queue
appendix, 39, 214
sequel, 65
row, 69
Quibble
sophistry, 477
equivocate, 544
absurdity, 497
wit, 842
Quick
rapid, 274
transient, 111
active, 682
haste, 684
early, 132
skilful, 698
irascible, 901
feeling, 821, 822
Quick-sighted
quick-eyed, 441
sagacious, 498
Quick-witted
wit, 842
clever, 498
Quicken
hasten, 132
animate, 163
vivify, 359
operate, 170
urge, 615
excite, 824
promote, 907
violence, 173
Quicksand
pitfall, 667
Quicksilver
velocity, 274
Quid
tobacco, 298A
money, 800
Quid pro quo
compensation, 30

payment, 807
exchange, 794
interchange, 148
Quiddity
essence, 1, 5
quibble, 477
wit, 842
Quidnunc
curiosity, 455
Quiescence
cessation, 142
inertness, 172
inactivity, 683
rest, 265
Quiet
rest, 265
silent, 403
calm, 174, 826
dissuade, 616
peace, 714
Quietism
piety, 987
heresy, 984A
Quietus
death, 360
downfall, 732
Quill
writing, 590
Quill-driver
writing, 590
Quinary
number, 98
Quincentenary
see Quingentenary
Quinary
number, 98
Quincunx
number, 98
Quingentenary
celebration, 883
Quinquagesimal
fifty, 98
Quinquefid
number, 99
Quinquereme
ship, 273
Quinquesection
number, 99
Quint
number, 98
Quintessence
essence, 5
importance, 642
Quintet
five, 98

Quintuple
number, 98
Quip
wit, 842
amusement, 840
ridicule, 856
satire, 932
Quirites
non-combatant, 726A
Quirk
caprice, 608
evasion, 617
wit, 842
Quisling
traitor, 742
Quit
depart, 293
relinquish, 624
loss, 776
neglect, 927
pay, 807
Quite
greatness, 31
Quits
equality, 27
atonement, 952
Quittance
forgiveness, 918
atonement, 952
reward, 973
payment, 807
observance, 772
Quitter
coward, 862
shirker, 623
Quiver
agitate, 315
vibrate, 314
shiver, 383
fear, 860
affect, 821
store, 636
arm, 727
Quixotic
imaginary, 515
rash, 863
enthusiastic, 825
Quiz
to ridicule, 856
inquiry, 461
Quizzical
ridiculous, 853
Quocumque modo
means, 632
Quod

prison, 752
Quodlibet
sophism, 477
subtle point, 454
enigma, 461
wit, 842
Quondam
preterition, 122
Quorum
assembly, 72
Quota
apportionment, 786
Quotation
imitation, 19
citation, 82
price, 812
Quote
cite, 82, 467
bargain, 794
Quotidian
period, 108, 138
Quotient
number, 84

R.A.
artist, 559
R.I.P.
burial, 363
Rabbet
junction, 43
Rabbi
clergy, 996
Rabble
mob, 876
bad man, 949
assemblage, 72
Rabelaisian
coarse, 961
Rabid
insanity, 503
headstrong, 606
angry, 900
feeling, 821
Race
to run, 274
contest, 720
course, 622
career, 625
torrent, 348
lineage, 11, 69
kind, 75
people, 372
Racehorse
horse, 271

fleetness, 274
Racer
horse, 271
fleetness, 274
Racial
ethnic, 372
Rack
frame, 215
physical pain, 378
moral pain, 828
to torture, 830
punish, 975
purify, 652
refine, 658
cloud, 353
Racket
noise, 402, 404
brawl, 713
roll, 407
bat, 633
plan, 626
Raconteur
narrator, 594
Racy
strong, 171
pungent, 392
feeling, 821
style, 574
Radar
direction, 693
Raddle
weave, 219
red, 434
Radiant
diverging, 291
light, 420, 423
beauty, 845
glory, 873
Radiator
fire, 386
Radical
cause, 153
algebraic root, 84
complete, 52
intrinsic, 5
reformer, 658
revolution, 146
Radically
thorough, 31
Radio
hearing, 418
publication, 531
news, 532
wireless, 599B
Radioactivity
light, 420

Radiogram
  hearing, 418
  news, 532
Radioscopy
  light, 420
Radiotherapy
  light, 420
Radius
  length, 200
  degree, 26
Radix
  cause, 153
Raff
  refuse, 653
  rabble, 876
Raffia
  tape, 45
Raffish
  vulgar, 851
Raffle
  chance, 156, 621
Raft
  ship, 273
Rafter
  support, 215
Rag
  shred, 51
  clothes, 225
  escapade, 497
  to tease, 830
  joke, 842
  deride, 929
  revile, 932
Ragamuffin
  rabble, 876
Rage
  violence, 173
  fury, 825
  wrath, 900
  desire, 865
  fashion, 852
Ragged
  bare, 226
Ragout
  food, 298
Ragtag
  commonalty, 876
  bad man, 949
Raid
  attack, 716
  robbery, 791
Rail
  enclosure, 232
  fence, 666

  imprison, 752
Rail at
  disapprove, 932
Rail-car
  vehicle, 272
Rail in
  circumscribe, 231
Raillery
  ridicule, 856
Railroad
  way, 627
Railway
  road, 627
Raiment
  dress, 225
Rain
  river, 348
Rainbow
  variegation, 440
Raise
  elevate, 307
  increase, 35
  produce, 161
  excite, 824
Raison d'être
  cause, 253
  motive, 615, 620
Raj
  authority, 737
Rajah
  master, 745
Rake
  cultivate, 371
Rake-off
  payment, 809
Rake up
  collect, 72
  extract, 301
  recall, 504
  excite, 824
Rakehell
  intemperate, 954
Rakish
  intemperate, 954
  licentious, 961
Rally
  ridicule, 856
  joke, 842
  recover, 658
  stand by, 707
  pluck up courage, 861
Ram
  impel, 276
  press in, 261
  insert, 300

Ram down
  condense, 321
  fill up, 261
Ramadan
  fasting, 956
Ramble
  stroll, 266
  wander, 279
  diffuse, 572
  delirium, 503
  folly, 499
Rambler
  traveller, 268
Ramification
  branch, 51, 256
  divergence, 291
  posterity, 167
Rammer
  plug, 263
  impeller, 276
Ramp
  rise up, 307
  slope, 217
Rampage
  violence, 173
  excitement, 825
Rampant
  violent, 173
  vehement, 825
  licentious, 961
  free, 748
  rearing, 307
Rampart
  defence, 717
Ramrod
  stopper, 263
Ramshackle
  imperfect, 651
Ranch
  farm, 780
Rancid
  fetid, 401
  rotten, 653
Rancour
  malevolence, 907
  revenge, 919
Randem
  row, 69
Random
  casual, 156, 621
Random
  uncertain, 475
Ranee
  noble, 875
  chief, 745

Range
space, 180
extent, 26
draw up, 58
to collocate, 60
roam, 266
direction, 278
series, 69
term, 71
class, 75
freedom, 748
Range-finder
lens, 445
Ranger
keeper, 753
Rangy
lank, 203
Rank
degree, 26
thorough, 31
collocate, 60
row, 69
term, 71
luxuriant, 365
fetid, 401
bad, 649
to estimate, 480
nobility, 875
glory, 873
Rankle
animosity, 505, 900
Rannygazoo
fraud, 545
Ransack
seek, 461
plunder, 791
Ransom
price, 812
deliverance, 672
liberation, 750
Rant
nonsense, 497
speech, 582
acting, 599
style, 573, 577
Rantipole
fool, 499, 501
Rap
knock, 276
snap, 406
beat, 972
Rap out
voice, 580
Rapacious
avaricious, 819

greedy, 865
predatory, 789
Rape
violation, 961
seizure, 791
Rapid
velocity, 274
Rapids
river, 348
danger, 667
Rapier
arms, 727
Rapine
spoliation, 791
evil, 791
Rapparee
thief, 792
Rappee
tobacco, 298A
Rapscallion
sinner, 949
Rapt
thought, 451
pleasure, 827
Rapture
emotion, 821
bliss, 827
Rara avis
unconformity, 83
Rare
infrequent, 137
few, 103
exceptional, 83
excellent, 648
Raree-show
sight, 448
amusement, 840
Rarefy
expand, 194
render light, 322
Rascal
sinner, 949
knave, 941
Rascality
vice, 945
improbity, 940
Rase
see Raze
Rash
reckless, 863
careless, 460
disease, 655
Rasher
layer, 204
Rasp

grate, 330, 331
Rat
tergiversation, 607
Rataplan
roll, 407
Ratchet
sharpness, 253
Rate
degree, 26
speed, 274
measure, 466
estimation, 480
price, 812
to abuse, 932
Rathe
early, 132
Rather
somewhat, 32
choice, 609
Ratify
consent, 762
affirm, 488
compact, 769
Ratio
relation, 9
proportion, 84
degree, 26
Ratiocination
reasoning, 476
Ration
apportion, 786
Rational
sane, 502
intellectual, 450
reasoning, 476
judicious, 480, 498
Rationale
cause, 153
attribution, 155
answer, 462
interpretation, 522
Rationalist
sceptic, 989
Rations
food, 298
Rats
rubbish, 643
Rattan
scourge, 975
Ratting
tergiversation, 607
Rattle
noise, 407
prattle, 584
discompose, 458

Rattle off
speech, 582
Rattlesnake
bane, 663, 913
Rattletrap
imperfect, 651
Raucous
hoarse, 581
Ravage
destroy, 162
evil, 619
despoil, 649
Rave
madness, 503
excitement, 825
love, 897
Ravel
entangle, 219
convolution, 248
difficulty, 704
untwist, 44, 61
Raven
black, 431
gorge, 296
Ravenous
desire, 789, 865
Raver
madman, 504
Ravine
pass, 198, 203
dike, 259
Raving
mad, 503
violent, 825
Ravish
emotion, 824
ecstasy, 829
rape, 961
Raw
immature, 123
unprepared, 674
unskilful, 699
cold, 383
sensitive, 378
Raw-boned
gaunt, 193, 203
ugly, 846
Ray
light, 420
Rayless
darkness, 421
Raze
level, 308
obliterate, 552
demolish, 649

Razor
sharp, 253
Razz
ridicule, 856
Razzle-dazzle
frolic, 840
Re
concerning, 454
Reabsorb
reception, 296
Reach
length, 200
river, 348
degree, 26
distance, 196
fetch, 270
arrive at, 292
grasp, 737
React
recoil, 277
revert, 145
counteract, 179
sensibility, 375
relapse, 661
Reactionary
mulish, 499
reversion, 145
Read
interpret, 522
learn, 539
Readable
intelligible, 518
Reader
teacher, 492, 540
clergy, 996
Reading
meaning, 516
Reading-glass
lens, 445
Readjust
equality, 27
Readmit
reception, 296
Ready
prepared, 673
capable, 157
willing, 602
useful, 644
eager, 682
dexterous, 698
early, 132
cash, 800
Ready money
payment, 807
Reagent

criterion, 467
test, 463
Real
existing, 1
substantial, 3
true, 494
Realism
truth, 494
Realistic
description, 594
Reality
existence, 1
Realize
attribute, 155
produce, 161
substantiate, 494
be aware of, 450
imagine, 515
price, 812
Really
very, 31
indeed, 870
Realm
region, 181
property, 780
land, 372
Reanimate
revivify, 163
refresh, 689
reinstate, 660
Reap
cultivate, 371
acquire, 775
succeed, 731
take, 789
Reaping-hook
sharpness, 253
Reappear
repetition, 104, 163
frequency, 136
Rear
back, 67, 235
erect, 161, 307
sequel, 65
bring up, 537
room, 191
privy, 653
Rearrange
arrangement, 60
Reason
cause, 153
motive, 615
intellect, 450
evidence, 467
argue, 476

wisdom, 498
moderation, 174

Reasonable
judicious, 498
right, 922
equitable, 924
probable, 472
sane, 502
moderate, 174
cheap, 815

Reasoning
logic, 476

Reasonless
fool, 499

Reassemble
gather, 72

Reassure
hope, 858

Reasty
foul, 653
fetid, 401

Réaumur
thermometer, 389

Rebate
moderate, 174, 813

Rebeck
musical instrument, 417

Rebel
disobey, 742

Rebellion
resistance, 719
revolution, 146

Rebellow
ululation, 412

Rebound
recoil, 277, 283
revert, 144
react, 179

Rebours
regression, 283

Rebuff
refuse, 764
repulse, 732
resist, 719
recoil, 277, 325

Rebuild
reconstruct, 163
restore, 660

Rebuke
disapprove, 932

Rebus
secret, 533

Rebut
answer, 462
confute, 479

deny, 536
counter-evidence, 468

Rebutter
lawsuit, 969

Recalcitrant
disobedient, 742

Recalcitrate
'resist, 276, 719
counteract, 179

Recall
recollect, 505
cancel, 756

Recant
retract, 607
repent, 950
deny, 536
resign, 757

Recapitulate
summary, 596
describe, 594
repeat, 104
enumerate, 85

Recast
plan, 626, 660
refashion, 146

Recede
move back, 283
move from, 287
decline, 659

Receipt
money, 810
recipe, 697

Receive
admit, 296
take in, 785
include, 76
acquire, 775
learn, 539
believe, 484
welcome, 892, 894
money, 810

Received
ordinary, 82
habitual, 613

Recension
revision, 457
improvement, 658

Recent
past, 122
new, 123

Receptacle
recipient, 191
store, 636

Reception
arrival, 292

comprehension, 54
inclusion, 76
ingestion, 296
conference, 588
admission, 785
visit, 892, 894

Receptive
intelligent, 498

Recess
place, 182
regression, 283
ambush, 530
holiday, 685
interval, 106
retirement, 893

Recession
motion from, 287
motion backwards, 283

Réchauffé
copy, 21
improve, 658

Recherché
goodness, 648

Recidivism
relapse, 661
reversion, 145
vice, 945

Recidivist
criminal, 949
turncoat, 607

Recipe
remedy, 662
precept, 697

Recipient
receptacle, 191
receiving, 785

Reciprocal
mutual, 12
quantity, 84
interchange, 148

Reciprocation
retaliation, 718

Recital
music, 415

Recitative
music, 415

Recite
narrate, 594
speak, 582
enumerate, 85

Reck
care, 459

Reckless
rash, 863
excitable, 825

careless, 460

Reckon
count, 85
measure, 466
believe, 484

Reckon upon
expect, 507

Reckoning
accounts, 811
price, 812

Reclaim
restoration, 660

Réclame
advertisement, 531
self-advertisement, 884

Recline
lie flat, 213
rest upon, 215
repose, 687
lowering, 308

Recluse
seclusion, 893, 955

Recognizable
visible, 446

Recognizance
security, 771

Recognize
see, 441
know, 490
assent, 488
remember, 505
discover, 480A
acknowledge, 535

Recognized
received, 82
habitual, 613

Recoil
repercussion, 277, 325
revert, 145
shun, 623
reluctance, 603
dislike, 867
hate, 898
reaction, 179

Recollect
remember, 505

Recommence
repetition, 104

Recommend
advise, 695
approve, 931
induce, 615

Recompense
reward, 973
payment, 809

Reconcile
agree, 23
content, 831
pacify, 723
forgive, 918

Recondite
obscure, 519
hidden, 529

Reconnaissance
survey, 441

Reconnoitre
see, 441
remodel, 146
restore, 660

Reconvert
restore, 660

Record
note, 551
list, 86

Recorder
recorder, 553
judge, 967

Recording
copy, 21

Recount
description, 594

Recoup
restore, 660, 790
reward, 973

Recourse
use, 677

Recovery
reinstatement, 660P
improvement, 658
recruit, 689

Recreant
coward, 862
base, 940, 945
apostate, 941
wretch, 949

Recreation
amusement, 840

Recrement
unclean, 653

Recrimination
accusation, 938
reprobation, 932
retaliation, 718

Recrudescence
recurrence, 104, 136

Recruit
refresh, 689
reinstate, 660
health, 654
repair, 658

aid, 707
provide, 637
strengthen, 159
beginner, 674
fighter, 726

Rectangle
angularity, 244

Rectify
straighten, 246
improve, 658
re-establish, 660

Rectilinear
straightness, 246

Rectitude
virtue, 944
right, 922
probity, 939

Recto
dextrality, 228

Rector
clergy, 996
director, 694

Rectory
office, 995
house, 1000

Reculons
regression, 283

Recumbent
horizontal, 213
oblique, 217

Recuperation
restitution, 790
improvement, 658
restore, 660
refresh, 689

Recur
repeat, 104
frequent, 136
periodic, 138

Recurvation
curvature, 245

Recusant
denying, 536
dissenting, 489
disobedient, 742
unwilling, 603
refusing, 764
heterodox, 984A
impenitent, 951

Red
redness, 434

Red book
list, 86

Red cent
trifle, 643

648

Red-handed
  murderous, 361
  action, 681
Red-hot
  heat, 382
Red lamp
  brothel, 961
Red letter
  indication, 550
Red light
  signal, 550
Red tape
  custom, 613
Red-tapist
  director, 695
Redaction
  publication, 531
  improvement, 658
Redargue
  confute, 479
Redcoat
  combatant, 726
Redden
  flush, 821
Reddition
  restoration, 790
Redeem
  reinstate, 660
  deliver, 672
  liberate, 750
  fulfil, 772
  atone, 952
  compensate, 30
  restore, 790
Redemption
  salvation, 976
Redintegrate
  reinstate, 660
  renovate, 658
Redolence
  odour, 398
  fragrance, 400
Redouble
  duplication, 90
  repeat, 104
  increase, 35
Redoubt
  defence, 717
Redoubtable
  fear, 860
Redound
  conduce, 176
Redress
  remedy, 662
  rectify, 658

restore, 660
reward, 873
Reduce
  lessen, 36
  contract, 195
  shorten, 201
  lower, 308
  weaken, 160
  convert, 144
  subdue, 731
  impoverish, 804
  in number, 103
Reductio ad absurdum
  confutation, 479
Reduction
  arithmetical, 85
Redundant
  ample, 641
  diffuse, 573
  remaining, 40
Reduplication
  imitation, 19
  doubling, 90
Re-echo
  imitate, 19
  repeat, 104
  reduplication, 90
  sound, 404, 408
Reechy
  uncleanness, 653
Reed
  musical instrument, 417
Re-educate
  teach, 537
Reef
  slacken, 275
  shoal, 346
  danger, 667
Reek
  hot, 382
  fume, 334
Reel
  rock, 314
  agitate, 315
  rotate, 312
  cinema, 599
  dance, 840
Re-embody
  combine, 43
  junction, 48
Re-entrant
  angle, 244
Re-establishment
  restoration, 145, 660
Refashion

remodel, 146
Refection
  refreshment, 689
  meal, 298
Refectory
  room, 191
Refer
  attribute, 155
  relate, 9
Referee
  judge, 480, 967
  adviser, 695
Referendum
  vote, 609
  inquiry, 461
Refinement
  elegance, 845
  fashion, 852
  taste, 850
  discrimination, 465
  improvement, 658
  wisdom, 498
  sophistry, 477
Refit
  repair, 658
  reinstate, 660
Reflect
  think, 451
  imitation, 19
Reflect upon
  blame, 932
Reflecting
  thoughtful, 498
Reflection
  maxim, 496
  likeness, 21
  imitation, 19
  blame, 932
Reflector
  optical instrument, 445
Reflet
  variegation, 440
Reflex
  regress, 283
  recoil, 277
Reflux
  regress, 283
  recoil, 277
Refocillate
  refresh, 689
  restore, 660
Reform
  improve, 658
  change, 140
Reformatory
  school, 542

Refraction
deviation, 279
angularity, 244
Refractor
optical instrument, 445
Refractory
resisting, 719
obstinate, 606
disobedient, 742
difficult, 704
Refrain
avoid, 623
reject, 610
unwilling, 603
abstain, 616, 681
temperance, 953
repetition, 104, 415
Refresh
cool, 385
relieve, 834
refit, 658
restore, 660
strengthen, 159
Refresher
fee, 809
Refreshing
pleasing, 377, 829
Refreshment
food, 298
pleasure, 827
recruiting, 689
Refrigeration
refrigerate, 385
Refrigeratory
cold, 387
Reft
disjoin, 44
Refuge
refuge, 666
Refugee
escape, 671
Refulgence
light, 420
Refund
restore, 790
pay, 807
Refurbish
improve, 658
Refuse
decline, 764
reject, 610
remains, 40
offscourings, 643
Refute

confute, 479
Regain
acquisition, 775
Regal
authority, 737
Regale
feast, 298
pleasing, 377, 829
Regalia
sceptre, 747
Regard
esteem, 931
respect, 928
love, 897
compliment, 894
view, 441
judge, 480
conceive, 484
credit, 873
Regarding
relation, 9
Regardless
inattention, 458
Regatta
amusement, 840
Regency
commission, 755
Regenerate
reproduce, 163
restore, 660
piety, 987
Regent
deputy, 759
governor, 745
Regicide
killing, 361
Regime
authority, 737
circumstance, 8
conduct, 692
Regimen
diet, 298
remedy, 662
Regiment
army, 726
assemblage, 72
Regimentals
dress, 225
Region
region, 181
Register
record, 551
list, 86
to arrange, 60
range, 26

to coincide, 199
ventilator, 351
fire-place, 386
Registrar
recorder, 553
Regorge
restitution, 790
Regrater
merchant, 797
Regress
regression, 283
Regressive
reversion, 145
Regret
sorrow, 833
penitence, 950
Regular
orderly, 58
complete, 52
rule, 80, 82
symmetric, 242
periodic, 138
soldier, 726
Regulation
arrangement, 60
direction, 693
usage, 80
order, 741
law, 963
Regurgitate
return, 283
flow, 348
restore, 790
Rehabilitate
reinstate, 660
restore, 790
Rehash
repetition, 104
improvement, 658
Rehearse
repeat, 104
trial, 463
describe, 594
prepare, 673
dramatic, 599
Reify
materialize, 3
Reign
authority, 175, 737
Reimburse
restore, 790
pay, 807
Rein
moderate, 174
check, 179

slacken, 275
restrain, 616
hold, 737
Reincarnation
reproduction, 163
Reindeer
carrier, 271
Reinforce
strengthen, 159
aid, 707
add, 37, 39
Reinforcement
supplies, 635, 637
Reinstate
restore, 660
Reinvigorate
restore, 660
refresh, 689
Reiterate
frequent, 136
repeat, 104, 535
multitude, 102
Reject
decline, 610
refuse, 764
exclude, 55
eject, 297
Rejoice
exult, 838
gratify, 829
cheer, 836
amuse, 840
Rejoinder
answer, 462
evidence, 468
lawsuit, 969
Rejuvenate
restore, 660
Rekindle
ignite, 384
motive, 615
Relapse
reversion, 145
retrogression, 661
Relate
narrate, 594
refer, 9
Relation
relation, 9
Relative
consanguinity, 11
Relax
weaken, 160
soften, 324
slacken, 275

unbend the mind, 452
repose, 687
leisure, 685
amuse, 840
lounge, 863
loose, 47
misrule, 738
relent, 914
Relaxing
unhealthy, 657
Relay
materials, 635
Release
liberate, 750
deliver, 672
discharge, 970
restore, 790
exempt, 927A
repay, 807
death, 360
Relegate
transfer, 270
remove, 185
banish, 55
Relent
moderate, 174
pity, 914
relax, 324
Relentless
malevolent, 907
wrathful, 900
revengeful, 919
flagitious, 945
impenitent, 951
Relevancy
pertinence, 9
congruity, 23
Reliable
believable, 484
trustworthy, 939
Reliance
confidence, 484
hope, 858
Relic
remainder, 40
reminiscence, 505
token, 551
sacred, 998
Relict
widow, 905
Relief
sculpture, 557
convexity, 250
aid, 707
Relieve

comfort, 834
refresh, 689
help, 707
improve, 658
Religion
theology, 983
belief, 484
piety, 987
Religiosity
sanctimony, 988
Religious
exact, 494
pious, 987
Relinquish
a purpose, 607, 624
property, 782
to discontinue, 142
Reliquary
rite, 998
Relish
like, 377, 827
taste, 390
savoury, 394
desire, 865
Relucent
luminous, 420
transparent, 425
Reluct
resist, 719
Reluctance
dislike, 867
unwillingness, 603
dissuasion, 616
Reluctation
resistance, 719
Relume
light, 384
Rely
confidence, 484
expectation, 507
hope, 858
Remain
endure, 106, 110
exist, 1
to be left, 40
rest, 265
continue, 141
Remainder
left, 40
property, 780
Remains
corpse, 362
vestige, 551
Remand
restraint, 751

delay, 133

Remark
observe, 457
assert, 535

Remarkable
important, 642

Remarkably
greatness, 31

Remedy
cure, 662
salubrious, 656
to restore, 660, 834

Remember
recollect, 505

Remembrance
compliment, 894

Remembrancer
recorder, 553

Remigration
egress, 295

Remind
recollect, 505

Reminiscence
remember, 505

Remiss
neglectful, 460
idle, 683
reluctant, 603
laxity, 738

Remission
see Remit

Remit
relax, 174
forgive, 918
restore, 790
discontinue, 142
pay, 807

Remnant
remainder, 40

Remodel
conversion, 140, 144
improve, 658

Remonstrate
dissuade, 616
expostulate, 932

Remorse
penitence, 950

Remorseless
resentment, 900
revenge, 919

Remote
distant, 196
not related, 10

Remotion
see Remove

Remove
displace, 185
retrench, 38
depart, 293
recede, 287
transfer, 270
extract, 301
term, 71

Removed
distant, 196

Remunerate
reward, 973
pay, 810

Renaissance
revival, 660

Renascent
reproduction, 163

Recontre
see Rencounter

Rencounter
fight, 720
meeting, 197, 292

Rend
disjoin, 44

Render
give, 784
restore, 790
interpret, 522
music, 415

Rendezvous
focus, 74
assemblage, 72

Rending
loud, 404
painful, 830

Rendition
surrender, 782
interpretation, 522

Renegade
apostate, 742, 941
turncoat, 144, 607

Renew
repeat, 104
reproduce, 163
frequent, 136
newness, 123
repair, 658
restore, 660

Reniform
curvature, 245

Renounce
relinquish, 624
property, 782
recant, 607
resign, 757

deny, 536
repudiate, 927
exempt, 927A

Renovate
reproduce, 163
newness, 123
restore, 660

Renown
repute, 873

Rent
fissure, 44, 198
hire, 788, 794
receipt, 810

Renter
possessor, 779

Rentier
wealth, 803

Renunciation
see Renounce

Reorganize
conversion, 144
restore, 660

Repair
mend, 658
refresh, 689
restore, 660, 790
atone, 952

Repair to
journey, 266

Reparation
compensation, 973

Repartee
wit, 842
answer, 462

Repast
food, 298

Repatriation
egress, 295

Repay
payment, 807
recompense, 973

Repeal
abrogation, 756

Repeat
iterate, 104, 143
imitate, 19
duplication, 90
frequent, 136
multiplied, 102

Repeater
watch, 114

Repel
repulse, 289
defend, 717
resist, 719

Rescind
cut off, 44
abrogate, 756
refuse, 764
Rescission
see Rescind
Rescript
order, 741
letter, 592
answer, 462
Rescue
deliver, 672
preserve, 670
aid, 707
Research
inquiry, 461
Reseat
restore, 660
Resection
disjunction, 44
Resemblance
similarity, 17
Resent
resentment, 900
Reservation
concealment, 528
silence, 585
shyness, 881
store, 636
Reserve
concealment, 528
silence, 585
shyness, 881
caution, 864
store, 636
Reservoir
store, 636
receptacle, 191
lake, 343
Reside
inhabit, 184, 186
Residence
abode, 189
location, 184
Resident
inhabitant, 188
emissary, 758
Residue
remainder, 40
Resign
give up, 757
relinquish, 624, 782
submit, 743
Resignation
endurance, 826
content, 831

Resignation
abdication, 757
humility, 743, 879
renunciation, 872
Resilient
elasticity, 325
rebound, 283
Resin
semiliquid, 352
Resist
withstand, 719
disobey, 742
refuse, 764
oppose, 179
tenacity, 327
Resistant
tough, 327
Resistless
strength, 159
Resolute
determined, 604
brave, 861
Resolution
decomposition, 49
investigation, 461
solution, 462
topic, 454
determination, 604
courage, 861
Resolve
purpose, 620
to liquefy, 335
decompose, 49
investigate, 461
discover, 480A
interpret, 522
Resonant
sonorous , 402
ringing, 408
Resorb
reception, 296
Resort
employ, 677
converge, 290
focus, 74
assemble, 72
frequent, 136
move, 266
dwell, 189
Resound
be loud, 402, 404
ring, 408
praises, 931
Resourceful
skill, 698

Resourceless
inactive, 683
Resources
means, 632, 780
wealth, 803
Respect
deference, 928
fame, 873
salutation, 894
observe, 772
reference, 9
Respectable
repute, 873
upright, 939
tolerable, 651
Respecting
relation, 9
Respective
speciality, 79
apportionment, 786
Respectless
inattention, 458
Respire
breathe, 359
repose, 687
Respite
pause, 265
intermission, 106
rest, 142, 685, 687
escape, 671, 672
reprieve, 970
Resplendent
luminous, 420
splendid, 845
Respond
agree, 23
sensibility, 375, 822
Respondent
accused, 938
Response
answer, 462
verbal, 587
rites, 998
Responsible
duty, 926
liable, 177
Responsive
see Respond
Rest
quiescence, 265
repose, 687
leisure, 685
remainder, 40
remain, 141
pause, 142

Retroaction
recoil, 277
regression, 283
counteraction, 179
Retrocession
recession, 287
Retrocognition
thought, 451
Retrograde
motion, 283
declension, 659
relapse, 661
reversion, 145
Retrogression
see Retrograde
Retrospect
memory, 505
thought, 451
past, 122
Retroversion
inversion, 218
Return
regression, 283
arrival, 292
frequency, 136
to restore, 790
reward, 973
report, 551
list, 86
appoint, 755
profit, 775
proceeds, 810
Reunion
junction, 43
assemblage, 72
party, 892
Revanchist
revenge, 919
Reveal
·disclosure, 529
Reveille
signal, 550
Revel
enjoy, 827
amuse, 840
dissipation, 954
Revelation
disclosure, 529
theological, 985
Revelry
cheerful, 836
Revenant
ghost, 980
Revendication
claim, 765
recovery, 660

Revenge
revenge, 919
Revenue
wealth, 803
receipts, 810
Reverberate
sound, 408
recoil, 277
Reverberatory
fire, 386
Reverence
respect, 928
salutation, 894
piety, 987
worship, 990
title, 877
Reverend
clergy, 996
Reverie
train of thought, 451
imagination, 515
Reversal
inversion, 218
Reverse
antiposition, 237
contrary, 14
change, 140
cancel, 756
evolution, 313
inversion, 218
misfortune, 830
adversity, 735
Reversion
possession, 777
property, 780
transfer, 783
Revert
recur, 104, 136
go back, 283
deteriorate, 659
Review
consider, 457
memory, 505
judge, 480
criticism, 595
rectify, 658
display, 882
Reviewer
writer, 590
Revile
abuse, 932
blaspheme, 988
Revise
consider, 457
improve, 658

restore, 660
proof, 21, 591
Revisit
presence, 186
Revitalize
restore, 660
Revival
worship, 990
Revivalist
clergy, 996
Revive
live, 359
restore, 660
refresh, 689
Revivify
reproduction, 163
restore, 660
Revoke
recant, 607
deny, 536
cancel, 756
refuse, 754
Revolt
resist, 719
revolution, 146
disobey, 742
shock, 830, 932
Revolting
vulgar, 851
Revolution
rotation, 312
change, 140, 146
periodicity, 138
Revolve
meditate, 451
Revolver
arms, 727
Revue
drama, 599
Revulsion
recoil, 277
Reward
reward, 973
Rhadamanthine
severe, 739
Rhapsody
discontinuity, 70
nonsense, 497
fancy, 515
music, 415
Rhetoric
speech, 582
Rhetorical
ornament, 577

Rheum
humour, 333
water, 337
Rhine
ditch, 350
Rhino
money, 800
Rhomb
angularity, 244
rhombohedron
angularity, 244
Rhomboid
angularity, 244
Rhombus
angularity, 244
Rhumb
direction, 278
Rhyme
poetry, 597
similarity, 17
Rhymeless
prose, 598
Rhythm
harmony, 413
regularity, 138
poetry, 597
Rib
ridge, 250
banter, 256
wife, 903
Ribald
vile, 874, 961
vulgar, 851
maledictory, 908
impious, 988
abuse, 932
Ribbed
furrow, 259
Ribbon
filament, 205
tie, 45
trophy, 733
decoration, 877
Rich
wealthy, 803
abundant, 639
savoury, 394
adorned, 847
style, 577
Richly
great, 31
Rick
store, 636
accumulation, 72
Rickety

weak, 160
imperfect, 651
ugly, 846
Rickshaw
vehicle, 272
Ricochet
recoil, 277
reversion, 145
Rid
loss, 776
relinquish, 782
abandon, 624
deliver, 672
Riddle
enigma, 533
obscurity, 519
question, 461
confute, 479
sieve, 260
arrange, 60
Ride
move, 266
get above, 206
road, 627
Rider
equestrian, 268
corollary, 480
appendix, 39
Ridge
narrowness, 203
projection, 250
Ridicule
deride, 856
depreciate, 483
disrespect, 929
Ridiculous
grotesque, 853
vulgar, 851
absurd, 497
silly, 499
trifling, 643
Riding
region, 181
Ridotto
gala, 840
rout, 892
Rifacimento
recast, 660
Rife
ordinary, 82
frequent, 136
prevailing, 175
Riff-raff
rabble, 876, 949
dirt, 653

Rifle
to plunder, 791
arms, 727
Rifleman
combatant, 726
Rift
separation, 44
fissure, 198
Rig
dress, 225
prepare, 673
frolic, 840
deception, 545
adorn, 845
Rigadoon
dance, 840
Rigescence
hardness, 323
Rigging
gear, 225
cordage, 45
Right
just, 922
privilege, 924
duty, 926
honour, 939
straight, 246
true, 494
suitable, 646
Righteous
virtuous, 944
just, 922
Rigid
hard, 323
exact, 494
strict, 772
severe, 739
stubborn, 606
regular, 82
Rigmarole
nonsense, 497, 517
unintelligible, 519
Rigour
severity, 739
compulsion, 744
exactness, 494
Rile
irritate, 830, 900
alienate, 898
Rill
river, 348
Rim
edge, 230
Rime
cold, 383

Rind
  covering, 222
Ring
  circle, 247
  sound, 408
  arena, 728
  party, 712
  syndicate, 778
Ring-fence
  enclosure, 232
Ringleader
  master, 745
  director, 694
Ringlet
  circle, 247
Rink
  arena, 728
Rinse
  cleanness, 652
Riot
  violence, 173
  revolt, 719, 742
  confusion, 59
  luxuriate, 377, 827
Rip
  tear, 44
  rush, 274
  sensualist, 954
  rascal, 949
Riparian
  and, 342
Ripe
  preparation, 673
Riposte
  answer, 462
Ripping
  excellent, 648
  delightful, 827
Ripple
  shake, 315
  murmur, 405
  wave, 348
Rise
  ascend, 206, 305
  slope, 217
  resist, 719
  revolt, 742
  spring, 154
  grow, 35
Risible
  laughable, 828
  ridiculous, 853
  witty, 842
Risk
  danger, 665

chance, 621
Risky
  improper, 961
Rite
  law, 963
  religious, 998
Ritornello
  frequency, 136
Ritual
  rite, 998
  ceremony, 882
Rival
  emulate, 720
  envy, 921
  oppose, 708
  competitor, 710, 726
Rive
  disjoin, 44
Rivel
  fold, 258
River
  water, 348
Rivet
  to fasten, 43, 150
  fastening, 45
Rivulet
  water, 348
Road
  way, 189, 627
  direction, 278
Road-hog
  selfishness, 943
Roadhouse
  inn, 189
Roadstead
  anchorage, 189
  gulf, 343
  refuge, 666
Roadster
  carrier, 271
Roadway
  way, 627
Roam
  journey, 266
Roan
  variegation, 271
Roar
  sound, 404
  cry, 411
  weep, 839
Roast
  heat, 384
  ridicule, 856
  deride, 929
  persecute, 830

censure, 932
Rob
  plunder, 791
Robber
  thief, 792
Robe
  dress, 225
Robin Goodfellow
  imp, 980
Robot
  automaton, 601
Robust
  strength, 159
Roc
  monster, 83
Rock
  hardness, 323
  land, 342
  to oscillate, 314
  pitfall, 667
Rock-and-roll
  melody, 413
Rock-bottom
  base, 211
Rockery
  garden, 371
Rocket
  signal, 550
  arms, 727
  light, 423
  space ship, 273A
  rise, 305
  rapid, 274
Rocky
  unsteady, 149
Rococo
  fantastic, 853
Rod
  sceptre, 747
  scourge, 975
  bane, 663
  measure, 466
  divining, 992
  gun, 727
Rodomontade
  rant, 497
  unintelligible, 519
  boasting, 884
Rogation
  worship, 990
Rogue
  cheat, 548
  knave, 941
  scamp, 949

Roguery
vice, 945
dishonour, 940
Roguish
sportive, 842
Roily
opaque, 426
Roister
insolence, 885
Role
business, 625
drama, 599
Roll
rotate, 312
move, 264
push, 284
flow, 348
smooth, 255
sound, 407
cylinder, 249
convolution, 248
fillet, 205
record, 551
list, 86
Roll-call
number, 85
Roll in
abound, 639
Roller
rotundity, 249
Rollicking
frolicsome, 836
blustering, 885
Rolling-stock
vehicle, 292
Rolling stone
traveller, 268
Roly-poly
size, 192
Roman
type, 591
Roman Catholic
Christian religion, 983A
Romance
fiction, 515
falsehood, 544
absurdity, 497
fable, 594
love, 897
Romantic
sentimental, 822
Romp
leap, 309
Rompers
dress, 225

Rondeau
poem, 597
Rondo
music, 415
Roof
summit, 210
height, 206
cover, 222
house, 189
Roofless
divestment, 226
Rook
deceiver, 548
swindle, 791
Rookery
abode, 189
Room
space, 180
occasion, 124
chamber, 191
Roommate
friend, 891
Roomy
space, 180
Roost
abode, 186, 189
Root
cause, 153
base, 211
word, 562
algebraic, 84
to place, 184
Root for
commend, 931
Root out
destroy, 162
displace, 185
eject, 301
discover, 480A
Rooted
fixed, 265
permanent, 141
old, 124
habitual, 613
Rope
cord, 205
fastening, 45
Ropy
demiliquidity, 352
Roral
moisture, 339
Rosary
rite, 998
garden, 371
Roscid

moisture, 339
Roscius
actor, 599
Rose
redness, 434
beauty, 845
spout, 350
Rosette
cluster, 72
ornament, 847
Rosicrucian
heathen, 984
Rosin
semiliquid, 352
Roster
list, 86
record, 551
Rostrum
beak, 234
pulpit, 542
Rosy
red, 434
auspicious, 858
Rot
disease, 655
decay, 659
decompose, 48
putrefy, 653
nonsense, 497, 517
to banter, 856
Rota
periodicity, 138
list, 86
record, 551
Rotate
rotation, 312
Rote
memory, 505
Rotor
navigation, 267
ship, 273
Rotten
foul, 653
fetid, 401
Rotter
knave, 949
Rotund
fat, 192
round, 249
Rotunda
abode, 189
Rotundity
roundness, 249
Roturier
commonalty, 876

Roué
scoundrel, 949
sensualist, 954
libertine, 962
Rouge
red, 434
ornament, 847
Rouge-et-noir
chance, 156, 621
Rough
uneven, 256
shapeless, 241
pungent, 392
sour, 397
austere, 395
violent, 173
windy, 349
sound, 410
unprepared, 674
ugly, 846
churlish, 895
brute, 913
bad man, 949
to fag, 686
Rough and ready
transient, 111
provisional, 673
Rough-grained
texture, 329
Rough-hewn
rugged, 256
unprepared, 674
Rough-house
disorder, 59
Roughcast
unprepared, 674
Roughly
near, 197
Roughneck
ruffian, 949
Rouleau
cylinder, 249
money, 800
Roulette
engraving, 558
gambling, 621
Round
circular, 247
rotund, 249
assertion, 535
periodicity, 138
song, 415
fight, 720
rung, 71
work, 625

Round-house
prison, 752
Round on
attack, 716
peach, 529
Round robin
record, 551
request, 765
Round-shot
arms, 727
Round-shouldered
distorted, 243
Round up
assemblage, 72
capture, 789
Roundabout
circuitous, 31
way, 629
circumlocutory, 566, 573
Roundelay
poetry, 597
Roundlet
circular, 247
Roundly
exertion, 686
Roup
sale, 796
Rouse
stimulate, 615
passion, 824
Roustabout
labourer, 690
Rout
discomfort, 732
assembly, 892
rabble, 876
Rout out
destruction, 162
Route
method, 627
direction, 278
Route march
journey, 266
Routine
order, 58
uniformity, 16
cycle, 138
rule, 60
custom, 613
work, 625
Rove
wander, 266, 279
Rover
traveller, 268

Row
series, 69
navigate, 267
violence, 173
brawl, 713
riot, 720
din, 404
Rowdy
violent, 173
vulgar, 851
Rowel
sharpness, 253
stimulus, 615
Royalty
authority, 737
receipt, 810
Rozzer
police, 664
Rub
friction, 331
difficulty, 703
Rub-a-dub
roll, 407
Rub down
pulverulence, 330
Rub out
disappear, 449
efface, 552
Rub up
improve, 658
Rubber
elasticity, 325
shoe, 225
pry, 455
Rubberneck
spectator, 444
curiosity, 455
Rubbing
copy, 21
Rubbish
inutility, 645
nonsense, 497, 517
Rubble
unimportance, 643
Rube
peasant, 876
Rubefy
red, 434
Rubicon
limit, 233
passage, 303
undertaking, 676
Rubicund
red, 434

Rubric
precept, 697
liturgy, 998
Rubricate
red, 434
Ruby
red, 434
gem, 650
ornament, 847
Ruche
fold, 258
Ruck
fold, 258
commonalty, 876
Rucksack
receptacle, 191
Rudder
guidance, 693
Ruddle
red, 434
Ruddy
red, 434
Rude
violent, 173
vulgar, 851
uncivil, 895
disrespectful, 929
ugly, 846
shapeless, 241
uncivilized, 876
Rudiment
beginning, 66
cause, 153
smallness, 193
non-preparation, 674
Rudiments
elementary knowledge, 490
beginning, 66
school, 542
Rue
regret, 833
repent, 950
Rueful
doleful, 837
Ruffian
maleficent, 913
scoundrel, 949
vulgarity, 851
Ruffle
derange, 61
fold, 258
edge, 230
discompose, 830
excite, 824

anger, 900
Rufous
red, 434
Rug
covering, 222
Rugged
rough, 256
ugly, 846
churlish, 895
style, 579
Rugose
wrinkled, 256
Ruin
decay, 659
failure, 732
evil, 619
debauch, 961
impoverish, 804
adversity, 735
ruins, 40.
Ruinous
painful, 830
Rule
regularity, 80
length, 200
measure, 466
government, 737
precept, 697
custom, 613
law, 963
to decide, 480
Rule out
exclude, 77
Ruler
master, 745
Rum
odd, 853
Rumba
dance, 840
Rumble
noise, 407
understand, 518
Rumbustious
violent, 173
Ruminate
thought, 451
chew, 296
Rummage
seek, 461
Rumour
publicity, 531
report, 532
Rump
rear, 235
remnant, 40

part, 51
Rumple
fold, 258
derange, 61
rough, 256
Rumpus
confusion, 59
din, 404
violence, 173
brawl, 713
contention, 720
Run
move quickly, 274
move out, 295
recurrence, 104, 136
flow, 109, 333
continue, 143
operate, 680
conduct, 692, 693
smuggle, 791
Run across
encounter, 292
Run after
pursue, 622
Run away
escape, 671
avoid, 623
from fear, 862
recede, 287
Run down
censure, 932
depreciate, 483
weakness, 160
Run high
violence, 173
Run in
insert, 300
arrest, 751
Run into
become, 144
Run low
decrease, 36
Run on
continue, 143
Run out
elapse, 122
waste, 638
Run over
redundant, 641
describe, 594
count, 85
examine, 457, 596
Run riot
violence, 173

Run through
peruse, 539
squander, 818
Run up
expend, 809
increase, 35
Runabout
vehicle, 272
Runaway
fugitive, 623, 671
Rundle
circle, 247
convolution, 248
rotundity, 249
Rune
writing, 590
Runlet
receptacle, 191
Runnel
river, 348
Runner
courier, 268
messenger, 534
Runner-up
sequel, 65
Running
continuously, 69
Runt
littleness, 193
Rupture
break, 44, 713
Rural
country, 189, 371
Ruralist
recluse, 893
Rurbania
suburbs, 227
Ruse
cunning, 702
deception, 545
Rush
rapidity, 274
haste, 684
violence, 173
to pursue, 622
trifle, 643
Rushlight
light, 423
Russet
red, 433
Rust
decay, 659
sluggishness, 683
canker, 663
red, 434
Rustic

rural, 189, 371
clown, 876
vulgar, 851
Rusticate
expel, 185
exclude, 55
Rustication
seclusion, 895
Rusticity
inurbanity, 895
Rustle
noise, 405, 409, 410
rob, 791
Rustler
robber, 792
Rusty
sluggish, 683
old, 128
unserviceable, 645
dirty, 653
deteriorated, 659
Rut
groove, 259
habit, 613
Ruth
pity, 914
Ruthless
pitiless, 907
revenge, 919
angry, 900
Rutilant
light, 420
Ruttish
impurity, 961
Ryot
commonalty, 876

S.A.
charm, 829
S O S
signal, 550
alarm, 669
Sabbatarian
bigot, 988
heterodoxy, 984A
Sabbath
rest, 685
Sable
black, 431
Sabot
dress, 225
Sabotage
damage, 649
Sabre

weapon, 727
to kill, 361
Sabretache
bag, 191
Sabulous
pulverulence, 330
Saccharine
sweet, 396
Sacerdotal
clergy, 995
pietism, 988
Sachem
master, 745
Sachet
fragrance, 400
Sack
bag, 191
to ravage, 649
havoc, 619
plunder, 791
dismiss, 297, 756
Sackcloth
asceticism, 955
atonement, 952
mourning, 839
Sacrament
rite, 998
Sacred
holy, 976
pious, 987
books, 986
inviolable, 924
Sacrifice
destroy, 162
offering, 763
self-denial, 942
atonement, 952
worship, 990
Sacrilege
irreligion, 989
impiety, 988
Sacristan
churchman, 996
Sacristy
temple, 1000
Sacrosanct
inviolable, 924
Sad
dejected, 837
mournful, 839
bad, 649
painful, 830
Saddle
clog, 706
add, 37

662

Safe
secure, 664
cupboard, 191
Safe-conduct
safety, 664
passport, 631
Safeguard
safety, 664
Safety-valve
means of safety, 666
Saffron
yellowness, 436
Sag
obliquity, 217
Saga
description, 594
Sagacious
intelligent, 498
foreseeing, 510
skilful, 698
Sagittate
angular, 244
Sahib
title, 877
Saic
ship, 273
Said
precedence, 62
priority, 116
repetition, 104
Sail
navigate, 267
set out, 293
Saint
holy, 948
pious, 987
spirit, 977
St. Luke's summer
autumn, 126
St. Martin's summer
autumn, 126
Saintly
virtuous, 944
pious, 987
angelic, 977
Sake
cause, 615
Salaam
respect, 743, 928
bow, 308
Salacity
impurity, 961
Salad
mixture, 41
Salamander

furnace, 386
Salary
pay, 809
Sale
merchandize, 796
Salesman
merchant, 797
representative, 758
Salient
projecting, 250
sharp, 253
manifest, 525
important, 643
Saline
pungent, 392
Saliva
excretion, 299
lubricant, 332
Sallow
yellow, 436
pale, 429
Sally
issue, 293
attack, 716
wit, 842
Salmagundi
mixture, 41
Salmon-coloured
red, 434
Salon
room, 191
Saloon
room, 191
vehicle, 272
Salt
pungent, 392
condiment, 393
wit, 842
preserve, 670
Saltation
dancing, 309
Saltatory
leap, 309
agitation, 351
Saltimbanco
quack, 548
Salubrity
health, 656
Salutary
salubrious, 656
remedial, 662
Salute
compliment, 894
kiss, 902
address, 586

firing, 882, 883
Salvage
tax, 812
discount, 813
reward, 973
acquisition, 775
to save, 672
Salvation
deliverance, 672
preservation, 670
religious, 976
Salve
to relieve, 834
remedy, 662
Salver
dish, 191
Salvo
exception, 83
condition, 770
excuse, 937
plea, 617
explosion, 406
salute, 882
Samaritan
benefactor, 912
Samba
dance, 840
Sambo
mixture, 41
Same
identity, 13
Sameness
monotony, 841
Samiel
wind, 349
Samovar
vessel, 191
Sampan
ship, 273
Sample
specimen, 82
San fairy ann
indifference, 456
neglect, 460
Sanatorium
salubrity, 656
Sanatory
improvement, 658
remedy, 662
Sanctify
authorize, 924
piety, 987
Sanctimony
hypocrisy, 988
falsehood, 544

Sanction
  authority, 924
  approbation, 931
  permission, 760
Sanctity
  piety, 987
Sanctuary
  refuge, 666
  altar, 1000
Sanctum
  holy, 1000
  room, 191
Sand
  pulverulence, 330
  manliness, 604
  courage, 861
Sand-blind
  dim-sighted, 443
Sand-shoe
  dress, 225
Sandal
  dress, 225
Sandalwood
  fragrance, 400
Sandbag
  defence, 717
  arms, 727
Sandpaper
  smooth, 255
Sands
  pitfall, 667
Sandwich
  interpose, 228
Sandy
  pulverulence, 330
Sane
  intelligent, 498
  rational, 502
Sang-froid
  insensibility, 823
  inexcitability, 826
  caution, 864
Sanguinary
  brutal, 907
Sanguine
  expectant, 507
  hopeful, 858
Sanhedrim
  tribunal, 696
Sanies
  fluidity, 333
Sanitary
  salubrity, 656
Sanity
  rationality, 502

health, 654
Sans
  absence, 187
Sans cérémonie
  modesty; 881
  sociality, 892
  friendship, 888
Sans façon
  modesty, 881
  sociality, 892
Sans pareil
  superiority, 33
Sans phrase
  frankness, 543, 566
Sans souci
  pleasure, 827
  content, 831
Sansculotte
  rebel, 742
  commonalty, 876
Santon
  hermit, 893
  priest, 996
Sap
  juice, 333
  inbeing, 5
  to destroy, 162
  damage, 659
  fool, 501
Sapid
  tasty, 390
Sapient
  wisdom, 498
Sapless
  dry, 340
Sapling
  youth, 129
Saponaceous
  soapy, 355
Sapor
  flavour, 390
Sapphire
  ornament, 847
Sappy
  juicy, 333
  foolish, 499
Saraband
  dance, 840
Sarcasm
  satire, 932
  disrespect, 929
Sarcastic
  irascible, 901
  derisory, 856
Sarcoma

disease, 655
Sarcophagus
  interment, 363
Sardonic
  contempt, 838
Sartorial
  dress, 225
Sash
  central, 247
Satan
  devil, 978
Satanic
  evil, 649
  hellish, 982
  vicious, 945
Satchel
  bag, 191
Sate
  see Satiate
Satellite
  follower, 281
  companion, 88
  space ship, 273A
Satiate
  sufficient, 639
  redundant, 641
  cloy, 869
Satiety
  see Satiate
Satin
  smooth, 255
Satire
  ridicule, 856
  censure, 932
Satirist
  detractor, 936
Satisfaction
  duel, 720
  reward, 973
Satisfactorily
  well, 618
Satisfy
  content, 831
  gratify, 827, 829
  convince, 484
  fulfil a duty, 926
  an obligation, 772
  reward, 973
  pay, 807
  suffice, 639
  satiate, 869
  grant, 762
Satrap
  ruler, 745
  deputy, 759

Satrapy
province, 181
Saturate
fill, 52, 639
soak, 337
moisten, 339
satiate, 869
Saturated
greatness, 31
Saturnalia
amusement, 840
intemperance, 954
disorder, 59
Saturnian
halcyon, 734, 829
Saturnine
grim, 837
Satyr
ugly, 846
demon, 980
rake, 961
Sauce
mixture, 41
adjunct, 39
abuse, 832
Sauce-box
impudence, 887
Saucepan
stove, 386
Saucer
receptacle, 191
Saucy
insolent, 885
flippant, 895
cheerful, 836
Saunter
ramble, 266
dawdle, 275
Sauve qui peut
speed, 274
recession, 287
avoidance, 623
escape, 671
cowardice, 862
Savage
violent, 173
brutal, 876;
angry, 900
malevolent, 907
a wretch, 913
Savanna
plain, 344
Savant
scholar, 492
wisdom, 500

Save
except, 38, 55, 83
to preserve, 670
deliver, 672
lay by, 636
economize, 817
Savings certificates
treasury, 802
Saviour
Deity, 976
benefactor, 912
Savoir faire
tact, 698
manners, 852
Savoir vivre
sociality, 892
breeding, 852
Savour
taste, 390
fragrance, 400
Savour of
similarity, 17
Savourless
insipid, 391
Savoury
palatable, 394
delectable, 829
Savvy
know, 490
Saw
jagged, 257
saying, 496
Sawder
flattery, 933
Sawdust
pulverulence, 330
Sawney
fool, 501
Saxophone
musical instrument, 417
Say
speak, 582
assert, 535
attention, 457
about, 32
Saying
assertion, 535
maxim, 496
Sayonara
departure, 293
Scab
traitor, 941
Scabbard
receptacle, 191, 222
Scabby

improbity, 940
Scabrous
rough, 256
indelicate, 961
Scaffold
frame, 215
preparation, 673
way, 627
execution, 975
Scald
burn, 384
poet, 597
Scalding
hot, 382
burning, 384
Scale
slice, 204
skin, 222
order, 58
measure, 58
measure, 466
weight, 319
series, 69
gamut, 413
to mount, 305
attack, 716
Scale, on a large
greatness, 31
Scale, on a small
small, 32
Scale, turn the
superiority, 33
Scallop
convolution, 248
notch, 257
Scalp
trophy, 733
to criticize, 932
Scalpel
sharpness, 253
Scamp
rascal, 949
to neglect, 460
Scamper
velocity, 274
Scan
vision, 441
inquire, 461
metre, 597
Scandal
disgrace, 874
vice, 945
news, 532
Scandalize
disgust, 932

665

Scandent
climb, 305
Scansion
metre, 597
Scant
narrowness, 203
smallness, 32
Scanties
dress, 225
Scantling
dimensions, 192
example, 82
small quantity, 32
scrap, 51
prototype, 22
Scanty
smallness, 32
narrow, 203
few, 103
insufficient, 640
Scapegoat
blame, 952
substitute, 147
Scapegrace
vice, 949
Scapular
vestments, 999
Scar
blemish, 848
Scaramouch
humorist, 844
buffoon, 857
Scarce
insufficiency, 640
infrequent, 137
Scarcely
little, 32
rare, 137
Scare
frighten, 860
Scarecrow
ugly, 846
bugbear, 860
Scaremonger
news, 532
Scarf
dress, 225
Scarf-skin
covering, 222
Scarify
torment, 830
Scarlet
red, 434
Scarp
slope, 217

Scarper
escape, 671
Scat
expel, 297
Scathe
evil, 619
bane, 663
injury, 659
badness, 649
Scatheless
secure, 664
saved, 672
Scathing
censorious, 932
Scatology
uncleanness, 653
Scatter
disperse, 73
diverge, 291
derange, 59
Scatter-brained
foolish, 499
Scattered
discontinuous, 70
Scatty
insane, 503
Scavenger
clean, 652
Scenario
plan, 626
cinema, 599A
Scene
appearance, 448
surroundings, 227
arena, 728
painting, 556
drama, 599
Scenery
vista, 448
Scent
smell, 398
knowledge, 490
suspect, 485
trail, 551
Scent-bag
smell, 400
Scentless
absence of smell, 399
Scepticism
doubt, 485, 497
religious, 989
Sceptre
sceptre, 747
Schedule
list, 86

record, 551
draft, 554
Scheme
plan, 626
draft, 554
Schemer
plot, 626
Scherzando
music, 415
Scherzo
music, 415
Schesis
state, 7
Schism
discord, 713
dissent, 489
heresy, 984A
Schizophrenia
insanity, 503, 504
Schmalz
sentiment, 822
flattery, 933
Scholar
learner, 541
erudite, 492
Scholarship
school, 490
learning, 539
Scholastic
learning, 490, 539
Scholiast
interpreter, 524
Scholium
interpretation, 496, 522
School
teach, 537, 542
flock, 72
belief, 484
School-days
youth, 127
Schoolboy
pupil, 541
Schooled
trained, 698
Schoolfellow
friend, 890
Schooling
teaching, 538
Schoolman
scholar, 492
sage, 500
theologian, 983
Schoolmaster
teacher, 540

Schoolmistress
  teacher, 540
Schooner
  ship, 273
Schottische
  dance, 840
Schwärmerei
  imagination, 515
Sciamachy
  absurdity, 497
Science
  knowledge, 490
  skill, 698
Scientific
  exact, 494
Scientist
  scholar, 492
Scimitar
  arms, 727
Scintilla
  small, 32
  spark, 420
Sciolism
  smattering, 491
Sciolist
  smatterer, 493
Scion
  child, 129
  posterity, 167
Scire facias
  inquiry, 641
Scission
  cut, 44
Scissors
  sharpness, 253
Sclerosis
  hardness, 323
Scobs
  pulverulence, 330
Scoff
  ridicule, 856
  deride, 929
  impiety, 988
Scold
  abuse, 932
  vixen, 936, 901
Scollop
  see Scallop
Sconce
  summit, 210
  mulct, 974
  candlestick, 423
Scoop
  depth, 208
  depression, 252

  perforator, 262
  profit, 775
  news, 532
Scoot
  hurry, 274, 684
  escape, 671
Scooter
  locomotion, 266
Scope
  degree, 26
  extent, 180
  intention, 620
  freedom, 748
Scorch
  burn, 384
  hurry, 684
Score
  mark, 550, 842
  furrow, 259
  motive, 615
  price, 812
  accounts, 805, 811
  record, 551
  twenty, 98
  musical, 415
  to count, 85
  to succeed, 731
Scoriae
  unimportance, 643
  uncleanness, 653
Scorify
  calefaction, 384
Scorn
  contempt, 930
Scorpion
  bane, 663, 913
  painful, 830
Scot-free
  gratuitous, 815
  deliverance, 672
  exemption, 927A
Scotch
  maltreat, 649
  stop, 706
  notch, 257
Scotch mist
  rain, 348
Scotomy
  dim-sightedness, 443
Scotticism
  language, 560
Scoundrel
  vice, 949
  evildoer, 913
Scour

  rub, 331
  run, 274
  clean, 652
Scourge
  whip, 972, 975
  bane, 663
  painful, 830
  bad, 649
Scourings
  refuse, 643
Scout
  messenger, 534
  servant, 746
  watch, 664
  to disdain, 930
  deride, 643
Scowl
  frown, 895
  complain, 839
  anger, 900
Scrabble
  fumble, 379
  nonsense, 517
Scraggy
  narrow, 203
  ugly, 846
Scram
  go away, 287, 293
  escape, 671
  repel, 289
  ejection, 297
Scramble
  confusion, 59
  haste, 684
  difficulty, 704
  mount, 305
Scrannel
  stridulous, 410
  meagre, 643
Scrap
  piece, 51
  small portion, 32, 193
  disuse, 678
  contention, 720
  to fight, 722
Scrap-book
  collection, 596
Scrape
  difficulty, 704
  mischance, 732
  abrade, 330, 331
  bow, 894
  save, 817
Scrape together
  collect, 72

get, 775
Scratch
  groove, 259
  mark, 550
  write, 590
  daub, 555
  abrade, 331
  hurt, 619
  to wound, 649
Scratch out
  obliteration, 552
Scrawl
  write, 590
Scrawny
  lean, 193, 203
Scream
  cry, 410
  complain, 839
Screech
  cry, 410
  complain, 839
Screech-owl
  noise, 412
Screed
  speech, 582
Screen
  concealment, 528
  asylum, 666, 717
  ambush, 530
  to shield, 664
  sieve, 260
  sift, 652
  inquire, 461
  discriminate, 465
  sort, 42, 60
  exclude, 55
  shade, 424
  cinema, 599A
Screened
  safe, 664
  invisible, 447
Screever
  artist, 559
Screw
  fasten, 43
  joining, 45
  instrument, 267, 633
  rotation, 312
  salary, 809
  miser, 819
Screw-steamer
  ship, 273
Screw up
  strengthen, 159
Screwball

madman, 504
Screwed
  drunk, 959
Scribble
  write, 590
  unmeaning, 517
Scribe
  writer, 553, 590
  priest, 996
Scrimp
  shorten, 201
  stint, 640
  save, 817
Scrip
  receptacle, 191
Script
  writing, 590
  radio, 599B
Scriptural
  Christian, 983A
Scripture
  revelation, 985
  certain, 474
Scrivener
  writing, 590
Scroll
  record, 551
  convolution, 248
Scrounge
  steal, 791
Scrub
  clean, 652
  plant, 367
Scrubby
  vulgar, 876
  shabby, 940
  bad, 649
  trifling, 643
  small, 193
  rough, 256
Scrumptious
  pleasing, 829
Scrunch
  pulverulence, 330
Scruple
  doubt, 485
  dissuasion, 616
  smallness, 32
Scrupulous
  careful, 459
  incredulous, 487
  exact, 494
  reluctant, 603
  punctilious, 939
  virtuous, 944

Scrutator
  inquiry, 461
Scrutinize
  examine, 457, 461
Scud
  speed, 274
  sail, 267
  shower, 348
  haze, 353
Scuffle
  contention, 720
Scull
  navigation, 267
Scullery
  room, 191
Scullion
  servant, 746
Sculp
  produce, 161
Sculptor
  artist, 559
Sculpture
  carving, 557
  form, 240
Scum
  dregs, 643, 653
Scunner
  disgust, 395
Scupper
  conduit, 350
Scurf
  uncleanness, 653
Scurrility
  ridicule, 856
  malediction, 908
  detraction, 934
  disrespect, 929
Scurry
  hasten, 274, 684
Scurvy
  bad, 649
  base, 940, 945
Scut
  tail, 235
Scutcheon
  standard, 550
  honour, 877
Scuttle
  tray, 191
  opening, 260
  to destroy, 162
  hasten, 274, 684
Scythe
  angularity, 244
  sharpness, 253

Sea
water, 341
blue, 438
Sea-nymph
sea, 341
Seaboard
edge, 342
Seal
to close, 67, 261
sigil, 550
mould, 22
evidence, 467
record, 551
compact, 769
security, 771
authority, 747
Seal up
shut up, 231, 751
Seam
junction, 43
Seaman
mariner, 269
Seamanship
conduct, 603
Seamstress
see Sempstress
Séance
council, 696
Seaplane
aircraft, 273A
Sear
burn, 384
deaden, 823
Search
seek, 461
pursuit, 622
Searching
thorough, 52
Searchless
unintelligible, 519
Seared
impenitent, 951
Seascape
spectacle, 448
Seaside
edge, 342
Season
time, 106
opportunity, 134
pungent, 392, 393
to preserve, 670
prepare, 673
accustom, 613
Seasonable
opportune, 134

expedient, 646
agreement, 23
Seasonal
period, 108
Seasoning
mixture, 41
pungency, 171, 393
Seat
abode, 189
position, 183
to place, 184
support, 215
Seaworthy
useful, 644
fit, 673
Sebaceous
unctuous, 355
Secateurs
sharpness, 253
Secede
dissent, 489
disobedience, 742
Seclude
restrain, 751
Seclusion
retirement, 526, 893
Second
of time, 108
instant, 113
abet, 707
auxiliary, 711
duplication, 90
Second-best
imperfection, 651
inferiority, 34
Second-hand
borrowed, 788
indifferent, 651
imitated, 19
Second-rate
imperfection, 651
inferiority, 34
Second sight
prediction, 510
intuition, 477
witchcraft, 992
Secondary
following, 63
consignee, 758
deputy, 759
inferior, 34, 643
imperfect, 651
Secondly
bisection, 91
Secret

latent, 526
hidden, 528
riddle, 533
Secretary
recorder, 553
writer, 590
Secrete
hide, 528
Secretive
reserved, 528
Sect
division, 75
Sectarian
dissenter, 984A
theology, 983
Section
part, 51
division, 44
class, 75
chapter, 593
Sector
part, 51
circularity, 247
Secular
number, 99
laity, 997
Secularism
heterodoxy, 984A
Secure
fasten, 43
safe, 664
engage, 768
gain, 775
retain, 781
confident, 858
Security
pledge, 771
warranty, 924
Sedan
vehicle, 272
Sedan chair
vehicle, 272
Sedate
thoughtful, 451
calm, 826
grave, 837
Sedative
calming, 174
sleep, 683
remedy, 662
Sedentary
quiescence, 265
Sederunt
council, 696

Sediment
dregs, 653
remainder, 40
Sedition
disobedience, 742
Seduce
entice, 615
vice, 945
impurity, 961
love, 897
Seducer
libertine, 962
Seducing
charming, 829
Seduction
impurity, 961
Seductive
attractive, 829, 845,
897
Sedulous
active, 682
See
view, 441
look, 457
bishopric, 995
See to
manage, 693
Seed
cause, 153
posterity, 167
Seedling
youth, 129
Seedy
weak, 160
ailing, 655
worn, 651
Seek
inquire, 461
pursue, 622
Seem
appear, 448
Seeming
semblance, 448
Seemly
expedient, 646
proper, 927
handsome, 845
Seepage
egress, 295
Seer
veteran, 130
oracle, 513
sorcerer, 994
Seesaw
oscillation, 314
Seethe

boil, 382, 384
Segar
tobacco, 298a
Segment
part, 51
circularity, 247
Segnitude
inactivity, 683
Segregate
exclude, 55
separate, 44
safety, 664
not related, 10
incoherent, 47
Seignior
master, 745
Seisin
possession, 777
Seismometer
impulse, 276
Seize
take, 789
rob, 791
possess, 777
Seizure
weakness, 160
disease, 655
Seldom
infrequency, 137
Select
choose, 609
good, 648
Selection
part, 51
Self
special, 13
Self-abasement
humility, 879
Self-accusation
penitence, 950
Self-admiration
pride, 880
Self-advertisement
boasting, 884
Self-applause
vanity, 880
Self-assertion
effrontery, 885
Self-centred
selfish, 943
Self-communing
thought, 451
Self-complacency
conceit, 880
Self-conceit

conceit, 880
Self-confidence
conceit, 880
Self-conquest
restraint, 953
Self-consciousness
knowledge, 490
modesty, 881
Self-contempt
humility, 879
Self-control
restraint, 942
Self-deceit
error, 495
Self-defence
defence, 717
Self-delusion
credulity, 486
Self-denial
disinterestedness, 942
temperance, 953
Self-evident
clear, 478
certain, 474
Self-examination
thought, 451
Self-existing
existence, 1
Self-forgetful
disinterested, 942
Self-importance
vanity, 880
Self-indulgence
selfishness, 943
intemperance, 954
Self-love
selfishness, 943
Self-opinionated
foolish, 499
vain, 880
obstinate, 606
Self-possession
caution, 864
discretion, 498
resolution, 604
Self-praise
vanity, 880
Self-regarding
selfish, 943
Self-reliance
security, 604
courage, 861
Self-reproach
blame, 950
regret, 833

Self-reproof
blame, 950
Self-respect
virtue, 944
pride, 878
Self-restraint
self-control, 942
Self-sacrifice
unselfishness, 942
Self-satisfied
vanity, 880
Self-seeking
selfishness, 943
Self-styled
pretence, 544
Self-sufficient
vanity, 880
Self-supporting
freedom, 748
Self-taught
knowledge, 490
Self-tormentor
dejection, 837
Self-willed
obstinate, 606
Selfish
selfishness, 943
Selfless
unselfish, 942
Sell
sale, 796
deception, 545
Sell short
detract, 284
Selvedge
edge, 230
Semantics
interpretation, 522
Semaphore
sign, 550
Sematology
sign, 550
Semblance
likeness, 19
Semeiology
sign, 550
Semi-
half, 91
Semicircle
roundness, 247
Semicolon
stop, 142
Semi-diaphanous
semi-transparent, 427
Semifluid

semiliquidity, 352
Semiliquid
semiliquidity, 352
Semilunar
curvature, 245
Seminary
school, 542
Semi-opaque
semitransparent, 427
Semitransparent
semi-transparency, 427
Semmit
dress, 225
Semper idem
identity, 13
Sempiternal
duration, 112
Sempstress
dress, 225
Senary
number, 98
Senate
council, 696
Senator
adviser, 695
Send
propel, 284
transfer, 270
errand, 755
affect, 824
Send down
expel, 893
Send up
ridicule, 856
Seneschal
master, 745
Seneschalship
power, 737
Senile
age, 128
Seniority
age, 128
Señor
title, 877
Sendation
physical, 375
affective, 820
excitement, 824
Sensational
exaggerated, 549
Sensationalism
vulgarity, 851
Sense
intellect, 450
wisdom, 498

meaning, 516
Senseless
foolish, 499
absurd, 497
insensible, 376
unmeaning, 517
Senses
feeling, 375
Sensibility
physical, 375
moral, 822
Sensible
material, 316
wise, 498
Sensitive
physical, 375
morally, 822
Sensorium
intellect, 450
Sensual
intemperance, 954
libertine, 962
Sensuous
perception, 375
Sentence
phrase, 566
maxim, 496
judgment, 969
condemn, 971
decision, 480
Sententious
concise, 572
pompous, 577
energetic, 574
Sentient
feeling, 375, 821, 822
Sentiment
opinion, 484
maxim, 496
idea, 453
Sentimental
sensibility, 822
affectation, 855
Sentinel
guardian, 664
keeper, 753
watch, 668
Sentry
see Sentinel
Separate
simple, 42
to disjoin, 44, 91, 198
exclude, 55
diverge, 291
divorce, 905

671

Sepia
brown, 433
Sepoy
combatant, 726
Sept
class, 75
Septenary
seven, 98
Septentrional
opposite, 237
Septet
number, 98
Septic
insalubrity, 657
Septuagint
revelation, 985
Septum
partition, 228
Septuple
seven, 98
Sepulchral
sound, 408, 410
Sepulchre
interment, 363
Sepulture
interment, 363
Sequacious
following, 63
servile, 886
Sequel
following, 65
in time, 117
addition, 39
Sequence
in order, 63
in time, 117
motion, 281
Sequester
take, 789
hide, 526
seclude, 893
confiscate, 974
Sequestrate
take, 789
condemn, 971
confiscate, 974
Seraglio
harem, 961
room, 191
Seraph
angel, 977
saint, 948
Seraphic
blissful, 829
virtuous, 944

Seraskier
master, 745
Serenade
music, 415
compliment, 902
Serendipity
windfall, 618
Serene
calm, 826
content, 831
Serf
clown, 876
slave, 746
Serfdom
subjection, 749
Sergeant
master, 745
Seriatim
continuity, 69
order, 59
speciality, 79
continuance, 144
Series
sequence, 69
book, 593
Serio-comic
ridiculous, 853
Serious
great, 31
important, 642
dejected, 837
resolved, 604
Serjeant
judge, 967
Sermon
dissertation, 595
lesson, 537
speech, 582
pastoral, 998
Serosity
fluidity, 333
Serpent
tortuous, 248
Satan, 978
deceiver, 548
cunning, 702
evil, 663
Serpentine
convolution, 248
Serrated
angular, 244
notched, 257
Serried
crowded, 72
dense, 321

Serum
lymph, 333
water, 337
Servant
servant, 711, 746
Serve
aid, 707
obey, 743, 749
work, 625, 680
suffice, 639
Serve out
apportion, 786
punish, 972
Service
good, 618
use, 677
utility, 644
worship, 990
servitude, 749
warfare, 722
Serviceable
useful, 644
good, 648
Servile
obsequious, 886
flattery, 933
Servitor
servant, 746
Servitude
subjection, 749
Sesqui-
number, 87
Sesquipedalia verba
ornament, 577
Sesquipedalian
long, 200
Sessions
legal, 966
council, 696
Sestina
poetry, 597
Set
condition, 7
group, 72
class, 75
firm, 43
to place, 184
establish, 150
prepare, 673
sharpen, 253
solidify, 321
leaning, 278
gang, 712
lease, 796
habitual, 613

Set about
begin, 676
Set apart
disjoin, 55
Set aside
disregard, 460
annul, 756
release, 927A
Set-back
hindrance, 706
adversity, 735
relapse, 661
Set down
humiliate, 879
censure, 932
slight, 929
rebuff, 732
Set fire to
burn, 384
Set foot in
ingress, 294
Set forth
publish, 531
tell, 527
show, 525
assert, 535
describe, 594
Set forward
depart, 293
Set in
begin, 66
tide, 348
approach, 286
Set off
depart, 293
compensate, 30
adorn, 845
Set-off
foil, 14
Set on
attack, 615
Set out
begin, 66
depart, 293
decorate, 845
Set right
reinstate, 660
Set sail
depart, 293
Set-square
angularity, 244
Set-to
combat, 720
Set to work
begin, 676

Set up
raise, 307
prosperous, 734
Set-up
state, 7
structure, 329
plan, 626
Set upon
attack, 716
desire, 865
willing, 602
determined, 604, 620
Setaceous
rough, 256
Settee
support, 215
Setting
surroundings, 227
Settle
decide, 480
be fixed, 141
be stationary, 265
place, 184
dwell, 186
sink, 306
arrange, 60
pacify, 723
defeat, 731
consent, 762
pay, 807
give, 784
bench, 215
Settlement
location, 184
colony, 188
dregs, 653
compact, 762, 769
property, 780
Settler
inhabitant, 188
Seven
number, 98
Seventy-four
ship, 273
Sever
disjoin, 44
Several
repetition, 102
special, 79
Severally
one by one, 44, 79
sharing, 786
Severe
harsh, 739
energetic, 171

painful, 830
unadorned, 576, 849
critical, 932
greatness, 31
Sew
join, 43
Sewer
drain, 295, 350
cloaca, 653
Sex
kind, 75
women, 374
Sex-appeal
charm, 829
Sexagesimal
sixty, 98
Sexcentenary
celebration, 883
Sext
worship, 990
Sextant
angularity, 244
roundness, 247
Sextet
number, 98
Sextodecimo
book, 593
Sexton
church, 996
interment, 363
Sextuple
number, 98
Sforzando
music, 415
Sgraffito
see Graffito
Shabby
mean, 819, 874
bad, 649
disgraceful, 940
trifling, 643
smallness, 32
Shack
abode, 189
Shackle
to tie, 43
hinder, 706
restrain, 751
fetter, 752
Shade
darkness, 421
shadow, 424
colour, 428
degree, 26
difference, 15, 41

small part, 32, 51

Shawl
dress, 225

Sheaf
assemblage, 72

Shear
subduction, 38
take, 789

Shears
sharpness, 253

Sheath
receptacle, 191
envelope, 222

Shed
building, 189
to emit, 297
scatter, 73
diverge, 291

Shed tears
weep, 839

Sheen
light, 420

Sheepfold
enclosure, 232

Sheepish
foolish, 881

Sheep's eyes
ogle, 902

Sheer
vertical, 212
simple, 42
complete, 52
smallness, 32

Sheer off
departure, 293

Sheet
layer, 204
paper, 593

Sheet-anchor
refuge, 666

Sheik
ruler, 745
priest, 996
philanderer, 902

Shelf
support, 215

Shell
cover, 222
arms, 727
attack, 716

Shell out
expend, 809

Shelter
refuge, 666, 717
safety, 664

Shenanigans
caprice, 608

Shelty
horse, 271

Shelve
slope, 217
locate, 184
neglect, 460
relinquish, 624
disuse, 678

Shemozzle
row, 713
contention, 720

Shepherd
director, 694
pastor, 996

Sheriff
jurisdiction, 965

Sherlock Holmes
inquiry, 461

Shibboleth
indication, 550
criterion, 467

Shield
defend, 717
safety, 664
buckler, 666

Shift
move, 264
change, 140, 144
substitute, 147
transfer, 270
expedient, 626, 634
evasion, 546
plea, 617
difficulty, 704
dress, 225

Shifting
transient, 111
moving, 270

Shiftless
unprepared, 674
inhabile, 699, 951

Shifty
dishonest, 544

Shikar
pursuit, 622

Shillelagh
club, 727
impact, 276

Shilly-shally
irresolution, 605

Shilpit
weak, 160

Shimmer

lustre, 420

Shin
climb, 305
kick, 276

Shindig
prank, 840

Shindy
violence, 173
contention, 720
din, 404

Shine
to emit light, 420
glory, 873
beauty, 845

Shintoism
religions, 984

Ship
vessel, 273
to deliver, 270

Shipload
cargo, 31
abundance, 639

Shipment
transference, 270

Shipshape
order, 58
conformity, 82

Shipwreck
failure, 732
to defeat, 731

Shire
county, 181

Shirk
avoid, 623
disobey, 742

Shirt
dress, 225

Shirt-waist
dress, 225

Shirty
angry, 900

Shivaree
uproar, 404

Shiver
shake, 315
cold, 385
layer, 204
fragment, 51
filament, 205
to divide, 44
destroy, 162

Shoal
shallow, 209
assemblage, 72, 102
danger, 667

Shock
  concussion, 276
  violence, 173
  sheaf, 72
  contest, 720
  affect, 821
  move, 824
  pain, 830
  inexpectation, 508
  dislike, 867
  hate, 898
  scandalize, 932
Shocking
  ugly, 846
  vulgar, 851
  fearful, 860
  painful, 830
  considerable, 31
Shoe
  dress, 225
Shogun
  master, 745
Shoogle
  oscillate, 314
Shoot
  propel, 284
  dart, 274
  kill, 361
  grow, 194
  attack, 716
  pain, 378
  offspring, 167
Shoot up
  increase, 35
  ascend, 305
  prominent, 250
Shop
  mart, 799
  buy, 795
  workshop, 691
Shopkeeper
  merchant, 797
Shoplifting
  stealing, 791
Shopman
  merchant, 797
Shopwalker
  director, 694
Shore
  support, 215
  land, 342
  edge, 230
  sewer, 653
Shoreless
  space, 180

Shorn
  deprived, 776
  reduced, 36
Short
  not long, 201
  concise, 572
  incomplete, 53
  unaccomplished, 730
  insufficient, 640
  brittle, 328
  uncivil, 895
Shortfall
  deficit, 204
Short-lived
  youth, 111
Short of
  inferiority, 34
Short-sighted
  myopic, 443
  foolish, 499
Short-tempered
  irascible, 901
Short-witted
  foolish, 499
Shortage
  insufficiency, 640
Shortcoming
  failing, 304
  fault, 651
Shorten
  diminish, 36
Shorthand
  write, 590
Shortly
  soon, 132
Shorts
  dress, 225
Shot
  missile, 284
  weapon, 727
  variegated, 440
  changeable, 149
  guess, 514
Shoulder
  projection, 250
  support, 215
  to shove, 276
Shout
  loudness, 404
  cry, 411
  voice, 580
Shove
  impulse, 276
Shovel
  vehicle, 272

  to transfer, 270
  receptacle, 191
Show
  manifest, 525
  appear, 446, 448
  evince, 467
  demonstrate, 478
  parade, 852, 882
  drama, 599
Show-down
  disclosure, 529
  opportunity, 134
Show of
  similarity, 17
Show up
  accuse, 874, 938
  appear, 446
Shower
  rain, 348
  abundance, 639
  liberality, 816
  assemblage, 72
Showman
  interpreter, 524
Showy
  coloured, 428
  gaudy, 847, 882
  vulgar, 851
Shrapnel
  arms, 727
Shred
  bit, 51
  filament, 205
Shrew
  vixen, 901
Shrewd
  intelligent, 498
  wise, 490
  clever, 698
  cunning, 702
Shriek
  cry, 410, 411
Shrill
  noise, 410
Shrimp
  little, 193
Shrine
  altar, 1000
  interment, 363
Shrink
  shrivel, 195
  narrow, 203
  decrease, 36
  small, 32
  recoil, 287, 898

avoid, 623
unwilling, 603
Shrive
penitence, 950
atonement, 952
Shrivel
decrease, 36
shrink, 195
small, 193
Shroud
funeral, 363
shelter, 666
safety, 664
hide, 528
Shrub
plant, 367
Shrubbery
agriculture, 371
Shrug
hint, 527, 550
dissent, 489
Shrunken
little, 193
Shucks
contempt, 643, 930
Shudder
fear, 860
aversion, 867
hate, 898
cold, 383
Shuffle
mix, 41
disorder, 59
derange, 61
interchange, 148
agitate, 315
toddle, 266, 275
evasion, 544, 546
cunning, 702
irresolution, 605
disgrace, 940
Shuffler
deceiver, 548
Shun
avoid, 623
dislike, 867
Shunt
turn aside, 279
shelve, 460, 678
Shut
close, 261
Shut down
cease, 142
Shut off
disconnect, 44

Shut out
exclude, 55
prohibit, 761
Shut up
enclose, 231
imprison, 751
close, 261
Shut up
confute, 479
Shutter
shade, 424
Shuttlecock
irresolute, 605
Shy
avoid, 623
suspicious, 485
unwilling, 603
modest, 881
fearful, 862
propel, 276, 284
Shylock
usurer, 805
Shyster
knave, 941
Sib
relation, 11
Sibilant
hiss, 409
Sibilation
decry, 929
censure, 932
Sibling
relation, 11
Sibyl
oracle, 513
ugly, 846
Sibylline
prediction, 511
Sic
imitation, 19
word, 562
Sick
ill, 655
tired, 841
Sicken
weary, 841
nauseate, 395
fall ill, 655
disgust, 830, 867
hate, 898
Sickle
instrument, 244
sharpness, 253
Sickly
ill, 655

weak, 160
Sickness
disease, 655
Side
laterality, 236
party, 712
affectation, 855
insolence, 878, 885
Side-car
vehicle, 272
Side-kick
friend, 890
associate, 88
partner, 711
Side-slip
deviation, 279
Side-track
set aside, 678
Side with
aid, 707
Sideboard
receptacle, 191
whisker, 256
Sideburns
whiskers, 256
Sidelight
interpretation, 522
Sidelong
lateral, 236
Sidereal
world, 318
Sideways
oblique, 217
lateral, 236
Sidle
oblique, 217
deviate, 279, 291
lateral, 236
Siege
attack, 716
Siesta
inactivity, 683
Sieve
perforation, 260
to sort, 60
Sift
to sort, 60
winnow, 42
clean, 652
inquire, 461
discriminate, 465
Sigh
lament, 839
Sigh for
desire, 865

Sing out
cry, 411
Sing-song
untuneful, 414
concert, 415
repetition, 104
Singe
burn, 384
Singer
musician, 416
Single
unit, 87
unmixed, 42
secluded, 893
unmarried, 904
Single-handed
unaided, 708
Single-minded
honest, 543
Single out
select, 609
Singlet
dress, 225
Sing Sing
prison, 752
Singspiel
drama, 599
Singular
exceptional, 79, 83
one, 87
remarkable, 31
Sinister
left, 239
bad, 649
discourtesy, 895
menacing, 909
vicious, 945
Sink
descend, 306
lower, 308
submerge, 310
deep, 208
fail, 732
destroy, 162
decay, 659
fatigue, 688
cloaca, 653
depressed, 837
droop, 828
conceal, 528
neglect, 460
in the memory, 505
Sinless
good, 946
Sinner

sinner, 949
impiety, 988
Sinuous
curved, 245
convoluted, 248
Sinus
concavity, 252
Sip
drink, 296
smallness, 32
Siphon
conduit, 350
Sir
respect, 877
Sirdar
master, 745
Sire
elder, 166
Siren
musician, 416
indication, 550
alarm, 669
seducing, 615
sea, 341
demon, 980
evildoer, 913
Sirocco
wind, 349
heat, 382
Sissy
weakness, 160
Sister
kindred, 11
likeness, 17
Sisterhood
assembly, 72
party, 712
Sisyphean
difficulty, 704
Sit
repose, 215
lie, 213
lowering, 308
Site
situation, 183
Sitting
consultation, 696
Situate
location, 184
Situation
circumstances, 8
place, 183
business, 625
Siva
deity, 979

Six
number, 98
Six-shooter
gun, 727
Sixth sense
intuition, 477
Size
magnitude, 31, 192
grade, 60
glue, 45, 352
quantity, 25
Size up
measure, 466
estimate, 480
scrutinize, 457
Sizy
sticky, 350
Sjambok
scourge, 975
Skate
locomotion, 266
Skean
arms, 727
Skedaddle
escape, 671
go away, 293, 287
Skein
knot, 219
disorder, 59
Skeleton
corpse, 362
frame, 626
small, 193
lean, 203
imperfect, 651
essential part, 50
Skelp
impact, 276
punishment, 972
Sketch
painting, 556
description, 594
plan, 626
Sketcher
artist, 559
Sketchy
imperfect, 53, 651
Skew
obliquity, 217
Skew-whiff
oblique, 217
Skewbald
variegation, 440
Skew
vinculum, 45

Ski
locomotion, 266
Skid
deviation, 279
hindrance, 706
Skiff
boat, 273
Skiffle
melody, 413
Skill
ability, 450, 698
Skim
move, 266
rapid, 274
attend lightly, 458, 460
Skimp
shorten, 201
stint, 640
save, 817
Skin
tegument, 222
to peel, 226
Skin-deep
shallow, 220
Skinflint
miser, 819
Skinful
fullness, 52
Skinny
small, 193
slender, 203
tegumentary, 222
Skip
jump, 309
neglect, 460
omit, 773
escape, 671
dance, 840
Skipjack
upstart, 734, 876
Skipper
master, 745
Skirl
shriek, 410, 411
lamentation, 839
Skirmish
fight, 720, 722
Skirt
edge, 230
appendix, 39
pendent, 214
circumjacent, 227
woman, 374
Skirting-board
base, 211

Skit
parody, 856
satire, 932
Skite
boast, 884
Skittish
capricious, 608
bashful, 881
excitable, 825
timid, 862
Skivvy
servant, 746
Skoal
drink, 959
Skulk
hide, 447, 528
coward, 860
flock, 72
Skull
head, 450
Skunk
fetid, 401
bad man, 949
Sky
world, 318
air, 338
summit, 210
Sky-line
outline, 229
Sky-rocket
ascent, 350
Skylark
frolic, 840
Skylight
opening, 260
Skymaster
aircraft, 273A
Skyscraper
height, 206
Slab
layer, 204
flatness, 251
record, 551
Slabber
ejection, 297
Slack
loose, 47
weak, 160
slow, 275
inert, 172
inactive, 683
unwilling, 603
laxity, 738
to moderate, 174
retard, 706

calm, 826
Slacken
relax, 687
Slacker
evasion, 623
Slacks
dress, 225
Slag
refuse, 40
dirt, 653
Slainté
drink, 959
Slake
quench, 174
indulge, 954
gratify, 831, 865
satiate, 869
Slam
shut, 406
slap, 276
Slander
detraction, 934
Slanderer
detractor, 936
Slang
neology, 563
language, 560
Slant
obliquity, 217
Slap
to strike, 276
hit, 972
try, 675
instantaneous, 113
quick, 274
haste, 684
Slapdash
careless, 460
hasty, 684
reckless, 863
Slapstick
drama, 599
Slash
cut, 44
notch, 257
Slashing
vigour, 574
Slat
strip, 205
Slate
writing-tablet, 590
covering, 222
to criticize, 934
Slate-coloured
grey, 432

Slating
  roof, 210
Slattern
  negligent, 460
  dirty, 653
  awkward, 701
Slatternly
  vulgar, 851
  unskilful, 699
Slaughter
  to kill, 361
Slave
  servant, 746
  to toil, 686
Slaver
  slobber, 297
  ship, 273
Slavery
  servitude, 749
Slavey
  servant, 746
Slavish
  imitative, 19
Slay
  kill, 361
Sledge
  vehicle, 272
Sledge-hammer
  impel, 276
  engine, 633
Sleek
  smooth, 255
  pretty, 845
Sleep
  inactivity, 141, 683
  insensibility, 376
Sleeper
  support, 215
  vehicle, 272
Sleeping-bag
  bed, 215
Sleeping-car
  vehicle, 272
Sleepless
  active, 682
Sleepy
  inactive, 683, 823
  slow, 275
  weary, 841
Sleet
  rain, 383
Sleeve
  dress, 225
Sleight
  cleverness, 698

Sleight of hand
  quickness, 146, 545
Slender
  narrow, 203
  small, 32
  trifling, 643
Sleuth-hound
  inquiry, 461
  pursuit, 623
Slice
  layer, 204
  part, 44, 51
  swerve, 279
Slick
  dexterous, 698
  smooth, 255
Slicker
  dress, 225
Slide
  pass, 264
  relapse, 661
  descend, 306
  elapse, 109
  become, 144
  skate, 266
Slide-rule
  numeration, 85
  measurement, 466
Slight
  small, 32
  slender, 203
  tenuous, 322
  trifle, 643
  to neglect, 460, 927
  to dishonour, 929
Slim
  thin, 203
  cunning, 702
Slimy
  viscous, 352
  dirt, 653
Sling
  hang, 214
  project, 284
  weapon, 727
Slink
  recede, 287
  prowl, 528
  escape, 671
Slip
  descend, 306
  strip, 205
  part, 51
  transfer, 270
  fail, 732

  liberate, 750
  workshop, 691
  guilt, 947
  smallness, 32
  dress, 225
  scion, 167
Slip away
  escape, 287, 671, 750
Slip cable
  departure, 293
Slip of tongue
  mistake, 495
  solecism, 568
Slip on
  dress, 225
Slip over
  cover, 460
Slipover
  dress, 225
Slipper
  dress, 225
Slippery
  smooth, 255
  uncertain, 475
  changeable, 149
  dangerous, 665
  not trustworthy, 940
Slipshod
  untidy, 653
  ungrammatical, 568
Slipslop
  affected, 855
  absurd, 497
  style, 573
Slit
  to divide, 44
  chink, 198
  groove, 259
Sliver
  part, 51
  strip, 205
Slobber
  slop, 337
  emit, 297
  soil, 653
Sloe
  colour, 431
Slog
  hit, 277
Slogan
  indication, 550
  defiance, 715
  war, 722
  maxim, 496
Sloop
  ship, 273

Slop
water, 337
insipid, 391
emit, 297
dirt, 653
police, 664

Slope
oblique, 217
flee, 623

Sloppy
wet, 337
disorder, 59
slovenly, 699
maudlin, 822

Slops
dress, 225

Slot
opening, 260
track, 551
degree, 26

Sloth
inactivity, 683
inertness, 172

Slouch
oblique, 217
low, 207
inactive, 683
ugly, 846

Slouch-hat
dress, 225

Slough
difficulty, 704
quagmire, 345
residuum, 40

Sloven
drab, 653
careless, 460
awkward, 699
bungler, 701
vulgar, 851

Slovenly
style, 573
disorder, 59

Slow
sluggish, 275
tardy, 133
dull, 843
wearisome, 841
inert, 172
inactive, 683

Slubberdegullion
knave, 941, 949
commonalty, 876

Sludge

mud, 653

Slug
slow, 275

Sluggard
slow, 275
sleepy, 683

Sluggish
slow, 275
inert, 172
sleepy, 683
callous, 823

Sluice
conduit, 350
outlet, 295
river, 348
to wash, 652

Slum
abode, 189
dirt, 653

Slump
fall, 306

Slur
stigma, 874
gloss, 937
reproach, 938

Slur over
neglect, 460
inattention, 458
conceal, 528
exclude, 55

Slush
pulp, 354
dirt, 653

Slut
hussy, 962

Sluttish
unclean, 653
neglect, 460

Sly
cunning, 702
false, 544

Smack
blow, 27
ship, 273
taste, 390
mixture, 41
small quantity, 32
kiss, 902

Small
in degree, 32
in size, 193

Smaller
inferiority, 34

Smart pain, 378
grief, 828

active, 682
clever, 498, 698
cunning, 702
to feel, 821
witty, 842
neat, 845
fashionable, 852

Smash
destroy, 162
failure, 732

Smashing
pleasing, 829
good, 648

Smatterer
ignoramus, 493

Smattering
ignorance, 491

Smear
daub, 222
ugly, 846
vilify, 483, 932, 934

Smeddum
courage, 861

Smell
odour, 398

Smelt
heat, 384

Smile
risible, 838

Smile upon
approve, 894

Smirch
soil, 653
blacken, 431

Smirk
grin, 838

Smirr
rain, 348

Smite
strike, 276
punish, 972
bad, 694

Smith
workman, 690

Smithereens
fragments, 51

Smithy
workshop, 691

Smitten
love, 897

Smock
dress, 225

Smog
mist, 353
dimness, 422

Smoke
cloud, 334
dimness, 422
heat, 382
trifle, 643
dirt, 653
preserve, 670
Smoke-stack
funnel, 351
Smooth
not rough, 16, 255
to calm, 174
lubricate, 332
easy, 705
to flatter, 933
cunning, 702
Smooth-bore
gun, 727
Smooth-faced
falsehood, 544
Smooth-spoken
falsehood, 544
Smooth-tongued
falsehood, 544
Smother
kill, 361
repress, 174
calm, 826
silence, 581
suppress, 528, 585
Smoulder
burn, 382
inert, 172
latent, 528
Smout
littleness, 193
Smudge
dirt, 653
blemish, 848
Smug
affected, 855
Smuggle
contraband, 791
introduce, 294
Smuggler
thief, 792
Smut
dirt, 653
black, 431
blemish, 848
impurity, 961
Smutch
blacken, 431
Snack
participate, 778

food, 298
Snaffle
restraint, 752
Snag
danger, 667
difficulty, 704
hindrance, 706
sharp, 253
projection, 250
Snail
slow, 275
Snake
miscreant, 913
Snaky
winding, 248
Snap
noise, 406
brittle, 328;
break, 44
be rude, 895, 900
seize, 789
vigour, 574
easy, 705
Snappy
concise, 572
Snare
trap, 667
Snarl
growl, 412
angry, 900
rude, 895
threaten, 909
disorder, 59
Snatch
to seize, 789
opportunity, 134
part, 51
Sneak
servility, 886
basement, 940
to hide, 528
retire, 287
Sneakers
shoes, 225
Sneer
contempt, 930
blame, 932
disparage, 929
Sneeze
snuffle, 409
blow, 349
Snick
part, 51
Snickersnee
weapon, 727

Snide
false, 544
Sniff
odour, 398
Sniff at
despise, 930
Sniffy
contemptuous, 930
Snigger
laugh, 838
Snip
cut, 44
Snip-snap
discord, 713
Sniper
fighter, 726
Snippet
smallness, 32
Snivel
cry, 839
Snivelling
servile, 886
Snob
commonalty, 876
sycophant, 886
Snood
dress, 225
fastening, 45
Snooper
spectator, 444
curiosity, 455
inquire, 461
Snooty
insolence, 885
Snooze
sleep, 683
Snore
noise, 411
sleep, 683
Snort
noise, 411
sleep, 683
drink, 298
Snout
prominence, 250
Snow
ice, 383
white, 430
Snow-shoe
locomotion, 266
Snowball
collection, 72
Snowk
sniff, 398
Snub
bluster, 885

Snub
blame, 932
refuse, 764
abash, 874
short, 201

Snuff
odour, 398
tobacco, 298A

Snuff-box
receptacle, 191

Snuff out
die, 360

Snuff up
inhale, 296

Snuffle
hiss, 409
blow, 349
stammer, 583

Snug
comfortable, 377, 831
safe, 664
latent, 526
secluded, 893

Snuggery
room, 189

Snuggle
draw near, 286
cuddle, 902

So-and-so
euphemism, 565

So-called
miscall, 565

So long
departure, 293

So-so
unimportant, 643
imperfection, 651
smallness, 32
tolerable, 736

Soak
immerse, 300
water, 337
moisture, 339

Soaker
drunkenness, 959

Soap
oil, 356
cleanness, 652

Soapy
unctuous, 355
servile, 886
flattering, 933

Soar
rise, 305

height, 206
great, 31
fly, 267

Sob
weep, 839

Sober
moderate, 174
temperate, 953
abstinent, 958
sane, 502
wise, 498
calm, 826
grave, 837

Sober-minded
wise, 502
calm, 826

Sobranje
council, 696

Sobriquet
misnomer, 565

Sociable
friendly, 892

Social
friendly, 888, 892

Socialism
participation, 778
philanthropy, 910
authority, 737

Society
man, 372
friendly, 892
party, 712
fashion, 852

Sociology
mankind, 372
philanthropy, 910

Sock
stocking, 225
drama, 599

Socket
receptacle, 191, 252

Socrates
sage, 500

Socratic method
quiz, 461

Sod
turf, 344

Soda-water
bubble, 353

Sodality
fraternity, 712
association, 892
friendship, 888

Sodden
wet, 339

overcharged, 641

Sofa
support, 215

Soft
not hard, 324
marshy, 345
moderate, 174
sound, 405
smooth, 255
weak, 160
silly, 499
irresolute, 605
timid, 862
lenient, 740
compassionate, 914
tender, 822

Soft currency
money, 800

Soft mark
dupe, 547

Soften
soothe, 826
mitigate, 834
palliate, 937
subdue, 824

Softy
wool, 501

Soggy
wet, 337

Soi-disant
deceiver, 548
misnomer, 565
boaster, 884

Soil
land, 342
dirt, 653
spoil, 659
deface, 846
tarnish, 848

Soiled dove
courtesan, 962

Soirée
assemblage, 72
reception, 892

Sojourn
abode, 189
inhabit, 186
settle, 265

Sol-fa
melody, 413

Solace
relief, 834
comfort, 827
condolence, 915
recreation, 840

Solar
world, 318
Solatium
recompense, 973
Soldan
master, 745
Solder
cohere, 46
join, 43
cement, 45
Soldier
combatant, 726
warfare, 722
Sole
alone, 87
base, 211
Solecism
ungrammatical, 568
sophistry, 477
Solemn
awful, 873
sacred, 987
grave, 837
pompous, 882
positive, 535
important, 642
Solemnity
parade, 882
rite, 998
dullness, 843
Solemnize
celebrate, 883
Solfeggio
melody, 413
Solicit
induce, 615
request, 765
desire, 865
Solicitor
law, 968
Solicitude
anxiety, 860
care, 459
desire, 865
Solid
complete, 52
dense, 321
certain, 474
true, 494
firm, 604
wise, 498
Solidify
coherence, 46
density, 321
Soliloquy

speech, 589
Solitary
alone, 87
secluded, 893
Solitude
see Solitary
Solmization
melody, 413
Solo
music, 415
Soloist
musician, 416
Solomon
sage, 500
Solon
sage, 500
wise, 498
Soluble
dissolve, 335
Solution
dissolving, 335
explanation, 462
interpretation, 522
Solve
explain, 462
discover, 480A
Solvency
wealth, 803
Somatics
material, 316
Sombre
dark, 421
grey, 432
black, 431
melancholy, 837
Some
a few, 100
Somebody
one, 87
man, 373
celebrity, 873
Somehow
manner, 155
Somersault
inversion, 218
Somerset
inversion, 218
Something
thing, 3
small degree, 32
Sometimes
frequency, 136
Somewhat
small, 32
Somewhere

place, 182
Somnambulism
imagination, 515
Somniferous
sleepy, 683
weary, 841
Somnolence
sleepy, 683
weary, 841
Son
relation, 167
Sonance
sound, 402
Sonata
music, 415
Song
music, 415
Song, old
unimportant, 643
Songster
musician, 416
Soniferous
sound, 402
Sonnet
poetry, 597
Sonorous
sound, 402
loud, 404
Sonsy
fat, 102
Soon
early, 132
transient, 111
Soot
black, 431
dirt, 653
blemish, 846
Sooth
truth, 494
Soothe
allay, 174
calm, 826
relieve, 834
Soothsay
predict, 511
Soothsayer
omen, 513
magician, 994
Sop
bribe, 615
reward, 973
wet, 337
Sophism
bad logic, 477
absurdity, 497

Sophisticate
mix, 41
mislead, 477
debase, 659
Sophistry
false reasoning, 477
misteaching, 538
Sophomore
learner, 541
Sophy
ruler, 745
Soporific
sleepy, 683
boring, 841
Sopping
moist, 339
Soprano
music, 413
high note, 409, 410
Sorcerer
sorcerer, 994
Sorcery
occult arts, 992
Sordes
uncleanness, 653
Sordid
mean, 819
base, 876
Sordine
silencer, 417
damper, 403
Sore
pain, 378
grievance, 828
painful, 830
angry, 900
Sorehead
discourtesy, 895
Sorely
greatness, 31
Sorites
reasoning, 476
Sororicide
killing, 361
Sorrel
redness, 434
Sorrow
pain, 828
Sorry
grieved, 828
penitent, 950
pitiful, 914
bad, 649
mean, 876
trifling, 643

smallness, 32
Sort
kind, 75
degree, 26
rectify, 658, 660
to arrange, 60
simplify, 42
Sortes
chance, 156, 621
prediction, 511
Sortie
attack, 716
Sortilege
sorcery, 992
prediction, 511
chance, 621
Sorting
arrangement, 60
Sostenuto
music, 415
Sot
fool, 501
drunkard, 959
Sotto voce
faintness, 405
aphony, 581
stammering, 583
Sou
money, 800
Soubrette
actress, 599
servant, 746
Sough
conduit, 350
cloaca, 653
wind, 349
Soul
intrinsic, 5
intellect, 450
affections, 820
man, 373
important part, 50, 642
Soulful
feeling, 821
Soulless
insensible, 823
Sound
noise, 402
healthy, 654
perfect, 650
good, 648
great, 31
to measure, 466
to investigate, 461
true, 494

wise, 498
orthodox, 983A
bay, 343
gap, 198
Sounder
herd, 72
Sounding-rod
depth, 208
Soundings
deep, 208
Soundless
deep, 208
silent, 403
Soundly
great, 31
Soup
food, 298
pulp, 354
Soup-and-fish
dress, 225
Soupçon
little, 32, 193
mixture, 41
Sour
acid, 397
uncivil, 895
misanthropic, 901
to embitter, 835
Source
origin, 66, 153
Sourdine
silencer, 417
Souse
immerse, 300
water, 337
Soutane
canonicals, 999
Souteneur
libertine, 962
South
opposite, 237
Souvenir
memory, 505
Sou'wester
dress, 225
Sovereign
great, 31
superiority, 33
strong, 157
ruler, 745
Sovereignty
authority, 737
Soviet
council, 696

Sow
scatter, 73
cultivate, 371
prepare, 673

Sozzled
drunk, 959

Spa
salubrity, 656
remedy, 662

Space
room, 180
separate, 44

Space ship
aircraft, 273A

Space travel
voyage, 267

Spacious
roomy, 180

Spade
sharpness, 253

Spaewife
oracle, 513

Spahi
combatant, 726

Spalpeen
bad man, 949

Span
distance, 196
nearness, 197
length, 200
measure, 466
time, 106
duality, 89

Spandule
demon, 980

Spangle
spark, 420
ornament, 847

Spaniel
servile, 886
flatterer, 935

Spank
impact, 276
beat, 972

Spanking
size, 192

Spar
discord, 713
contention, 720, 722

Spare
meagre, 203
scanty, 640
to give, 784
relinquish, 782
disuse, 678

exempt, 927A
refrain, 623
pity, 914
frugal, 953
economic, 817

Spare
superfluous, 641
in reserve, 636

Spare time
leisure, 685

Sparge
sprinkle, 73

Sparing
temperate, 953
small, 32
economic, 817

Spark
light, 420
fire, 382
fop, 854
court, 902

Sparkle
glisten, 420
bubble, 353

Sparkling
vigorous, 574

Sparse
scattered, 73
tenuous, 322
few, 103

Sparsim
non-assemblage, 73

Spartan
severe, 739

Spasm
fit, 173
throe, 146
pain, 378, 828

Spasmodic
fitful, 139

Spat
quarrel, 713

Spatial
space, 99

Spatter
dirt, 653
damage, 659

Spatterdash
dress, 225

Spatula
layer, 204
trowel, 191

Spawn
dirt, 653
offspring, 167

Spray
sterilize, 169

Speak
speech, 582

Speak fair
conciliate, 615

Speak of
mean, 516

Speak to
allocution, 586

Speak out
disclose, 529

Speaker
speech, 582
teacher, 540
interpreter, 524
president, 745

Spear
lance, 727
to pierce, 260
pass through, 302

Spearman
combatant, 726

Special
particular, 79
peculiar, 5

Special pleading
sophistry, 477

Specialist
adviser, 695
doctor, 662
proficient, 700

Speciality
intrinsic, 5
particular, 79

Specie
money, 800

Species
kind, 75
appearance, 448

Specific
special, 79

Specification
description, 594

Specify
name, 564
tell, 527

Specimen
example, 82

Specious
probable, 472
sophistical, 477
plausible, 937

Speck
dot, 193

small quantity, 32
blemish, 848
Speckle
variegated, 400
blemish, 848
Spectacle
appearance, 448
show, 882
prodigy, 872
Spectacles
optical instrument, 445
Spectator
spectator, 444
Spectre
vision, 448
ugly, 846
ghost, 980
Spectroscope
optical, 445
colour, 428
Spectrum
colour, 428
appearance, 448
Speculate
think, 451
suppose, 514
chance, 621
venture, 675
traffic, 794
view, 441
Speculum
mirror, 445
Speech
speech, 582
Speechless
silence, 581
Speed
velocity, 274
activity, 682
haste, 684
to help, 707
succeed, 731
Speedometer
velocity, 274
measure, 466
Speedwalk
way, 627
Speer
ask, 461
Spell
interpret, 522
read, 539
period, 106
charm, 993
necessity, 601

motive, 615
exertion, 686
Spellbound
motive, 615
Spelling
letters, 561
Spencer
dress, 225
Spencerism
causation, 153
Spend
expend, 809
waste, 638
Spendthrift
prodigal, 818
Spent
exhausted, 688
Spermaceti
oil, 356
Spew
ejection, 297
Sphere
ball, 249
region, 181
world, 318
rank, 26
business, 625
Spheroid
round, 249
Spherule
round, 249
Sphinx
oracle, 513
monster, 83
Spice
small quantity, 32
mixture, 41
pungent, 392
condiment, 393
Spick and span
clean, 123
Spicule
sharp, 253
Spidery
narrowness, 203
Spiflicate
trounce, 972
Spike
to pierce, 260
plug, 263
pass through, 302
sharp, 253
Spile
stopper, 263
Spill

filament, 205
fuel, 388
to shed, 297
waste, 638
splash, 348
disclose, 529
lavish, 818
misuse, 679
fall, 306
Spin
rotation, 312
excursion, 266
velocity, 274
reject, 610
Spin out
prolong, 200
protract, 110, 133
style, 573
Spindle
rotation, 312
Spindle-shanked
thin, 193, 203
Spindrift
spray, 353
Spine
sharpness, 253
Spineless
vicious, 945
weak, 160
irresolute, 605
Spinet
musical instrument, 417
Spinney
plant, 367
Spinster
celibacy, 904
Spiracle
air-pipe, 351
Spiral
convolution, 248
Spire
peak, 253
height, 206
soar, 305
Spirit
essence, 5
immateriality, 317
intellect, 450
affections, 820
resolutions, 604
courage, 861
ghost, 980
style, 576
activity, 682
to stimulate, 824

Spirit-level
  horizontal, 213
Spirited
  brave, 861
  generous, 942
Spiritless
  torpid, 823
  dejected, 837
  timid, 862
Spirits
  cheerfulness, 836
  intoxicant, 959
Spiritual
  immaterial, 317
  mental, 450
  divine, 976
  piety, 987
Spiritualism
  occult arts, 992
Spirituel
  witty, 842
Spirituoso
  music, 415
Spirt
  see Spurt
Spissitude
  density, 321, 352
Spit
  eject, 297
  pierce, 302
  rain, 348
  bar, 253
Spite
  malevolence, 907
  enmity, 889
  notwithstanding, 179
Spitfire
  fury, 173, 901
Spittle
  excretion, 299
Spittoon
  receptacle, 191
Spiv
  knave, 941
  bad man, 949
  cheat, 548
  swindler, 792
Splanchnic
  interior, 221
Splash
  affuse, 337
  spill, 348
  spatter, 653
  sully, 846
  parade, 882

  publicity, 531
Splatter
  wet, 337
Splay
  angularity, 244
Splay-footed
  distorted, 243
Spleen
  melancholy, 837
  hatred, 898
  anger, 900
  discourteous, 895
Spleenless
  good-natured, 906
Splendid
  beautiful, 845
  glorious, 873
  excellent, 648
Splendour
  light, 420
Splenetic
  sad, 837
  ill-tempered, 895
  irascible, 901
Splice
  join, 43
  entwine, 219
  marry, 903
Splinter
  divide, 44
  brittle, 328
  bit, 51, 205
Split
  divide, 44, 91
  quarrel, 713
  fail, 732
  laugh, 838
Split hairs
  argue, 465
  sophistry, 477
Split-new
  new, 123
Splosh
  money, 800
Splurge
  ostentation, 882
Splutter
  stammer, 583
  haste, 684
  energy, 171
  spitting, 297
Spoil
  vitiate, 659
  hinder, 706
  plunder, 791

  booty, 793
  injure, 649
  indulge, 740
  satiate, 869
Spoke
  tooth, 253
  radius, 200
  obstruct, 706
Spokesman
  interpreter, 524
  speaker, 582
Spoliate
  plunder, 791
  evil, 619
Spondulicks
  money, 800
Sponge
  clean, 652
  despoil, 791
  porous, 322
  oblivion, 506
  petitioner, 767
  parasite, 886
Spongy
  soft, 324
Sponsion
  security, 771
Sponson
  support, 215
Sponsor
  security, 771
  evidence, 467
Spontaneous
  voluntary, 600, 602
  free, 748
  impulsive, 612
Spoof
  deception, 545
Spook
  ghost, 980
Spoon
  receptacle, 191
  ladle, 272
  club, 276
  to make love, 902
Spoonerism
  blunder, 495
  inversion, 218
  ridiculousness, 853, 856
Spoonful
  quantity, 25
Spoony
  fool, 499
  amorous, 897

689

Spoor
track, 551
Spore
particle, 330
Sporran
pouch, 191
Sport
amusement, 840
gaiety, 836
wit, 842
enjoyment, 827
contention, 720
subjection, 749
abnormality, 83
Sports car
vehicle, 272
Sportsman
courage, 861
game, 840
good man, 948
Spot
place, 182
decoloration, 429
blemish, 848
to sully, 846
blot, 874
disgrace, 940
to detect, 457, 480A
Spotless
innocent, 946
clean, 652
good, 648, 650
fair, 845
Spotty
spotted, 440
Spousals
marriage, 903
Spouse
married, 903
companion, 88
Spouseless
celibacy, 904
Spout
conduit, 350
egress, 295
flow out, 348
speak, 582
act, 599
Sprain
strain, 160
Sprawl
lie, 213
leap, 309
Spray
sprig, 51
plant, 367

cover, 222
sprinkle, 337
sprinkler, 348
Spread
enlarge, 35
expand, 194
disperse, 73
diverge, 291
expanse, 180
publish, 531
Spread-eagleism
boasting, 884
bombast, 577
Spree
frolic, 840
intemperance, 954
Sprig
part, 51
scion, 167
Sprightly
cheerful, 836
witty, 842
Spring
early, 125
cause, 153
arise from, 154
ensue, 151
strength, 159
velocity, 274
leap, 309
rivulet, 348
instrument, 633
store, 636
Spring back
elastic, 325
recoil, 277
Spring tide
flow, 348
abundance, 639
Spring up
grow, 194
Springe
snare, 667
deception, 545
Sprinkle
mix, 41
disperse, 73, 291
omit, 297
wet, 337
Sprinkler
spray, 348
Sprinkling
smallness, 32
little, 193
Sprint

velocity, 274
Sprite
ghost, 890
Sprocket
tooth, 257
Sprog
recruit, 674
Sprout
grow, 35
expand, 194
arise from, 154
offspring, 167
Spruce
neat, 652
beautiful, 845
Spry
active, 682
healthy, 654
clever, 698
cheerful, 836
Spume
foam, 353
Spunk
courage, 861
Spur
sharp, 253
incite, 615
ridge, 250
Spurious
false, 544
erroneous, 495
illegitimate, 925
Spurn
disdain, 866, 930
refuse, 764
Spurt
impulse, 612
haste, 684
swift, 274
gush, 348
Sputnik
space ship, 273A
Sputter
emit, 297
stammer, 583
Spy
see, 441
spectator, 444
emissary, 534
Spy-glass
optical instrument, 445
Squab
large, 192
short, 201
broad, 202

recumbent, 215

Squabble
quarrel, 713

Squabby
broad, 202
short, 201

Squad
assembly, 72

Squadron
navy, 726
army, 273
assemblage, 72

Squadron-leader
master, 745

Squalid
dirty, 653
unattractive, 846

Squall
cry, 411
win, 349
violence, 173

Squalor
see Squalid

Squamous
scaly, 204
covering, 222

Squander
waste, 638, 818

Squandermania
waste, 818

Square
number, 95
buildings, 189
congruity, 23
expedience, 646
justice, 924
honour, 939
form, 244
prig, 855
to equalize, 27
to bribe, 784, 795

Square-toes
butt, 857

Squash
destroy, 162
check, 706
throw, 276
soft, 324
water, 337

Squashy
pulpy, 352

Squat
to encamp, 186
sit, 308
short, 201

broad, 202
flat, 213
ugly, 846

Squatter
inhabitant, 188

Squatting
horizontal, 213

Squaw
marriage, 903

Squawk
cry, 411, 412
complain, 839

Squeak
cry, 411, 412
complain, 839

Squeal
cry, 410, 411, 412
blab, 529
complain, 839

Squeamish
fastidious, 868
censorious, 932

Squeeze
contract, 195
narrow, 203
condense, 321
extort, 789
copy, 21

Squeeze out
extraction, 301

Squelch
squash, 162

Squib
sound, 406
lampoon, 932

Squiffy
drunk, 959

Squiggle
convolution, 248

Squint
dim-sighted, 443
look, 441

Squire
gentry, 875
possessor, 779
attendant, 746

Squirm
wriggle, 315

Squirrel
velocity, 274

Squirt
eject, 297
spurt, 348

Stab
pierce, 260

attack, 716
kill, 361
injure, 649, 659

Stable
house, 189
at rest, 265
immutable, 150
resolute, 604

Stable-boy
servant, 746

Staccato
music, 415

Stack
assembly, 72

Stadtholder
master, 745

Staff
support, 215
instrument, 633
weapon, 727
impact, 276
sceptre, 747
retinue, 746
party, 712
hope, 858

Stage
degree, 26
term, 71
step, 58
layer, 204
forum, 542
vehicle, 272
arena, 728
drama, 599

Stage effect
drama, 599
ostentation, 882

Stage-play
the drama, 599

Stager, old
proficient, 700

Stagger
totter, 314
slow, 275
agitate, 315
doubt, 485
dissuade, 616
affect, 824
astonish, 508, 870

Stagnant
quiescent, 265
unchanging, 141
insert, 172
inactive, 683

Stagy
  affected, 855
  ostentatious, 882
Staid
  steady, 604
  calm, 826
  wise, 498
  grave, 837
Stain
  colour, 428
  adorn, 847
  deface, 846
  blemish, 848
  spoil, 659
  disgrace, 874
  dishonour, 940
Stainless
  clean, 652
  innocent, 946
Stair
  way, 627
Stake
  wager, 621
  payment, 807
  danger, 665
  security, 771
  property, 780
  execution, 975
Stalactite
  lining, 224
Stalagmite
  lining, 224
Stale
  old, 124
  vapid, 866
  weary, 841
Stalemate
  non-completion, 730
Stalk
  follow, 266
  pursue, 622
Stalking-horse
  plea, 617
  deception, 545
Stall
  lodge, 189
  mart, 799
  theatre, 599
  cathedral, 1000
  delay, 133
Stallion
  horse, 271
Stalwart
  strong, 159
  large, 192
Stamina

strength, 159
resolution, 604
Stammel
  redness, 434
Stammer
  stutter, 583
Stamp
  character, 7
  form, 240
  mould, 22
  to impress, 505
  mark, 550
  record, 551
  complete, 729
  security, 771
Stampede
  flight, 287
  fear, 860, 862
Stance
  footing, 175
Stanch
  dam up, 348
  stop, 658
Stanchion
  support, 215
Stand
  to be, 1
  rest, 265
  be present, 186
  to continue, 141, 143
  endure, 110
  station, 58
  rank, 71
  support, 215
  resistance, 719
Stand against
  resist, 719
Stand by
  near, 197
  be firm, 604
  befriend, 707
  auxiliary, 711
Stand for
  represent, 550
  signify, 516
Stand-in
  substitute, 147, 634
  deputy, 759
  assistant, 711
Stand in with
  participation, 778
Stand off
  distance, 196, 287
Stand-offish
  unsociable, 893

Stand on
  support, 215
Stand out
  project, 250
  appear, 446
  opposition, 708
Stand still
  stop, 265
  remain, 141
Stand over
  lateness, 133
Stand up
  vertical, 212
  elevation, 307
  disappoint, 509
Stand up for
  vindicate, 937
Stand up to
  courage, 861
Standard
  rule, 80
  measure, 466
  degree, 26
  pupil, 541
  colours, 550
  good, 648
  prototype, 22
Standard-bearer
  combatant, 726
Standardize
  conformity, 82
Standing
  footing, 8
  term, 71
  situation, 183
  degree, 26
  repute, 873
  vertical, 212
Standpoint
  aspect, 453
Stanza
  poetry, 597
Staple
  whole, 50
  peg, 214
  mart, 799
Star
  luminary, 423
  decoration, 877
  ornament, 847
  glory, 873
  actor, 599, 599A
Star Chamber
  jurisprudence, 966
Star-gazer

astronomer, 318
Starbeam
   light, 420
   dimness, 422
Starbord
   dextrality, 238
Starch
   viscidity, 352
Starchy
   stiff, 323
   proud, 878
   affected, 855
Stare
   look, 441
   curiosity, 455
   wonder, 870
Staring
   visible, 446
Stark
   stiff, 323
   stubborn, 606
Starless
   dark, 421
Starlight
   light, 420
   dimness, 422
Stars
   celestial, 318
   necessity, 601
Stars and Stripes
   flag, 550
Start
   depart, 293
   begin, 66
   desultory, 139
   jump, 139
   arise, 151
   suggest, 514
   from surprise, 508
   from fear, 860
   from wonder, 870
Start up
   project, 250
   appear, 446
Starting-point
   beginning, 66
   departure, 293
Startle
   unexpected, 508
   wonder, 870
   fear, 860
   doubt, 485
Starve
   fast, 956
   with cold, 383, 385

want, 804
Starved
   lean, 193
   insufficient, 640
Starveling
   pinched, 203
   poor, 804
   famished, 540
State
   condition, 7
   nation, 372
   ostentation, 882
   property, 780
   to inform, 527
   assert, 535
   describe, 594
State trooper
   police, 965
Stateless
   displaced, 185
Stately
   pompous, 882
   proud, 878, 873
Statement
   information, 527
   assertion, 535
Stateroom
   chamber, 191
Statesman
   master, 745
Statesmanship
   direction, 694
Statics
   gravity, 319
Station
   stage, 58
   term, 71
   place, 182, 183
   to locate, 184
   stopping-place, 292
   rank, 26, 873
Stationary
   quiecence, 265
Stationery
   writing, 590
Statist
   statesman, 745
Statistics
   numeration, 85
   list, 86
Statue
   sculpture, 557
   representation, 554
Stature
   height, 206

Status
   standing, 8, 71
   situation, 183
   order, 58
   rank, 873
Status quo
   reversion, 145
Statute
   law, 697, 963
Staunch
   spirited, 604
   trusty, 939
   healthy, 654
Stave
   verse, 597
Stave in
   open, 260
   concavity, 252
Stave off
   defer, 133
Stay
   wait, 133
   continue, 141
   exist, 1
   support, 215
   refuge, 666
   rest, 265;
   prevent, 706
   dissuade, 616
   corset, 225
Stead
   utility, 644
Steadfast
   resolved, 604
   stable, 150
   quiescent, 265
   thought, 451
Steading
   farm, 189
Steady
   resolved, 604
   cautious, 864
   still, 265
   constant, 138, 150
   normal, 82
Steady as she goes
   caution, 864
Steal
   rob, 791
   creep, 275, 528
Steal away
   evade, 671
Stealth
   concealment, 528

Steam
  vapour, 334, 353
  to sail, 267
Steamboat
  ship, 273
Steamer
  ship, 273
Steam-roller
  compel, 744
Stearic
  unctuous, 355
Stearin
  fat, 356
Steed
  horse, 271
Steek
  close, 261
Steel
  strength, 159
  sharpener, 253
  inure, 823
Steel-cut
  engraving, 558
Steeled
  resolved, 604
Steelyard
  scale, 466
  weight, 319
Steep
  slope, 217
  height, 206
  immerse, 300
  soak, 337
  clean, 652
Steeple
  spire, 253
  high, 206
Steeplechase
  race, 274
  pursuit, 282, 622
Steer
  guide, 693
Steer for
  direction, 278
Steersman
  director, 694
Steganography
  writing, 590
Stegophilist
  climber, 305
Stele
  record, 551
Stellar
  heavens, 318
Stem
  origin, 153

  result, 154
  front, 234
  to oppose, 708
  to resist, 718
Sten
  gun, 727
Stench
  fetor, 401
Stencil
  copy, 556
Stenographer
  secretary, 553
Stenography
  writing, 590
Stentorian
  loud, 404
Step
  degree, 26
  station, 58
  term, 71
  near, 197
  support, 215
  motion, 264, 266
  measure, 466
  expedient, 626
  means, 632
  action, 680
Steppe
  plain, 344
Stepping-stone
  link, 45
  way, 627
  preparation, 763
  resource, 666
Stercoraceous
  unclean, 653
Stereoscope
  optical, 445
Stereoscopic
  visible, 446
Stereotype
  printing, 591
  engraving, 558
Stereotyped
  ordinary, 82
  habitual, 613
  fixed, 141, 150
Sterile
  unproductive, 169
  useless, 645
  clean, 652
Sterling
  true, 494
  good, 648
  virtuous, 944

  money, 800
Stern
  back, 235
  severe, 739
  forbidding, 895
Stern-wheeler
  ship, 273
Sternutation
  sneeze, 349
  sound, 409
Sternway
  navigation, 267
Stertorous
  sound, 411
Stet
  unchanged, 150
Stetson
  hat, 225
Stevedore
  doer, 271, 690
Stew
  confusion, 59
  fluster, 821
  difficulty, 704
  heat, 382
  cook, 384
  perplex, 828
  bagnio, 961
Steward
  director, 694
  agent, 690
  treasurer, 801
Stewardship
  charge, 693
  conduct, 692
. **Stick**
  adhere, 46
  stop, 142
  continue, 143
  staff, 215
  to stab, 260, 830
  pierce, 302
  difficulty, 704
  fool, 501
  scourge, 975
Stick at
  demur, 603
Stick in
  insert, 300
  locate, 184
Stick-in-the-mud
  inactivity, 683
Stick out
  project, 250
  erect, 212

Stick up
project, 250
erect, 212, 307
rob, 791
Stickit
failure, 732
Stickle
haggle, 769
barter, 794
reluctant, 603
Stickler
obstinacy, 606
severity, 739
Sticky
cohering, 46
semiliquid, 352
Stiff
rigid, 323
resolute, 604
difficult, 704
restrained, 751
severe, 739
dear, 814
affected, 855
haughty, 878
pompous, 882
ugly, 846
style, 572, 579
Stiff-necked
obstinate, 606
resolute, 604
Stifle
silence, 403
conceal, 528
destroy, 162
kill, 361
sound, 405
Stigma
disgrace, 874
blame, 932
Stigmatize
accuse, 938
Stile
way, 627
Stiletto
piercer, 262
dagger, 727
Still
ever, 112
silent, 403
quiet, 174
quiescence, 265
photograph, 556
calm, 826
notwithstanding, 179

compensation, 30
vaporizer, 336
Still-born
failure, 732
dead, 360
Stilted
bombastic, 577
affected, 855
Stilts
support, 215
height, 206
journey, 266
boasting, 884
Stimulate
incite, 615
violence, 173
energize, 171
passion, 824
Stimulus
zest, 615
Sting
pain, 378
sensation, 380
pungent, 392
suffering, 824, 830
provoke, 900
Stingy
mean, 817
Stink
stench, 401
Stinkard
stink, 401
Stinking
bad, 649
Stinko
drunk, 959
Stint
degree, 26
limit, 233
scanty, 640
parsimony, 819
Stipend
salary, 809
Stipendiary
receiving, 785
subjected, 749
magistrate, 967
Stipple
engraving, 558
variegation, 440
Stipulate
conditions, 770
bargain, 769
Stir
move, 264

agitation, 315
activity, 682
energy, 171
emotion, 824
discuss, 476
prison, 752
Stir up
mix, 41
excite, 615
violence, 173
Stirrup-cup
departure, 293
intoxicant, 959
Stitch
work, 680
to join, 43
pain, 828
Stiver
money, 800
Stock
cause, 153
store, 636
materials, 635
provision, 637
property, 780
money, 800
merchandise, 798
collar, 225
offspring, 166
relation, 11
quantity, 25
habitual, 613
Stock-still
immovable, 265
Stockade
defence, 717
Stocking
dress, 225
Stockpile
store, 636
provide, 637
Stocks
funds, 802
punishment, 975
restraint, 752
Stocky
short, 201
broad, 202
Stoic
insensible, 823
inexcitable, 826
disinterested, 942
Stole
dress, 225

Stolid
dull, 843
stupid, 499
Stomach
pouch, 191
taste, 390
liking, 865
Stomacher
dress, 225
Stone
dense, 321
hard, 323
materials, 635
missile, 284
weapon, 727
kill, 361
Stone-blind
blind, 442
Stone-coloured
grey, 432
Stone-wall
hinder, 706
Stonk
bombardment, 716
Stony broke
poor, 804
Stony-hearted
cruel, 900
Stooge
substitute, 147
assistant, 711
deputy, 759
loaf, 683
Stook
assemblage, 76
Stool
support, 215
Stool-pigeon
deceiver, 548
informer, 527, 529
Stoop
bow, 308
slope, 217
humble, 879
servile, 886
porch, 191
Stoor
see Stour
Stop
close, 67, 261
halt, 265
lodge, 186
prevent, 706
silence, 403
continue, 141
discontinue, 142

Stopcock
stopper, 263
Stopgap
shift, 626
substitute, 634
Stopgap
deputy, 759
plug, 263
Stopper
stopper, 263
Store
magazine, 636
provision, 637
shop, 799
the memory, 595
greatness, 31
Storehouse
store, 636
Storey
layer, 204
rooms, 191
Στοργή, love, 897
Storm
wind, 349
violence, 173
agitation, 315
passion, 825
convulsion, 146
anger, 900
to attack, 716
assemblage, 72
Storm-stayed
hindered, 706
restraint, 751
Story
narrative, 582, 594
news, 532
lie, 546
Stot
rebound, 277
Stound
wonder, 870
Stour
dust, 330
dirt, 653
Stout
strong, 159
lusty, 192
brave, 861
Stove
furnace, 386
Stow
locate, 184
desist, 142

Stow it
silent, 585
Stowage
space, 180
location, 184
Strabismus
dim sight, 443
Straddle
sit, 215
stride, 266
trim, 607
Stradivarius
violin, 417
Strafe
punish, 972
maltreat, 649
attack, 716
Straggle
stroll, 266
deviate, 279
disjunction, 44
disorder, 59
Straggler
rover, 268
Straight
rectilinear, 246
vertical, 212
direction, 278, 628
undiluted, 42
Straightforward
artless, 703
honest, 939
true, 543
style, 576
mid-course, 628
Straightway
time, 111
Strain
effort, 686
violence, 173
fatigue, 688
sound, 402
melody, 413
clean, 652
to clarify, 658
percolate, 295
transgress, 304
poetry, 597
voice, 580
misinterpret, 523
kindred, 11
style, 569
Strainer
sieve, 260

Strait
 maritime, 343
 gap, 198
 difficulty, 704
 want, 804
 narrow, 203
Strait-laced
 severe, 739
 censorious, 932
 haughty, 878
 stiff, 751
 fastidious, 868
Strait waistcoat
 restraint, 752
Straitened
 poor, 804
Stramash
 agitation, 315
 contention, 720
Strand
 shore, 342
Stranded
 difficulty, 704
 fixed, 150
 failure, 732
Strange
 exceptional, 83
 wonderful, 870
 ridiculous, 853
Stranger
 extraneous, 57
 ignorant, 491
Strangle
 choke, 361
Strap
 to tie, 43
 ligature, 45
 scourge, 975
Strap-oil
 punishment, 972
Strappado
 punishment, 972
Strapping
 large, 192
 strong, 159
Stratagem
 plan, 626
 artifice, 702
 deception, 545
Strategy
 conduct, 692
 skill, 698
 warfare, 722
 plan, 626
Strath

 valley, 252
Strathspey
 dance, 840
Stratification
 layer, 204
Stratocracy
 authority, 737
Stratocruiser
 aircraft, 273A
Statoliner
 aircraft, 273A
Stratosphere
 air, 338
Stratum
 layer, 204
Straw
 light, 320
 trifling, 643
Straw-coloured
 yellow, 436
Straw vote
 inquiry, 461
Stray
 wander, 266
 deviate, 279
 exceptional, 83
Streak
 colour, 420
 stripe, 440
 furrow, 259
 narrow, 203
 intersection, 219
Stream
 flow, 347
 river, 348
 of light, 420
 of time, 109
 of events, 151
 abundance, 639
Streamer
 flag, 550
Streaming
 incoherent, 47
Streamlet
 river, 348
Street
 buildings, 189
 way, 627
Street arab
 commonalty, 876
Street-car
 vehicle, 272
Streetscape
 spectacle, 448
Streetwalker

 libertine, 962
Strength
 vigour, 159
 power, 157
 greatness, 31
 energy, 171
 tenacity, 327
 degree, 26
Strengthen
 to increase, 35
Strenuous
 active, 682, 686
 resolved, 604
Strepitoso
 music, 415
Stress
 weight, 642
 intonation, 580
 strain, 686
Stretch
 increase, 35
 expand, 194
 lengthen, 200
 space, 180
 distance, 196
 exertion, 686
 encroachment, 925
 misinterpret, 523
 exaggeration, 549
Stretcher
 vehicle, 272
 support, 215
Strew
 spread, 73
Stria
 spot, 440
 furrow, 259
Striate
 furrowed, 259
 spotted, 440
Stricken
 hurt, 828
Strict
 severe, 739
 exact, 494
Stricture
 disapprobation, 932
Stride
 walk, 266
 motion, 264
Strident
 harsh, 410
Stridulous
 shrill, 410
Strife
 quarrel, 713, 720

Strike
hit, 276
luck, 618
beat, 649, 972
revolt, 719, 742
inaction, 681
impress, 824
wonder, 870
operate, 170
music, 415

Strike off
exclude, 55

Strike out
invent, 515
plan, 626
efface, 552

Strike up
begin, 66

Striking
manifest, 525

String
continuity, 69
to tie, 43
fibre, 205
ligature, 45
to arrange, 60

String up
kill, 361

Stringendo
music, 415

Stringent
severe, 739
compulsory, 744

Stringy
narrow, 203
tough, 327
viscous, 352

Strip
to divest, 226
rob, 789, 791
narrowness, 203
filament, 205

Stripe
length, 200
blow, 972
mark, 550
type, 75
variegation, 440

Stripling
youth, 129

Stripped
poor, 804

Strive
exert, 686

endeavour, 675, 676
contend, 720

Stroke
impulse, 276
mark, 550
work, 680
expedient, 626
success, 731
disease, 655

Stroll
walk, 266

Strong
powerful, 159
energetic, 171
vigorous, 574
tenacious, 327
pungent, 390, 392
cogent, 467
feeling, 821

Strong-box
treasury, 802

Strong-room
treasury, 802

Strong-willed
resolute, 604

Stronghold
defence, 717
refuge, 666
prison, 752

Strongly
great, 31

Strop
sharpen, 253
rub, 331

Strophe
poetry, 597

Structure
state, 7
texture, 329
building, 189

Struggle
contend, 720
exert, 686

Strum
music, 415

Strumpet
libertine, 962

Strut
parade, 882
boast, 884
pride, 878
support, 215

Stub
part, 51
end, 67

check, 550

Stubble
remainder, 40
rough, 256

Stubborn
obstinate, 606
unmanageable, 704

Stubby
short, 201
broad, 202
ugly, 846

Stucco
cement, 45
covering, 222

Stuck fast
difficulty, 704
stopped, 265

Stuck-up
vanity, 880

Stud
knob, 250
hanging, 214
point, 253
horses, 271

Studded
spotted, 440

Student
learner, 541
scholar, 492

Studied
intentional, 620

Studio
workshop, 691

Studious
thoughtful, 451
docile, 539

Studiously
purposely, 600

Study
thought, 451
learning, 539
research, 461
privacy, 893
intention, 620
copy, 21
music, 415

Stuff
substance, 3, 329
matter, 316
materials, 632
absurdity, 497
trifle, 643
to feed, 296
to line, 224
cram, 104

hoax, 545
Stuffing
contents, 190
Stuffy
musty, 401
hot, 382
Stultified
failure, 732
Stultify
counteract, 708
muddle, 699
Stultiloquy
absurdity, 497
Stumble
fall, 306
fail, 732
unskilful, 699
flounder, 315
Stumble upon
ascertain, 480A
Stumbling-block
difficulty, 704
hindrance, 706
Stumer
money, 800
Stump
trunk, 51
remnant, 40
to step, 266
speech, 582
Stumped
penniless, 804
Stumpy
short, 201
ugly, 846
Stun
stupefy, 376, 823
affect, 824
deafen, 419
astonish, 508, 865
loud, 404
Stunning
beauty, 845
Stung
pain, 828
Stunt
feat, 680
task, 625
Stunted
small, 193
contracted, 195
Stupefy
stun, 376, 823
wonder, 870
Stupendous

great, 31
large, 192
wonderful, 870
Stupid
dull, 843
credulous, 486
foolish, 499
Stupor
lethargy, 823
insensibility, 376
Sturdy
strong, 157, 159
Stutter
stammer, 583
Sty
dirt, 653
pen, 189
Stygian
infernal, 982
dark, 421
diabolic, 945
Style
state, 7
time, 114
fashion, 852
taste, 850
beauty, 845
to name, 564
diction, 569
pencil, 559
Stylet
arms, 727
Stylish
fashionable, 852
Stylist
style, 569
Stylite
recluse, 893
Stylograph
writing, 590
Stymie
to hinder, 706
Styptic
remedy, 662
contracting, 195
Suasion
persuade, 615
Suavity
courtesy, 894
Sub
loan, 787
advance, 809
Sub judice
inquiry, 461
Subacid

acid, 397
Subahdar
master, 745
Subalpine
height, 206
Subaltern
plebeian, 876
inferior, 24
officer, 726, 745
Subaqueous
depth, 208
Subastral
terrestrial, 318
Subcommittee
committee, 696
Subconsciousness
intellect, 450
Subcontrary
antiposition, 237
Subcutaneous
interiority, 221
Subdeacon
church, 996
Subdean
church, 996
Subdititious
substitution, 147
Sublimation
see Sublimate
Sublime
high, 206
beauty, 845
glory, 873
lofty, 574
magnanimous, 942
Subliminal
subconscious, 450
Sublunary
world, 318
Submachine-gun
arms, 727
Submarine
depth, 208
ship, 273
Submerge
immerse, 300
steep, 337
sink, 162, 208
plunge, 310
Submission
surrender, 725, 879
Submissive
humble, 725, 879
enduring, 826

Submit
surrender, 725
obey, 743
Subordinate
inferior, 34
unimportant, 643
servant, 746
subjection, 749
Subordination
order, 58
Suborn
hire, 795
bribe, 784
Subpoena
mandate, 741
Subscribe
assent, 488
agree to, 762, 769
give, 707, 784
Subscription
donation, 809
Subsequent
in time, 117
in order, 63, 65
Subservient
utility, 644
intermediate, 631
aiding, 707
servility, 886
Subside
sink, 306
cave in, 252
decrease, 36
calm down, 826
Subsidiary
tending, 176
means, 632
auxiliary, 707
Subsidy
pay, 809
gift, 784
aid, 707
Subsist
existence, 1
life, 359
continuance, 141
Subsistence
food, 298
livelihood, 803
Subsistence money
loan, 787
advance, 809
Subsoil
earth, 342
interior, 221
Substance

thing, 3
matter, 316
interior, 221
quantity, 25
texture, 329
compendium, 596
meaning, 516
important, 642
wealth, 803
Substantial
dense, 321
existence, 1
true, 494
Substantially
intrinsically, 5
Substantiate
demonstrate, 478
make good, 494, 924
Substantive
substance, 3
Substitute
means, 634
deputy, 759
Substitution
change, 147
Substratum
substance, 3
interior, 221
layer, 204
base, 211
support, 215
materiality, 316
Subsumption
inclusion, 76
Subterfuge
lie, 546
sophistry, 477
cunning, 702
Subterranean
underground, 208
Subtilize
sophistry, 477
Subtle
cunning, 702
wise, 498
rare, 322
light, 320
texture, 329
Subtract
retrench, 38
diminish, 36
arithmetical, 84
to take, 789
Subtrahend
deduction, 38

number, 84
Suburban
environs, 227
distance, 197
Subvention
aid, 707
gift, 784
Subvert
invert, 218
depress, 308
change, 140
destroy, 162
Subway
road, 627
Succedaneum
substitute, 147, 634
Succeed
answer, 731
follow, 63
Succès d'estime
approbation, 931
Success
success, 731
Succession
sequence, 63
transfer, 783
continuity, 69
of time, 109
lateness, 117
Successor
sequel, 65
posterior, 117
Succinct
concise, 572
Succour
help, 707
Succubus
demon, 980
Succulent
juicy, 333
edible, 298
semiliquid, 352
Succumb
yield, 725
obey, 743
fatigue, 688
Such
similarity, 17
Suck
imbibe, 296
deprive, 789
Sucker
dupe, 547
Suckling
youth, 129

Suction
  imbibition, 296
Sudatorium
  furnace, 386
Sudden
  early, 132
  abrupt, 508
  transient, 111
Suds
  froth, 353
Sue
  demand, 765
  at law, 969
Suet
  fat, 356
Suffer
  physical pain, 378
  moral pain, 828
  to endure, 821
  to allow, 760
  disease, 655
  experience, 151
Sufferance
  permission, 760
Sufficient
  enough, 639
Suffix
  sequel, 65
  adjunct, 39
Sufflation
  wind, 349
Suffocate
  choke, 361
Suffragan
  church, 996
Suffrage
  vote, 609
  prayer, 990
Suffragist
  dueness, 924
Suffuse
  mix, 41
  feel, 821
  blush, 874
Sufism
  religions, 984
Sugar
  sweet, 396
  to flatter, 933
Sugarloaf
  convexity, 250
Suggest
  suppose, 514
  advise, 695
  inform, 527

  recall, 505
  occur, 451
Suggestio falsi
  equivocalness, 520
  falsehood, 544
Suggestion
  plan, 626
Suggestive
  impure, 961
Sui generis
  special, 79
  unconformity, 83
Sui juris
  freedom, 748
Suicide
  kill, 361
Suit
  accord, 23
  class, 75
  expedient, 646
  series, 69
  clothes, 225
  courtship, 902
  at law, 969
Suit-case
  receptacle, 191
Suite
  series, 69
  adjunct, 39
  sequel, 65
  retinue, 746
Suiting
  accord, 23
Suitor
  love, 897
Sulcated
  furrow, 259
Sulky
  discourteous, 895
  bad-tempered, 901
  gloomy, 837
Sullen
  discourteous, 895
  bad-tempered, 901
  gloomy, 837
  misanthropical, 911
Sully
  deface, 846
  dirty, 653
  dishonour, 874, 940
Sulphur
  colour, 436
Sultan
  master, 745
  noble, 875

Sultry
  heat, 382
Sum
  total, 50
  number, 84
  to reckon, 85
  money, 800
Sum up
  description, 594
Sumless
  infinity, 105
Summary
  transient, 111
  early, 132
  concise, 572
  compendium, 201, 596
Summation
  numeration, 85
Summer
  heat, 382
  support, 215
Summer-house
  abode, 189
Summit
  top, 210
  climax, 33
Summon
  command, 741
  accuse, 938
Summon up
  evoke, 824
Sump
  marsh, 345
  sink, 653
Sumptuary
  expenditure, 800, 809
Sumptuous
  ostentation, 882
Sun
  luminary, 423
Sun-bonnet
  dress, 225
Sun-up
  morning, 125
Sunbeam
  light, 420
Sundae
  food, 298
Sunday
  rest, 685
Sunder
  disjoin, 44
Sundown
  evening, 126

Sundowner
 tramp, 268, 876
 loafer, 683
Sundries
 oddments, 51
Sundry
 multitude, 102
Sunk
 low, 208
 vice, 945
Sunless
 dark, 421
Sunlight
 light, 420
 cheerful, 836
 pleasing, 827
 prosperous, 734
Sunny
 see Sunlight
Sunshade
 shade, 424
Sunshine
 see Sunlight
Sup
 eat, 296
 drink, 298
Super
 good, 648
Superable
 facility, 705
Superabundant
 sufficient, 641
Superadd
 addition, 37
 increase, 35
Superannuated
 age, 128
Superannuation
 pension, 803
Superb
 proud, 845
Supercargo
 overload, 694
Supercherie
 deception, 545
Supercilious
 haughty, 878
 insolent, 885
 contemptuous, 929
Superdreadnought
 ship, 273
Supereminence
 repute, 873
Supererogation
 uselessness, 645
 superfluity, 641

 activity, 682
Superexalted
 repute, 873
Superexcellent
 goodness, 648
Superfetation
 addition, 37
Superficial
 shallow, 209, 220
 ignorant, 491
Superficies
 face, 220
Superfine
 best, 648
Superfluity
 excess, 641
 remainder, 40
Superfortress
 aircraft, 273A
Superhuman
 divine, 976
 perfect, 650
 great, 31
Superimpose
 cover, 220
Superincumbent
 above, 206
 weight, 319
 resting, 215
Superinduce
 production, 161
 change, 140
 addition, 37
Superintend
 direction, 693
Superintendent
 director, 694
Superior
 greater, 33
 important, 642
 good, 648
Superlative
 perfect, 650
 great, 31
Superman
 hero, 948
Supernal
 lofty, 206
Supernatant
 overlying, 206
Supernatural
 deity, 976
 spiritual, 317
Supernumerary
 redundant, 641

 remaining, 40
 actor, 599
Superpose
 addition, 37
 cover, 222
Superscription
 mark, 550
 writing, 590
 evidence, 467
Supersede
 disuse, 678
 substitute, 147
Superstition
 credulity, 486
 heresy, 984A
Superstratum
 exteriority, 220
Superstructure
 completion, 729
Supertax
 tax, 812
Supervacaneous
 useless, 645
 redundant, 641
Supervene
 happen, 151
 succeed, 117
 addition, 37
Supervise
 direction, 693
Supervisor
 director, 694
Supine
 horizontal, 213
 inverted, 218
 inert, 172
 sluggish, 683
 torpid, 823
 indifferent, 866
Supper
 food, 298
Supplant
 substitution, 147
Supple
 soft, 324
 servile, 886
Supplement
 adjunct, 39
 completion, 52
 addition, 37
Suppletory
 addition, 37
Suppliant
 petitioner, 767
Supplicant

petitioner, 767
Supplicate
 beg, 765
 pity, 914
 worship, 990
Supplies
 materials, 635
 aid, 707
Supply
 give, 784
 provide, 637
 store, 636
Support
 sustain, 215
 operate, 170
 evidence, 467
 aid, 707
 preserve, 670
 endure, 821, 826
Supporter
 prop, 215
Suppose
 supposition, 514
Supposing
 provided, 469
Supposition
 supposition, 514
Supposititious
 false, 544, 925
 non-existing, 2
Suppository
 remedy, 662
Suppress
 conceal, 528
 silence, 581
 destroy, 162
Suppurate
 fester, 653
Supra
 priority, 116
Supranatural
 spiritual, 317
Supremacy
 superior, 33
 authority, 737
 summit, 210
Supremely
 great, 31
Surcease
 cessation, 142
Surcharge
 redundance, 641
 dearness, 814
Surcingle
 fastening, 45

Surd
 number, 84
Sure
 certain, 474
 assent, 488
 consent, 762
 safe, 664
Sure-footed
 careful, 459
 skilful, 698
Surely
 wonder, 870
Surety
 security, 771
 evidence, 467
Surf
 foam, 353
 tide, 458
Surf-riding
 navigation, 267
Surface
 exterior, 220
Surfeit
 satiety, 869
 redundance, 641
Surge
 ocean, 341
 rotation, 312
 swell, 305
 wave, 348
Surgery
 remedy, 662
Surly
 gruff, 895
 unkind, 907
Surmise
 supposition, 514
Surmount
 rise, 305
 tower, 206
 overcome, 731
Surmountable
 facility, 705
 possible, 470
Surname
 nomenclature, 564
Surpass
 superior, 33
 grow, 194
 go beyond, 303
 repute, 873
Surpassing
 greatness, 31
Surplice
 gown, 225

canonical, 999
Surplus
 remainder, 40
 store, 326
 redundance, 641
Surprise
 wonder, 870
 non-expectation, 508
 disappoint, 509
Surprisingly
 great, 31
Surrealist
 artist, 559
Surrebutter
 lawsuit, 969
 reply, 462
Surrejoinder
 lawsuit, 969
 reply, 462
Surrender
 submit, 725
 obey, 743
 relinquish, 782
Surreptitious
 false, 544
 furtive, 528
Surrogate
 consignee, 758
 deputy, 634, 759
Surround
 circumjacence, 227, 231
Surtout
 dress, 225
Surveillance
 care, 459
 direction, 693
Survey
 view, 441
 measure, 466
Survive
 remain, 40
 continue, 141
 endure, 110
Susceptible
 liable, 177
 impressible, 822
 excitable, 901
Suscitate
 cause, 153
 produce, 161
 induce, 615
 excite, 825
 stir up, 173
Suspect
 doubt, 485

suppose, 514
Suspend
hang, 214
continue, 141
discontinue, 142
defer, 133
stop, 265
Suspense
doubt, 485
uncertainty, 475
expectancy, 507
hesitation, 603
irresolution, 605
Suspicion
doubt, 485
incredulity, 487
uncertainty, 475
fear, 860
particle, 32, 193
mixture, 41
Suspiration
lamentation, 839
Sustain
support, 215
strengthen, 159
aid, 707
operate, 170
preserve, 670
continue, 143
Sustenance
food, 298
Sustentation
provision, 637
Susurration
whisper, 405
Sutler
trader, 797
provision, 637
Suttee
religion, 991
burning, 384
killing, 361
Suture
joint, 43
Suzerainty
authority, 737
Svelte
lissom, 324
Swab
cleanness, 562
dry, 340
Swaddle
dress, 225
Swag
hang, 214

lean, 217
oscillation, 314
drop, 306
booty, 793
Swag-bellied
wollen, 194
Swagger
boast, 884
bluster, 885
smart, 845
Swaggerer
blusterer, 887
Swagman
tramp, 268
Swain
rustic, 876
Swallow
gulp, 296
believe, 484
destroy, 162
Swamp
marsh, 345
destroy, 162
Swamped
failure, 732
Swan-song
end, 67
death, 360
Swank
ostentation, 882
boasting, 884
pride, 878
affectation, 855
Swap
interchange, 148
barter, 794
Sward
plain, 344
Swarm
crowd, 72
sufficiency, 639
multitude, 102
to climb, 305
Swarthy
black, 431
Swash
spurt, 348
affuse, 337
Swashbuckler
fighter, 726
Swastika
cross, 219
Swat
blow, 276
Swatch

part, 51
Swathe
clothe, 225
fasten, 43
Sway
power, 157
influence, 175
authority, 737
induce, 615
oscillate, 314
agitate, 315
Sweal
calefaction, 384
Swear
promise, 768
affirm, 535
malediction, 908
Sweat
transude, 348
heat, 382
excretion, 299
labour, 686
to fatigue, 688
Sweater
dress, 225
Sweep
space, 180
degree, 26
curve, 245
rapidity, 274
clean, 652
displace, 185
destroy, 162
devastation, 619, 649
blackguard, 949
Sweeping
wholesale, 50
complete, 52
indiscriminate, 465A
Sweepings
refuse, 653
trifle, 643
Sweet
saccharine, 396
agreeable, 829
lovely, 897
melodious, 413
Sweetheart
love, 897
Sweetie
sweetheart, 897
Sweetmeat
sweet, 396
Swell
increase, 35

expand, 194, 202
bulge, 250
tide, 348
fop, 854
personage, 875
emotion, 821, 824
extol, 931
swagger, 885
good, 648
Swell mob
thief, 792
Swelled head
vanity, 880
Swelling
bombastic, 577
Swelter
heat, 382
Swerve
deviate, 279
diverge, 291
irresolution, 605
tergiversation, 607
Swift
velocity, 274
Swig
drink, 296
tope, 959
Swill
drink, 296
tope, 959
Swim
float, 305
navigate, 267
vertigo, 503
Swim in
abound, 639
Swim-suit
dress, 225
Swimming
successful, 731
buoyant, 320
Swimmingly
easily, 705
prosperously, 734
Swindle
peculate, 791
cheat, 545
Swindler
defrauder, 792
sharper, 548
Swing
space, 180
hang, 214
play, 170
oscillate, 314

rhythm, 138, 413
freedom, 748
Swinge
punish, 972
Swingeing
great, 31
Swinish
intemperance, 954
gluttony, 957
Swink
work, 686
Swipe
blow, 276
Swish
hiss, 409
Switch
scourge, 975
shift, 279
whisk, 311, 315
Switchback
obliquity, 217
Swivel
hinge, 312
cannon, 727
Swivel-eye
squint, 443
Swollen
proud, 878
expanded, 194
Swoon
fainting, 160
inactivity, 683
fatigue, 688
Swoop
seizure, 789
descent, 306
Swop
see Swap
Sword
arms, 722, 727
sharpness, 253
Swordsman
combatant, 726
Swot
to study, 539
scholar, 492
Sybarite
intemperance, 954
Sybo
condiment, 393
Sycophant
servility, 886
assent, 488
adulation, 933
flatterer, 935

Syllable
word, 561
Syllabus
list, 86
compendium, 596
Syllogism
logic, 476
Sylph
sprite, 979
Sylvan
woody, 367
Symbol
sign, 550
metaphor, 521
mathematical, 84
Symmetry
form, 252
order, 58
beauty, 845
equality, 27
Sympathy
kindness, 906
love, 897
friendship, 888, 891
pity, 914
Symphonic
harmony, 413
Symphony
music, 415
Symposium
feast, 299
festivity, 840
discussion, 461
Symptom
sign, 550
Synagogue
temple, 1000
Synchronism
time, 120
Syncopate
shorten, 201
Syncopation
rhythm, 413
Syncope
cut, 160
conciseness, 572
Syncretism
heresy, 984A
Syndic
master, 745
Syndicalism
participation, 778
Syndicate
partnership, 712, 797
co-operation, 709

Synecdoche
  metaphor, 521
  substitution, 147
Synod
  council, 696
  church, 995
  assemblage, 72
Synonym
  nomenclature, 564
  identity, 13
Synonymous
  equal, 27
  interpretation, 522
Synopsis
  arrangement, 60
  compendium, 596
Synovia
  lubricant, 332
Syntax
  grammar, 567
Synthesis
  combination, 48
  reasoning, 476
Synthetic
  imitation, 19
Syphon
  see Siphon
Syren
  see Siren
Syringe
  spray, 348
Syrup
  sweet, 396
Systaltic
  pulse, 314
System
  order, 58, 60
  plan, 626
Systole
  pulse, 314
  contraction, 195
Syzygy
  contiguity, 199

T.N.T.
  arms, 727
T-square
  angularity, 244
T.V.
  radio, 599ʙ
Ta
  thanks, 917
Ta ta
  departure, 293

Tab
  adjunct, 39
Tabby
  variegated, 440
Tabernacle
  temple, 1000
Tabid
  morbid, 655
  shrivelled, 195
  noxious, 649
Table
  stand, 215
  layer, 204
  flatness, 251
  list, 86
  record, 551
  repast, 298
Table-cloth
  covering, 222
Table-d'hôte
  food, 298
Table-talk
  talk, 588
Table-turning
  occult, 992
Tableau
  painting, 556
  scene, 824
Tableland
  plain, 344
  flat, 213
Tablet
  record, 551
  layer, 204
  flatness, 251
Taboo
  spell, 992, 993
  prohibition, 761
Tabor
  music, 417
Tabouret
  support, 215
Tabula rasa
  oblivion, 506
Tabulate
  arrange, 60, 69
  register, 86
Tace
  silence, 403
Tachometer
  velocity, 274
Tachygraphy
  writing, 590
Tacit
  hidden, 526

Taciturn
  silent, 585
Tack
  direction, 278
  nail, 45
  to turn, 279
  change course, 140
Tack to
  add, 37
  join, 43
Tackle
  gear, 633
  fastening, 45
  to undertake, 676
  encounter, 720
  impact, 276
Tacky
  sticky, 46
Tact
  skill, 698
  wisdom, 498
  taste, 850
  discrimination, 465
Tactician
  proficient, 700
Tactics
  conduct, 692
  plan, 626
  skill, 698
  warfare, 722
Tactile
  touch, 379
Taction
  touch, 379
Tactless
  foolish, 499
  discourteous, 895
Tactual
  touch, 379
Tadpole
  young, 129
Tag
  add, 37, 39
  fastening, 45
  part, 51
  smallness, 32
  end, 67
  sequel, 65
  point, 253
  maxim, 496
Tail
  end, 67
  back, 235
  adjunct, 37, 214
  sequel, 65

follow, 281, 461
Tailor
dress, 225
Tailpiece
rear, 235
sequel, 65
end, 67
adjunct, 39
Taint
disease, 655
decay, 659
dirt, 653
stink, 401
fault, 651
disgrace, 874
Taintless
pure, 652
Take
to appropriate, 789
receive, 785
eat, 296
believe, 484
understand, 518
please, 829
Take aback
surprise, 508, 870
Take after
similarity, 17
Take away
remove, 38, 789
Take back
retract, 607
Take care
caution, 864
Take down
swallow, 296
note, 551
lower, 308
humiliate, 879
Take effect
agency, 170
Take heed
attention, 457
Take hold
taking, 789
Take in
include, 64
· admit, 296
realize, 450
understand, 518
cheat, 545
Take it
believe, 484
suppose, 514
Take off

remove, 185
divest, 226
imitate, 19
personate, 554
ridicule, 856
jump, 305
Take on
anger, 837
undertake, 676
Take out
extract, 301
obliterate, 552
Take part with
aid, 707
Take place
happen, 151
Take root
dwell, 186
Take tent
care, 459
Take the mickey out of
ridicule, 856
Take to
like, 827
Take up
inquire, 461
Take up with
sociality, 892
Take wing
departure, 293
Taking
vexation, 828
anger, 900
acquisition, 775
pleasing, 829, 897
Tale
narrative, 582, 594
counting, 85
Tale-teller
tell, 534
Talebearer
tell, 534
Talent
skill, 698
intellect, 450
intelligence, 498
Talisman
spell, 993
Talk
speak, 582
rumour, 532
conversation, 588
Talkative
talk, 584
prolix, 573

Talkie
cinema, 599A
Tall
height, 206
Tallboy
receptacle, 191
Tallow
fat, 356
Tally
agreement, 23
numeration, 85
record, 551
check, 550
Talmud
revelation, 985
Talons
claw, 633
authority, 737
Talus
slope, 217
Tam-o'-shanter
hat, 225
Tambourine
music, 417
Tame
inert, 172
moderate, 174
feeble, 575
calm, 826
domesticate, 370
teach, 537
Tamis
strainer, 260
Tammy
hat, 225
Tamper with
change, 140
meddle, 682
bribe, 615
Tan
yellow, 433
to thrash, 972
Tandem
journey, 266
sequence, 69
Tang
taste, 390
Tangent
contiguity, 199
Tangible
touch, 379
real, 1
material, 316
Tangle
derange, 61

Tangled
disordered, 59
matted, 219
Tango
dance, 840
Tank
recipient, 191
reservoir, 636
fighter, 726
arms, 727
vehicle, 272
Tankard
receptacle, 191
Tanker
ship, 273
Tanner
money, 800
Tantalize
entice, 615
disappoint, 509
tease, 830
tempt, 865
Tantalus
receptacle, 191
desire, 865
Tantamount
equal, 27
identical, 13
synonymous, 516
Tantara
loudness, 404
roll, 407
Tantrum
passion, 900
excitability, 825
Taoism
religions, 984
Tap
hit, 276
opening, 260
channel, 350
plug, 263
noise, 406
to let out, 297
to intercept, 789
Tape
joint, 45
Tape recorder
mechanical instruments, 417
Taper
narrow, 203
sharp, 253
candle, 423
Tapestry

art, 556
ornament, 847
Taps
signal, 550
Tar
mariner, 269
semiliquid, 352
Taradiddle
untruth, 546
Tarantella
dance, 840
Tardy
dilatory, 133
slow, 275
Tare and tret
discount, 813
Target
object, 620
laughing-stock, 857
Tariff
price, 812
Tarn
lake, 343
Tarnish
discoloration, 429
deface, 846
spoil, 659
dirt, 653
disgrace, 874, 940
Tarpaulin
covering, 222
Tarry
remain, 110
continue, 141
late, 133
expect, 507
rest, 265
Tart
acid, 397
rude, 895
irascible, 901
courtesan, 962
Tartan
dress, 225
variegated, 440
ship, 273
Tartar
irascible, 901
Tartarus
hell, 982
Tartuffe
hypocrite, 544, 548
impiety, 989
Task
business, 625

to put to use, 677
function, 644
Taskmaster
director, 694
Tassel
ornament, 847
pendant, 214
Taste
sapidity, 390
to experience, 821
discrimination, 850
small quantity, 32
Tasteless
vapid, 391
unattractive, 866
Tasty
savoury, 394
delicious, 829
Tat
knit, 43
Tâtonnement
trial, 463
Tatter
part, 51
Tatterdemalion
commonalty, 876
Tattle
talk, 588
Tattler
newsmonger, 532
Tattoo
roll, 407
variegate, 440
Taunt
reproach, 938
ridicule, 856
hoot, 929
Tautology
repetition, 104
identity, 13
diffusiveness, 573
Tavern
inn, 189
Tawdry
vulgar, 851
colour, 428
Tawny
yellow, 436
brown, 433
Tax
impost, 812
to accuse, 938
require, 765
impose, 741
employ, 677

Taxi
vehicle, 272

Tea
food, 298

Tea-gown
dress, 225

Tea-room
food, 298

Teach
teaching, 537

Teach-in
lecture, 595

Teachable
learning, 539

Teacher
instructor, 540

Team
group, 69
party, 712

Teamster
director, 694

Tear
separate, 44
destroy, 162
violence, 173
move rapidly, 274
weeping, 839

Tear out
extract, 301

Tease
annoy, 830

Teaser
poser, 533, 704

Teat
convexity, 250

Technique
skill, 698
musical, 415

Technology
skill, 698

Techy
see Tetchy

Teddy bear
plaything, 840

Teddyboy
bad man, 913, 949

Tedium
fatigue, 841

Teem
abound, 639
numerous, 102
productiveness, 168

Teeming
assemblage, 72

Teenager

youngster, 129

Teeny-weeny
little, 193

Teepee
abode, 189

Teeter
oscillate, 314

Teetotalism
sobriety, 958
temperance, 953

Teetotum
rotation, 840

Tegument
covering, 222

Telecast
radio, 599B

Teledu
stink, 401

Telegenic
radio, 599B

Telegnosis
occult, 992

Telegraph
signal, 550
news, 532

Telegraphic
concise, 572
velocity, 274

Telekinesis
occult, 992
thought, 451

Teleology
intention, 620

Telepathy
occult, 992
thought, 451

Telephone
hearing, 418
news, 532

Teleprompter
radio, 599B

Telescope
optics, 445

Teleview
radio, 599B

Television
publication, 531
radio, 599B

Tell
inform, 527
count, 85
influence, 175
speak, 582
describe, 594

Tell of

mean, 516

Tell off
count, 85
reprimand, 932

Telltale
evidence, 467
divulge, 529

Telly
radio, 599B

Temerity
rashness, 863

Temper
nature, 5
state, 7
elasticity, 323
affections, 820
to moderate, 174
soften, 324, 826
prepare, 673
irascibility, 901

Temperament
nature, 5
tendency, 176
disposition, 820
music, 413

Temperance
moderation, 953

Temperate
moderate, 174
mild, 826

Temperature
heat, 382

Tempest
violence, 173
wind, 349
agitation, 315
excitement, 825

Tempestivity
occasion, 134

Temple
church, 1000
side, 236

Tempo
melody, 413

Temporal
transient, 111
material, 316
laical, 997

Temporary
transient, 111

Temporize
cunning, 702
policy, 698
diuturnity, 110
delay, 133

Terrier
list, 86
Terrific
frightful, 830
great, 31
Terrify
affright, 860
Territory
region, 181
realm, 780
Terror
fear, 860
Terrorist
enemy, 891
evildoer, 913
Terse
concise, 572
Tertian
periodicity, 138
Tertiary
triality, 92
Tertium quid
difference, 15
mixture, 41
Terza rima
poetry, 597
three, 92
Tessara
four, 95
Tessellated
variegation, 440
Test
experiment, 463
Test-tube
receptacle, 191
Testament
revelation, 985
Tester
support, 215
Testify
evidence, 467, 560
Testimonial
record, 551
gift, 784
Testimony
evidence, 467
Testy
irascible, 901
rude, 895
Tetchy
irascible, 901
Tête-à-tête
duality, 89
chat, 588
Tether

fasten, 43
moor, 265
restrain, 751
Tetrad
number, 95
Tetragon
four, 95
Tetrahedron
angularity, 244
four, 95
Tetralogy
four, 95
Tetrarch
master, 745
Text
meaning, 516
prototype, 22
theme, 454
printing, 591
Text-book
lesson, 537
synopsis, 596
Texture
condition, 7
fabric, 329
roughness, 256
Thalassic
ocean, 341
Thalassotherapy
remedy, 662
Thalia
the drama, 599
Thane
master, 745
Thankful
gratitude, 916
Thankless
ingratitude, 917
painful, 830
Thanks
gratitude, 916
worship, 990
Thatch
cover, 210
Thaumatrope
optical, 445
Taumaturgy
occult arts, 992
Thaw
melt, 335
heat, 384
mollify, 826
relent, 914
Theatre
drama, 599

arena, 728
school, 542
spectacle, 441
amusement, 840
Theatrical
ostentatious, 882
affected, 855
Theft
steal, 791
Theism
piety, 987
Theme
topic, 454
dissertation, 595
music, 415
Themis
right, 922
Then
time, 121
Thence
cause, 155
departure, 293
Thenceforth
time, 121
Thenceforward
time, 121
Theocratic
deity, 976
Theodolite
angle, 244
Theology
theology, 983
Theopathy
piety, 987
Theorbo
musical instrument, 417
Theorem
proposition, 535
Theorise
suppose, 514
Theory
knowledge, 490
attribution, 155
Theosophy
theology, 983
Therapeutics
remedy, 662
There
place, 186
Thereabouts
nearly, 32
near, 197
Thereafter
time, 117
Thereby
instrumentality, 631

Therefore
reasoning, 476
attribution, 155
motive, 615
Therein
interiority, 221
Thereof
relation, 9
Thereupon
posteriority, 117
Therewith
accompany, 88
Theriac
remedy, 662
Thermal
heat, 382
Thermometer
heat, 382, 389
Thersites
envy, 921
Thesaurus
store, 636
words, 562
Thesis
theme, 454
dissertation, 595
affirmation, 535
Thespis
drama, 599
Thetis
ocean, 341
Theurgy
occult arts, 992
Thew
strength, 159
Thick
broad, 202
dense, 321
semiliquid, 352
turbid, 426
dirty, 653
numerous, 102
Thick-coming
frequent, 136
Thick-skinned
insensitive, 376, 823
Thicket
plant, 367
Thief
robber, 792
Thievery
stealing, 791
Thimble
instrument, 633

Thimbleful
littleness, 193
smallness, 32
Thin
small, 193
narrow, 203
rare, 322
scanty, 640
few, 103
to subduct, 38
Thin-skinned
sensitive, 375, 872
Thing
substance, 3, 316
event, 151
parliament, 696
Thingumbob
trifle, 643
euphemism, 565
Think
cogitate, 451
believe, 484
Think of
intend, 620
Think out
plan, 626
Think upon
remember, 505
Thinker
reasoning, 476
sage, 500
Third degree
inquiry, 461
Third part
number, 94
Third-rate
imperfect, 651
Thirdly
number, 93
Thirst
desire, 865
Thisness
speciality, 79
Thistle
sharpness, 253
Thistledown
light, 320
Thither
direction, 278
Thole
feeling, 821
Thong
join, 45
Thor
god, 979

Thorn
sharp, 253
painful, 830
pain, 378
Thorny
difficult, 704
Thorough
completeness, 52
Thorough-bass
music, 413
Thorough-going
greatness, 31
Thorough-paced
great, 31
complete, 52
Thoroughbred
manners, 852
Thoroughly
great, 31
Thorp
abode, 189
Though
counteraction, 179
compensation, 30
opposition, 708
evidence, 468
Thought
reflection, 451
maxim, 496
small quantity, 32, 193
idea, 453
Thoughtful
reflecting, 451
wise, 498
Thoughtless
incogitant, 452
careless, 460
foolish, 499
improvident, 674
unskilful, 699
Thousand
number, 98
Thowless
inactive, 683
Thraldom
slavery, 749
Thrall
slave, 746
Thrapple
air-pipe, 351
Thrash
beat, 972
Thrash out
inquire, 461

Thrasonical
boast, 884
Thread
tie, 45
filament, 205
continuity, 69
file, 60
to pass through, 302
Thread one's way
journey, 266
experiment, 463
Threadbare
bare, 226
imperfect, 651
Threat
threaten, 909
Threaten
future, 121
doom, 152
alarm, 669
danger, 665
Three
number, 92
Three-master
ship, 273
Threefold
number, 93
Threnody
lament, 830
Thresh
see Thrash
Threshold
beginning, 66
Thrice
number, 93
Thrift
success, 731
prosperity, 734
economy, 817
Thriftless
prodigal, 818
Thrill
touch, 379
affect, 821, 824
Thriller
story, 594
Thrilling
tingling, 380
charming, 829
Thrive
succeed, 731
prosper, 734
health, 654
Throat
opening, 260

air-pipe, 351
Throb
agitate, 315
emotion, 821
Throe
violence, 173
agitation, 146, 315
pain, 378, 828
Throne
seat, 215
abode, 189
authority, 747
Throng
assembly, 72
Throttle
seize, 789
occlude, 261
suffocate, 361
Through
passage, 302
instrument, 631
owing to, 154
end, 66
Throughout
totality, 50
time, 106
Throw
propel, 284
eject, 297
exertion, 686
Throw away
lose, 776
relinquish, 782
Throw-back
reversion, 145
Throw down
destroy, 162
overthrow, 308
Throw in
add, 300
Throw off
eject, 297
do with ease, 705
Throw over
desert, 624
Throw up
resign, 757
desert, 624
Thrum
music, 415
Thrush
musician, 416
Thrust
push, 276
eject, 297

attack, 716
Thrust in
insert, 300
interpose, 228
Thud
noise, 406
Thug
thief, 792
bad man, 949
Thuggism
killing, 361
Thumb
finger, 379
Thumb-nail
little, 193
Thumbscrew
scourge, 975
Thump
beat, 276
punish, 972
noise, 406
Thumping
great, 31
Thunder
noise, 404
roar, 411
violence, 173
threaten, 909
Thunder-box
toilet, 191, 653
Thunder-storm
violence, 173
Thunder-struck
awe, 870
Thunderbolt
prodigy, 872
Thunderclap
prodigy, 872
Thundering
size, 192
Thurible
rite, 998
Thus
reasoning, 470
Thus far
smallness, 32
Thwack
beat, 276
punish, 972
Thwart
obstruct, 706
intersect, 219
Tiara
diadem, 747
ornament, 847

canonicals, 999

Tick
sound, 407
oscillation, 314
indicate, 550
credit, 805

Tick off
reprimand, 932

Ticket
indication, 550
permission, 760
plan, 626

Tickle
touch, 380
please, 377, 829
laugh, 838

Tickled
amused, 827

Ticklish
difficult, 704
uncertain, 475
dangerous, 665

Tiddly
drunk, 959

Tide
ocean, 341
flood, 348
abundance, 639

Tidings
news, 532

Tidy
clean, 652
trim, 673

Tie
relation, 9
fasten, 43, 45
security, 771
equality, 27
obligation, 926
contention, 720

Tie-beam
support, 215

Tier
continuity, 69
layer, 204

Tiff
discord, 713
anger, 900

Tiffin
food, 298

Tiger
violence, 173
courage, 861
servant, 746
wretch, 913

miscreant, 949

Tight
fast, 43
closed, 261
smart, 845
drunk, 959

Tight-lipped
taciturn, 585

Tike
commonalty, 876

Tile
covering, 222
hat, 225

Till
to cultivate, 371
coffer, 191, 802
up to the time, 108

Tilt
slope, 217
tumble, 306
cover, 222

Tilt at
attack, 716

Tilt over
obliquity, 218

Timber
materials, 635

Timbre
music, 413

Timbrel
musical instrument, 417

Time
period, 106

Time-ball
indication, 550

Time-server
servility, 886
apostate, 941
cunning, 702
expedient, 646
irresolution, 605
versatile, 607
selfish, 943

Time-worn
old, 124
exhausted, 659

Timelessness
never, 107

Timely
early, 132
opportune, 134

Timepiece
chronometer, 114

Timid
fearful, 860

cowardly, 862
humble, 881

Timon of Athens
recluse, 893

Timorous
see Timid

Timpanist
musician, 416

Tin
money, 800
to preserve, 670

Tin hat
defence, 717

Tin-opener
open, 260

Tinct
colour, 428

Tincture
mixture, 41
to colour, 428

Tinder
burn, 388

Tine
sharpness, 253

Ting
ring, 408

Tinge
colour, 428
mix, 41

Tingle
pain, 378, 828
feeling, 821

Tingling
titillation, 380

Tink
resonance, 408

Tinker
improve, 658

Tinkety-tonk
departure, 293

Tinkle
resonance, 408
faint sound, 405

Tinsel
ornament, 847
glitter, 420
display, 882
tawdry, 851
false, 544

Tint
colour, 428

Tintinnabulation
resonance, 408

Tiny
little, 32

small, 193

Tip
summit, 210
end, 67
hint, 527
to give, 784, 809
reward, 973
of iceberg, 193

Tippet
dress, 225

Tipple
drink, 296, 298
drunkenness, 959

Tipstaff
police, 965

Tipsy
drunk, 959

Tiptoe
high, 206
curiosity, 455

Tiptop
summit, 210
first-rate, 648

Tirade
disapproval, 932
declamation, 582

Tire
weary, 841
worry, 830
fatigue, 688

Tiresome
wearisome, 841

Tiro
see Tyro

Tirrivee
agitation, 315

Tissue
texture, 329

Tit
small, 193
pony, 271

Tit for tat
retaliation, 718
compensation, 30

Titanic
greatness, 31, 192

Titbit
dainty, 829

Tithe
tenth, 99
dues, 812

Titillate
touch, 380
please, 377, 838

Titivate

dress, 225
beautify, 845

Title
distinction, 877
name, 564
mark, 550
property, 780
right, 924

Title-page
beginning, 66, 593

Titter
laugh, 838

Tittle
small quantity, 32
little, 192

Tittle-tattle
chat, 588
news, 532

Tittup
frisk, 266, 274

Titubation
fall, 306
failure, 732

Titular
title, 564

Toad
ugliness, 846

Toad-eater
servile, 886
flatterer, 935

Toady
to flatter, 933

Toast
roast, 384
celebrate, 883

Tobacco
tobacco, 298A

Toccata
music, 415

Tocsin
alarm, 669
indication, 550

Toddle
walk, 266
limp, 275

Toddler
child, 129

Toe
base, 211

Toehold
support, 215

Toff
notability, 642
fop, 854

Toffee

sweet, 396

Toffee-nose
proud, 878

Toga
dress, 225

Together
added, 37
simultaneous, 120
accompanying, 88

Tohu-bohu
tumult, 315

Toil
exertion, 682, 686
trap, 667

Toilet
dress, 225
room, 191

Toilsome
difficult, 704

Token
sign, 550

Toledo
arms, 727

Tolerable
endurable, 651

Tolerant
patient, 826

Tolerate
endure, 821
permit, 760
licence, 750
lenity, 740
laxity, 738

Toll
sound, 407
tax, 812

Tollbooth
mart, 799
prison, 752

Tolling
interment, 363

Tomahawk
arms, 727

Tomb
interment, 363

Tomboy
vulgar, 851

Tome
volume, 593

Tomfoolery
absurdity, 497
ridiculous, 856
amusement, 840

Tommy
soldier, 726

Tommy-gun
arms, 727
Tompion
stopper, 263
Tom-tom
drum, 416, 722
Ton
taste, 852
Tonality
melody, 413
Tone
state, 7
affections, 820
strength, 159
sound, 402
melody, 413
minstrelsy, 415
colour, 428
Tone down
modify, 174, 469
discoloration, 429
Tone-poem
music, 415
Tong
guild, 712
Tongs
grip, 781
Tongue
language, 560
Tongue-tied
dumb, 581
Tongueless
dumb, 581
Tonic
remedy, 662, 656
refresh, 689
music, 413
Tonnage
size, 192
Tonsure
canonicals, 999
Tontine
income, 810
Too
addition, 37
Too much
redundance, 641
Tool
instrument, 631, 633
adorn, 847
Toot
sound, 408
intemperance, 954
Tooth
projection, 250

notch, 257
sharp, 253
link, 45
taste, 390
Toothache
pain, 378
Toothbrush
clean, 652
Toothful
smallness, 32
Toothsome
savoury, 394
agreeable, 829
Tootle-oo!
departure, 293
Top
summit, 210
good, 648
to surpass, 33
Top-boot
dress, 225
Top-hamper
hindrance, 706
Top-heavy
inverted, 218
dangerous, 665
tipsy, 959
unbalanced, 28
Top-hole
excellent, 648
Top-sawyer
proficient, 700
Topaz
yellow, 436
ornament, 847
Toper
drunkard, 959
Tophet
hell, 982
Topi
hat, 225
Topic
topic, 454
Topical
situation, 183
apt, 23
Toplofty
contempt, 930
Topmast
height, 200
Topmost
great, 33
high, 210
Topography
situation, 183

Topping
excellent, 648
Topple
fall, 306
ruin, 659
Topple over
inversion, 218
Topsy-turvy
upside down, 218
nonsensical, 497
Toque
hat, 225
Torah
revelation, 985
Torch
light, 423
Torchlight
light, 420
Toreador
combatant, 726
Torment
physical, 378
moral, 828, 830
Tornado
violence, 173
wind, 349
Torpedo
weapon, 727
wreck, 732
car, 272
Torpedo-boat
ship, 273
Torpedo-boat destroyer
ship, 273
Torpedo-net
defence, 717
Torpid
inert, 172
insensible, 823
inactive, 683
Torrefy
burn, 384
Torrent
flow, 348
violence, 173
Torrid
heat, 382
Torsion
twist, 311
Torso
part, 51
Tort
wrong, 923

Tortoise
slow, 275
Tortoise-shell
variegation, 440
Tortuous
twist, 248
dishonest, 939
style, 571
Torture
physical, 378
moral, 828, 830
Tosh
nonsense, 517
Toss
throw, 284
oscillate, 314
agitate, 315
derange, 61
Toss-up
chance, 156, 621
Tosspot
drunk, 959
Tot
dram, 298
Tot up
numeration, 85
accounts, 811
Total
whole, 50
Totalitarian
authority, 737
Totalizator
numeration, 85
Totem
indication, 550
Toto coelo
contrariety, 14
difference, 15
greatness, 31
completeness, 52
Totter
limp, 275
droop, 160
oscillate, 314
agitate, 315
decay, 659
Tottering
dangerous, 665
imperfect, 651
Totting
retrieve, 775
Touch
tact, 379
contiguity, 199
to relate to, 9

music, 415
mix, 41
small quantity, 32, 39
act, 680
treat of, 516, 595
excite, 824
pity, 914
test, 463
borrow, 788
Touch-and-go
uncertainty, 475
danger, 665
Touch up
improve, 658
Touched
feeling, 821
Touching
relation, 9
Touchstone
evidence, 467
Touchwood
fuel, 388
Touchy
irascibility, 901
sensitive, 822
Tough
strong, 327
violent, 173
difficult, 704
brute, 913
bad man, 949
Toupee
wig, 225
roughness, 256
Tour
journey, 266
Tourer
vehicle, 272
Touring-car
vehicle, 272
Tourist
traveller, 268
Tournament
combat, 720
Tourney
combat, 720
Tourniquet
stopper, 263
hindrance, 706
Tournure
outline, 229
appearance, 448
beauty, 845
Tousle
derange, 61

Tousled
disorder, 59
Tout
solicit, 765, 767
publicity, 531
Tout ensemble
whole, 50
Touter
eulogist, 935
solicitor, 767
Toutie
ill, 655
Tow
pull, 285
Towards
direction, 278
Towel
clean, 652
Tower
height, 206
building, 189
defence, 717
to soar, 305
Towering
great, 31
passion, 900
Town
city, 189
fashion, 852
Town crier
publicity, 531
Town talk
news, 532
Township
region, 181
Townsman
inhabitant, 188
Toxic
poisonous, 657
Toxicology
poison, 663
Toxin
poison, 663
Toy
amusement, 840
trifle, 643
Tracasserie
discord, 713
Trace
inquire, 461
discover, 480a
vestige, 551
Trace to
discover, 155

Tracery
lattice, 219
ornament, 847
Traces
harness, 45
Trachea
air-pipe, 351
Tracing
copy, 21
representation, 554
Track
way, 627
trail, 551
to trace, 461
Trackless
difficult, 704
space, 180
Tract
region, 181
dissertation, 595
Tractable
easy, 705
willing, 602
obedient, 743
malleable, 324
dutiful, 926
Tractile
easy, 705
malleable, 324
Traction
drawing, 285
transmission, 270
Trade
business, 625
traffic, 794
Trade mark
indication, 550
Trader
merchant, 797
Tradition
record, 551
description, 594
Traditional
old, 124
Traduce
detract, 932, 934
Traffic
barter, 794
business, 625
Traffic warden
police, 965
Tragedy
drama, 599
disaster, 830
Tragelaph
unconformity, 83

Tragic
distressing, 830
Tragi-comedy
ridicule, 856
Tragi-comic
the drama, 599
Trail
sequel, 65
pendent, 214
slow, 275
drag, 285
odour, 398
indication, 551
pursue, 622
to track, 281, 461
Trailer
cinema, 599asa
Train
series, 69
sequel, 65
sequence, 281
retinue, 746
appendix, 39
traction, 285
vehicle, 272
teach, 537, 540
cultivate, 375
tame, 370
accustom, 613
drill, 673
Train-bearer
servant, 746
Train oil
oil, 356
Trained
skill, 698
Trait
appearance, 448
lineament, 550
Traitor
knave, 941
disobedient, 742
Trajectory
path, 627
Tram
vehicle, 272
Tram-car
vehicle, 272
Trammel
fetter, 752
restrain, 751
hinder, 706
Tramontana
wind, 349
Tramontane

distant, 196
alien, 57
Tramp
to stroll, 266
stroller, 268
commonalty, 876
ship, 273
Trample
violate, 927
bully, 885
spurn, 930
Tramway
way, 627
Trance
lethargy, 823
insensibility, 376
inactivity, 683
Tranquil
calm, 174, 826
peaceful, 721
quiet, 165
to pacify, 723
Tranquillizer
drug, 662
Transact
conduct, 692
traffic, 794
Transaction
event, 151
Transalpine
distance, 196
Transatlantic
distance, 196
Transcend
go beyond, 303
Transcendent
great, 31, 33
spiritual, 317
perfect, 650
good, 648
glorious, 873
Transcendental
recondite, 519
spiritual, 317, 450
Transcribe
write, 590
copy, 21
Transcript
write, 590
copy, 21
Transcursion
trespass, 303
Transept
of church, 1000
crossing, 219

Transfer
things, 270
property, 783
remove, 185
Transfiguration
change, 140
divine, 998
Transfix
perforate, 260
Transform
change, 140
Transformation
wig, 225
Transfuse
transfer, 270
mix, 41
translate, 522
Transgress
go beyond, 303
infringe, 773
violate, 927
sin, 947
Tranship
transfer, 270
Transient
passing, 111
Transilient
transcursion, 303
Transistor
radio, 599
Transit
conversion, 144
motion, 264
transference, 270
Transition
motion, 264
conversion, 144
transference, 270
Transitive
passing, 111
Transitory
passing, 111
Translate
interpret, 522
transfer, 270
promote, 995
Translucent
transparent, 425
Transmigration
change, 140
conversion, 144
Transmission
moving, 270
of property, 783
passage, 302

Transmitter
hearing, 418
Transmogrify
change, 140, 144
Transmute
change, 140
conversion, 144
Transparent
pellucid, 425
obvious, 518
perspicuous, 570
Transpicuous
transparent, 425
Transpierce
pierce, 260
Transpire
appear, 525
disclose, 529
Transplant
displace, 185
transfer, 270
Transpontine
drama, 599
Transport
transfer, 185, 270
punish, 972
ship, 272
feeling, 821, 824
please, 827, 829
Transpose
displace, 185
invert, 218
transfer, 270
exchange, 148
Transubstantiation
rite, 998
Transude
ooze, 295
pass through, 302
exude, 348
Transverse
oblique, 217
Trap
snare, 667
vehicle, 272
Trap-door
escape, 671
pitfall, 667
Trapes
journey, 266
Trappings
clothes, 39, 225
gear, 633
ornament, 847
property, 780

Trash
absurdity, 497
nonsense, 517
trifle, 643
Travail
work, 686
Travel
journey, 266
motion, 264
Traveller
traveller, 268
Traverse
move, 266
pass, 302
investigate, 461
obstruct, 706
Travesty
copy, 21
to imitate, 19
misinterpret, 523
burlesque, 856
Travolator
way, 627
Tray
receptacle, 191
Treachery
deceit, 940
Treacle
sweet, 396
semiliquid, 352
Tread
journey, 266
motion, 264
Treadle
instrument, 633
Treadmill
punishment, 975
wearisome, 841
Treason
revolt, 742
treachery, 940
Treasure
money, 800
goodness, 648
perfection, 650
windfall, 618
Treasurer
treasurer, 801
Treasury
treasury, 802
store, 636
Treat
manage, 692
bargain, 769
amuse, 840

please, 827
Treatise
book, 595
Treatment
action, 692
remedy, 662
painting, 556
Treaty
agreement, 769
Treble
number, 93
music, 413
Tree
plant, 367
execution, 975
Trefoil
three, 92
Trek
journey, 266
Trellis
cross, 219
Tremble
agitate, 315
waver, 149
with cold, 385
with fear, 860
with emotion, 821
Tremendous
great, 31
fearful, 860
Tremolo
quaver, 407
Tremor
agitation, 315
feeling, 827
fear, 860
Tremulous
stammer, 583
Trench
furrow, 259
defence, 717
Trench on
nearness, 197
encroach, 303, 925
Trenchant
keen, 171
sharp, 253
disapproving, 932
style, 574
Trencher
plate, 191
layer, 204
Trend
direction, 278
curve, 245

tendency, 176
Trendy
fashion, 852
Trepan
deceive, 545
perforator, 262
Trepidation
agitation, 315
emotion, 821
excitability, 825
fear, 860
Trespass
go beyond, 303
sin, 947
Tress
hair, 256
Trestle
support, 215
Trey
number, 92
Triad
number, 92
Trial
experiment, 463
essay, 675
difficulty, 704
suffering, 828
lawsuit, 969
Triality
number, 92
Triangle
angularity, 244
triality, 92
musical instrument, 417
Triangulate
measurement, 466
Tribe
class, 75
kindred, 11
assemblage, 72
Tribrach
verse, 597
Tribulation
pain, 828
Tribunal
tribunal, 966
Tribune
officer, 745
Tributary
giving, 784
river, 348
Tribute
donation, 784
reward, 973
approbation, 931

Tricar
vehicle, 272
Trice
instantaneous, 113
Trichotomy
trisection, 94
Trick
deception, 545
contrivance, 626
skill, 698
cunning, 702
speciality, 79
to dress, 225
adorn, 845
Trickery
artifice, 702
Trickle
ooze, 295
drip, 348
Trickster
deceiver, 548, 702
thief, 792
Tricksy
sportive, 840
Tricolour
variegation, 440
flag, 550
Trident
ocean, 341
Tried
employed, 677
trusty, 939
Triennial
periodical, 138
Trifid
number, 94
Trifle
unimportant, 643
small, 32
loaf, 683
Trifle away
idle, 683
Trifle with
neglect, 460
disparage, 483
Triform
number, 92
Trig
beauty, 845
Trigeminal
triple, 93
Trigger
instrument, 633
Trigonal
angularity, 244

Trilateral
side, 236
Trilby
hat, 225
Trill
sound, 407
resonance, 408
music, 415
Trilogy
triality, 92
Trim
state, 7
form, 240
dress, 225
ornament, 845, 847
order, 58
to adjust, 27
prepare, 673
beat, 731
scold, 932
change sides, 607
Trimmer
fickle, 605, 607
apostate, 941
Trimming
edge, 230
ornament, 847
Trinal
number, 92
Trine
triplication, 93
Trinity
Deity, 976
Trinket
ornament, 847
Trinkgeld
gift, 784
Trinomial
triality, 92
triplication, 93
Trio
number, 92
Triolet
poetry, 597
Trip
jaunt, 266
to fall, 306
hasten, 274
mistake, 495
fail, 945
guilt, 947
Trip up
overthrow, 731
deceive, 545
Tripartition

trisection, 94
Triphthong
letter, 561
Triple
triplication, 93
Triplet
triality, 92
poetry, 597
Triplicate
triplication, 93
Tripod
support, 215
Tripper
traveller, 268
Tripping
nimble, 682
failing, 495
Triquetra
triality, 92
Trireme
ship, 273
Trisect
tripartition, 94
Triste
dejected, 837
Tristful
dejected, 837
Trisulcate
tripartition, 94
furrow, 259
Trisyllable
letter, 561
Trite
old, 82
hackneyed, 496
unimportant, 643
Tritheism
heathen, 984
Triturate
pulverulence, 330
Triumph
success, 731
trophy, 733
exult, 838
boast, 884
celebrate, 883
Triumphant
elated, 836
Trivet
support, 215
Trivial
trifling, 643
useless, 645
flimsy, 477
smallness, 32

Trochee
verse, 597
Troglodyte
seclusion, 893
Troll
roll, 312
sing, 415
fairy, 980
Trolley
vehicle, 272
Trolley-bus
vehicle, 272
Trollop
libertine, 962
Trombone
musical instrument, 417
Troop
army, 726
assemblage, 72
Troop-ship
ship, 273
Trooper
combatant, 726
ship, 273
Trope
metaphor, 521
Trophy
triumph, 733
record, 551
Tropical
heat, 382
metaphor, 520
Tropology
metaphor, 520
Tropopause
air, 338
Troposphere
air, 338
Trot
run, 266
velocity, 274
Trot out
manifestation, 525
Troth
truth, 494
promise, 768
belief, 484
Trothless
faithless, 940
false, 544
Troubadour
musician, 416
Trouble
derange, 61
evil, 619, 649

adversity, 735
pain, 828, 830
exertion, 686
Troubleshooter
mediator, 724
Troublesome
difficulty, 704
Troublous
disorder, 59
Trough
conduit, 250
trench, 259
hollow, 252
Trounce
censure, 932
punish, 972
Trousers
dress, 225
Trousseau
dress, 225
Trow
think, 451, 484
know, 490
Trowel
instrument, 191
Truant
absent, 187
fugitive, 623
idle, 683
Truce
pacification, 723
suspension, 141, 142
Truck
vehicle, 272
barter, 794
summit, 210
Truckle to
submission, 725
Truculent
malevolence, 907
Trudge
slowness, 275
True
real, 1, 3
veracious, 543
good, 648
faithful, 772
orthodox, 983A
True-love
love, 897
Truepenny
probity, 939
Truism
absurdity, 497
Trull

impurity, 962
Truly
really, 31
assent, 488
verily, 494, 543
Trump
good man, 939, 948
Trump card
device, 626
success, 731
Trump up
falsehood, 544
Trumpery
unimportance, 643
nonsense, 517
Trumpet
musical instrument, 417
to publish, 531
roar, 412
war-cry, 722
Trumpet-tongued
publication, 531
Trumpeter
messenger, 534
Truncate
shorten, 201
incomplete, 53
subduct, 38
Truncheon
club, 727
staff of office, 747
mace, 633
Trundle
roll, 312
propel, 284
Trunk
whole, 50
origin, 153
paternity, 166
box, 191
Truss
join, 43
support, 215
packet, 72
Trust
credit, 805
belief, 484
credulity, 486
hope, 858
Trustee
consignee, 758
treasurer, 801
Trustless
improbity, 940
Trustworthy

probity, 939
certainty, 474
Trusty
probity, 939
Truth
truth, 494
Truthful
veracity, 543
Truthless
falsehood, 544
Try
experiment, 463
endeavour, 675
use, 677
annoy, 830
judge, 967
Try-out
trial, 463
Trying
difficult, 704
Tryst
party, 892
Tsar
see Czar
Tu quoque
retaliation, 718
Tub
vessel, 191
to bathe, 337
Tub-thumper
ranter, 584
Tuba
wind instrument, 417
Tubby
corpulent, 192
Tube
opening, 260
way, 627
Tubercle
convexity, 250
Tuberosity
convexity, 250
Tubular
opening, 260
Tuck
fold, 258
dagger, 727
Tuck in
insert, 300
eat, 296
locate, 184
Tuft
rough, 256
collection, 72

Tuft-hunter
  sycophant, 886
  flatterer, 935
  time-server, 943
Tug
  pull, 285
  effort, 686
  ship, 273
Tuition
  teaching, 537
Tulip
  variegation, 440
Tumble
  fall, 306
  derange, 61
  spoil, 659
  fail, 732
  agitate, 315
Tumbledown
  deterioration, 659
Tumbler
  glass, 191
  buffoon, 844
Tumbrel
  vehicle, 272
Tumefaction
  expansion, 194
Tumid
  swollen, 194
  bombastic, 549, 577
Tumour
  swelling, 194
  convexity, 250
Tumult
  disorder, 59
  violence, 173
  agitation, 315, 825
  resistance, 719
  revolt, 742
  emotion, 825
Tumultuous
  disorder, 59
Tumulus
  interment, 363
Tun
  large, 192
  drunkard, 959
Tunable
  harmony, 413
Tundra
  space, 180
  plain, 344
Tune
  music, 415
  melody, 413

  to prepare, 673
Tune, out of
  irrelation, 10
  disagreement, 24
Tuneful
  harmony, 413
Tuneless
  discord, 414
Tunic
  cover, 222
  dress, 225
Tuning-fork
  musical, 417
Tunnage
  size, 192
Tunnel
  opening, 260
  way, 627
Turban
  dress, 225
Turbid
  opaque, 416
  foul, 653
Turbinate
  convolution, 248
  rotation, 312
Turbine
  navigation, 267
  ship, 273
  instrument, 633
Turbo-jet
  aircraft, 273A
Turbulence
  disorder, 59
  violence, 173
  agitation, 315
  excitation, 825
Tureen
  receptacle, 191
Turf
  plain, 344
Turgescent
  expanded, 194
  exaggerated, 549
  redundant, 641
Turgid
  swollen, 194
  exaggerated, 549, 577
  redundant, 641
Turkish bath
  furnace, 386
Turmoil
  confusion, 59
  agitation, 315
  violence, 173

Turn
  state, 7
  juncture, 134
  form, 240
  period of time, 138
  curvature, 245
  deviation, 279
  circuition, 311
  rotation, 312
  journey, 266
  change, 140, 144
  translate, 522
  purpose, 630
  bout, 680
  aptitude, 698
  emotion, 820
  nausea, 867
Turn away
  diverge, 291
  dismiss, 756
Turn down
  reject, 610
Turn off
  dismiss, 756
  execute, 361
Turn out
  happen, 151
  eject, 297
  strike, 742
  equipage, 852
Turn over
  invert, 218
  reflect, 451
Turn round
  rotation, 312
Turn tail
  retreat, 283, 287
Turn the scale
  superiority, 33
Turn the tables
  contrariety, 14
Turn turtle
  inversion, 218
Turn up
  happen, 151
  chance, 156, 621
  arrive, 292
  appear, 446
Turncoat
  tergiversation, 607
  irresolution, 605
  renegade, 144
  knave, 941
Turnkey
  keeper, 753

Turnpike
hindrance, 706
Turnpike road
way, 627
Turnstile
hindrance, 706
Turpitude
dishonour, 940
wrong, 923
disgrace, 874
Turquoise
blue, 438
Turret
height, 206
defence, 717
Turtle-dove
love, 897
Tush
contempt, 930
Tusk
sharpness, 253
Tussle
contention, 720
Tutelage
safety, 664
subjection, 749
learner, 541
Tutelary
safety, 664
Tutor
teacher, 540
to teach, 537
cultivate, 375
Tuxedo
dress, 225
Twaddle
absurdity, 497
nonsense, 517
loquacity, 584
Twain
duplication, 90
Twang
taste, 390
sound, 402, 410
voice, 583
Tweak
squeeze, 195, 203
punish, 972
Tweeds
dress, 225
Twelve
number, 98
Twenty
number, 98
Twerp

bad man, 949
Twice
duplication, 90
Twiddle
rotation, 312
Twig
part, 51
plant, 367
to notice, 457
comprehend, 518
Twilight
morning, 125
evening, 126
grey, 432
Twill
fold, 258
Twilled
crossing, 219
Twin
duplicate, 90
accompaniment, 88
similar, 17
Twine
thread, 45
fibre, 205
intersect, 219
convolution, 248
cling, 46
Twinge
bodily pain, 378
mental, 828, 830
Twinkle
light, 420
Twinkling
moment, 113
Twirl
agitation, 315
convolution, 248
turn, 311, 312
Twist
cord, 45
distort, 243
falsehood, 544
obliquity, 217
convolution, 248
bend, 311
imperfection, 651
prejudice, 481
Twit
disapprove, 932
ridicule, 856
slight, 929
Twitch
pull, 285
convulsion, 315

pain, 378
mental, 828
Twitter
agitation, 315
cry, 412
music, 415
emotion, 821
Two
duality, 89
Two-by-four
trifling, 643
Two-seater
vehicle, 272
Two-step
dance, 840
Twofold
duplication, 89, 90
Twopenny
paltry, 643
Tycoon
master, 745
Tyke
commonalty, 876
Tympanum
hearing, 418
Tympany
expansion, 194
Tynewald
council, 696
Type
pattern, 22
class, 75
nature, 5
person, 372
man, 373
rule, 80
indication, 550
printing, 591
Typewriting
writing, 590
Typhoon
violence, 173
rotation, 312
wind, 349
Typical
ordinary, 82
special, 79
Typify
indication, 550
Typography
printing, 591
Tyrannicide
killing, 361
Tyranny
severity, 739

authority, 737
Tyrant
  master, 745
Tyro
  learner, 541
  novice, 674

Uberty
  sufficiency, 639
Ubiety
  presence, 186
Ubiquitous
  presence, 186
Udder
  teat, 250
Ugly
  ugliness, 846
  cantankerous, 895
  formidable, 860
Uh-huh
  assent, 488
Ukase
  order, 741
  law, 963
Ukelele
  stringed instrument, 417
Ulcer
  disease, 655
  care, 830
Ulema
  judge, 967
Ullage
  deficiency, 53
Ulster
  coat, 225
Ulterior
  in space, 196
  in time, 121
Ultimate
  end, 67
Ultimatum
  conditions, 770
Ultimo
  priority, 116
Ultimogeniture
  descent, 167
Ultra
  superiority, 33
  greatness, 31
  extremist, 604
Ultramarine
  blueness, 438
Ultramontane
  authority, 737

alien, 57
Ululation
  cry, 412
Ulysses
  cunning, 702
Umber
  brown, 433
Umbilical
  centrality, 223
Umbra
  darkness, 421
Umbrage
  shade, 424
  darkness, 421
  offence, 900
  enmity, 889
  grudge, 898
Umbrella
  shelter, 666
Umpire
  judge, 480, 967
Umpteen
  plurality, 100
Unabashed
  bold, 861
  haughty, 873, 878
  insolent, 885
  conceited, 880
Unabated
  great, 31
Unable
  impotence, 158
Unacceptable
  painfulness, 830
Unaccommodating
  disagreeing, 24
  uncivil, 895
  disobliging, 907
Unaccompanied
  alone, 87
Unaccomplished
  incomplete, 730
Unaccountable
  obscure, 519
  wonderful, 870
  arbitrary, 964
  irresponsible, 927A
Unaccustomed
  unused, 614
  unskilled, 699
  unusual, 83
Unachievable
  difficult, 704
  impossible, 471
Unacknowledged

ignored, 489
  unrequited, 917
Unacquainted
  ignorant, 491
Unactuated
  unmoved, 616
Unadmonished
  unwarned, 665
Unadorned
  simple, 849
  style, 575
Unadulterated
  simple, 42
  genuine, 494, 648
Unadventurous
  quiet, 864
Unadvisable
  inexpedient, 647
Unadvised
  unwarned, 665
  foolish, 699
Unaffected
  callous, 376
  genuine, 494
  sincere, 543
  simple, 576, 849
  elegant, 578
  in good taste, 850
Unafflicted
  serene, 831
Unaided
  meak, 160
Unalarmed
  courage, 861
Unalienable
  dueness, 924
Unallayed
  strength, 159
Unallied
  irrelative, 10
Unallowable
  wrong, 923
Unalluring
  indifference, 866
Unalterable
  identical, 13
  unchanged, 141
  unchangeable, 150
Unamazed
  expectance, 871
Unambiguous
  intelligibility, 518
Unambitious
  indifference, 866
Unamiable
  ill-natured, 907

725

Unanimity
accord, 714
assent, 488
Unannexed
disjoined, 44
Unannounced
inexpectation, 508
Unanswerable
demonstrative, 478
certain, 474
irresponsible, 927ʌ
arbitrary, 964
Unappalled
courage, 861
Unapparent
invisible, 447
latent, 526
Unappeasable
violence, 173
Unapplied
disuse, 678
Unapprehended
unknown, 491
Unapprehensive
courage, 861
Unapprised
ignorance, 491
Unapproachable
distant, 196
great, 31
Unapproved
disapprobation, 932
Unapt
incongruous, 24
expedient, 647
unskilful, 699
Unarmed
weak, 158, 160
Unarranged
in disorder, 59
unprepared, 674
Unarrayed
simplicity, 849
Unascertained
ignorance, 491
Unasked
voluntary, 602
Unaspiring
indifferent, 866
modest, 881
Unassailable
safety, 664
Unassailed
freedom, 748

Unassembled
non-assemblage, 73
Unassociated
disjunction, 44
Unassuming
modesty, 881
Unatoned
impenitence, 951
Unattached
disjunction, 44
Unattackable
safety, 664
Unattainable
difficult, 704
impossible, 471
Unattained
failure, 732
Unattempted
avoidance, 623
Unattended
alone, 87
Unattended to
neglect, 460
Unattested
counterevidence, 468
unrecorded, 552
Unattracted
dissuasion, 616
Unattractive
indifference, 866
Unauthentic
uncertainty, 475
Unauthenticated
counter-evidence, 468
erroneous, 495
Unauthorized
undue, 738, 925
wrong, 923
lawless, 964
prohibited, 761
Unavailing
useless, 645
failure, 732
Unavoidable
necessary, 601
certain, 474
Unavowed
dissent, 489
Unawakened
inactivity, 683
Unaware
ignorant, 491
unexpecting, 508
impulsive, 601
Unawed

courage, 861
Unbalanced
inequality, 28
Unballasted
mutable, 149
foolish, 499
Unbar
liberate, 750
Unbearable
pain, 830
Unbeaten
success, 731
Unbecoming
undue, 925
disgraceful, 874, 940
incongruous, 24
Unbefitting
undue, 925
disgraceful, 940
incongruous, 24
Unbegotten
inexistence, 2
Unbeguile
disclosure, 529
Unbegun
unprepared, 674
Unbeheld
invisibility, 447
Unbelief
doubt, 485
infidelity, 989
incredulity, 487
Unbelievable
improbable, 473
Unbeliever
heathen, 984
Unbeloved
hate, 898
Unbend
straighten, 246
repose, 687
the mind, 452
Unbending
hard, 323
resolute, 604
Unbeseeming
base, 940
Unbesought
willingness, 602
deprecation, 766
Unbewailed
disapprobation, 932
Unbiased
wise, 498
impartial, 480

726

Unclose
opening, 260
Unclothe
divestment, 226
Unclouded
light, 420
joyful, 827
Unclubbable
unsociable, 893
Uncoif
divestment, 226
Uncoil
straighten, 246
evolve, 313
Uncollected
non-assemblage, 73
Uncoloured
achromatism, 429
Uncombed
vulgarity, 851
Uncombined
single, 47
Un-come-at-able
difficult, 704
Uncomely
ugliness, 846
Uncomfortable
annoyed, 828
annoying, 830
in pain, 378
Uncommendable
bad, 945
blamable, 932
Uncommon
unconformity, 83
greatness, 31
infrequency, 137
Uncommunicative
close, 585
concealing, 528
Uncompact
rarity, 322
Uncompelled
voluntary, 600
free, 748
Uncomplaisant
discourtesy, 895
Uncomplying
refusing, 764
disobedient, 742
Uncompounded
simpleness, 42
Uncompressed
light, 320

rare, 322
Uncompromising
strict, 82
severe, 739
resolved, 604
truthful, 543
Unconceived
unmeaning, 517
unintelligible, 519
Unconcern
indifference, 866
Unconcocted
non-preparation, 674
Uncondemned
acquittal, 970
Unconditional
absolute, 768A
Unconfined
freedom, 748
Unconfirmed
uncertainty, 475
Unconformable
irrelation, 10
disagreeing, 24
Unconformity
irrelation, 10
irregular, 16A, 83
Unconfused
clear, 518
methodical, 58
Unconfuted
true, 494
demonstrated, 478
Uncongealed
fluidity, 333
Uncongenial
disagreeing, 24
insalubrious, 657
Unconnected
irrelative, 10
discontinuous, 70
disjoined, 44
Unconquerable
power, 157
Unconquered
resistance, 719
Unconscionable
excessive, 31
unprincipled, 945
Unconscious
insensible, 823
mind, 450
involuntary, 601
ignorant, 491
Unconsenting

refusing, 764
unwilling, 603
Unconsidered
incogitancy, 452
Unconsolidated
single, 47
Unconsonant
disagreement, 24
Unconspicuous
invisible, 447
Unconstitutional
lawful, 925
Unconstrained
free, 748
willing, 600
unceremonious, 880
Unconsumed
remaining, 40
Uncontested
certainty, 474
Uncontradicted
true, 488
Uncontrollable
violent, 173
emotion, 825
Uncontrolled
unrestrained, 748
Uncontroverted
agreed, 488
Unconventional
unconformity, 83
unhackneyed, 614
Unconversant
ignorant, 491
unskilled, 699
Unconverted
dissent, 489
Unconvinced
dissent, 489
Uncopied
non-imitation, 20
Uncork
liberation, 750
Uncorrected
imperfection, 651
Uncorrupted
disinterested, 942
innocent, 946
Uncouple
disjunction, 44
Uncourteous
rude, 895
Uncourtly
rude, 895

Uncouth
ugly, 846
ridiculous, 853
style, 579
rude, 851
Uncovenanted
unsecured, 768A
Uncover
open, 260
denude, 226
disclose, 529
bow, 894
Uncreated
inexistence, 2
Uncropped
whole, 50
Uncrown
abrogation, 756
Unction
emotion, 824
piety, 987
extreme,
rite, 998
Unctuous
oily, 355
hypocritical, 988
flattering, 933
servile, 886
Unculled
untouched, 678
relinquished, 782
Uncultivated
ignorant, 491
unprepared, 674
Uncultured
ignorant, 491
Uncurbed
freedom, 748
Uncurl
straightness, 246
Uncut
whole, 50
Undamaged
goodness, 648
Undamped
dryness, 340
Undated
waving, 248
time, 115
Undaunted
courage, 861
Undazzled
wisdom, 498
Undebauched
innocence, 946

Undecayed
goodness, 648
Undeceive
inform, 527, 529
Undeceived
knowledge, 490
Undecided
in question, 461
uncertain, 475
irresolute, 605
indifferent, 610
Undecipherable
unintelligible, 519
Undecked
simplicity, 849
Undecomposed
simpleness, 42
Undefaced
beauty, 845
Undefended
submission, 725
Undefiled
innocence, 946
purity, 960
Undefinable
unmeaning, 517, 519
uncertain, 475
Undefined
see Undefinable
Undemolished
tire, 50
good, 648
Undemonstrative
modesty, 881
Undeniable
certainty, 474
Undeplored
hate, 898
Undepraved
innocence, 946
Undeprived
retention, 781
Under
below, 207
less, 34
Under-bodice
dress, 225
Under breath
faintness, 405
Under-reckon
depreciation, 483
Underbid
bargain, 794
Underbred
rude, 861

Undercharge
cheap, 815
Undercover
secret, 534
Undercurrent
stream, 347
latency, 526
Underestimate
depreciation, 483
Undergo
feeling 821
Undergraduate
learner, 541
Underground
low, 207
deep, 208
way, 627
Undergrowth
plant, 367
Underhand
hidden, 528
false, 544
base, 940
Underlie
latent, 526
Underline
mark, 550
emphatic, 642
Underling
servant, 746
Underlying
lowness, 207
Undermanned
insufficiency, 640
Undermine
burrow, 252
counteract, 706
damage, 659
Undermost
base, 211
Underneath
lowness, 207
Underpin
support, 215
Underplot
plan, 626
Underprivileged
forfeit, 925
Underprize
underrate, 483
Underprop
support, 215
Underquote
bargain, 794

Underrate
depreciation, 483
Undersell
sale, 796
Undersized
littleness, 193
Understaffed
insufficiency, 640
Understand
know, 490
meaning, 516
intelligible, 518
Understanding
intellect, 450, 498
agreement, 714
compact, 769
Understatement
falsehood, 544
Understood
implied, 516
metaphorical, 521
Understrapper
servant, 746
Understudy
deputy, 159, 634
substitute, 147
Undertake
promise, 768
pursue, 622
endeavour, 676
Undertaker
interment, 363
Undertaking
enterprise, 676
business, 625
Undertone
faintness, 405
Undertow
danger, 667
Undervalue
depreciation, 483
Underwear
dress, 225
Underworld
commonalty, 876
Underwood
plant, 367
Underwrite
insure, 769, 771
Undescribed
unconformity, 83
Undescried
invisible, 447
Undeserved
undueness, 925
Undesigned

necessity, 601
chance, 621
Undesigning
artlessness, 703
Undesirable
unpleasant, 830
unattractive, 866
inexpedient, 647
Undesirous
indifference, 866
Undespairing
hope, 858
Undestroyed
whole, 50
persisting, 141
existing, 1
Undetermined
irresolute, 605
untried, 461
uncertain, 475
obscure, 519
chance, 156
Undeterred
resolute, 604
Undeveloped
latent, 526
Undeviating
progressing, 282
straight, 246
direct, 278
mid-course, 628
unchanged, 150
Undevout
irreligion, 989
Undigested
unarranged, 59
crude, 674
Undiluted
strength, 159
purity, 42
Undiminished
whole, 50
great, 31
increase, 35
Undine
sprite, 980
Undirected
deviating, 279
casual, 621
Undiscerned
invisibility, 447
Undiscerning
blind, 442
stupid, 499
Undisciplined

unskilfulness, 699
Undisclosed
concealment, 528
Undiscoverable
concealment, 528
Undisguised
sincere, 543
true, 494
Undismayed
courage, 861
Undispersed
assemblage, 72
Undisposed of
disuse, 678
retention, 781
Undisputed
certainty, 474
Undissolved
entire, 50
dense, 321
Undistinguished
indiscrimination, 465A
Undistorted
straight, 246
true, 494
Undistracted
attention, 457
Undisturbed
quiet, 265, 685
calm, 826
orderly, 58
Undiverted
resolution, 604
Undivided
whole, 50
Undivulged
concealment, 528
Undo
untie, 44
do away with, 681
counteract, 179, 706
reverse, 145
Undoing
ruin, 735, 830
Undone
non-assemblage, 73
incomplete, 730
foiled, 732
hapless, 828
Undoubted
certainty, 474
Undraped
nudity, 226
Undreaded
courage, 861

Undreamed
incogitancy, 452
Undress
nudity, 226
morning dress, 225
Undressed
unprepared, 674
unadorned, 849
Undrilled
unprepared, 674
unaccustomed, 699
Undriven
willing, 602
Undrooping
activity, 682
Undue
wrong, 923, 925
Undulate
oscillate, 314
wave, 248
Undutiful
vice, 945
Undyed
achromatism, 429
Undying
perpetual, 112
immutable, 150
Unearth
manifestation, 525
discovery, 480A
inquiry, 461
Unearthly
immaterial, 317
heavenly, 981
pious, 987
Uneasy
pain, 828
Uneatable
unsavoury, 395
Unedifying
misteaching, 538
Uneducated
ignorant, 491
unprepared, 674
unskilful, 699
Unembarrassed
manners, 852
Unemployed
inactive, 683
not used, 678
Unencumbered
easy, 705
exempt, 927A
Unending
infinite, 105

long, 200
Unendowed
impotence, 158
Unendurable
painfulness, 830
Unenjoyed
weary, 841
Unenlightened
ignorant, 491
foolish, 499
Unenslaved
free, 748
Unenterprising
caution, 864
Unentertaining
dullness, 843
Unentitled
undueness, 925
Unequal
inequality, 28
unable, 158
unjust, 923
Unequalled
superior, 33
Unequipped
non-preparation, 674
Unequivocal
sure, 474
clear, 518
Unequivocally
greatly, 31
Unerring
certain, 474
true, 494
innocent, 946
Unespied
invisible, 447
hidden, 526
Unessayed
disuse, 678
Unessential
unimportance, 643
Uneven
rough, 256
unequal, 28
irregular, 16A, 83
Unexaggerated
truth, 494
Unexamined
neglect, 460
Unexampled
unconformity, 83
Unexceptionable
good, 648
legitimate, 924

innocent, 946
Unexcited
inexcitability, 826
Unexciting
moderate, 174
Unexecuted
non-completion, 730
Unexempt
liability, 177
Unexercised
unused, 678
unprepared, 674
unskilled, 699
Unexerted
inertness, 172
Unexhausted
vigorous, 159
abundant, 639
Unexpanded
contraction, 195
Unexpected
unlooked-for, 508
sudden, 132
wonderful, 870
Unexpensive
cheapness, 815
Unexplained
latent, 526
unknown, 491
Unexplored
latent, 526
unknown, 491
Unexposed
latent, 526
Unexpressed
latent, 526
Unextended
immateriality, 317
Unextinguished
violent, 172
burning, 382
Unfaded
colour, 428
fresh, 648
Unfading
perpetuity, 112
Unfailing
constant, 141
Unfair
unjust, 923
dishonourable, 940
false, 544
Unfaithful
faithless, 940

Unfaltering
resolution, 604
Unfamiliar
unconformity, 83
Unfashionable
vulgarity, 851
abnormal, 83
Unfashioned
formless, 241
unwrought, 674
Unfasten
disjunction, 44
Unfathomable
deep, 208
infinite, 105
unintelligible, 519
Unfavourable
obstructive, 708
out of season, 135
Unfearing
courage, 861
Unfeasible
impracticable, 471
Unfed
fasting, 956
deficient, 640
Unfeeling
insensibility, 823
impenitence, 951
Unfeigned
veracity, 543
Unfelt
insensibility, 823
Unfeminine
vulgarity, 851
manly, 373
Unfetter
unfasten, 44
release, 750
Unfettered
spontaneous, 600
Unfinished
non-completion, 53, 730
Unfit
inappropriate, 24
incapacitate, 158
inexpedient, 647
Unfix
disjoin, 44
Unfixed
irresolute, 605
mutable, 149
Unflagging
activity, 682
resolution, 604
Unflattering

sincere, 543
true, 494
Unfledged
unprepared, 674
young, 129
Unflinching
resolute, 604
bravery, 861
persevering, 682
Unfoiled
success, 731
Unfold
evolve, 313
straighten, 246
disclose, 529
interpret, 522
Unforbidden
permission, 760
Unforced
free, 748
willing, 602
Unforeseen
unexpected, 508
surprising, 870
Unforfeited
retention, 781
Unforgettable
importance, 642
Unforgivable
vice, 945
Unforgiving
revenge, 919
Unforgotten
memory, 505
Unformed
non-preparation, 674
Unforthcoming
unsociable, 893
Unfortified
weakness, 160
Unfortunate
failure, 732
adversity, 735
unhappy, 828
untimely, 135
Unfounded
falsehood, 544
Unfrequent
seldom, 137
Unfrequented
seclusion, 893
Unfriended
weak, 160
enmity, 889
Unfriendly

enmity, 889
opposed, 708
malevolent, 907
Unfrock
disqualify, 925
punish, 972
dismiss, 756
Unfruitful
unproductiveness, 169
Unfulfilled
non-observance, 773, 925
Unfurl
evolution, 213
Unfurnished
unprepared, 674
insufficient, 640
Ungainly
ugly, 846
rude, 895
Ungarnished
unadorned, 849
Ungathered
disuse, 678
Ungenerous
stingy, 819
selfish, 943
Ungenial
insalubrious, 657
uncivil, 895
Ungenteel
vulgar, 851
rude, 895
Ungentle
rude, 895
violent, 173
Ungentlemanly
vulgar, 851
rude, 895
dishonourable, 940
Un-get-at-able
distant, 196
Ungird
disjunction, 44
Unglue
disjunction, 44
incoherence, 47
Ungodly
irreligion, 989
Ungovernable
violent, 173
disobedient, 742
passion, 825
Ungoverned
freedom, 748

Ungraceful
ugly, 846
inelegant, 579
vulgar, 851
Ungracious
uncivil, 895
unfriendly, 907
Ungrammatical
solecism, 568
Ungrateful
ingratitude, 917
Ungratified
pain, 828
Ungrounded
error, 495
Ungrudging
liberality, 816
Unguarded
neglected, 460
improvident, 674
dangerous, 665
spontaneous, 612
Unguent
oil, 356
Unguided
ignorant, 491
unskilful, 699
Unhackneyed
desuetude, 614
Unhallowed
irreligion, 989
profane, 988
Unhand
liberation, 750
Unhandsome
ugly, 940
Unhandy
unskilfulness, 699
Unhappy
pain, 828
Unhardened
tender, 914
penitent, 950
innocent, 946
Unharmed
safety, 664
Unharness
disjoin, 44
liberate, 750
Unhatched
non-preparation, 674
Unhazarded
safety, 664
Unhealthy
ill, 655

unwholesome, 657
Unheard-of
ignorant, 491
exceptional, 83, 137
impossible, 471
improbable, 473
wonderful, 870
Unheeded
neglected, 460
Unheralded
inexpectation, 507
Unheroic
cowardly, 862
Unhesitating
resolution, 604
Unhewn
formless, 241
unprepared, 674
Unhindered
free, 748
Unhinge
weaken, 169
derange, 61
Unhinged
unsettled, 605
insane, 503
Unholy
evil, 989
Unhonoured
disrespect, 874
Unhook
disjoin, 44
Unhoped
unexpected, 508
Unhouse
displace, 185
Unhurt
uninjured, 670
Unicorn
monster, 83
prodigy, 872
Unidea'd
unthinking, 452
Unideal
true, 494
existing, 1
Uniform
homogeneous, 16
simple, 42
orderly, 58
regular, 82
symmetrical, 242
livery, 225
insignia, 550
uniformity, 23

Unify
combine, 48
make one, 87
Unilluminated
dark, 421
ignorant, 491
Unimaginable
inconceivable, 519
Unimaginative
dull, 843
Unimagined
truth, 494
Unimitated
original, 20
Unimpaired
preserved, 670
sound, 648
Unimpassioned
inexcitable, 826
Unimpeachable
innocent, 946
irrefutable, 474, 478
inalienable, 924
perfect, 650
Unimpeded
facility, 705
Unimpelled
uninduced, 616
Unimportant
insignificant, 643
Unimpressionable
insensible, 823
Unimproved
deterioration, 659
Uninfluenced
unbiased, 616
obstinate, 606
Uninfluential
inert, 172
Uninformed
ignorance, 491
Uninhabited
empty, 187
solitary, 893
Uninitiated
unschooled, 699
Uninjured
good, 648
preserved, 670
healthy, 644
Uninquisitive
indifferent, 456
Uninspired
unexcited, 823
unactuated, 616

Uninstructed
ignorant, 491
Unintellectual
ignorant, 452
imbecile, 499
Unintelligent
foolish, 499
Unintelligible
difficult, 519
style, 571
Unintentional
change, 621
Uninterested
incurious, 456
inattentive, 458
indifferent, 823
weary, 841
Uninteresting
wearisome, 841
dull, 843
Unintermitting
unbroken, 69
durable, 110
continuing, 143
active, 682
Uninterrupted
continuous, 69
unremitting, 143
Uninvestigated
unknown, 491
Uninvited
exclusion, 893
Uninviting
unattractive, 866
unpleasant, 830
Union
junction, 43
combination, 48
concord, 23, 714
concurrence, 178
marriage, 903
Union Jack
flag, 550
Unique
special, 79
alone, 87
exceptional, 83
dissimilarity, 18
non-imitation, 20
Unison
agreement, 23
concord, 714
uniformity, 16
melody, 413
Unisonant

harmony, 413
Unit
number, 87
troop, 726
Unitarian
heterodoxy, 984A
Unite
join, 43
agree, 23
concur, 178
assemble, 72
converge, 290
league, 712
Unity
singleness, 87
integrity, 50
concord, 714
Universal
general, 78
Universe
world, 318
University
school, 542
Unjust
wrong, 923
Unjustified
undue, 925
Unkempt
careless, 653
slovenly, 851
Unkennel
turn out, 185
disclose, 529
Unkind
malevolent, 907
Unknit
disjoin, 44
Unknowable
concealment, 528
Unknown
ignorant, 491
latent, 526
to fame, 874
Unlaboured
unprepared, 674
style, 578
Unlace
disjoin, 44
Unlade
ejection, 297
Unladylike
vulgar, 851
rude, 895
Unlamented
disliked, 898

unapproved, 932
Unlatch
disjoin, 44
Unlawful
undue, 925
illegal, 964
Unlearn
forget, 506
Unlearned
ignorant, 491
Unleavened
non-preparation, 674
Unless
circumstances, 8
qualification, 469
condition, 770
Unlettered
ignorant, 491
Unlicensed
unpermitted, 761
Unlicked
clownish, 876
vulgar, 851
unprepared, 674
Unlike
dissimilar, 18
Unlikely
improbable, 473
Unlimited
infinite, 105
space, 180
great, 31
Unlink
disjoin, 44
Unliquefied
solid, 321
Unlit
darkness, 421
Unload
unpack, 297
disencumber, 705
transfer, 270
Unlock
unfasten, 44
explain, 462
Unlooked-for
unexpected, 508
Unloose
unfasten, 44
liberate, 750
Unloved
hate, 898
Unlovely
ugly, 846

Unlucky
  inopportune, 135
  failing, 732
  unfortunate, 735
  luckless, 828
  painful, 830
  bad, 649
Unmade
  non-existent, 2
Unmaidenly
  ill-mannered, 851
Unmaimed
  uninjured, 654
Unmake
  reversion, 145
Unmanageable
  perverse, 704
  unwieldy, 647
Unmanly
  improbity, 940
  effeminate, 374
  cowardly, 862
Unmanned
  weak, 160
  sad, 837
Unmannerly
  rude, 895
Unmarked
  neglect, 460
Unmarred
  sound, 654
  preserved, 670
Unmarried
  celibacy, 904
Unmask
  show, 525
  disclose, 529
Unmatched
  different, 15
  unparalleled, 20
  dissimilar, 18
Unmeaning
  nonsense, 517
Unmeasured
  abundant, 639
  infinite, 105
  undistinguished, 465A
  casual, 621
Unmeet
  undue, 925
Unmelodious
  discord, 414
Unmelted
  density, 321
Unmentionable

unseemly, 961
Unmentioned
  latency, 526
Unmerciful
  malevolence, 907
Unmerited
  undueness, 925
Unmethodical
  disorder, 59
Unmindful
  inattention, 458
  neglect, 460
  forgetful, 506
  ungrateful, 917
Unmingled
  simpleness, 42
Unmirthful
  dejection, 837
Unmissed
  neglect, 460
Unmistakable
  clear, 518
  visible, 446
Unmitigated
  greatness, 31
  complete, 52P
Unmixed
  simpleness, 42
Unmodified
  permanence, 141
Unmolested
  content, 831
  safe, 664
Unmoral
  vice, 945
Unmourned
  hate, 898
Unmoved
  quiescent, 265
  resolute, 604
  obstinate, 606
  torpid, 823
  uninduced, 616
Unmusical
  discord, 414
Unmuzzled
  freedom, 748
Unnamed
  misnomer, 565
Unnatural
  unconformity, 83
Unnecessary
  inutility, 645
  superfluous, 641
Unneeded

inutility, 645
Unneighbourly
  unsociable, 893
Unnerved
  impotence, 158
  weakness, 160
Unnoted
  neglected, 460
  ignoble, 874
Unnoticed
  neglected, 460
  ignoble, 874
Unnumbered
  infinity, 105
Unobjectionable
  goodness, 648
Unobscured
  vision, 420
Unobservant
  inattention, 458
Unobserved
  unseen, 460
Unobstructed
  unopposed, 709
  free, 748
  clear, 705
Unobtainable
  impossibility, 471
Unobtained
  loss, 776
Unobtrusive
  modesty, 881
Unoccupied
  vacant, 187
  solitary, 893
  unthinking, 452
  inactive, 683
Unoffending
  innocuous, 648
  innocent, 946
Unofficial
  unauthorized, 925
Unopened
  closure, 261
Unopposed
  co-operation, 709
Unorganized
  mineral, 358
  unprepared, 674
Unornamental
  ugly, 846
Unornamented
  simple, 849
  style, 576

Unorthodox
heterodox, 984A
abnormal, 83
Unostentatious
modesty, 881
Unpacified
discord, 713
Unpack
ejection, 297
Unpaid
debt, 806
gratuitous, 815
Unpaid-for
credit, 805
Unpalatable
unsavoury, 395
disagreeable, 830, 867
Unparagoned
perfection, 650
Unparalleled
great, 31
superiority, 33
exceptional, 83
unmatched, 20
Unpardonable
vice, 945
Unpatriotic
selfish, 911
Unpeaceful
warfare, 722
Unpeople
displacement, 185
exclusion, 893
Unpeopled
empty, 187
Unperceived
latent, 526
neglected, 460
unknown, 491
Unperformed
non-completion, 730
Unperjured
probity, 939
Unperplexed
wisdom, 498
Unpersuadable
obstinacy, 606
dissuasion, 616
Unperturbed
impassive, 823
Unphilosophical
folly, 499
Unpick
disjunction, 44
Unpierced
closure, 261

Unpin
disjunction, 44
Unpitying
ruthless, 907
angry, 900
Unplagued
content, 831
Unplayable
difficult, 704
Unpleasant
pain, 830
Unplumbed
deep, 208
Unpoetical
prose, 598
Unpolished
rude, 895
vulgar, 851
unprepared, 674
Unpolluted
goodness, 648
Unpopular
disliked, 830
Unpossessed
loss, 776
Unpractical
inactivity, 683
Unpractised
unskilfulness, 699
disuse, 614
Unprecedented
unconformity, 83
dissimilarity, 18
infrequency, 137
Unprejudiced
judicious, 480
wise, 498
Unpremeditated
impulsive, 612
unprepared, 674
Unprepared
non-preparation, 674
Unprepossessed
wisdom, 498
Unprepossessing
unpleasing, 829
ugly, 846
Unpresentable
vulgarity, 851
Unpretending
modesty, 881
Unpretentious
modest, 881
Unprincipled
vice, 945

Unprivileged
undueness, 925
Unproclaimed
latency, 526
Unprocurable
impossibility, 471
Unproduced
non-existent, 2
Unproductive
barren, 169
useless, 645
Unprofessional
non-observance, 614
Unprofitable
useless, 645
inexpedient, 647
bad, 649
unproductive, 169
Unprogressive
unchanged, 141
Unprolific
barren, 169
Unpromising
hopeless, 859
Unprompted
impulse, 612
Unpromulgated
latent, 526
Unpronounced
latent, 526
Unpropitious
hopeless, 859
inauspicious, 135
Unproportioned
disagreement, 24
Unprosperous
adversity, 735
Unprotected
danger, 665
Unproved
sophistry, 477
Unprovided
scanty, 640
unprepared, 674
Unprovoked
uninduced, 616
Unpublished
latency, 526
Unpunctual
tardy, 133
untimely, 135
irregular, 139
Unpunished
exempt, 960

Unpurified
uncleanness, 653
Unpurposed
chance, 621
Unpursued
relinquishment, 624
Unqualified
inexpert, 699
unentitled, 925
unprepared, 674
complete, 52
Unquelled
violence, 173
Unquenched
violence, 173
burning, 382
Unquestionable
certainty, 474
Unquestioned
certainty, 474
assent, 488
Unquiet
excitement, 825
Unravaged
undamaged, 648
Unravel
untie, 44
straighten, 246
unfold, 313
decompose, 49
solve, 462, 480A
interpret, 522
disembarrass, 705
arrange, 60
Unravelled
arranged, 58
Unreachable
distance, 196
Unreached
shortcoming, 304
Unread
ignorance, 491
Unready
non-preparation, 674
incompleteness, 53
Unreal
non-existing, 2
erroneous, 495
imaginary, 515
Unreasonable
foolish, 499
exorbitant, 814
unjust, 923
impossible, 471
erroneous, 495

Unreasoning
material, 450A
instinctive, 477
Unreclaimed
impenitence, 951
Unreconciled
discord, 713
Unrecorded
obliteration, 552
Unrecounted
exclusion, 55
Unrecovered
deterioration, 659
Unrectified
imperfection, 651
Unredeemed
greatness, 31
Unreduced
greatness, 31
Unrefined
vulgarity, 851
Unreflecting
impulse, 612
Unreformed
impenitence, 951
Unrefreshed
fatigue, 688
Unrefuted
demonstrated, 478
true, 494
Unregarded
neglected, 460
unrespected, 929
Unregistered
unrecorded, 552
Unrehearsed
impulse, 612
Unrelated
irrelation, 10
Unrelaxed
unweakened, 159
Unrelenting
malevolent, 907
revengeful, 919
Unreliable
dubious, 475, 485
untrustworthy, 940
Unrelieved
aggravation, 835
Unremarked
neglected, 460
Unremembered
forgotten, 506
Unremitting
continuing, 69, 110

industrious, 682
Unremoved
location, 184
Unremunerative
inutility, 645
Unrenewed
unchanged, 141
Unrepealed
unchanged, 141
Unrepeated
fewness, 103
unity, 87
Unrepentant
impenitent, 951
Unrepining
patient, 831
Unreplenished
insufficient, 640
Unreported
untold, 526
Unrepressed
violent, 173
Unreproached
innocence, 946
Unreproachful
forgiveness, 918
Unreproved
innocence, 946
Unrequited
owing, 806
ingratitude, 917
Unresented
forgiven, 918
Unresenting
enduring, 826
Unreserved
frank, 543
Unresisting
obedience, 743
Unresolved
irresolute, 605
Unrespected
disrespect, 929
Unresponsive
insensibility, 823
Unrest
moving, 264
change, 140
changeable, 149
Unrestored
deterioration, 659
Unrestrained
free, 748
unencumbered, 705
Unrestraint
intemperance, 954

Unrestricted
undiminished, 31
free, 748
Unretracted
affirmation, 535
Unrevealed
concealed, 528
Unrevenged
jealousy, 920
Unreversed
permanence, 141
continuance, 143
Unrevoked
continuance, 143
Unrewarded
debt, 806
ingratitude, 917
Unrhymed
prose, 598
Unriddle
solve, 462
interpret, 522
disclose, 529
Unrighteous
evil, 945
Unrip
uncover, 260
Unripe
unprepared, 674
Unrivalled
goodness, 648
Unrivet
disjoin, 44
Unrobe
divest, 226
Unroll
straighten, 246
evolve, 313
display, 525
unravel, 47
Unromantic
true, 494
Unroof
divest, 226
Unroot
pull up, 162
Unruffled
calm, 174
placid, 826
unaffected, 823
quiet, 265
orderly, 58
Unruly
disobedient, 742

obstinate, 606
violent, 173
Unsafe
dangerous, 665
Unsaid
unspoken, 581
untold, 526
Unsanctified
unholy, 988, 989
Unsanctioned
undue, 925
Unsanitary
insalubrious, 657
Unsated
desire, 865
Unsatisfactory
discontent, 832
displeasing, 830
Unsatisfied
discontent, 832
Unsavoury
unsavouriness, 395
Unsay
retract, 607
Unscanned
neglected, 460
Unscathed
health, 654
Unschooled
illiterate, 491
uneducated, 699
Unscientific
ignorant, 495
unskilled, 699
Unscoured
unclean, 653
Unscreened
danger, 665
Unscrew
disjoin, 44
Unscriptural
heterodoxy, 984A
Unscrupulous
evil, 940
Unseal
disclosure, 529
Unseam
disjoin, 44
Unsearched
neglect, 460
Unseasonable
intempestivity, 135
inexpedient, 647
inappropriate, 24
Unseasoned

unprepared, 674
unaccustomed, 614
Unseat
dismiss, 756
Unsecured
uncovenanted, 768A
Unseemly
undue, 925
vicious, 945, 961
vulgar, 851
ugly, 846
inexpedient, 647
Unseen
invisible, 447
unprepared, 674
neglected, 460
Unselfish
generous, 942
Unserviceable
useless, 645
Unset
disjoin, 44
Unsettle
derange, 61
irresolute, 475, 605
mutable, 149
insane, 503
Unsevered
whole, 50
Unshackle
free, 748
liberate, 750
untie, 44
Unshaken
strong, 159
resolute, 604
Unshapely
ugly, 846
Unshapen
amorphous, 241
ugly, 846
Unshared
possession, 777
Unsheathe
uncover, 226
Unsheltered
danger, 665
Unshifting
continuance, 143
Unshocked
unmoved, 823
Unshod
divestment, 226
Unshorn
whole, 50

Unshrinking
resolution, 604
courage, 861
Unsifted
neglected, 460
Unsight
hinder, 706
Unsightly
ugly, 846
Unsinged
uninjured, 670
Unskilful
unskilled, 699
useless, 645
Unslaked
desire, 865
Unsleeping
activity, 682
Unsociable
exclusive, 893
Unsocial
exclusive, 893
Unsoiled
clean, 652
Unsold
possessed, 777
Unsolder
disjoin, 47
Unsoldierly
cowardly, 862
Unsolicited
willing, 602
Unsolicitous
indifferent, 866
Unsolved
secret, 526
Unsophisticated
genuine, 494
simple, 42, 849
good, 648
innocent, 946
Unsorted
unarranged, 59
Unsought
avoided, 623
unrequested, 766
Unsound
imperfect, 651
unhealthy, 655
sophistical, 477
Unsounded
deep, 208
Unsown
unprepared, 674
Unsparing

ample, 639
Unspeakable
great, 31
wonderful, 870
Unspecified
general, 78
Unspent
unused, 678
Unspoiled
goodness, 648
Unspoken
unsaid, 581
Unsportsmanlike
improbity, 940
Unspotted
clean, 652
innocent, 946
beautiful, 845
Unstable
mutable, 149
irresolute, 605
Unstained
untouched, 652
honourable, 939
Unstatesmanlike
unskilful, 699
Unsteadfast
irresolute, 605
Unsteady
mutable, 149
irresolute, 605, 607
dangerous, 665
Unstinted
plenteous, 639
Unstirred
unmoved, 826
calm, 265
Unstitch
disjoin, 44
Unstopped
open, 260
continuing, 143
Unstored
unprovided, 640
Unstrained
unexerted, 172
relaxed, 687
turbid, 653
Unstrengthened
weak, 160
Unstrung
weak, 160
Unsubdued
free, 748
Unsubjugated

free, 748
Unsubmissive
disobedient, 742
Unsubstantial
unsubstantiality, 4
rare, 322
texture, 329
imaginary, 515
erroneous, 495
Unsubstantiated
erroneous, 495
Unsuccessful
failure, 732
Unsuccessive
discontinuous, 70
Unsuitable
incongruous, 24
inexpedient, 647
time, 135
Unsuited
see Unsuitable
Unsullied
clean, 652
honourable, 939
guiltless, 946
Unsummed
infinity, 105
Unsummoned
voluntary, 600
Unsung
untold, 526
Unsunned
dark, 421
Unsupplied
insufficiency, 640
Unsupported
weak, 160
Unsuppressed
persisting, 141
Unsurpassed
great, 31
superior, 33
Unsusceptible
unfeeling, 823
Unsuspected
latent, 526
Unsuspicious
credulous, 484, 486
hopeful, 858
Unsustained
weak, 160
Unswayed
uninfluenced, 616
Unsweetened
unsavoury, 395

Unswept
dirty, 653
Unswerving
straight, 246
direct, 278
determined, 604
Unsymmetrical
disorder, 59
distortion, 243
Unsympathetic
unfriendly, 907
Unsystematic
disorder, 59
Untack
disjoin, 44
Untainted
healthy, 654
pure, 652
honourable, 939
Untalented
unskilled, 699
Untalked-of
latency, 526
Untamed
rude, 851
ferocious, 907
Untangled
order, 58
Untarnished
probity, 939
innocence, 946
Untasted
taste, 391
Untaught
ignorant, 491
Untaxed
cheap, 815
Unteach
misteach, 538
Unteachable
unskilled, 699
Untempered
greatness, 31
Untempted
uninfluenced, 616
Untenable
weak, 160
undefended, 725
sophistical, 477
Untenanted
empty, 187
Untended
neglected, 460
Untested
neglected, 460

Unthanked
ingratitude, 917
Unthankful
ungrateful, 917
Unthawed
solid, 321
cold, 383
Unthinkable
impossible, 471
Unthinking
thoughtless, 452
Unthought-of
neglected, 460
unconsidered, 452
Unthoughtful
neglectful, 460
Unthreatened
safe, 664
Unthrifty
prodigal, 818
unprepared, 674
Unthrone
dismiss, 756
Unthwarted
unhindered, 748
Untidy
in disorder, 59
slovenly, 653
Untie
loose, 44
liberate, 750
Until
time, 106, 108
Untilled
unprepared, 674
Untimely
ill-timed, 135
Untinged
simple, 42
uncoloured, 429
Untired
refreshed, 689
Untiring
active, 682
Untitled
commonalty, 876
Untold
secret, 526, 528
countless, 105
Untouched
disused, 678
insensible, 376, 823
Untoward
bad, 649
inopportune, 135

unprosperous, 735
unpleasant, 830
Untraced
latency, 526
Untracked
latency, 526
Untrained
unskilled, 699
unprepared, 674
unaccustomed, 614
Untrammelled
free, 705, 748
Untranslated
misinterpretation, 523
Untravelled
quiescent, 265
unknown, 491
Untreasured
unstored, 640
Untried
undetermined, 461
Untrimmed
simple, 849
unprepared, 674
Untrodden
new, 123
not used, 678
impervious, 261
Untroubled
calm, 174, 721
Untrue
false, 544
Untrustworthy
dishonest, 940
erroneous, 495
uncertain, 475
dangerous, 665
Untruth
falsehood, 544, 546
Untunable
discord, 414
Unturned
straight, 246
Untutored
ignorant, 491
Untwine
unfold, 313
Untwist
straighten, 246
evolve, 313
separate, 44, 47
Unurged
spontaneous, 600
Unused
unaccustomed, 614, 699

Upbraid
disapprove, 932
Upbringing
teaching, 537
Upcast
elevation, 307
Upgrow
height, 206
Upgrowth
ascent, 305
Upheave
elevation, 307
Uphill
activity, 217
ascent, 305
difficult, 704
Uphold
support, 215
evidence, 467
aid, 707
continue, 143
Upholster
cover, 222
furnish, 637
Upkeep
preservation, 670
Uplands
height, 206
Uplift
elevation, 307
Upper
height, 206
Upper hand
authority, 737
success, 731
Upper storey
brain, 450
Uppermost
height, 206, 210
Uppish
self-assertive, 885
Upraise
elevation, 307
Uprear
elevation, 307
Upright
vertical, 212
honest, 939
virtuous, 944
Uprise
ascent, 305
Uproar
noise, 404
turmoil, 173
Uproar

disorder, 59
Uproot
destruction, 162
extraction, 301
Upset
throw down, 308
disorder, 59
derange, 61
change, 140
invert, 218
destroy, 162
Upshot
end, 66
total, 50
Upside-down
inversion, 218
Upstage
affected, 855
supercilious, 930
proud, 878
Upstairs
height, 207
Upstart
plebeian, 876
prosperous, 734
Upturn
inversion, 218
Upwards
height, 206
Uranology
world, 318
Urban
abode, 189
Urbane
courtesy, 894
Urchin
small, 193
child, 129
wretch, 949
Urge
impel, 276
incite, 615
solicit, 765
hasten, 684
accelerate, 274
violence, 173
Urgent
important, 642
required, 630
Uriah Heep
servility, 886
Urinal
room, 191
privy, 653
Urinate

excrete, 299
Urn
vase, 191
funereal, 363
kettle, 386
Usage
custom, 613
rule, 80
use, 677
Usance
debt, 806
Use
employment, 677
waste, 638
utility, 644
habit, 613
rule, 80
Used up
worn, 651
surfeited, 869
Useful
use, 644
Useless
misuse, 645
Usher
teacher, 540
servant, 746
announce, 511
receive, 296, 894
begin, 66
precede, 62, 280
prior, 116
Ustulation
heating, 384
Usual
ordinary, 82
customary, 613
Usufruct
use, 677
Usurer
merchant, 797
Usurp
assume, 739
dethrone, 738
seize, 789
illegality, 925
Usury
debt, 806
Utensil
instrument, 633
Utilitarian
philanthropy, 910
Utilize
use, 644, 677

Utmost
superior, 33
Utopia
visionary, 515
hopeful, 858
Utter
extreme, 31
to speak, 580, 582
disclose, 529
publish, 531
distribute, 73
money, 800
Uttermost
greatness, 31
Uxorious
love, 897

V.I.P.
importance, 642
V.1
bomb, 727
Vacant
void, 4
absent, 187
thoughtless, 452
foolish, 499
scanty, 640
Vacate
absence, 187
Vacation
leisure, 685
Vaccination
injection, 300
Vacillation
changeableness, 149
undulation, 314
uncertainty, 475
wavering, 605
Vacuity
void, 4, 180
absence, 187
inexistence, 2
imbecility, 499
Vacuous
empty, 187
Vade-mecum
teaching, 537
school, 542
Vagabond
rogue, 949
wanderer, 268
pauper, 804
Vagary
whim, 608

absurdity, 497
imagination, 515
antic, 856
Vagrant
moving, 264
roving, 266
fickle, 149
devious, 279
traveller, 268
tramp, 876
Vague
uncertain, 475
obscure, 519
style, 571
Vails
expenditure, 809
reward, 973
Vain
unreal, 2
unprofitable, 645
conceited, 880
unvalued, 866
Vainglorious
haughty, 878
boasting, 884
vain, 880
Valance
edge, 230
Vale
concavity, 252
Vale
departure, 293
Valediction
departure, 293
courtesy, 894
Valentine
courtship, 902
Valet
servant, 746
Valetudinarian
disease, 655
Valhalla
interment, 363
Valiant
courage, 861
Valid
strong, 159
powerful, 157
influential, 175
cogent, 467
logical, 476
Valise
receptacle, 191
Valley
concavity, 252

Vallum
defence, 717
Valour
courage, 861
Value
price, 812
goodness, 648
importance, 642
to measure, 466
estimate, 480
Valueless
inutility, 645
Valve
stop, 263
conduit, 350
Vamoose
go away, 287
Vamp
repair, 658
improvise, 612
music, 415
flirt, 902
cinema, 599A
Vamp up
furbish, 673
Vampire
bane, 663
evildoer, 913
demon, 980
Van
front, 234
beginning, 66
wagon, 272
Vandal
commonalty, 876
evildoer, 913
Vandalism
vulgarity, 851
Vane
indication, 550
wind, 349
Vanguard
front, 234
beginning, 66
Vanish
disappear, 449
perish, 2, 4
transient, 111
Vanity
conceit, 880
folly, 499
worthlessness, 645
Vanity-case
receptacle, 191
Vanquish
success, 731

Vanquished
failure, 732
Vantage-ground
influence, 175
Vapid
insipid, 391
unattractive, 866
style, 575
Vaporize
vaporization, 336
Vapour
gas, 334
bubble, 353
insolence, 885
boasting, 884
chimera, 515
rare, 322
Vapour bath
furnace, 386
Vapours
dejection, 837
Variable
changeable, 149
irresolute, 605
Variance
difference, 15
disagreement, 24
discord, 713
Variation
non-imitation, 20
irrelation, 10
music, 415
Varied
different, 15
Variegation
colour, 440
Variety
difference, 15
multiformity, 16A
exception, 83
class, 75
Variform
difference, 15
variety, 81
Various
different, 15
many, 102
variation, 20
Varlet
sinner, 949
Varnish
coat, 222
decorate, 845, 847
semiliquid, 352

sophistry, 477
falsehood, 544
excuse, 937
Vary
differ, 15
diversify, 18
modify, 20
change, 140
fluctuate, 149
Vasculum
botany, 369
Vase
receptacle, 191
Vassal
servant, 746
Vassalage
subjection, 749
Vast
in quantity, 31
in size, 192
Vat
receptacle, 191
Vatican
temple, 1000
Vaticide
killing, 361
Vaticination
prediction, 511
Vaudeville
the drama, 599
Vault
cellar, 191
sepulchre, 363
to leap, 305, 309
Vaulting
superiority, 33
Vaunt
boasting, 884
Vaurien
sinner, 949
Veda
sacred books, 986
Vedette
safety, 664
warning, 668
Veer
regression, 283
change, 140
deviate, 279
change intention, 607
Vegetable
vegetable, 365
plant, 367
Vegetarian
temperance, 953

Vegetate
grow, 194
exist, 1
inactivity, 683
insensibility, 823
quiescence, 265
Vehemence
violence, 173
emotion, 825
Vehicle
vehicle, 272
instrumentality, 631
Vehmgericht
illegality, 964
Veil
mask, 530
to conceal, 528
shade, 424
covering, 225
Veiled
invisible, 447
latent, 526
Vein
humour, 602
tendency, 176
cast of mind, 820
mine, 636
Veined
variegation, 440
Velleity
will, 600
Vellum
writing, 590
Velocipede
locomotion, 266
Velocity
swiftness, 274
Velour
smooth, 255
rough, 256
Velvet
smooth, 255
rough, 256
ease, 705
physical pleasure, 277
moral pleasure, 827
profit, 618
Velveteen
smooth, 255
rough, 256
Venal
parsimony, 819
mercenary, 812, 943
Vend
sell, 796

Vendetta
feud, 713
revenge, 919
Vendible
sale, 796
Vendor
merchant, 797
Veneer
covering, 222
ostentation, 882
Venerable
old, 128
Veneration
respect, 928
piety, 987
worship, 990
Venery
chase, 622
Venesection
ejection, 297
Vengeance
revenge, 919
(with a),
greatness, 31
Vengeful
revenge, 919
Venial
excusable, 937
Venom
bane, 663
malignity, 907
Venomous
evil, 649
malignant, 907
Vent
air-pipe, 351
opening, 260
emit, 295
disclose, 529
Vent-peg
stopper, 263
Ventilate
perflate, 349
air, 338
clean, 652
discuss, 595
examine, 461
publicity, 531
Ventilator
wind, 349
Ventricle
receptacle, 191
Ventriloquism
voice, 580
Venture

chance, 156
to try, 621, 675
danger, 665
courage, 861
Venturesome
brave, 861
rash, 863
Venue
place, 182
Venus
goddess, 979
beauty, 845
love, 897
Veracity
truth, 494, 543
Veranda
portico, 191
Verb. sap.
advice, 695
Verbal
word, 562
Verbatim
imitation, 19
interpretation, 522
word, 562
Verbiage
diffuse, 573
nonsense, 497
Verbose
diffuse, 573
loquacious, 584
Verdant
green, 435
vegetation, 367
credulous, 486
ignorant, 491
Verd-antique
green, 435
Verdict
opinion, 480
sentence, 969
Verdigris
green, 435
Verdure
green, 435
plant, 367
Verecundity
modesty, 881
humility, 879
Verge
brink, 230
to tend, 278
contribute, 176
Verger
churchman, 996

Veridical
truthful, 543
Verify
test, 463
demonstrate, 478
judge, 480
warrant, 771
Verily
positively, 32
truly, 494
Verisimilitude
probable, 472
Veritable
truth, 494
Verity
truth, 494
Verjuice
sourness, 397
Vermicular
convolution, 248
Vermiform
convolution, 248
Vermilion
redness, 434
Vermin
base, 876
unclean, 653
Vernacular
language, 560
familiar, 82
Vernal
early, 123
spring, 125
Vers de société
poetry, 597
Vers libre
poetry, 597
Versatile
changeable, 605
skilful, 698
Verse
poetry, 597
Versed
skill, 698
Versicolour
variegation, 440
Versifier
poetry, 597
Version
interpretation, 522
Verso
left hand, 239
Vert
change belief, 144, 484
green, 435

Vertex
summit, 210
Vertical
verticality, 212
Vertigo
insanity, 503
Verve
imagination, 515
feeling, 821
Very
great, 31
Very light
light, 423
Vesicle
cell, 191
globe, 249
Vespers
rite, 990, 998
Vespertine
evening, 126
Vessel
recipient, 191
ship, 273
tube, 260
Vest
dress, 225
give, 784
Vestal
purity, 960
Vested
legal, 963
Vestibule
entrance, 66
room, 191
Vestige
record, 551
Vestments
canonicals, 999
Vestry
conclave, 995
church, 1000
Vesture
dress, 225
Veteran
old, 130
adept, 700
fighter, 726
Veterinary
remedy, 662
taming, 370
Veto
prohibit, 761
refuse, 764
Vetturino
director, 694

Vex
painful, 830
Vexation
pain, 828
Vexatious
painful, 830
Via
way, 627
direction, 278
Via media
mean, 29
middle, 68
Viability
life, 359
Viable
practicable, 470
Viaduct
way, 627
Vial
bottle, 191
wrath, 900
Viands
food, 298
Viaticum
rite, 998
Vibrate
fluctuate, 149
oscillate, 314
Vicar
clergy, 996
deputy, 759
Vicarage
office, 995
house, 1000
Vicarious
substituted, 149, 755
Vice
guiltiness, 945
imperfection, 651
deputy, 759
grip, 781
vinculum, 45
Vice versa
correlation, 12
contrariety, 14
interchange, 148
Vicegerency
agency, 755
Vicegerent
consignee, 758
deputy, 759
Vice-president
master, 745
Viceroy
deputy, 759

Vicinity
nearness, 197
Vicious
fallacious, 477
faulty, 651
immoral, 945
Vicissitude
change, 140
mutable, 149
Victim
injured, 732
dupe, 547
sufferer, 828
Victimize
deceive, 545
baffle, 731
Victoria
vehicle, 272
Victory
success, 731
Victualling
provision, 637
Victuals
food, 298
Videlicet
namely, 522
specification, 79
Video
radio, 599B
Viduity
widowhood, 905
Vie
emulate, 648
contend, 720
View
sight, 441
appearance, 448
to attend to, 457
landscape, 556
opinion, 484
intention, 620
radio, 599B
View-finder
optical, 445
Viewless
invisible, 447
Viewy
caprice, 608
Vigesimal
twenty, 98
Vigil
watch, 459
eve, 116
Vigilance
attention, 457

care, 459

Vigils
worship, 990

Vignette
engraving, 558

Vigour
strong, 159
healthy, 654
activity, 683
energy, 171
style, 574

Viking
pirate, 792

Vile
bad, 649
odious, 830
valueless, 643
disgraceful, 874, 940
plebeian, 876

Vilify
censure, 932
defame, 934
scold, 908
shame, 874

Vilipend
censure, 932
defame, 934
shame, 874
disrespect, 929

Villa
abode, 189

Village
abode, 189

Villager
inhabitant, 188

Villain
vice, 945
knave, 941

Villainage
subjection, 749

Villainy
vice, 945
improbity, 940

Villanelle
poetry, 597

Villous
roughness, 256

Vim
energy, 171, 682
style, 574

Vincible
weakness, 160

Vinculum
junction, 45

Vindicate

justify, 924, 937

Vindictive
revengeful, 919
irascible, 901

Vinegar
sourness, 397
condiment, 393

Vineyard
agriculture, 371

Vintage
agriculture, 371

Viola
musical instrument, 417

Violate
disobey, 742
engagement, 773
right, 925
duty, 927
a usage, 614

Violence
physical, 173
arbitrariness, 964

Violently
great, 31

Violet
purple, 437

Violin
musical instrument, 417

Violinist
musician, 416

Violoncello
musical instrument, 417

Viper
bane, 663, 913
miscreant, 949

Virago
irascibility, 901
fury, 173

Virescent
green, 435

Virgin
girl, 129
celibacy, 904
purity, 960

Virginal
musical instrument, 417

Virginia
tobacco, 298AA

Viridescent
green, 435

Viridity
green, 435

Virile
manly, 373
adolescent, 131

strong, 159
style, 574

Virtu
taste, 850

Virtual
real, 1
potential, 2

Virtually
truth, 494

Virtue
goodness, 944
right, 922
probity, 939
purity, 960
power, 157
courage, 861

Virtueless
vice, 945

Virtuosity
taste, 850
skill, 698

Virtuoso
taste, 850
performer, 416
proficient, 700

Virulence
insalubrity, 657
poison, 663
malignity, 649
page, 900
malevolence, 907

Virus
poison, 663
disease, 655
insalubrity, 657

Visage
ront, 234
appearance, 448

Vis-à-vis
front, 234
opposite, 237

Viscera
interior, 221

Viscid
semiliquid, 352

Viscount
noble, 875
master, 745

Viscounty
title, 877

Viscous
semiliquid, 352

Visé
indication, 550

Vishnu
deity, 979

Visible
visibility, 446
Vision
sight, 441
imagination, 515
apparition, 980
Visionary
erroneous, 495
imaginary, 515
impossible, 471
heterodox, 984A
Visit
sociality, 892
frequent, 136
arrival, 292
Visitation
pain, 828
disease, 655
calamity, 830
Visiting-card
indication, 560
Visitor
arrival, 292
director, 694
Visor
concealment, 528
Vista
point of view, 441
prospect, 448, 507
Visual
vision, 441
Vital
importance, 642
Vitality
life, 359
strength, 159
Vitals
interior, 221
Vitiate
deteriorate, 659
debase, 945
Vitreous
density, 321
Vitrify
density, 321
harden, 323
Vitriolic
malevolent, 907
Vituperate
disapprove, 932
scold, 908
Viva
honour, 873
Viva voce

speech, 582
Vivacious
active, 682
sensitive, 822
cheerful, 836
Vivarium
taming, 370
Vive
honour, 873
Vivid
light, 420
colour, 428
lively, 375
energetic, 171
style, 574
Vivify
life, 359
Vivisect
anatomize, 44
Vixen
scold, 901
fury, 173
Viz.
meaning, 516
Vizier
deputy, 759
Vizor
see Visor
Vocable
word, 562
Vocabulary
word, 562
Vocal
voice, 580
loudness, 404
music, 415
Vocalist
musician, 416
Vocalize
speech, 580
Vocation
business, 625
Vociferate
cry, 411
loudness, 404
voice, 580
Vogue
fashion, 852
custom, 613
repute, 873
Vogue word
neology, 563
Voice
speech, 580
grammar, 567

sound, 402
cry, 411
choice, 609
affirmation, 535
opinion, 484
Void
vacuum, 2, 4
absence, 187
to emit, 297
invalidate, 964
Voivode
master, 745
Volant
flight, 267
Volapük
language, 560
Volatile
vaporizable, 336
changeable, 149
irresolute, 605
Volatility
caprice, 608
Volcanic
violence, 173
excitable, 825
Volitation
flight, 267
Volition
will, 600
Volley
impulse, 276
attack, 716
violence, 173
collection, 72
Volplane
descent, 306
Volte-face
recantation, 607
Voluble
loquacity, 584
Volume
bulk, 192
quantity, 25
greatness, 31
book, 593
Voluntary
willing, 600, 602
music, 415
Volunteer
endeavour, 676
offer, 600, 763
Voluptuary
libertine, 962
Voluptuous
sensual, 954

pleasure, 377
joy, 827
delight, 829
Volute
convolution, 248
Vomit
ejection, 297
Vomitory
opening, 260
Voodooism
occult arts, 992
Voracity
appetite, 865
gluttony, 957
Vortex
rotation, 312
whirlpool, 348
Votary
devotee, 840, 865
Vote
choice, 609
affirmation, 535
Vote for
assent, 488
Votive
promise, 768
Vouch
testify, 467
assert, 535
Voucher
evidence, 467
record, 551
security, 771
Vouchsafe
permit, 760
consent, 762
ask, 765
deign, 879
Vow
promise, 768
assert, 535
worship, 990
Voyage
journey, 267
motion, 264
Voyageur
boatman, 269
Voyeur
curiosity, 455
Vraisemblance
probability, 472
Vulcan
god, 979
Vulgar
unrefined, 851

discourteous, 895
commonalty, 876
Vulgarism
solecism, 568
language, 560
Vulgate
revelation, 985
Vulnerable
danger, 665
Vulpine
cunning, 702
Vulture
bane, 663

W.C.
lavatory, 653
Wabble
oscillation, 314
Wacky
mad, 503
Wadding
lining, 224
softness, 324
stopping, 263
Waddle
slowness, 275
oscillation, 314
Wade
swim, 267
Wafer
layer, 204
Waft
transfer, 270
blow, 267, 349
Wag
oscillate, 314
agitate, 315
wit, 844
Wage war
contention, 720
Wager
chance, 621
Wages
expenditure, 809
Waggery
wit, 842
Waggish
merry, 836
Waggle
oscillation, 314
agitation, 315
Wagon
vehicle, 272
Wagonette

vehicle, 272
Waif
outcast, 893
Wail
lamentation, 839
Wain
vehicle, 272
Wainscot
lining, 224
base, 211
Waist
narrow, 203
Waistcoat
dress, 225
Wait
tarry, 110, 133
expect, 121, 507
inaction, 681
Wait on
accompany, 88
help, 707
call on, 894
Waiter
servant, 746
Waits
musicians, 416
Waive
relinquish, 624, 782
dispense with, 678
Wake
sequel, 65
back, 235
trace, 551
to excite, 824
funeral, 363
lamentation, 839
Wale
ridge, 250
Walk
move, 266
slowness, 275
region, 181
business, 625
way, 627
conduct, 692
arena, 728
Walkie-talkie
hearing, 418
radio, 599B
Walkover
easy, 705
Wall
lining, 224
circumscription, 231
enclosure, 232

749

prison, 752
asylum, 666
defence, 717
obstacle, 705

Wall-eyed
dim-sighted, 443

Wallet
receptacle, 191
purse, 802

Wallop
thrash, 972

Wallow
lie low, 207
rotation, 312

Waltz
dance, 840
music, 415

Wan
achromatism, 429

Wand
sceptre, 747

Wander
roam, 264, 266
deviate, 279, 291
circuit, 629
delirium, 503

Wanderer
traveller, 268

Wane
decay, 659
decrease, 36
contract, 195

Wangle
falsify, 544
steal, 791
plan, 626
cunning, 702

Want
desire, 865
require, 630
be inferior, 34
scant, 640
poverty, 804
imcomplete, 53

Wanting
witless, 499
imperfect, 651

Wantless
sufficiency, 639

Wanton
unrestrained, 748
motiveless, 616
impure, 961

War
warfare, 722

War-cry
indication, 550
defiance, 715

War-horse
carrier, 271

War loan
treasury, 802

War-whoop
indication, 450

Warble
music, 415

Ward
restraint, 751
safety, 664
asylum, 666

Ward off
defend, 717
avert, 706

Warden
guardian, 664
deputy, 759
master, 745

Warder
keeper, 263, 664, 753

Wardmote
tribunal, 966

Wardrobe
dress, 225
receptacle, 191

Wardship
safety, 664

Ware
merchandise, 798

Warehouse
store, 636
mart, 799

Warfare
war, 722

Warlike
contention, 720
courage, 861

Warlock
spirit, 980
sorcerer, 994

Warm
hot, 382
to heat, 384
ardent, 821, 824
angry, 900
irascible, 901
violent, 173

Warming-pan
heater, 386
preparation, 673

Warmth

heat, 382
emotion, 821
passion, 900

Warn
admonish, 695
forebode, 511

Warning
warning, 668
omen, 512
alarm, 669

Warp
narrow, 203
deviate, 279
prejudice, 481
imperfect, 651
texture, 329

Warrant
evidence, 467
order, 741
permit, 760
protest, 535
money-order, 800
security, 771
to authorize, 737
justify, 937

Warrantable
defensible, 937

Warranty
surety, 771
sanction, 924

Warren
den, 189

Warrior
combatant, 726

Warship
ship, 273

Wart
convexity, 250

Warts and all
unflattering, 544

Wary
cautious, 864
careful, 459

Wash
cleanse, 652
colour, 428
water, 337
marsh, 345

Wash out
obliterate, 552

Wash-out
fiasco, 732

Washerwoman
cleaner, 652

Washy
watery, 337
weak, 160
valueless, 645
style, 573
Wasp-waisted
thin, 203
Waspish
discourteous, 895
irascible, 901
Wassail
feast, 840
Waste
decrease, 36
contract, 195
expend, 638
destroy, 162
vacant space, 180
plain, 344
misuse, 679
useless, 645
prodigality, 818
refuse, 643
loss, 776
Waste-pipe
conduit, 350
Wasted
weakness, 160
Wasteful
useless, 645
prodigal, 818
Wastrel
outcast, 893
prodigal, 818
Watch
observe, 441
attend to, 457
expect, 507
sentinel, 753
clock, 114
Watch-fire
indication, 550
Watch-tower
warning, 668
Watcher
spectator, 444
Watchet
blue, 438
Watchful
care, 459
Watchman
safety, 664
Watchword
indication, 550
Water

fluid, 337
to weaken, 160
Water-cart
spray, 348
Water-clock
chronology, 114
Water-closet
room, 191
lavatory, 653
Water-gate
conduit, 350
Watercourse
conduit, 350
Watered
variegated, 440
Waterfall
river, 348
Watering-can
spray, 348
Waterlogged
difficulty, 704
Waterproof
dryness, 340
safe, 664
dress, 225
Watershed
summit, 210
Waterspout
river, 349
rotation, 312
Watertight
closed, 261
Wattle
plaiting, 219
Wave
of water, 348
the sea, 341
sinuous, 248
oscillate, 314
hint, 527
curl, 245
salute, 894
Waver
unwilling, 603
hesitate, 475, 605
fluctuate, 149
Wavy
convolution, 248
Wax
become, 144
increase, 35
soft, 324
semiliquid, 352
unctuous, 355
lubricate, 332

substance, 356
rage, 900
Waxcloth
covering, 222
Way
road, 627
space, 180
passage, 302
conduct, 692
habit, 613
Wayfarer
traveller, 268
Wayfaring
journey, 266
Waylay
deception, 545
Ways and means
means, 632
Wayward
obstinate, 606
capricious, 608
discourteous, 895
changeable, 149
Wayworn
fatigue, 688
Wayzgoose
picnic, 298
festivity, 840
Weak
feeble, 160
powerless, 158
insipid, 391, 575
small in degree, 32
foolish, 499
irrational, 477
irresolute, 605
compassionate, 914
vicious, 945
Weak-headed
fool, 499
Weak-hearted
coward, 862
Weak-kneed
irresolute, 605
Weak side
vice, 945
Weaken
enfeeble, 160
decrease, 36
invalidate, 468
impair, 659
Weal
good, 618
ridge, 250

Weald
plant, 367
plain, 344

Wealth
rich, 803

Wean
change habit, 614
change opinion, 484
infant, 129

Weapon
instrument, 633
arms, 727

Weaponless
impotent, 158

Wear
decrease, 36
decay, 659
use, 677
clothe, 225
alter course, 279

Wear and tear
waste, 638
injury, 619

Wear off
diminish, 36
cease, 142
habit, 614

Wear out
damage, 659
fatigue, 688

Wearisome
fatigue, 688
painful, 830
ennui, 841

Weary
fatigue, 688
ennui, 841
uneasy, 828

Weary Willie
loafer, 683

Weasand
air-pipe, 260, 351

Weather
air, 338
succeed, 731
disintegrate, 330

Weather-beaten
weak, 160

Weather-bound
restraint, 751

Weather-glass
measure, 466
air, 338

Weather-ship
air, 338

Weather-wise

prediction, 511
air, 338

Weathercock
irresolute, 605
mutable, 149

Weave
interlace, 219
wind, 248
produce, 161

Web
texture, 329
intersection, 219

Wed
marriage, 903

Wedded to
habit, 613
opinion, 484
obstinate, 606

Wedge
angular, 244
intervention, 228
instrument, 633
to insert, 300
locate, 184
join, 43
ingress, 294
flock, 72

Wedlock
marriage, 903

Wee
small, 32, 34

Weed
rubbish, 643, 645
plant, 367
cultivate, 371
reduce, 103
mourning, 225, 839
widow, 905
reject, 55
tobacco, 298A

Weedy
thin, 203

Weekly
period, 108, 138
publication, 531

Weeny
little, 193

Weep
lament, 839

Weigh
heavy, 319
ponder, 451
measure, 466
lift, 307
influence, 175

Weigh anchor
depart, 293

Weigh down
aggrieve, 649

Weigh with
motive, 615

Weighbridge
weight, 319

Weight
influence, 175
gravity, 319
importance, 642

Weightless
levity, 320

Weir
hindrance, 706
dam, 350

Weird
strange, 83
wonderful, 870
prediction, 511
supernatural, 980
destiny, 601

Welcome
grateful, 829
sociality, 892
reception, 894
friendly, 888

Weld
coherence, 46
join, 43

Welfare
prosperity, 734

Welkin
world, 318

Well
water, 343
to flow, 348
much, 31
healthy, 654
deep, 208
store, 636
origin, 153

Well-behaved
good, 944

Well-being
prosperity, 734
gratification, 827

Well-born
patrician, 875

Well-bred
courteous, 894
genteel, 852

Well-conducted
good, 944

Well-disposed
friendly, 707, 888
Well-doing
virtue, 944
Well done
approbation, 931
Well enough
imperfection, 651
Well-favoured
beauty, 845
Well-founded
probable, 472
Well-groomed
adornment, 847
Well-grounded
knowledge, 490
Well-informed
knowledge, 490
Well-intended
virtue, 944
Well-judged
intelligence, 498
Well-knit
strength, 159
Well-mannered
courtesy, 894
Well-meant
benevolent, 906
Well-off
prosperity, 734
wealth, 803
Well out
egress, 295
Well-proportioned
symmetry, 242
Well-set
strength, 159
Well-spent
success, 731
Well-tasted
savoury, 394
Well-timed
opportune, 134, 646
Well-to-do
prosperity, 734
Well-wisher
friend, 890
Welladay
lamentation, 839
Wellington
boot, 225
Wellnigh
almost, 32
Welsh
to cheat, 545

Welsher
deceiver, 548
swindler, 792
defaulter, 808
Welt
edge, 230
Welter
rotation, 312
agitation, 315
Weltschmerz
weariness, 841
Wen
convexity, 250
Wench
young girl, 129
woman, 374
Wend
journey, 266
Werewolf
demon, 980
Wersh
tasteless, 391, 866
insipid, 575
West
side, 236
Wet
water, 337
moisture, 339
Wet-nurse
to pamper, 954
Whack
blow, 276, 972
share, 786
try, 675
Whacked
exhausted, 160
Whacker
size, 31, 192
Whale
monster, 192
Whaler
ship, 273
Wham
impact, 276
Whang
impact, 276
Wharf
anchorage, 189
Whatnot
receptacle, 191
What's-his-name
euphemism, 565
Wheedle
flatter, 933
coax, 615

endearment, 902
Wheel
circle, 247
circuition, 311
deviation, 279
rotation, 212
instrument, 633
means, 632
money, 800
torture, 378, 975
pain, 830
execution, 972
Wheel-chair
vehicle, 272
Wheelbarrow
vehicle, 272
Wheen
plurality, 100
multitude, 102
Wheeze
blow, 349
hiss, 409
joke, 842
Whelm
redundance, 641
Whelp
young, 129
When
time, 119
Whence
attribution, 155
inquiry, 461
reasoning, 476
departure, 293
Whenever
time, 119
Whensoever
time, 119
Where
presence, 186
Whereabouts
situation, 183
nearness, 197
Whereas
reason, 476
Wherefore
reason, 476
attribution, 155
inquiry, 461
motive, 615
Whereupon
futurity, 121
Wherever
space, 180
Wherewith
instrument, 631

753

Wherewithal
means, 632
money, 800
Wherry
boat, 273
Whet
excite, 824
incite, 615
sharpen, 253
desire, 865
meal, 298
Whey
fluid, 337
Whiff
wind, 349
Whiffy
smelly, 401
Whigmaleerie
trifle, 643
While
duration, 106, 120
Whilom
preterition, 122
Whim
caprice, 608
prejudice, 481
desire, 865
imagination, 515
wit, 842
Whim-wham
trifle, 643
Whimper
lamentation, 839
Whimsical
fancy, 515, 608
ridiculous, 853
Whimsy
desire, 865
Whine
cry, 411
complain, 839
Whinny
animal cry, 412
Whip
to beat, 276, 972
scourge, 975
rapidity, 274
driver, 694
trouble, 830
Whip-hand
success, 731
Whip off
escape, 671
Whip-round

giving, 784
Whip up
snatch, 789
Whipper-in
director, 694
servant, 746
Whippersnapper
youth, 129
Whippet
chase, 622
Whipping-post
scourge, 975
Whirl
rotation, 312
Whirligig
rotation, 312
Whirlpool
vortex, 312
eddy, 348
danger, 667
confusion, 59
Whirlwind
wind, 349
vortex, 312
agitation, 315
Whirlybird
aircraft, 273A
Whirr
roll, 407
Whisk
rapidity, 274
circuition, 311
agitation, 315
Whisker
hair, 256
Whisky
vehicle, 272
Whisper
faint sound, 405
stammer, 583
tell, 527
prompt, 615
remind, 505
Whist!
silence, 403, 585
Whistle
hiss, 409
music, 415
instrument, 417
Whistle at
depreciate, 483
Whit
point, 32
part, 51
small, 193

White
whiteness, 430
eye, 441
White feather
coward, 862
White horses
wave, 348
White lie
equivocalness, 520
plea, 617
White-livered
cowardice, 862
Whitewash
whiten, 430
adorn, 847
vindicate, 937
acquit, 970
insolvency, 808
Whither
tendency, 176
direction, 278
Whittle
disjoin, 44
abbreviate, 201
Whiz
sibilation, 409
expert, 700
Whizz-kid
go-getter, 682
Whodunit
story, 594
Whole
entire, 50
complete, 52
healthy, 654
Whole-hearted
cordial, 602
Wholesale
greatness, 31
whole, 50
indiscriminate, 465A
plenty, 639
barter, 794
Wholesome
salubrity, 656
Wholly
great, 31
whole, 50
Whoop
cry, 411
loud, 404
weep, 839
Whoopee
merry, 836

Whopper
untruth, 546
Whopping
size, 192
Whore
libertine, 962
impurity, 961
Why
reason, 615
inquiry, 461
cause, 155
Wicked
vice, 945
improbity, 940
Wicker
crossing, 219
Wicket
entrance, 66
opening, 260
Wide
broad, 202
Wide-awake
hat, 225
Wide of
distance, 196
Widen
expand, 194
Widespread
dispersed, 73
Widow
widowhood, 905
Width
breadth, 202
Wield
use, 677
brandish, 315
Wife
marriage, 903
Wifeless
celibacy, 904
Wig
dress, 225
to scold, 932
Wiggle
oscillate, 314
Wight
man, 373
Wigwam
abode, 189
Wild
violent, 173
mad, 503
excited, 825
rash, 863
licentious, 954

foolish, 499, 699
useless, 645
desert, 344
Wilderness
space, 180
useless, 645
seclusion, 893
Wildfire
heat, 382
Wile
cunning, 702
stratagem, 545
Wilful
obstinacy, 606
Will
volition, 600
resolution, 604
Will-o'-the-wisp
light, 423
phantom, 515
Willing
acquiescent, 488
voluntary, 600, 602
Willow
lamentation, 839
Willowy
pliant, 324
Willy-nilly
compulsion, 744
necessity, 601
Willy-willy
vortex, 312
Wily
sly, 702
Wimble
perforator, 262
Wimple
dress, 225
Win
get, 775
steal, 791
succeed, 731
engage, 897
Win over
conciliate, 831
Wince
flinch, 860
feel, 821, 825
pain, 378, 828
Winch
instrument, 633
raise, 307
Wind
blast, 349
circuition, 311

convolution, 248
rapidity, 274
Wind-bound
hindrance, 706
restraint, 751
Wind up
screw up, 159
end, 67
complete, 729
fear, 860
Windbreaker
dress, 225
Windcheater
dress, 225
Windfall
good, 618
luck, 621
success, 731
Winding
curved, 245
undulating, 248
Winding-sheet
shroud, 363
Windlass
instrument, 633
raise, 307
Windmill
rotation, 312
Window
opening, 260
Windpipe
air-pipe, 351
Windy
air, 338
verbose, 573
Winebag
drunken, 959
Winebibber
drunken, 959
Wing
side, 236
limb, 633
troop, 726
asylum, 666
move, 267
Wing-commander
master, 745
Winged
rapid, 274
Wink
blind, 442
nictitate, 443
hint, 527
indicate, 550

Wink at
  permit, 760
  overlook, 460
Winning
  pleasing, 829
  courteous, 894
  lovely, 897
Winnow
  sift, 42
  exclude, 55
  clean, 652
  inquire, 461
  pick, 609
Winsome
  pleasing, 829
  lovely, 897
Winter
  cold, 383
Wintry
  cold, 383
Wipe
  clean, 652
  dry, 340
  strike, 276
Wipe off
  non-observance, 773
Wipe out
  obliterate, 552
  demolish, 162
Wire
  filament, 205
  ligature, 45
  message, 532
Wiredrawn
  lengthy, 200
  thin, 203
  style, 571
Wireless
  message, 532
  publication, 531
  hearing, 418
  radio, 599B
Wireworm
  bane, 663
Wiry
  tough, 327
Wisdom
  wisdom, 498
  intellect, 450
Wise
  wisdom, 498
  way, 627
Wise to
  knowing, 490
Wiseacre
  sage, 500

Wisecrack
  wit, 842
  maxim, 496
  phrase, 566
Wish
  desire, 865
Wishbone
  spell, 993
Wish joy
  congratulation, 896
Wishing-cap
  spell, 993
Wishy-washy
  insipid, 391
  absurd, 497
  feeble, 575
  trifling, 643
Wisp
  assemblage, 72
Wistful
  thoughtful, 451
Wit
  intellect, 450
  humour, 842
  wisdom, 498
  humorist, 844
Witch
  oracle, 513
  proficient, 700
  sorceress, 994
  bad woman, 949
Witchcraft
  sorcery, 992
Witchery
  attraction, 615
  charm, 829
  sorcery, 992
With
  addition, 37
  accompanying, 88
  instrumental, 631
Withal
  addition, 37
  accompanying, 88
Withdraw
  subduct, 38
  recede, 283, 287
  diverge, 291
  deny, 536
  depart, 293
  retire, 893
Withe
  fastening, 45
Wither
  shrink, 195

decay, 659
Withering
  disapproving, 932
Withershins
  rotation, 312
Withhold
  retain, 781
  conceal, 528
  stint, 640
  prohibit, 761
  dissuade, 616
Within
  interior, 221
Without
  unless, 8
  absence, 187
  exterior, 220
  subduction, 38
  exception, 83
  circumjacent, 227
Withstand
  resist, 719
  oppose, 179, 708
Withy
  fastening, 45
Witless
  ignorant, 491
  neglectful, 460
  imbecile, 499
Witling
  fool, 501
Witness
  evidence, 467
  voucher, 550
Wits
  intellect, 450
Witticism
  wit, 842
Wittingly
  purposely, 620
Witty
  wit, 842
Wive
  marriage, 903
Wizard
  sorcerer, 994
  oracle, 513
  good, 648
Wizardry
  occult, 992
Wizened
  withered, 193, 195
Wobble
  oscillate, 314

Woden
god, 979
Woe
pain, 828
evil, 619
Woebegone
pain, 828
dejection, 837
Woeful
painfulness, 830
Wold
plain, 344
Wolf
to devour, 296
alarm, 669
philanderer, 902
Woman
woman, 131, 374
Womanish
cowardly, 862
Womanly
weakness, 160
Womb
interior, 221
cause, 153
Wonder
astonishment, 870
prodigy, 872
Wonderfully
great, 31
Wonderment
prodigy, 872
Wondrous
wonder, 870
Wonky
imperfect, 651
Wont
habitual, 613
usual, 82
Woo
desire, 865
courtship, 902
Wood
plant, 367
Wood-note
animal cry, 412
Woodcut
engraving, 558
Woodcutter
forester, 371
Wooer
love, 897
Woof
texture, 329
Wool

hair, 256
Wool-gathering
folly, 499
inattention, 458
madness, 503
Woolsack
pillow, 215
authority, 747
tribunal, 966
Wop
alien, 57
Word
vocable, 562
intelligence, 532
promise, 768
revelation, 985
Deity, 976
maxim, 496
Wording
expression, 566
style, 569
Wordless
aphony, 581
Words
quarrel, 713
Wordy
diffuseness, 573
Work
product, 154
agency, 170
to use, 677
shape, 240
adorn, 847
action, 680
book, 593
Work in
introduce, 37
Work off
get rid of, 545, 672
Work out
conduct, 692
achieve, 729
Work up
incite, 615
inflame, 824
Work upon
influence, 175
Workhouse
poverty, 804
Working
activity, 682
Workman
agent, 690
originator, 164
Workmanlike

skill, 698
Workmanship
produce, 161
handiwork, 680
Workshop
workshop, 691
World
universe, 318
mankind, 373
fashion, 852
events, 151
great, 31
Worldling
selfish, 943
Worldly
selfish, 943
irreligious, 989
Worldwide
world, 318
Worm
small, 193
animal, 366
spiral, 248
Worm in
insert, 300
interpose, 228
Worm out
ascertain, 480A
Wormeaten
imperfect, 651
decayed, 659
Wormwood
unsavoury, 395
Worn
imperfect, 651
decayed, 659
Worry
vexation, 828
to tease, 830
harass, 907
Worse
badness, 649
Worsen
deteriorate, 659
Worship
religious, 990
title, 877
servility, 886
Worshipful
repute, 873
Worst
defeat, 731
Worsted
defeated, 732

Worth
goodness, 648
value, 644
virtue, 994
price, 812
Worth while
utility, 644
Worthless
useless, 645
profligate, 945
Worthy
virtuous, 944
good, 648
saint, 948
Wot
knowledge, 490
Wound
evil, 619
badness, 649
injure, 659
hurt, 900
Wrack
evil, 619
Wraith
spirit, 980
Wrangle
dispute, 713
reason, 476
Wrangler
scholar, 492
Wrap
cover, 222
circumscribe, 231
Wrapped in
attention, 457
Wrapper
cover, 222
dress, 225
Wrapt
see Rapt
Wrath
anger, 900
Wreak
inflict, 918
Wreath
trophy, 733
ornament, 847
honour, 877
Wreck
remainder, 40
destruction, 162
failure, 732
Wrecker
thief, 792
Wrench
extract, 301

seize, 789
twist, 243
draw, 285
Wrest
seize, 789
twist, 243
distort, 523, 555
Wrestle
contention, 720
Wrestler
combatant, 726
Wretch
sinner, 949
apostate, 941
Wretched
unhappy, 828
bad, 649
contemptible, 643
petty, 32
Wriggle
agitation, 315
cunning, 702
Wright
workman, 690
Wring
pain, 378
to torment, 830
distort, 243
Wring from
taking, 789
Wrinkle
fold, 258
hint, 527
Writ
order, 741
in law, 969
Write
writing, 590
Write off
cancel, 552
Write up
praise, 931
detail, 594
Writer
lawyer, 968
Writhe .
agitate, 315
pain, 378, 828
Writing
book, 593
Writing-case
receptacle, 191
Wrong
evil, 619
badness, 649

erroneous, 495
vice, 945
immoral, 923
to injure, 907
Wrong-headed
foolish, 499
obstinate, 606
Wrongdoer
sinner, 949
evildoer, 913
Wrought up
excitation, 824
Wry
oblique, 217
distorted, 243
Wunderbar
wonder, 870
Wynd
abode, 189
Wyvern
monster, 83

Xanthin
yellow, 436
Xanthippe
shrew, 901
Xebec
ship, 273
Xylography
engraving, 558
Xylophone
musical instrument, 417

Y
bifurcation, 91
Yacht
ship, 273
navigation, 267
Yahoo
commonalty, 876
Yak
carrier, 271
Yammer
cry, 411
complain, 839
Yank
jerk, 285
Yap
animal cry, 412
Yard
workshop, 691
abode, 189
support, 215

Yardstick
measure, 466
Yarn
filament, 205
prate, 584
story, 594
exaggeration, 549
Yashmak
dress, 225
Yataghan
arms, 727
Yaw
deviate, 279
Yawl
ship, 273
Yawn
open, 260
gape, 198
fatigue, 688
insensible, 823
Yawp
cry, 411
Yea
assent, 488
Yeah
assent, 488
Year
period, 108
Yearly
periodical, 138
Yearn
desire, 865
pine, 828
pity, 914
love, 897
sad, 837
Yeast
bubble, 353
Yegg
evildoer, 913, 949
thief, 792
Yell
cry, 411
complain, 839
Yellow
yellow, 436
cowardly, 862
Yelp
animal cry, 412
Yen
desire, 865
Yeoman
man, 373
commonalty, 876
farmer, 371

Yeomanry
army, 726
Yep
assent, 488
Yes
affirmation, 488
consent, 762
Yes-man
assent, 488
Yesterday
preterition, 122
Yet
exception, 83
time, 106, 122
counteraction, 179
compensation, 30
Yield
submit, 725, 826
regress, 283
obey, 743
consent, 762
relinquish, 624
furnish, 784
produce, 161
gain, 810
price, 812
facility, 705
Yippy
hippy, 183
Yodel
music, 415
Yoga
asceticism, 955
Yogi
priest, 996
Yoke
join, 43
vinculum, 45
couple, 89
bond, 752
subjection, 749
Yokel
clown, 876
Yonder
distance, 196
Yore
preterition, 122
Yoshiwara
brothel, 961
Young
age, 127
Young man
lover, 897
Youngster
youth, 129

Younker
youth, 129
Youth
age, 127
newness, 123
lad, 129

Zadkiel
oracle, 513
Zany
fool, 501
Zarathustra
religious founder, 986
Zareba
defence, 717
Zeal
activity, 682
feeling, 821
desire, 865
Zealot
active, 682
resolute, 604
obstinate, 606
Zealotry
obstinacy, 606
Zebra
variegation, 440
Zenana
apartment, 191
Zend-Avesta
sacred books, 986
Zenith
summit, 210
climax, 33
Zephyr
wind, 349
Zeppelin
aircraft, 273A
Zero
nothing, 4
naught, 101
Zest
relish, 390, 394
enjoyment, 827
Zetetic
inquiring, 461
Zeus
god, 979
Zigzag
angle, 244
obliquity, 217
deviation, 279
oscillation, 314
circuit, 629

Zion
heaven, 981
Zipper
pendent, 214
Zither
musical instrument, 417
Zodiac
outline, 229
universe, 318
Zoilus
envy, 921
Zollverein
compact, 769

Zombie
fool, 501
Zone
circle, 247
belt, 229
region, 181
layer, 204
Zoography
zoology, 368
Zoological garden
taming, 370
Zoology
zoology, 368

Zoom
deviation, 279
ascent, 305
Zoophyte
animal, 366
Zootomy
zoology, 368
Zoroaster
religious founder, 986
Zouave
combatant, 726
Zymotic
insalubrity, 657